FROMMER

COMPREHENSIVE TRAVEL GUIDE

AUSTRIA & HUNGARY '91-'92

by Darwin Porter
Assisted by Danforth Prince

PRENTICE
HALL
PRESS

NEW YORK • LONDON • TORONTO • SYDNEY • TOKYO • SINGAPORE

FROMMER BOOKS
Published by Prentice Hall Press
A division of Simon & Schuster Inc.
15 Columbus Circle
New York, NY 10023

ISBN 0-13-338005-X
ISSN 0899-3297

PRENTICE
H A L L
PRESS

Manufactured in the United States of America

CONTENTS

PART ONE

AUSTRIA

PART TWO

HUNGARY

MAPS

Inflation Alert

In researching this book we have made every effort to obtain up-to-the-minute prices, but even the most conscientious researcher cannot keep up with the current pace of fluctuating prices. As we go to press, we believe we have obtained the most reliable data possible. Nonetheless, in the lifetime of this edition—particularly its second year (1992)—the wise traveler will add 15% to the prices quoted throughout these pages.

FROMMER'S AUSTRIA & HUNGARY

This book is about two small countries in Central Europe that were once the seat of a great empire. The territories and lands of both countries have been reduced by a roller-coaster ride from the heights to the depths. Austria, for example, only regained its full sovereignty as late as July 27, 1955, whereas Hungary lost much of its territory, including Transylvania, to neighboring countries in World War II. It took until 1989 before it began to reassert itself as a republic.

1. The Reason Why

Even after the loss of its former colonies, Austria was left with a land of scenic grandeur and soaring alpine peaks. There are those (and perhaps I join them) who say that, taken as a whole, Austria is the most beautiful country on earth.

A great world power in the 18th and 19th centuries, Austria still preserves reminders of its past in its epic monuments and grandiose baroque buildings.

The Federal Republic of Austria consists of nine fairly autonomous provinces, called Bundesländer: Vienna (of course), Upper Austria, Lower Austria, Salzburg, Tyrol, Vorarlberg, Styria, Carinthia, and tiny Burgenland. Each of these provinces contains geographical and cultural differences, and it is the lucky visitor who gets to see all of Austria, which, though small, takes many weeks to visit in its entirety (and even then you'll have only skimmed the surface).

Austria is a sports-oriented country (and not just for skiers). It's also rich in music and drama, in art, museums, galleries, churches, and cathedrals.

West Germany, with which it once had an ill-fated alliance in the late 1930s and war-torn '40s, lies to the northwest. To the northeast is Czechoslovakia, to the east is Hungary, and to the southeast lies Yugoslavia—three countries that Austria used to dominate in part. Of course, Italy is to the south, and to Austria's west is Switzerland, with which it often fought battles until that even tinier country fully gained its independence from Habsburg domination.

Austria is peaceful today, and if it thinks of empire, it is only nostalgically (I've talked to many older Viennese who remember the last parade in their city of the

Austro-Hungarian Empire). Nowadays its German-speaking populace (English is virtually a second language) are among the most hospitable in Europe.

Austria, like Switzerland, no longer sends its soldiers marching across other frontiers but is itself invaded in both summer and winter. Austria is a true biseasonal country, enjoying both a huge summer and winter tourist industry. The new invaders are tourists, and they come to seek out the grandeur of "the roof of Europe." About 75% of Austria is mountainous. Austria today has about 7.5 million in population, a people associated with gemütlichkeit, a warm, contented, friendly feeling generated by those who appreciate the good life.

This is best summed up by the popular saying, "In Germany everything is *verboten* that is not expressly permitted, and in Austria everything is permitted that is not expressly forbidden!"

An increasing amount of freedom exists in the Hungary of today. More than in any other country of Eastern Europe, Hungary is welcoming visitors as never before. It has made border crossings easier (visas are now granted at the frontier), and it is sprucing up its monuments and building better hotels and finer restaurants to receive its millions of annual visitors.

Austria itself is expensive, but Hungary is so cheap that the Austrians who live on its border sometimes cross over just to get their hair done.

These two countries, which once formed the heart of the Austro-Hungarian Empire, have long been separated by the tides of history caused by two world wars. But—and only for the purposes of this guidebook—we will join them for a reunion once more. Vienna, now more than ever, is the gateway to Budapest.

FROM THE ALPS TO THE DANUBE

The scenery of Austria is more varied than that of Switzerland, combining rich agricultural plains along the Danube, alpine peaks and lakes, and castles (often in ruins) that evoke the Middle Ages. All that, combined with acres and acres of vineyards, has made Austria a tourist mecca since the 19th century.

The name Austria, or Osterreich, means "Eastern Empire," a designation given to the far-eastern sector of the lands conquered by Charlemagne. But from prehistoric times, the part of Europe centering around present-day Austria has been a crossroads, with the Danube Valley allowing traverse both by land and water.

During the "twilight of the Habsburgs," culminating in 1918, Austria, poised between the West and the East, lost much of its territory and later faced international humiliation.

Memories of Hitler—who turned their country into a virtual colony of the Third Reich, in spite of the sentiment of many Austrians at the time who wanted to "amalgamate" with Nazi Germany—and of the succeeding partial Soviet occupation are still strong in the minds of many Austrians. However, despite reverses that may well be credited to the *hubris* of their rulers, Austria has recovered.

This country, once reaching from czarist Russia to the Adriatic, now smaller than the state of Maine, is still a land of music. Its festivals, such as the world-famous one at Salzburg, its skiing, and those monumental baroque edifices already referred to hold an appeal that I, along with thousands of others, find irresistible.

Vienna is the most distinguished capital city in the German-speaking world, but though they share a common language, Austria and Germany are two very different countries. A visit to one will hardly be like a visit to the other.

Austria has one of the lowest inflation rates in Europe, and among the trio of big skiing countries, it's cheaper than either Switzerland or France.

As fat as this book is—probably the single biggest guide ever published on the hotels and restaurants of Austria—you should know that it represents only a fraction of the actual facilities available. What I'm sharing with you are my favorites. Perhaps, using the book as your seed core, you'll find dozens more on your own.

Likewise, this was the first major guide in English to describe in any detail the hotels, restaurants, shops, and nightclubs of Hungary, along with its many tourist attractions. And not only those found in Budapest but also in the country's provinces, which take in the famed Danube Bend, Lake Balaton, and the Great Hungarian Plain.

THE BEST OF AUSTRIA AND HUNGARY

I have set for myself the formidable task of seeking out Austria and Hungary at their finest and condensing them between the covers of a book. The best towns, villages, cities, and sightseeing attractions are documented, as well as the best hotels, restaurants, bars, cafés, shops, and nightspots.

But the best need not be the most expensive. My ultimate aim—beyond that of familiarizing you with the offerings of Austria and Hungary—is to stretch your dollar power . . . to reveal to you that you need not pay scalper's prices for charm, topgrade comfort, and gourmet-level food.

In this guide I'll devote a lot of attention to those old tourist meccas—Vienna, Salzburg, Innsbruck, Budapest—focusing on both their obvious and their hidden treasures. But they are not the full "reason why" of this book. Important as they are, they simply do not fully reflect the widely diverse and scenic countryside of Austria and Hungary. To discover that, you must venture deep into the Tyrolean country or perhaps to the windswept *puszta* (flat steppe) of the Great Hungarian Plain.

---

2. About This Book

In brief, this is a guidebook giving specific details—including prices—about Austrian and Hungarian hotels, restaurants, bars, cafés, sightseeing attractions, nightlife, and tours. Establishments in many price ranges have been documented and described, although I am constantly searching for bargains. Along with the deluxe citadels, I am more interested in the family-run *gasthof*-type place where you can often bask in gemütlich warmth but at low prices. In every case, deluxe or budget, each establishment was measured by a strict yardstick of value. If it measured up—meaning if it was among the best in its category—it was included.

Now, more than ever, one needs an accurate guidebook that includes tips for saving money. By careful planning and selecting from my listings, you'll find the true Austrian or Hungarian experience while remaining within a reasonable budget. This applies to independent travelers as well as those who visit Austria or Hungary on a tour. If you're one of the latter, and have already obtained your flight ticket and hotel, you'll still need a guide to direct you to restaurants, nightlife, and sightseeing attractions rarely covered on a package tour. If you're given a car, then you'll be in the market for suggestions of where to go in the country once you leave either Vienna or Salzburg, whichever is your "gateway" city.

SOME WORDS OF EXPLANATION

No restaurant, inn, hotel, nightclub, shop, or café paid to be mentioned in this book. What you read are entirely personal recommendations; in many cases the proprietors never knew their establishments were being visited or investigated for inclusion in a travel guide.

Unfortunately, although I have made every effort to be as accurate as possible, prices change, and they rarely go downward.

When checking into a hotel, always inquire about the rate and agree on it. That policy can save much embarrassment and disappointment when it comes time to settle the tab. If the prices quoted are not the same as those mentioned in this book, remember that my prices reflect those in effect at the time this edition was researched.

This guide is revised cover to cover every other year. But even in a book that appears with such frequency, it may happen that that cozy little wine tavern of a year ago has changed its stripes, blossoming out with cut-velvet walls, crystal chandeliers, and dining tabs that include the decorator's fee and the owner's new villa. It may further develop that some of the people or settings I've described are no longer there or have changed in this fast-moving world.

All that leads up to the next major point—

AN INVITATION TO READERS

Like all the books in the series, *Frommer's Austria & Hungary* hopes to maintain a continuing dialogue between its author and its readers. All of us share a common aim, I'm sure, and that is to travel as widely and as well as possible, at the lowest possible cost. In achieving that goal, your comments and suggestions can be of aid to other readers.

Therefore if you come across a particularly appealing hotel, restaurant, shop, or bargain, please don't keep it to yourself.

Comments about existing listings are always helpful. The fact that a hotel or restaurant (or any other establishment) appears in this edition doesn't mean that it will necessarily appear in future editions if readers report that its service has slipped or that its prices have not only risen drastically but unfairly.

Even if you like a place I've recommended, your comments are especially welcome—and have been known to brighten many a gray day.

Send your comments or finds—and, yes, those inevitable complaints that always arise—to Darwin Porter, c/o Frommer Books, Prentice Hall Trade Division, 15th Floor, 15 Columbus Circle, New York, NY 10023.

Here's how *Frommer's Austria & Hungary* sets forth its information:

In Part One, **Chapter I** explores the methods of "getting to" and "getting around" Austria. The most obvious means of reaching it would be by air from America, or perhaps you'll go by car after your exploration of Germany, Italy, or Switzerland. But my coverage of transportation within Austria will focus mainly on the railway lines and bargain passes.

Chapter II provides a general discussion of the country and a brief historical survey, along with a description of its people, customs, hotels, and cuisine. Alternative and special-interest travel is also previewed. Winter and summer sports and practical facts about the country conclude this chapter.

Chapter III wings in on Vienna, one of the great tourist attractions of Europe, and covers all hotel categories—deluxe, first class, middle bracket, inexpensive— and a large number of pensions (boarding houses). Restaurants, coffeehouses, and cafés are also surveyed.

Chapter IV continues the exploration of Vienna, focusing on sightseeing attractions, shops, and nightlife.

Crisscrossed by the Danube, Lower Austria, covered in **Chapter V,** is a land of castles and vineyards. Hotels are generally inexpensive, of the *gasthaus* type, but many first-class resorts exist in such spots as Baden. The chapter explores the Wienerwald (Vienna Woods), along with the wine villages. An itinerary, with sights, food, and inns along the "Wine Road," is presented. The major winter sports and mountain-air resorts in the high peaks of Semmering and Schneeberg are described. This chapter also explores another wine district, Weinviertel, north of Vienna, lying between the Danube and Czechoslovakia. Although the chapter deals with trips on Danube paddleboat steamers, the most space is devoted to castles and abbeys in the area—some in ruins, some turned into hotels, others into sightseeing attractions. Chief among these is the Benedictine abbey at Melk, the largest in Lower Austria.

Burgenland, described in **Chapter VI,** is known for its gardens, castles, and fortresses. We'll visit the mysterious Neusiedler See, a shallow saltwater lake. This chapter adds a little paprika to the book, because the area is much like Hungary. Spa and castle hotels will be surveyed, along with more modest guesthouses. Burgenland is one of the great bargain areas of Austria and is rich in sights.

Chapter VII, on Salzburg, takes in the "city of Mozart," whose annual Mozart Festival is described. A full range of hotels, from deluxe to inexpensive, is surveyed, including some special ones in the environs. Likewise, restaurants range from inexpensive brewery-operated establishments to first-class selections serving an international cuisine. Special restaurants in the environs, including some with terraces and belvederes overlooking the Alps, are covered. Attractions range from Mozart's birthplace to the Hohensalzburg Fortress, along with details of how to get about, including by aerial cable railway. Nightlife takes in the casino, and there's also a sports section, as the Gaisberg mountain lies on the outskirts of the city.

Chapter VIII describes Land Salzburg, that area of sports and spas—famous the world over—lying within easy reach of Salzburg. Our selection of hotels ranges from the deluxe ones at Badgastein to modest mountain lodges. The great High Alpine Hwy., the Grossglockner Road, is described, with peaks at 12,000 feet and views at 8,000-foot levels. The towns near Radstädter Tauern Pass, one of the most prestigious ski areas in Land Salzburg, and such famous resorts as Zell am See, are covered as are their accommodations.

Chapter IX goes into Upper Austria, which is crossed in part by the Danube. Here the Salzkammergut, the lake country, is the most popular area with visitors. Major attention is devoted to Linz, the capital of Upper Austria, and its many sights nearby. The baroque Augustinian abbey of St. Florian, with its Bruckner organ and lavishly decorated imperial rooms, is one of the chief sights of the country. The highlights of this province emphasize attractions along the Danube. Little-known places are spotlighted, including Enns, the oldest town in Austria. The outstanding castles and abbeys of the area include Kremsmünster Abbey, founded in A.D. 777. A special section is devoted to Bad Ischl, the fashionable spa and winter-sports center where Franz Joseph held summer court in the heyday of Imperial Austria.

Chapter X turns to Innsbruck and Tyrol, the favorite part of Austria for nearly all visiting Americans. The obvious attention goes to the capital, baroque-style Innsbruck, acclaimed by many as one of the loveliest towns of Europe. Innsbruck's sights, hotels, restaurants, shops, and nightlife are followed by such sights in the environs as the winter-sports center at Igls. The Stubai Valley is previewed, both as a summer center and a winter ski mecca, with its glacier and mountains. A section includes one of Tyrol's most exciting events, an excursion along the Karwendel railway, traveling by electric train along the Austrian-Bavarian border. Winter-sports centers such as Seefeld are surveyed. Lienz, called by many "the prettiest little city in Europe," is given a special bouquet, and Kitzbühel, one of the best-known towns in Austria, is cited for exceptional ski facilities. The chapter includes information on the famous Zugspitze, from which at nearly 10,000 feet one can see the Swiss Alps and part of Bavaria. The valleys of Tyrol, including Achen, Tuxer, and Ziller, are surveyed, along with a full range of Tyrolean hotels and restaurants, plus shopping for such specialties as dirndls, lederhosen, woodcarvings, and those famous Tyrolean hats.

Austria's westernmost province, Vorarlberg, unfolds in **Chapter XI.** It's much like Switzerland. Here we'll center mainly at Bregenz, a little town on the Bodensee (Lake Constance), and we'll explore the Bregenz Forest, a land of lovely woods, alpine meadows, and highlights. For the most part, hotels and restaurants in the area are small, family-type operations. *Stube* taverns and restaurants—some of them centuries old—are presented.

Carinthia, in **Chapter XII,** is the southernmost part of Austria, bordering Italy. Framed by high mountains, it's a land of lakes and narrow valleys. Its best-known summer resorts lie around Wörther See, and the most fashionable spot on the lake, Velden, has first-class hotels and boarding houses, including one of the finest in Austria, the baroque Schloss Velden. Winter-sports resorts, such as Kanzelhöhe, known for its "perfect snow" and sunshine, are covered as well. There is a heavy emphasis on sports: boat races, waterskiing, swimming, and sailing.

The "green state," Styria, covered in **Chapter XIII,** in the southeastern part of the country, has Graz as its capital. The Styrian gray-and-green hunting suits are known all over the world. It is the Styrian version of the dirndl that is most popular. Its skiing terrains, publicized by the Alpine World Skiing Championships, are also covered. Old Graz is cited as one of the best bargain areas of Austria, in both restaurants and hotels. Other towns include Bad Aussee, an important spa and winter-sports center, and the summer resort of Altausee, in the Styrian sector of the Salzkammergut. The province has many well-known hotels along with the relatively undocumented old inns. *Weinstuben* are also important here, along with cafés and pastry shops. A small number of museums are previewed, including the old buildings of the Landesmuseum Joanneum and the Styrian Museum of Folklore.

Chapter XIV takes us into Hungary, introducing you to its history, people, food, drink, art, culture, and sports.

Chapter XV visits one of the most exciting tourist destinations in Europe—the lively capital of Hungary, Budapest, which is 1,000 years old. You'll be introduced to its many attractions, ranging from the beauty of its six bridges spanning the Danube to gulasch parties. Hotels, restaurants, shopping, and day- and nighttime entertainment will be suggested.

The main sightseeing targets of the country outside Budapest are visited in **Chapter XVI,** ranging from the Danube Bend to Lake Balaton to the Great Plain and puszta region, where horseback riding is the way to go. Great spas, a paprika factory, and vineyards from which come the famous wines of the country will be explored.

In Appendix I, Austrian (German) words and phrases for basic vocabulary use are listed, as well as menu listings you will find helpful.

Appendix II lists Hungarian vocabulary and menu terms.

---

3. A Word About Cost

Austria has had a low inflation rate when compared to some of the other countries of Western Europe. This has made the country one of the better buys in Europe. But it is far from cheap.

Vienna and Salzburg are the two most expensive cities, with Innsbruck a runner-up. But one of the reasons for that is that these are the three cities the typical American visitor has heard of and therefore heads for. So I have a suggestion. If you have only a few days for Austria, don't spend all your time in these high-priced tourist meccas, but head instead for a night or two in such old and historic cities as Graz and Linz, where the hoteliers and the restaurateurs are not as tab-happy.

As for restaurants, the main meal of the day in Austria is taken at noon. That's when most restaurants, wanting to attract local business (not just the tourist), offer a fixed-price menu, often at a modest price. So when in Austria, do as the Austrians do and enjoy a most filling and reasonably priced lunch, perhaps ordering a much lighter dinner or supper when the tabs are likely to be much higher.

Sometimes, particularly if you're planning to tour a province such as the Tyrolean country, it's better to anchor into just one place in the countryside and take day trips. Chances are, you'll get a much better rate, especially on half-board arrangements, than you would by hotel-hopping, and because Austria is a small country, you can still explore everything that a province has to offer.

Whenever possible, try to book into a country inn on the half-board plan, which can mean discounts for you. Half board means one main meal a day, along with breakfast. You're free to have lunch outside, and if you've planned your itinerary well, you can easily be back at your hotel for dinner in the evening.

If you'd like to see a part of Austria—any part, since all of them are fascinating —and economy is a major concern in your case, then there are some spots in Austria that are extremely reasonable. Chief among these is Burgenland (see Chapter VI), a province much sought out and known to Europeans, but little known to most

North Americans. Isolated, remote, almost forgotten (but not abandoned), East Tyrol is another such spot, as are certain sections of Styria and Carinthia.

Of course, if you can adjust your schedule, off-season travel can be quite a bargain in Austria. Sometimes hotel prices are lowered as much as 30%. In Tyrol, for example, especially at ski resorts, guests are often granted 30% to 50% reductions at hotels in summer. However, in Vienna and Salzburg, high season is the summer months, when the steepest prices are in effect. Rates are often lowered in these cities from autumn to spring.

Costs have been rising greatly in Hungary, but after a trip through Western Europe it will come as a great relief to your pocketbook. As a quick rule of thumb, if you've traveled "second class" in most of the nations of Western Europe, you'll find that you can afford "first class" or deluxe (which exists mainly in Budapest) once you cross the border. Budapest, naturally, is the most expensive destination, and once you're out of that city into the countryside of Hungary, you'll encounter prices you haven't seen in the last decade or so.

TIME OUT FOR A COMMERCIAL

On your tour of Austria or Hungary, you will come close to many major attractions in other countries that you may want to explore. Since I had to set some limitation on the number of pages in this book, it was impossible to devote separate chapters to neighboring attractions.

I'll cite only an example or two to prove my point. For example, when you visit southern Austria you're close to the many attractions of Italy, including Venice. At Salzburg you're on the doorstep of exciting Bavaria. In Vorarlberg you're next door to Switzerland and Liechtenstein, that tiny principality left over from the Habsburg Empire.

Because of the geography of Austria and, again, depending on which sections of that country you plan to travel in, you may want to take along some of our sister guides as traveling companions.

Specific ones that might appeal to you include:

Frommer's Switzerland and Liechtenstein
Frommer's Germany
Frommer's Italy
Frommer's Eastern Europe and Yugoslavia on $25 a Day

---

4. Frommer's Dollarwise Travel Club—How to Save Money on All Your Travels

---

In this book we'll be looking at how to get your money's worth in Austria and Hungary, but there is a "device" for saving money and determining value on *all* your trips. It's the Frommer's Dollarwise Travel Club, now in its 31st successful year of operation. For information about the Club write to the Club Secretary, Frommer's Dollarwise Travel Club, 15 Columbus Circle, New York, NY 10023. For order forms listing all Prentice Hall travel guides, turn to the last two pages of this book.

PART ONE

AUSTRIA

PART ONE

GETTING TO AND AROUND AUSTRIA

Deep in the heart of Central Europe, Austria is not as remote as it may seem at first. It can easily be reached by plane from North America, and for many vacationers it's becoming a travel destination in its own right in both winter and summer. The time is long past when Austria was given only a quick stopover on a whirlwind visit to Europe.

1. Traveling to Austria

Although Austria is serviced by a number of airlines, most of them require a transfer and a change of aircraft in other European capitals, such as Frankfurt, before continuing to Vienna. But that changed in 1989. **Austrian Airlines,** the national carrier of Austria, inaugurated nonstop service from New York to Vienna. Since then, Austrian Airlines has established itself as a world-class airline, offering the fastest and most frequent service from North America to Vienna, as well as the airline with some of the best connections to Eastern Europe (more about that later).

Austrian Airlines operates six days a week from New York's JFK Airport. Departures are daily except Tuesday, and they're scheduled for the early evening, with arrivals in Vienna the next morning. Your immersion in Austrian culture begins the moment you step aboard. Flight attendants offer an array of newspapers, in-house movies, food and wine, and other comforts. Best of all, Austrian Airlines' A-310 Airbuses have around 23 fewer seats in them than do similar aircraft operated by other airlines. This is welcome news for long-legged passengers.

The flight to Vienna is timed to connect to a wave of other Austrian Airlines flights leaving for Eastern or Southeast Europe.

Austrian Airlines operates one of the most modern fleets in the industry, with the average age of each aircraft being six years.

Austrian Airlines is not alone in flying to Vienna. Its only competitor, in terms of nonstop flights from North America, is an airline you might not have thought of: **Royal Jordanian Airlines,** the national carrier of the Hashemite Kingdom of Jordan. From New York, that airline operates two nonstop flights a week from New York to Vienna, departing late at night. The flights then continue to Amman, the capital of Jordan. The airline also flies twice a week from Chicago to Vienna. One of these flights is nonstop, the other touching down in New York.

All of the U.S.-based carriers flying into Austria require a stopover in some other European capital. **Pan American,** for example, flies from New York to Budapest twice a week, from which connections can be arranged to Vienna.

American Airlines arranges nonstop service from New York into Zurich, and then transfers onto an Austrian Airlines flight bound for Vienna, which departs 90 minutes later.

These and other options can best be discussed with a telephone sales agent for one of the airlines or a travel agent. Toll-free reservations and information numbers: for Austrian Airlines, 800/843-0002; for American Airlines, 800/433-7300; and for Pan Am, 800/221-1111. In New York City, call Royal Air Jordanian at 212/949-0050, or toll free 800/223-0470 outside the city.

THE LESS EXPENSIVE FARES

Obviously, you'll save money by determining your departure date in advance. Many travelers prefer the security of advance reservations in hotels, which, of course, is impossible unless you pre-reserve your airline ticket.

The least expensive airfares at Austrian Airlines, for example, are called PEX (not to be confused with APEX), and these require a purchase of 30 days in advance and a European stopover of between 7 and 21 days.

A slightly different, slightly more expensive ticket is Advance Purchase Excursion Fare, or APEX, which requires a purchase of only seven days in advance and a stopover of between seven days and three months.

Austrian Airlines also offers a break to anyone between the ages of 12 and 25. Its round-trip Youth Fare requires only that it be reserved and purchased three days or less before departure. The return half of the ticket can be used any time within a year of departure.

Excursion Fares

Excursion fares differ from PEX or APEX in that no advance purchase is necessary. For this type of ticket, Austrian Airlines offers a $50 discount on the round-trip of a midweek flight but makes no restrictions about early reservations or minimum time logged abroad. The return half of the ticket is valid for a year after departure.

FULL-FARE TICKETS

If you want to arrange multiple stopovers, choose coach class with no restrictions. For this kind of travel it's better to discuss the options with an airline reservations agent, since a combination of options and other benefits might be available, depending on your itinerary.

Austrian Airlines, like Pan Am and American, offers special advantages and comforts to first-class and business-class travelers willing to pay the higher fares. Both have upgraded food and beverage service, with seats that recline more than in coach class. First class offers special service with lots of extras, including seats that fold down almost horizontally.

ALTERNATIVE FARES TO AUSTRIA

There are several other flight options that you may want to consider.

Charter Flights

Strictly for reasons of economy, some travelers may wish to accept the numerous restrictions and possible uncertainties of a charter flight to Austria. Charters require that passengers strictly specify departure and return dates, and full payment is required in advance. Any changes in flight dates are possible (if at all) upon payment of a stiff penalty. Any reputable travel agent can advise you about fares, cities of departure, and most important, the reputation of the charter company.

Do-It-Yourself Fares

You may also put together your own combination tickets to Vienna by flying to another European destination—London, for example—and then flying from there to Vienna. This *can* save dollars, but not always. This latter point cannot be emphasized too strongly, since fares from one Western European country to another are notoriously overpriced, not at all like the low-cost domestic fares in the United States. (To illustrate the point, one Frenchman once calculated that he could fly from Paris to New York cheaper than he could wing his way from Paris to Lyon in his own country.) For the first leg of your flight, assuming it is to some European destination before Austria, you should shop around for the best airfare bargains through your newspaper or travel agent.

You can, for example, fly **British Airways, Virgin Atlantic,** or **Continental Airlines** to London's Gatwick Airport from New Jersey's Newark Airport. This particular routing to London sometimes costs less than flights to the more prestigious Heathrow in London, with departures from New York's JFK. You can then arrange for a flight to Austria on **Austrian Airlines** or on any one of the many European airlines servicing the London-to-Vienna route, including British Airways. The money you save may not be that great, but you'll have the option of, say, adding England to your vacation plans before journeying on to the Alps. For information about flights from North America and London, call British Airways (toll free 800/247-9297), Continental Airlines (toll free 800/525-0280), or Virgin Atlantic (toll free 800/862-8621).

Once you're in Europe, Austrian Airlines (toll free 800/862-8621) offers more flights into Austria from such cities as London, Munich, and Paris than any other carrier. Tickets purchased in North America, especially if part of a package deal including transatlantic passage, usually cost less than intra-European tickets bought once you're abroad.

GATEWAY TO EASTERN EUROPE

Vienna has now emerged as the major gateway to Eastern Europe, where nations are finding that newfound freedom includes travel abroad.

From Vienna, Austrian Airlines is the principal carrier to this fast-rising market, as it often wings to what was once its country's empire. From Vienna, the airline services such cities as Moscow, Warsaw, Budapest, Prague, Bucharest, Sofia, and Belgrade, even Istanbul.

---

2. Traveling Within Austria

By boat, plane, rail, car, or bicycle, Austria is well served by transportation possibilities. The major ones are surveyed below.

BY CAR

All main roads in Austria are hard-surfaced. Between Salzburg and Vienna there is a four-lane autobahn (two lanes in either direction), and between Vienna and Edlitz the autobahn has six lanes. Part of the highway system includes mountain roads, and in the alpine region drivers face gradients of 6% to 15%.

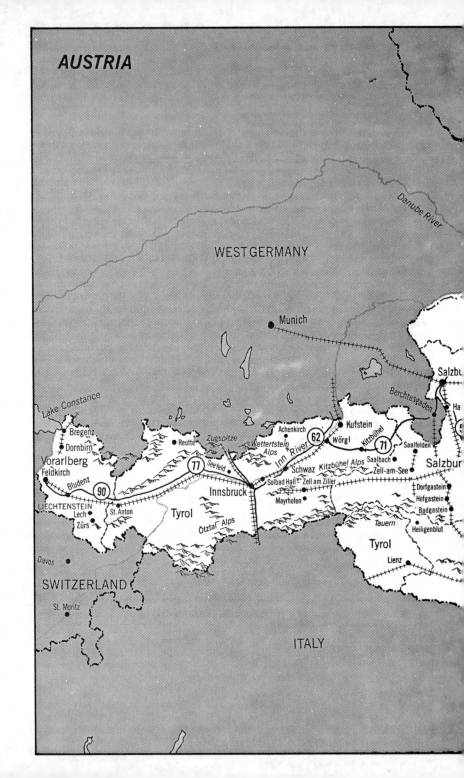

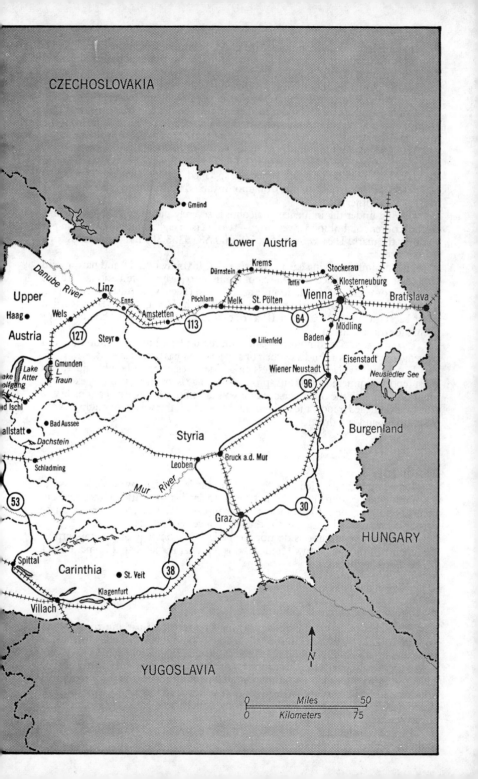

In summer, driving conditions are good, but in winter, from December to March, motorists must reckon with snow on roads and passes at higher altitudes. Roads at altitudes of up to 5,580 feet are kept open in winter, although they may be temporarily closed because of heavy snowfall or avalanche danger. If you're planning to drive in Austria in winter, snow tires or chains will be needed.

Don't take chances. Ask about road conditions before you start on a trip. This information is available in English seven days a week from 6am to 8pm from the Austrian Automobile Club (tel. 0222/72-99-7 or 0222/71-19-97 in Vienna).

Traffic regulations are similar to those in other European countries where you drive on the right. The speed limit is 50 kilometers per hour (31 m.p.h.) in built-up areas within the city limits unless otherwise specified. Out of town, the limit is 130 kilometers per hour (80 m.p.h.) on motorways, 100 kilometers per hour (62 m.p.h.) on all other roads.

Driving under the influence of alcohol is severely punished. The permissible alcohol content of the blood is very low—two beers or eight ounces of wine can put you over the mark. The *minimum* fine is 5,000 AS ($363.50) and possible loss of a driver's license.

The minimum driving age in Austria is 18. If you're over 18 and have a valid United States driver's license, you're not required to have an International Driver's License. However, you should inquire at your travel agency, an Austrian consulate, or an Austrian National Tourist Office (addresses in the U.S. and Canada are listed in "Fast Facts for Austria," Chapter II) as to official validation of your home driver's license for use in Austria.

Use of seatbelts is compulsory, and children under 12 may not sit in the front passenger seat unless a child's seatbelt or a special seat has been installed.

If you are involved in or witness an accident resulting in bodily injury, you must report it immediately. If only property damage is involved, you may exchange identification with the other person, or if you can't find the owner of a vehicle you may have damaged, report the incident to the police. Otherwise, you might be considered a hit-and-run driver.

Motor Fuel

Regular-grade unleaded *(blei-frei)* motor fuel is generally available in Austria. Premium-grade gasoline is still leaded, but with smaller quantities of that environmentally suspect metal. This means that you can now take an American car to Austria without modification to the catalytic converter/exhaust system.

Austrian service stations do not accept U.S.-oil-company or general-purpose credit cards, although you will find stations with names familiar at home: Exxon, Mobil, Shell, and Texaco.

Parking

A number of Austrian cities and towns have restricted parking zones, where you can park for 90 minutes in specially marked "blue zones," so called because of blue lines on the road.

In Vienna, Graz, Linz, Klagenfurt, Innsbruck, and other major towns, you must use a parking voucher to stop in limited-parking zones. You must purchase a voucher and when you park, write in the time you arrived and display it on the dashboard inside the windshield. You can buy vouchers at banks, gas stations, or tobacconists.

Parked vehicles that are obstructing traffic are towed away in a very short time, at the owner's or driver's expense.

Automobile Clubs

ÖAMTC (Österreichischer Automobil-, Motorrad- und Touringclub), Schubertring 3, A-1010 Vienna (tel. 0222/71-19-97), is the leading auto club of Vienna.

You may also want to avail yourself of the services of ARBÖ (Auto-, Motor- und Radfahrerbund Österreichs), Mariahilferstrasse 180, A-1150 Vienna (tel. 0222/853-53-57).

Motorcycles

The same requirements as for operating cars in Austria hold for operating motorcycles.

Both drivers and passengers of motorcycles must wear crash helmets. Lights must be kept on when the vehicle is being driven.

Car Rentals

Many visitors to Austria say that the only thorough way to see the landscape is with a car, and in a country where the most scenic valleys are sometimes inaccessible by train, you'll find that renting a car is usually the best way to travel once you get there.

If you're a skier, you needn't worry about driving in Austria even in winter. Access to the mountain ski resorts is so important to the nation's economy that Austria maintains some of the best snow-removal equipment in the world. Of course, you should exercise increased caution and slower speeds on alpine roads, but the truth is that most of the major highways are free of snow even in the dead of winter.

Renting a car is easy. All drivers in Austria must have been in possession of a valid driver's license for at least one year prior to the rental of the vehicle. They must also present a valid passport at the time of signing the rental agreement. Drivers not in possession of a major credit card must pay a minimum deposit, plus the estimated cost of the rental and the estimated tax in advance.

Budget Rent-a-Car is one of the least expensive major car-rental companies and has more than a dozen locations throughout Austria. These include all of the country's major airports, such as Vienna, Innsbruck, and Salzburg, as well as convenient locations within such major cities as Innsbruck, Klagenfurt, and Linz. The cheapest car available at press time is a two-door Ford Fiesta, with manual transmission and room for up to four passengers. If a car is reserved at least two business days in advance, the rate is $159 per week with unlimited mileage, plus 21% tax. This price does not take into account the seasonal price reductions often publicized for the summer months, which may be in effect at the time of your trip.

A word about insurance: Like its competitors, Budget will offer you an optional insurance policy known as a collision damage waiver (CDW). If you accept it, you'll be charged around $8.65 per day. Its advantage is that it allows you to waive any financial responsibility for eventual damage to your car (even if it isn't your fault) in the event of an accident. Clients who choose not to take the extra precaution (I always take it) are liable for the first $600 worth of damage if an accident does occur. The amount of potential liability for uninsured renters at Hertz and Avis is almost twice that amount, and the price of the CDWs is higher than that for the same waiver at Budget. For more information, contact Budget by calling their 24-hour toll-free number, 800/527-0700, and ask for the international department.

Hertz maintains 25 offices in Austria. To qualify for the cheapest rates, clients must book a car in advance. For up-to-date tariffs and more information, call toll free 800/654-3131 within the U.S. or 800/268-1311 in Canada (in Toronto, dial 416/245-2211).

Avis has some 24 locations in Austria, as well as a toll-free reservations number for U.S. residents: 800/331-2112. Its rates are competitive with Budget's and Hertz's. Canadians should call toll free 800/268-2310.

National, through its affiliate, **Europcar,** offers 12 locations in Austria, many of them at airports. If given sufficient notice, the staff will make arrangements to have cars delivered to reasonable locations within Austria. For information in the U.S. and Canada, call toll free 800/CAR-RENT.

BY TRAIN

Rail travel is superb in Austria, with fast, clean trains taking you through scenic regions. If you don't have a car, this is the preferred way to travel, as trains will take you to nearly all places in Austria, except for remote hamlets tucked away in almost inaccessible mountain districts. Many other services tie in with railroad travel, among them car or bicycle rental at many stations, bus transportation links, and package tours, including boat trips and cable-car rides.

On the 3,600-mile railroad system linking Austria with all of Europe, fares are based on mileage, with the ticket tariff being different for local and express trains. Main lines are electrified and mainly, except in rough mountain areas, double track. Branch lines are diesel-powered on single tracks. Some private short lines and narrow-gauge railroads still use steam power. Most trains have both first- and second-class seating arrangements, first-class travel costing about 50% more than second. Seats can be reserved in advance.

If you travel by train in Austria, chances are you'll take an Inter-City Express Train, which connects Vienna with all major cities in the country, including Salzburg, Klagenfurt, Graz, and Linz. A train trip from Salzburg to Vienna takes about three hours.

Eurailpass

Both Hungary and Austria are part of the Eurail system, and a Eurailpass is good for unlimited trips on all routes of the Austrian Federal Railways and on many Danube boats. For many years travelers to Europe have been taking advantage of the Eurailpass, one of the continent's great travel bargains. The ticket entitles bona fide North American residents to unlimited first-class travel over the 100,000-mile national railroad networks of Western European countries, except Great Britain. Passes may be purchased for as short a period as 15 days or for as long as three months.

The pass cannot be purchased in Europe, but you can buy yours before you go from travel agents in all towns and from railway agents in such major cities as New York, Montréal, Los Angeles, and Chicago. The Eurailpass is also available at the offices of CIT Tours Corp., the Swiss National Railways, the German Federal Railroads, and the French National Railroads, all of which have offices in major U.S. cities.

The Eurailpass is valid for first-class travel. Vacationers planning a trip can secure the pass for $320 for 15 days, $398 for 21 days, $498 for one month, $698 for two months, and $860 for three months.

Fifteen-day or one-month tourists have to estimate the rail distance to determine if such a pass is to their benefit. To obtain full advantage of the ticket for the shorter periods, you'd have to spend a great deal of time on the train. Obviously, the two- or three-month traveler gets the greatest economic benefits, making the Eurailpass ideal for extensive trips.

The advantages are tempting: no tickets, no supplements—simply show the pass to the ticket collector, then settle back to enjoy the scenery. Seat reservations are required on some trains. Many of them have couchettes (sleeping cars), for which an additional fee is charged.

Eurail Saverpass is a good money-saving ticket offering discounted 15-day travel, but only if groups of three people travel constantly and continuously together between April and September, or if two persons travel constantly and continuously together between October and March. The price of a Saverpass, valid all over Europe and good for first class only, is $230 per person.

Eurail Youthpass is a single, convenient card designed for passengers under 26 years of age. It gives you one or two months of unlimited second-class (coach) rail travel in Eurailpass countries. Rates are $360 for one month and $470 for two months.

Eurail Flexipass is a time-flexible Eurailpass ticket giving travelers 9 days of first-class rail travel that can be used either consecutively or otherwise in 17 countries within one 21-day period. It costs $340 and assures 9 days of travel of your choice without the feeling you're losing travel days after you have validated your pass, if you elect to stay in one place a little longer.

Austrian Rail Passes

You can hop around Austria by rail using a **Rabbit Card,** which is valid for 10 days from purchase and can be used on any 4 travel days of your choice within that period on all Austrian Federal Railways. You can buy vouchers at all major railroad stations in such countries as West Germany, the Netherlands, Switzerland, and Italy, among others, which will be exchanged for a Rabbit Card at your first stop in Austria. You pay in the currency of the country where you pick up the voucher.

For second-class travel, adults pay 890 AS ($64.75); for first class, 1,290 AS ($93.75). Juniors, 6 to 26, are charged 490 AS ($35.50) in second class and 690 AS ($50.25) in first class.

By the way, Rabbit Cards are also good on some buses and on boats plying the Danube within Austria. Inquire when you pick up your voucher.

A network pass, **Bundesnetzkarte,** is sold in one-month versions (also one year, but that's a lot of traveling!). The one-month network pass costs 3,100 AS ($225.25) in second class and 4,650 AS ($338) in first class.

Families or friends traveling together (up to six persons) can make use of the discount mileage pass, known locally as **Kilometerbank.** You buy and prepay for 2,000 kilometers (1,243 miles) of rail transportation for 1,700 AS ($123.50), which can be used by adults and children in second or first class for any trip of more than 44 miles one way. The conductor on the train will deduct mileage from your balance for each passenger using the pass, depending on the length of the trip (up to a maximum of 600 kilometers, or 372 miles—if you travel farther, your additional mileage is free). You are charged only half mileage for a child 6 to 15. A premium factor of 1.5 applies for first-class travel. Discount mileage books are sold only within Austria.

Senior Citizens' Discount

In Austria, women 60 years of age and over and men 65 and over, regardless of nationality, can travel on half-fare passes valid on the Austrian Federal Railways and on the bus systems of the Federal Railways and the Postal Service. The reduction is not applicable on municipal transit lines such as subways, streetcars, or buses, even in towns where the Postal Service operates the local bus service.

To purchase a half-fare ticket, a **Railway Senior Citizen's Identification** must be obtained in advance. This is issued at all railroad stations, at certain major post offices, and at the central railroad stations (Hauptbahnhof) in Frankfurt and Munich, Germany, as a service to foreign visitors using these cities as their air-travel gateways who wish to continue their trip to Austria by rail. In Zurich, Switzerland, both the Senior Citizen's and the Austrian Network passes are available at the rail station at the Zurich airport. At the main rail station, Zurich Hauptbahnhof, you can purchase only the Senior Citizen's pass. This makes it possible to take a train into Austria without having to break your trip at the border.

The price of the identification is 200 AS ($14.50), and it is valid from January 1 to December 31. A passport photo is required, and you must present your passport to prove your age. With this Senior Citizen's Identification, not available in the

United States, you can buy tickets for your half-fare travel in Austria. The reduction is also granted for express trains, first-class tickets, and for checked luggage. If a TEE (Trans European Express) train is used, any supplement must be paid in full.

You can obtain the senior identification by mail from Austria. Send a photostat of your passport (the page with the picture stating your age), one passport photo, and a $25 traveler's check. Write to OeBB—Verkehrseinnahmen- und Reklamationsstelle, Mariannengasse 20, A-1090 Vienna, Austria. With this pass, it is then possible to buy tickets for train and bus travel at half fare. On trains, the 50% reduction is also granted for express trains, first-class tickets, and for checked luggage. EC surcharges, if applicable, have to be paid in full if an EC train is used.

Other Railway Data

For information on short-distance round-trip tickets, cross-country passes, and passes for all lines in the individual provinces, as well as piggy-back transportation for your car through the Tauern Tunnel, check with the Austrian National Tourist Office, Austrian Federal Railways, 500 Fifth Ave., New York, NY 10110 (tel. 212/944-6880).

Bicycle Rental

From the beginning of April until the beginning of November, you can rent a bicycle at leading Austrian railroad stations.

A photo identification must be presented at the time of rental. The charge is 80 AS ($5.80) per day, which is reduced to 40 AS ($2.90) if a railroad ticket to the point of rental is held. You can reserve a bicycle in advance. The vehicle can be returned where it was rented or to any other Austrian railroad station during business hours.

BY BUS

This is the third major means of getting about in Austria, although it is perhaps less desirable than traveling by car or train. Nevertheless, the country has adequate bus or motor-coach services run by federal and local authorities as well as by private companies. There are about 1,800 scheduled lines, including charter trips and excursions originating in tourist centers. The buses of Austria have an enviable safety record.

The motor-coach system of the **Austrian Postal Service** will take you into remote mountain hamlets. On a nearly 19,000-mile network of lines, the 1,500 Postal Buses go almost everywhere. Whether you're going to a ski resort at the height of the winter season or in the busy summer, I advise you to make reservations for Postal Bus travel. Information about Postal Service motor-coach travel is given in the Austrian Motor Coach Schedule (Kursbuch), or you may ask at Postal Travel Agencies in Vienna, Linz, and Graz; post offices in tourist areas; or the Austrian Federal Railways.

Buses will take longer to reach your destination than do the trains, but this has advantages, giving you the chance to sit back and see some of the most beautiful scenery in Europe. Routes, timetables, and prices are to be found in the Austrian Bus Guide.

Europabus offers excursions and tours with guaranteed departures. They are Circular Tour of Austria, a five-day trip; the Royal Monarchy Tour, eight days; Hungarian Rhapsody, three days; and Excursion to Budapest, two days. Information on Europabus is available at Generaldirektion der Österreichischen Bundesbahnen, Kraftwagendirektion, Elisabethstrasse 9, A-1010 Vienna (tel. 0222/7501 or 0222/71101), and at Blaguss Travel International, Wiedner Haupstrasse 15, A-1040 Vienna (tel. 0222/501-80, ext. 125).

BY AIR

The flag carrier of Austria, **Austrian Airlines** (AUA), has a modern and well-maintained fleet of planes linking Vienna not only to the capitals of Europe but also to leading cities in Austria, including Salzburg, Linz, and Graz. Linz to Frankfurt, Germany, is a convenient run if, for instance, you have a return ticket on a line such as Lufthansa from Frankfurt to New York.

If you want information on Austrian Airlines before you leave home, check with their office at 15 W. 50th St., New York, NY 10017 (tel. 212/307-6226, or toll free 800/843-0002 outside New York State).

Austrian Air Services (A.A.S.) has daily scheduled domestic flights connecting Vienna with several capitals of federal provinces: Graz, Klagenfurt, Linz, and Salzburg. The timetable for these flights is adjusted to the schedule of international flights. Austrian Airlines is the general representative for A.A.S.

Tyrolean Airways' regular flight network consists of up to four flights per day between Innsbruck and Vienna and daily flights between Innsbruck and Frankfurt and Innsbruck and Zurich, as well as four flights per week between Innsbruck and Graz. Tyrolean services are included in computerized reservation systems. Therefore, reservations are accepted in travel agencies as well as by Austrian Airlines, Lufthansa, Swissair, and other IATA airlines, and at the Tyrolean offices at Innsbruck Airport (tel. 0512/81-77-70) and in Vienna at Opernring 1 (tel. 0222/56-36-74). All published IATA fares to and from Innsbruck are applicable on Tyrolean Airways service. Tyrolean's Frankfurt, Zurich, and Vienna service provides ideal international connections with those gateways.

BY BOAT

Why not take a boat trip on the Danube or on one of Austria's beautiful lakes?

Passenger boats are operated by the **First Danube Steamship Co.** (Erste Donau-Dampfschiffahrts-Gesellschaft, or DDSG), with main offices at Handelskai 265, A-1021 Vienna (tel. 0222/21-75-00). Regular trips are made by the company's White Fleet on a daily schedule from April to October. Special excursions are also available. A 20% reduction in fare is yours if you purchase a round-trip ticket. Also, a family of either two adults and one child or one adult and two children is entitled to a 50% discount. Children under 6 ride free, and those from 6 to 15 go for half fare. International railroad tickets are valid on the Danube River boats, but with a supplement added. You must present your rail ticket at the DDSG ticket counter before embarking. These boats do not transport cars.

There are also scheduled trips between Vienna and Budapest, Hungary, but you must have a valid passport and a visa.

Austrian Federal Railways has scheduled boat service, usually operating between May and September, on the following Austrian lakes: Wörther See, Ossiacher See, Millstätter See, Traunsee, Mondsee, Hallstätter See, Grundlsee, Attersee, Zeller See, Achensee, Plansee, and Bodensee (Lake Constance).

The Lake Constance boats visit the most popular tourist destinations daily from May to October. A special ticket, the **Bodenseepass,** is valid for 15 days. On 7 of the 15 days, you can go on excursions on any scheduled boat. Also, during the time the pass is valid, the holder can purchase tickets at reduced fares for any railroad, bus, and cable-car trips in the Lake Constance area.

Information on Lake Constance offerings is available at Schiffshafen, A-6900 Bregenz (tel. 05574/22-868).

On Lake Wolfgang in the Salzkammergut lake district, Austrian Federal Railways boats connect villages around the lake. A one-day pass permits repeated trips in any direction.

---

3. The Grand Tour of Austria

If your time is severely limited and you can only skim the surface of the attractions of this alpine country, you may want to take a grand tour of its highlights. Our trip begins with the assumption that you're coming from either Germany or Switzerland, perhaps having already traveled with our companion guides, *Frommer's Germany* and *Frommer's Switzerland and Liechtenstein*.

Allow 15 days for this tour and be prepared for some fast traveling.

Day 1: We begin at Bregenz on Lake Constance, with city sightseeing, exploring the old quarter, and taking in the medieval gates and walls. In the afternoon, take an excursion to Pfaender by cable car for a view of the lake or else take a boat trip on Lake Constance. Remember that the Bregenz Festival is from mid-July to mid-August.

Day 2: Still based in Bregenz, you have a choice of three different excursions. You can go on a full-day bus ride to Schröcken or take a circular bus trip to the Bregenz Forests, the Flexen Pass, Bludenz, and Feldkirch. Another possibility is to take a circular bus trip to Partenen, the Silvretta mountains, Landeck, and the Arlberg.

Day 3: Take the morning train to Innsbruck, passing through some of Europe's most magnificent alpine scenery. Spend the afternoon sightseeing in Innsbruck, exploring the medieval city at the foot of the majestic Nordkette mountain range. Visit the Hofkirche with its impressive tomb of Emperor Maximilian I, the imperial palace, the old town, the Goldenes Dachl, the Ferdinandeum Tyrol Museum, the Tyrol Museum of Popular Art (housing the best collection of this kind in the world), and Ambras Castle. In the evening, see a folklore performance.

Day 4: Still based in Innsbruck, take the morning cable car to Hafelekar at 7,400 feet for a panoramic view of the Tyrolean Alps. In the afternoon, go from nearby Igls by cable car to Patscherkofel at 7,370 feet, or else take a half-day excursion to the Alps: the Ziller Valley, the Gschnitz Valley, perhaps the Stubai Valley or Achensee.

Day 5: In the morning, take the train from Innsbruck to Salzburg, the four-hour trip taking you past green valleys and beautiful Austrian villages. Spend the afternoon sightseeing in one of the most colorful cities of Europe, where Mozart was born in a building that is among the featured attractions. In addition, see the cathedral, St. Peter's Abbey with its 4th-century catacombs, the impressive Renaissance and baroque churches, the Festival Halls, the Mirabell Palace with its verdant gardens. If possible, attend the Salzburg Festival, which runs from late July until the end of August. Or you can see a show of the marionettes, perhaps attend a concert or a folkloric program in the evening.

Day 6: In the morning, while still based in Salzburg, visit the Hohensalzburg Fortress, the huge fortified castle that dominates the skyline, and walk through the numerous courtyards and arcades. Take a guided tour through the attractive collections in the state rooms (45 minutes). In the afternoon, visit Hellbrunn Palace on the outskirts of the city, a magnificent baroque structure with formal gardens and trick fountains; or take a half-day excursion to one of the following areas: Gaisberg, the Salzkammergut lake district, or the salt mine of Dürnberg near Hallein.

Day 7: In the morning, take an express train from Salzburg to Linz on the Danube (1½ hours). See the center of this interesting, lively city, and later, still in the morning, take the riverboat down to Vienna (a 10-hour trip). The First Danube Steamship Company operates this service from May to September, in other seasons, take the train from Linz to Vienna (3 hours). Along the Danube, you'll see magnificent abbeys, ancient towns, and historic ruins.

Day 8: Spend the morning sightseeing in Vienna, visiting such landmarks as St. Stephen's Cathedral, the Hofburg Palace, the Church of the Capuchin Friars (housing the burial vault of the Habsburg emperors), and the Museum of Fine Arts, one of the world's four ranking collections of paintings and archeological treasures. In the afternoon, stroll through the old streets of the Inner City, having a close look at the churches and palaces, and go to Belvedere Palace and walk through its sprawling gardens. Treat yourself to a relaxed hour in that singularly Viennese institution—a coffeehouse where you can sample a delicious pastry and have a cup of coffee with a top hat of whipped cream. In the evening, go to the opera or attend a theater performance, perhaps a concert. Note that the Vienna Festival is from late May to late June.

Day 9: In the morning, while you're still in Vienna, pay a visit to the summer residence of the Habsburg emperors with its splendid state rooms and its beautiful gardens, or attend the morning practice of the white Lippizaner stallions at the Spanish Riding School. In the afternoon, make a half-day excursion into the surroundings of Vienna, stopping over at the ancient Cistercian abbey of Heiligenkreuz and the convent of Mayerling, the site of the tragic death of Crown Prince Rudolph. Continue through romantic Helenental to the spa and holiday resort of Baden before returning to Vienna. In the evening, go to one of the *heurigen* in Grinzing, where fun-loving people eat, drink, and sing along with Schrammel musicians.

Day 10: Take a full-day excursion—on your own or else arranged by one of the various travel agencies. The most interesting for the immediate environs is a bus trip through the Wachau. You can visit the old town of Melk and its Benedictine abbey. This is the world's largest monastic edifice, with a church, library, and elegant state rooms. You can go by boat down the Danube to Dürnstein, the ancient town between the river and the vineyards, with the ruins of a historic fortress high up on a hill, and then take the bus to Göttweig, the superb abbey with its fine architecture and rich collections. Have dinner in a vaulted restaurant before returning to Vienna.

Day 11: In the morning, take a train from Vienna to Graz, a journey of 3½ hours, going via the Semmering Pass, the oldest mountain railroad line in Europe. In the afternoon, take a walk through the center of Graz to see the old main streets and the major square. Go up to Schlossberg by funicular and see the Clock Tower and the old fortifications. Stroll by the Landhaus with its arcaded Renaissance courtyard and past Emperor Ferdinand II's mausoleum, then ride out to Eggenberg Palace and visit the Hunting Museum and the game preserve in the palace grounds.

Day 12: In Graz in the morning, visit the Joanneum Museum of the Province of Styria, with its prehistoric collection, and the armory, the richest of its kind in the world. In the early afternoon, take a train to Villach, passing through the forests and mountains of Styria, which is called the green province. The ride takes 5 hours.

Day 13: In the morning, stroll through the old quarter of Villach, seeing the Town Hall and Paracelsus House. In the afternoon, take an excursion to Kanzelhöhe and Ossiacher See or visit the mountain resort of Mallnitz.

Day 14: In the morning, take the train from Villach to Lienz (3 hours), going through the valley of the Drau River. In the afternoon, walk through the old streets of town, shop for souvenirs, and visit the museum of Bruck Castle. Go by chair lift to Hochstein or by cable car to Zettersfeld.

Day 15: Take one of the most rewarding full-day excursions in Austria by exploring the Grossglockner, that high alpine road to Heiligenblut, one of the most scenic villages in all the Alps. Then go on to Franz-Josefs-Höhe at the flank of the country's highest mountains (12,470 feet).

Day 16: Armed with our companion guide, *Frommer's Italy,* head for the sunny south and such resorts as Cortina d'Ampezzo or such major art cities as Venice.

But know that you will have only skimmed the surface of the attractions of Austria, and hope that surely there will be a second trip or perhaps a third.

TOURS

Is this the year for your trip to Europe? Or has fluctuating currency made you afraid that if you go, you might have to stay in undesirable hotels and search long and hard for inexpensive eating places in order to see the things you've wanted to in the country or countries of your choice?

Don't despair. It is still possible to make affordable trips to see the highlights of many European countries and stay in first-class hotels, dine well, and visit the outstanding attractions by going on a tour. With all the features provided by a good tour group, you can know ahead just what your visit will cost, and you won't be bothered with such matters as having to arrange your own transportation in the countries where language might be a problem, look after your luggage, and other requirements of travel that can make or break your enjoyment of a European journey.

Whether you have a few days or several weeks for your trip, don't put off your European travel just because you're timid or because of economic uncertainty. Your tour will be paid for in advance, so currency changes can't make it cost more.

Consult a travel agent for the best offerings in effect at the time of your visit.

An investment in travel is an investment in memories that will last you all your life.

---

4. Alternative and Special-Interest Travel

Mass tourism of the kind that has transported vast numbers of North Americans to the most obscure corners of the map has been a by-product of the affluence, technology, and democratization that only the last half of the 20th century was able to produce.

With the advent of the 1990s, and the changes they promise to bring, some of America's most respected travel visionaries have perceived a change in the needs of many of the world's most experienced (and sometimes jaded) travelers. There has emerged a demand for specialized travel experiences whose goals and objectives are clearly defined well in advance of an actual departure. There is also an increased demand for organizations that can provide like-minded companions to share and participate in esoteric travel plans.

This yearning for a special-interest vacation might be especially intense for a frequent traveler whose expectations have already been defined by earlier exposure to foreign cultures.

With that in mind, the author of this guide hopes to enhance the quality of his readers' travel experiences by including the following section.

SENIOR CITIZEN VACATIONS

One of the most dynamic organizations in the world of postretirement studies for senior citizens is **Elderhostel,** 80 Boylston St., Boston, MA 02116 (tel. 617/426-7788). Established in 1975 by Martin Knowlton, a retired engineer and professor of political science, it is, quite simply, one of the most creative forces in the lives of senior citizens. Today, Elderhostel maintains a wide array of programs throughout Europe and the world, including Austria and Hungary. Most courses last for around three weeks, representing remarkable value, considering that airfare, hotel accommodations in student dormitories or modest inns, all meals, and tuition are included. Currently, three weeks with all of these included cost a surprisingly low $2,650 to $2,925 for a program in St. Pölten, for example. Courses involve no homework, are ungraded, and focus on the social and political sciences. Even field trips are related to the academic discipline being studied in the classroom.

In no way is this to be considered a luxury vacation, but rather an academic fulfillment of a type never possible for senior citizens until several years ago. Participants must be over the age of 60. However, if a pair goes as a couple, only one needs to be older than 60. Meals are the kind of solid, no-frills fare most college undergraduates know only too well. A frequently unpublicized side benefit of this program is the safety in which many older single women can travel. Some 70% of the participants are women, who understandably prefer to travel with a goal, an orientation, amid like-minded individuals waiting for them at the end of their transatlantic airplane ride.

Anyone interested in participating in one of Elderhostel's programs should write for their free newsletter and a list of upcoming courses and destinations.

One company that has made a reputation exclusively because of its all-inclusive tours for senior citizens is **SAGA International Holidays.** Established in the 1950s as a sensitive and highly appealing outlet for aged (mature) tour participants, they prefer that joiners be at least 60 years old or older.

For more information, get in touch with SAGA International Holidays, 120 Boylston St., Boston, MA 02116 (tel. toll free 800/669-7242).

EDUCATIONAL AND STUDY TRAVEL

Although many Austrian people have a knowledge of English, it is always a greater pleasure to travel in their country if you can speak, even read, their language, which is primarily German. The reputation of Austrian educational institutions is outstanding. Universities, technical colleges, and private schools in various cities offer summer courses for students from all over the world.

You can enroll in programs embracing such subjects as the German language and Austrian culture, the literature of Austria (in German), social sciences, and international law. Other languages are also offered, such as Russian and Serbo-Croatian, with introductions to the cultures of these countries. Extensive music seminars and courses are available, and sports programs include camps for young people interested in soccer, skiing, and tennis, with language as an adjunct.

Information on Austrian summer schools can be obtained from the **Austrian Culture Institute,** 11 E. 52nd St., New York, NY 10022 (tel. 212/759-5156). Copies of a summer schedule are available from the **Austrian Press & Information Service,** 31 E. 69th St., New York, NY 10021 (tel. 212/288-1727).

Other language courses are offered, ranging from two to six weeks in length, during the summer. In Vienna and Salzburg, in small classes, students can become proficient in speech communication and enrich their appreciation of Austrian culture and the Austrian way of life. Business German is an option. Included in the cost of such a course is bed-and-breakfast, with lunch available.

For information on these latter classes, depending on the city that interests you, write to the **Salzburg International Language Center,** Moosstrasse 106, A-5020 Salzburg (tel. 0662/84-44-85), or to **SPIDI** (Spracheninstitut der Industrie), Lothringerstrasse 12, A-1031 Vienna (tel. 0222/752-506-23).

SPAS AND HEALTH RESORTS

Austrians have long been aware of the therapeutic faculties of mineral water, thermal springs, and curative mud within their own country. More than 100 spas and health resorts are to be found here, including the Oberlaa Spa Center on the southern hills of Vienna, utilizing the hidden resources of nature to cure and prevent physical ailments and in pursuit of therapy and rehabilitation. These spas and health centers are comprehensive and offer many-sided aspects of contemporary medical care, from the skin in.

You can "take the waters" at baths (*baden*), with springs ranging from thermal brine to thermal sulfur water, some rich in iodine or iron, some with radon. Users of these facilities have found them effective in treatment of digestive troubles, rheumatism, cardiac and circulatory diseases, and gynecological and neurological ills, to name just a few of the many physical ailments that are eased at various health centers.

Information about these spas and the treatment to be found is available from **Österreichischer Heilbäder- und Kurorteverband,** Josefplatz 6, A-1010 Vienna (tel. 0222/512-19-04). Ask for a copy of their brochure, *Nature the Healer: Spas and Health Resorts in Austria.* You can also learn about "Kneipp Cures," a method developed in the 19th century as a restorative treatment and still hailed as "a magic formula in the world of natural medicine."

MILEAGE BETWEEN AUSTRIA'S MAJOR CITIES
Distance in Miles

	Arlberg	Bregenz	Brenner	Eisenstadt	Graz	Innsbruck	Kitzbühel	Klagenfurt	Linz	Salzburg	VIENNA	Zell am See
Arlberg		58	93	394	369	71	130	283	262	189	365	161
Badgastein	193	251	143	272	168	123	63	81	139	63	243	32
Bad Ischl	224	282	174	194	143	154	86	139	62	35	165	87
Bregenz	58		151	452	404	128	188	340	319	247	423	223
Brenner	93	151		344	297	23	80	233	212	127	315	115
Eisenstadt	394	452	344		109	321	253	183	145	206	31	254
Feldkirch	34	23	128	429	381	105	164	317	296	224	399	199
Graz	369	404	297	109		276	217	87	150	178	123	186
Innsbruck	71	128	23	321	276		59	212	191	119	294	94
Kitzbühel	130	188	80	253	217	59		153	124	51	227	35
Klagenfurt	283	340	233	183	87	212	153		168	158	195	131
Krems	339	397	289	88	141	269	201	207	90	154	47	202
Linz	262	319	212	145	150	191	124	168		77	116	137
Salzburg	189	247	127	206	178	119	51	158	77		186	52
Spielfeld	399	435	328	131	31	299	248	88	181	209	144	200
Villach	259	316	209	200	111	188	129	24	185	120	219	89
VIENNA	365	423	315	31	123	294	227	195	116	186		228
Zell am See	161	223	115	254	186	94	35	131	137	52	228	

OPERA TOURS

On a cultural note, **Dailey-Thorp Travel,** 315 W. 57th St., New York, NY 10019 (tel. 212/307-1555), has been in business since 1971. It is probably the best-regarded organizer of music and opera tours in America. Because of its "favored" relation with European box offices, it's often able to purchase blocks of otherwise unavailable tickets to such events as the Salzburg Festival, the Vienna, Milan, Paris, and London operas, or the Bayreuth Festival in Germany. Tours range from 7 to 21 days, including first-class or deluxe accommodations and meals in top-rated European restaurants. Dailey-Thorp is also known for its breakthrough visits to operas in Eastern Europe and regional operas of Italy.

SETTLING INTO AUSTRIA

Austria has almost a split personality. The side it has turned to the world—and perhaps the best known—is the glittering life of Vienna in its heyday, a world of romance and gaiety, the city of the Blue Danube (which isn't always so blue), of the waltz and the operetta. No person perhaps evokes this nostalgia for 19th-century Vienna more than Johann Strauss the Younger (1825–99), whose best-known work is, naturally, "The Blue Danube Waltz."

But there's quite a different side to Austria, far removed from the life that revolved around the imperial court in Vienna's heyday. That is the spirit of the mountains, especially in Tyrol, a land of rugged individuality and independence, where man and woman in days gone by had to confront a harsh nature and control it to survive.

To understand Austria is to know the baroque. In this sense baroque isn't a mere architectural style: it defines the people as they lived. It suggests the condition of their soul at the time. Just as the architecture is flamboyant and theatrical, so were the people of Vienna. Much of that same style lives on today.

The theater has been an important part of the life of Vienna since the 18th century. Even with electricity shortages in those dark and dim days of foreign occupation following their defeat in World War II, the Viennese still considered the lights of the theater essential, some ranking this as important as providing power to hospitals.

The Austrians have worked hard to rebuild their country in the aftermath of war and occupation. In some ways they are becoming as efficient as the Swiss. And how unlike their legendary character!

While Germans (except in southern Germany) greet you by saying "Guten morgen" or "Guten tag," in Austria the traditional greeting is "Grüss Gott," which translates more or less as "May God greet you." It's used by everyone—religious or not.

Nearly all Austrians worthy of the name still maintain part of their traditional dress. Some of these designs have not changed for centuries. You'll still see men in loden jackets (most often Styrian gray with green lapels) and shorts made of stout leather and called lederhosen. Felt hats are adorned with a feather or, more macho, a tuft of chamois hair. Women are known for their dirndl, a style that long ago came to America. Austrians view their national dress as part of their inheritance, to be passed on from one generation to the next.

They wisely have come to blend a respect for their proud traditions and former greatness with a kind of benign tolerance for the realities the present world has brought to them.

Today, like Switzerland, Austria is a neutral country, and maybe for that very reason the people can be more relaxed and hospitable to strangers, knowing as they do that their hour has come and gone upon the world stage. From Vienna to remote East Tyrol, the Austrian is now prepared to enjoy life on his or her own terms, without some emperor or dictator determining the course of the land.

1. The Austrians

In this section, you will be introduced to a fascinating people, the Austrians, as we present a brief survey of their history, religion, government, language, music, literature, and art and architecture.

HISTORY

Austrian history seems to have been preordained by the country's geographical location centering along the Danube, which made it a crossroads and a battleground even in prehistoric times and the meeting point of three cultures—Romanic, Germanic, and Slav. Archeological finds have shown that even before the Iron Age numerous tribes passed through this territory, and about 1000 B.C. the Indo-European Illyrians of the Hallstatt Culture established a high level of barbarian civilization in the upper regions of what is now Austria, followed by the Celts, who moved into the lower alpine areas about 400 B.C. and founded the kingdom of Noricum, with other tribes settling the west in regions now divided between Austria and Switzerland.

The Romans wrested the region from the Celts and other tribal settlers in about 15 B.C., establishing military garrisons and settlements at such strategic locations as Vindobona (Vienna), Juvavum (Salzburg), and Lentia (Linz), with resultant rapid economic and cultural development of the alpine and Danube regions. Roads were built, vineyards and wine making introduced, and Roman law instituted. The spread of Christianity began in about A.D. 300.

The decline of Roman power, culminating in removal of settlers in the 5th century, was speeded by the entrance into the region of Germanic tribes. The mass migration of the Romans left empty lands that were the target of repeated invasions as Teuton rule gave way to that of Huns, Avars, and then Magyars, until the region was taken over by the Bavarians from the northwest, under Frankish leadership. When Charlemagne became king of the Franks in A.D. 768, he established peace with his sword and achieved a more civilized culture.

After Charlemagne's death, the region again became a battleground, with a staggering number of claimants, ranging from Moravian to Magyar (ancestors of today's Hungarians). Finally, the first Austrian dynasty, the Babenbergs, gained control. It was this royal family who fastened onto the fact that territory could better be gained by treaty, inheritance, marriage, and politics than through war, so that the population of the region they controlled grew, with farming, trade, and cities thriving. The aristocracy built their castles at strategic points, and by the end of the 10th century the region was already being mentioned as Ostarrichi, later replaced by the German name, Österreich (Austria).

Following the dying out of the Babenberg dynasty, with the resultant political and military maneuvering by hopeful successors, the Habsburgs moved into the picture, inaugurating an era that lasted more than 600 years after the crowning of Rudolph I in 1273. The Habsburgs, too, suffered the vicissitudes of rulerdom, but during their long reign, although their power was concentrated in Austria, they were to be Holy Roman Emperors and rulers of Austria, Hungary, Germany, Bohemia, Italy, Belgium, Spain, the Netherlands, and other nations and territories in Europe and the New World. The sphere of control of the Habsburgs waxed and waned, while their troops were involved in every conflict that erupted in Europe, with other nations being sometimes ally, sometimes adversary. During their dynastic supremacy the Habsburgs ruled over a wide diversity of ethnic groups as well as geographical areas. Under their umbrella came, at various times, the Slavs, Germans, Magyars, Romanians, Czechs, Poles, Ruthenes, Slovenes, Croats, and Serbs, plus other smaller cultural entities.

During the years of rule by the Habsburg House of Austria, there were 20 emperors and kings, and there was a time, at the height of their dynastic influence, when the sun never set on the Habsburg Empire. Through the family's Spanish line, territories of the New World had been added in the 16th century, thus extending Habsburg possessions despite a breakaway from the dynasty's hegemony by the Swiss in the 14th and 15th centuries. Later, of course, Spain and the Netherlands were to be governed by a different branch of the Habsburg line, separating those countries from Austrian control.

The defeat of the Turks, who moved westward and even laid unsuccessful siege to Vienna in the late 17th century but were finally driven out of Central Europe in 1697, saw Austria begin to emerge as a major European power.

During the reign of Maria Theresa moderate and durable reforms were carried out, and her son, Joseph II, continued her work but with a more radical approach. However, two significant changes were his: the abolition of serfdom and the introduction of complete freedom of religion.

Napoleon, of course, played his part on the stage of Austrian history: French victories brought about the loss of Lombardy, Tuscany, provinces on the Rhine, Italian provinces, Bavaria, Baden, and Württemberg, the last three losses meaning that Germany was withdrawn from the Habsburg Empire. The decimation of Austrian holdings led to the renunciation by Franz II of the title Holy Roman Emperor in 1806, which was just as well, since loss of Salzburg, Inviertel, Galicia, and the Slav lands soon followed.

Under the leadership of Prince von Metternich as foreign minister, and later chancellor, of Austria, after the abdication of Napoleon, many of the Polish and Italian territories lost during this tumultuous era were regained at the Congress of Vienna in 1814–15, and Austria regained its niche as a world power, only to lose it, perhaps irrevocably, through backing the wrong side in World War I and being grabbed by Hitler in the dark days before World War II.

In the mid-19th century, national revolutions tore the Austrian Empire asunder, and many dominions were lost—among them those in Italy and Germany—and Hungary almost went too. But a form of government was declared in 1867 under which Emperor Franz Joseph became ruler of a "Dual Monarchy," Austria and Hungary. This dualism saw Hungary become a constitutional monarchy of which Franz Joseph was king, while Austria remained a full monarchy of which he was emperor. This situation held until 1918, although the rumbles of dissatisfaction among minority national groups within the Dual Monarchy became ever louder. It was not until after the collapse of the Central Powers—Austria, Germany, Turkey, and Bulgaria—in World War I that the last Habsburg abdicated the throne on November 11, 1918, the monarchy was dissolved, and Austria and Hungary became separate republics.

From this review you may have gained the impression that the history of Austria has been somewhat muddled—and you're right. Many historians, in describing the

Holy Roman Empire, have said that it wasn't holy, it wasn't Roman, and it wasn't an empire. But it was in accord with the love of color, pageantry, titles, and the "follow the leader" nature of the Austrian people.

Since World War II and re-establishment of the Austrian republic, withdrawal of occupation forces in 1955 marked the beginning of coalition governments, leading to a stable economy. On the departure of the Soviets in 1955, and the return of property seized as German assets in 1945 and administered for 10 years by Moscow, Austria was given back major industrial plants, oilfields and installations, and the assets of the Danube Steamship Company, in return for money and goods as reparations to the Russians.

In the peace treaty of 1955, the Austrian State Treaty, signed by the United States, Great Britain, France, and the Soviet Union, Austria was recognized as a sovereign, independent, and democratic state, with the four powers declaring they would respect its independence and territorial integrity. The pre-1938 frontiers were guaranteed, political or economic union with Germany was prohibited, human rights and the rights of the Slovene and Croat minorities and of democratic institutions were pledged, and all National Socialist and Fascist organizations were dissolved. The Allied powers guaranteed Austrian neutrality, but this was not mentioned in the treaty.

However, the Austrian federal government passed a constitutional law declaring the country's permanent neutrality and stating that Austria would never in the future accede to any military alliances nor permit the establishment of military bases by foreign states on its territory.

Austria has seen days of glory and of tragedy, and today its people live in the peaceful, neutral, forward-looking remnant of an area chopped out of a once far-flung domain. But you won't find the Austrians mourning the lost empire. The fascinating mélange of nationalities, each of which has infused its racial characteristics and behavior patterns into the rich tapestry of Austria, gives this country an important place in the world.

RELIGION

In a country rife with conflicts of various sorts, it would be odd if there had been no dissension on religious beliefs, and of course there were in Austria. The Protestant Reformation began during the reign of Charles V in the 16th century and spread rapidly during the early years, being accepted by many German princes. Charles wasn't in favor of abandoning Catholicism, but he was too busy with other wars to check the spread of reform. Under Ferdinand I, Austria became a leader in the Catholic Counter-Reformation, a religious conflict that led to the Thirty Years War (1618–48) involving Europe's Catholic and Protestant rulers. Although the Treaty of Westphalia, which ended the war, recognized the right to existence of Protestant states and also the rights of Protestants in Catholic states, this latter guarantee did not include the Austrian Protestants.

Catholicism is still the dominant faith in Austria, although Joseph II, son of Maria Theresa, introduced religious freedom in the closing days of the 18th century.

The Jewish population of Austria was 200,000 in 1934, but, after the Holocaust, that figure had shrunk to 11,000 in 1951. Most Jewish Austrians live in Vienna, as do most of the country's Protestants, the latter once estimated at only 6.2% of the population. Today religious freedom is practiced throughout the country.

GOVERNMENT

The country is a parliamentary democracy, and the head of the Austrian state is the federal president. The country's main legislative bodies are the houses of the Nationalrat and the Bundesrat. They form what is known as the federal assembly. The federal government is headed by a chancellor who, along with cabinet members, conducts any government affairs that are not the responsibility of the president.

In today's government, personal liberty is guaranteed, and the federal constitution prohibits discrimination on the grounds of sex, birth, class, religion, race, status, or language.

The political scene is dominated by the Socialist Party and the People's Party, each of which has achieved varying majorities.

LANGUAGE

The sole official language of the country is, of course, German. But, surprisingly, not everybody speaks it.

Austrians also speak Slovene, Croatian, Czech, or Hungarian. The largest group is the Croatian minority, who live for the most part in Burgenland. The second sizable group is the Slovenes, concentrated generally in southern Carinthia. Thousands of Hungarians live in Burgenland, and the smallest group of all, the Czechs, reside primarily in Vienna.

The difference in dialects between one part of Austria and another is considerable. Sometimes people who live "just across the valley" from each other find it hard to communicate. The Viennese accent is known for its soft lilt (often satirized by Prussian Germans). Many Austrians have what is called a Bavarian accent.

THE PEOPLE

Ethnically, it is estimated that some 98% of the country's population is German. But there has been such a mixture of blood that pure representatives of a single race would be rare exceptions. Taken as a whole, the country is a mixture of Nordic and Dinaric (to a much smaller degree, Mediterranean and Baltic types).

Over the centuries each Austrian province from Burgenland to Tyrol has developed an ethnic and cultural identity. A lot of this had to do with geography. There's a vast difference between life in the alpine regions in the west and in the vineyards that flourish along Austria's eastern border with its former satellite, Hungary. The widely different range in climate and vegetation led to different ways of life, as well as customs and regional apparel.

MUSIC

In music, Austria has had a great history. In the heyday of baroque splendor in the 17th century, the imperial court at Vienna was a flourishing center of musical culture. Even the emperors themselves composed music! It was the most fruitful period of the Habsburg dynasty.

Opera, crossing the Alps from Italy, became an important part of the Viennese court. Vienna quickly established itself as the center of opera in the German-speaking world.

In the final years of the 18th century Vienna became the rendezvous point for the great composers of orchestral music: Wolfgang Amadeus Mozart, Joseph Haydn, Ludwig van Beethoven. Franz Schubert, the fourth of these great composers, was actually a native of Vienna and has been called the most Viennese of composers. In time they would be followed by Anton Bruckner (1824–96), Johannes Brahms, and Hugo Wolf, along with Gustav Mahler (a pupil of Bruckner) and Franz Schmidt.

The operetta, introduced in the second half of the 19th century, was to become something pointedly Viennese in the history of the musical theater. Thus began what was known as the Golden Age of Operetta. The so-called silver age began around 1900, a movement led by Franz Lehár, a Hungarian who is known chiefly for his *Merry Widow*.

Today such events as the Festival of Vienna, the Salzburg Festival, and the Bregenz Festival continue to make Austria a center of world culture.

ART AND ARCHITECTURE

The artistic heritage of Austria, reflecting German, Mediterranean, and Eastern European influences, can be traced from prehistoric times through the Roman era, the Middle Ages, the Renaissance, and up to modern times. Art objects from the late Bronze and early Iron Ages have been found, as well as such examples of Roman art as mosaics and murals from the 2nd to the 4th centuries A.D. The coming of Christianity to the country led to the flourishing of ecclesiastic art, the earliest samples extant being illuminated manuscripts that show Scottish-Irish influence.

Stylized figures in the Byzantine style (8th century) gave way to Romanesque stone and wood sculptures carved to decorate the abbeys and churches that flourished in medieval Austria. Frescoes can be seen in centers of worship throughout the country, along with richly carved and painted altarpieces, panel paintings, and Gothic-style illuminated manuscripts. The influence of the Italian Renaissance is seen in both art and architecture of the later Middle Ages. Tombs of the royalty and nobility became increasingly ornate, as did art in all forms created for the glorification of abbeys and palaces. Trinity columns, statuettes, and busts joined the parade of artistic output during the 16th, 17th, and 18th centuries.

Painting was not of great merit in Austria in the 19th century, but some great art has originated in the country since the dawn of the present century. Such painters as Kokoschka, Klimt, and Schiele are recognized as among the best, with many promising followers springing up in modern times.

In the realm of architecture, when the Turks retreated, failing to capture Vienna, the flowering of the baroque burst across Austria, beginning in Salzburg. The architect Johann Bernhard Fischer von Erlach (1656–1723) brought this style to its zenith. He designed part of the Hofburg, the imperial palace of Vienna. He was rivaled by Lukas von Hildebrandt (1668–1745), who designed the summer palace of Prince Eugene, the Belvedere, which marked the peak of the baroque and rococo in Austria.

During the reign of Maria Theresa (1740–80), the late baroque Theresian style came into its own, and seemingly everybody in the country painted new buildings in Maria Theresa ochre, a color that remains popular to this day.

In time baroque and rococo gave way to neoclassicism, and the period between the Congress of Vienna (1814–15) and the March revolution of 1848 was the Biedermeier period (called the Vormärz).

In the heyday of Franz Joseph I, the famous Ringstrasse, or "Vienna Ring," was developed as a symbol of the wealth and national pride of the Austro-Hungarian Empire.

In spite of war damage, many of the great buildings of Vienna, and Austria in general, remain to delight the generations of today. One glory of the Ringstrasse, the famed Staatsoper (State Opera), was hit by bombs on the night of March 13, 1945, in the closing days of World War II. It was long ago rebuilt.

LITERATURE

Neither the poetry and prose nor the dramatic work of Austrian writers has made much impact on the English-speaking world, perhaps primarily for the very reason that the literary productions of Austria do not translate into our language with the power of the original writing. From the minnesingers of the 12th to the 15th centuries came the great German epic, *The Niebelungenlied,* but even in Austria, such works based on the period of chivalry were little known among the common people. Many later literary efforts are so political in flavor as to preclude wide acceptance outside their own country.

Theater flourishes in Vienna, with the dramatic work of Austrian playwrights being popular even in the festival periods, when many foreigners are likely to be in the audiences, striving to understand the German language.

2. Food and Drink

Cooking has never been ruled by treaties or dates. With the empire gone and the country today a small, neutral republic in Central Europe, Austrian cuisine has survived as one of the last remnants of a vanished empire. The culinary arts not only of Austria but also of Hungary, Yugoslavia, and Czechoslovakia have influenced the cookery you'll eat today.

In the heyday of the empire, the "love thy neighbor" policy was in vogue, perhaps overdone by some Austrian women. Many preferred to take as husband—or as lover—a handsome Hungarian, Yugoslav, or Czech. Perhaps the stunning uniform, especially that of the Hussars, had something to do with the choice. When the women of Vienna started to cook for their men, and the lovers requested dishes like Mama made back in Budapest or Prague, the cuisine of the empire was born. Today Austria has one of the world's most lavish, lighthearted (but not light in calories!), and enthusiastic cuisines.

It's pointless to argue whether a dish is of Hungarian, Czech, Austrian, or even Serbian origin. Sometimes it's virtually impossible to tell which chef stole from the other. Personally, I've always been more interested in my palate's response to the taste than in the province in which a dish originated. And my palate responds well to *Wiener küche* (Viennese cooking), which is the result of centuries of borrowing from foreigners combined with home concoctions.

Paprika and gulasch came from Hungary; dumplings, a mainstay of Viennese cookery today, originated in Bohemia, as did several sauerkraut dishes; Wiener schnitzel may have first pleased diners in Milan. Each province of Austria, from Tyrol to Carinthia, has its own specialties. For example, the Styrians are fond of corn cake and chicken. In Tyrol you'll have the chance to sample one of the area's most popular dishes, groestl (minced veal with onions and potatoes).

Meals in this country are big and hearty, and the Austrians like to eat, taking as many as six meals or snacks a day. These include not only breakfast, with milk, butter, jam, and coffee, but also a *gabelfrühstück* (fork breakfast) at ten o'clock, which usually includes meat, perhaps little finger sausages. Lunch at midday is normally a big, filling repast, and the afternoon *jause* consists of coffee, open-faced sandwiches, and the luscious cakes that Austrian cooks make so well. Dinner may be a large meal, although many Austrians prefer a light repast then. The nightlife crowd often takes supper—perhaps *après théâtre*—before retiring. In other words, Austria is not a dieter's delight.

FOOD

Austrians eat mainly meat dishes, except for fresh fish from the lakes and rivers. Among these, my personal favorite is the salmon trout of the Salzkammergut lake district.

Wiener schnitzel (breaded veal cutlet) is Vienna's most famous meat dish outside Austria. The most authentic local recipes insist that the schnitzel be fried in lard; others prefer butter or at least a combination of the two. On one point everybody agrees: the schnitzel should have the golden-brown color of a Stradivari violin.

The main meat specialty in Austria is boiled beef, or **tafelspitz**, said to reflect "the soul of the empire." It is the *specialité de la nation*. In fact, you won't find a single discriminating Viennese who hasn't, at least once in his or her life, eaten this celebrated dish. Try it at Sacher's in Vienna, or if the price there is too high, then the boiled beef can be ordered at a much cheaper *beisel*, the cousin of a French bistro. Of course, the tafelspitz at Sacher's will probably be served to you at a table graced by a silver candelabrum; at a beisel, the decorative note is likely to be an empty wine bottle holding a candle.

Boiled beef originated during the reign of Franz Joseph I, who liked it for his midday meal. The rest of the kingdom followed his example, and before World War II the most celebrated people of Vienna ordered boiled beef at Meissl and Schadn's, the best-known beef restaurant in Austria in the pre-Nazi era. There, one could choose from two dozen different cuts of beef. It became a ritual to order your favorite cut, and you had really arrived in status if the waiter knew your preference without having to ask. Alas! Meissl and Schadn's—that venerated landmark where the Austrian composer Gustav Mahler used to dine in 1897, when he was chief conductor of the Vienna State Opera—is no more. It was destroyed by Allied bombs during World War II.

Roast goose is served in Austria on festive occasions such as Christmas, but at any time of the year you can order *eine gute fettgans,* a good fat goose. After such a rich dinner, you may want to relax over some wonderful, strong coffee, followed by schnapps.

Soups are usually good in Austria and quite inexpensive. Among the favorites are gulyassuppe (a gulasch soup of—you guessed it—Hungarian origin) and leberknödlsuppe (meat broth with round dumplings containing chicken liver). There are infinite varieties of gulasches, both Austrian and Hungarian. These are usually stews of beef or pork, spiced with paprika. The Austrian version, Wiener gulasch, is usually less highly seasoned with paprika than the Hungarian.

Austrian bread, especially that baked in the ovens of Vienna, is considered among the best in the world. It comes in all shapes, sizes, and colors, made with many different grains and flours. Strudels, too, come in all shapes, sizes, and flavors. I often enjoy a poppyseed yeast strudel. In the baking line, the Lillie Langtry of Vienna, Katharine Schratt, an actress at the Burgtheater, was reported to make a special old Vienna coffee cake, alt Wiener gugelhupf, which was so good that the Emperor Franz Joseph I fell in love with her!

Austrians generally are exceedingly fond of **desserts,** and all over the country you will have the chance to sample Salzburger nockerln, a taste-tempting frothy soufflé. Viennese pastries are also renowned, including chocolate saddle of venison cake, a delightful chocolate-almond concoction.

Even if you're not addicted to eating sweets, there's a gustatory experience you mustn't miss in the city of its origin: a **Sacher torte** in Vienna. This dessert is known all over the world, and many gourmets claim to have the original recipe for the "king of tortes," *die echte.* Master pastry baker Franz Sacher created the Sacher torte for Prince von Metternich, and tourists would often ask Madame Sacher for the recipe but she never gave it to them. Where else but in Vienna would a cake lead to a lawsuit? Demel's sued the Sacher Hotel, each insisting that it had the authentic recipe. The suit became a *cause célèbre.* But the hotel and Demel's still make Sacher torte today and ship it all over the world. You decide for yourself which does it better.

Madame Sacher helped cultivate the legend of Vienna as a citadel of gourmet cuisine. In Robert E. Sherwood's play *Reunion in Vienna,* this fabulous, cigar-smoking hostess was played by Helen Westley. The spirit of Madame Sacher lives on in Vienna and in the hotel she made famous.

DRINK

Austria is celebrated for its wine production—and consumption!—and for having brought the drinking of coffee to a fine art.

Beer, Wine, and Liquors

Austria imposes few restrictions on the sale of alcohol, so except in alcohol-free places, you should be able to order beer or wine with your meal—even if it's 9 in the morning, or earlier, when many Austrians have their first strong drink of the morning, some preferring beer to coffee as a bracer to get them trucking.

In general, Austrian wines are served when new. Most of them are consumed where they are produced and are not known outside the region where they are grown. I generally prefer the white wine to the red, and perhaps you will too.

More than 99% of all Austrian wine is produced in vineyards in eastern Austria, principally Vienna, Lower Austria, Styria, and the youngest province of the country, Burgenland.

The most famous Austrian wine, **Gumpoldskirchen,** comes from Lower Austria, not only the largest province but the biggest wine producer. The center of the Baden wine district—called in Austria the Südbahnstrecke—is the village of Gumpoldskirchen, which gives the wine its name. This white wine is heady and rich, and just a little sweet.

An outer district of Vienna, **Klosterneuburg,** an ancient abbey on the right bank of the Danube, produces what is—arguably—the finest white wine in Austria. Monks have been making wine at this Augustinian monastery for centuries.

The ancient town of Krems, on the left bank of the Danube, produces very popular table wines, including **Kremser Sandgrube.**

The Wachau district, lying to the west of Vienna, also produces some fine wines known for their delicate bouquet, including **Loibner Kaiserwein** and **Duernsteiner Katzensprung.** These wines are fragrant and fruity.

By far the best red wine, and on this there is little disagreement, is **Vöslauer** from Vöslau. It's strong but, even though red, not quite as powerful as Gumpoldskirchen and Klosterneuburger.

From Styria comes Austria's best-known rosé, **Schilcher,** which is slightly dry, fruity, and sparkling.

Because many Viennese visiting the *heurigen* outside their capital didn't want to get too drunk, they started diluting the new wine with club soda or mineral water. Thus the **spritzer** was born, a drink that swept Europe and North America as well. The mix is best with a very dry wine. If you use a sweetish wine, you're likely to get what Marlene Dietrich once called "weak lemonade."

In all except the most deluxe places it is possible to order a carafe of wine (called *offener wein*), which will be much less expensive.

Austrian beers are relatively inexpensive and quite good, and they are sold throughout the land. **Gösser,** produced in Styria, is one of the most favored brews. It comes in both light and dark. In Salzburg, **Augustiner Bräu** is famous, and in Innsbruck, **Adambräu.** The country brews most of its own beer (Vienna is a major production center, and **Schwechater** is the finest beer made in the city).

Two of the most famous liqueurs—beloved by the Austrians—include **slivovitz** (a plum brandy which originated in Croatia) and **barack** (made from apricots, of Hungarian origin).

Imported whisky and bourbon are likely to be lethal in price. When you're in Austria, it's a good rule of thumb to drink the "spirit of the land." In this case, that means wine and beer. It'll be far easier on your budget than Chivas Regal or whatever it is you drink back home.

The most festive drink, in my opinion, is **bowle** (pronounced bole). Austrians, especially the Viennese, often serve this at a party. It was first made for me by the great chanteuse Greta Keller, and I've been a devotee of it ever since. She preferred the lethal method of soaking berries and sliced peaches overnight in brandy. She would then pour three bottles of dry white wine over the fruit and let it stand for another two to three hours. Before serving, she'd pour a bottle of champagne over it! In her words, "You can drink it as a cocktail, during and after dinner, and on . . . and on . . . and on!"

The Heurigen

In 1784 Joseph II decreed that each vintner in the suburbs of Vienna could sell his own wine right on his doorstep to paying guests. And thus a tradition was born which has continued to this day.

Heurig means new wines or, more literally, "of this year." These taverns lie on the outskirts of Vienna, mainly in Grinzing but also in Nussdorf and Sievering. The latter two make a wine so full-bodied that the legend is "one has to bite them!" Most of the heurigen are in a rustic style, with wooden benches and tables. Much of the drinking, however, takes place in vine-covered gardens in fair weather. A green branch hanging above the doorway usually designates a heurige. In some of the more old-fashioned places, on a nippy night there's a crackling fire in an often flower-bordered ceramic stove.

Schmaltzy Viennese songs are often featured. Naturally, there's likely to be not only a gypsy violin but perhaps an accordion or even a zither (remember the movie *The Third Man?*).

Many heurigen today are in fact quite elaborate restaurants; others are still simple, and it's quite acceptable in these to bring your own snacks or else drink the "new wine" with cheese and sausage you buy on the premises.

The wine is surprisingly potent, in spite of its innocent taste.

Once the Viennese came out to the wine districts just after the harvest. Nowadays the heurigen are year-round institutions.

The Ritual of Coffee Drinking

Although it may sound heretical, Turkey is credited with establishing the tradition of the famous Viennese coffeehouse. The Imperial City was successful in fending off two Turkish invasions, one in 1529 and another in 1683. The Turks, in their hasty retreat, left behind bags of coffee, and a legend was born.

It is said that the first coffeehouse opened in Vienna in the mid-17th century. The proprietor of this inaugural *Wiener kaffeehaus* was Frantz Kolschitzky, a notorious rogue.

In the heyday of Vienna, the literati gathered at the Café Central. There you might have encountered Karl Kraus, an ugly little man, almost a hunchback, who was as aggressive as his writings. Or perhaps Stefan Zweig, the man who became known throughout the world for his psychological tales such as *Amok* and *Kaleidoscope.*

In Vienna, jause is a 4pm coffee-and-pastry ritual. Naturally, you select your favorite cake or pastry and, of course, one must not drink Viennese coffee in a café that doesn't evoke memories of Schubert, Mozart, Suppé, Lehár, Strauss, or Beethoven.

On your second visit to a Viennese coffeehouse, the *herr ober* should know at once which table you prefer (your *stammtisch)*, and how you like your coffee!

You can order your coffee several ways—everything from almost milk-pale *(verkehrt)*, which is one part coffee to four parts milk, to mocha (ebony-black coffee served in a delicate demitasse). *Kaffee mit schlagobers* is the easiest, simplest, and most traditional method of preparing coffee in Vienna. Whipped cream is served with it. You might even order *doppelschlag* (double whipped cream).

Turkish coffee is also brewed authentically in Vienna.

---

3. Sports, Summer and Winter

For information about sports to watch or to participate in, contact the **Austrian National Tourist Office,** Margaretenstrasse 1, A-1040 Vienna (tel. 0222/58-72-00). The staff there can put you in touch with the right persons or organizations to help you plan your vacation if you tell them what sports you are interested in.

SUMMER

The mountains and lakes provide plenty of opportunities for all kinds of sports and pastimes.

Hiking and Mountaineering

With more than 70% of Austria's total area taken up by mountains of all shapes and sizes, it's no wonder that outdoor-oriented visitors find the Alps to be a paradise for walking, hiking, and mountain climbing. Paths and trails are marked and secured, guides and maps are available, and there's an outstanding system of huts to shelter you. Austria has more than 450 chair lifts or cable cars to open up the mountains for visitors.

Certain precautions are essential, foremost being to inform your innkeeper or host of the route you plan to take. Also, suitable hiking or climbing shoes and protective clothing are imperative. Camping out overnight is strongly discouraged here because of the rapidly changing mountain weather and the established system of keeping track of hikers and climbers in the mountains. More than 700 alpine huts—many of which are really full-service lodges with restaurant facilities, rooms, and dormitories—are fixed points spaced about four to five hours apart, so that you can make rest and lunch stops. Hikers are required to sign into and out of the huts and to give the destination of the day before setting off in the morning. If you don't show up at a hut as planned, search parties go into action.

If you're advised that your chosen route has difficulties, be wise. Hire a mountain guide or get expert advice from some qualified local person before braving the unknown. Certified hiking and climbing guides are based in all Austrian mountain villages and can be found by looking for their signs or by asking at the local tourist office.

Above all, *obey signs*. Even in summer, if there's still snow on the ground you could be in an area threatened by avalanches. There are other important rules to follow for your own safety if you're going walking, hiking, or mountaineering. You can obtain these from the Austrian National Tourist Offices, from bookstores in Austrian cities, at the branches of various alpine clubs, or at local tourist offices in villages throughout the Alps.

For information about any of the alpine clubs, the principal organization is **Verband alpiner Vereine Österreichs,** Backerstrasse 16, A-1010 Vienna (tel. 0222/52-54-88).

Schools of mountaineering are found in at least three dozen resorts, in all Austrian provinces except Burgenland, with regular courses, mountain tours, and camps for all ages. Distinction is made between summer and winter mountaineering, of course.

Camping

Austria has some 400 campsites placed in its most beautiful areas. If you want to park away from a public campground, you must have the consent of the property owner. Also, you can't park your camp trailer on or beside a public highway unless you have a traction vehicle and obey parking regulations. Some mountain roads are either closed to or not recommended for campers. For details on camping opportunities and the cost at various campsites, ask for the camping list available at the National Tourist Office.

Water Sports

Austria has no seacoast, but from Lake Constance (Bodensee) in the west to Lake Neusiedl (Neusiedl See) in the east, the country is rich in lakes and boasts some 150 rivers and streams.

Swimming is, of course, possible year round if you wish to use an indoor pool or to swim at one of the many health clubs in winter. Recent major developments of swimming facilities at summer resorts, especially those on the warm waters of Carinthia, where you can swim from May to October, and in the Salzkammergut lake district between Upper Austria and Salzburg province, have seen this sport increase greatly in popularity.

The beauty of Austria underwater is attested to by those who have tried **diving** in the lakes. Most outstanding, I am told, are the diving and underwater exploration possibilities in the Salzkammergut lake district and in the Weissen See in Carinthia. You can receive instruction and obtain necessary equipment at both places.

If you prefer to stay on top of the water, you can go sailing, windsurfing, or canoeing on the lakes and rivers.

The sailing (yachting) season lasts from May to October, with activity centered on the Attersee in the Salzkammergut lake district, on Lake Constance out of Bregenz, and on the Lake Neusiedler, a large shallow lake in the east. Winds on the Austrian lakes can be treacherous, but a warning system and rescue services are alert. For information on sailing, get in touch with **Österreichischer Segel-Verband,** Grosse Neugasse 8, A-1040 Vienna (tel. 0222/587-86-88). A recognized sailing license, required for Lake Constance, can be acquired upon examinations through the Chief District Office in Bregenz.

Most resorts on lakes or rivers where **windsurfing** can be safely enjoyed have equipment and instruction available. This sport is increasing in popularity and has been added to the curriculum of several sailing schools, especially in the area of the Wörther See in Carinthia, warmest of the alpine lakes.

If you're interested in shooting the rapids of a swift mountain stream or just paddling around on a placid lake, don't miss the chance to go **canoeing** in Austria. Possibilities vary from slow-flowing lowland rivers such as the Inn or Mur to the wild waters of glacier-fed mountain streams suitable only for experts. Special schools for fast-water paddling operate from May to September at the village of Klaus on the Steyr River in Upper Austria, at Opponitz in Lower Austria on the Ybbs River, and at Abtenau in Salzburg province.

White-water rafting on the Inn River is offered by Feelfree, Gasthaus Zum Löwen, Magerbach, A-6425 Haiming, in Tyrol (tel. 05266/661). An all-inclusive price provides you with equipment such as a wetsuit, waterproof jacket, life jacket, and crash helmet. Participants must be at least 14 years old, in good health, and able to swim.

Austria is a fishing paradise, offering as it does many clear, unpolluted streams, deep rivers, and lakes. You can angle for trout, char, pike, sheat-fish (monster catfish), and pike-perch in well-stocked mountain streams. In the right-hand tributaries of the Danube, you might catch huck, a land-locked salmon that is an excellent fighter and a culinary delight, usually fished for in late fall. The waters of Wörther See in Carinthia sometimes yield the North American big-mouth black bass, with which an owner of Velden Castle once stocked the lake by accident. Intended for a pond on his estate, one barrel fell into the lake and burst, introducing the immigrants from America to a new happy home.

A Sports Potpourri

Hunters find game of all sorts both in the mountains and the lowlands of Austria. If you're a passable shot, you may want to try your skill as a Nimrod here. Who knows? You might bag a roebuck, a marmot, or a chamois in season. For wild boar, foxes, polecats, wild rabbits, and weasel, it's open season all year, but you can't hunt without a license. For the latest information on whether you can bring your sporting guns and ammunition into the country, or where you can secure such equipment, plus facts about where and how to get a hunting license, check with the National Tourist Office.

Golfing, once a pursuit only of a privileged few, has become a sport for everybody who takes the time to learn. One of the country's most outstanding 18-hole courses is at the Murhof in Styria, near Frohnleiten. Others are the Igls/Rinn near Innsbruck, Seefeld-Wildmoos in Seefeld, Dallach on the shores of the Wörther See in Carinthia, Enzefeld and Wiener Neustadt-Foehrenwald in Lower Austria, and the oldest of them all, Vienna-Freudenau, founded in 1901. There are numerous nine-hole courses throughout the country. The season generally extends from April to October or November.

Tennis courts are to be found at most resort hotels and at sports centers.

Ask at a local office of tourist information, at a railroad station, or at your resort hotel if you'd like to rent a bicycle. **Cycling** tracks and paths are laid out so that you can ride across the country untroubled by vehicular traffic.

For a change from land and water sports, why not take to the air? **Gliding,** for which Austria is well suited, can be arranged at many airfields, and instruction is available at Spitzerberg, some 30 miles east of Vienna; at Zell am See in Salzburg province; at Niedr-Oblarn and Graz in Styria; and at Wiener-Neustadt.

Hang-gliding continues its popularity. Facilities for this daredevil sport are spread across the country.

Hot-air **ballooning** is available at Puch near Weiz in Styria.

Personally, I'll stick to **horseback riding,** for which you can rent a mount for one ride or spend your holiday on an Austrian-style ranch.

Besides all these sports in which you can participate, Austria has a wealth of spectator sports, ranging from auto racing to soccer to boat racing to horse racing, plus much more.

Also in the world of sports to be enjoyed in summer, there's **grass skiing,** which doesn't require snow and can be practiced by those who don't care to go high into the Alps to ski on snow. Ask at the Austrian National Tourist Office for a list of resorts providing this sport, as well as for details about centers offering summer snow skiing. As for winter snow sports, read on.

WINTER

The winter-sports scene in Austria is snow-white, with the towering peaks of the Alps, snow-blanketed pastures and forests, and smooth ice on lakes providing such attractions as downhill and cross-country skiing, hot-dogging, ice skating, tobogganing, curling, bobsledding, sleigh riding, and mountaineering for the sturdy hiker.

Skiing

It may have lost world-power status with the death of the empire, but Austria today has world renown for its uphill transportation, which whisks skiers to the snow slopes for their downhill ski runs. Some 3,500 facilities transport passengers on rides of scenic splendor to sites where they can begin their enjoyment of the approximately 12,500 miles of marked runs. Intricate networks cover whole mountainsides so that you don't have to take a step uphill on your own. Ski "circuses" allow skiers to move from mountain to mountain, and a ski "swing" opening up opposite sides of the same mountain ties villages in different valleys into one big ski region.

Shuttle buses, usually free for those with a valid lift ticket, take you to valley points where you board funiculars, gondolas, aerial trains, or chair lifts. Higher up, you may leave the larger conveyance and continue by another chair lift or, even higher up, by surface lift, probably by T-bar.

Austria made its way into winter-sports history through the selection of Innsbruck twice for the site of the Winter Olympics. But skiing here is not the monopoly of stars. It's a popular leisure activity of young and old, mainly because of the climate and topography. Compare the vast ski area transportation network today with that of 1945, when the country had only a dozen cableways, eight mountain railways, and six ski lifts.

The Austrian Ski School is noted for its fine instruction and practice techniques, available in many places: Arlberg; the posh villages of Zürs and Lech/Arlberg, where jet-setters gather; the Silvretta mountains; and Hochgurgl, Obergurgl, Hochsölden, and Sölden in the Tyrolean Ötztal, to name a few. Year-round skiing is possible in the little villages of the Stubaital, through use of a cableway on the Stubai glacier, more than 10,000 feet above sea level. Known to all top skiers in the world is Kitzbühel, another lure to the jet set, as is Seefeld.

Skiing is a family sport in Europe, and ski centers usually have gentle slopes and instruction for youngsters, plus baby-sitting services for the very small. Many places have something extra to offer, since Austria's ski resorts have been working villages for centuries, while skiing facilities are relative newcomers. The Valley of Gastein was known for its medicinal thermal springs long before it became a ski center. The people of Schladming, in the Dachstein mountains, wore their local costumes and lodens before the first cross-country skier came to the high plateau of the little, unspoiled village of Ramsau.

Among the most attractive large-scale skiing areas are the Radstädter Tauern region and Saalbach/Hinterglemm in Salzburg province. Here, as in most of the winter-sports areas, you'll find ski huts with crackling fires in the grates and hot spiced wine or perhaps Jägertee, hot tea heavily laced with rum.

Hot-dogging is an American import to Austria and is a special kind of skiing involving acrobatics, trick skiing, artistic skiing, and ski "ballet." Organized hot-dogger activities usually occur early in the season in such places as Bad Kleinkirchheim, Badgastein, the Kitzsteinhorn near Zell am See, or the Stubai glacier.

Cross-country skiing is popular among those who want to enjoy the winter beauty in quiet. Many miles of tracks are marked for this sport, and special instructors are available.

Other Winter Sports

Tobogganing, called the *luge* in the Winter Olympics, requires no special skills and is a thrill sport for amateurs. Many towns have special runs, and some mountain roads are closed to allow sledding.

Eisschiessen is the alpine form of **curling.** Instead of stones, "sticks" are used—weighted wooden disks with handles.

You can ride horseback in the snow, but it's more romantic to go in a one- or two-horse open **sleigh** to huts in the winter forest for a mug of hot spiced wine.

Whether you wish to indulge in any of these activities in the bracing alpine air or not, at most resorts you can enjoy swimming in an indoor pool, basking in a sauna, playing tennis or ninepins, trying your skill on a rifle range, or working out in the exercise room or gymnasium.

And there's always après-ski festivity, the main drawing card for some winter vacationers.

For the spectator, there are many competitive winter-sports events held at the resorts and elsewhere.

---

4. Austria for Children

If you're undecided as to whether to take your children with you on a visit to Austria, hesitate no longer. Of all the countries I have visited, I recommend Austria as at or near the top of the list of ideal vacation places to share with the young—even the *very* young. The pleasures available for children (which most adults enjoy just as fully) range from seeing the magnificent Lippizaner stallions go through their "airs above the ground" paces at the Spanish Riding School in Vienna, to exciting cable-car and chair-lift rides (to ski or not to ski), boat trips on the Danube, zoos and castles, fortresses and dungeons.

In Vienna, besides the wonders of the Spanish Riding School (which you and your children may have seen in the Disney movie *The Miracle of the White Stallions*), an outstanding attraction is the Prater amusement park, with its giant Ferris wheel, roller coasters, merry-go-rounds, games arcades, and tiny railroad. Even if your kids aren't very interested in the state chambers of palaces, take them to Schönbrunn, where the coach collection and the zoo will surely be enjoyed. In summer, beaches along the Alte Donau (an arm of the Danube) are suitable for swimming. And there's always the lure of the *konditorei,* those shops where scrumptious Viennese pastries are sold.

Salzburg's Hohensalzburg Fortress, complete with dungeon, vies with the trick fountains and zoo at the palace of Hellbrunn on the outskirts as a pleasurable experience for the young. Folklore evenings and performances of the marionettes at the Marionetten Theater hold their own fascination. A children's grotto railway with dwarf and fairytale scenes at Linz, a visit to a salt mine or to ice caves, excursions to the Salzkammergut lakes, yodelers and an alpine zoo at Innsbruck are just a few of the fun things for persons of all ages.

These are rivaled if not topped by Minimundus on the outskirts of Klagenfurt at Wörther See in Carinthia. This "small world," set on a broad stretch of land, has more than 100 miniature models of the best-known buildings of the world, ranging from the Suleiman Mosque in Istanbul to the famous Moulin Rouge nightclub in Paris to the Taj Mahal. Minimundus lets you go around the world in 80 minutes, more or less.

Everywhere in Austria are facilities for summer sports—swimming, boating, mini-golf, hiking—what have you. Perhaps most outstanding, however, are the winter programs for children at ski resorts. At Austria's ski schools former world champions and other racing celebrities take time for the younger pupils, helping them become used to snow, first through play and then through learning to ski. In many winter resorts, ski kindergartens take children from the age of 3 up.

Information on children's ski activities is available from travel agencies and from representatives of the Austrian National Tourist Office (see "Information Before You Go" in the "Fast Facts for Austria," below). Nurseries and play areas are available, so you don't have to worry about your child being kept hard at work on skis the entire day. Most schools have equipment to rent.

Baby-sitting services are available through most hotel desks or by applying at the Tourist Information Office in the town where you are staying. Many hotels have children's game rooms and playgrounds.

---

5. Fast Facts for Austria

What follows is a round-up of data to help ease your adjustment into the country, beginning with—

BANKING: Foreign and Austrian money can be brought into the country without any restrictions, and there is no restriction on taking foreign money out of the country either. Foreign currency and traveler's checks can be exchanged at all banks, savings banks, and exchange counters at airports and railroad stations at the official exchange rate of the day as given out by the Austrian National Bank.

BANKING HOURS: In the federal provinces, banking hours vary according to the region. The exchange counters at airports and railroad stations are generally open from the first to the last plane or train, usually from 8am to 8pm every day. For banking hours in Vienna, see "Fast Facts" in Chapter III.

CLIMATE: At the center of Europe, Austria has a temperature that varies greatly depending on the location. The national average ranges from a low of 9°F in January to a high of 68°F in July. However, in Vienna the January average is 32°F, while for July it's 66°F. A New Yorker who lived in Austria for eight years told me the four seasons were "about the same." In a subalpine climate it's neither very, very hot nor, on the other hand, is it Siberian cold. Snow falls in the mountainous sectors by mid-November. Road conditions in winter can be very dangerous in many parts of the country. The winter air is usually crisp and clear, with many sunny days. The winter snow cover lasts from late December through March in the valleys, from November through May at about 6,000 feet, and all year at above 8,500 feet. The ideal times for visiting Vienna are spring and fall, which have mild, sunny days. "Summer" season generally means from Easter until about mid-October.

CLOTHING: In spring and fall, a few warm pieces and a topcoat or raincoat are advisable. In winter, you'll need a sweater and an all-purpose raincoat, as evenings are cool, especially in the mountain areas. You'll be wise to plan your wardrobe according to where you'll be staying. Vienna is fairly dressy, especially in the evening. Mountain country demands some woollies and sturdy walking shoes, and if you get into alpine activities you'd better have a heavy sweater and a down parka. Don't forget to have boots or shoes with slip-proof soles for winter walking.

CONSULATES AND EMBASSIES: The main building of the **U.S. Embassy** is at Boltzmanngasse 16, A-1090 Vienna (tel. 0222/31-55-11). However, the consular section is at Gartenbaupromenade 2, A-1010 Vienna (tel. 0222/51-451). Lost passports, tourist emergencies, and other matters are handled by the consular section. Embassy and consulate hours are Monday to Friday from 8:30am to noon and 1 to 4:30pm.

The **Canadian Embassy** is at Dr.-Karl-Lueger-Ring 10, A-1010 Vienna (tel. 0222/533-36-91), and is open Monday to Friday from 8:30am to 12:30pm and 1:30 to 3:30pm. The **Australian Consulate,** Mattiellistrasse 2-4, A-1040 Vienna (tel. 0222/512-85-80), receives from Monday to Friday from 9am to 1pm (for visa applications) and 2 to 5pm (for lost passports and other matters). The **British Embassy** is at Jaurèsgasse 12, A-1030 Vienna (tel. 0222/713-15-75), but most tourist emergencies are handled by the British Consulate Section of the British Embassy, Jaurèsgasse 10, A-1030 Vienna (tel. 0222/75-61-17), next door. The consulate is open Monday to Friday from 9:15 to 11:30am.

CRIME/SAFETY: Whenever you're traveling in an unfamiliar city or country, stay alert. Be aware of your immediate surroundings. Wear a money belt and don't sling your camera or purse over your shoulder; wear the strap diagonally across your body. This will minimize the possibility of your becoming a victim of crime. It's your responsibility to be aware and be alert even in the most heavily touristed areas. In recent years, however, Vienna has been plagued by purse-snatchers. In the area around St. Stephen's Cathedral, signs (in German only) warn about pickpockets and purse-snatchers. Small foreign children often approach sympathetic adults and ask for money. As the adult goes for his wallet or her purse, adults rush in and grab the money, fleeing with it. Unaccompanied women especially are victims of this type of thievery; they should never open a purse in public, but hold on to it tightly.

CURRENCY: The basic unit of currency is the Austrian **schilling** (AS), which contains 100 **groschen.** There are coins with denominations of 2, 5, 10, and 50 groschen and 1, 5, 10, and 20 schillings, and banknotes with denominations of 20, 50, 100, 500, and 1,000 schillings. As a general guideline the price conversions in this book have been computed at the rate of 13.75 AS = $1 U.S. (1 AS = 7¢ U.S.).

As for all European countries, the international exchanges are far from stable, and this ratio might be old hat when you go to Austria. As a guide, however, I'm including the following exchanges at the rates given above.

Schilling	U.S.$	Schilling	U.S.$
1	.07	500	36.35
5	.35	600	43.60
10	.75	700	50.90
25	1.80	800	58.15
50	3.65	900	65.45
100	7.25	1,000	72.70
150	10.90	1,100	79.95
200	14.55	1,200	87.25
250	18.20	1,300	94.50
300	21.80	1,400	101.80
400	29.10	1,500	109.05

CUSTOMS: Austrian officials are fairly lenient (and the most tolerant people in the world if you're just arriving from one of the Communist countries, where they really check your luggage!). The duty-free limit is 400 cigarettes or 80 cigars or a pound of tobacco, if you're over 17 and you come from a non-European country. However, if you fly to Austria from the Continent, the limit is reduced to 200 cigarettes or 50 cigars or 250 grams of tobacco. You can also bring in two liters of wine and a liter of liquor (but only .75 liter from a country in Europe). Likewise, you're allowed 10 ounces of cologne and 2 ounces of perfume, along with $100 worth of souvenirs. Most items such as cameras, tape recorders, portable typewriters, sports equipment, or whatever, intended for your personal use, are allowable.

Upon leaving Austria, you're allowed to bring back $400 worth of merchandise into the U.S. without paying additional tax. The duty-free limit on gifts sent home from abroad has been raised to $50.

ELECTRIC CURRENT: Austria operates on 220 volts AC, with the European 50-cycle circuit. That means that U.S-made appliances will need an adapter-converter. Many Austrian hotels stock adapter plugs but not power converters. Electric clocks, record players, and tape recorders, however, will not work well even on converters.

GAMBLING: Casinos are found in at least 11 locations in Austria: Vienna, Velden am Wörther See in Carinthia, Graz, Baden near Vienna, Badgastein in Salzburg province, Salzburg, Seefeld and Kitzbühel in Tyrol, Linz, and Bregenzaand Riezlern/Kleinwalsertal in Vorarlberg. Each has its own style, giving the opportunity to try your luck in a historic downtown palace, a nostalgic spa pavilion, or a rustic alpine mansion, as well as in modern settings.

GUIDES: In the federal provinces, guides are available through the Provincial Tourist Boards or the various city tourist offices.

HOLIDAYS: Bank holidays in Austria are as follows: January 1, January 6 (Epiphany), Easter Monday, May 1, Ascension Day, Whitmonday, Corpus Christi Day, August 15, October 26 (Nationalfeiertag), November 1 and 26, and December 25 and 26.

INFORMATION BEFORE YOU GO: Your travel agent can supply you with the information you wish, or get in touch with the **Austrian National Tourist Office,** whose U.S. representatives are at: 500 Fifth Ave., New York, NY 10110 (tel. 212/ 944-6880); 500 N. Michigan Ave., Suite 544, Chicago, IL 60611 (tel. 312/644-5556); 4800 San Felipe St., Suite 500, Houston, TX 77056 (tel. 713/850-9999); and 11601 Wilshire Blvd., Suite 2480, Los Angeles, CA 90025 (tel. 213/477-3332). In Canada, 1010 Sherbrooke St. West, Suite 1410, Montréal, Québec H3A 2R7 (tel. 514/849-3709); 2 Bloor St. East, Suite 3330, Toronto, ON M4W 1A8 (tel. 416/967-3381); and Suite 1220-1223, Vancouver Block, 736 Granville St., Vancouver, BC V6Z 1J2 (tel. 604/683-5808 or 683-5809).

INFORMATION IN AUSTRIA: Dispensing information for the entire country, the **Austrian National Tourist Office** is at Margaretenstrasse 1, A-1040 Vienna (tel. 0222/58-86-60). It cannot, however, make reservations for you. As you travel throughout the towns and villages of Austria, you'll see signs indicating a fat "i." Most often that will stand for "information," and you'll be directed to a local tourist office where, chances are, you can obtain maps of the area and might even be assisted in finding a hotel should you arrive without a reservation.

LANGUAGE: German is the official language of Austria, but since English is taught in the high schools, it is commonly spoken throughout the country, especially in tourist regions. Certain Austrian minorities speak Slavic languages, and Hungarian is commonly spoken in Burgenland.

METRIC CONVERSIONS: In Austria, you face a whole new way of measuring. Even the temperature will be expressed in Celsius. The conversions below will show you how to change kilometers into miles, grams into pounds, meters into yards, and liters into ounces. Once you get the hang of it, it isn't as hard as it first appears.

THE METRIC SYSTEM—IN A NUTSHELL

LENGTH
1 millimeter = 0.04 inches (*or* less than 1/16 inch)
1 centimeter = 0.39 inches (*or* just under 1/2 inch)
1 meter   = 1.09 yards (*or* about 39 inches)
1 kilometer = 0.62 mile (*or* about 2/3 mile)

To convert kilometers to miles, take the number of kilometers and multiply by .62 (for example, 25km × .62 = 15.5 miles).

To convert miles to kilometers, take the number of miles and multiply by 1.61 (for example, 50 miles × 1.61 = 80.5 km).

CAPACITY
1 liter = 33.92 ounces
        = 1.06 quarts
        = 0.26 gallons

To convert liters to gallons, take the number of liters and multiply by .26 (for example, 50 l × .26 = 13 gal).

To convert gallons to liters, take the number of gallons and multiply by **3.79** (for example, 10 gal × 3.79 = 37.9 l).

WEIGHT
1 gram   = 0.04 ounce (*or* about a paperclip's weight)
1 kilogram = 2.2 pounds

To convert kilograms to pounds, take the number of kilos and multiply by **2.2** (for example, 75kg × 2.2 = 165 lbs).

To convert pounds to kilograms, take the number of pounds and multiply by **.45** (for example, 90 lb × .45 = 40.5kg).

AREA
1 hectare (100m² = 2.47 acres

To convert hectares to acres, take the number of hectares and multiply by **2.47** (for example, 20ha × 2.47 = 49.4 acres).

To convert acres to hectares, take the number of acres and multiply by **.41** (for example, 40 acres × .41 = 16.4 ha).

TEMPERATURE

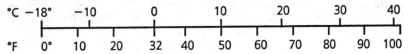

To convert degrees C to degrees F, multiply degrees C by 9, divide by 5, then add 32 (for example 9/5 × 20°C + 32 = 68°F).

To convert degrees F to degrees C, subtract 32 from degrees F, then multiply by 5, and divide by 9 (for example, 85°F − 32 × 5/9 = 29°C).

PASSPORTS AND VISAS: Citizens of the U.S. or Canada need only a valid passport to enter Austria. No visa is required.

PHOTOGRAPHY: You'll want to take lots and lots of photographs in Austria, as it is one of the most beautiful countries on earth. However, take along as much film as you can because film sold in Austria, although readily available, carries a heavy tax.

RADIO: The Austrian Radio network (ÖRF) has English news broadcasts at 8:05am daily. "Blue Danube Radio" broadcasts daily in English from 7 to 9am, noon to 2pm, and 6 to 7:30pm only in the Vienna area. The Voice of America broadcasts have news, music, and feature programs on AM (middle wave here) from 7am to 1pm and in the midafternoon and early evening. It is at 1197 on the dial.

SHOPPING: A large variety of quality items is available to the shopper in Austria. You'll find jewelry, including costume jewelry, leather goods, needlepoint articles, traditional-costume-inspired fashions, knitwear, sportswear and equipment, novelties, and hunting rifles among the many Austrian-made goods offered.

SHOPPING HOURS: In many Austrian stores, hours are 8am to 6pm Monday to Friday and 8am to noon on Saturday. Many stores close for two hours during the middle of the day.

STAYING IN A PRIVATE HOME: If you want to meet the Austrian people at home, sleep in comfortable rooms at moderate rates, and travel without a set itinerary, look for signs that say "Zimmer Frei" attached to the front of a house or to a short post at the front yard gate or driveway. This means the proprietors rent rooms on a bed-and-breakfast basis to travelers. You'll encounter these signs along Austria's highways, and even more so, along some of the most scenic byways.

Such accommodations have hot and cold running water in the bedrooms, although private bath and toilet facilities are rare. (There's usually a toilet on every floor and one bathroom in the house.) A Continental breakfast is served.

Rates for such rooms vary considerably, depending on the type of accommodation provided, but on the average, the charge is from 200 AS ($14.50) per person daily with breakfast included.

Few such homes accept advance reservations, so you just stop in and inquire. When the rooms are filled, the sign is taken down or covered. You can find help in securing accommodations of this kind through the local tourist office.

You may need a few words of basic German, as only a few such proprietors speak a little English. If you're staying for only one night, you may be asked to pay your bill in advance, and it must be paid in Austrian schillings.

Whole families or traveling parties can have the experience of staying on a farm, renting several rooms or even a wing of the house, but generally a stay of at least a week is required and advance reservation through a local tourist office or regional tourist board is necessary. The correct form of address for the local offices is *Verkehrsverein*, then the name of the town near which you wish to stay, and the name of the country, Austria. Regional boards should be addressed by writing to *Landesfremdenverkehrsamt*, followed by the name of the capital of the respective Austrian province, and the name of the country. Your reservation will be confirmed upon receipt of a deposit.

TAXES: A 20% value-added tax (VAT) is included in the list of items sold in Austria. Tourists must pay this VAT at the time of purchase, but can obtain a tax refund on purchases totaling more than 1,000 AS ($72.75) or more per store if the merchandise is taken out of the country unused. You will show the VAT (*MWSt*) as a separate item or will say that the tax is part of the total price. To get the refund, you must fill out a form, U-34, which is available at most stores patronized by tourists. A sign will say "Tax-free Shopping." Get one for ÖAMTC quick refund if you plan to use the option of getting your money at the border. Check whether the store gives refunds itself or uses a service. Sales personnel will help you fill out the form and will affix the store identification stamp. Keep your U-34 forms handy when you leave the country and have them validated by the Austrian Customs officer at your point of departure.

After returning home, mail the validated U-34 form or forms to the store where you bought the merchandise, keeping a copy of each form. The store will mail to your home address a check, bank draft, or international money order covering the amount of VAT refund due you. Information and help in expediting some steps of this process are available at the Austrian Automobile and Touring Club (ÖAMTC), which has instituted methods of speeding up your receipt of the refund. Ask at its offices at major highway checkpoints or at a bank or travel agency handling its arrangements. Check with the Austrian National Tourist Office at one of its North American offices before you go. Ask for the ÖAMTC brochure "Tax-free Shopping in Austria."

TAXIS: In large Austrian cities, taxis are equipped with officially sealed taximeters, which show the cost of your trip in schillings. If a rate change has recently been instituted, there may be a surcharge added to the amount shown on the meter, pending adjustment of the taximeter. Surcharges will be posted in the cab. A supplement is charged for luggage carried in the vehicle's trunk. Zone charges or set charges for standard trips are the rule in most resort areas. Tip the driver 10% of the fare.

TIME: Austria operates on Central European Time, which makes it six hours later than U.S. Eastern Standard Time. It advances its clocks one hour in summer, however.

TIPPING: A service charge of 10% to 15% is included on hotel and restaurant bills, but it's a good policy to leave an additional 5% to 10% (preferably the latter) for waiters and 25 AS ($1.80) per day for your hotel maid.

Railroad station, airport, and hotel porters get 20 AS ($1.45) per piece of luggage, plus a 10-AS (75¢) tip. Your hairdresser should be tipped 10% of the bill, and the shampoo person will be thankful for a 20-AS ($1.45) gratuity. Hatcheckers and toilet attendants are usually given 10 AS (75¢).

TOBACCO: Tobacco is a state monopoly in Austria and sale is through shops and kiosks marked "Austria Tabak," as well as by vending machines and in hotels, restaurants, cafés, and inns. A number of specialty tobacconist shops sell foreign tobacco products. Hobby, Milde Sorte, Memphis Light, Dames, and Falk are some of the most popular Austrian cigarette brands. In 1784 Joseph II founded the Österreichische Tabakregie, the oldest tobacco-processing concern in Europe.

YOUTH HOSTELS: Austria has about 100 youth hostels distributed throughout the provinces. Rates for bed-and-breakfast range from 80 AS ($5.75) to 130 AS ($9.50) per person daily. Some hostels lock their doors between 10pm and 6am to discourage late arrivals. Dormitories must be empty between 10am and 5pm. You must have an International Youth Hostel Federation membership card for use of Austria's youth hostels, and advance reservations are recommended.

In Austria, you can get information regarding hostels from **Österreichischer Jugendherbergsverband,** Schottenring 29, A-1010 Vienna (tel. 0222/533-53-53). A detailed brochure is available at the Austrian National Tourist Office (see "Information in Austria" above) and its representatives abroad.

VIENNA

City of music, cafés, waltzes, parks, pastries, and gemütlichkeit—that's Vienna. The capital city of Austria has long held an enchantment for visitors, gaining much of its charm even during times of great upheaval in the long reign of the Habsburgs and retaining it in the dark days of World Wars I and II, a charm that is present today.

Vienna is a true cosmopolitan city, with a blend throughout its history of tribes, races, and nationalities all becoming assimilated through the centuries, with countless, constant additions of foreigners of all backgrounds fusing their customs, ideas, and culture to become the witty, charming, and cynical Viennese.

From the time the Romans selected the site of a Celtic settlement for location of one of its most important Central European forts, Vindobona, the city that grew up in the Vienna Basin of the Danube has played a vital role in European history. Austria grew up around the city and developed into a mighty empire, but the Viennese character formed during the long history of the country can only be said to be a rich amalgam of the blending of cultures that have made Vienna what it still is today: a city whose people devote themselves to enjoyment of the good life.

Music, art, literature, theater, architecture, education, food, and drink (perhaps wine from the slopes where the Romans had vineyards in the 1st century A.D.)—all are a part of the gemütlichkeit of Vienna.

The splendor and brilliance of Habsburg Vienna were seen in the court panoply, where uniforms, decorations, gems, and precious metals made a dazzling, if sometimes tiring, show. Before some of the city's brilliance was dimmed by the fall of the empire, it was described as a "royal palace amidst surrounding suburbs."

The roster of renowned Viennese, either born in the city or spending much of their creative lives there, is endless—endless, that is, in that more names are added constantly as more Viennese make their appearance on the stage of cultural and professional life and become world-renowned.

Whenever I watch the boat traffic flow past on the Danube (not as beautiful and blue as Johann Strauss Jr. described it but still an important, navigable Central European waterway), I am always a little awed at the thought of the immortal music and musical dramas that had their inception here. Mozart, Lehár, Schubert, Beethoven, the Strausses (all of them), Suppé, Gluck, Mahler, Brahms, Liszt, Lanner, Haydn, Weber, Schoenberg—in the music world alone these are some of the outstanding names that were known during the days of empire.

Another name familiar in Vienna toward the latter days of the Habsburgs is Biedermeier. This is not the name of a real person but of a character in a book, and is the appellation used to describe a period and a style. The name Freud, however, is that of a real Viennese.

But I am not nostalgic for that era, because I know that talent, even genius, still burgeons in this beautiful country. Many personalities, especially theatrical, have come out of Vienna in recent decades and gone on to world acclaim: Erich von Stroheim, Hedy Lamarr, Curt Jurgens, Oskar Werner, Magda Schneider, Josef von Sternberg, Fritz Lang, O. W. Pabst, Maria Schell, Paula Wessely, and Greta Keller, to name a few.

The Viennese have always been hospitable to foreigners, but there was a time at the end of the 18th century when the emperor felt that tourists might spread pernicious ideas, and all non-Austrians were limited to a one-week stay in the capital. This, of course, is no longer so, nor has it been for nearly 200 years. Now you can laugh, play, feast, and sightsee—enjoy all the offerings of the city to the fullest—with the smiles of the Viennese welcoming you to gemütlich Vienna.

The face of the city has been altered by many occurrences—war, siege, victory, defeat, death of an empire, birth of a republic, bombing, occupation, and the passage of time—but Vienna is still the happy, cosmopolitan "Queen of the Danube."

AN ORIENTATION

First, you'll need a very good and detailed map to explore Vienna, as it covers more than 158 square miles and has some 1,500 miles of streets (many of them only narrow alleyways).

Most visitors will spend all their time in the **Inner City,** or Innere Stadt, of Vienna, its First District. This is that famed section encircled by the Ringstrasse and the Danube Canal. Most of the city's best-known churches, baroque palaces, galleries, historic monuments, hotels, and museums lie within this much-frequented district.

The **Ringstrasse** runs along the line of the old city walls for about 2½ miles. My suggestion is that you take a tram along the Ring before you do any actual exploring. That way, you'll get a feel for monumental Vienna before taking it on block by block.

The Ringstrasse on your map will come under a number of different names: sometimes it's called the Opernring, or the Schottenring, or else the Burgring or the Dr. Karl-Lueger-Ring. After an interruption by the Danube Canal, the Ringstrasse resumes with such names as the Stubenring, the Parkring, the Schubertring, and the Kärntner Ring.

The **Graben,** once the southwestern frontier of Vienna, is hardly that now. Absorbed by the city, it is today a major shopping artery. But if Vienna has a "main" street, it is surely the **Kärntnerstrasse,** which is jam-packed with pedestrians during the day. It extends as far as the **Karlsplatz.** Along the way, you'll find some of Vienna's best-known hotels and cafés.

Beyond the Danube Canal is the Second District, with the famous amusement park, the **Prater.** In the Third District, you'll find the **Belvedere Palace,** and in the Eighth District, **Schönbrunn Palace.**

1. Getting Around in Vienna

Whatever means of transportation you may select for your visit to the Austrian capital and its environs, these basic suggestions may help make your visit a happy one.

AIRPORT

Vienna's international airport is **Wien Schwechat,** about 12 miles from the city center, which can be reached either by bus or by train. There is a regular **bus** service between the airport and the City Air Terminal (Wien Mitte), at the Hotel Hilton. Buses run every 30 minutes from 6 to 8am and every 20 minutes from 8am to 7:20pm, and to accommodate flights arriving after 7:30pm. The one-way fare is 55 AS ($4). There's also a service between the airport and the railroad stations, Westbahnhof and Südbahnhof, leaving Westbahnhof every 30 minutes between 6am and 7pm (reaching Südbahnhof 15 minutes later) and starting from the airport every 30 minutes between 7am and 7pm. A **train** service runs between the airport and the City Air Terminal and Wien Nord (Praterstern) from 7:30am to 8:30pm. Trains run about every hour. A **minibus** service will shuttle you between the airport and your hotel. Seats may be reserved at the airport, at your hotel, or with your airline. A one-way **taxi** ride from the airport into the Inner City is likely to cost 300 AS ($21.75) to 400 AS ($29). Therefore, it's better to take the bus.

The official **Vienna Tourist Information Office** in the arrival hall of the airport is open October to May daily from 9am to 10pm, June to September from 9am to 11pm.

RAILROAD STATIONS

Vienna has two main railway stations, Südbahnhof and Westbahnhof. Südbahnhof, Südtirolerplatz, A-1100 Vienna (tel. 0222/222-15-53 for train information), services all trains heading south, which includes parts of eastern Italy, all of Yugoslavia, the southern Austrian provinces of Styria, Carinthia, Burgenland, and the city of Wiener Neustadt. Westbahnhof, Europaplatz, A-1150 Vienna (tel. 0222/222-15-52), services all trains heading west, including those to Salzburg, Innsbruck, all of Germany, and any connections to Italy that are made through Salzburg via the Brenner Pass. Train information for both stations will be given if you call 0222/17-17.

PUBLIC TRANSPORTATION

Whether you want to visit historical buildings or the Vienna Woods, museums, theaters, the Prater, or the heurigen, the **Vienna Transport** (Wiener Verkehrsbetriebe), with its network of facilities covering hundreds of miles, can take you there—by U-Bahn (underground), streetcar, or bus.

Vienna has a uniform rate, allowing the same tickets to be used on all these means of transportation as well as on the Schnellbahn (Rapid Transit) of the Austrian Federal Railways in the Vienna area and on some connecting private bus lines.

There are no conductors on most buses and streetcars, which means you must have the correct change, 20 AS ($1.45), when you get your ticket at a vending machine at the station or aboard the vehicle you choose. A ticket from the machine will be stamped with the date and time of purchase. It's wiser to buy your tickets in advance at a Tabak-Trafik (tobacconist shop) or at an advance-sales office. Tickets purchased in advance must be stamped before you start your ride by the machine on conductorless streetcars or at the platform barriers of the underground or Stadtbahn. Once a ticket is stamped, it may be used for any one trip in one direction, including changes.

You can ride directly into the Inner City on the underground U-1 or on city bus 1-A, 2-A, or 3-A. The underground runs daily from 6am to midnight and the buses Monday to Saturday from 6am to 10pm and on Sunday from 6am to 8pm.

Further information, all types of tickets, and maps of the transportation system are available at Vienna's Transport's main offices at Karlsplatz (tel. 0222/587-31-86) or at St. Stephen's Square underground stations (tel. 0222/582-42-27) Mon-

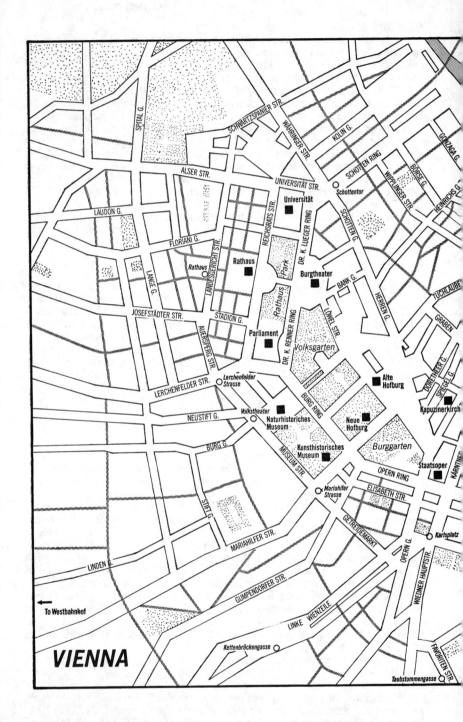

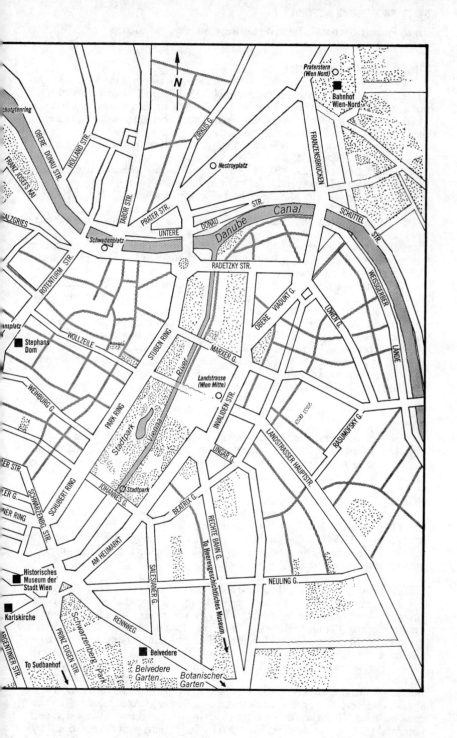

day to Friday from 8am to 6pm, on Saturday, Sunday, and holidays from 8:30am to 4pm.

Three-Day Vienna Ticket

One of the city's best deals for tourists is Vienna Transportation's Special Sightseeing Pass, a three-day rover ticket costing 102 AS ($7.40). You can use not only the public transportation network (underground, streetcars, and buses), which covers hundreds of miles, but also the Schnellbahn in the Vienna area and buses carrying the letter "B," for as many rides as you like.

The three-day ticket is available at Vienna Public Transport Information Centers at the following locations:

□ Karlsplatz (tel. 0222/587-31-86), open Monday to Friday from 8am to 6pm, on Saturday, Sunday, and holidays from 8:30am to 4pm.

□ Stephansplatz (tel. 0222/582-42-27), open the same days and hours as Karlsplatz.

□ Praterstern (tel. 0222/24-93-02), open Monday to Friday from 10am to 6pm.

All advance-sales offices of Vienna Public Transport are open Monday from 6am to noon, on Tuesday and Wednesday from 6:30am to 12:30pm, on Thursday and Friday from 12:30 to 6:30pm.

You can also get the three-day ticket at tourist information offices: Vienna West (on the Autobahn from Salzburg, Autobahnstation Wien-Auhof) and Vienna South (on the Autobahn from Graz, exit Zentrum, Triesterstrasse 149).

Other places selling the tickets are at the airport in the arrival hall next to where you pick up your baggage; at the DDSG landing pier, Reichsbrücke; and at the information offices of the Austrian Travel Agency (Österreichisches Verkehrbüro) at the main railway stations. The one at Westbahnhof is found in the upper hall and at Südbahnhof in the lower hall.

The three-day ticket is valid on three consecutive days, including the day it is stamped.

TAXIS

Taxi stands are marked by signs, or you can call for a radio cab by phoning 31-300, 43-69, 60-160, or 91-01. Fares are indicated on an officially calibrated taxi meter. The fare for trips outside the Vienna area, for instance to the airport, should be agreed on with the driver in advance.

HORSE-DRAWN CARRIAGES

Vienna's *fiakers,* or horse-drawn carriages, have transported people around the Inner City for some 300 years. You can clip-clop along in one for about 20 minutes at a cost of 600 AS ($43.50). In the First District, you'll find a fiaker for hire at the following sites: north side of St. Stephen's, on Heldenplatz near the Hofburg, and in front of the Albertina on Augustinerstrasse.

DRIVING AND TRAFFIC REGULATIONS

In general, Austria's traffic regulations do not differ much from those of other countries where you drive on the right. In Vienna the speed limit is 50 kilometers per hour, about 30 m.p.h. Honking car horns is forbidden everywhere in the city. From December 15 to March 30, between 8pm and 5am, parking is prohibited on all streets where streetcars run. You are allowed a maximum stop of 10 minutes even though parking is forbidden. In limited-parking areas you may park on weekdays between 8am and 6pm only if you have a valid ticket, allowing parking for up to 1½ hours. The parking tickets may be obtained from the ticket offices of the Vienna Public Transport, from many gasoline stations, from tobacconists, and from most bank branches. The tickets are canceled by having marked on them the year, month, date, and time of day. *Warning:* The "No Parking" signs with the additional sign

"Kurzparkzone" (Limited-Parking Zone) are displayed only at the beginning and end of the zones. Special maps indicating location of hotels, one-way streets, and parking facilities in the First District are available at the official tourist offices. If you have car trouble, 24-hour service is offered by ARBÖ (tel. 0222/78-25-25) and ÖAMTC (tel. 0222/95-40).

2. Fast Facts

AMERICAN EXPRESS: The office is at Kärntnerstrasse 21-23 (tel. 0222/515-40).

BABY-SITTER SERVICES: Call Academische Gästedienst, Mühlgasse 20, A-1040 Vienna (tel. 0222/587-3525). Most of the sitters here are students who charge 100 AS ($7.25) per hour for sitting at your hotel. Another service is Babysitter's Centrale, Herbst Strasse 6, A-1160 Vienna (tel. 0222/95-11-35).

BANKS: The open hours of Vienna banks and savings banks are 8am to 3pm on Monday, Tuesday, Wednesday, and Friday, to 5:30pm on Thursday (branch offices are closed from 12:30 to 1:30pm). Monday through Saturday you can **change money** in many travel agencies, and daily in the exchange offices of the Westbahnhof from 7am to 10pm, and the Südbahnhof from 6:30am to 10pm. At the airport the exchange windows are open from 6:30am to 11pm; in the City Air Terminal (Wien Mitte) from 8am to 12:30pm and from 2 to 6pm.

CHURCH SERVICES: For information on services held by the religious group of your choice, call one of the following numbers: tel. 0222/48-50-55 for Catholic; tel. 0222/512-83-92 for Lutheran, with headquarters at Dorotheergasse 18, A-1010 Vienna; tel. 0222/84-10-475 for Baptist, with headquarters at Mollardgasse 35, A-1060 Vienna; tel. 0222/531-04 for Jewish, with headquarters at Seitenstättengasse 4, A-1010 Vienna; and tel. 0222/713-15-75 for Anglican, with headquarters at Jaurèsgasse 17-19, A-1030 Vienna.

CLOTHING: For concerts and theaters, dark suits and cocktail dresses are recommended. For specially festive occasions such as opera premieres, receptions, and balls, tails and dinner jackets are the preferred dress for men and evening dresses for women. You can rent men's evening wear, as well as carnival costumes, from several places in Vienna, which you will find in the telephone directory classified section (the *Yellow Pages* in the U.S.) under "Kleiderleihanstalten." I've learned that it's a good idea to take a light topcoat when I go out in the evening, even in summer.

DOCTORS: A list of physicians can be found in the telephone directory under Ärzte. If you get a sudden illness during the night and need an emergency doctor, call 141 daily from 7pm to 7am. For dental problems during the night or on Saturday and Sunday, call 512-20-78.

EMERGENCY: If you're faced with an emergency in Vienna, help is available. Depending on the nature of the situation, you may call: fire brigade (tel. 122), police (tel. 133), or ambulance (tel. 144).

HEALTH CLUBS: Even if you're not registered at the Hilton, you are welcome to use the popular health club, Tu Was (tel. 0222/75-41-81), on the third floor of this deluxe hotel at Am Stadtpark. After registering at the desk, you'll be given a locker key, a towel, and access to the sauna, cold baths, and showers; women and men share the facilities equally. After a sauna, guests relax, draped in towels, beside the TV of the clubroom. Entrance fees for a sauna visit are 220 AS ($16). The club is open daily from 10am to 10:30pm. Women who prefer to have their sauna alone are directed to a private room.

LOST AND FOUND: A lost property office is maintained at Wasagasse 22 (tel. 0222/31-66-11-0), open Monday to Friday from 8am to 1pm. Items found on trains are taken to the central lost property office at Westbahnhof. Items left on buses and streetcars are passed on to the Wasagasse office after three days. If you miss something as soon as you get off the bus, you can pick it up (providing it is returned) at Wiener Stadtwerke (Verkehrsbetriebe; tel. 0222/501-30-0) without waiting three days.

PHARMACIES: Drugstores (chemist's shops) are open Monday through Friday from 8am to noon and 2 to 6pm, and on Saturday from 8am to noon. At night and on Sunday you'll find the names of shops whose turn it is to be open at those times listed on a sign outside every shop.

POST AND TELEGRAPH OFFICES: Addresses for these can be found in the telephone directory under "Post." Post offices are generally open Monday through Friday from 8am to 6pm. The central post office, Fleischmarkt 19, and all railroad station post offices are open at night and on Sunday. Postage stamps are available at all post offices and at tobacco shops, and there are stamp vending machines outside most post offices. For information, phone 0222/02-29-02. The central telegraph office is at Börseplatz 1.

TOURIST INFORMATION: The official **Vienna Tourist Information Office** is at 38 Kärntnerstrasse 38 (tel. 0222/513-40-15), which is open daily from 9am to 7pm. Tourist information is dispensed here, and room reservations are made.

3. Where to Stay

Finding a room in Vienna, in spite of its great number of hotels, can be a problem, especially in August and September (the latter the time of the Vienna Fair), if you should arrive without a reservation. Vienna has some of the greatest hotels in Europe, more than 300 recommendable ones. If you arrive without a reservation in the peak visiting months, you may have to stay on the outskirts of Vienna, in the Grinzing or the Schönbrunn district, for example, and commute to the Inner City by streetcar, bus, or underground.

In Vienna a five-star hotel such as the Imperial is decidedly luxurious and expensive. A four-star hotel is first class. Two- and three-star hotels are in the middle bracket, and a little one-star is the lowest of the lot, often no more than a boarding house (but often comfortable and quite clean).

When calling a hotel in Vienna from outside the city, dial the **city telephone code,** 0222, then the hotel's number. Inside Vienna, don't use the area code.

THE DELUXE HOTELS

The grandest hotel in Vienna is the **Hotel Imperial,** Kärntner Ring 16, A-1010 Vienna (tel. 0222/50-11-00), evoking memories of the Austro-Hungarian Empire and Strauss waltzes in practically everyone who visits it. Luminaries from around the world use this as their headquarters, especially musical stars who prefer the location two blocks from the State Opera and one block from the Musikverein. Wagner stayed here with his family for a few months in 1875 (some scholars claim that he worked out key sections of both *Tannhäuser* and *Lohengrin* during that period). Other artists who have soothed their opening-night jitters in one of the rooms include Domingo, Caballé, Carreras, Fonteyn, Ormandy, Fürtwangler, and Karajan, along with the thousands of music-lovers who have traveled to Austria to see and hear them.

The 158-room hotel was built in 1869 as the private residence of the Duke of Württemberg. The Italian architect Zanotti designed the façade like an almost overwhelmingly massive governmental building with a heroic frieze carved into the triangular pediment below the roofline. It was converted into a private hotel in 1873. The Nazis commandeered it as their headquarters during World War II, and the Russians requisitioned it in 1945, turning it into a shadowy ghost of its former self. Since Austria regained its independence, massive expenditures have returned it to the glory of its former beauty.

On the staircase leading up from the glittering salons you'll see archways supported by statues of gods and goddesses, along with two Winterhalter portraits of Emperor Franz Joseph and his wife, Elizabeth. Everything is outlined against a background of polished red, yellow, and black marble, crystal chandeliers, Gobelin tapestries, and fine rugs. For many, the favorite rooms are the salons whose arched ceilings are painted with intricately designed garlands of fruit, ornate urns, griffins, and the smiling faces of sphinxes. Some of the royal suites are palatial, but all the rooms today are soundproof and air-conditioned, contain private bath, and are generally spacious. Rates include a 15% service charge and run from 2,500 AS ($181.75) to 4,100 AS ($298) daily for a single and from 3,300 AS ($240) to 4,900 AS ($356.25) for a double.

In the elegant restaurant, with a turn-of-the-century atmosphere, antique silver, portraits of Franz Joseph, and superb service, the cuisine offers traditional Austrian dishes done with a light touch and excellent flavor. A café downstairs plays Viennese music, while the hotel's bar is an intimate rendezvous point.

Hotel Bristol, Kärntner Ring 1, A-1010 Vienna (tel. 0222/515-16). You probably won't notice that this Vienna landmark looks any different from many other grand buildings in town from the outside. But connoisseurs of Austrian hotels maintain that this is a superb choice, with a decor evoking the full power of the Habsburg Empire. The hotel was constructed in 1894 next to the State Opera, in the ultimate of luxury, and it's been updated to give its clients the benefit of black-tile baths and modern conveniences. Many of the architectural embellishments rank as objets d'art in their own right, from the black carved marble fireplaces and the oil paintings in the salons to the corkscrew baroque columns of rare marble in the Bristol restaurant, the Korso, which is, by the way, one of the best in Vienna. Even the chairs are crafted in a style that, depending on your mood, can be identified as either shield-back or heart-back Hepplewhite. The modern Rôtisserie Sirk and the elegant Café Sirk are other meeting places for gourmets.

The *après-théâtre* ambience is a Viennese legend. The hotel's music room has a resident pianist who fills the ground floor with waltzlike melodies on the Grand Boesendorfer. On your way to the sumptuously appointed bedrooms, you'll see grandfather clocks in the corridors, most of them giving accurate time. The club floor offers luxurious comfort, enhanced by period furnishings in the style of the hotel's *fin-de-siècle* architecture. The Bristol Club Rooms in the tower, for club floor guests only, have comfortable chairs, an open fireplace, a self-service bar, library, TV, video recorder, stereo deck, and sauna. Each club accommodation consists of a bedroom with a living room area, and many have a small balcony providing a rooftop view of the Vienna State Opera and the Ringstrasse.

Prices for the hotel's 152 rooms include a 15% service charge. Singles cost from

2,500 AS ($181.75) to 2,700 AS ($196.25) daily, with doubles ranging from 3,800 AS ($276.25) to 4,500 AS ($327.25).

Wien Hilton, Am Stadtpark, A-1030 Vienna (tel. 0222/75-26-50), is one of this international chain's most handsome European properties, offering the plush accommodations and the predictably good service for which Hilton is known. Its modern design, soaring atrium lobby, and nighttime activity might come as a relief after "Olde World" Vienna. The health club on the third floor, Tu Was, is filled with youthful members of the outside community, and the hotel's desirable location on the Stadtpark, a 10-minute walk from Vienna's cathedral, guarantees the establishment's popularity with business people and sightseers alike.

The Hilton is attached to the City Air Terminal, which is the drop-off point for buses coming in at frequent intervals from the airport. The hotel offers 622 air-conditioned and comfortably upholstered rooms in styles ranging from modern to baroque, from Biedermeier to art nouveau. Singles range from 1,800 AS ($130.75) to 3,000 AS ($218) daily, with twins and doubles costing 2,500 AS ($181.75) to 4,000 AS ($290.75). The hotel has converted 42 guest rooms and one suite to provide extra comfort and facilities to guests on an executive floor. The extra amenities, tailored to the needs of business people, include hairdryers, toiletries, and additional phones. There is also an executive lounge on this floor offering Continental breakfasts, afternoon coffee, snacks, and cocktails on a complimentary basis. This floor also provides special assistance by the staff as well as a no-stop checkout system and pickup by private limousine at the airport upon request.

The adjacent Stadtpark is connected to the hotel by a bridge, which strollers and joggers use during their excursions into the landscaped, bird-dotted expanses of the most famous park of Vienna. Even the glass-lined exterior is filled with bronze and aluminum balustrades, designed in a style reminiscent of art nouveau pioneer Gustav Klimt, whose other designs fill large expanses of the hotel's interior.

The Prinz Eugen restaurant (see my dining recommendations) is a gourmet bastion of fine food, acclaimed by many as the finest in Vienna. Since the Hilton towers over the city skyline, it affords very good views from the top floors. The Café am Park has a large open terrace where, in summer, you'll want to enjoy a Viennese coffee.

Hotel Sacher, Philharmonikerstrasse 4, A-1010 Vienna (tel. 0222/514-56). When the Sacher was built in 1876, Vienna, the empire, and the world were all very different places from what they are today. Nevertheless, much of the glory of the Habsburgs is still evoked during a walk through the public rooms. The décor of red velvet, crystal chandeliers, traditional wallpaper, and brocaded curtains gives a nostalgic feeling of old Vienna. The façade is appropriately grand, with enough neoclassical detailing to make a Roman feel at home, a striped awning over the sidewalk café, and flags from seven nations displayed near the caryatids on the second floor. You might sense an undercurrent of espionage here. Enough novelists have used it in settings for their spy stories to evoke that image, yet despite that, both the crowned heads of Europe and the deposed heads (especially those of Eastern European countries) have dined and lived here.

In addition to intrigue, the Sacher has produced culinary creations that still bear its name. Franz Sacher, the celebrated chef, left the world a fabulously caloric chocolate cake called the Sacher torte, which has appealed to virtually everybody over the years.

The 124-room hotel charges 1,000 AS ($72.75) for a single without bath, 1,500 AS ($109) to 2,000 AS ($145.50) for a single with bath. Doubles, all with baths, cost from 2,700 AS ($196.25) to 4,500 AS ($327.25) daily. Rates include breakfast, service, and tax. Demi-suites and chambers with drawing rooms are more expensive. Half- or full-board terms can be arranged. The reception desk is fairly flexible about making arrangements for salons, apartments, or joining two rooms together, if it is possible to do so.

The Sacher, especially its elegant coffeehouse, is the logical music-lover's choice in Vienna. You'll hear some kind of lilting classical music there in the afternoon, just as you had probably fantasized. All of the interior is a rococo splendor. The concierge, for a fee, can probably produce "unobtainable" theater and opera tickets.

Plaza Wien, Am Schottenring 11, A-1010 Vienna (tel. 0222/31-39-0), is Hilton's newest "grand hotel." It rises imposingly for 10 stories in the center of the city, opening onto the Ringstrasse just opposite the stock exchange. Because of its location in the financial district, it draws many business clients from around the world; but is also suitable for visitors, as it is near such attractions as the State Opera, the Burgtheater, City Hall, and the Kunsthistorisches and Naturhistorisches museums. Designed with style and flair, with the discriminating modern visitor in mind, the luxury hotel offers 252 spacious guest rooms and suites. Each is equipped with three-speed, individually controlled air conditioning, three direct-dial phones, color TV with remote control, minibar, and private safe, along with floor-to-ceiling windows and a large marble bathroom fitted with hairdryers, phone, and radio. The hotel also offers a penthouse floor with balconies and a nonsmoking floor. Singles range from 1,750 AS ($127.25) to 2,650 AS ($192.75) daily, with twins and doubles renting for 2,250 AS ($163.50) to 3,050 AS ($221.75). Suites are more expensive, of course.

Drinking and dining facilities are special features of the hotel, with its three restaurants, piano bar, cocktail lounge, sidewalk terrace, and, of course, 24-hour room service. You might begin with a champagne breakfast in Le Jardin or, in the afternoon, enjoy apfelstrudel in the Plaza Café. La Scala restaurant features the cuisine of northern Italy. To top the evening, you can order a nightcap in the Plaza Bar. Other facilities include a business center, health and fitness club (with sauna, massage, gym, whirlpool, solarium, and health bar), and free underground parking for hotel guests. Airport limousine service is free for individual guests.

Hotel im Palais Schwarzenberg, Schwarzenbergplatz 9, A-1030 Vienna (tel. 0222/78-45-15), just off the State Opera in the heart of the city, hidden within 15 acres of beautiful gardens, is the preferred retreat of those who cherish a noble and elegant atmosphere. The palace was built 300 years ago by Lukas von Hildebrandt and Fischer von Erlach, masters of baroque architecture, and has kept its splendid original touches since that time. It was gutted during the Nazi era but was completely reconstructed after the Soviet occupation of Vienna. Today the same ambience of high ceilings with striated marble, crystal chandeliers, mythical beasts, oval mirrors, and gilt—lots of it—fills the public rooms between painted murals of festive deities. Guests enjoy the two-level bar and the terrace restaurant overlooking the private park.

The 38 bedrooms and suites contain exquisite objets d'art and antique pieces. Luxuriously furnished and handsomely decorated, each accommodation has a private bath and phone. These double rooms rent for 4,000 AS ($290.75) to 5,000 AS ($363.50) daily.

Hotel Ambassador, Kärntnerstrasse 22, A-1010 Vienna (tel. 0222/514-66), a renowned hotel whose façade has been restored to the elegance it knew before World War II, stands on the square facing the Donner Fountain, with the shop-lined Kärntnerstrasse on the other side. Mark Twain stayed here, as have a host of diplomats and celebrities, including Theodore Roosevelt. The trademark of the hotel has always been the color red, either in the silk wall coverings, the bedspreads, the upholstery, or the long carpet that is sometimes unrolled to the waiting limousine of some person known in world headlines. The wall-to-wall carpeting is, as you guessed, scarlet, relieved often by a discreet pattern of forest foliage. The public rooms have many, many chandeliers, which, in contrast to the vivid colors of everything else, appear sometimes as the most prominent furnishings. The Ambassador couldn't be better located: it's between the State Opera and St. Stephen's Cathedral.

High-season rates, charged from late March to mid-November and during the Christmas to New Year's season, are 2,000 AS ($145.50) daily for singles, 2,400 AS ($174.50) to 3,500 AS ($254.50) for doubles. The rest of the year, singles cost

1,700 AS ($123.50) to 1,800 AS ($130.75), with doubles going for 2,000 AS ($145.50) to 3,000 AS ($218). The 107 sumptuous accommodations contain TVs, radios, and air conditioning. Rates include buffet breakfast. This hotel is an ideal choice for devotees of rococo *fin-de-siècle* décor.

Vienna Marriott, Parkring 12A, A-1030 Vienna (tel. 0222/51-51-80), is one of the newest hotels in the capital and also one of the most dramatically designed. Its fan-windowed Mississippi riverboat façade displays expanses of tinted glass broken into glistening rectangles in an exterior of finely wrought enameled steel. When it was originally built on the site of a covered garage, its designers allocated a third of the building for offices of the American Consulate and a few private apartments. The remainder contains 304 comfortably modern bedrooms, some of which are larger than those in the other contemporary palaces of Vienna. Singles range from 1,875 AS ($136.25) to 2,600 AS ($189) daily, with doubles costing 2,290 AS ($166.50) to 3,300 AS ($240).

Opposite the Stadtpark, the hotel enjoys an ideal location for visitors, as it lies only a few minutes' walk from such famous landmarks as St. Stephen's Cathedral, the State Opera, and the Hofburg Palace.

The public rooms are elegant, and on my most recent visit one of the rooms was the site of a reception for the most prominent socialites of Vienna. The hotel's lobby culminates in a stunning stairway whose curved sides frame a splashing waterfall and masses of plants. Both in-house bars offer live entertainment at cocktail hour, while a pair of top-quality restaurants feature appetizing and well-prepared Viennese and international specialties. In the gourmet restaurant, the Symphonika, an array of plushly pastel-colored banquettes clusters around a magnificent copy of a Hoffman-designed art nouveau chandelier. Exercise buffs appreciate the basement-level swimming pool, sauna, and Jacuzzi.

THE UPPER BRACKET

Called the "guesthouse of the kaisers," **Parkhotel Schönbrunn,** Hietzinger Hauptstrasse 10-20, A-1131 Vienna (tel. 0222/82-26-76), is today part of the Steigenberger reservations system. It has had a long history since Franz Joseph I made possible its construction in 1907. On this same site the first performances of "Loreleyklänge" by Johann Strauss Sr. and of "Die Schönbrunner," the famous waltz by Josef Lanner, took place. Through its heyday, guests have ranged from Thomas Edison to Walt Disney.

Today the hotel is modern and updated, although its original core is still used for public rooms. Contemporary wings and annexes house many present-day guests. The newer additions include the Stöckl, Residenz, and Maximilian, together with a villa formerly inhabited by Van Swieten, the personal doctor of the Empress Maria Theresa.

In all, 400 well-furnished guest rooms in this complex are available, the décor ranging from classical to modern. Each accommodation is equipped with a private bath or shower, color TV, radio, phone, and minibar. An annex, the Hotel Viktoria, with 60 well-equipped rooms, completes the picture of this, the largest hotel site in Vienna. Doubles at the five-star Parkhotel range from 1,950 AS ($141.75) to 3,000 AS ($218) daily, with singles costing 1,050 AS ($76.25) to 1,850 AS ($134.50). However, rooms at the three-star Viktoria are 1,450 AS ($105.50) in a double and from 750 AS ($54.50) in a single.

Inside the complex is a coffeehouse furnished almost entirely with Biedermeier tables and chairs, along with a series of lavishly outfitted public salons. The Jagerstübl is traditionally decorated in forest colors. There is also a French restaurant, plus a winter garden restaurant, a gypsy tavern, and two bars. A pool area is one of the best equipped of any hotel in Vienna, with a fitness center, sauna, and solarium. The establishment lies 1½ miles from the West Station, 3 miles from the City Air Terminal. Opposite Schönbrunn Castle and its park, it is a 12-minute underground ride to the center.

Hotel de France, Schottenring 3, A-1010 Vienna (tel. 0222/34-35-40), has been a long-enduring favorite, attracting its share of celebrities over the decades. Its carefully chiseled gray stone façade looks basically as it did when it was first erected beside the Ringstrasse in 1872. Inside, however, much modernization has transformed its ambience into a savory choice. Nowadays you get comfortable, tasteful, and unobtrusively conservative décor. In such a quietly subdued and appealing ambience, you often encounter businesspeople from all over the world. They like the high-ceilinged public rooms with their dozens of Oriental carpets, their generously padded armchairs, even a full-dress portrait of Franz Joseph, who was the leader of the empire when the hotel was built.

The 220 bedrooms are among the finest in their price range in the capital. Each is well furnished with many amenities along with such regular features as a private bath, radio, TV, minibar, safe, and phone. Singles range from 1,300 AS ($94.50) to 2,000 AS ($145.50) daily, with doubles renting for 2,000 AS ($145.50) to 3,700 AS ($267), depending on the room assignment.

The hotel offers two restaurants, one the Bel Étage, where you can enjoy such dishes as filet in Roquefort and whisky sauce, tafelspitz (the favorite dish of the emperor), and fogas, the famous fish from Lake Balaton in Hungary. There is also a French bistro as well as a sophisticated and elegant atrium bar.

Hotel Römischer Kaiser, Annagasse 16, A-1010 Vienna (tel. 0222/512-77-51), a Best Western affiliate, is housed in a national trust building that has seen its share of transformations. It was constructed in 1684 as the private palace of the imperial chamberlain and later housed the Imperial School of Engineering before becoming a *fin-de-siècle* hotel. Among its attractions is a sidewalk café whose tables are shaded with flowers and umbrellas. The hotel rents 24 romantically decorated rooms (my favorite has red satin upholstery over a chaise longue and white and gold paint with plenty of curlicues). In Vienna all this is not only acceptable but perfectly charming. The red-carpeted sidewalk café with bar service evokes memories of what Vienna was like as an imperial capital.

Singles rent for 1,600 AS ($116.25) daily, with doubles costing 2,400 AS ($174.50). Every room includes breakfast, private bath, radio, phone, minibar, and color TV.

SAS Palais Hotel, Heihburggasse 32, Parkring, A-1010 Vienna (tel. 0222/51-51-70), is one of Vienna's grandest renovations, an unused neoclassical palace converted into a hotel in 1985. Owned by SAS, the Scandinavian airline, it has a cream-colored façade adorned with cast-iron railings, reclining nymphs, red banners, and elaborate cornices. In its imaginatively decorated lobby you'll find arching palms, a soaring ceiling, plushly upholstered chairs, and a cubbyhole bar with music.

An elegant basement-level restaurant decked out with peach-colored upholstery and a white ceramic stove offers beautifully presented food. Exercise buffs sometimes jog in the adjacent city park before relaxing in the hotel's sauna and whirlpool. The hotel contains 165 compact but cozy rooms, each efficiently organized and comfortably furnished, with lots of alluring extras. Rooms come in various sizes with different amenities, ranging in singles from rooftop to Business Club and in doubles from Business Club to Royal Club. Singles cost 1,990 AS ($144.75) to 2,600 AS ($189) daily, with doubles ranging from 2,900 AS ($210.75) to 3,650 AS ($265.25). Rates include tax and service.

Hotel König von Ungarn, Schulerstrasse 10, A-1010 Vienna (tel. 0222/515-84), is on a narrow street near the cathedral, a choice site. In the business of receiving paying guests for more than four centuries, this is Vienna's oldest accommodation that has been in business continuously. In an early 17th-century building, it was once a *pied-à-terre* in this city for Hungarian noble families during their stays in the Austrian capital. The 32-room hotel also has Mozart connections through the building in which its kitchen operates. The composer reportedly died here in 1791. He wrote some of his immortal music when he resided in an apartment upstairs, where a Mozart museum is to be found.

The interior is filled with interesting architectural details, such as marble columns supporting the arched ceiling of the King of Hungary restaurant, one of the finest in the city, a high-ceilinged mirrored solarium/bar area with a glass roof over the atrium, and a live tree growing out of an opening in the pavement. There are comfortable chairs, Venetian mirrors, and an atmosphere of old Vienna in the tall hinged windows overlooking the old town. Everywhere you'll find low-key luxury, old tradition, and modern convenience.

The hotel charges from 1,300 AS ($94.50) to 1,600 AS ($116.25) daily in a single and 1,750 AS ($127.25) to 2,000 AS ($145.50) in a double, including a buffet breakfast. All accommodations have minibars, phones, radios, and color TVs.

Hotel Kaiserpark-Schönbrunn, Grünbergstrasse 11, A-1120 Vienna (tel. 0222/83-86-10). Not everyone can walk out his or her front door and stare immediately at Schönbrunn Palace, but if you stay here that's precisely what you'll do. This elegant hotel is outfitted with lots of dark paneling and red velvet. The 54 bedrooms are as comfortable as you'd expect from an establishment of this quality; each of them has a private bath, phone, TV, and radio. The hotel charges from 1,150 AS ($83.50) daily for a single and 1,800 AS ($130.75) for a double, including a buffet breakfast. A public swimming pool in Schönbrunn Park is only a short walk away, and a subway will take you into the center of Vienna in seven minutes.

Hotel Tyrol, Mariahilferstrasse 15, A-1060 Vienna (tel. 0222/587-54-15), is a privately owned hotel that is conveniently located in the center of town near the Hofburg Palace. The interior is decorated with a combination of upholstered chairs and couches, plus a few select pieces of antique furniture. Each of the 37 up-to-date rooms offers a bath, phone, radio, and TV, and there's a garage in the immediate vicinity. Rates in the soundproof rooms are 1,050 AS ($76.25) daily for a single and 1,550 AS ($112.75) for a double.

Hotel Europa, Neuer Markt 3, A-1010 Vienna (tel. 0222/51-59-40). The welcoming parapet of this glass-and-steel hotel extends over the sidewalk almost to the edge of the street. You'll find it midway between the State Opera and the main cathedral, St. Stephen's. It offers 102 comfortable rooms, a Viennese café, and a first-class restaurant, Zum Donnerbrunnen, with evening zither music. The Europa Bar is elegant. Bedrooms are spacious, with lots of light coming in from the large windows; they are also air-conditioned and contain private baths. Singles cost 1,380 AS ($100.25) daily, with doubles renting for 1,990 AS ($144.75).

Hotel Amadeus, Wildpretmarkt 5, A-1010 Vienna (tel. 0222/63-87-38), is only two minutes away from the cathedral and within walking distance of practically everything else of musical or historical note within the city. The hotel maintains its 30 bedrooms and carpeted public rooms in tip-top shape. Some of the walls of the reception area are papered over with enlargements of old engravings of the Vienna of young Wolfgang Amadeus Mozart's era. The bedrooms offer baths, phones, radios, minibars, and TV hookups. Singles rent for 1,150 AS ($83.60) daily, with doubles costing 1,500 AS ($109).

Hotel Prinz Eugen, Wiedner Gürtel 14, A-1040 Vienna (tel. 0222/505-17-41), displays a façade of identical soundproof windows with balconies facing toward a residential section of Vienna favored by diplomats. The 110-room hotel is immediately opposite Belvedere Palace and the rail station of Vienna South. Subways will carry you quickly to the downtown section, and there are good highway connections. Inside you'll find a restaurant, a warmly paneled bar, and a series of conference rooms and salons that are often in demand by the local business community. The décor is a mixture of traditional pieces, a few antiques, some Oriental rugs, and such glitzy touches as glass walls with brass trim, adaptations of crystal chandeliers, and blowups of 18th-century illustrations of everyday life in Austria. Singles rent for 1,015 AS ($73.75) to 1,250 AS ($91) daily, with doubles costing 1,550 AS ($112.75) to 2,050 AS ($149), including breakfast.

Hotel Bellevue, Althanstrasse 5, A-1091 Vienna (tel. 0222/34-56-31). The sandstone façade of this five-story, 160-room hotel reminds me a little of the Flatiron Building in Manhattan, as it's set on the acute angle of a street corner one block away from the Franz-Josefs Bahnhof. The Italianate embellishments seem to converge at a point on the fifth floor where the statues of two demigods support the corner of the roofline. Inside, the many renovations have stripped the former detailing, leaving a clean series of lines; there are high ceilings, wood paneling, and a limited number of antiques. Bedrooms are functionally furnished with low beds, utilitarian desks and chairs, and padded armchairs. Singles rent for 1,180 AS ($85.75) daily, with doubles costing 1,630 AS ($118.50). Guests can use a sauna.

Hotel Astoria, Kärntnerstrasse 32-34, A-1015 Vienna (tel. 0222/515-77), is for nostalgia buffs who want to experience life as grandly lived in the closing days of the Austro-Hungarian Empire. A first-class hotel, the Astoria has an eminently desirable location, lying on the shopping mall close to St. Stephen's Cathedral and the State Opera. Decorated in a turn-of-the-century style, the hotel offers 108 well-appointed and traditionally decorated bedrooms. Of course, it has been renovated over the years, but the old style has been respected, and management seems genuinely concerned in offering a good standard for what in Vienna is considered a reasonable price. Singles cost 1,300 AS ($94.50) daily, with doubles ranging from 1,700 AS ($123.50) to 2,500 AS ($181.75); all rates include a breakfast buffet, service, and tax. The Astoria has long been a favorite with visiting performers such as Leonard Bernstein. The restaurant is so special it deserves (and gets) a special recommendation.

Hotel Erzherzog Rainer, Wiedner Hauptstrasse 27-29, A-1040 Vienna (tel. 0222/50-11-10), is housed in an old-fashioned building with rows of gently curved bay windows rippling across the façade. It's only five minutes on foot to the State Opera and the Kärntnerstrasse, with a subway stop only a few steps away. The hotel is a well-run family business. Peter Nedomansky, the managing director, supervises the polite staff in their duties throughout the 84 well-decorated rooms, in which you'll find color TVs, radios, phones, and private baths. A booking service for opera and theater tickets operates out of the lobby, while Austrian specialties are served in the attractive restaurant, Serviette. A cozy bar is modishly decorated in accents of black and brass. Other services offered include 10-hour cleaning Monday to Friday. Singles cost 980 AS ($71.25) to 1,400 AS ($101.75) daily, and doubles 1,750 AS ($127.25) to 1,950 AS ($141.75).

Hotel am Parkring, Parkring 12, A-1010 Vienna (tel. 0222/51-480), is a first-class hotel situated on the top three floors of a massive modern construction on the edge of Vienna's best-known city park. From many of the windows you'll have views of St. Stephen's Cathedral less than a block away, and have much of the rest of Vienna laid at your feet. The 64 air-conditioned units, including seven suites, all have direct-dial phones, minibars, and color TVs. The Himmelstube restaurant and the Coffee-Bar give an ambience that is unmistakably Viennese, particularly with the skyline spread out before you. An elevator from the streetside private entrance leads directly to your floor. Singles cost 1,100 AS ($80) daily, with doubles going for 1,900 AS ($138.25).

Hotel Maté, Ottakringer Strasse 34-36, A-1170 Vienna (tel. 0222/43-61-33). Many of the ceilings of this modern hotel are fashioned of handcrafted hardwood planks fastened together for an effect of visual interest. In one of the conference rooms the ceiling looks like an inverted topographical map of some Austrian mountain range, finished in natural wood grains. The rest of the public rooms are fitted with marble floors, comfortable upholstery, and—in the case of the bar area—a combination of natural woods that frame the magenta and red panels on the walls and ceilings. An indoor swimming pool rests under a roofline that is shaped into a continuous barrel vault, with cutouts of Polynesian-style fish, potted palms, and rattan furniture. The outside of this 250-room hotel has decorative geometric designs on the streamlined façade, and there's a protective parapet. Bedrooms are comfortably furnished and well maintained. The cost is from 950 AS ($69) daily for a single, rising to 1,550 AS ($112.75) for a double.

Theater-Hotel in der Josefstadt, Josefstädter Strasse 22, A-1080 Vienna (tel. 0222/42-36-48), one of Vienna's newer hotels, lies next to the Theater in der Josefstadt within walking distance of the monumental city center and the major historic sights. A first-class hotel, it offers 54 tastefully furnished bedrooms and suites, each equipped with bath, satellite color TV, direct-dial phone, and kitchenette. Singles rent for 1,250 AS ($91) daily, with doubles costing 1,900 AS ($138.25). The hotel also offers a good restaurant, the Theater-Restaurant with a bar attached, as well as the Theater-Café. Facilities include a sauna and a solarium.

Hotel Kummer, Mariahilferstrasse 71A, A-1060 Vienna (tel. 0222/588-95), looks as highly ornamented as any public monument constructed during the height of the empire. Delightfully baroque, the façade is richly embellished, from Corinthian capitals with what look like acanthus-leaf bases to balustrades shaped like urns to four deities staring down from under the eaves. While the modern public rooms inside are not as delightful as the exterior, they are nevertheless comfortable and satisfactory in every way. The 106 rooms, within walking distance of the Vienna West train station, are all equipped with baths and soundproof windows. Singles rent for 1,000 AS ($72.50) to 1,250 AS ($91) daily, with doubles costing 1,550 AS ($112.75) to 2,050 AS ($149), with breakfast included. The carpeted restaurant and the bar area are attractive places.

Hotel President, Wallgasse 23, A-1060 Vienna (tel. 0222/599-90), was designed with enough angles in the façade to allow each of the bedrooms to have an irregular shape, usually with two windows in each unit, both facing toward different skylines. The façade is white and bronze, and there's a rooftop terrace where many guests sit sipping drinks in summer, separated from the buildings of old Vienna by an eight-story drop-off and a barrier of green plants. Aside from the views, each of the 77 bedrooms has a complete bath, comfortable furnishings, phone, radio, TV, air conditioning, minibar, and minisafe. Singles cost from 1,250 AS ($91) daily, with doubles going for 1,850 AS ($134.50). Studios for two are available at 2,200 AS ($160). The Restaurant Casserole serves Viennese and international cuisine in an informal setting every night till 11.

Hotel Royal, Singerstrasse 3, A-1010 Vienna (tel. 0222/51-568), is on one of the more prestigious streets of the old city. The outside presents a restrained dignity to the older buildings around it. The hotel lies less than a block from St. Stephen's Cathedral. Each of the 81 rooms is differently furnished, with some good reproductions of antiques and even an occasional original. The entire facility was built in 1960 and rebuilt in 1982. Each unit has a private bath, radio, minibar, phone, and TV, plus room service if you want it. Singles cost 900 AS ($65.50) to 1,350 AS ($98.25) daily, with doubles going for 1,300 AS ($94.50) to 1,900 AS ($138.25).

THE MODERATE RANGE

Hotel Kaiserin Elisabeth, Weihburggasse 3, A-1010 Vienna (tel. 0222/52-26-26), a few blocks from the cathedral, is perfectly located. The first thing you might notice about the interior is the number of beautiful Oriental rugs lying on top of well-maintained marble or wood floors. The main salon has a pale-blue skylight suspended above it, with mirrors and half-columns in natural wood. If you should select one of the hotel's 66 rooms, you'll be interested to know that Richard Wagner, Franz Liszt, and Edvard Grieg all spent at least one night here. The rooms have been considerably updated since then, and although some parts of the building date from the 14th century, what you're likely to see in your private space is an up-to-date décor of polished wood, clean linen, and perhaps another Oriental rug. In the breakfast room you'll see a portrait of the Empress Maria Theresa above the fireplace. Each accommodation contains a private bath, phone, radio, color TV, and minibar. Singles cost 800 AS ($58.25) to 1,150 AS ($83.50) daily, with doubles going for 1,050 AS ($76.25) to 1,700 AS ($123.50).

Fürst Metternich Hotel, Esterházygasse 33, A-1060 Vienna (tel. 0222/588-70). Pink and gray paint and ornate stone window trim identify this solidly built hotel, which began life as an opulent private house. While many of the building's grander architectural elements were retained, including a pair of red stone columns in the entrance vestibule, as well as an old-fashioned staircase guarded with griffins, the high-ceilinged bedrooms were given a conservatively neutral decor during renovations completed in 1985.

With the cost of breakfast included, the 57 bedrooms cost 700 AS ($51) to 990 AS ($72) daily for a single and 1,100 AS ($80) to 1,540 AS ($112) for a double, depending on the season. Each unit contains a tile bath, color TV, radio, and a phone. Over morning coffee, your view will encompass colorful lithographs from the changing exhibition of pop art hanging in the breakfast room. One of the neighborhood's most stylish bars, the Offiziers Casino, is accessible from the lobby. The location is near the Mariahilferstrasse, about a 20-minute walk from the cathedral.

K & K Palais Hotel, Rudolfsplatz 11, A-1010 Vienna (tel. 0222/533-13-53). When its severely dignified façade was built in 1890, it sheltered the affair of Emperor Franz Joseph and his celebrated mistress, Katherina Schratt. Occupying a desirable position near the river, it remained unused for two decades until members of the Best Western chain renovated it in 1981.

Today, vestiges of its imperial past remain, in spite of the warmly contemporary décor that fills the airy lobby and the lattice-covered bar and coffeeshop. The public rooms are painted a shade of Austrian Imperial yellow, and one of Ms. Schratt's antique secretaries occupies a niche near a white-sided tile stove. Otherwise, the 66 bedrooms are comfortably outfitted with contemporary furniture, TVs, radios, minibars, and private baths. Charges are from 1,500 AS ($109) daily for a single and from 1,850 AS ($134.50) for a double, with breakfast, taxes, and service included.

K & K Hotel Maria Theresia, Kirchberggasse 6-8 (Breitegasse 5), A-1070 Vienna (tel. 0222/93-56-16). The initials of its name stand as a reminder of the dual monarchy (Kaiserlich und Königlich—"by appointment to the Emperor of Austria and King of Hungary"). Even the surrounding neighborhood, near the major museums and the center of the city, reminds its guests of the days of Maria Theresa. The location is within the artists' colony of Spittelberg, within walking distance of the Winter Palace gardens, the Volkstheater, and the famous shopping street, Mariahilferstrasse.

The hotel offers 123 comfortably contemporary rooms, each with private bath, phone, radio, and TV. Singles rent for 930 AS ($67.50) daily, with doubles going for 1,200 AS ($87.25).

Hotel am Stephansplatz, Stephansplatz 9, A-1010 Vienna (tel. 0222/53-40-50). You'll walk out of your door and face the front entrance to Vienna's cathedral if you stay in this 62-room hotel, with its unadorned façade. The public rooms are done in a mixture of modern and traditional, and some of the bedrooms contain painted reproductions of rococo furniture and red-flocked wallpaper. Each of the units has bath or shower and toilet, direct-dial phone, color TV, radio, and minibar. Single rooms cost from 1,250 AS ($91) daily, with doubles renting for 1,850 AS ($134.50). A buffet breakfast, service, and taxes are included in the tariffs. A typical Viennese coffeeshop, the first-floor Dom Café, is a well-known rendezvous spot.

Hotel Opernring, Opernring 11, A-1010 Vienna (tel. 0222/587-55-18), a hotel affiliate of Best Western, sits on the Ringstrasse directly opposite the State Opera. The comfortable 33-room hotel has up-to-date furnishings, such as reclining upholstered armchairs on chrome bases, wall-to-wall carpeting, and subtly patterned draperies. Aside from the décor, however, you'll quickly find that the efforts of the owner, Mrs. Susie S. Riedl, more than justify this as a choice for your stay in Vienna. If you write to her far enough in advance, she will forward the schedule for both of Vienna's opera companies, and even arrange for ticket purchases for guests who live in foreign countries. Doubles cost 1,680 AS ($122.25) to 2,080 AS ($151.25) daily. Summer singles aren't available, but they can be rented off-season for 1,050 AS ($76.25) to 1,200 AS ($87.25) daily. Tariffs include breakfast, and some of the rooms are large enough to accommodate three to four guests.

Hotel Albatros, Liechtensteinstrasse 89, A-1090 Vienna (tel. 0222/34-35-08), lies close to the U.S. Embassy and the Franz-Josefs Bahnhof, some distance to the north of the Rathaus. The hotel was built in 1971, offering a total of 70 bedrooms. If any reader associates an albatross with bad luck, you'll need to change your thinking about this one. The comfortable bedrooms are cheerfully decorated, clean, and well furnished. Singles rent for 950 AS ($69) daily, with doubles costing 1,400 AS ($101.75). Tariffs include breakfast, and the hotel also offers an indoor swimming pool and sauna.

Hotel Austria, Wolfengasse 3, A-1010 Vienna (tel. 0222/515-23). The staff of this hotel always seems willing to tell you where to go in the neighborhood for a good meal or a glass of wine, and often distributes carefully typed sheets explaining the medieval origins of this part of Vienna. This unpretentious family-owned establishment sits on a small street whose name will probably be unfamiliar to many taxi drivers, although a corner building on the adjoining street, Fleischmarkt 20, is the point where you'll turn into the narrow lane. The staff maintains the comfortable furnishings in the lobby and in the chandeliered breakfast room in tip-top condition.

The hotel offers a total of 51 bedrooms, 40 of which contain private baths or showers. Including a buffet breakfast, service, and tax, singles range from 715 AS ($52) to 1,015 AS ($73.75) daily, with doubles renting for 980 AS ($71.25) to 1,450 AS ($105.50).

Hotel Wandl, Petersplatz 9, A-1010 Vienna (tel. 0222/53-45-50). Stepping into this hotel is like stepping into a piece of another family's history since it's been in the same ownership for generations. The establishment lies in the Inner City and offers views of the steeple of St. Stephen's Cathedral from many of its windows, which often open onto small balconies with railings. The breakfast room is a high-ceilinged two-toned room with hanging chandeliers and lots of ornamented plaster, while the bedrooms usually offer the kind of spacious dimensions that went out of style 60 years ago. The hotel faces St. Peter's Church. Each unit—there are 138 in all—has a private bath or shower as well as a phone. Singles range from 800 AS ($58.25) to 850 AS ($61.75) daily, with doubles costing 1,300 AS ($94.50) to 1,400 AS ($101.75). Rates include breakfast, service, and tax.

Hotel Stefanie, Taborstrasse 12, A-1020 Vienna (tel. 0222/21-15-00), is an updated 130-room hotel across the Danube Canal from the cathedral, in an area easily accessible to the rest of the city. The interior is decorated in part with beautifully finished wall paneling in geometric designs and gilded wall sconces. Although upon closer examination much of the décor is reproduction, the hotel still gives a hint of the rococo splendor of 19th-century Vienna. A bar area is filled with black leather armchairs on chrome swivel bases and concealed lighting that throws an azure glow over the artfully displayed rows of bottles. All rooms have baths or showers, channel TVs, direct-dial phones, radios, minibars, and partial air conditioning. Singles cost 1,120 AS ($81.50) to 1,380 AS ($100.25) daily, with doubles renting for 1,420 AS ($103.25) to 1,820 AS ($132.25).

Hotel Post, Fleischmarkt 24, A-1010 Vienna (tel. 0222/51-58-30), lies in what was the slaughter-house district in the Middle Ages and what is today an interesting section full of hotels and restaurants. The dignified front of this hotel is constructed of gray stone, with a façade of black marble covering the street level. The manager is quick to tell you that both Mozart and Haydn frequently stayed in a former inn at this address. Those composers would probably be amused to hear recordings of their music played in the coffeehouse/restaurant attached to the hotel. About half of the 107 bedrooms have private baths. Bathless singles cost 350 AS ($25.50) to 410 AS ($29.75) daily, and singles with showers go for 720 AS ($52.25). Doubles without baths cost 340 AS ($24.75) per person, and doubles with baths are priced at 480 AS ($35) to 570 AS ($41.50) per person, including breakfast.

Hotel Kärntnerhof, Grashofgasse 4, A-1010 Vienna (tel. 0222/512-19-23), advertises itself as a *gutbürgerlich* family-oriented hotel, which, depending on your tastes, might suit you perfectly. The décor of the public rooms is tastefully arranged around Oriental rugs, well-upholstered chairs and couches with cabriole legs, and an occasional 19th-century portrait. The bedrooms are more up-to-date, usually with the original parquet floors and striped or patterned wallpaper set off by curtains. Many of the private baths glisten with tile walls and floors. The owner of this hotel supervises the maintenance of the 43 rooms and does what he can to be helpful, directing guests to the post office and other nearby Vienna landmarks. The cathedral is only a four-minute walk from the hotel. Singles cost from 650 AS ($47.25) to 950 AS ($69) daily, with doubles renting for 950 AS ($69) to 1,550 AS ($112.75). An apartment for three persons costs 1,950 AS ($141.75).

Hotel Graben, Dorotheergasse 3, A-1010 Vienna (tel. 0222/512-15-31). Elegant is the only word I'd use to describe the façade of this Inner City which housed, among other great names, Franz Kafka. The establishment lies on the Graben, which leads into the St. Stephansplatz, in a district loaded with antiques dealers and on a street that insists on "pedestrians only" during most of the day. The hotel is graced with such ornaments as carved marble fireplaces, Oriental rugs, and gilded chandeliers. In addition to the period antiques, you'll find a lot of art nouveau gracefully decorating the 46 bedrooms, all equipped with baths, radios, telephones, and minibars. The rate for a single ranges from 850 AS ($61.75) to 1,300 AS ($94.50) daily, with doubles costing 1,500 AS ($109) to 1,700 AS ($123.50). Many of these doubles are decorated in an art nouveau style or else with reproduction period antiques. Tariffs include a buffet breakfast, taxes, and service.

Hotel Regina, Rooseveltplatz 15, A-1090 Vienna (tel. 0222/42-76-81), was established in 1896 in a format that every Viennese would instantly recognize, the "Ringstrasse" style. The façade is appropriately grand for its neighborhood, close to the Votive Church, and looks a lot like a French Renaissance palace. The tree-lined street is usually calm, especially at night. It's an old-world hotel with red salons and interminable corridors. All 130 bedrooms have either a private bath or a shower. Singles cost from 950 AS ($69) to 1,350 AS ($98.25) daily, with doubles renting for 1,350 AS ($98.25) to 1,950 AS ($141.75).

Hotel Savoy, Lindengasse 12, A-1070 Vienna (tel. 0222/93-46-46). You'll find a hotel called "the Savoy" in many European capitals, and this one is worthy of bearing that illustrious name. Built within walking distance of the Ringstrasse, the hotel is centered in one of Vienna's principal shopping districts known both for wholesale and retail purchases. Each of the 43 rooms is tastefully decorated in a low-key ambience guaranteed to make you feel at home, using such cosmetic touches as ruffled bedspreads, along with big-windowed views of the city. Each bedroom has its own private bath, as well as radio and TV. Singles cost 1,050 AS ($76.25) daily, with doubles renting for 1,500 AS ($109). All tariffs include breakfast, service, and taxes. Garages and streetcar and bus stops are all in the immediate vicinity.

SOME BUDGET HOTELS

A low-key hostelry near the City Air Terminal, **Hotel Goldene Spinne,** Linke Bahngasse 1A, A-1030 Vienna (tel. 0222/712-44-86), is managed by Theophil Böck, who maintains the corner building with charm. His English-speaking staff are glad to advise guests about nearby sights. Of its 42 units, 34 contain private baths—either tubs or showers—while still others contain complete bathrooms. Rates for singles, depending on the plumbing, range from 430 AS ($31.25) to 530 AS ($38.50) daily, with doubles costing 675 AS ($49) to 830 AS ($60.25). Triples, ideal for families, cost 1,200 AS ($87.25) with shower; and four-bedded rooms, also with bath or shower, go for 1,530 AS ($111.25). Breakfast and taxes are included in the tariffs.

Zur Wiener Staatsoper, Krugerstrasse 11, A-1010 Vienna (tel. 0222/513-12-74). You'll probably stop to admire the elaborately baroque façade of this family-run hotel even if you don't plan to stay there. With 22 clean and comfortable rooms, plus an elevator, the Staatsoper is convenient to most Inner City monuments. All rooms have private showers (but no baths) and toilets. With breakfast, tax, and service included, singles rent for 700 AS ($51) daily, with doubles costing 950 AS ($69).

Hotel Graf Stadion, Buchfeldgasse 5, A-1080 Vienna (tel. 0222/42-52-84), is one of the very few genuine Biedermeier hotels left in Vienna. Charging moderate prices, it is located right behind the Rathaus, within a 10-minute walk from most of the central monuments. The façade evokes the building's early 19th-century elegance, with triangular or half-rounded ornamentation above many of the windows. The 40 bedrooms (36 doubles and 4 singles) have been refurnished, and each has a private bath. Singles rent for 650 AS ($47.25) daily, doubles for 950 AS ($69), triples for 1,250 AS ($91), and quads for 1,600 AS ($116.25). All rates include a Continental breakfast.

Hotel Rathaus, Lange Gasse 13, A-1080 Vienna (tel. 0222/43-43-02). You enter the Rathaus through a wrought-iron gate. The corridors are tiled and decorated in a functional style, as are the 40 bedrooms, each with private bath or shower, radio, and direct-dial phone. Singles cost 630 AS ($45.75) daily, with doubles renting for 920 AS ($67). An additional bed can transform a double into a triple for 260 AS ($19). Breakfast is included in all tariffs. This is a no-frills type of place, but because it's so well situated near the university and Parliament, and because its prices are so reasonable, I consider it a worthy choice.

Hotel-Pension Museum, Museumstrasse 3, A-1070 Vienna (tel. 0222/93-44-26), was originally built in the 17th century as the home of an aristocratic family. But its façade was altered around 1890 into the elegant art nouveau look you see today. It is located across from the Imperial Museums, and there are enough palaces, museums, and monuments nearby to keep you occupied for several days. You'll appreciate the spacious proportions inside many of the 20 bedrooms, each with private bath, TV, and radio. With breakfast, service, and tax, singles rent for 760 AS ($55.25) daily, with doubles costing 1,200 AS ($87.25).

Hotel Schneider, Getreidemarkt 5, A-1060 Vienna (tel. 0222/588-38), sits at the corner of a well-known street, the Lehárgasse, in the center of Vienna between the State Opera and the flower market. The hotel is a modern five-story building with panoramic windows on the ground floor and a red-tile roof; the façade is painted a baroque yellow. The interior is warmly decorated with 19th-century antiques, in part, and comfortably upholstered chairs. Musicians, singers, actors, and other artists form a part of the loyal clientele. This is one of Vienna's better small hotels, renting 71 rooms, each with private bath or shower. Singles go for 1,060 AS ($77) daily, with doubles costing 1,240 AS ($90.25), including a breakfast buffet.

A Summer Budget Hotel Chain

Academia Hotels, with headquarters at Pfeilgasse 3A, A-1080 Vienna (tel. 0222/42-25-34, ext. 77), is a chain of budget accommodations all of which are reserved for university students during the term and operated as fully licensed and categorized hotels every summer between July 1 and September 30, offering comfortable rooms for tourists at reasonable rates. These hotels are among the best bargains in town, especially since all of them are within walking distance of the city center, only a few minutes by streetcar J or underground no. 2 from the opera. They are mainly group hotels, but offer good value for individual travelers as well. The chain also has hostelries in Graz and Salzburg.

Rates at the Academia accommodations all include a Continental breakfast.

Hotel Academia, Pfeilgasse 3A, A-1080 Vienna (tel. 0222/42-25-34), has 368 bedrooms, each with complete bath. Singles rent for 620 AS ($45) daily, twins for 400 AS ($29) per person, and triples for 320 AS ($23.25) per person. Lunch or dinner costs 130 AS ($9.50).

Hotel Atlas, Lerchenfelderstrasse 1-3, A-1070 Vienna (tel. 0222/93-45-48), is a 181-room establishment with complete baths in all units. Singles go for 690 AS

($50.25) daily, with twins renting for 450 AS ($32.75) per person and triples for 390 AS ($28.25) per person. Lunch or dinner costs 130 AS ($9.50).

Hotel Avis, Pfeilgasse 4, A-1080 Vienna (tel. 0222/42-63-74), offers 72 rooms, each with private bath. Singles cost 500 AS ($36.25) daily, with twins going for 350 AS ($25.50) per person and triples for 280 AS ($20.25) per person. Lunch or dinner costs 130 AS ($9.50).

The fourth in the quartet of hotels is **Hotel Aquila,** Pfeilgasse 1A, A-1080 Vienna (tel. 0222/42-52-35), which receives summer guests in its 72 bedrooms, each equipped with a shower. Singles rent for 470 AS ($34.25) daily, with doubles going for 310 AS ($22.50) per person and triples for 250 AS ($18.25) per person. Lunch or dinner costs 130 AS ($9.50).

THE BEST OF THE PENSIONS

In a corner building, **Hotel-Pension Elite,** Wipplingerstrasse 32, A-1010 Vienna (tel. 0222/533-25-18), is next to the Vienna stock exchange. The neighborhood is appropriately grand for this edifice, which looks like a former private palace. You'll be near the university, the Burgtheater, and the cathedral. The public rooms are tastefully furnished with a mixture of antiques and modern pieces, crystal chandeliers, lots of well-oiled paneling, green-tile fireplaces, and Oriental rugs. The family-run establishment lives up to its name and deserves a high recommendation for good service in a refined framework. The hotel offers 28 bedrooms, 14 of which contain private baths or showers. Depending on the plumbing, singles range from 475 AS ($34.50) to 780 AS ($56.75) daily, with doubles going for 800 AS ($58.25) to 1,300 AS ($94.50). Breakfast, included in the rates, is served in the elegantly upholstered and carpeted dining room.

Hotel-Pension Arenberg, Stubenring 2, A-1010 Vienna (tel. 0222/512-52-91), is an old-world pension in the most prestigious section of downtown Vienna, on the Ringstrasse near all the museums and palaces, three minutes away from the air terminal and close to the canal. Rooms are soundproof and often contain Oriental rugs, interesting art, and good furniture. The entire establishment boasts only 23 rooms, with room service available during the dinner hour only. All units have baths or showers. With breakfast, tax, and service included, singles cost 890 AS ($64.75) daily, with doubles renting for 1,580 AS ($114.75). There is a restaurant in the same building.

Pension Sacher, Rotenturmstrasse 1, A-1010 Vienna (tel. 0222/533-32-38 from 8am to 1pm or 0222/461-03-05 after 1pm), is a well-run hostelry whose regular clients return year after year, partially because the pension's location on the Stephansplatz is a choice one. Although it is not now connected to the famous hotel with the same name, the Pension Sacher is owned by the great-grandson of the man who invented the Sacher torte in 1832. Carl Sacher's ancestor was the cook for Prince Metternich when the luscious dessert was first introduced to Viennese palates. His son, Edward, founded the Hotel Sacher, and his grandson, father of the owner of the pension, also named Carl, founded the Hotel Sacher in Baden near Vienna in 1881. The present Carl and his three sons, the only male descendants of the line, still have an interest in the Baden hotel and in an apartment facility in Baden.

The pension consists of eight apartments, each with kitchenette, bathroom, and direct-dial phone. There is no staff other than a maid who comes in Monday to Saturday to tidy the rooms. You must book for at least two nights. Charges for a single go from 600 AS ($43.50) to 650 AS ($47.25) daily, with doubles ranging from 700 AS ($51) to 1,000 AS ($72.75), the latter with a sitting room. The pension is on the seventh floor of the building. It's best to write well ahead of time for a reservation.

Pension Wiener, Seilergasse 16, A-1010 Vienna (tel. 0222/512-48-160), is a well-recommended 11-room pension, run by the Atnas family and occupying the third floor of a 19th-century apartment house (with an elevator) in a downtown section about two blocks from the cathedral. You're made to feel like a guest in a private home at this tranquil oasis with plenty of up-to-date conveniences and old-fashioned hospitality. All units come with private baths, radios, color TVs, phones, and refrigerators. Singles rent for 820 AS ($59.50) daily, while doubles cost 1,150 AS ($83.50), all including breakfast served in your room.

Pension Reimer, Kirchengasse 18, A-1070 Vienna (tel. 0222/93-61-62), is reached by walking from the Opernring up Mariahilferstrasse, one of the two main shopping streets of the city. The 14-room pension is quiet, despite its central location. Rooms are large and clean, with modern furniture, and most of them are equipped with showers. The price charged for a single (bathless) is 275 AS ($20) daily. Double rooms, depending on the plumbing, range from 600 AS ($43.50) to 700 AS ($51).

Pension Nossek, Graben 17, A-1010 Vienna (tel. 0222/533-70-41). Mozart lived in this centrally located building in 1781 and 1782, writing the *Haffner* Symphony and *The Abduction from the Seraglio.* The establishment lies a few blocks from such major sights as St. Stephen's Cathedral. In 1909 the building was converted into a guesthouse by the grandmother of one of the present owners, and it has long been a good bet for clean, comfortable accommodations. Most of the 28 bedrooms have been renovated, all but a few containing private baths or showers and private toilets. With breakfast included, singles cost 500 AS ($36.25) to 700 AS ($51) daily, with doubles going for 700 AS ($51) to 1,100 AS ($80). The pension is managed by the charming sisters, Miss Bernad and Mrs. Gundolf, who are part-owners. Dr. Renato Cremona, the other part-owner, lived in Florida for many years before returning to Vienna.

Pension Neuer Markt, Seilergasse 9, A-1010 Vienna (tel. 0222/512-23-16), is housed in a white baroque building with an interesting elliptical façade facing a square with an ornate fountain, near the cathedral. The carpeted rooms are clean and well maintained in an updated motif of white walls and vibrant color accents. Some of the beds are set into niches, and many of the windows are large. Each of the 37 units comes with bath, phone, and central heating. Singles peak at 1,050 AS ($73) daily, with doubles renting for 1,150 AS ($83.50).

Altwienerhof, Herklotzgasse 6, A-1150 Vienna (tel. 0222/83-71-45), is a highly acclaimed restaurant, one of the finest and most expensive in the city. But it is also a reasonably priced hotel, with 23 bedrooms furnished in traditional style. The place oozes with old-world charm, an atmosphere carefully generated by the owners, Rudolf and Ursula Kellner, and their helpful and welcoming staff. Singles with hot and cold running water, or else private showers, range from 430 AS ($31.25) to 490 AS ($35.50) daily. Doubles range from those with hot and cold running water to units with private baths, costing 750 AS ($54.50) to 800 AS ($58.25). Some apartments are even more expensively priced.

Pension Dr. Geissler, Postgasse 14, A-1010 Vienna (tel. 0222/533-28-03), is an attractively informal guesthouse offering unpretentious lodgings at reasonable prices to visitors who find themselves near the well-known Schwedenplatz at the edge of the Danube Canal. The 24 bedrooms are furnished with simple blond headboards and a few utilitarian pieces. A double with bath or shower ranges from 960 AS ($69.75) to 1,020 AS ($74.25) daily, including breakfast. You can order hot meals à la carte at any time of the day.

Pension Zipser, Lange Gasse 49, A-1080 Vienna (tel. 0222/42-02-28), is situated within a five-minute walk of the Rathaus. It offers 50 rooms—many overlooking a private garden—which are reached by the elevator. They come with private baths, phones, wall-to-wall carpeting, and central heating, and are efficiently managed by the Austerer family. The façade is ornamented with carved shell motifs above the third floor. Much of the renovated interior is tastefully adorned with wood detailing. Singles rent for 580 AS ($42.25) daily; doubles or twins for 950 AS ($69) to 1,050 AS ($76.25); and triples for 1,200 AS ($87.25) to 1,400 AS ($101.75). Breakfast buffet, service, and tax are included.

Hotel-Pension Barich, Barichgasse 3, A-1030 Vienna (tel. 0222/712-12-73), might be the choice for guests who prefer quiet residential surroundings. Northeast of the Südbahnhof, behind an unpretentious façade, is a small, quiet, and well-furnished hotel. The proprietors, Ulrich and Hermine Platz, who manage the establishment, speak fluent English. All 16 bedrooms are soundproof and have private showers or baths, toilets, direct-dial phones, radios, color TVs with in-house videos, minibars, hairdryers, electric trouser presses, and safes. Singles rent for 720 AS ($52.25) to 890 AS ($64.75) daily, with doubles costing 1,120 AS ($81.50) to 1,380 AS ($100.25), including breakfast and tax. Garage space is available on request.

4. Where to Dine

What you'll find in Vienna are restaurants of all types, serving not only Austrian cuisine, but Yugoslavian, Hungarian, and Czechoslovakian as well, along with Chinese, Italian, Russian, or whatever.

There are also many classic dishes of the Wiener küche that you'll want to try. Before dining out, refer to the notes on Austrian cookery in Chapter II under "Food and Drink."

Unlike many capitals of Western Europe, Vienna has not kept abreast of changing times, and Sunday closing times (marked by "Sonntag Ruhetag" signs) still predominate. Watch also for those summer holiday closings, when chefs would rather rush to the seashore or lakeside than cook for Vienna's visiting hordes.

THE UPPER BRACKET

Korso bei die Oper, Mahlerstrasse 2 (tel. 0222/515-16), is a citadel of gastronomic chic. It is reached by walking across Aubusson carpets and past the antiques of the Hotel Bristol lobby, or else through a street entrance. In the restaurant, expensive paneling, scarlet-colored carpeting, fountain-shaped crystal chandeliers, Sheraton shield-backed armchairs, and baroque corkscrew-shaped columns flanking a pink marble fireplace create an opulent atmosphere.

Chef Reinhard Gerer, one of the finest in Vienna, prepares an alluring mixture of both traditional and nouvelle cuisine for a discriminating clientele. Your meal might include tafelspitz as Franz Joseph liked it, roast veal kidneys in a burgundy sauce, a rack of lamb with aromatic spices, medallions of beef with a shallot-flavored butter sauce and Roquefort-flavored noodles. Your first course might have been oysters, accompanied by one of the selections from an extensive wine list. Full meals cost from 700 AS ($51), and reservations are important. The restaurant's hours are noon to 3pm and 7 to 11pm daily except Saturday lunch. It is also closed for the first two weeks of August.

Rôtisserie Prinz Eugen, Hilton Hotel, Am Stadtpark (tel. 0222/75-26-52, ext. 355), is one of the finest restaurants of Vienna. The setting is like that of an operetta version of a baronial château, filled with every comfort imaginable and certain to impress with its overlay of charm. There are three rooms, each one embellished in the style of Belvedere Palace, itself dating from the 18th century. You might dine in a salon decorated in muted beige and gold, honoring the musical heritage of the Austrian capital. A second salon is the Baronial Hall, a grill, with scenes from the prince's battles adorning the walls, furniture, and oak paneling. The waiters serve international specialties from the open grill. The final room is the Belvedere Library, the bookshelves holding hundreds of antique volumes. It has dark-wood paneling.

Eduard Mitsche, from Carinthia, is one of the founders of nouvelle cuisine Viennoise. As such, he is one of the leading chefs of Austria. Each day he creates a special gourmet menu based on the freshest ingredients available in the market, many of which he has had brought to Vienna for the purpose, supervising his staff of 75 persons in preparation and service, which are superb. Try his "variations of sweets," which look like works of art. Each dish is prepared for a discriminating palate. This place is an exclusive Viennese haunt, drawing both locals and foreign patronage, each group of which seems to appreciate its excellent wine cellar. You can order from the international menu weekdays from noon to 2:30pm. Business lunches, consisting of two courses and coffee, cost from 300 AS ($21.75). Dinner is served daily from 7 to 11:30pm. Gourmet menus cost from 730 AS ($53), with à la carte items beginning at 500 AS ($36.25).

Gottfried Restaurant, Untere Viaduktgasse 45 at Marxergasse 3 (tel. 0222/713-82-56), one of the best two or three restaurants in Vienna, was established in 1985 on a commercial street near the City Air Terminal. It revels in the kind of décor that many less successful restaurants would like to emulate, combining a perfectly controlled ambience with superb food. The pure-white walls and lace-covered windows are flatteringly offset with ruby-colored Oriental carpets, pink napery, and unglazed terra-cotta floors. Add to this about a dozen polite and uniformed waiters, verdant plants, and comfortably contemporary armchairs covered in pastel-tinted upholstery, and you get an idea of what Gottfried is all about.

Considering the quality of the cuisine, set menus are reasonably priced at 250 AS ($18.25) and 420 AS ($30.50) at lunch, and 720 AS ($52.25) and 880 AS ($64) at dinner. A la carte meals cost from 550 AS ($40). Your meal might begin with potato soup with truffles or include carpaccio, a salad of lobster with fresh asparagus, a salad of wild duck, and a provençale fish soup so rich it could almost be considered a relish. Carinthian-born Josef Fadinger is the experienced chef whose meals are worth the expense. The establishment is open for lunch Sunday to Friday from noon to 2pm and for dinner daily from 6 to 11pm. Reservations are necessary.

Zu den Drei Husaren, Weihburggasse 4 (tel. 0222/512-10-92), is an enduring favorite among restaurants serving an inventive and classic Viennese cuisine. Some consider it as much an institution as St. Stephen's Cathedral, which stands nearby. Few social or business leaders would consider a trip to Vienna without a dinner here. Over the years, it has entertained the famous (the Duke and Duchess of Windsor) and the infamous. Just off the Kärntnerstrasse, it has a large plate-glass window with plaster mannequins of the Hungarian officers who established the place after World War I. An interior view reveals Gobelin tapestries, antiques, fine rugs, and masses of flowers.

The establishment is expensive and select, with a delectable cuisine that has been rated by practically everyone as the best traditional food in Vienna. To the background music of gypsy melodies, you dine on such dishes as lobster cream soup with tarragon, stewed rumpsteak with white cabbage and noodles, freshwater salmon with pike soufflé, breast of guinea fowl, and an array of sole dishes. The chef specializes in veal, including his deliciously flavored kalbsbrücken Metternich. The place is celebrated for its repertoire of more than 40 hors d'oeuvres, served from a trolley rolled through its elegant precincts. A dessert specialty is the Husaren pfannkuchen (Hussar's pancake), as well as a form of cheese-filled crêpe which, as if that weren't enough, has a chocolate sauce poured over it (the recipe is known only to the chef). Meals cost from 400 AS ($29) to 1,200 AS ($87.25). The restaurant serves dinner nightly from 6pm to 1:30am. It's often closed for a month in parts of July and August.

Sacher Hotel Restaurant, Philharmonikerstrasse 4 (tel. 0222/81-4-56), is a famous, famous restaurant, serving the epitome of Viennese cookery. Long an enduring favorite—either before or after the opera—it has few detractors. Seemingly all celebrities who come to Vienna eventually are seen in the red dining room, where they're likely to order the restaurant's most famous dish, tafelspitz, the Viennese boiled beef platter that was fit for an emperor. The chef serves it with a savory, herb-flavored sauce. Of course, that emperor was not Franz Joseph I: Madame Sacher annoyed him by encouraging liaisons between archdukes and the attractive young members of the Vienna Opera Ballet.

Wear your finest for dinner here, and make sure you show up before 11pm, even though opening hours are from noon to 1am. Count on spending from 600 AS ($43.50) up for a sumptuous meal. Waiters will often suggest various Austrian wines to accompany your dinner. For dessert, the Sacher torte enjoys world renown. It is said to have been created in 1832 by Franz Sacher while he served as Prince Metternich's apprentice. The Sacher torte is the most famous pastry in Vienna. It's primarily a chocolate sponge mixture. After it's baked, it's sliced in half and filled with apricot jam.

Palais Schwarzenberg Restaurant, Schwarzenbergplatz 9 (tel. 0222/78-43-15), has one of the most elegant backgrounds of any restaurant in the city. It lies in a famous hotel (see the previous recommendation). The owner is Prince Karl Johannes von Schwarzenberg, scion of one of the country's most aristocratic families. Take your time over an apéritif in the deluxe cocktail lounge, where the waiter will most likely recite the daily specialties of the chef. In summer you can dine on a terrace considered the most beautiful in Vienna. Dining in such an imperial setting might cause you to imagine you are a Habsburg. The cuisine is refined, with many French dishes, and the service is first class and very old-world. The wine cellar is superb, and the chef is a man of many talents. He seasonally adjusts his menu and therefore has many specialties, including goose liver gulasch and medallions of veal with crabmeat and pearl onions. Dinner costs from 500 AS ($36.25) to 1,000 AS ($72.75). The restaurant is open daily from noon to 2:30pm and 6pm to midnight, year round. Reservations are essential.

König von Ungarn (King of Hungary), Schulerstrasse 10 (tel. 0222/512-53-19), is a beautifully decorated restaurant inside the famous hotel of the same name, which is housed in a 16th-century building. You dine in an atmosphere of crystal, chandeliers, antiques, marble columns, and a vaulted ceiling. The service here is superb, with a masterful menu of Viennese and international dishes. If you're in doubt about what to order, try the tafelspitz, the savory boiled beef dish that we've already sampled at the Sacher Hotel. It's elegantly dispensed from a trolley that makes the rounds through the richly decorated place. Other menu choices, which change frequently according to what is seasonal, include a ragoût of seafish with fresh mushrooms, tournedos with a mustard and horseradish sauce, and a stunning collection of appetizers that might include scampi in a caviar sauce. À la carte dinners average 400 AS ($29) to 600 AS ($43.50), and considering what you get, that's not an overpriced check. The restaurant is open daily except Saturday from 11:30am to 3pm and 6:15pm to midnight.

Steirereck, Rasumofskygasse 2 (tel. 0222/713-31-68), means "corner of Styria," which is exactly what Heinz and Margarethe Reitbauer have created in the rustic décor of this intimate restaurant (acclaimed by some Viennese as the best in the city), which lies on the Danube Canal between the Central Station and the Prater. The Reitbauers have used original beams and archways brought from an old castle in Styria to enhance the ambience of their establishment, with murals adding to the cozy feel. They offer both traditional Viennese dishes and nouvelle cuisine selections. For example, tafelspitz might be served in the old-fashioned way or else in a more modern manner, with a warm cranberry sauce. Other dishes are likely to include veal with Calvados and wild rice, rack of lamb Styrian style, and soufflé of trout with sorrel noodles. The menu is wisely limited and well prepared, changing daily depending on the fresh produce available at the market. Expect to pay from 680 AS ($9.50) for a meal of six courses. The restaurant is closed on Saturday and Sunday and holidays but open otherwise from 11:30am to 3pm and 7 to 11pm, which makes it popular with after-theater diners.

Leupold's Kupferdachl, Schottengasse 7 (tel. 0222/63-93-81), has been directed by the Leupold family for the past 40 years. Today it specializes in the Austrian equivalent of nouvelle cuisine, but the chef also prepares more conservatively traditional dishes. Specialties of the house are fish, lamb, and game dishes. The rustically elegant interior has lots of paneling, a scattering of Oriental rugs, and a cozy ambience of banquettes and elegantly detailed straight-backed chairs. Lunch averages around 350 AS ($25.50), while dinner costs from 450 AS ($32.75) and up. The restaurant is open Monday to Friday from noon to 3pm and 6pm to midnight. On Saturday it's open only for dinner, and is closed from late July until mid-August.

At **Kervansaray & Hummer Bar,** Mahlerstrasse 9 (tel. 0222/512-88-43), you get a sense of the historic link between the Habsburgs and their 19th-century neighbor, the Ottoman Empire. The place actually contains three different restaurants on the same premises (the deli is reviewed separately). The two remaining restaurants occupy two different floors, but each is committed to serving an array of delectable seafood flown in frequently from the North Sea or from the Bosphorus.

On the ground floor, in the Kervansaray, a team of polite waiters, many from Turkey, announce a changing array of daily specials. They also serve tempting salads from an hors d'oeuvres table. Perhaps the true visual treat of the evening is upstairs in the Lobster Bar, where, in a spacious series of interconnected rooms dotted with Oriental carpets, guests enjoy the bounties of the sea.

A meal in either section of the restaurant often begins with a champagne cocktail and is followed by one of many appetizers, including a lobster and salmon caviar cocktail. Main courses include a short list of meat dishes, including filet steak with Roquefort sauce, but they consist mainly of seafood, such as grilled filet of sole with fresh asparagus, bouillabaisse, a Norwegian salmon with horseradish and champagne sauce, and, most definitely, lobster. Full meals cost 500 AS ($36.25) to 800 AS ($58.25) if you stick to the standard fare. But if shellfish is your weakness, a tab could run much higher. The restaurant is open daily except Sunday from noon to 3pm and 6pm to 1am.

Restaurant Mitsukoshi, Albertinaplatz 2 (tel. 0222/512-27-07). Upstairs, the Café Mozart is a model of baroque elegance, but in the basement diners experience a cross-cultural shock in discovering the most elegant and sophisticated Japanese restaurant in Austria. It was established in 1985 when one of Tokyo's best-known department stores, Mitsukoshi, upgraded the décor of the café and opened the basement restaurant. Opalized marble, Japanese cypress, carefully arranged lighting, and Noh masks were incorporated into what is a showplace of Mitsukoshi design and style.

First, visitors enjoy a cup of Japanese tea or sake in a restrained lounge where the severe angles of a black granite fountain are softened with carefully arranged flowers, and then a kimono-clad waitress from Japan escorts visitors down a flight of steps to the alluringly simple dining room. There you can order an à la carte Japanese meal for 550 AS ($40) or a fixed-price menu, ranging from 500 AS ($36.25) to 900 AS ($65.50). Sushi, imported from Italy or Turkey, is followed by a full-service meal in a ritualized format on lacquer dishes with fresh vegetables. The establishment is closed Sunday. Between Monday and Saturday, meals are served from noon to 2pm and 7 to 10:30pm. Reservations are suggested. The main entrance to this establishment is around the corner from the Albertinaplatz on the Maysedergasse.

Landhaus Winter, Simmeringer Lände 262 (tel. 0222/76-23-17), is a century-old country house surrounded with flowers in summer and decorated inside with rustic artifacts. It sits at the edge of the Danube Canal, providing a refuge for those Viennese who wish to escape the congestion of their city. The terrace is particularly pleasant on a summer day, although the interior is cozily paneled and elegant. Well-prepared fish is one of the specialties here, and a selection might include perch or eel, both cooked in a number of ways, or Greenland salmon, French oysters, Portuguese mussels, and a young brook trout from local waters. Meat dishes might include medallions of roebuck, tournedos with mushrooms, lamb steak with fennel, and filet of beef in a cabbage cream sauce. Meals range from 350 AS ($25.50) to 750 AS ($54.50). Reservations are suggested, and the restaurant is closed on Sunday evening and all day Monday. Lunch is from noon to 3pm, dinner from 6pm to midnight (but the last orders go in at 10pm). To reach the restaurant, you must drive or ride 20 minutes east of Vienna, exiting at the autobahn Simmerringer Heide exit.

Altwienerhof, Herklotzgasse 6 (tel. 0222/83-71-45), near Schönbrunn Palace, is one of the premier dining spots in Vienna. Rudolf and Ursula Kellner bring sophistication and charm to the wood-paneled, subduedly lit establishment, which has a winter garden. The chef prepares a *cuisine de marché,* based on shopping for only the freshest and highest-quality ingredients, which go into the preparation of the luxurious dinners served at beautifully laid tables. Since the menu changes frequently, I can't recommend specialties, but the maître d' is always there to assist. Regional specialties are the pride of the kitchen staff. Each night the chef prepares a six-course *menu de dégustation,* giving you a sampling of the best dishes. The wine list consists of some 700 items, and the cellar houses 18,000 bottles; each of the wines is selected by Mr. Kellner himself. A fixed-price lunch is offered for 425 AS ($31), whereas dinners cost from 675 AS ($49) to 940 AS ($68.25). Hours are 11:15am to 3pm and 6pm to midnight daily except Sunday.

Steinerne Eule (Stony Owl), Halbgasse 30 (tel. 0222/93-22-50), is the exclusive haunt of some of the most prestigious gourmets of Vienna. With the prices it charges—between 320 AS ($23.25) and 650 AS ($47.25) for a fixed-price meal— you can see why. À la carte dinners cost less, from 225 AS ($16.25). The chef blends an attractive synthesis of nouvelle Austrian cuisine with traditional Viennese recipes. The menu changes according to the season and the market availability. Therefore, depending on this, you might get venison terrine with fresh goose liver, zucchini filled with goose liver pâté, or veal delicacies sometimes served with spinach noodles. For an innovative dessert, the chef occasionally features an avocado mousse with fresh strawberries, or perhaps an apple parfait with kiwi fruit. The restaurant serves daily except Sunday and Monday from 11am to 3pm and 6pm to 1am.

Hauswirth, Otto-Bauer-Gasse 20 (tel. 0222/587-12-61). The imposing entrance to this restaurant is under a rectangular corridor with a well-polished fan window at the far end. You'll push open the leaded-glass door to enter this art nouveau enclave, which has become a stamping ground of well-dressed habitués. The summertime gardens are lovely, but in winter you'll probably eat in a paneled ambience of dark wood and crystal chandeliers. The chef adheres to *neue Wiener küche.* He seasonally adjusts his menu, which might include quail, venison, asparagus, lots of fresh berries, goose liver, sweetbreads, well-prepared steaks and fish specialties, plus a tempting array of homemade pastries. À la carte meals range from 350 AS ($25.50) to 600 AS ($43.50), while a set menu is offered for 500 AS ($36.25). The cellar holds not only a large variety of the best of Austrian wines but also a well-chosen assortment of some of the best European vineyards. The place is open daily except Saturday and Sunday from noon to 3pm and 6pm to midnight.

Restaurant Fischerhaus, an der Höhenstrasse (tel. 0222/44-13-20), in the Vienna Woods, is popular with members of Vienna's diplomatic community and the city's business elite. Celebrities who have dined here include Arnold Schwarzenegger, Robert Mitchum, and Elizabeth Taylor. The cellars read like an international directory of fine wines, especially those from the Napa Valley of California. The establishment is housed in a century-old farmhouse surrounded by greenery, with an outdoor terrace and an interior with a wintertime fireplace and a collection of antique firearms and hunting memorabilia. Since its opening in 1954, the restaurant has lured the Viennese with its hearty Austrian and international fare. Fixed-price menus begin at 450 AS ($32.75), with à la carte dinners costing from 380 AS ($27.75). Meals are served continuously from noon to 10pm daily except Sunday night and Monday. Annual closing is in January and February.

THE MEDIUM-PRICED RANGE

Restaurant Stiebitz (Zum Schwarzen Kameel), Bognergasse 5 (tel. 0222/63-81-25), dates from 1618 and has remained in the same family. A delicatessen against one of the walls sells wine, liquor, and specialty meat items, although most of the action takes place among the chicly dressed clientele in the café. On a Saturday morning the café section is packed with weekend Viennese recovering from a late night out with massive doses of caffeine. Everyone stands here, drinking the beverages that the uniformed waiters bring on trays, and selecting open-face sandwiches from the trays on the black countertops.

The restaurant beyond the café is a perfectly preserved art deco room. Jeweled copper chandeliers hang from beaded strings, with illumination beaming through their etched-glass globes. The walls are a combination of polished paneling, yellowed ceramic tiles, and a dusky plaster ceiling frieze of grape leaves. The vine theme is repeated in the machine-age marquetry in several kinds of hardwoods, which graces many of the room dividers. The restaurant contains only 11 tables, and it might be a perfect place for a nostalgic lunch or dinner in Vienna. The international cuisine features specialties such as herring filet Oslo, potato soup, tournedos, Roman saltimbocca, and an array of daily fish specials. Meals range from 300 AS ($21.75). The restaurant is open Monday to Friday from 9am to 7pm, on Saturday from 9am to 2:30pm; closed Sunday.

The first-floor restaurant inside the previously recommended **Hotel Astoria,** Kärntnerstrasse 32—entrance is at Führichgasse 1 (tel. 0222/526-58-50)—remains the premier authentic Jugendstil dining room of Vienna, dating from 1911. The foyer is filled with portraits of opera stars, and the appropriately grand décor boasts a handsome marble fireplace. One food critic once wrote, "If Tadzio and his mummy [a reference to the Thomas Mann characters in *Death in Venice*] had lunch here on their way to Venice, it must have looked very much like it does today." An opera menu is offered either before or after the performance at the nearby Staatsoper, and there is a wide selection of Austrian and international food. Typical dishes include tafelspitz; saddle of veal, old Vienna style; and tournedos with morel sauce. Meals cost from 200 AS ($14.50) to 450 AS ($32.75), so the dining room appeals to a wide range of pocketbooks. Service is daily from noon to 9:30pm.

Franz Zimmer Schubertstüberln, Schreyvogelgasse 4 (tel. 0222/63-71-87). Awnings shelter the café chairs set onto a raised platform above the pink begonias and cobblestones of the quiet street near the Burgtheater. From looking at it, you'd never guess that the inside is as big as it is, but once you pass through the small garden entrance, you'll see a series of rooms that have been elevated to a high pitch of the modern decorator's art. You'll find a room here for practically every taste, from the plushly modern bar with horseshoe-shaped banquettes to a rustically informal eatery called the Bistro. Entered on the left, this is the least expensive place to go for lunch. My favorite rooms in the main restaurant: two salons in pastel-colored, high-ceilinged elegance. The distinguished chef has prepared several menus, letting diners select from such dishes as Hungarian fish soup, filet Stroganoff with rösti, and filet of veal "Old Vienna" (that is, with a goose liver and sour cream sauce). To finish, why not sample the cheese strudel? Meals cost from 150 AS ($11) to 400 AS ($29). The Bistro is open Monday to Friday from 9am to midnight, and the main restaurant serves from 11am to 3pm and 6pm to midnight; closed Saturday and Sunday. Annual closing is from the end of August until late September.

Abend-Restaurant Feuervogel, Alserbachstrasse 21 (tel. 0222/34-10-392). For some 80 years this has been a Viennese landmark, bringing Russian cuisine to a location across the street from the palace of the Prince of Liechtenstein. You'll eat in romantically Slavic surroundings with gypsy violins playing Russian and Viennese music in the background. Specialties include chicken Kiev, beef Stroganoff, veal Dolgoruki, borscht, and many other dishes that taste as if they came right off the steppes. Your hors d'oeuvres might be sakkuska, a variety platter popular in Russia. For dessert you might select a Russian ice cream called plombier. An average meal will cost from 250 AS ($18.25); however, you can also order a 500-AS ($36.25) "gourmet kreml dinner," with five courses. The restaurant is open every day except

Sunday from 6pm to 1am. It's closed from mid-July until after the first week of August.

Rôtisserie Sirk, Kärntnerstrasse 53 (tel. 0222/515-16), is a plushly modern restaurant conveniently near the State Opera on the second floor of the Hotel Bristol. The kitchen prepares conservative but flavorful meals with flair and gusto, and the Sirk represents good value, especially when compared to the higher-priced citadels around it. On the lower street level is an art nouveau café, complete with rich pastries, beveled glass, and big windows. Most diners, however, head immediately for the stairwell leading up to the second floor. Every night a traditional three-course opera supper, with a varied choice of components, is offered for 350 AS ($25.50). Otherwise, full à la carte meals cost from 400 AS ($29). Specialties include "3 Kleine Filets" (beef, pork, and veal) served with mushrooms, spinach, and a pepper cream sauce; roast duck crisp from the oven with red cabbage and bread dumplings; medallions of venison in a goose liver sauce; and saddle of veal with morels. Meals are served daily from noon to 3pm and 7pm to midnight. The café downstairs is open from 10am to midnight.

Firenze Enoteca, Singerstrasse 3 (tel. 0222/513-43-74), is the premier Tuscan restaurant of Vienna. In the heart of the monument district, near St. Stephen's Cathedral, it is furnished in a Tuscan Renaissance style, with copies of frescoes by Benozzo Gozzoli. Along with a wide array of classic Chianti and other wines from all over Italy, the kitchen turns out superb Italian cuisine, specializing in homemade pasta served with zesty sauces. Diners begin by making a selection from the antipasti table, then choose among such dishes as spaghetti with "fruits of the sea"; penne with salmon; veal cutlet with ham, cheese, and sardines; and perhaps filet of beef with a tomato-and-garlic sauce. Meals, costing from 350 AS ($25.50), are served daily from 11:30am to 3pm and 6pm to midnight. The location is next to the Royal Hotel. It's best to call for a reservation.

Restaurant Stadtkrug, Weihburggasse 3 (tel. 0222/512-79-55), a long-enduring favorite, attracts the visiting cultural celebrity (Leonard Bernstein) or the visiting out-of-work politician (Richard Nixon). Its dining rooms are in the formal scarlet-colored Middle European tradition, and service is equally formal. The restaurant occupies the site of a Sakristei room dating from the 14th century, and it stands across from the even more famous (and more expensive) Zu den Drei Husaren. In the evening, pianists or a gypsy band entertains you. Lunch is served daily from 11:30am to 3pm and dinner from 6pm to midnight, with meals costing from 350 AS ($25.50). The cookery is traditionally Viennese, with such dishes as oven-roasted goose with white-wine cabbage and bread dumplings, boiled rib of beef with dill sauce, medallions of venison, and veal stew in a paprika cream sauce.

The pine-paneled **Marco Polo,** Wehrgasse 9 (tel. 0222/587-83-65)—owned by an Italian/Austrian team, Edgardo (Edy) Marco de Polo and his delightful wife, Olga Schmid—is one of the warmest refuges in an otherwise nondescript neighborhood. With its immaculate napery, tiny bar, and simply decorated rooms, the place is a modest trattoria, yet it attracts such stars as Raf Vallone. The real star of the place, however, is English-speaking Olga. The food is superb, especially the homemade ravioli, which is worth a culinary award. The homemade pesto is always available, and meats, flavored with garlic and Italian herbs, are grilled to perfection. Other recommendable courses include gnocchi with Gorgonzola, risotto ai frutto di mare, green tagliatelle with salmon, saltimbocca, scaloppine marsala, and, for dessert, zabaglione with marsala. Each dish is freshly prepared. Full meals cost from 360 AS ($26.25). The restaurant is open daily except Sunday from 11am to 2:30pm and 6pm to midnight. Because the place is small, reservations are important.

Restaurant Bukarest, Bräunerstrasse 7 (tel. 0222/512-37-63), serves Balkan —mainly Romanian—specialties in a tunnel-like room with old vaulting and an exposed charcoal grill. A café in front offers sidewalk tables for guests who prefer to be outdoors. Specialties include Serbian bean soup, grilled sirloin steak stuffed with chopped meat, and a Jamaican pepper and garlic dish. Another dish of which the chef is proud is his mixed grill, and his baklava is outstanding. Expect to spend from 300 AS ($21.75) per person. The restaurant serves daily except Monday from 11:30am to 2:30pm and 6pm to midnight.

Sailer, Gersthoferstrasse 14 (tel. 0222/47-21-21), near the Türkenschanzpark, is tastefully decorated in an old Vienna style, with wood paneling, Biedermeier portraits, and in one of the cellar rooms, antique chairs, each hand-carved in a different design. The art nouveau exterior is lit with spots at night, revealing an interior where clients are seated on two different levels, according to their choice. Specialties of the house include deer and elk, wild boar, pheasant, and partridge, each prepared according to classic and time-honored Viennese recipes, along with a tempting collection of tortes and pastries. The third-generation owners acquiesce to the demands of an updated light cuisine with daily specials that depend on the availability of produce in the marketplace. They serve Monday to Saturday from 11:30am to 2:30pm and 6 to 11pm; the restaurant is closed on Sunday and holidays. Meals average 250 AS ($18.20) at lunch, going up to 400 AS ($29.10) at dinner.

Niky's Kuchlmasterei, Obere Weissgerberstrasse 6 (tel. 0222/72-44-18). The bill, when it comes after a long and pleasant meal, will arrive in an elaborate box suitable for jewels, along with an amusing message in German (if you can read it) that offers a tongue-in-cheek apology for cashing your check. The restaurant has a décor of old stonework, with modern innovations both in the architecture and in the cuisine. The large menu, the well-prepared food, the welcoming ambience, and the lively crowd of loyal habitués make it a good choice for an evening meal. Its summer terrace is among the most exclusive in Vienna. The cookery is basically Viennese and French, with meals costing 200 AS ($14.50) to 400 AS ($29). It is open Monday to Saturday from 10am to midnight.

Restaurant Serviette, Wiedner Hauptstrasse 27 (tel. 0222/50-11-10), is an intimately elegant dining room attached to the Hotel Erzherzog Rainer. The building, constructed in 1912, has been renovated into an attractive place for both lodging and meals (see previous recommendation). Its well-run restaurant offers food items such as tafelspitz with applesauce, horseradish, chives, and sautéed potatoes; a tender Wiener schnitzel; and grilled fogosch with anchovy butter. Many of their specialties are based on the produce of the season, which is likely to include fresh strawberries or raspberries and, inevitably, summer vegetables. In the autumn they feature hare, deer, venison, and wild boar. Dessert might be shredded pancakes with stewed plums or a Salzburg-style soufflé. Fixed-price meals range from 300 AS ($21.75) to 475 AS ($34.50), à la carte dinners from 250 AS ($18.25) to 400 AS ($29). Lunch is served daily from noon to 3pm and dinner from 6 to 11pm. A less expensive brasserie on the premises offers an inexpensive quick meal with beer on tap and tempting pastries. Brasserie hours are daily from noon to 3pm and 6pm to 12:30am.

Griechenbeisl, Fleischmarkt 11 (tel. 0222/533-19-41), was established in 1450 and today is still one of the leading restaurants of Vienna. It has a labyrinthine collection of at least seven different dining areas on three different floors, all of them with low vaulted ceilings, smoky paneling, wrought-iron chandeliers, and Styrian-vested waiters who scurry around with large trays of food. This is a long-enduring favorite with the Viennese, and especially the foreign colony, who appreciate its mellow antique atmosphere and its dozens of charming touches. As you enter from the street, look down at the grate below your feet for an illuminated view of a pirate counting his money. As you go in, be sure to see the so-called inner sanctum, with signatures of such former patrons as Mozart, Beethoven, and Mark Twain.

The Pilsen beer is well chilled and the food is *bürgerlich,* meaning hearty, ample, and solidly bourgeois. Menu items include deer stew, both Hungarian and Viennese gulasch, sauerkraut garni, and braised leg of venison. À la carte meals cost from 350 AS ($25.50) and are served daily from 10am to 12:30am. The restaurant features nighttime accordion and zither music.

Mathias Keller, Maysedergasse 2 (tel. 0222/52-21-67), evokes memories of the old Austro-Hungarian Empire. This is the Vienna outpost of the much more famous (and much larger) Mathias Keller in Budapest, which is probably the most famous restaurant in that city. In Vienna the cellar restaurant is decorated in Czardas style and features gypsy music. From noon to midnight daily, you can enjoy its Hungarian fare, all the typical dishes so well known across the border: stuffed cabbage, gulasch soup, perhaps a mixed grill for two preceded by smoked trout. Meals cost from 225 AS ($16.25). Perhaps as a good sign, visiting Hungarians always seek out this keller during their Vienna rounds.

THE BUDGET RESTAURANTS

In the medieval section of town, **Ofenlock,** Kurrentgasse 8 (tel. 0222/533-88-44), is a well-reputed eating house of old Vienna. The waitresses wear Biedermeier costumes and will give you a menu that looks more like a magazine. Some of the mock medieval illustrations inside are funny, and when you get around to reading the food items, you'll be prepared for the gutbürgerlich aspect of many of them. Specialties include two kinds of schnitzel, pork, noodle, and hearty soup dishes, as well as salads and cheese platters. For smaller appetites, there's a page devoted to one-dish meals, any of which would go well with the wine and beer consumed in quantities here. A robust three-course meal will cost from 200 AS ($14.50). The restaurant is open daily except Sunday and holidays from 10am to midnight.

Restaurant Kardos, Dominikaner Bastei 8 (tel. 0222/512-69-49), serves Hungarian and mixed-grill specialties. However, the menu is adjusted seasonally so that the chef can turn out well-prepared foods using the freshest ingredients available to him. Regional recipes familiar to many Eastern Europeans are featured. Barack, an apéritif made from apricots, is offered, as well as piquant little rolls known as grammel. They're seasoned with pork and hot spices. The décor is brightly Hungarian, with contrasting sunny colors, elaborate pine detailing cut into country baroque patterns, and a cellar locale with gypsy music in wintertime. Full meals cost as little as 150 AS ($11), but 250 AS ($18.25) is more average. Service is from 11:30am to 2:30pm and 6 to 11pm. Closed Sunday night and Monday.

Zwölf-Apostelkeller, Sonnenfelsgasse 3 (tel. 0222/512-67-77), is an old wine tavern, parts of its walls predating the year 1561. Rows of wooden tables stand under vaulted ceilings, with illumination provided partially by the streetlights that have been set into the masonry floor. This place is popular with students, partly because of its reasonable prices and partly because of its proximity to St. Stephen's. It's so deep you feel you're entering a dungeon. The tavern is open daily from 4:30pm to midnight. In addition to beer and wine, the establishment serves hearty Austrian fare. Specialties include Hungarian gulasch soup, meat dumplings, and a Schlachtplatte (a selection of hot black pudding, liverwurst, pork, and pork sausage with a hot bacon and cabbage salad). Meals cost from 100 AS ($7.25).

The sophisticated delicatessen, **Do & Co.,** Akademiestrasse 3 (tel. 0222/512-64-74), next to the State Opera, is to Vienna what Fauchon is to Paris. Depending on the season, the asparagus might have been flown in from Paris or Argentina, while the shellfish may have come from either the North Sea or the Bosphorus. Regardless of the origin, the rich display of food fills sprawling rows of glass cases laden with pâtés, seafood salads, and Viennese pastries. The establishment is connected by a corridor to the already-recommended Kervansaray & Hummer Bar.

Visitors can carry their purchases away with them or move to one of the tiny, somewhat cramped tables scattered near the entrance. You can order a salad or else a portion of Norwegian lobster thermidor, one of three shrimp platters, salmon quiche, or filet of turbot. The place is likely to be packed, especially at lunchtime, with young and demanding gastronomes willing to sacrifice space and ambience for a slice of the good life. You can spend anywhere from 180 AS ($13) to celestial heights for an elegant snack, depending on your appetite and budget. The establishment is open daily except Sunday from 8:30am to 6:30pm.

Restaurant Siddhartha, Fleischmarkt 16 (tel. 0222/513-11-97), is at the end of a covered arcade in the old city, in a crowded, clean ambience of white stucco, candlelight, fresh flowers, and vaulted ceilings. This restaurant serves only vegetarian food. It's very popular, and you'll be fortunate to get a seat during peak serving hours. It's open daily except Sunday from 11:30am to 3pm and 6 to 11pm. Menu specialties include ratatouille, quiche Lorraine, a Siddhartha plate for two persons (mixed specialties), many curry dishes, Roquefort crêpes, piccata milanese (with imitation veal), mushrooms Romanoff, and mangos in port. Meals cost from 125 AS ($9) to 275 AS ($20).

Alte Backstube, Lange Gasse 34 (tel. 0222/43-11-01), is worth visiting just to admire the baroque sculptures that crown the top of the doorway leading into what was originally built as a private home in 1697. Four years later it was transformed into a bakery, with wood-burning stoves installed in various parts of the ground floor. For more than 2½ centuries the establishment served the baking needs of the neighborhood, and then, in 1963, the Schwarzmann family added a dining room, a dainty front room for drinking beer and tea, and a collection of baking-related artifacts. The passageway leading into the cozily vaulted dining room is lined with documents, antique troughs, and tools related to baking, as well as baroque sculptures.

Once seated, you can order wholesome, robust Teutonic specialties such as braised pork with cabbage, Viennese-style gulasch, and roast venison with cranberry sauce and bread dumplings. There's an English-language menu if you need it. Try the house special dessert of cream cheese strudel with hot vanilla sauce. Full meals cost from around 225 AS ($16.25). The charming staff serves meals every day except Monday. Tuesday through Saturday the restaurant is open from 8am to midnight; on Sunday and holidays, hours are 2pm to midnight. Closed in August.

La Crêperie/Le Bistro, Jasomirgottstrasse 5 (tel. 0222/533-55-07). Despite its location on a crowded street several blocks from the cathedral, parts of its woodsy décor evoke a country tavern high in the Alps. As you enter from the street, the first area to greet you is a rustically nostalgic Bistro, with dark unvarnished walls and a predictable array of pastas and pizzas. The most interesting part, however, lies at the top of steep stairs. There, a labyrinth of carefully decorated rooms is filled nightly with dozens of clients chattering, drinking, and eating. Choose among the rooms, with their thick, sloping ceiling beams evoking a 19th-century barn, or else with stained-glass ceilings and Toulouse Lautrec–style murals. In any event, keep walking until you find your preferred décor. Food is served daily from 11:30am to 3pm and 6pm to midnight. Full meals cost 200 AS ($14.50), including Marseilles-style fish soup, cassoulet, scampi provençal, mussels marinara, and a wide assortment of the chef's specialty, crêpes and galettes, named after such evocative references as Pigalle, Nice, and Provence.

Dubrovnik, Am Heumarkt 3 (tel. 0222/713-27-55), is a Balkan restaurant where the staff wears the regional garb of the different provinces of Yugoslavia. It's set up in three rooms on either side of a central vestibule filled with busy waiters rushing in and out of the kitchen, which you can see through an open door at the far end. The menu lists many Yugoslav dishes, including Serbian bean soup, as well as specialties from the grill, including pork kidney. Among the fish dishes, the most exotic is the Serbian fogosch (a kind of whitefish), served with potatoes and garlic. Dessert could be baklava or both Bulgarian and Serbian cheese if you'd like to finish with a savory. Meals average 175 AS ($12.75). The restaurant is open daily from 11am to 3pm and 6pm to midnight.

Figlmüller, Wollzeile 5 (tel. 0222/512-61-77), in the Inner City, is considered one of the most famous beisels in Vienna. The passageway down which it's located leads to a site that is about 500 years old. Inside, the relaxed ambience is one of good and simple Viennese cookery, with a Wiener schnitzel that is by now legendary. It sprawls across (and off) your plate, it's so big. You'll also find an excellent selection of Viennese sausages, along with tafelspitz and about ten fresh salads. Daily specials are written on a blackboard, and are served Monday to Friday between 8am and 11pm and on Saturday from 8am to 3pm. The wines are excellent, and the restaurant is usually packed at the peak serving hours. Meals cost 150 AS ($11) to 300 AS ($21.75). Figlmüller is closed in August.

Wein-Comptoir, Bäckerstrasse 5 (tel. 0222/51-21-760), is one of the most charming of the wine-tavern restaurants in the old town. You can visit just to sample a wide selection of wines, mostly Austrian, which are enjoyed at tables on the street level. It is also possible to descend the steps into the brick-vaulted cellar, where tables are arranged for meals. There, waiters run up and down the steep steps, serving not only wine but platters of Austrian and international food. Since most dishes are cooked to order, prepare yourself for a long wait. Full meals cost from 225 AS ($16.25), and might include such dishes as breast of venison in a goose liver sauce, tafelspitz, or breast of pheasant with bacon. You might precede your main course with either a rich potato soup flavored with bacon bits or else a terrine of pike and zander. The restaurant is open daily except Sunday from 11:30am to 3pm and 6 to 11pm.

Gösser Bierklinik, Steindlgasse 4 (tel. 0222/533-33-36), also known as the Güldene Drache (Golden Dragon), serves what is reportedly the finest beer in the city. It's brewed in Styria. This is an ancient rustic institution in a building that, according to tradition, dates from Roman times. An inn was opened here in the early 16th century, way back during the reign of Maximilian I. With such a tradition, naturally the décor seems strictly from the Middle Ages, and the cuisine is quintessentially Viennese. The waitresses always seem to be carrying ample mugs of Gösser beer, and are often rushed and harassed. When you finally get their attention, you can order such hearty fare as veal chops with dumplings, plus a wide variety of gutbürgerlich ribstickers. You will likely spend from 225 AS ($16.25) for a full meal. The restaurant serves daily except Sunday and holidays from 9am to 11:30pm.

Thomaskeller, Postgasse 2 (tel. 0222/512-74-46), lies just off the Wollzeile, in the cellars of a Dominican monastery. It's one of the finest wine taverns in Vienna, with a casual atmosphere and carafes of excellent wine from Haugsdorf. Gutbürgerlich food is served in a gutbürgerlich setting under a tall vaulted ceiling of dark-red brick. Flags from the different parts of "the Empire" hang above the wrought-iron wall sconces and the two antique streetlights set into the brick floor. No one puts on airs. The waiters seem to have a sense of humor, and the daily specials are written on a blackboard. You'll find bargain dining in an authentic setting. A fixed-price evening meal costs from 125 AS ($9), and might include schweinebraten with sauerkraut and apple strudel. Service is daily from 5pm to midnight.

Zum Weissen Rauchfangkehrer, Weihburggasse 4 (tel. 0222/512-34-71), is more than 125 years old, the former guildhall of Vienna's chimney sweeps. In fact the name of the place, translated as the "white chimney sweep," comes from a blackened wretch who terrified his neighbor, the city baker, by falling into a drunken sleep in a kneading trough and emerging the next day like a ghost, covered with flour. The interior is rustic, with pine banquettes that look vaguely like church pews, deer antlers, and fancifully crafted chandeliers. Stained glass is set into the dividers separating the many niches and cubbyholes, while big street-level windows let in lots of light. A piano in one of the inner rooms provides nighttime music. The menu offers such specialties as Viennese fried chicken, both a Tyrolean and a paprika schnitzel, veal gulasch, wild game specialties, bratwurst, and several kinds of strudel. You should reserve a table, and you'll certainly want to finish with the house specialty, a fabulously rich chocolate cream puff whose long German name I won't give for reasons of space. You can dine here for 250 AS ($18.25). The place is open daily from noon to 3pm and 6pm to 1am.

Glacisbeisel, Messepalast (tel. 0222/96-16-58), is housed inside the walls of what were once the imperial stables. To reach it, you'll have to traverse imperial courtyards before coming to its door. Climb one flight above ground level to a wood-sheathed atmosphere filled with tin cake molds and regional pottery. The location is near the English Theater, inside a maze of palatial buildings whose entrances lie on Museumstrasse. The restaurant serves Wiener schnitzel, other Viennese specialties such as tafelspitz (boiled beef with potato rösti), plus a milk and cream strudel with vanilla sauce. Meals are priced from 225 AS ($16.25). In summer the restaurant seats more than 300 diners on an open-air terrace constructed right into the ramparts of what used to be a vineyard. Service is daily except Sunday and holidays from 11am to midnight. Annual closing is for one week in January.

Augustinerkeller, Augustinerstrasse 1 (tel. 0222/533-10-26), lies in the basement of a palace that shelters the Albertina Collection in the Hofburg complex. It has a lively group of patrons from all walks of life, and sometimes they get boisterous, especially when the Schrammel music goes on late into the night. This place offers one of the best values for wine tasting in Vienna. The ground-floor lobby lists in big letters the prices of vintage local wines by the glass. Drinkers take a taste from the hundreds of bottles near the stand-up stainless-steel counter.

You enter a vaulted brick room with a worn pine-board floor and wooden banquettes. This long and narrow room is usually packed with people and atmosphere, and often it features strolling accordion players. An upstairs room looks much the same as the one below, although it's less crowded, much quieter, and usually doesn't have music. Aside from the wine and beer, the establishment serves food daily from 10am to 11pm. The cooking is simple, including roast chicken on a spit, schnitzel, and Viennese tafelspitz. Meals cost from 125 AS ($9).

Antiquitäten-Keller, Magdalenenstrasse 32 (tel. 0222/587-64-61), offers a well-prepared but limited menu in an antique cadre of local beerhall style with nightly classical music. It's open daily from 6pm to 1am, with an annual closing sometime in August. A main meal of typical Viennese food goes for around 150 AS ($11). There are three rooms inside, so feel free to walk around a bit before selecting a place to sit. It can be reached from the Vienna State Opera on the U4 in about five minutes.

Rathauskeller, Rathausplatz 1 (tel. 0222/42-12-19), has Neo-Gothic rooms decorated with arched ceilings and stained-glass chandeliers. In the heart of Vienna in the cellar of the City Hall, it serves a variety of typically Viennese food as well as an international cuisine. As a special attraction, the cellar offers its clients a Viennese music soiree—a ramble through the world of operetta, waltz, and Schrammel music. The whole package with dinner costs 298 AS ($22.75), Tuesday to Saturday at 8pm; on the other hand, the Knight's Hall presents music daily after 7pm. The Rathauskeller is open daily except Sunday from 11:30am to 3pm and 5:30 to 11pm. An average three-course meal costs from 250 AS ($18.25).

Buffet Trześniewski, Dorotheergasse 1 (tel. 0222/512-32-91). Everyone in Vienna knows about this place, from the most hurried office worker to the city's most elite hostesses. Franz Kafka lived next door and used to come here for sandwiches and beer. It's unlike any buffet you may have seen, with a crowded format of six or seven cramped tables and a rapidly moving queue of clients who jostle for space next to the glass countertops. You'll indicate to the waitress the kind of sandwich you want, and if you can't read German signs, you just point.

Most people come here for at least six or seven of the delicious finger sandwiches, which include 18 combinations of cream cheese, egg and onion, salami, mushroom, herring, green and red peppers, tomatoes, lobster, and many more. You might also want to order small glasses of fruit juice, beer, or wine with your snack. If you want something to drink, the cashier will give you a rubber token which you'll present to the woman at the far end of the counter (again, you'll jostle your way through the crowd). Each of the sandwiches costs 7 AS (50¢) and warm pastries go for 14 AS ($1). The buffet is open Monday to Friday from 9am to 7:30pm and on Saturday from 9am to 1pm.

Piaristenkeller, Piaristengasse 45 (tel. 0222/42-91-52), is a wine tavern where Erich Emberger has successfully renovated and reassembled the centuries-old vaulted ceilings into a vast cellar room. The place was originally founded in 1668 by

Piarist monks. This is a worthwhile establishment to visit to try all the traditional Austrian culinary specialties created from original recipes in the kitchen, which once served the cloisters of which the cellar was a part. Meals cost from 250 AS ($18.25). The tavern is open daily from 5pm to midnight, with zither music played from 7:30pm. In summer the garden at the church square is open from 11am to midnight. Lunches are served daily if you order in advance. Wine and beer are available whenever the cellar is open.

5. Coffeehouses, Tea Rooms, and Cafés

The café has been called the most traditional Viennese institution. Today they come in all shapes and sizes. Many are modern, while others have clung more to their traditional past. Some Viennese still use the cafés as their living room, where they meet and entertain their friends, especially if their apartments are too small. Others, however, have deserted the café completely, preferring to stay home these days and watch television.

In theory at least, you're never rushed—even if you occupy a table for hours and order only one cup of coffee. Your coffee is always brought with a glass of water on the side. Most Viennese order a pastry to go with their coffee. Even though service is included in your tab, it is customary to leave an extra tip.

It's also possible to order simple meals in most of the establishments here recommended. You can almost always get a hearty bowl of gulasch soup, and if not that, certainly sausage and hard-boiled eggs, along with good bread and cheese.

Café Demel, Kohlmarkt 14 (tel. 0222/533-55-16). The windows of this much-venerated establishment are filled with fanciful spun-sugar creations of characters from folk legends. When I was last there, Lady Godiva's five-foot tresses sheltered a miniature village of Viennese dancers. Inside you'll find a splendidly baroque Viennese landmark of black marble tables, cream-colored embellished plaster walls, elaborate half paneling, and crystal chandeliers covered with white milk-glass globes. Dozens of different pastries are offered every day, including pralinentorte, Senegal torte, truffle torte, sandtorte, Nelsontorte, as well as cream-filled horns (kugelhupfs), plus a mammoth variety of elegant tea sandwiches made of smoked salmon, egg salad, caviar, or shrimp, among other ingredients.

You'll select what you want from the glass cases before going in to seat yourself on one of the bentwood chairs or upholstered love seats. The counterwoman will give you a ticket that you'll keep. Another waitress will bring the confection to your table, along with whatever beverage you select. At the end of your visit you'll pay the waitress for the bill she'll calculate from the ticket stubs you've accumulated from the counterwoman.

If you want to be traditional, ask for a Demel-Coffee, which is filtered coffee served with milk, cream, or even whipped cream. Coffee costs 42 AS ($3.05), and those tempting cakes begin at 39 AS ($2.85). Hours are from 10am to 6pm daily.

Café Central, Herrengasse 14 (tel. 0222/533-37-63), stands in the center of Vienna just across from the Hofburg (the imperial winter palace) and the Spanish Riding School. This grandly proportioned café offers an insight into 19th-century Viennese life. The décor shows the splendor of the late Empire style and is a nostalgic remembrance of things past. The café was the center of Austrian literature and the meeting place of the country's best-known writers. Even Lenin, under an assumed name, is said to have plotted the Russian Revolution here. The café offers a variety of Viennese coffees and a vast selection of pastries and desserts, costing from 35 AS ($2.55). For lunch, there is a restaurant offering both Viennese and provincial recipes. The Central is open daily except Sunday and holidays from 10am to 8pm.

Café Landtmann, Dr.-Karl-Lueger-Ring 4 (tel. 0222/63-06-21), is one of the great cafés of the Ringstrasse, with a history that goes back more than 110 years and a view overlooking the Burgtheater. It has traditionally drawn a colorful mixture of politicians, journalists, and actors. It was also Freud's favorite. The original chandeliers and the prewar chairs have been refurbished, and you can read Austrian and foreign newspapers in a spot that some VIP probably just vacated. An hour here might be an attractive way to spend part of a day in Vienna. A large coffee costs 32 AS ($2.35), and full meals are available if you want them.

Café Leopold Hawelka, Dorotheergasse 6 (tel. 0222/512-82-30), just off the Graben, was one of the most famous rendezvous points for poets, artists, and the literati in days gone by. Nowadays it is the most frequented café in Vienna for young people from around the world. With its marble-topped tables and bentwood chairs, the setting is unmistakably Middle European. Waiters in formal dress scurry from the well-stocked bar with drinks on small silver trays. If the service is slow, which it usually is, you can amuse yourself by reading the bulletin board of artistic events near the entrance. Coffee costs from 28 AS ($2.05). Hours are 8am to 2am (opens at 4pm on Sunday); closed Tuesday.

Café Imperial, Kärntner Ring 16 (tel. 0222/50-110-389), is associated with the deluxe hotel covered earlier in the guide. The café was a favorite of Gustav Mahler and a host of other celebrated cultural figures. Imperial Toast is a good snack here, and if you want a main meal you can always order the famed boiled beef dish of Austria, tafelspitz. Meals begin at 250 AS ($18.25), and are served daily from 7am to 11pm.

Café Mozart, Albertinaplatz 2 (tel. 0222/513-30-07). There are at least five Mozart cafés in Vienna, but this one is the most famous of all of them. It attracts affluent members of the business community, along with opera singers and university professors. There's been a café named Mozart on this spot since 1794, although the current establishment was founded in 1840. Japanese interests renovated it into the plushly streamlined format you see today, which is certainly elegant but without the baroque detailing you might have hoped for. Fourteen different coffees are served, with prices starting at 22 AS ($1.60), and you can also order a Wiener schnitzel with salad for 138 AS ($10). The menu is in English. Scenes from *The Third Man*—that thriller starring Orson Welles and Joseph Cotten—were shot here. The café is open daily from 9am to midnight.

Café/Restaurant Prückel, Stubenring 24 (tel. 0222/512-61-15), was built at the turn of the century, and in 1955, when Austria had just regained its independence, the place was renovated. Nothing has changed since. It is open daily from 9am to 10pm, playing host to an offbeat coterie of arts-conscious clientele who sit in the Sputnik-era chairs. Masses of dog-eared newspapers lie scattered about, and it's the kind of place where you can read half a Tolstoy novel for the cost of a cup of coffee. The owner, Christl Sedlar, offers 20 different kinds of coffee, including the house favorite, Maria Theresia, which is a large black coffee with orange liqueur and whipped cream, costing 60 AS ($4.35).

Café Tirolerhof, Tegetthoffstrasse 8 (tel. 0222/512-84-33), is convenient after you've visited the Albertina Collection or been to the Spanish Riding School. Under the same management for decades, it is open Monday to Saturday from 7am to 9pm and on Sunday from 7am to 8pm. A slice of apple strudel costs 30 AS ($2.20), and a mélange of coffee and cream goes for the same price.

Café-Restaurant Arabia, Kohlmarkt 5 (tel. 0222/533-09-29), serves specialties such as asparagus in season, venison, fresh strawberries, and delectable Viennese pastries. An average meal costs 125 AS ($9) to 175 AS ($12.75). Centrally located, the café is open daily from 7am to 8pm.

Restaurant-Café Carrousel, Krugerstrasse 3 (tel. 0222/512-73-97), in the middle of the city, a few blocks from the Vienna State Opera, offers 220 seats in a modernized art nouveau format of bright colors, bentwood chairs, and an occasional statue of a merry-go-round horse. A sidewalk terrace extends the seating capacity of the restaurant. The menu features the usual café drinks, such as coffee, tea, wine, and beer, plus good Viennese cookery with a few international dishes thrown in for variety. Meals cost 60 AS ($4.25) to 160 AS ($11.75). Hours are 10am to midnight daily.

Demmer's Teehaus, Mölkerbastei 5 (tel. 0222/533-59-95), serves 30 different kinds of tea, plus dozens of pastries, cakes, toasts, and English sandwiches. Demmer's is under the management of the previously recommended Buffet Trześniewski; however, the teahouse gives you a chance to sit down and enjoy your drink and snack. Teas begin at 30 AS ($2.20). The establishment is open Monday to Friday from 10am to 6pm.

SIGHTS, SHOPS, AND NIGHTLIFE OF VIENNA

1. WHAT TO SEE
2. WHERE TO SHOP
3. VIENNA AFTER DARK

"**A**sia begins at the Landstrasse." Prince von Metternich, the Austrian states-man who arranged the marriage of Napoleon and Marie-Louise of Austria, made that now-famous remark to suggest the power and influence of the far-flung Austri-an Empire, whose destiny was linked with that of the Habsburgs from 1273 to 1918.

After deliverance from the dreaded plague and the equally dreaded Turks, Vien-na entered into a period of great power and prosperity that reached the zenith of empire under the long reign of Maria Theresa from 1740 to 1780. Many of the sights I'll describe shortly are traced directly to that great empress of the Age of En-lightenment. She welcomed Mozart to her court at Schönbrunn when he was only six years old, a child prodigy indeed.

At the collapse of the Napoleonic Empire, Vienna took over Paris's long-held position as "the center of Europe." The crowned heads of Europe met for the now-legendary Congress of Vienna in 1814–15. But so much time was devoted to galas that a remark made by Prince de Ligne became famous in its day: "The Congress doesn't make progress, it dances."

In this chapter we'll explore this city of gemütlichkeit, beginning first with its many sightseeing attractions—most of which are a holdover from its days of empire—and going on to take in its many shopping possibilities as well as its nightlife and heurigen, or wine taverns.

1. What to See

Vienna stands today, as it always has, as a crossroads between West and East (it's only 44 miles from the Hungarian border). After New York and Geneva, it's the third city of the United Nations. It's also the home of many international organiza-tions.

You can spend a week here and you'll have just touched the attractions of this multifaceted international city. I'll skim only the highlights, and even seeing what's listed below will take more than a week of some fast-paced walking.

Many readers will not have the time to spend seeing Vienna as it deserves to be seen. Some visitors will have only a day or two, and with those people in mind, I've compiled a list of the major attractions a first-time traveler will want to seek out, however brief the stay in Vienna. If this guidebook awarded stars, I'd rate each of the following sights three stars, the highest accolade: the Inner City, Ringstrasse, Schönbrunn Palace, Hofburg Palace, Belvedere Palace, Kunsthistorisches Museum, and St. Stephen's Cathedral.

These top-rated sights are each previewed below, together with others I consider the two- or one-star attractions of Vienna. But before we visit them in detail, let's skim the highlights of Vienna's sights on a walking tour.

A WALKING TOUR OF IMPERIAL VIENNA

There are hundreds of potential itineraries through the architectural wonders of Vienna. However, this two- to three-hour walking tour will give you at least an exterior view of many of them. Place names in boldface are explained in detail in other sections of this guide. This tour is mainly designed to reveal lesser-known sights best seen from the outside, on foot. Later, you can pick and choose the attractions you most want to revisit.

Our tour begins at the southernmost loop of the beltway, the **Ringstrasse,** which encircles most of the historic core of the city. From a stance in front of the most obvious symbol of Viennese culture, the **Staatsoper** (State Opera), proceed one block northward on the most famous pedestrian street of Austria, the Kärntnerstrasse. This tour will eventually take you past this street's rows of glamorous shops and famous houses, but, for the moment, turn left behind the arcaded bulk of the State Opera onto the Philharmonikerstrasse. On the right-hand side, you'll see the lushly carved caryatids and globe lights of Vienna's best-known hotel, the **Sacher.** If you're interested, a confectionary store with a separate streetside entrance sells portions of the hotel's namesake, the Sacher torte, which can be shipped anywhere in the world.

A few steps later you'll find yourself amid the irregular angles of the Albertinaplatz, where you can enjoy a "mélange" of coffee with a cap of whipped cream at the **Café Mozart,** lying just a few storefronts off to the right. Immediately opposite the café, behind an undistinguished façade, is one of Vienna's best-known buildings, the headquarters of the **Albertina Collection.** A monumental staircase built into its side supports the equestrian statue that dominates the square. Its inspiration was Field Marshal Archduke Albrecht in honor of a battle he won in 1866. One of the many baroque jewels of Vienna, the Lobkowitz Palace lies adjacent to the Albertinaplatz at Lobkowitzplatz 2. (Its position is confusing because of the rows of buildings partially concealing it. To get there, walk about 50 paces to the right of the Albertina Collection.)

At the far end of the Lobkowitzplatz, take the Gluckgasse past a series of antiques shops filled with art deco jewelry and silverware. At the end of the block, at the Tegetthoffstrasse, go left. About 40 paces later, you'll be in front of the deceptively simple façade of the Church of the Capuchin Friars (see **Tombs of the Habsburgs**). Originally constructed in the 1620s, its façade was rebuilt in a severely simple design following old illustrations in 1935. Despite its humble appearance, the church contains the burial vaults of every Habsburg ruler since 1633. The heavily sculpted double casket of Maria Theresa and her husband, Francis I, is flanked with weeping nymphs and skulls, but capped with a triumphant cherub uniting the couple once again in love.

The portal of this church marks the beginning of the Neuer Markt, whose perimeter is lined with rows of elegant baroque houses. The square's centerpiece is the partially dressed river goddess of the Donner fountain. Holding a snake, she is attended by four laughing cherubs struggling with fish. The waters flowing into the basin of the fountain are provided by four allegorical figures representing nearby tributaries of the Danube. The fountain is a copy of the original, which was moved to Belvedere Palace. It was commissioned by the City Council in 1737, executed by Georg Raphael Donner, but judged obscene and immoral when viewed for the first time by Maria Theresa. Today it is considered one of Austria's masterpieces of baroque sculpture.

Now take the street stretching west from the side of the fountain, the Plankengasse, where a yellow baroque church fills the space at the end of the street. As you approach it, you'll pass arrays of shops filled with alluringly old-fashioned merchandise. Even the pharmacy at the corner of the Spiegelgasse has a vaulted ceiling and rows of antique bottles. The store at Plankengasse 6, as well as its next-door neighbor at the corner of Dorotheergasse, is well stocked with museum-quality antique clocks, many of which ticked their way through the dying days of the early 19th century. Turn left when you reach the Dorotheergasse, past the turn-of-the-century Italianate bulk of no. 17. Therein lies one of the most historic auction houses of Europe, the **Dorotheum**, established in 1707.

About a half block later, turn right into the Augustinerstrasse, whose edge borders a labyrinth of palaces, museums, and public buildings known as the **Hofburg**. The grime-encrusted grandeur of this narrow street is usually diminished by the traffic roaring past its darkened stone walls. Despite that modern intrusion, this group of buildings is the single most impressive symbol of the former majesty of the Viennese Habsburgs. In about half a block you'll arrive at the Josefsplatz, where a huge equestrian statue of Joseph II seems to be storming the gate of the Palffy Palace (no. 5). Its entrance is guarded by two pairs of relaxed caryatids who seem to be discussing the horseman's approach. Next door, at no. 6, is another once-glittering private residence, the Palavicini Palace. A few steps later, a pedestrian tunnel leads past the **Spanish Riding School.** The district becomes increasingly imperial, filled with slightly decayed vestiges of a long-ago empire whose baroque monuments are flanked with outmoded streets and thundering traffic.

Michaelerplatz now opens to your view. Opposite the six groups of combative statues struggling with their own particular adversaries is a streamlined building with rows of unadorned windows. Known as the Loos House (Michaelerplatz 3), it was designed in 1910 and immediately became the most violently condemned building in town. That almost certainly stemmed from the unashamed contrast between the lavishly ornamented façade of the Michaelerplatz entrance to the Hofburg and what contemporary critics compared to "the gridwork of a sewer." Franz Joseph himself hated the building so much that he used the Michaelerplatz exit as infrequently as possible so that he wouldn't have to look at the building, which faced it.

A covered tunnel that empties into the center of the square takes you beneath the Hofburg complex. Notice the passageway's elaborate ceiling where spears, capes, and shields crown the supports of the elaborate dome. Cars seem to race beside you, making this one of the most heavily embellished traffic tunnels in the world. An awesomely proportioned series of courtyards reveal the Imperial Age's addiction to conspicuous grandeur. Continuing straight through the passageway, you'll eventually emerge beneath the magnificent curves of the Haldenplatz. Its carefully constructed symmetry seems to dictate that each of the magnificent buildings bordering it, as well as each of its equestrian statues and ornate lampposts, seems to have a well-balanced mate.

Gardens stretch out, flowering in summer, in well-maintained splendor. Enjoy the gardens if you want, but to continue the tour, put the rhythmically spaced columns of the Hofburg's curved façade behind you and walk catercorner to the far end of the palace's right-hand wing. At the Ballhausplatz, notice the Chancellery at no. 2. It's an elegant building, yet its façade is modest in comparison with the ornamentation of its royal neighbor. The events that transpired within influenced the course of European history hundreds of times since the building was erected in 1720.

Here, Count Kaunitz plotted with Maria Theresa again and again to expand the influence of her monarchy. Prince Metternich used these rooms as his headquarters during the Congress of Vienna in 1814 and 1815. Many of the decisions made here were responsible for the chain of events leading to World War I. In 1934 Dollfuss was murdered here. Four years later Hermann Göring, threatening a military attack, forced the ouster of the Austrian cabinet with telephone calls made to an office in this building. Rebuilt after the bombings of World War II, this battle-scarred building has housed Austria's Foreign Ministry and its Federal Chancellor's office since 1945.

Walk along the side of the Chancellery's adjacent gardens, along the Lowelstrasse, until you reach the **Burgtheater,** the national theater of Austria. Notice the window trim of some of the buildings along the way, each of which seems to have its own ox, satyr, cherub, or Neptune carved above it. At the Burgtheater, make a sharp right-hand turn onto the Bankgasse. The ornate beauty of the Palais Liechtenstein, completed in 1706, is on your right, at no. 9. A few buildings farther on, stone garlands and glimpses of crystal chandeliers are visible at the Hungarian Embassy, at no. 4-6 on the same street.

Now retrace your steps for about a half block until you reach the Abraham a Sancta Clara Gasse. At its end, you'll see the severe Gothic façade of the **Church of the Minorites** in the Minoritenplatz. Its 14th-century severity contrasts sharply with the group of stone warriors struggling to support the gilt-edged portico of the baroque palace facing it.

Walk behind the blackened hulk of the church to the curve of the building's rear. At this point, some maps of Vienna might lead you astray. Regardless of the markings on your particular map, look for the Leopold-Figl-Gasse and walk down it. You'll pass between two sprawling buildings, each of which belongs to one or another of the Austrian bureaucracies, which are linked with an above-ground bridge. A block later, turn right onto Herrengasse. Within a few minutes, you'll be on the by-now-familiar Michaelerplatz. This time you'll have a better view of **St. Michael's Church,** where winged angels carved by Lorenzo Mattielli in 1792 fly above the entranceway and a single pointed tower rises. Turn left (north) along the Kohlmarkt, noticing the elegant houses along the way: no. 14 houses **Demel's,** the most famous coffeehouse of Vienna; no. 9 and no. 11 bear plaques for Chopin and Haydn, respectively. At the Graben, turn right. The plague column you see in the center has chiselled representations of clouds piled high like whipped cream, dotted profusely with statues of ecstatic saints fervently thanking God for relief from the plague.

A few feet before the plague column, turn left onto the Jungferngasse and enter what is probably my favorite church in Vienna, **St. Peter's,** or Peterskirche.

Return to the Graben, passing the papal tiaras at the base of the plague column. A few steps later, pass the bronze statue of a beneficent saint leading a small child in the right direction. You might, at this point, want a sandwich at the famous **Buffet Trześniewski,** Dorotheergasse 1, off to the right. Continue your way down the Graben to Stock-im-Eisen. Here two pedestrian thoroughfares, the Graben and the Kärntnerstrasse, meet, both under the spire of **St. Stephen's Cathedral.** To your right, notice the sheet of curved Plexiglass bolted to the corner of an unobtrusive building at the periphery of the square. Behind it are the preserved remains of a tree that used to grow nearby. In it, 16th-century blacksmiths drove a nail for luck each time they left Vienna for other parts of Austria. Today the gnarled and dusty log is still covered with an almost uninterrupted carapace of angular nails.

Now, first encircle and then enter the soaring Gothic majesty of St. Stephen's Cathedral. When you exit, turn left after passing through the main portal, passing once again the nail-studded stump in Stock-im-Eisen, and promenade down the pedestrian thoroughfare of the Kärntnerstrasse. Notice especially the exhibition of art objects on the second floor of the world-famous glassmaker, **Lobmyer,** at no. 26.

If you still have the energy, make a two- or three-block detour off the Kärntnerstrasse, turning left on the Johannesgasse. The severe façade of no. 8 contains an exhibition of religious folk art. A few steps farther, baroque carvings that include stone lions guard the 17th-century portals of the Savoy Foundation for Noble Ladies (no. 15), where well-born damsels sometimes struggled to learn "the gentle arts of womanhood."

As you retrace your steps back to the shops of the Kärntnerstrasse, you might hear the strains of music cascading into the street from the Vienna Conservatory of Music, which also lies within the Johannesgasse. Turn left as you reenter the Kärntnerstrasse, enjoying the views until you eventually return to the point of origin, the State Opera.

THE INNER CITY

The Inner City (Innere Stadt) is the tangle of streets of the old town from which Vienna grew in the Middle Ages. Much of your exploration will be confined to this area. It is encircled by the boulevards of "The Ring" and the Danube Canal. The main street of the inner city is the Kärntnerstrasse, most of which is a pedestrian mall. The heart of Vienna is the Stephansplatz, the square on which St. Stephen's Cathedral sits.

RINGSTRASSE

In 1857, seeing no further need for the old walls that had girdled old-town Vienna for several centuries, Emperor Franz Joseph ordered them torn down and replaced by a series of grand buildings and a wide promenade. Ringstrasse, or Ring Boulevard, was laid out between 1858 and 1865, an elegant horseshoe curve 2½ miles long, one of the grand boulevards of Europe, overhung with leafy trees. The emperor got his wish—a boulevard worthy of an empire that controlled some 50 million people.

A cross-section of architectural styles was used in constructing the buildings on the Ringstrasse, ranging from Greek to Gothic. The street name changes eight times around the boulevard, and along it you'll pass the Stadtpark, the State Opera, the Burggarten, the Hofburg Palace, the Volksgarten, the Parliament, the Rathaus, the Burgtheater, the University of Vienna, and the Museum of Fine Arts. The Viennese call this pastiche of architecture *Ringstrassenstil*. They refer to the Ringstrasse simply as "The Ring."

You can circle the boulevard by public transport, but some people walk from one end to the other. If you wish to do that, the starting point is Aspernplatz by the Danube Canal. Along the way—for a rest—you can stroll into one of the parks (perhaps the Stadtpark), where you might hear Viennese music in summer as you relax at an outdoor café.

THE PALACES OF VIENNA

On your sightseeing tour of Vienna, I suggest you start with the once-royal palaces, perhaps first—

Schönbrunn Palace

A Habsburg palace of 1,441 rooms, Schönbrunn (tel. 0222/811-13-0) was designed by those masters of the baroque, the von Erlachs. It was built between 1696 and 1712, ordered by Emperor Leopold I for his son, Joseph I, with Leopold directing the architects to design a palace whose grandeur would surpass that of Versailles. However, Austria's treasury, drained by the cost of wars, would not support the ambitious undertaking, and the original plans were never carried out.

When Maria Theresa became empress, she had the original plans changed greatly, and Schönbrunn looks today much as she conceived it, with delicate, feminine rococo touches designed for her by Austrian Nikolaus Pacassi. It was the imperial summer palace during Maria Theresa's 40-year reign, from 1740 to 1780, being considered by the empress as a fit place for her 16 children, 6 of whom did not live to grow up. Schönbrunn was the scene of great ceremonial balls and lavish banquets.

During the Congress of Vienna, in 1814–15, fabulous receptions were held here. At the age of six, Mozart performed in the Hall of Mirrors before Maria Theresa and her court, and the empress held secret meetings with her chancellor, Prince Kaunitz, in the round Chinese Room.

Franz Joseph was born at Schönbrunn, and the palace was the setting for much of the lavish court life carried on when he was emperor. He spent the last years of his life at Schönbrunn. The last of the rulers of the House of Habsburg, Karl I, signed his abdication document here on November 11, 1918.

Napoleon, when Emperor of France, stayed here in 1805 and 1809. A melancholy footnote to the connection between the arrogant Bonapartes and the House of Habsburg is revealed in the brief life history of the son of the Emperor Napoleon and his second wife, Marie-Louise, daughter of Franz I of Austria. The boy, hailed by his father as "King of Rome" but officially known as the Duke of Reichstadt, lived at Schönbrunn—but not entirely from choice. The Austrian minister of foreign affairs, Metternich, who had for his own Machiavellian reasons arranged the marriage of Napoleon and Marie-Louise, ordered what was tantamount to imprisonment for the young duke—house arrest at Schönbrunn. The palace was no doubt the best of all possible worlds in which to be incarcerated, but the "King of Rome" was still in custody there upon his death in one of the splendid guest rooms at the age of 21.

Schönbrunn Palace was damaged in World War II by Allied bombs, but restoration has obliterated the scars.

In complete contrast to the grim, forbidding-looking Hofburg, Schönbrunn Palace, done in "Maria Theresa ochre," has **formal gardens,** laid out in 1705, embellished by the Gloriette, a marble summerhouse topped by a stone canopy on which the imperial eagle is mounted. The so-called Roman Ruins consist of a collection of marble statues and fountains, dating from the late 18th century, when it was fashionable to simulate the ravaged grandeur of Rome. The park, which can be visited until sunset daily, was laid out by Adria van Steckhoven and contains many fountains and heroic statues, often depicting Greek mythological characters.

The **State Apartments** are the most stunning display within Schönbrunn Palace. Much of the interior ornamentation is in 23½-karat gold, and many porcelain tile stoves are in evidence. Of the 40 rooms that you can visit, particularly fascinating is "The Room of Millions," decorated with Indian and Persian miniatures and considered to be the grandest rococo salon in the world. Much of the palace is in the rococo style, done in reds, white, and gold. You get to see the apartments once lived in by Franz Joseph and his ill-fated empress, Elizabeth, and the lavish rooms in which guests of the royal family were housed. Three of the reception rooms were decorated by the painter Joseph Rosa. You'll be shown the bleak chamber and the spartan iron bedstead in which the aged Franz Joseph died in 1916.

Guided tours lasting 45 minutes are narrated in English but only at the indicated times given on the timetable. The apartments are open in summer daily from 8:30am to 5:30pm (winter hours run from 9am to 4pm). Admission for adults is 50 AS ($3.65). Young people up to 27 years pay only 25 AS ($1.80), and children up to 15 years, 10 AS (75¢). One should tip the guide.

Evening tours combined with a concert are given at special rates in July and August, beginning at 7:15pm. For detailed information about the concerts, including programs, times, and sales of tickets, get in touch with Kulturamt der Stadt Wien, Friedrich Schmidt Platz 5 (tel. 0222/428-00, ext. 2085).

On the ground floor of the east wing of the main building are the **Bergl Rooms** and the **Crown Prince Rooms.** These consist of four rooms with wall and ceiling murals by Johann Bergl, a painter in the second half of the 18th century, and three rooms in which an exhibit traces the history of Schönbrunn Palace. Hours are from 9am to noon and 1 to 5pm from May 1 to late October. The price of admission depends on whatever temporary exhibition happens to be on view. Costs usually range from 15 AS ($1.10) to 25 AS ($1.80) per person.

The palace is closed January 1, November 1, and December 24.

Well worth seeing is the **Schlosstheater,** or Palace Theater, which is still the setting for performances in summer. Marie Antoinette appeared on its stage in pastorals during her happy youth, and Max Reinhardt, the theatrical impresario, launched an acting school here.

Adjacent to the palace is the **Wagenburg,** a carriage museum (tel. 0222/82-32-44) with a fine display of imperial coaches from the 17th, 18th, and 19th centuries. The coronation coach of Karl VI (Charles, 1711–40), which was pulled by eight white stallions, is here. It was used for a total of seven Habsburg coronations. Also to be seen are coaches ridden in by Franz Joseph and his wife, Elizabeth, and by Napoleon and his wife, Marie-Louise. The grim funeral coach of Franz Joseph is also on display. The children's phaeton you will see was built for Napoleon's son. The Wagenburg is open from 10am to 5pm (until 4pm in winter), costing 30 AS ($2.20) for admission. It is closed Monday.

The oldest zoo in Europe, **Tiergarten Schönbrunn** (tel. 0222/811-13-0), dating from 1752, is on the grounds of Schönbrunn Palace, open daily from 9am to 6pm at the latest, changing with the seasons. Maria Theresa liked to take breakfast here.

The Schönbrunn **botanical gardens** are also open to visitors.

To reach the palace, take the underground U-4 green line to the Schönbrunn stop. For the zoo, get out at the Hietzing stop.

Hofburg Palace

The winter palace of the Habsburgs, known for its vast, impressive courtyards, the Hofburg (tel. 0222/587-55-54) sits in the heart of Vienna. To reach it (you can hardly miss it), head up the Kohlmarkt into Michaelerplatz, which is decorated with two enormous fountains embellished with statuary. This complex of imperial edifices, the first of which was constructed in 1279, grew and grew as the empire did, so that today the Hofburg Palace is virtually a city within a city. The earliest parts were built around a courtyard, the **Swiss Court,** named for the Swiss mercenaries who used to perform guard duty here. This most ancient part of the palace is at least 700 years old.

Hofburg's complexity of styles, not always harmonious, is the result of each emperor's having added to it according to his own tastes and taking away some of the work of his predecessors. So grand were the architect's plans for the 20th-century changes that the empire had ended before they could be carried out. The palace, which has withstood three major sieges and a great fire, is called simply *die Burg,* or "the palace," by Viennese. Of its more than 2,600 rooms, fewer than two dozen are open to the public.

The Imperial Treasury, the **Schatzkammer** (tel. 0222/533-60-46), reached by a staircase from the Swiss Court, is considered the greatest treasury in the world. It is divided into two sections: the Imperial Profane and the Sacerdotal Treasuries. One part displays the crown jewels and an assortment of imperial riches, and the other, of course, contains ecclesiastical treasures.

The most outstanding exhibit in the Schatzkammer is the imperial crown, which dates from 962. It is so big that even though padded, it was likely to slip down over the ears of a Habsburg at a coronation. Studded with emeralds, sapphires, diamonds, and rubies, this 1,000-year-old symbol of sovereignty is a priceless treasure, a fact recognized by Adolf Hitler, who had it taken to Nürnberg in 1938 (the American army returned it to Vienna after World War II ended). Also on display is the imperial crown worn by the Habsburg rulers from 1804 to the end of the empire. You will see the saber of Charlemagne and the holy lance from the 9th century. The latter, a sacred emblem of imperial authority, was thought in medieval times to be the weapon that pierced the side of Christ on the cross. The Agate Bowl was once believed to be the Holy Grail.

Among great Schatzkammer prizes is the Burgundian Treasure seized in the 15th century, rich in vestments, oil paintings, gems, and robes. This loot is highlighted by artifacts connected with the Order of the Golden Fleece, that romantic medieval order of chivalry. You will also see the coronation robes of the imperial family, some of which date from the 12th century. The cradle of the "King of Rome," son of Napoleon and his Austrian second wife, Marie-Louise, is in the Empire style in silver, pearl, and gilt.

The Schatzkammer is open Monday, Wednesday, and Friday from 10am to 6pm, and on Saturday and Sunday from 9am to 6pm (it closes at 4pm in winter). Admission is 45 AS ($3.25).

The Hofburg complex also includes the **Reichskanzleitrakt,** or Imperial Chancellery, where the emperors and their wives and children lived on the first floor. To reach the **Kaiserappartements** (Imperial Apartments), you enter via the rotunda of the Michaelerplatz. The apartments are richly decorated with tapestries, many from Aubusson. The court tableware and silver are magnificent, revealing the pomp and splendor of a bygone era. Leopoldinischer Trakt, or Leopold's apartments, date from the 17th century. You can't visit the quarters once occupied by Maria Theresa, as they are now used by the president of Austria.

These Imperial Apartments seem to be more closely associated with Franz Joseph than with any other emperor, probably because of his long reign. His wife, Elizabeth of Bavaria, lived here too when she wasn't traveling, which actually was most of the time until her fatal stabbing by an assassin in Switzerland. Elizabeth believed in keeping fit and had a room where she worked out. She was a vain empress, refusing to sit for portraits after she turned 30. You'll see the "iron bed" of Franz Joseph, who claimed he slept like his own soldiers. Maybe that explains why his wife spent so much time elsewhere!

The Kaiserappartements are open year round, Monday to Saturday from 8:30am to 4:30pm; on Sunday, hours are 8:30am to 1pm. A German-language guided tour costs 20 AS ($1.45). English-language tours aren't available unless you hire one of the freelance tour guides loitering around the entryway, or else prearrange one with the Vienna Tourist Information Office.

Construction of **Die Burgkapelle** (Palace Chapel) in the Gothic style started in 1447 during the reign of Emperor Frederick III, but it was subsequently massively renovated. From 1449 it was the private chapel of the royal family. Today the Burgkapelle is the scene of the Hofmusikkapelle, an ensemble consisting of the Vienna Boys' Choir and members of the Vienna State Opera chorus and orchestra, performing works by classical and modern composers. Masses (performances) are held every Sunday and on religious holidays at 9:15am from January to mid-June. Written applications for reserved seats should be sent at least eight weeks in advance of the time you wish to attend, but send no checks or money. The cost per seat ranges from 50 AS ($3.65) to 180 AS ($13). For reservations, write to Verwaltung der Hofmusikkapelle, Hofburg, A-1010 Vienna. If you failed to reserve in advance, you may be lucky enough to secure tickets from a block sold at the Burgkapelle box office every Friday from 5pm on, but the queue starts lining up at least a half hour before that. Or you might settle for standing room (it's free).

The Vienna Boys' Choir boarding school is at Palais Augarten, Obere Augartenstrasse.

Neue Burg, called the New Château, was the most recent addition to the Hofburg complex. Construction was started in 1881 and continued until work was halted in 1913. The palace was the residence of Archduke Franz Ferdinand, the nephew and heir apparent of Franz Joseph, whose assassination at Sarajevo set off the chain of events that led to World War I.

One collection in the Neue Burg is devoted to arms and armor, considered second only to that of the Metropolitan Museum in New York. It is in the **Hofjagdlund Rüstkammer** on the second floor of the New Château. On display are crossbows, swords, helmets, and pistols, plus armor, mostly the property of the emperors and princes of the House of Habsburg. Some of the exhibits, such as scimitars, were captured from the Turks as they fled the scene of their losing sieges of Vienna. Of bizarre interest is the armor worn by the little Habsburg princes, who had to learn the martial arts at a very early age. Hofjagdund Rüstkammer is open Monday to Friday from 10am to 4pm and on Saturday and Sunday from 9am to 4pm, charging an admission of 30 AS ($2.20).

Another section, called **Musikinstrumentensammlung,** is devoted to old musical instruments, mainly from the 17th and 18th centuries, but with some from the 16th. Some of the instruments, especially pianos and harpsichords, were played by Brahms, Liszt, Mahler, and Beethoven. The hours and admission charge are the same as for the Collection of Arms and Armor.

In the **Ephesos-Museum** (Museum of Ephesian Sculpture), Neue Burg 1, Heldenplatz, entrance behind the Prince Eugene monument (tel. 0222/93-45-41), you'll see numerous high-quality finds from Ephesus in Turkey and the Greek island of Samothrace. It is in the Neue Hofburg, an annex of the Collection of Greek and Roman Antiquities of the Kunsthistoriches Museum. Here the prize exhibit is the Parthian monument, the most important relief frieze from Roman times ever found in Asia Minor. It was erected on the occasion of the victorious conclusion of the Parthian wars (A.D. 161–65) to commemorate Emperor Lucius Verus, commander of the Roman forces. The museum is open Monday, Wednesday, and Friday from 10am to 4pm and on Saturday and Sunday from 9am to 4pm, charging an admission of 30 AS ($2.20).

Visit the **Museum für Völkerkunde** (Ethnographical Museum) (tel. 0222/ 93-45-41) if for no other reason than to see "Montezuma's treasure," three flamboyant feather robes that the mighty Aztec emperor is supposed to have given Cortés when the Spanish conquistador went to Mexico. Also displayed, however, are Benin bronzes, Cook's collections, and Indian and Asian exhibits. The museum, charging an entrance of 30 AS ($2.20), is open Monday, Thursday, Friday, and Saturday from 10am to 1pm and on Wednesday from 10am to 5pm. Sunday hours are 9am to 1pm.

Also in the Hofburg complex is the **Österreichische Nationalbibliothek,** or Austrian National Library, Josefplatz 1 (tel. 0222/534-10), where you'll see an equestrian statue of Joseph II. The royal library of the Habsburgs dates back to the 14th century; the library building, developed on the premises of the court from 1723 on; is still expanding to the Neue Hofburg. The Great Hall was ordered by Karl VI and designed by those masters of the baroque, the von Erlachs. Its ornate splendor and the frescoes of Daniel Gran are impressive. The complete collection of Prince Eugene of Savoy forms the core of the precious holdings shelved herein. With its heritage of manuscripts, rare autographs, globes, maps, and other memorabilia, it is among the finest libraries in the world.

The Great Hall (Prunksaal) can be visited Monday to Saturday from 10am to 4pm and on Sunday from 10am to 1pm, May to October. Off-season, it is open Monday to Saturday from 11am to noon but closed on Sunday. Admission is 30 AS ($2.25).

The **Albertina Collection** (tel. 0222/53-48-30), entrance at Augustinerstrasse 1, is another Hofburg museum, this one showing the development of graphic arts since the 14th century. Housing one of the world's greatest graphic collections, the museum was named for a son-in-law of Maria Theresa. The most outstanding treasure in the Albertina is the Dürer collection, although what you will usually see are copies, the originals being shown only on special occasions. See, in particular, Dürer's *Praying Hands,* which has been reproduced throughout the world. The some 20,000 drawings and more than 250,000 original etchings and prints include work by such artists as Poussin, Fragonard, Rubens, Rembrandt, Michelangelo, and Leonardo da Vinci. Prince Eugene of Savoy collected many of the graphics displayed here. There are many changing exhibitions of both old and modern drawings and prints. The entrance fee is 16 AS ($1.15), and the museum is open daily except Friday from 10am to 6pm.

Augustinerkirche (Church of the Augustians), entrance on Josefplatz, was constructed in the 14th century as part of the Hofburg complex to serve as the parish church of the imperial court. In the latter part of the 18th century it was stripped of its baroque embellishments and returned to the original Gothic features. The Chapel of St. George, dating from 1337, is entered from the right aisle. The chapel is open Monday to Thursday from 8 to 8:45am and on Friday from 8 to 8:45am and from 9:30am to noon. The tomb of the favorite daughter of Maria Theresa, Maria Christina, is also here, but there's no body in it. The princess was actually buried in the Capuchin Crypt, which I will describe later in this section under "Tombs of the Habsburgs." The richly ornamented empty tomb here was designed by Canova and is considered one of his masterpieces.

This church is a place of death but also of life. Maria Theresa married François of Lorraine here in 1736, and the Augustinerkirche was the site of other royal weddings: Marie Antoinette to Louis XVI of France in 1770, Marie-Louise of Austria to Napoleon in 1810 (by proxy—he didn't show up), and Franz Joseph to Elizabeth of Bavaria in 1854. Some of the great church music of Vienna is performed at this church on Sunday at 11am.

A bittersweet nostalgia seems to permeate the **Spanische Hofreitschule** (Spanish Riding School), Hofburg, Josefsplatz, a reminder of the fact that horses were an important part of both imperial and everyday life for many centuries, with their care and training a matter of pride and honor. The school is in the white, crystal-chandeliered ballroom in an 18th-century building of the Hofburg complex, designed by J. E. Fischer von Erlach. There I always marvel at the skill and beauty of the sleek Lippizaner stallions as their adept trainers put them through their paces in a show that is the same now as it was four centuries ago. These are the world's most famous and most classically styled equine performers. Many North Americans have seen them in the States, but to watch the Lippizaners move to the music of Johann Strauss or a Chopin polonaise in their "airs above the ground" dressage in this, their home setting in Vienna, is a pleasure you should not miss.

Performances usually take place on Sunday at 10:45am and on Wednesday at 7pm, except in January, February, July, August, and December. Between mid-April and June and in September and October, short performances are held at 9am on Saturday. Reservations must be made in advance, as early as possible. Order your tickets for the Sunday and Wednesday shows at Michaelerplatz 1 (tel. 0222/533-90-31), or through a travel agency in Vienna. (Tickets for Saturday shows can be ordered only through a travel agency.) Prices for seats are 200 AS ($14.50) to 600 AS ($43.50); for standing room, 135 AS ($9.75) to 150 AS ($11); and for short performances, 150 AS ($11). Children under 3 are not admitted, but those from 3 to 6 can attend free with adults.

Training sessions may be visited daily except Sunday in February, except Sunday and Monday from March till June and September till November. Tickets with no advance reservations for the training sessions can be purchased at door 2, Josefsplatz, costing 50 AS ($3.65) for adults and 15 AS ($1.10) for children.

Tombs of the Habsburgs

Kaisergruft (Capuchin Crypt), Neuer Markt (tel. 0222/512-68-53), was the burial place of the imperial family of Habsburgs for some three centuries. The vault is below the Kapuziner Church, which was built between 1622 and 1632. Capuchin friars guard the final resting place of the Habsburgs, where 12 emperors, 17 empresses, and dozens of archdukes are entombed. But only their bodies are here. Their hearts are in urns in the St. George Chapel of the Augustinerkirche in the Hofburg complex, and their entrails are similarly enshrined in a crypt below St. Stephen's Cathedral.

Most outstanding of the imperial tombs is the double sarcophagus of Maria Theresa and her consort, Emperor Francis I (François of Lorraine). Before she joined him on a permanent basis, the empress used to descend into the tomb to visit the gravesite of her beloved Francis. The "King of Rome," the ill-fated son of Napoleon and Marie-Louise of Austria, was buried here in a bronze coffin after his death at the age of 21. (Hitler managed to anger both the Austrians and the French by having the remains of Napoleon's son transferred to Paris in 1940.)

Emperor Franz Joseph was interred here in 1916, a frail old man who outlived his time and died just before the final collapse of his empire. His wife, Empress Elizabeth, was buried in the crypt following her assassination in Geneva in 1898, as was their son, Archduke Rudolf, who committed suicide at Mayerling. Archduke Franz Ferdinand, heir apparent to Franz Joseph at the time of his assassination at Sarajevo, and Karl I, the last of the Habsburg rulers, were not entombed in the Kaisergruft. Karl I was buried in Madeira, where he lived in exile after the fall of the Habsburgs. Countess Fuchs, the governess who practically reared Maria Theresa, lies in the crypt, although she was not a Habsburg. (The empress bestowed this burial honor on the countess.)

The crypt may be visited daily from 9:30am to 4pm for an admission of 30 AS ($2.20). To find Kaisergruft, head for Neuer Markt. The entrance is to the left of Kapuziner Church.

Belvedere Palace

Lying to the southeast of Schwarzenberg Palace on a slope above Vienna, approached through a long garden with a huge circular pond, Belvedere Palace was designed by Johann Lukas von Hildebrandt, who is considered the last major Austrian baroque architect. Built as a summer home for Prince Eugene of Savoy, Belvedere consists of two palatial buildings, the design of which foretokens the rococo. The pond reflects the sky and palace buildings, which are made up of a series of interlocking cubes. The interior is dominated by two great, flowing staircases. The office for administration is at Prinz-Eugen-Strasse 27 (tel. 0222/78-41-58).

Unteres Belvedere (Lower Belvedere), entrance at Rennweg 6, was constructed from 1714 to 1716. **Oberes Belvedere** (Upper Belvedere) was started in 1721 and completed in 1723. It is entered at Prinz-Eugen-Strasse 27.

The Gold Salon in Lower Belvedere is one of the most beautiful rooms in the palace. Anton Bruckner, the composer, lived in one of the buildings until his death in 1896, and the palace was the residence of Archduke Franz Ferdinand, who was slain in 1914. In May 1955 the peace treaty recognizing Austria as a sovereign state was signed in Upper Belvedere by foreign ministers of the four powers that occupied this country at the close of World War II — France, Great Britain, the United States, and the Soviet Union.

Today visitors can come to the splendid baroque palace, enjoying the superb view of the Wienerwald (Vienna Woods) from the terrace and passing the regal formal French-style garden to go between Unteres and Oberes Belvedere to see the art collections now open to the public in both.

Lower (Unteres) Belvedere has a wealth of sculptural decorations and houses the **Österreichisches Barockmuseum** (Museum of Baroque Art). Here are displayed the original sculptures from the Neuer Markt fountain, the work of Georg Raphael Donner, who died in 1741. During his life, Donner dominated the development of Austrian sculpture of the 18th century, well founded in Italian art. On the fountain, four figures represent the four major tributaries of the Danube. Works by Franz Anton Maulbertsch, an 18th-century painter, are also exhibited. Maulbertsch, strongly influenced by Tiepolo, was considered the most original and the greatest Austrian painter who lived in his century. He was best known for his iridescent colors and flowing brushwork.

Another section is the **Museum mittelalterlicher Österreichischer Kunst** (Museum of Medieval Austrian Art) in the Orangery. Here you'll see works from the Gothic period. One Tyrolean Romanesque crucifix dates from the 12th century. Outstanding works include seven panels by Rueland Frueauf, scenes from the life of the Madonna and the Passion of Christ.

Upper (Oberes) Belvedere was turned into **Österreichische Galerie des 19. und 20. Jahrhunderts** (Austrian Gallery of 19th- and 20th-Century Art) in 1954.

In a large salon decorated in red marble you can see the 1955 peace treaty, mentioned above. Many paintings of the Biedermeier period in Austria are in this gallery. The west wing is devoted to art turned out during the long reign of Franz Joseph. Among outstanding works is *The Entrance of Charles V into Antwerp*, painted by Hans Makart. Also on display are many pictures by Gustav Klimt, who died at the end of World War I at the very collapse of the Austro-Hungarian Empire. Klimt was a founder of the Secession movement in art. See *The Kiss*, one of his most celebrated works. Klimt's student Egon Schiele, who died the same year as his teacher (1918), is also represented. *Death and the Girl* is one of his better-known paintings.

The work of one of Austria's most noted artists, Oscar Kokoschka, can be seen here. Although most of the painter's life was spent in Britain, to which he fled when the Nazis entered Vienna in 1938, becoming a naturalized citizen of the United Kingdom, Kokoschka is viewed as the greatest contemporary Austrian artist. He attempted to express psychological confusion and the solitude of women and men. The artist died in 1980.

Belvedere Palace is open Tuesday to Sunday from 10am to 4pm; closed Monday. Admission is 30 AS ($2.20). One-hour guided tours in English are conducted in summer.

THE MUSEUMS OF VIENNA

There are those who say that all of the Inner City of Vienna is virtually a museum. That's true. Much of the city is to be enjoyed by strolling through its streets enjoying the monuments and squares, but in some cases you'll want to find out what's behind those grandiose façades, what hidden treasures they protect. The many buildings actually operating as museums will let you do just that.

Admission to all municipal museums is free throughout the year. Children up to the age of 14 are admitted free to most national museums. From September 1 to April 30, admission is free on Saturday, Sunday, and public holidays; from October 1 to March 31 at the Museum of Fine Arts (Kunsthistorisches Museum) and the Museum of Military History (Heeresgeschichtliches Museum).

If your schedule allows for a visit to only one, make it the—

Kunsthistorisches Museum

The **Museum of Fine Arts,** the Kunsthistorisches, Burgring 5, across from the Hofburg Palace (tel. 0222/93-45-41), is housed in a huge building that contains many of the fabulous art collections gathered by the Habsburgs when they added new territories to their empire. Acquisitions highlight the art of ancient Egypt and Greece. The museum is rich in works of Dutch, German, Flemish, French, and Italian painters, with representation of many of the greatest European masters, such as Velásquez and Titian.

Among notable works from the German, Dutch, and Flemish schools are Roger van der Weyden's crucifixion triptych, a Memling altarpiece, and Jan van Eyck's portrait of Cardinal Albergati. But it is the works of Pieter Brueghel the Elder for which the museum is renowned. This 16th-century Flemish master is known for his sensitive yet vigorous landscapes. He did many lively studies of peasant life, and his pictures today are almost a storybook of life in his time. See especially his *Children's Games* and *Hunters in the Snow*, one of his most celebrated works. Don't confuse this artist with his son, Pieter Brueghel the Younger, also a painter.

Many visitors go to the gallery that displays the work of Van Dyck, especially to see his *Venus in the Forge of Vulcan*. Rubens, naturally, comes in for a big, lavish display. You'll see his *Self-Portrait* and *Woman with a Cape*, for which he is said to have used the face of his second wife, Helen Fourment. Rubens brings a robust Flemish enthusiasm to the museum's galleries in both religious and allegorical works. Great pride is, of course, taken in the Rembrandt collection, which includes two remarkable self-portraits as well as a moving portrait of his mother and one of his son, Titus

Holbein the Younger, who lived in England, painted *Jane Seymour,* third wife of Henry VIII.

For me, other than revisiting the works of Brueghel, the thrill of any trip to Vienna is seeing the Kunsthistorisches Museum's aggregation of the works of Albrecht Dürer, the German painter and engraver (1471–1528), known for his imaginative art and his painstakingly detailed workmanship. Here you will see his noted *Blue Madonna.* He was also known for his realistic landscapes, as best seen in *Martyrdom of 10,000 Christians.* Dürer was a true Renaissance man.

The glory of the French, Spanish, and Italian schools is also to be seen in this Vienna museum, having often come into Habsburg hands as "gifts." Represented are Titian by his *A Girl with a Cloak,* Veronese by the *Adoration of the Magi,* Caravaggio by his *Virgin of the Rosary,* Raphael by *The Madonna in the Meadow,* and Tintoretto by his painting of Susanna caught off guard in her bath when the Peeping Tom elders came along. One of my all-time favorite painters is Giorgione, and here I can gaze long at his *Trio of Philosophers.* If you have only a short time to spend in this museum, I suggest that you skip many galleries if necessary just to see the work of Velásquez, the 17th-century Spanish artist often referred to as a "painter's painter." Some of his pictures of the court of Philip IV of Spain are exhibited.

One whole section of galleries is devoted to the works of ancient Egypt, Greece, and Rome. Don't miss seeing the tiny Egyptian hippopotamus. There is a noteworthy assemblage of cameos in onyx, some of which belonged to Emperor Augustus. There are also Etruscan antiquities on display.

In a sculpture and applied arts section, you can drool over the celebrated gold salt cellar by Benvenuto Cellini, which was made for Francis I and is a Renaissance goldwork masterpiece. Here you'll also see ivory horns from the 9th century. Perhaps you'll fancy a rococo breakfast service used by Maria Theresa and her big brood of young Habsburgs. Finally, there's a numismatic exhibit, with many medals left over from the Austro-Hungarian Empire.

The museum is open Tuesday to Friday from 10am to 6pm, on Saturday, Sunday, and holidays from 9am to 6pm. The galleries are open late on Tuesday and Friday from 7 to 9pm. All are closed Monday. Admission is 45 AS ($3.25).

On Maria-Theresien-Platz, where the Kunsthistorisches Museum is situated, stands a glorious concoction, a memorial constructed in 1888 to honor the long reign of Maria Theresa, with important statesmen clustered at the feet of the empress.

Uhrenmuseum der Stadt Wien

The Municipal Clock Museum, Schulhof 2 (tel. 0222/533-22-65), has a wideranging assemblage of timepieces, some ancient, some modern, some in between. Housed in what was once the Obizzi town house, the museum dates from 1690 and displays clocks of all shapes and sizes. Clock collectors from all over Europe and North America come to gaze and perhaps to covet. See Rutschmann's astronomical clock made in the 18th century. There are many cuckoo clocks and a gigantic timepiece that was once mounted in the tower of St. Stephen's.

The museum is open Tuesday to Sunday from 9am to 12:15pm and from 1 to 4:30pm.

Historisches Museum der Stadt Wien

The Historical Museum of Vienna, on the Karlsplatz (tel. 0222/505-87-47), is a fascinating but apparently little-visited collection. History buffs seek it out, however, finding here the full panorama of the history of the old city unfolded, beginning with the settlement of prehistoric tribes in the Danube basin. Roman relics, artifacts from the reign of the dukes of Babenberg, and a wealth of leftovers from the Habsburg sovereignty are here, as well as arms and armor from various eras. A scale model shows Vienna as it looked in the Habsburg heyday. You'll see pottery and ceramics from the Roman era forward, 14th-century stained-glass windows, mementos of the

Turkish sieges of the city in 1529 and 1683, and even Biedermeier furniture. There's also a section on Vienna's art nouveau.

The museum is open daily except Monday from 9am to 4:30pm.

Akademie der bildenden Künste

When I'm in Vienna, I always make at least one visit to this academy of fine arts, Schillerplatz 3 (tel. 0222/588-16), to see the *Last Judgment* triptych by the incomparable Hieronymus Bosch. In this work, the artist conjured up all the demons of the nether regions for a terrifying view of the suffering and sins that mankind must go through. There's more here than that, however, and you'll have the opportunity to see many Dutch and Flemish paintings, some from as far back as the 15th century, although the academy is noted for its 17th-century art. The gallery boasts works by Van Dyck, Rembrandt, Botticelli, and a host of other artists. There are several works by Lucas Cranach the Elder, outstanding being his *Lucretia,* completed in 1532, which some say is as enigmatic as *Mona Lisa.* Rubens is represented here by more than a dozen oil sketches. You can see Rembrandt's *Portrait of a Woman* and scrutinize Guardi scenes from 18th-century Venice.

Hours are 10am to 2pm Tuesday to Friday (except Wednesday, when the gallery is open from 10am to 1pm and 3 to 6pm). On Saturday and Sunday it is open from 9am to 1pm. It is closed Monday. Admission is 15 AS ($1.10).

Niederösterreichisches Landesmuseum

That polysyllabic name simply identifies the Museum of Lower Austria, Herrengasse 9 (tel. 0222/533-10). The museum has exhibits of the geology, flora, and fauna of the area surrounding Vienna. These exhibits are displayed in a palace dating from the 17th century.

Normally, the museum is open Tuesday to Friday from 9am to 5pm, on Saturday from 9am to 2pm, and on Sunday from 9am to noon; closed on Monday and from mid-July to September. Admission is 25 AS ($1.80).

Österreichisches Museum für angewandte Kunst

The Museum of Applied Art, Stubenring 5 (tel. 0222/711-36), has a rich collection of tapestries, some from the 16th century. Of special interest is a Persian carpet depicting *The Hunt.* The most outstanding assemblage of Viennese porcelain in the world is here, as are some 13th-century Limoges enamels. Exhibits include much Biedermeier furniture and other antiques, glassware and crystal, an Oriental display, outstanding objects of "Wiener Werkstätte," and large collections of lace and textiles. One hall is devoted to art nouveau.

You can see these displays of applied art Wednesday to Monday from 11am to 6pm for 30 AS ($2.20).

Museum Moderner Kunst

The Museum of Modern Art, Fürstengasse 1 (tel. 0222/34-12-59), was opened in 1979. Built between 1698 and 1711, the edifice, one of the most splendid in Vienna, was the home of the Prince of Liechtenstein. It is lavish with baroque adornment on the first floor. The permanent collection shows works of international modern art from 1900 to the present and is especially rich in surrealism, object art, photo-realism, and abstract art.

Hours are daily from 10am to 6pm (except Tuesday). Admission is 30 AS ($2.20).

Museum des 20 Jahrhunderts

This modern museum lying in the Schweizergarten (tel. 0222/78-25-50) was opened in 1962 in the pavilion built for the 1958 World's Fair in Brussels by Karl Schwanzer. Now it is used for ever-changing exhibits of international modern art, and there is an important sculpture garden outside the museum.

Hours are daily from 10am to 6pm except Wednesday, when it is closed. Admission varies according to the exhibit being shown, ranging from 30 AS ($2.20) to 50 AS ($3.65).

Heeresgeschichtliches Museum

Vienna's Museum of Military History, Arsenal 3 (tel. 0222/78-23-03), is the oldest state museum building in Vienna, constructed from 1849 to 1856. Mostly, of course, the military history of the Habsburgs—their glittering triumphs and their defeats—is delineated.

A glass case in the center of the Hall of Glory (Ruhmeshalle) contains the six orders of the House of Habsburg that Franz Joseph wore on all public occasions. The colors are faded and the pins and other fasteners almost worn away from use. I find fascinating the Sarajevo room, with mementos of the assassination of Archduke Franz Ferdinand and his wife on June 28, 1914, the event that ignited the smoldering kindling and set off the deadly bonfire of World War I. The archduke's bloodstained uniform is displayed, along with the bullet-scarred car in which the royal couple rode on that fateful day. Many exhibits relating to the navy of the Austro-Hungarian Empire may be seen. Frescoes depict important battles, including those fought with the Turks in and around Vienna.

The museum is open daily from 10am to 4pm (except Friday). A 30 AS ($2.20) admission is charged.

THE CHURCHES OF VIENNA

The houses of worship are so inviting that even nonbelievers may want to attend on their Vienna visit, if not for the rich baroque decoration of crystal chandeliers and trompe-l'oeil ceilings, then for the magnificent music of Mozart, Bach, Haydn, perhaps Bruckner. Many former Gothic churches have a massive baroque overlay, although some have been relieved of this decoration and put back to their original simpler style. If you spent a week visiting the churches of Vienna, you still wouldn't have seen them all. If your stay here is relatively brief, I suggest you look at the first two recommended below, and then see others if you have more time. I'll begin with the king of them all—

St. Stephen's Cathedral

Lying in the very heart of the city, at Stephansplatz 1, a bustling intersection where legend has it that if you wait long enough you'll see anybody you're looking for in the city, St. Stephen's Cathedral (tel. 0222/515-52-563) was founded in the 12th century in what even in the Middle Ages was the town's center. The church was the result of a new basilica being built on the site of a Romanesque sanctuary.

Stephansdom (the German name for this church) was virtually destroyed in a 1258 fire that swept Vienna, and toward the dawn of the 14th century the Romanesque basilica gave way to a Gothic building. The cathedral suffered terribly in the Turkish siege of 1683 but then was allowed to rest until the Russian bombardments of 1945, with the Germans bringing more destruction when they continued to fire on Vienna from the outskirts as they fled the city. During these most recent depredations the wooden roof of St. Stephen's was heavily bombed, but it has been replaced with a steel structure. The steeple, rising to some 450 feet, has come to symbolize the very spirit of Vienna. Reopened in 1948 after restoration from war damage, today the cathedral is considered one of the greatest Gothic structures in Europe, rich in woodcarvings, altars, sculptures, and paintings.

The west door, in the Romanesque style, called Giants' Doorway (Riesentor), is one of the oldest parts of the main building, having been spared from the 1258 fire. It is richly embellished with statuary. The mammoth bell of St. Stephen's,

Pummerin or Boomer Bell, largest in the country, was originally cast from cannons left behind by the fleeing Turks after their failed siege of 1683. I'm sure the bell was sufficiently blessed to remove any heretical taint from the metal. Or perhaps some tinge remained, to be released in the fire of 1945, for the bell fell and shattered then, since replaced by a bell donated by Upper Austria.

The 352-foot-long cathedral is inextricably linked with Viennese and Austrian history. It was here that mourners attended Mozart's "pauper's funeral" in 1791, and it was on the cathedral door that Napoleon posted his farewell edict in 1805.

The pulpit of St. Stephen's was carved from stone by Anton Pilgrim, his enduring masterpiece. But the chief treasure of the cathedral is the carved wooden Wiener Neustadt altarpiece dating from 1447, richly painted and gilded, found in the Virgin's Choir. See also the curious tomb of Emperor Frederick III in the Apostles' Choir. Made of a pinkish Salzburg marble in the 17th century, the tomb is carved with hideous little hobgoblins trying to enter and wake the emperor from his eternal sleep. The entrance to the catacombs or crypt is on the north side next to the Capistran pulpit. You can visit it daily from 10 to 11:30am and 2 to 4:30pm for 25 AS ($1.80). In the crypt, you'll see the funeral urns that contain the entrails of 56 members of the Habsburg family. (As I noted earlier, the hearts are inurned in St. George Chapel of the Augustinerkirche and the bodies entombed in the Capuchin Crypt of the Kapuzinerkirche Church.)

You can climb the 344-step south tower of St. Stephen's, which dominates the Viennese skyline and from which you have a view of the Vienna Woods. Called Alter Steffl (Old Steve), the tower with its needlelike spire was built between 1350 and 1433. From it, watchkeepers of earlier days kept vigil over the city. So well known is Old Steve that the Viennese refer to the entire cathedral as Alter Steffl. If you're game to climb the tower, you can do so from March to October, 9am to 5pm, and from the middle of December through the first week of January, 9am to 4:30pm. Admission is 15 AS ($1.10).

The north tower (Nordturm) was never finished to match the south one, but was crowned in the Renaissance style in 1579. You can reach it by elevator from April to the end of September, 9am to 6pm, and from October to the end of March, 8am to 5pm; the charge is 30 AS ($2.20). You view a panoramic sweep of the city and the Danube.

St. Maria am Gestade

This church at Passauer Platz, the Church of Our Lady of the Riverbank, was once just that, with an arm of the Danube flowing by it, making it a favorite place of worship for fishermen. But the river was redirected, and now the church draws people by its beauty. A Romanesque church on this site was rebuilt in Gothic style between 1394 and 1427. The western façade is in the flamboyant Gothic style, with a seven-sided Gothic tower surmounted by a dome that culminates in a lace-like crown. This tower has long been an Old Town landmark.

The church's most remarkable treasure is in the Chapel of St. Clement, an altarpiece made in 1460. See the panels depicting the Coronation of the Virgin and the Annunciation. In the interior are many pieces of Gothic statuary and superb woodcarving.

St. Maria am Gestade was much damaged during Turkish sieges, both in 1529 and 1683.

Church of the Teutonic Order

Die Deutschordenkirche and its treasury, Schatzkammer des Deutschen Ordens, both at Singerstrasse 7 (tel. 0222/512-10-65), will stir thoughts of the Crusades in the minds of history buffs, but the relics of vanished glory may make some visitors wish they had been among the nobility of the Middle Ages.

The Order of the Teutonic Knights was a German society founded in 1190 in the Holy Land. In 1205 the Order came to Vienna, but this church they built dates from 1395. The building didn't fall prey to the baroque madness that swept the city following the Counter-Reformation, so you see it pretty much as it was originally, a Gothic church dedicated to St. Elizabeth. A choice feature is the 16th-century Flemish altarpiece standing at the main altar, which is richly decorated with woodcarving, much gilt, and painted panel inserts. Many knights of the Teutonic Order are buried here, their heraldic shields still mounted on some of the upper walls.

In the treasury of the knights on the second floor of the church, you'll see mementos such as seals and coins illustrating the history of the order, as well as a collection of arms, vases, gold, crystal, and precious stones. These were very wealthy knights. Also on display are the charter given to the Teutonic Order by Henry IV of England and medieval paintings. A curious exhibit is a Viper Tongue Credenza, said to have the power to detect poison in food and render it harmless.

Treasury hours are 10am to noon daily and 3 to 5pm on Tuesday, Wednesday, Friday, and Saturday. Admission is 50 AS ($3.65).

St. Peter's Church

Called Peterskirche, this church dominates Peterplatz. It's the second-oldest church in Vienna, but the spot on which it stands may well be the *oldest* Christian church site. Many places of worship have stood here, the first believed to date from the second half of the 4th century. Charlemagne is credited with having founded a church on the site (late 8th or early 9th century).

The present St. Peter's, the most lavishly decorated baroque church in Vienna, was designed in 1702 by Gabriel Montani. Von Hildebrandt, the noted architect who designed the Belvedere Palace, is believed to have finished the building in 1732. The fresco in the dome is a masterpiece by J. M. Rottmayr, depicting the Coronation of the Virgin. The church contains many frescoes and much gilded carved wood, plus altarpieces that are the work of many well-known artists of the time.

St. Rupert's Church

The oldest church in Vienna, Ruprechtskirche stands at Ruprechtsplatz, where it has been since 740, although much that you see now, such as the aisle, is newer— from the 11th century. It's believed that much of the masonry from a Roman shrine on this spot was used in the present church. The tower and nave are Romanesque, the rest Gothic. St. Rupert is the patron saint of salt merchants of the Danube.

The church is not always open to the public, so if you really want to see it, I suggest you attend service on Saturday at 5pm or on Sunday at 10:30am.

Church of St. Charles

Construction on Karlskirche, opening onto Karlsplatz, dedicated to St. Charles Borromeo, was begun in 1716 by order of Emperor Charles VI. Black plague swept Vienna in 1713, and the emperor made a vow to build the church if the disease would abate. Work on the structure was begun by that master of the baroque, Johann Bernard Fischer von Erlach, who labored from 1716 to 1722. His son, Joseph Emanuel, completed it between 1723 and 1739. The lavishly decorated interior was given to the people by the father-and-son leaders in the baroque field.

The well-known ecclesiastical artist J. M. Rottmayr painted many of the frescoes inside the church from 1725 to 1730. The green copper dome of Karlskirche is a lofty 236 feet high, a dramatic landmark on the Viennese skyline. Two columns, spin-offs from Trajan's Column in Rome, flank the front of the church, and there is also a statue by Henry Moore.

Church of the Jesuits (Universitätskirche)

Built at the time of the Counter-Reformation, this church at Dr.-Ignaz-Seipel-Platz 1 (tel. 0222/525-23-233) is rich in baroque embellishments—no surprise, as it was constructed between 1624 and 1631, when the baroque craze in churches was sweeping the city. This was the university church, dedicated to the Jesuit saints Ignatius of Loyola and Franciscus Xaverius. It was built at the order of the emperor, Ferdinand II. The rich high-baroque decorations (galleries, columns, and the trompe-l'oeil painting on the ceiling, which gives the illusion of a dome) were added from 1703 to 1705, after the Thirty Years' War and the Turkish siege of Vienna had ended. The embellishments were the work of a Jesuit lay brother, the Roman Andrea Pozzo, at the orders of Emperor Leopold I. The redecorated church was dedicated to the Assumption of the Virgin. See Pozzo's painting of Mary, behind the main altar.

In July the church is a central point of the **Spectacvlvm,** a summer festival held by the Society for Music Theater in the Old University District. Baroque operas and contemporary ballets are performed in the church, with other segments of the Spectacvlvm performed elsewhere. Information about this event is available from the **Society for Music Theater,** Türkenstrasse 19, A-1090 Vienna (tel. 0222/34-06-99).

Church of St. Michael

Michaelerkirche on Michaelerplatz can date some of its Romanesque portions to the early 1200s. The exact date of the chancel is not known, but it is probably from the mid-14th century. Over its long history this church has felt the hand of many architects and designers, resulting in a medley of styles, not all harmonious. Perhaps only the catacombs would be recognized by droppers-in from the Middle Ages.

Most of the present look of St. Michael's dates from 1792, when the façade was done in the neoclassical style typical of the time. The spire, however, is from the 16th century. The main altar is richly decorated in baroque style, and the altarpiece, entitled *The Collapse of the Angels,* is the last major baroque work done in Vienna. The year was 1781.

Church of the Minorites

If you're tired of baroque ornamentation, visit Minoritenkirche, Minoritenplatz 2A (tel. 0222/533-41-62), a church of the Friar Minor Capuchins, a Franciscan order also called the Minorite friars (inferior brothers, so called to emphasize their humility). This church, begun in 1250 but not completed until early in the 14th century, had its tower damaged by the Turks in their two sieges of Vienna, and then it fell prey to baroque architects and designers in the 18th century. But in 1784 Ferdinand von Hohenberg ordered that the baroque additions be removed and the simple lines of the original Gothic church returned, complete with Gothic cloisters. Inside you'll see a mosaic copy of da Vinci's *The Last Supper.*

The church is open to visitors Monday to Saturday from 9am to noon and 3 to 6pm. Masses are said on Sunday at 8:30 and 11am.

Church of the Piarist Order

Work on Piaristenkirche, on Jodok-Fink-Platz, which is more popularly known as Piaristenplatz, was launched in 1716 by the Roman Catholic teaching congregation known as Piarists (fathers of religious schools), but the church was not consecrated until 1771. Some of the designs submitted during that long period are believed to have been drawn by von Hildebrandt, the noted architect who designed Belvedere Palace, but many builders had a hand in things during the decades between construction start and consecration.

Despite the time lag and the many alterations during construction, this church is noteworthy for its fine classic façade. Frescoes by F. A. Maulbertsch, done in 1752, adorn the inside of the circular cupolas.

Church and Court of the Scots

Heinrich, a Babenberg ruler who died in 1177, during his reign founded a "monastery of the Scots," Schottenhof in Freyung, in 1155. The monks were in fact

Irish, but who was inclined to point out an error to a medieval monarch? So Schottenhof was and still is the "Courtyard of the Scots" and Schottenkirche the "Church of the Scots." Although it suffered much damage in the late Middle Ages, the church always bounced back and has survived massive alterations done in the 17th century, plus a major facelift that gave it its present appearance in 1880, the heyday of the empire. In the art gallery in the abbey, you'll see paintings showing Vienna in the Middle Ages.

Kirche am Hof

This most exuberantly baroque of all Vienna's churches is called "The Church of the Nine Choirs of Angels." With the Germanic penchant for expressing a name by stringing all the words together, I'm glad they simply call this church by its am Hof location rather than using a literal translation.

The church was constructed between 1386 and 1403 by Carmelite monks in the Gothic style. However, when the Jesuits took it over early in the time of the Counter-Reformation, they made many architectural changes, so that today it bears a simple baroque façade, which was completed in 1692. In a chapel inside the church you can see a fresco by Franz Anton Maulbertsch, perhaps the greatest and most original of the 18th-century Austrian painters.

Kirche am Hof has a place in history. It was here that Franz II, seeing the end of the Holy Roman Empire approaching, proclaimed the Austrian Empire in 1804. It was well that he did. Just two years later the Holy Roman Empire, brought forth with great fanfare in 962, ceased to exist.

VIENNA WOODS

Yes, dear reader, there really are Vienna Woods. They weren't simply dreamed up by Johann Strauss Jr. as the subject of musical tales in waltz time. The Wienerwald is a land of gentle paths and trees several thousand acres in size in a delightful hilly landscape. If you stroll through this area, a weekend playground for the Viennese, you'll be following in the footsteps of Strauss and Schubert. Beethoven, when his hearing was failing, claimed that the chirping birds, trees, and leafy vineyards of the Wienerwald made it easier for him to compose.

A round-trip through the woods, which lie to the south and west of Vienna, takes about 3½ hours by car, a distance of some 50 miles. You leave the city on the Eichenstrasse. Even if you don't have a car, the woods can be visited relatively easily on your own. Board trolleycar no. 1 near the State Opera, going to Schottenring. There you must switch to tram no. 38 (the same ticket is valid) going out to Grinzing, the village that is the site of the famous heurigen, or wine taverns. At Grinzing you can board a bus that goes through the Wienerwald to Kahlenberg (see below). The whole trip takes about 1½ hours each way. You might rent a bicycle nearby to make your own exploration of the woods.

Many of the attractions of the Wienerwald are described in Chapter V, "Lower Austria."

When you go to the Vienna Woods by public transportation, after you reach Grinzing (if you can resist the heurigen), you board bus no. 38A up the hill to **Kahlenberg** on the northeasternmost spur of the Alps (1,585 feet). If the weather is fair and clear, you can see all the way to Hungary and Czechoslovakia from here. At the top of the hill is the small Church of St. Joseph, where King John Sobieski of Poland stopped to pray before leading his troops to the defense of Vienna against the Turks. For one of the best of all views overlooking Vienna, go to the right of the Kahlenberg restaurant. From the terrace there, you'll have a panoramic sweep, including the spires of St. Stephen's.

Many Austrian visitors from the country, a hardy lot, walk along a footpath to the suburb of Nussdorf and Heiligenstadt, perhaps along the very path Beethoven trod when he lived there. At Nussdorf, it's possible to take a trolleycar, designated D, which will return you to the heart of Vienna.

THE PARKS OF VIENNA

When the weather is fine, the typical Viennese shuns city parks in favor of the Wienerwald, brought to the notice of the world by Johann Strauss Jr. in his celebrated work, "Tales from the Vienna Woods." But if you're an aficionado of parks, you'll find some magnificent ones in Vienna, where there are more than 4,000 acres of garden and parks within the city limits and no fewer than 770 sports fields and playgrounds. You can, of course, visit Schönbrunn Park and Belvedere Park when you tour those once-royal palaces.

City Parks

Of the parks of Vienna, tastefully laid out by municipal authorities, I will highlight only the most popular, beginning with—

STADTPARK This lovely garden is on the site of the slope where the Danube used to overflow into the Inner City, before the canal was constructed. It can be reached from the Ring or from Lothringer Strasse. Many memorial statues stand in the park, perhaps the best known being the one to Johann Strauss Jr., composer of operettas and waltzes, including "The Blue Danube Waltz." (His father was also a noted musician.) Here, too, are monuments to Franz Schubert and to Hans Makart, a well-known artist whose work you'll see in churches and museums.

The Kursalon, an elegant café-restaurant, stands at the south end of the Stadtpark. Here you can sit at a garden table and often enjoy a concert of Viennese music as you sip the local wine.

VOLKSGARTEN Next to the Burgtheater, visited elsewhere in this book, the people's park was laid out on the site of the old city wall fortifications and can be entered from Dr.-Karl-Lueger-Ring. It's the oldest public garden in Vienna, dating from 1820. Here, too, there are many monuments. One to Franz Grillparzer, the poet, was sculpted in 1889. A memorial to the assassinated Empress Elizabeth dates from 1907. Construction of the so-called Temple of Theseus, a copy of the Theseion in Athens, was begun in 1820.

BURGGARTEN From the Burgring, you can enter this former garden of the Habsburg emperors, built soon after the Volksgarten was completed. There is a monument to Mozart in this park as well as an equestrian statue of Franz I, beloved husband of Maria Theresa. The only open-air statue of Franz Joseph in all Vienna is here. The Burggarten lies next to the Neue Hofburg. There's a statue of Goethe at the park entrance.

BOTANISCHER GARTEN Exotic plants from all over the world, many extremely rare, are found in the Botanical Garden of the University of Vienna at Rennweg 14 (tel. 0222/78-71-01), next to Belvedere Park, from which it can also be entered. The Botanical Garden grew out of a place where medicinal herbs were planted on orders from Maria Theresa. The garden may be visited daily from mid-April until the first of October, 9am to dusk, but always call before going if the weather is inclement, as the garden may be closed. No admission is charged.

DONAUPARK The entrance to the Danube Park, laid out in 1964 between the Danube and the Old Danube (which was diverted from its original course), is on Wagramer Strasse. The 247-acre park was converted from a garbage dump by municipal authorities to become a recreation park with flowers, shrubs, and walks, as well as a bird sanctuary. Within the park are a bee house, a birdhouse with native and exotic specimens, a small-animal paddock, a horse-riding course, playgrounds, and games.

An outstanding feature of the park is the **Donauturm** (Danube Tower), Donauturmstrasse 4 (tel. 0222/23-53-68), an 828-foot tower with two rotating café-restaurants from which you have a panoramic view of Vienna. One restaurant is at a 528-foot level, the other at 561 feet. International specialties and Viennese cuisine are served in both, with meals costing from 250 AS ($18.25). A sightseeing terrace at 495 feet can be visited if you don't come here to dine. Two express elevators take people up in the tower, which in summer is open from 9am to midnight, and in winter, from 10am to 10pm. The charge for the elevator ride is 40 AS ($2.90) for adults and 30 AS ($2.20) for children.

The Prater

Since 1766, when Emperor Joseph II opened the Prater to the public, this extensive tract of woods and meadowland lying between the Danube River and the Danube Canal has been Vienna's favorite recreation area. Joseph, son and co-ruler of Maria Theresa, a liberal reformer and humanist, didn't always come up with changes everybody liked, but when he declared that "everybody shall be allowed to walk, ride, and drive in the Prater at their pleasure," he came up with a winner. Before that the area had been used mostly as a hunting preserve and riding ground for the aristocracy. People still hunted in the wooded section until the reign of Franz Joseph.

Perhaps the coming of too many people drove all the game away, because from the time it was opened to the public, a collection of booths, amusements, and restaurants sprang up in the Prater and drew many visitors. In its early years it was a gathering place for the carriage trade too. Even the emperor and empress came here —when they could get in!

The Prater is considered the birthplace of the waltz. It was first heard here in 1820, introduced by Johann Strauss Sr. and Josef Lanner. However, it was under Johann Strauss Jr., who became known as "the king of the waltz," that this music form reached its greatest popularity.

The best-known part of the huge park is at the end nearest the entrance from the Ring. Here you'll find the **Riesenrad,** the giant Ferris wheel, one of the landmarks of Vienna, constructed in 1897, 220 feet at its highest point. If you saw the film *The Third Man,* you may recall this Ferris wheel in the scene where it appeared that Orson Welles was going to murder Joseph Cotten.

Just beside the Riesenrad is the terminus of the Lilliputian railroad, the 2.6-mile narrow-gauge line that operates in summer using vintage steam locomotives. The amusement park, right behind the Ferris wheel, has all the typical entertainment facilities—roller coasters, merry-go-rounds, tunnels of love, games arcades, whatever.

The Prater is not a fenced-in park, but not all amusements are open all year. The season lasts from March or April until October, but the Riesenrad operates from the beginning of March until November 1. Some of the more than 150 booths and restaurants stay open in winter, including the pony merry-go-round and the gambling places.

In the **Prater Museum,** Hauptallee 2 (tel. 0222/24-94-32), you'll find historical exhibits, including carousel figures and posters, illustrating the 200-year-old history of the park. Located in the Planetarium building near the Ferris wheel, the museum is open on Saturday, Sunday, and public holidays from 2 to 6:30pm. It is closed in August. Admission is 15 AS ($1.10) for adults and 5 AS (35¢) for children.

The Prater is also a sports center, with swimming pools, riding schools, and race courses here and there between woodland and meadows. International soccer matches are held in the Prater stadium.

To reach the Prater, take either streetcar no. 1 from the Ring or the U1 subway to Pratersten. If you drive here, don't forget to observe the "No Entry" and "No Parking" signs, which apply from 3pm on daily. The place is usually jammed on Sunday afternoon in summer. I suggest you schedule your visit at some other time.

HOMES OF FAMOUS PEOPLE

Many of the residences once occupied by celebrated personages in Vienna, most often composers, have been made into museums and opened to the public. It's a privilege for the music-lover to see the rooms once lived and worked in by his or her particular favorites. But dwelling places of noted persons outside the music world are also preserved. For instance, you may visit the apartment where the originator of psychoanalysis wrote of his revolutionary studies.

If you're a Beethoven fancier and want to see where this genius lived, you'll have to do a bit of footwork, as he seems never to have stayed long in one place. He was evicted from several of his dwellings because of a habit he had of composing at 3 o'clock in the morning. His music may have been heavenly, but it probably came off as pretty hellish to neighbors who preferred to spend the night hours sleeping.

You can visit one of his residences where the landlord was tolerant (or the neighbors deaf), the **Pasqualati House**, Mölker Bastei 8 (tel. 0222/63-70-665). The building dates from the 1790s, and Beethoven lived there—on and off—from 1804 to 1814. He is known to have composed his Fourth, Fifth, and Seventh Symphonies here, as well as *Fidelio* and other works.

There isn't much to see except some family portraits and the composer's scores, but you may feel it's worth the climb to the fourth floor (there's no elevator). You may visit the apartment daily except Monday from 11am to 12:15pm and 1 to 4:30pm.

Once a fairly remote and isolated wine-growing village, Heiligenstadt is really a suburb of Vienna today. It is visited chiefly for its connection with Beethoven, who came here hoping that a sulfur spring to which miraculous powers were attributed could help him recover his hearing. In 1802 the composer wrote a letter, the "Testament of Heiligenstadt," in the house at Probusgasse 6; in it he painfully documented his hopelessness about his rapidly approaching deafness. The house is open Tuesday to Friday from 10am to 4pm, on Saturday from 2 to 6pm, and on Sunday from 9am to 1pm; closed Monday.

For a few months in 1817, Beethoven lived at Pfarrplatz 2 in a 17th-century house that has been turned into a heurige.

Haydns Wohnhaus (Haydn's House), Haydngasse 19 (tel. 0222/596-13-07), is where Franz Josef Haydn conceived and wrote his magnificent later oratorios *The Seasons* and *The Creation*. He lived here from 1797 until his death in 1809. Haydn gave lessons to Beethoven here. There's also a room in this house, which is a branch of the History Museum of Vienna, honoring Johannes Brahms. Hours are 10am to 12:15pm and 1 to 4:30pm Tuesday through Sunday. There's no admission charge.

You'll discover the **Mozart-Wohnung** (Figarohaus), or Mozart Memorial, at Domgasse 5 (tel. 0222/513-62-94), a 17th-century house called the House of Figaro because Mozart composed his opera *The Marriage of Figaro* here. The composer's life in this house from 1784 to 1787 covered a relatively happy period in what was otherwise a rather tragic life. It was here that he often played chamber music concerts with Haydn, whose home we have just visited. Later, Mozart was not to have such a fancy address as this one on Domgasse. Over the years he lived in a dozen houses in all, which became more squalid as he aged. He died in poverty and was given a blessing at St. Stephen's Cathedral in 1791, then buried in St. Marx Cemetery.

The Domgasse apartment has been turned into a museum. Hours are 10am to 12:15pm and 1 to 4:30pm daily except Monday.

The **Schubert Museum** (Schubert's birthplace) is at Nussdorferstrasse 54 (tel. 0222/34-59-924). The composer, son of a poor schoolmaster, was born in 1797 in a house built earlier in that century. Many Schubert mementos are on view. The house is open daily except Monday from 10am to 12:15pm and 1 to 4:30pm. Schubert's last residence was in his brother's house, Kettenbruckengasse 6 (tel. 0222/57-39-072), and the room in which he died at the early age of 31 has been made into a memorial.

"The king of the waltz," Johann Strauss Jr., lived at the **Johann-Strauss-Wohnung,** Praterstrasse 54 (tel. 0222/24-01-21), for a number of years, composing "The Blue Danube Waltz" here in 1867. Now part of the History Museum of Vienna, the house is open daily except Monday from 10am to 12:15pm and 1 to 4:30pm.

At the **Sigmund Freud Museum,** Berggasse 19 (tel. 0222/31-15-96), with its dark furniture (only part of it original), lace curtains, and collection of antiquities, you get the feeling that the doctor might walk in at any moment and tell you to make yourself comfortable on the couch. His velour hat, dark walking stick with ivory handle, and other mementos are to be seen in the study and waiting room he used during his life here from 1891 to 1938. When Hitler staged his takeover of Austria, the so-called Anschluss, Freud fled these quarters to seek safety in London.

You may visit the museum daily from 9am to 3pm. Admission costs 30 AS ($2.20) for adults and 15 AS ($1.10) for children above the age of 10. The museum also has a bookshop where souvenirs are available, including a variety of postcards of the apartment, books by Freud, posters, prints, and pens.

TOURS

The two Vienna sightseeing companies, **Cityrama Sightseeing Tours** and **Vienna Sightseeing Tours,** offer a wide range of trips for visitors. If sufficient notice is given, you can be picked up at your hotel for all but the minitours.

Cityrama conducts nonstop tours lasting about 1½ hours each at 9:45am and 2:45pm daily from Stephansplatz and at 10am and 3pm daily from Johannesgasse.

Vienna Sightseeing Tours (Wiener Rundfahrten), Stelzhamergasse 4-11 (tel. 0222/72-46-83), offers many tours, ranging from a 1½-hour Vienna-Getting Acquainted trip to a one-day luxury excursion to Budapest. The get-acquainted tour costs 160 AS ($11.75) for adults and 60 AS ($4.35) for children, and is a favorite with visitors who are pressed for time and yet want to see the most important sights of the city. It takes you past the historic buildings of the Ringstrasse—the State Opera, Hofburg Palace, museums, the House of Parliament, City Hall, Burgtheater, the university, and the Votive Church—and into the heart of Vienna to St. Stephen's Cathedral, as well as Belvedere Palace, St. Charles Church, and the Musikverein (Vienna Philharmonic Orchestra building). Tours leave the State Opera daily at 10:30 and 11:45am and at 3 and 4:30pm.

Vienna Woods–Mayerling, another popular excursion, lasting about four hours, leaves from the State Opera and takes you to the towns of Perchtoldsdorf and Mödling, passing by the Höldrichsmühle, where Franz Schubert composed many of his beloved Lieder, going to the Abbey of Heiligenkreuz, a center of Christian culture since medieval times. The commemorative chapel in the village of Mayerling reminds visitors of the tragic suicide of Crown Prince Rudolph, only son of Emperor Franz Joseph, and his mistress. The tour also takes you for a short walk through Baden, the spa once a favorite summer resort of the aristocracy. Tours cost 360 AS ($26.15) for adults and 110 AS ($8) for children.

A Grand City Tour, which includes a visit to Schönbrunn and Belvedere Palace, leaves the State Opera daily at 9:30am and 10:30am, and again at 2:30pm, lasting about three hours and costing adults 320 AS ($23.25) and children 120 AS ($8.70).

A visit to the Spanish Riding School, where the world-renowned Lippizaner horses are trained, is offered on Saturday and Sunday in connection with city tours conducted by Vienna Sightseeing Tours, leaving from the State Opera at 8:30am. Adults are charged 260 AS ($19) and children 120 AS ($8.70). The stop at the riding school allows you to see a half-hour performance by the Lippizaners. The Sunday tour ends at the school.

Perhaps you'll have time to make an eight-hour trip along the Danube, going to Wachau by bus and boat and tasting the wines produced in this area since Roman times. From the end of March until October 31 this tour leaves daily at 9:30am, cutting the schedule to every Thursday and Sunday from November 1 to March 31. The price is 850 AS ($61.75) for adults and 480 AS ($35) for children.

2. Where to Shop

Visitors find much of interest to buy or just to look at in Vienna's shops, where you'll see handcrafts produced in a long-established tradition of skilled workmanship. Popular for their beauty, quality, and reasonable prices are petit-point items, hand-painted Wiener Augarten porcelain, work of gold- and silversmiths, handmade dolls, ceramics, enamel jewelry, wrought-iron articles, leathergoods, and many other items of value and interest.

The main shopping streets are in the city center (First District). Here you'll find **Kärntnerstrasse,** between the State Opera and Stock-im-Eisen-Platz; the **Graben,** between Stock-im-Eisen-Platz and Kohlmarkt; **Kohlmarkt,** between the Graben and Michaelerplatz; and **Rotensturmstrasse,** between Stephansplatz and Kai. There are also **Mariahilferstrasse,** between Babenbergerstrasse and Schönbrunn, one of the longest streets in Vienna; **Favoritenstrasse,** between Südtiroler Platz and Reumannplatz; and **Landstrasser Hauptstrasse.**

Shops are normally open Monday through Friday from 9am to 6pm and on Saturday from 9am to noon. Small shops close between noon and 2pm for lunch. Railroad station shops in the Westbahnhof and the Südbahnhof are open daily from 7am to 11pm, offering groceries, smoker's supplies, stationery, books, and flowers. These two stations also have hairdressers, public baths, and photo booths.

Vienna's antiques shops hold what seems to be a limitless treasure trove, and you can find valuable old books, engravings, etchings, and paintings in second-hand shops, bookshops, and picture galleries.

The state-owned **Dorotheum,** Dorotheergasse 17 (tel. 0222/51-56-00), is the oldest auction house in Europe, dating from 1707, when it was founded by the Emperor Joseph I as an auction house where impoverished aristocrats could fairly (and anonymously) get good value for their heirlooms. If you're interested in what is being auctioned off, you give a small fee to a *Sensal,* one of the licensed bidders, and he or she will bid in your name. The Dorotheum is also the scene of many art auctions, and there are 16 subsidiaries in other districts, plus large private galleries and antique dealers.

You may find a little of everything at the **Flohmarkt,** or flea market, in the vicinity of the Naschmarkt, near the Kettenbrückengasse underground station. It is held every Saturday from 8am to 6pm except on public holidays. Naturally it's customary to haggle over the price, and the Viennese have perfected that skill.

The **Naschmarkt** itself is a vegetable and fruit market, the "Covent Garden of Vienna," which has a lively scene every day. To visit it, head south of the opera district. It's at Linke and Rechte Wienzeile.

Ö.W. (Österreichische Werkstatten), Kärntnerstrasse 6 (tel. 0222/512-24-18), is a big, well-run store that sells hundreds of handmade art objects from Austria. You'll find an especially good selection of pewter, along with enameled jewelry, glassware, brass, baskets, ceramics, and serving spoons fashioned from deer horn and bone. Be sure to keep wandering through this place, as there are three floors and a friendly staff. Even if you skip the other stores of Vienna, check this one out.

Popp & Kretschmer, Kärntnerstrasse 51 (tel. 0222/512-78-01). The staff here is usually as well dressed and elegant as the clientele, and will, if you appear to be a bona fide customer, offer coffee, tea, or champagne as you scrutinize the carefully selected merchandise. The store contains three carpeted levels of dresses for women, along with shoes, handbags, and a small selection of men's belts, briefcases, and travel bags. The establishment is opposite the State Opera, near many of the grand old hotels of Vienna.

Lanz, Kärntnerstrasse 10 (tel. 0222/512-24-56), is a well-known Austrian store specializing in haute couture in Austrian folkloric clothing. It has a rustically elegant format of wood paneling and brass chandeliers. Most of their stock is for women, although they do offer a limited selection of men's jackets. Clothes for toddlers begin at sizes appropriate for a 1-year-old child, while women's apparel begins at size 36 (American size 7).

Gerold and Co., Graben 31 (tel. 0222/533-50-140), is a good bookstore in Vienna for English-language publications. The sales personnel are helpful, and you can often pick up many titles not readily available elsewhere.

Another good bookstore is **Morawa,** Wollzeile 11 (tel. 0222/515-62), which is huge and rambling, occupying a labyrinth of vaulted rooms a short walk from St. Stephen's Cathedral. They sell both English- and German-language books.

J. & L. Lobmeyr, Kärntnerstrasse 26 (tel. 0222/512-05-08). If during your exploration of Vienna you should happen to admire a crystal chandelier, there's a good chance that it was made by this company. It was designated in the early 19th century as a purveyor to the Imperial Court of Austria, and it has maintained an elevated position ever since. The company is credited with designing and creating the first electric chandelier in 1883. It has also designed chandeliers for the Vienna State Opera, the Metropolitan Opera in New York, even the Assembly Hall in the Kremlin.

Behind its art nouveau façade on the main shopping street of town, you'll see at least 50 chandeliers of all shapes and sizes. The store also sells hand-painted Hungarian porcelain, along with complete breakfast and dinner services. They'll also engrave your family crest on a wine glass if you want it, or sell you one of the uniquely modern pieces of sculptured glass from the third-floor showroom. The second floor is a museum of some of the outstanding pieces the company has made since it was established in 1823.

Mary Kindermoden, Graben 14 (tel. 0222/533-60-97), is—at last!—an inexpensive store specializing only in children's clothing with a regional twist. If you've thought about buying a pair of lederhosen for your nephew or a dirndl for your niece, this is the place to go. In the heart of the old city, near St. Stephen's Cathedral, the establishment has two floors of well-made garments, which even include lace swaddling clothes for a christening. Most garments are for children aged 10 months to 14 years, although lederhosen (which are adorable if you can get junior to wear them) are available for children 10 months to 8 years. The staff speaks English and seems to know how to deal with children. The company also has 26 other shops the Vienna area.

Loden Plankl, Michaelerplatz 6 (tel. 0222/533-80-320), was originally established in 1830 by members of the Plankl family, who continue the ownership today. This is the oldest, best-established, and perhaps the most reputable outlet in Vienna for traditional Austrian clothing. You'll find a collection of Austrian loden coats, trousers, dirndls, jackets, lederhosen, and suits for men, women, and children. The building that contains the store dates from the 17th century, and the location is opposite the Hofburg. Children's clothing usually begins with items for two-year-olds, and women's sizes range from 7 to 20 (American). Large or tall men won't be ignored either, as sizes go up to 58.

Albin Denk, Graben 13 (tel. 0222/512-44-39), is the oldest remaining porcelain store doing continuous business since its establishment in 1702. Its clients have included the Empress Elizabeth, who saw the shop in almost the same format you'll see it in today. The décor of the three low-ceilinged rooms is beautiful, as are the thousands of objects from Meissen, Dresden, and other regions. With such a wealth of riches, it's hard to make a selection, but the staff will help you.

The jewelry store, **A. E. Köchert,** Neuer Markt 15 (tel. 0222/512-58-28), is where the fifth generation of the family that served as court jewelers until the end of the House of Habsburg maintains the same fine workmanship of their ancestors. The store, founded in 1814, is in a 16th-century building protected as a monument. The firm has designed many of the crown jewels of Europe, but the staff still gives attention to customers looking only for such minor purchases as charms for a bracelet.

3. Vienna After Dark

Come to the cabaret . . . or the heurige or the disco or the casino—whatever turns you on in the nightlife scene. Vienna has a little bit of everything and a lot of some late-evening entertainment activities to pursue after you've been to the theater or opera and perhaps topped it off with a fine dinner. Now you're ready to play. You can dance, go to shows, gamble, listen to music, and smile a lot in gemütlich nighttime Wien.

Liquor costs pretty much the same in all the clubs. Sometimes a cover charge is imposed, especially when live entertainment is offered. Financially, it's better to drink beer in nightspots than hard liquor, as the latter is expensive.

FASHIONABLE BARS
Eden Bar, Liliengasse 2 (tel. 0222/512-74-50), is the chic rendezvous spot in Vienna, often drawing local society figures in evening dress. The setting is one of 19th-century grandeur. You enter a spacious room with a small mezzanine. Tables and private boxes surround the dance floor, or you can find a seat at the half-moon-shaped bar. It is open nightly from 10pm to 4am, but if you show up much before midnight, you may have the place to yourself. The Eden is a popular *après-théâtre* stop, and if there's a foreign celebrity in Vienna, he or she is likely to visit here. A live band plays for dancing, and the music is of the best nightclub variety played in Vienna. Drinks cost from 90 AS ($6.55).

Galerie-Bar, Singerstrasse 7 (tel. 0222/512-49-29). Vienna is known for its fashionable bars, and one of the best is found at this address. In a warmly outfitted ambience of burl walnut, original artwork, and vaulted ceilings, the bar attracts visitors nightly except Sunday from 7pm to 4am. The location is in the neighborhood of St. Stephen's Cathedral. A mixed drink such as vodka and tonic costs 90 AS ($6.55).

Around the corner a slightly younger crowd is drawn to **Chamäleon,** Blutgasse 3 (tel. 0222/513-17-03), which is decorated in a tongue-in-cheek style, taking its theme from the elusive chameleon. This champagne and cocktail bar—there is recorded music—has one of the widest ranges of mixed drinks in Vienna, everything from the famous Singapore Sling to "The Bronx." Drinks cost from 70 AS ($5.10), and the club is open nightly except Sunday from 5pm to 2am.

DISCOS
Queen Anne, Johannesgasse 12 (tel. 0222/512-02-03), has attracted lots of interesting people to its nightclub and disco, the leading one in town. Patrons have included David Bowie, German playboy Gunther Sachs, the Princess of Auersperg, and "Deep Purple." The club has a big collection of the latest Stateside and Italian records, as well as occasional musical acts performed by singers ranging from Mick Jagger lookalikes to imitations of Watusi dancers. The brown doors with brass trim are open from 9pm to 6am. Sometimes a cover charge, perhaps 120 AS ($8.70), is imposed. A Scotch and soda goes for 105 AS ($7.65).

Atrium, Schwarzenbergplatz 10 (Schwindgasse 1) (tel. 0222/505-35-94), lies within a five-minute walk of its original location, where it was Vienna's first disco. Today it caters to a young crowd who gather here nightly from Thursday to Sunday from 8pm to 4am. There's a 30-AS ($2.20) cover charge, but on Thursday and Sunday women are admitted free from 8 to 9pm. Also, every Thursday and Sunday drinks are half price. Otherwise, a large beer costs 38 AS ($2.75).

Chattanooga, Graben 29A (tel. 0222/533-50-00), offers one of the most popular sidewalk cafés along the Graben in summer. Inside, the décor of its restaurant is like that of a railroad car in the Gay '90s, with formally dressed waiters working feverishly behind glass counters. They serve cheeseburgers and simple meals upstairs, but the real reason for coming here is the disco downstairs. You'll get a modernized view of the generous proportions of old Vienna in the wide mirrored staircase leading to the half-rounded room with its maroon velvet niches. Stylized white tree trunks sprout from the floor to the sophisticated décor of the ceiling (displays are likely to change for certain musical acts). The entrance fee is usually 20 AS ($1.45). Beer starts at 65 AS ($4.75). This is the only dining establishment in the city that is open seven days a week from 8am to 2am (to 4am on Saturday), during which time all items on the menu are available.

It's called **New Scotch Club,** but except for the whisky you might drink, there's not much Scottish ambience at this disco and coffeehouse at Parkring 10 (tel. 0222/512-94-17), in Vienna's most fashionable area, next to the Hilton. The establishment, open daily from 11am to 6am, is a popular place for society figures and others to meet. Furnished luxuriously, it has sophisticated technical equipment, including a hydraulic stage and fancy lights. The establishment has three floors, and near one of the three downstairs bars you'll find a monumental waterfall. Upstairs, the coffeehouse is cozy, and on the second floor is a famous cocktail bar. Drinks cost from 90 AS ($6.55).

For a change, drop in at **Confetti,** Wiesingerstrasse 8 (tel. 0222/513-32-71), which has similar high standards and is under the same management as New Scotch Club. In addition, it serves Italian specialties. It is open daily from 11:30am to 2:30pm and 5:30pm to 4am, with light meals costing from 250 AS ($18.25).

JAZZ

Right next door to the members-only Take Five is the **Tenne,** Annagasse 3 (tel. 0222/512-57-08), where live groups play jazz music for listening or for dancing on a floor with a circle of boxes hovering above. Tenne has a log cabin ambience, with lots of farm equipment, such as ox yokes, making up the décor. The club is open nightly except Monday from 8pm to 3am. Entrance is 20 AS ($1.45), and a large beer goes for 60 AS ($4.35).

ROCK

Papa's Tapas, Schwarzenbergplatz 10 (tel. 0222/65-03-11), at the same location as the previously recommended disco, the Atrium, attracts rock and roll fans. It plays host to a changing venue of visiting rock stars, whose arrival is always heralded in the Vienna newspapers. Entrance fees range from 30 AS ($2.20) to 150 AS ($11), depending on the event. When there's no live music, the place operates as a bar, with a large beer costing 35 AS ($2.55). In a corner is the Wurlitzer Bar, with its American-made jukebox. For 5 AS (35¢), you get three back-to-back singles, all vintages '50s stuff, including Elvis. The club is open nightly from 8pm to 4am. Viennese-born Helmut Fink is the impresario of the place.

EROTIC NIGHTLIFE

Moulin Rouge, Walfischgasse 11 (tel. 0222/512-21-30), has for years been the leading nightclub of Vienna. If you're window-shopping, you can see pictures of the "artists" who will later disrobe for you during a show in this "red mill" modeled after the original Moulin Rouge in Paris, with curved walls, clapboard siding, and windmill. In the pictures you view from the sidewalk the women are stark naked, so there's no surprise awaiting you if you decide to go into the club's lavishly decorated room, which has two tiers of seating. The show is presented nightly from 11pm to

2:30am, with the bar open from 10pm to 6am. The entrance fee is 75 AS ($5.45). Once you're inside, a beer costs 200 AS ($14.50) or a hard drink 250 AS ($18.25). If you're a halfway presentable single male and willing to pay the price, you won't have to wait long for companionship.

WINE CELLARS

A famous drinking spot is **Esterházykeller,** Haarhof 1 (tel. 0222/533-25-67), where the ancient bricks and scarred wooden tables are permeated with the aroma of endless pints of spilled beer. An outing here isn't recommended for everyone, although to its credit no one ever feels sloppily dressed at the Esterházykeller. If you decide to chance it, choose the left-hand entrance (while facing it from the street), grip the railing firmly, and begin your descent. A promenade through this establishment's endless recesses and labyrinthine passages could provide views of the faces you may have thought appeared only in movies. Wine, a specialty, costs from 18 AS ($1.30) a glass. Order a bottle if you plan to stay a while. The place is open Monday through Friday from 10:30am to 10pm. On Saturday and Sunday, hours are 4 to 10pm.

St. Urbani-Keller, Am Hof 12 (tel. 0222/63-91-02), named after the patron saint of wine making, is one of the most historic and deepest cellars in Vienna. Carl Hipfinger renovated the cellar as a public gathering place in 1906. Many of the artifacts inside, from the paneling in the German Romantic style to the fanciful wrought-iron lighting fixtures, were designed by one of Austria's most famous architects, Walcher von Molthein, who rebuilt Vienna's Kreuzenstein Castle at the beginning of the century. The cellar has brick vaulting dating from the 13th century, and sections of solid Roman walls you can admire while listening to the folkloric music at night.

The most popular room is the one on the lowest level, so be sure to continue your descent down the steep stairs until you reach the room with the thick oak tables at the bottom. There you'll find enough art, including numerous crucifixes and a Renaissance chandelier of St. Lucretia, to keep anyone interested. Many kinds of wine are served, but the featured vintage comes from the vineyards of the owner's family. That wine has been offered as gifts to everybody from the famous General Rommel (the so-called Desert Fox) to the president of Austria.

The establishment is open daily from 6pm to 1am, with hot food served until midnight. Meals cost from 255 AS ($18.50), but if you've already eaten, no one will mind if you drop in just for a drink. Watch your step on the way up or down.

GAMBLING

For games of chance, **Spiel-Casino Wien,** Esterházy Palace, Kärntnerstrasse 41 (tel. 0222/512-48-36), opened in 1968, is the place to go. The entrance fee is 170 AS ($12.25). In exchange for that you receive 200 AS ($14.50) worth of chips. You can charge up to 7,000 AS ($509) on your Diners Club, MasterCard or VISA credit cards. You'll need to show your passport to get in. There are gaming tables for French or American roulette, blackjack, and chemin de fer. The club is open daily from 3pm to 3am.

THE HEURIGEN

These wine taverns on the outskirts of Vienna were introduced in Chapter II, under "Food and Drink." These gardens of vintners lie principally in Grinzing (the most popular district) or in Sievering, Neustift, Nussdorf, or Heiligenstadt. They have been celebrated in operettas, films, and song.

In some of the more basic taverns the schilling-wise Viennese bring their own *heurigenpackerl,* a picnic composed mainly of cold cuts, cheese, some chicken, always a sausage, and hard-boiled eggs. But many of these so-called heurigen have grown into elaborate restaurants.

If you don't want to pack your own lunch or dinner but wish to economize, you can bring along inexpensively priced picnic packages sold at many a deli in Vienna. However, you can bring your own lunch only into the simpler, workingman's type of wine cellar, where the proprietor is content just to sell wine. Often his wife and family prepare food that they'd like to sell, however.

The most-visited section, **Grinzing,** lies at the edge of the Vienna Woods. Once it was a separate village until it was overtaken by the ever-increasing city boundaries of Vienna. Much of Grinzing remains unchanged, looking as it did in the days when Beethoven lived nearby and composed music. It's a district of crooked old streets and houses, their thick walls built around inner courtyards that are often grape arbors sheltering gemütlich Viennese wine-drinkers on a summer night. The playing of zithers and accordions lasts long into the night.

Which brings up another point. If you're a motorist, don't drive out to the heurigen. Police patrols are very strict, and you're not to be driving with more than 0.8% alcohol in your bloodstream. It's much better to take public transportation. For example, to go to Grinzing from the heart of Vienna takes only about half an hour.

Take trolley line no. 38 to Grinzing; no. 41 to Neustift am Wald; or no. 38, the same as for Grinzing, to Sievering, which is also reached by bus 39. Heiligenstadt is reached by underground line U-4.

I'll lead off with some of my favorites.

Passauerhof, Cobenzlgasse 9 (tel. 0222/32-63-45). One of Vienna's well-known wine taverns maintains an old-fashioned ambience little changed since the turn of the century. Some of its foundations date from the 12th century. Menu specialties include such familiar fare as tafelspitz, an array of roasts, and plenty of strudel. You can order a glass or bottle of wine, perhaps a meal costing from 125 AS ($9). The establishment is open Monday to Saturday from 4pm to midnight and on Sunday from 11am to midnight. Music is played from 7 to 11:30pm.

Grinzinger Hauermandl, Cobenzlgasse 20 (tel. 0222/32-20-444), in Grinzing, is a rustic inn where many of the guests are lively Viennese escaping their city for an evening in the suburbs. You'll enter through a garden where you'll notice a gypsy wagon perched on the roof. The farm-style cookery includes noodle soup with liver dumplings, as well as a selection of dishes so hearty they could fortify you for a day's work in the vineyards. A quarter liter of wine (about two glasses) costs 29 AS ($2.10), while à la carte meals range from 130 AS ($9.50) to 320 AS ($23.25). The tavern is open daily except Sunday from 5:30pm to midnight.

Altes Presshaus, Cobenzlgasse 15 (tel. 0222/32-23-93), is the oldest heurige in Grinzing, with an authentic cellar you might ask to see. The interior is filled with wood paneling and antique furniture, giving the place character. It's open Tuesday to Saturday from 4pm to midnight; it's closed not only on Sunday and Monday but from November through February. The garden terrace blossoms throughout the summer. Meals cost from 130 AS ($9.50) to 280 AS ($20.25).

Mayer, Am Pfarrplatz 2 (tel. 0222/37-12-87), in Heiligenstadt, is a historic house, some 130 years old when Beethoven composed sections of his Ninth Symphony while living here in 1817. Today Viennese music replaces the melodies that may have filled the house during Ludwig's era. However, the same kind of fruity dry wine is still sold to guests in the shady courtyard of the rose garden. Menu items, aside from the new wine, include grilled chicken, savory pork, and a buffet of well-prepared country food. Reservations are suggested. It's open daily from 4pm to midnight. The innkeepers, the Mayer family, sell wine for 25 AS ($1.80), with meals costing from 200 AS ($14.50).

Alt Sievering, Sieveringer Strasse 63, Sievering (tel. 0222/32-58-88), is one of several attractive heurigen in this Vienna suburb. The owner, Walter Slupetzky, not only serves excellent new wine but prepares such specialties as game, lamb, fish, soufflés, dessert pancakes, strudels, and cakes. A fixed-price menu, which you can eat in summer under the shade trees, costs from 85 AS ($6.25), with à la carte meals ranging from 175 AS ($12.75). The restaurant is open from 9am to 11pm except

Tuesday and Wednesday. If you prefer beer, the house keeps three different types on tap.

CULTURAL VIENNA

The cultural life of Vienna is set to music. This has been true for a couple of centuries or so, and the city has been a lure to composers and librettists, musicians and music-lovers even up to today. There's plenty of room for music in Vienna, and you can find places to enjoy everything from chamber music to pop, from waltzes to jazz. You'll find small discos and large concert halls, as well as musical theaters. And if you should (how could you?) tire of tuneful, atonal, or whatever musical sounds, then there's drama from classical to modern to avant-garde, among other attractions. Below I'll describe just a few of the better-known spots for cultural recreation. There are many others for you to find on your own if you're in Vienna long enough.

The four state theaters—Staatsoper (State Opera), Volksoper, Burgtheater (National Theater), and the Akademietheater—are all reached by the same phone number. Reservations and information for all four theaters can be obtained by calling an office whose purpose is to unite all four theaters into a coherent system not only for reservations but for information. To reach that office—and the number is likely to be busy—call either 51444-2959 or 51444-2960. Many tickets are issued, even before the box office opens, to subscribers. Box office sales are made only one week before each performance at each theater. The season is generally from September until June. Tickets for all state theater performances, including the opera, are available by writing to the **Österreichischer Bundestheaterverband,** Goethegasse 1, A-1010 Vienna, from points outside Vienna. Orders must be received at least two weeks in advance of the performance to be booked. No one should send money through the mails. Advance orders from Vienna are not accepted. Otherwise, you can purchase your ticket at the box office, the **Bundestheaterkasse,** Hanuschgasse 3, which is open Monday to Saturday from 9am to 5pm and on Sunday from 9am to noon.

A highlight of the cultural season is the **Vienna Festival,** usually from May 20 to June 20. During this important European event, Vienna is likely to stage at least 1,000 performances. This is not just a music festival—theater and other activities are offered too. For instance, Clown Town at the Prater draws entertainers from all over the Continent. The State Opera is the centerpiece of the festival. The Theater an der Wien is the official festival house, and there's a good chance you'll get to see Beethoven's *Fidelio* here.

Austrian State Theaters

If your German is halfway passable, try to see a play by Arthur Schnitzler if one is being staged during your visit. This mild man, who died in 1931, was the most characteristically Viennese of the Austrian writers. Through his works he gave the Imperial City the charm and style more often associated with Paris. Whenever possible I attend a revival of one of his plays, such as *Einsame Weg* (The Solitary Path) or *Professor Bernhardi.* My favorite is *Reigen,* on which the film *La Ronde* was based. Schnitzler's plays are often performed at the Theater in der Josefstadt (see below).

Staatsoper, or State Opera, Opernring 2 (tel. 0222/51444-26-55), is considered one of the three most important opera theaters in the world, and the upkeep is apparently a necessity to the Austrians, as its operation is estimated at a cost to the taxpayers of some million schillings a day. When the State Opera was originally built in the 1860s, criticism of the structure so upset one of the architects, Eduard van der Nüll, that he killed himself. In 1945, at the end of World War II, despite other pressing needs such as that for public housing, Vienna started restoration work on the theater, finishing it in time to celebrate the country's independence from occupation forces in 1955.

With the Vienna Philharmonic Orchestra in the pit, some of the leading opera stars of the world perform here. In their day, Richard Strauss and Gustav Mahler worked as directors. Daily performances are given from the first of September until the end of June. Prices range from 50 AS ($3.65) to 1,800 AS ($130.75), depending on your seat selection. For special events, these prices could go even higher. Guided tours of the Staatsoper can also be arranged, especially in summer, when the opera is not playing. The cost is 30 AS ($2.20), and information about these tours can be obtained by calling 0222/51444-29-55.

Volksoper, Währingerstrasse 78 (tel. 0222/51444-26-57), the folk opera house, presents lavish productions of Viennese operettas and other musicals from the first of September until the end of June on a daily schedule. Tickets cost from 50 AS ($3.65) to 600 AS ($43.50). Tickets go on sale at the Volksoper itself only one hour before performance.

Burgtheater, or National Theater, Dr.-Karl-Lueger-Ring 2 (tel. 0222/51444-26-56), produces classical plays in German. Work started on the original structure in 1874, but the theater was destroyed in World War II and later rebuilt. It is the dream of every German-speaking actor to appear here.

Akademietheater, Lisztstrasse 3 (tel. 0222/51444-26-58), the largest theatrical concern in Europe, specializes in contemporary works. The Burgtheater company often performs here.

Other Theaters

Theater an der Wien, Linke Wienzelle 6 (tel. 0222/588-30 or 0222/905-40 for tickets), opened on the night of June 13, 1801, and ever since that time fans have been able to enjoy both opera and operetta presentations here. Today it specializes in musical productions such as *Cats*. This was the site of the premiere of Beethoven's *Fidelio* (then called *Leonore*) in 1805; in fact, the composer once lived in this building. The world premiere of Johann Strauss Jr.'s *Die Fledermaus* was also given here. Invariably, every year an article appears in some newspaper proclaiming that Theater an der Wien was the site of the premiere of Mozart's *The Magic Flute*—a neat trick, considering that the first performance of that great work was in 1791, while this theater did not exist until 1801. During the years of occupation after World War II, when the Staatsoper was being restored after heavy damages, the Vienne State Opera made Theater an der Wien its home. Tickets for performances cost 90 AS ($6.55) to 540 AS ($39.25).

Schlosstheater at Schönbrunn Palace, mentioned earlier, is a gem of a theater in a regal setting, which opened in 1749 for the entertainment of the court of Maria Theresa. The architecture is a medley of baroque and rococo, and there's a large, plush box where the imperial family sat to enjoy the shows. The theater belongs to Hochschule für Musik und darstellende Kunst and is used for performances of the Max Reinhardt Seminar (theater productions) and opera productions throughout the year. No phone number is available for the theater, because a wide array of different art groups, each responsible for its own ticket sales, perform here.

Volkstheater, Neustiftgasse 1 (tel. 0222/93-35-01), opened in 1889 and has a long tradition of classical repertoire, from Ibsen to Strindberg, Nestroy, and Raimund. Modern plays and comedies are also presented. The season runs from September until the end of June. Tickets cost from 50 AS ($3.65) to 350 AS ($25.50).

Vienna English Theater, Josefsgasse 12 (tel. 0222/42-12-60), is the only English-speaking theater in Vienna. It was established in 1963 and proved so popular that it's been around ever since. Many international celebrities have appeared on the stage of this neobaroque theater building, and many British actors perform here. Princess Grace of Monaco played here, before her tragic death, in a performance to raise money for charity. Occasionally works of American playwrights are presented.

Theater in der Josefstadt, Josefstädter Strasse 26 (tel. 0222/42-51-27), is a typically Viennese theater, which presents, among other works, contemporary social comedies and classical plays. Under the aegis of Max Reinhardt, who took it over in 1924, this became one of the most outstanding theaters in the German-speaking world.

Count yourself fortunate if you get to hear a concert by the Wiener Philharmoniker at the **Musikverein,** Dumbastrasse 3 (tel. 0222/65-81-90). The Musikverein has two concert halls, one of them the famous Golden Hall known all over the world because of various TV productions. Some 600 concerts per season (September to June) are presented. Only 10 to 12 of these concerts are played by the Vienna Philharmonic, and these are subscription concerts. It is sometimes difficult to obtain tickets for these concerts. The box office at Karlsplatz 6 (tel. 0222/65-81-90) is open Monday to Friday from 9am to 6pm and on Saturday from 9am to noon. Ticket prices range from 20 AS ($1.45) for standing room—available for almost every concert—up to 1,000 AS ($72.75) for special concerts.

Konzerthaus, Lothringerstrasse 20 (tel. 0222/712-46-860), is another major concert hall, this one with a trio of auditoriums. The "Concert House" was built just before the outbreak of World War II.

LOWER AUSTRIA

"The cradle of Austria's history," Lower Austria, or Niederösterreich, is the biggest of the nine federal states that make up the country today. This province, crisscrossed by the Danube, is in fact named *Lower* Austria because the great river flows east into it. It may seem to you more like *Upper* Austria because of its geographic location, much of it being north of the rest of the country. The 7,402 square miles of the state are bordered on the north and east by Czechoslovakia, on the south by the province of Styria, and on the west by Upper Austria. It lies virtually on the doorstep of Vienna, the state capital of this province of 1½ million living souls as well as the nation's capital.

This historic nucleus of the Austria of today was once a heavily fortified land, as some 550 fortresses and castles—many still standing but often in ruins—testify. The medieval dynasties of the Kuenringers and the Babenbergers had their hereditary estates here, and it was through Lower Austria that the legendary Nibelungen passed. Many monasteries and churches, ranging from the Romanesque and Gothic eras up to the much later baroque abbeys, are found here.

The province is filled with vineyards, and in summer it's rich in festivals, not only of music and operetta but also of classical and contemporary theater.

It's relatively inexpensive to travel in Lower Austria, with a drop of at least 30% below the prices you encounter in Vienna, just visited, or in such places as Salzburg and Innsbruck, which will be explored further on in this book. This price differential explains why many people, especially those from other Austrian provinces, visit in Vienna but stay at one of the neighboring towns in Lower Austria. Parking is also accessible in the outlying towns. However, you mustn't expect always to have a private bath if you want to check into an old inn.

Lower Austria is divided into five distinct districts, the best known being the Wienerwald (Vienna Woods) completely surrounding Vienna.

Another district, **Alpine Lower Austria,** lies about an hour's drive south of Vienna. With mountains up to 7,000 feet high, this area has been greatly developed in the past few years and has a system of mountain railways, chair lifts, and cable cars, as well as hundreds of miles of hiking paths.

The foothills of the Alps, beginning about 30 miles west of Vienna, comprise a district extending to the borders of Styria and Upper Austria. This area has some 50 open-air swimming pools that are busy in summer and nine chair lifts that go up to the higher peaks, such as Ötscher and Hochkar, each around 6,000 feet.

A celebrated section is the **Waldviertel-Weinviertel,** a viertel being a traditional division of Lower Austria. The viertels in this case are the woods (*wald*) and wine (*wein*) areas. They contain thousands of miles of marked hiking paths and, of course, many mellow old wine cellars.

Another district, **Wachau-Nibelungengau,** is of historical and cultural significance. In fact, it's considered one of the most historic valleys in Central Europe. It is a land of castles and palaces, of abbeys and monasteries. For centuries it has also been known for its wine making. Lying on both banks of the Danube, this area begins about 40 miles west of Vienna.

Some 60% of the grape harvest of Austria is produced in Lower Austria, stretching from the rolling hillsides of the Wienerwald to the terraces of the Wachau. Many visitors to the country like to take a "wine route" through the province, stopping off at cozy taverns to sample the vintages from Krems, Klosterneuburg, Dürnstein, Langenlois, Retz, Gumpoldskirchen, Poysdorf, and other spots.

Lower Austria has 12 spa resorts, of which Baden is the most celebrated. Innkeepers make families with children especially welcome at these resorts. Most hotels accommodate children up to 6 years old free. Between ages 7 and 12, they are given 50% reductions on the listed prices for adults. Many towns and villages have facilities designed especially for the amusement of children.

In short, Lower Austria is a good place to go for a family holiday.

---

1. The Wienerwald

The Vienna Woods—romanticized in operetta, literature, and the Strauss waltz—have already been introduced in the sightseeing section of Vienna. The woods stretch all the way from Vienna's city limits to the foothills of the Alps to the south.

You can hike through the woods along marked paths or else drive through at a leisurely pace, stopping off at country towns to sample the wine and the local cuisine, usually hearty, filling, and reasonable in price. The woods are filled with wine taverns and cellars, and on weekends with Viennese and a horde of foreign tourists, principally German. I advise you to make any summer visit on a weekday. Perhaps the best time of year to go is September and October, the months when the grapes are harvested from the terraced hills.

If you don't want to go on your own, a popular tour out of Vienna will take you to the Wienerwald and Mayerling. It goes through the Vienna Woods to the Castle of Liechtenstein and the old Roman city of Baden, with an excursion to Mayerling, where Crown Prince Rudolf and his mistress died violent deaths. You'll also go to the Cistercian abbey of Heiligenkreuz-Höldrichsmühle-Seegrotte. A boat ride on Seegrotte, the largest subterranean lake in Europe, is included.

This tour is operated by **Vienna Sightseeing Tours,** Stelzamergasse 4 (tel. 0222/72-46-83). It runs from April 1 to October 31 at 9:30am and 2:30pm and from November 1 to March 31 at 9:30am only, taking about four hours. The cost is

380 AS ($27.75) for adults and 120 AS ($8.70) for children. The price includes admission fees and a guide.

KLOSTERNEUBURG

Lying on the northwestern outskirts of Vienna within easy reach of the capital, Klosterneuburg is an old market town in the major wine-producing center of Austria. The Babenbergs founded the town practically at the gates of Vienna in the eastern foothills of the Vienna Woods, making it an ideal spot to enjoy the countryside and also to participate in the cultural and entertainment activities of Vienna, 7 miles southeast.

A Roman stronghold occupied the site of the town in the 1st century A.D.

Klosterneuburg Abbey (Stift Klosterneuburg) (tel. 02243/6210), which lies to the east of the Upper Town, is considered the most significant abbey in Austria. The abbey church dates from 1114, but the first of the Gothic west towers was not constructed until the end of the 14th century. The magnificent stained-glass windows also date from that century. The altar of the church is from 1181 and contains more than 50 biblical scenes in enamel, but the most outstanding exhibit in Stift Klosterneuburg is the altarpiece by Nicolas of Verdun in the Chapel of St. Leopold. The abbey apartments are richly furnished with many empire antiques.

You can visit the abbey Monday to Saturday from 9am to noon (last guided tour at 11am) and 1:30 to 6pm (last guided tour at 5pm). On Sunday there's a guided tour at 11am. Admission is 30 AS ($2.20) for adults and 10 AS (75¢) for children.

The abbey came into its glory when the ruling family of Austria, the Babenbergs, moved here from Melk and built a grand residence, remnants of which are preserved in the Albrechtsberger Abbey. After the royal residences were moved to Vienna, the abbey declined in power and prestige, but it was revived in the 18th century by Emperor Charles VI, who came up with an ambitious architectural scheme—to build a pompous residence and monastic edifice that would rival El Escorial, the celebrated palace built by Philip II of Spain on the outskirts of Madrid. This grandiose building scheme was never completed, but the monastery was finally finished in the 19th century, looking as you will see it today.

The abbey has an old restaurant, **Stiftskeller** (tel. 02243/2071), where you can dine well for 300 AS ($21.75), enjoying such classic and traditional Austrian specialties as tafelspitz. Service is from 10am to midnight Monday to Friday and from 10am to 10pm on Saturday and Sunday. The restaurant has a historic wine cellar.

If you don't choose to eat here, you can patronize one of several heurigen in the district, enjoying good wine and country food.

Austrians and tourists gather in Klosterneuburg annually to celebrate St. Leopold's Day on November 15.

Food and Lodging

Hotel-Restaurant Josef Buschenreiter, Wienerstrasse 188, A-3400 Klosterneuburg (tel. 02243/2385), is a modern white-walled hotel with metal window frames and a mansard roof above the balcony on the fourth floor. A terrace on the roof and an indoor swimming pool provide diversion for hotel guests, who will also find a contemporary bar in contrasting earth-colored patterns. The hotel rents 40 rooms with private baths or showers. Singles cost 420 AS ($30.50) to 460 AS ($33.50) daily, with doubles renting for 750 AS ($54.50) to 1,100 AS ($80).

Hotel Schrannenhof, Niedermarkt 17-19, A-3400 Klosterneuburg (tel. 02243/2072), in a building originally dating from the Middle Ages, was completely renewed and equipped for modern comfort in 1986. It rents nine units, including apartments with large living and sleeping rooms, small kitchens, color TVs, and phones, as well as quiet and comfortable double rooms with showers, color TVs, and phones. Singles range from 650 AS ($47.25) to 700 AS ($51) daily, with dou-

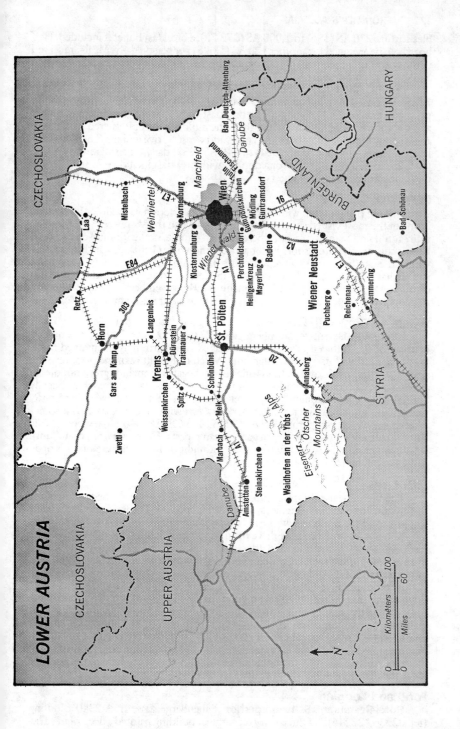

bles costing 770 AS ($56) to 1,000 AS ($72.75); a breakfast buffet is included. Half board can be arranged for another 120 AS ($8.75) per person daily. Meals are served in the hotel's café-restaurant next door. The kitchen includes both typically Austrian and international dishes.

Pension Alte Mühle, Mühlengasse 36, A-3400 Klosterneuberg (tel. 02243/7788), is housed in an uncomplicated two-story, 30-bed building. It is reasonable in price and gracious in hospitality. The breakfast room offers a rich morning buffet, and a comfortable restaurant-café in the same building has upholstered banquettes and a sunny modern décor of bright colors and conservative designs. The Veit family, the owners, charge 330 AS ($24) to 440 AS ($32) daily for a single and 540 AS ($39.25) to 800 AS ($58.25) for a double, with breakfast included. In summer the pleasant garden is a lure for guests.

PERCHTOLDSDORF

This old market town with colorful buildings, referred to locally as Petersdorf, is one of the most visited spots in Lower Austria when the Viennese make the wine tour. You'll find many heurigen, where you can sample local wines and enjoy good, hearty cuisine. Perchtoldsdorf is not as well known as Grinzing, which is actually within the city limits of Vienna, but many discriminating visitors find it less touristy. It has a Gothic church, and part of its defense tower is from the early 16th century. A vintners' festival is held annually in early November. Local growers make a "goat" from grapes for this festive occasion, which attracts many Viennese.

Where to Drink and Eat

Landhaus Killermann, Sonnbergstrasse 22 (tel. 0222/86-81-81), very much a heurige for the 20th century, is a well-managed and charmingly maintained rustic *weinstube* filled with farmer's implements. Much of the allure of the place revolves around its charismatic owner, Luki Killermann. Specialties include green noodles in a cream and ham sauce, filet of venison in a wine sauce, roasted zander, and many bürgerlich specialties designed to go well with the wine and the live guitar music. The place might be considered an upmarket *stüberl* with a bit of pizzazz. It is somewhat expensive, charging from 340 AS ($24.75) to 640 AS ($46.50) per person (the latter price only for those seeking a gargantuan repast). Hours are from 6pm "until whenever the guests leave," often around midnight or 1am. The restaurant is open daily, but call first to be sure.

MÖDLING

The Viennese use this place as a resort. Quite old, it lies at the beginning of the Brühl Valley and still has a medieval core, the Hauptplatz. The Rathaus (Town Hall) dates from 1548. Beethoven wrote his *Missa Solemnis* here in 1818.

About a 15- to 18-minute drive from Mödling is **Schloss Liechtenstein.** The castle was built originally in the 12th century, but that one was largely demolished in one of the Turkish sieges. Construction on the present schloss began in 1820. You can visit a relic of the old castle, however, a Romanesque chapel dating from 1165.

Another popular excursion from Mödling is to **Schloss Laxenburg,** a short drive to the east. In the complex, surrounded by a baroque park, are an old castle from the 14th century and a new one. The Neues Schloss, once used by the Habsburgs as a summer residence, has been turned over to an institute. Yet another mock Gothic castle from the 19th century has been converted into a restaurant. Mainly, however, the place is visited for its park, once the hunting ground of the dukes of Austria but now the home of protected wild game. True to the baroque ideal, the park is studded with statuary and "temples."

Food and Lodging

Hotel-Restaurant Babenbergerhof, Babenbergergasse 6, A-2340 Mödling (tel. 02236/22246), is a three-story rectangular building painted a deep Maria Theresa ochre with a garden restaurant in back. On a summer night the owner, Karl

Breyer, stretches lights below the large trees in the garden, while in winter the indoor ambience is one of well-maintained modernity. Rooms, 48 in all, are comfortably furnished and well maintained. Thirty-five of them have either a private bath or a shower. Singles range from 220 AS ($16) to 530 AS ($38.50) daily, with doubles costing 420 AS ($30.50) to 850 AS ($61.75), including breakfast.

HINTERBRÜHL

Instead of staying in Mödling, you might prefer to drive to the neighboring hamlet of Hinterbrühl, where you'll find a good hotel and food. The village is only a 20-minute ride from Vienna. This is no more than a cluster of bucolic homes, much favored by the Viennese who want to escape the city for a long weekend. Hinterbrühl holds memories of Schubert, who wrote "Der Lindenbaum" here.

Food and Lodging

Hotel/Restaurant Höldrichsmühle, Gaadner Strasse 34, A-2371 Hinterbrühl (tel. 02236/26274), has been painted a pastel pink since the era when Schubert stayed here, and it still has much of its old allure. The hotel rents 20 bedrooms, each with private bath or shower. Singles cost 510 AS ($37) to 690 AS ($50.25), whereas doubles rent for 960 AS ($69.75) to 1,400 AS ($101.75). Prices depend on the plumbing and the size of the accommodation. The restaurant connected to the hotel is one of the best in the village. Viennese often come here to eat under the linden trees of the restaurant's terrace. In winter they find the Biedermeier-filled interior cozy and inviting. Specialties of the chef include fresh trout, roast veal with corn salad, an array of venison dishes in season, and many varieties of fish, including eel.

GUMPOLDSKIRCHEN

From Mödling, you can take the wine road, or *weinstrasse*, to Gumpolds-kirchen, a town celebrated for its Gumpoldskirchner wine, a Viennese favorite. Along the main street are heurigen. Like Perchtoldsdorf, this village is preferred by many Viennese to Grinzing. Go to any of the wine taverns whose doors are open, and chances are you'll be served not only delectable white wine of the town but food as well, all at reasonable prices.

Where to Dine

Weinstadl, Jubiläumsstrasse 42 (tel. 02252/62218), is a rustically cozy estab-lishment with wood tables, big flasks of local wine, and a warm, welcoming atmosphere. The room here is vast, usually with live music, in a building that in old-en days was used to store the abundant harvests that came from this region. You can sit in an upper level if it's open on the night you happen to visit, which might be a good idea since the music near the bandstand can be rather loud. The chef is known for his grills, turning out an especially good tournedos. The produce is fresh, and the food is well presented. À la carte meals range from 170 AS ($12.25) to 350 AS ($25.50). The restaurant is closed from January 10 to February 10 and on Sunday. It's open only in the evening, from 6pm to midnight, and reservations are suggested.

GUNTRAMSDORF

In your search for a charming place to stay in the Wienerwald, with the atmos-phere typical of the area, the following recommendation near Gumpoldskirchen might be considered. The hamlet lies at the very doorstep of the Wienerwald.

Food and Lodging

Landhotel Jagdhof, Hauptstrasse 41, A-2353 Guntramsdorf (tel. 02236/52-2-25). The hotel is identified by a wrought-iron bracket hanging over the front door, with a medieval sign announcing the locale. The 34 rooms here are tastefully decorated and comfortable. Singles go for 480 AS ($35) to 700 AS ($51) daily, with doubles costing 600 AS ($43.50) to 900 AS ($65.50), breakfast included. All units have private baths.

Much of the reputation of the establishment, however, revolves around its well-known restaurant. Under the vaults of an old farmhouse, it abounds in rustic atmosphere, and offers a cuisine so well prepared that many clients are repeaters. Here you get good, reliable Austrian food. The restaurant, charging 250 AS ($18.25) for meals, is open daily except Sunday from noon to 2:30pm and 6 to 11pm.

TULBINGER-KOGEL

This hamlet is a short drive from Vienna. Its main virtue seems to be its wooded rolling hills and the autumn foliage, which can be spectacular. Dozens of Viennese make the drive here to escape the congestion of their capital.

Food and Lodging

Berghotel Tulbinger Kogel, A-3001 Tulbinger-Kogel (tel. 02273/7391), sprawls like an 18th-century château across a wide vista of forested land with a distant view of the Alps. Its walls are white, and the symmetrically sloping roofline comprises a single row of prominent gables. An outbuilding with surrounding balconies provides modern accommodations as well as a calm and beautiful view of the nearby region. The hotel rents 32 bedrooms, each with private bath, and charges 680 AS ($49.50) to 830 AS ($60.25) per person daily. It has the finest restaurant in the area and one of the most copious wine lists in the country. Closed in February.

HEILIGENKRUEZ

This most ancient Cistercian abbey in Austria, dating from 1133, lies about 10 miles to the north of the spa in Baden and 15 miles to the west of Vienna. Called the Abbey of the Holy Cross, the church, founded by Leopold III, was built in the 12th century, but there has been an overlay of Gothic and baroque in subsequent centuries, with some stained glass from the 13th and 14th centuries still in place. The abbey was once ravaged by the Turks, but much of the complex was reconstructed in the 17th and 18th centuries. However, the Romanesque and Gothic cloisters date from 1240, with some 300 pillars of red marble, a striking display. Some of the dukes of Babenberg were buried in the 1240 chapter house, including Duke Friedrich II, the last of his line, who died in 1246. Heiligenkreuz has more relics of the Holy Cross than any other site in Europe except Rome.

The Nazi regime did not succeed in suppressing the abbey, and today a vital community of 50 Cistercian monks lives in Heiligenkreuz. In summer at noon and 6pm visitors can attend the solemn choir prayers of the monks. Tours are conducted Easter through October, but only on Saturday, Sunday, and holidays. Tours leave every 30 minutes from 1:30 to 5pm. Admission is 40 AS ($2.90).

Heiligenkreuz lies only a mile from Mayerling, and Mary Vetsera, the mistress of Archduke Rudolf, who died with him in 1889 (see below), is buried in the abbey churchyard.

MAYERLING

This beautiful spot in the heart of the Wienerwald, to the west of Baden and 2½ miles from Heiligenkreuz, was the setting in 1889 for a grim tragedy that altered the line of succession of the Austro-Hungarian Empire and shocked the world. On a snowy night, Archduke Rudolf, only son of Emperor Franz Joseph and Empress Elizabeth, and his mistress, Maria Vetsera, were found dead in the hunting lodge at Mayerling and called suicide victims.

Rudolf was locked into an unhappy marriage, and neither his father nor Pope Leo XIII would allow, through annulment, breaking the matrimonial bonds. At the time of his death Rudolf was 30 years old. He had met Maria at a German embassy ball when she was only 17. Because of the young archduke's liberal leanings and sympathy for certain Hungarian partisans, he was not popular with his country's aristocracy, which of course gave rise to lurid speculation about the deaths, not only in the press but also in books and in films, as to whether the couple actually killed themselves or were the victims of cleverly designed assassination.

Franz Joseph, grief-stricken at the loss of his only son, ordered the hunting lodge torn down and had built the Carmelite nunnery that still occupies the lodge site.

As it turned out, if Rudolf had lived he would have succeeded to the already-tottering Habsburg throne in 1916 in the middle of World War I, shortly before the collapse of the empire.

Food and Lodging

Hotel-Restaurant Marienhof, A-2534 Mayerling (tel. 02258/2379), is a belle époque–style establishment in the midst of the hunting territory most preferred by Crown Prince Rudolf. The original part is a three-story structure with white stucco walls and a brown-tile roof with matching shutters, somewhat removed from the other buildings of the village. The owners, Johann and Cäcilia Hanner, have enlarged their place by adding a new building, bringing the room total to 72, with 33 units in the new structure. In the new part, all rooms come with complete baths, radios, TVs, phones, minibars, and balconies. Singles rent for 610 AS ($44.25) daily, while the rate for a double room ranges from 490 AS ($35.50) per person. The hotel has such amenities as a sauna, a solarium, a tennis court, and table-tennis facilities. Guests can enjoy Austrian specialties such as homemade sweets and coffee on the sunny terrace. The hotel also has two restaurants and a bar where you can spend the evening in an agreeable and cozy atmosphere.

---

2. Baden bei Wien

Czar Peter the Great of Russia is credited with ushering in the golden age of Baden as a spa around the dawn of the 18th century. The Soviet army used the resort city as its headquarters from the end of World War II to the end of the Allied occupation of Austria in 1955. But there's not much Russian about Baden, the dowager empress of health spas in Europe.

The Romans, who didn't miss many of the natural attractions in sections of Europe into which they moved, began in A.D. 100 to visit and enjoy what they called Aquae, with 15 thermal springs whose temperatures reach 95°Fahrenheit. You can still see the Römerquelle (Roman Spring) in the Kurpark, which is the center of Baden today.

This lively casino town and spa in the eastern sector of the Vienna Woods was at its most fashionable in the early part of the 18th century, but its appeal for royalty, aristocracy, sycophants, musicians, and intellectuals continued for much of the 19th century. For years the resort was the summer residence of the Habsburg court. In 1803, when he was still Francis II of the Holy Roman Empire, the monarch (who became Francis I of Austria when the vast empire originated by Charlemagne ended in 1806) began annual summer moves to Baden, a practice that ended only at his death in 1835.

Where the court went, there went the most outstanding musicians and artists of the age. Even before the spa was "discovered" by Emperor Francis, however, Mozart spent time in Baden, and it is here that he is said to have composed his *Ave Verum*. Schubert is supposed to have done creative work at this spa, and Beethoven, who lived in Baden for three summers, worked on his Ninth Symphony in this peaceful town surrounded by forests and vineyards.

At **Beethoven's House,** Rathausgasse 10 (tel. 02252/86800-550), a little museum has been set up. Summer hours are 9 to 11am and 3 to 5pm daily except

Thursday, and winter hours are 9 to 11am on Thursday and 3 to 5pm Tuesday to Saturday. Admission is 10 AS (75¢).

During the Biedermeier era (mid to late 19th century), Baden became known for its Schönbrunn yellow (Maria Theresa ochre) Biedermeier buildings, which still contribute to the spa city's charm. The Kurpark, Baden's center, is handsomely laid out and beautifully maintained. Public concerts performed here keep alive the magical music of the great Austrian composers.

The bathing house complex was constructed over the location of more than a dozen sulfur springs. In the complex are some half dozen bath establishments, plus two outdoor thermal springs.

Emperor Karl made this town the Austrian army headquarters in World War I, but a certain lightness of heart persisted in the Austrians and in the life of Baden. It was the presence of the Russians during the post–World War II years that brought about the lowest ebb in the resort's fortunes. The Soviets did little to encourage luxurious spa resort vacations and casino gambling.

Among sights in Baden, there is the celebrated death mask collection at **Städtisches Rolletmuseum,** Weikersdorfer-Platz 1 (tel. 02252/48255). The museum is open from May 1 until the end of October, on Wednesday and Saturday from 3 to 6pm and on Sunday from 9am to noon. Admission: 12 AS (85¢).

The **Trinity Column** at the Hauptplatz commemorates the lifting of the plague that swept over Vienna and the Wienerwald in the Middle Ages.

The resort (officially named Baden bei Wien to differentiate it from other Badens *not* near Vienna) is some 15 miles from the capital city. An old streetcar still makes its slow and tedious way here. However, the resort is also more efficiently connected to Vienna by rail and bus lines.

FOOD AND LODGING

A place where comfort and a sense of history go hand in hand is the **Grand Hotel Sauerhof zu Rauhenstein,** Weilburgstrasse 11-13, A-2500 Baden bei Wien (tel. 02252/41251). Ludwig van Beethoven once took Karl Maria von Weber to lunch here "in happy and joyful spirits." It was once a recreational center for Austria's imperial officers. The exterior has been restored to its former grandeur. It rambles across a wide expanse of lawn in a three-story neoclassical format with steeply sloping slate roofs. Few of the original furnishings remain, although the management has collected a handful of vintage Biedermeier sofas and chairs to fill the starkly elegant public rooms, where portraits of Franz Joseph in all stages of his life decorate the pure-white walls. There's a collection of Russian icons in glass cases and a series of medieval halberds along the walls of the richly decorated, farmer's-style restaurant.

In the depths of this historic building is a wine cellar, as well as a copy of a Roman covered courtyard whose vaulted ceiling is supported by eight chiseled columns. A plaque announces that Beethoven wrote his "Wellington Sieg" here and that the premises served as a sanitorium in World War I and as a Russian headquarters after World War II.

All the 87 bedrooms contain private baths and comfortable modern décor. Depending on the season and the accommodation, single rooms range from 1,100 AS ($83.50) to 1,300 AS ($94.50) daily, while doubles cost 1,500 AS ($109) to 1,800 AS ($130.75), daily, with breakfast included. Half board costs an additional 190 AS ($13.75) per person. On the premises are a beauty farm, two tennis courts, and a jogging course. A golf course is located nearby. Under the brick vaulting of one of the older sections, the management has installed a 40-foot swimming pool.

Clubhotel Baden (Schloss Weikersdorf), Schlossgasse 9-11, A-2500 Baden bei Wien (tel. 02252/48301), has all the massive beams you'd expect in such an old building, along with arched and vaulted ceilings that are sculpted into unusual sinuous patterns. The oldest part of the hotel has an Italianate loggia stretching toward the manicured gardens, and an inner courtyard with stone arcades and a flagstone pavement. Even the rooms in the newer section have repeated the older section's arches and high ceilings, with a constant reappearance of ornate chandeliers and antique (or reproduction) furniture. The nearby sports facility has an indoor swimming pool, tennis courts, a sauna, a whirlpool, and massage facilities. On the premises are a charming baroque bar and two restaurants. Accommodations are handsomely furnished and most comforatable. There are 76 bedrooms in the main house, plus 26 in the annex. Singles range from 750 AS ($54.50) to 950 AS ($69) daily, with doubles costing 620 AS ($45) to 820 AS ($59.50) per person daily. Breakfast is included in these rates, and all units contain a private bath.

Hotel Gutenbrunn, Pelzgasse 22, A-2500 Baden bei Wien (tel. 02252/48171). If what you want is an elegant old-world hotel with lots of original architectural features, this might be the one for you. The pink-and-white façade has a hexagonal tower at one of its corners, and a slate roof capped with a baroque steeple. The interior has a skylit reception area with a double tier of neoclassical loggias, all of them focusing on the hanging chandelier in the center. The 80 bedrooms are well furnished and maintained. Singles rent for 1,000 AS ($72.75) daily, while doubles cost 1,500 AS ($109) to 2,300 AS ($167.25), with breakfast included. A sauna and a swimming pool are on the premises, plus a good restaurant. The hotel is connected to the city spa facilities by a passage.

Hotel Herzoghof, Theresiengasse 5, A-2500 Baden bei Wien (tel. 02252/48395), is an elegant cream-colored hotel across from the city park. The complicated detailing of its 19th-century façade hints at the old-fashioned décor inside, where Oriental rugs, stained glass, and high ceilings evoke another era. On the premises are both an indoor and an outdoor swimming pool, a sauna, a garden terrace, and a dining room capped with a skylight. The hotel also offers an array of hydrotherapy and spa facilities.

The conservatively comfortable accommodations of the 118-bed hotel contain a scattering of reproductions of antiques, as well as private baths. Half board costs 170 AS ($12.25) per person in addition to the room rate. High-season tariffs are 1,400 AS ($101.75) daily in a double and 900 AS ($65.50) in a single, with breakfast included. Off-season reductions are granted.

Parkhotel, Kaiser-Franz-Ring 5, A-2500 Baden bei Wien (tel. 02252/44386), is an elegantly contemporary 90-room hotel in the middle of an inner-city park dotted with trees and formal statuary. The high-ceilinged lobby is contemporary, with a marble floor padded with thick Oriental carpets and ringed with richly grained paneling. Most of the sunny bedrooms have their own loggia overlooking scores of century-old trees. Each contains a private bath, radio, TV, and minibar. Singles cost 830 AS ($60.25) to 1,100 AS ($80), while doubles are priced at 1,200 AS ($87.25) to 2,200 AS ($160), with breakfast included. Half board is another 200 AS ($14.50) per day. The hotel also contains a heated indoor swimming pool, two Finnish saunas, a restaurant, a coffeeshop, and a concrete terrace overlooking the park. Private parking is available. Anna-Maria Merzl, the manager, is familiar with American guests because of the contingents of visitors from Los Angeles who come here every year.

Krainerhütte, A-2500 Baden bei Wien (tel. 02252/44511), stands 5 miles west of Baden at Helenental, on its own tree-filled grounds. Run by Josef Dietmann and his family, it's a large A-frame chalet with rows of wooden balconies stretching across the front. The interior has well-worked wooden surfaces and more detailing than you might expect in such a modern hotel. There are separate children's rooms and play areas. Depending on the season, singles cost from 1,100 AS ($80); doubles run from 860 AS ($62.50) to 940 AS ($68.25) per person. All tariffs include half board. In the cozy restaurant or on its terrace, you can dine on international and Austrian cuisine, with fish and deer from the hotel grounds offered on the menu. On the premises is an indoor swimming pool, plus a tennis court, a sauna, and an exercise room. Hiking in the owner's forests, hunting, and fishing are possible. Bus service to Baden is available all day.

A COFFEEHOUSE AND RESTAURANT

Badner Stüberl, Gutenbrunnstrasse 19 (tel. 02252/41232), an old-fashioned coffeehouse and restaurant in the center of the older section of Baden, is filled with black and red upholstery and unusually designed lighting fixtures. Specialties of the house include generous proportions of a Stroganoff dish that is searched out by visitors from Vienna, along with a green salad garnished with chicken, and pork and beef steaks grilled to savory tenderness. À la carte meals range from 130 AS ($9.50) to 250 AS ($18.25). The establishment is open daily except Tuesday from 12:30 to 2pm and 6 to 10pm.

NIGHTLIFE

The major attraction, of course, is the **Casino Baden** in Spa Park (tel. 02252/44496). Here you can play roulette, ponta banca, blackjack, baccarat, poker (seven-card stud), money-wheel, and slot machines. Many visitors from Vienna come down to Baden for a night of gambling, eating, and drinking; on the premises are two bars and a restaurant. Guests are often most fashionably dressed, and you'll feel more comfortable if you are too. (Men should wear jackets and ties.) Visitors must show a passport when paying the 170 AS ($12.25) entrance fee. In exchange for that, they receive 200 AS ($14.50) worth of free chips. The casino is open daily from 3pm to 3am.

---

3. Wiener Neustadt

When you head south from Vienna on the Südautobahn, Wiener Neustadt, a former imperial city, might be your first stopover. Called Allzeit Getreue because of its loyalty to the throne, this thriving business city between the foothills of the Alps and the edge of the Pannonian lowland has a strong historical background.

Unfortunately, Wiener Neustadt was a popular target for Allied bombs during World War II, because it lay at the point where the routes from Vienna diverge, one going to the Semmering Pass and the other to Hungary via the Sopron Gate. The presence here of a military academy that turned out officers for the Austrian army for some 200 years may have been an added attraction to bombers. German Gen. Erwin Rommel, "the Desert Fox," was the academy's first commandant during the Nazi era. At any rate, bomb the city the Allies did—more than any other town in the country. It's estimated that some 60% of its buildings were leveled.

The town was founded in 1192, when its castle was built by Duke Leopold V of the ruling house of Babenberg. He had it constructed as a citadel to ward off attacks of the Magyars from the east. From 1440 to 1493 Austrian emperors lived at this fortress in the southeast corner of what is now the old town. Maximilian I, called "the last of the knights," was born here in 1459 and lies buried in the Church of St. George in the castle. It was Maria Theresa who in 1752 ordered that the structures comprising the castle be turned into a military academy.

You can visit the **Church of St. George** (St. Georgskirche), Burgplatz 1, daily from 8am to 4pm. The gable of the church is adorned with more than 100 heraldic shields of the Habsburgs. It's noted for its handsome interior, decorated in the late Gothic style.

Neukloster, a Cistercian abbey, was founded in 1250 and reconstructed in the 18th century. The New Abbey Church (Neuklosterkirche), on Ungargasse near the Hauptplatz, is Gothic with a beautiful choir. It contains the tomb of the Empress Eleanor of Portugal, wife of Friedrich III and mother of Maximilian I. Mozart's *Requiem* was first presented here in 1793.

Liebfrauenkirche, on the Domplatz, was once the headquarters of an episcopal see. It's graced by a 13th-century Romanesque nave, but the choir is Gothic. The west towers have been rebuilt.

In the town is a **Recturm,** a tower in the Gothic style said to have been built with the ransom money paid for Richard the Lion-Hearted.

WHERE TO STAY

The best hotel in town is **Hotel Corvinus,** Bahngasse 29-33, A-2700 Wiener Neustadt (tel. 02622/24134), which has a color scheme of white and weathered bronze. It sits in a quiet neighborhood near the city park. Its 68 bedrooms, each with private bath, have modern comforts in a décor of solid colors. Singles rent for 490 AS ($35.50) daily, with two persons paying 1,360 AS ($98.75); a buffet breakfast is included. Children under 12 stay in their parents' room free. All units have TVs, and hotel guests can use the sauna, Turkish bath, and whirlpool. Also on the premises are a modern bar area, a parasol-covered sun terrace, and a lightheartedly elegant restaurant serving Austrian and international dishes.

Hotel/Restaurant Forum, Heimkehrerstrasse 2, A-2700 Wiener Neustadt (tel. 02622/24918), is a comfortable 36-room hotel near the railway and bus stations. Bedrooms are cheerfully papered and usually high-ceilinged, while the outdoor terrace restaurant and the indoor bar area are attractive gathering spots. Singles with baths or showers cost 340 AS ($24.75) daily, with doubles going for 540 AS ($39.25).

FOOD AND DRINK

Restaurant Porsche, Neuenkirchnerstrasse 90 (tel. 02622/359144). Years ago a garage mechanic opened a small restaurant above his shop so that his clients would have a place to wait. Today the shop is the biggest Volkswagen-Porsche workshop in the city, and the restaurant has evolved into a high-quality and popular eatery filled with garage and race-car memorabilia (the silverware, for example, is engraved with the initials V.W.). The daily menus are solid, hearty, and what the Austrians call "honest." The savory and uncomplicated selections include veal steak Ticino style, a nourishing beef soup, and a wide range of generously served gutbürgerlich dishes. À la carte dinners range from 120 AS ($8.75) to 300 AS ($21.75). Open daily from 8am to 9pm, the Porsche doesn't "run" on Saturday.

Witetschka, Allerheiligenplatz 1 (tel. 02622/23109). This small and tasteful café was long ago used by Austrian Protestants as a meeting place. Today it's a hangout on one of the city's most beautiful squares. Much of the menu is devoted to café items, including ice cream, elaborate pastries (try the crêpes Suchard), and coffee drinks. Coffee is priced from 18 AS ($1.30), with pastries costing from 20 AS ($1.45). The café stays open from 7:30am to 8pm Monday to Friday, closing at 3pm on Saturday and all day Sunday.

---

4. Semmering/Puchberg

One of the best-known places for skiing in Austria, **Semmering,** at an elevation of 3,200 feet sheltered by forests of firs and mountain ranges, is a little more than an hour by car or train from Vienna. It's a romantic spot in summer and a choice location for winter sports when snow blankets the area. The resort, built on terraces, is perched around the Semmering Pass, which divides Lower Austria from Styria.

An international resort, called by the Austrians a *kurort,* a fresh-air spot rather than a mineral springs spa, Semmering is considered by doctors to be ideal for the health of patients, and there are many rest homes in the vicinity.

In winter guests ski at the centers at Semmering-Hirschenkogel or Spital am Semmering. In this region, Raxalpe and Schneeberg are two of the highest mountains in Lower Austria. They are separated by the Höllental, or Valley of Hell. This misnamed valley is really a lovely, wild spot, lying to the northwest of Semmering. The Schwarza River creates the gap between the two mountains.

If you don't want to stay right in Semmering, accommodations are found in **Puchberg** and **Reichenau,** which is like a summer spa. It has a direct cable-car hookup that will take you up to the **Rax.**

Puchberg, at the foot of the Schneeberg, is a tranquil place with a rack railway that takes you right into the mountain range. It requires a full day for an excursion up to Schneeberg. The train from Puchberg climbs to the Hochschneeberg terminus in about an hour and 20 minutes. A hotel (see below) is perched on the mountainside. From the terminus, you can go by foot to the Kaiserstein (6,760 feet), from which you're rewarded with a vista of the Alps and a panoramic sweep of the Raxalpe, a limestone massif that attracts many climbers. It is riddled with tunnels. From its upper belvedere you can see a sweep of the Semmering mountains to the south, the Kaiserstein to the north, and the Valley of Hell, also to the north.

Departures from Puchberg on the mountain railway from April to October are six times a day.

FOOD AND LODGING

I'll survey a range of accommodations in different price brackets at all three resorts, beginning with the most popular—

At Semmering

Hotel Panhans, Hochstrasse 32, A-2680 Semmering (tel. 02664/8181). The sprawling white façade of this hotel shelters both the most glamorous and the highest accommodation in town. Capped with a green roof, and filled with marble and an elaborate re-creation of art nouveau detailing, it contains 70 well-furnished bedrooms as well as dozens of privately owned apartments. The establishment was built in 1888, and completely reconstructed in 1982 in an art nouveau style. Today it often hosts conventions from throughout Austria.

On the premises are an indoor pool, exercise room, a restaurant, and a coffeehouse, along with a cocktail bar and disco outfitted with Oriental trappings. Depending on the season and the view, singles cost 700 AS ($51) to 1,000 AS ($72.75) daily, while doubles go for 1,100 AS ($80) to 1,600 AS ($116.25), with breakfast included.

Kurhaus Dr. Stühlinger, A-2680 Semmering (tel. 02664/447), receives guests in a four-story building with large arched windows on the ground floor, horizontal rows of wooden balconies, an angular modern extension sided with glass, and landscaping that makes it seem taller than it actually is. You'll enter through the grand loggia extending off the front of the building. The public rooms are streamlined, filled with curved lines and big windows. A basement swimming pool and a host of health facilities are available, sometimes for an extra charge, to guests. The rooms are clean and filled with wooden furniture and lots of natural light. With half board included, the per-person rate ranges from 550 AS ($40) to 950 AS ($69) daily. The hotel rents 44 bedrooms, 39 with private baths or showers.

Gartenhotel Alpenhiem, Villenstrasse 55, A-2680 Semmering (tel. 02664/322), open from December to October. A well-designed 25-room chalet with a modern annex extending toward the downhill side of a forested hill, it contains both an indoor swimming pool and a comfortable bar area with upholstered chairs and rustic details. All units have private baths or showers, phones, radios, and TV outlets. Your hosts, Frank and Rudolfine Steiner, charge from 420 AS ($30.50) to 520 AS ($37.75) per person daily for half board.

Pension Daheim, A-2680 Semmering (tel. 02664/382), is a gracefully embellished chalet with green shutters and a series of gables that look out over the valley below. The interior is filled with pleasant wooden furniture and warmly patterned fabrics. The establishment is directed by the Hahnl-Steeger family, who charge 350 AS ($25.50) to 420 AS ($30.50) per person daily for half board. They have six single and six double rooms, each with shower and TV. The price difference depends on the view.

Hotel/Pension Belvedere, Hochstrasse 60, A-2680 Semmering (tel. 02664/270). This four-story building has a gabled roofline and a series of arches repeating themselves in the ground-floor windows and in the second-floor loggias. A formal garden grows abundantly off to one side, while a café with parasols lies near the stone walls of the ground floor. On the premises you'll find a small swimming pool and sauna. Rooms with private baths range from 410 AS ($29.75) to 480 AS ($35) per person daily, while bathless units cost around 280 AS ($20.25) per person. Breakfast is included in all the tariffs. The Englschall family, your congenial hosts, welcome guests from December to October into their 19-room hotel.

At Puchberg

Forellenhof Wanzenböck, Losenheim 132, A-2734 Puchberg (tel. 02636/220511). From the front, you'll see a curved series of windows capped with a sloped roof and an upper-level terrace. A more conventional modern wing stretches off to the side, accented with flagstone walls and blue-green fir trees. The interior has wrought-iron wall sconces, pine paneling with arched niches for religious art, and lots of hunting trophies. The 25 earth-toned bedrooms are filled with comfortable contemporary furniture. An in-house swimming pool with a sauna has imaginative metal cut-outs of giant fish fastened to one of the brown tile walls. As the name of the hotel would imply, the Wanzenböck family are the owners. They charge from 500 AS ($36.25) per person daily for a room and full board during the ski season.

Hotel Puchbergerhof, A-2734 Puchberg (tel. 02636/2278), is a mellow old building with a stucco façade highlighted with golden illustrations, slate gables, and wooden shutters. The backyard is filled with flowers and well-kept greenery, while the interior has wooden paneling that is sometimes stenciled with regional designs. The 20 cozy bedrooms sometimes have wooden ceilings and an occasional carved headboard. Edith Resch, the charming hostess, receives guests from December to October, charging them from 380 AS ($27.75) to 440 AS ($32) daily for half board.

Berghaus Hochschneeberg, A-2734 Puchberg (tel. 02636/2257), is a solidly built masonry house reachable only by a cog railway on a path up through alpine meadows. The hotel is perched over a steep cliff, and might be an ideal place to get away from it all. There are up to seven trains a day in peak season, two at most other times from the terminal at Puchberg, which go to a station (Hochschneeberg) five minutes away from the hotel. They leave at 9 and 11:40am. On Friday and Saturday there's a train at 3:45pm as well. The train ride to the hotel takes an hour and a half. Guests are received from mid-May to the end of October, and are charged from 200 AS ($14.50) per person daily for bed-and-breakfast.

At Reichenau

Alpenhotel Knappenhof, A-2651 Reichenau (tel. 02666/3633), is an alpine chalet covered with yellow stucco and wooden slats. Its shutters are forest green, and from the parasol-dotted sun terrace you'll have a view of the rock-covered mountains in the distance. Aside from the sauna and indoor swimming pool, there's a choice of a wide range of health facilities, including underwater massage and diet therapy. The 26 bedrooms, each with private bath or shower, phone, and radio, have modern furnishings and cheerful colors. Most guests stay here on half-board terms, paying from 520 AS ($37.75) per person daily.

Gasthof Flackl, A-2651 Reichenau (tel. 02666/2291). In summer the balconies of this country chalet hotel are filled with flowers. In winter skiers check in, enjoying the warmly inviting traditional atmosphere: green ceramic stove, chalet chairs, wooden ceilings. The Flackl family, your hosts, rent 43 bedrooms, 32 with private baths or showers. Half-board charges range from 250 AS ($18.25) to 365 AS ($26.50) per person daily. The rooms are simply furnished but well maintained, and the food served is wholesome and filling.

5. The Marchfeld

When you travel through Lower Austria in the autumn, you see signs at little inns advertising wild game on the menu, with such graphics as a defenseless stag cornered by hunting dogs. Or you might see pheasant and quail strung up for proper aging. A lot of this game comes from the Marchfeld, a rich agricultural plain lying to the east of Vienna. The Marchfeld, called "the fertile granary of Austria," was under Soviet domination during the occupation years.

The "fertile granary" lies roughly between the River March and the Danube, which, with all due respect to Strauss, is a muddy brown rather than a beautiful blue. The plain lies on the border between Lower Austria and the Slovakia section of Czechoslovakia. The Marchfeld is not one of the scenic sections of Austria, but it is historically significant, having been a battleground on many occasions. Here the Austrians fought the Magyars (Hungarians), the Turks, and even the forces of Napoleon.

While you're still based in Vienna, you can explore much of this area on a long morning's drive, leaving the city on the right bank of the Danube via Rte. 9 and heading toward Bratislava in Czechoslovakia. You'll have to have a visa as well as your passport if you cross the border.

On your drive, a good dining stopover might be—

FISCHAMEND

I suggest you explore in the morning and return to this town for lunch, as it's the site of the oldest fish restaurant in Austria. Many Viennese make culinary pilgrimages here to partake of its cuisine (see below). A market town with an early 16th-century tower, Fischamend lies on the Fischa River.

Where to Dine

Fischrestaurant Merzendorfer (tel. 02232/314) is supposed to be the oldest restaurant in Austria specializing in fish, all of which are deliciously and conscientiously prepared. If you've wanted to try eel (with fennel or dill sauce, for example) or fish from the Danube, as well as carp, Serbian-style fogasch, trout, sheat-fish, or pike-perch with anchovy butter, this is the place to come. You might begin your meal with an Austrian roe soup. À la carte meals begin at 250 AS ($18.25). The restaurant is small and cozy, with an outdoor terrace filled with plants in summer. Lunch is served from 11am to 2pm, and dinner from 5:30 to 10pm. The restaurant is closed Sunday evening, all day Monday, and from the day before Christmas until January 6. It's also closed during all of August.

For your next sightseeing stop, you might take a look at some Roman ruins by driving to—

PETRONELL-CARNUNTUM

The **open-air museum in Petronell-Carnuntum** (tel. 02165/2480) presents the excavations of the Roman city of Carnuntum, which thrived between the 2nd and 4th centuries, with some 45,000 inhabitants. Also shown are the reconstructions of a temple of Diana and a street portico, which provide information about the ancient architecture of Pannonia. Guided tours are given daily from 9am to 5pm, costing 20 AS ($1.45).

BAD DEUTSCH-ALTENBURG

In this spa town, a neighbor of Petronell, stands the **Museum Carnuntinum.** Near the spa complex, the museum contains the most interesting of the Roman artifacts excavated at Carnuntum (see above). The building and the collection of exhibits are open daily from 9am to 5pm, charging 30 AS ($2.20) admission.

ROHRAU

Four miles on from Petronell stands **Schloss Rohrau,** A-2471 Rohrau (tel. 02164/2253), where an 18th-century castle houses one of the most important private art collections in Austria. Called the Harrach Gallery, it has an impressive aggregation of art and is particularly rich in paintings from the Spanish and Neapolitan baroque period. The gallery is open to the public April through October, daily except Monday from 10am to 5pm. Admission is 40 AS ($2.90).

Music-lovers come to Rohrau because it was here that Joseph Haydn, son of a wheelwright, was born in 1732. Haydn wrote 104 symphonies, perfecting the classical sonata form. The **Haydn House,** Rohrau 60 (tel. 02614/2268), a modest thatched cottage, contains mementos, including original scores. It is open daily except Monday from 10am to 5pm, charging an admission of 20 AS ($1.45).

Even if you're not going on to Czechoslovakia, you might want to continue toward the border to the old town of—

HAINBURG

As nations developed and boundaries between countries were fixed, border towns naturally became defensive citadels. Hainburg was no exception. Its great moment in history was long ago, during the Middle Ages, but it still has a ruined castle and some fortified gateways, and part of the 13th-century wall that circled the town still stands. The Wiener Tor gateway is also from the 13th century. There are many vintage houses, in Gothic, Renaissance, and the ubiquitous baroque style.

Haydn attended school in this town, which lies between two cone-shaped hills overlooking the Danube. A fountain is dedicated to the composer.

GROSSENZERSDORF

If you don't want to drive back to Vienna for the night, you can stay in this hamlet north of the Danube, in an area immediately east of the capital city. The village is partially enclosed by its former fortified wall, and nearby battlefields haunt the communal memory—at Aspern in 1809 Napoleon suffered his first defeat in the field, and through this sector the Red Army and the retreating Nazis fought in the closing weeks of World War II in Europe.

Food and Lodging

Hotel am Sachsengang, A-2301 Grossenzersdorf (tel. 02249/29010), is a rambling building with a gently sloping roof and an elegantly crafted wood-trimmed interior. The indoor swimming pool is sunny and spacious, with scattered café tables to permit you to take coffee beside the water. An outdoor terrace faces a tree-lined canal. The hotel has a sauna, an indoor swimming pool, a whirlpool, a massage, and a tennis club. There are 54 comfortable bedrooms, all with private baths or showers, direct-dial phones, and minibars. Singles rent for 660 AS ($48) to 700 AS ($51) daily, and doubles for 900 AS ($65.50) to 990 AS ($72).

Taverne, Hotel am Sachsengang (tel. 02249/29010). This elegant restaurant boasts wood detailing and handsomely rustic touches, and is a part of the above-named hotel. Many of the featured dishes come in puff pastry, including Hungarian fogosch and rack of lamb. Other specialties include veal Parma, wild venison, and a wide range of desserts, all of them served on blue-and-white porcelain. Fixed-price meals range from 190 AS ($13.75) to 460 AS ($33.50), while à la carte meals cost anywhere from 195 AS ($14.25) to 360 AS ($26.25). From May to October, live gypsy music is played in the restaurant. Hours are daily from 11am to 3pm and 6 to 9:30pm in winter, till 10pm in summer.

Farther along, still on the north bank of the Danube, you can visit—

ECKARTSAU

This hamlet has had its moment in history. It was to an imperial hunting lodge here that Emperor Karl I and the royal family fled in the last days of the empire, when the Habsburg sovereignty collapsed in 1918. The baroque lodge was built in 1722. You are allowed to stroll through the gardens and some display rooms, run by the Federal Forestry Administration; for information, phone 02214/2240. The villa and its grounds are open from mid-March until the end of October but only on Saturday, Sunday, and holidays. Tours are at 11am and 1pm, and the admission cost is 20 AS ($1.45).

DEUTSCH-WAGRAM

Should you become fascinated by the Marchfeld, you can drive along a more northerly route from Vienna, reaching the village of Deutsch-Wagram in about 20 minutes. Many memories of Napoleon are here, especially at the hotel recommended below.

Food and Lodging

Hotel Marchfelderhof, Bockflieserstrasse 31, A-2232 Deutsch-Wagram (tel. 02247/2243), is a beautiful 33-bed hotel with a lot of atmosphere. Established in 1912, and replete with historic artifacts, valuable paintings, and rustic detailing, it is directed today by the Bocek family. Some of their rooms come with private baths or showers, and you pay more for these, of course. It's customary to stay here on half-board terms, since the hotel has a well-known restaurant (see below). Half-board terms cost from 350 AS ($25.50) to 450 AS ($32.75) per person daily. The hotel also has an art nouveau café.

Restaurant Marchfelderhof (tel. 02247/2243) is one of the best restaurants in the region. It has a gemütlich and cozy décor of polished wood, hunting artifacts, warmly tinted textiles, and oil paintings, all of which add an elegant and rustically appropriate note. Some of the accessories, such as a mandolin and a coal miner's lamp hanging from the ceiling, add a lighthearted touch. A garden terrace with a cherub-capped fountain is pleasant on a summer afternoon. Specialties on any given night might be avocado sections with oysters in a spicy sauce, filet of wild venison, all the meat dishes you can think of, and a satisfying array of desserts. Portions are more than generous. Fixed-price meals range from 150 AS ($11) to 475 AS ($34.50), with à la carte dinners starting at 200 AS ($14.50). Hot food is served continuously throughout the day from 11am to 11pm; closed Monday. Reservations are suggested. The annual vacation for both the hotel and restaurant is from December 28 to mid-February.

6. The Weinviertel

The Weinviertel, or wine district, referred to in my introduction, lies to the north of Vienna, a rich wine-growing territory between the Danube and the Austria-Czechoslovakia border. On one of the most pleasant drives to be made in the environs of Vienna, you not only go through the vineyard district but you also pass many castles, often in ruins, which evoke the tumultuous Middle Ages.

You can stop in somnolent old market towns that seem light-years removed from bustling Vienna. Many of the little towns have beautiful churches, and scenic views abound. The people who inhabit the district appear to lead relaxed and peaceful lives.

Your tour might take you to—

KORNEUBURG

This town, like Vienna, has a landmark column commemorating deliverance from the plague. It also has the Augustinerkirche, a rococo church built in 1773. A tower from the 15th century crowns the Rathaus (Town Hall).

A short distance from the town center is a castle fortress, **Burg Kreuzenstein,** rebuilt after being virtually demolished by the Swedes in 1645. Reconstruction was launched in 1874 and carried on into the 20th century. Some objets d'art are on exhibit. The castle is open daily except Monday from 9am to 5pm for a 50-AS ($3.65) admission. You can enjoy the café and restaurant, from which a fine vista unfolds.

From Korneuburg, I suggest you continue to the little town of—

EGGENBURG

One of the most beautiful little towns in the Weinviertel, Eggenburg, lying on the Schmida, was encircled by fortified walls in the 15th century. You can still see the defense towers and gates. Its castle, now in ruins, evokes thoughts of past grandeur. The parish church, dedicated to St. Stephen, has two Romanesque towers. On the main square, the Hauptplatz, stands a pillory dating from the 16th century. It's only there to look at today. Look for the **Gemaltes Haus** (Painted House). The Krahuletz Museum, which has some prehistoric relics, is only of minor interest.

Towns near the border might intrigue you. One is—

RETZ

This well-known wine village lies near the Thaya Valley, almost in the Bohemian hills of Czechoslovakia. Retz is distinguished by fortified towers and ramparts, two gate towers dating from the 13th century. The center of this wine-district town is the main square, or Hauptplatz, where a stately column dedicated to the Holy Trinity stands. The houses on the square are much photographed. The Rathaus (Town Hall) was reconstructed in the 16th century. The church, a Gothic Dominican structure, is noteworthy. The town also has an 18th-century windmill.

Many Viennese drive to Retz, mostly on Sunday, to take tours of the **wine cellars** of the town. Tours are conducted daily at 2pm for an admission charge of 35 AS ($2.55). For bookings and information, call 02942/2700.

If you head east along the Thaya River, you come to—

LAA

This 13th-century town, very near the Czechoslovakian border, was once heavily fortified. Some of its walls still stand, as do the ruins of an ancient fortress. Also to be seen are an early Gothic parish church and a castle with an armor collection from the 15th century.

Close by are some wine-growing towns, including **Poysdorf,** which is quite near the once heavily fortified but now quite open border between Austria and Czechoslovakia.

On the way back to Vienna from Laa, you might enjoy a stopover at—

MISTELBACH

This charming old town, not far from Czechoslovakia, is in the northeast corner of Austria. Its Gothic-style parish church is from the 15th century. The *karner* (charnel house or bone house) is even older, from the 12th century. Mistelbach also has a baroque castle, built in 1725.

Food and Lodging

Zur Goldenen Krone, Oberhofer Strasse 15, A-2130 Mistelbach (tel. 02572/ 27295). Walter Heindl is the engaging owner of this wine tavern and 11-room hotel. The outside has a faded ochre façade and tall, old-fashioned windows, which let in lots of light. Singles range from 270 AS ($19.75), while doubles cost 220 AS ($16) to 260 AS ($19) per person daily. The wood-paneled restaurant has a wall-size illustration of one of Austria's royal families, and lots of comfortably intimate nooks and crannies. Specialties include game and veal dishes, all of them cooked in a regional style. À la carte meals range from 125 AS ($9) to 300 AS ($21.75).

---

7. The Wachau-Danube Valley

If you plan to journey along the Danube, I recommend taking a paddleboat steamer in summer. You can travel by armchair, lounging on the deck along this longest river in Central Europe. (The Volga holds "longest river" title for the Continent.)

If you're really "doing the Danube," as some travelers do, you can begin your trip at Passau, West Germany, and go all the way to the Black Sea and across to the Crimean Peninsula, stopping over at Yalta, scene of the famous, now controversial, meeting of Roosevelt, Churchill, and Stalin. However, the Vienna to Yalta portion of the trip alone takes nearly a week and few travelers have that kind of time to devote to it.

Therefore, most visitors limit themselves to a more restricted look at the Danube, taking one of the many popular trips offered in Vienna. If you go westward on the river, your first stop might well be at Klosterneuburg, which was previewed as an excursion in the environs of Vienna (see section 1 in this chapter).

Vienna Sightseeing Tours, Stelzhamergasse 4-11 (tel. 0222/75-11-42) in Vienna, offers Wachau-Danube Valley tours daily from April 1 to October 31, starting at 9:30am, and on Sunday from November 1 to March 31, also departing at 9:30am. The eight-hour trip costs 850 AS ($61.75) for adults, 480 AS ($35) for children. It takes you from Vienna to Krems, with the boat trip on the river taking about two hours. Arriving at Melk, you have lunch and then visit the abbey. From there, a bus takes you to Dürnstein before your return to Vienna.

Of course, you can do a Wachau-Danube Valley land tour in your own car. Some of the sights lie a few miles from the river, so if you're a serious sightseer an automobile will give you far more freedom to explore on your own.

Actually, the Wachau is that part of the Danube Valley lying between Krems and Melk, about 50 miles to the west of Vienna. It's possible to reach this far-western tip of the Wachau, where many visitors come to see Melk Abbey, by taking a train from Vienna to Melk and then a river trip between Melk and Krems.

Scenic experts consider the Wachau one of the most beautiful parts of Austria, where competition for top rating is keen. Throughout this part of the Danube Valley you'll pass ruins of castles reminiscent of the Rhine Valley.

Stopovers along your route by car could include some of the following places, beginning with—

TULLN

This is one of the most ancient towns in Austria, originally being the naval base, Comagena. Later a center for the Babenbergs, who ruled Austria before the Habsburgs, Tulln, on the right bank of the Danube, is called "the flower town" because of the masses of blossoms you'll see in spring and summer. It is the place, according to the saga of the Nibelungen, where Kriemhild, the Burgundian princess of Worms, met Etzel, king of the Huns.

The twin-towered *pfarrkirche* (parish church) grew out of a 12th-century Romanesque basilica dedicated to St. Stephen, as was the cathedral in Vienna. Its west portal is from the 13th century. A Gothic overlay added in its early centuries gave way in the 18th century to the baroque craze that swept the country. A 1786 altarpiece commemorates the martyrdom of St. Stephen. Ogival vaulting was used in the chancel and the nave. Adjoining the church is the **karner** (charnel house or bone house). This funereal chapel is actually the major sight of Tulln, considered the finest of its kind in the entire country. Built in the mid-13th century in the shape of a polygon, it is richly decorated with capitals and arches. The Romanesque dome is adorned with frescoes.

Food and Lodging
Hotel/Restaurant Römerhof Stoiber, Langenlebarnerstrasse 66, A-3430 Tulln an der Donau (tel. 02272/2954), was built in 1972 near the station. It has a simple modern façade of white walls and unadorned windows, with a prominent sign announcing its name. The interior is warmly outfitted with earth colors, a macramé wall hanging, and pendant lighting fixtures. The 50 comfortable bedrooms rent for 330 AS ($24) single and 540 AS ($39.25) double. All units have private showers and toilets, phones, and TVs. A wood-ceilinged restaurant serves well-prepared meals in an attractively rustic setting; specialties include Wiener schnitzel and roast beef in sour cream sauce. Complete meals are offered for as little as 100 AS ($7.25). Hot food is served from 7am to 10pm (till 8pm on Sunday). The hotel is closed on Monday. There is a little beer garden as well as a car park for the use of guests in front of the building.

Hotel zur Rossmühle, Hauptplatz 12, A-3430 Tulln an der Donau (tel. 02272/2411), lies a 30-minute drive west of the center of Vienna. Motorists coming from Germany should exit from the autobahn at St. Christophen. The entrance to the hotel—a yellow building on the central square of this historic village—stands under a rounded arch protected with a wrought-iron gate. The interior attractively combines antique furniture and crystal chandeliers. The 56 bedrooms are decorated somewhat in a baroque style. Singles cost 610 AS ($44.25) daily, with doubles renting for 480 AS ($35) per person. The hotel, also one of the best places in the area for dining, serves Austrian cuisine daily from noon to 2pm and 7 to 10pm; meals cost from 250 AS ($18.25).

Farther along, you come to—

TRAISMAUER
This old market town hardly merits a stopover, but it does have a ring of town walls, partially preserved, and a Renaissance castle that was once the property of the archbishops of Salzburg. Its Wiener Tor dates from the 16th century.

A drive of about 7 miles will take you to a more interesting spot, the—

HERZOGENBURG MONASTERY
Founded in the early 12th century by a German bishop from Passau, this Augustinian monastery (postal code A-3130 Herzogenburg) has a long history with some illustrious highlights. Located 10 miles south of the Danube, the present complex of buildings comprising the church and the abbey was reconstructed in the baroque style. That master of baroque, Fischer von Erlach, designed some of the complex. The art painted in the high altar of the church is by Daniel Gran, and the most outstanding art owned by the abbey is a series of 16th-century paintings on wood, displayed in a room devoted to Gothic art. The monastery is known for its library containing more than 80,000 works.

Guided tours lasting an hour take visitors through the monastery daily from the first of April until the end of October, from 9 to 11am and 1 to 5pm for an admission of 30 AS ($2.20). There's a wine tavern in the complex where you can eat platters of Austrian specialties and drink the product of local grapes.

ST. PÖLTEN
Most guidebooks omit St. Pölten, which is today mainly an industrial town and rail link on the line from Linz to Vienna. But this is not only an important rail junc-

tion, it's also a city of culture and tradition, its origins going back to the time it was a Roman village known as Aelio Cetio. It lies on the left bank of the River Traisen, which connects to the Danube 12½ miles to the north, passing along Traismauer, visited above.

The cultural heyday of St. Pölten—an episcopal see in the province, which lies in the foothills of the Alps—was the 18th century, but many devotees today appreciate its special treasures. Daniel Gran, the painter, and Jakob Prandtauer, the architect, lived here and some of their works remain. These two loom large in the annals of Austrian art and architecture.

For your tour of the old town, head for the Domplatz, which, as its name indicates, is dominated by a **cathedral** of early Gothic style. The present structure supplanted a Romanesque church built on the site in the mid-12th century. However, some of the original edifice remains. One of the cathedral's towers is crowned by a baroque onion-shaped dome. Prandtauer worked on designs for the interior, and there are ceiling paintings by Gran.

The second most important square in the old town is the **Rathausplatz**, where you will of course find the Rathaus (Town Hall), dating from the 16th century, and also a colony of baroque houses. To the north of the square is a Franciscan church known for outstanding altarpieces by Kremser Schmidt, the noted baroque artist from Krems (see below).

Another interesting sight is the **Institute of the English Maidens** (Institut der Englischen Fräulein) on the Linzerstrasse. The charming baroque building dates from 1715. A portrait of the Virgin by Lucas Cranach the Elder is exhibited in one of the altars.

Where to Dine

Maria Kern, Harlandeserstrasse 41 (tel. 02742/31-1-17). Establishments like this hold few illusions about innovative menus. The place remains much as it was years ago, with a conservatively flavorful menu featuring such dishes as huntsman's soup, an array of roasts, and stuffed roll of pork, along with traditional Austrian desserts. À la carte meals cost from 150 AS ($11). The establishment is open for lunch and dinner daily except Wednesday, with hot food served continuously from 7am to 11pm.

Back along the Danube, continue to one of the major sightseeing targets of the Wachau-Danube Valley—

KREMS

In the eastern part of the Wachau on the left bank of the Danube lies Krems, a city some 1,000 years old. The city today encompasses Stein and Mautern, once separate towns.

Krems is a mellow town of courtyards, old churches, and ancient houses in the heart of the vineyard country, with some partially preserved town walls. Just as the Viennese flock to Grinzing and other suburbs to sample new wine in heurigen, so do the people of the Wachau come here to taste the vintners' products, which are new in Krems earlier in the year than in the Vienna area.

The most interesting part of Krems today is what was once the little village of **Stein.** Narrow streets are terraced above the river, and the single main street, Steinlanderstrasse, is flanked with houses, many from the 16th century. The Grosser Passauerhof, Steinlanderstrasse 76, is a Gothic structure decorated with an oriel. Another house, at Steinlanderstrasse 84, which combines Byzantine and Venetian elements among other architectural influences, was once the imperial toll house. In a troubled era, the aristocrats of Krems barricaded the Danube and extracted heavy fines from the river traffic. Sometimes the fines were more than the hapless victims could pay, so the townspeople just confiscated the cargo.

The parish church (pfarrkirche) of Krems is somewhat overadorned, rich with gilt and statuary. Construction on this, one of the oldest baroque churches in the province, began in 1616. In the 18th century Martin Johann Schmidt painted many of the frescoes you'll see inside the church. In the Altstadt, or Old Town, the **Steiner Tor,** a 1480 gate, is a landmark. The town's Rathaus (Town Hall), from 1549, has an oriel.

You'll find the **Historisches Museum der Stadt Krems** (Historical Museum of Krems; tel. 02732/2511, ext. 339) in a restored Dominican monastery. The abbey is in the Gothic style from the 13th and 14th centuries. It has a painting gallery displaying the works of Martin Johann Schmidt, a noted 18th-century artist better known as Kremser Schmidt (mentioned earlier). The complex also has an interesting **Weinbaumuseum** (Wine Museum), exhibiting artifacts, many quite old, gathered from the vineyards along the Danube.

The Historical Museum is open from around Easter until the middle of November. Hours are 9am to noon and 2 to 5pm (9am to noon on Sunday). It's closed on Monday. Admission is 25 AS ($1.80).

Where to Stay

Parkhotel Krems, Edmund-Hofbauer-Strasse 19, A-3500 Krems (tel. 02732/7565), is a large glass-walled 60-room hotel with a wooden canopy stretching over the front entrance. After registering in a paneled reception area, you'll be able to choose between a meal in the airy café, on its terrace, or in one of two restaurants. One serves typically Austrian food, the other, Greek specialties. The waitresses, all of whom wear regional garb, will bring you wine from the Wachau district. Singles rent for 350 AS ($25.50) daily, doubles for 580 AS ($42.25), with breakfast included. All units contain private baths. The hotel's fitness center includes a sauna and solarium.

Hotel-Restaurant am Förthof, Donaulände 8, A-3500 Krems (tel. 02732/3345), in the Stein sector of the city, is a big-windowed building with white stucco walls between each of its flower-covered wooden balconies. A rose garden surrounds the base of an al fresco café, while the inside is decorated with Oriental rugs and a scattering of antiques amid the newer furniture. On the grounds is an outdoor swimming pool bordered in stone. The 20 high-ceilinged bedrooms, each with complete bath or shower, foyer, phone, and shared balcony, rent for 650 AS ($47.25) to 700 AS ($51) per person daily for half board. At dinner, hotel guests have a choice of main dishes that include contemporary cuisine or traditional Austrian cooking.

Where to Dine

Restaurant Bacher, Südtiroler Platz 208, A-3512 Mautern (tel. 02732/2937), 2½ miles from Krems. This excellent restaurant-hotel, with an elegant dining room and a well-kept garden, is operated by Lisl and Klaus Wagner-Bacher. Lisl cooks à la Paul Bocuse, serving an imaginative array of the freshest possible ingredients. Specialties include crabmeat salad with nut oil, zucchini stuffed with fish, and two kinds of sauces, plus a changing collection of creatively prepared foods. Dessert might be beignets with apricot sauce and vanilla ice cream. She has won awards for her cuisine, as her enthusiastic clientele will tell you. À la carte meals range from 250 AS ($18.25) to 650 AS ($47.25) for a "menu dégustation." The wine list includes more than 600 vintages, with tastings of 16 different wines from the surrounding regions. The restaurant is open Wednesday to Sunday throughout the year; annual closing occurs during three weeks in February. Hours are 11:30am to 2pm and 6:30 to 9pm, with reservations strongly advised.

Eight double and five single rooms are offered. Rooms contain TVs, minibars, phones, and radios; each is attractively furnished. The cost: 725 AS ($52.75) daily in a single, 525 AS ($38.25) to 695 AS ($50.50) per person in a double.

DÜRNSTEIN

Less than 5 miles from Krems is the loveliest town along the Danube, Dürnstein, which draws throngs of tour groups in summer. Terraced vineyards mark this as another Danube wine town. The town was once fortified, and its walls are partially preserved.

The ruins of a castle fortress, 520 feet above the town, are a link with the Crusades. It was here that Leopold V, the Babenberg duke ruling the country at that time, held Richard the Lion-Hearted of England prisoner in 1193. It seems that Richard had insulted the powerful Austrian duke in Palestine during one of the frequent religious forays of the Middle Ages to get the Holy Sepulcher and its appurtenances into Christian custody. The story goes that when Richard was trying to get back home, his boat went on the rocks in the Adriatic and he tried to sneak through Austria disguised as a peasant. Somebody probably turned stool pigeon, but at any rate, the English monarch was arrested and imprisoned by Leopold.

For quite some time nobody knew exactly where Richard was incarcerated in Austria, but his loyal minstrel companion, Blondel, had a clever idea. He went from castle to castle, playing on his lute and singing Richard's favorite songs, particularly where it seemed as if somebody important might be held prisoner. The tactic paid off, the legend says, and at Dürnstein Richard heard the voice of the minstrel singing and took up the lyrics in reply. This discovery forced Leopold to transfer the English king to another castle, this one in the Rhineland Palatinate, but by then everybody knew where he was, so Leopold set a high ransom on the Plantagenet head, which was eventually met and Richard was set free.

The castle was virtually demolished by the Swedes in 1645, but you can visit the ruins if you don't mind a vigorous climb (allow an hour). The castle isn't so much, but the view of Dürnstein and the Wachau is more than worth the effort.

Back in the town, take in the principal artery, Hauptstrasse, which is flanked by richly embellished old residences. Many of these date from the 1500s and have been well maintained through the centuries. In summer the balconies are filled with flowers.

The 15th-century pfarrkirche (parish church) also merits a visit. The building was originally an Augustinian monastery and was reconstructed when the baroque style swept Austria. The church tower is considered the finest baroque example in the whole country. There is also a splendid church portal. Kremser Schmidt, the noted baroque painter mentioned earlier, did some of the altar paintings.

Food and Lodging

Hotel Richard Löwenherz, A-3601 Dürnstein (tel. 02711/222), is built into what was once an abbey. Classified today as one of Austria's "Romantik" hotels, it's filled with antiques, Renaissance sculpture, and elegant chandeliers. The vaulting of some of the ceilings rests on exposed stone columns, while the paneling in other rooms is well polished and mellow. An arbor-covered sun terrace with restaurant tables extends toward the Danube, and will give you a chance to see the other residents of the hotel enjoying the view. Best of all, the hotel offers a swimming pool where you'll be able to see the reflection of the apse of a medieval church in its waters. The spacious bedrooms, especially those in the balconied modern section, are tastefully filled with lighthearted furniture and cheerful, unobtrusive colors. Singles range from 1,000 AS ($72.75) to 1,100 AS ($80) daily, while doubles cost 1,250 AS ($91) to 1,600 AS ($116.50) daily, with buffet breakfast included. The restaurant offers excellent local wines as well as fish from the Danube among its many regional specialties. The dining room is open daily from 7am to midnight.

Hotel Schloss Dürnstein, A-3601 Dürnstein (tel. 02711/212). The baroque tower of this Renaissance castle rises above one of the most scenic parts of the Danube. It used to be owned by the princes of Starhemberg, but today it's one of the best-furnished hotels in Austria, with a series of intricate architectural details. It contains white ceramic stoves, vaulted ceilings, parquet floors, Oriental rugs, gilt mirrors, and oil portraits of elaborately dressed courtiers. Below the ochre façade of one of the wings, an ivy-covered wall borders the water of a swimming pool. The real beauty of the grounds, however, is found on the shady terrace a stone's throw from the river, whose traffic stimulated the construction of this building more than 350 years ago.

The restaurant is outfitted with velvet armchairs with cabriole legs. Here you'll be served well-prepared dishes from the kitchen of an experienced chef. The hotel rents 37 bedrooms, each with private bath or shower. Half board ranges from 1,050 AS ($76.25) to 1,550 AS ($112.75) per person daily, the most expensive price being for one of the hotel's most elegant rooms (rare antiques, beautiful upholstery, and beds worthy of Napoleon). The Schloss Dürnstein receives guests from April to October.

Gartenhotel Pfeffel, A-3601 Dürnstein (tel. 02711/206), is a black-roofed, white-walled hotel whose angularity is partially concealed by well-landscaped shrubbery. The public rooms are furnished with modern pieces, and all but two of the 30 bedrooms contain private baths or showers. Open from March to November, the hotel rates as one of the best bargains in this much-frequented tourist town. With half board included, the rate per person ranges from 350 AS ($25.50) to 600 AS ($43.50) daily. Leopold Pfeffel is your host.

Gasthof-Pension Sänger Blondel, A-3601 Dürnstein (tel. 02711/253). Lemon-colored, charmingly old-fashioned, with green shutters and clusters of flowers gathered at the windows, this hotel derives its name from the faithful minstrel who searched the countryside until he found Richard the Lion-Hearted imprisoned at Dürnstein. Aside from the good and reasonably priced restaurant, Sänger Blondel offers 18 rooms to travelers, costing 495 AS ($36) for a single and 370 AS ($27) per person for a double, with breakfast included. All rooms have showers or baths and toilets. The hotel is open from March to November.

After exploring Dürnstein, most visitors rush to Melk, but if you have more time to spend in this beautiful area, there are other sights in the immediate vicinity. These include—

WEISSENKIRCHEN

This is a celebrated wine town in the heart of the vineyards of Wachau, which lie along the Danube. You'll see many old houses, but Weissenkirchen's main attraction is its fortified Gothic **pfarrkirche,** or parish church, from the 15th century. The builders had the church fortified in 1531, fearing that the Turks would take Vienna and pose a threat to areas to the west of the capital. From one of the belvederes here you have an excellent view of the Danube Valley. A car-ferry crosses the river here.

The **Wachaumuseum** (Wachau Museum; tel. 02715/2268) also merits a visit. The Teisenhofer-Hof, once a patrician house, was also fortified in the 16th century. It has a charming courtyard and arcades extending out to support a canopied gallery. The museum is devoted to the history of the region. It's open from the first of April to the end of October from 10am to 5pm, except Monday. Admission is 20 AS ($1.45) for adults and 10 AS (75¢) for children.

Weissenkirchen has some of the finest food in the Wachau (see below), so you may want to schedule a luncheon stop here.

Food and Lodging

Raffelsbergerhof, A-3610 Weissenkirchen (tel. 02715/2201), the former headquarters of one of the river's traffic controllers, has been renovated to some of its Renaissance integrity—and converted into a tastefully decorated hotel, with a pretty garden and contemporary touches in the 12 comfortable bedrooms, each with private bath. The Anton family, your hosts, charge 400 AS ($29) to 600 AS ($43.50) per person daily. The hotel is closed from November until April.

Florianihof, at Wösendorf (tel. 02715/2424), is a beautifully old-fashioned house decorated with taste and rustic furniture. Specialties of the house include such gutbürgerlich dishes as blutwurst and sauerkraut, zucchini and chicken cream soup, and cabbage noodles with ham. You can also order wine-cream soup, tafelspitz, and several kinds of schnitzels. A four-course fixed-price menu costs 230 AS ($16.75), with à la carte dinners beginning as low as 175 AS ($12.75). Closing day is Thursday. Otherwise, the place is open on weekdays from 1 to 8pm, on Saturday from 10am to midnight, and on Sunday from 10am to 9pm. Next door is a café serving drinks, desserts, champagne, Austrian wine, and snacks.

SPITZ

Southward along the Danube in the direction of Melk lies Spitz, a sleepy little market town known for its grapes and characterized by its terraced vineyards. It is at its most beautiful in spring when hundreds of fruit trees are in bloom.

Spitz has the ubiquitous ruined castle and is noted for its ancient houses, many owned by vintners. Balconies of the houses are filled with masses of geraniums in spring and summer. A walk along the Schlossgasse will permit you to see some of the town's finest buildings. The Gothic pfarrkirche (parish church) is from the 15th century. The well-known baroque painter Kremser Schmidt worked on the altar.

Food and Lodging

Hotel Wachauer Hof, A-3620 Spitz (tel. 02713/2303), a large, white gabled structure situated near vineyards and other buildings, is a good choice should you desire to stay overnight along the Danube in the vicinity of Melk. Of the 55 attractively furnished bedrooms, 30 come with private baths or showers. The hotel is closed from November 20 to Easter. Otherwise, it charges from 220 AS ($16) daily for a single, going up to 550 AS ($40) for a double, a good bargain.

Mühlenkeller, Auf der Wehr 1 (tel. 02713/2352). Some of the foundations of this wine restaurant date from the 11th century. From the thickness of some of the walls, you can imagine that much of the rest of the building is almost as old. Menu items include a conservative but flavorful medley of Teutonic specialties, including roast pork with noodles and cabbage, tafelspitz, and veal gulasch, along with grilled blood sausage and a fattening array of strudels. Menus begin at 75 AS ($5.50), with à la carte dinners costing from 100 AS ($7.25). Of course, you can spend far more. Dinner is nightly except Wednesday from 4pm to midnight. Lunch is sometimes offered, but only occasionally (call to make sure). The restaurant takes a long Christmas break.

From here, a car-ferry will take you and your vehicle over to the Danube's right bank.

SCHÖNBÜHEL

On the right bank of the Danube in one of the most idyllic settings of the Wachau, some 3 miles before you reach Melk, stands the castle of Schönbühel, built in the early 1800s. It was erected on a rocky ledge commanding a view of the valley and of Melk. An architect was allowed to create a fantasy of onion-shaped domes and "pepperpot" towers on the castle.

Finally, you arrive at one of the chief sightseeing goals of every pilgrim to Austria—

MELK

Some 55 miles from Vienna on the right bank of the Danube, Melk marks the west terminus of the Wachau. **Melk Abbey** (tel. 02752/2312), one of the finest baroque buildings in the world, and the **Stiftskirche**—the abbey church—are the major attractions today. However, Melk has been an important place in the Danube Basin since establishment of a Roman fortress on a promontory looking out onto a tiny "arm" of the Danube. Melk also figures in *The Nibelungenlied,* in which it is called Medelike.

The rock-strewn bluff where the abbey now stands overlooking the river was the seat of the Babenbergs who ruled Austria from 976 until the Habsburgs took over. In the 11th century Leopold II of the House of Babenberg presented Melk to the Benedictine monks, who turned it into a fortified abbey. It became known as a center of learning and culture, and its influence spread all over Austria, a fact that is familiar to readers of the *The Name of the Rose,* by Umberto Eco. However, it did not fare well during the Reformation, and it felt the fallout from the 1683 Turkish invasion, although it was spared from direct attack when the armies of the Ottoman Empire were repelled at the outskirts of Vienna. The construction of the new building began in 1702, just in time to be given the full baroque treatment.

Most of the design of the present abbey was by the baroque architect Jakob Prandtauer. Its marble hall, called the Marmorsaal, contains pilasters coated in red marble. A richly painted allegorical picture on the ceiling is the work of Paul Troger, whose work is distinguished by his blue coloring. The library, rising two floors, again with a Troger ceiling, contains some 80,000 volumes. The Kaisergang, or emperors' gallery, 650 feet long, is decorated with paintings of the rulers of Austria, the most notable of which is the prominently displayed likeness of Maria Theresa.

Despite all this adornment in the abbey, it still takes second place in lavish glory to the Stiftskirche, the golden abbey church, damaged by fire in 1974 but now almost completely restored, even to the regilding with gold bullion of statues and altars. Richly embellished with marble and frescoes, the church has an astonishing number of windows. Many of the paintings are by Johann Michael Rottmayr, but Troger also had a hand in decorating the church. The Marble Hall banquet room next to the church was also damaged by the fire but has been restored to its former ornate elegance.

Visitors can make arrangements to tour the monastery on their own by phoning, but the best opportunity to see it is to take a tour with an English-speaking guide. Melk is still a working abbey, and you may see black-robed Benedictine monks going about their business or schoolboys rushing out the gates.

Guided tours of the abbey complex are given daily from 9am to noon and 1 to 4pm in April, May, and October, until 5pm in summer. Otherwise, its tours are at 11am and 2pm. Admission is 30 AS ($2.20) for adults and 15 AS ($1.10) for children.

Everyone heads for the terrace for a view of the river. Napoleon probably used it for a lookout when he made Melk his headquarters during the campaign against Austria.

Food and Lodging

Hotel Stadt Melk, Hauptplatz 1, A-3390 Melk (tel. 02752/2475), is a four-story beflowered hotel with a gabled roof, white stucco walls, and a position just below the yellow baroque walls of the town's palace. The pleasant restaurant has leaded-glass windows in round bull's-eye patterns of greenish glass, while the simply furnished bedrooms are clean and comfortable. There's a sauna on the premises. The hotel rents 15 bedrooms, each with private bath or shower. Singles rent for 510 AS ($37) daily, with doubles costing from 600 AS ($43.50) to 800 AS ($58.25), with breakfast included.

---

8. The Nibelungengau

Austrians call one section of the Danube Valley the Nibelungengau, a name that brings a nostalgic "Once upon a time . . ." feeling even to those only vaguely familiar with the legend of Siegfried and his struggle to steal the treasure of the

Nibelungen, a tribe of dwarfs, and awaken the enchanted princess, Brunhild. *The Nibelungenlied* is the German epic poem, probably written about A.D. 1200, which set down household legends that had been centuries in the making. After the gold hoard was taken from the dwarfs, the name Nibelungen was given to the followers of Siegfried, the Burgundian kings who acquired the treasure after Siegfried's death. In Teutonic tradition, the epic of the Nibelungen enjoys a renown equaled only by that of King Arthur in England.

The Nibelungengau is that part of the Danube Valley lying beyond the Wachau to the west. Here you'll find—

PÖCHLARN

This river town, which still has remnants of its medieval walls, is today a focal point of tourist attention in June. Visitors from all over Europe and America come to attend a festive pageant, complete with bonfires, that briefly turns back the clock to the Middle Ages. In *The Nibelungenlied*, Pöchlarn was Bechelaren, where the margrave, Rüdiger, entertained the Burgundian kings, who were going east to face the king of the Huns (really Attila). The Erlauf River flows into the Danube at Pöchlarn.

Two miles north of the town stands **Hohenstein Castle** at Arstetten. The baroque chapel here, a parish church since the 17th century, contains the tombs of two people who figured prominently and tragically in the history of the 20th century—Archduke Franz Ferdinand, heir to the throne of Austria, and his wife. Their assassinations at Sarajevo (now a Yugoslavian city) on June 28, 1914, touched off events that led to World War I.

MARBACH

A ferry connects this little village with the right bank of the Danube. Summer tourists visit it, but otherwise it's a fairly sleepy little market town.

However, from here you can take a steep 2¼-mile drive up to—

MARIA TAFERL

At this little summer resort, a fantastic view of the Nibelungengau unfolds. The hamlet is known for its pilgrimage church, designed by Jakob Prandtauer, the architect of Melk Abbey. A Celtic sacrificial stone can be seen outside.

If you'd like to anchor in this bucolic little spot, I have the following recommendations:

Food and Lodging

Hotel Krone, A-3672 Maria Taferl (tel. 07413/6355), has an elegantly detailed pseudo-baroque façade stretching out in two separate wings, each of them with a modernized mansard roof. The interior has a paneled bar area—where you might decide to have a before-dinner drink below the glowing brass chandeliers—plus an opulent dining room with a splendid view of the Danube. The 49 bedrooms are rustic and comfortable, costing 390 AS ($28.25) to 650 AS ($47.25) per person daily, based on double occupancy. Occupants of singles pay a 100-AS ($7.25) daily supplement. An indoor swimming pool, a rooftop sun terrace, and a whirlpool and sauna are part of the facilities.

Hotel Kaiserhof, A-3672 Maria Taferl (tel. 07413/6355), under the same management as its sister hotel, the Krone, has a large outdoor swimming pool within sight of the twin baroque towers of a nearby church. The façade is pleasantly simple, with attractive shrubbery and flowerboxes, an imposing entrance area, and a summer cold buffet that is sometimes served on the spacious lawns outside. An outdoor terrace offers panoramic views of the Danube. The Kaiserhof offers 16 well-furnished bedrooms with private shower. Prices are the same as for the Hotel Krone.

PERSENBEUG

Near the end of the Nibelungengau is Persenbeug, a market town across the river from Ybbs, with a bridge connecting the towns. Persenbeug was built in 1617 on a rocky ledge overlooking a loop of the Danube. Persenbeug Castle, a Habsburg imperial residence, was the birthplace of "the last of the Habsburgs," Karl I, who died in exile in Madeira in 1922. The river you can see from here has been dammed by a power station.

If you take the bridge across the dam, you'll arrive at—

YBBS

On the right bank of the Danube, this old town lies near the mouth of the Ybbs River. You can still see the remains of its medieval walls. The town, which may or may not have grown up on the site of a Roman fort, has a Gothic church.

Gourmet Dining

Villa Nowotni, Trewaldstrasse 3 (tel. 07412/2620). The imaginative chef of this well-known restaurant likes to combine the tenets of modern French cuisine with traditional Austrian ingredients. The result is a gastronomic citadel that attracts diners from all over Europe and America. In a décor filled with art nouveau accessories, a team of well-trained waiters serves such specialties as trout Stroganoff with fresh asparagus, variations on quail, and deliciously prepared dishes from the mainstream of Austrian cuisine. The offerings change frequently, but the menu de dégustation gives appreciative diners small portions of an almost unending variety of imaginative courses, based upon the availability of ingredients. Set menus cost from 400 AS ($29) to 550 AS ($40), with à la carte meals beginning at 250 AS ($18.25) and going up. The restaurant is open daily except Sunday dinner and Monday, and reservations are most important. Franz and Evelyn Nowotni quickly become "Franz and Evelyn" to their satisfied guests.

9. The Ybbs and Erlauf Valleys

In the far-western section of Lower Austria are two little-known—at least to North Americans—valleys containing a number of charming old towns and villages as well as beautiful scenery. To explore the Erlauf Valley, called "one of the few backwaters left in Europe," you can head south from Ybbs, going toward the Styrian resort of Mariazell.

Your first stop along this route might be at the brewery town of **Wieselburg,** which has an old church and castle.

If you continue along the same route, soon you'll reach **Pürgstall,** which also has an old church and castle.

In a short time you'll approach **Scheibbs,** which is bigger than either Wieselburg or Pürgstall. Remnants of the town walls have survived ever since the Middle Ages, and a tower gate and some houses date from the Renaissance. The parish church is in the Gothic style, and—you guessed it—there's a castle, this one from the 16th century.

From Scheibbs, you can drive to **Gaming,** a little summer resort noted for its former Carthusian monastery, Marienthorn, built in 1330 and dissolved by order of Emperor Joseph II in 1782. The church, from 1332, is in the "high Gothic" style.

At Erlauf Lake you can take a road that connects with the upper part of the Ybbs Valley. I recommend heading for **Lunz am See,** a market town and small summer resort on Lunzer Lake. It has a Gothic parish church from the early years of the 16th century.

Along the Ybbs River, about 6½ miles from Lunz, lies **Göstling,** a tiny summer resort. Many travelers pass through, going another 5¼ miles to Lassing, where they connect with the **Hochkar Alpine Road.** This is less than 6 miles long and reaches a height of 4,720 feet. At the end of the road you can go the rest of the way by chair lift almost to the summit of Hochkar at 5,931 feet. From this vantage point you'll have a panoramic view of the countryside.

Your chief target in the Ybbs Valley should be—

MAIDHOFEN AN DER YBBS

This mellow old place in the lower part of the valley got its city charter in 1288. The early economy of the town was based on work in the forges with iron mined in the Erzberg. Many houses here are from the 1400s and 1500s. Gables and oriels were common in early house construction, as were arcaded courtyards.

The Rathaus, or Town Hall, has such an arcaded court. The parish church, built in 1510, is in late Gothic style. The **stadtturm** (tower) was erected in 1542 to commemorate the town's victory over the Turks. The exact moment of the Turkish defeat, shortly before noon, was "frozen for eternity" in the tower's clock dial. A nearby castle was the summer home of the Baron de Rothschild for some years of the 19th century.

The pilgrimage church of **Sonntagberg,** rising 5 miles north of the town, is the most distinguishing landmark to be seen in the Ybbs Valley. The church was built in 1706 by Jakob Prandtauer, the noted baroque architect.

STEINAKIRCHEN AM FORST

For one of the most spectacular accommodations not just in the valley but in all of Austria, consider the following 12th-century castle, which lies in a forest setting in the foothills of the Alps with a superb view of the Danube Valley.

Ernegg, the site of the castle, is a satellite of Steinakirchen, lying about 10 miles south of the Vienna/Salzburg motorway (take the Ybbs exit). It's about a 90-minute drive from Vienna. By railroad, take the train to Amstetten.

Food and Lodging

Schloss Ernegg, A-3261 Steinakirchen am Forst (tel. 07488/214) is about 12½ miles southwest of Ybbs. It's hard to imagine a more idyllic hotel: it's isolated from the nearest village, which is just a mile away. From the outside it looks like a cross between a medieval fortress and a baroque pleasure palace, and once you're inside you'll realize that it's actually a bit of both. Constructed originally in the 12th century, it has an inner courtyard whose three floors of arcades rest on chiseled granite columns, elaborate public rooms whose salmon-colored walls reflect off the white tile ceramic stoves, and an impressive collection of rugs, antiques, and oil paintings. The dining room has a high ceiling, pink napery, well-prepared food, and a collection of hunting trophies.

The hotel maintains a private stable, whose horses are available for the use of guests. There are also tennis courts and a heated swimming pool in the nearby village. The 9-hole golf course, situated on the slope behind the castle with a magnificent view over the Erlaug and Danube valleys, is not an easy one; the hotel also has an 18-hole course on either side of the river below the castle. Clay pigeon shooting and trout fishing can be arranged nearby.

There are only 20 bedrooms in the castle open to the public. For these, the daughter of the last Count of Auersperg, who is in charge of the hotel, charges 490 AS ($35.50) to 650 AS ($47.25) per person daily, based on double occupancy, with half board included. Occupants of a single pay a supplement of 120 AS ($8.75) per day. The castle is open from the first of May until October.

AMSTETTEN

This busy commercial town of light industry on the Ybbs River makes a convenient stopover in this part of the province, as it has some fine accommodations and good food. Its parish church is from the 14th century.

Where to Stay

Hotel Hofman, Bahnhofstrasse 2-4, A-3330 Amstetten (tel. 07472/2516), is an imposing 19th-century hotel whose combination of Victorian and baroque elements renders it grandly imperial in a faded sort of way. It has a square cupola above a complicated roofline, plus well-embellished laurel wreaths crowning the top of the single third-floor lunette window. Some of the inside rooms still have rustic timbers and old-fashioned décor, although the 57 bedrooms have been modernized into a contemporary format. Near the train station, the hotel has a country-style dance bar popular with local residents on weekends. Forty-five of the bedrooms contain either private baths or showers. Bed-and-breakfast costs from 280 AS ($20.25) to 475 AS ($34.50) per person daily. There's a garage on the premises if you're driving.

Hotel-Restaurant Gürtler, Rathausstrasse 13, A-3300 Amstetten (tel. 07472/2765), is a central hotel with boldly outlined windows and a stucco façade. The interior has paneling, wrought-iron detailing, and strong but pleasing colors. The contemporary bedrooms have patterned wallpaper and comfortable beds. The hotel rents 74 accommodations, both with and without private bath. The daily bed-and-breakfast rate ranges from 250 AS ($18.25) to 400 AS ($29) per person. Streetside rooms tend to be noisy, so get a unit facing the courtyard if possible. The restaurant serves well-prepared specialties, including, for example, grilled and pan-fried seafish, plus a daily menu that often has nouvelle cuisine touches. Try the pork cutlet with a spicy orange and apricot sauce, a variety of velvety-smooth cream soups, and a tempting list of pastries. À la carte meals begin at 150 AS ($11).

HAAG

Sometimes called Stadt Haag, this is my most remote recommendation in the province. It lies in the far-western reaches of Lower Austria. Actually, it's not inconvenient, being just off the autobahn to Linz. You might prefer to stop here instead of going on into busy Linz. Haag is only a short drive from Amstetten (visited above), and it may well suit your taste if you're looking for an overnight stay in an "undiscovered" Austrian village.

Where to Dine

Schafelner, Hauptplatz 11 (tel. 07334/2411), is a lime-green baroque building with white trim and steeply sloping tile roof. The interior has both a dining room with elegantly upholstered straight-back chairs clustered beneath vaulted arches, and a less formal weinstube paneled in wood with chairs that might be called "country Biedermeier." Restaurant specialties include mousse of smoked trout, lamb sausages on lentils, saddle of venison with bread dumplings and cranberries, filet of veal with morels and roast potatoes, and sweetbreads in Austrian white wine sauce. Desserts might include soufflé of cottage cheese in orange sauce and coffee mousse with rum sauce. A four-course fixed-price meal costs 345 AS ($25), with à la carte dinners beginning at 250 AS ($18.25). Lunch is from 11am to 2pm and dinner from 6 to 10pm daily except Monday and on Tuesday at lunch. The place is closed for two weeks in July and two weeks in January.

---

10. The Ötscher Mountains

To the south of St. Pölten, lying between the Eisenerz Alps and the Vienna Woods, are alpine foothills known as the Ötscher mountains or massif. The Austrians jealously guard for themselves this popular area, which is unspoiled and certainly not yet overbuilt or filled with tourist lures. If you appreciate beautiful scenery and a tranquil way of life, you'll enjoy this area.

After leaving St. Pölten, the first stop will be—

LILIENFELD

This was once a huge Cistercian abbey in the Traisen Valley, founded by one of the Babenberg dukes named Leopold in 1202, when Romanesque was in flower; but many baroque architects worked on it through the years. The tomb of that Leopold is here. Lilienfeld has one of the most celebrated libraries in Lower Austria, dating from 1704. Inside the abbey is an art gallery, and the cloisters have 13th-century pillars of red marble. Some of the stained glass is from the 14th century. The abbey church is Gothic. A park surrounds the complex.

Tours are conducted from 8 to 11am and 2 to 5pm for a fee of 30 AS ($2.25).

At Freiland, an industrial town at the confluence of the Turnitz and the Traisen, you can take one of the area's most scenic drives.

ANNA BERG

This hamlet lies at the top of a pass. It is known for its church of pilgrimage dating from the 14th century. The church later received, as did practically every other building in Austria, a baroque overlay.

---

11. The Waldviertel

To the north of the Wachau and the "land of the Nibelungen" lies the Waldviertel, not to be confused with the already-visited Weinviertel. That was a trip to the land of the grapes. In the Waldviertel you'll meet forests. From Krems, in the Danube Valley, you can begin your exploration of this history-rich region, much of which can be visited in a day's sightseeing trip, and return to Krems or nearby Dürnstein for the superior food and lodging as night falls.

The area abounds with castles, many in ruins. Two rivers, the Thaya and the Kamp, cross it. Waldviertel means forest sector, and the region lives up to its name, with many wooded uplands as well as river valleys.

Your first stop might be at—

LANGENLOIS

Standing at the top of the Valley of the Kamp, Langenlois, 6 miles from Krems, is known for vineyards from which a good dry white wine called Schluck is made. In this old market town, complete with Gothic church, you should visit the old buildings of the Altstadt (Old Town), taking in, among other attractions, a column built in the 13th century to commemorate deliverance from the plague. Many houses dating from the 16th century have arcaded courtyards. Others are from the 17th and 18th centuries, and you'll note differences in building styles. Often the houses are richly painted in pastels, including Maria Theresa ochre.

Where to Eat

Brundlmayer, Walterstrasse 14 (tel. 02734/2383), is a heurige-style restaurant serving the local vintage of Gruner Veltliner. You can enjoy such wines as Riesling, both white and blue burgundies, and many others. The restaurant is in a Renaissance-era house, and many guests come here not just for the wine but for the richly ample buffet. You can enjoy meat-stuffed strudels, wurst with sauerkraut, several preparations of ham, and many other items. À la carte meals cost from 80 AS ($5.75) to 170 AS ($12.25). Hours are 11:30 to 2:30pm and 6 to 9:30pm. The restaurant is closed Monday, Tuesday, and Wednesday; it also shuts down from mid-December until the end of February.

From Langenlois, the road heads north through the Kamp Valley to—

GARS AM KAMP

This market town, perched on the east bank of the river, enjoys a modest summer visitor traffic. The Rathaus (Town Hall) is from the late 16th century.

A much more appealing destination is the romantic town of—

HORN

The major business hub of the eastern Waldviertel, Horn has many buildings of historic interest, including a castle built in the Middle Ages that was given a much later architectural overlay. Armed with a good map, you can set out on many excursions from Horn, especially if you're interested in castles.

Rosenburg Castle, Schlossplatz 1 (tel. 02982/2911), built in the 12th century, has a large courtyard where tournaments were held when knighthood was in flower. Apartments of the edifice, which stands on a rocky slope, contain antiques and much weaponry. Visitors are allowed through only on conducted tours, which are held daily from 9am to noon and 1 to 5pm. Performances of birds of prey are staged. Admission is 50 AS ($3.65).

Even more important is the nearby **Abbey of Altenburg,** founded in 1144. Reconstruction on this Benedictine religious house began in 1650 and lasted for almost a century. The design of the abbey was the masterpiece of Joseph Mungenast. As the taste for baroque swept the land during that time, the abbey was of course not spared, with the result that some parts of the façade, with onion-shaped domes, appear Byzantine. The lowest point in the abbey's history was when it was used as a barracks for Soviet soldiers during 1945 and 1946.

The abbey cupola was frescoed by the noted baroque painter Paul Troger, whose work I have already mentioned in this chapter. In the crypt are macabre paintings illustrating *The Dance of Death*. You can also visit the treasury with its antiques, objects in gold and silver, and statuary. A combined ticket to both the abbey church and its treasury is 40 AS ($2.90). The abbey is open daily from April to October, 9am to noon and 1 to 5pm.

From Fuglau, a road leads to **Greillenstein Castle,** which dates from the 14th century, although the present structure is more 16th century. Contained within is a Criminal Law Museum, with exhibits of instruments of torture. The property has been the traditional seat of the counts of Kuefstein. You can visit the castle daily from April through October, 9am to noon and 1 to 5pm. Admission is 30 AS ($2.20).

For your final visit in the Waldviertel, I suggest—

ZWETTL

Many remains of the old city walls, studded with towers and gates, can still be seen in this major hub of traffic and business lying at a loop of the Kamp River near the Ottenstein Dam in the northern sector of the Waldviertel. Two miles northeast of the town lies **Zwettl Abbey** (tel. 02822/3181), a Cistercian religious house founded in 1138, now an architectural mélange of Romanesque, Gothic, and baroque. Its choir, in the late Gothic style, is one of its chief treasures. The cloister is intriguing, with both Romanesque and Gothic touches. The church, whose baroque tower pierces the sky, was built in the 14th century but now has 18th-century overlays.

Such noted artists as Jörg Breu are represented here (see his pictures on the famous late Gothic winged altarpiece from 1500). Paul Troger has many paintings in the church, refectory, and library, including some notable frescoes. J. M. Götz is best seen in his sculptures of the high altar, and J. I. Egedacher designed the organ in 1728.

The abbey is open from May 1 until the end of October. Guided tours are conducted at 10am, 11am, 2pm, and 3pm. In July, August, and September there is also a guided tour at 4pm. On Sunday, tours leave at 11am, 2pm, and 3pm. Admission is 30 AS ($2.20).

BURGENLAND

The Easternmost and the newest province of Austria, Burgenland is a little border region between East and West that came into being in 1921, formed of German-speaking border areas of what had been Hungary in the Austro-Hungarian Empire and for centuries before that. It's the start of a large, flat steppe (puszta) that reaches almost to Budapest, but it also lies practically on the doorstep of Vienna. The province shares a western border with Styria and Lower Austria, and its long eastern boundary separates it from its former fatherland, Hungary.

This area has suffered greatly from wars over the centuries—from tribal ages through long years when it was a part of the Roman Central European country of Pannonia, to efforts to add it to the Ottoman Empire, and up to the war-torn times in this century. Burgenland joined Austria after a vote of its citizens in the aftermath of World War I, although when the vote was taken in 1919, its capital, Ödenburg, now called Sopron, chose to remain with Hungary. This accounts for the narrow corridor between the northern and southern parts of the province. The Hungarian city of Sopron actually lies to the west of Lake Neusiedl (Neusiedler See, in German), an important part of Burgenland. Sopron represents a far penetration of what used to be called the Iron Curtain into Austria. The Russians occupied Burgenland from 1945 to 1955, and few, if any, of its citizens seemed sorry to see them depart.

Called "the vegetable garden of Vienna," Burgenland is mostly an agricultural province, also growing such products as wheat and fruit. It is noted for its wines, producing more than one-third of all the wine made in Austria. The province is a point where the Great Hungarian Plain gradually modulates into the foothills of the eastern Alps, 29% of its area being covered by forest and 7% of its agricultural lands composed of vineyards. Its Pannonian climate means hot summers with little rainfall, but the winters are moderate. For the most part you can enjoy sunny days from early spring until late autumn.

Besides the 2% of the Burgenland population that is Hungarian, many other citizens of the province are not typically Austrian. Some 10% belong to the Croat ethnic group that settled here in the 16th century after fleeing their southern Slav homes before the advance of Turkish armies. For hundreds of years the Croats, Hun-

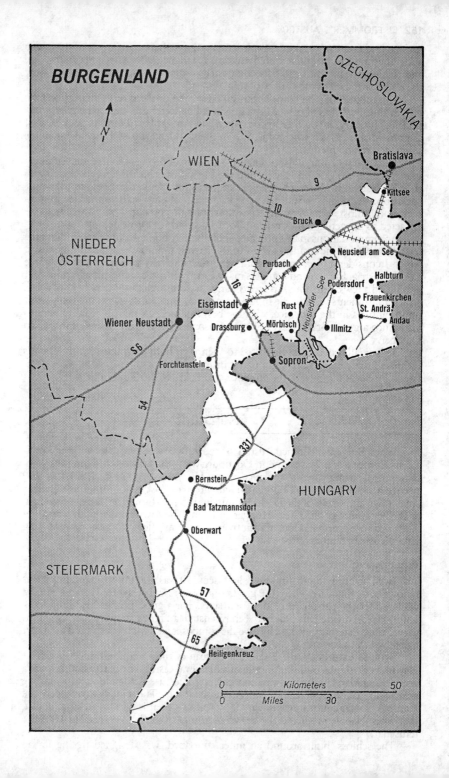

garians, and German-speaking people have lived together in this area, but the ethnic and religious variety is still reflected in customs, language, dress, legends, folk songs, and folklore. Many Burgenlanders interested in maintaining their traditions wear the traditional garb of their ancestors on Sunday.

This mixture of ethnic stock has resulted in a regional cookery that is among the best in Europe. It has of course been heavily influenced by its eastern neighbors, especially Hungary, as you'll appreciate when you savor gulasches and strudels, as well as goose dishes. Much wild game lives in the wooded areas of Burgenland and is often featured on menus.

The capital of Burgenland, **Eisenstadt,** a small provincial city, was for many years the home of Joseph Haydn, and the composer is buried here. Each summer there's a festival at **Mörbisch,** using **Lake Neusiedl** (Neusiedler See) as a theatrical backdrop. Neusiedl is the only steppe lake in Central Europe. If you're here in summer, you'll most certainly want to explore it by motorboat. Lots of Viennese are attracted to Burgenland on weekends for sailing and/or birdwatching.

Accommodations in this province are extremely limited, but they're among the least expensive in the country. The area is relatively unknown to North Americans, which I consider a pity, and I recommend that you add it to your itinerary. Like Lower Austria, Burgenland contains many fortresses and castles, often in ruins, but you'll find a few castle hotels in the romantic style, as well as some rather high-class spa establishments with all the modern amenities. **Bad Tatzmannsdorf** is the most important spa in the province, with the best facilities. Or perhaps you'll prefer to settle into a gasthof-type place. The spa season in Burgenland lasts from April to October.

This small province is connected to Vienna by both train and bus services. It's estimated that you can drive through it in about 2½ hours. You can also travel between Eisenstadt, capital of the province, and Lake Neusiedl by bus.

1. Eisenstadt

When Burgenland joined Austria in the 1920s, it was a province without a capital, its former seat of government, Ödenburg (now the far-western Hungarian city of Sopron), having voted to remain a part of Hungary. In 1924, realizing that they needed a provincial capital, Burgenlanders agreed on Eisenstadt for the honor. This small town at the foot of the Leitha mountains is only 31 miles southeast of Vienna, at the beginning of the Great Hungarian Plain. The town is surrounded by vineyards and forests and has lots of fruit trees. It's a convenient stopover for exploring Lake Neusiedl, 6 miles to the east.

THE SIGHTS

Even before assuming its new role, Eisenstadt was not unknown. Mainly it was renowned as the place where the great composer Joseph Haydn lived and worked while under the patronage of the Esterházys. For a good part of his life (1732–1809) Haydn divided his time between Eisenstadt and the Esterházy Castle in Hungary. Prince Esterházy eventually gave the composer his own orchestra and a concert hall in which to perform.

Schloss Esterházy, the Eisenstadt château of the Esterházy princes in which Haydn worked, was built on the site of a medieval castle. The Esterházy clan was a great Hungarian family with vast estates who ruled Eisenstadt and its surrounding area. They claimed descent from Attila the Hun. The Esterházys helped the Habsburgs gain control in Hungary. So great was their loyalty to Austria, in fact, that when Napoleon offered the crown of Hungary to Nic Esterházy in 1809, he refused it.

The schloss, built around an inner courtyard, was designed by the Italian architect Carlone, and fortified because of its strategic position. Carlone started work on the castle in 1663, but subsequently it was remodeled by many other architects, resulting in sweeping alterations to its appearance. In the late 18th and early 19th centuries it was given a baroque pastel façade. On the first floor, the great baronial hall was made into the Haydnsaal, where the composer conducted the orchestra Prince Esterházy had provided for him and often performed his own works before the Esterházy court. The walls and ceilings of this concert hall are elaborately decorated, but the floor is of bare wood, which, it is claimed, is the cause of the room's acoustical perfection.

A complete tour of Esterházy Palace takes 45 minutes, whereas a tour of Haydnsaal lasts about 20 minutes. Both tours are conducted for a minimum of 10 persons. In summer, hours are 9am to 5pm daily. In winter, hours are 9am to 4pm Monday to Friday. Admission is 20 AS ($1.45) for adults and 10 AS (75¢) for children.

Haydn House, Haydn-Gasse 21 (tel. 02682/2652), the little Eisenstadt home of the composer from 1766 to 1778, is now a museum honoring its former tenant. It is open May to October daily from 9am to noon and 1 to 5pm. Admission is 15 AS ($1.10). Although he appeared in court nearly every night, Haydn actually lived very moderately when he was at home. However, the home wasn't exactly bleak, as he had a little flower-filled courtyard. The museum has collected mementos of Haydn's life and work.

If you want to pay your final respects to the memory of Haydn, follow Hauptstrasse, which will connect you to Esterházystrasse leading to the **Bergkirche** (Church of the Calvary), containing Haydn's tomb, built of white marble.

Until 1954 only the composer's headless body was here. His skull was in the Music Museum in Vienna, where curious spectators were actually allowed to feel it. Haydn's head was stolen a few days after his death and did not get back together with his body for a total of 145 years! The story of how the head traveled from one owner to another—eventually even being sold—before finally, I hope, coming to rest with the other part of Haydn's remains at Eisenstadt is a long and complicated one.

To honor another composer, Franz Liszt, you can leave Eisenstadt going south on the road to the small village of **Raiding.** There the **Liszt Geburtshaus** (Franz Liszt's birthplace; tel. 02619/7220), is now a museum containing many mementos of the composer's life, including an old church organ he used to play. Liszt's father worked as a bailiff for the princes of Esterházy, and this was his home when little Franz was born in 1811. The museum is open from Easter until the end of October, 9am to noon and 1 to 5pm, charging an admission of 15 AS ($1.10).

Near Eisenstadt at **St. Margarethen,** there is an outdoor sculpture gallery at a quarry. Sculptors have done monumental carvings on the site instead of taking the material for their artwork back to their studios. The outdoor sculpture gallery is open to the public, but there is an admission fee to the quarry; adults pay 15 AS ($1.10) and children 10 AS (75¢). The quarry is open in summer from 9am to 6pm and in winter from 10am to 4pm. For more information, call 02680/2188.

As in Oberammergau, there are Passion plays at the quarry every five years. The next performance is in 1991.

FOOD AND LODGING

Hotel Burgenland, Schubertplatz, A-7000 Eisenstadt (tel. 02682/5521), a contemporary hotel, is designed with a modified mansard roof, white stucco walls, and big windows. The comfortable bedrooms have lots of light, wood-grained headboards, and functional furniture. A swimming pool, a sauna, two restaurants, and a café are on the premises. With breakfast included, singles rent for 750 AS ($54.50) daily, while doubles cost 1,040 AS ($75.75), depending on the season. All accommodations have private baths, TVs, radios, and minibars. Half board is another 140 AS ($10.25) per person daily.

One of the best restaurants in Burgenland is the hotel's **G'würstöckl,** open daily from 11:30am to 2:30pm and 6 to 10pm. Of bright, airy, modern design, it specializes in such dishes as cabbage soup, veal steak with fresh vegetables, and a host of other platters sometimes influenced strongly by the kitchens of Hungary. Fixed-price menus cost 145 AS ($10.50) to 160 AS ($11.75), with à la carte meals running from 120 AS ($8.75) to 220 AS ($16). Reservations are suggested.

Parkhotel Mikschi, Haydn-Gasse 38, A-7000 Eisenstadt (tel. 02682/4361), is a modern 56-room hotel in the center of town. Its prominent balconies shelter big windows and look out over a sunny garden. Inside, the contemporary public rooms have a wintertime fireplace encased in brick with a copper hearth. Singles rent for 650 AS ($47.25) daily, with doubles going for 900 AS ($65.50), including a buffet breakfast. Each of the well-furnished rooms has a bath, refrigerator, phone, and wall-to-wall carpeting.

Hotel Eder zum Goldenen Adler, Hauptstrasse 25, A-7000 Eisenstadt (tel. 02682/2645). This cozily decorated 19-room family-style guesthouse—filled with wooden furniture, deer antlers, and iron chandeliers—has a garden terrace surrounded with a thick wall of greenery. The simple bedrooms are clean and comfortable. Singles rent for 310 AS ($22.50) to 340 AS ($24.75) daily, while doubles range from 440 AS ($32) to 490 AS ($35.75). The hotel's restaurant serves hot and cold Austrian and Hungarian specialties at reasonable prices. It is closed Friday.

---

2. Lake Neusiedl

This lake, called Neusiedler See in German, is a true steppe lake lying in the northern part of Burgenland. It has been described as strange and mysterious, and is certainly like no lake familiar to North Americans. It was part of a body of water that once blanketed all of the Pannonian Plain. Today it's only about 6 feet deep at its lowest point, and the wind can shift the water dramatically, causing parts of the lake to become dry at times. A broad belt of reeds encircles the huge expanse of lake, about 115 square miles. It's between 4¼ and 9¼ miles wide, and about 22 miles long. If you're tall enough you could walk across it, but I'm not recommending that!

Because of the curvature of the earth, the middle of the lake is about 80 feet higher than the longitudinal axis. The Neusiedler See possesses no natural outlets. Its water is slightly salty, and the plants and animal life here are unique in Europe. This is the meeting place of alpine, Baltic, and Pannonian flora and fauna. Some 200 different species of birds inhabit the lake area, resting on its reeds, including the Rust stork.

Destinations along the lake include:

ILLMITZ

This old puszta (steppe) village lying on the east side of the lake has grown into a town that does a slight tourist business in summer. This is steppe country, and a tourist brochure issued by the town pictures the most characteristic part of the landscape, a traditional rural Hungarian-type well with long wooden poles used to draw up water.

Area Sights

Leaving Illmitz and heading toward the border, you come to the village of **St. Andrä bei Frauenkirchen,** where you'll see thatch houses. The little town is known for its basket-weaving, so you might want to drive here for a shopping expedition.

A short drive farther will take you to **Andau,** which became the focus of world attention in 1956 during the Hungarian uprising. It was through this point, almost on the border, that hundreds of Hungarians dashed to freedom in the West, fleeing the grim massacres of Budapest.

Starting in the late 1940s, the border with Hungary was closely guarded, and people who tried to escape into Austria were shot from the Communist-controlled watchtowers. But now all that has changed. In 1989 the fortifications were rendered obsolete as hundreds of East Germans fled across the border to freedom in the West. Before the year was out, their own Berlin Wall came tumbling down and they didn't need this means of escape anymore.

The surrounding marshy area of this remote sector of Austria, called **Seewinkel**, is a haven for birds and contains many rare flora, plus many small puszta animals. This is a large natural wildlife sanctuary. You'll see a few windmills and expanses of reeds, which are used to make roofs and shelters.

This area, very different from the celebrated Austria of alpine and Wienerwald lore, is little known to North Americans, and therefore a visit here can qualify as an offbeat adventure. For devotees of geography, it's a fine part of Central Europe for exploration, with sights you won't see elsewhere.

Food and Lodging

Heurigenrestaurant/Pension Rosenhof, Floriangasse 1, A-7142 Illmitz (tel. 02175/2232), is a charming baroque building in an agricultural area a block from the main highway running through the center of town. The arched gateway piercing its gold-and-white façade takes visitors into a rose-laden courtyard filled with arbors. A tile-roofed sister building, capped with platforms for storks' nests, contains 14 cozy bedrooms. Daily per-person rates range from 180 AS ($13) to 210 AS ($15.25).

In an older section you'll find a wine restaurant whose star attraction is the recent vintage produced by the Haider family's wine presses. Many of your fellow diners live in the neighborhood, and they enjoy the Hungarian and Burgenlander specialties as much as you do. In the evening, musicians fill the air with gypsy music. The place is open from March until the end of October, with meals served daily from 11am to 3pm and 5 to 10pm.

HALBTURN

North of St. Andrä, if you go through Frauenkirchen you reach the hamlet of Halbturn, which lies within a stone's throw of the Austria-Hungary border. Here you'll find a lovely baroque concoction designed by the architect Lukas von Hildebrandt, which was used as a summer palace by Empress Maria Theresa and her large brood. It's surrounded by well-laid-out park grounds forming a handsome setting for this landmark of luxurious imperial living, standing in curious contrast to the sparsely settled, bleak villages in the far-western extremities of Hungary.

Originally a hunting lodge destroyed by the Turks during the siege of 1683 and rebuilt by Hildebrandt in the 18th century, the building was again partially burned in 1949, when it was part of the Soviet-occupied zone. In the central hall is a ceiling painted by F. A. Maulbertsch, done in 1765 and considered his masterpiece.

PODERSDORF

If you head west from Frauenkirchen, you reach Podersdorf am See, one of the finest places for swimming on the mysterious lake, as its shoreline is relatively free of reeds. This attracts visitors, and the little town has become a modest summer resort. The parish church in the village is from the late 18th century. You'll see many storks nesting atop chimneys, and some of the cottages have thatch roofs. The Viennese like to drive out here on a summer Sunday to go for a swim and also to purchase wine from the local vintners.

Food and Lodging

Haus Attila, Strandplatz 1, A-7141 Podersdorf (tel. 02177/2415), the best place to stay (of a modest lot), receives visitors from April to October. Its light-grained balconies are concealed by a brake of trees. Each of the 21 bedrooms has a private bath or shower, and accommodations are clean, comfortable, and filled with utilitarian furniture. With half board included, the daily rate ranges from 480 AS ($35) to 520 AS ($37.75) per person daily. In the basement is a well-stocked wine cellar where a member of the Karner family might take you for a look.

An excellent two-star choice, **Seehotel Herlinde,** Quergasse 9, A-7141 Podersdorf (tel. 02177/2445), is a holiday hotel on the beach of Lake Neusiedl away from the main highway. The hotel rents 40 bedrooms, each with its own balcony; the best ones open onto views of the lake. Bed-and-breakfast costs range from 250 AS ($18.25) to 300 AS ($21.75) per person daily. The food and wine are plentiful, the latter often enjoyed on a 200-seat terrace.

Gasthof Seewirt, Strandplatz 1, A-7141 Podersdorf (tel. 02177/2415). Standing close to the previously recommended Haus Attila (it shares the same phone number), this 16-room hotel sits at the edge of the lake, with a wide expanse of marshland close by. The bedrooms are comfortable, and the public rooms include a rustically modern restaurant, a café terrace, and a sauna. The rates range from 350 AS ($25.50) to 375 AS ($27.25) per person for bed-and-breakfast. The hotel is open February through November.

KITTSEE

On to the north in the direction of Bratislava, Czechoslovakia, is the Austrian border town of Kittsee, where a Count Esterházy (of the same family that ruled in Eisenstadt and sponsored the composer Haydn there) had a baroque castle erected, beginning in 1730. Toward the southeast sector of the village is the Czechoslovakian frontier.

En route to Bratislava is a colony of residential houses with a startling name for this area—**Chicago.** It was named by an emigré who likened the pace of construction to what he'd known as a laborer in Chicago, Illinois.

NEUSIEDL AM SEE

At the top of Lake Neusiedl on the north bank lies this stopover, which is likely to be crowded on summer weekends. Water sports prevail here, and sailboats can be rented. The parish church, in the Gothic style, is noted for its "ship pulpit." A watchtower from the Middle Ages still stands guard over the town, although it's no longer manned. Many vineyards cover the nearby acreage. If you plan to be here on a weekend in summer, I advise you to make a reservation ahead.

Food and Lodging

Hotel Wende, Seestrasse 40, A-7100 Neusiedl am See (tel. 02167/8111). Its walls are dotted with maps of Burgenland, and many menu items in its dining room are recipes from the region. The place is actually a complex of three sprawling buildings, interconnected by rambling corridors that open into conference rooms. Set at the edge of town, on the road leading to the water, the hotel is almost a village unto itself. The aura proves to be one of clean but slightly sterile propriety, although the indoor pool and sauna, along with the glass-enclosed clubhouse, add notes of diversion. The well-known in-house restaurant offers such dishes as wild game in season, rumpsteak Hotel Wende, several pork specialties, veal piccata, and roast beef Esterházy style. Full meals cost from 380 AS ($27.75). The hotel has 105 well-furnished bedrooms, each with private bath or shower. Charges range from 470 AS ($34.25) to 550 AS ($60) per person daily, breakfast included. Both the hotel and restaurant are closed for the last week in January and the first week in February.

Gasthof zur Traube, Hauptplatz 9, A-7100 Neusiedl am See (tel. 02167/423), stands on the bustling main street of town. The pleasant restaurant on the ground floor is illuminated with leaded-glass windows and filled with country trim and wrought-iron table dividers. You can stop in for a meal or else book one of the cozy upstairs bedrooms for an overnight stay (you have to register at the bar in back of the restaurant). Franz Rittsteuer and his family are the owners. With breakfast included, their prices go from 240 AS ($17.50) to 280 AS ($20.25) per person daily. The place is small, with only 20 beds. Seven of the bedrooms have private showers.

The best food at the resort is served at **Barth-Stuben,** Franz-Liszt-Strasse 37 (tel. 02167/2625). The owner, a truly charming man named Gerhard Garth, works as hard as his staff, and does so daily except Monday from 11am to 11pm. In the center of the resort, the restaurant has a décor of art nouveau swirls designed to attract the vacationing Viennese on an outing. The predominant color is pink, with lots of light-grained wood. The food is original, often invented by the owner-chef himself. It includes a few nouvelle Hungarian dishes as well as time-tested Austrian favorites, including zander filet with Riesling, filet of eel with garlic sauce, Hungarian fish soup, and tafelspitz. The fish comes from a nearby lake. Meals range in price from 100 AS ($7.25) to 375 AS ($27.25). The restaurant is closed for two weeks in November and for two weeks in both January and February.

PURBACH AM SEE

If you take the road south from the area around the northern tip of Lake Neusiedl, your first stopover might be in this little resort village, which has some decent accommodations. Purbach is also a market town, and you can buy Burgenland wine in the shops. Some of the town walls, built against invading Turks, still stand.

Food and Lodging

Am Spitz, A-7083 Purbach am See (tel. 02683/5519). The main building of this 17-room hotel has baroque embellishments rounding out the angular sections of the frontal gable. When you enter you'll see stucco detailing in the rounded columns of the restaurant and bar area, lots of weathered timbers and ceiling beams, and a scattering of antiques. The Hölzl-Schwarz family are your hosts here, charging 400 AS ($29) to 420 AS ($30.50) per person daily for half board. Many of the accommodations have panoramic views of the lake, and they also contain private showers. The adjoining restaurant, rustically decorated, is one of the best places in the region for Burgenland cookery. Specialties include chicken soup, bacon salad, lamb cutlets with potatoes and spinach, and an array of local wines. À la carte meals cost from 150 AS ($11) to 320 AS ($23.25). Reservations are suggested, and the gasthof receives guests from March to December.

Nikolauszeche (tel. 02683/5514). In a niche high above the rest of the baroque décor, someone has placed a statue that looks more like the Madonna than the namesake of this establishment, Saint Nicholas. The food, however, is authentically regional, attracting a wide cross section of Austrians, many of whom travel from Vienna. Once here, from 12:30 to 3pm and 6 to 11pm, they can order the rich bouillon or cabbage soup, the Hungarian fogosch, and the chef's special ham crêpes, as well as select from a well-chosen wine list. Renaissance guitar music is played. If you seek privacy and quiet, you can gravitate to an interior courtyard, finding a quiet corner for an intimate conversation. The restaurant is closed Tuesday, and à la carte meals cost from 400 AS ($29). Reservations are suggested.

Leaving Purbach and taking the road south toward Eisenstadt, you can veer off on a secondary road southeast along the lakeshore to our final destinations, which are also provided with limited accommodations. The first stopover is at—

RUST

This colorfully named summer resort—famous for its stork nests built on chimneys throughout the town—stands right on the lakeshore. The heart of Rust is an old-town section that is well preserved and immaculately ready for your inspection. Its walls were built in 1614 as protection against the Turks.

The little resort has a gemütlich atmosphere, especially on weekends. Summers are often hot, and the water of the lake is warm. Sailboats and Windsurfers are rented for touring the Neusiedler See, where the shallowness of the waters alleviates fear of drowning, except for small children.

Rust might be called the capital of the Burgenland lake district. The town lies in a rich setting of vineyards that produce the Burgenlander grape. If it's available, you should try the Blaufränkisch, a red wine that seems to be consumed entirely either locally or by the Viennese, who flock to the area and often return home with bottles of the vintage of the region. Sometimes you can go right up to the door of a vintner's farmhouse, especially if a green bough is displayed, and sample wine and buy it on the spot, as at a heurige.

On my last visit during August, the taverns in the town had lively gypsy music. Some local residents, when the wine is in their blood, like to dance in regional costume wearing high boots. You're left with the distinct impression that you're in Hungary.

Food and Lodging

Seehotel Rust, A-7071 Rust (tel. 02685/381), one of the most attractive hotels in the lake district, is well designed and modern, set on a grassy lawn at the edge of the lake. It has an appealing series of connected balconies, rounded towers that look vaguely medieval, and a series of recessed loggias set into the slope of the roofline. The ceiling beams of the big-windowed restaurant sweep up toward the central lighting fixture, while a series of floor-mounted lamps curve over many of the tablecloths like spokes of an umbrella. Food items include tafelspitz with chive sauce, calves' brains with a honey vinegar, watercress soup, and sole meunière. Meals in the restaurant begin at 300 AS ($21.75). A gypsy band sometimes provides the evening's entertainment.

The hotel rents 89 pleasantly furnished bedrooms, each equipped with private shower or bath. With half board included, per-person rates go from 720 AS ($52.25) to 780 AS ($56.75) daily. On the premises of the hotel are an indoor swimming pool, a sauna, two tennis courts, and a bar area.

Hotel-Restaurant Sifkovits, Am Seekanal 8, A-7071 Rust (tel. 02685/276), offers a concrete-and-stucco façade fashioned into sloping rows of well-planted balconies. An older wing has a format of red-tile roofs and big windows (which sometimes cover entire walls). The bedrooms get a lot of sun and are comfortably streamlined. Other facilities include a sauna, an exercise room, a café, a sun terrace, and outdoor tennis courts. Rooms range from 250 AS ($18.25) to 520 AS ($37.75) per person; prices, of course, depend on the season and the accommodation. Food is served daily from 11am to 10pm.

MÖRBISCH

Our final stopover along the lake, near the Hungarian border, is this charming little, typical Burgenlander lakeside hamlet. There are both a small bathing beach and mineral springs, the water of which is bottled for sale. The town fills up in August, when the lakeside outdoor theater presents operettas such as *The Merry Widow*. Wine-tasting festivals are also a Mörbisch feature, especially on Sunday, when the Viennese drive here from the capital.

Food and Lodging

Hotel Steiner, Hauerstrasse 1, A-7072 Mörbisch (tel. 02685/8444), has an attractive cream-colored façade with one recessed balcony covered with flowers. With 50 rooms, the place is big enough to usually have an empty accommodation, but quiet enough to afford relaxing comfort. The Steiner family, your hosts, rent rustically modern bedrooms, and have such facilities as a sauna, a heated swimming pool, and an appealing restaurant. From April until the end of November, they charge 450 AS ($32.75) to 500 AS ($36.25) daily for a single, 780 AS ($56.75) to 1,000 AS ($72.75) for a double, with half board included. Each room has a private bath or shower.

3. Forchtenstein

After leaving the lake district, you can head south from Eisenstadt toward the narrow "waistline" of the province, a small corridor between north and south Burgenland created when Ödenburg, then the capital (now the Hungarian far-western frontier city of Sopron), voted to remain with the fatherland and be ruled by Budapest. Many of the people of Forchtenstein grow fruit.

AREA SIGHTS
Visitors come here chiefly to look at **Forchtenstein Castle** (tel. 02626/81212), lying in Burgenland, 9 miles southeast of Wiener Neustadt in Lower Austria. From a belvedere here you can see as far as the Great Plain of Hungary. The castle was constructed on a rock on orders of the counts of Mattersdorf in the 13th century. The Esterházy family had it greatly expanded around 1636.

The castle saw action in the Turkish sieges of Austria, both in 1529 and in 1683. You can see a handsome collection of armory here, some captured from the fleeing Turks. But they didn't all get away. Turkish prisoners carved out of the rock the castle cistern, more than 450 feet deep. There's also a display of "memorabilia of the hunt," as it is described here.

Admission is 35 AS ($2.50), and the castle is open daily from April to October, 8 to 11:30am and 1 to 4pm. In March and November, it is open only on Saturday and Sunday (same hours). The rest of the year, it is closed.

FOOD AND LODGING
A long, grangelike building, **Gasthof Sauerzapf,** Rosalienstrasse 9, A-7212 Forchtenstein (tel. 02626/81217), has two stories of weathered stucco, renovated windows, and a roofline that's red on one side and black on the other. The updated interior is cozy and appealing, albeit simple, and is kept immaculate. Franz Sauerzapf and his family charge 175 AS ($12.75) to 195 AS ($14.25) per person daily for half board. Rooms are modestly furnished, and reasonably comfortable for the price. The restaurant serves good food and an array of local wines.

Gasthof Wutzlhofer, Rosalia 12, A-7212 Forchtenstein (tel. 02626/81253). The view from the rooms of this family-run stucco guesthouse encompasses all of the valley and many square miles of forested hills.

For his 17 beds, Herbert Wutzhofer, the owner, charges from 180 AS ($13) daily for a single and from 320 AS ($23.25) for a double, with breakfast included. This place is one of the bargains of the area—good food and comfort—and it remains open year round. Many guests prefer to take half board, enjoying the hearty regional cooking.

Reisner, Hauptstrasse 141 (tel. 02626/63139), serves garden-fresh vegetables in a rustic setting. The main dining room is perfectly acceptable, but my favorite is the cozily rustic stüberl, which seems to be preferred by the locals as well. Besides the especially good steaks, you might enjoy trout filet served with a savory ragoût of tomatoes, zucchini, potatoes, and basil, or else sautéed sweetbreads with beans and a yogurt-vinaigrette dressing over cabbage. À la carte meals range from 120 AS ($8.75) to 350 AS ($25.50). Hours are 11:30am to 3pm and 6 to 10pm daily except Wednesday. Reservations are suggested.

4. Bernstein

This little market village lying in the Valley of the Tauchen is known for its castle, which provides the most dramatic accommodations in Burgenland (see below). Bernstein is also known for its serpentine stone, a jet-green stone sometimes called Bernstein jade. Workers polish the stone here, and it can be purchased in the shops, although much of it is shipped around the world. It's shaped into ornaments of many different types.

WHERE TO STAY

Rich in history, **Hotel Burg Bernstein,** A-7434 Bernstein (tel. 03354/220), is in a castle initially constructed during the era of Charlemagne (around A.D. 800). Most of the castle you see today, however, was built in the 13th century, with thick stone walls and towers, plus small windows along the outer walls. The owners were so preoccupied with defending themselves from invaders that they even surrounded the 395-foot-deep well with a defensive stone tower.

In 1953 this piece of history was converted into a 10-room hotel and furnished with antiques appropriate to its status as a historic monument. Its dining room has a stone floor and an ornate baroque ceiling. Most of the bedrooms are baronial and are filled with beautiful pieces of craftsmanship.

The castle is said to have a resident ghost. Its long-ago former owner, a medieval lord, Graf Uilaky, reportedly returned home from a siege somewhere in Hungary, only to discover his wife in bed with one of the male servants. He slashed out the heart of the hapless servant, but for his adulterous wife he showed he was no women's liberation advocate. He sealed her up in her bedroom and left her there to die of thirst and starvation. Her "ghost" is still reported to roam the place on dark nights.

The bed-and-breakfast rate for a room with private bath is 600 AS ($43.50) per person nightly, or else you can stay here on full-board terms, costing from 760 AS ($55.25).

---

5. Bad Tatzmannsdorf

The best-known spa of the province, 9 miles south of Bernstein, lies in a heavily forested valley. Its springs and baths, said to be beneficial both for certain cardiac conditions and for female ailments, have been used for centuries. Many Hungarians from Budapest spent part of their summers here in earlier times.

Naturally, the resort has a Kurpark, where on a summer evening there's likely to be entertainment. There's also an open-air museum containing many ancient structures moved from the surrounding valley.

FOOD AND LODGING

Constructed in a modern format, **Parkhotel,** A-7431 Bad Tatzmannsdorf (tel. 03353/8220), has several different beige-and-white sections connected by a flowering garden. Many of the rooms have private balconies, which open out of the comfortable and pleasing sleeping areas (lots of paneling and tasteful furniture). The public rooms boast built-in banquettes near big windows, while an outdoor café affords a relaxing getaway on a warm day. The Anderle family are the distinguished owners of this hotel, charging 455 AS ($33) to 520 AS ($37.75) daily for a single and 775 AS ($56.25) to 925 AS ($67.25) for a double, with breakfast, taxes, and service included. The hotel rents 26 singles, 24 doubles, and four apartments.

Hotel zum Kastell, Josef-Haydnplatz 6, A-7431 Bad Tatzmannsdorf (tel. 03353/8428). On a summer day, guests at this 30-room hotel gather on the sun terrace or on one of the private balconies attached to their bedrooms. Seats in the dignified restaurant are usually fashioned in banquette format around circular tables, with cluster chandeliers hanging near the arched windows. A less formal restaurant is cozily outfitted with terra-cotta tiles and upholstered wooden chairs. Many of the summertime guests have moved in for a week or more as part of their annual vacations, but if you want to stay for just a night, rates run from 440 AS ($32) to 480 AS ($35) per person daily. The hotel offers 30 bedrooms, each with private bath or shower. Guests are received from March to November.

Hotel-Pension Sonnenhof, Parkstrasse 33, A-7431 Bad Tatzmannsdorf (tel. 03353/417), is a big-windowed, balconied, 25-bed hotel set on a hillside with a view of several farmhouses in the distance. Janisch Albert is the kindly owner of this well-maintained establishment. Guests can stay here on half-board terms, ranging from 375 AS ($27.25) to 415 AS ($30.25) daily for a single and 630 AS ($45.75) to 730 AS ($53) for a double.

---

6. Heiligenkreuz

If you're looking for a tranquil hideaway, look no further! No one will ever find you in this, one of the most remote places I've recommended (not to be confused with Heiligenkreuz, the Cistercian abbey west of Baden). This little town lies in the far-southern tip of Burgenland, right next to the Hungarian frontier, near the confluence of the Raab and the Lafnitz. There are many thatch houses in the area, which is known and treasured by the Austrians. If a North American turns up here, it's considered a rarity.

Heiligenkreuz is near a battle site where General Montecuccoli defeated the Turks in 1664, a fact honored by Rainer Maria Rilke, the noted German lyric poet, in *The Cornets*.

From this peaceful town you can head for nearby Hungary or Yugoslavia, although a visa is required to enter either country.

FOOD AND LODGING

Gasthof Edith Gibiser, A-7561 Heiligenkreuz 81 (tel. 03325/216), is for those who'd like to soak up some authentic Burgenland atmosphere. Edith Gibiser rents 40 beds in 13 rooms, each with private bath or shower, as well as five cozy thatch-roofed cottages in the garden. All the rooms are comfortably and attractively furnished. Singles range from 280 AS ($20.25) to 400 AS ($29) daily, doubles from 220 AS ($16) to 360 AS ($26.25) per person, breakfast included. For half board, charges go from 380 AS ($27.75) to 420 AS ($30.50) per person. The restaurant is well known for its Pannonian specialties, including Hungarian cabbage soup, Burgenländische garlic soup, genuine Hungarian goose liver, "gypsy meat," and outstanding desserts, including the house special, Somlauer Nockerl. Meals cost from 75 AS ($5.50) to 340 AS ($24.75), and are served daily from 11am to 10pm except Monday in the off-season (November to May).

SALZBURG

A baroque city on the banks of the Salzach River, Salzburg, set against a mountain backdrop, is the beautiful capital of the Austrian province of Land Salzburg. The city and the river were so named because many of the early residents earned their living in the salt mines in the region. The site of Salzburg was once the Roman town of Juvavum.

This "heart of the heart of Europe" is the city of Mozart, who was born here in 1756. The composer's association with the city beefs up tourism even today, providing major revenue to the area.

This fact carries a certain irony, because Mozart wasn't all that appreciated in Salzburg in his lifetime. But since his death just 200 years ago, his image seems to be everywhere. A square bears his name. A statue in its center honors him. A music academy is named for him. And of course his music dominates the Salzburg Festival. Too bad he couldn't have been more honored when he was still around to enjoy it. He died in Vienna on December 5, 1791, and the sad truth is that the body of the 35-year-old musical genius was carried in a pauper's hearse to a common grave in the cemetery of St. Marx in the Austrian capital.

The Old Town lies on the left bank of the river, where a monastery and bishopric were founded in 700. From that start, Salzburg grew in power and prestige, becoming an archbishopric in 798. In the heyday of the prince-archbishops, the city became known as the "German Rome." The little province known as **Land Salzburg,** of which Salzburg is the capital, still occupies much the same space in the mountains of west-central Austria as shown on maps of the Middle Ages designated as "church lands." It was in the Holy Roman Empire, a part of Germany until it was joined to Austria in 1816 after the Congress of Vienna.

Salzburg is a city of 17th- and 18th-century houses, and for the most part has a worldwide reputation for the grandeur of its architecture. Much of that work was done by those masters of the baroque, Fischer von Erlach and Lukas von Hildebrandt.

As well as being the scene of the celebrated Salzburg Festival, this is where Max Reinhardt staged Hugo von Hoffmannsthal's adaptation of the morality play *Everyman* (*Jedermann,* in German) in 1920, an event that has become a tradition.

Salzburg lies a short distance from the Austrian–West German frontier, so it's convenient for exploring many of the nearby attractions of Bavaria (see *Frommer's Germany*). On the northern slopes of the Alps, the city is at the intersection of traditional European trade routes and is well served today by air, autobahn, and rail.

AN ORIENTATION

Most visitors head for the **Altstadt,** or Old Town, which lies on the left bank of the Salzach, that part stretching from the river to the Mönchsberg. This is a section of narrow streets (many from the Middle Ages) and slender houses. This part of Salzburg is in complete contrast with the town constructed by the prince-archbishops, which lies between the Neutor and the Neugebäude. The bishops created a town of magnificent buildings and large, airy squares.

The heart of the old section, on the left bank of the Salzach, is the **Residenzplatz,** with its splendid Unterberg marble baroque fountain.

The newer part of town is on the right bank of the Salzach, below the **Kapuzinerberg,** which is the right-bank counterpart of the Mönchsberg. This peak rises 2,090 feet, and is a lovely woodland.

Mönchsberg itself, to the west of Hohensalzburg, is a mountain ridge slightly less than two miles long. It rises over the old town.

---

1. Fast Facts

Here is a collection of data to help ease your adjustment into the practicalities of life in the city of Mozart.

AMERICAN EXPRESS: The office, located at Mozartplatz 5 (tel. 0662/84-25-01), is open Monday to Friday from 9am to 5:30pm and on Saturday from 9am to noon.

BANKS: The city's banks are open Monday to Friday from 8am to noon and 2 to 4:30pm. Money can be exchanged at the mail railway station daily from 7am to 10pm and at the airport from 9am to 4pm.

CAR BREAKDOWN SERVICE: Try SAMTC (Salzburg Automobile Service), Alpenstrasse 102 (tel. 0662/20-5-01), or ARBO (Motorists Association), Münchner Bundesstrasse 102 (0662/33-6-01), day or night. The emergency number is 120.

CONSULATE: The United States has a consulate office in Salzburg. It's the U.S. Consul General, Giselakai 51 (tel. 0662/28-6-01). The office is open Monday to Friday from 9 to 11am and 2 to 4pm.

EMERGENCY NUMBERS: Information on various problems or answers to emergency needs are available by telephone as follows: police—133; fire—122; ambulance—144.

LAUNDRY: If you need to wash your clothes, you'll find laundrettes available opposite the main rail station. They are Constructa, Kaiserschützenstrasse 10 (tel. 0662/76-2-53), and Westinghouse, Kaiserschützenstrasse 18 (tel. 0662/733-90).

MEDICAL HELP: For information on doctors, specialists, and dentists, call Ärztekammer für Salzburg, Schrannengasse 2 (tel. 0662/71-3-72 or 0662/71-3-28). The Medical Emergency Center, Paris-Lodron-Strasse 8A (tel. 0662/141), is open from 7am Saturday to 7am Monday. It is also open on public holidays.

PHARMACIES: These are open Monday to Friday from 8am to 12:30pm and 2:30 to 6pm, on Saturday from 8am to noon. For night or Sunday service, shops display a sign giving the address of the nearest pharmacy open.

POSTAL CODES: Salzburg, A-5020; Anif, A-5081; and Bergheim, A-5101.

POST OFFICES: The main post office is at Residenzplatz 9 (tel. 0662/84-41-21). The post office at the main railway station is open all year 24 hours a day.

RAILWAY STATION: The main station is at Südtiroler Platz (tel. 0662/71-5-41).

TELEPHONE AREA CODES: The area code for Salzburg is 0662. For Anif, it is 06246, and for Bergheim, 0662 (the same as Salzburg).

TOURIST INFORMATION: For information about Salzburg or Land Salzburg, consult the following offices: the Salzburg City Tourist Office, Auerspergstrasse 7, A-5020 Salzburg (tel. 0662/8072), and the Salzburg State Board of Tourism, Alpenstrasse 96, A-5033 Salzburg (tel. 0662/205-06).

TRANSPORTATION: A quick, comfortable service is provided by **city buses** through the center of the city from the Nonntal car park to Sigsmundsplatz, the city-center car park. Service is Monday to Friday from 9am to 6pm, on Saturday from 9am to noon. Fares are 17 AS ($1.25) for one ride for an adult, 8.50 AS (60¢) for children.

Reduced-fare tickets may be purchased at the local railway station (opposite the main railway station), at the ticket counter of the cable train up to Hohensalzburg Fortress, from conductors of the lift to Mönchsberg, and in 91 tobacco shops in the city that are specially marked. These tickets are sold in blocks of 5 and 10 at a reduction of 20% off the regular fare.

For information on transportation, call 0662/71-2-10. Be warned: Buses stop running at 11pm.

You'll find **taxi ranks** scattered at key points all over the city center and in the suburbs. The Salzburg Funktaxi-Vereinigung (radio taxis) office is at Rainerstrasse 2 (tel. 8111). To order a taxi in advance, call 74-4-00.

There are **horse-drawn cabs** (fiakers) at Residenzplatz. Four persons pay 320 AS ($23.25) for a half-hour ride, 620 AS ($45) for an hour's jaunt.

---

2. Where to Stay

Some of the finest accommodations, particularly the schloss hotels or even converted farmhouse pensions, lie on the outskirts of Salzburg, within an easy drive of the city. However, for the most part they're suitable only for motorists. If you don't

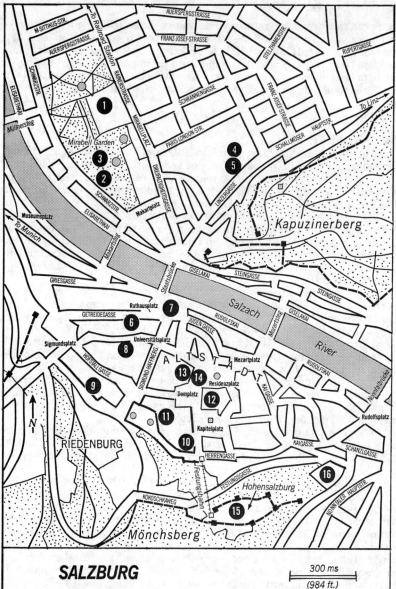

SALZBURG

300 ms
(984 ft.)

KEY TO NUMBERED SITES

1. Mirabell Palace
2. Mozarteum
3. Magic Flute House
4. Friedhof St. Sebastian
5. St. Sebastian's Church
6. Mozart Museum
7. Altes Rathaus
8. Kollegienkirche
9. Festival Hall
10. St. Petersfriedhof
11. Stiftskirche St. Peter
12. Salzburg Cathedral
13. Residenz
14. Franciscan Church
15. Hohensalzburg Fortress
16. Nonnberg Convent

have a car, then you may want to consider one of the hostelries right in the city—within walking distance of all the major sightseeing attractions. If you're driving, you may want to read Chapter VIII before selecting a hotel. Since the hotels of Salzburg are often very crowded in summer (and are impossibly booked during the Salzburg Festival in August), many travel-wise Europeans reserve one of the less expensive accommodations in Land Salzburg, from which they then drive into Salzburg.

THE DELUXE CHOICES

The award as the finest hotel in Salzburg goes to **Goldener Hirsch**, Getreidegasse 37, A-5020 Salzburg (tel. 0662/84-85-11). It's so steeped in legend and history that the mention of its name in Austria evokes instant recognition. It sits in an enviable position in the Old Town, a few buildings from Mozart's birthplace. The 71-room hotel is composed of four medieval town houses, three of which are joined together in an intimate labyrinth of rustically elegant hallways and staircases. A fourth, called "The Coppersmith's House," is across the street, containing 17 charming and elegant rooms, each with a marble bathroom and lots of space. Sections of the thick walls date from 1407 and required extensive renovations after Count Emmanuel and Countess Harriet von Walderdorff took over the buildings after World War II.

Today their son, Johannes, is the alert general manager, whose clientele is considerably more sophisticated than it was when the place was set up as an inn in 1564. The hotel is built on a small scale, yet it absolutely reeks of patrician elegance, which is enhanced by the superb service of the staff, many of whom are dressed in gray and forest-green Styrian suits. The décor throughout the hotel, from its huntsman-style bar to its impeccably elegant restaurant (see my dining recommendation), includes alpine antiques, stag horns, and well-crafted wood and stone detailing.

This is the kind of hotel where you can dial a staff member for virtually anything from flowers to theater tickets. If you arrive by car, you can double-park in front of the Getreidegasse entrance or at the Sigmundsplatz entrance, and a staff member will take your vehicle to the hotel's garage.

Rooms are beautifully furnished and maintained, costing 1,600 AS ($116.25) to 3,100 AS ($225.25) daily for a single, 3,100 AS ($225.25) to 4,300 AS ($312.50) for a double. All tariffs are slightly higher at the time of the Salzburg Festival.

Salzburg Sheraton Hotel, Auerspergstrasse 4, A-5020 Salzburg (tel. 0662/79-32-10), one of the crown jewels in the Sheraton chain, opened in 1984 in a desirable location about 10 pedestrian minutes from the Mozartplatz. An older hotel was demolished to make room for the dignified new structure, half of whose 165 bedrooms, including 21 suites, look out over the formal Mirabell Park. The Austrian architect who designed this place took pains to incorporate it into its 19th-century neighborhood, specifying that the exterior be capped with a mansard roof and that the casement windows be ringed with elaborate trim. As you enter, the lobby opens to reveal a plushly intimate piano bar outfitted in alluring designs of burnished brass, richly grained wood, art nouveau trappings, and sun-flooded views of the garden. What might be the best-valued luncheon buffet in town is served in the cream-and-crystal Mirabell Room, which is rapidly earning its place among the best restaurants of Salzburg. A less formal bistro offers daily specials, wine, and beer in wood-lined cubbyholes illuminated with iron street lamps.

Each bedroom contains its own private bath, with floor-to-ceiling tiles designed by Valentino, built-in headboards, concealed minibar, thick wall-to-wall carpeting, color TV, radio, direct-dial phone, and air conditioning. The exclusive Junior, Queen, and President suites have silky wallpaper and are filled with elegant copies of Biedermeier furniture.

The Sheraton is the largest five-star hotel in Salzburg, but because of its personalized service you feel at home. The hotel is connected by a corridor to the city swimming pool, which has a sauna. Winter rates range from 1,300 AS ($94.50) to 2,100 AS ($152.75) daily for a single, from 1,800 AS ($130.75) to 2,600 AS ($189) for a double. Summer prices are 2,000 AS ($145.50) to 2,600 AS ($189) for a single, 2,500 AS ($181.75) to 3,100 AS ($225.25) for a double. Tariffs increase at festival time, but a buffet breakfast is always included.

Hotel Bristol, Makartplatz 4, A-5020 Salzburg (tel. 0662/73-5-57), is a traditional five-star hotel consisting of 20 single rooms, 50 double or twin rooms, and 10 apartments. Though built in 1890, it has been renovated many times since to keep it up to international deluxe hotel standards. It lies close to the Mirabell Gardens, encompassing a view of Hohensalzburg Fortress. The bedrooms range from upper-class functional to opulently baroque, with embellished ceilings and crystal chandeliers. Rates for a single range from 1,960 AS ($142.50) to 2,700 AS ($196.25) daily, with doubles going for 2,300 AS ($167.25) to 5,000 AS ($363.50); tariffs include breakfast, service, and tax. The hotel's restaurants include the Polo Lounge, seating 40, as well as the Crystal Room, seating 80. The piano bar has terrazzo floors and Oriental rugs, concealed lighting, paneling, and discreet music. Comfortably upholstered armchairs in the public rooms afford a vantage point for viewing the large paintings, some of which look as if they belong in a museum. The hotel receives guests from April to December.

Hotel Schloss Mönchstein, Mönchsberg Park 26, A-5020 Salzburg (tel. 0662/848555), a Teutonic-style manor house, stands on top of a rocky outcropping above the center of Salzburg. Because of its height it affords panoramic views of the city, which you might enjoy from one of the well-appointed salons after a day of sightseeing. The ochre exterior is a pastiche of watchtowers, step gables, and big windows, some of which curve in the direction of the elaborate gardens.

Also on the premises are an elegant restaurant and bar, Paris Lodron, with leaded-glass windows, a tennis court, a wedding chapel, and a garden terrace overlooking a statue of Apollo in the private park.

Each of the 17 bedrooms has a private bath, direct-dial phone, color TV, radio, minibar, and hairdryer; each suite has an electronic safe. Singles range from 1,600 AS ($116.25) to 2,200 AS ($160), while doubles go from 1,800 AS ($130.75) to 3,600 AS ($261.75), with breakfast included. Half board costs 600 AS ($43.50) per person per day.

Hotel Kobenzl, Gaisberg 11, A-5020 Salzburg (tel. 0662/217760), is a country-style inn on Gaisberg mountain, about 7 miles from the heart of Salzburg. If your intention is to stay outside the crowded city, this is a good choice. Its exterior has half-timbered detailing, fieldstone masonry, big windows with a panoramic view over Salzburg, and weathered wooden balconies. The air here is mountain pure, the amenities are top-notch, and the décor is tasteful and attractive, with use of antiques. The 36 bedrooms contain baths, TVs, safes, phones, clock radios, and hairdryers. Charges, which include a buffet breakfast, are 1,600 AS ($116.25) to 2,400 AS ($174.50) daily for a single, 2,400 AS ($174.50) to 4,000 AS ($290.75) for a double, tax and service included.

The Herzog family prepares a savory cuisine, which has appealed to everybody from Richard Nixon to Margaret Thatcher to Arnold Schwarzenegger, plus many other celebrities whose patronage is attested by autographed pictures in the lobby and nameplates on many of the chairs in the dining room. À la carte meals are also served on the terrace, from which you have a sweeping view of snow-capped peaks across the valley of the Salzach River and the forests. Terrace dining is not confined just to good weather, as picture windows and awnings can be quickly placed if necessary. The hotel has a heated indoor pool with a masseuse, a sauna, and a fitness room. A public bus runs to and from the city. The hotel is open from March to the end of October.

Hotel Österreichischer Hof, Schwarzstrasse 5-7, A-5020 Salzburg(tel. 0662/7-25-41), is a palatial white hotel on the right bank of the Salzach. It has a magnificent view across the water to the Old Town, plus an interior décor of wrought iron, grand staircases, potted palms, Biedermeier and Victorian antiques, big windows, and Oriental rugs. Built about a century ago, it has attracted a clientele that has numbered some of the most powerful figures in Europe.

Among the restaurants inside, my favorite is the wood-paneled Zirbelzimmer, whose craftsmanship is admirable. Other facilities include a piano bar and a garden terrace. The 120 well-furnished rooms range in price from 1,750 AS ($127.25) daily for a single, from 1,750 AS ($127.25) to 3,600 AS ($261.75) for a double.

Haus Ingeborg, Sonnleitenweg 9, A-5020 Salzburg (tel. 0662/21-7-90). This small and luxurious alpine chalet in a secluded area northeast of the Old Town has a slope-roofed façade of reddish-colored wood and white stucco. The interior is outfitted with well-crafted details such as exposed ceiling beams, a riserless staircase of hardwood, and a geometrically paneled ceiling. Some of the bedrooms are furnished with special accessories such as baronial beds. Each of the 12 handsomely equipped and furnished bedrooms has a private bath. Singles rent for 1,800 AS ($130.75) daily, with doubles costing 3,300 AS ($240) to 3,600 AS ($261.75). Your hosts, the Oberrauch family, open the hotel from March to October and in December and January. They have an outdoor swimming pool and a sauna.

Schloss Kavalierhaus Klessheim, A-5071 Siezenheim (Salzburg) (tel. 0662/85-08-77), one of the most unusual and special retreats of Austria, was originally a neoclassical villa built for the brother of Franz Joseph in 1882. After Hitler took over Austria, he ordered that the palace be fixed up for him as a private retreat, perhaps intending to journey over from Berchtesgaden, but those plans never worked out. Later, the place was used as a vacation retreat for top-ranking military brass during the American occupation of Austria. Since 1957 it has been a beautiful castle hotel, and it has received, among others, former presidents Richard Nixon and Gerald Ford. Its 21 bedrooms are rented only in July and August, at a cost of 450 AS ($32.75) to 900 AS ($65.50) per person daily, depending on the plumbing. The rest of the year, the hotel is used as a conference and banqueting center, and is the headquarters of the largest hotel training school in the region. The location is near the airport, about 2½ miles northwest of the center of Salzburg.

FIRST-CLASS HOTELS

At the foot of Gaisberg stands the **Hotel Fondachhof,** Gaisbergstrasse 46, A-5020 Salzburg-Parsch (tel. 0662/20-9-06), one of the most pleasing hotels in the area. Built 200 years ago as a baroque manor house with mustard-yellow walls and a steep tile roof, it was made into a 28-room hotel in 1950, and today affords secluded lodgings to guests from April to October. Many of the bedrooms look down on a gazebo set close to the flowered sun terrace. On the grounds are sculpted fountains, a heated swimming pool, and a sauna. Many of the accommodations are furnished with antiques, while the architectural detailing inside includes stone columns and decorative ceramic stoves. Singles range from 1,000 AS ($72.75) to 1,400 AS ($101.75) daily, doubles from 1,950 AS ($141.75) to 3,000 AS ($218), breakfast included. Prices depend on the season.

Maria Theresien Schlössl, Morzgerstrasse 87, A-5020 Salzburg-Hellbrunn (tel. 0662/84-12-44). An archbishop ordered this castle built in the early part of the 17th century, and there's still a vague ecclesiastical feeling in the proportions of the lemon-colored baroque façade with curved gables. The place became a hotel about three years before Hitler annexed Austria. Lying 2½ miles from the center on the town's southern outskirts, it is more a manorial home than an actual castle; in fact, it was once an outbuilding of the neighboring Hellbrunn Palace. The hotel is set in spacious parklike grounds, through which guests wander freely, inspecting the well-manicured gardens. Of the 16 bedrooms, 13 have private baths. Singles cost from 1,600 AS ($116.25) daily, with doubles going for 2,800 AS ($203.50). The helpful staff serves good food, including Austrian, German, and French specialties.

Hotel Kasererhof, Alpenstrasse 6, A-5020 Salzburg (tel. 0662/2-12-65), is composed of two mustard-colored baroque buildings connected by a low passageway. The main building was constructed in 1642 on land that had previously belonged to an archbishop. A nearby chapel, which is part of the hotel, was erected 35 years later, and is still filled with museum-caliber pieces from the 18th century. The public rooms are outfitted with cozily contrasting patterns of flowered upholstery over Oriental rugs. The Kasererhof is open all year except in February. It rents 51 comfortably furnished bedrooms, each with private bath or shower. Rates range from 1,200 AS ($87.25) daily for a single, with doubles peaking at 4,200 AS ($305.25), including a buffet breakfast. Less expensive doubles are rented for 3,000 AS ($218). The hotel also has a good restaurant, open daily except Saturday and Sunday.

Hotel Winkler, Franz-Josef-Strasse 7-9, A-5020 Salzburg (tel. 0662/7-35-13), can be recognized by the huge sign stretching above the honeycomb concrete of its rectangular façade. The 103 contemporary bedrooms are outfitted with discreet colors, big windows, and such romantic touches as gilded headboards in baroque patterns. Each of the bedrooms has a private bath or shower. Singles range from 1,100 AS ($80) to 1,800 AS ($130.75) daily, doubles from 2,000 AS ($145.50) to 3,300 AS ($240). The hotel is located in a commercial district outside the Old Town, near many 19th-century buildings. It accepts tour groups, who have their own dining room.

Bayerischer Hof, Kaiserschützenstrasse 1, A-5020 Salzburg (tel. 0662/54-1-70). Set within a two-block walk of the railway station, this streamlined hotel often hosts groups visiting from other parts of the Teutonic world. The attractively modern lobby is paneled with light-grained oak and carpeted. The 60 bedrooms are well-insulated refuges from the surrounding commercial neighborhood. The establishment opened in 1985, and since then has done a thriving business in each of the three in-house dining rooms. Each room has a private bath or shower. Singles begin at 750 AS ($54.50) daily, with doubles climbing to 1,800 AS ($130.75).

THE MIDDLE RANGE

The comfortable, contemporary **Hotel Stieglbräu,** Rainerstrasse 14, A-5020 Salzburg (tel. 0662/77-6-92), is within a five-minute walk of the main train station, in the Mirabell section of Salzburg. Facilities include two pleasant restaurants and a salad bar for light snacks. The 50 bedrooms are simply furnished, with big windows, clean sheets, snug beds, and private baths. The hotel has its own parking lot, which will solve at least one of your problems in traffic-congested Salzburg. Singles begin at 700 AS ($51) daily, with doubles beginning at 1,350 AS ($98.25).

Novotel, Franz-Josef-Strasse 26, A-5020 Salzburg (tel. 0662/88-20-41). This welcome addition to Mozart's city brings a successful chain format to Salzburg. Unlike most Novotels (which tend to be on the outskirts of cities, appealing to motorists), however, this one is centrally located, lying within walking distance of many of the major sights. It offers 140 well-furnished double rooms, each with two beds, along with private bath or shower, toilet, direct-dial phone, color TV (satellite TV in four languages), and minibar. Doubles cost 1,450 AS ($105.50) to 1,800 AS ($130.75) daily. A sofa in each room can easily serve as a bed for a child. Geared to early or late arrivals, a restaurant, bar, and café are open daily from 6am to midnight.

Hotel Mozart, Franz-Josef-Strasse 27, A-5020 Salzburg (tel. 0662/72-2-74), open March through October only, angles itself around a street corner a few blocks from the train station. However, it is in a quiet neighborhood. Buff-colored stucco covers the six-story façade. Inside, the decoration contains Oriental rugs and a number of "budget baroque" frills, along with modern furniture and often sunny bedrooms, 33 in all. Each accommodation has a private bath or shower and phone (some contain TVs and minibars). The rate in a double room ranges from 650 AS ($47.25) to 830 AS ($60.25) per person daily, including breakfast. The hotel, which has a real family atmosphere (the staff is helpful), contains many thoughtful touches, such as drawings of the old city of Salzburg.

Hotel Pitter, Rainerstrasse 6-8, A-5020 Salzburg (tel. 0662/78-5-71), has an impressive gray stucco façade, angling around a curve in its street, and lower floors with restrained neoclassical detailing around their windows. The huge lobby area boasts beautifully polished square columns of red porphyry and a marble floor. One of the three inviting restaurants contains a wood-paneled bar, while a daytime café provides a place to read the local newspapers. The Fellner family are the owners of this hotel, where attractively furnished singles or doubles rent for 750 AS ($54.50) to 910 AS ($66.25) per person daily, depending on the season. The hotel offers 207 bedrooms, each with private bath or shower. In summer the garden restaurant is an inviting place to relax and have lunch or dinner.

Hotel Restaurant Gablerbräu, Linzer Gasse 8, A-5020 Salzburg (tel. 0662/73-4-41), is an inviting hotel built in three six-story sections. The end sections are rust-colored with white trim, while the center part has been painted a beige pink, with arched windows on the ground floor and wrought-iron detailing on its imposing façade. Inside are three restaurants: one with vaulted ceilings and green and yellow murals, another covered with wrought-iron detailing, and a third—the least formal of all—which is a beer hall. Not far from the right bank's Markartplatz, the hotel offers 52 bedrooms, each with private bath or shower. Singles begin at 650 AS ($47.25) daily, with doubles starting at 1,300 AS ($94.50).

Hotel Kasererbräu, Kaigasse 33, A-5020 Salzburg (tel. 0662/84-24-45), has a distressed stucco façade and baroque ornamentation around each of its windows. It's in one of the Old Town's most colorful neighborhoods, a few blocks from the cathedral. The building has sections dating from the 13th century, plus a collection of baroque and Biedermeier furniture that goes well with the Oriental rugs and embellished plaster ceilings. The dining room is rustically alpine, while some of the bedrooms have painted regional furniture covered with provincial floral motifs. Each of the 43 bedrooms has a private bath or shower. Singles begin at 850 AS ($61.75) daily, with doubles going for 2,000 AS ($145.50).

Hotel Johann Strauss, Makartkai 37, A-5020 Salzburg (tel. 0662/344430), is an ochre-colored hotel on a pedestrians-only square near the river. You might want to rest after a day of sightseeing on its flower-covered terrace, which offers a view of the Old Town. All of the 22 simple contemporary bedrooms have private baths or showers. Singles cost from 780 AS ($56.75) daily, with doubles renting for 1,500 AS ($109) and up. The dining room is not overly decorated, serving well-prepared food at reasonable prices.

Hotel Wolf-Dietrich, Wolf-Dietrich-Strasse 7, A-5020 Salzburg (tel. 0662/71275), is composed of two neoclassical town houses joined together by an updated ground-floor façade. The lobby area boasts a profusion of Oriental rugs, and its unbroken modern paneling is accented with brass detailing. The 30 smallish bedrooms are appealing and cozy, and all units have TVs, refrigerators, and private baths or showers. Alpine carving and graceful pine detailing adorn one of the two restaurants, while mirrors and unusual murals of Neptune chasing a sea nymph decorate the indoor swimming pool. Comfortably furnished doubles cost 1,050 AS ($76.25) to 1,480 AS ($107.50) daily, with singles ranging from 690 AS ($50.25) to 850 AS ($61.75); a breakfast buffet is included.

Hotel Auersperg, Auerspergstrasse 61, A-5020 Salzburg (tel. 0662/71-72-10). This moderately priced 59-room hotel with a pleasant garden is centrally located near the train station. Each of its rooms has such amenities as a private bath or shower, toilet, phone, radio, and TV. Rates range from 540 AS ($39.25) to 990 AS ($72) daily for a single, from 495 AS ($36) to 800 AS ($58.25) per person for a double, with a breakfast buffet included, as well as tax and service. The difference in price depends on the season. The hotel also offers a comfortable bar and a good restaurant with an Austrian atmosphere. Parking can be arranged for your car.

Hotel Stein, Staatsbrücke, A-5024 Salzburg (tel. 0662/74-3-46), has a renovated stucco-and-stone exterior, disguising the fact that an inn has stood on this site since 1399. The interior is the kind of spacious and airy place where you'll feel at ease; one of the favorite spots is the rooftop terrace, where you can drink coffee or wine. The 80 bedrooms are conservatively furnished in comfortable chairs and sofas. Rooms are rented with or without private bath or shower. Singles cost 560 AS ($40.75) to 770 AS ($56) daily, with doubles going for 880 AS ($64) to 1,260 AS ($91.50).

Hotel Europa, Rainerstrasse 31, A-5020 Salzburg (tel. 0662/73-391-0), is an angular, tall concrete building rising from a tree-dotted area a short walk from the main station. On the 14th floor lies a panoramic restaurant serving an international cuisine, while a less expensive snackbar on the ground floor might be a good stop-over for lunch. The contemporary bedrooms are tastefully decorated, with vivid color schemes whose tones are sometimes repeated on the ceilings. Each of the 104 rooms has its own private bath, as well as radio, minibar, and TV. Singles cost 910 AS ($66.25) to 1,080 AS ($78.50) daily, with doubles going for 1,270 AS ($92.25) to 1,730 AS ($125.75).

Hotel Drei Kreuz, Vogelweiderstrasse 9, A-5020 Salzburg (tel. 0662/72-7-90), has a ground-floor series of aluminum-framed windows set into the kind of po-rous rock that Salzburg is built of. The upper floors are a two-toned combination of yellow stucco and terra-cotta–colored panels. At the reception area you'll be greeted with a wall-size illustration of medieval Salzburg. The restaurant has some of the most massive beams I've seen in this part of Austria, along with a cozy bar and a gemütlich décor of rustic tables and chairs. The name of the hotel derives from the three crosses of the Kapuzinerberg nearby, which was the site of public executions centuries ago. The 20 bedrooms are tasteful and well furnished, each with a private bath or shower. Singles cost from 890 AS ($64.75) daily, with doubles renting for 1,600 AS ($116.25) and up.

BUDGET HOTELS

Near the Rathaus in the Old Town, **Hotel Elefant,** Sigmund-Haffner-Gasse 4, A-5020 Salzburg (tel. 0662/84-33-97), is a well-established family-run hotel. It is in one of the most ancient buildings of Salzburg, a house more than 700 years old, in a quiet alley off Getreidegasse. In the lobby, you'll see a pink-and-white marble checkerboard floor as well as a 400-year-old marquetry cabinet. One of my favorite rooms is the vaulted Bürgerstüberl, where high wooden banquettes separate the ta-bles and where the chairs are comfortably curved. You might like to dine in the historic Ratsherrnkeller, a room that in the 17th century was called the wine cellar of Salzburg. The 36 well-furnished and high-ceilinged bedrooms all have baths or showers, toilets, phones, radios, TVs, hairdryers, and minibars. They rent from 700 AS ($51) daily for a single and from 1,400 AS ($101.75) for a double.

Hotel Pension Fuggerhof, Eberhard-Fugger-Strasse 9, A-5020 Salzburg (tel. 0662/641-290-0). This family-run boarding house stands on the south slope of the Kapuzinerberg. From the outside it looks like the secluded mountain home of a wealthy industrialist, with three stories of curved walls, stone detailing, and cone-shaped roofs. A kidney-shaped swimming pool is set among pine trees near the ho-tel's entrance. The furnishings are comfortably rustic, often painted in regional designs or richly grained with baroque carvings. Each of the 20 bedrooms has a pri-vate bath, refrigerator, phone, and radio. Herta Kammerhofer, your congenial hostess, charges 900 AS ($65.50) daily for a single; doubles cost 1,100 AS ($80) to 2,000 AS ($145.50), the higher price for a suite. Breakfast is included in all tariffs. The hotel has an elevator, a laundromat, and a sauna.

Hotel Weisse Taube, Kaigasse 9, A-5020 Salzburg (tel. 0662/84-24-04). The reception area lies behind a stone-trimmed wrought-iron–and–glass door a few steps from the Mozartplatz. The hotel is in the pedestrian area of the Old Town, but you can drive up to it to unload baggage. Car parking is possible in a garage about a four-minute walk away at special prices for hotel guests. Constructed in 1365, the Weisse Taube has been owned by the Haubner family since 1904. Some of the public rooms maintain the massive ceiling beams of their original construction, but the 30 bedrooms, all with baths or showers, are for the most part renovated and comfortably streamlined. Depending on the season and the plumbing, singles cost 390 AS ($28.25) to 600 AS ($43.50) daily, with doubles ranging from 700 AS ($51) to 1,500 AS ($109). Breakfast is included. The hotel has an elevator, a TV room, and a bar.

Hotel Blaue Gans, Getreidegasse 43, A-5020 Salzburg (tel. 0662/84-13-17), is a 500-year-old building with a long tradition. "The Blue Goose" has an ash-colored façade and a convenient location in the Old Town near the underground garages of the Mönchsberg. On the ground floor lies an informal beer hall and a café-restaurant. The hotel's 50 bedrooms are cozy and comfortable, and all but four have private baths or showers. Each as a phone as well. Charges for a single range from 400 AS ($29) to 500 AS ($36.25) daily, with doubles costing 800 AS ($58.25) to 1,500 AS ($109), including breakfast, service, and tax.

THE BEST OF THE GUESTHOUSES

A pension or guesthouse in Salzburg does not necessarily indicate economy. They can be luxurious, with a five-star rating, or of a more modest class, comparable to (but often better than) a third-class hotel. I'll lead off with the most expensive. If you're on a strict budget, read from the bottom of the list.

Dr. Wührer's Haus Gastein, Ignaz-Rieder-Kai 25, A-5020 Salzburg (tel. 0662/22-5-65), is a prosperous-looking Teutonic villa, built as a private home in 1953. It lies in calm green scenery on the bank of the Salzach River. Only a few minutes from the center of the town's oldest boroughs, the house offers a true Salzburg atmosphere. The establishment is officially classified as a hotel; however, a stopover in one of its 12 ample bedrooms is similar to a stay in an upper-class private home. During the annual music festival the place is likely to be filled with musicians, some of them well known, who appreciate the spacious flowering garden, a stage setting for breakfast or afternoon tea. You can spot colonies of ducks paddling behind a screen of riverside saplings.

The interior is sparsely but pleasantly furnished, with conservative pieces and Oriental carpets. The bedrooms contain cozy Salzburg furniture created by artists from the city who have made their reputations worldwide. All the units have bathrooms, phones, radios, and minibars, and many have private balconies. The owner, Hans L. Wührer, charges 1,200 AS ($87.25) daily for a single and 1,800 AS ($130.75) for a double, including breakfast, service, and tax.

Haus Arenberg, Blumensteinstrasse 8, A-5020 Salzburg (tel. 0662/77-1-74). Staying in a place like this gives you the chance to enjoy the best of the Austrian countryside while being a short car ride from the Old Town. On a fieldstone foundation, the two balconied stories have a format of white stucco and wood detailing. Parts of the interior are completely covered in blond paneling, while the panoramic breakfast room is accented with hunting trophies and Oriental rugs. The view from the comfortable bedrooms usually encompasses the nearby city. All 12 units have private baths. Singles cost from 700 AS ($51) daily, with doubles renting for 1,300 AS ($94.50) and up.

Hotel-Pension am Dom, Goldgasse 17, A-5020 Salzburg (tel. 0662/84-27-65), is one of the best-run hotels in its category in the city. It contains only 13 bedrooms, so reservations are important. A double room with bath and toilet, plus breakfast, costs 960 AS ($69.75) to 1,040 AS ($75.50) daily; with shower and toilet, the double charge is 880 AS ($64) to 940 AS ($68.25). The Bachleitner family operate this rustically decorated guesthouse, which lies only a few steps from the Residenzplatz. Their building is a reconstruction of a 14th-century structure. The restaurant specializes in grill dishes, and there is also a snug little cellar room open daily from 11am to midnight.

Pension Wolf, Kaigasse 7, A-5020 Salzburg (tel. 0662/84-34-530), near the Mozartplatz, dates from 1429. It's built of stucco, with big shutters, and is ideally located. Red polished stone steps lead to the wood-ceilinged first-floor reception area. The interior is rustically cozy, with a few baroque touches, such as an embel-lished ceiling. Since the 12-room hotel is usually full, even in off-season, reservations are imperative. The sunny bedrooms, each with a private bath or shower, cost 700 AS ($51) daily for a single, rising to 1,000 AS ($72.75) to 1,300 AS ($94.50) for a double. All rates include breakfast.

Pension am Eschenbach, Hellbrunner Strasse 21, A-5020 Salzburg (tel. 0662/20-3-47). One of the best features of this 10-room country-style guesthouse is the welcome provided by the kindly owner, Michael Elwischger. The public rooms are filled with an eclectic mixture of 19th-century paintings, formal sculp-ture, and cozy contemporary furniture, while the high-ceilinged bedrooms have painted designs on the furniture and are outfitted in cheerful colors. Singles cost 420 AS ($30.50) to 500 AS ($36.25) daily, with doubles going for 650 AS ($47.25) to 750 AS ($54.50). Bungalows for two rent for 900 AS ($65.50) to 1,100 AS ($80). Also available: an apartment for six persons (minimum of four) with its own kitchen and shower, costing 1,800 AS ($130.75) to 2,500 AS ($181.75). A one-week minimum rental is required on the apartment, and breakfast is included in the price. The pension is an eight-minute walk from the center of the city.

Pension Helmhof, Lieferinger Hauptstrasse (Kirchengasse 29), A-5020 Salz-burg (tel. 0662/33-0-79), is an appealingly rustic 16-room stucco chalet with flowery balconies and a stone-trimmed sun terrace. Rooms, 12 with private bath or shower, are comfortably furnished and well kept, and the staff is hospitable. Singles cost from 400 AS ($29) daily, with doubles renting for 500 AS ($36.25) to 720 AS ($52.25), breakfast included.

Pension Adlerhof, Elisabethstrasse 25, A-5020 Salzburg (tel. 0662/75-2-36). Only the second and third floors of this guesthouse near the train station retain their original baroque embellishments. The windows of the first and fourth floors have been stripped and recovered with polished marble and gray stucco, resulting in a pastiche of styles. The high-ceilinged but cozy interior has wooden furniture with occasional painted designs, plus lots of folkloric touches (an occasional hunting tro-phy, for example). The Pregartbauer family charges 250 AS ($18.25) to 390 AS ($28.25) daily for a single, and 460 AS ($33.50) to 620 AS ($45) for a double, breakfast and taxes included. Prices depend on the season and the plumbing. About half of the 25 units have private showers, and all have direct-dial phones.

Pension Goldene Krone, Linzer Gasse 48, A-5020 Salzburg (tel. 0662/72-3-00). My favorite part of this family-run guesthouse is the ivy-covered walls of its big sun terrace, where a member of the Egger family will serve you coffee after a tiring day in the city. Only a few minutes from the Staatsbrücke, the hotel offers 27 com-fortably outfitted bedrooms with patterned carpeting and wooden furniture; 22 of the rooms come with private baths or showers. Singles cost 375 AS ($27.25) daily, with doubles going for 800 AS ($58.25). Breakfast is included in these rates.

Food and Lodging at Anif

Romantik Hotel Schlosswirt, Halleiner Brundesstrasse 22, A-5081 Anif (tel. 06246/2175), is a country inn on the outskirts of Anif, 4 miles from the center of Salzburg and a half mile from the autobahn's exit at Salzburg-Süd. It was founded in 1607, and with its flagstone floors, thick walls, and a collection of local artifacts and hunting trophies, has done a thriving business ever since. It's so well known that Austrians sometimes drive all the way from Innsbruck to dine here.

The bedrooms, whether in the main building or in the L-shaped annex, are fur-nished mainly with Biedermeier furniture, with patterned wallpaper and flower-boxes at the windows. If you're a late riser, be warned that traffic beginning at 7am might disturb you if you're housed in the annex, which is right on the highway. All 32 rooms have private baths and are well equipped. Singles cost from 700 AS ($51) daily, with doubles renting for 1,200 AS ($87.25) to 1,400 AS ($101.75). Rooms come with a generous breakfast buffet of wurst, cheese, and coddled eggs.

Dinner is an elegant experience. Menu items include matjes herring with dill, an array of wild game in season, duckling in orange sauce, and many traditional fish dishes. A kindly English-speaking hostess in regional dress will help you with translations. Meals begin at 220 AS ($16) and go up. The hotel closes in February.

Hotel Friesacher, A-5081 Anif (tel. 06246/2075), is an elegant 100-bed chalet with a hipped roof, a long expanse of gables, and natural-grained wooden balconies covered with flowers. It has an older building a few steps away, which serves as a well-furnished annex to the main hotel, with flowering lawns scattered in between. The entrance hall to the main building has an intriguing variety of blue-gray and rust-colored marble covering the floor, and a wooden ceiling muting the light from the big windows. Throughout the hotel you'll find unusual artifacts, intimate corners, and service provided by the Friesacher family. The spacious bedrooms, each with its own bath, cost 640 AS ($46.50) to 780 AS ($56.75) daily for a single and 980 AS ($71.25) to 1,180 AS ($85.75) for a double. Apartments, double occupancy, rent for 1,380 AS ($100.25).

The hotel also has a country-style dining room, with rustic artifacts, which is considered one of the finest in the area. In summer, guests can also patronize an open-air terrace. The food is served daily except Wednesday from 11:30am to 2:30pm and 6 to 9:30pm, so you may want to drive out for an evening here even if you aren't staying in Anif. Prices range from 120 AS ($8.75) to 270 AS ($19.75). Specialties are typically Austrian, including tafelspitz and dumpling soups, along with such classic Austrian sweets as topfenstrudel (made with cottage cheese) and palatschinken (dessert crêpes). Closed from Christmas to mid-January.

Food and Lodging at Aigen

Gasthof-Hotel Doktorwirt, Glaserstrasse 9, A-5026 Salzburg-Aigen (tel. 0662/22-9-73), a chalet with prominent gables, a red-tile roof, and white stucco walls, lies on the southern edge of Salzburg, within 10 minutes by car or trolley from the Old Town. The adjoining restaurant produces many of the sausages it serves, as well as a collection of tempting pastries. The décor is rustic, sunny, and pleasant, with lots of wood detailing. On the premises is an outdoor swimming pool with a view of the mountains, and there are also a sauna and solarium. The 39 cozy bedrooms—all with baths or showers, direct-dial phones, TVs, and radios—rent for 500 AS ($36.25) to 750 AS ($54.50) daily for a single and 750 AS ($54.50) to 1,200 AS ($87.25) for a double, breakfast included. By car, exit from the autobahn at Salzburg-Süd, or else take city bus line 49.

Food and Lodging at Bergheim

Hotel Gasthof Gmachl, Dorfstrasse 12, A-5101 Bergheim (tel. 0662/52-1-24), lies 4 miles from the center of Salzburg. It looks like a private chalet home of a prosperous businessperson, with an interior embellished with carved stone and octagonal ceiling panels. In one of the public rooms, a massive hearth burns under a stone-and-stucco overhang. The 75 beds are contained in cozy rooms, some of them with sloping paneled ceilings and lots of homey individualized touches. Singles begin at 800 AS ($58.25) daily, while doubles rent for 1,450 AS ($105.50). On the grounds are three sand tennis courts, an indoor heated swimming pool, and a sauna; 2½ miles away is a riding stable.

---

3. Where to Dine

Salzburg has a wide variety of restaurants in several price ranges. But two special desserts you'll have to sample while there include the famous Salzburger nockerln, a light mixture of stiff egg whites, as well as the elaborate confection known as the

Mozart-Kugeln, with bittersweet chocolate, hazelnut nougat, and marzipan. You'll also want to taste the beer in any one of the numerous Salzburg breweries.

THE UPPER BRACKET

Even if the **Goldener Hirsch,** Getreidegasse 37 (tel. 0662/84-85-11), served only the clients of its adjoining hotel (see my hotel recommendation), it would still attract the brightest luminaries of the international music and business community. The fact is, however, that dozens of the fans of this place travel a long distance to eat in the authentically renovated ambience of an inn established in 1407. It's staffed with a superb team of chefs and waiters in an atmosphere of elegantly restrained simplicity. Specialties include parfait of smoked trout in a mustard dill sauce, grilled hare, veal in saffron sauce, and many more dishes, all impeccably prepared and beautifully served. À la carte meals range from 280 AS ($20.25) to 550 AS ($40). The restaurant is open from noon to 2:30pm and 6:30 to 9:30pm daily, and reservations are suggested.

Weinrestaurant Alt-Salzburg, Bürgerspitalgasse 2 (tel. 0662/84-14-76), is one of the bastions of formal Austrian service. The predominant colors are red and white, in a wood-ceilinged room crafted to reveal part of the chiseled rock of Mönchsberg. The crystal here shines, the waiters are formally dressed (often better than the clients), and the food choices include tomato mousse with shrimp, parfait of calves' liver, quenelles of veal kidneys Calvados in a chervil sauce, and saddle of hare with mushrooms. Meals generally cost from 400 AS ($29). The restaurant is open from 11:30am until 2pm and 6:30 to 11pm (till midnight during August). The restaurant is closed on Sunday, and reservations are needed on other nights of the week. It's also closed in February.

Zum Eulenspiegel, Hagenauerplatz 2 (tel. 0662/84-31-80), is housed in a white- and peach-colored building at one end of a quiet cobblestone square in the Old Town. Inside, guests face a choice of five rooms on three different levels, all of them rustically but elegantly decorated. Management seems to have no problem with allowing clients to pick their favorite rooms, so feel free to look around if all the tables aren't full. A small bar area on the ground floor is a pleasant place for an apéritif.

After that, you climb a stone staircase whose stucco walls are filled with art objects. Upstairs, the menu features a table d'hôte priced from 156 AS ($11.25) to 250 AS ($18.25). It might include cream of zucchini soup, along with many classic dishes such as tafelspitz, perch filet, and Salzburger nockerln. À la carte meals cost approximately the same as the set dinners. The restaurant is open from 11:30am to 2pm and 6 to 11pm, and the bar is open from 10am to midnight daily. Walter and Gabi Ritzberger-Wimmer are the polite owners of this place. They keep it open year round, except in February, and reservations are always vital.

THE MIDDLE RANGE

Some 60 years ago, **G'würzmühl,** Leopoldskronstrasse 1 (tel. 0662/84-63-56), was a spice mill (that's what its name means in German). Today it is one of the best-known restaurants in Salzburg, featuring an array of typically Austrian and international specialties. The kitchen also serves a children's menu. Charging from 150 AS ($11) for a meal, the restaurant is open daily except Tuesday from 11:30am to 3pm and 6pm to midnight. In August, it remains open every day. The location is about five minutes from the center of town.

Hagenauerstuben (Stranz & Scio), Universitätsplatz 14 (tel. 0662/84-26-57). Melodies composed by this building's most famous occupant might accompany your before-dinner drink in this restaurant. It's accessible from the rear entrance of the building where Mozart was born. Many visitors never get beyond the street-level bar, where snacks and drinks are served in a 14th-century room with stone floors and a vaulted ceiling, plus a changing exhibition of modern lithographs and watercolors. At the top of a narrow flight of stone steps you'll discover an austere trio of thick-walled rooms decorated with a ceramic stove and wooden armoires. A central serving table holds an array of salads and hors d'oeuvres, which are served by a brigade of waiters.

If you can find a free table, you can dine informally in the downstairs bar. The upstairs rooms are so popular that reservations are essential. Both an international and a regional Austrian kitchen is featured here, with meals costing from 250 AS ($18.25). Wines are available by the glass, carafe, or bottle. The restaurant is open daily except Sunday from 9am to midnight; however, it closes on Saturday at 2pm.

Stiftskeller St. Peter (Peterskeller), St.-Peter-Bezirk 1-4 (tel. 0662/84-12-680). There's a legend that says that Mephistopheles met with Faust in this tavern, which isn't that far-fetched considering that it was established by Benedictine monks in A.D. 803. In fact, it's the oldest restaurant in Austria, and is housed in the abbey of the church that supposedly brought Christianity to Austria. Aside from a collection of baroque banqueting rooms, open only for special occasions, the establishment contains an inner courtyard with vaults cut from the living rock, a handful of dignified wood-paneled rooms, and a brick-vaulted cellar with a tile floor and rustic chandeliers.

In addition to the wine fermented from the abbey's vineyards, the tavern serves such menu items as cheese soup with white wine and ham, filet of pork in a Roquefort cream sauce with rice, roast duckling, and a combination plate of sausages, pork chops, semolina dumplings, potatoes, and sauerkraut. An unusual dessert might be curd dumplings with plum jam. Meals cost 175 AS ($12.50) to 300 AS ($21.75). The restaurant is open daily except Monday until 1am, but hot food is served only from 9am to 11pm. The Stiftskeller is closed from the first of November until just before Easter.

Restaurant Hohensalzburg, Hohensalzburg Schloss (tel. 0662/84-17-80), offers a chance to dine at the former stronghold of the prince-archbishops of Salzburg (see the sightseeing attractions). The restaurant is in the castle, which is perched on a block of Dolomite rock. You are 400 feet above the Salzach, and naturally you'll have a panoramic view.

This gutbürgerlich restaurant is host to a folkloric music group that performs every Tuesday and Friday from 8:30 to 10:30pm. Also, during the summer, evening concerts of Mozart's music are presented daily. All week long, clients enjoy such specialties as grilled pork, grilled steak with pearl onions and pepperoni, veal dishes, schnitzels, fish, and fowl. The restaurant, charging 100 AS ($7.25) to 250 AS ($18.25) for a typical meal, is open daily from March until the end of October from 10am to 6pm (until 11pm at the time of the festival in July and August, and until 9pm in June and September).

Purzelbaum, Zugallistrasse 7 (tel. 0662/84-88-43). During the Salzburg Festival, you're likely to see some of the most dedicated music-lovers in Europe congregating around the small square tables of this sophisticated bistro. Located in a residential neighborhood not frequently visited by tourists, it's near a duck pond at the bottom of a steep incline leading up to Salzburg Castle. There's a cramped corner of the bar reserved for visitors who only want to drop in for a drink. Most guests, however, reserve a table in one of the trio of rooms containing marble buffets from a French buttery, an art nouveau ceiling from a now-defunct café in Paris, and panels painted blue-green.

Habitués begin their meal with one of the daily champagne-based cocktails, then order a glass or a bottle of vintage wine that the owners import from five different countries. A set menu costs 380 AS ($27.75), with à la carte meals costing from 500 AS ($36.25).

Restaurant K & K (Stiegl-Bräu-Keller), Waagplatz 2 (tel. 0662/84-21-56), is on a giant square in the Old Town near the cathedral. It has three different sections, each with a separate ambience. From the street you'll see an elaborate wrought-iron and gilt bracket holding a sign. You'll go down a massive stone staircase to reach the bierkeller, which is a marvel of another time's masonry (it was built 900 years ago). The stube on the ground floor is candlelit, with a wood-paneled ambience.

Upstairs is the restaurant, which is divided by a flagstone-covered hallway into three separate eating areas, with dozens of stone accents crafted from both the porous rocks of Salzburg and slabs of salmon-colored marble. The diners here tend to be better dressed, and the atmosphere is slightly more formal. The three restaurants serve warm food—a medley of imaginative and traditional Austrian dishes—daily from 11am to 2pm and 6 to 10pm. They're also open for drinks and snacks from 9am to midnight in summer and 10am to midnight in winter. Fixed-price meals cost 185 AS ($13.50) and 325 AS ($23.75). Menu items in the three restaurants include such specialties as perch, trout, roast filet of beef in a cognac cream sauce with fresh mushrooms and green peppercorns, tafelspitz, and breast of chicken in a curry cream sauce, along with grilled lamb and an array of shellfish.

THE BUDGET RANGE

Krimpelstätter, Müllner Hauptstrasse 31 (tel. 0662/32-2-74), is a 500-year-old restaurant that stands in a neighborhood bustling with traffic, but inside a visitor can enjoy a décor virtually untouched by the modern world. Unlike other establishments, which were originally built as private houses, this one was designed and constructed as an inn, with chiseled stone columns to support the vaulted ceilings and heavy timbers grown dark with smoke. In summer the roses and trellises of the establishment's beer garden attract up to 300 visitors at a time.

If you want a snack, a beer, or a glass of wine, head for the paneled door marked "Gastezimmer" in the entry corridor. If you're looking for a more formal, less visited area, a trio of cozy antique dining rooms sits at the top of a flight of narrow stone steps. The menu offers the same dishes in each of the different areas. The restaurant features a Land Salzburg regional kitchen, with such specialties as homemade sausages and wild game dishes. Meals cost from 175 AS ($12.75). Service is every day except Monday, and drinks and snacks are available during all open hours. Full meals, however, are served only from 11:30am to 2pm and 6 to 10:30pm, when it would be wise to make a reservation.

Hotel Stadtkrug, Linzer Gasse 20 (tel. 0662/75-54-5), located on a narrow street in the Old Town, has a rustic and attractive restaurant. The layout is unusual, with a kitchen opening off the hotel's reception area and with a dining room that contains a stone staircase leading from the back to the large arched window in front. Wooden tables are set on two tiers, illuminated by gilded wooden chandeliers with pink shades. Typical dishes include mixed grills, gulasch, peppersteak, and Salzburger nockerl. One of the featured specialties is trout meunière, the ingredients of which come from the exposed trout tank that bubbles in the entrance vestibule. There are also daily blackboard specials. Meals cost 120 AS ($8.75) to 225 AS ($16.25). The restaurant is open daily from 11am to 11pm.

Zum Mohren, Judengasse 9 (tel. 0662/84-23-87). A statue of an exotic-looking Moor sits atop the wrought-iron sign announcing the entrance to this restaurant. The house that contains it was built in 1423, with much of the original masonry still showing. You'll have to descend a flight of gray stone steps to reach the three distinctly different eating areas, the best of which is on the right as you enter. The ceilings are made either of vaulted stucco or of well-crafted paneling. You'll see many replicas of Moors, with or without a gold earring, either in bas-relief or in full-rounded sculpture. A third area, on the left as you enter, is more cavelike, with an orange ceramic stove and a low ceiling. Meals, which range in price from 125 AS ($9) to 210 AS ($15.25), might include entrecôte Parisian style, filet mignon with broccoli and béarnaise sauce, grilled lamb chops, a good selection of cheese, and lots of rich desserts. The restaurant is open every day but Sunday from 11am to midnight, and the chef stops serving hot food after 11pm. Zum Mohren is closed in November.

Sternbräu, Griesgasse 23 (tel. 0662/84-21-40). You'll enter this establishment through a cobblestone arched passageway leading off a street in the Old Town. The place seems big enough to have fed half of the old Austro-Hungarian army, with a series of rooms that follow one after the other in varying degrees of formality. The Hofbräustübl is a rustic fantasy combining square masonry columns with a massive format of hand-hewn beams and wood paneling. The other rooms have such accessories as sea-green tile stoves, marble columns, and oil paintings. In addition to the different rooms, you'll also be able to eat in the chestnut-shaded beer garden, which is usually packed on a summer's night, or else under the weathered arcades of an inner courtyard.

Daily specials, which are served by a battalion of aproned waiters, include typically Austrian dishes such as Wiener schnitzel, some trout recipes, cold marinated herring, Hungarian gulasch, hearty regional soups, and lots of other gutbürgerlich selections. À la carte meals begin at 175 AS ($12.75), and the restaurant is open daily from 8am to midnight.

Mundenhamer Bräu, Rainerstrasse 2 (tel. 0662/75-6-93). As you enter this warm-hued restaurant, located near the main train station, you'll pass by an elongated stainless-steel counter that almost looks as if it came from a delicatessen. There are several different seating areas, of which my favorite is the big-windowed section with a view of a city park. In season, game is a specialty; otherwise, menu items are likely to include Salzburger cream schnitzel, paprika cutlets, mushroom ragoût, and a specialty of the house called Mundenhamer potpourri, a mixed grill for two diners. The menu is in English and the portions are large, meals costing 120 AS ($8.75) to 250 AS ($18.25). Hours are 9am to midnight; closed Sunday.

s'Herzl, Sigmundsplatz 7 (tel. 0662/84-85-17), has an entrance on this famous square, as well as next door to the glamorous Goldener Hirsch, of which it is a part. Because it offers such good value, it attracts a mixture of both visitors and locals. From Sigmundsplatz, you descend a few steps from the sidewalk into a pair of cozily proportioned rooms, one of which is paneled and timbered. You'll see photographs of musicians who have come here to dine while performing at the annual Salzburg Festival. From 11am to 2:30pm and 6 to 9pm daily, waitresses in dirndls serve an appetizing array of food, which is likely to include roast pork with dumplings, various grills, game stew (in season), and, for the trencherperson, a farmer's plate of boiled pork, roast pork, grilled sausages, dumplings, and sauerkraut. House specialties are served on heart-shaped tin platters, the heart theme coming from the restaurant's name. Meals cost from 175 AS ($12.75).

Bastey-Brasserie & Crêperie, Kaigasse 7 (tel. 0662/84-11-80). Its location on the ground floor of the Pension Wolff, a short walk from the Mozartplatz, is ideal. Its leaded windows look out just above the level of the sidewalk, illuminating an alpine décor of exposed wood and scarlet napery. In many ways the place is perfect for seekers of a light meal unencumbered with heavy sauces and starches. It prepares 13 different kinds of crêpes, ranging from zucchini with tomato to chili with cheese. The kitchen also makes special salads (everything from Caesar to niçoise), homemade pastas, and vegetarian food. Meals cost from 120 AS ($8.75). The establishment is open daily except Sunday from noon to 2:30pm and 6pm to midnight.

Jugoslawisches Restaurant, Hotel Weisses Kreuz, Bierjodlgasse 6 (tel. 0662/84-56-41), has a façade of stone blocks that is almost hidden on a small villagelike street just south of the cathedral. A grape arbor shelters the front terrace, where in summer tables have been set out for relaxed guests. The cuisine is both Viennese and Balkan, and includes Serbian bean soup, boiled beef, mutton chops, roast beef in a cream and onion sauce, and peppersteak. More exotic specialties include Serbian gulasch soup, moussaka, fried mincemeat loaf Serbian style with pickled peppers, and Dalmatian steak with Serbian rice and stuffed cabbage, along with a Serbian-style risotto. An average meal costs from 180 AS ($13), and the restaurant is open from 11am to midnight.

In the four-bedroom hotel, each accommodation has a complete bath. Singles begin at 580 AS ($42.25) daily, with doubles costing from 840 AS ($61). All tariffs include breakfast, tax, and the use of the garage.

Zipfer Bierhaus, Sigmund-Haffner-Gasse 12 (tel. 0662/84-31-01), is a long-enduring favorite, often popular with the after-concert crowd since it serves daily until midnight (it opens at 10am). It is closed on Sunday in winter. The décor is in the familiar beerhouse tradition, and the food is also familiar if you've been in Austria for a while: noodle casserole with ham in a cream sauce, breaded and fried filet of plaice or trout, veal gulasch, and a spicy paprika salad with wurst and cheese. Meal prices start at a most reasonable 175 AS ($12.75). Not only is the food well prepared, but the portions are generous.

Yuen, Getreidegasse 24 (tel. 0662/84-37-70), is one of the better Chinese restaurants of Salzburg, of which there are quite a few. The Austrians call this *ausländische küche,* or foreign cuisine, but its offerings will be familiar to most North Americans. The location is in an alley and courtyard off the main shopping street of Salzburg. You climb some stone steps to reach its precincts, and once inside you'll think you've been transported back to Old Singapore. Under a wood ceiling, Chinese lamps provide soft lighting, and the service is polite and efficient. Everyone aims to please. Most à la carte meals cost from 250 AS ($18.25), or you can go for the bargain—a menu for two persons costing from 300 AS ($21.75). You might begin with a spring roll or Chinese fish soup and proceed to crispy duck Szechuan style or chicken with mango. The chef also caters to vegetarians and prepares several kinds of chop suey. Hours are 11:30am to 11:30pm daily.

---

4. The Cafés of Salzburg

Cynics in the festival city sometimes complain that there isn't a lot to do in Salzburg except drink endless cups of thickened coffee while waiting for someone at the next table to be brilliant about art or music.

But that isn't the perception of everyone. A hometown friend of mine told me that the peak emotional experience of her trip to Europe happened while seated at a café table in the Mozartplatz. The combination of the baroque setting, the strains of a string orchestra, the Austrian pastry half eaten on her plate, and the companionship of a close friend made her realize that she was suddenly living her fantasy of what culture, art, and beauty are all about.

Don't leave Salzburg without some significant time in one of the world-famous cafés of the inner city. Descriptions of some of my favorites immediately follow.

Café Tomaselli, Alter Markt 9 (tel. 0662/84-44-88), was established in 1705. It opens onto the cobblestone pavement of one of the most charming squares of the Altstadt. Aside from the summer chairs placed outdoors, you'll find a high-ceilinged square room with many tables, small crystal lighting fixtures, and lots of what look like elegant conversations. Another, more formal room to the right of the entrance has oil portraits of well-known 19th-century Salzburgers in oval frames hung one above the other. The crowd is haute bourgeoisie. A waiter will probably show you a pastry tray filled with 40 different kinds of cakes, which you are free to order or not as you see fit. Other menu items include omelets, wursts, ice cream, and a wide range of drinks. Pastries cost from 25 AS ($1.80) and coffee from 20 AS ($1.45). The café is open daily from 7am to 9pm and on Sunday and holidays from 8am to 9pm.

Restaurant Café Winkler, Am Mönschberg 32 (tel. 0662/84-12-15), reached by the elevator (*aufzug*), offers a magic view of the Old Town, excellent traditional cuisine and cellar, and good service. Lunch, coffee and cake, afternoon tea, and dinner are offered, with dance music during the summer, in the contemporary surroundings of this typical continental first-class restaurant. Lunch costs from 200 AS ($14.50), with set dinners priced from 350 AS ($25.50). You can also visit during the day for coffee and cake. The establishment is open Tuesday to Sunday from 11am to midnight.

Kaffeehäferl, Universitätsplatz 6 (tel. 0662/84-32-49), is constructed in a gray-and-white format of stucco walls set onto columns made of the porous rock that supports many of the buildings of Salzburg. This establishment attracts members of both the business and art communities of the city. The interior is simpler and more modern than you'd expect. Masses of ceramic pots are displayed in cases on one of the far walls. A specialty of the house is fleckerl with ham, which is served in addition to the wide selection of coffee, wine, and pastries. Coffee costs from 20 AS ($1.45), with the price the same for the average pastry. The café is open Monday to Friday from 9am to 7pm, on Saturday to 6pm, and on Sunday in summer from noon to 6pm (in winter, Sunday hours are 2 to 6pm).

Schatz-Konditorei, Getreidegasse 3 (tel. 0662/84-27-92), is an oldtime Austrian confectioner. The cobblestones in front of its 19th-century wood-and-glass façade are from the 14th century. Almost everything is made from traditional recipes, my favorite of which is the well-known Mozart-Kugeln, a combination of pistachio, marzipan, and hazelnut nougat, all of it dipped in chocolate. Clients are free to try any of the pastries with coffee at an indoor café table or to purchase them for consumption elsewhere. Pastries cost from 15 AS ($1.10), with coffee averaging 25 AS ($1.80). Some varieties of pastry, including the Mozart-Kugeln, are mailed around the world. The Konditorei is open Monday to Friday from 8:30am to 6:30pm and on Saturday from 8am to 1:30pm. During festival performances in summer, they are open full time on Saturday and in December.

Konditorei Ratzka, Imbergstrasse 45 (tel. 0662/70-9-19). This small shop lies 10 minutes from the center of town. Herwig Ratzka is the owner and pastry chef, and by all accounts he's a master at his craft. He uses the freshest ingredients to produce about 30 different pastries. Since the cakes are made fresh every day, much of the selection is gone by late afternoon. So for an insight into what's for sale, go early in the day. The best ones cost 35 AS ($2.50). Mr. Ratzka requests that clients not smoke in the shop, which is open Wednesday to Friday from 8am to 12:30pm and 1:30 to 5pm (on Sunday, from 9am to 5pm). It's closed on Monday and Tuesday and for two weeks in January, two weeks in June, and two weeks in September.

Café-Restaurant Glockenspiel, Mozartplatz 2 (tel. 0662/84-14-03). Its location on one of the most colorful squares of Salzburg has made this café the most popular and the most frequented in the city. Management keeps about 100 tables with well-maintained armchairs in front of the café. If the day is warm enough, you might want to spend an afternoon in one of the chairs, particularly on the days when there is live chamber music. Immediately after entering you'll find yourself face to face with a glass case filled with every high-calorie delight west of Vienna.

The rooms opening on either side contain big arched windows overlooking the statue in the square. A restaurant upstairs, with an even bigger pastry case than the one downstairs, is tastefully decorated in browns and beiges, with a big balcony. The restaurant offers such specials for lunch as gulasch of veal with dumplings, boiled rump of beef with roast potatoes and a chive sauce, and roast sausages with sauerkraut. Midday meals cost from 150 AS ($11). For dinner, you can sit on the balcony and look over Salzburg's famous buildings while you enjoy Austrian regional and international specialties that cost from 250 AS ($18.25). Many people, however, come here just for the drinks and pastries. Coffee costs from 28 AS ($2.05), and it comes in many varieties of coffee, including Maria Theresa, which contains orange liqueur. The café is open daily from 9am to midnight in summer and from 10am to 8pm the rest of the year. The restaurant serves food from 11am to 11pm in summer and from 11am to 6pm otherwise. Though the café is open daily all year, the restaurant closes for part of the autumn and winter.

Café Bazar, Schwarzstrasse 3 (tel. 0662/74-2-78), is as deeply entrenched in Salzburg's social life as practically anything else in town. Its regular clientele includes people from all walks of Austrian life, many of whom usually sit in the same section of the café and order practically the same item every time they visit. It's housed in a pink stucco palacelike building with many baroque features across the river from the main section of the Old Town. The inside is high-ceilinged and vaguely art deco, with light-grained wooden walls covered with marquetry designs. You'll occasionally see someone with a Franz Joseph mustache wearing a gray flannel Styrian suit with loden trim, but a growing number of the clients are young and fashionable, and would probably be much at home at a café in London or Paris.

Menu items include an array of salads, sandwiches, and omelets. Coffee prices range from 20 AS ($1.45), while pastries go for 18 AS ($1.25) to 30 AS ($2.20). The café is open from 7:30am to 11pm; closed Sunday.

---

5. What to See

The Old Town lies between the left bank of the Salzach River and the ridge known as Mönchsberg, which rises to a height of 1,650 feet and is the site of Salzburg's gambling casino. The main street of the old town is **Getreidegasse,** a narrow little thoroughfare lined with five- and six-story burghers' buildings. Most of the houses along the street are from the 17th and 18th centuries. Mozart was born at no. 9 (see below). Many lacy-looking wrought-iron signs are displayed, and a lot of the houses have carved windows.

You might begin your tour at the **Mozartplatz,** with its outdoor cafés. From here you can walk to the even more spacious **Residenzplatz,** where torchlight dancing is staged every year, along with outdoor performances.

The **Residenz,** Residenzplatz 1 (tel. 0662/80-42-26-90). This opulent palace, just north of the Domplatz, was the seat of the Salzburg prince-archbishops after they no longer felt the need of the protection afforded in the gloomy Hohensalzburg Fortress West of Mönchsberg (see below). The Residenz dates from 1120, but work on the series of palaces in its present form, which comprised the ecclesiastical complex of the ruling church princes, began in the late 1500s and continued until about 1782. The lavish rebuilding was originally ordered by Archbishop Wolfgang (usually called "Wolf") Dietrich. The Residenz fountain, from the 17th century, is one of the largest and most impressive baroque fountains to be found north of the Alps.

The child prodigy Mozart often played in the Conference Room for guests. In 1867 Emperor Franz Joseph received Napoleon III here, and in 1871 Kaiser Wilhelm I was also a state guest at the Residenz. More than a dozen state rooms, each richly decorated, are open to the public. Conducted tours are given through these rooms daily in July and August from 10am to 4:30pm. From September to June, hours are 10am, 11am, noon, 2pm, and 3pm. Admission is 30 AS ($2.20) for adults, free for children.

On the second floor you can visit the **Residenzgalerie Salzburg** (tel. 0662/8042, ext. 2270), an art gallery founded in 1789, now containing European paintings from the 16th to the 19th centuries, displayed in 15 historical rooms. The paintings on exhibition are from the following schools: Dutch, Flemish, French, Italian, Austrian baroque, and Austrian 19th century. Gallery hours are 10am to 5pm daily. Admission is 30 AS ($2.20) for adults, 20 AS ($1.45) for students, and free for children up to the age of 15.

Across from the Residenz stands the celebrated **Glockenspiel,** Mozartplatz 1 (tel. 0662/80-42-26-81), with its 35 bells. You can hear this 18th-century carillon at 7am, 11am, and 6pm. A 20-minute conducted tour (minimum of three persons) is conducted daily at 10:45am and 5:45pm. Admission is 20 AS ($1.45). In winter, tours are conducted only from Monday to Friday, and there are no tours in bad weather.

At the south side of the Residenzplatz, where it flows into the **Domplatz** (here you'll see a 1771 statue of the Virgin), stands the Dom, **Salzburg Cathedral,** world-renowned for its 10,000-pipe organ. The original building from 774 was super-seded by a late-Romanesque structure erected from 1181 to 1200. When this edifice was destroyed by fire in 1598, Prince-Archbishop Wolf Dietrich followed up the start of work on the Residenz by commissioning construction of a new cathedral. His overthrow prevented the finishing of the project. His successor, Archbishop Markus Sittikus Count Hohenems, commissioned the Italian architect Santino Solari to build the present cathedral, which was consecrated in 1628 by Archbishop Paris Count Lodron.

Considered by some people the "most perfect" Renaissance building in the Germanic countries, the cathedral has a marble façade and twin symmetrical towers. The mighty bronze doors were created in 1959. The themes are Faith, Hope, and Love. The interior is in rich baroque style with elaborate frescoes, the most impor-tant of which, along with the altarpieces, were designed by Mascagni of Florence. In the cathedral you can see the Romanesque font at which Mozart was baptized. The dome was damaged during World War II and restored by 1959. In the crypt, traces of the old Romanesque cathedral that once stood on this spot have been unearthed. The cathedral is open daily from 8am to 5pm and can be visited free. However, in order to see the excavations—open daily from Easter to mid-October, 9am to 5pm —you must pay an admission of 10 AS (75¢).

The treasure of the cathedral and a parade of the "arts and wonders" the arch-bishops collected in the 17th century are displayed in the **Dom Museum** (tel. 0662/84-41-89), entered through the cathedral. The museum is open Monday to Saturday from mid-May to mid-October and on Sunday and holidays from 11am to 5pm. Admission is 25 AS ($1.80).

The allegorical play *Everyman,* in an adaptation by Hugo von Hoffmannsthal, is performed in the Domplatz at the Salzburg Festival.

Stiftskirche St. Peter is the church of St. Peter's Abbey and Benedictine Mon-astery, founded in 696 by St. Rupert, whose tomb is here. The church, once a Romanesque basilica with three aisles, was completely overhauled in the 17th and 18th centuries in an elegant baroque style. The west door dates from 1240. The church is richly adorned with art treasures, some altar paintings being by Kremser Schmidt. The Salzburg Madonna in the left chancel is from the early 15th century.

St. Peter's Cemetery (Petersfriedhof, in German), St. Peter Bezirk (tel. 0662/84-45-78), lies at the stone wall that merges into the rock called Mönchsberg. Many of the aristocratic families of Salzburg lie buried here as well as many other noted persons, including Nannerl Mozart, sister of Wolfgang Amadeus. Four years older than her better-known brother, Nannerl was also an exceptionally gifted musi-cian. You can see the Romanesque Chapel of the Holy Cross and St. Margaret's Chapel, dating from the 15th century. The cemetery and its chapels are rich in nos-talgia, monuments to a way of life long vanished.

The church is open daily from 9am to 5pm. It is also possible to take a tour through the early Christian catacombs in the rock above the church cemetery. Tours are conducted daily from May to September, 10:30 to 11:30am and 1:30 to 5pm. Admission is only 10 AS (75¢).

Kollegienkirche, or Collegiate Church, opening onto Universitätsplatz, an open-air marketplace, was built between 1694 and 1707 for the local (Benedictine) university founded in 1622, designed by the great baroque architect Fischer von Erlach. The university, disbanded in 1810, was refounded in 1962 as the University of Salzburg, whose main campus is in the suburb of Nonntal. There are a few other old university buildings in the area of the church, including a fine library and read-ing room. This is von Erlach's finest and largest Salzburg church and one of the most celebrated baroque churches in Austria (and that's saying a lot). Altar paintings are by Rottmayr.

Hohensalzburg Fortress, Mönchsberg 34 (tel. 0662/80-42-21-23), strong-hold of the ruling prince-archbishops before they moved "downtown" to the

Residenz, towers 400 feet above the Salzach River on a rocky Dolomite ledge. The massive fortress crowns Festungsberg and literally dominates Salzburg. Work on Hohensalzburg began in 1077 and was not finished until 1681, during which time many builders of widely different tastes and purposes had a hand in the construction. This largest completely preserved castle left in Central Europe has bastions for the cannons needed in the strife-torn Middle Ages, when the odor of sanctity was often mixed with the odor of gunpowder. Functions of defense and state were combined in this fortress for six centuries.

The elegant state apartments once lived in by the prince-archbishops and their courts are on display. Coffered ceilings and much intricately constructed ironwork are of interest. See, in particular, an early 16th-century porcelain stove in the Golden Room.

The **Burgmuseum** is distinguished mainly by its collection of medieval art. Plans and prints tracing the growth of Salzburg are on exhibit, as well as instruments of torture and many Gothic artifacts. The Salzburger Stier, or Salzburg Bull, an open-air barrel organ built in 1502, plays melodies by Mozart and his friend Haydn in daily concerts following the Glockenspiel chimes. The **Rainermuseum** has displays of arms and armor. The beautiful late Gothic St. George's Chapel, dating from 1501, has marble reliefs of the apostles.

Conducted tours go through the fortress daily, but hours depend on the season: from November to February, 9:30am to 3:30pm; March, 9:30am to 4pm; April and October, 9:30am to 4:30pm; May, June, and September, 9am to 5pm; and July and August, 9am to 5:30pm. The Rainermuseum is open only from May 1 to October 8. Adults pay 35 AS ($2.55), and children are charged 20 AS ($1.45).

You should visit Hohensalzburg even if you're not interested in the fortress, just for the view from the terrace. From the Reck watchtower you get a panoramic sweep of the Alps. Also, the Kuenberg bastion has a fine view of the domes and towers of Salzburg, looking from here like a riot of baroque architecture.

There are several ways to reach the fortress. If you're athletic you can follow one of the paths or lanes leading to it, or you can come on foot from Kapitelplatz by way of Festungsgasse or else from Mönchsberg via the Schartentor. I like to take the funicular from Festungsgasse at the station in back of the cathedral. The round-trip costs 25 AS ($1.80) for adults and 12.50 AS (90¢) for children. The funicular runs every 10 minutes during daylight hours (the trip takes 6 minutes). You can't go to the fortress by car.

West of Hohensalzburg Fortress is **Mönchsberg**. This heavily forested ridge extending for some 1½ miles above the old town has fortifications dating from the 15th century. Several panoramic vistas can be seen from it, and a lovely view of Salzburg is possible from Mönchsberg Terrace just in front of the Grand Café Winkler, where the casino is located. Express elevators leave from Gstättengasse 13 (tel. 0662/205-51-15) daily from 7am to 3pm. A return fare costs 10 AS (75¢) for adults and 5 AS (35¢) for children.

The **Mozart Museum,** Mozart's Gerburtshaus (Mozart's birthplace), Getreidegasse 9 (tel. 0662/84-43-13), is a typical old burgher's house. Leopold Mozart lived on the third floor of this structure from 1747 to 1773, and it was here that Wolfgang Amadeus was born on January 27, 1756, a date all Salzburgers know.

The apartment contains a number of mementos. The child prodigy Mozart, who began composing at the age of four, wrote his early works here. You can see the small violin on which he played and his childhood spinet.

You can visit this birthplace of Salzburg's most renowned citizen from May 1 to October 8 daily from 9am to 7pm. Off-season hours are daily from 9am to 6pm. Admission is 50 AS ($3.65) for adults and 15 AS ($1.10) for children.

It's also possible to visit the **Mozart Wohnhaus,** Makartplatz 8 (tel. 0662/71-776), with its multivision show. This residence of the Mozart family from 1773 to 1787 was rebuilt after World War II damage. All that remains of the original are the entrance and the Tanzmeistersaal (dance master's hall). It is open daily from June 1 to September 30, charging an admission of 35 AS ($2.55) for adults and 5 AS (35¢) for children aged 6 to 14.

Museum Carolino Augusteum, Museumplatz (tel. 0662/84-41-89), consists of both a main museum reflecting Salzburg's cultural history and several ancillary collections. Founded in 1834 and destroyed by a 1944 bombing, it was reconstructed in 1966. Of the several collections then brought together under one roof, that devoted to archeology contains some well-known pieces, such as the Dürnberg beaked pitcher, as well as Roman mosaics. The flowering of art in 15th-century Salzburg is on view, including a rich trove of Gothic panel painting, and there are many paintings from the Romantic Period, as well as works by Hans Makart, who was born in Salzburg in 1840. Hours are Tuesday from 9am to 8pm, and Wednesday to Sunday from 9am to 5pm, with an admission cost of 30 AS ($2.20).

Mirabell Gardens, on the right bank of the river, laid out by Fischer von Erlach and now a public park, are the finest baroque gardens in Salzburg. They are studded with statuary and reflecting pools. Some of the marble balustrades and urns were also designed by von Erlach. There's also a natural theater. As you wander in the gardens at your leisure, be sure to visit the bastion with fantastic marble baroque dwarfs and other figures, by the Pegasus Fountain in the lavish garden west of Schloss Mirabell (coming up). From the gardens you have an excellent view of Hohensalzburg Fortress. The marble statues make Mirabell Gardens virtually an open-air museum.

Mirabell Palace (Schloss Mirabell) was built originally as a luxurious private residence called Altenau. Prince-Archbishop Wolfgang Dietrich had it constructed in 1606 for his mistress and the mother of his children, Salome Alt. Not much remains of the original grand structure. Lukas von Hildebrandt rebuilt the schloss in the first quarter of the 18th century, and it was modified after a great fire in 1818. The official residence of the mayor of Salzburg is now in the palace, which is like a smaller edition of the Tuileries in Paris. The ceremonial marble "angel staircase" with sculptured cherubs, carved by Raphael Donner in 1726, leads to the Marmorsaal, a marble and gold hall used for concerts and weddings. Candlelit chamber music concerts are staged here.

Admission is free to both the gardens and the palace, which lie just off the Makartplatz.

You can also visit the **Salzburger Barockmuseum** (tel. 0662/77-4-32) in the orangery of the Mirabell Gardens. Here European art of the 17th and 18th centuries is displayed, with works by Giordano, Rottmayr, Bernini, and Straub, among other artists in the Rossacher collection. Hours all year are 9am to noon and 2 to 5pm. Tuesday to Saturday, 9am to noon on Sunday and holidays. Admission is 30 AS ($2.20) for adults and 15 AS ($1.10) for children.

Friedhof St. Sebastian (St. Sebastian Cemetery) in Linzergasse was commissioned by Prince-Archbishop Wolf Dietrich in 1595, to be laid out like an Italian *campo santo*. Tombs of Mozart's wife, who endured many hardships, and of his father, Leopold, are here. In the middle of the cemetery is St. Gabriel's Chapel, wherein lies the mausoleum of the now-notorious Dietrich. The interior of his sarcophagus is lined with multicolored porcelain.

To reach the cemetery, you take steps modeled after those in the Italian style up from **St. Sebastian's Church.** The original late Gothic edifice dated from the early 16th century. It was rebuilt and enlarged in 1749, decorated in the rococo style. Destroyed by fire in 1818, it was later reconstructed. The 1752 rococo doorway remains from the old church building. Paracelsus, the Renaissance doctor and philosopher who died in 1541, is entombed here.

Nonnberg Convent, reached by a flight of steps at the end of the Kaigasse, is the oldest existing convent on earth. It was founded about 700 as a Benedictine nunnery by St. Rupert, and St. Rupert's niece, St. Erentrudis (or Ehrentrude), was the first abbess. The convent is a storehouse of treasures, with elaborate woodcarvings. There's also a museum of sacred relics. In the abbey church, in late Gothic style, is the tomb of St. Erentrudis. The St. John Chapel over the gateway displays a Gothic altarpiece from the late 15th century. An underground passage leads from the convent to Hohensalzburg Fortress.

The **Franciscan Church** (Franziskanerkirche), near the Domplatz, was built to replace St. Mary's parish church, which was destroyed by fire in 1167. The present edifice was consecrated in 1223, the Romanesque nave dating from that year. In the 17th century the house of worship was rebuilt, and now is one of the most interesting churches of Salzburg stylistically, having Romanesque and Gothic styles as well as rococo and baroque elements in its architecture and decoration.

The **Festspielhaus** (Festival Hall), Hofstallgasse 1 (tel. 0662/8045), was once the court stables, designed by Wolf Dietrich and built in 1607. Today it is the center for the major musical events of Salzburg, cultural activity reaching its peak during the August festival. The modern hall seats 2,300 spectators, and the major concerts and big operas are performed here. Many outstanding Austrian artists contributed to the decoration of the modern Festival Hall.

Conducted tours (45 min.) are held in May and June, Monday to Friday at 11am and 3pm, Saturday at 11am; in September, Monday to Friday at 11am and 3pm; from October to April, Monday to Friday at 3pm, Saturday at 11am. During the Easter Festival (March–April) tours are Monday to Saturday at 2pm. No tours are conducted during the summer festival in July and August. Admission is 30 AS ($2.20) for adults and 12 AS (85¢) for children.

On the right bank of the Salzach, at Schwarzstrasse 26, is the **Mozarteum** (tel. 0662/73-154), founded almost a century after the composer's birth. In this building (constructed just before World War I), concerts of the Salzburg Festival have been performed since 1921. There are two concert halls and a vast library of works about and by the composer. In the garden stands the **Magic Flute House,** a little wooden structure in which Mozart composed *The Magic Flute* in 1791. It was shipped here from the Naschmarkt in Vienna. In 1971 the Mozarteum was designated as the College of Music and the Performing Arts.

Tours through the Magic Flute House are conducted from July 1 to August 31, Monday to Friday from 11am to noon, for 60 AS ($4.35) per person.

Also on the right bank is the "other hill" of Salzburg, the **Kapuzinerberg,** a forested area rising more than 2,000 feet. Today this area is a lovely park. A Capuchin friary was built here in the closing year of the 16th century, constructed inside an old fortification from the Middle Ages. On the south side of the hill is a handsome street, Steingasse, from medieval times, and the Steintor, which was once a gate in the walls of Salzburg. The author of "Silent Night," Joseph Mohr, was born here in 1792.

From vantage points on the Kapuzinerberg you can see into Bavaria.

IN THE ENVIRONS

The environs of Salzburg are outstanding, and to explore them fully you'll need to refer to the information contained in Chapter VIII of this book, "Land Salzburg." The area is a setting of beautiful old romantic castles, charming villages, glacial lakes, salt mines, ice caves, and some of the most spectacular alpine scenery in Europe. But before going on to Land Salzburg, I'll describe a few attractions to be found right on the doorstep of the city.

Schloss Hellbrunn (Hellbrunn Palace), about 3 miles south of the city, is a popular spot for outings from Salzburg. It's at the end of Hellbrunnerstrasse off Alpenstrasse. Also to be seen here is the Hellbrunn Zoo. The palace dates from the early 17th century, built as a hunting lodge and summer residence for Prince-Archbishop Marcus Sitticus. The zoo was formerly the palace deer park.

The palace gardens, one of the oldest baroque formal gardens in all Europe, are known for their trick fountains. As you walk through, take care. You may be showered when and from a source you least suspect. In some of the contrived fountain play, spurts of water shoot out from unlikely spots, such as from antlers. Some 265 figures in a mechanical theater are set in motion by a clockwork movement to the music of an organ, powered by water.

The rooms of the schloss are furnished and decorated in 18th-century style. See, in particular, the banqueting hall with its trompe-l'oeil ceiling. There's also a domed octagonal room that was used as a music room and reception hall.

Conducted tours of the castle, trick fountains, and folklore museum are given during these hours: 9am to 4pm from April 1 to April 15; to 5pm from April 16 to April 30 and September 1 to September 15; to 5:30pm from May to August. From September 16 to September 30, hours are 9am to noon and 1 to 4:30pm, to 4pm in October. Admission is 39 AS ($2.85) for adults and 19 AS ($1.40) for children. The gardens, orangery, and pheasantry may be visited free.

A **Folk Museum** (part of Museum Carolino Augusteum) is in the Monatsschlösschen, overlooking Hellbrunn Park, and can be visited from Easter to November 1 daily from 9am to 5pm for an admission of 15 AS ($1.10) for adults and 10 AS (75¢) for children. The collection, assembled by Archbishop Markus Sittikus in 1615, is spread over three floors. Reflecting a cross section of local folk art, displays depict popular religious beliefs, folk medicine, and the traditional costumes of Land Salzburg.

In the same setting, a natural gorge forms the **Stone Theater,** where the first opera performed in the German-speaking world was presented in 1617. A Hellbrunn Festival is held in the gardens, palace, and theater in August.

In 1960 the **Hellbrunn Zoo** (tel. 0662/84-11-69) was opened, stretching around the western slope of the hill, with low fences allowing the public close views of the zoo's mainly alpine animal denizens. As this was the deer park for the prince-archbishops, there are still large herds of stags and their families grazing on their ancestral acres. The zoo is open all year. Daily visiting hours are 9am to 4pm from October to March, and 9am to 6pm from April to September. Admission is 35 AS ($2.55) for adults and 15 AS ($1.10) for children.

It's only about a 20-minute drive from the heart of Salzburg to Hellbrunn Palace, and if the weather is good, many visitors prefer to walk the 3 miles. If you drive, turn off Alpenstrasse at the Mobil gas station. Or you can take a 55 bus, which makes the run in about 18 minutes.

About 10 miles east from the center of Salzburg is **Gaisberg,** which at 4,250 feet is one of the best places for views of the Salzburg Alps. Much of the road leading here is hewn out of rock. You can take a bus to the Gaisbergspitz, or summit, from which you see almost a full panorama. On a clear day you can see into Chiemsee in West Germany and to the Dachstein massif. In summer the bus leaves Mirabellplatz daily at 10:30am and 2pm, the trip taking about an hour.

To reach **Untersberg,** about 7½ miles from Salzburg, you head south out of the city toward Berchtesgaden in West Germany, the retreat of Hitler during his days of power. At the St. Leonhard junction, turn right and drive to the platform of a cable-car station. The funicular goes to the Untersberg summit (6,020 feet), from which you have a panoramic view of the Salzburg Alps. A marked path leads to the Salzburger Hochtron (6,100 feet), highest Austrian peak in the Untersberg massif.

Funicular service runs March 1 to June 30 and September 16 to October 31 from 9:15am to 4:45pm; July 1 to mid-September from 8:30am to 5:30pm, and December 25 to February 28 from 10am to 4pm. The fare is 150 AS ($10.90) for a round-trip ticket, 80 AS ($5.80) for children.

The **Church of Maria Plain,** about 2½ miles north of Salzburg, is the most important pilgrimage church in the vicinity of the city. Construction on the twin-towered baroque church started in 1671, and it's lavishly embellished. To reach Maria Plain you head out Plainstrasse, eventually turning right onto Plainbergweg. If you take the tram it's about 45 minutes farther on foot. Many people prefer the view from here at night.

From Maria Plain you can continue on about 9 miles northwest to another pilgrimage church at **Oberndorf.** This village lying on the Salzach River is where Father Joseph Mohr wrote the carol "Silent Night" on Christmas Eve in 1818. A memorial chapel was built here in 1937.

Mattsee, 14 miles from Salzburg, is a small resort for city residents, on the shores of Niedertrumer See, Obertrumer See, and Grabensee. Many tombstones from the 14th century have been found in the cloister of a 13th-century collegiate church here. To get to Mattsee, head out on Plainstrasse and the Itzlinger Hauptstrasse. You'll go through the hamlets of Bergheim, Lengfelden, and Elixhausen to reach it.

In the Tennengau, a division of the Salzach Valley south of Salzburg, a major attraction is—

Hallein

The second-largest town in Land Salzburg (visited in detail in the upcoming chapter), Hallein, once a center for processing the salt from the mines of Dürnberg, was a prize possession of the prince-archbishops of Salzburg. Today it's an industrial town on the Salzach River, and tourists pass through it on the way to the Dürrnberg mines.

On the north side of the Hallein parish church are the former home and tomb of the man who composed the music for Mohr's carol, Franz-Xaver Gruber, a schoolteacher, who died in 1863.

The Dürrnberg Salt Mines are the big lure, forming one of the most popular attractions in Land Salzburg, usually visited on day trips from Salzburg. On guided tours, visitors walk downhill from the ticket office to the mine entrance, then board an electric mine train that takes you deep into the caverns. From there, you go on foot through deep galleries, changing levels by sliding down polished wooden slides. You exit the mine on the train that brought you in. An underground museum traces the history of salt mining back into remote time.

Hallein is connected to Salzburg, 10 miles away, by both train and bus service. From here there's a cable railway to Dürrnberg, although many Germans and Austrians prefer to walk to the mines, the trip taking about an hour.

Tours lasting 1½ hours are conducted daily from 9am to 5pm, May to September, and from 10am to 2pm in October. Admission is 85 AS ($6.20) for adults and 45 AS ($3.25) for children. The round-trip cable-car ride is 56 AS ($4.05) per person. Phone 06245/5394 for more information. The tourist office is at Unterer Markt 1, A-5400 Hallein. There is a modern road from Hallein directly to a large parking lot near the ticket office to the mines.

Also in the Salzburg environs is the Pongau basin, described in the Land Salzburg chapter coming up, a division of the Salzach Valley. An outstanding attraction, most often visited on day trips from the city, is the—

Eisriesenwelt

Some 30 miles south of Salzburg by train is the "World of the Ice Giants," the largest known ice caves in the world. The caves, opening at some 5,500 feet up, stretch for about 26 miles, although only a portion of that length is open to the public. You'll see fantastic ice formations at the entrance, extending for half a mile.

To reach the Eisriesenwelt, head for Werfen, a village that is the center for exploring the ice caves. It also contains **Castle Hohenwerfen,** which was founded in the 11th century and frequently reconstructed. It is one of the most important castles in Land Salzburg and is visible for miles around. It's open in summer to visitors.

If you come by train from Salzburg, you can take a taxibus from Werfen's Hauptplatz (main square), going 3½ miles by mountain road to the same point you'll reach if you're traveling in your own car, rising from 1,600 feet to 3,000 feet. You have to take a cable car to the entrance of the caves, which involves a 15-minute walk along a shady path with stunning views to the lower station. The round-trip cable-car ride costs 85 AS ($6.20) for adults and 45 AS ($3.25) for children to this point.

Tours begin at Dr.-Friedrich-Oedl-Haus at 5,141 feet, from which you walk to the actual entrance. Tours take about two hours and cost 65 AS ($4.75) for adults and 35 AS ($2.55) for children. Conducted tours are given every hour, 9:30am to 3:30pm, from May to October. In July and August the schedule is accelerated if demand justifies it. For information, telephone 06468/7603.

Eisriesenwelt is on the western cliffs of the Hochkogel, towering over the Salzach Valley. You can imagine you're in the kingdom of the Ice Queen as you pass through this underground ice wonderland, which looks as if fairies had decorated their frozen precincts, adorning them with icy figures and frozen waterfalls. The climax of this chill underworld tour is the spectacular Ice Palace. It's too bad visitors can't explore the entire 26-mile length of the cave, but such a venture is extremely dangerous and cannot be permitted.

Allow about 5½ hours for the entire trip from Werfen and back. Dress warmly, and wear shoes appropriate for hiking.

Even if you don't want to go underground, I recommend making the drive as far up toward the caves as you can go, as the scenery along the way is splendid.

TOURS

If you have very limited time in Salzburg and want to see as much as possible, consider an organized tour. The best ones are offered by **Panorama Tours & Travel,** Schrannengasse 2 (tel. 0662/716-18-0), which is the Gray Line company for Salzburg.

The original **Sound of Music Tour** combines the Salzburg city tour with an excursion to the lake district and the places where the film with Julie Andrews was shot. The English-speaking guide shows you not only highlights from the film but also historical and architectural landmarks of Salzburg, as well as a part of the Salzkammergut countryside. Departure is daily at 9:30am and 2pm, and the cost is 180 AS ($13) for the morning tour and 250 AS ($18.25) for the afternoon tour.

You must take your passport along for any of three trips into Bavaria in West Germany. One of these—called the **Eagle's Nest Tour**—takes visitors to Berchtesgaden and on to Obersalzberg, where Hitler and his elite followers had a vacation retreat. Departure is daily at 9am, May 15 to October 20, with the tour lasting 4½ hours and costing 480 AS ($35).

Among other tours offered, one takes in charming castles and the surrounding Land Salzburg landscape. Departure is daily at 1pm. The tour lasts five hours and costs 480 AS ($35).

Bookings are possible at the bus terminal at Mirabellplatz/St. Andrä Kirche (tel. 0662/74029).

6. Where to Shop

Salzburg, being a much smaller city, obviously doesn't have the wide range of merchandise that Vienna does. However, if you're not going on to the Austrian capital, you may want to patronize some of the establishments recommended below, most of them opening at 9am and staying open until 6pm. Note that a number of them, especially the smaller places, take a one- or two-hour break for lunch. The stores also close down on Saturday afternoon and all day on Sunday.

Good buys in Salzburg include souvenirs of Land Salzburg, dirndls, lederhosen, petit point, and all types of sports gear. **Getreidegasse** is a main shopping thoroughfare, but you'll also find some intriguing little shops on the **Residenzplatz.**
Alois Wenger & Co., Getreidegasse 29 (tel. 0662/84-16-77), offers one of the

finest selections of Austrian loden and traditional costumes in Salzburg. It's a member of a chain of stores stretching across Austria, but this is one of its most stylish shops. It sells adaptations of traditional dresses such as the kind of alpine-inspired dirndl, crafted in satin and velvet, that a woman might wear to a fashionable party. The staff is also available to give advice.

Jahn-Markl, Residenzplatz 3 (tel. 0662/84-26-10), is a small and elegant store with a forest-green façade trimmed with brass and wrought-iron detailing. In the center of the Old Town, it has been in the same family for four generations. It carries lederhosen for all sizes, leather skirts, and a full line of traditional Austrian coats and blazers. The less expensive items are usually sold off the racks that stretch high above the clients' heads. More expensive items are usually made to order in four weeks and can be mailed anywhere in the world for an additional charge. Some children's clothing is available as well, along with hats, belts, and gloves.

Salzburger Heimatwerk, Am Residenzplatz 9 (tel. 0662/84-41-19), is one of the best places in town to buy native Austrian handcrafts. It's a dignified stone building in the least crowded section of the Residenzplatz, with a discreet (and hard to see) sign announcing its location. Items for sale include Austrian silver and garnet jewelry, painted boxes, candles, woodcarvings, copper and brass ceramics, tablecloths, and patterns for cross-stitched samplers in alpine designs. A special section sells dressmaking materials such as cotton and silk, with dressmaker patterns that can be adapted for the eventual size of the garment. Wherever you go in this interesting store, be sure to keep exploring until you've seen every room.

Sporting Goods Dschulnigg, Griesgasse 8 (tel. 0662/84-23-76), is an uppercrust emporium for clothes, guns, fishing equipment, overcoats for both men and women, intricately patterned sweaters in alpine colors, a collection of fur-lined hats, and many kinds of sporting goods. Queen Elizabeth II and Prince Phillip have been photographed on a shopping expedition here. You can get hunting rifles in Austria without a license (but not pistols or revolvers), although the Customs officers back home might present a problem. Be sure to climb to the second floor if you're interested.

Slezak, Makartplatz 8 (tel. 0662/73-5-68), in Mozart's second house, sells gloves, skirts, leather goods, umbrellas, suitcases, sweaters, belts, and hand-embroidered evening jackets and purses, and has a good selection of all these items. Slezak has a branch shop at the Salzburg Sheraton.

Schatz-Konditorei, Getreidegasse 3 (tel. 0662/84-27-92). Already covered in the café section of this chapter, this establishment is an excellent pastry shop and one of the few in Salzburg that will mail cakes to foreign clients. The specialty of the store is the highly acclaimed Mozart-Kugeln, a concoction of pistachio, marzipan, and hazelnut nougat, dipped in chocolate. It might make a nice present for the friends or relatives you left behind. Packages of this gourmet delight can be air mailed to North America.

Gollhofer Herrenmode, Getreidegasse 10 (tel. 0662/84-21-75), is a large store selling quality clothing for men and women. It has a high-ceilinged, spacious format with lots of modern paneling and a collection of merchandise that includes sports jackets, leather garments, and women's shoes. This is more of a large downtown store than an intimate boutique.

Brüder Fritsch, Getreidegasse 42-44 (tel. 0662/84-75-51 for the shoe store, 0662/84-17-93 for the leather shop and women's boutique), sells high-quality shoes, luggage, leather goods, petit point, and women's fashions to an upmarket clientele. Both Laura Biagiotti and Yves Saint Laurent are represented here.

Musikhaus Pühringer, Getreidegasse 13 (tel. 0662/84-32-67), sells all kinds of classical musical instruments, especially those that are popular in Central Europe, as well as a large selection of electronic instruments (including synthesizers and amplifiers). There's a choice of folk-music records and tapes, plus many classical recordings, especially those by Mozart. The store is appropriately located a few buildings away from the composer's birthplace.

Lobmeyr, Schwarzstrasse 20 (tel. 0662/73-1-81), is the Salzburg branch of the famous store in Vienna. Among a wide range of crystal goblets and elegant china, it includes some of the prettiest breakfast services I've seen, many of them made in Hungary.

Lanz, Schwarzstrasse 4 (tel. 0662/74-2-72), is a well-stocked store across the river from the Old Town. The format is rustically modern, with one of the widest collections of long-skirted dirndls in town, in dozens of different fabrics and colors. Men's clothing includes loden-colored overcoats. The store also sells dirndls for little girls, women's shoes, and hand-knitted sweaters.

J. B. Neumüller, Rathausplatz 3 (tel. 0662/1429). In winter this store sells children's toys. In summer the stock changes, the shelves filling up with handcrafted souvenirs such as mugs, cowbells, and rustic art objects.

---

7. Salzburg After Dark

The annual cultural events, which reach their peak at the Salzburg Festival (see below), overshadow any after-dark amusements such as discos and beerhalls. Clubs come and go in Salzburg fairly rapidly.

FESTIVAL

The **Salzburg Festival**—one of the premier music attractions of Europe—reached its 70th season in 1990. The composer Richard Strauss founded the festival, aided by the director Max Reinhardt and the writer Hugo von Hofmannsthal. Details on the festival are available by writing to the box office of the Salzburg Festival, P.O. Box 140, A-5010 Salzburg, Austria (tel. 0662/8045).

Festival tickets are in great demand, and there never are enough of them. Don't arrive expecting to get into any of the major events unless you've already purchased tickets. Travel agents can often get tickets for you, and you can also go to branches of the Austrian Tourist Office at home or abroad. Hotel concierges, particularly at the deluxe and first-class hotels of Salzburg, always have some tickets on hand, but they most often ask outrageous prices for them, depending on the particular performance you wish to attend. At first-night performances of the major productions, remember that evening dress is *de rigueur*.

An annual event is Hofmannsthal's adaptation of the morality play *Everyman*, which is staged outside the cathedral in the Domplatz. Concerts are likely to be conducted in the Rittersaal of the Residenz Palace (Mozart also conducted here) and in the marble salon of Mirabell Palace (Mozart's father, Leopold, conducted here). The Salzburger Marionette Theater (see below) also presents performances. Ballet is likely to be performed by the Vienna State Opera Ballet with the Vienna Opera Chorus and the Vienna Philharmonic. Operas (certainly by Mozart, and possibly by Richard Strauss and Beethoven) are accompanied by the Vienna Philharmonic. International soloists—such big names as Luciano Pavarotti—are invited annually, and the London Symphony or the Berlin Philharmonic is also likely to be invited.

The 1991 dates for the festival are July 27 to September 1. Tickets begin at 150 AS ($11) for standing room at one of the serenade concerts, going up to 1,700 AS ($123.50) for choice seats. Opera seats range from 700 AS ($51) to 3,300 AS ($240).

OTHER CONCERTS

The aforementioned **Salzburger Marionetten Theater,** Schwarzstrasse 24 (tel. 0662/7-24-06) presents shows from Easter through September (there are also special shows at Christmas). These puppets perform both opera and ballet and are a delight to adults and children alike. Usually they present Mozart operas. Seats are likely to range from 230 AS ($16.75) to 350 AS ($25.50). The theater was founded in 1913, and since that time has been one of the most unusual—and enjoyable—theatrical entertainments in Salzburg. You may forget that marionettes are onstage, it's that realistic.

Although the **Salzburger Landestheater,** Schwarzstrasse 22 (tel. 0662/7-40-86), doesn't always play for summer visitors, you can see its regular repertoire of operas (not just Mozart) and operettas if you're in Salzburg from September until some time in June. On one visit, for example, you might see a thrilling performance of Giuseppe Verdi's *La Traviata.* In August, performances are given for the Festival.

All year round you can go to the tourist office in Salzburg and pick up a list of musical events that are being presented when you're there, even if you should arrive in January. In fact, the annual **Mozart Week** is in January. Summer chamber music concerts are held throughout the city at major landmarks such as the Residenz.

Music, especially organ concerts, is also presented at the **Mozarteum,** Schwarzstrasse 26 (tel. 0662/7-31-54).

JAZZ

Jazzclub Urbanikeller, Schallmooser Hauptstrasse 50 (tel. 0662/70894), is the most popular jazz emporium in town. The entrance cost averages around 80 AS ($5.80), but this can vary or be nothing at all, depending on the popularity of the musicians on any given night. It is open only on Friday from 8pm to either 2 or 3am. Once you're inside, half a liter of beer goes for 40 AS ($2.90).

GAMBLING

Casino Salzburg, Mönchsberg (tel. 0662/84-56-56), sits alongside the Café Winkler. You reach it by an elevator at the bottom of the hill. Inside the casino, French and American roulette are played, as well as black jack and baccarat. Poker is also offered. You must take your passport, and you can visit daily from 3pm to 3am. In exchange for an entrance fee of 170 AS ($12.25), the management will give you lucky chips or gaming tokens worth 200 AS ($14.50). If you drive, there is free parking for casino guests for 12 hours in the Mönchsberg-Garage Nord.

LATIN AMERICAN MUSIC AND DINING

Mexicano Keller, Hotel Blaue Gans, Getreidegasse 43 (tel. 0662/84-24-91), is a popular evening spot in Salzburg. It offers Latin American music and Mexican food. The cuisine includes both enchiladas and chili con carne, along with five different steak dishes, including carne asada Acapulco. Fondue Mexicano is another specialty, served for two persons. Sangría is available as well, and meals cost from 175 AS ($12.75). The décor looks like a combination of an Austrian wine cellar and a ranch south of the (American) border, with a vaulted stone ceiling and rustic ranchero-style banquettes. The cellar is open from 8pm to 2am; closed Tuesday and Wednesday.

BEER GARDENS

Casinos not for you? My recommendation for one of the most enjoyable and authentic evenings in Salzburg is to pay a gemütlich visit to the **Augustiner Bräustübl,** Augustinergasse 46 (tel. 0662/3-12-46), the most famous beer garden of Salzburg. (The place got its name from an old Augustinian monastery.) In winter, guests retreat inside one of several large beerhalls, but in fair weather the beer-drinking fraternity spills into the leafy chestnut garden to "taste the brew." The brew, incidentally, is excellent, and it is served Monday to Friday from 3 to 11pm, on Saturday and Sunday from 2:30 to 11pm. The activity gets loud and raucous, especially when the young men from Munich invade on their summer tours south from neighboring Bavaria. To get here, you climb a steep, narrow cobblestone street and go through an austere stone entranceway, passing statues of ecstatic saints and happy cherubs.

After descending a baroque staircase whose ceiling frescoes evoke images of a

Habsburg palace, you'll come face to face with about a dozen kiosks, where you can buy carry-away portions of salads, wursts, sandwiches, and pretzels. Farther on, you choose one of the thick stoneware mugs from the drying racks and carry it to the beer tap, paying the cashier as you go. A full liter costs from 50 AS ($3.65), depending on the type of brew you select. Smaller mugs are available if you just want to sip and watch the crowd. You take your own mug to one of the trio of cavernous rooms (*saals*) nearby. This place has been known to squeeze in some 2,200 beer-drinkers (the busiest night on record).

Stiegelbräu Keller, Festungsgasse 8-10 (tel. 0662/84-26-81). To reach this place, you'll have to negotiate a steep cobblestone street that drops off on one side to reveal a breathtaking view of Salzburg. Part of the establishment is carved into the rocks of Mönchsberg mountain, so all that is visible from the outside is a gilded iron gate and a short stairway of porous stone. The cavernous interior is open only in summer when, along with hundreds of others, you can drink beer and eat traditional bierkeller food such as sausages and schnitzels. But, mainly, you can attend performances of the Alpinia Folkloric Club. Its members offer a "Salzburger Abend" every Wednesday and Saturday night at 8:15, which includes 2½ hours of yodeling and Schuhplattler dancing, all of which is accompanied with music from brass bands and zithers. Seats cost around 150 AS ($11) and should be booked in advance.

LAND SALZBURG

The geographic borders of Land Salzburg may appear to be a fantasy—the work of a mapmaker gone haywire—but actually the boundaries of this lofty province in the high Alps follow the dictates of Mother Nature. Craggy mountains, deep valleys, winding rivers, lakes, and rolling foothills, plus a little political expediency, all had their effect on the cartographers' pens. This Bundesland (state, or province) of Austria takes in some 2,762 square miles. It's known for its beautiful waterfalls, including the Krimml Falls, the most important cataract in the eastern Alps.

This is a land of both summer and winter sports, with such celebrated spas as Badgastein and such renowned ski resorts as Zell am See, Kaprun, and Saalbach. You can select resorts right on the lakeside or else mountain hotels at celestial levels. You'll be better suited to the activities of this province if you're athletic.

Instead of staying in Salzburg, especially during the crowded, hotel-scarce months of festival time, you might prefer to anchor into one of the resorts described below and commute to the province's capital city. You'll find the prices often cheaper and the living much easier if you don't mind the drive. (You won't necessarily have to go into the city *every* day.)

Accommodations are wide-ranging. If you want deluxe, you'll find it. If you want a mountain hut or just a *zimmer* (room) in one of the local houses—usually perched in some idyllic spot—these are available too. A few castle hotels, some of the finest accommodations in Austria, are found in Land Salzburg, to suit those who have traditional and romantic tastes and don't always demand the latest in plumbing fixtures.

The terrain directly around Salzburg is flat, but most of Land Salzburg is mountainous. Always inquire about local weather conditions before embarking for a day's sightseeing, particularly if you're going to be traversing one of those lofty alpine highways. The highest mountain range in Austria, the Hohe Tauern, lies on the southern fringe of Land Salzburg. A national park, the Hohe Tauern encompasses one of the most beautiful areas of the eastern Alps, still mainly undeveloped. The core of the park is formed of mighty mountains, steep rock faces, glaciers, and glacier streams, one of which contains the Krimml Falls mentioned above. The park's periphery comprises mountain meadows, alpine pastures, and protective woods. Visitors to the park are required to treat the plants and animals with respect.

The Tauern Hwy. is one of the most important roads going from north to south over the Alps. Vehicles pass through two tunnels while traversing the highway. The Tauerntunnel is 4 miles long and the Katschbergtunnel 3¼ miles.

Because many of the alpine highways are feats of engineering, requiring enormous investment of capital and paralyzingly expensive upkeep, tolls are charged. They're not excessive, but are vital to keeping some scenic splendors open to the public.

Of course, Land Salzburg is a skier's paradise. The season begins about 10 days before Christmas and usually lasts until Easter or beyond, depending on snow conditions. Skiing on some of the lofty plateaus is possible all year long.

Kaprun, Saalbach, and Zell am See are long-established *and* expensive resorts. However, in the true spirit of the Frommer guides, I've sought less familiar and even undiscovered places—many known only to the Austrians and an occasional German tourist—for this book. Many establishments we'll visit, particularly the smaller, off-the-beaten-track resorts, are making their debut in a guide (in any language).

Long cut off from the rest of the world but now accessible because of modern engineering achievements, some of the sections of Land Salzburg still cling tenaciously to their traditions. Old costumes and folklore still flourish in the province, although who can say whether the present generation—heavily influenced by U.S. styles, music, or whatever—will want to keep the traditional ways alive into the next century?

The quickest way to reach the province of Land Salzburg is to fly into Salzburg, then go by train, bus, or private car to one of the resorts. If you're really in a hurry, you can take an air taxi from the capital to either Zell am See or Badgastein.

Many excursions leave from Salzburg and go into Land Salzburg, but frankly I think it's much more fun if you do it on your own. Most of the people involved in tourist services speak English, and you can travel in relative security and comfort, perhaps making discoveries of your own. You might even prefer to take a Postal Bus which goes to *all* regions.

Of course, during your tour of Land Salzburg, you can easily stray toward the West German frontier. In many places you'll be very near the border, and in fact in your exploration you might have to cross that border once or twice. That should pose no problem. Often, if you don't look suspicious, the border guards will wave you across without even looking at your passport.

One of the most interesting sections to explore in west-central Austria is the Salzkammergut lake country. This is a narrow-waisted corridor in Land Salzburg between Bavaria and Upper Austria. Parts of it will be explored in other sections of this guide. Essentially, it's a land for those who like clear alpine air and blue mountain lakes, the country of *The Sound of Music*.

Salzkammergut, incidentally, means "domain of the salt office." Many parts of the area grew rich from mining salt—and also gold.

1. Badgastein

The premier spa of Austria and one of the great spa towns of Europe—that's Badgastein. The local tourist industry is said to have been founded by Frederick, Duke of Styria, who came here in the 15th century for treatment of a gangrenous

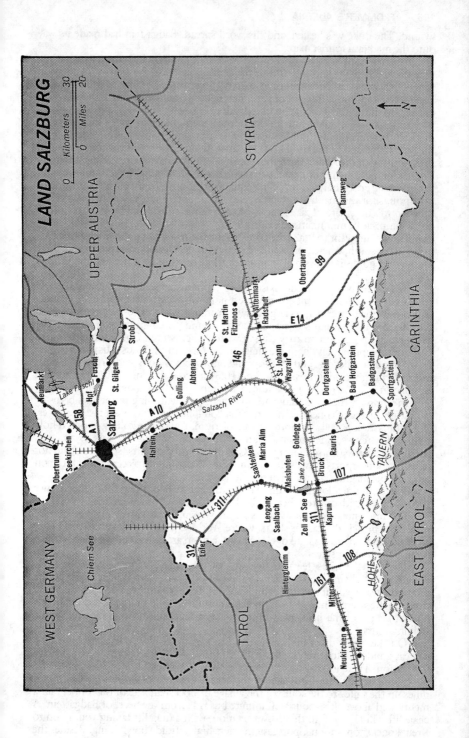

wound. The duke was healed, and the word spread. Badgastein had made its way onto the medieval tourist map.

In more modern times, royalty and aristocrats put it back on the spa map when they flocked here around the turn of the century to "take the waters." And good waters they are—radioactive springs with healing properties. The curative effect of Badgastein's springs is due not only to their natural heat from deep under the earth but also to the radium emanation called radon.

Badgastein lies on the north slope of the Tauern massif in one of the most dramatically beautiful spots in all of Austria. The spa town climbs steep hillsides split by the foaming waters of the tumbling Gasteiner Ache. Hotels, many with water piped in directly from the Ache, adorn the steep slopes formed by the cascading waterfall. The spa's indoor swimming pool is carved into a rock filled with the radon waters.

With its pristine alpine air, skiing equaling that of St. Moritz in Switzerland, 18 hot springs for thermal hydrotherapy, and a mountain tunnel that has been called "the world's only natural giant sauna," Badgastein is considered by many people to be the pinnacle of mountain spa resorts.

Those who want to "take the cure" in the natural sauna go to **Böckstein,** two miles to the south, where the thermal galleries (underground passageways) are in an abandoned goldmine. A small train takes those seeking treatment to the various chambers.

Badgastein began its resort existence as a summer retreat, but is now also a center for winter sports. It contains the finest hotels in Land Salzburg province, and a big convention center attracts large crowds from many places.

Besides the natural scenery of the town and its environs, you can see the **Nikolauskirche,** a 15th-century church with well-preserved Gothic frescoes, a late Gothic stone pulpit, and baroque altars and tombs. In the **Haus Austria,** you can view a mineral collection and see slides and photographs along with artifacts in mining and hunting exhibitions. Hours are 10:30am to noon and 3:30 to 6pm daily. Admission is 25 AS ($1.80) for adults. Children up to 10 years are admitted free.

In summer, there are things to do other than swimming in thermal baths or taking advantage of concomitant activities. You'll find an array of saunas, massages, and gymnastics, as well as sunning in the solarium. You can go golfing on an 18-hole course, play tennis, ride horseback, go on mountain outings, or make excursions, perhaps in a fiacre (horse-drawn trap). Cableways and chair lifts (see below) are not only for winter-sports crowds. In summer they'll take you to places from which you can view the magnificent world of the Hohe Tauern.

There's quite a lot of evening entertainment in Badgastein, both in summer and in winter, with cabaret, theater, folkloric events, and other activities.

In winter, however, most visitors are drawn here for the fine skiing possibilities, with three principal areas for skiers, where World Championships and World Cup races are held. In 1958 Graukogel, one of the main areas, was the site of the World Championships for skiers.

Graukogel (8,224 feet), to the east of the valley, is reached by bus from Badgastein. A chair lift takes skiers to the halfway station, from which they go the rest of the way by double-chair lift and drag lift. Expert European skiers prefer these slopes in the afternoon. A round-trip ticket costs 160 AS ($11.75). A mountain restaurant stands at the halfway station. This is a favorite starting point for alpine walking tours.

On the west side of the valley rises **Stubnerkogel** (7,310 feet), reached by a six-seat gondola. However, it takes a chair lift and a couple of drag lifts to reach the top station. There is a mountain restaurant with a marvelous view. Easy mountain walks are possible here. **Kreuzkogel** (8,800 feet) is at **Sportgastein,** which lies 5 miles up the valley to the south of the village of Böckstein, site of the tunnel sauna mentioned above. It's about a 20-minute bus ride from the heart of Badgastein. A chair lift will take you to the halfway station, with a drag lift taking you up on to Kreuzkogel's top station. Sportgastein offers high-altitude bowl skiing. Besides the well-equipped skiing facilities here, including cross-country runs, you can also enjoy indoor horseback riding or trekking, indoor tennis on sandy courts, alpine curling, ice skating, and walks on beautiful winter paths away from traffic.

You can drive from Badgastein to Sportgastein along the Gasteiner Alpenstrasse at elevations ranging from 3,000 to 4,766 feet. The toll charge is 40 AS ($2.90) per person; children under 15, free. In winter the ski season ticket includes the road toll.

UPPER-BRACKET HOTELS

Hotel Elisabethpark, A-5640 Badgastein (tel. 06434/2551). The ceilings of this five-star hotel are as varied and unusual as anything else you are likely to find in Austria. They include sections covered with heavily textured knotty pine as well as rooms crowned with Moorish patterns of geometric greens and reds. One of the sitting rooms has a white ceiling with iridescent gray-blue wallpaper and elegant marble detailing around the windows. The public rooms stretch on and on, which is not surprising since this hotel is a vast, sprawling collection of buildings, with a white exterior, lots of balconies, and a series of hallways that are often decorated with unusual paintings, hunting trophies, and regional antiques. A thermally heated swimming pool on the premises, a sauna, and a host of massage therapies are part of the health facilities here. In 115 well-furnished rooms and apartments, tariffs range from 1,050 AS ($76.25) to 1,200 AS ($87.25) daily for a single and from 1,900 AS ($138.25) to 2,200 AS ($160) for a double, including breakfast. The hotel is open from mid-December until April and from mid-May until mid-October.

Parkhotel Bellevue, A-5640 Badgastein (tel. 06434/25710), offers a vast expanse of covered balconies turned toward the most scenic part of the nearby mountains. Viewed from the downhill side, it looks like a glittering collection of windows and extensions, with a generous covering of ivy over the foundations of many of them. The 90-room hotel includes a 400-year-old alpine hut near the ski slopes, with a rustic bar area and a smoke bonnet supported by carved wooden posts. In the main building an elegant series of public rooms is tastefully filled with Oriental rugs, painted ceilings, and comfortable niches.

The bedrooms are spacious, well furnished, and sunny, usually with big balconies and beautiful lighting fixtures. In summer, rates range from 800 AS ($58.25) to 1,100 AS ($80) per person daily. In winter, charges go up to 1,400 AS ($101.75) per person daily. All prices include full board, featuring a bountiful breakfast buffet and a four-course dinner, along with free entrance to the hotel's indoor thermal swimming pool and free use of a chair lift to its Bellevue-Alm in winter. Prices are slightly higher between December 20 and January 6. An American-style bar offers live music, while an indoor thermal swimming pool is graced with copies of ancient Roman sculptures. A full range of massage therapies is available for an additional fee.

Villa Hess Hotel-Restaurant, Erzherzog-Johann-Promenade 1, A5640 Badgastein (tel. 06434/38280), attracts the most discerning (and well-heeled) visitor to the spa, as it is both a leading hotel and the premier restaurant of Badgastein (see below). To reach the place, you first have to negotiate a hilly road leading to Badgastein (watch for the signs pointing the way). Jörg Wörther, master chef, proves he's also adept at running a fine and elegant hotel—in this case an art nouveau villa. Reopened in 1987 after careful renovations, the hotel has a ground-floor restaurant with three different rooms and a bar. Upstairs, the so-called Bel Étage, there are six elegant double rooms, each with private bath, color TV, and direct-dial phone. Depending on the time of year, singles range from 750 AS ($54.50) to 1,050 AS ($76.25) daily, with doubles going from 1,200 AS ($87.25) to 1,800 AS ($130.75). Gourmet half board costs another 450 AS ($32.75), which is a really good value, considering the quality of the cuisine. The hotel closes in June and November.

Hotel Weismayr, A-5640 Badgastein (tel. 06434/2594), sits prominently in the center of town, rising grandly in a series of milk-white stories, each embellished with neoclassical ornamentation. The roof is fashioned of green copper, while the street level has been modernized to include cafés and kiosks. Both the main sitting room—a blend of browns and reds, with Oriental rugs, comfortable settees, and wing chairs—and the elegant high-ceilinged dining room are beautifully decorated. Parasols and plants dot the terrace café. The hotel, open from December to March and May to October, rents 76 bedrooms, each with private bath or shower. In winter, half board costs 960 AS ($69.75) to 1,060 AS ($77) per person daily; in summer, half board is 860 AS ($62.50) to 960 AS ($69.75) per person daily.

Hotel Wildbad, A-5640 Badgastein (tel. 06434/3761), stands out from the collection of buildings around it because of its dark-yellow façade and its flat-roofed construction of big windows and prominent balconies. Views from the 40 wood-detailed bedrooms usually offer splendid vistas of the valley; the public rooms are pleasant and up-to-date. On the premises is a sauna with a range of physical therapy services, as well as a terrace sundeck with chaises longues and café tables. In the center of the village, close to the indoor thermal pools and the ski lifts, the hotel charges 620 AS ($45) to 860 AS ($62.50) daily for a single and 560 AS ($40.75) to 860 AS ($62.50) per person for a double, with half board included. Gerhard Hörtnagl, owner and manager, sees to it that excellent food is provided, with a superb salad buffet and a buffet breakfast. The hotel is open from December to October.

MIDDLE-BRACKET HOTELS

Amid towering pine trees on a rise above the rest of the spa town, **Hotel Salzburgerhof,** A-5640 Badgastein (tel. 06434/2037), looks like a 19th-century balconied building with a later series of stories added on top, one of which holds an indoor swimming pool. Much of the interior, including the reception area and bar, is covered with paneling and small accents of vivid color. Anny and Helmut Lercher, the owners, charge 720 AS ($52.25) to 950 AS ($69) per person daily, with half board included, depending on the season. The 100 bedrooms, which are rented from December to March and May to September, contain either private baths or showers.

Hotel Straubinger, A-5640 Badgastein (tel. 06434/20120), is a 370-year-old traditional hotel in the center of town, where Franz Joseph, the emperor, used to stay. Inside, the 50-room hotel contains an American bar, two dining rooms, a sun terrace, a reading room with a small library, and a massage service. The food is well prepared, and the service, directed by Karl-Michael Rödhamer, is professional. In well-furnished rooms, singles range from 600 AS ($43.50) to 850 AS ($61.75) daily, and doubles cost 1,050 AS ($76.25) to 1,600 AS ($116.25), with half board included.

Kurhotel Miramonte, A-5640 Badgastein (tel. 06434/2577), sits on the landscaped side of an alpine hill, with a panoramic view of the valley from the hotel's downhill side. It's surrounded with wooden balconies in their full natural grain, which contrasts prettily with the white walls of the superstructure. A big terrace has sun umbrellas jutting up from the extended roof of the second floor. Inside, the public rooms are elegantly simple, with Oriental rugs that cover even the tile floors of the rustic bar and weinstube area. Sauna, massage, and hydrotherapy services are available for an additional fee. The hotel offers 36 comfortably furnished bedrooms, each with private bath or shower. With half board included, the daily per-person rate ranges from 675 AS ($49) to 750 AS ($54.50). Open from December to April and June to September.

Kurhotel Mirabell, Bismarckstrasse 4-6, A-5640 Badgastein (tel. 06434/3301), rises imposingly from a hillside location thick with old pines. This cream-colored 130-bed hotel is rated four stars by the government, and it's been enlarged and renovated several times since its original construction at the turn of the century. Inside, a pleasantly dowdy collection of Victoriana and lace curtains contrasts with modern tile surfaces and an array of spa facilities. Many guests check in here for the hydrotherapy cure, although others come only for the relaxation. With half board, doubles cost 570 AS ($41.50) to 680 AS ($49.50) per person daily, with singles requiring an additional 50 AS ($3.75) daily surcharge.

Hotel Grüner-Baum, A-5640 Badgastein (tel. 06434/2516-0), is a complex of five chalet buildings surrounding a grassy area in the Kötschach Valley on the outskirts of Badgastein. The oldest building has, during its long history, offered hospitality to Kaiser Wilhelm, Empress Elisabeth, the Shah of Iran, Arturo Toscanini, Arthur Schopenhauer, Charles Laughton, and King Ibn Saud. The oldest parts of the building are exquisitely crafted of local woods, sometimes with elaborate regional carving, with hunting trophies beneath the beamed ceilings.

The 94 bedrooms are cozily rustic, with wood paneling and sometimes a recessed sleeping alcove in some of the singles; all have baths or showers. The daily half-board rate ranges from 950 AS ($69) to 1,600 AS ($116.25) per person.

The hotel sits at the starting point for 2½ miles of cross-country ski trails and will rent equipment to guests. It has a beginner's slope nearby, with a T-bar lift, as well as facilities for bowling, curling, hunting (deer and chamois), shooting (woodcocks), tennis, boccie, and swimming (both indoor and outdoor heated pools). There's a dancing bar as well as organized weekly activities. Children are well kept in the Miniclub and ski kindergarten. The hotel is open from December to March and May to October.

Hotel Savoy, A-5640 Badgastein (tel. 06434/2588), is a roadside hotel with dramatic terraces and big expanses of glass covering some of the windows. Inside is a covered swimming pool, plus a sauna and a graceful series of public rooms with high ceilings, crystal chandeliers, and antiques. Some of the floors have marble coverings, others contain Oriental rugs, and most of the comfortably furnished rooms are tastefully filled with pleasing fabrics and colors. There are tennis courts nearby. The hotel rents 59 well-furnished bedrooms, of which 54 contain private baths or showers. The half-board rate ranges from 650 AS ($47.25) to 850 AS ($61.75) per person daily.

Hotel Schillerhof, A-5460 Badgastein (tel. 06434/2581), sits on the side of a forested hill overlooking Badgastein. Its symmetrical construction encompasses wings on either side of the main section, which is covered with horizontal rows of wooden balconies. The interior has big windows, warmly tinted public rooms, and a panoramic restaurant. An outdoor swimming pool is flanked with chiseled stone walls, while the bedroom walls are sometimes covered with light-grained planking. The 80-bed hotel has rooms both with and without private baths. Half board, depending on room assignments, ranges from 550 AS ($40) to 900 AS ($65.50) per person daily.

BUDGET HOTELS

An unusual hostelry designed in the 19th century, the **Hotel Mozart,** A-5640 Badgastein (tel. 06434/2686), has half-rounded stone projections extending toward the front, a long veranda on the ground floor, and a gabled mansard roof on top of which an additional story was later added. The inside has beautifully patterned Oriental rugs in muted colors covering the floor of the wood-paneled lobby area, as well as crystal chandeliers hanging from the detailed plaster ceiling. Some of the 70 comfortably furnished rooms have private baths, although there are thermally heated baths on each floor. Bed-and-breakfast costs 240 AS ($17.50) to 410 AS ($29.75) per person daily.

Kurhaus Alpenblick, A-5460 Badgastein (tel. 06434/2062), is a chalet with a side wing containing comfortable balconied bedrooms. These are decorated with eclectic furnishings, which include Oriental rugs, heavy wooden headboards, and richly upholstered chairs; big windows offer views of the mountains. Well-prepared meals are served in the timbered and beamed dining room. A swimming pool is located outside on the grounds near a small mountain stream. The hotel, open from

December to October, rents 38 rooms with private baths or showers. Half-board charges range from 470 AS ($34.25) to 620 AS ($45) per person daily.

BEST FOR DINING

Not only is **Villa Hess,** Erzherzog-Johann-Promenade 1 (tel. 06434/38280), the most acclaimed restaurant in Badgastein, but it is recognized by many critics as one of the eight best restaurants in all of Austria. Using style and flair to wake up the sleepy tastebuds of the old spa, Jörg Wörther concocts the best specialties here, each made from patrician ingredients. After a champagne cocktail, you can opt for a rack of lamb, goose liver terrine with brioche, wild trout with mushrooms, tafelspitz, calves' brains, or roast venison with kohlrabi. Dessert might be a Glacierter Nussschmarrn mit Fichtenhonigobers (the waiter will explain). À la carte meals range from 380 AS ($27.75) to 720 AS ($52.25), with fixed-price menus going for 420 AS ($30.50) to 780 AS ($56.75). The restaurant is closed in June and November, but otherwise open daily except Monday from noon to 2pm and 6pm to midnight.

AFTER DARK

The center of nightlife—and the chicest spot to be seen at the spa and winter-sports center—is the **Casino Badgastein** (tel. 06434/2465). Here you can play roulette, baccarat, poker, and blackjack, but you'll need a passport to get in. The entrance fee is 170 AS ($12.25), which entitles you to 200 AS ($14.50) worth of free chips. The casino is open daily, 7pm to 2am, from Christmas to April 1 and July to September 15.

Schi-Alm (tel. 06434/2036). By the light and heat of a blazing open fireplace, visitors of many generations enjoy dance music and the romantic alpine atmosphere of this popular dance hall. The featured activities, which change every night of the week, range from a cheese-and-knockwurst evening (Monday), to a re-creation of a heurige, complete with Austrian wines and music (Wednesday), to a candlelit dance (Saturday). Drinks cost from 50 AS ($3.65), and full meals are served daily from 5pm to 2am.

One of the most popular discos in town is at the already recommended **Hotel Weismayr.** This place attracts a young and affluent crowd.

Another popular disco is **Mühlhäusl,** considered the best in town. It's found beneath the Hotel Söntgen (tel. 06434/2235), a three-minute walk from the Cure and Congress Center. This is an intimate rendezvous point, also attracting a young crowd.

If you want more conventional dancing, head for the **Hotel Elisabethpark,** already recommended. This is an elegant nightlife retreat, and most of its patrons are well dressed.

Another elegant choice on the après-ski circuit is the also recommended **Parkhotel Bellevue,** where guests often linger in its alpine tavern, enjoying drinks, candlelight, and an open fire. Its American bar has live music in season, a band playing for dancing couples.

2. Bad Hofgastein

Lying 5 miles from Badgastein, halfway to Dorfgastein (coming up), is another resort, Bad Hofgastein (2,850 feet), an old established spa and long a rival of Badgastein for the tourist schilling.

Bad Hofgastein is tinier than Badgastein, but it's almost as charming. The little resort is actually almost a satellite of the larger spa, as the radioactive waters of Badgastein are pumped to its neighbor. Some hardy visitors like to follow a marked footpath between the two towns, the trip taking about 2½ hours. As a resort unit, Badgastein and Bad Hofgastein welcome at least as many visitors as does Salzburg—maybe more.

The **pfarrkirche** (parish church) of this tiny village is late Gothic, dating from the end of the 15th century, although it has a baroque altar. Some sights, such as old houses with turrets, evoke thoughts of the gold-mining days in the Gastein Valley. In the 16th century the nearby goldmines made Bad Hofgastein the rival of Salzburg in wealth. A rich mining family lived at the 15th-century **Weitmoserschlössl,** which has now been turned into a café.

Bad Hofgastein, about 55 miles south of Salzburg, is on the town railway and federal road 167 and is served by Postal Buses.

The Gastein Valley and Bad Hofgastein are attracting more and more wintersports fans to the area. Some 50 gondola cableways and ski lifts open up more than 150 miles of well-marked and well-groomed ski runs. Thanks to the high capacity of an updated funicular cableway, the monocable rotation gondola lift with cabins for six passengers, two quadruple-chair lifts, and a triple-chair lift, skiers don't have to wait in long lines but can get right to skiing. The Dorfgastein-Grossarl interconnection and that of Schlossalm via the Angertal and Jungeralm ski center up to the Stubnerkogel (the largest lift interconnection in Land Salzburg) provide some of the most enjoyable ski runs in the valley.

Also available are cross-country skiing on well-maintained tracks, tobogganing, skating, and riding in horse-drawn sleighs.

UPPER-BRACKET HOTELS

Rising majestically in a contemporary adaptation of a chalet, **Grand Park Hotel,** Kurgartenstrasse 26, A-5630 Bad Hofgastein (tel. 06432/6356), stands in its own birch-filled park, with a swimming pool and lawn chairs on the grassy lawns around it. The interior is filled with stone and polished-wood accents, plush carpets, and modern touches of bright colors and shining brass, all of which combine for a feeling of well-being. An indoor pool under a soaring timbered roof is only one of the many sports and health-oriented facilities. Handsomely furnished singles range from 750 AS ($54.50) to 1,300 AS ($94.50) daily, and doubles cost 650 AS ($47.25) to 1,200 AS ($87.25) per person, with half board included. The 95 bedrooms contain private baths and showers.

Hotel Palace Gastein, Alex-Moser-Allee 13, A-5630 Bad Hofgastein (tel. 06432/67150), is a 200-room luxury hotel with an elevator, situated in a quiet, sunny spot a few minutes' walk from the resort center. Guest rooms all have showers or baths and toilets, radios, telephones, and balconies. Half board in winter ranges from 950 AS ($69) to 1,200 AS ($87.25) per person daily; in summer, however, half board goes from 700 AS ($51) to 940 AS ($68.25). Facilities guests may use include the thermal indoor pool, sauna, solarium, Guerlain beauty farm, covered tennis courts, hotel ski bus to the Schlossalm funicular railway, hairdresser, cosmetic salon, and supervised kindergarten, plus bars, a Vienna coffeehouse, and a lively nightclub. There is a daily program of entertainment and activities. The hotel is open from December to October.

Hotel Carinthia, Dr.-Zimmermann-Strasse 2, A-5630 Bad Hofgastein (tel. 06432/83740), is a large, solid-looking chalet with flowered balconies on all sides and regional painted detailing on the corner mullions and around some of the windows. The interior has elegant and unusual touches, such as brass sheathing above the stone curves of the fireplace, the tucked-away corner bar, and modern chandeliers in the high-ceilinged dining room. The colors of the 40 spacious bedrooms are coordinated in pleasing combinations, such as reddish violet with beiges and browns, in a contemporary décor of style and comfort. In addition to the indoor swimming pool the hotel has a wide range of massage and hydrotherapy regimes. In winter, with half board included, singles rent for 820 AS ($59.50) daily, with doubles costing 690 AS ($50.25) per person. Half-board charges in summer are 630 AS

($45.75) daily for a single and 600 AS ($43.60) per person for a double. Open from December to March and May to October.

Kur- und Sporthotel Moser, Kaiser Franz-Platz 2, A-5630 Bad Hofgastein (tel. 06432/6209), on the main square of town, has sections dating back to the 12th century. You'd never know it from a quick glance at the façade, which is pleasantly balconied with pink accents above the red street-level awnings. The interior, however, is vaulted and cozy, with lots of old exposed wood, heavy beams, Oriental rugs, and a tapestry. The furnishings are rustic and regional, with lots of homey touches such as racks of pewter above the banquettes of the dining room. The 50 sunny bedrooms, each with private bath, rent for 650 AS ($47.25) to 750 AS ($54.50) per person daily, with half board included. The hotel has private parking, and guests enjoy a roof garden for sunning, hot-spring thermal baths in the old Roman health tradition, a sauna, and massage facilities. For evening relaxation, they can choose an intimate lounge and terrace dining, or they may prefer the cozy cellar for dining and dancing in winter. Open from December to March and May to September.

Hotel Norica, R.-Bachbauer-Gasse 1, A-5630 Bad Hofgastein (tel. 06432/8391), in the pedestrian zone, is dramatically designed in such a way that the flowered balconies angle themselves directly toward the sun. A spacious sun terrace is covered with potted shrubs. A rounded hearth inside illuminates the art objects and striped banquettes of one of the public rooms, while the dining room is spacious, with good service.

An in-house disco, a curved bar, an indoor thermal swimming pool, a sauna, and a Turkish bath, plus a wide range of other sports, offer plenty of distractions. The light-toned, good-sized bedrooms, all with baths/showers, toilets, phones, color TVs and radios, are done in wood accents. Full-board rates go from 800 AS ($58.25) to 1,340 AS ($97.50) daily for singles and from 720 AS ($52.25) to 1,290 AS ($93.75) per person for doubles, depending on the season. The hotel is open from December to April and May to October.

MODERATE AND BUDGET HOTELS

Hotel Sendlhof, Pyrkerstrasse 34, A-5630 Bad Hofgastein (tel. 06432/3510), has six big-windowed floors, each surrounded with balconies and potted flowers. An outdoor heated swimming pool lies across the lawn. The interior has heavily recessed rectangular designs in the ceiling's paneling, large windows, cozy fireplaces with masonry detailing, and lots of extra touches such as ceramic stoves and painted detailing below some of the massive arches. Management sometimes provides live zither music in the evening.

The 55 bedrooms are elegant and cozy, each of them with lots of exposed wood and a private bath. Most of the units have private balconies. The Sendlhof charges 550 AS ($40) to 900 AS ($65.50) per person daily for half board. Open from December to March and May to October.

Hotel Astoria, Salzburger Strasse 24, A-5630 Bad Hofgastein (tel. 06432/62770), is a generously proportioned five-story building with a simple white and wood-balconied façade and an interior that has been renovated into a contemporary format of streamlined furniture and warmly inviting colors. An indoor swimming pool is encircled with molded furniture. This four-star hotel rents 50 bedrooms, each with private bath or shower. Half-board charges range from 620 AS ($45) to 800 AS ($58.25) per person daily. Guests are received from December to October.

Hotel St. Georg, Dr.-Zimmermann-Strasse 7, A-5630 Bad Hofgastein (tel. 06432/6100), has an elegant country-house atmosphere, with attractive en suite bedrooms and family apartments designed for discerning guests. The 50 bedrooms have complete baths, plus phones and TV connections, and they rent for 830 AS ($60.25) to 930 AS ($67.75) per person daily, with half board. The surcharge for single occupancy is 125 AS ($9). Tariffs include a buffet breakfast, a four-course dinner, service, heating, and taxes. Tempting Austrian cuisine is served in the Salzburg country-style restaurant, with special diets being catered to. Guests have the use of an indoor swimming pool, sauna, solarium, steam bath, and massage and cosmetic treatments. Secure parking is available in the hotel garage. Open from December to October.

Kurhotel Österreichischer Hof, Kurgartenstrasse 9, A-5630 Bad Hofgastein (tel. 06432/62160). One of the many charming aspects about this 57-room family-run hotel is a regional portal, which is surrounded with yellow and gold painted detailing, a theme repeated around many of the chalet's windows. A balconied extension with the same detailing stretches out behind. Both sections have the added benefit of angled stone buttresses reaching as high as the second-floor windows. The interior contains a heated pool, a range of massage therapy rooms, warmly tinted public rooms, and comfortably furnished and attractive bedrooms, many of them with wood paneling. Sometimes they're surprisingly spacious, and often have good views over the valley. Singles range from 625 AS ($45.50) to 885 AS ($64.25) daily, doubles from 565 AS ($41) to 875 AS ($63.75) per person. Half board is included. The Kurhotel is open from December to March and May to September.

Kurhotel Germania, Kurpromenade 14, A-5630 Bad Hofgastein (tel. 06432/6232), is a modern 62-room hotel with some beautifully maintained Victorian antiques (including an exquisite collection of armchairs) filling some of the big-windowed public rooms. If your unit has a balcony—and many of the pleasant and sunny bedrooms here do—you'll have a view of the houses and barns of the valley below. The façade of the hotel rises in a symmetrical series of white walls and wooden balconies, with summer parasols adding colorful accents. A full range of massage and hydrotherapy services is available inside. With full board included, singles range from 580 AS ($42.25) to 830 AS ($61.75) daily, while prices for a double are 505 AS ($36.75) to 760 AS ($55.25) per person. Tariffs depend on the plumbing. The hotel is open from December to October.

Kur- und Sporthotel Alpina, Parkstrasse 11-17, A-5630 Bad Hofgastein (tel. 06432/84750), a fine-quality hotel just three minutes from the center and the ski lift, offers such facilities as a heated thermal indoor swimming pool, sauna, solarium, and first-class restaurant and bar. The hotel also has its own thermal baths, massages, and mud packs. It looks like a double chalet, with symmetrical rooflines that peak above rows of wooden balconies. The interior is as tasteful and warm as anything you'll find in town, with attractive color schemes. A heavily beamed ceiling covers the illuminated waters of the indoor pool, while the lobby area is lit with pin spotlights from overhead beams. Each of the 99 often sunny bedrooms comes with a private bath or shower. Half-board charges range from 700 AS ($51) to 1,000 AS ($72.75) per person daily. The hotel is open from December to October.

Kurhotel Völserhof, Pyrkerstrasse 28, A-5630 Bad Hofgastein (tel. 06432/8288), rises five balconied stories above a flowering garden near the edge of town. In summer the areas above the windows of the second-floor restaurant are covered with masses of red flowers, while the arched windows on the ground floor are surrounded with regional designs. Much of the interior alternates areas of white with full-grained areas of wood. The city's recreation center is a 5-minute walk from the 48-bed hotel, and the terminus of the funicular is 10 minutes away. The Lang family, your hosts, charge 500 AS ($36.25) to 700 AS ($51) per person daily for half board; they close the hotel from mid-October to mid-December.

WHERE TO DINE

Near the departure point of the Schlössalmbahn, **Café-Restaurant Weitmoser-Schlössl** (tel. 06432/6601), because of its position on a steep hillside, affords a good view of the city below. Parts of it date from the 14th century, although today you'll just be grateful for the warmth of the place in winter and for the shaded ash trees in summer. You can dine here on mainly Austrian specialties, with meals costing 120 AS ($8.75) to 160 AS ($11.75). If you want only coffee, tea, or afternoon schnapps, you'll find an array of these items. Coffee costs from 25 AS

($1.80), while pastries range from 26 AS ($1.90). The place is open daily except Monday from 9am to 9pm.

AFTER DARK

For your big night on the town, you can take a taxi from Bad Hofgastein to Badgastein to gamble at the **casino,** already recommended.

Otherwise, you can stay right in Bad Hofgastein, dancing at its discos, enjoying open fires in its taverns, or else dancing more formally at the hotels that import live bands in season. The tourist office will tell you the latest information about which hotels or clubs are likely to have nightlife at any given time, as schedules and programs fluctuate.

Among the hotels, one of the best centers for après-ski life is the **Hotel Norica** (see above). You can just drop in for a drink at its bar, or else patronize one of its restaurants, including the Schneckenthurm-Häusl, the Egghaus-Stübl, or the Kutscher Grill. The young at heart will go below to **Georgies Club,** a disco that opens nightly in season at 8:30pm (closing time depends on the crowd). There's no cover charge, but a large beer will cost about 30 AS ($2.20).

There's also dancing nightly in season to a live band at **Palace Gastein** (see above).

The most interesting disco in Bad Hofgastein is called **Sherwood** (tel. 06432/7328), which has a very modern décor and assesses no cover charge. A large beer costs about 30 AS ($2.20). It's best to go after 10pm. The club, depending on the crowd, stays open late.

You may also want to check out the action at **Tennistreff** (tel. 06432/8485). The place has two tennis courts and a squash court along with a bar and restaurant, and is open daily in season from 10am to midnight; the music is recorded. A glass of wine costs from 16 AS ($1.15).

---

3. The Pongau

Badgastein and Bad Hofgastein, already explored, are part of a section of Land Salzburg known as the Pongau. It's one of several parts of an alpine valley called Salzach. The Pinzgau section (coming up) of the Salzach Valley is in the southwest.

The Pongau's most frequented tourist route is through the **Gastein Valley,** of which Badgastein and Bad Hofgastein are a part. For many centuries the Gastein Valley has been known for its hot springs, and in more recent times it has also become a winter-sports center, this phase of activity developing mainly after World War II. As a consequence, many old spas such as Badgastein suddenly find themselves overrun with skiers in winter.

The **Radstädter Tauern** region is the second most popular section of the Pongau. It sprawls across five mountains and four valleys, with a mammoth expanse of skiable terrain from St. Johann to Obertauern. In between, you'll find that Wagrain, Flachau, Altenmarkt, and Radstadt are all well provided with hotels. You might find a car convenient in the Radstädter Tauern. However, most of it can be reached by lifts and runs.

DORFGASTEIN

This alpine village (2,750 feet) in the Gastein Valley is both a winter and a summer resort, its tranquil ambience attracting many who shun the more commercial atmosphere of Badgastein and Bad Hofgastein. It has an assortment of hotels and gasthof-type places, as well as an open-air swimming pool heated by solar energy.

Dorfgastein is popular with Austrian families who, in winter, can park the small fry all day at a ski kindergarten while the grownups enjoy the ski runs and slopes. In fact, the resort has many faithful habitués who resent its increasing popularity. The ski circus comprising Dorfgastein and Grossarl offers four chair lifts and 15 T-bar lifts to slopes of varying challenges, and there is also a natural toboggan run and a curling rink. A Gastein ski pass is valid for all cable cars and lifts in the Gastein Valley, and the ski bus is free.

The village has a **parish church** (pfarrkirche) "updated" in the baroque style but originally built in the 14th century.

You can take a bus from the heart of the village to the lower station of the chair lift, the trip taking less than an hour. The lift takes you to Wengeralm, and from there you can go by another lift to Kreuzkogel (6,690 feet).

Another popular attraction is the stalactite cavern, **Entrische Kirche,** 48 miles from Salzburg. Ascent from Klamstein takes more than half an hour to reach these partly water-bearing, stalactite, and dry caves. Total length is 2 miles on three levels. The caves are open daily except Monday from the end of April to October, 10am to 6pm. Conducted tours last an hour. Admission is 48 AS ($3.50) for adults and 24 AS ($1.75) for children.

Food and Lodging

Hotel Kirchenwirt, A-5632 Dorfgastein (tel. 06433/251), is a cozy and tastefully decorated 30-room chalet hotel a few steps from the village church. Its wood-paneled restaurant can be viewed through the arched stucco windows of the ground floor, while the public rooms are filled with Oriental rugs, comfortable chairs, and a coffered ceiling. The bedrooms are spacious and comfortable, often with unusual shapes and many wood accents. The bar area is denlike and intimately rustic, with provincial artifacts hanging from the walls. The building has its own elevator and is maintained by the Köstinger family. Rates range from 580 AS ($42.25) to 650 AS ($47.25) per person daily, with half board included. Prices depend on the season and the plumbing.

Hotel/Restaurant Römerhof, A-5632 Dorfgastein (tel. 06433/209), has four floors of well-built wood and stucco, designed like an expanded version of a chalet. Constructed in 1966, it sits near the site of a 12th-century tower that served after 1421 as a shelter for men and horses. The Hasenauer family maintains accommodations considerably more comfortable than those written about in the medieval annals.

The interior is decorated with wood beams, wrought-iron embellishments, and rustic furniture. The exterior walls of the wood-paneled restaurant are covered with painted floral designs. A public swimming pool and the departure point for the cable cars are each a five-minute walk from the hotel, whose 34 bedrooms come with private baths or showers. In winter, half-board rates range from 580 AS ($42.25) to 680 AS ($49.50) per person daily; in summer, from 440 AS ($32) to 480 AS ($35) per person daily. Visitors are received from December to October.

Après-Ski

When darkness falls on the slopes, the after-dark circuit starts buzzing. Nightlife (and there is some) is fairly restrained, taking place for the most part in the lounges and bars of the hotels, many of which have open blazing fires.

K-Keller, at the already recommended Hotel Kirchenwirt (tel. 06433/251), is the scene of the liveliest disco action in town. Open nightly from 9pm to 2am, it charges no admission. Once you're inside, a large beer goes for 27 AS ($1.95). Popular with young skiers, the cellar is open only in winter.

Also popular is the **Hotel Römerhof** (tel. 06433/209), recommended above. The Hasenauer family maintains a lively atmosphere.

GOLDEGG

Lying on a small lake dominated by a 14-century castle, Goldegg, reached by going through Schwarzach, is about an 18-minute bus ride from St. Veit im Pongau. Schwarzach is at the western end of the Pongau. Goldegg, both a winter- and a summer-sports resort, is known also for its peat baths. A nine-hole golf course is nearby.

Count Christoph of Schernberg bought the old **castle** of Goldegg in the 16th century and added the Rittersaal, a big hall now equipped with paintings of the Roman-German Empire, Renaissance ornaments, Christian images, and depictions of ancient myths. In 1973 the local municipality bought the building and began renovating it. The counts of Galen still live in the village.

In the castle is the **Pongau Folk Museum** (tel. 06433/81-1-70), the private property of Prof. Nora Watteck. It contains displays of old rural tools used in the everyday lives of those who once lived here, as well as local sports equipment from the past 300 years. The museum is open daily May 1 to September 30 from 3 to 4pm; however, in July and August it is open from 2 to 4pm. Off-season, it is open only on Thursday at 2pm. Adults pay 15 AS ($1.10) and children 8 AS (60¢).

Food and Lodging

Hotel Gesinger zur Post, A-5622 Goldegg (tel. 06415/81-0-30), consists of two country-style buildings, both with flowered balconies and window boxes, plus a pleasant lakeside location with a view of the mountains. The interior is outfitted with painted regional furniture, polished pine paneling, homey detailing, and lots of comfort. Under the rafters of what was probably a barn, the 40-room hotel has installed a dancing nightclub, complete with hanging lanterns and lots of intimate corners. Congenial hosts Raimund and Hertha Gesinger do everything they can to make guests comfortable. The cozy bedrooms are equipped with spacious private baths, and usually have enclosed sleeping compartments behind full-length curtains. Half-board rates range from 495 AS ($36) to 830 AS ($60.25) per person daily, based on double occupancy, depending on the season. In a single, a supplement of 150 AS ($11) daily is charged. Open from December to March and May to October.

Hotel Seehof, A-5622 Goldegg (tel. 06415/8137), is filled with the kind of rustic artifacts and local painted furniture that many of us could spend weeks looking for in antique shops. It sits on the lake, which reflects the chalet's forest-green shutters and the many flowerpots on the hotel's balconies. An outdoor terrace sports sun parasols. In summer many guests enjoy the private lakeside beach, while in winter the hotel rents ski equipment for the nearby slopes. A sauna and Turkish bath are on the premises. An in-season disco, filled with a décor of rustic beams and farmer's implements, affords a pleasant place for a drink. The 30 bedrooms are contemporary and warm, often with private balconies and sloping paneled ceilings; the modern private baths are tiled in autumnal colors, with wood detailing and big mirrors. Accommodations rent for 610 AS ($44.25) to 760 AS ($55.25) per person daily, depending on the season, with half board included.

The owner, Mr. Schellhorn, is director of the ski-tracking school of Goldegg, where you can find 36 miles of some of the best ski tracks in Land Salzburg. He is also director of the resort's golf course, and offers discounts to hotel residents on their greens fee.

Hotel/Pension Neuwirt, A-5622 Goldegg (tel. 06415/8114), sits on the side of a hill in the center of the village. The approach road to the hotel will take you around the back side of a miniature religious shrine. The big ground-floor windows let lots of light flood into the public rooms, and many guests enjoy a sun terrace built into stone columns above the downhill side of the building. The interior has lots of country charm, heavy ceiling beams, and handpainted murals set into wooden frames. The Mayr family, your hosts, rent 25 well-furnished bedrooms (each with private bath or shower), charging 440 AS ($32) to 500 AS ($36.25) per person daily for half board, which is available year round.

Hotel Lärchenhof, Weng 24, A-5622 Goldegg (tel. 06415/8169), with weathered balconies, is pleasantly surrounded with green lawns. The ground-floor restaurant has lots of exposed light-grained wood and big windows, while elsewhere on the premises you'll find a dancing bar as well as a rustic drinking area adorned with cut saplings stripped of their bark and nailed into rustic table dividers. The owner rents 34 bedrooms with private baths or showers, charging 370 AS ($27) to 450 AS ($32.75) per person daily for half board. The Lärchenof is open from December to March and May to October.

WAGRAIN

At 2,750 feet, Wagrain, in the vicinity of Salzburg, lies in a sunny valley amid green meadows and forests in summer and fine ski runs in winter. It's the hometown of the poet Karl-Heinrich Waggerl, whose memory is honored with a **folklore museum,** open June to September on Monday from 3 to 6pm, on Saturday from 4 to 6pm, and on Sunday from 10am to noon. Admission is free. This tiny resort is in the three-valley ski round point of Flachau–Wagrain–St. Johann, with open skiing ground protected against avalanches.

From mid-December to mid-April some 60 miles of mechanically prepared downhill runs are open, suitable for everybody from beginners to intermediates, and there's a ski school in the area. Three chair lifts and 11 drag lifts are available. The top station that can be reached is at 6,600 feet. You can go to Flachau, the neighboring resort, by chair lift.

For nonskiers Wagrain offers rambling trails, tobogganing, folkloric evenings, Austrian curling, and horse-drawn sleigh rides in winter. Summer visitors can use the chair lifts for sightseeing, and they can swim in a heated outdoor pool or take advantage of one of the four tennis courts.

Food and Lodging

Hotel Alpina, Kirchboden 108, A-5602 Wagrain (tel. 06413/8337), is a white stucco chalet with balconies and a low-lying extension that stretches off down the hillside. One of the public rooms contains a white-brick fireplace with a large metallic hood—a pleasant place for a drink if a fire is burning. On the premises is a rustic bar, as well as a sauna and an indoor pool with big glass windows looking out onto the snow-covered hillside. Your hosts, the Wiesbacher family, rent 30 sunny bedrooms, each with private bath or shower. In winter the half-board rates range from 690 AS ($50.25) to 750 AS ($54.50) per person daily; in summer they range from 380 AS ($27.75) to 440 AS ($32) per person daily. The hotel is closed from early October until the beginning of December, with special discounts available between early December and Christmas.

Hotel Wagrainerhof, A-5602 Wagrain (tel. 06413/8204). Local residents say that you can tell what time it is by the direction of the shadows that fall from the ornate eaves of this enlarged chalet. You'll enter through a pointed arch into which some craftsman has skillfully inserted a door of patterned brass. Inside is a high-quality series of cozy rooms with thick carpeting, burnished paneling, and art objects. A rustic bar often has live music, while the gemütlich restaurant is filled with homey touches. The in-house café has standing brass lamps and a cross-beam ceiling. In the center of the village, the hotel is owned by the Rotzer family, who open it from December to March and May to October. The summer half-board rate is only 350 AS ($25.50) per person; in winter, however, half board ranges from 550 AS ($40) to 590 AS ($43) per person daily. The 43 bedrooms come with private baths or showers.

Alpengasthof Kirchboden, A-5602 Wagrain (tel. 06413/8202), is a solidly constructed chalet with cut-out patterns on its three tiers of balconies, arched windows on its ground floor, and a flowered sun terrace with parasols. The interior is covered in many areas with natural-grained wood, while some of the thick beams are reinforced with wrought-iron straps. A fieldstone fireplace is capped with a timbered mantelpiece. The view encompasses most of the village of Wagrain. The establishment, open from December to September, rents 27 bedrooms, each with private bath or shower. In winter, half-board charges go from 480 AS ($35) to 550 AS

($40) per person daily. Summer half-board terms are 295 AS ($21.50) to 320 AS ($23.25) per person daily.

The adjoining restaurant is excellent. The well-prepared specialties tend to be regional (palatschinken, Pariser schnitzel), along with good appetizers and a fine selection of cheeses. The cost of meals begin at 150 AS ($11), going up.

Gasthof Grafenwirt, A-5602 Wagrain (tel. 06413/8230), is a three-story villa with white walls and lots of ivy growing up the side. A walled garden is a good place for a summer drink. The inside is accented with lots of paneling, rustic artifacts, and brightly contrasting patterns. The smallish bedrooms have painted furniture and a minimum of other decoration, but are comfortable nevertheless. A total of 17 bedrooms, all with private baths or showers, are rented from December to September. In winter, half-board tariffs go from 465 AS ($33.75) to 535 AS ($40) per person daily; in summer, from 350 AS ($25.50) to 400 AS ($30) per person daily.

The in-house restaurant is one of the better ones in the region. Colorfully decorated with pretty chandeliers and wrought-iron accents, it serves standard Austrian specialties such as liver noodle soup, beef gulasch, and Tyrolean-style liver. Menus begin at 150 AS ($11).

FLACHAU

This member of a trio of resorts that also includes Wagrain and St. Johann im Pongau is just 5 miles southwest of Altenmarkt, in a lovely position in the Enns Valley, on the motorway. From the village, you can go by cable car to Griesskareck at 6,530 feet.

Flachau, known heretofore mainly to Europeans, is just beginning to attract more international skiers. Hence the prices are fairly reasonable.

Food and Lodging

Alpenhotel Tauernhof, A-5542 Flachau (tel. 06457/23110), is considered the finest hotel in this mountain resort area. All of its various public rooms have rustic décor. There are several restaurants, a lounge and bar, a video room, a children's playroom, an indoor swimming pool with a sauna, a solarium, and a massage salon. The hotel also has tennis courts and a minigolf layout. In the 400-year-old chalet, Schusterhäusl, there is a farmer's-style bowling alley, plus a beer garden. For the 66 well-furnished bedrooms, each with private bath or shower, winter half-board tariffs are 585 AS ($42.50) to 895 AS ($65) per person daily, with summer half-board rates ranging from 470 AS ($34.25) to 685 AS ($49.75) per person daily. Both the buffet breakfast and four-course dinner included in the rates are excellent. The hotel is open from December to October.

Hotel Pongauerhof, A-5542 Flachau (tel. 06457/2242). The balconies of this stucco-and-wood chalet extend only part of the way across the façade, interrupted as they are by an extension stretching toward the front. This allows the cheerful bedrooms inside to be more spacious than those in the other hotels of the region. The public rooms are busily filled with contrasting patterns and designs, with lots of paneling and hanging light fixtures. The hotel is small and run in a personal manner. Guests are received from December to September in the 24 well-furnished bedrooms, which cost 510 AS ($37) to 570 AS ($41.50) per person daily, with half board included in winter. Summer travelers get a break when half board is lowered to 290 AS ($21) to 310 AS ($22.50) per person daily. The hotel has a sauna, a solarium, and a recreation room.

The in-house restaurant is often sought out by the local residents. Snails are a specialty of the chef, who also prepares a full line of snacks, including pizzas and various salads (often without lettuce) at the daily salad bar. Full meals are also available, and main courses are likely to include pork Wiener schnitzel and marinated roast pork (sometimes garnished with a cabbage salad). A wide variety of Austrian beer is on tap as well. Meals cost from 175 AS ($12.75).

Hotel Alpenhof, A-5542 Flachau (tel. 06457/205), has a pleasing exterior design, where the balconies have thick timbers running vertically up the front of the solidly constructed chalet. In summer the café terrace offers a resting point in the shadows of the flowers on these balconies. In winter guests prefer to bathe in the sunny indoor pool or enjoy the rustic wood-covered interior. The hotel, each of whose 28 bedrooms has a private shower or toilet, receives guests from December to October. In winter, half-board charges are 750 AS ($54.50) to 800 AS ($58.25) per person daily. In summer, half-board rates go from 500 AS ($36.25) to 550 AS ($40) per person daily. The restaurant is especially worth the visit, specialties of the house including grilled filet of pork in a cream sauce, as well as roast marinated pork and an array of veal dishes.

Forellenhof, A-5542 Flachau (tel. 06457/273), is a wood-and-stucco chalet with a gently sloping roof and a pleasing façade of recessed balconies and symmetrical detailing. From the café sun terrace, clients can look at the pink-and-white walls of the onion-domed church next door. The hotel interior is attractive and cozy, with lots of handcrafted paneling and dozens of extra touches, such as stained-glass inserts, hanging ornate lamps, and an occasional niche containing a statue. Under the heavy overhead beams of the ceiling you can enjoy well-prepared regional cuisine. An octagonal indoor swimming pool is sheltered below a wooden ceiling that is supported by an unusual series of curved laminated beams. A sauna and a whirlpool are also on the premises. The Forellenhof rents 49 comfortable and sunny bedrooms, each with private bath or shower. Half-board rates range from 750 AS ($54.50) to 780 AS ($56.75) per person daily in winter, lowered to 520 AS ($37.75) to 550 AS ($40) in summer. The Krauthauf family are your conscientious hosts.

ST. JOHANN IM PONGAU

The third of the three-valley trio of summer and winter resorts, including Wagrain and Flachau, St. Johann im Pongau (there's a larger St. Johann in Tyrol) lies 38 miles from Salzburg on the sun-drenched terrace on the right bank on the river. The town's twin-towered **parish church** (pfarrkirche) was built in 1855, but use of the site for a house of worship dates from the year 924.

The winter-sports season here lasts from December to April. There are more than 52 lifts and cable cars in the tri-resort area, plus some 60 miles of prepared runs. This best-known ski-lift network in the Salzburg mountains is called Drei-Taler-Skischaukel, or three-valley ski swing.

If you're a nature-lover, St. Johann is a good base for many excursions, such as to the **Grossarlbach Valley** to the south of the town and to the mouth of **Wagrainer Tal** to the north.

Just 3 miles south of St. Johann im Pongau is the most important gorge of the eastern Alps, the spectacular **Liechtensteinklamm,** which attracts more visitors to its ¾-mile length than any other such site. A path has been blasted through the gorge, and during about a 45-minute trek you can climb up a mammoth cauldron with rock walls some 1,000 feet high. At its tiny waist the gorge is only 12½ feet wide. A tunnel leads to the waterfall, with a drop of about 200 feet at the gorge's end.

To reach the Liechtensteinklamm, go 3 miles by road to Grossarl. The road to the gorge is marked. From there, count on about an hour by foot. The gorge may be visited from May 10 to the first Sunday in October from 8am to 5pm. Admission is 21 AS ($1.55) for adults and 13 AS (95¢) for children.

Food and Lodging

Alpenland, A-5600 St. Johann im Pongau (tel. 06412/70210), is the leading hotel at the resort. As its name implies, this wood-lined establishment offers the closest thing to a total alpine fantasy in town. Against a background of burnished pine, a corps of pretty waitresses in dirndls serve a wide selection of Austrian wines, beer from the tap, and well-prepared mountain dishes. Try, for example, a tangy peppersteak, veal Cordon Bleu with parsley potatoes, liver dumpling soup, and the homemade bread. À la carte meals cost from 175 AS ($12.75). The 270-bed hotel, open year round, offers attractively furnished and well-maintained bedrooms. In winter, the half-board rate is 1,010 AS ($73.50) per person daily, lowered in summer to 855 AS ($62.25). The staff is attentive and helpful at this four-star resort hotel with many amenities.

Pension Monika, Liechtensteinkammstrasse 2, A-5600 St. Johann im Pongau (tel. 06412/411), a 10-minute walk from the train station at the southern edge of St. Johann, has weathered pine siding and a double row of balconies festooned with flowers. The sunny interior has lots of wood trim and comfortable furniture. The cuisine is prepared by the owners themselves, the Rudolf Wedl family. They offer only 12 bedrooms, each snug and cozy, and each with private shower. Their half-board rate ranges from 280 AS ($20.25) to 300 AS ($21.75) per person daily.

RADSTADT

Between the Dachstein massif in the north and Radstädter Tauern to the south lies Radstadt, at the beginning of the 13½-mile Radstädter Tauern road to the pass, which has been used since Roman days as a way north through the mountains.

The town, built by a prince-archbishop of Salzburg, has many handsome patrician houses. Some other features of its past, including town walls, have been preserved. The skyline is distinguished by a trio of large towers built in the 16th century. Its **pfarrkirche** (parish church) is from the 14th and 15th centuries. In the churchyard stands the late Gothic **Schustersäule** (Cobbler's Column) from 1513.

Radstadt, for a long time a summer resort, now has been developed as a winter sports attraction. Many excursions from here are possible to the satellite resorts of Altenmarkt, Filzmoos, and Obertauern (coming up).

Food and Lodging

Sport Hotel Weissenbacher, Schlosstrasse 45, A-5550 Radstadt (tel. 06452/590), is skillfully landscaped into the side of an alpine meadow. A flight of stone-trimmed stairs will lead you first to the raised sun terrace, with its views of the many flowers surrounding the balconies, and then into the well-decorated public rooms. These are awash with comfortable niches, mellow paneling, and rustic conviviality. A full range of sporting pastimes lies within a short distance of the hotel. One of the foremost attractions is a network of some 9½ miles of freshwater streams in the region, which are said to be filled with an angler's dream of eel, trout, and carp. The hotel, which is closed from Easter to mid-May and November 1 to December 15, offers 30 bedrooms, each with private bath. Half-board prices in winter range from 560 AS ($40.75) to 785 AS ($57) per person daily; half-board tariffs in summer go from 430 AS ($31.25) to 620 AS ($45) per person daily. Nonguests are welcome at the hotel's restaurant, Lechenstubl, one of the best in the area. It is open daily from 11am to 2pm and 6 to 11pm, charging from 200 AS ($14.50) for a full meal.

Alpengasthof Seitenalm, A-5550 Radstadt (tel. 06452/490), is a well-designed complex of chalets 2 miles (via good roads) from the center of Radstadt. The main building has a dining room whose high ceiling is supported by massive vertical timbers. For skiers who want to be close to the slopes, or for mountain climbers in summer, the hotel rents rooms in its rustic Kurzenhof, which is about a mile and a half away, near the hotel's T-bar lift. An outdoor swimming pool and nearby horseback riding provide distraction, along with fishing, hiking, shooting, and table tennis. A sauna is on the premises. From December to April and June to September, the 24-room hotel rents individually decorated bedrooms, each with private bath or shower. Furnishings are in good taste, with many homelike touches. Half-board in winter ranges from 385 AS ($28) per person daily, while in summer it starts at 350 AS ($25.50). Sometimes in summer you might want to eat in the country-style Grill Hut, assembled from logs notched together, while zither music accompanies your meal. The Arnold family have been the owners for three generations.

Gasthof Pertill, Muezgrubweg 3, A-5550 Radstadt (tel. 06452/471), a small, family-run guesthouse, lies about 2 miles from the center. The view from the sun terrace encompasses the village and the valley. Inside, you'll find things as rustic and cozy as you'd expect from an alpine retreat. For bed-and-breakfast, Mr. and Mrs. Erich Kocher charge from 180 AS ($13) per person daily, summer or winter, in one of six twin bedrooms, three with shower. They also offer a three-bedroom unit for rent.

ALTENMARKT

Some 2 miles west of Radstadt lies this sleepy provincial hamlet, sometimes called Altenmarkt in Pongau (2,790 feet). It's popular with Austrian families who come here to take advantage of the good accommodations available at reasonable prices and to enjoy swimming, skiing, and other sports typical of the region.

Of interest is the **parish church** (pfarrkirche) with an 18th-century statue of the Virgin.

Food and Lodging

Pension Urbisgut, A-5541 Altenmarkt (tel. 06452/7227), is a symmetrical double chalet connected with a balconied center section. The exterior walls have been decorated in some areas with regional painted designs. The cozy interior has painted furniture in some of the bedrooms and a bar area that sometimes is one of the most active and convivial places in nighttime Altenmarkt. The Bittersam family, the convivial owners of this place, charge 470 AS ($34.25) to 500 AS ($36.25) per person daily for half board in winter in one of their 42 well-furnished bedrooms, each with private bath or shower. The summer half-board terms are lowered to 350 AS ($25.50) to 390 AS ($28.25) per person daily. Guests are received from December to October.

Gasthof Markterwirt, A-5541 Altenmarkt (tel. 06452/420), is one of my favorite places in town, located in a three-story chalet with weathered facing and white shutters. It's next door to the village's baroque church. Aside from having cozy and comfortable rooms, the gasthof serves as one of the village's social centers. The café has big windows and a woodsy modern décor, and you might want to stop here for coffee even if you're just driving through town. The Kellerstüberl has a vaulted ceiling, cozy ambience, and painted designs on the white plaster. In addition, the Alte Küche, the main dining room, and the Gaststube, as well as the outdoor sun terrace, are inviting places for a drink or a meal, with set menus priced from 125 AS ($9). The Schneider family are your hosts at this 900-year-old hotel, offering 31 bedrooms, each with bath or shower, phone, radio, and TV. They are open from December to October. Half-board charges in winter range from 490 AS ($35.75) to 580 AS ($42.25) per person daily, while summer charges are 320 AS ($23.25) to 370 AS ($27) per person daily for half board.

Lebzelter Stub'n, Marktplatz 79 (tel. 06452/503), is an accommodating restaurant whose prices are low enough for a large family and whose specialties are so varied that guests can enjoy a different dish every day of the week. Wednesday, for example, is fondue day. Tuesday is strudel day. In addition to that, the restaurant serves thick and savory steaks, tafelspitz, tiroler Gröst'l (sautéed potatoes, onions, boiled meat, and bacon), blutwurst, lamb, fish, and venison dishes. A member of the Kohlmayr family is always on the premises, serving, in addition to everything else, pizzas. À la carte meals range from 125 AS ($9) to 350 AS ($25.50). The restaurant is open daily from 11:30am to 3pm and 5 to 11pm, but closes in May and again in October.

FILZMOOS

A still-unspoiled resort 50 miles south of Salzburg, Filzmoos (3,465 feet) lies at the foot of the 8,000-foot Bischofmütze, a section of the Dachstein massif.

Filzmoos is a good starting point for many excursions, as well as for walking tours. In winter you can ride in horse-drawn sleighs (ask at your hotel), practice curling and ice skating, and go skiing. The resort has a good ski school, along with 16 ski lifts and many fine slopes, some of which are suitable for beginners, others for the most experienced of skiers. From here you can try the Dachstein Glacier runs about 7½ miles away, via the scenic Höhenstrasse.

Ski areas include **Rossbrand** (5,250 feet), which lies to the south of Filzmoos. This section is serviced by a drag lift. **Rettenstein** (5,380 feet), to the north of the resort, is the second most popular area. Its drag lift is in two stages.

The third ski section is **Grossberg** (4,590 feet), also to the north of Filzmoos, served by a chair lift. It has runs for all grades of skiers.

Food and Lodging

Sporthotel Filzmooserhof, Neuberg 85, A-5532 Filzmoos (tel. 06453/232), is the balconied chalet between the village church and the public swimming pool. Sports enthusiasts will find lots to do, since the public facilities for golf, minigolf, and tennis are close at hand, as well as access to the ski slopes. One of the hotel's exterior walls has a hand-painted illustration of a man carrying a child across a stream, which guests can study while sipping coffee on the sun terrace. The interior is cozy, rustic, and filled with sunny colors. The Webinger family rents attractively and comfortably furnished 36 bedrooms, each with private shower or bath, for 560 AS ($40.75) to 1,000 AS ($72.75) per person daily in winter for half board. Summer half-board tariffs cost 600 AS ($43.75) to 700 AS ($51) per person daily.

The adjoining restaurant is one of the better establishments in the village, serving international dishes such as scampi, steak, and schnitzel, and a collection of regional dishes that, even if you speak German, you'll have difficulty translating. The staff will help you, especially with the names of some of the Bosnian dishes, which include a sour cream soup with potatoes. Both the restaurant and the hotel are closed from Easter till mid-May and mid-October until mid-December.

Hotel Alpenkrone, A-5532 Filzmoos (tel. 06453/280). One of the best times to view this hotel is in summer, when masses of alpine flowers cluster in the meadow nearby. Constructed in two parts, the chalet hotel has balconies facing the jagged mountains and an interior decoration that makes ample use of light-grained wood paneling. The doors to the bar area are wrought of straps and plates of solid iron, strong enough to keep anyone in (or out) for a long time. The dancing bar is a popular local hangout. The 62 bedrooms are comfortable, clean, and well furnished, and guests are received from December to October. With half board included, winter rates are 370 AS ($27) to 410 AS ($29.75) per person daily, based on double occupancy. Summer tariffs range from 300 AS ($21.75) to 330 AS ($24) daily (per-person rates based on double occupancy). Singles pay a daily supplement of 60 AS ($4.35).

Hotel Hanneshof, A-5532 Filzmoos (tel. 06453/275). The bedrooms in this comfortable chalet hotel have windows as big as those in any hotel in town, as well as spacious balconies, lots of paneling, and a series of colorful public rooms designed around open hearths and ornate wrought-iron chandeliers. The hotel was constructed in 1974, with careful attention to all the modern amenities, including a big indoor pool and a sauna. In winter the well-furnished rooms range in price from 550 AS ($40) to 770 AS ($56) per person daily, half board included. The Hanneshof is open from December to April.

Après-Ski

In season, live bands are imported, and there is the inevitable collection of discos. The **Hotel Alpenkrone,** already recommended, is one of the most popular stops on the after-dark circuit. Young skiers especially are drawn to its Steve's Bar, a rustically alpine place. It is open in summer and winter daily from 4pm to 2am, charging 27 AS ($1.95) for a large beer.

If you want to dance, there are three nightlife places I'd recommend for music and rhythm. Each assesses no cover, and charges 27 AS ($1.95) for a large beer. Hours in each establishment in winter are from 8:30pm until around 2am, depending on the crowd.

These nightspots include the Hutten Bar, inside the already recommended **Sporthotel Filzmooserhof** (see above). Designed like the inside of a mountain hut, it has indestructible furniture and alpine accessories.

Mühlradl (tel. 06453/686) stands in the center of Filzmoos in the heart of a building that has a store selling sports equipment. It is a rustic place with free-flowing suds.

Alm-Bar, inside the **Hotel Hubertus** (tel. 06453/204), is another rustic spot attracting snow bunnies.

OBERTAUERN

This winter and summer resort at 5,930 feet lies at the top of an old Roman road dividing Land Salzburg from Carinthia (see Chapter XII). The unspoiled resort is about 60 miles from Salzburg. It can be reached by train from Radstadt or else by Postal Bus. A car isn't really necessary here, as you can easily get around on skis in winter and on foot in summer. The people of Obertauern are hospitable, and the tourist office is helpful.

In the vicinity is the **graveyard of the nameless ones,** the burial place of bodies recovered from the mountain area over the centuries, most of them victims of avalanches. The cemetery is near the Tauern Pass and dates from the 16th century.

One of the newest ski resorts in Land Salzburg, Obertauern has become an international sports center, with both ski and chair lifts, plus a cable car. A ski school is in business, with state-qualified instructors, and there are children's ski courses, plus a ski kindergarten.

The elevation at the top of the pass ensures that the snow is good and the season extra long. You can ski from November until the end of May at this "snow-proof" resort, with its ski circus. It's easier on one side, steep on the other, letting you ski all around the village.

Food and Lodging

Hotel Edelweiss, A-5562 Obertauern (tel. 06456/245). Once you sit down at the bar in this imaginatively decorated three-star hotel you're likely never to leave. That's because the bar stools hang from a ceiling beam like children's swings and, in addition, mold themselves to the contours of your back. Other niches within the hotel's public rooms include Hancock-style rocking chairs placed beside the rustic fireplace, whose semicircular metallic bonnet exposes the flames to three sides of the room. A heated swimming pool and sauna are places to relax in before dinner in the restaurant or the brasserie, which might be followed by nighttime dancing. The 65 contemporary bedrooms are sunny and filled with autumnal colors, and all have private baths or showers. The Edelweiss is open only for the winter season (December to April), when half-board charges range from 760 AS ($55.25) to 940 AS ($68.25) per person daily.

Alpenhotel Perner, A-5562 Obertauern (tel. 06456/236). There's so much variety to the many sections of this mountainside hotel that it almost gives the impression of a long series of balconied railroad cars strung together. The interior is appealingly outfitted with hewn beams and timbers, often with carved detailing, as well as accents such as stained-glass insets and both stone and wrought-iron embellishments.

The public swimming pool is connected to the hotel via an underground passage, and covered tennis courts are nearby. A four-star choice, Alpenhotel Perner rents 81 well-furnished bedrooms, each with private shower or bath. Guests are accepted from December to April and for a short summer season, July to September. Half-board charges range from 880 AS ($64) to 1,080 AS ($78.50) per person daily. The dancing bar sees a lot of winter action, often with live music.

Hotel Kristall, A-5562 Obertauern (tel. 06456/323), has a chalet façade and a two-story balconied extension angling attractively off to one side. The contemporary interior has lots of rustic touches, including a fireplace whose hood is fashioned from curved and textured stucco. The bedrooms usually have good views of the mountains, pleasing wooden furniture, and springtime colors in the curtains, bedspreads, and wall-to-wall carpeting. Guests enjoy well-prepared meals under the coffered ceiling of a panoramic dining room. Each of the 23 bedrooms has a private bath or shower. For bed-and-breakfast, charges are 380 AS ($27.75) to 430 AS ($31.25) per person daily. The hotel is open from December to April and in July and August.

Hotel Kärntnerland, A-5562 Obertauern (tel. 06456/271), is a 16-room balconied building with painted embellishments in regional patterns covering its stucco walls. It sees itself as more of a private club than a resort hotel, with attentive service provided by the Günter Kanduth family. Inside, guests enjoy a library, an open hearth, and two restaurants, one of them a rustic keller and the other a high-ceilinged paneled room with comfortable upholstered armchairs and colorful napery. The bedrooms are warmly intimate, often with contrasting patterns and cozy colors. Winter rates, with half board included, range from 450 AS ($32.75) to 600 AS ($43.75) per person daily, depending on the plumbing. In summer the bed-and-breakfast rate starts at 200 AS ($14.50) per person.

Hotel Kohlmayr, A-5562 Obertauern (tel. 06456/282). As you approach this well-run four-star hotel, it looks like a pleasantly situated chalet, with stucco walls and several rows of wooden balconies with matching shutters. You'll soon realize, however, that the entire construction rests on top of a glass-walled foundation that contains the heated swimming pool with its view of the mountains. The rest of the hotel is tastefully and rustically filled with paneling, cozy bric-a-brac, and pleasing colors. Also on the premises are a sauna and a fitness room. The 45 spacious sunny bedrooms look out over an alpine vista, and are sometimes divided into two sections by a full-length curtain (which you can close if you plan to sleep late); each room comes with a private bath or shower. Half-board charges in winter are 980 AS ($71.25) to 1,600 AS ($116.25) per person daily. In summer they are 410 AS ($29.75) to 690 AS ($50.25) per person daily. Open from December to April and June to September.

Après-Ski

Nightlife is very limited, but there is some. Many skiers, mostly European, go to bed by 10pm so they'll have an early chance on the slopes.

One of the best places for after-dark diversions is the **Alpenhotel Perner,** already recommended. In their Stage Coach, a dance band keeps the joint jumping.

The **Hotel Edelweiss,** again recommended previously, also occasionally has dancing to live music.

But the most fun is likely to be found at the **Gasthof Taverne,** A-5562 Obertauern (tel. 06456/229). In this converted cow barn, a ski expert, Mr. Oberhummer, and his sons welcome you in a real gemütlich atmosphere. They feature Tyrolean music and dancing along with yodeling. Set menus cost 100 AS ($7.25) to 120 AS ($8.75). The tavern also rents 20 rooms with showers and toilets, half board costing 350 AS ($25.50) per person daily in summer and rising to 480 AS ($35) in winter. The family pension is directly beside the ski and chair lifts and the ski school.

4. The Tennengau

The Tennengau, named for the Tennen massif, is one of the divisions of the Salzach Valley to the south of Salzburg. It's characterized by rolling hills and many woodlands. Often you'll see waterfalls, of which those outside the town of Golling are the most visited.

As you leave Salzburg going south on the left bank of the Salzach River, you'll pass through Anif, a section already previewed in the environs of Salzburg (Chapter VII). You'll find some excellent old romantic accommodations in Anif, if you'd like to live on the immediate outskirts of the provincial capital.

If you don't want to stay in the Tennengau region, you might consider it as a day's exploration from Salzburg, its chief sight being the Dürrnberg Salt Mines outside Hallein (see the previous chapter). However, if you'd like to anchor in the district—in either summer or winter—the town that is most blessed with accommodations in a wide range of prices is Abtenau (sometimes called Bad Abtenau), which for decades has been known mainly as a winter ski business.

Much of the Tennengau area, especially the houses with their gables and window boxes of geraniums, will remind you of Bavaria.

GOLLING

The major attraction drawing visitors to Golling, 7½ miles south of Hallein, is the **Gollinger Wasserfall** (Golling Waterfall), 1½ miles outside the little resort, plus about a 20-minute walk. The waterfall—between Golling and Kuchl, 17 miles from Salzburg—tumbles down more than 500 feet over a rock wall. Visits are possible all day from May to October, a tour taking about an hour. Admission is free.

You can also visit the **Salzach Gorge** near Golling. It's an hour's walk from Golling up to Pass Lueg. You can visit the gorge all day from May to October. Allow about an hour. Admission is 10 AS (75¢) for adults and 5 AS (35¢) for children.

In Golling you can visit the **castle** with its chapel and folklore collection. You'll see remains of cave bears, fossils, and copies of rock drawings, plus views of the village in old pictures. Visiting hours are June to September on Wednesday, Saturday, and Sunday from 9am to noon. Admission is 20 AS ($1.45) for adults and 5 AS (35¢) for children.

Many visitors use Golling as a base for enjoying the varied sports facilities in the nearby mountains.

Food and Lodging

Goldener Stern, Marktplatz 56, A-5440 Golling (tel. 06244/2200), sits in a row of picture-book houses in the center of the village. It has arched windows on the ground floor, three floors of embellished windows above that, and a wrought-iron bracket holding a sign out over the street. The interior is filled with rustically modern furniture, while the 40 bedrooms are cozy and comfortable, each with private bath or shower. The overnight bed-and-breakfast charge ranges from 220 AS ($16) to 330 AS ($24) per person.

Many of the region's gourmets know about the in-house restaurant. Its specialties include dried alpine beef, sliced wafer-thin and served with pearl onions and pickles, filet steak, filet Stroganoff, and an Austrian version of the Italian saltimbocca (veal schnitzel stuffed with ham and served with a savory sauce). There's also an array of seafood, including mussels prepared in several different ways. À la carte menus cost 150 AS ($11) to 500 AS ($36.25). The vaulted dining room is open from 8am to midnight; closed Monday. Reservations are suggested.

OBERALM

The main reason for visiting this hamlet, which lies near Hallein and Salzburg, is to stay at the castle hotel recommended below.

However, if you're sightseeing in the area you might want to stop to see the **parish church** (pfarrkirche), which is Romanesque with Gothic extensions. It has a magnificent high altar from 1707 by J. G. Mohr. The church is embellished with baroque furnishings and has heraldic tombstones. See the funeral shield from 1671.

Food and Lodging

Schloss Haunsperg, A-5411 Oberalm (tel. 06245/2662), is an early 14th-century castle, decorated with towers and interior ornamentation. The outside is restrained, with a yellow covering of stippled stucco with white trim. A small but ornate baroque chapel adjoining the hotel has a wrought-iron gate separating the vestibule from the inner sanctuary, along with plenty of gilt embellishments. The public rooms include a series of vaulted corridors, each furnished with antiques and rustic chandeliers, several salons with parquet or flagstone floors, and a collection of antiques. My favorite is the second-floor music salon. Many of the accommodations, which contain period furniture, are divided into suites of two or three rooms plus private bath, along with some doubles (also with bath). The owners, the von Gernerth-Mautner Markhof family, rent only eight bedrooms, costing 645 AS ($47) to 1,080 AS ($78.50) per person daily, with breakfast included. A tennis court is on the premises.

ABTENAU

Nestling at the foot of the Kogel, Abtenau is known for its Gothic church. The little town, 30 miles from Salzburg, can be reached by bus from Golling in the Salzach Valley. It does mostly a summer business, but some winter trade has been developing. The minor spa is closed in winter.

Summer holiday visitors enjoy touring through the mountain landscape, strolling on forest paths, canoeing, playing tennis, horseback riding, swimming, and watching folkloric entertainment. You can hire guides for climbs in the Tennengebirge, but allow a whole day for this activity. A chair lift goes from Abtenau to the Karkogel at 3,950 feet.

During the winter months guests often assist in feeding the deer. Abtenau offers skiing, tobogganing, horse-sledge rides, ice skating, and swimming in a covered pool. There are some 60 miles of quiet hiking trails and fitness runs.

Food and Lodging

Gasthof Roter Ochs, A-5441 Abtenau (tel. 06243/2259), sits on the village's central square, across from the church. The sides of the building are covered with red, gold, and gray geometric illustrations, while the front has paintings of village characters who appear to be dancing and leaping over the sides of the wooden balconies. The public rooms are modern and simple, and some of the comfortable bedrooms have carved headboards and rustic furniture. Live folkloric music and dancing are part of the entertainment provided in the beer and wine room, Zum Stacherl. A wide variety of accommodations is offered, the most desirable having minibars and TVs as well as private balconies. Forty-one rooms are rented, each with private bath or shower. Half board ranges from 540 AS ($39.25) to 760 AS ($55.25) per person daily.

Sporthotel Gasthof Moisl, A-5441 Abtenau (tel. 2232/06243), founded in 1764, is a prosperous-looking building in the middle of the town, with a back side dotted with short masonry columns and carriage lamps and a front side covered with regional paintings, wooden balconies, and heavily overhanging eaves. The interior is filled with heavy coffered ceilings, curved half timbering, rounded stucco columns, and an unusually shaped central fireplace in the baroque style. A scattering of carved regional antiques adds to the appeal of the hotel, along with an inviting collection of bar and restaurant areas. On the premises is an indoor shooting range, plus an indoor swimming pool with a big-windowed view of the rest of the village, along with a bowling alley and fitness room. The hotel rents 70 bedrooms, most of them doubles. Each has a private bath or shower. In winter, half-board rates go from

590 AS ($43) to 905 AS ($65.75) per person daily, while summer half-board tariffs range from 575 AS ($41.75) to 710 AS ($51.75) per person daily.

Windhofer's Hotel/Restaurant Post, A-5441 Abtenau (tel. 06243/2209), has lots of rustic artifacts scattered throughout its interior, including an ox yoke positioned below a hay-filled manger hanging from the ceiling of an intimate bar. The Windhofer family has placed an old iron-and-wood postal cart in the lobby, filling it with flowers. Summer guests might enjoy the terrace below the balconies of the 38-room chalet, whose smallish bedrooms are comfortable and clean. In winter, half-board rates, based on double occupancy, range from 450 AS ($32.75) to 575 AS ($41.75) per person daily. The summer the half-board, double-occupancy rates range from 350 AS ($25.50) to 450 AS ($32.75) per person daily. Singles pay a daily supplement of 60 AS ($4.35).

Breakfasts are buffet style and generous, but the evening meals are particularly inviting and well prepared, served in a gemütlich room with a big ceramic stove and lots of niches. Specialties include rumpsteak Tyrol, Indian-style veal, onion-flavored roast of beef, and fresh salads. À la carte meals in the restaurant cost from 150 AS ($11) to 300 AS ($21.75), and are served daily from 7am to 10pm. A covered swimming pool is nearby. A member of the family will sometimes organize bus excursions to sights in the area. The hotel is open from December to March and May to October.

---

5. The Pinzgau

The Pinzgau section of Land Salzburg stretches east from the Gerlos Pass to the Gastein Valley, with the Salzach River flowing through. To the south lies Hohe Tauern and to the north the Kitzbühel alpine region.

This is a very special area for skiing, especially the twin villages of **Saalbach** and **Hinterglemm,** which lie at the end of a valley ringed by a horseshoe of mountains laced with more than 40 ski lifts. The chief resort of the Pinzgau, **Zell am See,** is treated separately (see below). Another outstanding ski resort in the Upper Pinzgau region is **Kaprun.** The **Grossglockner Road** begins in Pinzgau (see below).

The Austrians call the Upper Pinzgau Valley the Oberpinzgau. This was one of the most isolated regions of the country until massive hydroelectric works opened it to the world. But the Upper Pinzgau area, from a tourist point of view, isn't as lively as the resorts, such as Saalfelden, of the Mittelpinzgau, or Middle Pinzgau. This area runs along the **Steinernes Meer,** or "Sea of Stone," marking the frontier of Bavaria, part of West Germany.

LOFER

Ideally situated in a setting of forests, valleys, and mountain rivers, Lofer is an old market town, with a **Bauerntheater** (Peasant Theater) and a Gothic-style **pfarrkirche** (parish church). The church tower dominates the town with its two onion-shaped domes. Many of the houses are decorated with oriels, as much of the architecture was inspired by nearby Bavaria.

Lofer is both a health resort and a ski center, offering hospitality as well as native tradition and rural charm. It's known for its peat-water and mud baths and its Kneipp cures. The fog-free area around Lofer is suitable for walking in both summer and winter. Sports facilities include a tennis court, skating rink, minature golf course, and enclosed swimming pool.

A ski school is operated here, and there are nine T-bar lifts. A chair lift will deliver you to the Sonnegg-Loderbühel at 3,290 feet and the upper station of the Loferer Alm, 4,600 feet. Rising in the background of the town are the Loferer Steinberge and the Reiter Steinberge.

A popular excursion is to the pilgrimage church, **Maria Kirchenthal** (see St.

Martin). You can also visit the **Lamprechtsofen Cavern,** Austria's deepest water-bearing cave, on the road from Lofer to Weissbach, about 37 miles from Salzburg by bus. A guided tour takes about 40 minutes. The cavern is open daily from 7am to 7pm, charging an admission of 25 AS ($1.80) for adults and 12 AS (85¢) for children.

Food and Lodging

Hotel Bräu, A-5090 Lofer (tel. 06588/2070), has a lemon-colored façade, white neoclassical ornamentation around each of the windows, and voluptuously curved wrought-iron balconies on the second floor. It's in the center of the village. If you don't see it as you approach it on the narrow flagstone-covered sidewalk, you'll recognize it by the ornate curved bracket (it's shaped like the garlanded head of a mythical bird) extending out over the pavement. Parts of the hotel were constructed in 1639, and from a view of the antiques inside it's easy to get a sense of the era of its construction. In the modern parts of the hotel, every effort has been made to offset the antique appearance of the older sections. A bar area is an unusual study in modern design, while the entrance hall is covered with marble floors and discreet geometric designs. The 28 bedrooms, each with private bath, are usually filled with painted alpine furniture and a romantic selection of colors. Rates range from 360 AS ($26.25) to 420 AS ($30.50) per person daily for bed-and-breakfast.

The garden restaurant is one of the most charming places in town for a meal, and you can easily move into the rustic dining room when it turns cold. Specialties include a delectable soup of smoked trout, roast pork in a Gorgonzola cream sauce served with green spätzle, and tafelspitz, while desserts might feature a variety of fresh strudels. Meals begin at 150 AS ($11), going up.

Haus Gertraud in der Sonne, A-5090 Lofer (tel. 06588/7303), is a wood-covered chalet with red and white shutters. It's set high on a mountainside, its solitary position among fir trees getting a lot of sunshine. Access to the hotel can be made via a winding alpine road, where Haus Gertraud is the last stop. The Blüml family maintains a private rope tow up a beginner's ski slope, or advanced skiers can reach more challenging slopes from the nearby ski lift. In winter or summer a terrace provides a wooden deck where guests can get a suntan. The colorful, cozy interior has a rustic bar area with rows of exposed shingles serving as a roof, and evenly spaced rows of honey-colored planks cover the walls of many of the 25 well-furnished bedrooms, 11 of which have private baths or showers. Half board ranges from 530 AS ($38.50) to 580 AS ($42.25) per person daily, depending on the season. Guests are accepted from December to April and June to October.

Hotel Gasthof Post, A-5090 Lofer (tel. 06588/3030), is a gracefully painted chalet with two-dimensional colored embellishments surrounding each of the façade's windows. It also has balcony railings, plus lots of flowers. Guests rarely check out of this place without having coffee on the street-level sun terrace, where a view of the village street life is presented just beyond the summer flowerbed. The décor inside contains lots of aged wood and a few well-placed ceramic stoves. Forty-four rooms are offered, 23 of which have private baths or showers. In winter, half board ranges from 380 AS ($27.75) to 620 AS ($45) per person daily. In summer, half board goes from 280 AS ($20.25) to 460 AS ($33.50) per person daily, depending on the plumbing.

The adjoining restaurant is filled with rustic detailing coupled with a gemütlich feeling. Specialties of the house include a ragoût of fresh venison, trout, pork cutlets, and a tempting array of further fish and meat dishes.

Hotel St. Hubertus, A-5090 Lofer (tel. 06588/266). You'd never guess that this beautifully painted chalet is as big as it is, but actually it stretches for dozens of yards behind the regional designs and balconies of its façade. The spotlessly clean interior has ceilings almost universally made of wood—at least in the public rooms —and an attractive décor of wooden chairs with upholstery. Each of the 52 comfortable bedrooms contains a private bath, and many of them have balconies. Rates in winter run from 590 AS ($43) to 620 AS ($45) per person daily for half board. Summer half-board rates go from 500 AS ($36.25) to 540 AS ($39.25) per person daily.

ST. MARTIN BEI LOFER

This tiny village is visited for its pilgrimage church, a large baroque edifice in a romantic setting called **Maria Kirchenthal**. The building was designed by the renowned master of the baroque J. B. Fischer von Erlach. The church has a museum displaying votive pictures from the 17th to the 19th centuries.

The church, a mile west of the village, is reached by a toll road open only in summer, or you can make an hour's walk from Lofer (see above).

The **Vorderkaser Gorge** can be visited from St. Martin. A 1½-mile road connects the gorge with the Mittelpinzgau Road near the Vorderkaser bus stop. The gorge may be seen daily from the first of May until the end of October from 9am to 5pm. Admission is 22 AS ($1.60) for adults and 11 AS (80¢) for children.

For information about the gorge, call the tourist office in St. Martin bei Lofer (tel. 06588/7345).

A restaurant at Prommer Rudolf, open daily in summer from 9am to 8pm, provides a good place to eat and drink. However, it is closed in winter.

SAALBACH AND HINTERGLEMM

This internationally known tourist resort, at an elevation of 3,290 feet, places emphasis on relaxation, recreation, and sports—both summer and winter.

From spring until late in the autumn, many quiet walks or more extended hikes are possible, as well as mountaineering, riding, bowling, minigolf, and tennis. You can swim in a nearby lake, where surfing and sailing are also possible. There are some 160 miles of well-laid-out footpaths. A kindergarten caters exclusively to children of people on holidays.

Saalbach has seen rapid growth as a winter-sports resort in recent years, with numerous lifts close to the center of town. There's one cable car big enough to carry 100 passengers, along with 40 tow and chair lifts. Tobogganing is popular too, as are ski-bobbing, sleigh rides, and curling in the clear, alpine winter. Many cross-country ski tracks emanate from here.

Saalbach is a twin resort to **Hinterglemm,** which lies about an eight-minute car ride to the west, at the head of the valley. Often the region is spoken of as a unit—the Saalbach-Hinterglemm ski area. The resorts are linked by a lift system and a ski bus. The area has a variety of well-groomed slopes and deep-snow runs. The major lift, the Schattberg cableway, leaves from the heart of Saalbach, taking skiers to the top station (6,560 feet), where an excellent restaurant boasts a suntrap terrace with a panoramic vista. Of course, summer visitors can also take the cableway to enjoy the scenery.

The Saalbach-Hinterglemm visitors' racing course is available to enthusiasts Tuesday to Sunday from 10am to noon and 2 to 4pm, with slaloms, giant slaloms, and parallel slaloms being held. Both resorts have ski schools and provide ski-circus runs.

Saalbach has fine shops where you can buy traditional Austrian clothing as well as chic apparel for dress or sports. Local arts and crafts shops are also of interest to visitors.

Saalbach can be a good center for exploring the neighboring resorts of Kaprun and Zell am See.

The Resort Hotels

Hotel Sonnleiten, A-5753 Saalbach (tel. 06541/402), is a multisectioned balconied hotel with a series of gently sloping rooflines and a format that looks like a greatly expanded chalet. It's on the ski slopes a short distance above the village, and parts of the hotel are attractively angled to create a varied façade of many different planes. Some sections of the interior have high modern ceilings supported by massive sloping beams. Management often has a fire going, even in summer, near the curved bar.

The dining room is large, with a paneled ceiling and wooden chairs. On the premises are tennis courts and an outdoor swimming pool, heated in winter. (Many guests take a warm dip, then roll around in the snow!) The hotel, open from December to September, offers 51 bedrooms, each with private bath or shower. With half board included, the per-person daily rate in winter ranges from 950 AS ($69) to 1,280 AS ($93). Summer half-board tariffs go from 630 AS ($45.75) to 850 AS ($61.75) per person daily.

Hotel Ingonda, A-5753 Saalbach (tel. 06541/262). Built as late as 1980, this hotel-restaurant exudes an aura of well-established, even antique, prosperity. It was named after the attractive brunette wife of the owner, Dietmar Scheyerer, who works hard to make the establishment one of the most comfortable at the resort. Aside from the Ingonda's five-star restaurant, the social center is a rambling pine-covered bar occupying an extended corner of the elegantly rustic lobby. There, an intricately crafted softwood ceiling casts a mellow glow over the leather chairs and Oriental carpets.

The hotel contains 47 well-furnished bedrooms, each with its own bath, TV, radio, phone, and balcony. Most residents at this December-to-October hotel opt for half board, costing 1,250 AS ($91) to 1,350 AS ($98.25) per person daily in winter. Summer half-board tariffs are 500 AS ($36.25) to 600 AS ($43.75) per person daily.

Skiers appreciate the proximity of the hotel to any of the village's trio of ski lifts, a one-minute skiborne trek from the entrance. The hotel has its own Jacuzzi, sauna, solarium, and massage facilities, not to mention its well-recommended restaurant. There, in a setting of chalet chairs and burnished paneling, guests enjoy such specialties as scampi flambéed in gin, filet of beef jambalaya, tender cuts of well-seasoned beef, and homemade strudels. Meals cost from 250 AS ($18.25) if you're dropping in to dine (reserve in season for a table, of course).

Hinterhag, A-5753 Saalbach (tel. 06541/7212), is an unusual and appealing hotel set on the side of an alpine hill a short distance from the center of town. You can ski from the hotel directly to and from the slopes. The Hinterhag is composed of at least five different sections, all of them balconied and built in a chalet style, connected into an architectural unit that might be your headquarters during your stay in Saalbach. In addition to a large collection of paneled and timbered public rooms, the hotel maintains a combination art nouveau café and art gallery.

The story of the construction of this oft-expanded 28-room hotel is documented in photographs on a wall in one of the public rooms. The cuisine ranks as the finest at the resort (see my dining recommendations coming up), and the varieties of light-hearted activities for wintertime guests also bring repeat business. Bedrooms have lots of exposed wood and an occasional wry touch, such as a nun's head extending over a bed's headboard, seeming to look down at whatever might be happening. Sepp and Evi Fersterer, both avid skiers, are your hosts. Their single- or double-occupancy charges run from 680 AS ($49.50) to 980 AS ($71.25) per person daily, with breakfast included; breakfast is actually a brunch served every day until noon. The hotel is closed every year from April to December.

Hotel Glemmtalerhof, A-5753 Hinterglemm (tel. 06541/7135), rises six stories, all of them in a chalet style, above the central street of the village. The street level of the hotel contains a few small shops as well as the front entrance. Inside, the hotel offers gemütlich and cozy public rooms, sometimes accented with fireplaces and lots of exposed wood. A covered swimming pool has big windows and sun chairs, while the public tennis courts are a few buildings away. The hotel is decorated in a combination of knotty-pine paneling and conservatively modern accessories for an attractive and appealingly rustic format. The 78 bedrooms, each with private bath or shower, are the kinds of places where you'll be tempted to linger; they're covered with mellow pine and invitingly lit. In winter, charges for half board range from 910 AS ($66.25) to 1,060 AS ($77) per person daily, while summer half-board tariffs go from 500 AS ($36.25) to 580 AS ($42.25) per person daily. The hotel, open from December to October, has a coffee shop, two bars, a night club, and a choice of restaurants.

Hotel Bauer, A-5753 Saalbach (tel. 06541/2130), presents lots of visual distraction. You'll see a mixture of colors and patterns, all of them invitingly cozy. In summer many guests sit on the flowered terrace in front, while in winter they move into the large and happily cluttered public rooms, which contain lots of niches for secluding oneself with a book or a friend. In the center of town, the hotel maintains a chalet annex a few minutes away, closer to the ski slopes. The annex contains rooms similar to the ones in the main buildings, as well as a snackbar that skiers find convenient. From December to September, the hotel receives guests in its 35 bedrooms, each with private bath or shower. Half-board rates range from 900 AS ($65.50) to 1,100 AS ($80) per person daily in winter. Summer half-board charges go from 420 AS ($30.50) to 520 AS ($37.75) per person daily.

Hotel Saalbacher Hof, A-5753 Saalbach (tel. 06541/7111), a traditional family establishment, has one of the town's prettiest chalet façades, embellished with heraldic paintings, masses of summer flowers, and on top of the lower of the two sloping rooflines, an open-sided stork's tower supported by a single stout post. The interior is dignified, restrained, and baronial, with a big stone fireplace in the attractively formal main salon, acres of chestnut-colored paneling, and pleasingly bold Oriental rugs. A wide grassy lawn with a view of the onion dome of the village church leads down to the outdoor heated swimming pool. There are also tennis courts.

The Dschulnigg family provides live music for dancing at five-o'clock tea and in the evening. There are three different restaurant and bar areas, my favorite of which has masonry walls and hanging lamps shaped like enormous pewter double-handled tankards. The accommodations in a nearby annex are similar to the ones in the main house, with 170 beds in all. In winter, half-board rates go from 850 AS ($61.75) to 1,450 AS ($105.50) per person daily, while in summer they range from 480 AS ($35) to 670 AS ($48.75) per person daily. Heating, service, and taxes are included in the prices.

Berger's Sporthotel, A-5753 Saalbach (tel. 06541/577). If you arrive in mid-winter, the ambience is almost like that of a giant, almost never-ending house party, the guests of which tend to be refugee urbanites celebrating their once-a-year vacation. On the premises are a boutique and dress shop, a small heated indoor swimming pool, a two-tiered restaurant and disco with a central marble-covered dance floor, a stüberl, and a cellar bar with live music and intimate lighting. In the center of Saalbach, the hotel can be recognized by its wooden balconies and its big yellow sign. All 55 rooms (about 100 beds) are equipped with baths or showers, phones, radios, color TVs, and minibars. Rates with half board are 450 AS ($32.75) to 550 AS ($40) per person daily in summer, rising to 850 AS ($61.75) to 1,400 AS ($101.75) per person daily in winter.

Hotel Kristiana, A-5753 Saalbach (tel. 06541/253), one of my favorite hotels in Saalbach, has a façade that bristles with jutting balconies, the horizontal supports of which have been intricately cut into pleasing patterns. On one corner, just above the sun terrace, an artist has executed a series of etched panels designating what might be the different seasons in Saalbach. The interior is a rustic fantasy of carved beams and well-polished paneling, several open fireplaces, and comfortable, well-planned rooms, each with its own private bath. A sauna is on the premises, while tennis courts and an indoor swimming pool are just around the corner. Johann Breitfuss and his family are your accommodating hosts at this 34-unit hotel. Depending on the season, prices are 460 AS ($33.50) to 920 AS ($67) per person daily for half board based on double occupancy. Singles pay a surcharge of 150 AS ($11) per day.

Alpenhotel Saalbach, A-5753 Saalbach (tel. 06541/666), is a big modern hotel with a design reminiscent of a chalet. It has painted detailing around some of the windows on the lower floors, lots of wooden balconies, and a façade divided into several different sections. A disco in the basement is one of the attractions, as well as a cozy, well-furnished interior. This includes a collection of country artifacts, several fireplaces (one of which juts pleasantly into the room and is capped with a conical stucco chimney), a popular bar with enough unusual details and enough people to make you want to linger, and a cellar with regional folk music. A long narrow indoor pool capped with what looks like hand-hewn ceiling beams is part of the sports facilities, along with a sauna, an exercise room, a whirlpool, and a solarium. Apartments are available for extended stays, sleeping two to six guests. Your hosts, the Thomas family, rent 100 bedrooms, all with the modern plumbing amenities. Rooms have been renovated and are better than ever. Some offer balconies with panoramic views. Rates for half board range from 975 AS ($71) to 1,465 AS ($106.50) per person daily, based on double occupancy. Singles pay a daily supplement of 100 AS ($7.25). The hotel is closed from mid-April to mid-May and November 1 to December 15.

Hotel Panther, A-5753 Saalbach (tel. 06541/227). When the flowers are out in full force, the balconies of this 60-room hotel are stunning. Even when they're not, the exterior is invitingly rustic, with solidly constructed wooden balconies, heavy overhanging eaves, and an open-sided tower, ideal for a stork's nest, crowning the roof. The interior is generously decorated with well-crafted paneling, tile floors, and Oriental rugs. The hotel—only a few steps from the cable car and within skiing distance of the bottom of the slopes—is open from December to March and May to October. In winter, with half board included, per-person rates (tax and service included) range from 1,020 AS ($74.25) to 1,070 AS ($77.75) daily. In summer, per-person rates for half board are lowered to 410 AS ($29.75) and 450 AS ($32.75).

Hotel Kristall, A-5753 Saalbach (tel. 06541/376), is a 40-room family-style chalet in the center of Saalbach. Its five stories contain well-furnished bedrooms, many of them papered in light patterns of gray and white, with furniture that sometimes looks as if it came from a private home. The public rooms are either rustic and heavily timbered or filled with modern and flamboyant colors and big windows. One area looks like a Victorian pub complete with globe lights. On the premises are an indoor pool, a sauna, a fitness room, and frequent live entertainment. The owners receive guests only from December 15 to Easter. For half board, the per-person rate ranges from 790 AS ($57.50) to 990 AS ($72) daily.

Gasthof Unterwirt, A-5753 Saalbach (tel. 06541/274), has a modern balconied addition set at right angles to the main house. The overall effect is pleasant and relaxed, a feeling helped by the rustic décor of the ceiling beams, ceramic tile stoves, and full-grained paneling. Kroll family members keep the guesthouse open from December to September. They rent 52 bedrooms, 44 of which contain private baths or showers. In winter, depending on the plumbing, half-board tariffs go from 560 AS ($40.75) to 890 AS ($64.75) per person daily. In summer, half board costs 300 AS ($21.75) to 410 AS ($29.75) per person daily.

Hotel Haus Wolf, A-5754 Hinterglemm (tel. 06541/346). If you're interested in ski lessons, this might be an ideal hotel since the local ski school makes its headquarters here. The hotel is right beside the Reiterkogel cable car in a 47-room chalet with wooden balconies and a first-floor sun terrace. The interior is covered with wood paneling, some of it crafted into curved and geometric designs, and the vertical columns supporting the ceilings are made either of wood or stone; homey touches include shelves with hand-painted plates just below ceiling level. In winter, fires burn beneath copper-sheathed chimneys, and guests often congregate in one of the several bars and restaurants. A smaller annex provides comfortable accommodations, often filled with painted furniture, a short distance away. Prices range from 620 AS ($45) to 920 AS ($67) per person daily; half board is included in the rates. All rooms contain baths or showers, phones, radios, and TVs. Facilities include an indoor swimming pool, a sauna, a solarium, and a sun terrace. The hotel is open from December to March and May to September.

Where to Dine

Hinterhag-Alm, Hotel Hinterhag (tel. 06541/7212), is considered by some gourmets to be among the best restaurants in Land Salzburg. The award-winning chef, Peter Huber, uses ingredients from the mountains that wouldn't ordinarily be used anywhere else. One example is a local variety of stinging nettles, which, when properly prepared, make a delicious flavoring for dumplings, salads, and soups. Some of his recipes are updated versions of very old local dishes. He uses large quantities of cabbage, reaching perfection in his cabbage soup. Dandelion greens, which are used in salads, as you'd expect, also might turn up in a honeyed dessert parfait. Specialties also include whortleberry omelets, sometimes suggested as an appetizer, as well as mountain roast mutton flavored with thyme.

The restaurant is open only from December to April. Lunch is served daily in season from 11am to 4pm, with prices ranging from 75 AS ($5.50) to 250 AS ($18.25). Dinner absolutely requires a reservation and is served from 7:30 to 10pm, costing from 500 AS ($36.25). The restaurant, located inside an alpine hut set near the edge of the ski slopes, is within a five-minute walk of this previously recommended hotel.

Gute Stube, Hotel Dorfschmeide, Hinterglemm (tel. 06541/7408), appears nondescript, scattered over several floors, but inside you'll find a Teutonic retreat of glowing pine, wrought iron, and gemütlich warmth. Portions are copious, flavorful, and worth the trip even if you're staying in Saalbach. You won't find anything very exotic, but the traditional dishes are satisfying. The peppersteak comes steaming and rich and might be followed by a richly caloric chocolate-flavored palatschinken. À la carte meals cost 150 AS ($11) to 350 AS ($25.50). The restaurant is open only from December to early April, offering food service daily from noon to 2pm and 6:30 to 9pm.

Après-Ski

Saalbach is one of the liveliest centers in Land Salzburg for après-ski and nightlife.

First, for coffee, tea, or pastries, you might drop in at one of the many cafés in town.

In the center of Saalbach, the **Galerie Café** (tel. 06541/242) is housed in a modernized white-stuccoed chalet on a sloping street across from the Hotel Ingonda. Inside, bentwood chairs, expositions of art, and tempting pastries lure visitors. The artworks change frequently, but you'll find that the caloric sweets are inevitably there. Coffee costs from 19 AS ($1.40), with pastries beginning at 24 AS ($1.75). Hours are daily from 9am to 10pm.

Saalbacher Fassl (tel. 06541/7309) is a café-restaurant with dance music. It is open daily in winter from 10am to 1am. Coffee costs from 19 AS ($1.40), and the house specialty is a combination of homemade ice creams in a bowl, costing from 36 AS ($2.60). The place lies behind the Hochalm lift at Hinterglemm.

At the previously recommended **Hotel Kristall** (tel. 06541/376), Visage is one of the best discos at the resort. It is open in winter only, nightly from 9pm to 3am, charging 35 AS ($2.55) for a large beer.

If you want more local entertainment, consider the Kuhstall Bar at the also-recommended **Alpenhotel Saalbach.** It's open nightly in winter only, from 9pm to 2am. There is no entrance fee, but both live and recorded music is presented for dancing. The décor is predictably rustic, and a large beer costs 30 AS ($2.20).

At the **Hotel-Gasthof Neuhaus** (tel. 06541/7151), one of my favorite spots, a two-man Zigeuner band in the Keller Bar entertains the skiers after a hard day on the slopes. This place was the original village inn. It begins its bar service every afternoon at 4, when a large beer costs 30 AS ($2.20).

Hinterhag-Alm (see previous recommendation) is a magnet in winter for about 500 skiers who head toward this rustic hut every afternoon at 4. Set a few paces from the edge of the slopes, it offers live music; guests dance in their ski boots. The preferred drink is a potent combination of schnapps and rum known as Jägertee. Drinks cost from 50 AS ($3.65). At 6pm, the place clears out as skiers get ready for the evening.

The Sportkeller Night Club at the recommended **Berger's Sporthotel** is for those who like their après-ski with a good band and a good drink (maybe more than one). Sportsmen are fond of the place.

The après-ski crowd shuttles back and forth between Saalbach and Hinterglemm, and after a few drinks the resorts merge into one.

In Hinterglemm, a good spot is the Knappenhof Knappenkeller of the **Knappenhof Tirolerhof** (tel. 06541/529). Strains of dance music from a live band are heard in winter, and there's recorded music in an adjacent disco. Sometimes Tyrolean music is interspersed with the more modern sounds. The place is open in summer and winter for lunch and dinner from noon to 3pm and 6pm to midnight. Grilled specialties are offered as well as Wiener schnitzels, pizzas, and Italian food, with meals costing from 200 AS ($14.50).

Also at Hinterglemm, the recommended **Hotel Glemmtalerhof** has perhaps the most gemütlich atmosphere of any place in the village. The Alm-bar, a small, intimate disco, stays open very late, and the Glemmerkeller Apéritif Bar is just the place to order a fondue any time before midnight. The show room, however, is Harlekin Dancing, where well-known international bands often appear in season.

If you're seeking a rustic, charming setting, try the previously recommended **Hotel Haus Wolf** at Hinterglemm. Some of the most attractive and fun-loving people in the area gather here around the fire. The décor might be called "Come to the Stable."

SAALFELDEN

An old market town in the Middle Pinzgau, Saalfelden is set against a background of towering mountains. Lying in a broad valley formed by the Saalbach River, this is a good center for touring the **Steinernes Meer**, or "Sea of Stone," a karstic limestone plateau that the Austrian government has turned into a nature reserve.

Although Saalfelden is primarily a summer resort, winter-sports areas in the mountains are within easy reach.

The town has a **pfarrkirche** (parish church) with a Gothic crypt beneath the choir and a late Gothic triptych in the presbytery.

At **Ritzen Castle,** which dates from 1563, a local museum (Heimat-museum) is devoted to life in the Pinzgau region. Here you'll see a rich collection of Christmas cribs by the artist Xandl Schläffer, exhibited in four rooms. Another hall displays a collection of pictures and ecclesiastical art. The museum is open Wednesday, Saturday, and Sunday from 2 to 4pm (daily in high season). Admission is 20 AS ($1.45) for adults and 10 AS (75¢) for children.

Food and Lodging

Hotel Dick, A-5760 Saalfelden (tel. 06582/2215), is a long four-story building with unusual geometric designs around the windows and heraldic paintings on the white front section. The reception hall has Louis XIII–style chairs and dark paneling, while the rest of the interior is graced with high coffered ceilings and bright colors. In the backyard a heated swimming pool is the gathering place in summer. The featured bedroom has 18th-century furniture and a painted ceiling, but the other units contain pleasant furniture quite a bit newer. In winter, half board ranges from 400 AS ($29) to 490 AS ($35.75) per person, lowered in summer to 390 AS ($28.25) to 420 AS ($30.50) per person. All 30 accommodations are equipped with private baths. The adjoining restaurant serves unusual specialties, such as Japanese gulasch, plus a wide variety of fresh fish. The hotel is open from December to October.

Restaurant Schatzbichl, Ramseiden 82 (tel. 06582/3281), is an alpine country house known for its cuisine. The recipes are usually derived from formulas used for generations by the area's grandmothers, and are served by local waitresses dressed in regional garb. Specialties are often placed in a copper pan directly onto your table, while members of your party dig in with forks and serving spoons. You might enjoy kasfarfeln (thick consommé with cheese, onions, chives, and dumplings) or schottnocken (served in a big pot with spätzle, smoked cheese, chives, and onions), or finally my favorite, erdäpfelgröstl (a big pot with potatoes, broth, sausages, onions, and chives). Menus range in price from 110 AS ($8) to 275 AS ($20). À la carte meals begin at 150 AS ($11), going up. Be sure to call ahead for a reservation. The restaurant is open daily from 10am to midnight. It's closed November 3, December 5, and in April.

You can get here by car, because the restaurant lies off a road dug into the valley of Maria Alm. But if you're adventurous, you can walk here in an hour and a half from Maria Alm, which might make a midday excursion.

LEOGANG

This is really an off-the-beaten-track hamlet known principally to the Austrians and Bavarians. In the general vicinity of Saalfelden, it's so undiscovered that you can enjoy quietness and tranquility here. Leogang is both a summer and a winter resort, lying at an elevation of 2,750 feet, in the Middle Pinzgau. Many day excursions are possible from here, including one to the "sea of stone" mentioned above.

Food and Lodging

Hotel Krallerhof, A-5771 Leogang (tel. 06583/246), is designed in a combination of antique rural styles (which include painted baroque detailing around some of the windows) and late 20th-century adaptations such as an A-frame roof over part of the front section. The result is a pleasing combination of old and new, with an interesting sprinkling of contemporary sculpture thrown in. Because of its isolation from other buildings in the village, you'll be able to imagine that the sun terrace stands at the edge of a virtual wilderness, which goes as far as the peaks of the nearby Leoganger Steinberge.

The popular double-tiered nightclub inside is appealingly decorated with lofty ceilings, sloping exposed stairways, and hand-carved paneling. Regional live music can often be heard. The 75 well-furnished bedrooms cost 800 AS ($58.25) to 1,000 AS ($72.75) daily for a single in winter, rising to 1,360 AS ($98.75) to 2,100 AS ($152.75) for a double or twin. Summer tariffs for a single range from 650 AS ($47.25) to 850 AS ($61.80) daily, going up to 1,200 AS ($87.25) to 1,680 AS ($122.25) for a double or twin. Charges include half board. On the premises are an indoor and outdoor swimming pool, plus a ski school and a small ski lift for beginners. The hotel is open from January to September.

KAPRUN

Both a summer resort and a winter ski center, as are most towns in the area, Kaprun is known for its high glacier skiing. The town is hardly the most attractive or the most atmospheric in Land Salzburg, but serious skiers don't seem to mind that. It's about a 12-minute run from Zell am See, which is easily reached by bus.

Area Attractions

The surrounding area takes in the Valley of Kaprun and its magnificent dams. It includes an ascent to the **Kitzsteinhorn** (9,612 feet), which can be quite complicated, involving Postal Buses, funiculars, and cableways. Always have your routes outlined at the tourist office with a detailed area map before you set forth. An English-speaking staff member there will supply the best possible routing and provide you with the most up-to-date hours, costs, and types of services likely to be available at the time of your visit. Also, you can learn about weather conditions from that source. For example, after mid-October, tours to the valley of the dams may not be possible. However, a visit to Kitzsteinhorn is an attraction in both summer and winter.

The Kitzsteinhorn will probably be first on your list of things to see. To reach the summit, you can go by cable car, transferring to the Salzburger Hütte at the Restaurant Alpincenter, where you can enjoy lunch with a view. The Alpincenter (8,020 feet), incidentally, is the largest ski area in Austria.

You can also reach the mountain by taking the underground funicular and changing at the Alpincenter. Don't forget that traffic gets very heavy here in winter.

The bottom station of this glacier railway is at an elevation of 2,784 feet and the top one is at 9,087 feet. Not only can you ski from the Alpincenter, but you can also take glacier and mountain tours.

It's best to purchase a day ticket—round-trip, naturally—for both the cable railway and the glacier lift, costing 180 AS ($13), as the railway goes only to the second platform of the cableway. You get off the train at that station and board a cableway, which will swing west, coming to a stop near the summit of the Kitzsteinhorn.

You'll find the Panoramatunnel cut through the mountains, as well as the Aussichtsrestaurant (talk about dining with a view!). You'll also be able to see Grossglockner, the neighboring mountain and the highest in Austria at 12,340 feet. The tunnel measures some 1,000 feet on the south side of the mountain, opening onto a panoramic gallery from which the view of Grossglockner is possible.

The **Kapruner Tal,** or Valley of Kaprun, is visited in summer to see its dams, which form a dramatic mountain sight. These dams, constructed in tiers, were originally built as part of the World War II recovery act, the U.S.-financed Marshall Plan. Experts from all over the world come here to study these hydroelectric constructions, considered brilliant feats of engineering genius. Trips are possible from the middle of May until around the middle of October, depending on weather conditions.

From Kaprun you can take a road to see the mammoth wall of the **Limbergsperre** (Limberg Dam). At the Gletscherbahn cable-car station, you can go all the way to the Kitzsteinhorn, already described. From the Limberg-stollen car park, you can take a shuttle bus to the lower station of the Lärchwand funicular. At the upper platform you'll have a magnificent view of the Limberg Dam rising nearly 400 feet. The dam holds back water to form the Lower Wasserfallboden reservoir (see below).

You can go along the valley by Postal Bus, passing through some 1½ miles of tunnels, to the Mooser Dam. A view of the Wasserfallboden lake reservoir (5,480 feet) is possible from here. The reservoir holds more than 18,500 million gallons of water.

You can see the two dams, the Moosersperre and the Drossensperre, which combine to form the Mooserboden reservoir, capable of holding nearly 19 billion gallons of water. These hydroelectric plants have reservoirs surrounded by glaciers of the Glockner range. An inclusive ticket to visit the plants costs 150 AS ($11). This covers the cost of transport from the Limbergstollen or Kesselfall car parks as far as the Mooserboden and back. The ice-covered peaks of the High Tauern can be seen from the dams.

Food and Lodging

Sporthotel Kaprun, A-5710 Kaprun (tel. 06547/8625), on the outskirts of the village, is a large chalet with a gently sloping roof and flowered balconies. It's near the cableway stations at the southern exit of Kaprun. Built in 1977, it has an attractive format of paneled ceilings, big windows, and spacious public rooms. These include a sauna, a children's playroom, and a game room. Exercise machines and table-tennis tables are nearby, plus at least one bar area. The 59 good-sized bed-rooms are modern, and some areas are covered with paneling; all rooms come with private baths or showers. In summer the half-board tariff is 490 AS ($35.75) per person daily, rising in winter to 575 AS ($41.75).

Hotel Orgler, A-5710 Kaprun (tel. 06547/8205), is a cream-colored house in the middle of the village. Slightly isolated from its neighbors, it offers peace, quiet, and a pleasantly rustic interior of high ceilings, heavy beams, and chalet furniture. Each of the 34 bedrooms has a private bath or shower, toilet, phone, radio, TV con-nection, balcony, and room safe. Half-board rates range from 470 AS ($34.25) to 550 AS ($40) per person daily in summer, from 650 AS ($47.25) to 820 AS ($59.50) per person in winter. Apartments with three or four beds are available for families. The hotel's dining room and restaurant are furnished in traditional Austri-an style, as are the cozy stubes and the bar with an open fireplace. On the premises are a Turkish steam bath, a sauna, a Jacuzzi, and a solarium, as well as a tennis center with indoor and outdoor courts, a squash court, and an 18-hole golf course. All of these facilities are open only from December to April and June to October.

Gasthof zur Mühle, A-5710 Kaprun (tel. 06547/8625), is a white-walled cha-let with wooden balconies and five floors of cozy, good-sized rooms. On a quiet road in an isolated part of the village, it contains a sauna, table-tennis facilities, and a com-fortable TV room. It's owned and operated by the Nindl family, who rent 37 bedrooms with private baths or showers. Winter half-board charges range from 385 AS ($28) to 525 AS ($31.25) per person daily. Summer half-board rates go from 305 AS ($22.25) to 390 AS ($28.25) per person daily.

Hotel Alpincenter, A-5710 Kaprun (tel. 06547/8300), is a sturdily built wood-and-concrete hotel near the terminus of the ski lift at the middle station of the Kitzsteinhorn railway, some 8,000 feet up the mountain. The interior is modern and rustic, with lots of heavy exposed beams, a central fireplace with curved stools pulled up in a circle around it, and a series of clean and attractive public rooms, usu-ally filled with sports enthusiasts. This hotel makes week-long offers that include a six- or seven-day ski pass, but for the daily rate, half board ranges from 420 AS ($30.50) to 465 AS ($33.75) per person, with single occupants paying a daily sur-charge of 80 AS ($5.75). Each of the 30 rooms has a private bath.

Zirbenstüberl (Hubertus) (tel. 06547/8504). Considered by many visitors a tempting refuge from the weather and the hordes of visitors who descend upon Kaprun, this popular pine-paneled spot is an all-encompassing pizzeria, spaghetti house, and Austrian food factory dispensing everything from Italian-inspired dishes to Pinzgau specialties. No lunch is served, but dinner is available nightly from 6:30 to 10pm. The place closes for two months in spring and again for two months in the slow autumn. Meals cost from 150 AS ($11) and up.

Après-Ski

Kaprun has its own relatively modest nightlife, but should you ever get bored you can always take the shuttle bus over to Zell am See for much more excitement. Nightlife reaches its peak in Kaprun on Friday and Saturday nights, and on other nights you might like to turn in with a good book . . . or whatever.

The **Sporthotel Kaprun,** already recommended, is the scene of the most ac-tion, offering dancing to either disco records (the latest hits from the U.S.) or else live bands, often imported from Italy. You might begin your evening with a Chinese fondue dinner or an Indonesian rijsttafel, that ceremonial feast of the Dutch colo-nists.

Your evening in Kaprun might begin relatively modestly—and early—by dropping in at **Morokutti** (tel. 06547/8424)—if you can find a seat—with its modern alpine décor. There is no disco here and no dancing; the main activity is drinking and talking. The place is open daily except Monday but only in winter, and hours are 10am to midnight. A glass of wine costs 31 AS ($2.25).

Baum Bar (tel. 06547/8216) has one of the most rustically alpine décors in town, and it hires live performers in season to provide dance music. Music begins in winter from 8pm, but there are plenty of drinkers there during the après-ski period beginning daily at 4pm. A large beer costs 35 AS ($2.55).

There's dancing at the **Dancing-Bar-Pub Nindl** (tel. 06547/8259). In high season, folkloric entertainment is often presented, along with live music and show bands. There is no entrance fee. Call to find out what's happening at the time of your visit.

Many skiers like to spend their evening sitting and drinking around an open fire. Nearly all hotels and pensions welcome outside guests.

MARIA ALM

The village of Maria Alm, 3 miles east of Saalfelden at an elevation of 2,600 feet, is both a summer and a winter resort. Lying at the foot of the Steineres Meer, the karstic limestone plateau called the "Sea of Stone," now a nature reserve, Maria Alm holds many attractions for warm-weather visitors, including chair-lift rides to heights presenting glorious alpine vistas, a 35-mile network of marked pathways for walks in shady woods and across wide romantic grassways, tennis, and minigolf.

The surrounding mountains attract skiers in winter. Together with Hintermoos and Hinterthal, Maria Alm forms a large avalanche-free winter-sports area, with continuous snow cover from the beginning of December to the end of April.

The church spire in Maria Alm rises to 276 feet.

Food and Lodging

Hotel Norica, A-5761 Maria Alm (tel. 06584/491), is a four-story roadside chalet with balconies and rustic detailing. The cozy interior features alpine timbers (some of them decorative), knotty paneling, and conference facilities. A heated indoor swimming pool and a sauna, along with a wind-sheltered sun terrace, are part of the facilities. The location of this hotel, near the ski lifts, makes it attractive to winter-sports enthusiasts. Each of the 81 comfortably furnished rooms has a bath. Singles range from 660 AS ($48) to 1,190 AS ($86.50), while doubles go from 520 AS ($37.75) to 1,000 AS ($72.75) per person, with half board included. Rates depend on the season.

The adjoining restaurant is definitely an above-average place at which to eat. Menu items include scampi Café de Paris, peppersteak Madagascar, and filet Stroganoff. The restaurant is open daily, and reservations are a good idea.

Restaurant Arcade, Hinterthal 9 (tel. 06584/828-235). The décor of this small and intimate restaurant, both inside and out, features regionally inspired handiwork. The clientele is local and loyal, although the establishment draws a large number of vacationers as well. Menu items include specialties such as filet of beef in a paprika-rosemary sauce, trout in a Riesling sauce, and turbot with a chive sabayon. Dessert items are too lengthy to list, but one of the most popular is the walnut parfait. Set menus cost from 250 AS ($18.25) and up, with à la carte meals beginning at about the same. Go from noon to 2:30pm or 6:30 to 9:30pm. Reservations are important. The restaurant is closed for all of May and from early October to just before Christmas.

Almer Heurigen Keller (tel. 06584/7615). Easy to find in the basement of a building right in the center, this country wine cellar has hosted many personalities whose names are known throughout the Teutonic world. It offers a good selection of wine and a solidly appealing cuisine prepared by Hans and Regina Haller. To accompany your bottle of wine, you might enjoy one of the house schnitzels, sausages with cabbage, or an array of snacks and salads from the buffet. The cellar is open every day except Tuesday from noon to 10pm. It's closed from mid-April to the end of May and from the end of October to mid-December. Set menus cost from 200 AS ($14.50), with à la carte dinners ranging from 175 AS ($12.75) to 400 AS ($29).

MAISHOFEN

This is actually a little satellite outpost of Zell am See where you might choose to anchor if you want to stay in the area, yet escape the frenetic pace that overtakes the larger resort in the height of both the winter and the summer seasons. Maishofen has convenience and tranquility, with all the sights and attractions of Zell am See at its doorstep.

Food and Lodging

Schloss Kammer, A-5751 Maishofen (tel. 06542/8202). From the outside, this place looks more like a prosperous bourgeois house than a castle. But for romantics, a small room in the main building might be a perfect hideaway. Most of the accommodations get lots of sun and are furnished with antiques or reasonably good copies, along with baroque fireplaces or ceramic stoves. Each has a shower and toilet. You can stay here for 370 AS ($27) per person daily for half board. Or, especially if you're a family, the Neumayer family will rent you an apartment in a neighboring annex, suitable for two to six persons.

In the main hotel the public rooms have old photographs and lots of carved statues. The dining room is one of the most sought-after in the region. Most of its plaster ceiling is supported by massive stone columns and old vaulting. A green ceramic stove provides heat to offset the winter winds blowing against the small-paned windows. The noodles are homemade, accompanying such main dishes as roast pork, roast venison, gulasches, and a variety of tempting stews. À la carte meals range from 100 AS ($7.25) to 185 AS ($13.50). The restaurant is open from noon to 2pm and 3 to 10pm; closed Tuesday in the off-season.

BRUCK AN DER GROSSGLOCKNERSTRASSE

The starting point for Grossglockner Road (coming up) is at this little mountain resort, which becomes a lure to skiers when the snow falls. In summer the Grossglocknerstrasse brings lots of vehicular traffic through the village, standing at an elevation of 2,485 feet. Bruck's **pfarrkirche** (parish church) is from the 19th century.

From here visitors go up to **Schloss Fischhorn** for one of the most celebrated views in the area. Another excursion is to **Taxenbach,** 7½ miles away. Some 15 minutes from that point, you reach **Kitzloch Gorge,** where you can take a 45-minute tour from May 1 until the end of October, daily from 8am to 6pm. The cost is 25 AS ($1.80) for adults and 5 AS (35¢) for children. For information, call 06545/295.

Food and Lodging

Hotel Lukashansl, A-5671 Bruck an der Grossglocknerstrasse (tel. 06545/458), has a façade of white stucco with shutters. The windows are small and are surrounded with detailing in country baroque. A member of the Peter Mayr family has cultivated a grape arbor near the café terrace, which is separated from the road by a row of potted shrubs. An annex with flowered balconies juts off to one side of the main building with parking space beside it. The hotel rents 150 well-furnished bedrooms, each with private bath. Guests stay here on half-board terms, which range from 400 AS ($29.10) to 450 AS ($37.75) per person daily. The hotel is especially popular in winter.

RAURIS

Motorists entering the Rauris Valley from Taxenbach come upon Rauris, which was a gold-mining town in the Middle Ages. Many of the elegant old houses in the town are from that era.

At the **Rauriser Talmuseum** (tel. 6253), in the Nationalparkgemeinde Rauris, you'll find popular art and artifacts left over from the gold-mining heyday of the town. The collection is in honor of Ignaz Rojacher, founder of the Sonnblick Observatory. The museum stays open all year, with guided tours daily at 10am and 4pm. Admission is 20 AS ($1.45) for adults and 10 AS (75¢) for children.

Rauris (2,600 feet) is a summer excursion and a winter ski resort. You can take chair lifts to the Kreuzboden at 4,280 feet and the Jack-Hochalm at 4,820 feet.

Food and Lodging

Sporthotel Rauriserhof, A-5661 Rauris (tel. 06544/6213). If you could see this large, modern hotel from the air, it would look like two huge chalets connected by a central corridor and a series of low-lying sports facilities. One of Europe's most popular American tennis camps, directed by international tennis specialists, is featured here. The tennis facility contains three outdoor and two indoor clay courts, an indoor swimming pool and sauna, three tanning stations, a sports physiotherapist, and a fitness center. At the end of a tiring day of sports and play, guests can enjoy a collection of cozily paneled bars, backgammon rooms, crackling fireplaces, and intimate corners. The place is fun, interesting, and could be a central point for a prolonged stay exploring the region's footpaths. The hotel rents 72 well-furnished bedrooms, each with private bath or shower. In winter, half-board terms range from 650 AS ($47.25) to 780 AS ($56.75) per person daily; in summer, from 550 AS ($40) to 660 AS ($48) per person daily.

The in-house restaurant is worth a special trip. Aside from its Austrian specialties, international fare includes snails, crabmeat soup, and entrecôte Café de Paris. Gutbürgerlich selections feature well-prepared game, schnitzels, roasts, and pork cutlets in vodka sauce. Meals range from 150 AS ($11) to 375 AS ($27.25), and are served daily from 7am to midnight, December to October.

Gasthof Schüttgut, Wörth (tel. 06544/6403), is authentic enough to make you feel like one of the prosperous local farmers. The restaurant used to be a rough-timbered farm building, constructed in the 16th century, until it was transformed into this charming establishment. The service is personalized, and you are likely to feel a gemütlich warmth before the end of your meal. Specialties are wholesome, filling, and regional. À la carte meals range from 85 AS ($6.25) to 225 AS ($16.25). It is open every day from noon to 9:30pm.

MITTERSILL

The major town of the Upper Pinzgau region (Oberpinzgau), Mittersill, at an elevation of 2,590 feet, is at the intersection of ancient trade routes, with buildings rich in tradition. Surrounded by three lakes and 30 miles of alpine brooks, with many beautiful paths for summer walking and hiking, the town is also a popular winter-sports center.

Skiers can go to the main skiing area of Pass Thurn-Kitzbühel, where one ski pass allows use of any of the 56 ski lifts and a ski bus.

The glaciers of Hohe Tauern south of the village are part of the national park system, which you can visit.

Mittersill has two churches built in the baroque style in the mid-18th century. Schloss Mittersill, from the 16th century, is privately owned and cannot be visited.

There's a local **museum** in the Felber Tower (tel. 06562/4441), where a varied collection of Pinzgau peasant furnishings is exhibited, as well as many minerals, tools, and other artifacts. It also shows ecclesiastical art. The museum is open from June 1 until the end of September—Monday to Friday from 9am to 5pm, on Saturday and Sunday from 1 to 5pm. Admission is 20 AS ($1.45) for adults and 5 AS (35¢) for children.

Food and Lodging

Schloss Mittersill, A-5730 Mittersill (tel. 06562/4523). The Gothic chapel attached to this prosperous-looking house is frequently used for marriage ceremonies, which eventually spill over into the main hotel. The hotel is about a 20-minute walk from the center of the village and is easily accessible by car. You'll recognize it by its patterned red and white shutters and its roofline with three tiers of small-windowed gables. The public rooms are stately, with vaulted ceilings and thick walls pierced with triple sets of arched Gothic windows. A library/sitting room has stone detailing and paneling darkened long ago by frequent polishing. My favorite room has a massively timbered ceiling, pure-white walls, a stone fireplace, and lots of hunting trophies.

Each of the bedrooms is individually furnished, sometimes with built-in closets of knotty pine. The 110-bed hotel, open from December to October, charges from 320 AS ($23.25) to 705 AS ($51.25) per person daily for half board.

Gasthaus Bräurup, A-5730 Mittersill (tel. 06562/216), is a historical white-walled house with four floors of wood-grained shutters and a surrounding grassy lawn. The interior's rustic touches include lots of burnished paneling, ceramic stoves with unusual hand-painted illustrations, shelves of antique pewter, and a scattering of large regional antiques. The 40 bedrooms are usually large and well furnished, with large windows. The elevator is big enough to accommodate wheelchairs. The rates per person range from 450 AS ($32.75) to 550 AS ($40) daily, including half board.

My favorite room is the richly paneled rectangular restaurant with the hand-carved baroque finials at the corner of the walls and ceiling. In the center is a round panel bristling with sheaves of grain carved into the glowing hardwoods. The gasthaus has a sauna, a steambath, and a solarium. The establishment is in the center of the village next to the church.

NEUKIRCHEN AM GROSSVENEDIGER

Lying near Wald in Pinzgau at an elevation of 2,800 feet, in a setting of alpine woods and meadows, fields and forest paths, Neukirchen's sunny terraces afford a view of 15 mountain peaks, including the Grossvenediger, the Kleinvenediger, and the Geiger. Many alpine hikes can be arranged by the Oberpinzgau school of mountaineering.

The village has a late Gothic church with a 14th-century fresco. You can also see the **Castle Hochneukirchen** here, dating from the 16th century. The present schloss was built on the site of a much older structure that was destroyed.

Like nearly all resorts in Land Salzburg, Neukirchen is a ski center in winter and a holiday resort in summer.

Food and Lodging

Hotel Gassner, A-5741 Neukirchen am Grossvenediger (tel. 06565/6232), is a large hotel built chalet style in two sections joined together by a series of balconied rooms. A sun terrace rests on massive stone columns above a parking lot, and the hotel is slightly outside the central part of the village. The interior is contemporary and rustic, with lots of comfortable banquettes and full-grained polished planking decorating the ceilings and walls. The indoor pool is big enough to swim laps in, while the spacious bedrooms are simple, cozy, and comfortable. Also on the premises is a sauna, and the hotel has easy access to the nearby ski slopes. Usually a crackling fire will be waiting for you after your return from a winter's day outdoors. From December to October, the hotel rents 65 cozily furnished bedrooms, charging from 370 AS ($27) to 440 AS ($32) per person daily for half board, depending on the season.

Gasthof/Pension Kammerlander, A-5741 Neukirchen am Grossvenediger (tel. 06565/6231), is a large, four-story hotel with a concrete exterior, painted white, wrap-around balconies, and heavy overhanging eaves. Not far from the village church, the gasthof is owned by the Kammerlander family, who welcome guests to their comfortable hotel. The interior includes masonry detailing, lots of wood, art objects, and a comfortably inviting restaurant and bar area with well-prepared Austrian-style food. From December to October, the hotel offers 40 bedrooms, charging winter half-board rates of 450 AS ($32.75) to 520 AS ($37.75) per person daily, and summer half-board rates of 360 AS ($26.25) to 420 AS ($30.50) per person daily.

WALD IM OBERPINZGAU

Wald, a summer and winter resort at a 2,900-foot elevation, occupies one of the most beautiful sites in the Upper Pinzgau. The village lies at the junction of the old road from the Gerlos Pass, and from it you can see the glacial peaks of the Grossvenediger massif. In its churchyard are gravestones carved out of rare minerals.

In summer, Wald is a good center for easy footpaths and climbs in the national park. From here, you can enjoy alpine hunting and trout fishing. Also, a hang-gliding school may attract you.

Skiing and other sports lure winter visitors. A ski school prepares you to try the 25 miles of slopes. About 18 major lifts reach three skiing areas where snow is virtually guaranteed well past Easter. Skiing is possible at elevations ranging from 4,800 feet to 6,500 feet. There are also any number of easy footpaths. Hotels here can organize toboggan runs, riding, horse-sleigh rides, and curling.

Food and Lodging

Jagdschloss Graf Recke, A-5742 Wald im Oberpinzgau (tel. 06565/6417). This elegant red-roofed mansion was built in 1926 as the personal hunting lodge of the Silesian family of the Count von der Recke. At the time they owned the hunting rights in what is today the nearby Austrian National Park of Hohe Tauern. The best time to see this place might be in summer, when a thick layer of wildflowers covers the grounds around it. A curved swimming pool lies just beyond the stone foundation. The famous guests who stayed here in the 1920s and 1930s would make a long (and perhaps notorious) list, although today the hunting trophies that fill the interior are the only reminder of their presence. Tennis, horseback riding, alpine hunting, and trout fishing, plus proximity to the miles of footpaths in the region, along with the dozens of ski lifts all around, are part of the benefits of this well-run hotel.

For its 31 rooms the management charges from 420 AS ($30.50) daily for a single, rising to 1,000 AS ($72.75) for a double. Full board ranges from 750 AS ($54.50) to 800 AS ($58.25) per person daily. Meals, costing from 150 AS ($11) and up, are served daily from noon to 2pm and 7 to 9pm.

Walderwirt & Märzenhof, A-5742 Wald im Oberpinzgau (tel. 06565/8216). Everyone has a choice in life, and in this case you'll be able to choose between two different buildings on either side of the street. The older of the two was built in 1770, and still maintains the vaulted ceilings, heavy timbers, and some of the painted antiques of the year of its construction. The modern section has streamlined wooden balconies, an indoor pool, tennis courts, lots of paneling, and an open fireplace whose massive hanging chimney is made of small plates of iron riveted together. Accommodations cost approximately the same in the two buildings, and they're connected by an underground passage in case you can't decide which you like better. The 40 comfortably furnished rooms cost 650 AS ($47.25) to 690 AS ($50.25) per person daily in winter, based on double occupancy. Summer charges range from 520 AS ($37.75) to 560 AS ($40.75) per person daily, based on double occupancy. All charges include half board.

The Strasser Restaurant, in the hotel's older section, is one of the best dining spots at the resort. It has old paneling, smallish windows, and a ceramic stove. The food comes in copious quantities, and is the kind of gutbürgerlich fare best enjoyed with a few beers. Many of the cheese selections come from the region. À la carte meals cost from 150 AS ($11) and up, and are served daily from 11am to 2pm and 6 to 9pm.

KRIMML

This village in the far-western extremity of Land Salzburg is visited mainly by those wishing to explore **Krimml Falls.** The German name for this scene of iridescent splendor is Krimmler Wasserfälle. These falls, the highest in Europe, are spectacular, dropping 1,250 feet in three stages. They lie to the south of the Gerlos Pass, which connects the Salzach Valley in Land Salzburg with the Siller Valley in the Tyrolean country. Krimml, mainly a summer resort, is the best base for exploring the falls. The village is in a heavily forested valley called Krimmler Ache, between the Kitzbühel Alps and the Hohe Tauern.

If you're coming from Salzburg, figure on some 95 miles by train. There's also bus service from Zell am See. If you're traveling by car, you have a choice of leaving your vehicle at the car park at the south of the village and making a 30-minute walk to the lower falls, or taking the Gerlos Pass toll road, open from June 1 to September 30. The falls are open daily from 8am to 6pm, charging adults 10 AS (75¢) and children 5 AS (35¢).

Most visitors allow about 3½ hours to explore the entire falls area. On a sunny day, try to visit the Wasserfälle around noon when they are at their most spectacular. On summer nights the waterfalls are likely to be floodlit on Wednesday, depending on weather conditions.

Wear good, sturdy shoes, and since viewing points are always shrouded in spray, a raincoat will come in handy.

After you've seen the lower falls, if you want to see the second stage, count on another 12-minute walk. From there it's only a five-minute jaunt to the third and final stage for viewing the cataracts. There are also paths leading to the fourth and fifth viewing points. The middle part of the falls can be seen at the sixth and seventh lookouts. At the Bergerblick you'll have your greatest view of the waterfalls, reached by continuing another 20 minutes from the seventh viewing point. If you wish, you can go on to the Schettbrücke (4,800 feet) for a look at the upper cascades.

Krimml is also visited in winter, because good skiing is offered at Gerlosplatte (5,600 feet), 7 miles away. The waterfalls lie under a deep ice layer during the winter.

Food and Lodging

Hotel Klockerhaus, A-5743 Krimml (tel. 06564/208). This peaceful 43-room double chalet has wooden balconies, gently sloping rooflines, and a central section two stories high. It's on the border of the Hohe Tauern National Park, with a magnificent view of the Krimml falls. The family hotel has well-furnished lounges and comfortable bedrooms with showers, toilets, TVs, phones, and balconies. Half board costs 380 AS ($27.75) to 460 AS ($33.50) per person daily. The kitchen serves Austrian and international specialties. The proprietors, Bruno and Margarethe Czerny, see to the well-being of their customers.

Hotel Krimmlerfalle, A-5743 Krimml (tel. 06564/203), is a pretty four-story house with sea-green shutters and wood siding covering the third and fourth floors. In summertime the balconies are covered with pink and red flowers. The dining room is laid out below a wooden ceiling whose planks are arranged in a circular pattern above the modern upholstered chairs. The 30 tasteful and comfortable bedrooms range in price from 295 AS ($21.50) to 370 AS ($27) per person daily, with half board included. Your congenial hosts are the Schöppl family.

6. The Grossglockner Road

Grossglocknerstrasse, the longest and most splendid alpine highway in Europe, and one of the outstanding tourist attractions on the Continent, will afford you one of the greatest drives of your life.

The hairpin turns and bends of the Grossglockner Road have been called "the stuff Grand Prix is made of." It's believed that this was the same route through the Alps used by the Romans, although this was forgotten until 1930, when engineers building the highway discovered remains of the work of their road-building predecessors done some 19 centuries earlier. The highway, representing engineering genius, was finished in 1935. It was the one that such countries as Switzerland and France copied years later when they built their own alpine highways.

It runs for nearly 30 miles, beginning at Bruck an der Grossglocknerstrasse (see above) at 2,483 feet, via Fusch/Grossglocknerstrasse, and heading toward Ferleiten, Hochmais, and Fuschtörl through Hochtortunnel, where the highest point is 8,220 feet, to Guttal and Heiligenblut (4,267 feet) in Carinthia.

The actual mountain part of the road stretches for some 13½ miles, usually at about 6,500 feet. It has a maximum gradient of 12%.

Many visitors prefer to take the bus over this spectacular stretch, but if you feel that your driving is good enough, you can do it by private car. Because of the high altitudes, the road is passable only from mid-May to mid-November. Always check with some authority about the road conditions before considering such a drive, especially in spring and autumn. A one-way trip for a passenger car brings a toll of 250 AS ($18.25), collected either at Ferleiten or at Heiligenblut. In summer, there is regular Postal Bus service running from such places as Zell am See and Salzburg.

After leaving Bruck, you enter the Fuscher Valley going south, and along the way you'll be rewarded with breathtaking alpine scenery. Four miles from the Hochtortunnel on the north side, you can branch off onto the Edelweiss-Strasse, going along for about 1½ miles to the car park at the **Edelweiss-Spitze** (8,433 feet). Here you'll see a panorama of 37 10,000-foot peaks. At Edelweiss-Spitze is an observation tower, going up to more than 8,450 feet.

One of the interesting detours along the road is to the stone terrace of the **Franz-Josefs-Höhe.** It's named for the emperor who once had a mansion constructed here in the foothills of the Pasterze Glacier. The stretch from Gletscherstrasse to Franz-Josefs-Höhe (7,770 feet) is some 5 miles long, branching off near Guttal. This road lies above the Pasterze Glacier, opposite the Grossglockner (12,430 feet). The Pasterze, incidentally, is the largest glacier in the eastern Alps, 5½ miles long.

If you're traveling in spring and autumn, it might not be possible to take detours to the Edelweiss-Spitze or the Franz-Josefs-Höhe if heavy snow falls. If you do take the side trip to the latter site, avoid arriving there around midday. On a bright sunny day in summer, the place is literally mobbed. It has an outstanding view of the majestic Grossglockner.

From May until the end of September, it's possible to descend from Freiwandeck to Pasterze Glacier by taking a funicular. Service is every hour daily from 8am to 4pm.

7. Zell am See

Founded by monks around the middle of the 8th century, the old part of Zell am See lies on the shore of the Zeller See (Lake Zell), with a backdrop of mountains. Zeller See is a deep glacial lake filled with clear blue alpine water. The town today is the most important resort in the Middle Pinzgau, a district that has already been previewed. Zell is popular and fashionable in both summer and winter. It's also a center for those who'd like to get an early start and travel the Grossglockner alpine highway, described above.

AREA ATTRACTIONS

Unlike most resorts in Land Salzburg, Zell am See has some old buildings worth exploring. These include **Kastnerturm,** or Constable's Tower, the oldest building in town, dating from the 12th century. It was once used as a grain silo.

The town's **pfarrkircke** (parish church) is an 11th-century Romanesque-style structure. It has, however, a late Gothic choir from the 16th century.

Castle Rosenberg is also from the 16th century. It was once an elegant residence in the South Bavarian style of the free state of Salzburg. Today it houses the Rathaus (town hall), with a gallery. There's a tower at each of the four corners, and a round tower.

The **folklore museum** is in the old tower, the Vogtturm, near the town square. The tower is about 1,200 years old. In the museum, old costumes are displayed, and many artifacts on exhibit show the traditional way of life in earlier Land Salzburg. From June to October, the museum is open Monday to Friday from 10am to noon and 3 to 5pm. In winter it is open Monday to Friday from 3 to 5pm. Admission is free.

Zell is as well equipped for summer as for winter sports, as are the competitive resorts of Kaprun and Saalbach.

For winter visitors, snow conditions in the Zell area are usually ideal from December all the way to the end of April. Zell am See attracts beginner and intermediate skiers, plus many nonskiers as well—people who like the attractions and bustling life of the winter resort even if they never take to the slopes. They do take the chair lift (sans skis) for the magnificent alpine scenery. Skiing is possible at elevations ranging from 3,000 to 9,000 feet.

Sports fans gravitate to the **Kur-und-Sportzentrum,** an arena northwest of the resort housing a mammoth indoor swimming pool as well as saunas and an ice rink. Sometimes in cold weather, the lake is frozen over.

Although known as a winter-sports center, Zell am See also attracts visitors in the peak summer months. **Lake Zell,** which has been called "the cleanest" lake in Europe, is warm, maintaining an average temperature of some 70° Fahrenheit in summer. The lake is 2½ miles long and 1 mile wide. Motorboats can be rented for tours. You can go along a footpath from the town to the bathing station at Seespitz, the walk taking about half an hour.

Schmittenhöhe, at 6,450 feet, towers to the west of Zell am See. You can go up the mountain in four different ways, with even more choices for ways to descend. In summer the hardy and hearty have been known to climb it in four hours. I suggest, however, that you take the cableway. The view from here is one of the finest in the Kitzbühel Alps, the majestic glacial peaks of the Grossglockner range being only part of the celestial heights you'll see on your excursion. You can have lunch at the Berghotel at the upper station.

From the west side of Zell am See you can take a four-seater cableway to the middle station. From here you can connect with several lifts that will take you to the upper platform. A sun terrace at the upper station is popular in both summer and winter. (Don't be surprised to see bare breasts even in February.)

It's about a mile up Schmittenhöhe. Figure on about 1¾ hours for your round-trip, plus another 18 minutes by cable car. In summer, service is every half hour.

You can also take the Sonnalm cableway (entrance near the Schmittenhöhe terminus) to Sonnalm at 4,540 feet. You'll find another restaurant here. From Sonnalm, it's possible to go by chair lift to Sonnkogel (6,020 feet) and by drag lift to Hochmais (5,665 feet). From the eastern part of Lake Zell you can take the chair lift up to Ronachkopf (4,875 feet).

From Zell am See you can also take a funicular to Kaprun (see above), at the foot of the Kitzsteinhorn, for glacier and year-round skiing. In fact, some of the most spectacular excursions possible from Kaprun can be made easily on tours from Zell am See (refer to the Kaprun description for more details).

FOOD AND LODGING

Hotel Salzburger Hof, Auerspergstrasse 11, A-5700 Zell am See (tel. 06542/2828). You'll get a glimpse of the handcrafted interior of this 60-room five-star hotel through the glass doors leading inside. A polychrome wood statue of what might be an archbishop is fastened to a background of carved pine in the lobby. The most elegant piece of wrought iron in town serves as the entrance to the dining room. In the salon a blazing fire is housed in an unusual brick-lined stucco fireplace, which guests enjoy under heavily timbered ceilings. The Holleis family maintains the pleasant outdoor garden with its sun terrace, where barbecues are enjoyed. Evening programs presented include dancing, zither playing, and folklorica.

The hotel, with a chalet design, stands near the lake. Accommodations include junior suites and suites with TVs, minibars, private saunas, baths, and open fireplaces. Half-board rates range from 690 AS ($50.25) per person daily in a double to 1,600 AS ($116.25) per person in a suite. A sauna, a Jacuzzi, and a heated indoor swimming pool are on the premises.

Mövenpick Grand Hotel, Esplanade 4, A-5700 Zell am See (tel. 06542/2388), is the third manifestation of a "Grand Hotel" that has stood on this site. Based on late Victorian models, it is a wedding cake of mansard roofs and cream-colored stonework whose elaborate cornices and moldings are reflected in the cold waters of the lake. Centrally located on its own semipeninsula, it has a private beach as well as a sun terrace. The hotel offers 69 comfortably furnished regular rooms, suites, and imperial suites, all with baths, TVs, direct-dial phones, and minibars. Most of them also have private saunas and/or hot whirlpools. Standard rooms rent for 550 AS ($40) to 800 AS ($58.25) per person nightly, with suites costing more, of course. Guests face a choice of three restaurants: the Mövenpick, with traditional specialties; the Esplanade, with fresh fish offered daily; and the Rendez-Vous, a cozy corner in the heart of the hotel. The Wünderbar is housed in a glass dome directly under the roof. Recreation instructors offer special programs featuring such sports as paragliding and river rafting as well as glacier skiing all year.

Hotel zum Hirschen, A-5700 Zell am See (tel. 06542/2447). The Pacalt family are the congenial and hardworking owners of this balconied hotel with its white walls, wood trim, and central location. You'll enter from the street through a double doorway angled into a corner of the building, whose renovated interior has lots of wood accents, a central heating stove in white stucco and dark-green tiles, along with a combination of modern furniture that blends well with the painted armoire in the main salon. A covered heated swimming pool has an unusual border of smooth river rocks, with a sauna and steambath close at hand. From December to October, the 44-room hotel offers half board at winter prices of 650 AS ($47.25) to 1,050 AS ($76.25) per person daily. In summer, half-board tabs range from 585 AS ($42.50) to 735 AS ($53.50) per person daily. Each bedroom has a private bath or shower.

Restaurant Zum Hirschen is connected to the hotel. The setting is one of light-grained paneling and wholesome rusticity. Specialties include fresh lavarits from the nearby lake, mountain game, and homemade pâté. If that doesn't appeal to you, you might try creamed chipped veal with the Swiss-style rösti, a range of schnitzels and pork dishes, as well as roast veal in a burgundy sauce or perhaps entrecôte Café de Paris. The chef also prepares that traditional Franz Joseph favorite, tafelspitz. À la carte meals range from 150 AS ($11) to 400 AS ($29) per person.

Hotel Porschehof, A-5700 Zell am See (tel. 06542/7248), is a charming 43-room chalet in a woodsy area a few minutes' drive from the center of town. The main salon has a gently vaulted ceiling, painted chests, and wrought-iron lighting fixtures. The building is graced with several attractive fireplaces, my favorite of which has a pleasingly scaled fieldstone construction with an arch for the fire itself and a tapering pyramid for the chimney. Other design features include ceramic ovens, beamed ceilings, rustically alpine dining room chairs, and an inviting bar area. On the premises are a solar-heated indoor pool, a sauna, a fitness room, and massage facilities. Rates range from 470 AS ($34.25) to 700 AS ($51) per person daily for bed-and-breakfast. Each of the comfortably furnished units has a private bath, and almost all accommodations contain private balconies.

Clima Seehotel, Esplanade 1, A-5700 Zell am See (tel. 06542/2504), is an imposing building with a crescent-shaped terrace above the curved windows of the panoramic first floor. The hotel sits directly on the water, with several floors of white walls and at least one well-placed skylight. The 43 bedrooms behind the mansard-style gables on the top floor have an especially good view, and all the well-furnished units have private baths or showers, toilets, radios, phones, and TV connections. From December to October, guests are accepted at half-board rates ranging from 700 AS ($51) to 750 AS ($54.50) per person daily in summer and 850 AS ($61.75) to 900 AS ($65.50) per person daily in winter.

Hotel St. Hubertushof, Thumersbach, A-5700 Zell am See (tel. 06542/31160). This large, sprawling hotel is designed like a collection of balconied chalets clustered in a single unit. The sober, elegant décor attracts many repeat visitors, and the flat-roofed dance bar (which juts forward into the parking lot) ranks as one of the area's popular nightspots. The hotel, located in one of the resort's sunniest spots, offers 103 large, comfortable, and rustic bedrooms. Owner Erna Hollaus closes the hotel from November 1 to mid-December. Otherwise, half-board prices range from 490 AS ($35.50) to 550 AS ($40) per person daily, based on double occupancy. Singles pay a year-round supplement of 100 AS ($7.25) daily. The menu in the adjoining restaurant includes specialties from around the world, as well as a few regional grandmother-style recipes. Meals are well prepared and beautifully served, and might be followed by one of the chef's flaming desserts.

Hotel St. Georg, Schillerstrasse 10, A-5700 Zell am See (tel. 06542/3533), will greet you with one of the prettiest façades in town. Roughly half of the front is devoted to finely drawn country baroque designs around the windows. The other half of the exterior has flowered balconies, curved awnings, and a parapet covered with thick cedar shingles. The rustically romantic interior is filled with beamed ceilings, antique wrought iron, and old painted chests. On the premises are an indoor swimming pool, a sauna, and several cozy bars.

The restaurant has vaulted plaster ceilings, hunting trophies, wrought-iron wall sconces, and a circular open fireplace that acts as a focal point for the entire room. For visitors not on the board plan, à la carte meals range from 120 AS ($8.75) to 500 AS ($36.25). Specialties include fresh fish from the Zellersee. From December to October, guests are drawn to the 37 bedrooms, each well furnished and containing a private bath. Half-board tariffs in winter cost 630 AS ($45.75) to 790 AS ($57.50) per person daily, lowered in summer to 700 AS ($51) to 790 AS ($57.50).

Sporthotel Alpin, A-5700 Zell am See (tel. 06542/357678), is a contemporary chalet whose balconies almost completely surround it. It was designed in such a way that cars can drive up to the front entrance on a concrete platform cantilevered above the hillside slope. The elegant and sporty interior has big sunny windows, a warmly tinted decorative scheme with wine-colored accents, and lots of beamed ceilings. On the premises are a large indoor pool, a sauna, and massage facilities. Since the hotel lies slightly outside the village, it has both an excellent view of the lake and easy accessibility to the ski lifts.

The well-proportioned doubles contain private baths, radios, phones, color TVs, and minibars. With half board included, the 80-bed hotel charges 830 AS ($60.25) to 1,400 AS ($101.75) per person daily, based on double occupancy. Singles pay 980 AS ($71.25) to 1,550 AS ($112.75). The restaurant has lots of plants and big windows. Specialties include both Austrian and international foods, ranging from wild game to nouvelle cuisine dishes. If you happen to be around during one of the suckling pig banquets or one of the elaborate farmer's buffets, a uniformed chef will stand behind the heavily laden table to assist you.

Hotel Waldhof, A-5700 Zell am See (tel. 06542/2853), is a country-style hotel with lots of weathered planking and balconies. Just outside the sun terrace lies an outdoor pool. A warmly decorated cellar bar, filled with alpine timbers and colored lights, often has dancing with live music both at 5pm and later in the evening. The other public rooms are tastefully filled with Oriental rugs, big windows, and wood accents. The hotel rents 52 bedrooms, each with private bath or shower, phone, radio, cable TV extension, and minibar. All rooms are doubles, costing a winter high of 500 AS ($36.25) to 680 AS ($49.50) per person daily, including half board.

Summer charges for half board range from 390 AS ($28.25) to 450 AS ($32.75) per person daily. Singles pay a daily supplement of 100 AS ($7.25), and reductions are granted for children. Other facilities include a sauna, a solarium, and a heated indoor swimming pool.

Hotel/Restaurant Neue Post, A-5700 Zell am See (tel. 06542/3773). One of the best parts of this hotel is the dozens of details carved into the wood of the heavy ceilings of both the public rooms and the bedrooms. The interior has cozy fireplaces and huge hanging chandeliers fashioned of wrought iron and gilt. The outside of the building has lots of balconies, an enlarged central gable, and a painted design under the side of the roof peak. The 46 bedrooms, each with private bath, at this four-star hotel are well maintained and comfortable. In winter, half-board rates are 550 AS ($40) to 950 AS ($69) per person daily; in summer, they go from 500 AS ($36.25) to 800 AS ($58.25) per person daily.

APRÈS-SKI

Zell am See has one of the liveliest après-ski scenes in Land Salzburg. No one puts on airs here, and the clubs and taverns are very informal and getmütlich.

Wünderbar, Grand Hotel (tel. 06542/2388). The canopy of glass that shelters this glamorous bar from the snow and rain is set at the pinnacle of the Grand Hotel's mansard roof. A less imaginative architect might have considered this eyrie to be little more than wasted space, but in this case it welcomes some of the most fashionable après-skiers in town. Sixty persons can sit comfortably here, enjoying the live piano music and watching the light change upon the rock face of the nearby mountains.

Hotel Waldhof, also recommended, has a typical tavern with regional artifacts. Often a local musician—attired in lederhosen and red stockings—will play for skiers (the women invariably wear pants) who like to dance on the small floor.

A typical Austrian Bierstüberl is at the **Gasthof Alpenblick,** Alte Landesstrasse 6 (tel. 06542/7161), lying in the satellite hamlet of Schüttdorf on the road to Kaprun. Zither music is usually played for your enjoyment every evening in season. Meals cost 100 AS ($7.25) to 150 AS ($11). The place opens daily in winter at 4pm, transforming itself into a disco at 8pm and closing at either 3 or 4am, depending on business. There's no cover charge for the disco, and a large beer costs 50 AS ($3.65).

Pinzgauer Diele (tel. 06542/2165) is a well-frequented cocktail lounge/café/disco, open in summer and winter from 4pm to 4am. In winter it fills with the après-ski crowd. But after 9pm, it becomes a disco, charging an admission price of 60 AS ($4.35), which includes the price of your first drink.

In addition to the above-mentioned establishments, there are countless taverns willing to welcome you around their open fire and offer you a mug of chilled beer or warm wine.

---

8. The Flachgau

One of the chief attractions of the Flachgau district is **Wolfgangsee** (Lake Wolfgang), which lies mainly in Land Salzburg, although its major center, St. Wolfgang, is in Upper Austria. The chief Land Salzburg resort on the lake is St. Gilgen. Many people visit Lake Wolfgang on day trips from Salzburg, as it lies within easy commuting distance.

The best-known lake in the Salzkammergut, Wolfgangsee is 6 miles long and 1¼ miles wide. The northwest shores are fairly inaccessible.

The Flachgau is a relatively flat area in the environs of Salzburg, dividing Styria, another Austrian province, from Bavaria in West Germany. This section, unlike many of the districts of Land Salzburg to which I've previously introduced you, is strictly a summer resort area for those who enjoy lakeside holidays.

FUSCHL AM SEE

Fuschlsee, of all the lakes in Land Salzburg, is closest to the festival city. It lies to the east of the provincial capital. Salzburgers frequent it heavily, particularly on summer weekends. You may choose to stay in Fuschl am See as an alternative to Salzburg at any time of the year but especially during the festival season. From here you can explore Wolfgangsee.

Lake Fuschl is ringed by woodland. In fact, sections bordering the lake comprise a nature reserve. The lake is only 2½ miles long and less than a mile wide. It lies to the northwest of Lake Wolfgang. Fuschl, strictly a summer resort, lies on the eastern strip of the lake.

Food and Lodging

Parkhotel Waldhof, Seepromenade, A-5330 Fuschl am See (tel. 06226/264), is a first-class chalet hotel with a sprawling façade of flower-bedecked balconies as well as a curved series of bay windows. The interior has wood detailing, stone columns, knotty-pine paneling, leaded windows set in diamond-shaped panes, and a crackling open fireplace. On the premises and grounds are a shooting gallery with rifles set on stationary tripods, a high-ceilinged swimming pool, a sauna, a grassy lawn with frontage on the lake, massage facilities, and table tennis. Guests go on guided nature walks, which often end up with the guide leading his charges to his local tavern.

Each of the 70 individually furnished bedrooms has its own bath or shower, as well as a collection of elegantly comfortable furniture. Half board ranges from 600 AS ($46.50) to 900 AS ($65.50) daily.

Sporthotel Leitner, A-5330 Fuschl am See (tel. 06226/208), and **Pension Stefanihof,** A-5330 Fuschl am See (tel. 06226/371), are both owned by the Leitner family. The older of the two is a hip-roofed, green-shuttered building with a prominent dining room jutting out toward the lake. The more modern of the two has a streamlined format of modern windows and a few wood-trimmed balconies. The Sporthotel Leitner offers 41 well-furnished bedrooms, each with private bath or shower. Half-board costs range from 420 AS ($30.50) to 520 AS ($37.75) per person daily in summer, while winter half-board tariffs go from 340 AS ($24.75) to 440 AS ($32) per person daily. The same prices are charged at the Pension Stefanihof, which offers 22 bedrooms, each with private bath or shower.

Brunnwirt, A-5330 Fuschl am See (tel. 06226/236), is one of the region's leading restaurants, serving light and well-prepared meals to vacationing gourmets from as far away as Vienna. Housed in a 15th-century building loaded with atmosphere, it receives a healthy business from urbanites who motor here on the autobahn. The cuisine is light-textured and inspired by Austrian regional recipes. The kitchen staff is directed by Frau Brandstätter, who insists on strictly fresh ingredients. Specialties include game dishes, veal, lamb, and a range of other foodstuffs that appear on the frequently changing daily menu. Portions are generous. Herr Brandstätter will probably help you select a wine, and the clientele seems to have a good time. Set menus cost from 350 AS ($25.50), with à la carte meals going for 250 AS ($25.50) and up, perhaps to 500 AS ($36.25) and beyond. Brunnwirt has an annual closing during the first two weeks of February and the first two weeks of October. Otherwise, hours are noon to 1:30pm and 6 to 9pm daily except Sunday.

HOF BEI SALZBURG

About 15 minutes from Salzburg on Lake Fuschl is this resort, which has long drawn the aristocrats of Salzburg because of its private hunting and fishing preserves. There's a nine-hole golf course. You can fish for trout or rent boats for a tour of the lake. The setting is one of mountains, woods, and alpine lake water. From here it's easy to explore not only Fuschlsee but also Wolfgangsee and Mondsee.

Like the suburb of Anif (see Chapter VII), Hof bei Salzburg might be considered for its traditional and romantic accommodations, especially at festival time in August, when hotel rooms are virtually impossible to obtain in Salzburg.

Food and Lodging

Hotel Schloss Fuschl, A-5322 Hof bei Salzburg (tel. 06229/22530). The main section of this castle built in 1450 has the proportions of a city building, with a simple façade of unadorned windows and a height that's greater than its width or depth. Among its former guests were Nehru, Eleanor Roosevelt, and Khrushchev. In World War II, von Ribbentrop selected the schloss as his headquarters; later, Mussolini came here to meet with Nazi leaders. It was the former hunting lodge of the prince-archbishops of Salzburg, who cultivated the gardens on the peninsula jutting into Lake Fuschl and who, over the course of time, gradually transformed it from a semifortress into a pleasure palace. The interior is dotted with elegant, in some cases baronial, fireplaces, along with timbered ceilings, stone columns, and handcrafted stonework. The swimming pool, dedicated to the mythical figure of Diana, is found under the plastered vaulting of the ground floor.

According to the price you want to pay, you can rent either a modern room inside the hotel, part of a cozy bungalow on the surrounding grounds, or a luxurious suite fit for a prince and studded with valuable antiques. Singles range from 1,400 AS ($101.75) to 1,800 AS ($130), while doubles cost 2,200 AS ($160) to 3,200 AS ($232.75). An apartment or a two-person bungalow costs 3,800 AS ($276.25) to 5,000 AS ($363.75). All 84 accommodations contain private baths or showers, and prices include a buffet breakfast. Half board is available for an additional 420 AS ($30.50) per person daily.

The restaurant is one of the most frequented and highly praised in Austria, with a clientele that includes many of the country's leading politicians and industrialists. They may dine in the winter garden or, in summer, on the terrace overlooking the lake. Designated long ago as a Relais & Châteaux, it has several elegant rooms from which to choose, all decorated in excellent taste with dozens of antiques and paintings. One of the rooms is outfitted in pale green and pink, not unlike a Viennese pastry. The view encompasses much of the lake and sometimes a vista of Salzburg.

Menu items from the handwritten carte include lobster terrine with caviar, homemade noodles with goose liver pâté, and summer truffles, plus a host of seasonally adjusted specialties. Klaus Fleischhacker is the chef, Martin Adlgasser is the wine steward, and their combined efforts produce meals that are known throughout the region. Reservations are almost essential. À la carte meals range from 360 AS ($26.25) to 950 AS ($69), and fixed-price dinners go for 380 AS ($27.75) to 980 AS ($71.25). The dining room is open daily from 12:15 to 2pm and 7 to 9pm. Another restaurant, the Imperial, is a classic with an innovative and modern haute cuisine in the best international style.

Jagdhof am Fuschlsee, A-5322 Hof bei Salzburg (tel. 06229/22530), was an outbuilding of a nearby feudal castle. Originally a 16th-century farmhouse, it's in the authentic style that many 20th-century Austrian buildings are modeled after. The public rooms have evenly spaced timbers supporting the massive ceiling beams, with many contemporary and practical updates such as comfortable chairs, hanging lights, tile floors, and glass display cases. Part of the decoration consists of masses of hunting trophies and some 1,000 pipes. Management has also added two bowling alleys and an indoor rifle range.

All 50 of the comfortably furnished bedrooms have private baths. Half-board rates (the most typical arrangement for staying here) range from 560 AS ($40.75) to 660 AS ($48) per person daily. The dining room is filled with rustic artifacts, heavy beams, and a loyal and conservative clientele. A specialty of the chef is pike terrine with green sauce, which could be followed by a wide variety of fish and game dishes. Set menus cost from 400 AS ($29), with à la carte dinners going for 280 AS ($20.25) and up.

Gasthof Nussbaumer, A-5322 Hof bei Salzburg (tel. 06229/2275), is a modern country hotel, set against an alpine meadow, with a big asphalt parking lot on two sides. On the premises are an indoor heated pool, a sauna, and comfortable public rooms with honey-colored ceiling paneling, inviting banquettes, and lots of sunny windows. An elevator is among the conveniences, as are outdoor tennis courts and a grassy children's playground. The hotel sits just beside a ski lift. Guests are received from December to October, and charged 370 AS ($27) per person daily for one of the 62 attractively furnished bedrooms.

OBERTRUM

Lying on the northern part of Lake Obertrum, about 10 miles to the north of Salzburg, Obertrum is a popular holiday resort, offering bathing in the lake, water sports, sailing, fishing, tennis, horseback riding, and in winter/ice sports. It's also a good center for many hikes and excursions in a beautiful district.

Incidentally, the lake virtually joins Mattsee and Grabensee, separated only by narrow tongues of land.

Food and Lodging

Bräugasthof Sigl, A-5162 Obertrum (tel. 06219/7700). This hotel, along with the nearby brewery, has been owned by the same family since 1775. In the center of the village, it's housed in a distinguished-looking hip-roofed building with lots of chimneys, a row of gables, and a distinctive yellow-and-white façade. In summer, flowers bloom in the boxes near the rounded tower at one of the corners and also in the arched windows on the ground floor. The interior has a very old carved clothing chest, along with a sprinkling of other antiques. The comfortable bedrooms usually have conservative furnishings and a scattering of homey touches. The hotel is open all year, charging 230 AS ($16.75) to 280 AS ($20.25) daily for a single, and 190 AS ($13.75) to 235 AS ($17) per person for a double, including breakfast. Reservations are important, as there are only 19 bedrooms.

If you're a beer-lover, you'll gravitate to the earthy, unpretentious restaurant adjoining this hotel. You'll have a chance to sample each of the beers brewed in the region, as well as the solid country cooking that goes with the brew. Management features weeklong specials of, for example, wild game, depending on the season and the availability of ingredients. Desserts are satisfyingly rich, often containing their share of schnapps. À la carte dinners go for 75 AS ($5.50) to 240 AS ($17.50).

Gasthof Neumayr, Dorfplatz 8, A-5162 Obertrum (tel. 06219/302), is a centrally located, hip-roofed guesthouse with a façade of yellow stucco, forest-green shutters, and an arched entryway leading into a rustically old-fashioned interior. The hotel has 30 rooms, most with private showers. Half board ranges from 340 AS ($24.75) to 380 AS ($27.75) per person daily. The food served in the rustic stube is good enough to attract diners from Salzburg. Specialties of the establishment include fish, especially trout. For an appetizer, you may prefer the matjes herring or liver noodle soup. Other main dishes include an onion-flavored roast beef. The dining room is open from 7am to midnight, except on Tuesday, from November to March.

ST. GILGEN

This leading lakeside resort of Land Salzburg lies at the western edge of Wolfgangsee. In the summer it's filled mainly with Austrians and Germans enjoying the indoor swimming pool and bathing beach.

Once St. Gilgen was one of the strongholds of the prince-archbishops of Salzburg, and in a sense the aristocratic tradition continues even today, as many of the fashionable and wealthy from Salzburg maintain mountain villas here. Parties at festival time tend to be lavish. You're lucky if you get an invitation.

The town has many Mozart connections. In the vicinity of the Rathaus (Town Hall) is the house in which Anna Maria Pertl was born in 1720. She was to become Mozart's mother. After the composer's sister, Nannerl, married Baron Berchtold zu

Sonnenberg, she also settled in St. Gilgen. The **Mozart Fountain,** built in 1927, stands on the main square in front of the Rathaus.

Food and Lodging

Parkhotel Billroth, A-5340 St. Gilgen (tel. 06227/217), a mile from town, sits imposingly on its own spacious grounds. One wing was designed in a white-walled villa style, with the main section looking more like an overblown chalet. The view from the bedrooms and from the parasol-dotted sun terrace takes in the lake and the mountains beyond. The hotel has its own lakeside beach, with a floating sun raft ideal for bathing (especially since it's connected to the shoreline). It has its own outdoor tennis courts and easy access to the ski lifts. Some of the public rooms are baronial, with dark paneling, Oriental rugs, and wide, gently sloping staircases. The 44 bedrooms are comfortably and attractively furnished, and each comes with private bath or shower. Half-board tariffs range from 600 AS ($43.75) to 830 AS ($60.25) per person daily.

Hotel zur Post, Mozartplatz 8, A-5340 St. Gilgen (tel. 06227/239), is the comfortably proportioned hotel on the main square of town. It was established in 1415, and aside from the charm of the thick walls and heavy timbers, it has a high level of comfort and service. The interior has been updated so frequently it's difficult in some places to see the original building. Everything is nonetheless comfortable, clean, and pleasant. Someone has painted murals of village life under some of the ceiling's vaults, while parts of some of the wood ceilings are ornately decorated with paint and inlays. A swimming pool with a lake scene on the far wall is part of the lure. Twenty-four well-furnished bedrooms are rented, 11 of which contain private baths. Half-board ranges from 290 AS ($21) to 520 AS ($37.75) per person daily. Guests are received from December to October. The in-house restaurant is worth a stopover. Aside from its view over the center of the resort, it has both a romantic ambience (a ceramic tile oven) and good food.

Café-Pension Nannerl (tel. 06227/368). An 18th-century name deserves an 18th-century ambience, and that's exactly what you'll see in this charming old-style coffeehouse named after Mozart's sister. The furnishings are something you might have found in a wealthy farmer's house around 1801, and the food served includes the most delicious (and most caloric) in the repertoire of Austrian pastries, including Sacher torte, poppy tart, and Malakoff tart, each mouthwatering, each baked fresh every day and served in generous slices. Pastries range from 27 AS ($1.95), while coffee costs from 25 AS ($1.80). The café is open daily except Monday from 9am to 6pm.

STROBL

The flower gardens along the shore of Lake Wolfgang make this small resort a potent lure in summer. Strobl lies on the southeast side of the lake, almost opposite St. Gilgen at the western end. For a relatively undiscovered little lakeside village it has much appeal, mainly because of its romantic setting. The road to St. Wolfgang in Upper Austria branches off here.

Food and Lodging

Hotel Stadt Wien, A-5350 Strobl (tel. 06137/381), is a modern hotel with floor-depth windows and stone detailing. The interior is attractively outfitted in tasteful colors and occasional rustic details such as a ceramic stove in the dining room. The 12 sunny and airy rooms—all with private baths or showers, toilets, radios, and balconies—rent for 440 AS ($32) to 500 AS ($36.25) per person daily for half board. Guests are received from December to February and May to October. The hotel is only about 300 feet from the lake.

Parkhotel Seethurn, A-5350 Strobl (tel. 06137/202). One side of this big balconied hotel faces the edge of the village, where residents can admire the elaborate regional designs painted on part of the façade. The other end looks out over a well-maintained lawn area. The roof of the swimming pool is supported by massive laminated timbers, while the rest of the public rooms are elegantly and rustically laid out with wood furniture, big fireplaces, and coffered ceilings. All 44 well-furnished accommodations contain private baths, toilets, radios, and phones. Half board costs 650 AS ($47.25) to 750 AS ($54.50) per person daily.

---

9. The Lungau

A heavily forested district in the southeastern part of Land Salzburg, the Lungau can be visited easily on a day trip. The section is beginning to develop as a winter-sports center now that the Tauern highway has opened up the valley. However, in spite of its at times sun-drenched slopes, the Lungau is one of the chilliest parts of Austria in winter.

TAMSWEG
The principal town of the Lungau, whose people show a healthy respect for tradition, is Tamsweg, with a 1570 Rathaus (Town Hall) and a baroque pfarrkirche (parish church). This was once a Roman town, and some ruins remain. The pilgrimage **Church of St. Leonard,** enclosed by defensive walls, is a Gothic edifice known for its stained glass, including a unique "golden window."

You can visit **Lungauer Folklore Museum** (tel. 06474/547), which has fine pieces of provincial furniture and collections of paintings and old weapons. The museum is open year round daily except Monday from 10am to noon and 2 to 5pm. Sunday hours are 2 to 5pm. Guided tours are given every hour. Admission is 20 AS ($1.45) for adults and 10 AS (75¢) for children.

From Tamsweg, you might want to visit **Moosham Castle** at Unternberg, first mentioned in documents in 1256. This was formerly a fortress of the prince-archbishops of Salzburg. Its most outstanding feature is the lower courtyard. Its schloss chapel has a late Gothic triptych. A folkloric museum in the castle is open from January 1 until mid-June and mid-September until the end of October, daily except Monday from 10am to 3pm. In summer, it is open from 10am to 4pm. Admission is 40 AS ($2.90) for adults and 20 AS ($1.45) for children.

MAUTERNDORF
This is an old market town going back 1,000 years, and today it's both a summer resort center and a mecca for skiers in winter. It lies on a highway to the northwest of the Tauern Pass. From here you can take a cableway to Speiereckhütte (6,805 feet).

Mauterndorf Castle, erected on the ruins of a fort that stood here in Roman times, dates from 1253. Parts of it were extended in the 14th and 15th centuries. It contains a chapel with frescoes from the 14th century and a winged altarpiece, circa 1450. You can visit the keep and a local museum. Opening hours in June and September are 3 to 5pm on Saturday and Sunday only. In July and August, hours are 10am to noon and 3 to 5pm Wednesday to Monday. Admission is 25 AS ($1.80) for adults and 10 AS (75¢) for children.

Mauterndorf's **pfarrkirche** (parish church) has a sumptuous baroque altar from 1702.

Food and Lodging
Hotel Elisabeth, A-5570 Mauterndorf (tel. 06472/7365). The position of this hotel at the edge of the village marks the beginning of acres of farmland, most of which you can see from the windows of 44 well-furnished bedrooms. The hotel is one of the most elegant in town, outfitted like a private home with lots of balconies, a pleasing hip-roof design, and alpine furniture. Your hosts, the Spreitzer-Widmayer

family, receive guests from June to October and December to April. They built the hotel in 1969, but have renovated it several times since. Each of the well-furnished bedrooms has a private bath or shower. Summer prices on the half-board plan go from 500 AS ($36.25) to 900 AS ($65.50) per person daily. The higher price is for a luxurious apartment, with balcony, phone, radio, TV, minibar, and safe. Winter half-board charges are 690 AS ($50.25) to 1,260 AS ($91.50) per person daily.

On the premises are a sauna, an indoor pool, a dancing bar, and a hairdresser. The hotel restaurant offers a wide range of flambés and fondues, as well as Austrian and international specialties.

Hotel Post, A-5570 Mauterndorf (tel. 06472/7316), the most atmospheric choice in town, is a four-story white building with a dignified façade and solid proportions. It is in a beautiful square close to the 12th-century castle and provides an excellent center for walking and motoring in the Lungau valleys and mountains. The hotel's interior has lots of 16th-century touches. The dining room, which serves international cuisine and local specialties, is elegant, with leather-upholstered chairs. In summer, guests retreat to a courtyard garden. The hotel rents 15 rooms with private baths or showers. Half board costs 390 AS ($28.25) to 440 AS ($32) per person daily.

Gasthof/Pension Neuwirt, A-5570 Mauterndorf (tel. 06472/7268), is announced by its wrought-iron bracket extending over the pavement in front of the mustard-colored façade. The 34 bedrooms in this three-star hotel are cozy, colorful, and warm. They contain private showers, and cost 390 AS ($28.25) to 470 AS ($34.25) per person daily for half board in winter. Summer half-board charges go from 280 AS ($20.25) to 330 AS ($24) per person daily. On the premises are a swimming pool and table-tennis facilities.

The best restaurant in the resort—in fact, one of the finest in Land Salzburg— is **Mesnerhaus,** Kirchenplatz 56 (tel. 06472/7595). This fine establishment is housed in a 15th-century monastery, a Knappenhaus, and is operated by a distinguished chef, Franz Fuiko, a soft-spoken and charming man. Lunch is from 11:30am to 2pm and dinner is from 6 to 10pm; closed all day Monday and Tuesday at lunch. The restaurant is also closed for three weeks in May and for another three weeks in November. Despite its antique origins, the restaurant evokes more than anything else in town a contemporary Italian flair. The chairs are in red leather, and the ambience is one of Milanese chic. Mr. Fuiko studied cuisine at restaurants ranging from Marseille to Colorado, and has melded his own brand of cookery into a sophisticated version of Austrian and French. Fixed-price meals are served both at lunch and dinner for 160 AS ($11.75) to 580 AS ($42.25), with à la carte meals costing 130 AS ($9.50) to 450 AS ($32.75).

MARIAPFARR

This little town, at an elevation of 3,675 feet, becomes lively in winter when it fills up with skiers. Mariapfarr lies in an area of Austria renowned for its variety of runs and for attracting cross-country skiers. There are some 80 miles of beautifully placed tracks. It's possible to rent heavy skis and boots on the spot in the town's shops.

Mariapfarr has long been known for its pilgrimage church, dating from the 13th and 14th centuries. This Gothic **pfarrkirche** (parish church) is decorated with wall paintings and has an exceptional winged altar in the late Gothic style. Its 14th-century frescoes include Saint Mary, Protectress with Man of Sorrows, the only known representation of its kind.

Food and Lodging

Hotel Haus Carinth, A-5571 Mariapfarr (tel. 06473/235). Karl-Peter Dindl is the accommodating owner of this pleasantly isolated 32-room double chalet. Both wings of the hotel have hip roofs, balconies, and impressive views. The interior has all the rustic comfort you'd expect, as well as an invitingly dark décor of masonry, wood wall coverings, and comfortable furniture. On the premises are a tennis court, heated outdoor pool, and a sauna. Rates, based on double occupancy, range from 480 AS ($35) to 600 AS ($43.75) per person daily in winter, from 420 AS ($30.50) to 500 AS ($36.25) per person in summer. Single rooms cost about 30% more than the per-person rate in a double. Also on the premises is an outstanding à la carte restaurant with an open fireplace, featuring a variety of local and international gourmet specialties.

UPPER AUSTRIA

Too often neglected by North Americans who may be unaware of its charms, Upper Austria contains some of the country's most beautiful scenery. It is a land of mountains, scenic valleys, and lakes, with Styria and Land Salzburg to its south and Bavaria on the west. Its northern parts border the Bohemian forest in Czechoslovakia. Its eastern neighbor is Lower Austria, traditionally called its twin. The Austrian name of this province is Bundesland–Ober Österreiche, since it lies nearer to the source of the Danube, which cuts across both provinces, than does Lower Austria.

Upper Austria has three different types of landscape. In the north are the granite and gneiss hills, which are separated in the center of the province by the Valley of the Danube. There are also the limestone Alps and the Salzkammergut lake district, about a 30-minute drive from Linz, which crosses into Upper Austria. Here you'll find the most breathtaking scenery in the entire area. You can center at the Attersee, the Mondsee, the Traunsee, and the Wolfgangsee, part of the latter being in Land Salzburg.

Boating is fine on these lakes (*sees*), but if you like to swim, know that the *see* water here is not as warm as you'll find in Carinthia (Chapter XII). There are farms and fruit trees in the lake district. The cider of the region is excellent and competes with wine for popularity among the local inhabitants.

Except for Linz, the provincial capital, Upper Austria is a choice location for nature-lovers. Most of its towns are small, and although there's much industry, it doesn't blight the province with grime. Industrial installations are often discreetly hidden away, as is usually the case in Switzerland.

Bad Ischl, once a retreat of the Austrian imperial court, is perhaps the most fashionable spa attraction. Most of the hotels are in the Salzkammergut region, but in all towns and villages you can find one or two moderately priced to inexpensive inns. There are few deluxe accommodations, although several old castles have been turned into "romantik" lodging places. Most of the hotels around the lakes are open only in summer months, and May is an ideal time to visit. These areas tend to be overrun with visitors, especially Germans, in the peak months of July and August.

The ski areas of Upper Austria are not much known to the North Americans visiting this country, as they lie for the most part in the southeast corner. The Dachstein is another major ski area. If you like to ski and don't demand massive facilities and a lot of après-ski festivity, you'll find the emerging ski resorts of this province far less expensive than the more celebrated resorts in the Tyrol and Zell am See in Land Salzburg.

If you're coming into the region, you can fly to the Linz international airport—served by planes from main points in Europe—or to Salzburg, from which train service is good into Upper Austria. To remote places where trains don't go, a local Postal Bus service takes over. If you're driving, you can reach the province easily by the autobahn from Vienna.

It's also possible to take steamer service on the Danube between Passau in West Germany and Linz, but these boats operate only in summer. By steamer, you can continue on from Linz along the Danube into Lower Austria, to Vienna, and on to Budapest or even the Black Sea, as mentioned earlier. At certain times of the year you can make an excursion on the Danube leaving from the Linz marina.

1. Linz

This provincial capital of Upper Austria, about 116 miles northwest of Vienna, is the third-largest city in the country after Vienna and Graz. It is the biggest port on the Danube, which widens out considerably here to become a majestic thoroughfare. Three bridges connect Linz with the suburb of **Urfahr,** on the left bank of the river. If you enter the country from Passau, West Germany, Linz might be your gateway to Austria.

Linz was the site of a Roman castle and settlement, Lentia, in the 1st century A.D., and by the Middle Ages it had become a thriving center of trade through its position on the river. Emperor Friedrich III lived here from 1489 to 1493. The city now lies also on a direct rail route between the Adriatic and Baltic seas. It was here that Austria's first railroad terminated. Because of these factors, Linz became an industrial and manufacturing center, with blast furnaces and steel factories. These were built up rapidly after Hitler seized Austria in 1938, and the Nazis also established chemical plants here. This industrial upsurge led to massive destruction by Allied bombs, with reconstruction being started after 1945.

Like Frankfurt in West Germany, Linz became known in the days of the empire for its trade fairs. It has been the seat of a bishop since 1785. Its heyday, at least with the aristocracy, came in the 18th century, after which it experienced a cultural decline.

Linz today, however, is one of the leading cultural centers of Austria, although nowhere near the level of Vienna and Salzburg. The city's name appears in numerous Germanic songs, and many notable figures have come from or been connected with Linz, including native son Anton Bruckner, the composer. Mozart composed and dedicated a symphony to the city, and Beethoven wrote his Eighth Symphony here. Franz Schubert described with pleasure his holidays in Linz. Goethe, who had a romance with a Linz fräulein, dedicated one of his most lyrical works "to the beautiful girls of Linz."

Napoleon lived here three times—in 1800, 1805, and 1809. The first steel airplane was constructed at Linz by the Schiessl brothers.

THE SIGHTS

The most popular shopping district in the city is the **Landstrasse,** filled with boutiques, sometimes with Victorian embellishments on the buildings.

The **Hauptplatz** was the original marketplace and is now one of the biggest and most beautiful squares in all Europe, with baroque and rococo façades surrounding it. On the east side is the Rathaus (Town Hall). In the heart of the square stands the **Trinity Column,** like the column in Vienna, built in 1723 to mark deliverance, in the case of Linz, from plague, fire, and invasion by the Turks. This marble column, the Dreifaltigkeitssaule, rises 85 feet.

Martinskirche, or St. Martin's Church, is the most ancient church in Austria in its original form. It was constructed by Charlemagne in the 8th century, near the castle on the remains of a Roman wall. Mention was first made of the church in written records in 788. St. Martin's is considered a good example of Carolingian architecture. Frescoes inside the church date from the 15th century, and it also contains masterpieces of baroque art. This edifice is in dramatic contrast with the modern buildings that surround it.

The concert hall, called **Bruckner Haus** in honor of Anton Bruckner, the Linz-born composer, has an elliptical façade of glass and steel with a wooden interior where a raised dais accommodates an orchestra whose conductors have included Leonard Bernstein and Herbert von Karajan. Concerts presented in this acoustically perfect hall have been transmitted throughout the world. The building was constructed from 1969 to 1973 as a cultural and conference center.

The most popular place of pilgrimage from Linz is to **Pöstlingberg,** 3 miles northwest of the city on the north bank of the Danube, up a very steep hill. You can get there by going out Rudolfstrasse on the left bank of the river and taking a right turn onto Hagenstrasse. If you don't have a car, take the electric railway.

Pöstlingberg has a botanical garden with exotic tropical plants, and the summit terrace is a riot of blooming flowers in summer. A defensive tower now houses a grotto with a miniature railway, which makes a hit with children. The pilgrimage church is visited because of an 18th-century carved wood Pietà, but most tourists make the ascent mainly to take in the view over the Danube Valley. Linz is spread out below. The panorama stretches all the way to the foothills of the Alps and to the Bohemian forest in Czechoslovakia.

The **Landhaus,** southwest of the Hauptplatz, is one of the most important landmark buildings of Linz and headquarters of the government of Upper Austria. The original structure was built in the latter 16th century with an arcaded courtyard around a fountain. The Landhaus was rebuilt in the early 19th century. In the 17th century this was the city's university, where Johann Kepler, noted astronomer and mathematician, taught and developed the theory of planetary motion. The present university of Linz, on the north bank of the Danube, bears Kepler's name.

The **Minoritenkirche,** or Church of the Minorite Brothers, is Gothic, dating from the 13th century, but with a rococo overlay done in 1758. An art masterpiece inside is the high altar by Bartolomeo Altomonte, depicting the Annunciation. There are three red marble side altars.

The **schloss** (castle), standing high above the river, was the residence of Emperor Friedrich III when he and his court resided in Linz in the 15th century. It was built for the emperor and rebuilt after a fire in the early 19th century. Today it houses the Provincial Museum of Upper Austria, which has exhibits ranging from prehistoric artifacts from the Roman era to the local art of the province. Weaponry is also displayed, and you'll see much popular art and folkoric exhibitions showing how the people of Upper Austria used to live. There's a gallery of paintings, none outstanding, from the 19th century. Many Gothic and Renaissance interiors have been reproduced. A railway museum is also to be seen at the castle.

You can visit the parts of the castle open to the public Wednesday through Sat-

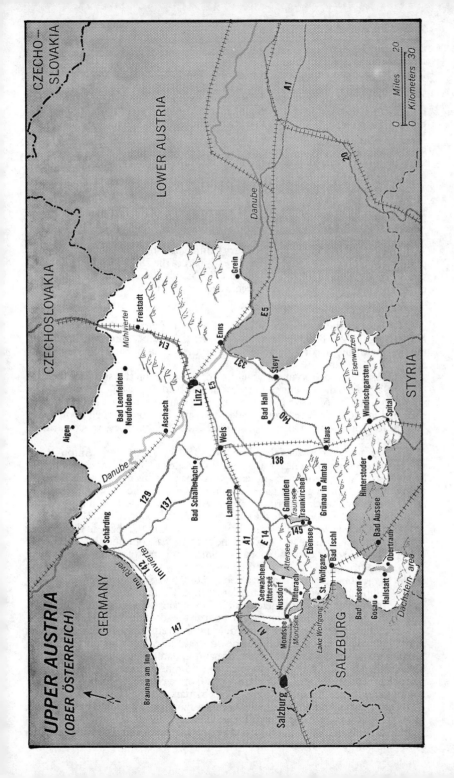

urday from 10am to 1pm and from 2 to 6pm, on Sunday from 9am to 1pm. It's closed Monday and Tuesday.

Alter Dom on Domgasse, the biggest baroque church in the city and formerly the cathedral of Linz, was constructed by the Jesuits around the latter part of the 17th century. You mustn't judge this church by its relatively simple exterior. The inside warms up considerably with pink marble columns, an intricately carved pulpit, and much statuary. The high altar is a concoction bedecked with marble images. Bruckner was the organist of this church for 12 years, and the annual Bruckner festival is centered here. Two other composers who worked in Linz are honored at the same time—Mozart, who composed his Linz symphony (No. 36 in C, K.425) here, and Beethoven, who wrote his Eighth in Linz.

The **Neue Galerie der Stadt Linz** (New Gallery), Blütenstrasse 15 (tel. 0732/ 2393-3600), is in the industrial suburb on the left bank, Urfahr, already referred to. Exhibited are paintings by German and Austrian artists of the 19th and 20th centuries. You can visit daily from 10am to 6pm, to 1pm on Sunday, and to 10pm on Thursday. Admission is 30 AS ($2.20).

Priesterseminarkirche, or Seminary Church, is a small place of worship dedicated to the Holy Cross. Dating from the early part of the 18th century, the building plans were the work of Johann Lukas von Hildebrandt, the celebrated architect. The church is worth a visit just to see its richly decorated interior.

EXCURSIONS

Of possible short trips out of Linz, the most popular is to the **Abbey of St. Florian** (tel. 07224/89030), about a 12-mile trek. The abbey, largest in Upper Austria, is one of the major attractions of the province, an outstanding example of baroque architecture.

Augustinians have occupied a building of some sort on this site since the 11th century, although the structures you see today are baroque, having been under construction from 1686 to 1751. St. Florian was a Christian martyr, killed by being drowned in the Enns River around 304. As a saint he is often called upon by the faithful to protect their homes against flood and fire. The abbey was constructed over his grave.

The greatest composer of church music in 19th-century Austria, Anton Bruckner, a native of Linz born near the present abbey site in 1824, became the organist at St. Florian as a young man and composed many of his masterpieces here. Although he went on to greater fame in Vienna, he was granted his wish to be buried at the abbey church underneath the organ he loved so well. You can visit the crypt, as well as the room where the composer lived for about a decade.

Carlo Carlone was originally in charge of rebuilding the abbey in the baroque style, the job being started in 1686, and the progress was continued by others.

The western exterior of the abbey is crowned with a trio of towers. The doorway is especially striking. As you enter the inner court, you'll see the **Fountain of the Eagle.** In the library, said to contain some 140,000 books and manuscripts, are allegorical ceiling frescoes by Bartolomeo Altomonte. The marble salon honors Prince Eugene of Savoy for his heroic defense of Vienna against a major siege by the Turks. The ceiling paintings here depict the Austrian victory over the "infidels."

The **Altdorfer Gallery** is the most outstanding feature of the abbey, surpassing even the Imperial Apartments. Well-known works of Albrecht Altdorfer, born in 1480, a master of the Danube school of painting, are displayed. Altdorfer was a warm, romantic contemporary of Dürer, to whom he is often compared. He did more than a dozen paintings for the abbey's Gothic church, his panels depicting, among other scenes, the martyrdom of St. Sebastian.

The **Imperial Apartments,** called the Kaiserzimmer, are reached by climbing a splendid staircase. Once Pope Pius VI stayed here. A whole host of royalty has occupied these richly decorated quarters, and you're allowed to visit the royal bedrooms of the emperors and empress.

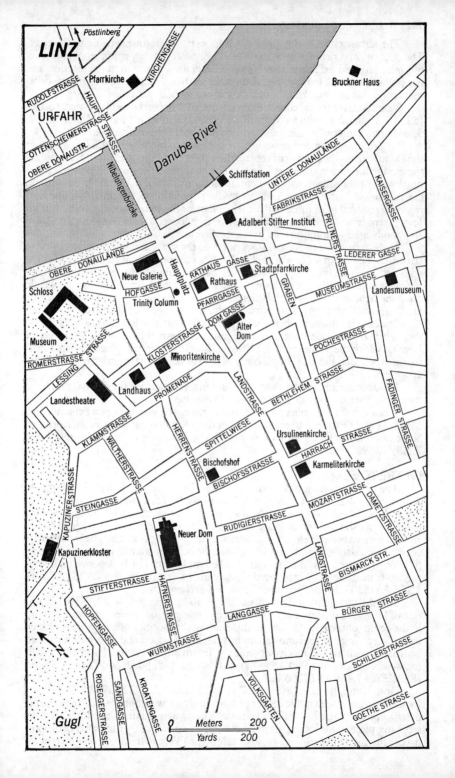

The **abbey church,** designed by Carlone, has twin towers rising to 260 feet. The decoration is rich—maybe too rich. It's distinguished by columns of pink marble, quarried near Salzburg. Lavish stucco decoration was used in the interior, and the pulpit is in black marble. The choir stalls are heavily gilded and rich with ornamentation and carving. You should allow about an hour for a tour.

Visitors can enter the church free, but guided tours of the monastery cost 30 AS ($2.20). Tours are conducted daily from April to October at 10 and 11am and at 2, 3, and 4pm. Otherwise, you must write to the abbey for permission to visit.

One of the most macabre outings from Linz is to **Mauthausen,** 16 miles down the Danube from the provincial capital, the village of the quarries that once supplied the granite for paving stones in Vienna. The Nazis used the quarters, about 2 miles northwest of the village, as a concentration camp in World War II. It was also an extermination center, where Austria's Jewish population was dramatically and horrifyingly reduced in number in the darkest days of the war. Not only were Austrian Jews exterminated at this camp but thousands of other so-called undesirables were also annihilated—homosexuals, gypsies, whatever.

The government of Austria does not hide the scene and its reminders of these atrocities. The camp's site was declared a national monument in 1949, and often schoolchildren are brought here and given descriptions of what went on in this notorious camp. Various countries who lost citizens have erected memorials outside the camp to honor the dead. It's believed that the Nazis killed some 200,000 victims here, although exact figures are not available. It may have been even more.

You can visit the huts where the condemned, most of whom almost surely knew their ultimate fate, were kept. You are also led down the infamous "Stairway of Death," which the prisoners took on their last walk. To visit the ghastly site is a shattering experience, but still people come here to be painfully reminded of a cruel and savage era.

Besides traveling to Mauthausen from Linz, you can visit the site via commuter train from Vienna, the ride taking about 45 minutes.

It takes about 1½ hours to take a tour of the camp, which is open February 1 to March 31 and October 1 to mid-December from 8am to 4pm daily. From April 1 to September 30, its hours are 8am to 6pm daily. For more information, telephone 7238/2269.

WHERE TO STAY

The most prestigious modern hotel in town is **Hotel Schillerpark,** Rainerstrasse 2-4, A-4020 Linz (tel. 0732/554050). It's a modern mirrored building at the entrance to the downtown's pedestrian zone, about 10 minutes on foot from the rail station. Inside is a gambling casino (the center of nightlife in Linz), along with two bars, an elegant restaurant, a sauna, and a solarium. The lobby area is covered with slabs of polished marble, while the bedrooms are airy, sunny, and tastefully filled with streamlined furniture. The hotel offers 111 bedrooms, each with private bath. Rated five stars by the government, it charges 795 AS ($57.75) to 1,475 AS ($107.25) per person daily for bed-and-breakfast.

Trend-Hotel, Untere Donaulande 9, A-4020 Linz (tel. 0732/2750750), is one of Linz's most prominent "skyscrapers," rising many stories above the ground in the center of the city. On the premises are all the facilities of a large urban hotel, including a range of bars and restaurants, an indoor pool, and 176 well-furnished bedrooms with all the modern comforts. International bands play at the hotel's nightclub. Singles cost 990 AS ($72) to 1,140 AS ($82) daily; doubles, 1,200 AS ($87.25) to 1,460 AS ($106.25).

Dom Hotel, Baumbachstrasse 17, A-4020 Linz (tel. 0732/278441), is ideally located in a quiet area in the center of town, only a few minutes' walk from the pedestrian precinct and the main rail station. The owners maintain the hotel as a cozy stopping place, with lots of atmosphere. All 44 comfortably furnished bedrooms have baths, direct-dial phones, radios, cable color TVs, and minibars. Singles rent for

940 AS ($68.25) daily, with doubles costing 1,300 AS ($94.50). Tariffs include a buffet breakfast, service, and tax. An apéritif bar is on the ground floor, and international specialties and Austrian dishes are served in the hotel restaurant. A sauna and solarium are available, as is free car parking.

Hotel-Restaurant zur Lokomotive, Weingartshofstrasse 40, A-4020 Linz (tel. 0732/54554), near the train station, the main highway, and the city center, is a completely renovated three-star hotel. All the 42 furnished bedrooms have baths or showers, TVs, phones, and central heating. The bed-and-breakfast rate ranges from 340 AS ($24.75) to 360 AS ($26.25) per person daily. The restaurant serves lunch and dinner, as well as snacks throughout the day. There is free parking.

Hotel Ebelsbergerhof, Wiener Strasse 485, A-4020 Linz (tel. 0732/311-733), a four-star hotel, stands in the suburb of Ebelsberg and is easy to find because of its vivid pink façade. The interior is woodsy and elegant, with thick curtains, thick beams, and an upper-class ambience of well-being and fine cuisine of Austrian specialties. The 38 well-furnished bedrooms are papered in flowered patterns, and each has its own bath and toilet, color TV, radio, and private minibar. They rent for 640 AS ($46.50) daily in a single, 970 AS ($70.50) in a double, with breakfast, sauna, and use of the solarium included. The hotel also provides a cellar dancing-bar.

Hotel Prielmayrhof, Weissenwolffstrasse 33, A-4020 Linz (tel. 0732/247-131), is housed in a distinguished-looking five-story building slightly outside the center of town. It can be reached from the main train station by public bus. Its exterior is painted terra-cotta with white trim, while its streamlined and comfortable interior has been renovated into a tasteful modern format of white walls and exposed wood. The hotel rents 32 bedrooms, each with private bath or shower. The overnight bed-and-breakfast rate is 360 AS ($26.25) per person daily. For 440 AS ($32) per person daily, you can take half board.

Hotel Wolfinger, Hauptplatz 19, A-4020 Linz (tel. 0732/2732910), is housed in a 500-year-old building on what is said to be the largest and best-preserved baroque square in Europe. Its entrance is through an arcade, a short distance from the Danube, in the middle of a pedestrian zone. Since 1975 it has been run by the Dangl family, with the help of an enthusiastic staff. Modern comfort has been added, but still there is a respect for tradition. All 27 bedrooms have private baths or showers and are furnished in part with antiques. Including breakfast, a double rents for 980 AS ($71.25) daily and a single goes for 720 AS ($52.25).

Hotel Mühlviertlerhof, Graben 24-26, A-4020 Linz (tel. 0732/272-268), has 28 comfortable rooms, all with a certain elegant rusticity and coziness, as well as private baths, phones, radios, and color TVs. The Zangerle family members maintain their centrally located hotel (only 50 steps to the Hauptplatz) with charm and efficiency. The bedrooms are immaculately kept and quiet, providing views of the garden. Rates range from 400 AS ($29) to 680 AS ($49.50) daily in a single, with doubles going for 360 AS ($26.25) to 600 AS ($43.75) per person.

WHERE TO DINE

Near the vegetable markets at the train station, **Restaurant Allegro,** Schillerstrasse 68 (tel. 0732/669800), is an elegant eating place serving modern Austrian cuisine. In addition to the live music that the management sometimes provides, the menu is set up like the movements of a musical work, labeled "Overture," "Intermezzo," "Theme and Variations," along with "Finale." A first course might be the house specialty of jamosala, mint sauce, and tonic (they call it "Allegretto"). Other introductory items include smoked salmon, pampas-style peppered ham, several kinds of salads, and snails. Main courses might be a steak potpourri or one of several fresh fish dishes. One of the best desserts is the homemade strudel. Fixed-price menus range from 375 AS ($27.25) to 520 AS ($37.75), with à la carte meals going for 170 AS ($12.25) to 375 AS ($27.25). Hours are 11:30am to 2pm and 6:30 to 10pm daily except Sunday. August is annual closing.

Restaurant Primo Piano, Hotel Wolfinger, Hauptplatz 19 (tel. 0732/

273291), is always decorated with fresh flowers. The menu is handwritten on a large sheet of handmade paper. The restaurant is one floor above ground level in this historic hotel building on the baroque main square of Linz, with a view over the spires of the two churches and the fountain in the center. An upright piano sits against one wall with a bowler hat and a piece of ragtime sheet music on top.

The rest of the room might be art nouveau or art deco, depending on where you look. However, if you gaze at the center of the plaster ceiling, the triple-cherub motif is pure baroque. Menu items include three kinds of spaghetti, trout meunière, peppersteak, veal piccata, saltimbocca, and excellent desserts. Meals range in price from 100 AS ($7.25) to 185 AS ($13.50). Hot dishes are served daily from 11am to 2pm and 5:30 to 10pm except Sunday, when only coffee and drinks are available.

Restaurant Niccolai, Klammstrasse 7 (tel. 0732/279028). For years, Linzers joked that this was the only pizzeria in town directed by a real Italian. This cozy restaurant, however, offers much more than pizza, even though there are a dozen kinds of this pie, ranging from fish to meat to cheese to just about everything good in the Mediterranean repertoire. You might want to try the Italian pastas (the tortellini à la casa is good), saltimbocca, a range of fish dishes, and a variety of tempting cheeses and dessert. À la carte meals cost 130 AS ($9.50) to 480 AS ($35). The restaurant is open Monday to Friday from 10:30am to midnight. Saturday hours are from 10:30am to 3pm; closed Sunday.

Wachauer Weinhaus, Pfarrgasse 29 (tel. 0732/274618). A baroque bas-relief of an ecstatic saint adorns the corner of this building near the old cathedral. The sign announcing this historic place is part of a wrought-iron bracket hanging over the cobblestone sidewalk. The smallest portion of any wine sold here is a quarter liter, which experience has taught me is about two full wine stems' worth. The wines from the Wachau region are featured, including five different kinds of white, four kinds of red, and one rosé, each priced from 13 AS (95¢) per glass. The establishment serves food from a limited menu priced from 175 AS ($12.75). Food items might include bean or gulasch soup, bratwurst, half a grilled hen, or free access to a self-service buffet. Wachauer Weinhaus is open daily except Sunday from 10am to midnight.

Steigelbräu Klosterhof, Landstrasse 30 (tel. 0732/273373). If you're not sure where you want to sit inside this large homey restaurant, you'll see photographs of the various eating areas posted in the vestibule. In some of the rooms formally dressed waiters serve food under high ceilings, while in other rooms blue-jeaned youths in leather jackets, along with a scattering of older people, fill the air with smoke and loud talk. An aquarium in the pink-and-white stone vestibule swarms with live trout. The place was once the library of Kremsmünster Abbey. Meals cost from 85 AS ($6.25) and are served daily from 11am to midnight.

Wienerwald, Promenade 22 (tel. 0732/271419), is a branch of the famous chain restaurant that does more than any other to offer gemütlich ambience and rustic settings on a mass scale. This particular branch has a dark, woodsy interior with big arched windows overlooking a summertime beer garden. Menu items include a quarter or half a fried chicken, plus a variety of schnitzels, gulasches, steaks, and braised beef with potato noodles. The staff also offers a children's menu, as well as beer and wine. Meals range from 85 AS ($6.25) to 110 AS ($8), and service is from 9:30am to 2am.

THE CAFÉS OF LINZ

Café Traxlmayr, Promenade 16 (tel. 0732/73353), is an old coffeehouse of the variety you might think died with World War I. It is next to a baroque palace on a wide ornamental boulevard, in a beige-and-brown building. Its outdoor sun terrace is protected by thick privets and geraniums in classical-style pots. It even has a fountain, designed to resemble a little boy playing with two gurgling fish, set into a wall out in front. The first thing you'll notice inside are the formally dressed staff (black and white tie are *de rigueur*), scurrying around with trays of coffee and cakes. The décor includes 1890s-style round marble tables, big mirrors, and crystal and gilt chandeliers. A rack of Austrian and foreign-language newspapers gives this place all the trappings of a Viennese coffeehouse, with elaborate pastries priced from 25 AS ($1.80); coffee also starts at 25 AS. During cold weather, hot dishes such as gulasch soup are served. The cafe is open daily except Sunday from 7:30am to 10pm.

Café-Konditorei Fritz Wagner, Landstrasse 15 (tel. 0732/271765). The orange-and-brown façade of this small shop might not be too impressive, but the Linzer torte and the other pastries sold inside are heavenly. Owned by the same family for almost 85 years, the coffeeshop maintains a limited number of outdoor café tables during the summer, with more than 40 more seats available indoors. It's open Monday to Friday from 8am to 7pm and on Saturday from 8am to 1pm; closed Sunday. Linzer torte can be mailed to any country in the world.

Café-Konditorei Tautermann, Klammstrasse 14 (tel. 0732/279686). The pastries from this small shop have won gold medals from contests held in places as far away as Brussels. You'll be able to buy fabulous-looking and tasting pastries, some of them with kiwi or regional fruits, from the ground-floor display cases. If you climb a simple flight of stairs, you can order coffee in a sunny upstairs room with a view of the cathedral's spire. The café is open daily except Tuesday from 9am to 7:30pm. Aside from pastries, the upstairs also serves the Linzer torte along with ice cream and small cold dishes. Coffee and pastries cost from 25 AS ($1.80).

Philipp Wrann, Hofgasse 6 (tel. 0732/273-288), is a well-known chain of pastry shops specializing in the Linzer torte—that heavenly concoction of butter, nuts, chocolate, and (in this case) gooseberry jam instead of raspberry jam—along with honey pies, candies, cakes, and chocolates. The company, which began in 1646, maintains five shops in Linz. Coffee starts at 21 AS ($1.50); pastries, range from 20 AS ($1.45) to 30 AS ($2.20). The shop is open daily from 8am to 8pm.

Café am Park, Hotel Schillerpark, Rainerstrasse 2-4 (tel. 0732/554050), seems to be the hottest place to go on a Sunday afternoon in Linz. If there's an equivalent of a sit-down singles bar, where everyone, and grandmother too, goes to watch, this is it. It's a big L-shaped room filled with belle-époque globe lights, upholstered bentwood chairs, and curtained glass windows overlooking the busy pedestrian traffic outside. You can get all the beverages you'd expect, as well as light snacks and wholesome meals, priced at around 160 AS ($11.75). The hours are daily from 8am to midnight.

WHERE TO SHOP

In an airy, sunny store, **O. Ö. Heimatwerk,** Landstrasse 31 (tel. 0732/2733760), has a stone floor, lots of handcrafted pine shelving, and a vaulted stucco ceiling dotted with pin spotlights. The entrance is under an arcade, although the shop windows face the busy pedestrian walkway of Linz's main shopping districts. Items for sale include local handcrafts such as pewter, intricately patterned silver, rustic ceramic pots, slippers, dresses, and a collection of dressmaking fabrics in regional patterns, many of them in polka-dot.

Trachten Feichtinger, Herrenstrasse 9 (tel. 0732/272884), has a décor of tasteful stucco curves and wood furnishings. The inventory includes a good selection of their own dirndls, skirts and jackets, and a full range of regional clothing, including sizes for men and women, girls and boys.

---

2. The Mühlviertel

This district of the Mühl River contains hills for exploring. The Mühl is a small river that flows into the Danube at a point above Linz. The district, or viertel, lies between the Upper Austrian capital and the border of Czechoslovakia. To visit the district, leave Linz on the road to Bad Leonfelden (coming up). The road you'll take is lofty at certain points, reaching an elevation of 2,800 feet, and you'll see places where the hills have been quarried for granite. The tourist office in Linz will outline a route for you through these hills, the entire round trip lasting some 4½ hours—longer if you want to take your time.

If you're touring and would like to stop over, the chief town of the Mühlviertel is—

FREISTADT

Once a thriving little town on the route followed by salt traders from the alpine districts to reach Bohemia, Freistadt lies in the northeastern section of the Mühlviertel. Remnants of the town's watchtowers, gates, and fortified walls can still be seen. On the large, rectangular main square, the **Hauptplatz,** the church of St. Catherine dates from the 14th century. A baroque overlay was added in the 17th century, but the church was rebuilt in the Gothic style. An onion-shaped dome crowns the parish church.

Schloss Freistadt, with a 175-foot-high keep, shelters the **Mühlviertler Heimathaus,** a provincial museum known for its collection of decorated glass engraved with gold.

Food and Lodging

Gasthof Deim (Zum Goldenen Hirschen), Böhmergasse 8, A-4240 Freistadt (tel. 07942/2258). The outside of this 23-room hotel has a series of neoclassical pilasters, corner mullions, and triangular window pediments, all clustered close together and accented with contrasting colors. The interior ceilings are usually vaulted, with stone ribs supported by massive masonry columns. Furnishings are rustic, and collections of hunting trophies and wrought-iron implements hang from the plaster walls. The cozy bedrooms have the kind of color schemes you can live with (mustards and russets) and lots of exposed wood. A garden sun terrace offers summer drinks. With half board included, rooms rent for 360 AS ($26.25) to 500 AS ($36.25) per person daily, depending on the plumbing.

KEPERMARKT

On the left bank of the Feldaist, north of the Danube, is the old town of Kepermarkt, about 6 miles south of Freistadt. A visit to the two towns can be ideally combined in a half-day excursion from Linz. Kepermarkt lies between the Mühlviertel and the Waldviertel, which was explored in the chapter on **Lower Austria.**

Kepermarkt is visited chiefly for its **Church of St. Wolfgang,** a Gothic edifice known for its altarpiece in the chancel, back of the main altar. You may be staggered at the size of it, as it appears to be about 42 feet high, with life-size figures. The carved part is of natural limewood. It's not only big, it's also beautiful to look at. Regrettably, the sculptor of this handsome work, dating from the latter part of the 15th century, is unknown. Otherwise, he would have earned a place for himself in books devoted to ecclesiastical art. It is believed that the altarpiece was originally painted, but that is not the case today.

BAD LEONFELDEN

A small spa 13 miles west of Freistadt, Bad Leonfelden is known for its mud baths and the Kneipp treatment. It's familiar mostly to Europeans, but you might want to make it a center for exploring Upper Austria. The spa has a pilgrimage church dating from the latter part of the 18th century.

A chair lift will take you to **Sternberg,** at 3,590 feet the loftiest point in the Mühlviertel. Once there, a lookout tower provides a panoramic sweep of the area.

The spa has been customarily visited by summer travelers, but lately some winter skiers have been seeking it out.

Food and Lodging

Gasthaus Böhmertor, A-4190 Bad Leonfelden (tel. 07213/429), was designed in a modern format using lots of glass and steel, with a balconied section containing 28 comfortable bedrooms, each with private bath or shower. The bed-and-breakfast rate ranges from 320 AS ($23.25) to 350 AS ($25.50) per person daily. The restaurants and bars are wood-paneled and cozy, with hanging lamps and lots of color. A large indoor pool and a sauna attract the athletic-minded or tired, and a range of massage facilities is also offered.

NEUFELDEN

Lying in the Grosse Mühl Valley, Neufelden has been a market town since the 13th century. Today it's known by the Austrians primarily as a little holiday resort in the Mühlviertel. The town has some lovely baroque buildings as well as a parish church from the 15th century. A wildlife park containing many different birds of prey is to the west of the town.

Food and Lodging

Mühltalhof, A-4120 Neufelden (tel. 07282/5787). Many of the balconies of this charming hotel look out over an artificial lake that comes close to the hotel's flowered sun terrace. A private beach extends right to the stone wall at the water's edge. On the premises are tennis courts, a children's playground, and a sauna. The inside is decorated with tasteful furniture, coffered ceilings, and lots of extra touches. This hotel is a good choice for families traveling with children, especially since the relaxed management does what it can to make your holidays pleasant. Each of the 25 comfortable rooms has its own bath. Singles start at 470 AS ($34.25) daily, while doubles range from 400 AS ($29) to 450 AS ($32.75) per person daily, with half board included. Prices depend on the season and the accommodation.

AIGEN IM MÜHLKRIES

A little market town enjoying a modest claim as a summer resort, Aigen lies in a forested area in the northwestern corridor of the Mühlviertel. From the resort, you can visit **Schlagl** (1,845 feet), an abbey built in 1218 and reconstructed centuries later. Its formerly Gothic church now flowers in the baroque style.

Aigen is surrounded by some of the most beautiful scenery in Upper Austria. From many of the panoramic belvederes you can look into Czechoslovakia.

Food and Lodging

Sporthotel Almesberger, A-4160 Aigen im Mühlkries (tel. 07281/8713). The Gruber family will be your hosts in this modern 56-hotel complex, which wraps itself around two sides of a grassy area with a fountain in the middle. The interior is cozily outfitted with wooden beams and timbers, tasteful upholstery, and rustic furniture. The spacious bedrooms often have wood-covered ceilings and attractively contrasting patterns. Charges for a bed and half board range from 460 AS ($33.50) to 620 AS ($45) per person daily, based on double occupancy. Single occupants pay a daily surcharge of 50 AS ($3.75). Terms include service and taxes.

3. Attersee and Mondsee

The noted Salzkammergut, to the northeast of Salzburg, is the most explored part of Upper Austria, although portions of it spill into other provinces. In fact, the parts we are about to consider are more often visited from Salzburg than from Linz.

Our first stopover will be at a warm lake and a cold one. First, the cold one—

ATTERSEE

The largest lake in the Austrian Alps, Attersee comes alive in summer with the sporting crowd, when visitors flock to the resort town that bears the lake's name. Frankly, in my opinion the lake is too cold almost all the time for swimming (although polar bear club members may disagree), but it's a great draw to boaters in summer. An Austrian sailing club has its headquarters here.

Those interested in fishing will be attracted to the lake's clear alpine waters, as it holds trout, char, and in little tributaries, brook trout. At many guesthouses along the shore you can have for dinner the fish you caught.

The blue-green *see* is 12½ miles long and about 1½ miles wide, with many orchards growing on its uplands. The government has built a road around the entire body of water. From the southern part of the lake, to the west of Burgau, you can take a 12-minute walk to a beautiful gorge, the **Burggrabenklamm,** with a waterfall, one of the most scenic sights along the Attersee.

Food and Lodging

Hotel Oberndorfer, A-4864 Attersee (tel. 07666/364), is a long, multi-sectioned hotel with a one-story extension stretching all the way to the edge of the lake. From the far edge of the sun terrace you can see the village church on the other side of the hotel. The 24 bedrooms are sunny, carpeted, and comfortable, while the public rooms have wood paneling and wrought iron. Bed-and-breakfast charges range from 430 AS ($31.25) to 720 AS ($52.25) per person daily. All units have balconies, private baths, self-dial phones, and radios, and most have color TVs and minibars. The most expensive doubles have better views and more elaborate plumbing. The hotel's restaurant serves daily from 11:30am to 2pm and 6 to 9pm. Open March to October and during December.

WEISSENBACH AM ATTERSEE

This tiny lakeside village and miniholiday resort lies on the southeastern corner of the lake. From here you can take a heavily forested, scenic road to a pass at **Weissenbach Sattel,** which has a chapel. Along this road you'll have a view of the Weissenbachklamm Gorge.

Food and Lodging

Hotel Post, A-4854 Weissenbach am Attersee (tel. 07663/240), is a balconied, 35-room hotel set at the edge of the lake. It's surrounded by trees, with a sun terrace stretching up to the edge of the water. Long rows of green-shuttered windows look out over iron railings onto the lake. In one of the public rooms stands a big ceramic stove with painted tiles. Modern furniture fills the tastefully appointed bedrooms, some of which have Oriental rugs as floor coverings. All units contain private baths. With half board included, the per-person rate ranges from 650 AS ($47.25) to 700 AS ($50) daily. On the premises are tennis courts, two bowling alleys, a sauna, and sailing facilities. You can rent equipment for waterskiing and other water sports.

UNTERACH AM ATTERSEE

This lakeside hamlet is so small it doesn't appear on most maps, but it occupies one of the loveliest positions on the lake. It's on the right bank, across from Weissenbach, and it can be a base for exploring either Attersee or Mondsee.

Food and Lodging

Hotel Georgshof, A-4866 Unterach am Attersee (tel. 07665/8501), is a wood-and-stucco chalet set on a hillside. If you walk out onto the backyard's sun terrace, you'll realize that the hotel is actually bigger than it appears from the road. The exteriors of many of the windows are embellished with regional designs in yellow and brown. Inside is a timbered and stuccoed bar area with chalet chairs and an angled serving area with alpine barstools. An indoor pool has a high ceiling and tile walls and floors. The 25 bedrooms, each with private bath or shower, are spacious and comfortable. The Hollerwöger family, your hosts, charge from 390 AS ($28.25) to 425 AS ($30) per person daily for half board.

SEEWALCHEN AM ATTERSEE

At the northern extremity of Lake Atter (Attersee) is this small village and holiday resort. It offers sailing and other water sports, but the main reason I'm recommending it is because of the following accommodation, one of the most pleasant stopovers in the Salzkammergut.

Food and Lodging

Gasthof Haüpl, A-4863 Seewalchen am Attersee (tel. 07662/8300), is one of the most elegant hotels in the region, and it remains open all year. From the street side it has a pleasing façade of white walls and a steeply sloped series of rooflines with long rows of interconnected gables. From the lake side the design literally blossoms into masses of flowers, set into boxes that hang from the handcrafted wooden balconies. The interior looks like a tastefully opulent private house. The paneling that covers many of the rooms glows softly in the reflected light from the wall sconces. In the light-grained bar the ceiling is crafted around baroque patterns and curves. The hotel rents 30 well-furnished rooms, each with private bath or shower. The bed-and-breakfast rate ranges from 580 AS ($42.25) to 850 AS ($61.75) per person daily.

The rustic dining room is said to be one of the best in the region. It's accented with graceful curves of wrought iron, and the chef prepares such delicacies as roast goose with baby vegetables in a savory sauce. This could be followed by a dessert parfait of fresh prunes in a caramel sauce. Frau Häupl, whose family has run this place for the past seven generations, does most of the cooking, assisted by an able group of chefs. Fixed-priced meals start at 350 AS ($25.50), while à la carte dinners cost from 150 AS ($11) to 475 AS ($34.50). The restaurant is closed Monday and in the period between October and April.

MONDSEE

"Moon Lake," or Mondsee, is considered one of the warmest lakes in the Salzkammergut. Crescent-shaped, it was named for the moon as long ago as Roman times. The Salzburg–Vienna autobahn runs along the south shores of this, the third-largest lake in the Salzkammergut district. In the background you can see the **Drachenwand** mountain and also the **Schafberg.**

The lake is sparsely settled, and if you want to find accommodations, you should head for the village that bears the lake's name, **Mondsee,** lying in the northwest corner. The village is popular in summer as a resort, with sailing schools and bathing beaches operating on the *see.*

Area Sights

A Benedictine abbey was once situated in Mondsee, dating from 748. However, Emperor Joseph II ordered the abbey dissolved in 1791, so the abbey church became the **parish church** (pfarrkirche), still a point of interest in the village. It's a 15th-century structure with an added baroque exterior, but its crypt is from the 11th century. The church was richly decorated by Meinrad Guggenbichler, a sculptor born in 1649. He designed seven of the more than dozen altars.

Part of the abbey is now the **Schloss Mondsee.** The castle is adjacent to the church. The wedding scene in *The Sound of Music* was filmed here.

The town has a museum in the former cloisters of the abbey, open from the first of May until the end of October from 9am to 6pm daily. Admission is 20 AS ($1.45) for adults and 10 AS (75¢) for children. The museum is in two sections: **Heimatmuseum,** where local artifacts are displayed related to life in the province in other days; and **Pfahlbaumuseum,** dedicated to prehistoric archeology. Exhibits trace local habitation by mankind from the time of Neolithic man's construction of houses on pilings in the lake. Discoveries from as far back as 3000 B.C. up to the disappearance of prehistoric man in 1800 B.C. include, among other things, Mondsee-Keramik pottery. For information, phone 06232/2270.

You may also visit the **Mondseer Rauchhaus,** or smokehouse, a rustic wood chalet flanked by outbuildings. Farmers from the district came here to dry their crops. There is no chimney above the vaulted hearth. The smokehouse is open from April until the end of October, 8am to 6pm. Admission is 20 AS ($1.45) for adults and 10 AS (75¢) for children.

Food and Lodging

Hotel/Restaurant Plomberg, St. Lorenz 41, A-5310 Mondsee (tel. 06232/3572), may remind you of a wealthy private home, but actually it's an alpine chalet three centuries old. Originally built as a coaching inn, it now contains 11 rooms plus one apartment. It's dotted in dozens of places—even the bedrooms—with Oriental rugs, thick curtains, and lots of tasteful accessories, which range from wrought-iron detailing to unusual art objects. The hotel sits above a stone wall that edges onto the lake. It's surrounded by deciduous trees and prosperous-looking villas. Bed-and-breakfast ranges from 500 AS ($36.25) to 900 AS ($65.50) per person daily. The hotel doesn't offer full- or half-board plans, because most of the guests make their own plans during the day.

The in-house restaurant serves outstanding food and is often considered among the best in Upper Austria. Karl and Monika Eschlböck have divided their restaurant into several cozy dining rooms, decorated with Oriental rugs and accented with heavy timbers and an occasional antique. The décor ranges from rustic to Jugendstil. Mr. Eschlböck was an apprentice at Troisgros in France and carries much of that establishment's expertise into his own restaurant. The menu is long and includes unusual adaptations of Austrian recipes as well as such items as veal liver with tomatoes, a salad of mâche and duck breast, and Corsican-style roebuck. À la carte meals range from 180 AS ($13) to 650 AS ($47.25), fixed-price dinners from 475 AS ($34.50) to 900 AS ($65.50). The restaurant is open daily from noon to 2pm and 7 to 10pm. Reservations are important. In summer many guests prefer to dine on one of two terraces. The establishment closes in January.

Hotel/Restaurant Weisses Kreuz, A-5310 Mondsee (tel. 06232/2254). The only spots of color a visitor will see against the bare white walls of this elegant place are the bouquets of flowers arranged by the employees of owner Gustav Lugerbauer. Of course, there's a view from the dining room out over a garden, but the main focus of this place is on the food. Your meal might include veal cutlets with "baby" vegetables and a potato strudel, a salad of marinated fish, or baby lamb cooked with rosemary. The cabbage and the richly flavored mushrooms used in the preparation of some of the recipes are likely to have been picked that very day in the restaurant's garden. Dessert might be crêpes stuffed with grapes and nuts or else a cream-flavored soufflé with strawberry sauce. Set menus range in price from 220 AS ($16) to 700 AS ($50), with à la carte orders starting at 175 AS ($12.75). Meals are served from 11:30am to 2pm and 6pm to midnight daily except Wednesday from September to July; reservations are necessary. The hotel/restaurant also rents 10 bedrooms, each well furnished and containing a private bath or shower. Bed-and-breakfast costs 400 AS ($29) to 600 AS ($43.75) per person daily.

Seehotel Lackner, Gaisberg 33, A-5310 Mondsee (tel. 06232/2359), is a clean, quiet hotel with colorful flowerboxes placed outside in summer. All 17 comfortably furnished rooms have balconies facing the lake and contain private showers and phones; they rent for 450 AS ($32.75) to 500 AS ($36.25) per person daily, including half board. You can enjoy the mountain view while dining on a terrace. The Lackner family are charming hosts, and they prepare Continental dishes; the Austrian desserts are made from family recipes. The hotel has a private beach for sunbathing or swimming, and the town and marina are but an easy walk from the door.

Grossgasthof Leitnerbräu, A-5310 Mondsee (tel. 06232/2219), has been owned by many generations of the Marschallinger family. You'll recognize it by its natural stucco façade with the white-and-pink geometric detailing around the windows. A wrought-iron bracket extends out over an awning, holding a depiction of two lions drinking from a barrel. The interior is cheerfully rustic, with a green ceramic stove in the restaurant and a scattering of painted antique furniture. Nine bedrooms are rented, six with private baths or showers; several of the rooms are spacious and sunny. Guests are received from December to October and charged 420 AS ($30.50) to 455 AS ($33) per person daily for half board.

La Farandole, Schössl 150 (tel. 06232/3457). Much of the allure of this restaurant derives from the years its owners spent learning their craft in the French section of Switzerland. You'll probably be greeted at the door by Madame Buchschartner, whose talented husband modestly remains behind the scenes in the kitchen. From your eyrie above the lake, you can enjoy an array of specialties that change with the seasons. Your meal might include a terrine of chicken livers with coarsely textured homemade bread, fresh asparagus with sweetbreads in puff pastry, marinated filet of salmon with leaves of lettuce, and filet steak with a pepper-flavored sabayon. Most of the vintages on the sophisticated wine list come from France and Austria. Fixed-price and à la carte dinners cost 365 AS ($26.50) to 595 AS ($43.25). Reservations are suggested. The restaurant is open from 11:30am to 2:30pm and 6pm to midnight except on Sunday evening, on Monday, and for lunch on Tuesday. The place is closed from the first week in January to the second week in February.

Café Frauenschuh (tel. 06232/2312) is an establishment so famous that it's known by sweet tooths throughout the region for its delectable pastries and chocolates. In the middle of the village, it offers racks of fruited and chocolate-covered confections, which you can eat on the spot or buy by the dozen to (supposedly) distribute among your friends back at the hotel. Coffee costs 22 AS ($2.20); pastries, from 20 AS ($1.45). From October to April, the café is open daily except Wednesday from 7:30am to 7pm; from May to September, it is open daily from 7:30am to midnight.

---

4. St. Wolfgang and Bad Ischl

The next two resorts, quite different in character, stand a short distance apart in the Salzkammergut.

St. Wolfgang lies on the Wolfgangsee, already visited in Chapter VIII on Land Salzburg. St. Gilgen in that province is a rival for St. Wolfgang, lying on the same lake but in Upper Austria. The province boundary crosses the lake.

Bad Ischl, once the summer residence of Emperor Franz Joseph, is the most fashionable spa in the lake district.

ST. WOLFGANG

In the midst of mountains in the Salzkammergut, Wolfgangsee is considered one of the most romantic lakes in Austria. Mountains and *see* join harmoniously to provide the setting for St. Wolfgang, a little holiday resort on the northeastern side of the lake below the Schafberg. Here in summer you can enjoy private bathing and other water sports, as well as frequent the beach cafés. Hiking is possible in many directions.

There's also winter skiing in the hills, with snow from December to midMarch. The ski slopes are free of avalanches. You'll find facilities here for skating, curling, and horse-drawn sleigh rides. Folkloric dancing is often presented as well.

In summer the resort is overrun with tourists, but there are two car parks at the entrance to the town. At certain times of the year I find it better to go to St. Wolfgang by boat, leaving from the landing stage at **Gschwendt** on the southern rim of the lake. Departures from mid-May to mid-October are usually hourly.

St. Wolfgang is the site of the celebrated **White Horse Inn** (see below), and the landscape has been called operetta-like—quite natural, as the inn was the setting for Ralph Benatzky's operetta *White Horse Inn,* which brought glory to the town.

Area Sights

Long before it was a holiday resort, St. Wolfgang was a renowned pilgrimage center, having been so since the 12th century. The **Church of St. Wolfgang** is said to stand on the spot where St. Wolfgang built a hermitage on a rocky spur of land. The church, from the latter 15th century, is highlighted by the Michael Pacher altarpiece, a magnificent work from 1481, pictured in many Gothic art books. Pacher's altarpiece is luxuriantly adorned with panel paintings and masterfully carved figures. The main panel depicts the Coronation of the Virgin. Thomas Schwanthaler designed the double altar of the patron saint, Wolfgang, and John the Baptist.

You can visit the church May to September daily from 9am to 5pm. Other months its hours are 10am to 4pm, from 11am on Sunday.

The most popular excursion from St. Wolfgang is to **Schafberg,** the view from the top being one of the best known and most sought in Upper Austria. Legend has it that you can see 13 lakes of the Salzkammergut from here, but I have never been able to do so. However, you're almost sure to have a good view of Mondsee and Attersee (which I've just introduced you to), and of course the entire Wolfgangsee. On a clear day you can see as far as the Berchtesgaden Alps. As a backdrop to the view, you can gaze at the peaks of the Hollengebirge and the Dachstein with its glacier caps.

The whole trip to Schafberg takes about 4½ hours, nearly half by rack rail called **Schafbergbahn,** which operates from mid-May to mid-October. Once you're there, allow for about 30 minutes' walking. Departures are hourly mid-May to mid-June from 8:30am to 4:30pm, mid-June to mid-September from 7am to 6:25pm, and mid-September to mid-October from 8:30am to 6:20pm. A round-trip fare costs 178 AS ($13) for adults and 89 AS ($6.45) for children. For more information, call 06138/2232. There's a hotel on the summit of the mountain, which rises to 5,850 feet.

Food and Lodging

Im Weissen Rössl (White Horse Inn), Im Stockl 74, A-5360 St. Wolfgang (tel. 06138/2306), was the setting used for a popular play (*Im Weissen Rössl am Wolfgangsee*) written in 1896 and adapted for the Berlin stage by a group of actors and directors who returned here to rewrite it in 1930. Actually, there has been an inn on this site since 1474, with continuous ownership by the Peter family since 1912.

This scene of the famous operetta absolutely reeks of romance and atmosphere. Its stippled yellow façade conceals a collection of carved antiques, which are clustered into intimate conversational groupings. The public rooms are large and sunny, usually wood-paneled and upholstered in cheerful colors. The indoor pool has direct access to the wide lakeside sun terrace with its view of the village church. On the premises are private tennis courts, a gymnasium, a sauna, sailing, waterskiing, and windsurfing facilities. In the evening the management usually provides live piano or zither music.

The restaurant of this Romantikhotel, serving both Austrian and international specialties, is considered one of the finest in the area. Meals start at 200 AS ($14.50). The hotel rents 68 bedrooms with private baths or showers. For bed-and-breakfast, singles cost 660 AS ($48) to 850 AS ($61.75) daily, with doubles going for 410 AS ($29.75) to 820 AS ($59.75) per person, depending on the room assignment. For half board, the charge is another 210 AS ($15.25) to 380 AS ($27.75) per person daily, depending on the room.

Sporthotel Wolfganger Hof, Pilgerstrasse 132, A-5360 St. Wolfgang (tel. 06138/22370), is a modern balconied guesthouse with two elongated sections set at right angles to each other. A summertime café has been set up under a tree just outside the entrance. Inside is a bar along with several restaurants, as well as a swimming pool, a sauna, and facilities for renting either bicycles or ski equipment. The hotel offers 56 attractively furnished bedrooms, each with private bath or shower. For bed-and-breakfast, singles cost 345 AS ($25) to 400 AS ($29) daily, and doubles cost 265 AS ($19.25) to 325 AS ($23.75) per person, plus another 110 AS ($8) per person for clients who want half board.

Seehotel Cortisen, A-5360 St. Wolfgang (tel. 06138/2376), is separated from the lake only by a solid stone wall, which supports a sun terrace and a short expanse of well-maintained lawn. From the street side the first thing you'll see are the illustrations of regionally dressed couples that cover parts of the façade. Inside, the décor is rustically elegant, with well-crafted woodwork, richly patterned Oriental rugs, and lots of antique knickknacks. The 28 cozy bedrooms often have private balconies and TVs and are tastefully furnished with lots of well-detailed pieces. The Ballner family are your hosts at this pleasant oasis. They charge 400 AS ($29) to 650 AS ($47.25) per person daily, based on double occupancy, with breakfast included. Singles pay a daily surcharge of 75 AS ($5.50). Prices depend on the exposure of your room and the season. Half board costs another 130 AS ($9.50) per person daily. The hotel shuts down from October to April.

Hotel Tirol, Robert-Stolz-Strasse 111, A-5360 St. Wolfgang (tel. 06138/23250), is a lakeside chalet rising four flower-covered stories above a grassy area that serves as a combination beach, sun terrace, and café. The interior has plenty of rustic ceiling beams and cozy alpine furniture, while many of the 16 comfortable bedrooms have carved headboards, paneled closet doors, and lots of atmosphere; some have private baths. The bar area is inviting, with bottles arranged in a wood, brick, and stucco combination that looks almost like a converted hearth. Bed-and-breakfast charges range from 320 AS ($23.25) to 460 AS ($33.50) daily for a single and 360 AS ($26.25) to 400 AS ($29) per person for a double, depending on the plumbing. For half board, the charge is another 140 AS ($10.25) per person daily. The hotel is open only from April to mid-October.

Gasthof/Pension Zimmerbräu, A-5360 St. Wolfgang (tel. 06138/2204), has the kind of façade that will make you want to stop in for coffee. A big-windowed restaurant extends partly into the street, while someone has installed lots of gingerbread under the eaves. You'll get the sense of a seaside town from the sun terrace of the two rustic beach huts whose foundations are built right into the lake. These also are accented with gingerbread and a wholesome sense of another era. The interior of the main hotel is simply and attractively furnished, with the kinds of floors that are easy to keep clean. The hotel, open from March to January, offers 24 comfortable bedrooms, each with shower and toilet; some of the accommodations open onto private balconies. The charges are 400 AS ($29) to 430 AS ($31.25) per person daily. Half board is included.

BAD ISCHL

The spa of Bad Ischl, one of the country's most fashionable watering places and the summer seat of Emperor Franz Joseph for more than 60 years, can be reached coming from Salzburg-Munich by leaving the motorway at Mondsee, heading along a well-constructed federal highway through the Salzkammergut, along Wolfgangsee and Mondsee. It's a 25-mile drive after you turn off the autobahn. Bad Ischl is easily accessible by daily bus and train service also. The spa establishments provide brine-sulfur mud baths for a variety of ailments.

Area Sights

The town, constructed on a peninsula between the Traun River and its tributary, the Ischl, still reflects a certain imperial conceit in its architecture, much of it left over from the heyday of the Austro-Hungarian Empire. The spa went into a decline after Franz Joseph stopped coming here in the first year of World War I, ending a practice he started in 1848 at the very beginning of his reign.

During imperial days the court was a magnet to musicians and artists, who depended on patronage from royalty and aristocracy for their bread and butter—and wine and caviar. Among those who made their way to Bad Ischl were Johann Strauss, Oscar Straus, Meyerbeer, Brahms, Bruckner, Lehár, Kálmán, Tauber, and Waldmüller.

Bad Ischl has chic shopping even today, as you'll note if you go along the **Pfarrgasse.** This street comes to an end at the **Esplanade,** a shaded promenade where the most famous figures in Europe once strolled. The smart set of the 19th century shunned the sun. Wealthy salt merchants once lived along this promenade, and Maximilian, ill-fated Emperor of Mexico, was born in a royal dwelling here in 1832.

The former **Pump Room,** dating from 1831, is in the middle of town on the Ferdinand-Auböck-Platz. Many of the buildings seen on the platz are in the Biedermeier style. The 1753 parish church was rebuilt when Maria Theresa was empress.

Many riverside walks are possible at this spa, and you'll see lovely gardens and villas attracting viewers. **Lehár Villa** (tel. 06132/6992) stands on the opposite bank of the Traun. Franz Lehár, the composer best known for his operetta *The Merry Widow,* lived here from 1912 until his death in 1948. The villa, now a museum, is open on Easter and from May to September 30 daily from 9am to noon and 2 to 5pm. Admission is 30 AS ($2.20).

The most important attraction of the town is the **Kaiservilla,** or Imperial Villa, in Kaiserpark (tel. 06132/3241), close to the downtown area. Emperor Franz Joseph used this Biedermeier palace for 60 summers as a residence and center for recreation. Highlights in the villa are the Gray Saloon, where the Empress Elisabeth lived and which she left on July 16, 1898, to begin her trip to Switzerland, where an assassin awaited her; and the emperor's study, where he signed the *Manifest,* a declaration of war sparking off World War I. Tours are conducted May 1 through 15 daily from 9:30am to noon and 1 to 4:30pm. Off-season, the villa is open Good Friday through Easter Monday and on Saturday and Sunday in April and October. Admission is 57 AS ($4.15).

Marmorschlössl (tel. 06132/4422), surrounded by the Kaiserpark, houses a photo-historic collection (Sammlung Frank). This tiny place was used by Empress Elizabeth as a tea pavilion. Hours are 9:30am to 4:30pm daily from April 1 to October 31. Admission to the park is 25 AS ($1.80) and to the museum another 20 AS ($1.45).

For a view of the overall area, you can take a cable car to **Katrin Mountain** (4,500 feet), a round-trip costing 120 AS ($8.70). It's an easy walk from the mountain station to the summit, where there are restaurants. From the mountain, you have a view into the Salzkammergut, with dozens of lakes and mountain heights, even glaciers. The cable car does not operate from early April to early May and late October to early December.

Another tour is south of the spa to the **salt mine** (tel. 06132/4231), which is open from mid-May to mid-September daily except Sunday from 9am to 5pm. Admission is 120 AS ($8.70), round-trip.

The **tourist office,** Bahnhofstrasse 6 (tel. 06132/3520), will give you complete directions and information about all the sights in the immediate environs if you'd like to stay in the spa and make some day trips.

Where to Stay

Kurhotel Bad Ischl, A-4820 Bad Ischl (tel. 06132/4271), in the center of town, is a modern hotel easy to recognize because of its multisectioned design of jutting angles and recessed balconies. Painted white, the hotel has a streamlined interior with neutral colors and lots of sunny, light-filled spaces. It was built between

1974 and 1976 with all the conveniences, including an underground garage, an indoor mineral water bath, a sauna, and a collection of restaurants, plus massage and therapy facilities. A heated corridor leads directly to the famous spa. Singles rent for 860 AS ($62.50) to 960 AS ($69.75) daily, while doubles cost 760 AS ($55.25) to 860 AS ($62.50) per person, including half board. Each of the 115 handsomely equipped accommodations has a private bath, phone, radio, color TV, and private balcony.

Zum Goldenen Schiff, Stifterkai 3, A-4820 Bad Ischl (tel. 06132/4241), is a leisurely five-minute walk from the spa facilities. The hotel is well situated, central but quiet, with a garden overlooking the Traun River and the Lehár Villa. The 55-room hotel offers all modern conveniences. An elevator, central heating, cozy dining rooms, and an excellent cuisine contribute to the allure. The riverfront rooms contain balconies and anterooms, and all units have baths or showers, color TVs, radios, minibars, direct-dial phones, and wall safes. Christine Gruber and her family try to satisfy all guests in this snug retreat. She charges 480 AS ($35) to 700 AS ($51) per person daily for bed-and-breakfast. A car park is also available.

Hotel Schenner, Schulgasse 9, A-4820 Bad Ischl (tel. 06132/6237-0), is imbued with a lot of Austrian charm and atmosphere. Positioned right in the center of the spa on a quiet street, the hotel (named for its family owners) is outfitted with stone detailing and plenty of exposed wood, as well as a conservatively rustic format that includes lots of wrought iron and several hunting trophies. Each of 28 cozy, comfortable bedrooms has a private bath or shower, radio, phone, color TV, and drink cabinet. Half board in a single ranges from 736 AS ($53.50) to 866 AS ($63) daily, with doubles costing 656 AS ($47.75) to 736 AS ($53.50) per person. The hotel also offers an outdoor solar-heated swimming pool, with a view over the roofs of Bad Ischl, along with a roof garden, a nudist sun terrace, and a small fitness area.

Hotel Goldener Stern, Kreuzplatz 30, A-4820 Bad Ischl (tel. 06132/3530), has one of the most memorable façades at the spa, covered with turquoise-colored stucco, white trim, and a white-walled rectangular tower jutting out from the corner. It's in the center of town, and while some of the public rooms have been renovated into a streamlined format of clean lines and modern paneling, the bedrooms retain much of their rustic allure. They're usually filled with painted furniture and wall-to-wall carpeting. Things are kept small around here, as only 15 rooms, each with private bath or shower, are rented. Singles begin at 460 AS ($33.50) daily, doubles at 390 AS ($28.25) per person, including half board.

Food and Drink

Weinhaus Attwenger, Lehárkai 12 (tel. 06132/3327), is the rustically decorated wine tavern purported to have been a favorite of Bruckner and Lehár. Its old-style décor is much imitated by more modern establishments. Many summer clients enjoy the riverside sun terrace, where on a pleasant day the savory coffee and delectable pastries seem even more tempting. If you want a full meal, the menu includes a wide range of Austrian and international dishes. These feature medallions of veal chef's style, mussels in a savory sauce, and several kinds of fish. Set menus cost 155 AS ($11.25) to 350 AS ($25.50), with à la carte dinners beginning at 200 AS ($14.50). The tavern is open daily from 10am to 2:30pm and 5:30pm to midnight. Reservations are a good idea.

Konditorei-Café Zauner, Pfarrgasse 32 (tel. 06132/3310), is the pastry shop (oldest in Austria) and coffeehouse that anyone with a sense of history usually heads for after viewing the summer playgrounds of the former Habsburg monarchs. The only Austrian coffeehouse more famous than this is Demel in Vienna. The imperial court used to order their pastries here, and it was said that the easiest way to listen to the heartbeat of the empire during July and August was to eavesdrop on a nearby table at Zauner. The café's guest book shows a clientele as rich and diverse as the pastry offerings. Among the names are those of Metternich, Kaiser Wilhelm II of Germany, Bismark, Brahms, Franz Lehár, Shirley MacLaine, and modern Austrian political figures such as the former chancellor Bruno Kreisky and the present head of state Kurt Waldheim.

You can buy pastries from the gold-and-white rococo showroom (which has been renovated to handle the flood of summer tourists) or eat at the small round-topped tables in an elegant series of inner rooms. Menu items include sandwiches and salads as well as an extensive assortment of exquisitely prepared pastries. The café is open daily in summer between 8:30am and 6pm. From October to March it closes on Tuesday. Many of the items can be mailed as gifts. Coffee costs 18 AS ($1.30) to 28 AS ($2.05), with pastries going for 15 AS ($1.10) to 30 AS ($2.20).

BAD GOISERN

This little spa town can be visited as an excursion from Bad Ischl, only 6 miles away, or else it can be used as a base for exploring this part of Upper Austria. Because it's much less well known than Bad Ischl, its prices are quite reasonable. Its little spa hotels offer good value for your schillings. The sulfurous spring waters of the spa contain iodine.

The resort attracts mainly Austrians and Germans who know of its quiet location in the Traun Valley. It's most popular in summer because of its good-sized open-air swimming pool, but it does some winter business, being convenient to a toboggan run and ski lifts. Hikers like to base here, from where they can go up **Hochkalmberg** mountain (more than 6,000 feet high) in 4½ hours and **Predigstuhl** (4,190 feet) in 3 hours.

Many travel-wise visitors use Bad Goisern as their center and then branch out during the day for sightseeing expeditions. The town lies in the middle of the most famous landscape in Austria, the Salzkammergut. It is easy to take expeditions to such centers as Bad Ischl, 6½ miles; St. Wolfgang, 17 miles; Hallstatt, 6½ miles; Obertraun (ice caves), 8½ miles; and Gosausee, 12½ miles.

Food and Lodging

Alpen-Apparthotel Mühlkogel, Unterjoch 38, A-4822 Bad Goisern (tel. 06135/7285-0), is the premier place to stay, rated four stars by the government. Arranged as a series of chalet-style buildings, it has an up-to-date array of amenities that appeals to the sporting crowd. The 120 comfortable units consist of both studio rooms and apartments (for those seeking longer stays), each with private bath, phone, private balcony, and lots of cozy corners. Depending on the season, two persons can stay here on half-board terms, costing 460 AS ($33.50) to 530 AS ($38.50) per person daily; the single supplement is 100 AS ($7.25) per day. Facilities include two good restaurants, as well as a coffee shop with a terrace. In the leisure center, you can enjoy an indoor swimming pool, a sauna and steam bath, a solarium, a bowling center, and table tennis, among other activities.

Kurhotel Jodschwefelbad, A-4822 Bad Goisern (tel. 06135/8305), is a sprawling hotel and sanitorium with a modern format and a 100-year-old history in the treatment of rheumatic and skin disorders, especially psoriasis. Maintaining resident dermatologists on the premises, the hotel offers good accommodations to patients and tourists alike. There is a range of outdoor activities in the region, and a thermally heated outdoor pool is on the premises. The hotel rents 65 bedrooms, 52 with private baths or showers. Half-board terms range from 650 AS ($47.25) to 700 AS ($51) per person daily. Closed in December.

Hotel Agathawirt, A-4822 Bad Goisern (tel. 06135/8341). In the nearby hamlet of St. Agatha is a romantic country hotel built in 1517. Today it has a humor-loving and friendly direction by the descendants of the family who bought it 200 years ago. It's designed with a steep hipped roof, lots of flowers, stone detailing around the entrance arch, and painted highlights around the corner mullions. The bedrooms inspire lingering and are suitable for other than just a good night's sleep. The headboards are often carved into regional patterns, and sometimes several kinds of wood are joined together for color contrast. If you're a light sleeper, avoid the units facing the street. Tennis, swimming, and ski facilities are all nearby. Of the 35 bedrooms, 20 come with private baths or showers. Half board ranges from 395 AS ($28.75) to 485 AS ($35.25) per person daily. The three-star hotel closes in November.

Hotel/Café Goiserermühle, A-4822 Bad Goisern (tel. 06135/8206). The second floor of this square-based building is crowned with a pyramid-shaped roof that comes to a point high above the lawns. The building is capped with a series of gables and a small tower surrounded by chimneys. The rooms have been renovated with all the modern comforts. The 40-bed hotel charges 320 AS to 340 AS per person daily, with half board included. The café serves well-seasoned steaks, schnitzels and fish, especially trout, in a homey and rustic setting. Open December to October.

---

5. Hallstatt

Hallstatt, a small market town south of Bad Ischl, considered one of the most beautiful villages in Austria, is my favorite place in this province. It stands on the left bank of the dark, brooding Hallstättersee in the Salzkammergut, on the southernmost tip of the province, right at the border of Land Salzburg (see Chapter VIII) and Styria (see Chapter XIII). You may well drive through a part of Styria to reach the lake, going via Bad Aussee.

To reach Hallstatt you take a road through a tunnel in the mountain. Leave your car in the car park and then go by foot past waterfalls to the town. There are several large cascades in the area.

Hallstättersee is a narrow lake, about 5 miles long and 1½ miles wide at its broadest expanse, almost completely surrounded by mountains. Its waters are so dark they're often called black.

Now a modern town, Hallstatt is considered the oldest still-inhabited village in Europe, owing its importance and its longevity to the local deposits of salt. Its perch against a mountain on a rocky terrace overlooking Hallstättersee seems like a curious place to build a town, but this was the site of an early Iron Age culture dating from 800 to 400 B.C. Many Iron Age relics have been unearthed in the area. The mining of salt from the mountain behind Hallstatt was known among pre-Celtic tribes of 1000 B.C. It died out in medieval times but was revived by the Habsburgs and continues today.

THE SIGHTS

The town of Hallstatt gave its name to one of the most important eras of prehistory. Some 1,000 tombs have been excavated in the area, which Austrians refer to as a "cradle of civilization." The 1,000 graves were of prehistoric people who constructed huts on piles in the lake. Many of the artifacts excavated here dating back to Neolithic times are displayed in the **Museum of Prehistory.** Also in the same building, the 14th-century Hallstatt-Markt, the oldest secular structure in the village, is the **Heimatmuseum.** It contains exhibits of local artifacts and details of the history of the region. The two museums are open daily from 9:30am to 6pm May to September, from 10am to 4pm October to April. Admission is 30 AS ($2.20) for adults and 20 AS ($1.40) for children.

The center of this beautifully situated village, with views of the Dachstein mountain massif, is the Market Square, which contains 16th-century buildings. The lakeside terrace is from the 18th century. Hallstatt's streets are narrow and often steep.

You can visit the **pfarrkirche** (parish church), which is romantically situated, with the churchyard bordering the dark waters of the lake. The house of worship is a large structure from the latter part of the 15th century. It has a squat tower, but its unusually designed roof with overhanging eaves evokes thoughts of Oriental buildings. The church's most outstanding art treasure is a big altarpiece, the gift of a salt merchant (obviously a rich one). Ten years in the making, beginning in 1505, the altarpiece depicts the Virgin with Saint Catherine and Saint Barbara.

Visitors can also go to the **Chapel of St. Michael,** a Gothic church next to the parish church. The cemetery was so small that this karner (charnel house or bone house) had to be used, starting in the 17th century. Some 12 to 15 years after a body had been buried in the ground the bones were transferred to the charnel house. Some skulls bear markings of the date of their owners' deaths. Other signs reveal the age of the dead, and sometimes markings show the cause of death.

Numerous cable cars and lifts are found in the town and surrounding area, as well as many walking paths or hiking trails. Mountain climbing is also possible, as Dachstein (9,820 feet) is in the vicinity, and the Dachstein Giant Ice Caves can be visited, although actually the mountain is more easily reached from nearby Obertraun (see below) than from Hallstatt. You can enjoy fishing on the Hallstättersee and in the Traun River, sailing, rowing, motorboating, swimming, and tennis. In winter Hallstatt is also a sports center, with snow from November to April. You can go skiing, sledding, curling, and ice skating, or hike along pleasant winter footpaths.

"Salt Mountain"

Lying above Hallstatt to the northwest is **Salzberg** (Salt Mountain), not to be confused with Salzburg, the city. The salt mines are still active and can be visited. Archeologists are constantly digging in this area and have unearthed many interesting finds.

To reach the mountain, you take the cableway from the Lahn and make a 20-minute walk after getting off. The funicular runs daily from 9am to 4:30pm during May and from mid-September to mid-October, from 9am to 6pm June to mid-September. A round-trip costs 70 AS ($5.10) for adults and 35 AS ($2.55) for children. Guided tours of the mines are conducted from 9am to 3pm during May and from mid-September to mid-October, and from 9am to 4:30pm June to mid-September. Tours cost 85 AS ($6.20) for adults and 40 AS ($2.90) for children over 4 (those under 4 not admitted). Dress warmly, and be sure to wear strong walking shoes for the 2½-hour mine tour.

There's a restaurant and snackbar with a terrace and a belvedere to let you take in the view. Hikers go all the way from here to the **Iron Age cemetery,** a trip taking about 1½ hours. If you like to hike, the tourist office will outline a series of walks in the area. One goes along the Echerntal to **Waldbachstrub** at the top of the valley, with lovely waterfalls. You can also climb to the **Tiergartenhütte,** which has a small inn, and on to the **Wiesberghaus,** 6,180 feet. After that, only the hardy continue to the **Simony-Hütte** at 7,230 feet, where there's another small inn lying at the foot of the Hallstatt Glacier. From Simony-Hütte, mountain climbers go up the **Hoher Dachstein,** the loftiest peak in the massif (9,820 feet), the climb taking 3½ hours.

The Dachstein Caves

These caves are among the most spectacular natural attractions of Upper Austria. To reach them, you can drive to Obertraun, where a sign in the vicinity will direct you to the lower station of the cableway that takes you to the caves. The cableway will deposit you at the intermediate platform (4,430 feet) on the Schönbergalm. From here it's about a 20-minute walk to the entrance to the caves.

Among the many attractions is the **Giant Ice Cave** (Rieseneishöhle), where even in summer the temperature is about 30° Fahrenheit. Be sure to dress for the cold. Among the ice cave's breathtaking features are the frozen waterfalls. You'll also see the so-called King Arthur's Cave and the Great Ice Chapel. The ice cave is open daily from the first of May until mid-October, 8:30am to 4:30pm; a guided tour costs 58 AS ($4.20). If you also wish to visit Mammoth Cave, a combined ticket costs 80 AS ($5.80). The Mammoth Cave has large galleries (subterranean passageways) cut through the rock by some ancient underground torrent. It takes about 1½ hours to go on a conducted tour of these caves. You're allowed to visit only a small part of the network of caves, which totals 23 miles in length, with a drop of 3,870 feet.

It's possible to go from the Schönbergalm station by cableway to the upper platform at a height of 6,920 feet. This is the **Hoher Krippenstein,** which offers an excellent panoramic view of the Dachstein massif. A chapel erected in the 1950s commemorates the accidental deaths here of 13 teachers and students. A round-trip to Krippenstein costs 190 AS ($13.75). Service is every 15 minutes daily from 9am to 4pm. You may have to queue up in summer, when many visitors make the trip.

From Krippenstein you can take a cable car down to **Gjaidalm** (5,880 feet).

Another cave can be visited in the area of Hallstatt, the **Koppenbrüllerhöhle,** or Koppenbrüller Cave. A torrent crosses the cave, and its activity causes continual enlargement of the cavern. The Austrians have made galleries that you can traverse for a glimpse of these turbulent underground waters.

The Koppenbrüller Cave is reached from Gasthaus Koppenrast, 2 miles upstream from Obertraun. You have to go on foot for about 10 minutes from the gasthaus. Guided daily tours, lasting an hour, are conducted through the cave from the first of May until the end of September from 9am to 5pm for a charge of 50 AS ($3.65).

The south wall of the Dachstein can also be explored. Take a cable car known as the Gletscherbahn (glacier road) up to **Hunerkogel.** To reach the cable car, leave from Schladming, going 10 miles via Ramsau on a toll road. The 12-minute cable-car ride leaves daily from 8am to 5pm. At the upper belvedere (8,840 feet) a magnificent view spreads out before you. You'll be able to see the Grossglockner as well as the Salzkammergut Alps. At Hunerkogel it's possible to ski in summer on the Schladminger Gletscher (small glacier).

FOOD AND LODGING

Seehotel Grüner Baum, A-4830 Hallstatt (tel. 06134/263), has a churchside location between the lake and a baroque fountain in the center of town. It's capped with a hipped roof of hammered copper and has an ochre-colored façade with white, heavily bordered windows. Its simple and comfortable rooms are accented with wood trim and often get lots of sunshine. The hotel's sun terrace extends out over the water on a pier, where you can go swimming or simply lie on a chaise longue with a drink if you want to. Later in the day you can sample local lake fish in the restaurant or on the terrace. There are 34 bedrooms, 25 with private baths or showers. Charges for half board range from 500 AS ($36.25) to 600 AS ($43.75) per person daily. The hotel is closed between mid-October and May.

Berghotel Krippenstein, A-4830 Hallstatt (tel. 06134/7129). Rarely have I seen such an inhospitable spot for a hotel—it stands on a rocky bluff that you can reach after taking three stages of the Dachstein cableway (see above). It's billed as the tourist attraction with the highest elevation in all of Upper Austria. It looks like a concrete fortress as you approach it from the lichen-covered rocks below. In winter it's ideally suited for skiers, although the views of the glacier in summer are well worth the trip here. The bedrooms, some with private baths or showers, cost 465 AS ($33.75) per person daily, with half board included.

Under the same management is the **Schönnberghaus,** A-4830 Hallstatt (tel. 06134/27323). This might be the ideal departure point for excursions to the ice caves of the Dachstein massif. Located at the end of the first stage of the Dachstein cableway, it's built entirely of wood, and offers a sunny terrace, a 100-seat restaurant, and 40 beds. Your neighbors in the next room might be members of one of the youth groups who sometimes rent out large blocks of beds for nature excursions. With half board included, the per-person rate is 320 AS ($23.25) daily.

GOSAU

This little village can be a happy alternative to staying at Hallstatt, as its prices are much more reasonable. Relatively little known, Gosau lies 6 miles west of Hallstättersee in the vicinity of the Gschütt Pass. Because it's in a ski region the village attracts winter business. Some of the Dachstein ski tours leave from here.

Gosau is also an ideal base for some summer touring. A road running south for about 5 miles leads to the Gosausee (Lake of Gosau), a mountain lake at 3,060 feet, encircled by steep rock walls. From here you can see the Gosau Glacier and the Dachstein (9,820 feet), surrounded by glaciers. The best view is from the lower lake.

It's popular to board a funicular going up to Gablonzer Hütte (5,200 feet), where you can enjoy snacks as you take in the view. The surrounding ski area is called the Swieselalm. A panoramic vista takes in the Hohe Tauern. Adventurers can climb to the top of Grosser Donnerkogel in about 2½ hours.

Food and Lodging

Sommerhof, A-4824 Gosau (tel. 06136/258), is separated from the road by a generous parking lot and a gracefully curved series of stone-flanked steps. From the sun terrace you can study the gold and white floral designs decorating the façade. You can also compare the artist's rendition to the masses of real flowers growing from the balconies. The interior has coffered wood ceilings painted in regional patterns, well-placed stone columns under beautifully illustrated arches, and 29 cozy, well-furnished bedrooms, all of which contain private baths. Half-board rates range from 460 AS ($33.50) to 490 AS ($35.75) per person daily. The hotel closes in November.

Hotel-Pension Koller, A-4824 Gosau (tel. 06136/207). The architecture of this Victorian-style building isn't the only unusual aspect about it. It sits on an expanse of lawn into which has been set a slate-ringed swimming pool. In the background rises a knife-edged series of jagged mountains. The hotel is built with arched loggias, recessed balconies, a series of hip and gabled roofs, and a feudal-style tower covered with cedar shingles. Forests come almost to the back door, but from the front the view is uninterrupted for several hundred feet. Inside, winter fireplaces give off a welcome warmth, plus there's a cozy weinstube and Sattelbar. The establishment offers 19 rooms with showers or baths, radios, and phones. Three apartments are suitable for families. Summer half-board prices range from 380 AS ($27.75) to 420 AS ($30.50) per person daily, with winter half-board charges going from 465 AS ($33.75) to 525 AS ($38.25) per person daily. Other facilities include a sauna and a solarium. Guests enjoy such special events as fondue evenings, candle-lit dinners, and zither evenings.

---

6. The Traunsee

One of the biggest lakes in the Salzkammergut, the Traunsee is about 7½ miles long and some 2 miles wide at its broadest expanse, and lies to the east of the two major lakes already explored: the Attersee and the Mondsee. Three mountain peaks —Traunstein, Hochkogel, and Eriakogel—make a silhouette which Austrians call *Schlafende Griechin* (Sleeping Greek Girl). Some sections of the Salzkammergut road run along the western edge of the lake.

The most dramatic part of this road is from Ebensee, at the southwestern tip of the lake, to Trauenkirchen. This spectacular corniche had to be hewn out of rock. The Traunsee is ringed with a number of resorts, the chief town being Gmunden. There's lake steamer service in summer. To reach this lake from Bad Ischl (see above), you drive northeast along the Traun River.

Your first stopover along the Traunsee will be at—

EBENSEE

This resort town on the southern Traunsee lakeside draws visitors by its scenic splendors and its mild, constant climate. It's a good base for excursions into the mountains or along the lake.

For summer visitors there are natural bathing beaches, trips to the **Gassi Stalactite Cavern,** windsurfing, diving, fishing, and boating. In winter the alpine plateau in the nearby Hollengebirge massif offers 15½ square miles of ski area with practice slopes, descents into the valley, and ski hikes. This avalanche-free region has snow from December until April. There are eight ski lifts.

You can reach Ebensee by road from Bad Ischl (see above) or by train.

Food and Lodging

Hotel Post, A-4802 Ebensee (tel. 06133/208), is set back from the street where it stands in the center of town near the Rathaus. Because it's like a dignified chalet, many of the 62 bedrooms have private balconies. The tasteful interior gives the impression of being older than it actually is. Parts of it have vaulted ceilings, lots of exposed wood, and wall murals. The streamlined bedrooms boast modern furniture and much comfort, including private baths. The bed-and-breakfast rate is 270 AS ($19.75) per day, rising to 370 AS ($26) for half board. Tariffs are based on double occupancy, and singles must pay a 60-AS ($4.25) daily surcharge.

TRAUENKIRCHEN

Built on a peninsula out into the Traunsee on the western shore is this little summer resort village, once the support facility for a Benedictine abbey at the peninsula's tip. After the Benedictines, the Jesuits occupied the abbey until the 17th century.

If time permits, visit the baroque **pfarrkirche** (parish church). Its pulpit is shaped like a sailing vessel, sculptured figures depicting the catching of fish by Christ's disciples. Nearby is the 17th-century **Chapel of St. Michael.**

Food and Lodging

Hotel Post, A-4801 Trauenkirchen (tel. 07617/2307), is a balconied hotel with a ground-floor series of rounded arches leading onto a popular daytime café terrace. Painted a pale yellow to set off the weathered balconies and the gray-and-white illustrations, the hotel sits on the main square of the village. The hotel rents 60 bedrooms, each with private bath or shower. Half board ranges from 450 AS ($32.75) to 500 AS ($36.25) per person daily.

GMUNDEN

This is one of the most popular summer resorts in the Salzkammergut, perched on the northern rim of the Traunsee with pine-green mountains as a backdrop.

Chestnut trees line the mile-long, traffic-free **Esplanade,** the town's chief attraction. You can walk from the **Rathausplatz** (Town Hall Square) to the **Strandbad** (the lakeside beach), watching the many majestic swans glide serenely along the lake. In days of yore, emperors and kings and members of the aristocracy strolled along the Esplanade and in the town's park, just as you can do today. The Welfen from Hannover, Württembergs, Bourbons, and diverse archdukes of Austria favored Gmunden as a pleasure ground, as did Franz Schubert, Friedrich Hebbel, and Johannes Brahms, among others.

The lake beaches are some of the best in the whole area, and in summer you can enjoy the varied lakeside activities, such as watching folkloric performances, dancing in discos, or relaxing in a cozy wine tavern or at an outdoor café. You can also bathe in the open-air swimming pool. Sailing, windsurfing, waterskiing, riding, and tennis are all available here. Perhaps you'd like to go mountaineering in the vicinity of this gemütlich town.

Gmunden, former center of the salt trade, has long produced Gmundner ceramics, and you'll see artistic work in faïence and green-flamed pottery.

A curiosity of the town is the **Orth Schloss,** or Palace of Orth, built on the Roman foundations of a small artificial island in the lake, connected to the town by a breakwater. Photographs of this palace are the most characteristic pictures taken of Gmunden, and one always graces the covers of tourist brochures luring visitors to the area. The gatehouse of the schloss, now the headquarters of an Austrian forestry school, is crowned by an onion-shaped dome. To reach the schloss, you walk across a 140-yard-long wooden bridge. Once there, you go into an inner courtyard flanked by arcaded galleries.

The palace got its name from its occupant, Johann Orth, the assumed name of Archduke Salvator, nephew of Emperor Franz Joseph. Growing bored with the court life in Vienna, the archduke came here in 1878 to take up life as Johann Orth. Johann or Salvator, whichever, he died mysteriously off the coast of South America in 1891.

The **parish church** (pfarrkirche) of Gmunden was built in the 15th century and given the inevitable baroque overlay in the 18th century. Thomas Schwanthaler carved the main altar with scenes of the Three Kings of Orient (the Magi) in 1678.

From Gmunden you can go by cableway in 12 minutes to the top of the **Grünberg,** where you have a view down the Traunsee, which has a fjordlike look at its southern end, with limestone rock faces rising almost vertically. The Dachstein completes the view. A round-trip ticket costs 90 AS ($6.55) per person. In winter, ski lifts, runs, and slopes on the Grünberg are easily reached. Also, curling, ice skating, and winter walks along the lake are available in Gmunden.

Where to Stay

Parkhotel am See, A-4810 Gmunden (tel. 07612/4230), is a long, low-lying 48-room building capped with a red-tile roof and an illuminated sign telling the name of the hotel. Between it and the lake someone has planted a rose garden and lots of begonias. The antiques inside include polychrome sculptures, painted double armoires, and gilt-covered 19th-century scroll-back chairs covered in pink satin.

One of my favorite rooms is the spacious lakeside restaurant. Here you can sit either indoors or on the covered balcony, where the first thing you'll see above your head is a verdant canopy of ivy. The Holzinger sisters maintain swimming facilities off a private pier. At the Victorian-style bar you might want to have a drink after returning from a five-minute walk to the center of town.

With full board included, singles rent for 660 AS ($48) to 950 AS ($69) daily, while doubles cost 680 AS ($49.50) to 880 AS ($64) per person, depending on the plumbing, the season, and the accommodation. All accommodations contain private baths or showers, phones, and minibars. The best rooms face the lake and have private balconies. The hotel is open from the middle of May to the end of September.

Schlosshotel Freisitz, A-4810 Gmunden (tel. 07612/4905), sits on a hill overlooking the lake. Its design looks like a combination of a baroque private house and a Victorian-style hotel. Its dozens of architectural oddities include a crenellated tower with tall arched windows, wrought-iron window bars, and jutting parapets over many of the balconied windows, and a stone terrace built into the slope of the grass-covered hill.

The interior has been renovated and today incorporates lots of modern building materials with the older stone-accented design. However, many of the original vaulted ceilings remain. The hotel offers 26 well-furnished rooms, each with bath or shower, and costs range from 380 AS ($27.75) to 650 AS ($47.25) per person daily, with breakfast. Open from April to October.

Seehotel Schwan, A-4810 Gmunden (tel. 07612/3391), is a beautifully detailed 19th-century hotel on the main square of town at the edge of the water. Its neoclassical design includes arched pediments above many of the windows, a gabled roof, and château-style corner towers. Painted white, like the bird it's named for, the hotel has a private mineral bath and a sauna on the premises. The well-furnished bedrooms are comfortable, and usually offer good views of both the town and the lake. Thirty-three of the 41 bedrooms come with private baths or showers. Half-board prices range from 490 AS ($35.75) to 990 AS ($72) per person daily.

Pension Haus Magerl, Ackerweg 18, A-4810 Gmunden (tel. 07612/3675), has a long, elegant façade whose white full-length shutters embellish a double row of balconied French windows. It sits in a grassy meadow with a view overlooking the lake. The clean and attractively simple public rooms have big, sunny windows and rustic wall coverings. On the premises are a sauna, an indoor pool, and a TV room. The establishment offers 40 bedrooms, simple but comfortable, each with private bath or shower. Half board ranges from 465 AS ($33.75) to 505 AS ($36.75) per person daily.

Where to Dine

Wandl-Stuben (tel. 07612/3884) lies in the center of town in a historic building with arcades. The inside is filled with dark paneling and lots of dimly lit niches, ideal for intimate conversations. By candlelight you read the menu, which offers one of the best assortments of food at the resort. Specialties include fresh lake fish, game, alpine lamb dishes, and a combination of old Austrian recipes and modern cuisine: oysters with mushrooms, butter, and onions, along with a host of regional specialties. Some of these feature savory and well-prepared meat dishes such as chateaubriand for two, medallions of pork in cream sauce, veal steak Luzern, and tournedos with a cognac cream sauce. Desserts include a range of warm sweets, such as banana flambé with chocolate sauce and walnut ice cream with plum-flavored whipped cream. Fixed-price menus range from 85 AS ($6.25) to 125 AS ($9), with à la carte dinners beginning at 260 AS ($19). Hot food is served daily except Sunday from 11:45am to 2:30pm and 6:30 to 10pm.

GRÜNAU IN ALMTAL

It's not on the Traunsee, but Grünau in Almtal, lying to the east of that lake, with good accommodations and restaurants as well as a wildlife park, might be a good stopover for you. It's often less crowded in summer than resorts on the Traunsee, and it occupies a beautiful position in the Alm Valley.

The wide valley lies about 9½ miles east of our last stopover, Gmunden. To reach Grünau, you will pass through **Scharnstein,** which has a 17th-century castle housing the Austrian Museum of Criminal Law. About 5 miles southward, you come to this summer holiday resort. **Kremsmünster Abbey** lies to the northeast, if you'd like to make a day's excursion.

Cumberland Wildlife Park (tel. 07616/8205) is 4 miles south of Grünau. Here you'll see otters, beavers, brown bears, and other animals. There's a restaurant at the park, plus a museum devoted to forestry.

If you continue on south along the Alm Valley, you'll reach Almsee, a lake at 2,810 feet.

Food and Lodging

Romantik Hotel und Restaurant Almtalhof, A-4645 Grünau in Almtal (tel. 07616/8204), offers a fairytale setting that should appeal to nostalgics around the world. The four-story solidly built chalet has masses of live flowers covering the window boxes and decorative flowers painted onto the regional furniture scattered throughout the hotel. The décor is romantic, charming, and worthy of an extended stay. The intimate bedrooms offer coffered ceilings, elaborate wrought-iron chandeliers, and pink bedding that contrasts with the light-grained pine of the wall paneling. Your hosts, the Leithner family, charge 500 AS ($36.25) to 550 AS ($40) for a single and 500 AS ($36.25) to 700 AS ($50) per person daily for a double, with breakfast included.

The large and elegant dining room has well-polished slats of vertical paneling, stained-glass window medallions, and a collection of old pewter and hunting trophies. Menu items are traditional and Austrian. They include schnitzels, roast beef, roast pork, pork cutlets with apples, a selection of wild game, and an unusual salad with a dressing of yogurt and marinated cabbage. À la carte meals range from 150 AS ($11) to 350 AS ($25.50), while fixed-priced dinners cost 220 AS ($16) to 450 AS ($32.75). Both the hotel and restaurant are closed between early October and about a week before Christmas, as well as from mid-March to the end of April.

Gasthof Deutsches Haus, A-4645 Grünau in Almtal (tel. 07616/8332), is a small, green-shuttered family-run hotel with two floors of bedrooms. The ground-floor dining room has alpine furniture and a green-tile oven under the beamed ceiling. The sun terrace looks out over a small lake, which is set in a restful location 6 miles from the nearest village. The restaurant serves home-style meals, with freshly caught lake trout prepared in several different ways. With half board included, per-person rates start at 300 AS ($21.75) per day. The hotel rents its homelike and comfortable rooms from the first of May until the end of September.

Restaurant Seehaus (tel. 07616/8366) occupies an idyllic lakeside spot 10 miles from the center of Grünau, which gives local residents the perfect excuse to make a midsummer excursion. Housed in a long, elegant building, the restaurant features gutbürgerlich regional fare served in generous portions, with meals costing 120 AS ($8.75) to 160 AS ($11.75). The place is open daily from 9am to 6pm.

---

7. Wels

A flourishing town in Roman times, Wels lies on the left bank of the Traun River in the center of a large farm belt and is known today for its agricultural fairs. It can be reached by heading north from Gmunden after your visit there. It's also an easy drive southwest from Linz. Wels is most often used as a base for exploring the hinterlands, although it has some attractions of its own. In about 1½ hours you can walk through the town, seeing its chief sights.

THE SIGHTS

The **Stadtplatz** is considered one of the most architecturally harmonious town squares in Austria, with beautifully decorated façades of old houses and an intricately carved fountain. It is broad and cobbled. Most of the houses date from the 16th to the 18th centuries. The baroque **Rathaus** (Town Hall), built in 1748, is one of the most ornate buildings in the old town. The **Ledererturm,** dating from 1618, is the only tower remaining of those that once studded the town walls. Many homes or shops in the old town are held up by arches and passageways with vaulted ceilings.

Emperor Maximilian I died in Wels in 1519, stricken as he was traveling from the Tyrolean country to Wiener Neustadt. The house in which he died is called the **Kaiserliche Burg.** On Burggasse, it has been turned into a museum of minor importance. You can see the room in which the emperor breathed his last.

The **Stadtpfarrkirche** (town parish church) has a 14th-century Gothic chancel and three stained-glass windows from that same century. The entire church was once Gothic until baroque architects went to work on it. The Romanesque inner doorway is surmounted by a tower with a bulbous dome, dating from 1732.

Across from the church stands the **Salome Alt house.** She was the mistress of, and mother of the dozen children of, Prince-Archbishop Wolf Dietrich, who is encountered so frequently in Salzburg history. Following the disgrace and overthrow of this ecclesiastic, he retired to Wels.

On the Ringstrasse you can see what is left of **Schloss Pollheim,** where, the story goes, the shoemaker-poet Hans Sachs lived. Wagner is said to have based his character in *Die Meistersinger von Nürnberg* on Sachs.

Wels is a town that has moved into the future industrially, as witness its chemical plants, but it also clings to its imperial past.

WHERE TO STAY

Hotel Greif, Kaiser-Josef-Platz 50, A-4600 Wels (tel. 07242/45361), has a substantial-looking masonry façade. The exterior hasn't been embellished in any way other than an occasional balcony, but the dining room inside has a renovated red-and-white Viennese-style décor of mirrors, crystal chandeliers, and high ceilings. The hotel rents 62 bedrooms, each with private bath or shower. Half-board charges range from 750 AS ($54.50) to 1,240 AS ($90.25) per person daily.

Gasthof Bayrischer Hof, Dr.-Schauer-Strasse 23, A-4600 Wels (tel. 07242/ 47214), is easy to recognize because of its elegant blue-and-white façade with neoclassical window treatments and a mansard tower extending upward from the building's exposed corner. The garden café is an inviting place to spend part of a warm midday. The well-equipped bedrooms all have private baths and showers, direct-dial phones, and TVs. Since 1949 the Platzer family has welcomed guests, charging from 330 AS ($24) to 420 AS ($30.50) daily for a single and 540 AS ($39.25) to 620 AS ($45) for a double, with a breakfast buffet included. One accommodation is ideal for honeymooners, with a private whirlpool bath and a "heaven-bed."

FOOD AND DRINK

Restaurant Wirt am Berg, Berg 6 (tel. 07242/45059), was established in 1630 and has been in the same family since 1881. Prominent diners have included the royal family of Monaco. About 2½ miles outside Wels, the three-story restaurant is painted a deep yellow-orange and opens into a series of rustically decorated dining rooms with hunting trophies.

On warm days you might prefer to eat under the chestnut trees on the brick-covered terrace. Wild game is the most popular item on the menu in hunting season, although at any time of year you can still enjoy an appetizer of carpaccio (cold filet) of venison with fresh fine herbs and a special salad marinated in walnut oil, or consommé of pheasant. This could be followed by venison ragoût or tafelspitz. Dessert might be curd dumplings with buttered bread crumbs and stewed plums. Meals cost 195 AS ($14.25) to 430 AS ($31.25). The restaurant also sells more than 800 kinds of wine. It is open daily except Sunday and Monday from 9am to 2pm and 5pm "till closing."

Café-Konditorei Urbann, Schmidtgasse 20 (tel. 07242/46051), is the best-known café in town, offering a tree-shaded summer garden where you're likely to see all kinds of people, many of them local residents who show up every day for their usual cup of coffee and favorite pastry. Near the train station, the café prepares freshly made specialties such as handmade chocolate truffles, marzipan and nut kugeln, homemade gingerbread (winter only), and homemade jams and ice creams.

The place prefers not to be classified as a restaurant, but nonetheless serves sandwiches, toast, and eggs. Coffee costs 18 AS ($1.30) to 28 AS ($2.05), with pastries averaging 25 AS ($1.80). The Urbann family has owned this place since 1853, and there was a candle and gingerbread shop on the premises from as early as 1630. The café is open Monday to Saturday from 8am to 7pm.

WHERE TO SHOP

Trachten-Feichtinger, Stadtplatz 18 (tel. 07242/47221), opposite the Stadtpfarrkirche, is in a 14th-century Stadtplatz house that is one of the most architecturally interesting buildings in Wels. It is known for the two marble Romans in the façade and has a planted arcade and a water fountain in the backyard. Inside there are carved wood furnishings as well as a cozy open fireplace in the dirndl department. Couturier made-to-order garments can be created from patterns and individualized fabrics within a few days, and alterations take only up to two hours.

Most of the stock is for women, including dirndls, brocade and silk combinations, loden costumes, skirts and blouses, overcoats, and dressmaking materials in a special section. Jackets are available for men, and dirndls for girls as young as one year are stocked here. Accessories include scarves, umbrellas, and belts. The shop is open Monday to Friday from 8:30am to noon and 2 to 6pm, and on Saturday from 9am to noon.

BAD SCHALLERBACH

This well-known Austrian spa lies 9 miles northwest of Wels and can easily be visited on a half-day excursion, unless you want to anchor here and "take the cure." The spa is known for its hot sulfur springs. It has both indoor and outdoor swimming pools and is visited mainly in the summer months by an essentially European clientele.

Food and Lodging

Grünes Turl, Gebersdorf, A-4701 Bad Schallerbach (tel. 07249/8163), was a farm complex first mentioned in a title deed in 1570. It was transformed by Herbert and Doris Ameshofer into a cozy restaurant that today combines well-prepared cuisine with an antique setting. It is set in an elongated white-walled building with two floors of flowered windows, a gently sloping roof, and a big sun terrace for afternoon meals. Food is usually served in the vaulted dining room, whose ceiling is supported by short stone columns. Your dinner might include generous portions of pork medallions in an herb sauce, an array of fresh fish, a platter of seasonal venison, and most definitely, an old Austrian favorite, cabbage cream soup. Desserts are homemade and satisfyingly caloric. Full meals cost 90 AS ($6.50) to 550 AS ($40).

This establishment is also a four-star hotel with 30 attractively furnished bedrooms. It offers much comfort from December to October, charging guests 485 AS ($35.25) to 510 AS ($37) per person daily for half board. Tennis is available, and fishing can be arranged.

TOURING THE ABBEYS

The two most popular excursions from Wels, to sites that are among the most outstanding sightseeing attractions of Upper Austria, will take you first to—

Lambach Abbey

In 1056 a Benedictine abbey was founded at Lambach (postal address A-4650 Lambach), 10 miles southwest of Wels and about 15 miles north of the Traunsee. It stands at a point where the Traun River meets its tributary, the Ager. The once Romanesque monastery (tel. 07245/351), which stands in the Marktplatz of the old market town, has changed its face since its early days, now showing a splendid baroque exterior. A towering marble gateway from 1693 leads into the first courtyard.

In the so-called ringing chamber, you can see one of the major attractions of the abbey, Romanesque frescoes from the 11th century. These works of art were once hidden but later discovered. They were restored in 1967 and put on public view, an event hailed by the Austrian press. The frescoes can be seen only on a guided tour from 9 to 11am and 2:30 to 5pm. Monday to Saturday, from 10 to 11am and 2:30 to 5pm on Sunday. Admission is 25 AS ($1.80).

The abbey's other attractions include a richly embellished library and a rather sumptuous refectory from the 18th century. The abbey church was built in the 1650s, and its main altar is believed to have been designed by the celebrated baroque architect J. B. Fischer von Erlach. The only surviving monastic theater in Austria, built in 1770, is reached by a stairway.

Kremsmünster Abbey

Near Bad Hall, between the emerging hills of the Alps and the Danube River, overlooking the Valley of Krems, this Benedictine abbey was founded in 777. Two domed towers of the abbey church dominate the local skyline. This abbey, lying 22 miles southwest of Linz, was founded by order of Tassilo III, a Bavarian duke whose son Gunther was killed by a wild boar during a hunt. The abbey was erected to honor the memory of the duke's son. It was, of course, Romanesque, but in the 17th and 18th centuries the old abbey was given the baroque treatment.

The most outstanding feature of a tour through Kremsmünster is the **Fischbehalter,** a fish pond made by the noted architect Carlo Antonio Carlone. It has five basins, each encircled by arcades, with statues that spout water. Figures depict everybody from Samson to Neptune.

In the cluster of abbey buildings the **Kaisersaal,** or Hall of the Emperors, has a collection of portraits of sovereigns of the Holy Roman Empire, painted by Altomonte at the end of the 17th century. One of the most outstanding works of art is a *Crucifixion* by Quentin Massys. The abbey still owns the chalice of Tassilo that was presented to the monks by the founding duke. It's the most ancient piece of goldsmith's work in either Austria or Bavaria, the duke's home. In the library is a celebrated manuscript, the *Codex Millenarius,* an 8th-century translation of the gospels.

An observatory tower rising nearly 200 feet has an exhibition of materials associated with astronomy and other sciences. This observatory has been called the first skyscraper in Europe.

Many noted men have been pupils at the abbey school, including the novelist Adalbert Stifter.

Tours are conducted through the abbey daily from Easter Sunday to the end of October at 9 and 10:30am, and again at 2 and 3:30pm. Allow about three hours for a tour of "the whole works," but there are also shorter tours. Admission is 55 AS ($4). For information, phone 07583-277216.

BAD HALL

After leaving Kremsmünster Abbey, if you drive 6 miles southeast you'll reach this well-known spa, whose iodine brine springs are among the most powerful in the heart of Europe. Its thermal park, covering nearly 90 acres, is beautifully landscaped.

You can visit the handsomely decorated **pfarrkirche** (parish church), from around the mid-18th century. Its vaulting is richly frescoed, and the baroque love of statues and cherubs is evidenced throughout.

On summer days, sacred-music concerts are presented here. You can learn the dates and hours of these recitals from the local tourist office.

Food and Lodging

Schlosshotel Feyregg, A-4540 Bad Hall (tel. 07258/2591), has been called one of the most beautiful castles in the pre-alpine regions of Austria. When it was built it served as the summer residence of the abbots from the monastery of Spital am Phyrn. The furnishings of the public rooms look as if they had come from a museum and are usually an accurate reflection of the castle's baroque origin. The 14 bedrooms are large and also beautifully furnished, each with private bath. Rates are 850 AS ($61.75) to 950 AS ($69) per person daily for half board.

Kurhotel, A-4540 Bad Hall (tel. 07258/2611), is composed of four elegantly designed villas a short distance away from one another in the middle of a 75-acre park just outside the center of town. This is the only hotel in Bad Hall with a complete inventory of cure facilities, administered by health care professionals. Each of the villas gives the impression that a grand duke will descend from a carriage in front of the portico at any moment. The interiors have been modernized but still evoke their former opulence, even though few of the original furnishings remain. The hotel rents 53 bedrooms, each with private bath or shower, charging 740 AS ($53.75) to 950 AS ($69) per person daily for half board.

Hotel Haller Hof, Hauptplatz 27, A-4540 Bad Hall (tel. 07258/2490), is a centrally located hotel designed around a concrete cube with a long, big-windowed extension stretching out back. The interior is filled with dated furniture, although everything is clean and well-maintained by the capable owner, Ferdinand Lindinger. From April to November, the hotel accepts guests in its 50 bedrooms, 42 of which contain private baths or showers. Half-board charges range from 350 AS ($25.50) to 375 AS ($27.25) per person daily.

8. The Southeast Corner

After visiting the renowned Kremsmünster Abbey and Bad Hall, you can head south along the Steyr River into a little-known area—the southeast corner of Upper Austria, bordering Styria. This section where many discoveries await you is known as **Pyhrn-Eisenwurzen.**

If you're ready for lunch, you might want to stop at either Molln or Klaus, coming up.

MOLLN

After traveling along the Steyr River, you can veer southeast off Rte. 140 at Leonstein to the hamlet of Molln and the very fine restaurant described below.

Where to Dine

Restaurant Martinsklause (tel. 07584/2916). The specialties here are numerous, served in generous quantities and delicately flavored. They include pâté of trout with toast, homemade spiced ham with apple horseradish, veal medallions with fresh tarragon, salt pork "Upper Austria" with bread dumplings, apple dumplings with nuts in an apple wine sauce, and many different kinds of strudel. Christine Köhler is the guiding hand behind this fine restaurant, noted for its traditional ambience and good service as well as its food. Set menus cost 100 AS ($7.25) to 175 AS ($12.75), with à la carte meals beginning at 100 AS ($7.25) but averaging 250 AS ($18.25). Service is daily except Wednesday from 11am to 1:30pm and 6 to 8pm. However, the place is open from 8am to midnight for drinks and snacks.

KLAUS

In the heart of the Pyhrn-Eisenwurzen district, Klaus is a village set in the midst of some of the most splendid scenery in Upper Austria.

The hamlet, just north of the Klauser See, a beautiful lake, has developed into a popular resort since construction of the reservoir for the hydroelectric power station Klaus. Now a paradise for wild-water enthusiasts as well as for those who prefer to canoe more quietly along the river, Klaus has a special school for kayaking and paddling.

Food and Lodging

Hotel Schinagl, A-4564 Klaus (tel. 07585/261). The painted illustration on the front of this partially balconied chalet is of a regionally dressed man and woman courting one another. On the premises is a rustically paneled stand-up bar, lots of big-windowed panoramas, and a series of comfortable chairs grouped into conversational units. Sporting facilities of the region will be described by Erich Mentil. The hotel offers 36 well-furnished bedrooms, each with private bath or shower, charging 400 AS ($29) to 525 AS ($38.25) per person daily for half board.

VORDERSTODER

After passing by the Klauser See, you can make a detour into the high mountain valley known as **Stodertal.** It lies directly east of the Totes Gebirge mountain range.

The upper part of the Steyr River flows through this scenic valley. You'll pass by the Stromboding Waterfall, which drops some 85 feet.

Food and Lodging

Pension/Restaurant Stockerwirt, A-4574 Vorderstoder (tel. 07564/8214), is beautifully situated on the slope of a hill with a view of the snow-covered mountains. The roof has a long expanse of interconnected gables, with a covering of red tile. The portico covering the entrance is fashioned of burnished sheet metal, hammered into graceful curves. The hotel on this site has been in the same family since 1664, although the format today has been significantly updated. A covered swimming pool is on the premises, as well as an immaculately clean kitchen serving well-prepared meals in a panoramic setting. Charges for the 19 comfortable, attractively furnished rooms, each with private bath or shower, are 360 AS ($26.25) to 390 AS ($28.25) per person daily, half board included. Guests are accepted from December to October.

HINTERSTODER

The Steyr River wends its way through Hinterstoder, the valley's chief resort, which is so remote it has no through traffic. It's about 4 miles from the principal Linz–Graz artery. Lying directly under the Totes Gebirge massif, the town has combined with Windischgarsten (coming up) and Spital am Pyhrn to become an emerging ski resort area in Upper Austria. Hinterstoder has the widest range of accommodations, but if you're selecting a hotel, you might want to consider the possibilities of the other two villages, since the three resorts are within easy reach of one another.

Hinterstoder, which is both a summer and a winter holiday village, has a good ski school. A chair lift will transport you to Hutterer Böden (4,550 feet), the middle station on the ascent, where several ski lifts await you as well as a hotel. From here you can take a chair lift to Hutterer Höss (6,230) feet, which has a mountain restaurant.

Another ski area, the Dietlgut-Bärenalm, lies about 2 miles from Hinterstoder at the far end of the valley. In winter a ski bus connects it to the center of the resort area. Once there you can take a double-chair lift to Bärenalm (3,950 feet), offering another mountain restaurant.

Food and Lodging

Berghotel Hinterstoder, Mitterstoder 200, A-4573 Hinterstoder (tel. 07564/5421-0), is shaped like a gently sloping pyramid, with flowered rows of parallel balconies in front of oversize bedroom windows. The hotel lies above Hinterstoder at the middle station of the cabin lift, which shuts down every day at 5pm. You can get there by car, but in winter—their high season—you must use chains. The hotel offers many sports and fitness facilities, including a gym, a sauna, and an indoor pool. Most of the private accommodations front a southern exposure and contain private baths, balconies, and a view of the well-maintained lawn that many of the guests use for midsummer sunbathing. The disco-keller, if it were located in your hometown, might become one of your preferred hangouts. This four-star hotel rents its 40 bedrooms from December to April and June to September. Summer half-board rates range from 390 AS ($28.50) to 520 AS ($37.75) per person daily, with winter half-board rates going from 530 AS ($38.50) to 760 AS ($55.25) per person daily.

Sporthotel Stoderhof, A-4573 Hinterstoder (tel. 07564/5266), is the major hotel in the village, right in the center, with a rambling modern format of white walls and a gently sloping gabled roof. A glass-walled greenhouse-type construction extends toward the sun terrace, behind which is an indoor swimming pool. The hotel lies only a few minutes' walk from the local ski area, site of World Cup ski racing, accessible by a gondola. The Fruhmanns provide 39 comfortably furnished bedrooms, each with private bath or shower. Winter half-board charges range from 560 AS ($40.75) to 710 AS ($51.75) per person daily, with summer half-board costs going from 510 AS ($37) to 580 AS ($42.25) per person daily.

Pension Dietlgut, A-4573 Hinterstoder (tel. 07564/5248), consists of one house with a series of adjacent outbuildings. Unabashedly romantic in style, with steep roofs, exposed cross-timbering, and an idyllic setting in a grassy area at the foot of a rocky cliff, it lies at the end of the valley. If you stay here it's best to have a car because of its distance from the village. The pension is known for its collection of hunting trophies, which cover the walls of one of the antique-filled public rooms. In one of the sitting rooms the amber-colored paneling is arranged in an unusual and attractive pattern of random vertical and horizontal lines. Rates for the 22 well-kept bedrooms range from 480 AS ($34) to 590 AS ($43) daily for a single, from 480 AS ($34) to 570 AS ($41.50) per person for a double. These prices include half board and depend on the plumbing and the season. The owners do much to make you comfortable.

WINDISCHGARSTEN

This resort lies in a sunny valley at an elevation of about 1,960 feet, about a half-hour drive from Hinterstoder, just visited. It's a typical Austrian village, with much old-fashioned charm and character, unspoiled so far by the inroads of modern tourism.

Skiing is limited in winter, as this is only an emerging ski resort. A single chair lift goes to the highest station at 2,800 feet. The après-ski life here is unpretentious and not highly organized, but some does exist, especially in the cellars of the hotels. However, if you'd like a change of pace you can take a bus ride and be deposited at Spital am Pyhrn (coming up) in just seven minutes.

With a lovely church spire piercing the winter sky and a blanket of snow covering the entire village for much of the winter, Windischgarsten is starkly idyllic, but I still prefer it in summer, when the valley is green, the sun reflects off the russet-colored roofs, and the towering, snow-capped mountains form a dramatic background.

Food and Lodging

Hotel Bischofsberg, Edlbach 31, A-4580 Windischgarsten (tel. 07562/8855), is a graceful collection of chalets set on the side of a hill with a view over the mountains. On the downhill side of the hotel lies a rose garden flanking an outdoor pool. From the front you'll notice the summertime café terrace and the painted embellishments around each of the windows. The inside is decorated with enough rusticity to make anyone feel at home. In the center of one of the sitting rooms, a stucco–and–ceramic tile oven gives off wintertime heat below the heavy beams of the paneled ceiling.

The light from the big windows against one wall of the spacious restaurant not only illumines the napery on your table, but nourishes the potted trees growing in the center of the room. The Löger family (which has so many members that it's almost like a village in itself) owns and manages this attractive hotel. With half board included, the charge is 475 AS ($34.50) to 530 AS ($38.50) per person daily. All the comfortably furnished rooms contain private baths, and there's also an indoor swimming pool.

Sporthotel Baumschlager, A-4580 Windischgarsten (tel. 07562/311), is a pretty chalet directed by Hans and Gerda Baumschlager, who rank among the region's most experienced hoteliers. Part of the establishment's ground floor is accented with an arched arcade, the roof of which supports a popular café terrace. The third- and fourth-floor balconies are festooned with flowers that are reflected in the glass of the doors leading into the attractive bedrooms. On the premises is a swimming pool, plus an outdoor tennis court, a sauna, a solarium, a bar, and a restaurant, the latter specializing in venison, fish, and regional recipes. In season it serves such delights as fresh asparagus and strawberries. This four-star hotel rents only 11 rooms, each with private bath or shower. Half-board rates range from 400 AS ($29) to 440 AS ($32) per person daily.

Hotel/Pension Schwarzes-Rössl, Linzer Strasse 39, A-4580 Windischgarsten. This long-established hotel in the center of town is housed in an elegantly symmetrical gray building with a gabled roof, an arched entrance, and cleverly painted trompe-l'oeil embellishments around each of the rectangular windows. Inside, many of the ceilings are vaulted or timbered, with a scattering of painted antiques and a restaurant—one of the best in town—filled with alpine furniture. The Löger family are your gracious hosts.

Food items in the restaurant are usually prepared in a temptingly old-fashioned style and served in big portions. Specialties include schnitzels in cream sauce with noodles, marrow soup, and an array of grilled meats and fish. Fixed-price menus range from 120 AS ($8.75) to 270 AS ($19.75), with à la carte dinners going from 130 AS ($9.50) to 270 AS ($19.75). Hours are 11:30am to 10pm daily; closed Wednesday in winter and for most of November.

SPITAL AM PYHRN

Spital was known as a stopover a long time ago on the ancient toll road that led over the nearby Pyhrn Pass on the road to Graz in Styria. The village, at 2,625 feet, lies close to Windischgarsten (see above).

In winter many skiers are attracted to Spital, where you can take a ski bus for about a mile to the foothills of the Pyhrn. There you board a mountain railway heading up Wurzeralm mountain and disembark at the Bergstation. The ride takes only eight minutes and the train can carry some 1,000 passengers per hour. The top station is at a lofty 4,700 feet. From Bergstation it's possible to go even higher, taking a double-chair lift to a height of 6,140 feet.

The **Alpenrose** is the center of most après-ski action. Otherwise, attractions are limited, but you can always go over to Windischgarsten, just recommended. Chances are, however, that you'll visit Spital am Pyhrn in summer, when it's at its most beautiful.

This village used to be the site of an abbey, and the **Stiftskirche** is well known. Work on this abbey church started in 1714 and continued for 16 years. Its baroque exterior is flanked by two towers. Kremser Schmidt did the paintings on the altarpieces of the side altars, and Altomonte painted some of the work on the colonnades in the then-fashionable trompe-l'oeil style.

Food and Lodging

Hotel Alpenrose, A-4582 Spital am Pyhrn (tel. 07563/225), is a well-established modern hotel with a two-story addition extending to the side of the main house. The public rooms are paneled and sunny, while the bedrooms are clean and filled with cheerful colors. An indoor swimming pool is five minutes away on foot. The Wesselitsch family are your hosts. Half-board rates (which in winter include free transportation from the hotel to the ski lifts) range from 250 AS ($18.25) to 300 AS ($21.75) per person daily. Half of the 24 comfortable bedrooms contain private showers. The hotel is open from December to October.

9. Steyr and Enns

For another look at Upper Austria, we'll leave the southeast corner, heading north again via a route that, if followed on, would lead to Linz. Instead, however, we'll detour along the Enns River to visit two of the most ancient patrician cities of Austria.

These cities bear the names of the rivers that flow through the area, known as the Donau-Paum. The first such city to which I'll introduce you is Steyr and the second is Enns.

Steyr

The old town of Steyr was built on a tongue of land that juts out between the Enns and the Steyr rivers. Three gates and a tower survive from the days when walls surrounded the town. The city's spread since its early days has taken it mainly along the Enns River. The boating crowd likes to visit here in summer, as this is the point of origin for many trips along both rivers.

Because of its name, visitors sometimes think that Steyr is in Styria, but even though that province also took its name from the Steyr River, the city is still very much in Upper Austria.

Steyr is the home of the well-known Steyr-Puch motorbike, and BMW trucks and bicycles are assembled here. But despite the factories, this is no grim industrial town. In its heyday it was considered a rival of Vienna, and the Old Town, particularly the major square with its many houses from the baroque era, makes it worth a stopover.

The Sights

The **Stadtplatz** (town square) is one of the best preserved in Upper Austria and the city's most attractive feature. The street takes the shape of a plaza, and you'll see arcades as well as several balconied houses in both the Gothic and Renaissance styles. Most outstanding are the **Rathaus** (Town Hall) at no. 27 and the **Bummerlhaus** at no. 32. Construction on the rococo Town Hall, crowned by a slender tower, began in 1765. The Bummerlhaus was a private mansion built in the Gothic style. If possible, you should try to see inside some of the courts that were built as a part of these magnificent houses.

The **Dominikanerkirche,** or Dominican Church, has a rich baroque interior, but it merits only a passing look. More intriguing is a street near the church, the colorful **Eisengasse,** which winds down to the Enns River.

The **Stadtpfarrkirche** (town parish church), on Pfarrgasse, dates from the middle of the 15th century, built in the Gothic style by the architect who designed St. Stephen's in Vienna, to which it bears a resemblance. The church has some quite old stained glass. You'll see many ancient gravestones nearby in the **pfarrhaus** (parish house), where Anton Bruckner composed his Sixth Symphony. A room in the house honors him.

You may also visit **Christkindl** (Christ Child), 2 miles west of Steyr, a well-known pilgrimage church in Austria. The baroque architects Carlone and Prandtauer designed Christkindl, which is painted a pinkish mauve. At Christmastime, children all over the world send letters to the *Wirtschaft,* a Christmas post office. If you send a self-addressed, stamped envelope, you'll receive a reply if your letter is addressed to Christkindl.

Food and Lodging

Hotel Minichmayr, Haratzmüllerstrasse 1-3, A-4400 Steyr (tel. 07252/23410). Views from the sun terrace of this old-world hotel encompass the confluence of the two rivers and much of the Old Town. The hotel offers good service, excellent cuisine (its kitchen ranks among the 200 best in Austria), and 51 comfortable bedrooms in a sunny format of taste and style. With a buffet breakfast included, rooms cost 410 AS ($29.75) to 605 AS ($44) per person daily. Guests have use of the sauna.

The Viertler family also runs the dining room, where specialties include fresh local river fish, a range of grilled and flambé-style meats, roasts, and an array of solid, regionally inspired recipes. Fixed-price menus cost 160 AS ($11.75) to 300 AS ($21.75). À la carte dinners cost 150 AS ($11) to 375 AS ($27.25).

Café Rahofer, Stadtplatz 9 (tel. 07252/24606), is an attractive modern café in the center of Steyr, open daily except Tuesday from 9am to 9pm. Serving pastries, wine, coffee, and snacks, it is a popular hangout for shoppers, lovers, and about everybody else in town. Coffee and pastries range from 18 AS ($1.30) to 25 AS ($1.80). The Rahofer is also an excellent restaurant, among the finest in the area, serving a meal of Austrian dishes beginning at 150 AS ($11) and going up.

ENNS

The oldest town in Upper Austria, Enns stands on what was once the site of a Roman camp and later was the Roman city of Lauriacum, on the left bank of the Enns River, a short distance from where its water flows into the Danube. Enns was granted its charter in 1212. The **Rathaus** displays many artifacts from the Roman days of the town.

The **Stadtturm** (Town Tower), constructed in 1564 on orders of Emperor Maximilian II, still stands on the principal plaza, along with several old patrician houses in the baroque style. From the tower you have an excellent view over the old town and the river.

The Gothic **pfarrkirche** (parish church) has a double nave flanked by only one aisle. Pillars divide it into two sections, then into a trio of sections.

To the north of the town stands **Ennsegg Castle,** dating from the 16th century. Some 5 miles to the west of Enns lies the renowned Augustinian Abbey of St. Florian. (For information, refer to the sights in the environs of Linz.)

Food and Lodging

Hotel Lauriacum, 5-7 Wienerstrasse, A-4470 Enns (tel. 07223/2315), presents a distinguished contemporary façade to a busy street in the center of Enns. The public rooms are filled with a combination of modern and rustic accessories, which include a ceramic tile oven, a coffered ceiling, and a collection of farm implements in one of the restaurants. Other rooms are invitingly contemporary. Management pays careful attention to its cuisine as well as to the well-being of its guests. The hotel rents 30 spacious and well-furnished bedrooms, each with private bath. Bed-and-breakfast charges range from 500 AS ($36.25) to 600 AS ($43.75) per person daily. A sauna is on the premises.

---

10. Stops Along the Danube

Many of the major stopovers along the Danube, including Linz, have been explored in other parts of this guide. Other sections on the great river have been visited in Lower Austria (Chapter V) and in Vienna. However, the Danube offers several rewarding stopovers in Upper Austria besides Linz, including the following towns and villages.

Assuming you are picking up this trail at Passau, a border city of West Germany, and driving through the Danube Valley, I'd recommend a visit first to—

ASCHACH

This Danube town has associations with Dr. Faust. (See the description of Faust Schlössl below, where you can order a meal or spend the night—if you dare.) A bridge in the town spans the Danube, and you may be able to see from your bedroom window steamers plying the river. Aschach has many baroque houses from the 18th century.

Directly south of Aschach, you can visit the small town of **Eferding,** which was mentioned in *The Nibelungenlied*.

Food and Lodging

Faust Schlössl, A-4082 Aschach (tel. 07273/7402). This medieval castle was used by tollkeepers of the powerful Schaumberg family, and later by a revolving series of noble families. The behavior of the residents so frightened the populace that it was soon rumored that the castle was not only haunted, but that it had been built by the devil for Dr. Faustus in a single night. In 1966 it was converted into a hotel. The interior is unpretentious, and except for a few of the original furnishings and an occasional rustic touch, the décor is modern. For the 30 rooms, each with private bath or shower, half-board rates range from 320 AS ($23.25) to 350 AS ($25.50) per person daily.

The arena of what had been a Roman theater was converted into the basin for an outdoor swimming pool. If you approach the castle from the river, it will appear more massive and foreboding than it actually is, although the many wings, arcades, towers, and balconies certainly make an impressive combination of yellow stucco and red tiles. Open February to December.

Bypassing Linz and Enns, already visited, I recommend that you drive along the Danube to the far-eastern border of Upper Austria. Here it's time for another stopover, this one in—

GREIN

Much of the economy of Grein, which lies on the left bank of the Danube, depends on shipping along the river. **Greinburg,** a schloss sheltering the Austrian Shipping Museum, stands to the west of the port. The castle, dating from the 15th century, has an inner court in the Renaissance style, with arcades.

In the **Stadtplatz,** a rococo theater from 1791, seating only about 150 spectators, has been preserved. This is the oldest-known theater in Austria. Also on the Stadtplatz are several turreted houses. The **parish church** of Grein has an 18th-century altarpiece by Altomonte.

A Coffeehouse

Kaffeesiederei Blumenstraussl, Stadtplatz 6 (tel. 07268/380), offers two separate dining rooms, both of them decorated in Biedermeier style. In summer the outdoor coffee garden is popular with almost everyone in town. The establishment lies close to the Rathaus, behind a well-preserved baroque façade. One of the rooms has a massive billiard table, a shiny ceramic stove. Empire-style hanging chandeliers, and country Biedermeier banquettes. You'll know when strawberries are in season by the wide range of pastries made with them as a primary ingredient. The Mozart torte is luscious, as well as the array of hot soups to warm up a cold day. Drinks, ice cream, and sandwiches are also available. Coffee costs 18 AS ($1.30) to 28 AS ($2.05), with pastries beginning at 28 AS ($2.05). The café's hours are 9:30am to midnight. It is closed on Monday year round and also on Tuesday in winter.

ST. NIKOLA

On both banks of the Danube near the point where it enters Lower Austria is this 800-year-old town, about two hours by autobahn from Vienna. It's a good base for visiting Melk, the Wachau, and many castles, churches, and medieval towns in the general area, all about an hour's drive from St. Nikola.

Food and Lodging

Hotel zur Post, A-4381 St. Nikola (tel. 07268/8140), is composed of the union of a 17th-century central building with a small onion dome attached to the corner tower, plus a modern balconied extension. The mostly contemporary furnishings inside are tasteful, clean, and rustic, and set in a pleasing combination of white plaster walls and horizontal paneling. The Danzer family are your hosts, charging a peak 320 AS ($23.25) to 360 AS ($26.25) per person for a single or double, with half board included. All 35 units contain private baths, toilets, radios, alarm clocks, and phones.

Hotel Donauhof, A-4381 St. Nikola (tel. 07268/8107). The service and attitude of the Aigner family make this an especially attractive starting point for touring this part of Austria. Parts of the hotel are more than 400 years old. The public rooms are attractively furnished with painted armoires, chalet chairs, and rustic timbers. The bar area stocks practically everything from homemade wines to vintage cognacs. The 18 bedrooms are comfortable enough to spend time in, and sometimes they have provocatively dark walls to accent the color scheme. Each has a private bath or shower. Bed-and-breakfast charges, depending on the season, range from 250 AS ($18.25) to 270 AS ($19.75) per person daily.

The restaurant bakes many of its own pastries fresh every day, while the menu items include both Austrian and international specialties. Guests are welcome to fish in the hotel-owned waters or in the Danube, and if they catch anything, the hotel will prepare it for supper. On the premises are a sauna, an exercise room, and a garden terrace overlooking the river.

---

11. Schärding and Braunau

From the far-eastern border of Upper Austria, most visitors will go on into Lower Austria, following the Danube until it reaches Vienna. However, since that territory has been explored previously, we'll jump across the province to highlight some stopovers along its western border before going into the Tyrolean country.

Some towns and villages that merit exploration in this section include—

SCHÄRDING

Because of its beautiful old buildings—painted in pastels of gold, pink, yellow, and turquoise—Schärding is often called the romantic city of the baroque. It lies above the Inn River, about 11 miles south of the West German city of Passau on the Danube, in a region of Upper Austria called the **Innviertel**. The Danube flows in the north, but in the west are the Inn and Salzach rivers.

If much of the area in and around Schärding reminds you of Bavaria, it's no wonder. The Innviertel was part of Bavaria until it was ceded to Austria in 1779.

Schärding was once a fortified town, and remnants of the old walls stand today, along with some gates and towers. Its **parish church** (pfarrkirche), like virtually every other old church in Austria, was once in the Gothic style but received a baroque overlay.

Food and Lodging

Hotel Forstinger's Wirthaus, Unterer Stadtplatz 3, A-4780 Schärding (tel. 07712/2302), has been a hotel since 1606 and has now attained four-star status. It is authentically rustic, and its comfortable accommodations were completely renovated in 1985. All 18 bedrooms have bathrooms, TVs, safes, phones, and minibars. Half-board charges range from 450 AS ($32.75) to 780 AS ($56.75) per person daily. The inn's restaurant, known throughout the region for its gutbürgerlich fare, is furnished with beautiful rustic furniture, and the service is efficient.

BRAUNAU AM INN

Lying on the right bank of the Inn River, Braunau, a very old town with several buildings from the Middle Ages still standing, has always been a frontier or border town. If you cross the bridge over the Inn you'll have to clear Customs, as you'll be in the small Bavarian village of Simbach.

The burghers' houses in Braunau date in part from the 16th and 17th centuries, but the most outstanding architectural treasure is **St. Stephen's Church,** with a large square tower rising 315 feet, the third-tallest tower in Austria. Inside you can visit the 15th-century Gothic chancel. In an adjacent chapel is the tombstone of a Passau bishop who died in 1485. See also its 16th-century baker's altar.

Braunau am Inn has the dubious distinction of being the birthplace of Adolf Hitler, although his name was Adolf Schicklgruber then. His father, Alois Schicklgruber, had been made a Customs inspector in Braunau in 1875. However, the town of Braunau was to be in the limelight much later in connection with its native son. When the Nazis were applying pressure on Austria before their complete takeover of the country, one of the most unlikely proposals made was that Braunau, because it was *Der Führer's Geburtsort* (native town), be ceded to Germany. Vague plans were in the air to turn it into a monument honoring the dictator's birth site.

After his takeover of Austria, Hitler made a "sentimental journey" to Braunau. He ordered his driver to take him to the Pommer Inn, in which he had been born, but his caravan had a difficult time reaching the building because cars full of onlookers jammed the road. Historians recorded that when his car reached Braunau, "a jubilant crowd struggled to touch the vehicle as if it were some religious relic."

Today, neo-Nazis have made the little town and the house at Salzburger Vorstadt 15, where Hitler was born in 1889, into a sort of pilgrimage goal for ultrarightists of Austria, although this is frowned on by the Austrian government. The former home of the Schicklgrubers is a brown-and-white building with a baroque façade.

Food and Lodging

Hotel Gann, Stadtplatz 23, A-5280 Braunau am Inn (tel. 07722/3206), is a distinctive-looking town house on the central square of the village. Its façade is painted a pearly gray-blue, while the heavy moldings around the neoclassical-style windows are pure white. The cellar bar is one of the most memorable places in town, partly because of the stone vaulting that soars over the striped chairs and partly because of the patronage of many of the locals. The 36 bedrooms have high ceilings and lots of cozily renovated comforts; 17 have private baths or showers. Bed-and-breakfast costs 270 AS ($19.50) to 340 AS ($24.75) per person daily.

INNSBRUCK AND TYROL

Land of ice and mountains, of dark forests and alpine meadows where wild-flowers bloom in the spring, of summer holidays and winter sports . . . that's Tyrol. Those intrepid tourists, the British, discovered its delights for holiday-makers and made it a fashionable destination for travelers in the last century. Now, however, the principal visitors are the Germans. Munich is only a few hours away, and even though Bavaria is itself one of the major tourist attractions of Europe, even the Bavarians head for Tyrol when they want a change of scenery.

Tyrol and its capital, Innsbruck, had an imperial heyday at the end of the Middle Ages, when the Habsburg, Maximilian I, often called "the last of the knights," was the Holy Roman Emperor. Castles dotted the countryside, many now only ruins.

With a population of about half a million Austrians occupying some 4,822 square miles, Tyrol was a much larger district at the turn of the century, until South Tyrol was lost to Italy in 1919. The lost portion was a large wine-growing area, considered the wealthiest part of Tyrol. This loss was a great blow for the Tyrolean people who remained in Austria, as it separated many of them from relatives, friends, and sometimes livelihood.

By the same post–World War I treaty, East Tyrol, whose capital is Lienz, was divided from its sister, North Tyrol, of which Innsbruck is capital. The two are separated by a protuberance of the portion of Tyrol given to Italy, which connects with a strip of Land Salzburg border. To the east of North Tyrol, the far larger portion of the split province, lies Land Salzburg. On its west is the Austrian province of Vorarlberg (to be visited in Chapter XI), to the north is Bavaria, West Germany, and to the south, Italy and a small part of Switzerland. East Tyrol is bordered by Carinthia on the east, Land Salzburg on the north, and Italy everywhere else.

Tyrol lies at the junction of several transcontinental links. The Valley of the Inn River, which I've divided into two sections, cuts across the northern part of the province. Many side valleys are offshoots of the major artery. The province is also known for its deep-blue alpine lakes, such as the Achensee and the Walchsee. The Drau River, rising in the Höhe Tauern Alps, runs through East Tyrol.

Tyrol is a province known for its folklore and colorful folk customs, including schuhplatter dancing, brass bands, and yodeling. It's also known for its Tyrol dress. Traditional garb topped off with tall hats (less common nowadays) used to be a special feature for both men and women, with the men being the more elaborately attired.

Today Tyrol is one of the most popular tourist regions of Europe, especially favored by Americans, who have to an extent supplanted the once firmly entrenched British holiday crowds. It didn't become a mecca for American tourists until shortly before World War I, when rail magnate J. Pierpont Morgan spent time in Innsbruck and publicized the area when he returned home. Since World War II, the resorts of this province have made it a popular destination for American skiers.

Tyrol is the most frequented winter playground in all Austria. Many prefer its ski slopes to those of Switzerland. It has also produced great skiers, and names such as Toni Sailer have become household words. Skiers flock here for many months, but especially from mid-December until the end of March, reservations are at their tightest at the most fashionable resorts.

Glacier tours around May and June are a big attraction, with mountain climbers appearing in the summer months. Trout fishermen work the waters until the first sniff of autumnal air. July and August bring the most visitors to the province, many of them North Americans, so reservations are essential.

I recommend a private car for getting around, if you can afford it, but only for spring, summer, and fall. If you're not an experienced alpine driver, the other months of the year—especially at some of the remote places—can be hazardous. However, the province is well served by rail and bus connections.

---

1. Innsbruck

The Tyrol capital, Innsbruck (elevation 1,880 feet and population nearly 150,000), is considered one of the most beautiful cities of Europe. It has long been a center of commerce and traffic, as it lies at the junction of two important routes across the central Alps—a north-south and an east-west highway. It's easily reached by rail, air, or road.

The name Innsbruck means "bridge over the Inn," the Inn, of course, being the river that flows through the city, which lies at a meeting place of the Valley of the

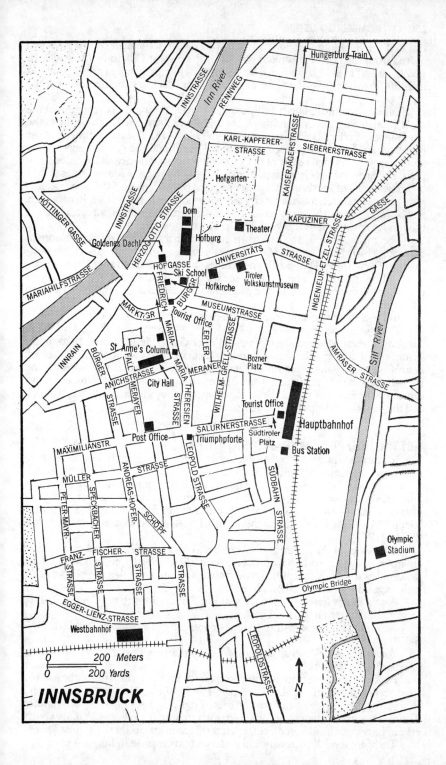

INNSBRUCK

Inn and the Sill Gorge. As long ago as 1180 a little settlement on the river was moved from the northern bank to the site of the present Old Town (Altstadt). In 1239, as a part of Swabia Bavaria, it was granted its own "rights and privileges," and in 1420, Tyrol being by then part of Austria, Innsbruck became the capital of the province.

The city became celebrated throughout Europe during the sovereignty of the Holy Roman Emperor Maximilian I, the Habsburg mentioned above, called "the last knight." Under Maximilian, whose reign (1490–1519) signaled the end of the Middle Ages, Innsbruck reached the height of its cultural and political importance, and it's still the cultural center of the Tyrolean country. The city had its second imperial heyday some 300 years later, during the 40-year reign of Maria Theresa.

The beauty of Innsbruck has been protected by town planners who have seen to it that new structures in the inner city are in harmony with the Gothic, Renaissance, and baroque buildings already standing. Modern urban development spreads along the Inn River east and west, away from the historic areas.

The main street of the old town historic district is the **Herzog-Friedrich-Strasse,** which becomes the Maria-Theresien-Strasse, the main axis of the post-medieval New Town. The Old Town becomes strictly pedestrian after 10:30am, but that's all right, since the only way to see that part of Innsbruck is on foot. For a more complete orientation to the monumental heartland of Innsbruck, refer to "The Sights."

In 1945 this city became the headquarters of the French zone of occupation.

Twice in a dozen years—in 1964 and 1976—the eyes of the world turned to Innsbruck when it hosted the Olympic Winter Games, leading to its becoming a winter-sports center with the most modern facilities. Skiers who come to Innsbruck benefit twice: they stay in a cosmopolitan city called the jewel city of the Alps, and they ski on some of the choicest slopes of the world. Nonskiers and summer visitors can enjoy the sights of the medieval old town, the shops with Tyrolean specialties, and the many excursions into the environs.

GETTING THERE AND TRANSPORTATION

Innsbruck is in the eastern Alps about 30 minutes from the Italian and 45 minutes from the German border. From the south, you can take the Brenner toll motorway. From the east, west, and north, the Inntal motorway brings you here. You can also come by train, as Innsbruck is connected with all parts of Europe by international railway links. There are scheduled flights from Frankfurt, Zurich, and Vienna. For flight information, check with **Tyrolean Airways** at Innsbruck (tel. 0512/81777).

A network of three tram and 25 bus lines covers all of Innsbruck and its close environs. Single tickets in the central area cost 15 AS ($1.10), and a booklet of five tickets goes for 47 AS ($3.40). You can also purchase a number of package deals, including a day ticket for 50 AS ($3.65).

Postal Buses leave from the Central Bus Station, next to the Central Railway Station, heading to all parts of Tyrol.

Taxi stands are in all parts of town, or you can call a radio car (tel. 0512/45-5-00).

You can take a ride in a **fiacre** (horse-drawn carriage) from in front of Tiroler Landestheater, Rennweg.

Parking: If you elect to use your own car for transportation in Innsbruck, you need to know something about parking. The fee for parking in the city center's short-term parking zones (marked by special signs) is 5 AS (35¢) for 30 minutes. The maximum length of time you can stay in one spot is 1½ hours. Parking vouchers can be bought in all post offices, at most tobacconists, and at the Tourist Office.

There are several multistory and underground car parks in Innsbruck.

FAST FACTS

AREA CODE: For Innsbruck and its nearby suburbs, the telephone area code is 0512.

AMERICAN EXPRESS: The office, Brixnerstrasse 3 (tel. 0512/582491), is open Monday to Friday from 9am to 5:30pm and on Saturday from 9am to noon.

BANKS: You can exchange money at banks in all parts of town Monday to Friday from 7:45am to 12:30pm and 2:30 to 4pm; at the Tourist Information Office (see below); and at the Central Railway Station (7:30am to 8:30pm daily).

CONSULATES: U.S. and Canadian visitors, as well as those from New Zealand and Australia, will have to use the consulate in Vienna. There's also an American Consulate in Salzburg. However, British citizens can go to the British Consulate, Mathias-Schmid-Strasse (tel. 0512/588320).

EMERGENCY NUMBERS: In case of trouble, call the following: 5900-0 for police; 59699 for fire; 575544 for an ambulance; and 582122 for mountain rescue.

HOTEL INFORMATION: It's available at the Central Railway Station (Hauptbahnhof) (tel. 0512/583-766-0).

LAUNDROMAT: You will find one at Münzwäscherei Hell, Amraserstrasse 15 (tel. 0512/41367), in the vicinity of the rail station. It's coin-operated. Closed weekends, but open Monday to Friday from 9am to 5pm.

MEDICAL SERVICE: Try University Hospital, located at Anichstrasse 35 (tel. 0512/5040).

PHARMACY: In the heart of Innsbruck, St.-Anna Apotheke, Maria-Theresien-Strasse 4 (tel. 0512/585847), is open Monday to Friday from 8am to 12:30pm and 2:30 to 6pm. As required by law, the pharmacy posts addresses of other pharmacies open on weekends or late at night.

POSTAL CODE: For Innsbruck and its nearby suburbs, the postal code is A-6020.

POST OFFICE: The Hauptpostamt (Central Post Office), Maximilianstrasse 2 (tel. 0512/5000), is open 24 hours a day. The post office at the Central Railway Station, Bruneckerstrasse 1-3, is open daily from 7am to 9pm.

TOURIST INFORMATION OFFICE: Located at Burggraben 3 (tel. 0512/

59850), it will supply you with a wealth of information that will aid you in your visit to Innsbruck and Tyrol. Open daily from 8am to 7pm.

SPORTS

Ski areas around Innsbruck are excellent for winter activity or for summer mountain walks and viewing. Five sunny snow-covered, avalanche-free areas around the capital of Tyrol are served by five cableways, 44 chair lifts, and ski hoists. More detailed information on skiing areas will appear later in this chapter.

In winter the city is also known for bobsled and toboggan runs and ice-skating rinks.

In summer in Innsbruck you can enjoy tennis at a number of courts, golf on either an 18-hole or a 9-hole course, horseback riding, mountaineering, gliding, swimming, hiking, and shooting.

HOTELS

Always arrive with a reservation, as Innsbruck is said never to be out of season. Accommodations are scarce from June until the end of summer and from about mid-December to mid-April.

The Upper Bracket

Hotel Europa Tyrol, Südtiroler Platz 2, A-6020 Innsbruck (tel. 0512/5931). The façade of this elegant hotel dating from 1869 was bombed in World War II and later rebuilt into the modern format you'll see today as you leave the train station. It has been renovated into what is often considered the best hotel in Innsbruck and is part of the Steigenberger Reservations System.

The lobby is a high-ceilinged, formally paneled room with an English-style bar at one end and accents of green marble. The upholstery on many of the chairs is made of leather, set off by the many Oriental rugs. This is a very formal but friendly hotel, with a public image so important that Queen Elizabeth II used it during her stay in Innsbruck. Other personalities who have stayed here have included King Ludwig of Bavaria, the Shah of Iran, General Patton, and everybody from the crew of *Apollo 14* to the original Harlem Globe Trotters.

The uniformed staff is helpful in every way and will usually be willing to show you the heavily ornate yellow-and-white Barock Saal, which the Tyrolean government uses for its most important functions. The ballroom was constructed by King Ludwig's Bavarian architects and builders. The hotel, incidentally, is the official residence for guests of the Tyrolean country government.

The Europa offers a total of 132 handsomely furnished rooms and suites with all the modern conveniences. The rooms are comfortable with Tyrolean or Biedermeier-style decorations. Each tasteful unit is equipped with color TV, minibar, radio, and direct-dial phone, along with a marble bathroom and a hairdryer. Singles range from 1,200 AS ($87.25) to 2,100 AS ($152.75) daily, with doubles going from 1,800 AS ($130.75) to 2,800 AS ($203.50), with breakfast, tax, and service included. The Restaurant Philippine Welser, considered one of the finest in Tyrol, is recommended separately.

Scandi Crown Hotel Innsbruck, Salurnerstrasse 15, A-6020 Innsbruck (tel. 0512/5935-0). Set two blocks from the rail station, the Scandi Crown occupies the tallest building in town, rising 14 stories. Its comfort and its capacity for conferences for up to 300 persons have turned it into one of the best hotels in Tyrol. A gracefully landscaped garden prefaces its russet-colored bulk. You register in a spacious modern lobby, whose walls are layered with a sheath of burnished brass trim and cherrywood. Facilities include both a Caffino-Bar and a top-notch restaurant (more about that later).

All of the 191 well-furnished bedrooms provide some kind of view over the baroque spires of Innsbruck and its ring-around mountains. They contain built-in furniture, tile baths, color TVs, phones, minibars, and all the extras you'd expect of a four-star hotel. With a buffet breakfast, singles cost 1,300 AS ($94.50) daily, with doubles going for 1,800 AS ($130.75). There is a heated swimming pool and a sauna.

Hotel Innsbruck, Innrain 3, A-6020 Innsbruck (tel. 0512/34511), lies on the border of the Altstadt near the Congress Center, fronting the Inn River. The government rates it 4½ stars (five stars is the maximum), which puts it in the celestial galaxy of Innsbruck, right after the Europa Tyrol and the Scandi Crown, already recommended. If you're driving, underground parking is available on the premises. The public rooms are not vast. You register at the main reception, a marble-floored area graced with Oriental carpeting and modern lighting fixtures. The 90 rooms tend to be handsomely furnished in a contemporary idiom, and the better ones have small sitting areas. Each has a private bath. Depending on the season, singles rent for 850 AS ($61.75) to 1,500 AS ($109), doubles for 1,200 AS ($87.25) to 2,200 AS ($160). Some apartments are even more expensive. Skiers returning from the slopes can relax at the small pool area. Later, they can enjoy both Austrian and international specialties in a choice of three dining rooms, the most interesting of which is decorated like a Tyrolean stube with dirndl-clad waitresses. The hotel also owns the less expensive Roter Adler (recommended below).

Romantikhotel-Restaurant Schwarzer Adler, Kaiserjägerstrasse 2, A-6020 Innsbruck (tel. 0512/58-71-09), is a nostalgic choice, preferred by many traditionalists to the Hotel Goldener Adler (see below). An appealing alternative to the modern hotels of Innsbruck, the Schwarzer Adler lies behind an antique façade of stucco, shutters, and a big-windowed tower. The Ultsch family, owners of the hotel, wisely respected its history when they furnished the interior in an authentic style with lots of Austrian charm. Aged paneling, vaulted ceilings, hand-painted regional furniture, antiques, and lots of gemülich clutter make for a cozy, intimate, and inviting ambience. The 26 bedrooms are virtually one of a kind, each with its special character and period décor, but each containing all the desired amenities of a modern hotel. The hotel rooms exude a feeling of comfort and hospitality, a sense of security enhanced by the helpful staff. Rates depend on the season: singles cost 650 AS ($47.25) to 950 AS ($69) daily; doubles, 500 AS ($36.25) to 800 AS ($58.25) per person. A few apartments are even more luxurious, but higher in price, of course.

Guests can dine in the original Tiroler Stube, with a history going back four centuries, or in the K. u K. (Kaiser and König) Restaurant, which has won awards for its modern Austrian cuisine. In fact, the restaurant is so popular that it's sometimes difficult to get a table reservation. Nevertheless, it's worth a try. Main courses include such dishes as veal filet Romantik with mushrooms and leaf spinach in puff pastry, venison medallions, and poached salmon or trout "any way you want it." Meals cost from 400 AS ($29), and service is daily except Tuesday from 11:30am to 2pm and 6 to 11pm.

Hotel Goldener Adler, Herzog-Friedrich-Strasse 6, A-6020 Innsbruck (tel. 0512/58-63-34). Even the phone booth near the reception desk of this 600-year-old hotel is outfitted in an antique style, concealed behind an old panel. Famous guests have included Goethe; the brother of Marie Antoinette (Joseph II, who arrived incognito in 1777); King Gustav III of Sweden (1783); the violinist Paganini, who cut his name into the windowpane of the room; and in 1573, Duke Albert V of Bavaria, who arrived with his son and a retinue of 416 people.

This hotel contains 31 rooms in a family-run format of leaded windows with stained-glass inserts, travertine floors, ornately carved Tyrolean furniture, and chandeliers where human figures are carved from ram's horns. The reception desk is on the first floor, above the heavy stone buttresses of the street level. Rooms are handsomely styled and furnished, costing 650 AS ($47.25) to 850 AS ($61.75) for a single, 1,000 AS ($72.70) to 1,600 AS ($116.30) for a double, the latter price for a deluxe accommodation. A buffet breakfast is included in the charges.

Hotel Central, Am Sparkassenplatz, A-6020 Innsbruck (tel. 0512/5920), is one of the most unusual hotels in town. It's housed in a hi-tech format of textured concrete with windows whose edges are beveled into angular glass-and-steel rectangles. The lobby floor is covered with hand-set mosaics of colored paving blocks arranged into pastel-colored circles. Above your head, it looks as if a bubble-making machine went crazy. Hundreds of glass balls hang from the high ceiling on golden strands of metal wire.

The management is capable, and will invite you to use the indoor pool and sauna on the top floor. For a total contrast to the rest of the hotel, guests can patronize a Viennese café with marble columns, sculptured ceilings, large gilt-and-crystal chandeliers, and a collection of international newspapers. The comfortable, modernized rooms—87 in all—evoke an almost Japanese sense of simplicity. Doubles range from 1,100 AS ($80) to 1,800 AS ($130.75), singles from 800 AS ($58.25) to 1,250 AS ($91), with breakfast included. Prices depend on the season.

Alpotel Tirol, Innrain 13, A-6020 Innsbruck (tel. 0512/57-79-31), is one of the leading four-star hotels of Innsbruck, lying right in the center of town, just a few walking minutes away from the historical district and the Maria-Theresien-Strasse. Even though the hotel has a choice location, it offers quiet rooms, facing either the garden or a courtyard. (It was built into an old convent.) All 73 rooms are furnished with private baths or showers, phones, radios, minibars, and color TVs. Most of them have terraces or balconies. Doubles, depending on the time of year, range from 600 AS ($43.50) to 720 AS ($52.25) per person daily. Singles pay a daily supplement of 200 AS ($14.50). Other facilities include a sauna, a sun bed, and underground parking. The hotel restaurant, Tiroler Stuben, is one of the best in town, offering clients a cozy, cultivated atmosphere. Guests are served not only typical Tyrolean food but specialties from France. Management also offers winter-sports guests free transportation to and from five different ski areas around Innsbruck.

Hotel Maria Theresia, Maria-Theresien-Strasse 31, A-6020 Innsbruck (tel. 0512/5933), behind an elegantly classic façade, is the best-known hotel on this famous shopping street a few blocks away from the winding alleys of the oldest parts of Innsbruck. A striking oil portrait of the empress herself hangs in the reception area. The helpful staff at this Best Western hotel will do everything possible to make you feel comfortable. Singles rent for 750 AS ($54.55) to 1,150 AS ($83.60) daily, with doubles costing 1,200 AS ($87.25) to 1,800 AS ($130.75); breakfast is included. All 104 rooms have been recently redecorated. Underground parking is available for guests.

Hotel Roter Adler, Seilergasse 4, A-6020 Innsbruck (tel. 0512/21069), is a renovated first-class hotel inside a 500-year-old house in the Altstadt. In the lobby, brightly covered banquettes curve around the antique stone arches that support the vaulted ceilings. The rest of the establishment has lots of exposed wood and cozy corners. Charges for the rooms range from 650 AS ($47.25) to 1,200 AS ($87.25) for singles and from 850 AS ($61.75) to 1,500 AS ($109) for doubles, the rate depending on the season. Breakfast is included. The 50 accommodations, for the most part, are commodious but simply furnished. The Roter Adler is under the same ownership as the more expensive Hotel Innsbruck, already recommended.

Hotel Grauer Bär, Universitätsstrasse 5-7, A-6020 Innsbruck (tel. 0512/5924), is located in the center of Innsbruck, next to the Imperial Gardens, the most interesting sights, and the shopping area. To the side of a large lobby is a persimmon-colored dining room with an ornate ribbed and vaulted white ceiling supported by a central stone column. The 115 rooms with private facilities cost 900 AS ($65.50) daily for a single and 720 AS ($52.25) per person for a double. A buffet breakfast is included. There is a cozy Tyrolean bar, and private car parking is available.

The Middle Bracket

Hotel Maximilian, Marktgraben 7-9, A-6020 Innsbruck (tel. 0512/59-967). Built in 1982, this inner-city hotel rates as one of the most attractive and up-to-date in Innsbruck. It sacrifices little of the antique charm of yesterday in its willingness to provide modern and convenient accommodations. The woodwork in the lobby is a beautifully crafted example of fine carpentry, while the reception desk is staffed with a bevy of helpful people. The 40 rooms are modern and comfortable. The most desirable ones look out over the back, where you'll have a closeup view of the shingled onion dome of the oldest church in Innsbruck (now used as the headquarters of a company that makes keys). Each of the rooms has an attractive bath and comes with breakfast included. For bed-and-breakfast, the cost ranges from 500 AS ($36.25) to 600 AS ($43.50) per person daily.

Villa Blanka, Weiherburggasse 8, A-6020 Innsbruck (tel. 0512/89-22-57), is a balconied modern hotel designed in a big-windowed rectangular format looking out over a well-planted park. It lies about 20 pedestrian minutes from the center of the city. The inside is filled with contoured leather chairs, big paintings, and a series of paneled rooms with coffered ceilings ranging from the contemporary to the rustically conservative. The long sun terrace is set on a balcony above the ground floor, with a view over the rare trees of the hotel's landscaping. The hotel rents 19 pleasantly and comfortably furnished bedrooms, each with private bath or shower. Bed-and-breakfast costs from 550 AS ($40) to 780 AS ($56.75) per person daily.

Hotel Mozart, Müllerstrasse 15, A-6020 Innsbruck (tel. 0512/59538), is a renovated 42-room hotel with a central location and a pleasant series of spacious bedrooms. Comfortably furnished singles rent for 560 AS ($40.75) to 820 AS ($59.50) daily, while doubles cost 630 AS ($45.75) to 1,000 AS ($72.75). All units contain private baths.

Hotel Greif, Leopoldstrasse 3, A-6020 Innsbruck (tel. 0512/58-74-01), is a five-story building with a light-brown façade and a desirable location near Innsbruck's Triumphal Arch. The vertical neon sign bolted to the side of the building illuminates the neoclassic pediments above each of the big windows. The modernized interior is filled with comfortable furniture, warm colors of beige, white, and crimson, along with adaptations of chalet chairs. The hotel rents 86 well-furnished bedrooms, each with private bath or shower. For bed-and-breakfast, the rate ranges from 500 AS ($36.25) to 650 AS ($47.25) per person daily. Several small dining rooms are decorated in Tyrolean style.

Hotel Royal, Innrain 16, A-6020 Innsbruck (tel. 0512/58-63-85), is a modern 20-room hotel with a riverside location convenient to everything in the city. Of interest to motorists, it has enough parking to give you a free spot (usually). The sunny dining room is pleasingly filled with carpeting and brightly colored walls. Each of the spacious and comfortable bedrooms is simply and attractively furnished, with its own private bath, small TV, phone, and radio. Doubles cost from 1,100 AS ($80), and singles rent from 720 AS ($52.25) daily, with breakfast included.

Tourotel Breinössl, Maria-Theresien-Strasse 12, A-6020 Innsbruck (tel. 0512/584165), lies behind an unusual blue-green façade on a major street of Innsbruck, next door to the famous Golden Roof. It's covered with flowered loggias and gently protruding bay windows. The inside is tastefully woodsy, with lots of hanging cloth lamps in the paneled restaurant, welcome touches of wrought iron and regional sculpture in the rustic restaurant, and attractively modern furniture in the 41 comfortable bedrooms. Singles range from 715 AS ($52) to 780 AS ($56.75), doubles from 1,080 AS ($78.50) to 1,180 AS ($85.75), with breakfast included. All accommodations contain private baths, phones, radios, minibars, and color TVs. In summer, guests enjoy a beer garden with music.

The Budget Range

Gasthof-Hotel Weisses Kreuz, Herzog-Friedrich-Strasse 31, A-6020 Innsbruck (tel. 0512/59479), lies on a street in the Old Town, which has changed little since 13-year-old Wolfgang and his father, Leopold Mozart, stayed here in 1769. Today the Josef Ortner family welcomes you to this famous old inn dating from 1465. The hotel's façade is relieved by an extended bay window, stretching from the second to the fourth floor. The ground floor is pierced by an arcade, while naïve stencils adorn the white stucco of the upper stories. A wrought-iron sign extending over the sidewalk holds the symbol of the hotel, a white cross.

You'll have to climb past two restaurants and a series of hand-painted ceramic plates set into the stucco of the stairway before arriving at the reception area. There you'll be pleasantly surprised by the carved stone columns, a TV room with an arched wood-covered ceiling, a collection of massive Tyrolean chests, and a carved balustrade worn smooth by the palms of generations of visitors. The hotel offers 39 bedrooms, 28 with private baths or showers. Singles range from 360 AS ($26.25) to 620 AS ($45) daily, doubles from 320 AS ($23.25) to 510 AS ($37) per person. For half board, add 115 AS ($8.25) per person daily to the rates.

Pension Stoi, Salurnerstrasse 7, A-6020 Innsbruck (tel. 0512/585434), is an unpretentious 12-room pension three minutes from the train station. Charges for the simply furnished rooms are 270 AS ($19.75) daily for a single, 420 AS ($30.50) for a double, 570 AS ($41.50) for a triple, and 680 AS ($49.50) for a quad. Service and taxes are included in the rates. Showers are free.

City-Hotel Goldene Krone, Maria-Theresien-Strasse 46, A-6020 Innsbruck (tel. 0512/58-61-60), is a baroque house with a green-and-white façade near the Triumphal Arch on Innsbruck's main street. All 35 rooms are modern and furnished with private showers; most of them have telephones. The hotel offers three-star comfort: an elevator, soundproof windows, and a Viennese-inspired coffeehouse, the Art-Gallery-Café, where an all-day salad buffet is set up every day from 11:30am to 2pm. The café is open daily except Sunday from 7am to 9pm. Single rooms cost 480 AS ($35) to 550 AS ($40), with doubles going for 380 AS ($27.75) to 450 AS ($32.75) per person, including breakfast buffet.

Staying at Hungerburg

Hotel Bellevue, Hochinnsbruck/Hungerburg, A-6020 Innsbruck (tel. 0512/89-23-36), is a large and rambling white-walled building with a well-maintained series of flowered balconies and grassy lawns. My favorite room has a red–and –blue-black Persian carpet and a high ceiling of honey-colored beams and brass chandeliers. On the premises are an indoor pool, a sauna, a solarium, a restaurant, a café, and the kind of bar you'd like to spend time in. From the windows of the spacious modern bedrooms you'll have a view of the mountains and the city of Innsbruck. The hotel offers 64 bedrooms, each with private bath or shower. Half-board terms range from 590 AS ($43) to 670 AS ($48.75) per person daily. Rates depend on the location of the units, each of which contains a private bath. The hotel is closed from late October to mid-December.

Hotel Pension zur Linde, A-6020 Hungerburg (tel. 0512/89-23-45), is a six-room Tyrolean inn with a complicated hipped and gabled roof covered in red tiles, plus a central slate-covered tower capped with a weathervane—usually pointing to the nearby mountains. The house is furnished with many antiques, plus original paintings and sculptures by regional artists. All the rooms have private balconies, which look down on the pleasant sun terrace. Most rooms have private showers and toilets. Prices for bed-and-breakfast are 280 AS ($20.25) to 480 AS ($35) per person daily, depending on the season. On the premises are gardens, a café, and a wine restaurant, as well as a private parking area and garages. The Patscheider family are the agreeable hosts.

Pension Alpina, Hungerburgweg 4, A-6020 Innsbruck (tel. 0512/892340). Botanists will love naming the varieties of flowers that grow from the window boxes attached to the three floors of balconies of this family-run hotel. Guests often choose to sit under the parasols on the lawn, sipping coffee and planning their next excursion to Innsbruck. The interior is paneled in light-grained pine, with alpine-style stools around the bar. The accommodating designer of this place surrounded the ceramic oven in the restaurant with a banquette. The Mair family prepares homemade pastries, the biggest in town, fresh every day in the café. The bedrooms, all with showers and toilets, rent for 350 AS ($25.50) daily for a single, 330 AS ($24) per person for a double, with breakfast included.

Lodging at Amras

Hotel Kapeller, Philippine-Welser-Strasse 96, Amras, A-6020 Innsbruck (tel. 0512/43106). You'll notice several pieces of polychrome church art scattered throughout the public rooms here, as well as a stone- and wood-trimmed décor of well-crafted rusticity. The hotel's restaurant is comfortable and serves good food, while the rest of the establishment is satisfactory and above average. It has a cozy bar in the lobby and a garden. The Happ family offers 36 well-furnished bedrooms, each with private bath or shower. Half board in winter ranges from 700 AS ($51) to 880 AS ($64) per person daily; in summer, from 740 AS ($53.75) to 920 AS ($67). The hotel stands near the church in the center of the village, about a mile and a quarter east of the town center of Innsbruck. Tram line no. 3 runs nearby.

WHERE TO DINE

This is never a problem in Innsbruck, as this alpine town has more than 150 restaurants, inns, and cafés, some of which offer entertainment at night. I suggest that if you're only going to be in Austria for a short time, you should stick to original Tyrolean specialties. However, if that doesn't suit you, an array of international cookery is offered as well.

The Leading Restaurants

Philippine Welser, Hotel Europa Tyrol, Südtiroler Platz 2 (tel. 0512/5931), in this already-previewed hotel, considered "the finest address in Innsbruck," is a distinguished restaurant. Against a delightful Tyrolean ambience, it serves both the guests of this five-star hotel as well as the general public. Traditional regional and creative cookery is the chef's motto, and he achieves his aim exceedingly well. The restaurant is dedicated to Philippine Welser, the "beautiful Augsburgerin" and wife of Archduke Ferdinand. She is known because of the greatest romance of the 16th century and also because of her handwritten cookbook, which made culinary history.

Typical dishes served today are likely to include marinated leg of lamb with a lentil salad, smoked venison with onions, and saddle of red deer in a ginger sauce. The crusty Philippine Welser pie contains sweetbreads, veal, tongue, and morels. Sometimes you can order a braised knuckle of veal. For dessert, you might try one of the specials such as a gingerbread soufflé with apple cream. Service is daily from 11:30am to 11pm. Fixed-price menus range from 200 AS ($14.50) to 250 AS ($18.25).

Scandiarama, Scandi Crown Hotel Innsbruck, Salurnerstrasse 15 (tel. 0512/5935-0), is one of the city's leading restaurants. One floor above the lobby level of this previously recommended four-star hotel, it is outfitted in a modern version of Jugendstil (art nouveau). It boasts a stained-glass skylight, a huge bank of curved windows overlooking the mountains, and a soothing pastel-tinted décor of soft pinks and creams. Dinner is served nightly from 6 to 11pm, costing from 320 AS ($23.25) on the à la carte menu. On Sunday and holidays, a Royal Swedish smörgåsbord is presented, a groaning buffet of freshly imported Swedish delicacies, costing from 230 AS ($16.75) per person. Service is from noon to 3pm at those times. Reservations are always important.

Domstuben, Pfarrgasse 3 (tel. 0512/33353), is located, as its German name implies, near the cathedral of St. Jakob. You can choose between the ground-floor and the upper-level restaurant, both of them rustically and tastefully filled with lots of wood and handcrafted details. The lower level has a vaulted ceiling. Hors d'oeuvres come from a well-stocked buffet. They might be followed by such delectable dishes as Bohemian veal gulasch with homemade egg noodles, Ticino-style venison, or grilled scampi. Look for the daily specials as well. To follow, you face a full range of desserts, perhaps kiwi mango salad in Grand Marnier with vanilla cream. À la carte meals range from 300 AS ($21.75). The restaurant is open daily from 11:30am to 2pm and 6 to 10:30pm, and reservations are suggested.

Bistro, Pradlerstrasse 2 (tel. 0512/46-3-19), is set in a turn-of-the-century house whose edge lies just a few paces from the Sil River. It requires a brisk but invigorating 10-minute walk from the center of the Old Town. There's a charming but cramped apéritif bar near the entrance where you can order a drink before heading into the soothingly pink dining room. The creative statement of Innsbruck-born Heinz Hagleitner, the restaurant contains 40 seats, plus a handful of tables set beside the river in summer. À la carte dinners range in price from 250 AS ($18.25) to 350 AS ($25.50); however, you can order a set menu at lunch for only 120 AS ($8.75). Specialties include an array of fresh fish such as zander, trout, salmon, and sole. You can also order such well-prepared dishes as chicken stuffed with ham, bread crumbs, and spinach, and many veal, lamb, and beef dishes. Full meals are served daily except Sunday from 11am to 2:30pm and 5pm to midnight.

Weinhaus Jörgele, Herzog-Friedrich-Strasse 13 (tel. 0512/57-11-55), is an attractive, historic wine house brimming with atmosphere and a rustic Tyrolean décor. H. P. Cammerlander, the proprietor, and his staff work hard to create an inviting ambience—successfully so, if you judge by the repeat customers. On the ground floor you can stop at the wine bar, with the wine cellar in the background; here you can taste some excellent Austrian and Italian vintages. Upstairs you enter a gemütlich restaurant, where traditional foods of the winelands are served. Meals are priced at around 200 AS ($14.50). With the extensive menu and wine list found here, you're sure to enjoy yourself. Hours are 10am to 1am daily.

Restaurant Goldener Adler, Herzog-Friedrich-Strasse 6 (tel. 0512/58-63-34), is the kind of Teutonic establishment that has a firm reputation and a loyal following. Visitors from other Austrian cities often plan ahead to eat here, in the same way that Goethe did when he visited Innsbruck so long ago. The menu is attractively old-fashioned, specializing in such Tyrolean dishes as braised beef, veal Tyrolean style, noodles with sauerkraut, cabbage soup with bacon, and a superb tafelspitz. There's also fondue, and for dessert, try the Salzburger nockerl. A full meal will cost from 350 AS ($25.50). You can dine in the Andreas-Hofer Stube or the Kaiser-Josef Stube on the second floor or in the Batzenhäusl or Goethe Stube downstairs. The latter is an evening restaurant, with meals accompanied by zither music. The same menu and prices apply to all the rooms. The place is open daily from 6:30am to midnight.

Picnic, Fallmerayerstrasse 12 (tel. 0512/23859), is a chic eatery, the kind of place where Liza Minnelli might feel at home singing "New York, New York." You climb a flight above street level to the slope-ceilinged restaurant, with terra-cotta floors, Oriental carpets, and exposed brick. The place exudes an aura of warmth even on the coldest nights. If you arrive early—and you should make a reservation—Innsbruck—you can stop for a drink in a bar below the restaurant, which attracts Innsbruck youth. The menu is sophisticated and international, with a wide selection of well-prepared dishes made from very fresh ingredients. You can, for example, select carpaccio, fish soup, French snails with garlic bread, or a perfectly done peppersteak or fresh salmon. The mixed fish platter is invariably good. Menus begin at 150 AS ($11), with many dinners averaging 420 AS ($30.50). The café-restaurant is open daily except Sunday from 11am to midnight.

Moderate to Budget Dining

Churrasco, Innrain 2 (tel. 0512/58-63-98), is a warmly decorated pizzeria housed in a pink stucco building at the riverside. Inside, you'll see an airy and comfortable décor, including a copper sculpture composed of vertical pipes of varying sizes welded together above the bar. You can sit in one of several rooms. You climb antique stairs to the second floor to reach the pizzeria, La Mamma. There you can enjoy such specialties as game alla carbonara, a mixed fish roast, and at least 16 pasta dishes and seven different meat specialties. In summer the management places tables outside at the edge of the river. Full meals range from 180 AS ($13) to 315 AS ($23), depending on what you order. Specialties on the ground floor are the same, except for the emphasis on grilled meats. The pizzeria is open daily from 9am to midnight.

Moby Dick, Adamsgasse (tel. 0512/57-35-80), near the train station, has a dimly lit ambience and a nautical theme, as its name would suggest. Although having little to do with historic Innsbruck, it's still a relaxing place to drop into for a drink, a snack, or a seafood dinner. The décor includes a horseshoe-shaped bar and lots of ship's lanterns and polished brass. Menu items run to quick lunches and all the seafood you'd expect. Full meals range from 180 AS ($13) to 315 AS ($23). The establishment is open all day from 7am to 11:30pm (on Sunday from 8am to 11:30pm).

Stiftskeller, Burggraben 31 (tel. 0512/58-34-90). This restaurant is housed in an 18th-century yellow-and-white palace, whose baroque detailing can be admired from the streetside beer garden. At night the garden is illuminated by lights attached to the shade trees. In cold weather you can, of course, dine inside. There, a crucifix of a tormented Christ hangs with other pieces of sculpture under a high wooden ceiling in one of the atmospheric rooms. There are several other seating possibilities down some of the tile corridors.

This place can get rowdy at night, but the management works hard cleaning up the next day to prepare for another onslaught. Meals are posted on a blackboard, and they usually include soup, a main course, and dessert for around 150 AS ($11). Typical menu items include spaghetti carbonara and venison schnitzel in a pheasant-flavored cream sauce, followed by fresh homemade apple strudel. The cellar is open daily from 9am to midnight.

Stiegl-Bräu, Wilhelm-Greil-Strasse 25 (tel. 0512/58-43-38), is a likable Tyrolean place in the center of town. Popular with locals because of its well-prepared homemade food, the restaurant offers three different wood-paneled rooms, plus copious amounts of wine and beer if you want that. Fixed-price meals range from 90 AS ($6.50) to 180 AS ($13), and are served daily from 8:30am to 10pm. In summer, guests can patronize a cozy beer garden.

Weisses Kreuz Restaurant, Herzog-Friedrich-Strasse 31 (tel. 0512/59-479), in Gasthof-Hotel Weisses Kreuz, is a good place to find typical Tyrolean food served in a country atmosphere generated by the painted façade and the happily cluttered, rustic interior. The restaurant on the second floor is open daily from 11am to 2:30pm and 5:30pm to midnight. During the summer season, a zither player entertains guests in the evening. On the first floor, a bar and a snack restaurant are open all day, as is a beer garden just in front of the hotel in Innsbruck's pedestrian area. In all the facilities, you can stop in just for a beer, but if you're hungry, you'll find a good selection of simply prepared fare, including Wiener schnitzel, rumpsteak with french fries, and grilled chicken. A full meal costs from 250 AS ($18.25).

Restaurant Kaffee Ottoburg, Herzog-Friedrich-Strasse 1 (tel. 0512/57-46-52), dating from the 13th century, is almost completely covered in wood and has brocaded chairs and Tyrolean music playing from near the well-stocked bar area. Beer comes in tall clear glasses without handles. Upstairs is a well-known restaurant, separated into four rooms on two different floors, each having the same menu. They have names such as Maximilian Stube and Herzogstube. Each room holds a maximum of five tables in a setting that might be called "19th-century Gothic." The décor includes paneling grown smoky with time, carefully notched ceiling beams, and irregular floor plans, which create nooks and out-of-the-way crannies for intimate dining.

A daily menu is offered for 150 AS ($11). Dishes include venison stew, a special mixed grill, pork chops with rice and carrots, and fried trout, the latter priced by the gram. The chef will also do a veal shank for two persons. The international menu emphasizes Tyrolean specialties, best seen in the dessert list, which offers two kinds of strudel and several other pastries. An average à la carte meal will cost from 180 AS ($13). Hours are 10am to midnight daily.

Altstadtstüberl, Riesengasse 13 (tel. 0512/58-23-47). Authentically gemütlich in cuisine and ambience, the restaurant is located on the street level of a building whose walls date from 1360. The flavorful food includes a salad buffet of fresh ingredients, along with several different kinds of wursts and sausages and such specialties as racks of lamb and roulades of beef and pork. You can dine here on many different price levels, ordering a simple meal for 100 AS ($7.25) or an elaborate spread for 500 AS ($36.25). Meals are served daily except Sunday from 11am to 3:30pm and 6 to 11pm.

Hirschen-Stuben, Kiebachgasse 5 (tel. 0512/58-29-79). The old-style décor of this Tyrolean restaurant encompasses two rooms, one with a beamed and one with a vaulted ceiling. You'll see hand-chiseled stone columns, brocade chairs, and a large stainless-steel bar dividing the two rooms. You'll have to go down a few steps from street level, but once you're there you can select an array of daily specials that might include fish soup, trout meunière, sliced veal in cream sauce Zurich style, veal steak with morels and cream sauce, beef Stroganoff, and peppersteak. In addition to Tyrolean dishes, the chef also prepares Italian specialties, including pastas, osso bucco, saltimbocca, and piccata milanese. A fixed-price lunch costs only 100 AS ($7.25), with à la carte dinners averaging 200 AS ($14.50). Lunch is served from 11am to 2pm and dinner from 6 to 11pm; closed Sunday. Reservations are suggested.

Basco, Anichstrasse 12 (tel. 0512/58-04-02). Set into a shop-lined street running into the busy Maria-Theresien-Strasse, this long and narrow restaurant stretches almost endlessly past an animated array of open kitchens and crowded bars. Many guests come here just for a drink, planting themselves with their friends and sometimes their dogs on one of the sun-flooded stools in front. A busy corridor leads past the open kitchens, where teams of uniformed chefs prepare the establishment's medley of Italian, Mexican, and Spanish cuisines. Dining tables are set in back amid a greenhouse décor of live plants, a bubbling fountain, and pinpoint lighting. Some of the menu items are meant for two persons, including paella and the fritto misto di mare. You can also try tortelloni tricolore, several kinds of enchiladas, a handful of fish dishes (including filet of sole), and an array of grills such as a juicy "Cattlemansteak." Full meals cost from 250 AS ($18.25). The restaurant is open daily from 7am to midnight, except on Sunday and holidays, when it is open from 8:15am to midnight.

Weisses Rössl, Kiebachgasse 8 (tel. 0512/58305). You'll enter this time-honored place through a stone archway opening onto one of the most famous streets of the old town. At the end of a flight of stairs with a crucifix at the top, you'll find two rooms with red-tile floors and about the most extensive set of stag horns (complete with the initials of the hunter and the date of the shooting) in Innsbruck. The simple menu offers daily specials and typical Tyrolean dishes usually served with pommes frites. Specials include saftgulasch with polenta, a grilled plate "alt insprugg" served for two persons, and a variety of schnitzels. Service is efficient, and meals range from 120 AS ($8.75) to 325 AS ($23.75). Hours are 7:30am to 3pm and 5pm to midnight; closed on Sunday and for all of November.

Wienerwald Breinössl, Maria-Theresien-Strasse 12 (tel. 0512/58-41-65). This chain might be called the Howard Johnson's of Austria. It offers chain-restaurant gemütlichkeit, generous portions, and hours that are usually longer than those of many smaller restaurants, including on Sunday. That is, from 8am to 1am. This particular branch is on one of the main inner-city streets of town. It encompasses a cavernous beer hall with a high ceiling, plus several smaller rooms. The simple and wholesome food includes four kinds of soup, three kinds of salad, six kinds of chicken, and three kinds of schnitzel, along with a sampling of beef and pork dishes. A children's menu is also offered, and beer and wine are served by the glass. The menu is in both English and German, and a meal usually ranges from 120 AS ($8.75) to 200 AS ($14.50), depending on what you order.

Some Leading Cafés

Café Munding, Keibachstrasse 16 (tel. 0512/58-41-18), on a quiet corner in the old town, is a comfortable-looking house built in 1720 in a baroque format of frescoes, carved bay windows, and lots of Tyrolean detailing. The interior has been modernized, offering an interconnected series of rooms, one of which has an ornate plaster ceiling and an abstract mural. The first thing you'll see when you enter is a pastry and chocolate shop. Food is served in the inner rooms; in addition to coffee priced from 25 AS ($1.80), it includes pizzas and toast, plus wine by the glass. The café is open daily from 8am to 10pm.

Stadtcafé, Rennweg 2 (tel. 0512/58-68-69). Between sips of your coffee, priced from 20 AS ($1.45), you can admire the attending nymphs and deities supporting the base of the equestrian statue in front of the elegantly modern café. It has a tall ceiling with starburst chandeliers, warmly tinted banquettes, and large photographs of theatrical scenes from the nearby Landestheater. It is open daily from 9am to midnight, with hot food served from 11am to 3pm and 5 to 11pm. In addition to coffee and pastries, you can also order full meals here, including grilled pork, veal, rumpsteak with poppyseed noodles, pasta, Tyrolean soups, and ham-and-cheese sandwiches. A menu of the day costs 150 AS ($11).

Alte Testube, Riesengasse 6 (tel. 0512/58-23-09), is the only teahouse of its kind in Tyrol. It offers 50 varieties of tea, costing from 18 AS ($1.30). Connoisseurs know that the best tea is brewed in a porcelain pot. The music that will probably accompany your beverage at this old-fashioned tea room might have pleased Mozart or one of his contemporaries. Any cup of tea goes well with the pastries glistening temptingly in the light from brass candlesticks. The location is one flight above a street-level restaurant in the center of the old town. The establishment is open every day except Sunday from 11am to 7pm.

Dining in the Environs

Restaurant Kapeller, Hotel Kapeller, Philippine-Welser-Strasse 96 (tel. 0512/43106), at Amras on the periphery of Innsbruck, about three-quarters of a mile from the town center, is set in a beautiful décor of modernized chalet chairs, Oriental rugs, and a tasteful combination of stone, stucco, and wood. Menu items are imaginatively light, including salads made with generous amounts of radicchio, avocados, mushrooms, and Gorgonzola. If you like soup, try the cream of fennel, and if you're looking for fish, sample the John Dory in white wine sauce or the fresh trout. Meat courses include venison in season, tafelspitz, filet of roast hare, and many veal and pork specialties. Set menus range from 200 AS ($14.50) to 550 AS ($40), with à la carte orders starting at 150 AS ($11). The owners, Johanna and Ferdinand Happ, open the dining room at 6am, closing it at midnight daily except Sunday and for all of January. Reservations for dinner are strongly suggested. There's open-air dining on the terrace in summer.

Gasthof Wilder Mann (tel. 0512/77387) at Lans. If you appreciate architecture, you'll enjoy studying the stucco tower attached to the corner of this elongated building with the half-timbered triangular section just under the sloping roofline. The interior is spacious and rustic, with good service and a series of well-prepared traditional specialties such as wine soup, venison pâté with cumberland sauce, and filet steak in a pepper-cream sauce. Dessert could be a Salzburger nockerl. Meals average about 320 AS ($23.25). The restaurant is open daily from 11am to 11pm. The Schatz and Schöpt families are the gracious owners of the place.

THE SIGHTS

As I mentioned above, **Maria-Theresien-Strasse,** which cuts through the heart of the city from north to south, is the main street of Innsbruck, a good place to begin your exploration. Often it's fascinating just to watch the passersby, especially when they're attired in the Tyrolean regional dress. Once this street was traversed by wayfarers heading over the Brenner Pass from Italy and on to Germany. Many 17th- and 18th-century houses line Maria-Theresien-Strasse.

On the south end of this wide street, a **Triumphpforte** (Triumphal Arch), modeled after those in Rome, spans the shopping street. Maria Theresa ordered it built in 1765 with a twofold purpose: to honor the marriage of her son, the Duke of Tuscany (later Emperor Leopold II), to a Spanish princess, and to mourn the death of her beloved husband, Emperor Franz I. From this arch southward the street is called Leopoldstrasse.

Going north from the arch along Maria-Theresien-Strasse you'll see **St. Anna's Column** (Annasäule), which every visitor seems to photograph. It enjoys the same renown in Innsbruck as the Eros statue does in Piccadilly Circus. Standing in front of the 19th-century Rathaus (the present Town Hall), the column was erected in 1706 in thanksgiving for the withdrawal in 1703 of invading Bavarian armies during the War of the Spanish Succession. On top of this Corinthian column a statue of the Virgin Mary stands on a crescent moon, with statues of the Saints Cassianus, Virgilius, George, and Anna surrounding the base.

Not far north of the Annasäule, the wide street narrows and becomes the Herzog-Friedrich-Strasse running through the heart of the **Altstadt** (Old Town), the medieval quarter. This street is arcaded and flanked by a number of well-maintained burghers' houses with their jumble of turrets and gables. Look for the multitude of dormer windows and oriels. Most of the buildings here are overhung with protective roofs to guard them against snowfalls.

Farther north stands the **Hofburg,** Rennweg 1 (tel. 0512/58-71-86), the 15th-century imperial palace of Emperor Maximilian I, rebuilt in rococo style in the 18th century on orders of Maria Theresa. Later it was to hold sad memories for the empress, as it was here that her husband died in 1765. The palace, the exterior of which is colored Maria Theresa ochre (a yellow that the empress favored) and flanked by a set of domed towers, is a fine example of baroque secular architecture. The structure has four wings and a two-story Riesensaal (Giant's Hall), painted in white and gold and filled with portraits of the Habsburgs. The rooms recall the power and heyday of that ruling family.

You can visit the state rooms, the house chapel, the private apartment, and the Riesensaal on guided tours, lasting about half an hour, daily from 9am to 4pm. The palace is closed Sunday from mid-October to mid-May. Admission is 20 AS ($1.45).

The Gothic-style **Hofkirche,** Universitätsstrasse 2 (tel. 0512/58-43-02), was built in 1553 by Ferdinand I. It's most important treasure is the cenotaph of Maximilian I, although his remains, alas, are not in this elegant marble sarcophagus glorifying the Roman Empire. He was never brought here from Wiener Neustadt, where he was entombed in 1519. The tomb, a great feat of the German Renaissance style of sculpture, has 28 bronze 16th-century statues of Maximilian's real and legendary ancestors and relatives surrounding the kneeling emperor on the cenotaph, with 24 marble reliefs on the sides depicting scenes from his life. Three of the statues are based on designs by Dürer. Tyrol's national hero, Andreas Hofer, is entombed here.

The Hofkirche has a lovely Renaissance porch, plus a nave and a trio of aisles in the Gothic style. One gallery contains nearly two dozen small statues of the saint protectors of the house of Habsburg. The wooden organ, dating from 1560, is still operational.

Another chapel, the Silberne Kapell, or Silver Chapel, was constructed between the church and the palace in 1578 on orders of Archduke Ferdinand II of Tyrol as the final resting place for him and his wife, Philippine Welser. The chapel takes its name from a silver Madonna. Silver reliefs on the altar symbolize the Laurentanian Litany. Alexander Colin designed the sarcophagi of Ferdinand and Philippine.

The Hofkirche and chapel are open from the first of May until the end of September from 9am to 5pm; otherwise, from 9am to noon and 2 to 5pm. Admission is 20 AS ($1.45).

The **Hofgarten,** a public park containing lakes and many shade trees, including weeping willows, lies north of Rennweg. Concerts are often presented at the Kunstpavillon in the garden in summer.

Perhaps Innsbruck's greatest tourist attraction, certainly its most characteristic landmark, is the **Goldenes Dachl,** or Golden Roof. It's a three-story balcony on a house in the old town, the late Gothic oriels capped with 2,657 gold-plated tiles. It was constructed for Emperor Maximilian I to serve as a royal box where he could sit in luxury and enjoy tournaments in the square below. Completed at the dawn of the 16th century, the Golden Roof was built in honor of Maximilian's second marriage, to Bianca Maria Sforza of Milan (Maximilian was a ruler who expanded his territory not by conquest but by marriage). Not wishing to alienate the allies gained by his first marriage, to Maria of Burgundy, which was ended by her death, he had himself painted on his balcony between the two women. But he is looking at the new wife, Bianca.

Inside the building you can visit the **Olympic Museum,** Herzog-Friedrich-Strasse 15 (tel. 0512/59100), where video films (in English) are shown of Innsbruck and the most interesting scenes from the 1964 and 1976 Olympic Winter Games, plus exhibits from the Olympics and an international Olympics stamp collection. The museum is open daily from 9am to 5pm, charging an admission of 20 AS ($1.45).

For the same ticket you can also visit **Stadtturm** (City Tower), Herzog-Friedrich-Strasse 21 (tel. 0512/575962). The tower dates from the mid-1400s and stands adjacent to the Rathaus. There was formerly a prison cell in the tower. From its top a splendid view opens onto the city rooftops and the mountain panorama beyond. It is open March 1 to October 31 daily from 10am to 5pm (until 6pm in July and August).

Take a look at **Helblinghaus,** on Herzog-Friedrich-Strasse opposite the Goldenes Dachl. It's a Gothic structure to which a rococo façade was added.

Dom zu St. Jakob (Cathedral of St. James), Domplatz 6 (tel. 0512/58-39-02), was rebuilt from 1717 to 1724 from designs by Johann Jakob Herkommer, a baroque architect. It has a lavishly embellished baroque interior, part of it done by the Asam brothers, and is roofed with domes. The church was heavily damaged during Allied bombing raids in World War II. One of its chief treasures is the painting *Maria Hilf* (Mary of Succor) painted by Lucas Cranach the Elder, on the main altar. In the north aisle, look for a 1620 monument honoring Archduke Maximilian II, who died in 1618. The church is open in winter daily from 7am to 6pm and in summer from 7am to 7pm. It is closed every Friday morning.

Tiroler Volkskunst-Museum (Tyrol Museum of Popular Art), Universitäts-strasse 2 (tel. 0512/58-43-02), is in the Neues Stift, or New Abbey, adjoining the Hofkirche on its eastern side. The abbey dates from the 16th and 18th centuries. The museum contains one of the largest and most impressive collections extant of the artifacts of life in Tyrol, ranging from handcrafts to religious and profane popular art, furniture, and national costumes. The three floors house a collection of Tyrolean mangers, or Christmas cribs, some from the 18th century. The Stuben (the finest rooms) are on the upper floors. Displays include a range of styles from Gothic to Renaissance to baroque, as well as a collection of models of typical Tyrolean houses. From May to September, the museum is open daily from 9am to 5pm (until noon on Sunday). From October to April, daily hours are 9am to noon and 2 to 5pm. Admission is 20 AS ($1.45).

Ferdinandeum Tyrol Museum (Tiroler Landesmuseum Ferdinandeum), Museumstrasse 15 (tel. 0512/59-489), has a celebrated gallery of Flemish and Dutch masters. This museum also traces the development of popular art in the Tyrolean country, with highlights from the Gothic period. You'll also see the original bas-reliefs used in designing the Goldenes Dachl. The museum is open daily from the first of May until the end of September, 10am to 5pm (also 7 to 9pm on Thursday). The rest of the year, the hours are 10am to noon and 2 to 5pm; closed on Sunday afternoon and all day Monday. Admission is 20 AS ($1.40).

From the **Alpenzoo,** Weiherburggasse 37 (tel. 0512/892323), lying on the southern slope of the Nordkette-below-Hungerberg plateau, you'll get a striking view of Innsbruck and the surrounding mountains. The zoo contains only those animals indigenous to the Alps, plus alpine birds, reptiles, and fish. It is open daily from 9am to 6pm, to 5pm in winter, with admission at 50 AS ($3.65) for adults and 25 AS ($1.80) for children.

EXPLORING THE ENVIRONS

Many of the satellite resorts such as Igls (coming up) can properly be considered day trips from Innsbruck. For the moment, therefore, I'll highlight only those attractions on the most immediate outskirts of the city.

Hungerburg

Hungerburg mountain plateau (2,860 feet) is considered by many to be the most beautiful spot in Tyrol, affording the best view of Innsbruck, especially on summer nights, when much of the city, including fountains and historic buildings, is floodlit. Some of the most scenic hotels in the Innsbruck environs are here, several of which I have recommended above.

You can drive to the plateau or else take the funicular, which departs about four times on the hour from 9am to 8pm, then about every 30 minutes until 10:30pm. There's an 11pm funicular on Friday and Saturday night. Round-trip fare is 40 AS ($2.90). For information, call 0512/53-070.

From the plateau, the Nordkette cable railway quickly takes you up to the Seegrube and the Hafelekar (7,655 feet) for a sweeping view of alpine peaks and glaciers. This is the starting point of high mountain walks and climbing expeditions. In summer the cable railway runs daily every hour from 8am to 6pm. A round-trip from Innsbruck to Hafelekar and back costs 226 AS ($16.50), while a trip between Hungerburg and Hafelekar goes for 186 AS ($13.50).

Schloss Ambras

This Renaissance palace, 2 miles southeast of the heart of Innsbruck on the edge of the Mittelgebirgsterrace, was built by Archduke Ferdinand II of Austria, Comte of Tyrol, in the 16th century. It is divided into a lower and an upper castle in the remains of a medieval fortress. This was Ferdinand's favorite residence and the center of the cultural life of his court. The lower castle was planned and constructed by the archduke as a museum for his various collections, including arms and armor, art and books, all of which can be seen today. The Spanish Hall, one of the first German Renaissance halls, was built to house the portraits of the counts of Tyrol.

The upper castle has a small but fine collection of medieval sculpture, black-and-white frescoes on the wall of the inner courtyard, the bathroom of Philippine Welser (first wife of Archduke Ferdinand), and a portrait gallery hung with dynastic paintings from the 14th to the 18th centuries. In some of the living rooms you can see 16th-century frescoes, 17th-century furniture, and wooden ceilings of the late 16th century.

Schloss Ambras (tel. 0512/48-446) is open from early May to the end of September daily except Tuesday, charging an admission of 30 AS ($2.20).

After viewing the interior, you can take a leisurely stroll through the castle grounds.

The Wilten Basilica

The southern district of Innsbruck where the Sill River emerges from a gorge, Wilten is one of the most dramatic landscapes in the environs of the city. It's an ancient spot that was once the Roman town of Veldidena.

Its parish church, constructed from 1751 to 1755, became a basilica in 1957. Built in a rich rococo style with twin towers, this is considered one of the most splendid houses of worship in the Tyrolean country. It's noted for its stucco work by Franz Xaver Feichtmayr. Matthaus Gunther is responsible for the frescoes on the ceiling. A sandstone figure depicting *Our Lady of the Four Columns* has been the subject of pilgrimage since the Middle Ages.

Across from the basilica is a cluster of baroque buildings that are the outgrowth of an abbey founded there in 1138. The abbey church, dating from the 1650s, merits a visit. It has a porch guarded by two stone giants and a grille from 1707 found in the narthex. This church was damaged by World War II Allied bombing.

Bergisel

If you're driving, head out the Brenner road to Bergisel (2,450 feet), a lovely wooded section in the environs ideal for leisurely strolls in the warm months. It lies near the gorge of the Sill River on the southern outskirts of Innsbruck, about a 20-minute walk from the Wilten Basilica. Here you'll see the ski jumps built for the 1964 and 1976 Olympic Winter Games. You'll have splendid views from the jumps.

The hill here is a historic site, scene of the 1809 battles in which Andreas Hofer led some Tyrolean peasants against French and Bavarian forces. He was later shot to death in Mantua on orders of Napoleon. Below the ski jump, on the north side, is the Andreas Hofer monument erected in 1893 to commemorate the battle. Tyroleans speak of this as their "field of remembrance," and it's filled with memorials and visitors. However, heroic though the local deeds may be, they may not interest North Americans. I recommend that you visit here just for the views and the relaxing walks.

TOURS

Sightseeing tours of Innsbruck, lasting about an hour, leave by bus daily from Hofburg at 10:15am, noon, 2pm, and 3:15pm.

A special two-hour bus tour leaves from Maria-Theresien-Strasse, the Central Railway Station, and Bozner Platz at 10am and 2pm.

Daily bus excursions from Innsbruck to the most beautiful part of Tyrol—Zillertal, Alpbach, and Kühtai—and to the favorite places in neighboring Italy and Germany and other parts of Austria, can be arranged at your hotel, a travel agency, or the tourist office.

SHOPPING

On their home turf, you can purchase such Tyrolean specialties as lederhosen, dirndls, leather clothing, woodcarvings, loden cloth, and all sorts of skiing and mountain-climbing equipment. You can stroll around such streets as the Maria-Theresien-Strasse, the Herzog-Friedrich-Strasse, and the Museumstrasse, ducking in and making discoveries of your own, perhaps finding some treasured gift or souvenir.

Here are a few of my recommendations if you're seeking something special:

Tiroler Heimatwerk, Meraner Strasse 2 (tel. 0512/58-23-20), is one of the best stores in Innsbruck for such handcrafted Tyrolean items as sculpture, pewter, textiles, woolen goods, hand-knitted sweaters, lace, and bolts of silk for do-it-yourselfers. You can purchase regionally inspired fabrics and dress patterns, which you can whip into a dirndl (or whatever) as soon as you get home. Also for sale are carved chests, mirror frames, and furniture. The elegant décor includes ancient stone columns and old, well-maintained vaulted ceilings.

Zinnreproduktionen Rudolf Boschi, Kiebachgasse 8 (tel. 0512/58-92-24). Using old molds discovered in abandoned Tyrolean factories, this imaginative company produces the finest reproductions of century-old pewter in the region. Mr. Boschi attends auctions throughout Europe, and after discovering rare pewter objects, he reproduces them in excellent quality at reasonable prices. Look for a copy of the 18th-century pewter barometer emblazoned with representations of the sun and the four winds or hand-painted ceramic mugs whose pewter lids keep suds from flowing over the top. Each of the items for sale is cast or molded in a nearby foundry south of Innsbruck.

Lanz, Wilhelm-Greil-Strasse 15 (tel. 0512/58-31-05), is a bright clothing store where the staff wear regional dresses and where the inventory includes everything you'd need to look authentically Tyrolean. Specific items include dresses, sweaters, dirndls, stockings, handkerchiefs, lederhosen, hand-knit sweaters, leather belts, sport coats, and overcoats. The store carries children's clothing and apparel for men too.

Lodenbaur, Brixner Strasse 4 (tel. 0512/58-09-11). This is the closest thing you'll find to a department store in Innsbruck devoted to regional Tyrolean dress. Most of the goods are made in Austria, including a full array of lederhosen, coats, dresses, dirndls, and accessories for men, women, and children. Be sure to check out the basement as well.

AFTER DARK

Innsbruck is more lighthearted about its nightlife than is Vienna. If you're in luck you'll get to attend a summer concert in the park or perhaps take in an operetta at the theater. You might retire to a beerhall to listen to brass bands and yodeling or be lulled by zither music at a restaurant.

Why not stroll through the Altstadt and, if it's a summer night, meander through the Hofgarten, which is lit? Perhaps you'd enjoy taking the funicular to Hungerburg for an overview of the night lights of Innsbruck, where many of the historic buildings and fountains are illuminated. Best of all, you can attend a Tyrolean folkloric evening or retreat to a typical local wine tavern offering entertainment.

It's wise to check with the tourist office as to current offerings, both theatrical presentations and folkloric ones. For example, in summer there's often a parade of a Tyrolean brass band in costumes, with a concert at the Goldenes Dachl. There are also likely to be concerts at Ambras Castle, ecclesiastical music at Wilten Basilica, organ concerts at the Igls parish church, and so on. Summer is the active season for this type of public entertainment.

If you want casino action, you have to drive to the resort of Seefeld (see attractions coming up), where the **Spiel-Casino** there offers roulette, baccarat, blackjack, or whatever daily from 5pm.

Many of the restaurants, in addition to food, offer Tyrolean evenings. That way, your dining choice also becomes your nightclub for the evening, which is a lot cheaper than going to a restaurant, then a separate nightclub.

Typical among these is the **Stiftskeller,** Burggraben 31 (tel. 0512/58-34-90). It presents a Tyrolean evening, beginning at 8. The folklore program offers an evening of country music, songs, yodeling, zither playing, hackbrett, xylophone, alphorn, singing saws, raffele, folk dancing, and schuhplatter. Entrance costs 100 AS ($7.25).

Club Filou, Stiftsgasse 12 (tel. 05222/580256), in the heart of the Old Town, is my favorite bar and nightclub in Innsbruck. In summer the tiny square in front of its façade blossoms with ivy-covered trellises, recorded music, and quadruplicate parasols, which protect the copper-covered outdoor bar. If you venture inside, past the antique cash register (whose zinc-plated drawers contain candy), you'll find an intimate and sophisticated hangout filled with Victorian settees and pop art. The right-angled bar is usually patronized by visiting musicians, athletes, and attractively trendy local residents. Food is available until 3am every night, and you can enjoy it at the bar or at one of the tiny tables. The house specialty is spareribs, although salads, soups, schnitzels, scampi, smoked salmon, and desserts are also available. A main course begins at around 95 AS ($7), but no one will mind if you order only a snack or just a drink. In a separate, very old room, the high ceiling of a disco is supported by medieval stone columns and ringed with a hi-tech steel balcony. There's no cover charge. Long drinks in both the café (which opens at 6pm) and the disco (which opens at 9pm) begin at around 45 AS ($3.25). Both sections close at 4am. Filou is open seven nights a week.

Casablanca Café Americain, Adolf Pichlerplatz 4 (tel. 0512/56-27-68). Anyone over 25 might feel that they've stepped into alien territory, but if you're the right age, on the make, and into rock, you'll fit in here. A marble foyer leads into a high-ceilinged room filled with mirrors, lattices, Bogart/Bergman memorabilia, a prominent bar, and dozens of tiny tables. Drinks begin at 30 AS ($2.20) and are served from 6pm to 1am Monday to Friday and from 5pm to 1am on Saturday and Sunday.

Queen Anne Club, Amraserstrasse 6 (tel. 0512/57-51-55), attracts nighttime prowlers who often stop for a drink at the neighboring Paulis Pub, where a crowd of convivial drinkers talk in a warmly masculine atmosphere of wood and olive-colored velvet. It opens nightly at 8pm. The Queen Anne disco in the basement opens at 9pm, imposing a cover charge of 30 AS ($2.20). The Queen Anne offers both live music (on occasion) and recorded disco (invariably). Scotch and soda in either section costs from 80 AS ($5.80). The club closes at 3am.

Nightclub Lady-O, Bruneckerstrasse 2 (tel. 0512/58-64-32), opposite the post office and near the train station, offers voyeuristic clients a collection of charming female artists. This is considered the only *real* nightclub in Innsbruck. Entrance is 20 AS ($1.45), with drinks beginning at 130 AS ($9.45). The club also has blue movies, a hot whirlpool, and a sauna. The club is open daily from 8:30pm to 4am, with shows beginning at 9:30pm and continuing nonstop until 4am.

Goethe Stube, Restaurant Goldener Adler, Herzog-Friedrich-Strasse 6 (tel. 0512/586334). Aside from the good food (see my restaurant recommendation), this place offers a nightly program that includes the zither and "jodlers." No admission is charged, but at least one drink is obligatory, costing from 50 AS ($3.65). Meals start at 150 AS ($11). It's open every night from 7pm to midnight.

Piano Bar, Scandi Crown Hotel, Salurnerstrasse 15 (tel. 0512/59-35-0), is set near the lobby of this previously recommended tallest hotel in town. The attractive, plushly sophisticated bar is one of the most desirable places in Innsbruck to meet for a drink, and is at its most popular daily from 5pm to 1am.

2. Igls and the Environs

This section, site of many of the Olympic Winter Games of 1964 and 1976, might be called "Olympic Innsbruck." It consists of a cluster of resorts, the best known of which is Igls, all lying within easy reach of the Tyrol capital, often with a commuting time of only half an hour. Each of these resorts perched on the slopes where the Olympics took place could be an alternative to staying in Innsbruck, which is often crowded.

A complete system of lifts opens up alpine scenery to everybody, from the beginner to the most advanced skier—or to the sightseer in warm weather.

IGLS

Lying on a sunny plateau in the alpine foothills at an elevation of 2,875 feet, Igls is the resort choice of many people who prefer to stay here—in either winter or summer—and commute to Innsbruck, 3 miles north. Although its number swells greatly with winter and summer visitors, the town has a population of fewer than 2,000 souls. Because it's so popular, Igls is certainly not the cheapest resort in Tyrol.

A streetcar from the Berg Isel station in Innsbruck will deliver you to Igls, 1,000 feet higher than the capital, in about 30 minutes. Buses on route "J" leave every 30 minutes on the hour and half hour from Igls and the main railway station in Innsbruck. The local train on the no. 6 line leaves Innsbruck at a quarter past each hour and Igls at a quarter to.

The outdoor air at Igls, long known as the "sun terrace" of Innsbruck, is never likely to be too hot, even on the hottest day in Austria. In fact, it feels air-conditioned outside even in summer. Although much of its world renown has been based on winter sports, this is a popular summer resort too, a place to rest or wander along alpine trails, to play golf on an 18-hole or a 9-hole course, to enjoy tennis, or whatever.

This is the favorite place for Innsbruckers to come to ski, and they're joined by throngs of visitors. Igls shared the Winter Olympics festivities and sporting competition with Innsbruck, and following the success of the 1976 event, this small resort town can boast a thrilling bobsled and toboggan run.

The major excursion from here is to take a cable car up to **Patscherkofel,** at an elevation of 6,430 feet, a ride covering about 2½ miles and taking about 18 minutes. Patscherkofel is the mountain that gives Innsbruck its vista. Many long ski descents from the mountain are possible.

A small kindergarten for children is in a log cabin in the **Kurpark,** a natural wooded area near the center of the village.

Where to Stay

Schlosshotel, A-6080 Igls (tel. 05222/77217), the most glamorous hotel in town, sits on its own grass-covered plateau at the end of a narrow street running into the main artery of the resort. It rises above its surrounding conifers, jutting an elaborate roofline of slate-capped spires, intricate chimneys, and baroque curves toward the nearby farming hamlet of Vils. The wrap-around veranda is graced with a pair of stone lions.

As the proportions of the outside imply, the bedrooms inside are high-ceilinged and spacious. They sometimes offer splendid views of the mountains, and always contain private baths. Forty rooms are rented, at half-board tariffs ranging from 1,610 AS ($117) to 2,030 AS ($147.50) per person daily. An excellent restaurant serves both traditional and international food in turn-of-the-century surroundings. The Schlosshotel is closed between November 1 and mid-December and during most of April, and it also offers both indoor and outdoor swimming pools.

Sporthotel Igls, A-6080 Igls (tel. 05222/77241), is a fancifully designed hotel built in a style that's a cross between a baroque castle and a mountain chalet. Some of the details include jutting bay windows, at least three hexagonal stone-trimmed towers with ornate detailing, and rows of flower-covered balconies. The spacious interior is dotted with antiques and conservative furniture, with plenty of gemütlich corners and sunny areas, both indoors and out.

The hotel has two restaurants, an à la carte grill room, two elevators, a bar, and a big indoor/outdoor swimming pool, plus a range of health and cure facilities. Horseback riding, golf, and tennis are close at hand. In winter the hotel offers a daily five o'clock tea dance. The hotel rents 90 bedrooms (a nearby annex handles the overflow) with private baths or showers. Half board costs 1,000 AS ($72.75) to

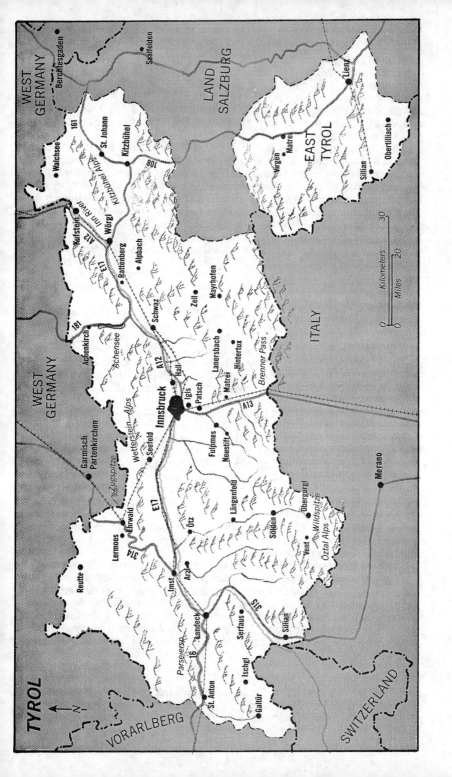

1,300 AS ($94.50) per person daily. Guests are received from December to March and May to October.

Hotel Alpenhof, A-6080 Igls (tel. 05222/77491). This tastefully furnished chalet has a salon, a warmly inviting bar area, and a sunny terrace where the owners serve well-prepared buffets. The hotel was modernized in 1980. Thirty-five carpeted and comfortable bedrooms, each with private shower, rent for 560 AS ($40.75) to 650 AS ($47.25) per person daily for half board. The Alpenhof is open from December to March and May to September.

Aegidihof, A-6080 Igls (tel. 05222/77108), is a rambling chalet near the Kurpark and the ski lifts. The interior has lots of hand-worked details, such as antique armoires set into niches designed especially for them, wrought-iron window bars and lighting fixtures, beamed ceilings, and Oriental rugs. The Skardarasy family, your hosts, charge 550 AS ($40) to 900 AS ($65.50) per person daily for half board at this 48-bed hotel, which is open from December to October.

Hotel Bon Alpina, Hilberstrasse 8, A-6080 Igls (tel. 05222/77219), is a tastefully designed chalet with Tyrolean atmosphere offering good food and service. In the center of the village, a five-minute walk from the ski lifts, the hotel has 94 bedrooms renting for 510 AS ($37) to 770 AS ($56) per person daily, based on double occupancy, with half board included. Singles pay a daily supplement of 160 AS ($11.75). Each room has a private bath or shower. The hotel has a sauna and a solarium as well as a sunny terrace.

Hotel Astoria, A-6080 Igls (tel. 05222/77481), is a wood and white-painted chalet near the center of Igls. The interior is darkly furnished with heavy wooden ceilings, autumnal colors, and hanging brass lamps. On the premises are a padded bar and a small swimming pool. The 42 light-colored bedrooms have private baths, southern balconies, phones, and TVs. The hotel is near the cable cars and is a three-minute walk from the public tennis courts. Winter half-board terms range from 600 AS ($43.50) to 700 AS ($51) per person daily, with summer half-board terms going from 480 AS ($35) to 580 AS ($42.25) per person daily.

Hotel Batzenhäusl, A-6080 Igls (tel. 05222/77104). The ornate paneling in the tavern is carved from what the locals call "stone pine," the glow from which beautifully complements the flowered carpets, leaded windows, and hand-worked lamps. The other sections of this comfortable hotel are crafted in a more modern style, still appealing and intimate, with ample use of heavy ceiling beams, flagstone floors, and Oriental rugs. The hotel is an antique chalet with a recently built addition more or less in the same style as the original intricately carved building. Dietrich Arnold and his attractive family, the owners, charge 570 AS ($41.50) to 1,230 AS ($89.50) per person daily for half board. They rent 35 well-furnished bedrooms, each with private bath. Even if you don't stay here, you may want to consider a dinner at its restaurant (see below), which is considered one of the best in the state. The hotel is open from December to October.

Hotel Tirolerhof, A-6080 Igls (tel. 05222/77194), has one of the prettiest façades in Igls. Designed in a rambling format of Tudor-style half-timbers, gabled red-tile roofs, and a long expanse of greenery rising on every side, the hotel offers apartment accommodations for two to eight people, as well as standard hotel rooms. In a wooded area four minutes from the center of town, this 75-bed hotel rents rooms with and without private baths, at half-board rates ranging from 440 AS ($32) to 500 AS ($36.25) per person daily. Its season is from December to September.

Where to Dine

Restaurant Batzenhäusl, Hotel Batzenhäusl (tel. 0512/77104). Gemütlich is a word to describe this carefully paneled antique-style dining room, where the chalet chairs are intricately carved and the service is good. A specialty of the house is flambé filet steak "Didi," a popular recipe prepared at your table. Other well-prepared dishes include such Austrian specialties as three kinds of meat on the same platter (covered in a mushroom cream sauce), apple strudel, and a series of savory meat-flavored soups. You might prefer the outdoor veranda or the garden in summer, although the dining room inside is most attractive. Meals range from 150 AS ($11) to 450 AS ($32.75). The dining room is open daily from 8am to midnight.

PÄTSCH

This small village above Igls stands on the sunny western slope of the Pätscherkofel, with a panoramic view of the Stubai Glaciers. Lying on the old Roman road below the Pätscherkofel peak, Pätsch is only a short distance from the mountain's Olympics slopes.

In winter, it attracts visitors with its skiing facilities, including cross-country runs, ice skating, and curling. The resorts offer a ski school. Horse-drawn sleighs take you along snow trails.

In summer you can go on hikes, swim, or play golf and tennis. Summer skiing is possible on the Stubai Glacier.

Food and Lodging

Hotel Grünwalderhof, A-6082 Pätsch (tel. 05222/77304), once the private hunting lodge of the Counts of Thurn and Taxis, is today operated by members of the Seiler family. The hotel stands on the site of an ancient Roman road. Proudly housed in one of the prettiest chalets in town, it has a relief of natural-grained lattice under the slope of its gabled roof, striped shutters, and a modern extension stretching out the back toward the secluded outdoor swimming pool. Inside, the ceiling vaults are covered with an artist's rendition of regional wildflowers, while the rest of the décor includes a scattering of antiques, lots of paneling, and leather-upholstered chairs in the spacious and comfortable dining room. On the premises are a small indoor pool, a sauna, and a tennis court. With half board included, rates range from 580 AS ($42.25) to 950 AS ($69) per person daily. Prices depend on the season and the accommodation; all rooms are comfortably furnished.

Hotel Altwirt, A-6082 Pätsch (tel. 05222/77637), enjoys a quiet location and an excellent view of the Stubai Glaciers. It was built around a carefully planned design incorporating heavy timbers, lots of wood, terra-cotta floor tiles, and well-chosen textiles. The 34 simple bedrooms have big baths, often tiled in somber tones of grays and blues, plus secluded balconies. The large indoor pool has sweeping views over the snow-covered mountains, which you can enjoy from the comfort of the heated water. Half board ranges from 430 AS ($31.25) to 500 AS ($36.25) per person daily. Children under 6 stay free in their parents' room, while youngsters aged 6 to 11 pay 20% of the adult rates.

Hotel Bär, A-6082 Pätsch (tel. 0512/77504), is an amply proportioned hotel that towers five stories above the alpine meadow where it sits a few hundred yards from the center of the village. The inside is covered with paneling tinted the same brown color as the hide of the animal the hotel is named after (a bear). It includes lots of attractive touches, such as big panoramic windows looking over the mountains, an antique ceramic stove surrounded by a warming bench, an indoor pool, warmly appealing restaurants, and a bar. The 37 cozy and well-furnished bedrooms cost 580 AS ($42.25) to 620 AS ($45) per person daily, with half board included. Prices depend on the plumbing and the season.

MUTTERS

On a sunny southern plateau above Innsbruck, Mutters is just 6½ miles from the Tyrolean capital. You can drive to the center of the city from here in about 15 minutes, or get there via the Stubaital railway in just 20 minutes. The village is separated from Innsbruck by a wide green forest belt lying above the city and the Inn Valley.

Mutters is in the skiing and recreation area of the Mutterer Alm and the Axamer Lizum, which were the central base for the sites of the 1964 and 1976 Olympic Winter Games. Mutterer Alm is the place for easy-going skiers. It can be reached by cableway.

Food and Lodging

Hotel Sonnhof, Burgstall 12, A-6162 Mutters (tel. 05222/573747), is a modern stucco-fronted chalet in a quiet country location a few minutes' walk from the center. The streamlined interior has big windows and colorful accessories, and includes an indoor pool, a sauna, and access to a flagstone-covered outdoor terrace. Members of the Ullmann family maintain the rustically modern bedrooms in top-notch condition; they also make every effort to perfect the savory cuisine served in the airy and attractive restaurant. They rent 28 good bedrooms from December to October, charging 490 AS ($35.50) to 580 AS ($42.25) per person daily for half board, depending on the plumbing and the season. The hotel is open from December to October.

Hotel Altenburg, Kirchplatz 4, A-6162 Mutters (tel. 0512/587053). The ground-floor entryway of this flowered 32-room chalet is sheltered with a three-arched arcade, which serves as an attractive backdrop for the summer café set up on the pavement outside. The interior is covered with horizontal planking, long ago sanded smooth and beautifully finished, while many of the ceilings are beamed and timbered and set with recessed pin lights. The elegant restaurant is filled with upholstered banquettes and conservative furniture, with big windows overlooking the mountains. Other facilities include a sauna, a steambath, and a solarium. Depending on the season, rates with half board included range from 460 AS ($33.50) to 570 AS ($41.50) per person daily. The hotel is closed from the end of September to mid-December and the end of March to mid-May. The Wishaber family are your genteel hosts.

Muttererhof, A-6162 Mutters (tel. 0512/587491), has a gabled roof and a dignified chalet façade—its balconies covered with flowers in season—within a few minutes' walk of the village center. On the premises are a covered swimming pool whose sliding glass doors remain open in summer; an elegantly paneled restaurant filled with carved chairs, leaded windows, and antique artifacts; and a verdant lawn with café tables in summer. Charges are 340 AS ($24.75) to 380 AS ($27.75) daily per person for bed-and-breakfast, depending on the season. Each of the 20 bedrooms has a private bath or shower. The Muttererhof is open from early December to April 25 and again from May 12 to October 25.

AXAMER LIZUM

This resort was created for the 1964 Olympic Winter Games. It's about a half-hour drive, 11 miles southwest from Innsbruck. The highest station on the system of funicular and lifts is at Hoadl (7,665 feet). You can also take a chair lift to Birgitzköpfl (6,700 feet).

In summer you can take pleasure in hiking on alpine footpaths and attending folkloric evenings. Winter brings the opportunity to participate in sports for the whole family. A variety of tracks and ski runs, a natural ice rink, and ski-bob runs are here, plus the longest natural toboggan run in Tyrol. Three chair lifts and four ski tows serve the skiers who come here. Experts find some of the slopes at Axamer Lizum especially challenging.

Food and Lodging

Hotel/Sportpension Lizumerhof, A-6094 Axamer Lizum (tel. 05234/8244), is an elongated 50-bed mountain building set on a forested hill within sight of the rocky bluffs around it. Near the ski lifts, the family-run hotel makes a cozy and attractive destination for lovers of summer and winter sports. The dining room has colorful napery, lots of sunshine, and what looks like an 18th-century group portrait. My favorite room has a sloped ceiling and an onion-shaped brick-and-plaster fireplace in the center. For half board, the charge ranges from 460 AS ($33.50) to 660 AS ($48) per person daily. Fondue evenings and special buffets with music and dancing are features of the hotel.

---

3. The Stubai and Wipp Valleys

One of the most beautiful valleys in Tyrol is the Stubaital, a 25-mile-long area with an endless vista of glacier tops and alpine peaks, some 10 miles from Innsbruck. From the Brenner Road you can fork off at Schönberg into the Stubaital, which has little villages such as Fulpmes and neighboring Neustift, both summer and winter playgrounds.

One of the first hamlets you'll encounter, and one of the most charming, is **Mieders** (3,120 feet). From here a chair lift goes up to Kopeneck at 5,350 feet.

If you decide to lodge in one of these little-known resorts, you'll find the prices favorable to your pocketbook. However, it's possible to stay in Innsbruck and drive through the valley, either by private car or on a bus, in a day. It's also possible to take a narrow-gauge electric train. If you travel by rail, you can go only as far as Fulpmes. After that, you must continue by bus.

The Wipp Valley, or Wipptal, is the valley of the Sill River, stretching from Innsbruck to the Brenner Pass. An autobahn—a great engineering feat—pierces the valley right on the outskirts of Innsbruck, going over **Europabrücke** (Europe Bridge), 625 feet high and 900 yards long. As you travel over it you'll literally feel that you're driving on a highway in the sky.

The **Brenner Pass,** known as the lowest gap in the major alpine chain, has been used since Roman times—and probably before. The pass marks the boundary between Italy and Austria.

Your first stopover in this section might be—

FULPMES

The major resort and the most ancient hamlet in the Stubai Valley is Fulpmes, surrounded by high mountains. Mention of a village here goes back to a document of 1344. The resort lies about halfway up the valley. Serles Mountain, to the south of Fulpmes, rises to a height of 8,900 feet. You might enjoy an excursion up to Telfes, slightly more than a mile by road above Fulpmes.

Most visitors see the Stubaital on day trips from Innsbruck, but the resort, a spot to visit in both summer and winter, offers a wide range of excellent hotels charging moderate prices, a winning combination. In summer there's an indoor heated swimming pool between Fulpmes and Telfes. Chair lifts operate in both summer and winter, one going from Fulpmes to Froneben at 4,430 feet and one to Kreuzjoch, at 6,900 feet.

If you're here at the right time you might enjoy a historical play presented about Tyrol's hero, Andreas Hofer, who led Bavarian and Tyrolean peasants against Napoleon and freed Tyrol from the French emperor's domination.

Food and Lodging
Sporthotel Alphof, Herrengasse 7A, A-6166 Fulpmes (tel. 05225/3163), is a four-story chalet on a quiet lane a short distance from the center of the village. Run by a family, it has an interior with plenty of rustic aspects: green ceramic stove,

knotty-pine paneling in one of the dining rooms, restaurant with formal chairs upholstered in mountaintop colors of evergreen and persimmon. There is a sauna on the premises, and both indoor and outdoor tennis courts are close at hand. The hotel rents 30 bedrooms, charging half-board tariffs ranging from 380 AS ($27.75) to 635 AS ($46.25) per person daily.

Hotel Pension Auenhof, A-6166 Fulpmes (tel. 05225/2763). The lobby of this chalet has gently arched ceiling beams, lots of carved wood, and white plaster walls dotted with antique farm utensils. The salon has an unusual country baroque armoire with four different portraits painted on its double doors, as well as a wood-trimmed fireplace that curves toward one of the conversation areas. On the premises are a sauna and an attractive restaurant, and access is possible to lots of ski and hiking trails. A ski bus makes frequent stops at the hotel on its way to the slopes. Pleasant and comfortable bedrooms, 25 in all, each with shower, are rented at winter half-board rates of 470 AS ($34.25) per person daily. Summer half-board terms are lowered to 400 AS ($29) per person daily.

Sporthotel Cristall, A-6166 Fulpmes (tel. 05225/3424), is a big-windowed chalet with four floors of attractively furnished wood-paneled bedrooms, 45 in all. The restaurant, which serves good food, has a green ceramic oven and a wholesomely alpine décor of wooden walls and ceilings. An intimate bar provides an inviting place to meet people. A summertime outdoor café is cantilevered above the slope of the hill into which this hotel is built, with an outdoor swimming pool visible from many of the flowered balconies. There's a sauna on the premises, as well as access to a host of sporting facilities. With breakfast included, doubles rent for 920 AS ($67) to 1,600 AS ($116.25) per person daily, singles for 540 AS ($36.25) to 820 AS ($59.50). Prices depend on the accommodation and the season.

Alpenhotel Tirolerhof, A-6166 Fulpmes (tel. 05225/2422). My favorite part of this beautifully embellished double chalet is the central fireplace near the reception desk. It looks like something that the witch would have used to lure Hansel and Gretel into her house if they had wandered into the enchanted forest on a winter's night. Its design of roughly applied stucco is curved around a widely splayed grate and fanciful andirons, and in winter it's usually kept burning most of the day. The rest of the hotel has dozens of elegantly rustic touches, such as the rich carving on some of the ceilings and the many rural artifacts strewn tastefully around the intimately lit interior. On the premises are an indoor pool, a hot whirlpool, a sauna, and access to the many nearby sports facilities. The hotel rents 43 well-furnished bedrooms, charging 540 AS ($39.50) to 670 AS ($48.75) per person daily in winter for half board. Half-board terms in summer cost 410 AS ($29.75) to 450 AS ($32.75) per person daily.

Hotel-Restaurant Holzmeister, A-6166 Fulpmes (tel. 05225/2260), has dozens of architectural details—which a team of craftsmen probably took months to complete. Many of the vaulted ceilings are embellished with painted regional designs, while the woodwork on the walls and ceilings is painstakingly polished and elegantly ornate. The balustrade on the stairwell leading to the upper floors is appropriate to the style of architecture, while each bedroom is a unique statement of comfort and rural charm. On the premises are a sauna and a solarium, and there's access to the many sports facilities of this alpine village. Under family ownership for many years, the hotel also offers a gemütlich Tyrolean stube. With a tasty breakfast buffet and a flavorful and nourishing evening meal included, half-board rates in summer range from 480 AS ($35) to 520 AS ($37.75) per person daily. In winter they cost 570 AS ($41.50) to 680 AS ($49.50) per person daily. The hotel rents 28 rooms, each with private bath or shower.

Sporthotel Brugger, Am Bichl 1, A-6166 Fulpmes (tel. 05225/2870), is a traditionally maintained four-story chalet with a combination of wood balconies, stucco walls, and a cozy interior with all the modern conveniences. In one of the restaurants someone has arranged a colorfully embroidered collection of cowbells on the wall, while in the main dining room the wood of the upholstered chairs matches the amber-colored paneling on the walls. The hotel rents 21 well-furnished and comfortable bedrooms, charging half-board rates in summer ranging from 350 AS ($25.50) to 460 AS ($33.50) per person daily. Winter half-board terms range from 455 AS ($33) to 635 AS ($46.25) per person daily.

NEUSTIFT

The name of this village means "new monastery" or "new church," and in fact it's a few centuries more recent than, say, the 12th-century *New* Forest in England. But Neustift dates back to 1505, when Emperor Maximilian I did some hunting here and had a chapel built, called *das neue Stift*. This village and others in the Stubai Valley have been in the tourist business since the 19th century, when mountain climbers discovered the area and made it accessible.

Neustift, about 3,000 feet above sea level, is surrounded by extensive hiking trails for summer visitors, leading up to the glaciers of the Stubai Alps. The Stubai Glacier lift will take you to a dizzying 10,050-foot height, where year-round skiing is pursued.

There are baby slopes here, served by T-bars, or you can take a chair lift from Neustift to Elferberg, a favorite with advanced skiers. Elferberg is also known for its panoramic view and long toboggan runs.

Where to Stay

Alpenhof Neustifterhof, A-6167 Neder Neustift (tel. 05226/2711), blends together a pair of Tyrolean chalets with an underground passage. They lie a few steps from the most modern indoor tennis courts in the region in an outlying hamlet (Neder Neustift), less than a mile east of the center of the resort. The sprawling interiors of these houses contain impressively crafted arrays of public rooms, each paneled in full-grained softwoods and filled with comfortable nooks and crannies. There is a pair of restaurants, along with an alpine bar with an adjacent cubbyhole of a firelit stüberl. The hotel was built in 1961, and since then has undergone three complete renovations, making it one of the best-maintained hotels at Neustift.

Each of the 60 balconied bedrooms is outfitted with a private bath and a modernized form of Tyrolean charm. Depending on the season and accommodation, half-board rates range from 510 AS ($37) to 720 AS ($52.25) per person daily. The buildings also contain a handful of apartments, which come with breakfast included in the price. The swimming pool has a timbered ceiling, its own sauna, and a big-windowed view over the surrounding countryside.

Sporthotel Neustift, A-6167 Neustift (tel. 05226/2509), is a 44-room wood-and-stucco chalet with ornamental eaves and painted country baroque patterns around the windows. The cozy interior has paneled rusticity, as well as wintertime fireplaces illuminating the well-prepared cuisine in the mountain dining room. The family owners of this engaging hotel charge 500 AS ($36.25) to 820 AS ($59.50) per person daily, with half board included. Prices depend on the season, and apartments are available for between two and four guests. Each room has a private bath, minibar, radio, and TV (upon request). A tennis court, an indoor swimming pool, a whirlpool, a sauna, and a solarium are on the premises.

Hotel Edelweiss, A-6167 Neustift (tel. 05226/2280). The grass-covered slope of an alpine hill separates this wood-trimmed chalet from an evergreen forest. Inside, a heavily timbered décor evokes mountainous Austria. Guests congregate beside a roughly plastered fireplace, within sight of leaded windows exposing the surrounding countryside and nearby village. An indoor swimming pool and an adjacent sauna are a few steps from a decorative fountain ringed with chaises longues. The 70 attractively furnished and comfortably appointed bedrooms, each with private bath or shower, rent for 480 AS ($35) to 550 AS ($40) per person daily for half board. You'll recognize this place at the edge of town by its country baroque window trim and jutting balconies.

Where to Dine

Restaurant Hoferwirt (tel. 05226/2201) is housed in a tastefully up-to-date hotel of the same name, which blends easily into the style of the structures around it. The interior's white walls act as a good foil for the cuisine served by a staff of efficient local residents. Specialties include baked lasagne, herb soup with shrimp, fondue bourguignonne for two, crab tails, and peppersteak. Meals range from 250 AS ($18.25). Hot food is served from 11am to 10pm. Reservations are suggested.

The outstanding dining room in the area is **Silberdistel,** Scheibe 124 (tel. 05226/3171), which serves only dinner, offered nightly except Monday from 6pm to midnight. (It also takes a two-week vacation sometime in summer.) The restaurant is set within a wood-walled chalet in the center of the resort. Inside, guests dine in one of a trio of wood-sided rooms redolent of alpine comfort and charm. Game dishes are featured in season, along with fresh fish and an array of international specialties. Tyrolean dishes are also in heavy demand. Meals cost 175 AS ($12.75) to 400 AS ($29).

STEINACH IM WIPPTAL

This little resort lies at the head of the Gschnitztal, another lovely valley cutting through the Stubai massif. Gschnitztal is most often visited from Steinach. If you take a fast train out of Innsbruck, you can be in Steinach im Wipptal in about half an hour. Be specific as to where you want to go, as there's another Steinach in Austria.

With well-tended ski trails and excellent runs, Steinach is attractive to winter visitors, but it may be that summer tourists have the best of it here, with the beauties of two valleys to explore.

From here you can travel to **Gries am Brenner,** along the Sill River. Some 15 miles from Innsbruck and 8 miles from the Brenner Pass, Gries, at an altitude of 3,810 feet, sits at the foot of the Padauner Kogel. This village, too, is both a summer and a winter resort. In the vicinity is the Brennersee, a beautiful lake.

To reach Gries you must go up a steep road. Roman soldiers marched along this route in ancient times, as it was their road to the colonies of Rome in the north. The railway line from here cuts deep into dark tunnels, piercing the Alps until it reaches the border of Italy.

Food and Lodging

Hotel Steinacherhof, A-6150 Steinach im Wipptal (tel. 05272/6241), a big elegant hotel, is a cross between a chalet and a private villa, its façade assembled from weathered planking and white-painted stucco. Architectural details include a row of arched windows stretching toward the rear gardens, plus a large curved extension whose sunny, attractive dining room often presents live music. The hotel has installed sun terraces atop two of the building's low-lying wings, although guests are free to roam through the gardens. Also on the premises are a big indoor swimming pool, a nearby café, an outdoor tennis court, a bar, and a Tyrolean restaurant with knotty paneling carved into neoclassical designs. All 60 accommodations contain private baths or showers, and the hotel charges 505 AS ($36.75) to 810 AS ($59) per person daily for half board. Guests are received from December to March and May to October.

Hotel Weisses Rössl, A-6150 Steinach im Wipptal (tel. 05272/6206), is in many ways the center of social life in the village. From one side the hotel presents a lime-green neoclassical façade with white detailing and weatherproof windows. The older section has such antique details as vaulted ceilings, regional memorabilia, and a collection of weapons and hunting utensils from another era. In the chalet addition that stretches off the back, members of the Jakober family have installed cozy alpine bedrooms with lots of custom-made carpentry. A stone-walled room on the premises contains an indoor pool, and nearby are a sauna and a fitness room. The large and sunny dining room welcomes passing visitors as well as hotel guests. For its 44 bedrooms, each with private bath or shower, the hotel charges 460 AS ($33.50) per person daily for half board in summer, with winter half-board terms ranging from 500 AS ($36.25) to 640 AS ($46.50) per person daily. Open from December to October.

4. Seefeld

Seefeld, 15 miles northwest of Innsbruck, is a member of Austria's "Big Three" of international rendezvous points for winter-sports crowds. The fashionable resort lies some 3,450 feet above sea level on a sunny plateau.

Seefeld hosted the 1964 and 1976 Nordic Events for the Olympic Games and the 1985 Nordic Ski World Championships.

Skiers are served with one funicular railway, two cable cars, three chair lifts, and 14 drag lifts. The beginners' slopes lie directly in the village center. The base stations of the lifts for the main skiing areas (known as Gschwandtkopt and Rosshutte/ Seefelder Joch) are at most a half mile away from the center, and are serviced by free daily nonstop bus service. There are 124 miles of prepared cross-country tracks.

Other winter activities offered here include curling, horse-drawn sleigh rides, outdoor skating (Ice Skating School, with artificial and natural ice rink), horseback riding, indoor tennis (Swedish Tennis School), tube sliding (you slide on rubber car tubes—lying or sitting), indoor golf facilities, paragliding, bowling, squash, hiking (60 miles of cleared paths), fitness studio, swimming, and saunas.

Summer visitors can enjoy swimming in three lakes, in a heated open-air swimming pool on the Seefeld Lake, or at the Olympia indoor and outdoor pools. Other summer sports facilities include tennis on 18 open-air and 8 indoor courts (Swedish Tennis School), riding (two stables with indoor schools), and golf on the 18-hole course, which has been rated by golf insiders as one of the 100 most beautiful courses in the world. Hiking on 124 miles of walks and mountain paths, cycling, minigolf, paragliding, and rafting can also be enjoyed.

Whatever time of year it is, you can try your luck at the casino, where roulette, baccarat, blackjack, seven-card stud poker, and slot machines are played.

While you're based in Seefeld, it's relatively easy to explore part of Bavaria in West Germany. (See *Frommer's Germany.*) You may or may not get to see little **Wildmoos Lake.** It can, and sometimes does, vanish all in a day or so, and then there may be cows grazing on what has become meadowland. However, the lake will suddenly come back again, and if conditions are right, it will become deep enough for swimmers. Wildmoos Lake comes and goes more frequently than Brigadoon.

The little German town of **Mittenwald,** one of the highlights of Bavaria, can easily be explored on a day trip from Seefeld.

THE RESORT HOTELS

The most unusual and most elegant hostelry in town is the **Hotel Klosterbräu,** A-6100 Seefeld (tel. 05212/26210). Constructed around a 16th-century cloister, the hotel combines so many architectural features that it's sometimes hard to believe that the views from the different angles are actually of the same building. The dramatic entrance is under a thick stucco arch only slightly wider than the rest of the arches that run along the ground floor. The interior contains soaring vaults supported by massive columns of the same kind of porous stone that built Salzburg (you can still see prehistoric crustaceans embedded in the stone). Posh accessories have been added, such as thick carpeting, Oriental rugs, intimate lighting, a scattering of antiques, and acres of beautifully furnished paneling, some of it carved into intricate designs. The modern sections blend discreetly into the older ones and give the added allure of, for example, a dome-shaped fireplace that juts gracefully into one of the well-furnished public rooms, as well as sweeping staircases and an occasional piece of old sculpture.

The 116 bedrooms are encased in a towering chalet behind the front entrance. The windows look out over the midsummer buffet set up near the outdoor sun terrace. The charge for staying at such a luxurious hotel is not cheap: rooms rent for 880 AS ($64) to 3,000 AS ($218) per person daily. These tariffs include half board in the hotel's renowned restaurant, and the prices vary according to the season and the room assignment. The hotel is open from December to March and June to September.

Restaurants on the premises include a country-style Bräukeller with regional furniture and live music; a rustically elegant Tyrolean room with carved ceiling beams, pewter candelabrum on each table, and impeccable service; and a more formal dining room where guests sit on wooden chairs upholstered in alpine patterns below ancient ceiling vaults. Dishes include a host of international and Austrian specialties. The person at the next table might be a vacationing celebrity from Germany traveling incognito. Fixed-price menus range from 300 AS ($21.75), while à la carte dinners go from 300 AS ($21.75) to 500 AS ($36.25). Reservations are necessary.

In the evening the chicly dressed patrons often drop in at Die Kanne nightclub, whose showgirls, comedians, and musical revues provide a high spot in the nightlife of the village. A daily afternoon tea dance in winter allows the hotel guests to meet one another. The big indoor swimming pool has a café area nearby, while an outdoor pool is visible from the sunny balconies of the well-furnished bedrooms, where you can enjoy breakfast if you want. Golf, tennis, mountain climbing, and skiing facilities are all within walking distance.

Hotel Astoria, A-6100 Seefeld (tel. 05212/22720), a luxurious five-star choice, stands on a beautiful elevated position in a large park, offering panoramic views of the surrounding mountain ranges. Because of its sunny and sheltered ambience, it is a favorite with well-heeled visitors in both summer and winter (open from December to March and June to September). Summer brings flowered terraces and gardens; winter, the open fireplace in the lounge bar and an indoor swimming pool. The hotel offers only 56 bedrooms, each with private bath and shower, phone, radio, color TV, and alarm clock. Winter half-board charges range from 1,250 AS ($91) to 2,290 AS ($166.50) per person daily; in summer they range from 790 AS ($57.50) to 1,350 AS ($98.25) per person daily. Saturday evenings are gala nights here—candlelit dinners and music from the house band—and once a week a Viennese heurige or a Tyrolean evening with traditional buffet is presented. Other facilities include parking, a sauna with a steam grotto, massage, a solarium, and a fitness room. There's also a wind-sheltered sun terrace. Weekly arrangements can be provided for golfers.

Hotel Wildsee-Schlössl, Innsbrucker Strasse 195, A-6100 Seefeld (tel. 05212/2390). What is today my favorite hotel in Seefeld was little more than a run-down pension until its owners rebuilt it in 1983. What emerged from their efforts was a radically reconstructed 40-room hostelry whose thick walls resemble those of a very ornate castle. A corner watchtower with a funnel-shaped roof was added, along with jutting balconies, step-fronted gables, and red-and-white-striped shutters. The location is across from the lake, along the side of the road leading into Seefeld from Innsbruck.

The beautifully appointed interior contains Austrian antiques, ticking grandfather clocks, alpine painted blanket chests, and dozens of comfortably upholstered cubbyholes to sink into with a drink. A blazing corner fireplace greets winter visitors near the reception desk. The in-house restaurant is covered separately. Accommodations lie at the top of a stairwell lined with hunting trophies. Furnishings are full-grained Tyrolean, with plush carpeting, timbered ceilings, and sun-flooded windows. Depending on the season, rates for half board range from 725 AS ($52.75) to 1,950 AS ($141.75) per person daily. In the basement are a sauna and a steambath.

Karwendelhof, A-6100 Seefeld (tel. 05212/2655), is one of the most elegant hotels in Tyrol. It's constructed in a chalet format with two distinct sections, the exterior walls of which are painted in regional designs. The 100-year-old Tyrolean parlors have parquet floors, heavily beamed ceilings, and lots of antique accents. The 42 personalized, well-maintained bedrooms are elegantly simple, often with at least one of the walls constructed of massive natural-grained planks; each bedroom has a private bath or shower. The engaging owners, the Wilberger family, offer their accommodations at summer half-board rates ranging from 450 AS ($32.75) to 1,200 AS ($87.25) per person daily. Winter half-board terms cost 600 AS ($43.50) to 1,300 AS ($94.50) per person daily. Prices vary according to the season and the accommodation.

The hotel restaurant, called Alte Stube, is completely covered in old paneling, by now burnished to a rich mellow glow. Menu items include beef, veal, and pork dishes, accompanied by fresh vegetables and followed by regional cheeses and home-baked pastries. Fixed-price menus go from 180 AS ($13) to 360 AS ($26.25), whereas à la carte dinners range from 220 AS ($16) to 450 AS ($32.75). Reservations are necessary.

The hotel's K-Keller is one of the social centers of the village. A casino in an adjoining building opens at 3pm every afternoon.

Lärchenhof Hotel, A-6100 Seefeld (tel. 05212/2383), is a luxurious five-star choice, with a well-cared-for look and a personal atmosphere, only a few minutes' walk from the pedestrian zone. The salons are big and sunny, permitting a vista from almost any point within. Intimate groupings of furniture are scattered throughout the paneled interior. The hotel offers 50 bedrooms, each with private bath or shower. In summer, half-board rates range from 800 AS ($58.25) to 1,300 AS ($94.50) per person daily; in winter, from 1,050 AS ($76.25) to 1,700 AS ($123.50) per person daily. The rooms mostly face south, with a living area, color TV, minibar, safe, and balcony; the décor is Tyrolean. Facilities include an indoor swimming pool, a sauna, massages, a solarium, and a lawn for sunbathing. The cuisine and the wine cellar enjoy a local reputation, and gala dinners and Tyrolean buffets with music and dancing are held one night a week. The Mayr family are the personable hosts, and they operate from December to March and June to September.

Alpenhotel Lamm, A-6100 Seefeld (tel. 05212/2464). The overhanging eaves of this elaborate hotel are supported by heavy beams that extend at an angle from the second floor to the outer edge of the roofline. The corners are rounded into protruding towers decorated with regional illustrations and designs, many of which are clearly visible from the village church next door. The cozy interior has ceiling beams, as well as an intimate bar, plus a scattering of rural artifacts and baroque sculpture. The most expensive bedrooms are fairly elegant and spacious. This 160-bed family-run hotel in the heart of the pedestrian zone charges 650 AS ($47.25) to 1,500 AS ($109) per person daily for half board, based on the season. Rooms have private baths, balconies, radios, TVs, and self-dial phones. Facilities include a fitness center with steambath, a panoramic sauna, a hot whirlpool, and a Kneipp facility. The hotel's restaurant, Zum Kirchenwirt, enjoys a good reputation among visitors, and dancing and music are offered daily in the Lammkeller.

Hotel Eden, A-6100 Seefeld (tel. 05212/2258), is a modern chalet with a façade covered with wooden balconies, a single painted illustration, and a wood-and-stucco extension jutting out from the front. An outdoor café contained within the natural windbreak of the hotel does a thriving business, both winter and summer. The interior has unadorned paneling, stone floors, big windows, and all the essential ingredients for the provision of comfort without excessive frills. You'll probably enjoy at least one drink at the curved wooden bar, or in one of its U-shaped banquettes, before retiring to one of the brightly colored bedrooms. These rent for 450 AS ($32.75) to 940 AS ($68.25) per person daily, with half board included.

Hotel Post, A-6100 Seefeld (tel. 05212/2201), is an imposingly tall chalet with two peaked roofs and evenly spaced rows of dark-toned balconies. You'll probably be greeted in the paneled reception area by a member of the Albrecht family, each of whom contributes to keeping this hotel running smoothly. The public rooms contain upholstered furniture and soft lighting. On the premises are a hotel disco, a shaded garden, two restaurants, and comfortable and 86 invitingly attractive bedrooms, most with private baths or showers. Half-board rates range from 460 AS ($33.50) to 1,200 AS ($87.25) per person daily.

Strandhotel Seespitz, A-6100 Seefeld (tel. 05212/2218), has a large, welcoming design that usually reminds everyone who sees it of the perfect vacation house. Designed like an oversized chalet, with lots of interesting angles and corners, it's separated from the lake only by a well-maintained lawn and a barrier of water-loving plants. The inside is heavily beamed, airy, and filled with light from the big panoramic windows. The 85-bed hotel is comfortable and tastefully furnished. Charges range from 470 AS ($34.25) to 920 AS ($67) per person daily for half board.

Hotel Wetterstein, A-6100 Seefeld (tel. 05212/2283). There's a delicacy to the wrap-around balconies of this unusual hotel that can't be found anywhere else in Seefeld. The hipped roofs of the original gray and white-trimmed core rise above a well-planned addition containing the oversized arched windows of the public rooms. The overall effect is appropriate to its location as the village's best viewpoint over the nearby tennis courts, which are transformed into a skating rink in winter. The sun terrace is popular in all seasons. The interior of the hotel is outfitted with a kind of no-nonsense masculinity that is unpretentious and appealing. Parts of the bedroom walls are usually covered with horizontal planking, while all 95 of them contain private baths. They range in price from 410 AS ($29.75) to 850 AS ($61.75) per person daily for half board. There are a Tyrolean Stüberl and, under the same management, a guesthouse behind the hotel with 20 beds. The Wetterstein lies directly next to the Olympia Sport and Congress Center, with a swimming pool and tennis courts.

Hotel Dreitorspitze, A-6100 Seefeld (tel. 05212/2952), is a six-story peak-roofed chalet whose comfortable bedrooms enjoy dramatic views of the mountains. The interior has a warmly appealing combination of honey-colored woods and subtle shades of red, which are contained both in the furniture's upholstery and in the vivid patterns of the dozens of Oriental rugs scattered throughout the public rooms. The hotel has an elevator, plus an indoor swimming pool, a sauna, a sun terrace, and a large garden with a putting green for outdoor golf practice. Forty-five of the 50 standard rooms contain private baths or showers, and there are apartments suitable for families. Summer half-board rates range from 620 AS ($45) to 850 AS ($61.75) per person daily, with winter half-board charges going from 850 AS ($61.75) to 1,200 AS ($87.25) per person daily. Open from December to March and June to September.

Hotel Tyrol, A-6100 Seefeld (tel. 05212/2221), is a modern alpine-inspired building, its three floors of white concrete faced with wooden shutters and balconies. The main dining room has Empire crystal chandeliers, patterned carpeting, and white-and-gold Louis XVI–style armchairs. A less formal restaurant is darkly paneled and rustically intimate, with cozy lighting and a woodsy kind of elegance. On the premises are both an indoor and outdoor pool, a sauna, a steambath, a Jacuzzi, a solarium, a disco bar, and a winter fireplace. The hotel offers 37 well-furnished rooms with private baths or showers, and tariffs range from 700 AS ($51) to 1,500 AS ($109) per person daily, with half board included. Prices depend on the accommodation and the season.

Hotel Diana, Klosterstrasse 97, A-6100 Seefeld (tel. 05212/2060), lies at the center of town, along a pedestrian zone close to the nightlife and sporting facilities. Guests congregate in the paneled warmth of the plant-lined public rooms. The Tyrolean restaurant contains a tile stove, while a less formal Stüberl serves snacks and drinks. Each of the 22 comfortably furnished bedrooms has its own phone and bath. Rates range from 440 AS ($32) to 850 AS ($61.75) per person daily, depending on the season; prices include half board. The hotel is closed in November.

Hotel Christina, A-6100 Seefeld (tel. 05212/2553), is a comfortable, contemporary 14-room chalet, with lots of exposed wood and a rustic, homelike character. It has an indoor pool accessible through big glass doors in the cellar, thanks to the hotel's location on the slope of a hill. Five pedestrian minutes from the center, the hotel charges 300 AS ($21.75) to 550 AS ($40) per person daily, based on double occupancy, the prices depending on the season. All units have private baths (many of them have balconies as well, and a buffet breakfast is included.

Waldhotel, Römerweg 106, A-6100 Seefeld (tel. 05212/2207-0), one of the oldest and most established hotels in Seefeld, has emerged from a total refurbishment with a 1930s flair combined with modern standards. Its location, at the edge of the resort adjoining the woods surrounding Seefeld, is about a seven-minute walk from the center of the village. All 26 rooms provide private baths or showers, balconies, radios, and direct-dial phones; superior rooms have sitting lounges and color TV. Winter rates range from 550 AS ($40) to 960 AS ($69.75) per person daily for half board, while summer half-board charges go from 390 AS ($28.25) to 690 AS ($50.25) per person daily. A panoramic garden restaurant and a terrace are favorite spots for lunch. In winter, there is a curling rink, and the hotel is just a three-minute walk from funicular and cable cars leading to the slopes. All year the place offers a variety of entertainment, such as a live Dixieland band or Tyrolean music.

Hotel Schönegg, A-6100 Seefeld (tel. 05212/2375), is a 35-room chalet hotel with a warm interior décor with contemporary paneling and furnishings. A bar, restaurant, and a sauna are on the premises. Close to the village center, the Schönegg is managed by the Schwenniger family, who charge 425 AS ($31) to 860 AS ($62.50) per person daily, depending on the season, with half board included.

WHERE TO DINE

Most guests book into a Seefeld hotel on the half- or full-board plan. But perhaps at least once you'll want to skip your hotel dining room to try one of the recommendations described below.

Restaurant Wildsee-Schlössl, Innsbrucker Strasse 195 (tel. 05212/2390), in the hotel previously recommended, emerges as one of the finest dining rooms in a region where competition is fierce. Contained within a re-creation of a Teutonic castle beside the lake, it consists of a trio of beautifully appointed rooms, lined with pieces of pewter. The first room as you enter is ringed with burnished paneling and canopied with a vaulted ceiling. Menu specialties are likely to include filet of sole in a saffron-flavored cream sauce, julienne of chicken with a bouquet of salad, a heavenly version of smoked wild salmon with a cranberry parfait, filet of lamb in an herb sauce, and veal medallions with fresh asparagus. Full à la carte meals cost 300 AS ($22.25) to 500 AS ($36.25), and are served daily from 11:30am to 2pm and 6 to 10pm. The restaurant closes in November.

Sir Richard (tel. 05212/2093), on the outskirts of town, creates an elegant aura of year-round Christmastime because of its masses of flowers, dozens of burning candles, and the immaculately pressed linen that covers the wood tables. Whether the menu items prepared by the chefs are Italian or Austrian, they are presented on delicate china with attentive service. You might begin your meal with watercress soup, followed by one of a variety of lamb, veal, or fish dishes, often accompanied by masterful sauces. Even the fresh leafy salads have just the right degree of tartness. À la carte dinners, starting at 380 AS ($27.75), are served from 11:30am to 2:30pm and 6:30pm to midnight. The restaurant is closed Monday from April to December.

Birklstüberl, Geigenbühelstrasse 79 (tel. 05212/2322), run by Robert Jenewein, is a straightforward restaurant serving Austrian dishes in a rustically traditional environment. Well-prepared specialties include fresh meats and vegetables, soups, cheeses, and homemade desserts, such as chocolate mousse. À la carte meals, served from noon to 2pm and 6pm to 9pm daily, cost 110 AS ($8) to 360 AS ($26.25). Reservations are suggested.

APRÈS-SKI

Seefeld in season bustles with typical wine and beer cellars, along with nightclubs and discos that come and go.

However, the major nighttime attraction is the **Spiel-Casino Seefeld,** Bahnhofstrasse (tel. 05212/2340), at the Hotel Karwendelhof, already recommended. It opens at 3pm, offering baccarat, blackjack, seven-card stud poker, a money wheel, American and French roulette, and 70 slot machines. Your admission is 140 AS ($10.25), for which you are given chips worth 200 AS ($14.50).

Hotel Klosterbräu, recommended previously, is the center of the most sophisticated nightlife on the après-ski circuit in Seefeld. Its nightclub, Die Kanne, presents an international orchestra and a floor show during its hours of 9pm to 3am daily. In winter the club also opens at 5pm for a *tanz-tee* (tea dance). The hotel also features international specialties in its restaurant, Ritter Oswald Stube, and a gemütlich atmosphere in its Bräukeller, open from 10am to midnight, presenting Stimmung music after 8pm.

LEUTASCH

If for some reason you don't wish to anchor for the night in Seefeld, you can drive northwest through the Valley of Leutasch (Leutaschtal), which is one of the most scenic valleys in northern Tyrol. It runs under the Wettersteingebirge to the border of Bavaria.

Among the villages in this valley, Leutasch has the best food and accommodations.

Food and Lodging

Hotel Kristall, A-6105 Leutasch (tel. 05214/6319), has elegant two-tone designs embellishing the outside window frames and long rows of flowered balconies. The interior is outfitted with amber-colored paneling, stone detailing, and a combination of traditional and rustically contemporary furniture. The gemütlich restaurant usually has live music, while the hotel bar is a popular rendezvous spot. On the premises are an indoor pool, a sauna, an exercise room, a solarium, along with Ping-Pong and pool tables. The Bader family offers 40 comfortably furnished bedrooms, each with private bath or shower, from December to September. Half-board charges in summer go from 470 AS ($34.25) to 820 AS ($59.50) per person daily. In winter, they range from 600 AS ($43.50) to 1,000 AS ($72.75) per person daily.

Hotel Leutascherhof, A-6105 Leutasch (tel. 05214/6208), is a three-story chalet with a big extension stretching out the back, plus a rounded bay window jutting out from one of the corners. The paneled interior is intimately lit, especially in the cozy bar and the dining room, where small framed pictures are scattered around for visual interest. The hotel was almost completely rebuilt in 1976, with private bathrooms added to each of the comfortable bedrooms. The Trasser family has operated this hotel as a family property since 1934, extending old-fashioned Tyrolean hospitality. Half board ranges from 620 AS ($45) to 785 AS ($57) per person daily. Facilities include a Finnish sauna, a solarium, and a fitness room.

5. Resorts Around the Zugspitze

The Zugspitze, part of the Wetterstein Alps, is a frontier mountain separating West Germany from Austria. The highest peak, almost 9,700 feet high, is in the neighbor country but can easily be seen from Tyrol. Its principal resorts are Garmisch-Partenkirchen in West Germany and Lermoos in Austria.

If you're exploring in this area, it's always wise to have your passport with you, as you'll cross the frontier if you follow my recommendations for this section of Tyrol.

Chances are, most readers of this guide will approach the Zugspitze from the Austrian side. If so, you can take a cableway, the Tiroler Zugspitzbahn, from Ehrwald-Obermoos, circling in a half moon through the Bavarian resort, Garmisch, and coming back to where you started. You can also take the trip by cog rail from Garmisch, perhaps departing from there, going up one side of the mountain and down the other, landing in Austria.

EHRWALD

With the most resort facilities of any place in the Tyrol section at the foot of the Wetterstein Alps, Ehrwald is popular in all seasons. It's one of a trio of resorts that includes Lermoos and Biberwier, sharing the same attractions (see below).

Bavaria, to the north, can easily be reached using Ehrwald as a base. Most visitors, however, just pass through Ehrwald to take the cable car for the ascent to the **Zugspitze,** one of the major attractions to be found in the west of Austria.

To reach the cable car, drive west from Ehrwald until you see a sign indicating Talstation Obermoos. Or you can take a bus from Ehrwald to that point. Here you board the Tiroler Zugspitzbahn, which will take you to the *mittelstation* at Gamskar (6,610 feet). From that point you go to the Zugspitzkamm station (9,203 feet), which had to be blasted out of the mountain rock. Your next stop is the summit of the Zugspitze, arriving at Zugspitzwestgipfel, 9,680 feet above sea level.

A busy restaurant at the summit has windows with one of the greatest panoramic views in all of Europe. From here you can see Grossglockner, the Dachstein, and the Bavarian Alps. To the north you're able to see as far as the Starnberger See, a lake in Bavaria.

The cable car is at its busiest during the summer months. Service is hourly from 8 to 11:30am and 1 to 5pm. It operates daily.

Food and Lodging

Hotel Alpenhof, Alpenhofstrasse 13, A-6632 Ehrwald (tel. 05673/2345). The big chimneys visible from the outside let you know that wintertime fires will probably be throwing off a welcome heat indoors. The main salon has a bar, a fireplace, a coffered ceiling, and a welcoming color scheme. Throughout this hotel are charming rustic touches, such as the ceramic stove in the alpine Stuben restaurant, the acres of paneling, and the thick walls sometimes set with leaded glass. There's also a more formal upholstered dining room.

In winter the management hosts a five o'clock tea dance with disco music in the café. The facilities include an outdoor tennis court, a sauna, and access to the village swimming pool. Most of the 46 attractively furnished bedrooms contain private baths; others offer showers. The accommodations are among the finest the resort has to offer. Rates for half board range from 520 AS ($37.75) to 710 AS ($51.50) per person daily, depending on the season and room assignment.

Hotel-Restaurant Spielmann, Wettersteinstrasse 24, A-6632 Ehrwald (tel. 05673/2225), is one of the best hotels at Ehrwald, and it is also generally cited as having the best cuisine. The establishment sits about a five-minute walk above the resort. In high season, it charges 580 AS ($42.25) to 670 AS ($48.75) per person daily for half board, depending on the accommodation. Singles pay a supplement of 100 AS ($7.25). Summer half-board prices range from 450 AS ($32.75) to 560 AS ($40.75) per person. There are a total of 30 comfortably furnished bedrooms, and the public rooms make effective use of Tyrolean furniture and Oriental carpets. A heated outdoor swimming pool is on the premises. Both the hotel and restaurant are closed from late October until mid-December and Easter till late May.

Connoisseurs throughout the region are attracted to the hotel restaurant, consisting of a quartet of rustically cozy rooms that share a blue-green *kachelofen* (ceramic tile stove) and open fireplace. Lunch is daily (when the hotel is open) from 11:30am to 2pm and 6 to 9pm. Food is both Austrian and French, and it's prepared by the Spielmanns' son, Christian, who is becoming increasingly well known as a chef. Nonresidents should call for a reservation and expect to pay 175 AS ($12.75) to 250 AS ($18.25) for set menus, with à la carte dinners ranging from 170 AS ($12.25) to 450 AS ($32.75).

Hotel Schönruh, A-6632 Ehrwald (tel. 05673/2332). From the flagstone-covered terrace on one of the upper floors, guests have a sweeping view of the fertile valley. This well-run hotel looks almost like a Mediterranean villa because of its curved walls, bay windows, and ornamental tower. Once you're inside, however, you'll know you're in a Tyrolean country house because of the crossbeam timbering, the roughly finished plaster walls, the ceramic stoves, and the mountain décor. The 85-bed hotel rents singles for 350 AS ($25.50) daily, with doubles peaking at 800 AS ($58.25). Full-board terms cost 550 AS ($40) to 700 AS ($51) per person daily. Open from December to March and May to September.

Hotel Sonnenspitze, Kirchplatz 14, A-6632 Ehrwald (tel. 05673/2208). Viewed from the front, this 30-room 19th-century hotel is charming enough to look almost like an oversize cuckoo clock. It has a symmetrical façade whose entrance you'll reach from a two-sided stairwell rising gracefully from the street-level outdoor café. The ornamental overhang of the eaves is crafted into a baroque curve that shelters the flowers on the wooden balconies.

There is a lot of decorative stonework inside, as well as big arched windows, a warmly inviting color scheme, and a scattering of old armoires and antique pewter. The Leitner family, owners of this congenial place, charge 540 ($39.25) to 865 AS ($63) daily for a single and 440 AS ($32) to 715 AS ($52) per person for a double, with half board included; the highest tariffs are charged in winter. All rooms have showers, toilets, phones, and balconies. English menu cards are available in the hotel's restaurant. The place is closed from mid-October to mid-December.

Alpenhotel, A-6632 Ehrwald (tel. 05673/2254), is a pleasantly designed chalet with the unusual added benefit of having the terminus for the Zugspitzbahn cable car attached to its side. If you stay here, you shouldn't miss riding to the top for a meal or a snack in what's considered an engineering marvel and a panoramic delight. Back at the bottom, your simply furnished room, with half board included, will cost 380 AS ($27.75) to 530 AS ($38.50) per person daily, depending on the season. All 24 accommodations contain private baths. Open from December to March and June to October.

LERMOOS

About a mile to the northwest of Ehrwald is Lermoos, a resort attracting visitors in both summer and winter—and it's not bad in spring and fall, either. It joins with Ehrwald and Biberwier to form a trio of resorts close enough together to allow you to take advantage of the facilities of all three. The threesome is linked by bus, with departures about every 30 minutes.

Warm-weather pursuits, besides going up the Zugspitze (see above), include hiking, mountain climbing, easy strolls through meadows and forests, swimming, minigolf, boating, fishing, cycling, riding in horse-drawn carriages (fiacres), and more.

When the snow falls, this becomes a white sports arena with, of course, downhill and cross-country skiing, ice skating, curling, tobogganing, winter walks, swimming in covered pools, and sunbathing (!). The carriage ride of summer is exchanged for a horse-drawn sleigh ride along snowy roads. Both Lermoos and Ehrwald have sleigh ranks on their church squares. You can reserve a vehicle for your ride between 10am and 4pm daily.

Whatever the weather, after dark you can enjoy Tyrolean evenings, learn to dance Tyrolean style, or just relax in a wine cellar or beer tavern.

Lermoos is well situated, set against the backdrop of the Zugspitze. You can take a chair lift to the side of the Grubigstein station (6,500 feet), from which you'll have a magnificent view of the mountain peak. Via the chair lift, you can eventually reach the top station at 7,215 feet above sea level.

Food and Lodging

Hotel Drei Mohren, A-6631 Lermoos (tel. 05673/2362), was built in 1806 and renovated in 1961. Its windows are crowned with regional embellishments, with a three-sided bay window extending toward the street from the white stucco façade. Management encourages its guests to go fishing for the region's trout, pike-perch, and carp. The hotel owns a small lake nearby, where guests can swim. Other facilities include an elegantly simple sitting room, with heavy ceiling beams and lots of exposed stone, a series of inviting public rooms with fireplaces, and two statues of Moorish attendants waiting in stylized poses beside the elevator doors.

The Drei Mohren's 50 bedrooms, all comfortably furnished and most with baths or showers, rent for 485 AS ($35.25) to 610 AS ($44.25) per person daily for half board, depending on the season. In the hotel restaurant, the Trout Room, which has a panoramic view, freshwater fish is the specialty of the chef. In season, the menu also includes wild game. The sunny café terrace has a view of the Zugspitze. Besides a playroom for children, there are a fitness room and a solarium. In winter the hotel stages fondue evenings.

Sporthotel Zugspitze, A-6631 Lermoos (tel. 05673/2630), is a 26-room chalet hotel run by the Scheiderbauer family, with painted designs around the windows, heavy overhanging eaves, and masses of flowers hanging from the balconies. Guests usually decide to spend some time on the sun terrace, which offers a view of the nearby mountains. The interior has big plate-glass windows, lots of exposed wood, and a rustic, homey feeling enhanced by Oriental rugs and light-grained furniture. In a restfully isolated position a few minutes from the center of the village, the hotel charges 560 AS ($40.75) to 895 AS ($65) per person daily for half board; all the rooms have baths or showers, toilets, safes, TVs, radios, and balconies. Facilities include a sauna and a solarium, and the kitchen prepares Tyrolean specialties.

Hotel Post, A-6631 Lermoos (tel. 05673/2281). The lobby of this hotel is decorated with antiques, including a baroque chest-on-chest with unusual legs. The décor includes beamed and coffered ceilings, a scattering of hunting trophies, a working ceramic stove, and a collection of contemporary and alpine chairs. The ambience is relaxed and attractively informal. A bar area often features evening dancing with live folkloric music. The hotel offers 125 comfortably furnished bedrooms, costing from 600 AS ($43.50) per person for a double, with singles starting at 650 AS ($47.25); half board is included. An indoor swimming pool is on the premises.

Hotel Tyrol, Oberdorf 10, A-6631 Lermoos (tel. 05673/2217), is a hillside chalet with a distinctive design that includes a big sun terrace set on top of a curved glass-walled extension. The warmly tinted décor includes multicolored flagstone floors, panoramic views over the village, and a convivial gathering place near the bar's hanging copper lamps. A few minutes from the train station, near the nursery slopes, the 45-room Tyrol charges 450 AS ($32.75) to 550 AS ($40) per person daily for half board in winter. In summer, guests pay 350 AS ($25.50) to 400 AS ($29) per person daily. Rooms are sunny and comfortable. The hotel is open from November to March and May to September.

Après-Ski

There's nothing fancy here in the way of nightlife, but Teutonic revelers seem to have a good, often rowdy time. If you like to dance, you might check out the already-recommended **Hotel Tyrol,** which often has a live group playing for your entertainment. The Kellerbar at the hotel occasionally stages Tyrolean folkloric evenings.

Live groups often play for dancing at the Taverna bar of the also-recommended **Hotel Post.** If there's no live action, you're likely to get disco music. The Post is also known for its Tyrolean folkloric evenings in season.

When I was last at the recommended **Hotel Drei Mohren,** they were having a beer-drinking competition, and I understand this is a regular feature. Here the action might be more Bavarian than Tyrolean . . . and a lot of fun.

When you return from the slopes after a hard day of skiing, you can join the throngs at the **Simon Konditorei** (tel. 05673/2419), which has the best and most mouthwatering pastries in town, along with Swiss hot chocolate wearing a "top hat" of whipped cream. In all but the slowest season, it's open daily from 9am to 6pm. (In the height of the ski season, it remains open until 10pm.) Coffee begins at 19 AS ($1.40), with pastries costing from 16 AS ($1.15) to 24 AS ($1.75).

BERWANG

In the far-northern reaches of the Tyrol country, very close to the West German border and encircled by mountains, is Berwang, an as-yet-unspoiled village with hospitable innkeepers. The little resort, at an elevation of 4,400 feet, has both an upper and a lower village. In winter people enjoy skiing here, with runs at varying stages of difficulty. The ski season usually ends in March.

You can reach Berwang by state road 189 from Innsbruck, or you may prefer to approach it by the main Bavarian highways heading south (for example, departing from Ulm via Kempten). From Garmisch in Bavaria, a good highway takes you here by way of Elbsee, crossing the border at Griessen and Lermoos. If you're traveling by train, the station to look for is Berwang-Bichlbach. Don't forget to bring your passport.

Food and Lodging

Sporthotel Singer, A-6622 Berwang (tel. 05674/8181), a four-star Relais & Châteaux, is an elegant chalet with two interconnected sections, each with a symmetrical peaked roof. The interior has the kind of fanciful rusticity that gives the feeling each object was carefully chosen by a skilled decorator. Many of the handsomely decorated bedrooms have beamed ceilings, and all have private baths and toilets, as well as phones. Some have TVs, and many have south-facing balconies. In all, 45 rooms are rented, costing from 840 AS ($61) to 1,180 AS ($85.75) per person daily for half board in winter. Summer half-board tariffs go from 640 AS ($46.50) to 930 AS ($67.50) per person daily.

The sports-minded hosts of this congenial hotel serve Berwang's finest cuisine in their restaurant, where there is a bar. A comfortable lounge with an open fireplace, sun terraces, and ample car parking add to the enjoyment of a stay here. The public salons are reinforced with massive timbers bolted and pegged into carefully finished paneling. Among sports facilities, the hotel offers a heated open-air swimming pool, an indoor pool, a children's play area, tennis courts, and minigolf, plus access to a fitness course.

Alpenhotel Berwangerhof, A-6622 Berwang (tel. 05674/8288), is a large, five-story hotel built in two interconnected sections. The generous balconies look out over the nearby village, the center of which is a few minutes away. The décor of the cozily rustic public rooms ranges from vintage Tyrolean to an up-to-date ambience of red upholstered chairs and vividly patterned carpeting. Overall, the effect is enhanced with Oriental rugs, massive wood detailing, and lots of alpine flavor. On the premises of the hotel is the largest indoor swimming pool in Austria. The manager invites guests to a daily five o'clock tea dance, often with live entertainment, after which they can move on to their choice of three bars and several restaurants. The main restaurant in this international hotel offers an intriguing combination of the designs of several different countries, with a tasteful emphasis on honey-colored woods, coffered ceilings, painted embellishments, and unusual accessories.

The 260-bed hotel rents accommodations with comfortable furnishings and private baths or showers. Full-board rates in summer range from 390 AS ($28.25) to 560 AS ($40.75) daily for a single and from 470 AS ($34.25) to 810 AS ($59) per person for a double. The high price is for occupancy of an apartment with balcony. In winter, singles range from 480 AS ($35) to 760 AS ($55.25) daily, with doubles going from 590 AS ($43) to 1,000 AS ($72.75) per person, including full board. The hotel is closed from mid-April to mid-May and from mid-October to mid-December.

Kaiserhof Sporthotel, A-6622 Berwang (tel. 05674/8285). The Kuppelhuber family are your hosts in this prosperous-looking chalet whose twin roofs and flowered balconies rise from a slight knoll at the edge of town. The modernized interior offers plenty of Tyrolean touches, including expanses of glossy paneling, light-grained ceilings, and a helpful staff outfitted in alpine costumes. On the premises are two restaurants, a tavern, and a coffeeshop; a dancing bar and a disco; an indoor swimming pool (with an adjacent paddle pool for children), a steambath, and a sauna; a pool table and a tennis court; a beauty salon; and a covered parking garage. The place makes an effort to accommodate families with small children. Bedrooms offer much comfort, with several homelike touches. Each of the 72 units contains a private bath, radio, TV connection, and balcony. With half board included, per-person rates range from 480 AS ($35) to 750 AS ($54.50) daily.

Après-Ski

The most popular place to go at night is the **Sporthotel Singer,** already recommended. Here a band plays for dancing. Live bands also appear regularly in season at the **Kaiserhof** and **Alpenhotel Berwangerhof** (see above). Of course, there's the usual round of kellers and stüberls. But what makes Berwang a bit exceptional is an array of varied entertainment staged weekly in season, ranging from torchlit processions on skis to beauty contests to amateur nights.

REUTTE

The capital of the Ausserfern district, Reutte lies in the Valley of the Lech, north of the Fernpass. Its location on the traffic route between Füssen in West Germany, the Fernpass, and the upper part of the Lech Valley brings a lot of summer traffic through the town. Reutte is also served by the same train as Lermoos and Ehrwald.

This is mostly a summer resort, with three nearby lakes popular for swimming in summer, although I find them too chilly for my personal comfort. The largest and most attractive of the three lakes is three-mile-long **Plansee,** a body of emerald-green water lying 4 miles to the east of Reutte. In the Tyrolean country, only the Achensee surpasses this lake in size. A short canal links the Plansee to the

Heitenwanter See, one of the most beautiful lakes in Tyrol. Included in the lake trio are the **Frauensee,** 2 miles northwest of Reutte, and the **Urisee,** about a mile to the northeast.

Many of the burghers' houses you'll see in Reutte are from the 18th century, most often with oriels and painted gables. The **pfarrkirche** (parish church) dates from 1691.

From Reutte you can explore the Lech Valley, which has developed a winter-sports trade.

Food and Lodging

Hotel Urisee, A-6600 Reutte (tel. 05672/2301), is a lakeside chalet with wood-trimmed loggias and monochromatic decorations around some of the frontal windows. It's surrounded by a wrap-around sun terrace, while the interior has over-head pin lights suspended from crisscrossed ceiling beams and rustically attractive furnishings. The 30-bed hotel rents rooms with baths or showers, most of the ac-commodations also having private balconies. Half-board rates range from 340 AS ($24.75) to 430 AS ($31.25) per person daily.

Alpenhotel Ammerwald, A-6600 Reutte (tel. 05672/8131), is big on local color. Located outside the town center, the 76-room hotel joins its two symmetrical sections by a connecting series of public rooms. The façade has big windows, cut-out shutters, and a long expanse of white stucco stretching toward the back. The cozy, warmly tinted interior has amber-colored paneling, lots of orange and brown field-stone detailing, and attractive textiles. The quiet and sunny rooms rent for 440 AS ($32) to 501 AS ($36.50) per person daily, with half board included. On the prem-ises are a sauna, a swimming pool, a bowling alley, and a bar that has become a fashionable rendezvous point.

The Fraundorfer family, your hosts, seem to know every colorful character in the region as well as dozens of international guests. Many of them enjoy the well-known restaurant, whose specialties include roast hare in pepper sauce, wild venison (in season) with mushrooms, and an array of fresh salads. Fixed-price meals cost 150 AS ($11) to 200 AS ($14.50), while à la carte dinners go for 150 AS ($11) to 500 AS ($36.25), depending on what you order. Reservations are suggested.

Hotel Tirolerhof, A-6600 Reutte (tel. 05672/2557), seems to be one of the few hotels in the Tyrol not designed like a chalet. It rises five stories above the center of town in a simplified baroque style. The curved roofline is covered in red sheet metal rimmed with fragile ice catchers. The interior has a décor of exposed wood, wrought-iron lighting fixtures, and attractive furniture. The hotel rents 37 bed-rooms, each with private bath or shower and each designed for comfort and convenience. Half-board charges range from 330 AS ($24) to 410 AS ($29.75) per person daily.

---

6. The Lower Inn Valley

The Valley of the Inn River, called Inntal in German, goes through Tyrol from the southwest to the northeast, a distance of some 150 miles, separating the Swiss frontier at the Finstermünz and the Bavarian border at Kufstein at the far side. For the purpose of convenience in touring I've divided the Inntal into the Upper Inn district (see below) and the Lower Inn Valley.

The heart of a popular tourist district of Austria is formed by the Lower Inn Valley, the Ziller Valley to the south, the Alpbach Valley, and the Achensee area in the north. The section abounds in villages and small towns whose lifts and cableways take visitors on panoramic trips high in the air with magnificent vistas spread out before them.

If you're planning to stay overnight or spend a longer time in the Lower Inn

Valley, you'll find the widest range—at least the best choice—of accommodations in Kufstein, the last Austrian town on the Inn before it enters Bavaria.

Your first stopover in the lower portion of the Inntal might be—

HALL IN TIROL

This old salt-mining town at the foot of the Bettelwurf massif, 5 miles along the river valley from Innsbruck, was a prize possession of the princes of Tyrol. No longer enjoying the prosperity of other days, Hall is now trying to make a name for itself as a spa to attract a tourist industry. You'll sometimes see it referred to as "Solbad Hall."

Even if you don't choose to stay overnight here, you may want to stop off for a view of Hall's **Obere Stadt,** or Upper Town. You begin your exploration at the center of the Lower Town, the Untere Stadtplatz. The heart of the old town, the Obere Stadtplatz, has many colorful buildings, often with oriels and grilles. Narrow little medieval streets branch off from the Upper Town square, which still functions in its age-old role as a marketplace. Two of the most charming of streets to seek out, really no more than cobbled alleyways, are the Sparkassegasse and the Arbesgasse.

The **parish church** (pfarrkirche), much improved in the 15th century, is in the late Gothic style, although the interior is rococo. The 15th-century Rathaus (Town Hall) has an attic like a pavilion.

SCHWAZ

About 17 miles northeast of Innsbruck, the old mining town of Schwaz, on the south bank of the Inn River, is even older than Hall in Tirol, just visited, going back to the 12th century. It came into prominence, however, from the 15th to the 17th centuries, when it grew fat and rich from copper and silver mines. Today it produces only mercury.

Many of the burghers' houses remain from the town's time of great prosperity. In the Stadtplatz (town square), you can see the much-photographed Gothic-style **Fuggerhaus,** with oriels, turrets, and an arcaded courtyard.

A Franciscan church, **Franziskanerkirche,** completed in 1515, has both Gothic and rococo touches and three naves. You can visit the cloister, which is pure Gothic. Here the church's treasure, nearly two dozen wall paintings depicting scenes from the Passion of Christ, is displayed.

The 15th-century **pfarrkirche** (parish church) of Schwaz is considered the largest Gothic hall church in Tyrol. It has a roof of some 15,000 plates of copper, worth a vast fortune. Inside you'll see a quartet of aisles and two parallel chancels. Seek out the altar dedicated to St. Anne in the south side aisle.

KUFSTEIN

A settlement at this site on the Inn River has existed for many centuries. Kufstein was first mentioned in a document near the end of the 8th century, and a Bavarian fortress was established here in 1205. In 1393 the settlement was raised to the status of a town by its ruling duke, Stefan III of Lower Bavaria. Emperor Maximilian I wrested the fortress from the Bavarians in 1504 and added Kufstein to the Austrian domain of the Habsburgs.

The old frontier fortress town has often suffered the ravages of hostilities between Bavaria and Austria through the centuries. The town was put to the torch in 1703, losing most of its early medieval character but not its fortress, which, although much added to and altered since the 13th century, still dominates the town, the last outpost of Austria in the Inn Valley.

Today only the memories of its turbulent past linger in this peaceful little holiday resort town, about 1,650 feet above sea level, surrounded by woods and lakes, with fields green in summer and snow-blanketed in winter. Much traffic between Bavaria and Tyrol passes through here, and it's a convenient touring point for the Kaisergebirge, the limestone range of the Alps.

Area Sights

A promenade runs along the waterfront in the lower part of Kufstein. An outstanding attraction of the town is the **Heldenorgel** (Organ of Heroes) in the Burgerturm. This is the world's largest open-air organ, having 4,307 pipes, and honors all the troops who died in the two World Wars.

Tours are conducted through the apartments from the first part of April until the end of October, daily from 9:30am to 4:45pm, costing 25 AS ($1.80).

The **Festung** (fortress) contains the Heimatmuseum, a local museum in which you can see artifacts from primeval life in the Inn Valley, rural implements, a wooden smoke kitchen (about 250 years old), a farmhouse room from 1638, a display of illustrations depicting the war-torn history of the castle and the town, many objects of ecclesiastical art, old national costumes worn by people of Kufstein from 1800 to 1850, a room of the old craftsmen, many stones and minerals from the surrounding area, a diorama of "Animals in the Mountains," and many examples of the birds and animals from this part of Austria, plus a museum-gallery of the arts.

Highlight of guided tours is the Kaiserturm, or Emperor's Tower, a massive edifice finished in 1522. You can visit cells in which prisoners were held captive. The fortress served as a state prison as late as 1865. The last part of the tour is the 230-foot-deep well going down to the groundwater of the River Inn.

For the best view of Kufstein, visit either **Pendling,** a mountain across the Inn River, or else **Heldenhügel** (Mountain of Heroes), where you'll see a memorial dedicated to Andreas Hofer, the Austrian patriot who led a band of peasants made up of Bavarians and his fellow Tyroleans against the forces of Napoleon in 1809.

One of the most interesting excursions from Kufstein is to take the **Ursprungpass Road,** which runs along for more than 15 miles, connecting Kufstein to Bayerischzell in West Germany (bring your passport). From Bayerischzell, you can begin your tour of the Bavarian Alps (see *Frommer's Germany*).

Another excursion can be made to **Thiersee,** a tiny lake at the foot of a mountain. The lakeside village presents a Passion play somewhat similar to the world-renowned one staged at Oberammergau in Bavaria.

Erl, another little town that merits a visit, lies about 7 miles down the Inn Valley from Kufstein, near the West German–Austrian border. A Passion play is presented here every 5 years, the next one coming up in 1993. This play originated here in 1613, but its production was abandoned for many years until its revival in 1959.

Food and Lodging

The four-star **Hotel Andreas Hofer,** Pirmoserstrasse 8, A-6330 Kufstein (tel. 05372/3282), in the center of Kufstein, is the most famous hostelry in town. Named for the Austrian patriot, it's operated by the Sappl family. Completely renovated, and now better than ever, it offers 95 bedrooms, each with private bath or shower, toilet, TV, radio, and phone. The double rate is 456 AS ($33.25) per person daily, with singles costing 556 AS ($40.50), including a big buffet breakfast. Facilities include a lounge room, a hotel bar, a Viennese cafeteria, a cozy restaurant with a fireplace in the middle, a Tyrolean room, four automatic bowling alleys, and a garage.

Gasthof Alpenrose, Weissachstrasse 47, A-6330 Kufstein (tel. 05372/2122), at the edge of town, is a modern 19-room stucco building designed like a chalet with balconies. Built in 1971 and renovated in 1985, it has a boxy extension (partially trimmed with wooden planking) stretching off to one side of the central core. The tastefully decorated alpine dining room has a beamed ceiling; its food is considered the best in the area, with the Telser family always using the finest ingredients (backed up by a good wine list). If you're touring in the area, you may want to call for a reservation. You can order set menus for 250 AS ($18.25) and up, with à la carte orders costing from 200 AS ($14.50).

Room rates, based on double occupancy, are 630 AS ($45.75) to 690 AS ($50.25) per person daily, with singles carrying a daily surcharge of 90 AS ($6.50). Half board is included in the room price, which varies according to the season and the plumbing.

---

7. The Achen Valley

One of the most famous lakes in Austria and the largest in Tyrol—some say the most beautiful too—is the **Achensee**. This body of water, usually a light-green color, is 5½ miles long and about three-quarters of a mile wide, surrounded by coniferous forests and with the majestic peaks of the Sonnwendgebirge and the Karwendelgebirge as a backdrop.

In summer the entire Achen Valley becomes virtually a holiday resort, with its little villages connected by a steamer that runs from one to another. This is of course the best way to see the lake. You'll notice lots of anglers trying their luck at fishing in the Achensee.

Although it's mainly known as a summer resort, the valley also attracts skiers in winter, with good snow conditions from December to April and five lifts with superb facilities for alpine skiing. More than 30 miles of well-tended cross-country courses take ski trekkers through woods and pastures into the Karwendel valleys. There are also cleared paths for long walks and rides in horse-drawn sleighs. Curling, skating, indoor tennis, bowling, and some minor après-ski activity make for a happy winter holiday.

How to get to the Achen Valley? It's not too difficult. At some point midway in your exploration of the Inn Valley you came to the town of **Jenbach,** on the north bank of the Inn. From there, it's possible to take a cog railway up to the lake. If you're driving you can head north from Jenbach along a road that winds around a lot at first, until it reaches Achensee. A bus also follows this route. If you're traveling by train you will be deposited at Maurach, at the southern tip of the lake.

Should you be seeking food and lodging, you'll find the most desirable accommodations in—

PERTISAU
This little village on the west side of the lake lies about 3 miles northwest of Maurach. It's the most frequented resort on the lake in summer, also doing a minor business in winter, attracting those who prefer a holiday in the snow.

Food and Lodging
Hotel Kristall, A-6213 Pertisau (tel. 05243/5490). During high season this tastefully decorated chalet is almost like a village within the village. Its elegant public rooms are filled with the kinds of ornamentation that impart a rich, full look. Details include old polychrome sculpture, lots of paneling, gracefully curved wrought iron, and touches of brasswork. There's an outdoor swimming pool on the grounds. The hotel rents 52 richly furnished bedrooms, each with private bath or shower. Half board ranges from 500 AS ($36.25) to 600 AS ($43.50) per person daily.

Hotel Rieser, A-6213 Pertisau (tel. 05243/5251), is a big chalet hotel surrounded by low-lying buildings that contain a pool, a sauna, a two-lane bowling alley, a table-tennis room, and a solarium. The hotel also has two indoor and six outdoor tennis courts, a squash court, minigolf, and a children's play area. The public rooms of the main building are richly filled with Oriental rugs, comfortable wood-framed chairs, heavy ceiling beams, and a scattering of carefully inlaid antique reproductions. The hotel rents 94 bedrooms with private baths or showers. Half board ranges from 560 AS ($40.75) to 890 AS ($64.75) per person daily. The color scheme throughout is woodsy and warmly tinted, especially in the dining room, where the chef prepares generous portions of tasty regional specialties.

Hotel Karlwirt, A-6213 Pertisau (tel. 05243/5206), is a five-story antique-style chalet with sun-bleached wood balconies and an interior décor filled with high ceilings, heavy beams, and cozy sitting areas (some of them near a stone fireplace). Franz Joseph came here on a hunting trip about a year before he was crowned emperor. The comfortably rustic dining room has elegant combinations of white plaster and light-grained wood, while in the 60 bedrooms large areas of pinewood usually cover at least one wall and part of the ceiling. With half board included, rooms rent for 640 AS ($46.50) to 670 AS ($48.75) per person daily. The hotel, open from December to October, is a few minutes' walk from the center of town. In a nearby building, under the ownership of the same family, is a popular restaurant, the Langlauf Stüberl, the tables of which are grouped around a central fireplace whose smoke rises through a metallic funnel. The place serves good, reasonably priced meals.

As an alternative to staying in Pertisau, you can drive north to—

ACHENKIRCH

A marvelously engineered road runs along the eastern shore of the Achensee, going through tunnels and affording delightful views of the lake—views you might otherwise miss unless you get to take the lake steamer that runs in summer. If you take this road north you'll reach the village of Achensee, lying at the north end of the lake of the same name.

If you're seeking a good and inexpensive place for a lakeside holiday, go on northwest from the village of Achensee for about 2 miles, which will bring you to Achenkirch. This little resort has a number of moderately priced hotels serving good, hearty food.

If you continue north from here for about 6 miles, you'll be at the Achen Pass and the Bavarian border.

Food and Lodging

Sporthotel Achenseehof, A-6215 Achenkirch (tel. 05246/6209). The façade of this hotel has an arched entrance, the shutters are painted in stripes of red and white, and many of the ground-floor windows are protected with decorative ironwork. The establishment sits in a parklike area whose edges form a gentle curve extending like a peninsula into the lake. The woodsy interior has lots of paneling, big windows, several fireplaces, and light-grained, heavily beamed ceilings. The owners, the Reiter family, rent 36 comfortable, attractive bedrooms, each with private bath or shower. Half-board charges range from 420 AS ($30.50) to 510 AS ($37) per person daily.

8. The Ziller Valley

Back at Jenbach in the Lower Inn Valley, from whence I suggested setting out northward to explore the Achensee Valley, I'll now take you south through the

Zillertal (the German name for the Ziller Valley) east of Innsbruck, a resort mecca in summer and a playground for lovers of winter sports.

Some say this is the most beautiful valley with the most rewarding scenery in all the Tyrolean country. You may wonder about this claim as you go through the first stretches of the Zillertal, but don't turn back. It gets more impressive the deeper you penetrate into the valley.

When you first enter the Zillertal, you'll pass rich meadowlands where cows are grazing (if it's spring, summer, or autumn), looking as sleek and healthy as those in Switzerland. On your west will be the Tux Alps and on the east the Kitzbühel Alps, to which I'll devote space later on in this chapter. As tempting as it may be to head for these alpine areas, I advise continuing for the time being deeper into the Ziller Valley, which will suddenly grow narrower, the scenery becoming more dramatic.

The people of the Zillertal are said to be the finest singers in Austria, generation after generation of valley families having inherited magnificent voices and making use of their talent.

I always pass through the first of the little villages and resorts, since in my opinion better ones are ahead.

The first town that merits a stopover is—

ZELL AM ZILLER

Don't confuse this resort with Zell am See in Land Salzburg. Zell am Ziller is the major town of the lower section of the Ziller Valley.

Once it was a gold-mining town, but those days are long gone. Today any gold mined here is from summer and winter visitors—but that's not meant to suggest that the resort is overpriced. Quite the contrary. Inns here are most reasonable in their prices, making Zell am Ziller a good choice for those seeking a budget holiday.

Like comparable Austrian villages, Zell has a **parish church** (pfarrkirche), this one dating from 1782. Constructed on an octagonal design, it's surmounted by a huge dome.

The best possible time to be in Zell am Ziller is on the first Sunday in May, when the residents of the Zillertal come together for one of the great folk events of Europe, the **Gauderfest.** This heavily attended occasion is like some huge May Day bash, honoring the ushering in of spring.

The glorious voices mentioned above fill the valley with song. It's very much like *The Sound of Music,* and you expect to see Julie Andrews come prancing over some hill or meadowland at any time. At this centuries-old Maytime festival you not only hear the people of the valley sing, you also get to watch and listen as they play their musical instruments, particularly harps and zithers.

Music isn't all that goes on at the Gauderfest. The beer drinking rivals that at the Oktoberfest in Munich. Just for this occasion, a powerful (I say lethal) malt drink, Gauderbier, is brewed and lavishly imbibed.

Once this village was known only as a summer holiday site, but in recent times it has become a winter sports resort as well. In 1978 the Kreuzjoch area was opened to skiers, and Zell am Ziller took its place on the tourist ski maps of Europe. In season a free ski bus stops at the major hotels to transport guests to these slopes.

You can go by gondola to a restaurant with a view of the **Gründalm** (3,350 feet), and then continue by chair lift to Rosenalm (5,775 feet), where another restaurant opens onto a panoramic view. From Rosenalm, a drag lift can take you to a lofty citadel 7,430 feet above sea level.

Another ski area, the **Gerlosstein,** more than 3 miles from Zell am Ziller, also has bus service, but not as frequently. From the bottom station, a cableway will lift you to 5,400 feet, where, if you wish to go on, you can take a chair lift up to 6,020 feet.

If you're coming directly to Zell am Ziller, you can fly to the nearest international airport, Munich, in West Germany, and arrange your further transportation there. A narrow-gauge railway runs from Jenbach in the Lower Inn Valley up the Zillertal to Zell.

Where to Stay

Alpenhof Zellerhof, Bahnhofstrasse 3, A-6280 Zell am Ziller (tel. 05282/2612). Its foundations date from the early 1900s, but a tasteful renovation in 1987 transformed this place into the glossiest and most stylish big-city hotel in town. Designed like an angular and modern adaptation of a traditional chalet, it contains acres of shimmering white marble, clusters of Tyrolean antiques, a sauna and health club snuggled up under one roof, and an array of wood-trimmed and lavishly accessorized bars and restaurants. This is the only hotel in Zell am Ziller with its own covered garage, its own ski-rental facilities, and a child-conscious design: murals of barnyard animals have been added to facilities intended for the tots. Half board in one of the 41 bedrooms costs 550 AS ($40) to 590 AS ($43) per person daily. Guests are received from December to October.

Hotel Bräu, A-6280 Zell am Ziller (tel. 05282/2313). At the edge of the most important crossroads of Zell am Ziller, this ample and comfortable chalet was originally built in the 15th century. The present building is much later, however—in fact, an extra wing was added in 1985. Rising five balconied stories, its ochre-colored façade is embellished with trompe-l'oeil frescoes, especially around the window frames and under the eaves. Inside, it contains three different dining Stubes (more about these later), along with a wide and old-fashioned entrance hall adorned with hunting trophies, Oriental carpets, and paneling. Each of the 36 comfortable bedrooms is outfitted with wood trim, private bath, and plenty of alpine charm. Depending on the season, the Herbst family charges 416 AS ($30.25) to 486 AS ($35.25) per person daily for half board. The hotel is closed between November 1 and mid-December and Easter and mid-May.

Hotel Tirolerhof, A-6280 Zell am Ziller (tel. 05282/2227), is a five-story balconied chalet with a desirable location in the commercial center. It was built in 1970 but expanded in the '80s. Today it's a clean modern building with Oriental carpets and lots of alpine charm. The 40 cozy bedrooms have concealed lighting, comfortable beds with thick quilts, and all the modern comforts. A member of the Waidhofer family, the owners, will quote you a half-board price ranging from 458 AS ($33) to 509 AS ($37) per person daily, depending on the season.

On the premises is a Tyrolean disco with thick wood walls and lots of rustic detailing, as well as an intimate country restaurant. Local residents are likely to gather in the evening for some serious beer drinking, and no one seems to mind if you join them. Other facilities include a sauna and solarium along with areas for massage. The hotel is an attractive choice for a holiday anytime except from mid-October to mid-December and mid-April to mid-May.

Where to Dine

Set on the second floor of Zell am Ziller's most stylish hotel, **Das Kleines Restaurant,** Hotel Alpenhotel Zellerhof (tel. 05282/2612), also serves some of the best food at the resort. This wood-sheathed gastronomic enclave mingles Tyrolean gemütlich with urban style. The main dining room contains a green ceramic stove, gracefully curved plank-covered vaulting, and big windows overlooking the busiest street. For even-greater doses of charm, ask for a table in the small and darkly intimate stübl where row upon row of antique photographs of almost-forgotten forebears adorn the paneling. Full meals cost from 350 AS ($25.50) to 600 AS ($43.50), but you can dine much more cheaply by ordering a set menu at 120 AS ($8.75).

You might begin with fried Camembert with cranberries, and follow with three kinds of schnitzels, or else trout or perch from the hotel's own fish hatcheries. One of the chef's specials is hunter's pie, made with venison and two kinds of wild mushrooms in a creamy sauce. A different special is featured every day of the week. The dishes are based on centuries-old alpine recipes such as pickled pork and boiled liver sausage. Lunch is daily from 11:30am to 2pm; dinner, 6 to 10:30pm.

Stübls, Hotel Bräu (tel. 05282/2313). Lined up edge to edge on the street level of this previously recommended hotel, this trio of authentic Tyrolean dining rooms compete with one another for the most regional charm. You might want to check out each of them before deciding. They're called Speisezimmer, Bräustübl, and Casino. Full meals cost around 300 AS ($21.75) and include a predictable array of solid Teutonic dishes, suitable for cold-weather days. Reservations are needed, and hours are 11:30am to 2pm and 6 to 9pm daily.

Après-Ski

Tanz Bar Dorfstadl, Hotel Alpenhof Zellerhof (tel. 05282/2612). Large, covered with pine paneling, and filled with furniture designed to handle hordes of hard drinkers, this popular nightclub caters to a crowd of celebrants who tend to be 30 years and older. Beneath heavy ceiling beams, you can order a large beer for 50 AS ($3.65) and listen to live bands play evergreen-inspired music. The place is open only in winter and midsummer, nightly from 8:30pm to 2:30am. Closing months are April, May, October, and November.

MAYRHOFEN

The road divides at Zell am Ziller, and to reach the next destination, you take the southwest route to the popular resort of Mayrhofen. After a visit there, I recommend that you return to Zell and then go southeast to Gerlos in the other direction.

But first, Mayrhofen.

This resort, standing at 2,075 feet, enclosed by towering alpine peaks and lying at the foot of the glaciers crowning the adjacent Alps, is a premier summer holiday spot and winter playground, the finest in the valley in terms of facilities and accommodations. Some of the best food in the area is served here.

For decades Mayrhofen has drawn summer holiday crowds with its endless opportunities for rambling and mountaineering, hang-gliding, shooting, tennis, fishing, swimming in a heated outdoor pool, minigolf, cycling, and even summer skiing in the Hinterlux glacier area at the top of the valley.

However, in recent years the resort village has come more and more into the picture as a ski center. Starting from scratch, you can learn to ski at the resort school. The children's ski training is especially good here, and a kindergarten makes this an ideal family resort.

Skiing is possible in the Penkenjoch section to the west of Mayrhofen, with a cableway taking you to nearly 6,000 feet. Mayrhofen has always offered good skiing for beginners and intermediates, but now there's also more for the experts. From the belvedere here you'll be rewarded with one of the most spectacular views of the Zillertal alpine range. A panoramic restaurant is here too.

You can also ski in the Ahorn area, to whose 6,250-foot height you're lifted by cableway departing from the south of Mayrhofen. At the top, seven drag lifts wait to serve you. Also at the top station is—guess what?—a restaurant with a panoramic view.

A wealth of other winter activities is available, including sledding on a natural toboggan run, alpine curling, ice skating, horse-drawn sleigh rides, horseback riding, and sports in an indoor arena.

Mayrhofen is a mecca for mountain climbers during nonskiing seasons, and you can find enjoyable nighttime entertainment ranging from tea dances to fondue evenings all year. You can also hear some of that famous Ziller Valley singing at folk festivals in July and August. The dates are different each year, so check at the tourist office.

Mayrhofen is reached by the Zillertal railroad, and one of the most popular diversions in summer is to take a ride on the narrow-gauge steam train between Zell am Ziller and Mayrhofen.

Area Attractions

From here you can also embark on some important excursions into the Alps around the Zillertal, where you'll be rewarded with some of the most spectacular scenery in Tyrol. By the time you reach Mayrhofen, the trail through the Zillertal that you've been following will have split up into four different parts, each one tempting. These valleys radiate off the Zillertal like blades of a big fan, reaching into the Alps. Three of them have the suffix *grund* (the German word for ground) on their names: the Stillupgrund, the Zemmgrund, and the Zillergrund. The latter takes its name from the alpine range.

You may not have time to explore all these valleys, but if you can make time for one, I suggest you make it the fourth of the quartet, the **Tuxertal,** or Tux Valley, the loftiest one, which cuts like a deep slash through the mountains. This valley comes to its terminus at several glaciers, including the Olperer, 11,400 feet high. You can take a bus from Mayrhofen to either the village of Lanersbach or on to Hintertux, both in the Tuxertal. The road runs west from Mayrhofen for some 13 miles to the end of the valley from which ski lifts branch off in several directions.

You come first to **Lanersbach,** the largest village in the Tuxertal, lying in a sunny, sheltered spot. From here you can take a chair lift to the Eggalm plateau with a restaurant at 6,560 feet. One of the most scenic panoramas of the Ziller Alps stretches before your eyes at this point.

Hintertux lies at the top of the valley, which of course is your ultimate destination. Once in this village you're virtually on the doorstep of magnificent glaciers. Views open in every direction. Because of thermal springs, Hintertux also enjoys a reputation as a spa. You may want to buy some woodcarvings here, as the craftsmen in the valley are well known for their skill.

You can ski on the glaciers in summer. A chair lift or a gondola from Hintertux will transport you to Sommerbergalm (6,800 feet). Once there, you can take a drag lift west to Tuxer-Joch Hütte (8,300 feet).

Where to Stay

Elizabethhotel, Einfahrt Mitte 432, A-6290 Mayrhofen (tel. 05285/2929), a five-star hotel and the most luxurious hostelry in town, is run by the Thaler-Moiggs family. The chalet façade has carefully detailed balconies, heavy overhanging eaves, a rounded stone entryway, painted designs, and a tower extending up from the center of the roof for whatever stork should build a nest there. The spacious and elegant interior is one of those tasteful places that only the right combination of money, taste, and skilled woodworkers can create. Each of the 36 bedrooms has a private bath, TV, radio, minisafe, and other modern conveniences. Half board in winter ranges from 1,150 AS ($83.50) to 1,295 AS ($94) per person daily. Half board in summer costs 800 AS ($58.25) to 895 AS ($65) per person daily.

Alpenhotel Kramerwirt, Am Marienbrunnen 346, A-6290 Mayrhofen (tel. 05285/2615), is a well-run hotel built Tyrolean style in the heart of the village near the church. There's been a hotel on this spot for the past 300 years, although the building you'll see today dates from around 1900. Its façade has stone trim around some of the windows, green shutters, a painted illustration of a medieval figure, and a towerlike construction high above the roofline. The rustic interior is paneled with dozens of examples of good woodwork, along with a scattering of Oriental rugs and antique painted chests.

Some of the 72 romantic bedrooms have four-poster beds and big marble-covered baths. Half board in winter costs from 629 AS ($45.75) to 729 AS ($53) per person daily, with summer half-board tariffs ranging from 579 AS ($42.25) to 679 AS ($49.50). On the premises is a small indoor pool, plus a sauna and a Turkish bath. A gemütlich nightclub, the Andreas Keller, is—obviously—in the cellar, containing exposed masonry, massive ceiling beams, checked tablecloths, and live musicians entertaining the drinkers and diners. Open December to October.

Hotel Neuhaus, Am Marktplatz 202, A-6290 Mayrhofen (tel. 05285/2203). Someone has lavished money and attention on the balconied exterior of this traditional hotel in the center of town. The forest-green shutters are well painted, while decorative talismans hang vertically from the slope of the slate-covered eaves. The 145-room hotel is actually a collection of large houses, all in the same style, connected with passageways and walkways. Both old and new sections make up the interior, with a décor that includes deep-relief carving, 19th-century hardwoods, and contemporary fireplaces. The dining room has an arched wooden ceiling, while the bar area might be a relaxed place for a drink before dinner. Spacious, well-furnished bedrooms rent for 625 AS ($45.50) to 725 AS ($52.75) per person daily for half board. Josef Moigg is the proprietor.

Hotel Neue Post, Hauptstrasse, A-6290 Mayrhofen (tel. 05285/2131). The older of the two buildings that form this hotel was built in 1626. It has a romantically paneled weinstube with an elaborately coffered ceiling and lots of atmosphere. The newer part contains comfortable bedrooms, lots of big, sunny windows, and modern amenities. Skiers tend to gravitate to the bar, open from 5pm to 12:30am, where music provides lively entertainment. Efficient service is provided against a rustically attractive décor. There's also an underground parking garage in the building. From December to October, the hotel rents 84 bedrooms, each with private bath or shower. Half board in winter ranges from 490 AS ($35.50) to 510 AS ($37) per person daily. Summer half-board charges go from 450 AS ($32.75) to 475 AS ($34.50) per person daily.

Gasthof Zillergrund, A-6290 Mayrhofen (tel. 05285/2377), is near a clear spring-water stream about a 5-minute drive (or a 30-minute walk) from the center of the village. The impressive entrance hall is accented with lots of wood and an intricate Oriental rug, while the dining room has a ceramic stove and exposed fieldstone. Rudolf Pfister is the congenial owner of this chalet hotel. The 24 comfortably appointed bedrooms, each with private bath or shower, cost from 438 AS ($32) to 468 ($34.25) per person daily for half board. The hotel has an indoor swimming pool, a lawn for sunbathing, a terrace, and a convivial Zirbenstube. A large outdoor café sometimes serves as a destination point for visitors who want to make the trek up from the village.

Where to Dine
Wirtshaus zum Griena (tel. 05285/2778) is strong on regional charm and cuisine. It is set amid a cluster of barns and outbuildings above Mayrhofen's main colony of resort hotels. To reach it, drive for about 10 minutes from the center to the uphill reaches of the resort into a secluded suburb. Fork left when you notice a fountain supported by a base of jagged fieldstones, then head several hundred feet down a one-lane road flanked by a fence of split railings. Inside the restaurant is a duet of dining rooms covered with unvarnished, frequently scrubbed pinewood planks which everyone says were installed 400 years ago. Even the tables are an uncoated series of smoothly sanded planks, on top of which rest large wooden bowls of pretzels.

Even if you speak German, you may find the menu tough going, as it's written in a little-used Tyrolean dialect. Many dishes are based on butter-and-egg alpine recipes, sometimes laden with cream from high-altitude cows. Several involve baking in a ceramic pot, including noodles layered with cream and cheese. Ever had beer soup? You might opt for the cheese platter, a bowl of polenta, or one of the meat dishes. The Wiener schnitzel, in the words of the apron-clad waitress, comes "fresh from the veal" and is "very, very pretty." Full meals, costing from 250 AS ($18.25), are served daily from 11am to 10pm.

GERLOS

It's not for the St. Moritz crowd, but Gerlos, a tiny resort in the Alps offering year-round pleasure, has its own special brand of warmth, hospitality, and fun, bringing repeat visitors, people who are not seeking the international limelight. Gerlos is in fact a secret that its devotees rather hope will stay that way. For majestic mountain scenery, Gerlos is hard to beat, set against a backdrop of the Kreuzjoch, looming over the resort from its 9,020-foot height.

To reach the resort, lying in a secluded, sunny valley at an elevation of 4,065 feet, you take a winding mountain road from Zell am Ziller. If you drive here in winter you'll need snowchains on your tires, but remember—no chains on the autobahn. If you're coming from Innsbruck, 48 miles away, for instance, you can get your chains put on as soon as you reach Zell. There's also a bus service from Zell am Ziller, the ride taking about 45 minutes, depending on road conditions. You should proceed cautiously on a drive to Gerlos even in warm weather, as the steep, winding road may be crowded with motorists.

Gerlos is a good ski resort, with runs ranging from beginners' slopes to those that challenge experts. You can take the Isskogel double-chair lift up to 5,500 feet, where you can see a sweep of five valleys, glaciers, and peaks of the Alps.

Summer visitors find a broad choice of pleasures, from hiking on the mountain trails to sailing, windsurfing, and fishing in the waters of the mammoth Durlassboder reservoir just outside the village. Horseback riding is offered in summer or winter, and when trails are snowy you can take a sleigh ride.

If you continue along the road to the east, you'll reach the Gerlos Pass and the Krimml waterfalls already visited in Chapter VIII on Land Salzburg. This Gerlos Pass road is one of the most scenic in Austria, linking the Ziller Valley with the upper Pinzgau region of Land Salzburg.

Food and Lodging

Hotel Gaspinerhof, A-6281 Gerlos (tel. 05284/5216), consists of three large chalets connected by underground passages and stairways. They're filled with antiques from the countryside, ranging from spinning wheels to grandfather clocks to just about the most beautiful painted armoires in the region. In one of the public rooms you might even stumble across a harp. On the premises are an indoor pool, a sexually mixed sauna, and romantically rustic bedrooms. An annex holds the overflow and costs less than the main building. The 150-bed hotel charges from 500 AS ($36.25) to 590 AS ($43) per person daily in summer for half board. In winter, half-board prices range from 685 AS ($49.75) to 980 AS ($71.25) per person daily.

Hotel Glockenstuhl, A-6281 Gerlos (tel. 05284/5217). The Eberl family are the owners of this wood-and-stucco chalet with overhanging eaves and neobaroque painting around some of the windows. A big-windowed café on the ground floor is a good place for coffee and snacks, and a rustic bar offers an inviting ambience. The dining room is spacious and outfitted with a large crucifix against one wall. The 28 big bedrooms have simple and attractive furniture, comfortable beds, and private baths or showers. They cost from 480 AS ($35) to 590 AS ($43) per person daily for half board in winter. Summer half-board tariffs range from 325 AS ($23.75) to 375 AS ($27.25) per person daily. The hotel is open from January to April and June to September.

Gasthof Pension Hubertus, A-6281 Gerlos (tel. 05284/5218), is a hillside chalet whose three upper floors are covered with aged wooden planks and relatively ornate balconies. The two bottom floors are made of white-painted stucco, with an arched entrance, big windows, and a wide veranda covered with a rustic porch. The interior has a yellow-and-white ceramic tile stove, painted antique furniture, and country curtains and ceiling beams. The hotel is small, offering only 20 bedrooms.

But these are spacious and have lots of exposed light-grained wood; all have private baths or showers. The half-board rate in winter ranges from 400 AS ($29) to 450 AS ($32.75) per person daily. Summer half-board prices go from 300 AS ($21.75) to 330 AS ($24) per person daily.

Après-Ski

For such a small village the nightlife in Gerlos is sophisticated, although it can be folkloric as well. Yodelers in lederhosen are likely to appear in any bar anytime, and chances are you'll definitely be entertained by a concert on an electric zither before you leave.

Gerlos has about eight clubs and dancing bars. Most of the nightlife activity takes place in the hotels, principally the already-recommended **Hotel Glockenstuhl** and the **Hotel Gaspinerhof.** Often you might find yourself dancing next to a visiting celebrity, including, on one occasion for me, Margaux Hemingway.

9. The Alpbach Valley

To tour another alpine valley, this one much smaller than the Zillertal, you can take the road north again, branching off to the east north of Schlitters and heading east again to Reith. Once there you can cut southeast to one of the most delightful valleys in the Tyrolean country. Thomas Wolfe wrote home to his mother of the Alpbachtal that "the valley has some of the most beautiful mountains and villages" he'd ever seen.

ALPBACH

One of the smallest valleys branching off from the Inn set among rich meadows, dark woods, rivers, and mountains, this was a copper- and gold-mining area ruled by the Fuggers in medieval times. The little settlement of Alpbach developed during that time. The town now enjoys minor renown as a meeting place of intellectuals, being the headquarters of the European Forum, an organization founded in 1945. Under its auspices, scientists, politicians, artists, and economists meet here to discuss the problems of the world.

From the village you can wander through meadows and forests to centuries-old farmhouses, nestling near high mountains, and enjoy warm hospitality and folkloric evenings in this tradition-steeped valley.

From nearby Brixlegg, a cableway will take you to the Grosser Galtenberg, a mountain 7,960 feet high.

Food and Lodging

Hotel Böglerhof, A-6236 Alpbach (tel. 05336/5227), has a history almost as old as that of the town itself. Built in 1470 as the home of a bowmaker, it became a hostel, a courthouse, and later a prison for the errant miners of the region. In 1936 Thomas Wolfe stayed here in what was at the time a farmhouse. The owner between 1945 and 1979 was the mayor of Alpbach, and he did everything he could to restore it to its rustic glory.

Today what you'll see are two symmetrical chalets with sun-bleached wooden balconies and elegantly embellished ground-floor windows. In summer thousands of geraniums and petunias virtually seem to set the chalet on fire because of their vivid colors. The interior has lots of old detailing such as massive ceiling beams, exposed carved stone, shiny paneling, and in the bedrooms romantically carved and painted furniture. On the premises is a double-level disco, plus an outdoor sun terrace, several bar areas, an indoor pool, an outdoor pool, a sauna, and a solarium. Tennis players can use the nearby outdoor courts free. The hotel has cozy restaurants where fresh-baked bread is served at every meal.

The Böglerhof rents 48 bedrooms, each with private bath or shower. In winter, half-board rates range from 700 AS ($50) to 1,100 AS ($80) per person daily, with summer half-board charges going from 650 AS ($47.25) to 900 AS ($65.50) per person daily. Guests can enjoy such weekly events as romantic dinners and wine tastings. Open from December to March and May to September.

Gasthof zur Post, A-6235 Alpbach (tel. 05336/5203), is a Tyrolean chalet surrounded by two tennis courts, a big outdoor pool, and masses of flowers. The interior contains a pub area popular with the après-ski crowd. The public rooms are filled with painted doorways and antique-style chests, along with lots of paneling and invitingly rustic detailing. A sauna offers a place to relax after a cold day outside. The Silberberger family, your hosts, rent 40 beds, charging from 470 AS ($34.25) to 720 AS ($52.25) per person daily for half board, depending on the room. Bedrooms are well furnished, functional, and modern. Open December to October.

Hotel Alpbacher Hof, A-6236 Alpbach (tel. 05336/5237). There's something streamlined and elegant about the simple interior of this 55-room hotel, almost as if the decorator wanted a lighter effect than is usually found in chalet hotels. Nonetheless, the design retains the rustic beauty of exposed wood. The main fireplace is flanked with red marble and built into a manorial-style format with a gently tapering plaster-covered chimney. The Andreas Bischofer family, the owners, have installed both an outdoor pool, along with modern baths in all the comfortable bedrooms. For bed and half board, rates range from 750 AS ($54.50) to 1,100 AS ($80) per person daily, depending on the season. The hotel is open from December to March and May to September.

Haus Angelika, A-6236 Alpbach (tel. 05336/5339), a super-bargain, stands in the center of the village, not too far from the local church. Built in 1970, it's a comfortable, well-managed alpine-style pension serving breakfast in a rustically paneled room with red and black accents. In the sitting room you'll often find a blazing fire. The 28-bed pension charges 250 AS ($18.25) to 310 AS ($22.50) per person daily for bed-and-breakfast. The Steinlechner family are your hosts. Open December to March and May to October.

REITH IM ALPBACHTAL

If you're seeking something more luxurious than tiny Alpbach offers, you can drive back to Reith and stay at the four-star hostelry recommended below.

Where to Stay

Hotel Kirchenwirt, A-6235 Reith im Alpbachtal (tel. 05337/2648), is a modern chalet with sunny windows and flowered balconies. The ceilings of the interior are elegantly geometrical and rather ornate, sometimes finished in attractive combinations of light and dark woods. Even the big indoor pool has a cross-beamed covering.

The accommodations at this 120-bed hotel are exceptionally good, with private plumbing and much comfort. Half board ranges from 510 AS ($37) to 740 AS ($53.75) per person daily for a double. Singles, also on the half-board plan, go from 615 AS ($44.75) to 865 AS ($62). On the premises are a sauna, a table-tennis and exercise room, and a children's playroom.

The neighboring town to Reith is—

RATTENBERG

This small border town of some 2,000 residents, once part of Bavaria, merits a stop just to look around the old quarter. Rattenberg, annexed by Maximilian I to be part of the Habsburg imperial holdings, was once a mining town, but the industry died out in the 17th century.

The old quarter still looks very much a medieval and Renaissance town. Many of the burghers' houses are from the 15th and 16th centuries, their oriels supplying the householders with a view of the comings and goings on the streets (a pursuit that has been replaced by television). Many of the old houses are coated with stucco, and a lot of the doors and some windows are framed in pink marble.

The same pink marble was used for finish in construction of the pfarrkirche (parish church), which dates from 1473.

As you walk down Hauptstrasse to see the old houses, you might also like to go on a shopping expedition, to purchase some of the glassware and local handcrafts for which Rattenberg is known.

You may want to go to the **Burg,** the fortified castle built on orders of Maximilian I when he confiscated the town from the Bavarians. The castle is in ruins, and it's about a half-hour walk from the town, but visitors go for the panoramic view of the area. Sometimes dramas are presented at the castle in summer.

---

10. The Kitzbühel Alps

Hard-core skiers and what are euphemistically called "the colorful people of the international leisure set" are attracted to this ski region. The Kitzbühel Alps are covered with such a dense network of lifts that they now form the largest skiing area in the country, with a series of superlative runs. The action centers at the town of Kitzbühel, but there are many satellite resorts that are much less expensive, including St. Johann in Tirol.

Kitzbühel is, in a sense, a neighbor of Munich, 81 miles away, whose municipal airport is used by most visitors who frequent the Kitzbühel Alps in wintertime.

KITZBÜHEL

Edward, Prince of Wales (you may remember him better as the Duke of Windsor), may have put Kitzbühel on the international map of fashionable ski resorts with his "discovery" in 1928 of what was then a town of modest guesthouses. Certainly, his return a few years later with Mrs. Simpson caused the eyes of the world to focus on this town, and the "upper crust" of England and other countries began flocking here, placing a stamp of elegance and sophistication on Kitzbühel.

At the time of this 20th-century renaissance, however, Kitzbühel was already some eight centuries old by documented history, settlement having been here much, much longer than that. Archeological finds have shown that during the Bronze Age and until the 9th century B.C. copper was mined and traded in nearby mountains. The settlement "Chizbuhel" is first mentioned in documents of 1165, the name being derived from the ruling family of Chizzo. Kitzbühel was a part of Bavaria until 1504, when it came into the hands of Holy Roman Emperor Maximilian I of Austria and became a part of Tyrol.

A second mining era began in Kitzbühel in the 15th century, this time copper and silver being the products, and the town became fat and prosperous for many decades. Numerous buildings from the mining days are still here, as are remnants of the town walls and three of the gates. In what used to be the suburbs of Kitzbühel you'll see some of the miners' cottages still standing.

What to See and Do

The town has two main streets, Vorderstadt and Hinterstadt, and unlike St. Moritz, where all the buildings are of modern vintage, Kitzbühel has preserved its traditional style of structures, at least in its core along these streets. You'll see three-story stone houses with oriels and scrollwork around the doors and windows, heavy, overhanging eaves, and Gothic gables.

The **parish church** (pfarrkirche) was built from 1435 to 1506 and renovated in the baroque style in the 18th century, restored again in 1951. The lower part of the **Church of Our Lady** (Liebfrauenkirche) dates from the 13th century, the upper part from 1570. Between these two churches stands the **Ölberg Chapel** (Ölbergkapelle) with a 1450 "lantern of the dead" and frescoes from the latter part of the 16th century.

In the **Heimatmuseum** (local museum), Hinterstadt 34, you'll see artifacts from prehistoric mining times in Europe and of the north alpine Bronze Age; a winter-sports section with trophies of Kitzbüheler skiing greats and displays showing the development of skiing here; and exhibits detailing the town's history. At one time this building was the town granary, built on the site of an early medieval castle. The center of the building is from the 13th century. The museum is open daily except Sunday from 9am to noon, charging 25 AS ($1.80) for adults and 5 AS (35¢) for children.

In winter the emphasis in Kitzbühel, 2,300 feet above sea level, is on skiing, and facilities are offered for everyone from novices to experts. The ski season starts just before Christmas and goes on until the beginning of April. With more than 62 lifts, gondolas, and mountain railroads on five different mountains, Kitzbühel has two main ski areas, the Hahnenkamm and the Kitzbüheler Horn. Cable cars are within easy walking distance, even in ski boots.

The linking of lift systems on the Hahnenkamm provides the celebrated **Kitzbühel Ski Circus,** which makes it possible to ski downhill for more than 50 miles, with runs that suit every stage of proficiency. Numerous championship ski events are held here, one being the World Cup event each January, when top-flight skiers pit their skills against the toughest downhill course in the world, a stretch of the Hahnenkamm especially designed and prepared for maximum speed. A ski pass entitles the holder to the use of all the lifts that form the Ski Circus.

Skiing became a fact of life in Kitzbühel as long ago as 1892, when the first pair of skis was imported from Norway and intrepid daredevils began to slide down the snowy slopes at breakneck speeds. Many great names in skiing have since been associated with Kitzbühel, perhaps the most renowned being Toni Sailer, a native of the town, who was the triple Olympic champion in the 1956 Winter Games.

Of course there are many other winter activities offered: curling, ski-bobbing, ski jumping, ice skating, tobogganing, hiking on cleared trails, and hang-gliding, as well as such indoor activities as tennis, bowling, and swimming. The children's ski school provides training for the very young. And don't forget the après-ski, with bars, nightclubs, and discos rocking from tea time until the wee hours.

Kitzbühel has summer too, with activities including walking tours, visits to the Wild Life Park at Aurach (about 2 miles from Kitzbühel), tennis, horseback riding, golf, squash, brass band concerts in the town center, cycling, and swimming. For the latter, there's an indoor swimming pool, but I recommend going to the Schwarzsee (Black Lake). This *see,* about a 15-minute walk from the center of town, is a peat lake and has bathing establishments, boats to rent, fishing, windsurfing, a waterski school, and restaurants.

On the sunny slopes of Kitzbüheler Horn, the **Alpine Flower Garden Kitzbühel** covers acres of ground at a height of some 6,000 feet. Alpine flowers can be seen in their natural environment of grass, shrubs, and rocks, with paths leading through the acreage. Admission to the garden is free. In either summer or winter, you can take the cable car that leaves for Kitzbüheler Horn (6,550 feet) every half hour.

Kitzbühel is not a cheap place to stay, but to make things easier on your pocketbook, the local tourist office, Hinterstadt 18 (tel. 05356/2155), has come out with

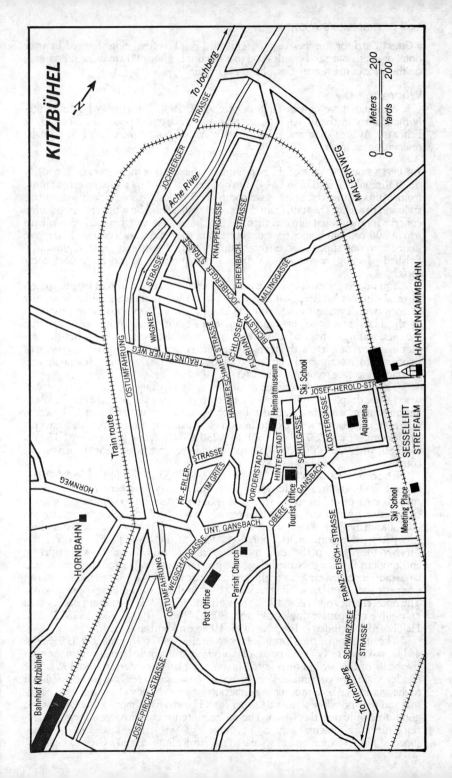

a **Guest Card** for summer visitors. This card is valid after being stamped by your hotel or guesthouse and entitles you to reductions, some of them quite substantial, on the price of many activities, plus some freebies.

Where to Stay

Although there's a wide range of hotels in Kitzbühel, reservations are absolutely mandatory in the high-season months, particularly the peak ski times such as February. As for Christmas in Kitzbühel, someone once wrote, "It's best to make reservations at birth."

THE UPPER BRACKET One of the best hotels at the resort is the **Hotel zur Tenne,** A-6370 Kitzbühel (tel. 05356/444). Owned and operated by a sophisticated family from Munich, this charming hotel combines Tyrolean gemütlichkeit with urban style and panache. The staff, from the general manager to the waiters, show genuine concern for their often devoted clientele. The hotel was created in the 1950s when a trio of 700-year-old houses (painted buttercup, terra-cotta, and cerulean blue) were joined into one superbly accessorized unit. You get yards and yards of gloriously finished paneling, re-creations of country baroque murals, and top-quality comforts.

You ride to your room in an elevator covered with depictions of laughing cherubs and summer landscapes, unless you want to ascend a staircase flanked at regular intervals with Tyrolean antiques and lighting sconces shaped into the imperial sign of the Habsburgs, the two-headed eagle. In addition to intimately decorated lounges, seating niches and nooks, the hotel sports the most luxurious health complex in town, complete with a tropically inspired cascade splashing within earshot of two hot tubs, a sauna, and a hot and cold foot bath. The Zur Tenne Restaurant and its Trader Vic's are recommended later on.

The 51 accommodations are as glamorous as anything in Kitzbühel: plenty of wood trim, deeply comfortable beds, eiderdowns, copies of or authentic Tyrolean antiques, minibars, phones, and fully accessorized private bathrooms. The suites each have a fireplace as well. Depending on the season, the bed-and-breakfast rates for singles ranges from 750 AS ($54.50) to 1,250 AS ($91); two persons pay 1,150 AS ($83.50) to 1,900 AS ($138.25). Studios and apartments are more expensive, of course.

The core of **Hotel Schloss Lebenberg,** A-6370 Kitzbühel (tel. 05356/4301), is a medieval knight's castle whose walls and turrets have been covered with a smooth layer of unblemished stucco. A modern extension looking vaguely like a cross between a villa and a chalet has been added nearby. The entire complex sits on a hill looking over the village, less than a mile from Kitzbühel, with dozens of mountain paths originating at its door. Very little of the castle's original décor has survived the passage of the years, and the interior is filled with wall-to-wall carpeting and modern furniture. Nonetheless, the hotel is comfortable and inviting, with a large indoor pool, a range of health and cosmetic facilities, a big sun terrace, and an energetic social program. The breakfast buffet in the elegant dining room is lavish. The hotel charges 680 AS ($49.50) to 1,605 AS ($116.75) per person daily, based on double occupancy; singles pay from 805 AS ($58.50) to 1,765 AS ($128.25). Half board is included in the price of the 109 rooms and apartments.

The ancestor of the **Hotel Goldener Greif,** A-6370 Kitzbühel (tel. 05356/4311), was built in 1271, and parts of it probably still remain buried within the massive walls of this well-known hotel. It was completely modernized in 1954. The façades' vivid series of trompe-l'oeil baroque frescoes give a realistic illusion of depth to the windows. From another angle the hotel is pure chalet style, with lots of balconies and red-and-white shutters. Owner Josef Harisch likes traditional charm with a good dose of luxury thrown in. The vaulted interior contains open fireplaces, antique furniture, Oriental carpets, a profusion of Tyrolean reverse-glass paintings, superb dining (recommended separately), a Tiroler Stüberl, and a Greif Keller in, of course, the cellar. The latter often presents folkloric entertainment in season. And this wouldn't be a first-rate Austrian hotel if it didn't provide a sauna with a pool, both of which are often packed at the height of the season. Herr Harisch and his family have one of the finest staffs in Kitzbühel.

The 56 bedrooms are especially attractive, some with canopied beds with scroll designs or wooden beds adorned with medieval reproduction statuary. If you want to splurge a bit, you can request one of the deluxe apartments, many in the hunting lodge motif, with their own Jacuzzis or private steambaths. Some of the apartments hold special charm in winter, having their own fireplaces. Winter half-board terms range from 850 AS ($61.75) to 1,700 AS ($123.50) per person daily, with summer half-board prices going from 520 AS ($37.75) to 820 AS ($59.50) per person daily. Each unit has a private bath, phone, radio, and TV connection.

In the heart of the old town next to the Spiel-Casino, this hotel is a traditional favorite for a lot of vacationers who prefer never to stay anywhere else. It lies 200 yards from the Hahnenkamm cable-car station and the nursery slopes. Open December to March and June to September.

Romantikhotel Tennerhof, A-6370 Kitzbühel (tel. 05356/3181)—in an elevated position on the outskirts of Kitzbühel, in the foothills of the mountains near the Hornbahn cable car and the golf course—is a comfortable 51-room chalet hotel descended from a centuries-old Tyrolean farmhouse. The whole place is furnished in alpine style with great care and taste, offering a touch of good living and complete relaxation in a lovely garden setting. Some of the public rooms have multicolored flagstone floors, ceramic-tile stoves, hunting trophies, and a collection of chalet chairs. The views from the outdoor café encompass the pool and the village. The restaurant (recommended separately) offers wholesome food, with vegetables and herbs straight from the hotel garden. The owners, Mr. and Mrs. Pasquali, take a personal interest in their guests and see that a high standard of service is maintained. Half board costs 890 AS ($64.75) to 1,850 AS ($134.50) daily for a single, depending on the season, and 710 AS ($51.50) to 1,505 AS ($109.50) per person for a double. If you are a traditionalist, try for one of the rooms in the original building, as they are the most intimate and cozy. All the accommodations are beautifully maintained, offering maximum comfort and many amenities. Open December to April and June to October.

Hotel Maria Theresia, A-6370 Kitzbühel (tel. 05356/4711), is a modern chalet with six stories of carefully applied decoration on its façade and an interior where much effort has been spent on creating a woodsy and quality-oriented décor. On the premises are a large bar area, a stone-trimmed lobby with an open fireplace, a Viennese café, and dining facilities (bountiful Austrian and international specialties). Much of the paneling is darkly tinted, even in the 105 comfortable bedrooms, which contain private baths or showers, phones, radios, and in some cases balconies. In winter, charges for a double range from 600 AS ($43.75) to 1,250 AS ($91) per person daily, with half board included. Summer prices, also with half board, are 489 AS ($35.50) to 630 AS ($45.75) per person. Singles pay a daily surcharge of 75 AS ($5.50).

A large fitness center on the fourth floor overlooks mountain views of the Hahnenkamm and Kitzbüheler Horn. In winter, facilities include massage, shiatsu, whirlpool, sauna, and solarium, along with a small bar/sitting area for relaxation. The hotel is operated in conjunction with the famed Goldener Greif and the Gasthof Schwarzer Adler.

Berghotel Ehrenbachhöhe, A-6370 Kitzbühel (tel. 05356/2151), is an attractively isolated first-class hotel at Hahnenkamm, which means it has to be reached by cable car. Its chalet façade looks out over a wide vista of mountains, while in the warmth of the interior you can swim in the indoor pool and enjoy good cuisine in the paneled dining room—or a few beers under the massively cross-timbered ceiling of the bar area. The 47 attractively detailed bedrooms rent for 700 AS ($51) to 750 AS ($54.50) per person daily in winter for half board. Summer half-board tariffs are 480 AS ($35) to 550 AS ($40) per person daily. The hotel is open from December to April and July to August.

THE MODERATE RANGE A 14th-century hunting lodge, **Schlosshotel Münichau,** Reither Strasse 32, A-6370 Kitzbühel (tel. 05356/2962), has red-and-white chevron shutters, at least three slate-roofed towers, and a severe medieval design. Lying 2½ miles from the center of Kitzbühel, the hotel commands an impressive view of the mountains from its location in the center of lush alpine meadows. An outdoor pool and a few medieval buildings are visible from the windows of the individually decorated bedrooms. The public rooms are embellished with unusual engravings and covered with vaulted ceilings. You'll find at least three open fireplaces, as well as a rustically elegant restaurant. With half board, the cost in winter ranges from 700 AS ($51) to 1,300 AS ($94.50) per person daily, depending on the plumbing. The cheaper units are in a comfortable modern annex a few steps away from the main building. Summer rates are slightly cheaper.

Hotel zum Jägerwirt, A-6370 Kitzbühel (tel. 05356/4281). The name of this place means "Hunter's Inn," and even if you don't like to hunt wild animals, you should love the blazing fires and the mellow paneling of this rustically attractive hotel. In a design of three small chalets joined with a central section, the hotel has a bar area with hewn overhead beams, as well as spacious bedrooms with lots of exposed wood. On the premises, a nightclub, the Halali, has an octagonal dance floor with dining tables set up around it and a timbered ceiling radiating out from the center like the spokes of a wheel. The restaurant is a member of the Chaîne des Rôtisseurs.

The 145-bed hotel charges from 1,200 AS ($87.25) per person daily for half board. Summer half-board charges go from 800 AS ($58.25) to 1,100 AS ($80) per person daily. Prices vary widely according to the season. A large sauna, a steambath, a fitness room, a solarium, and massage facilities are available. There are some apartments with hot whirlpool baths and color TVs. The hotel has a special movie room with many English-language video films. Both indoor and outdoor tennis courts are near the hotel, and a golf course is about a four-minute walk away.

Hotel Weisses Rössl, A-6370 Kitzbühel (tel. 05356/2541), was originally built in the 19th century as a coaching inn for the merchants passing through. Today, with the place run by the Hirnsberger-Klena family, it's difficult to detect the antique origins behind the weatherproof façade of chalet balconies. The hotel, radically renovated in 1987, is impeccably maintained, a haven from winter winds. It has a good staff and dozens of intimate and cozy seating niches for a retreat. One of the most prominent of these lies between the street-level reception desk and the in-house café. Winged with comfortable sofas, a fireplace provides midwinter cheer a few paces from the heavily trafficked hotel lobby. The fourth floor contains a small paneled room whose glass doors open onto a panoramic terrace with one of the best alpine views in town. The hotel, lying within a two-minute walk of the ski lifts, offers 70 snugly equipped bedrooms accented with pinewood trim, containing deeply comfortable furniture, private baths, phones, radios, TVs with videos, and minibars. In winter, half board ranges from 1,100 AS ($80) to 1,400 AS ($101.75) per person daily. In summer, half-board charges go from 900 AS ($65.50) to 1,100 AS ($80) per person daily. An à la carte restaurant, decorated with depictions of a white horse in etched glass, serves well-prepared Austrian and international dishes.

Hotel Tyrol, A-6370 Kitzbühel (tel. 05356/2468), is an attractively scaled chalet with five balconied stories and an open-sided wooden tower that the owners hope will eventually contain a stork's nest. In the center of town, the hotel has a simple décor and functionally practical bedrooms. On the premises is a large, somewhat bare dining room with a wood-paneled bar. The 85-bed hotel charges 550 AS ($40) to 650 AS ($47.25) per person daily for half board in winter, 490 AS ($35.50) to 550 AS ($40) per person daily for half board in summer.

Hotel Schweizerhof, A-6370 Kitzbühel (tel. 05356/2735), is a well-designed cross between a chalet and a mountain villa. It has a hipped tin roof, lots of balconies, and an exterior that looks different from practically every direction. The interior has some attractive antiques, Oriental rugs, and lots of beamed and paneled ceilings. All 42 bedrooms have phones, private baths and showers, and terraces among their many amenities. They are pleasing in décor, and those in the newer wing are more up-to-date, of course. The hotel has been enlarged in recent years. Singles rent for 550 AS ($40) to 1,150 AS ($83.50) daily, while doubles cost 620 AS ($45) to 1,000 AS ($72.75) per person, with half board included. The food is Tyrolean and international, and when you are booked on half board, you'll find the menu varied and interesting. On some winter evenings, the public rooms seem more like a house party than a hotel. Summer brings tables and umbrellas on the lawns. The hotel overlooks a children's ski school.

Hotel Klausner, A-6370 Kitzbühel (tel. 05356/2136), eight minutes from the center of town, is an ochre-colored twin-roofed building with a quiet location, a big parking lot, and a large garden with sun terrace close to the rear entrance. It's old and traditional, a familiar favorite. The interior has lots of stone detailing, both on its floors and in an occasional column supporting the wood-and-plaster ceilings. The 80 attractively simple bedrooms have high ceilings and functional furniture, and cost 740 AS ($53.75) to 840 AS ($61) per person daily for half board in winter. In summer, half-board tariffs go from 680 AS ($49.50) to 760 AS ($55.25) per person daily.

Sporthotel Bichlhof, A-6370 Kitzbühel (tel. 05356/4022). Slightly more than 2 miles south of the center of the resort, this hotel offers panoramic views over most of the valley. Its tasteful chalet format includes a big covered swimming pool, a sauna, and a steambath, as well as a décor of exposed paneling and patterned carpeting. The 30 spacious bedrooms sometimes have geometric grid patterns of dark wood against white walls that look almost Japanese in their simplicity. The price for half board ranges from 520 AS ($37.75) to 1,240 AS ($90.25) per person daily, depending on the accommodation and the season. Singles pay a surcharge of 100 AS ($7.25). The hotel is open from December to March and June to September.

SOME GOOD VALUES About a mile from the center of town, close to the Schwarzsee, is the **Hotel Bruggerhof,** A-6370 Kitzbühel (tel. 05356/2806), a countryside chalet with awnings covering its outdoor sun terrace. The interior has massively scaled ceiling beams, some of them carved into alpine patterns, and a warmly burning corner fireplace whose smooth stucco contrasts handsomely with the paneling around it. The dining room is graced with geometrically patterned wooden ceilings and wrought-iron chandeliers, while another section has ornate stucco columns supporting the full-grained ceiling. The owners, the Reiter family, run a well-maintained 55-bed hotel. Rooms are comfortable and cozy, with private baths or showers, toilets, and phones. Charges for half board are 730 AS ($53) daily per person in winter and 660 AS ($48) in summer. Open December to March and May to September.

Hotel Hahnenhof, A-6370 Kitzbühel (tel. 05356/2582), is an old-fashioned villa at the foot of the Hahnenkamm. Its interior has fresh colors, lots of wall-to-wall carpeting, a scattering of antiques, and exposed ceiling struts composed of heavy beams. The 16-room hotel is a gracious place to stay, very quiet because of its isolation from the village, which is about 10 minutes away. This would be a nice, romantic spot for a honeymoon, first or second. Rooms are comfortable and attractively furnished in Tyrolean style, with private baths. Prices for rooms with breakfast range from 250 AS ($18.25) to 600 AS ($43.50) per person daily, depending on the plumbing and the season. The hotel operates an à la carte restaurant serving Austrian specialties.

Gasthof Eggerwirt, A-6370 Kitzbühel (tel. 05356/2455), lies in Kitzbühel's lower altitudes, beside a steep street and a gurgling alpine stream whose waters have been channeled into a narrow prison of concrete. Highlighting the traditional stucco façade are country baroque designs that surround its windows with fanciful garlands of leaves and ribbons. Built in 1658, the place has been remodeled and much enlarged over the years, the last time as recently as 1984. Inside, the gasthof is clean, with well-maintained standards of simple, solid comfort. There's a charming dining room here, which will be recommended separately. The owners offer 20 bedrooms, each with private bath. Half-board terms in winter go from 620 AS ($45) to 740 AS ($53.75) per person daily. Summer half board costs 400 AS ($29) to 460 AS ($33.50) per person daily.

Where to Dine

Most guests stay at Kitzbühel on the half-board plan. It's also fashionable to dine around, checking out the action at the various hotels. With one or two exceptions, most notably the Unterberger Stuben, all the best restaurants are in hotels.

Wirtshaus Unterberger-Stuben (tel. 05356/2101) is a preferred hangout for the rich and famous who come every year to Kitzbühel. In addition to an occasional German-speaking film star (or whatever), you'll also find a scattering of athletes, urbanites, entwined couples, and hunters. Overall, the ambience is authentically Tyrolean. The owner, Mr. Unterberger, is the son of the town's most appreciated cook. Having learned to cook at his mother's stove, he and his wife decided to open this country-style inn in what had been his old family home.

In a setting of old paintings and rustic paneling, you are likely to be served one of your finest meals in the Tyrol. Try, if you see it on the menu, a poppyseed soufflé, or any of the specialties of the many countries that once belonged to the Austrian Empire. The fresh fish and the game are well prepared and savory. Dessert will probably feature (in summer) the succulent mountain berries of the region, or you might order the poached apples filled with white chocolate mousse.

An average meal will cost from 420 AS ($30.50), although the price could conceivably rise or fall depending on what you order. Reserve ahead and please be on time. The restaurant is open from 9am to midnight, with warm meals served only from noon to 1:30pm and 6:30 to 10pm. The chef takes off for all of June and all of November and on Tuesday from March 15 to June 30 and December 1 to 20.

Hotel Tennerhof Restaurant (tel. 05356/3181). You'll walk a short distance from the center of town before reaching this well-run Romantikhotel that looks like a balconied hunting lodge. The restaurant, rated by some critics as one of the 20 best in Austria, has a multicolored flagstone floor, a heavy beamed ceiling, and fern-green walls and tablecloths. Your attention will probably be directed toward the huge windows, whose view might give you pause between courses.

Specialties of the house include pungent lamb medallions, trout dishes, and a range of Tyrolean specialties, plus vegetables from the hotel garden when available. You'd better phone ahead for a table, since many of the guests staying at the hotel tend to fill up the dining room. Meals cost 300 AS ($21.75) to 500 AS ($36.25). Another restaurant at the Tennerhof caters especially to nonresidents of the hotel. The elegant interior is decorated with classic Tyrolean charm and atmosphere, and men are required to wear jackets and ties. The hotel dining room is open daily from 7:30am to midnight. Only dinner is served in the other restaurant.

Hotel Restaurant zur Tenne (tel. 05356/4444). Large, elegantly paneled, and accented with a corner bar, this is one of the top-notch restaurants of Kitzbühel, serving a sophisticated and well-prepared cuisine, definitely international in tone, using choice ingredients. A cooperative and polite young staff sees to your dining needs. Depending on the amount of sunlight streaming through the windows, the most popular seating area is often the glass-sided extension jutting out from the hotel into the stream of pedestrian traffic on the main street. The restaurant's cachet and its cuisine have been dramatically improved in recent years. It enjoys the same ownership as the prestigious Bayerischer Hof-Palais Montgelas in Munich, which has long been celebrated for its food. A delectable menu is likely to include carpaccio, a salad of juniper-smoked trout, filet of roast saddle of hare, medallions of venison, Hungarian gulasch, and chateaubriand. A popular favorite is the Tenne special steak, served with Idaho baked potatoes and sour cream. A dessert specialty is an iced soufflé flavored with Grand Marnier. Full meals, costing from 400 AS ($29), are served daily from 11am to 2pm and 6:30 to 10pm.

Tenne Stuben (Trader Vic's), Hotel zur Tenne (tel. 05356/4444). Its carefully polished panels, its large stone fireplace, and the centuries-old components that were used to craft its bar all evoke the Tyrolean Alps better than anything in town. Despite its décor (or because of it), the hotel management decided to create something here the likes of which Kitzbühel had never seen before. The menu format was borrowed from Trader Vic's in London, Munich, and New York, complete with tropical coladas and Polynesian flavorings. Only dinner is offered, nightly in winter from 5pm to 3am. You can order such time-tested favorites as filet of Szechuan beef, spiny Caribbean lobster thermidor, sweet-and-sour prawns, breast of duckling, banana fritters, and a full array of exotic drinks, some of which are served in a pineapple. Full meals cost from 400 AS ($29) and require a reservation.

Schloss Lebenberg (tel. 05356/4301). The royal family of Monaco has graced the dining room of this previously recommended hotel. If the elegant Gobelins Room in the old part is not to your liking, there are three other dining rooms nearby, all sharing the same menu. Fresh bread and butter are *de rigueur,* and specialties include cream of tomato soup with gin, calves' liver Tyrolean style, and a tempting array of fresh desserts, many of them made (in summer only) with whatever mountain berries are in season. Fixed-price meals go for 260 AS ($19) and 330 AS ($24), while à la carte dinners cost 180 AS ($13) to 450 AS ($32.75). The restaurant is open daily from noon to 9pm; closed from the end of October to December.

Goldener Greif (tel. 05356/4311), previously recommended as a hotel, offers some of the finest cuisine at the resort. Residents dine in a room looking out upon the slopes of the Hahnenkamm ski run. Nonresidents who make a reservation can also dine here in a room with vaulted ceilings supported by massive granite columns. A ceramic stove of orange tiles is the centerpiece, and the paneled walls display an impressive collection of 19th-century reverse paintings. Meals, costing from 350 AS ($25.50), include an array of Tyrolean and international specialties. You might, for example, order veal steak with fresh vegetables, peppersteak Madagascar, or venison. Many kinds of grilled steaks are regularly featured. A "Vienna pot" is one of the chef's specials, and fresh Tyrolean trout is offered daily. You might begin with a Serbian bean soup or else decide on a fondue bourguignonne. All the meat, sausages, and smoked meat come from the hotel's own butcher. In winter, food hours are daily from 11:30am to 2pm and 6:30 to 11pm (in summer, lunch hours are the same but the kitchen shuts down at 9pm).

Florianistube, Gasthof Eggerwirt (tel. 05356/2437), is contained in one of the less expensive and less ostentatious guesthouses at the resort, and it welcomes outsiders who call for a table. You dine in a cozy Tyrolean stube accented with paneling, white stucco, and alpine accessories. The menu is surprisingly comprehensive, international, and sophisticated for such a gasthof-type place. Full meals, costing from 250 AS ($18.25), might include porterhouse steak, tournedos with mushroom sauce, spaghetti with clam sauce, or fondue bourguignonne. Lunch is served daily from 11am to 2pm; dinner, 6 to 10pm. In summer a lunch or dinner buffet is sometimes served outside under the trees of the rear garden.

Après-Ski

Kitzbühel has about the best après-ski life in the Tyrolean country. Even before the approach of night, the activity has already begun in the mad dash for a seat at the **Café Praxmair,** Vorderstadt (tel. 05356/2646). This is one of the most famous pastry shops in Austria, and it's known for its florentines. Later on the Praxmair Keller pulsates with life. The owner, Toni Praxmair, brings in a piano player early in the evening. But if it's still five o'clock, the item to order is hot chocolate with a "top hat" of whipped cream. Coffee costs from 25 AS ($1.80), with pastries beginning at 20 AS ($1.45). Hours are 9am to 8pm daily.

The biggest after-dark attraction is the **Spiel-Casino** (tel. 05356/2300), located in the already-recommended Hotel Goldener Greif. Opening daily at 7pm, it has a restaurant and a bar, in addition to offering roulette, blackjack, and baccarat. Its summer season is from July 1 to mid-September, and its winter season lasts from Christmas until the end of March. It costs 170 AS ($12.25) to enter, and a passport is needed. It is recommended that men wear a coat and tie. There is no set closing time.

Tenne Night Club, Hotel zur Tenne (tel. 05356/4444). Its enormous popularity derives from more than its status as the only club in town with a live band. Multileveled and warmly rustic, it is known throughout Tyrol as the most convivial place to meet new companions in Kitzbühel. Up to 300 people at a time can crowd around the tables and the horseshoe-shaped bar. With live music, the place provides an opportunity for a lot of uninhibited fun. A limited menu includes schnitzels, rumpsteaks, and soups, but most guests come here just to drink and to party. A small cover charge is imposed only a few times per year when a truly outstanding band comes to play. The rest of the time the entrance is free, with hard drinks costing from 95 AS ($6.90). The club is open December to Easter and in August from 9am to 3am.

Take Five, Bichlgasse 3 (tel. 05356/3424), is considered the most popular and "most fun" disco in Kitzbühel. It is open nightly from 9pm to 3am, charging an entrance fee of 90 AS ($6.55). Hard drinks cost from 85 AS ($6.20). You'll find it near the stone archway leading over the main street of town opposite the Wienerwald restaurant.

Da Pepe, Hinterstadt 9 (tel. 05356/3331). The doors that shelter it from the snows outside are emblazoned with the kings and queens of hearts and spades. Inside, it offers a duet of bars, good music from several different eras, and a color scheme of emerald-green and white. This charming place where everybody meets everybody advertises itself as an "American Bar," and its drink list favors such tropical concoctions as planter's punch and piña coladas; five intriguing cocktails are made from champagne. Drinks cost from 25 AS ($1.80). If you're hungry, you can order homemade Hungarian gulasch or Italian pasta. Throughout the year, the bar is open daily from 5pm to 3am. However, on certain nights, especially in wintertime when the crowd has merited it, it's been known to close just before breakfast.

Drop-In, Hotel Weisses Rössl (tel. 05356/2541), is a well-frequented disco. Covered with mirrors, this place opens for drinks and music every winter night at 10pm. The club is also open for parts of July and for all of August. You can "drop in" any time before 5am. Sometimes a cover charge, ranging from 100 AS ($7.25), is imposed in the peak of the season.

Since most of the clubs of Kitzbühel are likely to be expensive, you might try the **Heurigenstadel Goldene Gams,** Vorderstadt (tel. 05356/2611), in the center of town. The décor is neo-Grinzing, and you can order both hot and cold food daily from 10pm to 2am. You're even allowed to grill your own steak. A zither player is likely to be on hand to play the *Third Man* theme.

Greif Keller, Hotel Goldener Greif (tel. 05356/4311), presents live music, often folkloric, but only in winter. In the cellar of this leading first-class hotel, it serves Tyrolean food but you can also come here just to drink, with most hard liquor costing 80 AS ($5.80) per drink. No cover is imposed, and hours are nightly from 7pm to midnight.

ST. JOHANN IN TIROL

St. Johann does not have the chic reputation of Kitzbühel, but neither does it have the high prices. Many "dollarwise" visitors stay here, taking advantage of the lower tariffs, and go to Kitzbühel, 6 miles to the south, to enjoy the facilities there.

This village, lying between two mountains, the Wilder Kaiser and the Kitzbüheler Horn, is both a summer holiday center and a winter ski resort. In summer it has a busy, open-air swimming pool, and in winter good ski runs appeal to both beginners and experts. A ski school and ski kindergarten, plus cross-country ski trails, add to the attractions. Bars in the snow are popular.

Many old Tyrolean houses fill the little town with charm, and some of the traditional inns have frescoed exteriors.

The Kaisergebirge, near St. Johann, draws many mountain climbers.

Where to Stay

Hotel Fischer, Kaiserstrasse 3, A-6380 St. Johann in Tirol (tel. 05352/2332), is a well-built chalet in the center of the village, with hanging vines flanking the sun terrace, plus evenly spaced rows of wooden balconies. The 35 sunny bedrooms are comfortable (albeit somewhat small), and they have private baths or showers and all the modern comforts. Half board in winter costs 750 AS ($54.50) to 850 AS ($61.75) per person daily. In summer, half board goes for 460 AS ($33.50) to 525 AS ($38.25) per person daily. The restaurant has a warmly intimate color scheme enhanced by the thick horizontal planks stretching across the walls. Typical dishes include North Sea salmon with dill sauce, schnitzels in cream sauce, and for dessert, a walnut parfait with marinated plums and kiwi. Open December to October.

Hotel Crystal, Hornweg 5, A-6380 St. Johann in Tirol (tel. 05352/2630), is a 45-room chalet, centrally located in the heart of the resort near the ski school. The interior is cozily outfitted with modern paneling and deep-seated chairs, with accents of wrought iron and modern textiles. The premises include a children's playroom and a sauna. The Lagler family, the hosts, charge winter half-board rates ranging from 690 AS ($50.25) to 940 AS ($68.25) per person daily. Summer half board costs 380 AS ($27.75) to 500 AS ($36.25) per person daily. The rooms are comfortably furnished in a traditional Tyrolean style, with all the necessary private facilities. Open from December to March and May to October.

Sporthotel Austria, Winterstrasse-Weg 3, A-6380 St. Johann in Tirol (tel. 05352/2507). This 50-room chalet has deeply recessed balconies and a rustically modern format of exposed wood and contrasting white stucco. The elegant interior has carefully crafted panelings on many of its ceilings, stone and tile accents, and brass chandeliers. The facilities include a big, attractive indoor pool with a bucolic mural covering one of the walls. Christine Mätzler, the hostess, charges winter half-board terms of 900 AS ($65.50) to 1,100 AS ($80) per person daily, with summer half-board prices ranging from 690 AS ($50.25) to 850 AS ($61.75) per person daily. The rooms are attractively decorated and comfortable. Open December to March and May to September.

Gasthof Post, Speckbacherstrasse 1, A-6380 St. Johann in Tirol (tel. 05352/2230), is about as solid a building as you'll find in Tyrol. It was first constructed in 1224, and parts of its original hewn ceiling beams are still in place. The façade is an elaborately ornate stucco surface where trompe-l'oeil baroque frescoes have been painted around each of the windows. The interior of the 45-room hotel, which stands a few buildings away from the village church, is replete with stone and wood columns, a painted ceiling, and lots of bucolic charm. The paneled bedrooms range from large to intimately small. With half board included, high-season rates cost 680 AS ($49.50) to 750 AS ($54.50) per person daily.

Hotel Park, Speckbacherstrasse 45, A-6380 St. Johann in Tirol (tel. 05352/2226), is a modern hotel that would look vaguely like a chalet except for its roofline, whose peak is broken into two distinct sections. My favorite feature in the contemporary sitting room is the copper-sheathed bonnet over the fireplace, which is built into a corner of two stucco walls. The 54 bedrooms, each with private bath or shower, are well maintained and of a high standard. Some of the cheaper units are "under the eaves." Half-board rates in winter range from 685 AS ($49.75) to 785 AS ($57) per person daily. Guests stay here on half board in summer for 455 AS ($32.25) per person daily. The hotel is open from December to March and May to October.

Hotel Europa, Achenallee 18, A-6380 St. Johann in Tirol (tel. 05352/2285), a charming hotel, lies next to the village sports center. Its façade is a 1960s-style pastiche of black-and-white detailing with weatherproof windows and Tyrolean balconies. The interior has coffered wooden ceilings, a hospitable bar area, a big sundeck, and a large open fireplace. The 50-bed hotel charges 705 AS ($51.25) to 820 AS ($59.50) per person daily for half board in winter. Summer half-board tariffs cost from 635 AS ($46.25) per person daily. Apartments are also available for two to five guests. Prices depend on the season, and all the well-furnished units contain private baths, phones, and balconies.

Where to Dine

Speckbacherstuben, Speckbacherstrasse 31 (tel. 05352/2843), is a local kind of restaurant popular with the residents of the village. It serves such items as bouillon with chives, warm cabbage salad with bacon bits, pork chops with garlic butter, and excellent salads using lots of fresh radiccio and leafy green lettuce. One of the chef's specialties is a mixed grill plate of veal, beef, and pork. Meals cost 150 AS ($11) to 300 AS ($21.75), and are served daily except Monday from noon to 2pm and 6pm to midnight. The restaurant is closed in May and November.

FIEBERBRUNN

This spa and well-known winter-sports resort lies in the Kitzbühel Alps in the Valley of the Pillersee-Ache, 7 miles southeast of St. Johann in Tirol. It can be reached by car or bus from St. Johann, about a 20-minute ride, depending on road conditions.

From here you can take a chair lift to **Lärchfilzkogel** (5,440 feet). In summer a popular excursion is to 2,730-foot-high **Lake Piller,** 6 miles north on the road to Waidring (see below).

Fieberbrunn has an outstanding schloss hotel, recommended below.

Food and Lodging

Schlosshotel Rosenegg, A-6391 Fieberbrunn (tel. 05354/6201). A hotel of charm and character, it has had a long history. Maria Theresa used it as a hunting lodge, and Napoleon's military staff used it as their headquarters. Its steeply sloping roof is studded with at least three rows of gables, as well as a collection of pointed towers. The Eberhardt family maintains a rustic restaurant in an adjoining low-lying modern building, which also includes a wine bar with an open hearth, Viennese music, and candlelight. When a second building behind the Schloss Rosenegg was acquired, its façade was renovated and its beautiful domed hall widened. It is now the site of the Rosenegg medieval banquets, held four times weekly. The banquet is an eight-course meal accompanied by a three-hour program of medieval dances, magicians, and fire-eaters. With drinks included, it costs 400 AS ($29) per person.

Within the castle are 30 beautifully appointed bedrooms, with another 50 units in the new building, which is joined to the hotel by a covered bridge. Rooms rent for 525 AS ($38.25) to 700 AS ($51) per person daily, including half board. Prices depend on the season and the accommodation.

Restaurant La Pampa, Rosenegg 61 (tel. 05354/6442). If you're in the mood for steaks and wouldn't mind taking a short excursion to a restaurant with a vaguely South American theme, this might be the place for you. It is run by the Erös family. The thick cuts of meat are grilled any way you prefer, and they're seasoned properly for maximum tenderness. Menu items include several kinds of soup (for instance, lobster bisque), roast beef Créole style, shrimp, and a wide range of salads. À la carte meals range from 180 AS ($13) to 350 AS ($25.50). The restaurant is open daily except Wednesday from 5:30 to 9:30pm, December to April and July to October.

WAIDRING

A Tyrolean village in the region where Tyrol, Bavaria, and Land Salzburg meet, Waidring is a popular holiday resort in summer and winter.

Summer visitors find 33 miles of well-tended walking paths, as well as high-altitude hiking trails on **Steinplatte** (6,000 feet). From December to mid-April, Steinplatte offers ideal skiing conditions, with a good lift system. You can go up the local mountain on the Waidring-Steinplatte mountain road if you prefer, although that's probably a better summer pursuit.

A ski school, illuminated natural toboggan run, curling, cross-country skiing, Tyrolean folklore evenings, and moonlight tobogganing add to the attractiveness of Waidring.

Food and Lodging

Sporthotel Tiroler Adler, A-6384 Waidring (tel. 05353/5311), is a large 35-room chalet in the middle of the village. Its balconies are covered in summer with masses of flowers, which contrast attractively with the weathered planking of parts of the façade. The interior has a woodsy contemporary décor that includes an elegant dining room and a slightly less formal restaurant with upholstered bar stools and light-grained paneling. Attractively furnished doubles range in price from 580 AS ($42.25), with singles costing from 360 AS ($26.25). Breakfast is included in these tariffs.

WESTENDORF

This charming Tyrolean village lies at an elevation of 2,575 feet on a sunny plateau in the Brizental (Brixen Valley) of the Kitzbühel Alps, undisturbed by through traffic. It's easily accessible by car, however, via the Inn Valley motorway to Wörgl and then the B70 Brixental road—but you'd better have heavy-tread tires on your car. You can also come here by train on the Innsbruck–Salzburg–Vienna railway.

Westendorf is surrounded by wooded mountains with walking and cycling trails, and summer visitors can ride the lifts up to the heights for views of the countryside.

For winter visitors the village has about 25 miles of prepared ski runs in use from the first of December until the middle of April, supervised by a well-organized mountain rescue service. Some 80 ski instructors are on hand to teach you how. Even tiny tots can learn to ski. The resort offers 15 chair lifts and T-bars, for which you need only one ski pass. There are good runs for both novice and intermediate skiers.

Other winter activities include sleigh rides, tobogganing, ice skating, curling, cross-country skiing, and after that, Tyrolean evenings complete with yodeling and whatever.

Food and Lodging

Hotel Briem, A-6363 Westendorf (tel. 05334/6310), sits quietly in a sunny meadow a few minutes away from the village center. Run by the Briem family, it's designed in an attractive chalet format of recessed balconies, clean white stucco, and lots of painted ornamentation around the weatherproof windows. The interior is rustic, with a simple dining room and a lounge/bar area. The hotel rents 42 rooms with private baths or showers, costing 400 AS ($29) to 490 AS ($35.50) per person daily in winter for half board. For half board in summer, rates range from 320 AS ($23.25) to 360 AS ($26.25) per person daily. Open from December to March and May to September.

Sporthotel Jakobwirt, A-6363 Westendorf (tel. 05334/6245). The Ziepl family are the owners of this charmingly traditional alpine hotel. The decorated building angles itself around an arcaded outdoor sun terrace with café tables and waitress service. The public rooms have massive ceiling beams, some of them carved, a hospitably rustic bar area, a scattering of antiques, and geometrically patterned tile floors in natural colors. Partly because of its location in the center of the village, the hotel's restaurants are popular throughout the year. These include an attractively formal dining room with upholstered chairs and a woodsy weinstube. Some of the best food at the resort is served daily from 11:30am to 2pm and 6 to 9:30pm. The hotel rents 49 bedrooms, all with private baths or showers. With half board included, the daily rate is 1,280 AS ($93) per person in winter and 1,040 AS ($75.50) in summer. Singles pay a daily surcharge of 80 AS ($5.75). The hotel has an indoor swimming pool, a sauna, and a solarium.

11. The Kaisergebirge

This nature reserve of Tyrol is known popularly by its nickname, "Kaiser." Lying to the north of the Kitzbühel alpine range (see above) and to the east of the Inn River, this is a land of coniferous forests and meadowlands filled in warm weather with contented-looking cows, a land of much beauty, ideal for hikers and climbers. It has towering mountain peaks and gorges of untamed beauty.

The Valley of the Kaiser connects with the Valley of the Inn at Kufstein. It divides the 6,560-foot-high Zahmer Kaiser (Tame Emperor) from the Wilder Kaiser (Wild Emperor), which has a jagged peak rising to 7,690 feet. Essentially, the Kaisergebirge is a limestone mountain range.

I will have two stopovers in this district, one in the southern part at Ellmau and another in the far-northern section, Walchsee, a lake-district retreat close to the Bavarian border. St. Johann in Tirol (see above) technically falls within this area, but because of its situation as a moderately priced resort near high-priced Kitzbühel, I included it in the district just visited.

ELLMAU

This holiday resort stands at 2,500 feet at the base of the Wilder Kaiser mountain and is considered the most beautiful spot in the valley. It lies in a triangle formed by Munich, Salzburg, and Innsbruck, within easy commuting distance of Kitzbühel. You can, of course, drive here. If you come by train, go to Kufstein, and from there a taxi will bring you to Ellmau.

In summer the little resort has an excellent hiking area and offers open-air concerts and Tyrolean evenings. It's also possible to take a cable car, the Hartkaiserbahn, for a panoramic sweep into the mountains.

Winter brings skiers to Ellmau, which has 10 lifts and well-maintained slopes. In addition, there are 52 more lift facilities in the surrounding area. In snow time you can participate in ice skating, curling, horse-drawn sleigh rides, cross-country skiing on well-kept courses, and of course, those Tyrolean evenings again.

Food and Lodging

Hotel der Bär, A-6352 Ellmau (tel. 05358/2395), is a winning combination of at least six different buildings clustered together in an isolated position a few minutes' walk from the village church. The furnishings of the interior run the gamut from rustically modern to 19th-century conservative, although the two styles compatibly merge with one another. On the premises are flagstone floors, Oriental rugs, comfortable settees, cafés, bar areas, and romantically furnished dining rooms. Everything is outfitted with taste and gemütlich comfort, with lots of visual stimuli to tease your aesthetic palate.

Each of the 46 upper-crust bedrooms is decorated individually, with ample use of rustic planking and subtle colors. Accommodations come in a wide variety of single or double rooms, including private outbuildings and apartments, some of them very luxurious. In winter, half-board charges range from 1,300 AS ($94.50) to 1,550 AS ($112.75) daily for a single, going up to 2,200 AS ($160) to 3,000 AS ($218) for a double. In summer, singles can take half board for 1,250 AS ($91) daily, with doubles paying 2,060 AS ($149.75) to 2,400 AS ($174.50). Suites are more expensive.

Some critics say that the best food in the province is served in the hotel's elegant restaurant. Americans will be flattered to see that the menu includes wines from California as well as Austria. Management invites guests to look into the kitchen, where an army of uniformed chefs prepares such dishes as cream of crayfish in a mustard and cucumber sauce, or rack of veal in a marsala sauce with leafy spinach. Desserts could include such delicacies as walnut ice cream with honeyed sour cherries. Prices for the elegant repasts, served daily from noon to 2pm and 6 to 9pm, range from 260 AS ($19) to 660 AS ($48). Reservations are important.

In a separate building is a pizzeria serving appetizing food in an informal setting. An outdoor pool is a short distance away, as well as an array of both summer and winter activities. Hotel guests have access to the tennis courts in the village and the golf course in nearby Kitzbühel. Also on the premises is a wide array of massage, beauty, and physical therapy facilities.

Hotel Hochfilzer, A-6352 Ellmau (tel. 05358/2501). The entrance to this lovely 54-room hotel stands under an archway painted around its edges with intricate designs of vines and flowers. Above that is a depiction of a handsome peasant and his pretty wife flanked by flowered balconies and tastefully monochromatic paintings. The façade is only a hint of the kinds of personalized attention and detailing available in this rambling hotel. The staff does everything it can to serve you at the thick-walled bar or in the cozy restaurant. The hotel has been owned by the Hochfilzer family since 1840, and in 1973 they added a modern chalet extension with lots of weathered wood and yellow shutters. In winter, half board costs 610 AS ($44.25) to 810 AS ($59) per person daily for a double with complete bath and TV, the price dropping to 420 AS ($30.50) to 480 AS ($35) per person in summer.

Berghotel Ellmau, A-6352 Ellmau (tel. 05358/2723), is a modern building with an unusual amount of big-windowed exposure toward the direct rays of the sun. Situated about 10 minutes from the center of the village, this efficiently managed 60-room hotel charges 550 AS ($40) to 650 AS ($47.25) per person daily for half board in winter. Summer half-board prices range from 380 AS ($27.75) to 420 AS ($30.50) per person daily. The attractively decorated rooms contain much modern comfort. Each has a phone, radio, and minibar. The hotel has a swimming pool, sauna, solarium, massage facilities, a game room, a bowling alley, and a TV room. A gemütlich atmosphere prevails here, and guests sometimes join in songfests.

WALCHSEE

Both a lake and a village lying close to the West German–Austrian border bear the name Walchsee. This is one of the most remote corners of the Tyrolean country, and although known to Austrians and Bavarians, it is little known to the average North American traveler. The lake, one of the largest and most beautiful in Tyrol, is set against a backdrop of alpine meadows and dark forests. In summer the Walchsee has many facilities for water sports. To reach the lake, you can drive or take a bus from St. Johann in Tirol or else from Kufstein.

The little resort village has excellent accommodations and food at moderate prices, which helps explain its popularity with European visitors.

If you develop "lake fever," you can also go to the smaller **Hintersteiner See,** facing the Wilder Kaiser at an elevation of 2,925 feet. However, the road to Lake Hinterstein is very poor.

Food and Lodging

Hotel Panorama, A-6344 Walchsee (tel. 05374/5661), is one of the most pleasant hotels in the region. It sits on a hillside, affording good views from behind the flowers covering the dozens of balconies. A parasol-dotted sun terrace has been set up just outside the eight-foot arches of the ground floor. The inside is elegantly woodsy, with lots of exposed wood and much detail. On the premises is a hospitable bar area, plus an indoor pool that leads into a form of stone grotto. There are plenty of health facilities, as well as helpful personnel. The hotel offers 48 comfortably furnished bedrooms, each with many amenities (including private bath). Half-board charges in winter are 700 AS ($51) per person daily, lowered in summer to 675 AS ($49). The Panorama, closed from the first of November to mid-December, is associated with a lakeside hotel, the Seehof, whose tariffs, opening dates, and management are the same. Even their phones and reservation service are the same. So if one is full, there may be space available at its affiliate. The hotels lie about 200 yards apart.

Hotel Schick, A-6344 Walchsee (tel. 05374/5331). The façade of this unusual hotel angles in a gentle curve toward an inner-village street. Sections of the white stucco are painted with soft shades of pink and blue into geometric regional designs. The interior has original uses of natural-grained pine, which acts both as a divider for the tables in one of the airy restaurants and as a warmly hospitable wall covering. Some of the décor includes half-timbered beams set into plaster walls, a round enclosure surrounding an open hearth, and lots of soft lighting. There are an indoor swimming pool, a wide range of health and beauty treatments, and access to nearby tennis courts with professional instruction. The hotel has 83 pleasantly furnished bedrooms, each with a private bath, for which it charges from 780 AS ($56.75) per person daily for half board in winter, and from 680 AS ($49.50) in summer.

---

12. The Upper Inn District

I've already introduced you to the Inn Valley that lies to the east of Innsbruck. Now on a much different excursion we'll go west from the Tyrolean capital in the direction of the remote western province, Vorarlberg. Along the way will be many detours and offshoots through valleys. At Landeck we'll depart from the westward trek, swinging directly south along the Inn, stopping off at the summer and winter resorts of Serfaus and Nauders as we head for the Italian frontier. Along the way, large mountains such as the Ötztal Alps rise on either side.

Heading west from Innsbruck, your first stopover might be—

ZIRL

Although Zirl, 8 miles to the west of Innsbruck, is usually visited as a luncheon stopover, the town does a busy tourist business, lying as it does at the crossing point of the main roads from Munich, the Brenner Pass, and Innsbruck.

Food and Lodging

Goldener Löwe, A-6170 Zirl (tel. 05238/2330), is a small, high-quality hotel whose 200-year-old alpine format was renovated into a woodsy style for 28 comfortable rooms, each of which has a private bath. There's nightly Tyrolean dancing in the restaurant. If that doesn't appeal to you, there are also two rustic weinstubes. The Plattner family works hard supervising and preparing the specialties in the restaurant, which include freshly caught trout with chives and wild mushrooms, a host of regional dishes prepared with wild berries and natural ingredients, and excellent desserts. Depending on the season, the bed-and-breakfast rate for double occupancy ranges from 440 AS ($32) to 490 AS ($35.50) per person daily. Singles pay from 550 AS ($40) to 620 AS ($45).

KÜHTAI

From Zirl, you can make a scenic detour, leaving the Valley of the Inn for a while. Head first for Kematen, a village at the entrance of the Sellrain Valley and then west along the Melach Gorge. You'll pass through the valley villages of Sellrain and Gries, which I don't view as meriting a stopover, although Innsbruckers like to escape the city in winter and come here to enjoy the mountain air. After passing another village, St. Sigmund, you'll be on your ascent to the plateau at Kühtai, a high-up summer and winter holiday center.

This village, on the land register of the counts of Tyrol in the 13th century, was later a resort of emperors. Maximilian I acquired the shooting rights in Kühtai in 1497, and an imperial hunting seat was built beginning about 1622, by Archduke Leopold. The Jagdschloss, or hunting lodge, remains from that time and is now one of the most delightful accommodations in this section of the guide (see below).

Kühtai offers winter recreation, including ski slopes for all stages of expertise, cross-country tracks, and ski-bobbing, with snow "guaranteed" from November to May. A ski school and ski kindergarten add to the attractions, with après-ski enjoyment provided.

Food and Lodging

Jagdschloss Kühtai, A-6183 Kühtai (tel. 05239/201). The charming and aristocratically elegant grandson of Kaiser Joseph, Count Stolberg-Stolberg, is the owner of this former hunting lodge, parts of which date from 1450. Archduke Leopold ordered a more recent version built on this site, incorporating parts of an older building. What you see today is a solidly constructed chalet with red-and-white chevron shutters and a stunning view over the countryside. Many of the massively paneled and timbered public rooms contain vaulted ceilings and furnishings dating back to the 17th century. These include very old chests, glistening brass chandeliers, antique engravings, and carefully grouped hunting trophies. The 60 accommodations are comfortable and cozy, and guests are accepted only from December 15 to Easter. The per-person rate, single or double occupancy, costs 1,300 AS ($94.50) per day, rising to 1,500 AS ($109) per person in an apartment. Half board is included. The rooms at the cheaper end of the price scale are sometimes located in the comfortable annex nearby.

The cozily rustic restaurant radiates atmosphere and style. The chefs use the best-quality meats to produce their specialties. The beef Stroganoff is heavenly. The leafy salads appear to have been picked minutes ago, and the desserts are richly satisfying combinations of chocolate, pastries, and fruit.

Hotel Mooshaus, A-6183 Kühtai (tel. 05229/277), is a homey, family-run hotel, Tyrolean style, which stands in the heart of the village not far from the ski lifts. Its public rooms include arched beamed ceilings, as well as wrought-iron accents dividing the congenial bar area from the rest of the establishment. The 48 attractively furnished rooms have all the conveniences, such as private baths and phones. Some of the units also contain private balconies. On the premises are a sauna, a solarium, and a sun terrace. In the Zirbenholzbar you'll be entertained by once-a-week dancing and special dinners. With half board included, rates are 730 AS ($53) to 950 AS ($69) per person daily in winter, 400 AS ($29) to 450 AS ($32) per person daily in summer.

From Kühtai the road continues into the Ötz Valley, which I will treat separately in an upcoming division. For the purposes of this section, however, I'll take you northwest from the town of Ötz to Imst, another major stopover along the Upper Inn region.

IMST

An old market town on a terrace above the river, Imst, at the mouth of the Gurgl Valley, is used as an overnight stop for many motorists as it lies at the junction of the Innsbruck–Landeck route. This is a good center for exploring the Pitz Valley and the Ötz Valley.

Imst is divided into an upper town (Oberstadt) and a lower town. If you're rushed, skip the lower one and visit Oberstadt. Its 15th-century **pfarrkirche** (parish church) was reconstructed after being swept by fire in 1822. The steeple of this large edifice is the highest in Tyrol, 300 feet. A large statue of St. Christopher stands outside the church. St. Michael's Chapel, next to the parish church, is a war memorial, with monumental frescoes by local artists inside.

Imst is especially known for its **Schemenlaufen** (Ghost Walk), a festival presented every few years. Schemenlaufen is a masked *fasching* (carnival) procession held two Sundays before Shrovetide. On Shrove Tuesday, the day before Ash Wednesday, the Auskehren, a masked carnival procession symbolizing the last fight between good and bad ghosts, takes place. Revelers wear carved masks, many of which are more than a century old. If you're not around at carnival time, you can see a collection of these masks in the local museum (**Heimatmuseum**) at Ballgasse 1.

Food and Lodging

Romantik Hotel Post, A-6460 Imst (tel. 05412/2554), the favorite of traditionalists who like a warm, cozy atmosphere, is composed of a 15th-century core and a more recent addition. The two main buildings, angled at 90 degrees from each another, are set in the midst of a park. The older of the two has an onion-dome tower and a steeply sloping gabled roof, as well as elegantly painted monochromatic embellishments. The Pfeifer family maintains a full-fledged array of sporting facilities around the 30-room hotel, including a covered swimming pool whose sliding glass doors open onto a view of the valley. The hotel's interior has an impressive collection of country antiques (some of them Biedermeier), wrought-iron doors, and carved paneling. With full board included, rates range from 580 AS ($42.25) to 780 AS ($56.75) daily for a single and from 520 AS ($37.75) to 760 AS ($55.25) per person for a double. Tariffs depend on the season. The hotel is closed from mid-October to mid-December.

Hotel Stern, A-6460 Imst (tel. 05412/3342). This well-run chalet has a sunny location on a grassy lawn. Inside, the woodsy public rooms are dotted with an informally cluttered collection of hunting trophies, cooking utensils, and other rustic artifacts. The 34 bedrooms, each with private bath or shower, are tastefully decorated and comfortable. From December to October, guests are accepted and charged from 555 AS ($40.25) to 615 AS ($44.75) per person daily for half board.

ARZL

The Pitz Valley is certainly not the most spectacular in Tyrol, but it's quite suitable if you're seeking a tranquil mountain valley like that which so delighted Thomas Wolfe decades ago. Arzl lies a short drive southeast of Imst on the south bank of the Inn River. From here you can continue your exploration by taking a curvy road that pierces the Pitztal (Pitz Valley), which runs south into the Ötztal Alps, lying between two other valleys—Ötzal on its eastern side and Kaumertal in the west.

If you take the road all the way to the end of the valley, passing through the hamlets of Trenkwald and Plangeross, you'll arrive at **Mittelberg** at the head of the valley. For your effort and time you'll be rewarded with a splendid view of the Mittelberg Glacier. The main town in the Pitztal through which you'll pass is St. Leonhard.

Food and Lodging

Hotel Post, A-6471 Arzl (tel. 05412/3111), a 59-room chalet, is filled with all the accoutrements you'd probably want in an alpine hotel, including a green ceramic stove, lots of paneling, and an open fireplace. Renovated in 1972, the hotel charges 350 AS ($25.50) to 450 AS ($32.75) per person daily for half board. Besides Tyrolean atmosphere, each of the comfortable and attractive accommodations has a private bath or shower. The food is good and plentiful.

LANDECK

Back on the main road after a detour into the Pitz Valley, continue your westward journey through the Upper Inn district, coming to a stop at Landeck, 15 miles west of Imst, lying at an elevation of 2,675 feet. Landeck is an industrial town, and hardly the most attractive one in the Inn Valley, but it's a convenient stopover choice.

The old town was built at the junction of the Inn and Sanna Rivers, and also the junction of the roads from the Reschen Pass and from Arlberg. It's on the rail line that leaves Innsbruck going toward the far-western Austrian province of Vorarlberg and points in eastern Switzerland. Landeck lies south of the Lechtal alpine range.

Schloss Landeck (tel. 05442/3202), a 13th-century castle, dominates the town and houses a museum. It is open daily from June to October, 10am to 5pm, and charges an admission of 20 AS ($1.45). More than the exhibits, the most striking feature is the view that unfolds from the castle precincts. The 1471 **pfarrkirche** (parish church) stands on a terrace almost as if it were at the foot of the schloss. It's one of the best-known Gothic buildings in the province. Inside, note the altarpiece from the 16th century. The winged altarpiece is in the late Gothic style.

In season, some of the hotels in Landeck present Tyrolean folkloric evenings.

Food and Lodging

Hotel Schrofenstein, A-6500 Landeck (tel. 05442/2395), operated by Peter and Gerlinde Volk, contains an elegantly antique entrance area, complete with an old beamed ceiling, marble floors, and Oriental carpets. On the premises is a rustic wine cellar, plus an attractive restaurant, and in summer you can take your meal below the chestnut trees in the garden. Sometimes there's live Tyrolean music. The Volks rent 60 well-furnished rooms with baths or showers, phones, and radios. Rates are 520 AS ($37.75) daily for a single and 920 AS ($66.90) for a double, including a breakfast buffet.

Hotel Schwarzer Adler, A-6500 Landeck (tel. 05442/2316), is a typical Tyrolean hostelry. The sunny interior gives off a feeling of solid tradition and security. With half board included, this family-run place rents 35 bedrooms, charging from 460 AS ($33.50) per person daily for half board. There are also eight apartments, accommodating two to four persons each, which are cozy, rustic, and quiet, overlooking the town. The owners, the Gapp family, are good hosts, providing much comfort in their bedrooms and good food at their table.

FISS

Fiss and its neighboring hamlet, Ladis, on the east side of the Inn River, may be reached by car or by taking the train to Landeck and going on by bus. Secure snow conditions, long ski runs, and concomitant winter activities are available here without the hustle and bustle of larger ski centers. Fiss has retained much of the originality of a Tyrolean mountain village.

Food and Lodging

Schlosshotel Fiss, A-6534 Fiss (tel. 05476/6557), looks like an updated version of a medieval fortress. Part of this effect is because of a square tower whose ground floor is pierced by an arched passageway, allowing cars to pass below it. The rest of the establishment stretches into the slope of a hill, which a guest can climb thanks to a series of flagstone steps flanked with carriage lamps. The rustic interior has massive ceiling beams, a scattering of antiques, and a dining room. The cozy bedrooms are outfitted with autumnal colors and lots of horizontal planking. In winter, half-board charges range from 540 AS ($39.25) to 740 AS ($53.75) per person daily. In summer, half board costs 365 AS ($26.50) to 415 AS ($30.25) per person daily. Singles pay a 50-AS ($3.75) daily surcharge. The hotel is open from December to April and June to September.

SERFAUS

Lying on the west bank of the Inn River, Serfaus is a convenient stopover between Landeck (see above) and Nauders (see below), if you're touring. This was once a farm village, but has been turned in recent years into a summer holiday retreat and winter-sports resort set against a backdrop of peaks crowned with icy white hoods. It has an exceptional range of good hotels at moderate prices.

Sunny slopes in an extensive skiing area span three mountain valleys and have cable car, chair lift, and surface lift transport. The skier faces intermediate and beginner ski runs, cross-country trails, and other winter-sports facilities.

Summer visitors can walk to centuries-old mountain farms, listen to brass bands, swim, and find relaxation in this hospitable spot.

The town is known for its two churches from the Middle Ages—one from the 14th century and the other from the dawn of the 16th century. Many buildings here still bear testimony to the ancient Rhaeto-Romanic cultural traditions of the area.

Food and Lodging

Hotel Cervosa, Herrenanger 150, A-6534 Serfaus (tel. 05476/6211), stands on the periphery of Serfaus. It's a large double chalet with lots of balconies and contains many facilities for the amusement of both summer and winter guests, including a typical Tyrolean restaurant, a sun terrace with chaises longues and waitress service, a hospitable bar, and a host of well-furnished public rooms. On the premises is a big indoor swimming pool, plus two saunas, two bowling alleys, a squash court, a fitness center, and a wide choice of massage and beauty facilities. The Westreicher family, the hosts, charge 610 AS ($44.25) to 910 AS ($66.25) per person daily in summer and 950 AS ($69) to 1,800 AS ($130.75) per person in winter for half board. The most expensive accommodations are apartments suitable for up to four persons. The 70 bedrooms are tastefully furnished, and most of them have private baths or showers; the better accommodations offer balconies with a southern exposure. The hotel is open from December to April and June to September.

Hotel Alpenhof, Herrenanger 149, A-6534 Serfaus (tel. 05476/6228), is an alpine chalet a four-minute walk from the center of the village. The interior has some of the most charming detailing around, much of it finished from light-grained knotty pine, well sanded, with a mellow glow. On the premises are dozens of charming extra touches, along with an indoor pool. The 96-bed hotel charges 720 AS ($52.25) to 1,350 AS ($98.25) per person for half board in winter. Summer half-board tariffs range from 350 AS ($25.50) to 450 AS ($32.75) per person daily. As a four-star establishment, the Alpenhof offers some of the best amenities at the resort, as reflected in its well-maintained and comfortable bedrooms.

Hotel Furgler, Untere Dorfstrasse 52, A-6534 Serfaus (tel. 05476/6201), is a 43-room modern chalet in the center of the village. Its public rooms contain lots of heavy ceiling beams, horizontal planking, and a blazing fireplace within a tapering plaster chimney. On the premises is a well-maintained dining room, filled with thick stucco walls and lots of light, where meals are served daily from noon to 2pm and 6 to 9pm. The rustically comfortable bedrooms rent for 950 AS ($69) to 1,200 AS ($87.25) per person in winter and for 520 AS ($37.75) to 590 AS ($43) per person in summer. Half board is included in these prices. The hotel has an indoor swimming pool (behind a large sun terrace), an indoor vapor bath, a solarium, and table tennis. There is a garage on the premises.

Hotel Löwen, Untere Dorfstrasse 21, A-6534 Serfaus (tel. 05476/6204). This attractively painted stone-trimmed chalet has gray and terra-cotta designs around its wood-framed windows. Inside, the hotel has lots of horizontal planking, a beamed dining room, a bar, a swimming pool, a sauna, and a billiard room, plus a flowered sun terrace. The modern bedrooms are pleasantly furnished with many amenities. In all, this place has a good atmosphere for a holiday. The price depends on when you stay here: half board in winter ranges from 1,000 AS ($72.75) to 1,450 AS ($105.50) per person daily, dropping in summer to 450 AS ($32.75) to 850 AS ($61.75). The Tschiderer family are your hosts. The hotel is open from December to April and June to September.

Schwarzer Adler, Untere Dorfstrasse 38, A-6534 Serfaus (tel. 05476/6491), is a five-story, square-based chalet with wood and regional designs accenting its façade. The interior has rustic touches, including heavy timbers and lots of light-grained paneling. On the premises is a health center containing a sauna, a whirlpool, a Turkish steambath, and a fitness center. The Luggen family take special care in the cuisine they serve. In winter this 80-bed hotel charges 650 AS ($47.25) to 970 AS ($70.50) per person daily for half board. Summer half-board tariffs range from 360 AS ($26.25) to 470 AS ($34.25) per person daily. For that, you get a good atmosphere, comfortable bedrooms, and good food. In addition to the dining room, there's also a well-stocked wine cellar.

Après-Ski

The hotels already recommended dominate this form of activity. The kellers and taverns of the hotels charge from 75 AS ($5.45) for hard drinks in most cases. In the peak season, **Hotel Cervosa** brings in live groups that entertain while patrons dance.

NAUDERS

This village of narrow streets, at an elevation of 4,585 feet, is known for its location near the Swiss, Austrian, and Italian frontiers, which has made it an international gathering place with some excellent hotels, charging reasonable prices.

About 12 minutes from the heart of Nauders you can take a drag lift to Stables (6,400 feet), then on to Stableschochboden (7,352 feet). There's also a chair lift to the west of the resort, called the Mutzkopf lift, going up to Rialsch at more than 6,000 feet. A restaurant with a panoramic terrace and a good view lies here on a belvedere.

For the most exalted view of all, you can take a trip by a gondola to **Bergkastel,** which rises some 2,625 feet from its point of origin at the Reschen area to the east of Nauders. From there drag lifts go to the Bergkastel summit at 8,530 feet.

Some 4 miles from Nauders you come to the Reschen Pass at 4,955 feet and the Italian border.

Food and Lodging

Hotel Astoria, A-6543 Nauders (tel. 05473/310), is a 25-room balconied chalet set in the middle of town. On the premises, directed by the Ernst Wiestner family, is a cozy collection of public rooms embellished with brass chandeliers and well-finished wood paneling. Guests can enjoy an attractively formal dining room and a slightly less formal weinstube. Everywhere here the colors are reminiscent of a woodsy mountaintop house, even though the establishment is set in the middle of the village. Facilities include an indoor pool, plus a sauna, a solarium, and a dancing bar where the management sometimes presents live musical entertainment. The hotel rents more than acceptably good bedrooms, each well maintained and containing a private bath or shower. Half-board tariffs in winter go from 720 AS ($52.35) to 790 AS ($57.45) per person daily. Summer rates range from 450 AS ($32.75) to 500 AS ($36.25) per person daily. Open from December to September.

Hotel Almhof, A-6543 Nauders (tel. 05473/313), is a tastefully rustic chalet with an arched entryway and generously proportioned balconies. The interior is a winning combination of plush Oriental rugs, massive ceiling beams, attractive lighting, and elegantly chosen accessories. Taking great pride in the establishment, the Kröll family have even had its name carved into one of the well-finished ceiling beams in the dining room. Attractions include a country weinstube, a hospitable bar, an indoor pool with a sauna, and a choice of health facilities, along with a children's playroom.

Although the hotel is in the center, the ski run comes almost to its doorstep. Open from December to April and June to October, the Almhof rents 44 bedrooms, each with private bath or shower. In winter, half-board terms range from 710 AS ($51.50) to 920 AS ($67) per person daily. In summer, half board costs 670 AS ($48.75) to 770 AS ($56) per person daily.

Hotel Margarethe Maultasch, A-6543 Nauders (tel. 05473/236). This rustic 120-bed hotel boasts lots of innate charm. Its stucco and shingle façade is composed of a series of curves and angled lines. The interior is a tasteful collection of mellow paneling and ceiling beams, some of which are arranged like spokes of a wheel around the top of a circular fireplace in one of the cozy sitting rooms. The facilities include an indoor swimming pool, a sauna, a solarium, and a table-tennis room. The Senn family are the owners, charging rates of 495 AS ($36) to 850 AS ($61.75) per person daily, with half board. Singles pay a daily surcharge of 70 AS ($5.10). Bedrooms are good-sized and well furnished, and most of them contain private baths or showers.

Hotel Schwarzer Adler, A-6543 Nauders (tel. 05476/6491), is a five-story square-based chalet with a prominent restaurant on the ground floor. The real appeal is on the inside, where some of the heavily timbered ceilings and walls are reinforced with angled cross-beams and accented with a happily cluttered ambience of contrasting fabrics and rustic details. You'll find an occasional antique blanket chest, as well as a blazing fireplace. The Tschiggfrey family are your hosts, charging from 750 AS ($54.50) to 790 AS ($57.50) per person daily for half board in winter. In summer, half-board tariffs are 470 AS ($34.25) to 500 AS ($36.25) per person daily. The hotel offers 28 bedrooms, each with private bath or shower.

Hotel Erika, A-6543 Nauders (tel. 05473/240), is capably managed by Essat and Ilse Mangalify, who make guests feel at home in their attractively rustic modern chalet. Built-in cabinets and wooden accents predominate throughout, the 45 bedrooms having lightly finished wood-plank ceilings in addition to their comfortable beds and private baths. Charges for a double range from 600 AS ($43.50) to 700 AS ($51) daily, including half board. Singles pay a daily surcharge of 55 AS ($4). Well-prepared Austrian specialties are served in the elegantly woodsy dining room.

Hotel Tirolerhof, A-6543 Nauders (tel. 05473/255), a six-story chalet, is a little taller than the other inner-village buildings surrounding it. From the upper-floor sun terrace and from the balconies guests can look down on the outdoor swimming pool. A brick-and-plaster exposed chimney provides winter heat to the comfortable chairs clustered around it. The furnishings of the tasteful public rooms include attractive woodsy pieces and lots of autumn-colored Oriental rugs. An indoor swimming pool is on the premises, and other features include a hospitable bar, a paneled weinstube, and a big sun terrace. Much of the clientele tends to be mildly athletic and sports loving. The Senn family are your hosts, charging from 750 AS ($54.50) to 790 AS ($57.50) per person daily for half board. Each of the 66 bedrooms has a private bath or shower. Open from January to April and June to October.

Après-Ski

It's not especially organized but relaxed and casual, the way most skiers prefer it.

Guests of the previously recommended **Hotel Almhof** are likely to be entertained by zither music in the late afternoon when they return from the slopes. A feature of the establishment is a grill room where you can cook your own meats to your desired perfection, just as you do back home.

One of your most elegant evenings with chic, convivial company is likely to be spent at the four-star **Hotel Astoria,** also recommended previously. It draws a fun-loving crowd to its bar, and later on guests can arrange to go on horse-drawn sleigh rides in the winter's night, returning in time for a body-warming glass of kirsch.

Also recommended before, the **Hotel Margarethe Maultasch** has a nightclub, Lady M, with music for dancing, and on occasion it also has fondue evenings.

---

13. The Ötz Valley

This next excursion into the Ötz Valley is actually an offshoot detour that can be made before you reach the midpoint of your tour of the Upper Inn district. Following the Valley of the Inn, you head west from Innsbruck, but before reaching Imst you can take a good but winding road (no. 186) south toward the Italian border. Along the way are many worthy stopovers, each town or village offering good food and hotels, again at reasonable prices.

The Ötztaler Ache flows through the valley, which extends for about 35 miles from the south bank of the Upper Inn. The mouth of the valley is at Ötz (spelled Oetz on some maps). Along the road you'll see many waterfalls as you ascend. I hope you'll be there on a sunny day, to marvel at the glaciers and peaks of the Ötztal Alps spreading before you. The valley cuts deep into the heart of some of the highest peaks in the eastern alpine range and leads into the midst of what has been called the "Tyrolean arctic," a glacier region of ethereal beauty. The mountain villages have glacier lifts for extensive skiing. Glacier skiing is possible from spring through fall on the gigantic Rettenbachferner.

This long valley has good skiing in its lower and outer reaches, but if it's summer and you're here just for the sightseeing, the inner or mid part is the most spectacular.

Our first stopover is at—

ÖTZ

Ötz (also spelled Oetz) is reached by going 3 miles south from the junction of the Inn River and the Ötztaler. A holiday center in both winter and summer, the resort, noted for its mild climate, is perched 2,695 feet high on a sunny slope. Ötz has many old buildings, often with traditional oriels and painted façades. A Gothic

pfarrkirche (parish church) dates from the 14th century, although it was enlarged centuries later.

Just two miles southwest of the town is a warm body of water, **Piburger Lake** (3,000 feet), which is popular in summer.

From Ötz, you can also make a 5½-mile trek south to the hamlet of **Umhausen,** the oldest village in the valley, now a holiday resort.

Food and Lodging

Sporthotel Habicherhof, Habichen 46 (at Habichen), A-6433 Ötz (tel. 05252/6248), has a striking design based on an alpine chalet. A six-story central section rises above rambling extensions containing the public rooms and a sun terrace, as well as a woodsily modern building with large windows and an indoor pool. The building blends attractively into the slopes of the hillside. The high-ceilinged interior contains lots of planking and coffered ceiling panels, as well as a bar area with alpine stools, cozy restaurants, and sitting rooms. The multilingual staff, directed by the Haslwanter family, creates a homey, informal atmosphere. The 32-room hotel sits on the main road leading into town, in the heart of the valley, surrounded by abundant snowfields. Rooms, each with private bath or shower, cost 490 AS ($35.50) to 700 AS ($51) per person daily in winter and 550 AS ($40) to 610 AS ($44.25) per person daily in summer.

Alpenhotel Oetz, Bielefeldstrasse 4, A-6433 Ötz (tel. 05252/6232), in the center of the village, is built on a stone foundation pierced with big arched windows. Visitors enjoying the view from the raised sun terrace are sheltered from the wind by the balconied hotel façade behind them. The interior has softly shining wood and parquet floors, paneled ceilings, and sunny colors—lots of homelike comfort. Solid, traditional cookery, usually well prepared, is available in the dining room. The Falkner family charges 380 AS ($27.75) to 480 AS ($35) per person daily for lodging in a single, double, or triple room, with half board included. Prices depend on the season, and each of the 41 comfortable units contains a private bath.

Hotel Drei Mohren, Hauptstrasse 54, A-6433 Ötz (tel. 05252/6301), one of the most distinctive structures in the village, dates from the turn of the century. The building is a baroque fantasy of onion domes, medieval towers, and hipped roofs, with dozens of arched windows piercing through the thick white walls. The chalet restaurant is done with old engravings and beautifully finished paneling. Most of the 20 grandly paneled bedrooms have private balconies and carved headboards. With half board included, the price is 500 AS ($36.25) per person daily. On the premises are an outdoor tennis court and a covered garage.

Gasthof zum Stern, Kirchweg 6, A-6433 Ötz (tel. 05252/6323). Parts of this 12-room inn date from 1611. Today the façade is opulently covered with bay windows painted with country baroque designs, and you'll recognize the hotel by the gilt and wrought-iron bracket hanging over the sidewalk, just below the cascades of summer geraniums. The paneled interior is filled with charm and rustic details, including a ceramic stove. The Griesser family, the accommodating owners, charge 300 AS ($21.75) per person daily, based on double occupancy, with singles paying a daily surcharge of 35 AS ($2.50), including half board. Rooms, furnished in a Tyrolean style, provide much comfort.

Café-Restaurant Heiner, Hauptstrasse 58, A-6433 Ötz (tel. 05252/6309). In high season this café and pastry shop has an avid collection of last year's fans waiting for a table. The family who runs this place is so well known that some of the locals simply call it by the family name, Haid. Aside from a wide collection of coffees and teas, the establishment sells eight combinations of yogurt, six kinds of refreshingly flavored milk, eight kinds of milkshakes (one of them with red wine), at least 10 kinds of flavored eggnog, and about 40 different concoctions that include ice cream in some way.

If you don't like sweets, you'll find about 15 kinds of carafe or bottled wine, as well as cognac. If dinner or lunch is on your mind, you can enjoy oxtail soup flavored with sherry, a crab cocktail, a host of omelets, and there are also children's platters. More filling are the various kinds of veal, beef, and pork dishes, as well as wild game served with tasty salads. À la carte meals begin at 90 AS ($6.50), going up to 400 AS ($29).

Continuing up the valley, your next stopover might be—

LÄNGENFELD

This major tourist resort, attracting both winter and summer visitors, is in the heart of the Ötz Valley, at the mouth of the Sulz Valley. The Fischbach torrent splits Längenfeld into two distinct parts. For miles around you can see the 240-foot high spire of the **pfarrkirche** (parish church) in upper Längenfeld.

If you base here, you might enjoy an excursion north to the **Stuibenfälle,** or Stuiben Falls, about 2 miles southeast of Umhausen. Perhaps the single most outstanding natural attraction of the Ötz Valley, the falls plunge down some 500 feet under a natural rock bridge. Wear your hiking shoes, as it's about a 20-minute walk from the road.

Food and Lodging

Gasthof zum Hirschen, at Oberlängenfeld, A-6444 Längenfeld (tel. 05253/ 5201), has been under the direction of the Gstrein family since 1860. Its chalet façade is embellished with stone detailing and a painted depiction of a jousting tournament. The interior is especially attractive. There's more paneling than you could shake a stick of knotty pine at. Nestled under some of the well-maintained plaster vaults, an alpine chest or a weathered crucifix appears. This is a pleasant place from which to explore the local foot trails. The 29-room hotel, open from December to October, charges 400 AS ($29) to 480 AS ($35) per person daily for half board in winter. In summer, half board costs 370 AS ($27) to 400 AS ($29) per person daily. Rooms are snug and cozy, especially on a winter night, and the hotel offers much comfort in any season. On the main road, its summer café restaurant is a potent lure.

Hotel Edelweiss, at Unterlängenfeld, A-6444 Längenfeld (tel. 05253/5206), is a fine little hotel with reasonable prices, lying on the main road that cuts through the valley. It has a large L-shaped floor plan that was created when a modern wing was added to an existing chalet, with baroque detailing around its windows. The interior is a combination of authentically rustic décor (as reflected by the weinstube) and a slightly more contemporary format of painted panels set between areas of natural-grain wood. The Engelbert Kuen family, the owners, charge from 350 AS ($25.50) to 420 AS ($30.50) per person daily for half board at this 50-bed hotel. Twenty-one of the simply but comfortably furnished rooms contain private baths or showers.

SÖLDEN

The capital of the inner Ötz Valley, Sölden, about 4,400 feet above sea level, draws visitors to this valley in summer, to the woods in spring and autumn, and to the heights in winter.

Sölden is the best-known village in the valley, linked by road, cable car, and ski lift to its higher sister village, **Hochsölden** (6,800 feet), a much more compact resort. Often winter visitors to Sölden on the half-board arrangement take lunch in Hochsölden when they visit it for the day. There's a ski kindergarten at Sölden.

You can take a cable car from Sölden, passing over glacial fields to some 10,000 feet on the **Geislacherkogel,** where from the upper station you'll be rewarded with a panoramic sweep of the Ötztal Alps. The Geislacherkogel from Sölden is the highest in Austria. A tunnel through the glacier connects the summer glacier resort of Rettenbachferner with the Tiefenbachferner, a large summer ski resort.

Sölden is also the beginning of the **Ötztal Glacier Road** (Ötztaler Gletscherstrasse), one of the loftiest roads in the Alps, rising to some 9,250 feet.

Food and Lodging

Hotel Central, A-6450 Sölden (tel. 05254/2260). This riverside chalet is designed around two big interconnected sections. The interior, constructed from high-quality building materials, features large quantities of beautifully grained timbers, big stucco arches, glowing wooden floors, and regional monochromatic detailing on some of the walls. Among the comfortable furnishings you'll find leather-covered settees, Oriental rugs, and woodcarvings prominently displayed on some of the vertical supporting beams. The 70 rooms are tasteful, opulent, and spacious, all of them containing private baths.

On the premises is a piano bar and a rustically intimate restaurant with excellent service and specialties. They include an array of light-textured international dishes such as calves' liver in a chanterelle cream sauce. Garnishes for some of the main courses are unusual and tasty—ginger crêpes, for example, or a sweet chestnut parfait in a Calvados and grape sauce. The price of a meal in the restaurant ranges from 210 AS ($15.25) to 695 AS ($50.50).

Guests of the hotel in winter pay from 940 AS ($68.25) to 1,100 AS ($80) per person daily for half board, based on double occupancy. Half-board rates in summer cost from 790 AS ($57.50) to 850 AS ($61.75) per person daily.

Hotel Sölderhof, A-6450 Sölden (tel. 05254/2317), is a contemporary chalet whose façade has maintained the rustic painted detailing of the region. The main salon contains a big curved bar, an attractively coffered ceiling, comfortable chairs and banquettes, and a collection of Oriental rugs covering the tile floor. On the premises is an informal stube as well as a more formal, elegantly appointed dining room. A hot whirlpool and sauna are part of the health facilities. The 42-bed hotel charges from 680 AS ($49.50) to 780 AS ($56.75) per person daily for half board in summer. Winter half-board charges range from 830 AS ($60.25) to 920 AS ($67) per person daily. The bedrooms are not overly fancy, but they are comfortable and well heated in winter.

Hotel Bergland, A-6450 Sölden (tel. 05254/2234). The Bergland's architect incorporated a chalet format with steep rooflines over an assembly of trapezoids, rectangles, and cubes. The result is a pleasing 165-bed hotel where guests are pampered. An upper-level sun terrace with dozens of parasols is one of the most popular places in town on a sunny day. This family-run hotel has an elegant interior covered with paneling below heavy ceiling beams; the public rooms contain a scattering of antique alpine chests, as well as beautifully appointed restaurants and bars (two of each). On the premises are a dancing bar with live music, an indoor pool, a sauna, and an engaging staff. The bedrooms are warmly intimate and are usually accented with well-finished planking. Summer half-board charges are 770 AS ($56) per person daily, and winter half-board tariffs range from 940 AS ($68.25) to 1,040 AS ($75.50) per person daily.

Hotel Sonne, A-6450 Sölden (tel. 05254/2203), is an attractive 115-bed chalet with mock-Tudor half-timbering and attentive management by members of the Gurschler family. Next to the chair lift to Hochsölden, the hotel has a rustically mellow interior filled with paneling, regional accessories, and modern comfort. On the premises are an attractive restaurant, an intimately lit bar area, and cozy paneled bedrooms (all with private baths). Rates are 450 AS ($32.75) to 600 AS ($43.50) per person daily. Half board is included in the prices, which rise over Christmas.

Hotel Alpina, A-6450 Sölden (tel. 05254/2202). Built into the slope of a hill and flanked by towering conifers, this 55-room hotel rises five stories above the alpine path running alongside it. Its windows are embellished with painted borders, and its attractive interior has lots of paneling and modern conveniences as reflected by the comfortable, cozy bedrooms. In summer, half-board charges range from 630 AS ($45.75) to 700 AS ($51) per person daily, going up in winter to 770 AS ($56) to 840 AS ($61).

Gasthof Waldcafé, A-6450 Sölden (tel. 05254/2319), a 25-room chalet on the side of the mountain, lies very close to most of the major ski runs. On the premises is a congenial restaurant, as well as simple but adequate bedrooms. The owners charge 315 AS ($23) to 530 AS ($38.50) per person daily, including half board.

Café-Restaurant Hermann, A-6450 Sölden (tel. 05254/2326). An alpine stream runs nearby, and the air couldn't be fresher than it is from the balconies of this capably managed 30-bed chalet set some distance above the village. The interior is accented with big windows (looking out over the forest), paneling, and regionally inspired detailing. The bedrooms have attractively wood-trimmed formats and modern comfort, as well as baths, phones, and, in some cases, balconies. Prices range from 450 AS ($32.75) to 580 AS ($42.25) per person daily, with half board included.

Après-Ski

There's quite a lot of nightlife, centering customarily around the major hotels. If you get bored, you can take the cableway up to **Hochsölden** and check out the more casual nightlife there.

You can drink at one of three bars and listen and dance to a live band at the already-recommended **Hotel Central,** the best spot for nightlife in Sölden. Chances are, you'll get to hear lederhosen-clad music-makers. At times, if the house count is right, the place takes on a carnival-like atmosphere.

The **Hotel Sonne** (see above) brings in live bands to play for dancing, and once a week the staff here stages a Tyrolean evening.

The other leading hotel for nightlife is the recommended **Hotel Bergland,** which often has some of the best bands in Sölden.

Young people are fond of the Alm Bar in the **Hotel Tyrolerhof** (tel. 2288), a modern hotel in the center of the resort.

HOCHSÖLDEN

This upper-level resort (6,800 feet), towering over just-visited Sölden, lies on a sunny alpine plateau and attracts visitors in both summer and winter. At first Hochsölden may not seem like a village at all, being more a cluster of modern hotels. It's connected to its lower sister by road, cable car, and ski lift. Because of the easy communication between the two resorts, the much larger facilities of Sölden, including the après-ski life, are available to guests at the Hochsölden hotels.

Its higher elevation makes it possible to ski at Hochsölden longer than at Sölden. Rettenbachferner and Tiefenbachferner, summer glacier skiing areas, are easily accessible to both resorts (see above).

Food and Lodging

Hotel Edelweiss, A-6452 Hochsölden (tel. 05254/2298), is an impressively designed hotel among a handful of other hostelries on the bleak alpine meadows near the top of the mountain ridge. Except for a curving glass-walled extension and a low-lying building containing a swimming pool, the structure looks like an oversize chalet. The paneled interior has lots of heavy beams and comfortable couches. On the premises are a bar and a restaurant, usually filled with an enthusiastic crowd of skiers. The woodsy bedrooms are accented with exposed planking. The 60-bed hotel charges 550 AS ($40) to 660 AS ($48) per person daily in summer. In winter, half board costs 850 AS ($61.75) to 950 AS ($69) per person daily. Visitors who are not hotel guests have access to the timbered nightclub through a separate door on the ground floor.

Sporthotel Schöne Aussicht, A-6452 Hochsölden (tel. 05254/2403), is one of the handful of chalet hotels in this ski village, with the ski area beginning right in front. The hotel has a popular day bar, a sauna, a solarium, a hairdressing salon, a TV room, and free care for babies and children. The 15 bedrooms all have attractive amenities, including bathrooms, phones, and radios, and the hotel charges 410 AS ($29.75) to 820 AS ($59.50) per person daily based on double occupancy, with half board included. Singles range from 490 AS ($35.50) to 910 AS ($66.25) daily.

Alpenhotel Enzian, A-6452 Hochsölden (tel. 05254/2252). On sunny days in late winter you're likely to see dozens of visitors stretched out on chaises longues on the big sun terrace of this elegant alpine hotel. Designed with curved corners, gables, and honey-colored exterior planking, the Enzian contains a modern interior with lots of exposed wood. On the premises are a billiard room, a bar and restaurant, a sauna, and simple, modern bedrooms. The Riml family, the owners, open the hotel from December to April and July to October. They rent 62 well-furnished bedrooms, each with private bath or shower. Summer half-board charges range from 450 AS ($32.75) per person daily, with winter half board costing 710 AS ($51.50) to 910 AS ($66.25) per person daily.

Hotel Alpenfriede, A-6452 Hochsölden (tel. 05254/2227), is a four-star hotel built in a wooded chalet style. Your hosts, the Lengler family, rent 54 comfortably furnished bedrooms, serviced by an elevator. All accommodations have showers or baths, radios, and phones, as well as balconies in most cases. With half board included, rates range from 540 AS ($39.25) to 930 AS ($67.50) per person daily, based on double occupancy. Singles pay a daily surcharge of 80 AS ($5.80). On the premises are a paneled sitting room and a warmly tinted bar area with heavy ceiling timbers and a stove with an open fireplace. Other facilities include a sun terrace, a sauna, a solarium, and steambath, plus a fitness room and a table-tennis room.

Après-Ski

As mentioned, you can avail yourself of the more active nighttime diversions of Sölden, down below, but you'll also find plenty of informal nightlife on your doorstep if you're based in a hotel in Hochsölden. Naturally, most of the après-ski nightlife centers around the major hotels. Even if you have your ski boots on, you can join the dancing throngs at the **Hotel Hochsölden** (tel. 05254/2229), which comes alive just as soon as skiers return from the slopes for the day and darkness falls. That means that the tea dance here is going strong by 4:30pm.

The **Hotel Edelweiss,** previously recommended, is one of the liveliest places on the after-dark circuit, with a live band playing for dancing.

More disco unfolds live at the also-recommended **Schöne Aussicht.** The dress here is wide-ranging—some men dress up in jackets and ties, others preferring sweaters.

OBERGURGL

This village with the funny-sounding name is part of a three-resort complex which includes Hochgurgl (see below) and Untergurgl. Obergurgl, lying less than 2 miles upstream from Untergurgl, is one of the loftiest villages in Austria, 6,322 feet, and the second-highest parish in Europe. This is where the Swiss physicist and aeronaut, Dr. Auguste Piccard, landed in his celebrated balloon.

This district is one of the major ski centers of the Tyrolean country. It's not well known among American skiers, although if you stay here you'll be virtually on the doorstep of the Ötztal Alps, surrounded by towering peaks and glistening glaciers. All of the ski runs end right in the village. A two-stage chair lift, leaving from the center of Obergurgl, services the principal ski area, the Gaisberg-Hohe-Mutt.

Food and Lodging

Hotel Austria, A-6456 Obergurgl (tel. 05256/314). Hans Steiner and his family are the congenial hosts of this pleasantly balconied chalet whose angled façade—located a short distance above the resort—provides lots of sunny terrace space. The tasteful interior is covered with beautifully grained panels and carved timbers, along with coffered ceilings, thick Oriental rugs, and lots of well-crafted architectural extras. On the premises are a sauna, a solarium, a hot whirlpool, and a Turkish steambath, as well as a bar area, a nightclub, and a baronial fireplace giving off winter heat. There's also an elegant restaurant with a subdued color scheme. The comfortably furnished bedrooms range from 700 AS ($51) to 1,500 AS ($109) daily for a single, from 550 AS ($40) to 1,450 AS ($105.50) per person for a double, the latter price for an apartment. Rates include half board. The hotel is open November to April and June to September.

Hotel Edelweiss & Gurgl, A-6456 Obergurgl (tel. 05256/224), is a famous old hostelry, with many years of tradition under the baton of the Scheiber family. It rises imposingly, a massive bulk of chalet-inspired balconies, wood trim, and bright windows. Its position close to the village church is prominent in the center of the resort. It's probably the best-accessorized, best-equipped, and most lavishly decorated hotel at Obergurgl, the dedicated life's work of the family members. Within its labyrinthine interior are dozens of Oriental carpets (which never seem to get damaged by ski boots) as well as a covered swimming pool with artificial waves and an adjacent sauna and solarium. Facilities include not only a covered garage and a satisfying array of bars for entertainment and après-ski possibilities, but restaurants and blazing fireplaces, plus cozy nooks and crannies. Each of its 97 bedrooms contains a suggestion of a beamed ceiling, pinewood panels interspersed with white plaster, deeply comfortable beds, big windows looking out over the nearby ski lifts, and a private bath or shower. Depending on the season, half board ranges from 470 AS ($34.25) to 1,050 AS ($76.25) per person daily. The hotel is a good choice for lunch or dinner, even if you're not staying there, as its table is among the finest in Obergurgl.

Fitnesshotel Gotthard, A-6456 Obergurgl (tel. 05256/335), is an attractive eight-story chalet sitting a five-minute walk above the center of the resort. The interior has carefully crafted wooden walls and ceilings, some of them rather elaborate, a Tyrolean collection of architectural extras such as a ceramic stove surrounded by a warming bench, a well-rated restaurant with panoramic views over the countryside, a bar, a fitness room, and a big indoor pool covered with an impressive set of timbers. The 50 rustically cozy bedrooms—each with a modern bath—rent for 730 AS ($53) to 1,050 AS ($76) per person daily, including half board. Open from November to April and July to September.

Hotel Hochfirst, A-6456 Obergurgl (tel. 05256/232), near the Festkogel gondola, is one of the biggest hotels in town with 84 rooms. Designed like an enormous slope-roofed chalet whose façade is tastefully divided into several different planes, the establishment benefits from a raised sun terrace and a jutting extension containing an indoor swimming pool. The interior has furniture upholstered in soft colors, half-timbered walls, heavy ceiling beams, and lots of paneling. On the premises are a restaurant and a bar, plus all the comforts you'd expect. Rates range from 525 AS ($38.25) to 1,400 AS ($101.75) daily for a single, while doubles go for 520 AS ($37.75) to 1,300 AS ($94.50) per person, with half board included. The wide price ranges are based on seasonal differences, winter being the more expensive season.

Hotel Josl, A-6456 Obergurgl (tel. 05256/205), is a 17-room chalet with a big sun terrace and a gently sloping alpine roof. A minute's walk from the center of the village, its rustic interior welcomes guests in both summer and winter—the Sport Café being popular with skiers and other lovers of the outdoors. The hotel charges 300 AS ($21.75) to 350 AS ($25.50) per person daily for half board in summer. In winter, prices are 480 AS ($35) to 780 AS ($56.75) per person daily for half board. Accommodations are cozily comfortable, with baths or showers, phones, and radios; some rooms have a south-facing balcony. Guests can relax in the sauna and later meet for drinks in the fireside lounge. The Josl-Keller is a lively après-ski rendezvous.

Hotel Alpina, A-6456 Obergurgl (tel. 05256/295), run by the Platzer family, is a six-story chalet with lots of wooden balconies angled toward the sunlight. The paneled interior has much regional detailing, including a green ceramic stove in the rustic knotty-pine-covered restaurant. A cozy bar and a formal dining room are also on the premises. The hotel rents 70 immaculately maintained and comfortable guest rooms, each with private bath or shower. In winter, half-board rates range from 850 AS ($61.75) to 1,350 AS ($98.25) per person daily; in summer, from 395 AS ($28.75) to 500 AS ($36.25) per person daily.

Gasthof Gamper, A-6456 Obergurgl (tel. 05256/238), owned and managed by the Gamper family, is a tastefully designed chalet lightly embellished with region-ally inspired painted illustrations. Near the Gaisberg lift, slightly away from the center of the village, the hotel has public rooms containing a crackling fireplace con-structed from large gray stones, plus comfortable banquettes, and well-finished ceiling panels; all this gives the establishment a cozily rustic feeling of well-being. The simple accommodations have various kinds of wood, including light-grained knotty pine covering some of the walls. The 60-bed hotel offers 31 rooms with pri-vate baths or showers. In winter, half board ranges from 550 AS ($40) to 820 AS ($59.50) per person daily, while in summer, half board costs from 320 AS ($23.25) to 370 AS ($26.90) per person daily. Open from November to April and June to September.

Hotel Regina, A-6456 Obergurgl (tel. 05256/221). Built in the early 1970s, this oasis is accented with country baroque wooden balustrades and a large exterior mural devoted to the "Snow King." In each of its details, it strives to be more than the usual cookie-cutter chalet, a goal encouraged and promoted by the genteel own-ers, the Schöpf family. Inside, mellow paneling and Oriental carpets lend warmth to a fine hotel choice. There are only 20 bedrooms, each equipped with private bath and several thoughtful extra touches. For half board, depending on the season, each guest pays 440 AS ($32) to 780 AS ($56.75) daily. Among the hotel's facilities are a sauna and steambath. The Regina lies on a hillside above the main congestion of the resort at the edge of a flat plateau used for cross-country skiing.

Après-Ski

There's quite a bit of après-ski life in Obergurgl, most of it relaxed and casual. After you return from the slopes, you might want to join your fellow skiers for drinks in the Josl-Keller at the already recommended **Hotel Josl.** This is a popular rendezvous spot, at least to begin your evening festivities. Local folk-music evenings are also presented here, but with no particular regularity. You'll have to inquire. Din-ner is served from 6:30 to 8:30pm, costing from 300 AS ($21.75).

The disco at the also-recommended **Hotel Austria** is one of the most sophisti-cated and expensive places for nighttime diversions.

There are not only two bars but frenetic dancing to disco music at the recom-mended **Hotel Hochfirst.** Tyrolean evenings are often presented at this hotel, and if so, you should reserve a table, as they're very popular.

HOCHGURGL

If Hochgurgl (7,050 feet) were actually a village, it would take the "loftiest vil-lage in Austria" title away from other claimants. However, Hochgurgl is really little more than a cluster of hotels, whose owners anxiously await the first snowfall each year. You can approach Hochgurgl from the Timmelsjoch Alpine Road. A ski bus runs back and forth between Hochgurgl and Obergurgl.

This is an area for dedicated skiers who want access to some of the highest peaks of Europe. A three-section chair lift, leaving from Untergurgl, just outside Obergurgl, will transport you to **Wurmkogl** at some 10,000 feet. At this lofty eleva-tion skiing is possible all year. From a restaurant at Wurmkogl you have a magnificent view of the Italian Alps.

Food and Lodging

Hochgurgl Hotel, A-6456 Hochgurgl (tel. 05256/266), an elegant chalet, glows at night from the many lights illuminating its rustically contemporary façade. The interior contains handsomely appointed apartments and private rooms, many of them filled with hand-worked paneling and comfortable furniture. Rates range from 1,090 AS ($79.25) to 1,750 AS ($127.25) per person daily for half board. The luxurious apartments are more expensive. The Tyrolean weinstube inside is filled with old paneling and rustic accessories, and has about the coziest ambience in town. The house specialty here is a savory roasted leg of venison, stuffed with bacon, onions, mushrooms, and lots of spices. This is served with a cream sauce made from apple schnapps, juniper berries, and raspberries. The other facilities at this accommodating hotel include a fitness center, a sauna, a massage room, a hairdresser, a dance bar, an elevator, and a big indoor pool, as well as a ski boutique on the ground floor.

Olymp Sporthotel, A-6456 Hochgurgl (tel. 05256/249), is a tastefully designed chalet lying at the end of the Ötztal "on the roof of the Tyrol." Right in the middle of the pists (ski trails), the Olymp welcomes guests with its spacious bedrooms and Tyrolean style, including Toni's Almhütte, a log hut made of 400-year-old wood with an open fireplace. Here you can order your hot Glühwein along with raclette and fondues; for a special dinner, you can grill your meat at the table on a hot stone. Twice a week there is live music, and dancing is nightly. A big sun terrace allows you not only to take an alpine sunbath but to absorb the mountain scenery; from your room you are likely to see 12 glaciers. The rate per person per night, with half board included, ranges from 700 AS ($51) to 1,400 AS ($101.75). The hotel has a lounge furnished in the Tyrolean style, along with several dining rooms. In the Badestube is an indoor swimming pool, as well as a sauna and Turkish bath. You can make your first ski run immediately outside the hotel door without using a lift.

Sporthotel Ideal, A-6456 Hochgurgl (tel. 05256/290), is a chalet set in a slightly isolated, sunny position just outside the village. The woodsy décor features horizontal planking, paneled and coffered ceilings, vivid colors, and comfortable furniture. Facilities include an indoor swimming pool, a sauna, a bar, a dining room, a weinstube, and a reading room, plus a well-stocked ski store. Rates in the comfortably furnished bedrooms range from 550 AS ($40) to 860 AS ($62.50) per person daily.

Hotel Riml, A-6456 Hochgurgl (tel. 05256/261), might have the most contemporary design in the village. With its gently sloping roof and an emphasis on horizontal lines, the hotel has big windows that open into woodsy bedrooms. The public rooms are covered with large amounts of light-grained paneling in an airy, sunny format. The Riml family are your hosts, charging from 530 AS ($38.50) to 930 AS ($67.50) per person daily for half board. Attractive hotel apartments are available for four to five guests. Children get discounts when sharing their parents' room. An indoor swimming pool, a restaurant, a bar, a sauna, and a bowling alley are on the premises.

Berghotel Angerer Alm, A-6456 Hochgurgl (tel. 05256/241), is an attractive wood-trimmed chalet built into the side of a sloping meadow. It required a team of craftspeople to complete the richly paneled interior, which was embellished with such details as a masonry fireplace that funnels its smoke through a beaker-shaped copper canopy built into the wall. Some of the furnishings of the public rooms include rustic alpine chests scattered among comfortable armchairs. On the premises are a bar area, a chalet restaurant, an indoor swimming pool, a popular sun terrace, and a Ping-Pong room. The comfortably rustic bedrooms rent for 700 AS ($51) to 1,200 AS ($87.25) per person nightly for half board.

Alpenhotel Laurin, A-6456 Hochgurgl (tel. 05256/227), has an attractive boxy design with most of the elements of a traditional chalet. Built into a hillside, the hotel does a thriving business on its raised sun terrace and in its comfortable, tastefully decorated restaurant. Menu items include regional and Austrian specialties, such as a collection of salads, schnitzels, well-prepared vegetables, and fruited desserts. Rooms are comfortable and tastefully furnished in an alpine style. Each has a private bath or shower and a balcony. In winter, half-board tariffs go from 500 AS ($36.25) to 950 AS ($69) per person daily, while summer half-board rates are 280

AS ($20.25) to 350 AS ($25.50) per person daily. The hotel is open from November to April and July to September.

VENT

This is the end of the valley—the end of the road, so to speak. Vent is small and unspoiled, and many discriminating visitors prefer it to Obergurgl and Sölden, which are likely to be overrun at the height of the ski season. However, always check road conditions when driving there in winter, because Vent has been cut off by the threat of avalanche activity.

Driving south from Sölden, you go first to the hamlet of Zwieselstein. There you fork in a southwesterly direction, proceeding for about 8 miles, passing through the Venter Tal, or Valley of Venter, with its magnificent alpine scenery, until you reach this mountain village (about 6,200 feet above sea level). If you don't want to drive, you can take a bus from Zwieselstein to Vent in summer, a favorite season for mountain climbers. Vent has not only a weather station but also a glacier observatory.

A wickedly steep mountain road, with gradients up to 30%—more suitable for mountain goats than for vehicles—will take you to **Rofenhöhe,** which at 6,606 feet is one of the loftiest villages in Austria with year-round residents. To the north is the **Wildspitze,** the tallest peak in the north Tyrolean country, at 12,375 feet. **Kreuzspitze,** 11,340 feet, looms on the right, and to the south is **Thalleitspitze,** 11,175 feet.

If you come to Vent to ski, a drag lift will transport you to the top station (8,850 feet).

Food and Lodging

Hotel Similaun, A-6458 Vent (tel. 05254/8104), its simplified chalet design having many concessions to late 20th-century building techniques, offers a panoramic view of the Alps. This is one of the finest places to stay at the resort. It has an interior decoration that is light and airy, with ample use of exposed wood. In winter the 26-room hotel charges 460 AS ($33.50) to 790 AS ($57.50) per person daily for half board, summer half-board charges going from 420 AS ($30.50) to 500 AS ($36.25) per person daily. The Tyrolean rooms are snug and comfortable. The most expensive seasons are Christmas, Easter, and spring carnival.

Hotel Post, A-6458 Vent (tel. 05254/8119). Directed by the Pirpamer family, this white-painted wood chalet has a big-windowed restaurant visible from the ground floor. Near the chair lift, the 40-room hotel contains a covered swimming pool, a sauna, a solarium, and an elevator. Each of the well-furnished bedrooms has a private bath and phone, and rents for 320 AS ($23.25) to 610 AS ($44.25) per person daily, depending on the season; breakfast is included.

---

14. The Paznaun Valley

In this snowy landscape 56 miles from Innsbruck, the postcard-pretty views are a dime a dozen. The valley is about 22½ miles long and lies between Landeck and Galtür. The Trisanna River is its waterway. To reach the Paznaun, head west from Innsbruck, then take a southwesterly route as signposted. At the head of the valley at Galtür is the Fluchthorn mountain peak.

Paznaun Valley offers superb skiing. The main village is Ischgl, which has put together a ski circus spilling over with runs and lifts across the border into Switzerland. Galtür, the second most important village, has lots of terrain on Ballunspitze and Seinisjoch. The valley is a choice starting point for ski mountaineering tours in the Silvretta glacier region and among the peaks of the Samnaun Alps.

You can even get a touch of the "winter wonderland" experience in summer by taking a highly recommended excursion deep into the Blue Silvretta mountain range, with towering peaks and glaciers as a backdrop.

ISCHGL

The major town of the Paznauntal is both a summer resort and a winter ski center, near the border of Switzerland. A most attractive village, Ischgl lies about halfway along the valley where the Trisanna Valley branches off. The resort, built on terraces at 4,600 feet, is about a half-hour drive from Landeck. It can also be reached by bus from Landeck.

West of town, you can take the Silvrettabahn cableway up to **Idalpe** (7,600 feet). The panoramic view from the lofty station is among the most impressive in the Austrian Alps. From the east part of Ischgl you can take yet another cableway to the Pardatschgrat station at 8,600 feet.

Food and Lodging

Hotel Elisabeth, A-6561 Ischgl (tel. 05444/5411), one of the most elegant hotels in the region, has a monumental curved façade covered with balconies, all of which face south. The well-appointed interior contains an attractively somber color scheme brightened with flashes of color from the many Oriental rugs and well-chosen upholstery fabrics. In the center of it all, masons have installed an open fireplace, with a conical chimney tapering gracefully up toward the ceiling.

On the premises are a café and pastry shop, a bar, a pizzeria, a covered pool and fitness center, and 57 spacious, luxuriously equipped bedrooms. These have all the modern comforts, including big color TVs, minibars, balconies with southern exposure, and a host of extras. The winter half-board rate ranges from 1,700 AS ($123.50) daily for a single or 1,550 AS ($112.75) per person, based on double occupancy. The hotel is open only from mid-December to early May.

The Marend restaurant has lots of space between its beautifully decorated tables and a soft color scheme of dusty rose, muted grays, and wood tones. Specialties are well prepared and ideal for an appetite whetted by mountain air (the roast beef is very tasty). À la carte meals range from 200 AS ($14.50) to 450 AS ($32.75) and are served daily from 10am to 9:30pm.

Hotel Madlein, A-6561 Ischgl (tel. 05444/5226), is another stylish alpine hotel, owned by the same people who run the previously recommended Elisabeth. If you look at it from a certain angle, you can count three wood-covered chalets that interconnect to form this well-situated hotel. Near the center of town, convenient to the cable cars, the 63-room hotel contains a swimming pool, lots of fitness facilities, and a cozy series of public rooms. These include a nightclub (which sometimes attracts well-known musical groups), two attractive restaurants, and a sitting room with an open fireplace built into a wall composed of massive gray rocks. High-season rates range from 1,350 AS ($98.25) per person daily for a double, and from 1,450 AS ($105.50) for a single, with half board included. A wide range of apartments suitable for up to four persons is also available. The bedrooms are up-to-date and well designed. Open January to April and June to September.

Hotel Post, A-6561 Ischgl (tel. 05444/5233). This imposing chalet hostelry is divided into several sections. The interior's rustic accents include lots of paneling, geometrically ornate ceilings, a central fireplace whose smoke rises through a stucco funnel, and a well-appointed dining room. The 62 cozy bedrooms rent for 700 AS ($51) to 1,400 AS ($101.75) per person daily. These tariffs, including half board, vary with the time of year and the plumbing assigned.

Hotel Garni Christine, A-6561 Ischgl (tel. 05444/5346), is a pleasant chalet whose rustic interior includes a bar and a central fireplace surrounded by banquettes. Rates in high season, with breakfast included, range from 440 AS ($32) to 700 AS ($51) per person daily. Prices vary according to the time of year, and all accommodations contain private baths.

Gasthof Goldener Adler, A-6561 Ischgl (tel. 05444/5217). No one knows exactly when this inn was built, but it was mentioned in a legal document in 1640. Later, in the 17th and 18th centuries, it served as the region's courthouse. Today it sits behind a six-story pastel-colored façade, with white trim and a solidly prosperous kind of ambience. The carved entrance is set with stained glass, while the panels of the interior range from full-grained natural wood to those painted in light colors with regional designs. The hotel has lots of rustic details and modern comfort. Johann Kurz and his family are the owners, and they rent 29 bedrooms, each with private bath or shower. In winter, half board costs 890 AS ($64.75) to 1,200 AS ($87.25) per person daily, in summer, half board goes for 460 AS ($33.50) to 600 AS ($43.50) per person daily. Open from December to April and June to September, the gasthof contains a Tyrolean restaurant serving well-prepared local specialties.

Alpenhotel Ischglerhof, A-6561 Ischgl (tel. 05444/5331), right by the valley station of the Silvretta cable car, is a comfortable hotel owned and managed by the Ludwig Kurz family. Its combination of different alpine styles includes a conical tower whose windows are surrounded with pink borders. The rambling surfaces of the rest of the hotel are covered for the most part with wooden balconies. The public rooms are elegantly decorated. A rustic and comfortable bar area has darkly intimate lighting and music, while one of the sitting rooms contains an open fireplace. The hotel offers 50 bedrooms, each with private bath or shower, and these are rented from December to April and June to September. In winter, half board costs 850 AS ($61.75) to 1,100 AS ($80) per person daily, in summer, half board goes for 350 AS ($25.45) to 420 AS ($30.55) per person daily. The accommodations are rustically furnished, with such modern amenities as private baths or showers, radios, direct-dial phones, and (in most instances) balconies with a view of alpine scenery.

Après-Ski

Après-ski begins early with a "tea dance" at the already-recommended **Hotel Garni Christine.** Here the owners, Rudolf and Anna Wolf, welcome not only their own guests but visitors from the other hotels to a lively atmosphere.

The **Hotel Elisabeth,** also recommended previously, has one of the most intimate and romantic candlelit dining and drinking atmospheres on the après-ski circuit.

One of the most elegant places to gather at night is the **Hotel Madlein** (see above). Head for the Almbar with its wooden beams, whitewashed brick, and attractive young patrons. This place is the undisputed nightlife centerpiece of the resort. Flamboyant in design (like many of its patrons), it was completely redecorated in 1987. Its large dance floor supports the most animated gyrations in town. Depending on what entertainment is offered on a particular evening, the entry fee ranges from 50 AS ($3.65) to 100 AS ($7.25) per person. The doors open every evening at 9 from December to May. Live bands rock through the night, at least until 3am.

GALTÜR

At the head of the Paznauntal and at the foot of the Silvretta Pass (closed to winter traffic) is Galtür, near the Swiss border and about an 18-minute drive from Ischgl, just visited. This relatively unspoiled resort, perched at a rather exalted 5,800 feet, has been well known for decades as a ski mountaineering center and a popular summer resort, attracting mountain climbers.

It has become better known in recent years for its downhill and its Nordic skiing. You can purchase the Silvretta ski pass, which entitles you to use the lifts at Ischgl as well as chair and drag lifts to take you from Galtür to the highest station at 7,260 feet. The Silvretta ski pass, incidentally, opens up a total of 67 lifts. Snow is good here from December to April.

There's a bus link between Galtür and Landeck, some 25 miles away.

Food and Lodging

Alpenhotel Tirol, A-6563 Galtür (tel. 05443/206), is a modern luxury chalet hotel a few minutes' walk from the center. Run by its owners, the Franz Lorenz family, the hotel has a welcoming, roomy hall with an open fireplace, a Spielerstube, and a large Zirbenstube paneled in knotty pine. All are furnished in traditional Tyrolean style. Such facilities as a whirlpool bath, sauna, solarium, and fitness room are available. The 45 bedrooms, which radiate coziness and contain baths or showers, rent for 850 AS ($61.75) to 970 AS ($70.50) per person daily for half board in winter. Summer half-board charges start at 550 AS ($40) per person daily. The hotel serves generous and well-prepared meals, including a buffet breakfast. Open December to April and June to September.

Hotel Ballunspitze, A-6563 Galtür (tel. 05443/214). The creative architect who designed this attractive hotel began with a clapboard house to which he added a modern balconied extension that ended up being about four times as big as the original house. Public rooms have been paneled and filled with comfortably rustic furniture. The owners, who open the hotel from December to October, rent 77 attractively furnished bedrooms, each with private bath or shower. Winter half-board charges go from 480 AS ($35) to 750 AS ($54.50) per person daily. In summer, half board costs 260 AS ($19) to 330 AS ($24) per person daily. The hotel sits at the edge of the village, within walking distance of most everything.

Hotel Fluchthorn, A-6563 Galtür (tel. 05443/202), is a tall alpine chalet whose form is slightly more streamlined than that of the others around it. It has monochromatic paintings and a warmly rustic interior. Fixtures include heavy ceiling beams, along with brass chandeliers, ceramic stoves, and comfortable easy chairs. On the premises are a dancing bar, a Tyrolean restaurant, and a sauna, as well as covered tennis courts and an indoor pool just a few steps down the street. The hotel rents 50 rooms (95 beds), all with baths or showers, direct-dial phones, radios, balconies, TVs, and minibars. In high season the overnight rate is 695 AS ($50.50) per person. Closed between the first of October and mid-December.

Hotel Pazmaunerhof, A-6563 Galtür (tel. 05443/234), has been owned and directed by members of the Lorenz family for the past century. Designed in a typical Tyrolean style with lots of balconies, this attractive hotel has been expanded to include a collection of rustically paneled rooms with chalet furniture and lots of cozy comfort in the bedrooms. The big-windowed dining room serves tasty, well-prepared Austrian specialties. Open from December to April and June to October, the hotel offers 76 bedrooms with private baths or showers. The half-board rate in winter ranges from 640 AS ($46.50) to 660 AS ($48) per person daily, with the summer half-board cost going from 360 AS ($26.25) to 390 AS ($28.25) per person daily.

Hotel Alpenrose, A-6563 Galtür (tel. 05443/201), is an attractive modern chalet whose simplified exterior sits against a backdrop of craggy mountains. The streamlined interior has taste and all the modern comforts, one of them being a well-recommended restaurant where the old-fashioned cookery honors butter, cream, and rich dishes as dietary staples. After a day in the mountains this might be exactly what you want. Rooms are well designed and streamlined for comfort. Rates range from 500 AS ($36.25) to 780 AS ($56.75) per person daily for half board.

Après-Ski

For such a small ski village the nightlife is more extensive and sophisticated than one might imagine.

The early evening begins with a tea dance at the **Hotel Wirlerhof-Almhof** (tel. 05443/346). The ski crowd here—still wearing their boots—arrive right from the slopes. Coffee, hot chocolate, beer, and tempting pastries are downed in a lively atmosphere of smoke, drink, and good times.

More in the center of town, the place to go is the **Hotel Post,** where there's a lively dance bar in the cellar that at some point seems to draw every skier in town.

---

15. The Arlberg (St. Anton)

There's no such thing as a sacred ski mountain—so far as I've ever heard—but if there were it would have to be the Arlberg, the mecca of the serious skier. Alpine skiing went out from here to conquer the world. On the east side of the Arlberg, 71 miles west of Innsbruck, is what's known as the cradle of alpine skiing. Here were born the names and the legends known to all dedicated skiers: the Ski Club Arlberg, the early Kandahar races, Hannes Schneider and his Arlberg method.

The Arlberg, with peaks that top the 9,000-foot mark, lures skiers with its vast network of cableways, lifts, runs stretching for miles, a world-renowned ski school, and numerous sporting amenities. Runs begin at the intermediate level, reaching all the way to the "nearly impossible."

The Arlberg, the loftiest mountain in the Lechtal range, marks the boundary between the settlers of the Tyrolean country and the Vorarlbergers, who live in the extreme western province of Austria. One of the Arlberg's most celebrated peaks is the Valluga, at 9,220 feet.

In 1825 a road was opened allowing vehicular traffic to travel to the Arlberg Pass. A 6-mile-long rail tunnel was opened in 1884, linking Tyrol and Vorarlberg, and finally in 1978 a new road tunnel linked the two provinces. Toll for the highway tunnel is 150 AS ($11). The road tunnel is the third longest in Europe. If you're not driving, you'll find the area serviced by the well-known Arlberg Express rail link.

ST. ANTON AM ARLBERG

Alpine skiing is no longer in the cradle, having come of age to the point where St. Anton is now more the citadel of this winter sport, for a modern resort has grown out of the old village on the Arlberg Pass that was the scene of ski history in the making. This is a center for a ski area considered among the finest in the Alps.

It was at St. Anton (4,225 feet) that Hannes Schneider, born here in 1890, evolved modern skiing techniques as a very young man and started teaching tourists how to ski in 1907. The Ski Club Arlberg was born here in 1901. In 1911 the Arlberg-Kandahar Cup competition came into being with donation of a valuable trophy to be awarded annually to the best alpine skier. Before his death in 1955 Schneider saw his ski school rated as the world's finest. Today the ski school, still at St. Anton, is one of the world's largest and best, with about 300 instructors, the majority of whom speak English.

The little town is on the main railway line at the end of the 6-mile Arlberg tunnel. It's a compact resort village, with a five-story cap on building. No cars are allowed in the business area, but sleds and skis are plentiful.

The snow in this area is considered perfect for skiers, and the total lack of trees on the slopes makes the situation ideal. The ski fields of St. Anton stretch over a distance of some 6 square miles. Beginners stick to the nursery slopes down below, and for the more experienced skiers there are the runs from the Galzig and Valluga peaks. A cableway will take you to **Galzig** (6,860 feet), where there's a self-service restaurant. You go from here to Vallugagrat (8,685 feet), the highest station reached. The peak of the Valluga, at 9,220 feet, commands a panoramic view. St. Christoph (see below) is the mountain annex of St. Anton.

In addition to the major ski areas I just mentioned, there are two other important sites attracting followers of the sport: the **Gampen/Kapall** and the **Rendl.**

St. Anton am Arlberg in winter is quite fashionable, popular with the wealthy and occasional royalty—a more conservative segment of the jet set than you'll see at other posh ski resorts. There are many other cold-weather pursuits than just skiing, including ski jumping, mountain tours, curling, skating, tobogganing, and sleigh rides, plus après-ski on the quiet side.

There's so much emphasis on skiing here that few seem to talk of the summertime attractions. In warm weather St. Anton is tranquil and bucolic, surrounded by meadowland. A riot of wildflowers blooming in the fields announces the beginning of spring.

At any time of the year, you can visit the **Ski + Heimat Museum** (Skiing and Local Museum), in the Arlberg-Kandahar House (tel. 05446/2475), where displays trace the development of skiing in the area pioneered by men of the Arlberg, as well as the history of the region from the days of tribal migrations in and around Roman times. The museum, in the imposing structure at the center of the Holiday Park in St. Anton, is open Sunday to Friday from 3 to 7pm. Admission is 20 AS ($1.45) for adults and 10 AS (75¢) for children.

The local library is also housed in the Arlberg-Kandahar House, and the park provides a variety of leisure activities, including minigolf, a woodland playground, a fishing pond, table-tennis facilities, open-air chess, and a curling rink.

Where to Stay

Most hotels in the peak season prefer Saturday-to-Saturday bookings.

Hotel St. Antoner Hof, A-6580 St. Anton am Arlberg (tel. 05446/2910), considered one of the best hotels in town, is the domain of the Raffl family. The balconied property sits at the edge of the main road running through St. Anton about a block from the historic center. Each accommodation contains a wood-ringed balcony, expanses of beautifully grained paneling, ceiling timbers, plush upholstery, and efficient modern bath. There are only 30 rooms, so advance reservations are important. Because of the small number of guests, personal service and attention are a hallmark of the hotel. At times a house-party atmosphere prevails. In winter, the hotel charges from 1,390 AS ($101) to 1,830 AS ($133) per person daily for half board. In summer, half board ranges from 680 AS ($49.50) to 780 AS ($56.75) per person daily. Some full apartments, with whirlpools and open fireplaces, are available.

Guests enjoy an array of public rooms, each of which seems awash with Tyrolean accessories, thick timbers, and collections of rustic implements guaranteed to dazzle the eye and warm the spirit. The staff seem good-natured here, doing their best to ensure a guest's comfort. A rock-ringed indoor pool, a Jacuzzi, a sauna, a solarium, a fitness studio, blazing fireplaces, and good cuisine are all part of an experience here. A handful of indoor tennis and squash courts lie adjacent to the hotel. The restaurant is recommended separately. The St. Antoner Hof is open from December to April and June to October.

Hotel Schwarzer Adler, A-6580 St. Anton am Arlberg (tel. 05446/22440), in the center of St. Anton, has been owned and operated by members of the Tschol family since 1885. The fresco-covered, exceptionally beautiful building that houses it was constructed as an inn in 1570, using stones taken from the ruins of Arlen Castle, one of the region's nearby little-visited medieval monuments. The inn became known for its hospitality to pilgrims crossing the treacherous Arlberg Pass and was eventually declared an "officially registered" hotel by Empress Maria Theresa. Until the advent of the ski boom, the hotel's most prosperous era was from 1880 to 1885, when more than 3,000 workers swelled the population of St. Anton during the construction of the Arlberg Tunnel. In 1932 layers of stucco were chiseled away during a restoration of the hotel's exterior to reveal 400-year-old frescoes whose designs were faithfully restored to their original grandeur. Of special interest is a country baroque depiction of a sundial whose shadow fills the space between the flying cherubs and beribboned flowers of the window trim.

The hotel's interior contains all the rustically elegant accessories you'd expect, including several blazing fireplaces, painted Tyrolean baroque armoires, and enough Oriental carpets to stock a small department store. Facilities also include a sauna and fitness center. There are 50 handsomely furnished and well-equipped bedrooms in the main hotel, plus 13 slightly less well-furnished (but less expensive) rooms in the annex. The annex, built in the 1960s, lies across the street above the hotel-owned Café Aquila. In high season, half board ranges from 1,150 AS ($83.50) to 2,500 AS ($181.75) per person daily. In summer, half board goes from 550 AS ($40) to 950 AS ($69) per person daily. Guests are received from December to April and June to September.

Hotel Alte Post, A-6580 St. Anton am Arlberg (tel. 05446/25530). The reception area's antique Tyrolean chest, which fills a specially made niche, is only one of the dozens of charming touches put into place by the owners, Claudia and Michael Zanner. Designed long ago in a rambling, four-story format of ochre-colored walls, green shutters, and jutting gables, the hotel can easily be reached from the town's rail station. It was originally built in the 17th century as a postal station. The renovations of 1984 retained most of the thick-timbered beauty and added plush upholstery as well as paneling.

Since it became a hotel in the 1920s, some prominent skiers and show business personalities have relaxed with lesser-known clients in the hotel's cozy niches, some of which are warmed with crackling fires. The hotel contains an excellent restaurant, a sauna, whirlpool, and fitness center. Its bar is covered separately as an après-ski attraction.

Open only from December to April, the hotel rents 45 bedrooms, charging from 980 AS ($71.25) to 1,580 AS ($115) for a single, from 1,420 AS ($103.25) to 3,960 AS ($288) daily for a double. Rooms combine old-fashioned paneling with modern comforts such as tiled and timbered private baths, phones, TVs, and sometimes very elegant accessories.

Hotel Arlberg, A-6580 St. Anton am Arlberg (tel. 05446/2210). The most fashionable way to arrive here in the dead of winter is by horse-drawn sleigh. This is a big, attractively styled modern chalet hotel, rated four stars by the government and containing a wood and stucco façade. About 10 minutes from the center, but only a block from the town church, it is removed from the often raucous part of town, but convenient nonetheless. Built in 1970, it has been run and owned by the Ennemoser family ever since, and they wisely employ a thoughtful staff, many of whom return year after year. This is one of the few hotels in town to have its own swimming pool, along with such facilities as a sauna or Turkish bath.

The warmly paneled interior contains an intimate Tyrolean restaurant, the Zinnstube, which is open to nonresidents who call for a table, and a larger restaurant reserved for half-board guests. Even in the latter, the menu is changed so frequently that if you stay here for two weeks in season you need not sample the same dishes. The spacious lounge, which gives off a warmly hospitable tinge, has a long sit-down bar, clusters of deeply comfortable armchairs, and a ceramic tile stove. The 65 bedrooms are not only comfortable but well appointed, each with Tyrolean cupboards, a minibar, eiderdowns, a private bathroom and balcony, a phone, and upon request, a TV. Depending on the room assignment and the season, the per-person half-board rate ranges from a low of 700 AS ($51) to a high of 1,580 AS ($115). The hotel also offers a popular winter disco, the Tenne.

Hotel Post, A-6580 St. Anton am Arlberg (tel. 05446/21130), has long been a traditional favorite, attracting men who wear loden coats and alpine hats. Today, however, they mix happily with, say, young women from England in skin-tight pants and huge fur boots. Noteworthy because of its sprawling dimensions and its wood-and-stucco façade, it sits in the most prominent position in St. Anton, the geographical center of the resort beside the main pedestrian thoroughfare. The location of this 120-bed hostelry is only three minutes from the lifts, however. It was originally built in the 19th century—hence, its old-fashioned name. From its earliest days, it established a reputation as one of the resort's most sports-oriented hotels.

It's never been a style setter, but it offers 65 bedrooms that are comfortably and conservatively equipped with eiderdowns, TVs, radios, phones, and lots of exposed wood—in all, cozy and appealing on a winter's night. The Alber family, your hosts, charge 1,150 AS ($83.50) to 1,520 AS ($110.50) per person daily for half board. The hotel contains a dimly lit and woodsy series of spacious public rooms, two dining rooms, and two of the most popular nightlife facilities in St. Anton, the Post Keller and Pub Piccadilly (more about these later).

Hotel Karl Schranz, A-6580 St. Anton am Arlberg (tel. 05446/25550), is a scenically located four-star hotel owned by the famed sportsman for whom it is named. In fact, part of the lobby of this spacious hotel is filled with trophies won by Karl Schranz. He runs the hotel with his wife, Evelyn, and the place is Tyrolean with a vengeance, as reflected by its alpine chairs, ceramic stove, gemütlich flavor, even its mounted stag heads, giving it somewhat the aura of a hunting lodge. When not heavy on alpine charm, the furnishings are often a streamlined modern. The 21 bedrooms are in a no-nonsense style, but comfortable nonetheless. The hotel, open only from December to April, charges 760 AS ($55.25) to 850 AS ($61.75) per person daily for half board. More expensive apartments, suitable for two to four persons, are also available. Each unit has a private bath, a phone, a radio, and (in most cases) an individual balcony. Facilities include a sauna, a fitness room, a restaurant, a sun terrace, a café, a garage, and a log fire.

Hotel Mooserkreuz, A-6580 St. Anton am Arlberg (tel. 05446/2230), a four-star hotel, lies on a hairpin turn fronting the winding road to St. Christoph and the Arlberg Pass on the outskirts of St. Anton. It is a generously sized mountain inn on the sunniest part of the slopes above the village. The Rahofer family will help to make your stay pleasant. Guests have free use of the indoor pool as well as the sauna, and the hotel bus makes frequent runs to the center of town and to the ski lifts. The hotel offers 42 attractively decorated and comfortable bedrooms, each with private bath or shower. Half board in winter costs 900 AS ($65.50) to 1,050 AS ($76.25) per person daily. In summer, half board goes for only 500 AS ($36.25) per person daily. Guests are accepted from December to October. You can have a lot of fun here in the deep of winter if the crowd is convivial and right, which it often is.

Sporthotel St. Anton, A-6580 St. Anton am Arlberg (tel. 05446/3111), is sprawling, contemporary, and prefaced with regular rows of weather-blackened balconies. It sits on the main pedestrian thoroughfare of St. Anton, ideal for "ski bunny" shopping, but it's a good choice for skiers, as it lies just three pedestrian minutes from the beginning of the chair lifts. You're greeted at the entrance with the sight of a bar and the music of a full-time organist, whose melodies add to the generous feeling that a happy ski holiday involves at least several cocktails per day. This establishment was built in the mid-1970s, and at least nominally pays allegiance to sports and its attendant demands, although many patrons come here just to enjoy its food and drink possibilities (more about both of these later). The hotel features an ozone-enriched swimming pool with a water cascade, along with a sauna and solarium. There are two competitive discos in the basement. The 53 intimately cozy bedrooms are comfortably contempotary in style, each with a balcony and at least a suggestion of exposed alpine pine, as well as a TV, phone, and private bath. In winter, half board costs 1,480 AS ($107.50) to 1,630 AS ($118.50) per person daily. In summer, half board goes from 750 AS ($54.50) to 850 AS ($61.75). Open from December to September.

Hotel Tyrol, A-6580 St. Anton am Arlberg (tel. 05446/2340), is not famous like some of its nearby competitiors, but it is a winning choice for a family vacation, nevertheless. Built some 18 years ago, it sits between the main highway running up to the Arlberg Pass and the onion-domed church that highlights the center of St. Anton. Graced with blackened balconies and a no-nonsense weather-resistant chalet exterior, it contains 58 well-furnished accommodations, of which 8 are singles; all have private baths. Many of the accommodations are good-sized, with sitting areas and balconies. It's a clean, well-maintained establishment, a hospitable choice because of the care offered by an English-speaking staff, under the direction of the Eberhard Falkner family. The hotel accepts guests from December to September. Half board in winter costs 800 AS ($58.25) to 1,200 AS ($87.25) per person daily. In summer, half board goes for 400 AS ($29) to 600 AS ($43.50) per person daily. One dining room is for guests on half board, but nonresidents can patronize the pine-paneled stube, which is loaded with Tyrolean charm and has an electrically fired kachelofen, or ceramic tile stove. There you can order from an international menu, including both fondue bourguignonne and fondue chinoise. You might prefer the double entrecôte instead. Meals cost from 300 AS ($21.75). In summer, café tables are placed outside, with views of the highway, a rushing river, and the mountains.

Berghaus Maria, A-6580 St. Anton am Arlberg (tel. 05446/2005). Attractively isolated in a quiet residential section named Oberdorf, this hotel is an address jealously guarded by its devotees. It lies on a hillside above the main touristic district of St. Anton, a steep 12-minute climb up the hill (and then only if you're hearty). A family-run hotel, it's known more for its restaurant than its accommodations, although its bedrooms are first-rate. Originally it was built in the 1950s, but has changed much over the years, with the last major expansion completed in 1987.

In winter you register within sight of a blazing corner fireplace whose cheer permeates even the stylish Tyrolean bar a few steps away. Each of the 26 snug and cozy bedrooms offers plenty of exposed wooden trim, functional not stylish furniture, and if you're lucky, a view over the Rendl ski slope. St. Anton is not noted as a cheap resort, but the Berghaus Maria keeps its prices reasonable. Open from December to October, it charges 720 AS ($52.25) to 1,190 AS ($86.50) per person daily for half board.

A hotel minibus takes visitors back and forth from the Berghaus to the center of St. Anton. For the cuisine, see my restaurant recommendations. The ingratiating owners, Hermann and Maria Spiss, who are state-certified ski instructors, also offer an indoor swimming pool with sauna and massage facilities. A spacious terrace is ideal for basking in the sun. As you approach, you'll recognize the hotel by its country baroque window trim and its position downhill from the road leading from St. Anton up to the alpine suburb of Moos.

Hotel Montjola, A-6580 St. Anton am Arlberg (tel. 05446/2302), lies about half a mile west of the center of the resort, high above the old road to the Arlberg Pass, called Alte Arlberg Strasse. It is a rustically appealing Tyrolean guesthouse with green-and-white striped shutters, lots of exposed wood, and an interior that has much charm. Throughout, you'll see heavy ceiling beams, a stone-rimmed fireplace, rustic knickknacks, and immaculately set dining room tables. Fondue is a specialty, and it's usually prepared by a member of the Nohl family. In summer, rates are 370 AS ($27) to 420 AS ($30.50) per person daily, with half board included. In winter, guests also book in here mainly on the half-board plan, which costs 760 AS ($55.25) to 920 AS ($67) per person, based on double occupancy. All 14 rooms contain private baths, toilets, and phones. Singles pay a daily surcharge of 50 AS ($3.75) to 75 AS ($5.50).

Hotel Rosanna, A-6580 St. Anton am Arlberg (tel. 05446/2011), is one of the least pretentious and most reliable middle-bracket hotels in St. Anton. Near the reception desk is a series of functionally comfortable sitting rooms, but most of the guests select a seat in the hotel's duet of restaurants as their preferred roost for socializing (more about eating and drinking here will be found in the après-ski section). Built in the 1960s and redecorated and modernized several times since then, the hotel contains 39 snugly comfortable bedrooms, each with a balcony, private bath, and TV on request. Open from December to October, the hotel charges 1,050 AS ($76.25) to 1,250 AS ($90) per person daily for half board in winter. In summer, half board costs 500 AS ($36.25) to 600 AS ($43.50) per person daily. The hotel has a sauna and a solarium on the premises, and extends a heartfelt welcome to its array of international guests.

Where to Dine

Raffl-Stube, Hotel St. Antoner Hof (tel. 05446/2910). It didn't exist until 1982. That's when members of the Raffl family enclosed a corner of their lobby and added some of the region's finest accessories. Today a table here is a much-sought-after commodity in a resort loaded with worthy competitors. Its primary décor statement involves the family's coat-of-arms, whose year of origin (1584) is emblazoned prominently across the entrance. Meticulously crafted pinewood panels from a local five-needle evergreen, the zirben, act as backdrops for the hunting trophies, antique pewter, and charmingly executed floral designs.

By intent, the place contains only 10 tables and in the peak of the season can get very exclusive, so reservations are imperative, especially if you're a nonresident. Overflow diners are offered a seat in a spacious but less special dining room across the hall. The hotel has long enjoyed a favored reputation for its cuisine, and somehow the food in the stube tastes even better than the regular dining room fare. Quality ingredients are always used, and the kitchen prepares tempting selections, including such specialties as roast goose liver with salad, cream of parsley soup with sautéed quail eggs, filet of salmon with wild rice, trout "prepared as you like it," and roast filet of pork, along with the ever-popular fondue bourguignonne. Full meals cost 300 AS ($21.75) to 800 AS ($58.50), and are served daily from 11 am to 2 pm and 6 to 10 pm.

Hotel Alte Post Restaurant (tel. 05446/25540). Outsiders are welcomed into this historic establishment's pair of antique dining rooms, where green ceramic stoves and intricately crafted wrought iron lend a mellow, graceful, and charming accent. Because of its limited number of tables, reservations are important. The kitchen chefs cook with flair at this place, turning out such classic dishes as rack of lamb, filet of beef, sweetbreads in often delightful ways, venison gulasch, fresh duckling, and fondue Bacchus. You'll be guided by a helpful, attentive staff through the menu, which costs from 300 AS ($21.75) for a full meal. Service is daily from 11:30 am to 2 pm and 7 to 9:30 pm. The restaurant lies behind a wooden door across from the reception area of this previously recommended hotel.

Berghaus Maria Restaurant (tel. 05446/20050) serves some of the finest food in the area—some say the best in St. Anton. It lies in the suburb of Oberdorf, high on a slope, in this previously recommended hotel. Although modernized, the hotel still retains dozens of charming antique Tyrolean touches and accents. Guests dine in one of a trio of alpine rooms, with ceramic tile stoves, Oriental carpets, rows of burnished pewter, and views over a snow-covered ski slope. Specialties include filet of venison in port wine sauce, dauphine potatoes, and marinated cabbage, or else stuffed squab, salmon in Riesling sauce, and for dessert, apple fritters in beer-flavored pastry with cinnamon. Full meals cost 400 AS ($29) to 450 AS ($32.75), and are served daily from 6:30 to 10 pm. Reservations are essential. The hotel's bar, which is warmed with a fire blazing in the nearby reception area, is open throughout the afternoon.

The Steakhouse, Sporthotel St. Anton (tel. 05446/3111). Some of the most attractive elements of this warmly decorated steakhouse include the fact that reservations aren't needed. You can watch your steak sizzling as you sip a drink in warm comfort. Some guests prefer one of the bar stools, whose perch will even allow more outgoing diners to communicate directly with the chef at the nearby grill about the preferred degree of doneness of their grilled meats. The steaks are just as good at one of the tables in the wood-trimmed dining room. Open daily from 11 am to midnight, the establishment serves meals costing from 350 AS ($25.50). Menu selections include Lyons-style onion soup, small and "giant" salads, grilled crayfish, filet of veal in mushroom sauce, filet of peppersteak, and if cholesterol is a problem, sliced roast turkey with pineapple on toast. Beer comes in foam-covered mugs, and wine is served not only in bottles but in less expensive carafes. The Steakhouse occupies part of the street level of the previously recommended Sporthotel St. Anton on the main pedestrian thoroughfare of the resort.

Hotel Schwarzer Adler Restaurant (tel. 05546/22440) is contained in the medieval walls of this previously recommended hotel. The restaurant prides itself on its Tyrolean authenticity, which reaches its zenith in one of its two wood-paneled *Stubes*, the preferred place to dine here. The darker of the *Stubes* boasts paneling said to be four centuries old. There, the lighting fixtures are especially noteworthy, each being designed from raw horns and fashioned into some mythical or allegorical figure from a Teutonic legend. In the center, a carved menagerie of animals is supported by a rounded motif not unlike a fanciful wagon wheel. For warmth, a ceramic tile stoves radiates a welcome heat.

Atmosphere aside, the real reason patrons come here is for the food. The kitchen brigade displays outstanding skills, which are best shown at one of the buffets. The menu tempts at every turn with such dishes as homemade salmon ravioli with a chervil-flavored cream sauce, medallions of saddle of venison with a juniperberry-flavored cream sauce, or medallions of anglerfish with ratatouille. The tafelspitz is another favorite. The cookery can be both straightforward and intricate. Meals, costing from 400 AS ($29), are served only at dinner—nightly from 6:30 to 10pm. Reservations are needed.

Restaurant Ferwall, An der Ferwall-Loipe (tel. 05446/3249), is ideal for a snowy night. Recognized as one of the best restaurants in the area, it lies on the slopes of a hill and is reached by taking the road to St. Christoph and the Arlberg Pass. At the previously recommended Hotel Mooserkreuz you can rent a horse-drawn sleigh to take you down a lane to the restaurant. Once there, you'll enter an alpine lodge with plenty of Tyrolean charm. Meals cost 175 AS ($12.75) to 350 AS ($25.50), the latter price for a mountain feast. You get traditional local dishes along with a few international specialties. In season, game is featured, including venison medallions. Deer sausages with sauerkraut are another specialty. The Ferwall serves dinner nightly between 7 and 8:30 (or 9) pm, depending on reservations, which are essential. Lunch, served only in summer, is daily from 11am to 2pm.

Restaurant Brunnenhof (tel. 05446/2293), in the neighboring resort of St. Jakob, is an authentic Arlberg farmhouse parlor dating from 1752. Its owners, the Wolfram family, are known for their well-prepared Tyrolean and international dishes. Guests who journey over here at night might begin, for example, with a cheese-noodle soup, then follow with tafelspitz with spinach and rösti. Meals cost 200 AS ($14.50) to 450 AS ($32.75) per person. The service is courteous and polite, and the house has a good wine list. It doesn't serve lunch, but offers dinner between December and April only, daily from 6 to 10pm.

Cafés and Stubes

Café Crispin (tel. 05446/3158) is a modern café set on the upper reaches of the resort's main pedestrian-only thoroughfare. Open daily from 9 am to midnight, it serves such standard dishes as soups (made fresh every day), schnitzels, and platters of beef. Wine can be ordered by the glass or by the carafe—even glühwein, which has been heated. Meals costing from 150 AS ($11) are among the most reasonable served at St. Anton. Of course, you can just sample the delectable Austrian pastries along with coffee or hot chocolate.

Café Aquila (tel. 05446/2245) achieved a certain kind of fame in the ski world as the Café Tschol. Now, under a new name, it lies just across the street from its daddy, the already-recommended Hotel Schwarzer Adler. This is an unusually pleasant café serving an array of light meals, beer, wine, tea, and several varieties of coffee. Full meals cost from 150 AS ($11), including such dishes as snails, tomato-flavored spaghetti, gulasch soup, spinach-stuffed ravioli, and a serve-yourself heaping selection of appetizers from a buffet. You can also visit just for coffee and Tyrolean pastries, perhaps a glass of wine. The latter goes for 20 AS ($1.45). The café is open daily from 9am to midnight.

Later in the evening, you may want to drink or eat inexpensively at the **Fuhrmannstube** (tel. 05446/2921). Warmly paneled, attractively rustic, and conveniently located near the town church on the main street, this café and restaurant serves reasonably priced meals costing from 150 AS ($11). It has a predictable but well-prepared array of such Teutonic specialties as rösti, spätzl, gulasch, farmhouse sausages with sauerkraut, and venison in season. It is open daily from 10am to 11pm.

Après-Ski

St. Anton's after-dark are among the most glittering in Tyrol. It'll be best if you like your fellow skiers, as in season it's likely to be elbow-to-elbow (or whatever) in most places.

One of the most alluring spots in town for a drink lies within the thick walls of the already recommended **Hotel Alte Post** (tel. 05446/25530). Off the lobby is a spacious and beautifully rustic room awash with alpine paneling, ceiling beams, comfortable banquettes, and some of the most attractive people at the resort. A pair of brass lions struggling with serpents flanks the blazing fire set near the entrance. An eight-sided bar offers roundabout seating near an intimate dance floor. Disco music makes the place animated later in the evening. The bar is open only between November and Easter. A large beer costs 40 AS ($2.90), and the bar is daily from 4pm to 2am.

Krazy Kanguruh (tel. 05446/2633). The core of this restaurant/disco was originally built as a stable, but today its earthy wood-sheathed ambience attracts the lion's share of the resort's restless and reckless. To reach it, you'll either have to ski from the resort's uppermost slopes, walk breathlessly up the steep hill from the village, or drive your car via the suburb of Moos along a winding and treacherously narrow road. A phone call in advance will apprise you of driving conditions and directions, whose complexity you'll appreciate only after you get there. Owned and operated by a dashing and entrepreneurial Swede, Gunnar Munthe, the place serves different functions depending on the hour of the day. From 11 am to 2 pm, lunches consisting of hamburgers, Wiener schnitzels, lasagne, and peppersteak are served by what some observers define as the most attractive corps of employees in Tyrol. Happy hour is raucous, rowdy, and loud. Be sure to ask for a shot of the pear-and-plum schnapps that a local farmer distills especially for the Krazy Kanguruh. Evening dinners are slightly more sedate, served nightly from 7:30 to 11pm. Lunches cost from 60 AS ($4.25), dinners from 250 AS ($18.25).

The basement disco is predictably energetic and arguably the most fun in town if you don't mind the cold-weather descent into town after the 3 am closing. Some of the more adventurous participants have dared slide back to town on the slippery edge of a plastic bag—and some partrons have ended up in the hospital doing this. There's no cover charge for the disco, and a beer costs from 29 AS ($2.10).

Post Keller, Hotel Post (tel. 05446/22130), is probably the most consistently energetic and bubbly nightspot in St. Anton. It lies in the basement of this previously recommended hotel, with a décor of pinewood paneling, unbreakable chairs and banquettes, and a long bar area—long ago permeated with spilled suds from countless mugs of foaming beer. There's never a cover charge for the place, which opens for "tea" from 4 to 6 pm every night—instead of tea, most guests order wine or schnapps. Food is served continuously from 6 pm to 2 am, and the bar finally closes for good at 3 am. No one will mind, however, if you drop in only for a drink, there to mingle and chatter. A large beer costs from 35 AS ($2.55), and live music is occasionally offered. Management creates an array of midwinter theme parties from time to time, including toga contests, "beach parties," carnival parties, and "black and white" parties. Full meals cost from 350 AS ($25.50) and might include such ski-resort fare as peppersteak, T-bone steak, and Wiener schnitzel.

Piccadilly Pub, Hotel Post (tel. 05446/22130), is, as its name suggests, an English-style pub. Painted a durable shade of green, and lined with photos of happy revelers enjoying "snow and suds," the place offers a stand-up format of rowdy fun and loud music. Special tongue-in-cheek events such as Australia Day see icons made of stuffed koala bears. The place lies off the main pedestrian thoroughfare of town behind etched-glass Victorian swinging doors. Hours are nightly from 9am till "very early the next morning." A large beer costs from 35 AS ($2.55).

Le Clou (tel. 05446/2017). Set beside the main pedestrian thoroughfare of the resort, this recent newcomer to the nightlife scene hides behind a harlequin-striped Tyrolean-inspired décor. It prides itself on opening just a few minutes later than many of its competitors, perhaps as a tongue-in-cheek satire on the rigidly maintained opening hours of many of the resort's fun spots. Happy hour, when drink prices are reduced, is daily from 4:36 to 6:37pm. After closing for a while, it reopens at 9:36 pm, shutting down at 2:59, or perhaps 3:01am.

Drop-In, Sporthotel St. Anton (tel. 05446/3111), competes with its neighbor, St. Anton bar, as the most popular, energetic, and desirable disco in town. A cover charge of 35 AS ($2.55) buys a patron a first drink, which is obtainable nightly from 9pm to 2am. The bar is round, allowing drinkers to casually check out their fellow imbibers across the assortment of bottles, glasses, and colored lights. The disco music is imported.

St. Anton Bar (Stanton Bar) (tel. 05446/2005-54). If you tire of Drop-In, its most aggressive competitor is only a few steps away. Amid a glittering décor that includes shimmering brass, lots of lights, and recently released music, it attracts patrons from all over the world who dance the night away from 9am to 3am. It features hits on video clips and a super light show, offering both drinks and snacks. Prices are the same as at Drop-In.

Rosanna Stüberl, Hotel Rosanna (tel. 05446/2011). This place is technically a restaurant, with a full array of tempting menu items for diners. However, it's still suitable as an après-ski choice, either for drinks or for a late-night pizza. You can choose from among three pine-sheathed rooms, one of which is dominated by what is said to be "the most skillful" pizza oven in town, offering 25 different varieties, ranging in price from 85 AS ($6.25) to 120 AS ($8.75). Food is served daily from 6pm to midnight. You can also order Italian saltimbocca, Indonesian-style beef, chop suey, or a paillard of veal if you don't want to settle for a pizza. Your choice of four kinds of noodles can be matched with your choice of six different kinds of sauces. Full meals cost from 200 AS ($14.50) unless you stick to pizza and beer.

Disco Klause, Hotel Schwarzer Adler (tel. 05446/22440). Hidden behind this hotel's 400-year-old exterior frescoes, which were rediscovered beneath layers of plaster and restored in 1932, lies a disco where holiday-makers unleash the last remnants of their energy after a day on the slopes. Visitors pay a 50-AS ($3.65) cover charge to dance the night away each evening from 9pm to 3am. A large beer costs from 30 AS ($2.20).

S'Fassl, Hotel Tyrol (tel. 05446/2340). The name of the place in German roughly translates as pub. On the street level of this previously recommended hotel, this place is not a major stop along the après-ski route, but it has plenty of devotees. Recorded disco plays in the background, but no one comes here to dance. The incentive to talk and laugh is usually a product of a charming staff. The barmaids make a special effort to welcome newcomers. Try for a seat on a padded banquette alongside one end of a four-sided bar. The place is open nightly from 5pm to 3am. A glass of beer costs from 30 AS ($2.20).

Underground (tel. 05446/2000), in the square at the end of the pedestrian zone, is a bistro/piano bar/club combination, offering a happy hour and tea dance from 4 to 6pm, a cocktail hour from 6 to 8pm, and bistro specialties including a salad bar and fondues, plus raclette, vegetarian dishes, and fish and chips, served from 7pm to midnight. Meals cost from 150 AS ($11). In the piano bar, from 9pm to 3am daily, you can listen to live jazz, blues, rock, and ballads, as well as dance to recorded music during the breaks. Hot snacks are available.

ST. CHRISTOPH

The mountain way station of St. Anton, St. Christoph (5,850 feet) is linked to the St. Anton terrain by a cableway at Galzig. It's on the road to the Arlberg Pass and has essentially the same ski facilities available as St. Anton, only here you're closer to the action. If you're not driving your own car, take the train to St. Anton, then go either by bus or taxi to St. Christoph.

A hospice, whose present reincarnation is described below, was originally established here in 1386 by a now-legendary saintlike mountain man, Heinrich of Kempten, whose self-imposed duty was to bury the remains of pilgrims who froze to death in the treacherous snowdrifts of one of the world's most unpredictable and temperamental mountain passes.

Because the Arlberg was the single most important route for commerce between northern Italy and the Teutonic world throughout the Middle Ages, literally hundreds of pilgrims froze to death at the pass or died of hunger, exposure, avalanches, or whatever. The church-related society and monastery that Saint Christopher established grew from the single efforts of one man into one of the most beneficent monastic orders of Europe. The monastery that grew up on the site accumulated artistic treasures talked about throughout Europe, many of them donated by grateful merchants whose caravans they had sheltered and saved.

Appropriately, the monastery was built several hundred feet on the Tyrolean side, from the uppermost heights of the frequently snowbound pass, amid a terrain so hostile that after the surrounding trees were felled for fuel, large carts were required to bring all the basic necessities into the community.

Throughout the Age of Enlightenment the hospice continued to recruit new members, whose main reason for being was to patrol the pass every morning and evening, searching for frozen bodies in anticipation of a decent burial, assisting wayfarers in trouble, and providing desperately needed accommodations for the thousands of caravans carrying merchandise across the pass.

By the late 19th century honorary membership in the Order of St. Christopher was granted to VIPs and charitably minded individuals around the world, frequently as a sign of political respect on the request of the Austrian government. Today its members are initiated with pomp, ceremony, and amused good humor, and have included such personalities as King Juan Carlos of Spain, the village postman, Queen Juliana and Prince Bernhard of the Netherlands, doctors, journalists, and artists.

As roads, phone lines, and helicopter rescue teams made passage over the Arlberg less treacherous, the Arlberg Pass developed into one of the world's leading ski resorts. In the 1950s the monastery, which had had difficulty recruiting new members, sold the complex to members of the Werner family. Under the guidance of the family patriarch, the monastery was modernized, upgraded, and brought into the 20th century with the addition of electricity and many of the era's creature comforts.

Tragically, only a few weeks after the completion of the improvements, a devastating fire destroyed all but a portion of the ancient monastery. Rumor had it that a maid, hired for the season, had started the fire in her room when a pair of stockings stretched to dry over an electric filament caught fire. The fire provided the opportunity to rebuild the first hotel recommended below.

Food and Lodging

Arlberg Hospiz, A-6580 St. Christoph (tel. 05446/26110). A world-class hotel, this 100-room hospice contains as much mystery, legend, and romance as any other hotel in Austria. Many of its most charming touches were lovingly and painstakingly re-created from old photographs and personal memories. Today what visitors see is a pink-walled building whose steep gabled roof looks strong enough to support even the heaviest blanket of snow. Inside, visitors are welcomed into this luxurious world, with more style and plush antique-oriented comfort than the medieval monks could have imagined. An equally luxurious annex, whose foundations once supported a building used to store salt, is connected to the main building by an underground passageway entirely sheathed in carefully finished pinewood.

The hotel is open only from November to May (groups book it solidly in summer). Guests can be assured in winter of almost constant snowfall, which they enjoy along with the superb food and array of in-house entertainment. The "party room," for example, changes its décor and nature from year to year. Once it was transformed into an ancient Roman tavern. The flagstones of the labyrinthine public rooms were imported from a crumbling French château. The valuable Persian carpets each seem to be antiques in their own right, and the hand-carved paneling in the different dining areas, about eight in all, could grace the living quarters of the wealthiest people on earth. In all, the hotel contains 80 plush and luxuriously furnished accommodations, with a host of amenities and perhaps the finest service in the Tyrol. Charges in winter range from 2,000 AS ($145.50) to 3,000 AS ($218) daily for a single, from 2,400 AS ($174.50) to 3,500 AS ($254.50) per person for double occupancy. Doubles are more impressive than singles—hence the higher charges.

Even if you don't stay here, consider having a meal; but reserve in advance. The hotel scatters its elegantly appointed Tyrolean table settings over the spacious main dining room, which seems to weave sinuously around an enormous hearth, with banks of windows, massive wooden posts, and salad buffets. International specialties change frequently. Meals cost 300 AS ($21.75) to 550 AS ($40). Hours are noon to 2pm and 7 to 10pm daily.

Hotel Arlberghöhe, A-6580 St. Christoph (tel. 05446/58251). Set at the base of a steep mass of snow-covered rocks, this modernized chalet hotel stands across the road from the more glamorous and expensive Arlberg Hospiz, just recommended. It was built around 1940, but has been modernized several times since then by the extended Tyrolean family who own and run it. Its rustic interior, heavy ceiling beams, and clusters of alpine antiques give the impression of far greater age. From its opening in late November until its closing in late April, skiers take warm refuge here, enjoying the well-scrubbed and conservative comfort, as the gales blow around the chalet's dark-stained balconies.

Management prefers to rent its 15 well-furnished bedrooms only by the week, and many single and married guests come here year after year, requesting a favorite chamber. Many of the bedrooms are quite spacious and heavy on wood tones, containing beautiful tile baths. With half board included, the per-person daily rate ranges from 1,100 AS ($80) to 1,200 AS ($87.25). The food is good and there's plenty of it, a medley of classic Austrian dishes, Tyrolean specialties, and international offerings. A Schischule (ski school) is on the ground level, and directly overhead skiers in their brightly colored outfits order drinks in the cold but invigorating air.

Gasthof Valluga, A-6580 St. Christoph (tel. 05446/2823). In its price bracket, this is probably the most charming and best-maintained hotel on the Arlberg Pass. It sits closest to the pass itself and has the most impressive views. In spite of its snowclad position, it lies only a short walk to the heart of the village. Guests register at a well-scrubbed, wood-clad bar of a café with warmly textured pinewood paneling. The German-speaking owner, Lydia Haueis, maintains only seven bedrooms, each impeccably proper. Two are suitable for up to four occupants. Each accommodation contains a wooden ceiling, lots of paneling, thick carpeting, a TV, phone, private bath, minibar, and lots of cozy charm. With half board included, per-person daily rates range from 900 AS ($65.50) to 1,080 AS ($78.50). Facilities include a sauna and a covered parking garage, along with the kind of exterior decoration familiar on alpine baroque buildings in the Engadine region of Switzerland. The hotel is open only from late November until May. Its restaurant is warmly accommodating, serving reasonably priced meals for 200 AS ($14.50) daily from noon to 2pm and 7 to 9pm.

16. East Tyrol

East Tyrol is like an afterthought—of, but not actually in, Land Tyrol. When Italy was ceded South Tyrol in 1919 in the aftermath of World War I, East Tyrol was like a refugee child separated from its mother and not reunited with her. This part of Tyrol was cut off from the rest of the province by a narrow projection of Italian land that connects to Land Salzburg.

Italy, including what used to be South Tyrol, lies to the south and west of East Tyrol, with Land Salzburg to the north and Carinthia to the east. The little subprovince, of which Lienz is the capital, is cut off from its neighbors on the north by seemingly impenetrable Alps. East Tyrol is known as Osttirol in German.

Because of its isolated position, East Tyrol tends to be neglected by the average North American tourist, which is a shame. The grandeur of its scenery and the warm hospitality of its people make it worth visiting. It's crowned by the magnificent peaks of the Hohe Tauern, the Grossvenediger, and the Grossglockner, and to the south lie the Lienz Dolomites, which invite exploration. The scenery along the Drau and the Isel valleys is spectacular. These two main valleys have many little side hollows worth exploring, especially the Virgental. You'll see a lot of alpine pastureland, meadows, relatively undiscovered valleys, and beautiful lakes.

The Romans occupied East Tyrol in ancient times. Later, the Slavs moved into the area as settlers and made it a section of Carinthia. It has known many rulers, from the Bavarians to the French. Even Great Britain had a hand in running things here, when the Allies made East Tyrol a part of the British-occupied sector of Austria from 1945 to 1955.

Since 1967 it's been possible to reach East Tyrol by taking the 3-mile-long Felbertauern Tunnel, a western route through the Alps. If you're driving, you can come from the east or the west. From the Grossglockner Road, you take the Felbertauern Road and the tunnel. If you're driving from the north to Lienz, the East Tyrol capital, you can take the Falbertauern Road from Land Salzburg, passing through the tunnel. In summer you may want to take the Grossglockner Road and the Iselberg Pass. This road runs along the boundary between East Tyrol and Carinthia.

It's also possible to take a train from Italy to East Tyrol. Corridor trains also operate between Innsbruck and Lienz. As you pass through Italy on this trip, the trains are locked and you don't have to show your passport or clear Italian Customs.

Woodcarving, long a pursuit in East Tyrol, is still practiced in tranquil chalets during the long winter months. You might like to shop for some pieces while you're here.

LIENZ

Don't confuse this city with *Linz*, the capital of Upper Austria. Lienz with an *e* serves as the capital of East Tyrol. It lies at the junction of three valleys—the Isel to the northwest, the Puster to the west, and the Drau to the east. The old town of Lienz stretches along the banks of the Isel River, with **Liebburg Palace,** a 16th-century building, now the seat of local government, overshadowing the Hauptplatz (main square).

Area Sights

The sights of Lienz are easy to see, taking no more than about 1½ hours. One of the main attractions is **Schloss Bruck** (Bruck Castle) with its **Osttiroler Heimatmuseum** (Museum of East Tyrol). This was the fortress of the counts of

Görz, who held sway over vast estates until they fell prey to the Habsburgs at the beginning of the 16th century. The castle stands at the head of the entrance to the Valley of Isel, less than a mile from the center of Lienz.

In the museum, much has been preserved of the life and times of the people of East Tyrol, including handcrafts and regional dress. The Rittersaal (Knight's Hall) shows how the castle looked in the Middle Ages. The most important feature of the museum is the Albin Egger-Lienz gallery, containing a magnificent collection of the art of this outstanding native painter, who died in 1926. Most often, he took the Tyrolean country and its people as his subjects. Another section displays artifacts unearthed at the archeological site of the Roman town of Aguntum (see below).

The museum is open daily from around Easter until the end of October from 10am to 5pm. Off-season, it is closed on Monday. Admission is 30 AS ($2.20), and there's a restaurant at the castle.

If you have time, visit **St. Andrä** (Church of St. Andrew), the outstanding feature of which is the collection of 16th-century tombstones carved of marble quarried outside Salzburg. The last of the counts of Görz is buried here. The church, consecrated in 1457, was restored in 1968, having fallen into a sad state of disrepair. During the restoration workmen uncovered murals, some dating from the 14th century. The nave is in the late Gothic style, and the church is considered the finest example of Gothic architecture in East Tyrol. A memorial chapel honors Lienz war dead. The renowned painter, Albin Egger-Lienz, mentioned above, is entombed here.

In winter Lienz at an elevation of 2,850 feet, attracts skiers to its two major ski areas: the **Hochstein** and the **Zertersfeld**, serviced by chair and drag lifts. The height of the top station is 7,225 feet.

In summer the town fills up with mountain climbers, mainly Austrians, who come to scale the Dolomites. This is a good base for many excursions in the area. For example, from Schlossberg, you can take a chair lift up to **Venedigerwarte** (3,335 feet). You can also explore the excavations of **Aguntum,** the Roman settlement, 3 miles east of Lienz. You can bathe in **Lake Tristacher,** 3 miles south of the city.

The **Dolomites,** actually the northwestern part of the Gailtal alpine range, lie between the Gail Valley and the Drau Valley. Their highest peak is the Grosse Sandspitze at more than 9,000 feet.

A Range of Hotels

Romantikhotel Traube, Hauptplatz, A-9900 Lienz (tel. 04852/64444). The location couldn't be more ideal, in the very center of town on a street lined with decorative trees. The distinctive façade is painted a vivid red, with forest-green shutters and a canopy covering part of the ground-level café. Furnishings in both the public rooms and the bedrooms are elegant and comfortable. On the roof is a covered swimming pool, while in the cellar a vaulted disco (often with live music) provides evening entertainment.

The décor of the 48 spacious bedrooms is conservatively modern, and many have views opening onto nearby mountains. Prices are 680 AS ($49.50) to 800 AS ($58.25) daily for a single, and 600 AS ($43.50) to 950 AS ($69) per person based on double occupancy, with a buffet breakfast included in the rates. For half board, there's a daily surcharge of 250 AS ($18.25) per person.

Hotel Sonne, A-9900 Lienz (tel. 04852/63311). Its modernized mansard roof and uncluttered windows rise from one end of the Südtirolerplatz. The 56-room hotel was originally built in the late 1960s, but almost completely renovated in 1978. Today, in addition to a charming staff, it contains terra-cotta floors, Oriental rugs, a sauna, and a very large bar with a timbered ceiling and fireplace, as well as a wood-trimmed and sun-flooded restaurant. The reservations system is tied in to the Best Western network. The cozy bedrooms are conservatively outfitted with modern furniture and occasional expanses of knotty-pine paneling. Each unit has a private bath, phone, radio alarm, and TV/video connection. Singles range from

610 AS ($44.25) to 680 AS ($49.50) daily, with doubles going from 510 AS ($37) to 580 AS ($42.25) per person. In an apartment for two, the per-person rate ranges from 680 AS ($49.50) to 750 AS ($54.50) daily. All rates include a buffet breakfast and are charged according to the season. The hotel has a roof garden and sun terrace, as well as an underground garage. A recreation and sport club program is offered, with tennis, squash, indoor and outdoor swimming pools, and use of a sauna.

Hotel Post, Südtirolerplatz 7, A-9900 Lienz (tel. 04852/62505). Most of the ground floor of this severe-looking hotel is filled with the wooden banquettes of the most popular café/bar in town. Under vaulted ceilings, in the light of a pair of small-shaded chandeliers, most of the active socializers of Lienz gather every evening after work. However, if you're interested in a hotel room, the reception area opens with its own entrance onto the square. A small lobby contains baronial settees heavily carved with cherubs and mythical beasts. There's a garden set up with café tables in back. Each of the 30 comfortably and well-maintained bedrooms contains a private bath, phone, and conservative furniture. The Lederer family charges 470 AS ($34.25) to 540 AS ($39.25) daily for a single with half board, or 410 AS ($29.75) to 470 AS ($34.25) per person for a double.

Gasthof-Pension Haidenhof, A-9900 Lienz (tel. 04852/62440), looks like an appealing cross between an alpine chalet and a Mediterranean villa. The windows of the hotel's central section are bordered with painted Tyrolean designs, while on either side symmetrical wings with strong horizontal lines stretch toward the surrounding forest. Views from the balconies of the well-furnished bedrooms encompass most of Lienz. On the premises is a sun terrace, along with a series of pastel-colored vaulted ceilings, plus a paneled restaurant. Prices range from 400 AS ($29) to 495 AS ($36) per person daily for a bed and half board. The hotel is open from December to October. It's about 20 minutes from the center of town.

Hotel Glöckturm, Pfarrgasse 2, A-9900 Lienz (tel. 04852/62164), is a sprawling old-fashioned 42-room hotel set in a wooded area beside the river. The façade looks as if three different buildings were welded into a single unit, all of them painted a baroque yellow with red–and–sea-green trim. The interior is simple and attractive, including the bedrooms. Rates range from 330 AS ($24) to 420 AS ($30.50) per person daily, with half board included.

Gasthof Goldener Fisch, A-9900 Lienz (tel. 04852/62132), about two minutes by car from the center of town, offers views of different mountains from practically every room in the house. The prosperous-looking façade is painted beige with brown shutters, tending to accent the jutting bay windows festooned in summer with flowers. The interior has lots of exposed paneling, a ceramic stove, and a hospitable bar and restaurant. Of the 35 bedrooms, 21 contain private baths or showers. The Egon Vergeiner family, the hosts, charge 280 AS ($20.25) to 350 AS ($25.50) per person daily for half board.

Where to Dine

Romantikhotel Traube, Hauptplatz (tel. 04852/64444). Amid Tyrolean accents of flowered banquettes, gilded wall sconces, and big arched windows, this airy restaurant offers elegant meals in comfortably paneled surroundings. Uniformed waiters present such well-prepared specialties as paprika-flavored chicken with sour cream sauce and buttered noodles, piccata of hare with ham-flavored spaghetti, local calves' liver with tomatoes, bacon, and roast potatoes, along with peppersteak in a cognac-flavor cream sauce. Set menus cost from 200 AS ($14.50) to 275 AS ($20), with à la carte meals ranging from 200 AS ($14.50) to 450 AS ($32.75). Food is served nightly from 6 to 10pm. Reservations are recommended. The restaurant is closed in November, for part of December, and for the last two weeks of April.

MATREI IN OSTTIROL

A winter-sports resort and summer-holiday retreat, Matrei in East Tyrol has much charm. From its location, winter visitors can avail themselves of two ski regions with well-prepared descents from above the 7,500-foot mark as well as interesting tracks for cross-country skiing and ski hiking. There are reliable snow conditions in the Goldried ski area (more than 6,500 feet) and at the runs near Matrei Tauernhaus and the Venedigerblick mountain railway.

In summer this is a choice spot for mountain climbing, walking, horseback riding, and tennis.

To reach Matrei by train, you can go to Lienz via Spittal or Innsbruck. From Lienz there's a Postal Bus connection. Of course, you can also come here by car. Just don't confuse Matrei in East Tyrol with another Matrei that you may have passed through in your exploration of the Wipp Valley.

Food and Lodging

Hotel Goldried, A-9971 Matrei in Osttirol (tel. 04875/6113), with its regularly spaced towers and alpine setting, looks much like a modernized version of a Teutonic fortress. Its dozens of balconies look out over a valley, combining access to good skiing with a pleasant, comfortable format. All the 50 accommodations in the main hotel and its annex, the Dependance Goldriedpark, are well-equipped apartments containing fireplaces, private saunas, children's rooms, kitchens, clothes washers and dryers, and up to three bedrooms, sometimes on two different levels.

Apartments vary in size and can accommodate up to eight people. Most visitors check in here for a week at a time. Depending on the season, an apartment for four ranges from 720 AS ($52.25) to 1,300 AS ($94.50) per day. A one-time cleaning charge, beginning at 560 AS ($40.75), is levied at the end of your stay.

There's an outdoor terrace with a pool, plus a Tyrolean bar, a kindergarten with child-sitting facilities, and an indoor pool. The hotel is only a few yards from a double-chair lift, the Höhe Tauern Süd, and the beginning of a network of almost endless cross-country ski tracks. Partly because the hotel is owned by a group of Swedish investors, it serves as the winter training ground for the Swedish national ski team.

Hotel Rauter, A-9971 Matrei in Osttirol (tel. 04875/6611), has an attractive modern façade. It looks like a combination of a beach resort house and an alpine chalet. The most distinctive feature is the huge simplified adaptation of an arched window from a Gothic church set into a curved area above the front entrance. The bedrooms have lighthearted elements that might be Japanese, art deco, or modified Gothic, depending on your whim. This is definitely a year-round hotel, containing facilities geared to sports of all seasons. These include a big indoor pool and a summer outdoor pool, as well as both in- and outdoor tennis courts. Horseback riding is nearby, and the hotel bus makes frequent winter runs to the ski slopes. Anglers will find rich fishing areas close to the hotel.

The Obwexer family charges 600 AS ($43.50) to 900 AS ($65.50) per person daily in a wide variety of accommodations, with half board included. A comfortable annex holds the overflow from the main hotel. The restaurant, considered one of the finest in East Tyrol, is tastefully outfitted with accessories. Specialties include medallions of spring lamb with a Calvados cream sauce and parsley apples and sweet corn. Meals range from 150 AS ($11) to 500 AS ($36.25).

Pension Alpengasthof Tauernhaus, A-9971 Matrei in Osttirol (tel. 04875/8802), is a rustic complex of at least three buildings, clustered in an alpine meadow about 9 miles from the center of Matrei. Technically it's up in the Tauerntal at about 5,000 feet. You can reach it by bus from Matrei if you want to spend some time in this isolated place. The accommodations house anywhere from one to six people in simple bedrooms accented with lots of wood. Forty rooms are rented, 29 with private baths or showers. Half-board rates range from 260 AS ($19) to 320 AS ($23.25) per person daily.

Gasthof Panzlwirt, Tauerntalstrasse 4, A-9971 Matrei in Osttirol (tel. 04875/6518), offers Tyrolean-style hospitality in an enlarged and modernized chalet. The house is one of the most decorative in the village, accented with regional designs around many of the windows and weathered wooden balconies. The hotel is owned and managed by members of the Panzl family, who are descendants of Johann Panzl, a fierce soldier and noted eccentric who fought for the freedom of the Tyrol in the wars against the French in the early 19th century. The Panzlwirt contains a bowling alley, a café, a restaurant, an underground garage, and a series of pleasantly furnished public rooms. Each of the 23 well-furnished rooms has a private bath, and most of them contain phones, radios, TVs, and kitchenettes. Some have balconies. With half board included, per-person rates range from 420 AS ($30.50) to 580 AS ($42.25) daily.

VIRGEN

This village in the Virgental (Valley of the Virgin) lies to the west of Matrei in Osttirol, visited above. The road through the valley is stunning, stretching for slightly less than 12 miles. Along it you pass through gorges and tunnels. Eventually you can see the 11,480-foot-high Dreiherrenspitze.

Food and Lodging

Gasthof Sonne, A-9972 Virgen (tel. 04874/5204), is a comfortable hotel built up on a terrace on the side of a hill in the center of the village. The main section has a hipped roof over white walls and a restaurant filling most of the big glass-walled extension on the first two floors. The interior has lots of rustic detailing and well-finished paneling. The Duregger family, your hosts, charge from 315 AS ($23) to 420 AS ($30.50) per person daily for half board. The 78-bed hotel is open from December to March and May to September.

SILLIAN

The highest village in the Valley of Puster (Pustertal), Sillian lies in the Dolomites a short distance from the Italian border. It's sunny and fog-free, even in winter, and has good snow conditions from December to March. Skiers will find the area serviced by chair and drag lifts. This unique landscape attracts nonskiers and summer visitors with its many beautiful walks.

On the outskirts of Sillian are the ruins of the 13th-century **Heimfels Castle,** once occupied by the powerful counts of Görz.

Food and Lodging

Hotel Post, A-9920 Sillian (tel. 04842/6273), was originally built more than 300 years ago as a changing and relay station for the postal service that traversed the busy routes between Austria and Italy. Today, behind a cream-colored stucco facade, it lies in the center of the village. The Post is owned by a prominent local family, the Atzwangers. Containing 50 simply furnished bedrooms, it charges year-round rates of 280 AS ($20.25) to 380 AS ($27.75) per person, with half board included. On the premises is a cozy restaurant serving from 11am to 2pm and 6 to 9pm, with meals costing from 125 AS ($9) if you'd like to patronize it as you pass through. There is also a popular and gemütlich wine cellar. The Post is closed from Easter to mid-May and for all of November until early December.

OBERTILLIACH

A short distance from Sillian, this hamlet near the Italian frontier might be an ideal stopping place in summer if you're gulping down all the beautiful scenery in the area, or in winter if you'd like to ski in the Lienz Dolomites.

Food and Lodging

Gasthof Weiler, A-9942 Obertilliach (tel. 04857/5202), has attractive proportions and simple lines. You'll reach it by climbing a curved stone staircase that ends at a stone-flanked sun terrace. The well-furnished interior is filled with warmly tinted colors and lots of exposed paneling, while the cozy contemporary bedrooms are outfitted with comfortable furniture and different shades of various earth colors. On the premises are a bar and a restaurant, serving regional cooking. The hotel, open from December to April and June to October, rents 21 bedrooms (each with private bath or shower), charging 464 AS ($33.75) to 520 AS ($37.75) per person daily for half board.

VORARLBERG

The westernmost province of Austria, and the smallest one other than Vienna, is Vorarlberg, a land of mountain villages and lakes, of deep valleys and meadowlands. This province is known for its natural beauty and scenery. In autumn, for example, one of the most beautiful spots on the European continent is the plain of the Rhine Valley near Dornbirn.

This is where Central Europe meets Western Europe, the Arlberg massif separating Vorarlberg from Tyrol. Essentially this province lies between Lake Constance and the Arlberg mountains. Local legend has it that this—not Mount Ararat in the Middle East—is where Noah landed with the ark after the flood waters had receded.

Of all the provinces of Austria, Vorarlberg is the most like Switzerland. In fact, at the end of World War I it almost became part of that neighbor country. Vorarlbergers speak the Alemannic dialect of German, which is more closely related to the language of the Swiss just across the border to the west than it is to that spoken elsewhere in Austria.

Bregenz, the province's capital, opens onto Lake Constance, which Austria shares with both West Germany and Switzerland.

Vorarlberg is supported by tourism and industry, mostly textiles. Outside its best-known and very expensive tourist centers, such as Zürs and Lech, prices in the province are quite reasonable, especially in gasthof-type accommodations.

This is the most highly industrialized province of Austria—after Vienna, of course—but industry rarely pollutes the air and somehow seems to blend in with nature for the most part. For instance, one of its major industries is hydroelectric installations in the mountains.

If you're traveling by train from Innsbruck (Chapter X), you can reach Bregenz in Vorarlberg in about 3½ hours.

1. Bregenz

The capital of Vorarlberg province, Bregenz, once the Roman town of Brigantium, sits on terraces rising above the water at the eastern end of Lake Constance (Bodensee, in German). One of the major tourist goals in the province, Bregenz is really a small, "two-in-one" place—a modern town along the shore of the lake with a traffic-free old town towering over it. In summer the promenade along the shoreline is popular.

THE SIGHTS

On lake vessels, you can travel the **Bodensee** district, venturing into West Germany and Switzerland, which share Lake Constance with Austria. For a panoramic view of the lake and the town, with Switzerland looming in the background, take the cable-car ride to Pfänder (see below).

Bregenz is at its liveliest in July at the time of its celebrated **music festival,** an event that rivals the festival at Salzburg. Many concerts are given, some open-air and some at the Festspiel-und-Kongresshaus. Most exciting are the elaborate productions of operas, operettas, and musical comedies presented on a large stage floating on the lake, with the audience watching from an amphitheater which seats 6,500 persons. You'll see ornate barges arriving with elaborately dressed actors and singers. The stage is on a series of islands anchored by pillars driven into the lake bottom.

The Unterstadt, or the **Lower Town,** is the shopping district, with traffic-free malls along the lake shore. In spring the quays of the Unterstadt blaze with color from flowerbeds as in some lakeside Swiss towns.

At the **Vorarlberger Landesmuseum** (Vorarlberg Regional Museum), Kornmarkt 1 (tel. 05574/46050), you'll find a rich repository of the artifacts and culture of a province. Exhibits include relics from prehistoric as well as Roman days. You'll see Romanesque and Gothic ecclesiastical works of art from the churches in the district. See, in particular, a portrait of the Duke of Wellington by Angelica Kauffmann. The museum is open daily except Monday from 9am to noon and 2 to 5pm, charging 15 AS ($1.10) for admission.

The **Upper Town** is called both Oberstadt and Altstadt. Once the stronghold of the counts of Bregenz and Montford, it is of interest to the lover of antiquity. If you're driving, head up Kirchstrasse, Thalbachgasse, and Amstorstrasse. Park and then stroll back into the Middle Ages, as you go along the quiet squares and narrow streets of the old quarter. Before the Upper Town was Roman Brigantium, it was the site of a Celtic settlement.

Among Oberstadt's attractions is **Martinsturm** (Tower of St. Martin) from the 13th century. On the upper floor of the tower is a local military museum. **St. Martin's Chapel,** founded in 1363, at the base of the tower, contains some murals from the 14th century. Far more interesting than any art, however, is the view of the surrounding area to be seen from the top of the tower.

The **pfarrkirche** (parish church) is dedicated to St. Gall. This 15th-century sandstone structure has a sunken nave from the 18th century.

The most important excursion in the environs is to **Pfänder,** to the east of Bregenz, reached by traveling 7½ miles on a narrow little twisting road through the mountains. To get there, head out of Bregenz along the road to Lindau, in West Germany, turning right in the direction of Lochau, where you pass a parish church. Make a right turn onto a secondary road leading to Pfänder. You'll come to a car park from which you go by foot to the Schwedenschanze belvedere, at nearly 3,500 feet. From the terrace you'll have a fine view of the town and the lake.

If you don't go by car, you can get to Pfänder from Bregenz by cableway. Go to

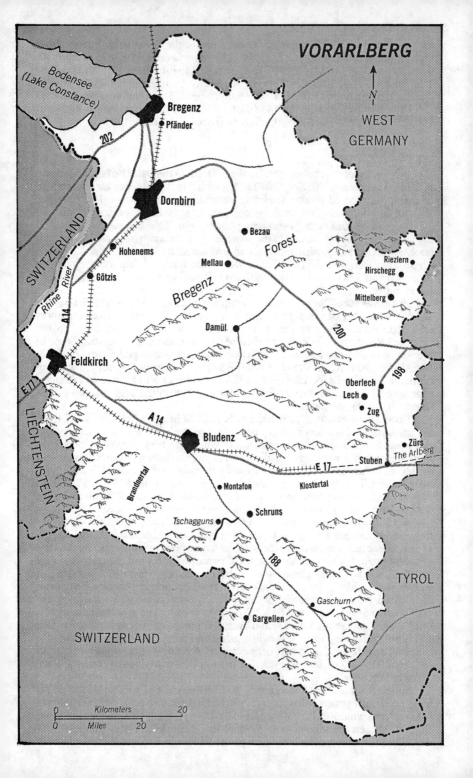

the lower station, which is about 500 yards east of the Kornmarkt. It takes about seven minutes to reach the summit. The cableway schedule: March 26 to April 30, 9am to 7pm; May 1 to May 31, 9am to 8pm; June 1 to June 30, 8:30am to 8pm; July 1 to August 31, 8:30am to 10:30pm; September 1 to September 23, 8:30am to 8pm; and September 24 to March 24, 9am to 6pm. The round-trip fare is 84 AS ($6.10) for adults and 56 AS ($4.05) for children. Information is available at Pfänderbahn, A-6901 Bregenz, Postfach 34 (tel. 05574/22160).

WHERE TO STAY

By most accounts the best hotel in Bregenz, the **Schwärzler Hotel,** Landstrasse 9, A-6900 Bregenz (tel. 05574/22422), lies within two minutes by car of the center of town. Such noted visitors as Arthur Ashe, Leonard Bernstein, José Carreras, Richard Claydermann, and Birgit Nilsson have all stayed at this elegant hotel. The 75 rooms all contain baths or showers, phones, color TVs, and minibars. Most of the rooms also have balconies. On the premises are a restaurant, a covered swimming pool, a flowered sun garden, a sauna, a steam bath, and a host of extras. Rates for a single range from 640 AS ($46.50) to 980 AS ($71.25), while prices for a double room go from 570 AS ($41.50) to 820 AS ($59.50) per person per day, with breakfast included.

Hotel Mercure, Platz der Wiener Symphoniker, A-6900 Bregenz (tel. 05574/26100), a member of a popular French hotel chain, is the town's newest and most up-to-date hotel. The emphasis is on comfort and convenience. Close to the Festspielhaus, it offers 94 well-furnished bedrooms with all the amenities. Some of the rooms open onto balconies, and two are specially equipped for the disabled. Rates range from 620 AS ($45) to 850 AS ($61.75) per person daily, including breakfast. The hotel's specialty restaurant is Le Gourmet, and it also operates an inexpensive cafeteria. Summer guests enjoy sitting out on the large, parasol-shaded terrace for drinks and food.

Hotel Weisses Kreuz, Römerstrasse 5, A-6900 Bregenz (tel. 05574/22489), is a graciously proportioned baroque building in the heart of town, with a green-and-white façade and a steeply pitched roof with three tiers of gables. Completely renovated in 1983, the interior is filled with painted armoires, elegant antiques, and conservative furniture. The 44 comfortably furnished bedrooms, all with private baths, radios, TVs, minibars, and phones, range in price from 640 AS ($46.50) to 740 AS ($53.75) daily for a single, from 1,040 AS ($75.50) to 1,280 AS ($93) for a double. Breakfast is included in the prices, which depend on the season.

Berghof Fluh, Fluherstrasse 7, A-6900 Bregenz (tel. 05574/24213), is a comfortable modern hotel designed almost like a spacious private home. Lying in Fluh, a small village just outside town, the hotel has a long flowered sun terrace with a view of the Swiss Alps. There are also a series of rustic public rooms, many of which are paneled, and a German-style tavern with a beamed ceiling, a handsome wooden bar, and an occasional visit by a local rock band. The 12 sunny and cheerful bedrooms, each with private bath, rent for 360 AS ($26.25) per person for bed-and-breakfast. Half board is another 140 AS ($10.25) per person daily. The in-house restaurant is often visited by German, Swiss, and Austrian urbanites. The small handwritten menu usually lists an assortment of fish, game, and crispy salads from both the Austrian and international repertoire of fine cuisine. À la carte meals range from 110 AS ($8) to 210 AS ($15.25). The restaurant shuts down Wednesday, and the hotel closes in February.

Gasthof Adler, Vorklostergasse 6, A-6900 Bregenz (tel. 05574/31788). This long, horizontal structure has a steeply pitched red-tile roof set above two floors of red-shuttered windows. Part of the façade has been covered with modern planking, although the rest of the hotel looks much older. The cozy interior contains a restaurant. The bedrooms are furnished with painted furniture and lots of exposed wood.

The 16-bed guesthouse charges 200 AS ($14.50) to 220 AS ($16) per person daily, with breakfast included. None of the rooms has a private bath, but the facilities in the hallways are adequate.

Hotel Heidelberger Fass, Kirchstrasse 30, A-6900 Bregenz (tel. 05574/ 22463), is an unusual baroque hotel in the center of town. Its façade is crowned with a big rococo gable with elaborately curved sides. The interior has lots of well-finished paneling, crisscrossed ceiling beams, and country-style accessories. The attractive restaurant serves well-prepared Austrian specialties. There are 17 comfortably furnished bedrooms. Singles cost 450 AS ($32.75) daily, while doubles go for 375 AS ($27.25) per person, with breakfast included.

WHERE TO DINE

Deuring-Schlössle, Ehre-Guta-Platz 4, A-6900 Bregenz (tel. 05574/27800), has been proclaimed as one of the finest restaurants of Austria. Through the efforts of its owners, the Huber family, this ivy-covered, stone-walled castle provides exceptional food and also hotel rooms within the center of old Bregenz. The establishment contains its share of half-timbered detailing, masses of fine silver and porcelain, and a Renaissance-era fireplace. Originally built in 1650, the castle is monumental and imposing. In its cellar is an impressive array of fine wines.

Food specialties are many and varied, including trout from Lake Constance, poached pike-perch with caper-flavored butter and vegetables, and a delicate appetizer of cannelloni stuffed with celery and served with a mousse of brook trout. You might also try a parfait of smoked eel with tomatoes or a gourmet salad of braised sweetbreads and artichoke hearts. Fixed-price menus range from 300 AS ($21.75) to 900 AS ($65.50), with à la carte dinners going from 235 AS ($17) to 600 AS ($43.50). Lunch is served daily from noon to 2pm, with dinner from 6:30 to 9:30pm.

Some guests prefer to spend the night in one of the luxurious bedrooms, 13 in all. With its garden ambience, the place is both stylish and relaxing. Prices of rooms, single or double occupancy, range from 1,050 AS ($76.25) to 2,500 AS ($181.75).

Ilge-Weinstube, Maurachgasse 6 (tel. 05574/23609), is an outstanding restaurant in the moderately priced category. Directed by the Reisinger family, it lies within the basement of a 300-year-old house sitting beside a historic street in the center of town. The décor is old-fashioned Vorarlberg, much like that you'd have found within a farmer's house. With meals starting at 300 AS ($21.75), the menu ranges from simple regional platters to full gala meals, with a superb wine list. The tafelspitz with rösti is especially delectable. Service is from 11am to 2:30pm and 6 to 11pm. On Sunday the restaurant is closed and on Monday it opens only for dinner.

Berghaus Pfänder, Auf dem Pfänder (tel. 05574/22184). From your panoramic eyrie in this lofty place, you'll be able to see both Germany and Switzerland. In an environment filled with exposed wood, you'll enjoy such specialties as roast calves' liver, fresh fish, or meat ragoûts, followed by delectable desserts. Meals cost from 175 AS ($12.75), and reservations are suggested. The restaurant is open daily except Monday from 7pm to midnight.

AFTER DARK

If you're in Bregenz on a summer night, you don't need nightlife: few smoke-filled clubs could compete with a walk along the lakeshore and a visit to a café. However, if you seek richer divertissements, you can visit the **Spiel-Casino Bregenz,** Platz der Wiener Symphoniker (tel. 05574/25127), where roulette, baccarat, and blackjack are played daily from 3pm to 3am. The parking garage is free. The entrance to the casino is 170 AS ($12.25), for which you receive chips worth 200 AS ($14.50).

2. The Bregenz Forest

From Bregenz you can make one of the most interesting scenic excursions in Vorarlberg—or in Austria, for that matter—deep into the Bregenzerwald, or Bregenz Forest. It's not as well known as the Black Forest of West Germany, but in my opinion it has just as much charm and character as its sister *wald* to the north.

The forest takes up the northern part of the Vorarlberg alpine range. A state highway splits the valley of the Bregenzer Ache River, making motoring easy, but the true charm of the forest lies off the beaten path in the little undiscovered valleys cut by tiny tributaries of the river. In spring the beautiful alpine meadows burgeon with wildflowers. In the background you can see the towering Alps.

Don't expect a proliferation of trees in the Bregenz Forest. The Austrians have cleared a lot of the woodlands to make meadows, where you'll see contented cows grazing, reminiscent of Switzerland.

One of the most frequented areas for sports and recreation is the **Bödele,** lying between the Valley of the Ache (don't you love that name?) and the Valley of the Rhine. Skiers are drawn to the highlands in winter.

The people who live in the forest are strong on keeping the old customs alive. If you're passing through the valley on a Sunday, you'll probably see some Vorarlbergers going to church in their traditional garb. The headdress of the women is often striking, ranging from small crowns to wide-brimmed black straw hats. Unlike most of the rest of Europe, the people of this area wear white for mourning rather than black.

BEZAU

The best-known village of the Bregenz Forest, Bezau is surrounded by a landscape that's beautiful in both winter and summer.

In the spring, summer, and autumn, you can hike, go mountaineering, swim, fish for trout, and play tennis or minigolf.

In winter there's alpine skiing, with the Hinterbregenzerwald ski ticket covering a range of more than 50 lifts and cable railways. There are some 35 miles of cross-country ski trails. You can also go tobogganing or play tennis at one of the three courts inside a hall.

A cableway from here will take you to the Baumgartenhöhe at 5,350 feet.

Food and Lodging

Hotel Schöne, A-6870 Bezau (tel. 05514/2207), is one of the loveliest hotels in the region. It's composed of two tin-roofed chalets covered with cedar shingles and flowery balconies. An elaborate wrought-iron sign extends over the driveway leading up to the hotel's location between a collection of houses and a big open field. This establishment was founded in 1850 as a link in the Austrian postal services. Renovated in 1989, the three-star hotel contains a blazing fireplace open to view on four sides, lots of rustic beams, tastefully discreet lighting, and a collection of alpine antiques.

The 42 bedrooms are country-style luxurious, and have many rustic details as well as modern baths and up-to-date comforts. The bed-and-breakfast rate ranges from 540 AS ($39.25) to 640 AS ($46.50) per person daily. On the premises is a heated indoor pool whose ceiling is a crafted wood-beamed marvel.

Gasthof Gams, A-6870 Bezau (tel. 05514/2220). This dignified-looking hotel rambles across a big lawn a few buildings away from the village church. The façade is an appealing combination of cedar shingles, white stucco, steeply pitched gables, and recessed balconies. Although the core of the hotel was built in 1648, guests find all the modern comforts, particularly the outdoor pool, whose entrance is through a low opening on the inside of the hotel. It is heated from May to October. Also on the premises are three outdoor tennis courts, a hot whirlpool, a sauna, a big garden, and several rustically antique-style sitting rooms. The 40-room hotel rents wood-paneled bedrooms, each with private bath or shower, at prices ranging from 550 AS ($40) to 700 AS ($51) per person daily, with half board included.

The restaurant, outfitted in an appealing style that originated years ago in the region, specializes in game, particularly venison. You'll also be offered seafood, such as a well-prepared filet of sole, along with filet steak, curry dishes, and desserts that include a variety of fresh mountain berries. Full meals cost 180 AS ($13) to 350 AS ($25.50).

DAMÜLS

This is one of the leading ski centers for winter sports in the Bregenz Forest, at an elevation of 4,680 feet. One skier who goes here every year describes it as being for connoisseurs. Hotels organize weekly après-ski programs, so check to see what the action is during your stay here. The village is small, so it's easy to get to know your fellow visitors.

Damüls is an area of great scenic beauty, making a summer visit also pleasant. This is the loftiest village in the forest.

Food and Lodging

Hotel Damülser Hof, A-6884 Damüls (tel. 05510/210), is a peacefully iso-lated collection of modern chalets interconnected by covered passageways. All of them sit in a sloping alpine meadow a short walk from the village church. The ele-gant interior has enough variety in its décor to please most guests. Each of the cozy public rooms is crafted from such top-quality materials as exposed bricks, carved and painted wooden ceilings, and intricately crafted wrought iron. There are inti-mate niches, soft lighting, and several fireplaces. On the premises are a bar area, an indoor pool, a sauna, a good restaurant, a bierstube/café, a dance bar, a sporting goods store, a bowling alley, and a big sun terrace. The Klauser family rents 50 bed-rooms, each paneled, well furnished, and equipped with bath or shower. In winter the half-board rate ranges from 760 AS ($55.25) to 870 AS ($63.25) daily for a sin-gle, from 700 AS ($51) to 800 AS ($58.25) per person for a double. Half-board singles in summer go for 560 AS ($40.75) to 650 AS ($47.25) daily, with doubles costing 450 AS ($32.75) to 560 AS ($40.75) daily.

Hotel Mittagspitze, A-6884 Damüls (tel. 05510/211), a short distance from the village church, is a pleasingly designed chalet with an angled façade of alternat-ing areas of white walls and weathered planking. The attractive décor emphasizes lots of amber-colored paneling, simple furniture, and tasteful accessories. Many of the 22 rooms have private balconies, and all have private baths or showers. Guests are accepted from December to October, and charged 500 AS ($36.25) to 680 AS ($49.50) per person daily for half board in winter. In summer, half-board charges range from 260 AS ($19) to 400 AS ($29) per person daily. The restaurant serves tasty and well-prepared food accompanied by excellent service.

MELLAU

One of the most charming and relatively unknown resorts in the Bregenz For-est is Mellau, a hamlet set against gently rolling mountains with plenty of woodland for walking. Trout fishermen find rewards in the Bregenzer Ache with its fast-flowing waters. Canoeing from here in the river's rapids is a thrilling sport. The vil-lage has a large, heated outdoor swimming pool.

Many folkloric evenings give visitors the chance to be entertained by groups wearing the traditional dress of the valley.

Food and Lodging

Hotel Pension Kreuz, A-6881 Mellau (tel. 05518/2208), is a modern five-story hotel with two distinct sections, each with a symmetrically peaked roof and lots of big-windowed balconies. The interior is dotted with rustic accessories, such as a stone-rimmed fireplace, heavy beams, hunting trophies, and brass chandeliers, and includes an attractive, up-to-date dining room. On the premises is an ozone-enriched swimming pool, plus a sauna, a collection of bar areas, a bowling alley, a dance hall, a reading room, and a daytime café with its own bakery. Hedwig Metzler, the owner, rents her 60 woodsy bedrooms, each with private bath or shower, for 500 AS ($36.25) to 910 AS ($66.25) per person daily for half board in winter. In summer, half board costs 300 AS ($21.75) to 725 AS ($52.75) per person daily. Open from December to March and May to October.

Hotel Engel, A-6881 Mellau (tel. 05518/2246). The oldest members of the Rogelböck family remember when their hotel was housed in a much older building whose picture you can see inside the modern chalet that replaced it. The cozy interior is accented with warmly designed textiles, blazing fireplaces, sunny and well-decorated restaurants, and a big indoor pool. The 31 well-furnished bedrooms, containing either a private bath or a shower, are open to guests from December to October. In winter, half-board charges range from 560 AS ($40.75) to 580 AS ($42.25) per person daily. In summer, half board is 510 AS ($42.25) per person daily.

---

3. Feldkirch and Dornbirn

Up to now I've assumed that you might enter Austria from Lake Constance if you're coming from either Switzerland or West Germany or directly from the Bavarian section of the latter country. However, you might also approach from another part of Switzerland, coming into Feldkirch. After visiting Feldkirch, I'll introduce you to the largest city of Vorarlberg, Dornbirn, which is even bigger than the provincial capital, Bregenz.

FELDKIRCH

This venerable town, considered "the gateway to Austria," lies on the road through the Arlberg. If you're traveling by rail from Switzerland, Feldkirch will be your first town in Austria. Unfortunately, many people rush on to other destinations, but it will be worth your time to get off the train and explore this town that goes back to medieval days.

Feldkirch was once a fortified town, growing up at the "heel" of Schattenburg Castle on a tributary of the Ill River and becoming known for its classical Latin school. The Old Town, which can be explored in about an hour, is the tourist attraction, the New Town lying to the northeast.

The heart of the Old Town is **Marktgasse** (Market Street), a rectangle with arcades. Many of the old houses are graced with oriels and frescoed façades. A popular wine festival is held here in July, with the town filling up with revelers.

Among the curiosities of the Old Town is the **Katzenturm,** or Tower of the Cats. The cats in this case were actually lions. The tower was named for a defense cannon here adorned with lion heads. The **Churertor,** or Chur Gate, is another Feldkirch landmark. Sights include the **Domkirche,** a cathedral church known for its 15th-century double nave. See the *Descent from the Cross,* a 1521 painting by Wolf Huber of the Danube school.

Schattenburg Castle, once a defense fortress and now a museum and restaurant, can be reached by car by heading up Burggasse, or you can climb the steps by the Schloss-Steig. Parts of the castle were built at the turn of the 16th century. From the castle precincts, you have a view of the Valley of the Rhine.

The **Heimatmuseum** in the castle exhibits a wealth of furnishings of the region, ranging from those that filled a farmer's shack to pieces that graced the hall of a nobleman. Also displayed are a large collection of art and an armor collection. The museum is open daily except Monday from 9am to noon and 1 to 5pm. Admission is 20 AS ($1.45). There is also a restaurant in the castle.

Where to Stay

Hotel Illpark, Leonhardsplatz 2, A-6800 Feldkirch (tel. 05522/24600), has the most strikingly contemporary façade in town. The drama of its format is enhanced by its location on a brick-covered square at the edge of the old quarter. The 92 tastefully decorated bedrooms have private baths, minibars, TVs, and radios. On the premises is a cafeteria, plus a beer cellar with an adjoining bowling alley (the perspective of which looks like a time tunnel from some space war), a dance bar, and an indoor swimming pool. Except for the rustic beer hall the décor is contemporary, with pin lighting and lots of attractively muted colors.

With breakfast included, rooms cost 650 AS ($47.25) per person daily. The international menu in the restaurant features week-long specials from many different countries. When I was last there the emphasis was on Provence, and the food items included a well-prepared Mediterranean fish soup. Meals range from 170 AS ($12.25) to 380 AS ($27.75). Reservations are suggested.

Central Hotel Löwen, Neustadt 15-19, A-6800 Feldkirch (tel. 05522/22070), has an ochre façade with an entrance beneath an arched street-level arcade. The interior is outfitted with a collection of rococo-framed mirrors, eclectically grouped chairs, and accessories, including what look like family portraits. The 64 bedrooms are pleasant and comfortable, their many amenities including private baths or showers. Half board costs from 420 AS ($30.50) per person daily.

Hotel Hochhaus, Reichsstrasse 177, A-6800 Feldkirch (tel. 05522/22479), a minute's walk from the train station, is in two separate balconied sections, one of which rises almost twice as high as the other. The hotel is painted a pastel yellow with neutral-toned balconies. On the premises is a ground-level sun terrace, and the comfortable accommodations have big windows and contemporary furniture. Nine of the 17 bedrooms contain private baths or showers. Rates range from 290 AS ($21) to 310 AS ($22.50) per person daily.

Where to Dine

Gasthof Lingg, Am Marktplatz, A-6800 Feldkirch (tel. 05522/22062), has a good local reputation—one it has enjoyed since 1878—and many of the town's official lunches take place here. The dining section is one floor above ground level in an old structure on the main square, whose medieval buildings are visible from the restaurant's windows. You could begin your meal with melon with shrimp, served in a homemade mayonnaise sauce, and then follow with one of several well-prepared meat, fish, or game specialties from the traditional Austrian kitchen. Full meals range from 125 AS ($9) to 350 AS ($25.50). The place is open daily except Monday from 9am to midnight. Reservations are suggested.

HOHENEMS

If you're in Vorarlberg the second half of June any year, you might go to Hohenems, between Feldkirch and Dornbirn, about 11 miles from Lake Constance. The little town has a well-attended **music festival** focused mainly, but not exclusively, on the works of Franz Schubert, although Schubert, who died at the age of 31, had no connection with Hohenems. It was selected as the site for the festival, called the Schubertiade Hohenems, by the noted German baritone Hermann Prey when he launched the event in 1976. The festival is presented in three places: the Rittersaal and the courtyard of the Palace of Hohenems and in the Stadthalle of the nearby city of Feldkirch.

For tickets, write to **Schubertiade Hohenems,** Schweizer Strasse 1, A-6845 Hohenems (tel. 05576/2091). Ticket prices range from 300 AS ($21.75) to 700 AS ($51). Festival brochures are available at all Austrian National Tourist Offices.

Some of the concerts of the Schubertiade Hohenems are held at Feldkirch.

It is possible to find accommodations at hotels in or near Hohenems. The tourist office (tel. 05576/4647) will provide more information, but it would be wise to make reservations as far in advance as possible. Since Hohenems itself does not always have sufficient hotel space, the Feldkirch Tourist Office (tel. 05522/23467) handles the overflow.

DORNBIRN

The "city of textiles," Dornbirn lies in the heart of Vorarlberg province, of which it is the largest town and the commercial center. A trade fair in mid-July ties in with the Bregenz Festival. Dornbirn, only 7 miles from the provincial capital, is at the outskirts of the Bregenz Forest on the edge of a broad Rhineland valley.

The city center is the Marktplatz (market square), graced by a 19th-century parish church in neoclassical style and by the **Rotes Haus** (Red House), a 1639 building that is now a restaurant.

The most exciting excursion in the environs is to **Karren** (3,200 feet), about 1½ miles from the heart of town. The sturdy of foot and shank will make the climb in about two hours, but you can take a cable car and get there in five minutes. For your trouble, you'll be rewarded with a magnificent view. From here you can hike down to the **Rappen Gorge,** with the Ache River flowing through it.

Food and Lodging

Sport & Tagungshotel Rickatschwende, Bödelstrasse, A-6850 Dornbirn (tel. 05572/65350), is a large modern hotel with lots of facilities, including an indoor swimming pool, a tennis court, a sauna, and a steambath. It also operates a health center, with its own doctor, for regeneration and weight loss. The hotel sits at the edge of a grassy field on the periphery of the town. Its 41 cozy bedrooms have warm colors, lots of exposed wood, and big sunny windows; all contain private baths, color TVs, radios, phones, and balconies. They rent for 540 AS ($39.25) to 900 AS ($65.50) per person daily, including breakfast. The supplement for half board is 185 AS ($13.50) per person daily.

Katharinenhof, Felder-Strasse 2, A-6850 Dornbirn (tel. 05572/62577), is a flat-roofed contemporary hotel with turquoise-and-white designs painted below some of the windows and a ground-floor extension stretching toward the street. The hotel has both a covered swimming pool and a sauna on the premises. Rates in the comfortably furnished rooms range from 345 AS ($25) to 375 AS ($27.25) per person daily, including breakfast. Eighteen rooms are rented, each with private bath or shower.

Gasthof Krone, Hatlerstrasse 2, A-6850 Dornbirn (tel. 05572/62720). The solidly constructed dining room is large enough to hold many hungry diners. The chef is skilled at his craft. Appetizers include avocado with crabmeat, which might be followed by a ragoût of venison with fresh spätzle. Your dessert might be an array of fresh sorbets or a praline soufflé with ice cream. Set meals range from 105 AS ($7.75) to 400 AS ($29); à la carte, from 110 AS ($8) to 320 AS ($23.25). The Rhomberg family, your hosts, keep the dining room open daily from 7am to 1am. They also rent 21 simple but adequate bedrooms, each well kept, costing 380 AS ($27.75) daily for a single and 640 AS ($46.50) for a double. Three of the rooms contain private baths and the rest have showers. The Krone is closed on Sunday and for part of Saturday.

---

4. Bludenz and Its Valleys

This little alpine town, at an elevation of about 2,000 feet, is at exactly the halfway point between Paris and Vienna on the main highway connecting the capital of the province, Bregenz, with the capital of the country, Vienna. Some of the houses in the town were here in the Middle Ages.

Bludenz is the gateway to five major mountain valleys: the **Klostertal,** the **Montafon,** the **Brandnertal** (Brand Valley), the **Grosswalsertal,** and the **Walgau.**

The Klostertal goes toward the east where lies the internationally renowned skiing territory of the Arlberg. The Montafon leads southward to the Silvretta alpine road, power stations, dams, artificial lakes, and the Silvretta-Nova ski center. The beautiful Brand Valley to the southwest has as a highlight the Lünersee, the largest lake in the eastern Alps. These three valleys are visited below.

Motorists pass through here, traveling the route from Lake Constance to the Arlberg and the Montafon Valley. Because of the valley's attractions, a variety of excursions are offered originating in Bludenz, including trips to some of Austria's finest skiing centers.

Besides the heavy tourist business engendered here, Bludenz also has an industrial side, with chocolate factories rivaling those of Switzerland, plus textile plants.

The town is surrounded by mountains, some of which reach a height of about 9,800 feet. Directly north of the town you can take a cableway to **Muttersberg** (4,635 feet), called the sun terrace of Bludenz.

FOOD AND LODGING

In the center of town, the **Schlosshotel,** Schlossplatz 5, A-6700 Bludenz (tel. 05552/63016), is built high up on the same rocky bluff as the castle and the baroque church. The hotel design is solidly conservative, with recessed balconies, red shutters, and a sprawling L-shaped format. The establishment encompasses well-maintained bedrooms in both the main building and the rambling annex a few steps away.

The interior décor has massive timbers, ornate chandeliers, and warmly textured colors. You might enjoy at least one meal on the sun terrace, or under the gently arched ceiling of the dining room. A bowling alley is on the premises, as well as a children's playroom and a putting green. The in-house café serves ice creams and pastries, while the restaurant offers well-prepared Austrian specialties. Your hosts, the Dörflinger family, charge 520 AS ($37.75) to 620 AS ($45) per person daily for half board. Each of their 36 bedrooms has a private bath or shower.

---

5. The Brand Valley

Often visited from Bludenz (see above), the Brand Valley (Brandnertal in German) is one of the most scenic valleys in Austria, a place of rare beauty surrounded by glaciers, with many side valleys. Romantic little villages and lush pastureland are set against a panoramic alpine backdrop. This is a valley with a wealth of inns and hotels, especially at Brand (coming up).

Skiers are attracted to the mountain ranges here, namely Niggenkopf and Palüd. The valley runs for almost ten miles before reaching Brand.

BRAND

A few centuries ago exiles from the Valais in Switzerland settled this village at the mouth of the Zalimtal near the Swiss border. At an elevation of 3,400 feet, Brand has long been a popular mountain health resort spread out along a mile stretch at the base of the Scesaplana mountain range. It's now a much-visited winter-sports center, the main resort of the Rätikon district of Vorarlberg.

You can take a cableway to the top of the Tschengla at 4,095 feet, as well as a chair lift to Eggen at 4,165 feet. From there, you can make connections to Niggenkopf at 5,235 feet.

A cable car also goes to the glacial **Lünersee** (Lake Lüner), a rather austere body of water which is the largest lake in the eastern Alps. It has been dammed and a reservoir created. The trip to Lünersee takes about two hours, 12 minutes of which is by cable car, which runs from June until mid-October. If you're at the lower station by 8am, you can catch the first car, but you must leave by 5pm.

Food and Lodging

Hotel Scesaplana, A-6708 Brand (tel. 05559/221), has a tasteful chalet design of wood accents, accommodating sun terraces, and balconied extensions angling out from the peak-roofed core. Managed by Ruth and Helmut Schwärzler, the hotel is in the center of the resort and has an attractively paneled interior. On the terrace is an indoor swimming pool, and there are indoor and outdoor tennis courts, a sauna, a solarium, a steam bath, whirlpool, massage, two restaurants, a bar, and a disco. A range of other sports is within easy access, including riding, fishing, skiing, and carriage drives (many of them cost an additional fee). Clients on the half-board plan receive a wide choice of specialties included with the evening meal.

The hotel offers 64 attractively furnished bedrooms in two categories. Type A includes cheerful twin rooms with modern furniture in the new part of the hotel (a third bed can be added); semisuites in the traditional core of the building also fall into this category. Type B includes standard rooms in the old building, most of which have balconies and sitting areas. All units have private baths, phones, safes, seven-channel TVs, and minibars. With half board included, per-person rates in summer range from 600 AS ($43.50) to 800 AS ($58.25) daily. In winter, tariffs on the same plan go from 650 AS ($47.25) to 1,400 AS ($101.75) per person daily (the highest tariff is charged at Christmas). Singles pay a daily supplement of 100 AS ($7.25).

Hotel Walliserhof, A-6708 Brand (tel. 05559/241), is a solidly built hotel with rows of recessed balconies and big windows looking out over the village church on one side and a long expanse of fields on the other. The public rooms are rustic, dotted with heavy timbers. On the premises is a covered pool, plus a sporting goods store and a sauna. Both indoor and outdoor tennis courts are nearby. The Meyer family, your hosts, charge 650 AS ($47.25) to 850 AS ($61.75) per person daily for half board in winter. Half board in summer costs 580 AS ($42.25) to 730 AS ($53) per person daily. Each of the 44 comfortable and attractively furnished bedrooms comes with a private bath or shower. The hotel is open from December to April and June to October.

Hotel Colrosa, A-6708 Brand (tel. 05559/225), is a popular stopover point for families and athletes, set in a quiet location on a forested hillside, not far from the center of town. Designed like a chalet, the four-star hotel contains 39 rustically pleasant rooms capped with beamed and paneled ceilings and accented with fireplaces. Capably managed by the Heinz Beck family, the hotel charges 620 AS ($45) to 820 AS ($59.50) per person daily, with half board included, for these well-kept, well-furnished bedrooms, each with private bath or shower.

Hotel Hämmerle, A-6708 Brand (tel. 05559/213), owned by a family of the same name, is a wood-trimmed chalet with a modern extension added on to a much older core. In the center of town, the hotel offers a big sun terrace, lots of grass-covered lawns for children's games, and a paneled interior illuminated by brass chandeliers sometimes accented by a depiction of a double-headed eagle. Many of the 24 cozy bedrooms have private balconies and views over the mountains; all have private baths or showers. Rates range from 200 AS ($14.50) to 470 AS ($37.25) per person daily, including breakfast.

Hotel Lagant, A-6708 Brand (tel. 05559/285), is a chalet hotel at the edge of the village, near the Niggenkopf chair lift. Built in 1970, the establishment contains an indoor swimming pool, an elevator, a big sun terrace, and cozily attractive public rooms. On the premises are a hospitable bar and a restaurant serving well-prepared Austrian specialties. The hotel, open from December to October, rents 75 up-to-date and well-maintained bedrooms; half-board charges range from 550 AS ($40) to 900 AS ($65.50) per person daily.

Après-Ski

Nightlife is very casual but fun at Brand, especially in the peak of the season.

The Scesa Taverna nightclub at the already-recommended **Hotel Scesaplana** is the major rendezvous point in town and has the most sophisticated entertainment. Tea dances usually get under way here at 4:30pm, and the Irish coffee is said to be the best in town. You'll also want to sample their fine draft beer later in the evening.

Special folkloric Vorarlberg evenings are also organized in season (ask at the tourist office to see what's featured at the time of your visit).

---

6. Little Walser Valley

The Kleinwalsertal (Little Walser Valley) is not to be confused with the Grosswalsertal (Big Walser Valley), mentioned above. Both take their name from the exiles who settled here from the Valais section of Switzerland. Little Walser lies in Vorarlberg, but is separated from the rest of the towns and hamlets of the province. The Allgäu Alps cut it off completely from the rest of Austria, so that although it's technically a part of this country, it's governed by West German customs and uses the West German mark instead of the Austrian schilling as the coin of its realm. As German-appearing as this valley may seem, however, you're reminded that you're still in Austria when you mail a letter, as Austrian stamps are necessary.

To say "completely" cut off isn't quite accurate, since Little Walser Valley *can* be reached directly from the rest of Austria, but you'd have to take a mountain goat trail to make the journey. Otherwise, to enter the valley you start at Oberstdorf at the border between West Germany and Austria.

The Breitach River runs through this broad valley, which is surrounded by limestone mountains. The valley is rich in tradition, and most of the old folk customs and dress are still kept alive by its people.

Little Walser Valley is both a summer and a winter resort. People come in summer to enjoy the pure mountain air, and they retreat here in winter for the snow.

RIEZLERN

This is the biggest hamlet in the valley, at the head of the Schwarzwassertal, or Black Water Valley. One of its most popular spots is its **Spiel-Casino Kleinwalsertal** (tel. 05517/5022). Germans flock over the border to play roulette, baccarat, and blackjack. The casino also has a restaurant and a bar. It opens at 5pm from Christmas to the end of March, 7pm the rest of the year. It usually closes around 3am, and the price of entrance is 23 DM ($13.75)—that's West German marks. For that, you get 30 DM ($17.75) worth of free chips.

South of the hamlet, you can take a cableway, the Kanzelwandbahn, to a mountain perch at 6,555 feet. Round-trip passage is 18 DM ($10.75) per person.

Food and Lodging

Hotel Stern, Walserstrasse 61, D-8984 Riezlern (tel. 08329/5208), has a lot of charm and oozes with tradition. The Althaus family, your hosts, like it that way. The hotel dates from 1936, but it was rebuilt in 1968 and has been renovated several times since. It is in the chalet style, with heavy eaves and regional decorations painted around the borders of the windows. On the premises is an excellent restaurant, plus a gemütlich bierstube, a dancing bar, a bowling alley, a fitness center, a sauna with massage facilities, and a children's play area. The bedrooms are attractively furnished and maintained, with doubles renting for 60 DM ($35.75) to 130 DM ($77.50) per person daily, half board included. Occupants of a single pay a surcharge of 20 DM ($12).

Gasthof Traube, Walserstrasse 56, D-8984 Riezlern (tel. 05517/5177), is a contemporary chalet whose attractively simplified façade still retains such oldtime accents as overhanging eaves and long wood-trimmed balconies. The hospitable interior includes dozens of ceiling beams and lots of rustic paneling. Half board costs from 65 DM ($38.75) to 105 DM ($62.50) per person daily for a double, rooms at the latter price having balconies. Singles pay 50 DM ($29.75) per day in rooms with showers, and also including half board. The Hugo and Christl Fischer family, your sports-loving hosts, do much to make your stay comfortable. Their concern is shown in their comfortably furnished and well-kept bedrooms.

HIRSCHEGG

If you blink you'll have passed through this hamlet. You can take a chair lift from here to the top station of the Heuberg at 4,500 feet, but the main reason for stopping in Hirschegg is the excellent accommodation described below.

Food and Lodging

Ifen-Hotel, A-6992 Hirschegg (tel. 05517/5071). Built in 1936, this hotel is approved by at least five European hotel associations, including Relais & Châteaux. Seen from a distance, the place looks like a marriage between a Mediterranean villa and a Teutonic piece of art deco. Architectural features include gently curving walls and distinctive struts extending at an angle from the exterior walls to the edge of the overhanging eaves. Views from the dozens of balconies encompass most of the village and the valley it sits in.

The elegant public rooms are filled with heavy beams, big windows, and rustic accessories, all in the framework of luxurious comfort. The sophisticated hotelier, Mrs. Renate Simon, welcomes an assortment of guests from around the world, charging 90 DM ($53.50) to 214 DM ($127.50) per person, depending on the season, for a room and half board. On the premises are a covered swimming pool, a bodybuilding studio, sunbeds, a beauty farm, a sauna, and a steambath. A team of chefs prepares elegant meals for the restaurant, which often features folkloric music.

---

7. The Montafon Valley

Montafon is a high alpine valley known for its powdery snow and sun. It stretches some 26 miles at the southern tip of Vorarlberg, with the Ill River flowing through on its way to join the Rhine. The valley, filled with mountain villages and major winter recreation areas, is encircled by the mountain ranges of Rätikon, Silvretta, and Verwall.

Montafon has been called a "ski stadium," so designated because it's a vastly integrated ski region. One ski pass covers unlimited use of 70 cable cars, chair lifts, and T-bars in all four main ski areas of the valley, as well as transportation between the resorts.

Hochjoch-Zamang has fine skiing in the back bowls and down the front, and is the main mountain at Schruns of Hemingway fame (see below). Tschagguns has Grabs-Golm for some easier runs. Silvretta-Nova at Gaschurn and St. Gallenkirch is a superb ski circus on several mountains, and the Schafberg of Gargellen is secluded in a side valley.

SCHRUNS/TSCHAGGUNS

These hamlets are so close together that they can be treated as one, being only about three-quarters of a mile apart. Schruns is the major town of the Montafon, lying on the right bank of the Ill River. Tschagguns, a smaller resort than Schruns, is on the left bank. Although known for winter sports, both are also popular in summer.

At Schruns you can go by cableway to the already-mentioned Hochjoch-Zamang. First, you go to Kapell at 6,025 feet, with its renowned restaurant. On the sun terrace here, people do everything from making love to getting an alpine suntan. A chair lift will take you from Kapell up to Sennigrat at 7,550 feet. It's finally possible to take a so-called Hochjoch taxi (really a lift) from Sennigrat to Kreuzjoch.

Above Tschagguns at Latschau, you can take a funicular or chair lift to Golm at 4,550 feet, a small but fascinating ski region with several lifts, including a four-person lift going up to 7,000 feet. These slopes attract both beginners and experts, and are known for World Cup races. In the area you can stop at a choice of a rustic little restaurant or a modern self-service one. After that, you can go by drag lift to Hochegga at 5,202 feet.

About Schruns, where he spent winters while he worked on *The Sun Also Rises,* Hemingway said that he preferred to go where the rain became snow.

Food and Lodging at Schruns

Hotel Alpenhof Messmer, A-6780 Schruns (tel. 05556/2664), presents a view of the valley and the mountains. The Messmer family has taken care to landscape this 35-room hotel into the hillside on which it sits, a short distance from the center of town. The interior has rustic accessories as well as an indoor pool (whose ceiling is supported by massive timbers), a hot whirlpool, and several open fireplaces. Most of the 39 bedrooms, decorated in a monochromatic delight of textiles, usually contain color TVs, private baths, and phones. In winter the rooms rent for 450 AS ($32.75) to 980 AS ($71.25) per person daily for half board. Half board in summer costs 450 AS ($32.75) to 850 AS ($61.75) per person daily.

Sport-Hotel Alpenrose, Silvrettastrasse, A-6780 Schruns (tel. 05556/2655), is a contemporary chalet, with lots of wood-accented balconies, stone retaining walls, and big windows. From the downhill side you'll notice a streamlined wood-and-glass extension looking out over the valley. The interior is loaded with rustic accessories, knotty paneling, and leather armchairs. On the premises are an indoor pool, a sauna, massage facilities, a children's playroom, a hospitable bar area, a reading lounge with an open fireplace, and a ceramic tile oven with its own warming bench. Ten minutes from the center, the hotel rents 39 well-furnished and comfortable bedrooms, each with private bath or shower. In winter, half board costs 450 AS ($32.75) to 980 AS ($71.25) per person daily, with summer half-board charges going for 450 AS ($32.75) to 850 AS ($61.75) per person daily. Open from December to October.

Löwen Hotel Schruns, Silvrettastrasse, A-6780 Schruns (tel. 05556/3141). The creative designers of this hotel decided to give guests the best of both worlds. They set a rambling chalet on top of a big lawn area in the center of town. The shrub-dotted lawn in front is actually poised on the top of the roof of a modern steel, glass, and concrete construction that contains an Olympic-size swimming pool. This is in many ways a social center of town, and except for outdoor recreation, it provides almost everything you need for a vacation. On the premises are five restaurants, a bar accented with flowered patterns that contrast nicely with the exposed wood, and a popular disco with live acts. Among the restaurants, the most appealing are the French restaurant and the Montafoner Stübe, where meals range from 290 AS ($21) to 500 AS ($36.25) or even more.

The 85 imaginatively designed bedrooms, each with private bath or shower, rent for 1,140 AS ($83) to 1,400 AS ($101.75) per person daily for half board in winter. In summer, half-board charges run from 900 AS ($65.50) to 1,050 AS ($76.25) per person daily.

Hotel Krone, A-6780 Schruns (tel. 05556/2255), is a peach-colored baroque building with white trim, black shutters, stone edging, and a hipped roof with at least one pointed tower. Owned by members of the Mayer family since 1847, the nine-room hotel has a shaded beer garden, a collection of rustic artifacts, and ornate paneling whose rich glow is reflected in the leaded windows. Management takes special care of its cuisine, which is well prepared and beautifully served. Half board in summer ranges from 420 AS ($30.50) to 500 AS ($36.25) per person daily; half board in winter costs 510 AS ($37) to 600 AS ($43.50) per person daily. Each of the pleasant bedrooms has a private bath. Nonresidents can also dine here.

Feuerstein (tel. 05556/2129) is the best-known place in town for ice cream and pastries. Housed in an antique building in the center, the establishment provides attractively decorated pastries. Some of them are miniature works of art. Coffee costs from 22 AS ($1.60), and pastries from 23 AS ($1.65). In midwinter, it is open daily from 10am to 11pm. Hours during the rest of the year are 10am to 7pm. Annual closing is from Easter until June and late October to mid-December.

Food and Lodging at Tschagguns

Hotel Montafoner Hof, A-6774 Tschagguns (tel. 05556/4400-0), is the premier resort at Tschagguns. The innkeepers at this 43-room four-star hotel, the Tschohl family, have already made a name for themselves in the valley. Known for the elegance of their accommodations and the warmth of their hospitality, they open this rather intimate hostelry from December to October. From its windows, many mountain vistas appear. A striking peach color on the outside, the Montafoner Hof is decorated inside with Austrian woods, notably pine, to give an authentic Tyrolean atmosphere; however, the hotel is completely modern in other respects, with some of the finest amenities in the area. All rooms come with private baths, radios, direct-dial phones, lounge corners, TV connections, and balconies. In winter, half board costs 960 AS ($69.75) to 1,020 AS ($74.25) per person daily. In summer, half board goes for 700 AS ($51) to 760 AS ($55.25) per person daily.

Skiers gravitate to the lounge bar or the pine-paneled rustic lounge, but in summer guests are likely to be found at the outdoor swimming pool or at one of the café tables placed outside. The cuisine served here ranks with the finest in the area; very fresh ingredients are deftly handled. Other facilities for sports-minded guests include an indoor pool, a spacious sauna, a steambath, a whirlpool, and an exercise room.

Cresta Hotel, A-6780 Tschagguns (tel. 05556/2395), looks like a skillfully blended collection of modern additions gradually added on to an older architectural core. The entrance is under a soaring concrete arch supported at one end by a masonry column. You can have a drink at the bar or a meal near the green tile stove in the Taverne. Here, daily specials include grilled veal steak, asparagus in season, a whole array of fresh salads, and desserts such as Viennese strudel. Meals range from 100 AS ($7.25) to 300 AS ($21.75), and include both fixed-price menus and à la carte selections. The bedrooms, often paneled with light-grained wood, are well-maintained and comfortable. Of the 37 rented, 28 come with private baths or showers. In winter, half board ranges from 520 AS ($37.75) to 610 AS ($44.25) per person daily, with half board in summer costing 460 AS ($33.50) to 540 AS ($39.25) per person daily. The hotel is open from December to March and May to September.

Sporthotel Sonne, A-6780 Tschagguns (tel. 05556/2333), is an attractive chalet, half of whose façade is decorated with shutters and the other half with wood-trimmed balconies. An older building, for some visitors even more charming, is connected to the new one with a covered passageway. The interiors are filled with variations of soft, well-matched colors, with big windows that flood the public rooms with sunlight. The accommodations have lots of space and rustic furnishings, some of them painted with floral designs. The owners rent 34 bedrooms, 28 with private baths or showers, and do so from December to March and May to September. With half board included, the per-person rate in winter ranges from 520 AS ($37.75) to 550 AS ($40) daily. In summer, half board costs 390 AS ($28.25) to 410 AS ($29.75) per person daily. A covered swimming pool and a sauna are on the premises.

Après-Ski

You can resort-hop, going back and forth between Schruns and Tschagguns, checking out whatever action appeals to you.

At Schruns, the already-recommended **Hotel Alpenrose** brings in a band every Saturday night in season to play for dancing. It also sponsors *schuhplättler* nights about twice a week.

The **Löwen Hotel,** also recommended, had the liveliest band on my last visit. Disco action is in the Löwen-Grube. Occasionally you can see folkloric shows here, as well as international shows. It's probably your best bet in town.

Tschagguns also is lively after dark in season. The moment they return from the slopes, skiers pile into the previously recommended **Cresta Hotel** and the **Sporthotel Sonne** (see above) for drinks, either hot chocolate or beer. Later, as the evening progresses, both of these places have dancing.

GASCHURN

This resort, reached by bus from either Bludenz or Schruns, lies at an elevation of 3,230 feet and is the starting point for the Silvretta-Nova winter-sports arena. Gaschurn and **Partenen,** a smaller resort, provide walking and climbing tours, and visitors can fish for trout in several rivers and storage lakes.

A gondola lift from Gaschurn takes you into one of the most beautiful ski regions in Austria, the **Silvretta-Nova.** In only 10 minutes this gondola lift transports guests in 128 six-person compartments to the top station at 6,590 feet. In addition, there are seven chair lifts and 21 T-bar lifts. This extensive lift system enables you to use the 50 miles of well-kept slopes, ranging from nursery runs to the most sophisticated slopes and touring routes. The ski school offers single and group lessons as well as cross-country skiing. There's also a ski kindergarten.

You can get further information at the tourist office of Gaschurn (tel. 05558/8201) or the tourist office of Silvretta Partenen (tel. 05558/8315).

Where to Stay

Sporthotel Epple, A-6793 Gaschurn (tel. 05558/8251), is a first-class vacation hotel in the center of town, designed in a contemporary format. The décor is luxurious, conservatively modern, and rustic, with lots of exposed wood and comfortable furniture. A covered swimming pool, a sauna, and tennis courts are on the premises. The 63 bedrooms, each with private shower and toilet, are well furnished and comfortable in the snug alpine tradition. In winter, half board costs 1,200 AS ($87.25) to 1,760 AS ($128) per person daily. In summer, half board goes for 650 AS ($47.25) to 730 AS ($53) per person daily. The hotel receives guests from December to April and July to September.

Zum Fässle, the adjoining restaurant, offers a welcome to visitors, as well as a varied menu specializing in Swabian specialties. These include juicy roast beef with onions, an array of crispy salads, homemade spätzle, and desserts such as tasty strudels. Full meals cost 200 AS ($14.50) to 450 AS ($32.75).

Posthotel Rössle, A-6793 Gaschurn (tel. 05558/8331). The older section of this 19th-century hotel has a weathered shingle façade, green shutters, and a gently sloping gabled roof. In 1966 the Kessler family added a bigger chalet section with modern comforts. These include both an indoor and outdoor pool, whose waters flow into one another, and a massive structure with soaring lintels and curved walls whose roof supports a sun terrace. The public rooms inside are universally rustic, accented with well-finished paneling, although the older section contains more colorful units. Also on the premises are a sauna, a bowling alley, and an open fireplace. The bedrooms, ranging from traditional to modern, rent for 580 AS ($42.25) to 1,060 AS ($77) daily for a single and 480 AS ($35) to 1,110 AS ($80.75) per person for a double, with breakfast included. Each of the 56 bedrooms has a private bath or shower. Open from June to April.

Hotel Pension Sonnblick, A-6793 Gaschurn (tel. 05558/8212), is a contemporary chalet set at the edge of the village near a steeply rising hill. The accommodating sun terrace is flanked with stone retaining walls, while the interior is outfitted in alpine modern, with an open fireplace, brass chandeliers, and rustic accessories. The bedrooms are somewhat on the small side, but are sunny and comfortable, sometimes giving a view of the village church and the hills beyond it. On the premises are an indoor pool, a sauna, a café, a day-bar, and an elevator. An older section is connected to the new part by a passage. For room and half board, doubles cost from 730 AS ($53) per person daily.

Where to Dine

Restaurant Alt Montafon (tel. 05558/8232) is the premier restaurant in the entire valley—perhaps, in the view of some food critics, the finest one in Vorarlberg. Covered throughout its two dining areas with thick panels and 19th-century farm implements, it offers about as much local flavor as you're likely to find in the region. The owner of this restaurant is an avid hunter, and the menu understandably includes the "antlered fruits" of the region. In addition, the homemade noodles are sometimes laced with pungent cheese, the garden vegetables are fresh and crispy, and the house specialty is roasted veal. Be sure to reserve a table because in winter this is one of the most popular places around. Fixed-price menus go from 210 AS ($15.25) to 300 AS ($21.75), with à la carte dinners ranging from 550 AS ($40) to 650 AS ($47.25). In summer, meals are offered continuously from 11am to 11pm daily. In winter, service is Tuesday to Friday from 5 to 11pm, on Saturday and Sunday from 11am to 11pm; the restaurant is closed on Monday throughout the year and from Easter to May and in November.

Après-Ski

Every two weeks the tourist office issues an information sheet to keep guests informed about what's going on in and around Gaschurn and Partenen.

At the **Landhotel Alpili** (tel. 05558/8759), you can dine to live music in the Tanzbar Sissi.

Every Tuesday and Thursday, the winners of the ski race for guests are honored —accompanied by live music—at the **Hotel Verwall** (tel. 05558/8206).

The best place for après-ski life is the Taverne of the already-recommended **Sporthotel Epple,** where in chic, snug surroundings you can enjoy zither music and dancing on most nights every week in season.

GARGELLEN

This is a charming mountain village at the end of the valley, with no through traffic. To reach the hamlet of Gargellen, you turn to the southwest—the road is marked—before you approach St. Gallenkirch. Gargellen lies between the Silvretta alpine range and the Rätikon. If you don't have a car, you can reach this resort by taking a bus from Schruns, after leaving St. Gallenkirch. You go 5 miles southwest through the Valley of the Gargellen to the village of Gargellen (4,675 feet).

Mountaineers flock to this well-patronized summer holiday resort. Trout fishing in the many fast-flowing mountain streams in the environs is another lure. You might enjoy a dip in the heated open-air swimming pool or taking a horseback ride.

In winter this is a ski place, with an extended ski area. Lifts link well-prepared runs for both beginners and experienced skiers. The resort offers a well-known ski school, a ski kindergarten, and cross-country slopes.

You can be transported to the resort's highest station, at 7,600 feet.

Food and Lodging

Alpenhotel Heimspitze, A-6787 Gargellen (tel. 05557/6319), is a chalet filled with a kind of heavy grace and dozens of handcrafted extras. Some of the ceiling beams look hand-hewn, and the knotty paneling attractively complements the autumnal colors of the finely patterned carpeting. You'll notice a scattering of carved alpine chests and polychrome statues, as well as soft lighting and a big fireplace trimmed with river rocks. The bedrooms sometimes contain flowered upholstery with white backgrounds and big sunny windows. The hotel is popular for both its rooms and its restaurant. The place just oozes with old-world charm, and connoisseurs of alpine inns rate this among the finest. The Thöny family are your hosts.

A Romantik hotel, Alpenhotel Heimspitze rents only 19 bedrooms, so reservations are imperative, especially in the winter season. Each of the spacious—at times even luxurious—rooms contains a private bath or shower. In winter, half board costs 760 AS ($55.25) to 1,100 AS ($80) per person daily, with half board in summer going from 600 AS ($43.50) to 890 AS ($64.75) per person daily.

Skiers and hikers will be glad to know that lunch on this plan can be taken either in the main hotel or in the Schafberg restaurant at the top of one of the chair lifts. A children's playroom is on the hotel premises, as well as a country restaurant whose tables are often decked with alpine roses. Specialties include fresh salads, tafelspitz, pork filet with buttered spätzle, and a wide choice of pastries. Set menus cost 150 AS ($11) to 650 AS ($47.25), with à la carte dinners ranging from 160 AS ($11.75) to 500 AS ($36.25). The restaurant is closed on Monday, and both the hotel and the restaurant are closed between early May and mid-June and between early October and mid-December.

Sporthotel Bachmann, A-6787 Gargellen (tel. 05557/6316), has an attractive chalet format constructed on top of a modern swimming pool set into the hillside. The interior is intimately cozy, combining lots of polished knotty paneling, ceramic tile stoves, open fireplaces, and rustically comfortable furniture. The dining room has massive beams supporting the ceiling. Also on the premises are an outdoor pool, a sauna, and tennis courts with a teacher. You have access to a host of wholesome alpine activities. At this sports-oriented hotel, you can rent one of 34 large and comfortably furnished bedrooms, most with private baths or showers, from December to April and June to September. Half board in winter ranges from 740 AS ($53.75) to 870 AS ($63.25) per person daily, in summer from 540 AS ($39.25) to 610 AS ($44.25).

Hotel Madrisa, A-6787 Gargellen (tel. 05557/6331), was the first hotel in Gargellen, and some locals will tell you that it was largely responsible for putting Gargellen on the tourist map. Early English skiers spread the word back home, and the rest was history; thousands have flocked here since. Even today the Madrisa has a devoted clientele. This is a much-changed four-star hotel, which the Hans Karl Rhomberg family has expanded and renovated for the comfort of guests until only the old gabled wing, considered a symbol of Gargellen, is an exterior reminder of its past, although much of the original paneling and carved wood has been preserved. All of the 65 well-furnished bedrooms contain private baths, toilets, radios, and phones, and many have their own balconies. The winter charge for half board ranges from 825 AS ($60) to 1,200 AS ($87.25) per person daily. In summer, half board costs 590 AS ($43) to 710 AS ($51.50) per person daily. A bar and an open fireplace are among the attractions in the reception area, and there is a pleasant dining room, as well as an indoor swimming pool, a cellar bar, a sauna, a solarium, massage facilities, and a gymnasium.

Hotel Alpenrose, A-6787 Gargellen (tel. 05557/6314), is a tastefully symmetrical chalet built into the side of an alpine meadow. Its façade is appealingly covered with weathered planking, and its interior provides rustic comforts, including a panoramic dining room with a woodsy décor, an agreeable bar area, a sauna, a whirlpool, a children's playroom, and physical fitness facilities. Rooms are fairly large and kept immaculately clean. Only nine bedrooms are rented, each with private bath or shower. In winter, half board ranges from 670 AS ($48.75) to 800 AS ($58.25) per person daily; in summer, from 490 AS ($35.50) to 570 AS ($41.50) per person daily. Guests are received from December to April and June to October.

---

8. Arlberg (Lech and Zürs)

The east side of Arlberg was visited in Chapter X on Innsbruck and Tyrol, so it's time for me to tell you the "west side story" of this massif that separates Vorarlberg from Tyrol.

This part of Austria is one of the major meccas for winter sports in Europe. Leading resorts on the Arlberg massif, the highest mountain range in the Lechtal Alps, include Lech and Zürs, and there's also rustic, tiny Stuben, with its own north-facing snow-catcher, the mighty Albona. An Arlberg ski pass allows the holder to use the 77 ski tows, chair lifts, and cable cars in the entire Arlberg region.

Up through the Flexen Pass, you come to Zürs, a chic, elegant, refined resort with skiing at Trittkopf and Mahdloch. Lech is larger, with easier skiing on Kriegerhorn and Mohnenfluh.

LECH

Founded in the 14th century by emigrés from the Valais district of Switzerland, Lech, on the northwestern flank of the Arlberg mountain range, still has its original **pfarrkirche** (parish church) from that era. This archetype of a snug alpine ski village is practically joined to Oberlech, a satellite resort a little farther up the mountain. Lech stands at 4,730 feet; Oberlech, at 5,600 feet.

Zürs, a sister village to Lech, is considered slightly more fashionable, but Lech has its own claim to fame: it has played host to Prince Charles and Princess Diana.

Lech is 8½ miles from Langen, and you can reach it and Oberlech by bus from either Langen or St. Anton am Arlberg. Langen lies on a major route and is the closest train station to Lech, which is serviced by good bus links.

In summer, visitors like to come here to tour the Upper Lech Valley, which stretches for about 35 miles to a lovely vale lying between the Lechtal and the Allgäu Alps.

Lech, Oberleck, and Zürs are linked by 34 lifts (as mentioned, the whole region has 77 lifts). All of these can be traveled on only one ski pass, making for a magnificent ski circus. Snow is advertised as guaranteed from the end of November until the end of April. Oberlech has a pedestrian zone with frequent cable-car connections. Lifts and runs are close together. It's possible to ski between Lech and Zürs. A cable car, whose last run is at 1am, connects Oberlech to the heart of Lech. You can take the Rüfikopf cable car from the heart of the resort to Rüfikopf (7,635 feet).

Regardless of which resort you stay in, I suggest you go to Oberlech if the day is sunny and find yourself a spot in one of the big sun-terrace restaurants there.

Where to Stay at Lech

Hotel Arlberg, A-6764 Lech (tel. 05583/21340), is a sprawling chalet well equipped for an alpine vacation in any season. In addition to a well-maintained lawn area, the grounds contain an outdoor pool, tennis courts, and a flowered sun terrace where waiters serve meals on well-ironed tablecloths. The interior offers beautiful regional antiques, some of them painted, carefully crafted paneling, and elegant accessories. Guests appreciate the intimate lighting in the bar after a day in the brilliant sunshine and also enjoy the warmth from the sitting room's baronial fireplace. The hotel rents 56 bedrooms, each with private bath or shower. In winter, half board

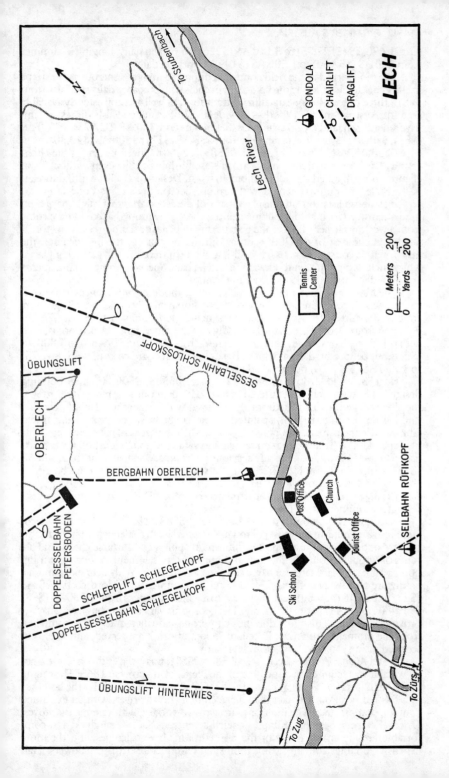

costs 1,690 AS ($122.75) to 3,110 AS ($226) per person daily, ranging in summer from 790 AS ($57.50) to 1,500 AS ($109) per person daily.

The food served in the richly outfitted dining room is as generous as the décor itself. The Schneider family directs a team of chefs who prepare a daily specialty from one of three or four European culinary traditions, as well as a consistently available array of Austrian-inspired foods—a wide array of game and fish dishes, cream-flavored gulasch, and cream schnitzels. Set menus cost 380 AS ($27.75) to 700 AS ($51), with à la carte dinners ranging from 235 AS ($17) to 600 AS ($43.50).

Gasthof Post, A-6764 Lech (tel. 05583/22060). Queen Beatrix of the Netherlands has been a frequent visitor to this establishment. But even without royal clientele it's still called the noblest hotel in town. Designed as a Romantik-Hotel, it has a chalet façade ornamented with trompe-l'oeil murals. This hotel long ago served as a postal station, and displays many of the accessories that might have been used a century ago, including alpine painted chests, furniture that could have come from a wealthy farmer's house, and a scattering of baroque sculpture. Clients fortunately get the best of the 20th century during their use of the indoor pool, the nearby tennis courts, the massage facilities, or any of the convivial gathering places, which include a popular sun terrace and several bars. Special summer arrangements are offered for fitness weeks and cooking courses.

The Moosbrugger family has installed all the modern conveniences in the bedrooms, which sometimes have elaborately painted headboards and refrigerators concealed in old chests. Accommodations include some units that are vast. The hotel, open from December to April and July to September, rents 41 bedrooms, each with private bath or shower. Half board ranges from 1,370 AS ($99.50) to 3,830 AS ($278.50) per person daily in winter. In summer, half board costs 850 AS ($61.75) to 1,700 AS ($123.50) per person daily.

Hotel Schneider Almhof, A-6764 Lech (tel. 05583/3500), is a huge building designed like several chalets clustered together. It opens onto the resort at the foot of the slopes. The interior is luxuriously outfitted with blazing fireplaces (including one beside the indoor pool), painted alpine cupboards, antiques, richly tinted fabrics, Oriental carpets, and polished stone. The international clientele who come here spend lots of time on the sun terrace and value the hotel's location near the ski lifts. The well-furnished, generally spacious bedrooms, 65 in all, rent for 2,500 AS ($181.75) to 3,400 AS ($247.25) daily in season for a single, with full board included. For a double, on the same plan, the charge is 2,800 AS ($203.50) to 2,900 AS ($210.75) per person. Small apartments cost more. Dining at the hotel merits a separate recommendation (see below).

Jagdhaus Monzabon, A-6764 Lech (tel. 05583/2104), is a tastefully decorated four-star hotel in the center of town. Designed like a chalet, it has public rooms that are outfitted with heavy beams, hunting trophies, comfortable chairs, and accents of wrought iron. On the premises are a beauty salon, an indoor swimming pool, a sauna, billiard tables, a bar, a café, and a restaurant. Willy Schneider and his family are the owners of this 55-bed hotel. In summer, half board costs 620 AS ($45) to 820 AS ($59.50) per person daily; in winter, it ranges from 1,280 AS ($93) to 1,980 AS ($144) per person daily. The bedrooms vary in style but have a happy, provincial feeling. This hotel does not compromise quality, and you're pampered from the moment you arrive. Excellent food and drink are served, and safely ensconced inside you can "let it snow, let it snow."

Hotel Krone, A-6764 Lech (tel. 05583/2551), was a chalet that became a hotel when it was acquired by a member of the Pfefferkorn family in 1865. The ceiling in the bar dates from about a century earlier (1741, to be exact). Today the hotel sits in a favored position between the village church and the river, with an expanded contemporary format. The interior is attractively woodsy, with ceramic tile stoves, Oriental carpets, beamed ceilings, paneled accents, a spacious sundeck, and comfortable fireside chairs. Many of the 54 bedrooms have balconies, and the more expensive doubles contain sitting rooms; all have private baths or showers. Half board in winter costs 1,440 AS ($104.75) to 1,860 AS ($135.25) per person daily. In summer, half board goes for 580 AS ($42.25) to 650 AS ($47.25) per person daily. Open from December to April and June to September.

Occupants of the hotel enjoy the evening dance bar, which is in an adjoining wing to avoid disturbing sleepers. Sometimes Tyrolean evenings are staged. On the premises is a modern fitness center with a sauna, a solarium, massage facilities, a hot whirlpool, and a Turkish steambath. A playroom exists for children. The big-windowed restaurant has a panoramic view and is given a separate recommendation under "Where to Dine."

Hotel Kristiania, A-6764 Lech (tel. 05583/2561-0). The most advanced of skiers are often attracted to this scenically located, tranquil retreat, perhaps because it is owned by Othmar Schneider, the Olympic ski champion. Once there, guests find 35 bedrooms, each with private bath or shower. The furnishings are comfortable, the rooms' many amenities make this four-star hotel worthy of its rating. It is open only from December to April, charging 1,490 AS ($108.25) to 1,950 AS ($141.75) per person daily for half board.

Built in 1968, the hotel was renovated in 1978. Rooms facing south have balconies and a view of the mountains, whereas units facing north have no balconies but a view of the village and the valley. The interior is filled with rustic Vorarlberg paneling and accessories. The hotel contains a restaurant for half-board guests, another one for à la carte nonresidents who call and reserve a table. The Kristiania sits within a three- to five-minute walk above the center of the resort, close to the rendezvous point for the cross-country ski school. Most guests leave their ski equipment at the skiraum in the center of town, where someone will prepare the skis with wax for the following day. They are thus relieved of the need to lug skis and poles up the hill to the hotel.

Tannbergerhof, A-6764 Lech (tel. 05583/2202), is an attractive shingled chalet with green shutters and lots of interior space. The atmosphere is conducive to helping both athletes and nonathletes appreciate sports and outdoor activities, although there's certainly enough inside to distract even the most ardent sportsperson. The public rooms are accented with well-finished paneling, a ceramic tile stove with a warming bench, soft lighting, and a blazing fireplace. On the premises is a popular evening disco, plus a lounge bar, and a restaurant serving specialties such as paprika gulasch and an array of veal dishes. The 51-bed hotel charges 1,430 AS ($104) to 2,440 AS ($117.50) per person daily for full board in winter. In summer, full board costs 620 AS ($45) to 880 AS ($64) per person daily. In a separate chalet, a three-minute walk from the hotel, the management maintains a covered swimming pool, a hot whirlpool, and a sauna.

Hotel Pension Lech, A-6764 Lech (tel. 05583/2289), is a pleasant 16-bedroom hotel composed of two chalets, five minutes away from the ski lifts. The interior is handsomely paneled and accented with soft lighting. On the premises are a sauna and a bowling alley. Each of the comfortably furnished bedrooms contains a private bath, and half board costs 900 AS ($65.50) to 1,190 AS ($86.50) per person daily. On this plan, you can enjoy a fondue evening and a rustic dinner with zither music, among special events. The hotel has a sauna, steambath, two bowling lanes, and a room for large-screen video programs. Open only from December to April.

Hinterwies, A-6764 Lech (tel. 05583/2531), is a white-walled, 27-room chalet with wood-grained shutters and baroque embellishments, a tranquil refuge above the resort. The interior is tastefully outfitted with lots of exposed wood, country furniture, Persian rugs, wall hangings, and various statuary and relics purchased on world sightseeing expeditions by the owners, the Schneider Adelheid family. One of my favorite parts is the flagstone back terrace, which leads up to the tapering chimney of a brick fireplace, protected by the overhang of the upper floors. The uncluttered bedrooms have lots of personalized and appealing touches. They are spacious, for the most part, up-to-date, and comfortable. With half board, tariffs range from 1,190 AS ($86.50) to 1,410 AS ($102.50) per person daily. The food is especially appealing and bountiful for en pension guests, as reflected by the weekly buffets. After a hearty Vorarlberg breakfast, guests can take the Hinterwies lift up to the slopes. Open only from December to April.

Hotel Pension Solaria, A-6764 Lech (tel. 05583/2214), is a partially shingled green-shuttered chalet set on a hillside at the edge of the village, a few minutes' walk from the center. The interior has attractively finished wood accents and lots of cozy comforts. There is easy access to the village's sporting facilities, including the nearby ski lifts, which you can reach by skiing a short distance downhill from the front door. Rooms at this 39-bed hotel are cozy and comfortable. In summer, half board costs 350 AS ($25.50) to 460 AS ($33.50) per person daily. In winter, half board goes for 650 AS ($47.25) to 1,250 AS ($91) per person daily. The Ender family, your hosts, will arrange for you to have breakfast served in your room if you wish.

Food and Lodging at Oberlech

Sonnenburg, A-6764 Oberlech (tel. 05583/2147), opening onto the village square, is a large double chalet with symmetrically peaked rooflines and alternating areas of white walls and wood-trimmed balconies covering the modern façade. In front the management has constructed a sun terrace looking down the hillside, while indoors the decor is warm, intimate, and woodsy. Many of the walls are accented either with brick or horizontal planking, with a scattering of regional antiques to augment the mellow glow from the paneling. On the premises is an indoor pool with a panoramic view, plus a kindergarten, two restaurants, and a collection of well-maintained bedrooms with modern comfort. A short distance away, and connected by an underground passage, stands the hotel's annex, Landhaus Sonnenburg, whose pleasantly furnished bedrooms rent for slightly less than those in the main building. Together, they offer a total of 70 bedrooms, available December to April. Each unit has a private bath or shower. With half board, charges range from 1,100 AS ($80) to 1,850 AS ($134.50) per person daily.

Hotel Montana, A-6764 Oberlech (tel. 05583/2460), above the village, has a large sun terrace looking out over Lech. It's designed like a light-grained chalet and has a stylish interior, making ample use of fuschia and pink as the appealing colors, which contrast well with the ruddy paneling. The in-house swimming pool is backed by an abstract mural, while the café/bar area is an attractive place for a midafternoon drink. The owner, Guy Ortlieb, an expatriate Frenchman, organizes weekly farmer buffets and cocktail parties, and does what he can to make his guests feel at ease in the sporty ambience of this hotel, which offers 27 rooms and 16 suites. Half-board rates in high season range from 955 AS ($69.50) to 1,650 AS ($112) per person daily, based on double occupancy. The hotel is open from December to April only.

Where to Dine at Lech

Gasthof Post Restaurant (tel. 05583/22060). The Moosbrugger family, owners of this previously recommended hotel, wisely hire some of the finest chefs in the Arlberg area for the superb meals served in this traditional hostelry. Their restaurant is a member of Relais & Châteaux, and serves food worthy of that designation. Step into an old-fashioned Austrian imperial world of antiques, alpine paneling, tile stoves, and hunting trophies. Many guests are on en pension terms, but nonresidents who make a reservation can select from two dining salons where they can make their food selections either from an à la carte menu or, perhaps more recommendable, from one of the chef's set menus. The latter range from 300 AS ($21.75) to 750 AS ($54.50)—a lot to pay, admittedly, but you get top-quality ingredients prepared with care and flair. À la carte meals run from 275 AS ($20) to 650 AS ($47.25).

The service and attention lavished on you here is among the finest in Lech, and, at your leisure over a drink, you can peruse the menu, which is a combination of both Austrian traditional and nouvelle cookery, along with international specialties.

In season, game is featured. Austrian classics are always there, including a tafelspitz that will help you understand why this was Franz Joseph's favorite dish. Other delicacies include lamb, fresh fish, rabbit pâté, and an impressive dessert list. Lunch is daily from noon to 2pm; dinner, 7 to 9pm.

Hotel Schneider Almhof Restaurant (tel. 05583/3500). There are those who consider this the finest restaurant at Lech, so you may want to escape your hotel dining room for at least one meal at this august establishment (see above). The more elegant of the hotel's restaurants is contained within a fine dining citadel, Wallisterstube, and its smaller and more intimate satellite salon, known simply as "The Stube." Both rooms open onto a view of the mountains and contain lots of antiques and well-oiled paneling, along with such touches as a blue-and-white ceramic stove. Accessories in the Walliserstube are mountain green, while those in the stube are sky blue.

Meals are offered only from November to April, 12:30 to 2pm and 6:30 to 11pm. During the rest of the year the Schneiders, the owners of the hotel, close the restaurant. Set menus cost 280 AS ($20.25) to 650 AS ($47.25), with à la carte dinners ranging from 250 AS ($18.25) to 500 AS ($36.25)—expensive but worth it. The most expensive menu, a gourmet repast, is served only in the evening. Guests might begin with snails in wine sauce with garlic butter or else a creamy garlic soup with bread croûtons. The chef invariably does homemade al dente noodles, and you can count on such Austrian classics as Wiener schnitzel or tafelspitz. Other dishes show imaginative flair and talent from the kitchen. Game is featured in season. You might interrupt your repast with a palate-cleansing kiwi sorbet and later follow with a delectable walnut parfait.

Hotel Montana Restaurant (05583/2460), in the previously recommended hotel, offers a dining spot, Zur Kanne, run by an expatriate Frenchman, Guy Ortlieb, who sets very high standards in the quality and freshness of his ingredients. The place has been elected to several prestigious rankings, including the Chaine des Rôtisseurs. It's known for serving the best fish in the valley, including salmon in a saffron sauce. You might begin, for example, with Alsatian wine soup, then follow with frogs' legs Provençal. Set menus, most recommendable, range from 250 AS ($18.25) to 500 AS ($36.25), with à la carte dinners costing 175 AS ($12.75) to 425 AS ($31). At the tables, the waiter will present a woman (if accompanied by a man) a menu with no prices indicated. Food is served daily from 11am to midnight.

Hotel Krone Restaurant (tel. 05583/2551) is located in the previously recommended hotel, but many nonresidents call to reserve a table. They enjoy not only its well-prepared food but its location in the center of the resort. It has an older section with a darkly weathered chalet façade dating from the turn of the century, with a modern addition from 1970. The Pfefferkorns, your hosts, are most charming. Most diners prefer a table in the main part of the restaurant, which has a curved row of large windows overlooking the river and, beyond it, the rendezvous point for the ski school. An additional pair of smaller and more intimate stubes are also available. One has paneling dating from 1741. Specialties of the chef include fish soup Provence style, roast veal in a chicken liver sauce, and several regional recipes. Set menus range from 200 AS ($14.50) all the way to 750 AS ($54.50). À la carte dinners range from 200 AS ($14.50) to 500 AS ($36.25) per person. The restaurant is open from 11:30am to 2pm daily, serving dinner from 6:30 to 9pm.

Hotel Berghof Restaurant (tel. 05583/2635) is deserving of its popularity. Peter Burger and his family welcome you to their four-star hotel dining room with the hopes you'll enjoy their fine cuisine. The décor has white walls, wood trim, a plank floor, and an antique cupboard, along with a collection of flowerpots. Big windows look out over the "baby lift" and the ski slopes. Specialties are light international and Austrian food. For example, a recent meal consisted of cream of cauliflower soup with a selection of main courses, including saddle of lamb or tafelspitz. You might, for example, enjoy a filet of chamois with salad greens and a red wine dressing or medallions of veal in Calvados with curried potatoes. For dessert, perhaps you'll sample a soufflé of curd cheese. Food is served daily from noon to 2pm and 7 to 9:30pm. Fixed-price menus range from 280 AS ($20.25) to 450 AS ($32.75). The hotel is closed from September to early December and from April until late June.

Dining at Zug

Gasthof Rote Wand (tel. 05583/2758). If you decide to try this appealing restaurant, you can feel safe in knowing that both Prince Rainier of Monaco and King Hussein of Jordan have tried it also. A specialty of the house is spätzle with cheese, which many diners enjoy almost as much as the roast veal and pork, the warm cabbage salad, or the tafelspitz. Some diners say that the real attraction, however, is the fondue bourguignonne or chinoise, which you could precede with a soup made from a purée of venison. If you're up for dessert, the hot curd strudel is heavenly. Meals range from 275 AS ($20) to 600 AS ($43.50), and reservations are suggested.

The interior includes massive ceiling beams as part of a rustically attractive alpine décor. The restaurant is next to the onion-domed village church. In winter, the owners arrange for a horse-drawn sleigh to pick you up in Lech, if you telephone. They are open daily from 10am to midnight from December 1 until around April 20, and again from July 1 until the end of September.

Auerhahn (tel. 05583/2754) means "game cock." Lying on the outskirts of Zug, this restaurant is housed in a building dating from the 1600s, when it was a farm family's home. Even today furnishings are in vintage farmer's style, and the ambience is warm and woodsy, with a likable hubbub coming from the crowded tables. Specialties include an array of fondues and, in honor of its namesake, wild game dishes. Desserts tend toward the traditional strudel smothered in vanilla sauce. Meals range from 300 AS ($21.75) but could run as high as 700 AS ($51). In winter the place is open daily from 11am to midnight; closed Monday at other times of the year. It shuts down entirely from early October to mid-December and in May and June. No credit cards are accepted, but clients can sign the bill and charge the expense to their rooms at any hotel nearby.

Après-Ski

Lech has perhaps the finest après-ski life in Vorarlberg, and if you ever get bored here, you can also check out the action at the satellite resorts or go over to Zürs.

Dedicated skiers always head for the Scotch Bar of the **Hotel Kristberg** (tel. 05583/2488), which is owned and run by Egon Zimmermann, a former Olympic racer. The bar is in the basement. The colors are pastel, and the place tries to be small and intimate, maintaining its Old Vorarlberg character. Disco music plays, and a live band might appear on special occasions. Scotch and soda begins at 85 AS ($6.20), but there's no cover charge. The bar is open nightly from 9:30pm to 2am.

The evening begins even earlier, however, with a tea dance at the **Hotel Tannbergerhof** (tel. 05583/2202), where Hilde Jochum welcomes you for a good time. Later in the evening, you can dance to disco music.

Situated in the **Hotel Krone** (tel. 05583/2551), the Kronen Bar is the only place in Lech with live music—well, almost. It opens at 9pm, closing at either 2 or 3am. There's no entrance charge, but a "music charge" is added to the drink tabs at the end of the evening, costing from 25 AS ($1.80).

"The Red Umbrella," at Oberlech, is the most famous afternoon rendezvous for skiers in the Lech area. Set on a raised wooden deck and operated by the December-to-April Petersboden Sport Hotel (tel. 05583/3232), this red umbrella is hydraulically operated. It is lowered each afternoon at four or five, depending on the business that day. It is demounted to avoid being destroyed by the nighttime mountain winds which rip up to the umbrella's location at Oberlech. Business otherwise is from 11am. The umbrella is 25 feet or so in diameter, with a circular bar for skiers. At a stool around this bar you can sit and order such drinks as Jägertee (laced with rum), Glühwein, or vodka feigen (with figs floating in it). Of course, schnapps in this cold remains the favorite drink. Food is simple and filling, including soups such as gulasch, potato salad with sausages, sandwiches, and lots of strudels, including apple. A popular item is Germknödel, a steamed jam-stuffed dumpling covered with poppy seeds. Meals cost from 120 AS ($8.75). If the weather is too bad, you'll have to retreat inside the hotel for drinking and eating, warming yourself beside a log fire.

Hubertusklause (tel. 05583/2316) is a nighttime bar open in season from 9:30pm to 2am nightly, and guests often sit entranced listening to zither music. Hubertusklause, incidentally, is considered one of the oldest après-ski gathering places in the Alps. It sits beneath a cluster of apartment units at the edge of Lech on the side of town facing Zürs. A large beer costs from 50 AS ($3.65).

ZÜRS

An immaculate resort lying about 2½ miles from Lech in a sunny valley, Zürs (about 5,600 feet) consists of half a mile of typical white stucco Vorarlberger buildings, with carved wood balconies. The resort, really a collection of hotels, is reached via the magnificent Flexen Road.

Unlike most of the places we've visited, Zürs is strictly a winter resort, and nearly all the hotels close in summer. This mountain village has an abundance of "guaranteed" snow. In fact, once Pierre Trudeau, then prime minister of Canada, was snowed in and missed a summit meeting. Because of its location Zürs is avalanche prone, but these potential snowslides do not deter the loyal habitués of Zürs. The snow here has been compared to talcum powder.

Zürs (pronounced "Seurs") is a favorite of monarchs and film stars. More formal than Lech, it's considered one of the most elegant resorts in the world, far more select than St. Moritz or Gstaad, although lacking their ostentation. The resort has 130 ski instructors. Many of the wealthy guests, often from South America, have their own personal teachers.

A chair lift east of Zürs takes you to **Hexenboden** (7,700) feet. A cable lift goes to **Trittkopf** (7,875 feet), with a mountain restaurant and sun terrace.

In the west, a chair lift will take you to **Seekopf** (7,175 feet). From the windows and terrace of the restaurant here, you can see the frozen Zurser Lake. From Seekopf a chair lifts goes to the top station at 8,035 feet.

Where to Stay

Hotel Zürserhof, A-6763 Zurs (tel. 05583/2513), is an exclusive private world unto itself. Five separate chalets combine forces in the shelter of an alpine valley to create this most luxurious of mountain refuges. This is the establishment that put Zürs on the tourist map, and is the preferred choice of King Hussein and his American-born queen, as well as the playground of VIPs from around the world. It grew from a house erected by the Count and Countess Valley Tattenbach in 1927, when they began to accept paying guests. When Hitler took over Austria, the Tattenbachs sold it and immigrated to Costa Rica. In 1955 the establishment was taken over by Ernst Skardarasy.

The accommodations usually consist of private apartments, many of which have stone fireplaces, bars, lots of space and opulent comforts, including open firplaces in some of them. The new apartments have Roman-style baths. Singles and apartments for one person range from 1,890 AS ($137.50) to 3,360 AS ($244.25) per day. Doubles and apartments for two cost 1,820 AS ($132.25) to 3,850 AS ($280), including full board. The hotel is open only from November to April. The public rooms are decked out with old panels, antiques, and Persian carpets. There's music almost every night in the cellar bar, and a wide assortment of even the most esoteric sports (an indoor driving range for golfers, for example). A tennis player's admirers can watch him or her volley on the indoor courts from the security of a café area and relax later in the sauna or whirlpool. There's a hotel-run kindergarten for children, plus free covered parking in a large underground lot.

Hotel Albona, A-6763 Zürs (tel. 05583/2341), is a contemporary 33-room five-star chalet with panoramic windows and a dramatic contrast between the light and dark areas of its façade. The interior is comfortably filled with velvet banquettes pulled around an open fireplace, rustic ceiling beams, and polished wood. On the premises are a range of health facilities (sauna, steambath, massage, and jet shower), indoor golf equipment, a cozy series of sitting rooms, a carefully decorated restaurant which exudes warmth, a popular farmer's-style bar and disco, and dozens of charming accents. With half board, rates range from 1,500 AS ($109) to 2,100 AS ($152.75) per person daily, depending on the season and the accommodation. The hotel is open only from December to April.

Sporthotel Lorunser, A-6763 Zürs (tel. 05583/22540). The late Princess Grace of Monaco used to send her children here, and today you're likely to spot two or three Princess Caroline look-alikes at the hospitable bar of this luxurious hotel. Queen Beatrix of the Netherlands sometimes prefers it for her winter holidays. Rustically designed with cedar shingles and regional paintings around the windows, the hotel has intricately carved ceiling beams, open fireplaces, well-finished paneling, and dozens of elegant accessories and furnishings, as well as 74 comfortable wood-trimmed bedrooms, each with private bath or shower. Half-board rates range from 1,390 AS ($101) to 2,480 AS ($180.25) per person daily. The hotel serves some of the best food at Zürs—some say the very best—but the dining room is open only to residents. Men most often wear jackets in the evening at the height of the season. The Lorunser is open only from December to April.

Alpenrose Post Hotel, A-6763 Zürs (tel. 05583/22710), was erected in the 19th century against the snowy bulk of the Arlberg, but has been much altered and added on to since then. Since 1898 it has been a family-run inn, and decades of family tradition is reflected in the place. From December to April only it receives guests, including the kinds of cachet, mink coats, and elegance Zürs attracts. It is a true sport hotel, yet many clients come not necessarily to ski, but instead to promenade, breathe the pure mountain air, and relax and visit with their grandchildren after they return from the slopes. The location is at the top of the town across from the Trittkopfbahn. Some of the 87 bedrooms are spacious, others are small; all come with private baths or showers. Furnishing can be quite grand, as reflected by canopied beds. South-facing rooms tend to get the sun and are therefore more desirable. Rates run from 1,330 AS ($96.75) to 1,580 AS ($114.75) per person daily.

The culinary fare tends toward the solid, substantial, and filling; however, a selection of elegant dishes is always offered in the dark and woodsy restaurant. The wine cellar is predictably good. Regional fare such as game is featured. You might begin with melon soup and follow with trout or one of the roasts. The pheasant is served with a choice of sauces, including a spicy orange and pepper.

Central Sporthotel Edelweiss, A-6763 Zürs (tel. 05583/2662). The imposing façade of this 74-room hotel, which is open only from December to April, incorporates white walls, cedar shingles, and painted embellishments. This is the oldest hotel in Zürs, although you'll find it hard to believe after looking at the brightly painted bedrooms, which seem to come in a rainbow assortment of vivid colors. Full-board rates for a single room range from 1,450 AS ($105.50) to 2,050 AS ($149) daily. For a double, per-person rates go from 1,350 AS ($98.25) to 1,980 AS ($144) daily. Tariffs vary according to the accommodation, and overflow guests are housed in the annex, the Hotel Edelweiss, where prices are slightly lower. The public rooms include open fireplaces, a small bar, a popular disco, a white dining room with occasional gilt accents, and a French restaurant painted an eye-catching forest green.

Thurnher's Alpenhof Sporthotel, A-6763 Zürs (tel. 05583/2191). This distinctive-looking chalet has vertical timbers running in uninterrupted lines from near the ground floor to the eaves. The attractive effect is almost like looking at a weathered gridwork stretched across the white façade. The interior is a tasteful collection of carved panels, polished wood, and warmly textured fabrics. The dining

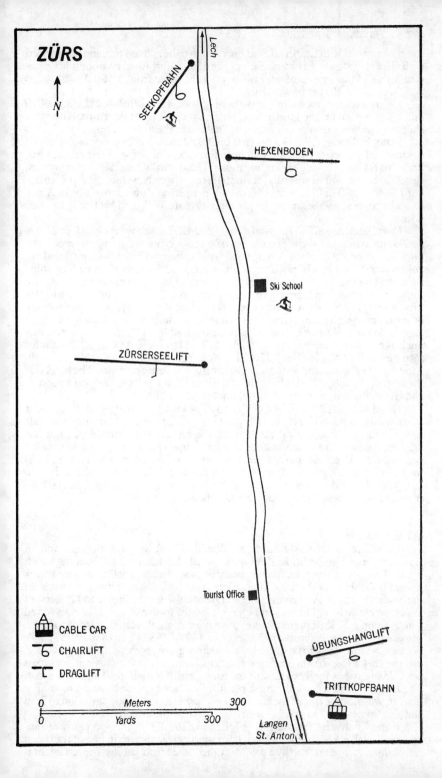

room is crowned with timbers almost big enough to be railroad ties, and is furnished with elegant upholstered chairs. Each of the 41 well-furnished bedrooms has a private bath and modern comfort. Half-board rates range from 1,650 AS ($120) to 3,250 AS ($236.25) per person daily.

On the premises are an indoor swimming pool, a fitness room, a sauna, a solarium, a sun terrace on the fourth floor, cinema with video, table tennis, billiards, a children's playroom, and one of the best kitchens in the Arlberg area.

Hotel Hirlanda, A-6763 Zürs (tel. 05583/2262), is a 26-room chalet with a rustically cozy interior containing an open fireplace, a farmer-style restaurant, a bar, and a collection of livable accommodations. These usually have dark wood accents, chalet furniture, and white walls. The hotel is open from November to April, charging 1,300 AS ($94.50) to 1,500 AS ($109) per person daily for half board. A sauna and a covered garage are on the premises. Oswald Wille and his family are your hosts.

Hotel Enzian, A-6763 Zürs (tel. 05583/22420), set above the bustle of Zürs is a 42-room symmetrical chalet with lots of wood accents and muted shutters. The interior is a tasteful combination of wood walls, coffered ceilings, warmly tinted upholstery, and open fireplaces where you can snuggle up for après-ski or perhaps enjoy a glass of Glühwein in the traditional alpine stube. On the premises are two dining rooms, a cozy bar, a sun terrace with waiter service, and a sauna where you can relax tired muscles after a day on the slopes. The Elsensohn family, your sports-loving hosts, do everything they can to create an informal ambience, providing a sauna, a tanning salon, and a game room. Guests are received from December to April, paying half-board rates ranging from 980 AS ($71.25) to 1,450 AS ($105.50) daily for a single and 920 AS ($67) to 1,350 AS ($98.25) per person for a double. The well-appointed bedrooms and apartments have many modern amenities. The hotel is at the edge of the village—on a hill behind the church and near the cable-car station—and you can ski directly from the front door to all the lifts.

Hotel Mara, A-6763 Zürs (tel. 05583/2644). The Hartinger family are your hosts at this 18-room chalet with its wood-paneled interior. Accents inside include lots of wrought iron, vertical planking on the walls of the intimate bar, and soft lighting. Unlike most hotels in Zürs, this one is open in summer, its whole season running from December to October. In summer, half board costs 375 AS ($27.25) to 420 AS ($30.50) per person daily. Winter half-board charges are 950 AS ($69) to 1,050 AS ($76.25) per person daily. The food served here is excellent, and each accommodation has a private bath, minisafe, phone, and TV.

Where to Dine

Hotel Zürserhof Restaurant (tel. 05583/2513) has high elegance and an Austrian-derived gemütlichkeit. A blue-blooded clientele (at least from the standpoint of money) dines here, often in black tie in season, especially for twice-a-week galas. The cuisine is of the finest international standard, and the service is considered the best at the resort. At the next table you are likely to see the Prince and Princess of Wales, certainly King Hussein and Queen Noor of Jordan. Even if the dish served here is among the least pretentious in the cuisine of rural Austria, it tends to be expensive (though well prepared). Dinners cost 450 AS ($32.75) to 850 AS ($51.75). For that, you are likely to be treated to something grand, perhaps roast suckling pig, but the chef also prepares Viennese roast chicken, roast veal, bratwurst, and roast pork. Many guests prefer to dine in the stube, which is traditional alpine in décor. The kitchen also prepares the most beautifully draped cheese buffet in town. For dessert, why not the one of the strudels with vanilla sauce? Hours are noon to 2pm and 7 to 9pm daily. The hotel is open from November through April.

Hotel Edelweiss Restaurant (tel. 05583/26620), in the previously recommended hotel, is known for its food. It's a sporty elegant place in one of the oldest establishments in Zürs, run by a pair of brothers, the Strolz family. The restaurant is decorated in kaiser gold and green. The area most popular with sports enthusiasts is the Palmers Stüberl. The ambience is stimulating on a winter's night, the table setting elegant. Several kinds of bread are offered before the meal begins. You can then, after ordering an appetizer, select such main courses as zander filet with a warm vinaigrette sauce or beef filet stuffed with goose liver and served with a sabayon of chives and quickly sautéed vegetables. Rösti is served as a side dish. You might also try the filet of sole from the grill, served with lemon-flavored butter. The chef also prepares a salad of fresh greens with goose liver slices. The cheese board is impressive, as is the wine list. A salad buffet is offered daily, along with whole-food selections for figure- and health-conscious guests. The hotel serves daily from noon to 2pm and 7 to 9pm, with set menus costing 400 AS ($29) to 550 AS ($40). À la carte dinners range from 200 AS ($14.50) to 500 AS ($36.25).

Hotel Hirlanda (tel. 05583/2262) is known for its warmly rustic, heavily beamed, and gracefully accessorized dining facilities, attracting clients avidly involved in skiing and its offshoot activities. The place is aggressively Austrian in its interior, which makes it a favorite of many ski instructors. The kitchen is known for its special preparation of hearty Vorarlberg dishes appealing to athletic vacationers. But it also presents gastronomically delicate dishes. There's a grill list of impressive proportions, and an equally impressive wine cellar. The grill is known for its medley of wood, which gives meats a pungent and most savory flavor. You might begin with onion soup served with cheese and croûtons or else lobster-stuffed ravioli. Spicy seasoned filet steaks are grilled on the wooden charcoal grill. Barbary goose with orange sauce is another delectable main course. Oven-baked potatoes come with an herb-flavored sour cream dressing that make them a delight. Desserts derive from the in-house pastry chef, who concocts different "surprises" every night, perhaps Málaga sabayon with mango slices. Lunch is served daily from noon to 2pm, dinner from 7 to 10pm. À la carte dinners cost 200 AS ($14.50) to 500 AS ($36.25) per person. The Wille family, the owners, keep the fireplaces blazing to take the chill off the coldest winter's night. The hotel is open from November to April.

Après-Ski

The most luxurious and elegant place to be seen at night is the already-recommended **Hotel Zürserhof,** where there's disco dancing.

For other discos, check out those at the **Hotel Albona** and the **Hotel Mara,** both previously recommended.

STUBEN

This little village and winter resort is almost a suburb of Lech, lying on the northern fringes of the larger village, on the west side of the Arlberg Pass. Stuben can be reached by bus, but the most romantic way to go from Lech is by horse-drawn sleigh.

The hamlet has been a way station for alpine travelers for many centuries, but in recent years it has become a modern ski area, with its own lift station on Albona. Stuben does not enjoy the chicdom that Zürs does, but its prices are much more reasonable, and it's in a fine location for skiers, having links with St. Anton in the Tyrol as well as with Lech and Zürs in the Arlberg region. In fact, the Arlberg ski pass mentioned above is valid for lifts and cars linking Stuben, St. Christoph, St. Anton, Zürs, and Lech.

Stuben is especially geared for family enjoyment, with children's ski courses, special meals, and hosts who help the small fry feel at home.

This was the birthplace of Hannes Schneider, the great ski instructor.

Food and Lodging

Hotel Mondschein, A-6762 Stuben (tel. 05582/511), is a 250-year-old country house with cascading window boxes and forest-green shutters. The interior is more contemporary, although the hospitality inside is pure old-fashioned Austrian.

The hotel offers much comfort in its 30 bedrooms, which are traditionally alpine, and come with private baths or showers. Winter half-board rates range from 840 AS ($61) to 880 AS ($64) per person daily. In summer, half board costs 420 AS ($30.50) to 440 AS ($32) per person daily. Facilities of the hotel include a bar, a solarium, a fitness center, and an indoor swimming pool, which the hosts, Werner Walch and his family, invite guests to use. Openly crackling fires are a wintertime lure, and secondary heating is provided by the traditional ceramic tile ovens, which create a warmly snug and cozy atmosphere.

Its restaurant is known for its cuisine, ranging from gutbürgerlich to haute gastronomy. The food includes a light and classical Austrian repertoire along with an impressive list of international specialties. Only the finest ingredients are used, including venison, beef, lamb, and fish. Some food critics, for example, claim its fish is the "best in the Arlberg." The wine list is also illustrious, stored in a centuries-old cellar—the special pride of its hardworking owner. Full meals cost from 250 AS ($18.25) and range toward heaven in price, depending on what you order. The dining room is open daily from 7:30am to midnight. The hotel closes every year for two weeks in May and for two weeks in late October and November.

Hotel Post, A-6762 Stuben (tel. 05582/761). When it was built in 1608, this 45-room hotel served as a shelter for tired mail-coach travelers. Today Nikolaus Fritz welcomes more up-to-date visitors in the rustically attractive public rooms, most of which have been designed in a pleasingly contemporary format of comfort and include open fireplaces and deep-seated chairs. On the premises are a restaurant and a bar, both of which offer welcome refreshment after a day outdoors. Just at the edge of the village, the hotel charges 600 AS ($43.50) to 870 AS ($63.25) daily, with half board included. Rooms at the nearby Hunting Lodge Post, or Jagdhaus, cost the same. Accommodations in the lodge are more spacious; they are decorated in a bright alpine style. Open December to April.

Hotel Albona, A-6762 Stuben (tel. 05582/712), is an attractive chalet with wooden shutters. On a narrow street in the center of the village, the hotel is outfitted with lots of exposed wood, alpine furniture, and sunny colors. On the premises are a hot whirlpool, a dancing bar, a restaurant, and a collection of 22 comfortable wood-trimmed bedrooms, each with private bath or shower. The hotel is open from December to April and June to September. Half-board rates in winter range from 590 AS ($43) to 750 AS ($54.50) per person daily. In summer, half-board charges go from 340 AS ($24.75) to 440 AS ($32) daily.

CARINTHIA

The southernmost province of Austria, Carinthia (Kärnten, in German) has been generously endowed by nature. Encircled by high mountains that give it fairly well-defined borders, it has been compared to a gigantic amphitheater, cut across by the Drau River (which becomes the Drava when it enters Yugoslavia). This province consists of mountainous Upper Carinthia in the west and the Lower Carinthian Basin region in the east. Because of its warm and sunny weather and lakes, which attract bathers and water-sports enthusiasts who don't go to ocean shores, a section of Carinthia is known as the Riviera of Austria. The Carinthian climate is the country's mildest.

Villach, to be previewed later, is the biggest road and rail junction in the eastern Alps, and Klagenfurt is the capital of Carinthia.

This is an ancient province, archeological discoveries in the area showing that it was known to the human race far back in unrecorded time. The Romans did not overlook it, their legions marching in to conquer alpine Celtic tribes of the kingdom of Noricum and establishing it as a Roman province.

For centuries this home of ethnic groups from Slovenia belonged variously to the kingdom of Germany and Avar-dominated Slavs from the east. Eventually the populace, hoping to fend off invasions, invited Bavaria to become Carinthia's protector. Thus it came to be ruled by Bavarians and was a part of the Holy Roman Empire. Bavarian settlers gradually assimilated with the Slav population.

When the Habsburgs took Kärnten as a part of their rapidly expanding empire, it was a duchy of the Holy Roman Empire under the Bohemian aegis, a situation resolved finally when Ferdinand I of Habsburg, soon to become emperor, married the heiress to Bohemia and made Carinthia an imperial duchy, later to be designated a province of Austria.

Yugoslavia claimed southern Carinthia after World War I, and in that confused time some of the territory was ceded to that country and more to Italy. All this land was later restored, and in 1920, after the collapse of the Habsburg Empire, a plebiscite was taken and a Slovenian minority in the south, along the Yugoslav border, voted to remain with Austria. A sizable minority of Carinthia's population of 600,000 today is Slovenian, but the majority of it is German.

The sunny weather and numerous idyllic lakes that are scattered among gentle hills and steep mountains make Carinthia mostly a summer tourist center. If you like water sports or just lazing in the sun, then a summer visit to this province might be in order. It's little known to or visited by North Americans, yet it's an ideal stopover point if you're heading south to Yugoslavia or Italy. The scenery is varied, and there is much beautiful countryside to be explored.

If you're athletic you can climb the gentle *Nocks* or else seek out the more demanding mountains. Fishing is a popular sport in this province, both in the lakes and the colder mountain streams. The region boasts more than 200 warm, clean lakes of varying sizes.

The "Carinthian Riviera" is the name given to the main lake area, including **Wörther See,** not far from Klagenfurt, the provincial capital. There are also Lake Ossiacher and Lake Millstätter. Weissensee, the fourth big lake, is less well known than the other three, but there are those who consider it the most beautiful. The best way to see the lakes in summer is to take one of the boats operating from April until the middle of October.

The best season to visit Carinthia if you want to enjoy the beauty and pleasure of the lakes is from the middle of May until the end of September, although the first two weeks in October are also ideal most years. In July and August hordes of tourists flock in, so if you plan to visit then, be sure you have reservations.

Although the warm lakes are the main drawing card for Carinthia, the province is making an increasing attempt to attract skiers to its mountains in winter. Skiing lasts from December until March, not April as in some parts of Austria farther north. As a ski center this province is much less expensive than Tyrol or Land Salzburg.

1. Klagenfurt

The provincial capital of Carinthia, Klagenfurt is a university town dating from 1161. Its charter was granted in 1252. The city lies only 38 miles from Italy and less than 19 miles from Yugoslavia. It is the cultural center of Carinthia.

Klagenfurt was destroyed by fire in 1514, but it was rebuilt and designated as the capital of the duchy in 1518. It was then a walled city, but the walls were torn down during the Napoleonic invasions in 1809. The center of the city is in quadrangular shape with four so-called rings, which are streets laid out along the former city walls. The center of this quadrangle and of the modern city is **Neuer Platz,** presided over by a fountain in the shape of a ferocious dragon called *Lindwurm,* the city's symbol.

It can get very hot in Klagenfurt in the peak of summer, but if you're there, do as the Klagenfurters do—retreat to nearby Wörther See (Lake Wörther) in the western sector of the city and linked to it by a canal.

THE SIGHTS

A major sight is the **Landesmuseum,** or provincial museum, Museumgasse 2 (tel. 04222/30552). On the grounds you can see Roman artifacts, including votive stones, gleaned from the excavations in Carinthia. The museum exhibits art and arti-

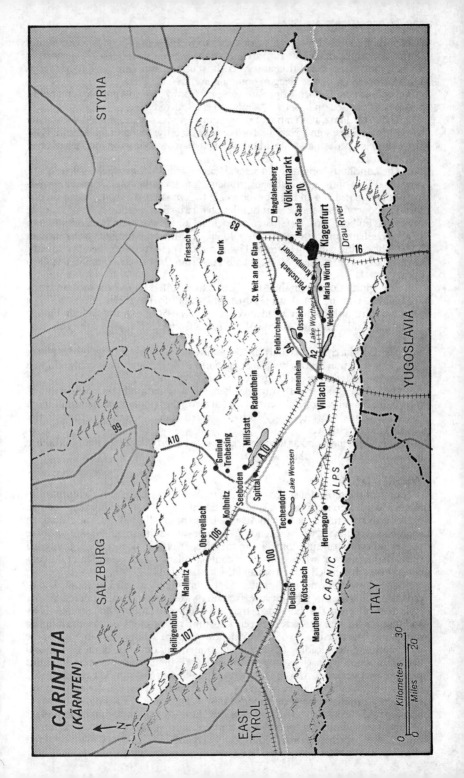

CARINTHIA
(KÄRNTEN)

facts of the province from prehistoric times to the present. The most outstanding feature is a display of ecclesiastical art. Also on view is a scale model of Klagenfurt as it was at the dawn of the 19th century. See the skull of a rhinoceros, said to have been a model for the renowned Dragon Fountain in the Neuer Platz.

The museum is open from 9am to 4pm, from 10am to 1pm on Sunday and holidays. It's closed on Monday. Admission is 15 AS ($1.10).

The **Alter Platz,** both a broad thoroughfare and a square, is lined with many baroque mansions, some from the 16th century. It is the center of the Altstadt (Old Town) and is a pedestrian zone. Many crooked, narrow little streets and alleys open off the square.

The **Landhaus,** originally an arsenal, later Carinthian state headquarters, and now the offices of the provincial government, stands on the Alter Platz. The building was begun in 1574 and completed in 1590. A moated castle once stood on this site. The courtyard of the present building has two-story arcades. A set of staircase towers has bulbous caps. Its Grosser Wappensaal, or Great Blazon Hall, dating from 1739, was handsomely decorated by Joseph Ferdinand Fromiller, who died in 1760. The ceiling painting of the hall is in trompe l'oeil. It has 665 heraldic shields. Great Blazon Hall is open Monday to Friday from 9am to 12:30pm and 1:30 to 5pm.

The **Trinity Column** in the Alter Platz is from 1681. One of the most interesting buildings on the square is the **Altes Rathaus** (Old Town Hall) from the 17th century. It has a three-story arcaded courtyard. The **House of the Golden Goose** (Haus zur Goldenen Gans) on the Alter Platz is from the final year of the 16th century.

The **Domkirche** (cathedral) of Klagenfurt lies to the southeast of the Neuer Platz. Construction on this building began in 1578. The interior is richly adorned in stucco and has ceiling paintings from the 18th century.

If you have children with you, take them by the **Minimundus,** a world in miniature, lying 2½ miles from Klagenfurt on Lake Wörther (see below). This minitown has building models which are 1/25th of their actual size, including not only castles but also the Eiffel Tower.

At landing stages, boats leave for trips on the lake in summer. A minigolf course lies nearby in Europa-Park.

WHERE TO STAY

One of the most unusual commercial buildings in Klagenfurt, the **Romantik-Hotel Musil,** Oktoberstrasse 14, A-9020 Klagenfurt (tel. 0463/511660), is probably the only structure of its kind in Austria. It was originally built in 1550 around an oval-shaped courtyard whose ascending balconies are vaulted from the side walls like the skylights in a baroque dome. From the street-level café, visitors can peer upward through three tiers of brickwork, whose counter-balancing stresses are carefully concealed beneath chiseled stonework and thick coats of plaster.

The engaging owners of this historic spot are Bernhard and Uta Musil. The façade that you'll see from the street was rebuilt in what might be called a Biedermeier style in 1860. From the shop-lined street outside, you'll enter an understated lobby and register at a desk midway between a bustling pastry shop, a coffeehouse, and a restaurant. The true beauty of the hotel, however, grows stronger with each of the winding stone steps leading upstairs. Each room opens onto one of the tiers of oval balconies, whose pinnacle is capped with a glass skylight. This is the best and most prestigious hotel in town, even though it contains only 16 rooms. The bedrooms are outfitted in an appealingly Austrian style, incorporating periods ranging from formal baroque to Biedermeier to farmer's baroque. Each contains a minibar, TV with a hookup to the "Skychannel" network of BBC news, and phone. Even the fuseboxes of this unusual hotel are concealed behind polychrome baroque statues. Room 8, my favorite, contains an ornate four-poster bed and parquet floors. With breakfast included, rates are 1,200 AS to 1,350 AS ($98.25) daily for a single and 1,500 AS ($109) to 1,700 AS ($123.50) for a double. The Musil-Stuben restaurant is recommended separately.

Hotel Moser Verdino, Domgasse 2, A-9020 Klagenfurt (tel. 0463/57878). The jutting tower of its elaborate pink-and-white façade was built in 1890 in a rich design of ornate cornices and trim. An insurance company occupies its top two floors, but the others are devoted to 78 well-scrubbed hotel rooms. Their furnishings vary widely, mingling a handful of modern pieces with groupings of antiques the owners have collected throughout Austria. Each accommodation contains a tiled and renovated bathroom, TV with BBC "skysatellite" news, and a minibar. A buffet breakfast is included in prices ranging from 850 AS ($61.75) to 1,300 AS ($94.50) daily for a single and 550 AS ($40) to 850 AS ($61.75) per person for a double. The most popular café in town, Café Moser Verdino, is near the oak-trimmed reception lobby.

Hotel Europapark, Villacher Strasse 222, A-9020 Klagenfurt (tel. 04222/21137), is designed in a low horizontal format that blends pleasingly into the landscaped garden around it. The sunny interior is filled with tasteful furniture, with a warmly appealing collection of abstractly patterned fabrics. The Meschnig family, your congenial hosts, charge from 580 AS ($42.25) to 720 AS ($52.25) daily for a single and 800 AS ($58.25) to 950 AS ($69) for a double at this 60-bed hotel. Their bedrooms are comfortable and well furnished, with a number of amenities.

Hotel Goldener Brunnen, Karfreitstrasse 14, A-9020 Klagenfurt (tel. 04222/57380), on the cathedral square in the heart of the city, is a peach-colored building with an arcaded courtyard filled with burgeoning plants. The management sets café tables there in summer. The hotel offers 27 comfortably furnished and well-maintained bedrooms, each with private bath or shower. Singles rent for 580 AS ($42.25) to 680 AS ($49.50) daily, with doubles costing 980 AS ($71.25) to 1,200 AS ($87.25).

Hotel Sandwirt, Pernhartgasse, A-9020 Klagenfurt (tel. 04222/56209). The neoclassical building that contains this historic hotel was originally built in the 1650s as a private house. Each of the Austrian presidents elected since 1945 has stayed here, enjoying the hospitality of Paul Jamek, whose ancestors bought the centrally located structure in 1899. You'll find portraits of those ancestors in the pine-paneled ground-floor stüberl, a few steps from the warmly decorated lobby. A series of wide steps leads to the 45 bedrooms. These vary widely in style, but they are usually high-ceilinged and comfortably old-fashioned. All but a few of the units contain private baths and minibars. Bed-and-breakfast costs 630 AS ($45.75) to 775 AS ($56.25) per person daily.

Kurhotel Carinthia, 8-Mai-Strasse 41, A-9020 Klagenfurt (tel. 04222/511645), is a modern hotel with six floors of two-tone concrete facing and big glass windows. The 28 conservatively but comfortably furnished bedrooms, each with private bath or shower, include flowered fabrics and an occasional 19th-century antique. Singles cost 550 AS ($40) to 900 AS ($65.50) daily, with doubles going for 380 AS ($27.75) to 700 AS ($51) per person. Centrally located but quiet, the premises contain a sauna, a hairdresser, a café, and a full range of health and massage facilities.

Hotel Garni Blumenstöckl, Oktoberstrasse 11, A-9020 Klagenfurt (tel. 04222/57793), is a very old hotel whose best feature might be the arcaded central courtyard. There you can sip drinks or coffee and admire the ornate wrought-iron balconies supported by the chiseled stone columns. Centrally located, the hotel offers 18 peaceful rooms, each of which has a private bath and shower. Singles range from 350 AS ($25.50) to 450 AS ($32.75) daily, with doubles costing 300 AS ($21.75) to 370 AS ($27) per person. The hotel is closed during part of September and October.

Hotel Wörthersee, Villacher Strasse 338, A-9020 Klagenfurt (tel. 0463/

21158). Set across the road from the lake, a few miles west of the center of town, this 34-room hotel looks like a cross between an Edwardian villa and a Teutonic castle. Its core was built by an Austrian nobleman as his lakeside house in 1840, then greatly enlarged in the ornate and timbered style of the day in 1892. A tunnel beneath the road leads to the hotel's grass-covered swimming area and a lakeside walkway stretching for several miles. The hotel is frankly at its best in summer when lakeside breezes ventilate the balconied rooms. Each of the wood-trimmed bedrooms contains a radio, alarm, phone, and private bath, and many also have minibars and balconies. Depending on the season, the accommodation, and the exposure, rates range from 390 AS ($28.25) to 840 AS ($61) per person daily for half board. Hildtraud Strohschein, the owner and chef, prepares a cuisine widely sought after in the area. His elegant repertoire includes such specialties as cream of broccoli soup with quail eggs, homemade pâté de foie gras, salads of smoked venison with marinated wild mushrooms, rack of baby lamb cooked in a shell of sea salt and egg yolks, and a white- and dark-chocolate mousse with a cocoa-cream sauce. À la carte meals cost 120 AS ($8.75) to 400 AS ($29), and the dining room is open daily except Monday from 7am to midnight.

WHERE TO DINE

Musil-Stuben, Hotel Musil, Oktoberstrasse 14 (tel. 0463/511660), has for years been the favorite restaurant of Klagenfurt, the place where people often go for family celebrations. Within its two intimately proportioned rooms, some of the most intensive restorations in town have reverted the décor to its 17th-century origins. One wall contains plaster casts of each of the building's owners, going back to 1660. Other accessories include hunting trophies and photocopies of historical documents, including bills of sale, affecting the hotel. If you decide to dine here, be sure to request a table in the *Stüber,* as it is more charming. Remember to reserve a table. The entrepreneurial owners have translated the regional menu into English. You can begin with Westphalian ham with cumberland sauce, or gulasch soup, following with three kinds of veal scallops, four kinds of filet steak, sole, trout, or game dishes. A serve-yourself salad bar offers arrays of seasonally adjusted produce. Full meals cost from 340 AS ($24.75), and are served daily from 11:30am to 2pm and 6:30 to 9:30pm.

Lido, Friedelstrand 1 (tel. 0463/261723), continues to receive favorable reviews from some readers. Enjoyable food and good wines make this place appealing, and it also seems a price-conscious bistro, one with a certain style. À la carte meals begin at 180 AS ($13), reasonable enough considering the quality of the food, although you could spend as much as 450 AS ($32.75) if you're extravagant. Quality ingredients are given serious attention in the kitchen, and often emerge looking like portraits on your plate. Try, for example, some of the fresh lake fish, perhaps beginning with a superb mousse of smoked eel. For your main course, try a classic dish such as filet of beef with a shallot-flavored red-wine sauce, finishing with a mousse of yogurt with fresh berries in the style of modern Austrian cuisine. The restaurant is open daily except Tuesday from 11:30am to 2:30pm and 6:30 to 9:30pm. Reservations are necessary.

Weinstube Kanzian, Kardinalplatz 2 (tel. 04222/512233), attracts a collection of amiable citizens who gather near the potted palms, chattering at tables separated from one another by screens. Specialties include Wiener schnitzels that are so big they hang over the edge of the plate, and an array of juicy meats with french fries. Your first course could be one of several kinds of soup, while the meal might not be complete without a piece of homemade torte for dessert. There's a wide selection of beer and wine as well. Menus cost 75 AS ($5.50) to 175 AS ($12.75), and are served from 11:30am to 2pm and 6:30 to 9:30pm. Closed Sunday.

Rote Lasche, Villacherstrasse 10 (tel. 0463/512059). Photographs from the great days of Hollywood fill the large windows of this restaurant, where your fellow diners are likely to be university students. The entrance lies off a busy boulevard. The main dishes are vegetarian specialties, but you can also order fresh trout, fresh shrimp, and special filets of beef, especially in the evening. The kitchen also serves freshly pressed fruit and vegetables juices, as well as many different kinds of herb tea. Meals range in price from 75 AS ($5.50) to 180 AS ($13). The restaurant is open Monday to Friday from 10am to midnight and on Saturday from 10am to 3pm. On Sunday it is closed.

THE CAFÉ LIFE

Other cafés in town might be older and more historic, but there's no question that **Café Moser Verdino,** Hotel Moser Verdino, Domgasse 2 (tel. 0463/57878), is the most popular and lighthearted gathering place. It seems to be constantly crowded with clients of all ages. In a décor ringed with Austrian marble, brass trim, and plush upholstery, you can gaze at rows of lithographs by artist Ernst Fuchs. Snacks, light meals, elegant pastries, wine by the glass, and beer are served daily from 6:30am to midnight. Coffee and pastries range from 21 AS ($1.55) to 36 AS ($2.60).

Café Musil, Oktoberstrasse 10 (tel. 0463/511660), inside the well-known hotel of the same name, is the best café in town. Patterned after a Viennese coffeehouse, the establishment serves a filling breakfast and an array of tortes and pastries that usually come fresh from the oven. Coffee costs from 21 AS ($1.55), with pastries going for 24 AS ($1.75). Open daily from 6:30am to midnight.

A SHOPPING NOTE

Kärntner Heimatwerk, Herrengasse 2 (tel. 04222/55575), is housed at the street level of a pink-and-white baroque building in the center of town. It offers the best collection in Klagenfurt of locally made handcrafts. Merchandise includes a selection of embroideries, ceramics, wrought iron, glassware, and textiles sold by the meter. Hours are daily except Sunday from 8:30am to 6pm.

EXCURSIONS FROM KLAGENFURT

The capital of Carinthia from 1170 until yielding the honor to Klagenfurt in 1518, **St. Veit an der Glan** was where the dukes of Carinthia held power when the province was an imperial duchy before the Habsburg takeover. The town was surrounded by high walls in the 15th century.

In the rectangular Hauptplatz (main square) at the center of town is a Trinity Column, dating from 1715, erected to mark the town's deliverance from the plague. Also on this square is the fountain called Schüsselbrunnen. The bottom part of this fountain is believed to have been excavated at the old Roman city of Virunum. A bronze statue crowning the fountain is a depiction of a miner from the 16th century, which St. Veit has adopted as its symbol.

The Rathaus (Town Hall) has a baroque exterior, but the building is from 1468. It has a lovely arcaded courtyard. Guided tours are conducted through the great hall of the Rathaus from 8am to noon and 1 to 4pm, except Wednesday afternoon. It's also closed Saturday and Sunday from November to April.

The pfarrkirche (parish church) is Romanesque with a Gothic choir. A circular karner (charnel house) is nearby. The baronial castle here served as an arsenal in the 16th century but has now been turned into a regional museum displaying artifacts of the area.

St. Veit an der Glan stands at the center of the most castle-rich section of Austria, with more than a dozen of the fortress complexes lying within a 6½-mile radius of St. Veit.

The best known and most visited is **Hochosterwitz Castle** (tel. 04213/2020), about 6 miles to the east of St. Veit, first mentioned in documents of 860. In 1209 the ruling Spanheims made the Osterwitz family hereditary royal cupbearers, and gave them Hochosterwitz as a fiefdom. When the last of that line was a victim of a Turkish invasion, the castle reverted to Emperor Frederick III and was subsequently passed by him to the governor of the area, Chrishof Khevenhüller. In 1570 Baron George Khevenhüller, also the governor, purchased the citadel and fortified it against the Turks, providing it with an armory and adding the gates, a task completed in 1586. Since that time the castle has been the property of the Khevenhüller family, left to them by Baron George, as shown on a marble plate in the yard dated 1576.

The castle, standing in a spectacular spot on a lonely, isolated hilltop 530 feet above the valley, gives an eagle's-eye view of the area around. It's considered the most striking castle in the country. To reach it, you go up a 16th-century approach ramp and through a total of 14 fortified gates. You can visit a number of rooms that have been opened to the public by the Khevenhüller family to show off the armor collection. In the private rooms you can also see a portrait gallery of the ancestors of the present owners.

Hochosterwitz Castle is open from Easter to October daily from 8am to 6pm. Admission is 35 AS ($2.55) for adults and 15 AS ($1.10) for children. A regional café and restaurant lies in the inner courtyard.

You can also strike out from St. Veit heading south again on the main road back to Klagenfurt. If you turn left after 4 miles and travel east, you'll reach the Ausgragungen, or **excavations at Magdalensberg,** at a distance of about 9 miles from St. Veit. Magdalensberg was a Celto-Roman settlement site and is considered the oldest Roman habitation north of the Alps. It is known that the Romans built a town here when they came this way to trade in the final century before the birth of Christ. In 1502 a farmer made the first discovery of a settlement here when he found a bronze statue, now called the *Magdalensberg Youth* (on display in Vienna).

However, it was not until the late 19th century that excavation work began. Even then collectors were mainly interested in discovering valuable Roman art objects. Serious archeologists began to work the site during the Allied occupation of Austria. As you explore the ruins, you can see the foundations of a temple as well as public baths and some mosaics. Tours are conducted from May to October daily from 8am to 6pm. Admission is 20 AS ($1.45) for adults and 10 AS (75¢) for children. For more information, call 04224/2255.

A celebrated pilgrimage, known as the "Four Hills Pilgrimage," starts from here every April. Complete with burning torches, the pilgrims race over four hills, and the run must be completed within 24 hours. This event is pagan in origin.

At the summit of the mountain the Austrians have erected a pilgrimage shrine honoring two saints: Mary Magdalene and Helen. From it a beautiful panoramic view of the encircling mountain range, including the Klagenfurt basin, unfolds before you.

Returning once more to St. Veit, you can head northeast along Rte. 83, which becomes E7. When you reach the junction with 93, turn west along the upper Gurk Valley road, passing through the hamlet of **Strassburg,** which was a walled town in the Middle Ages. Here there is a pfarrkirche (parish church) in the Gothic style, which you might want to visit if you have time. The Heilig-Geist-Spital Church, dating from the 13th century, has some lovely frescoes. Dominating the village is a castle built in 1147 but much changed over the centuries. Once this was the headquarters of the powerful prince-bishops of Gurk. It has been turned into a local museum.

The major goal of every pilgrim, however, lies 2 miles to the west—the **Cathedral of Gurk,** principal feature of the little market town in which it stands. From 1072 until 1787 this was the see of a bishop. The dom (cathedral) is a three-sided basilica erected from the mid-12th century to the beginning of the 13th, considered one of the most splendid examples of Romanesque ecclesiastical architecture in the country. A set of towers with onion-shaped domes rises nearly 140 feet.

The cathedral is rich in artwork, including the Samson doorway, an excellent example of Romanesque sculpture dating from 1180; some 16th-century carved panels that tell the story of St. Emma, an 11th-century countess who was canonized in 1938; the main 17th-century altar with dozens of statues; and a 1740 baroque pulpit. In the bishop's chapel you can see Romanesque murals—other than the main altar, the most important art objects in the cathedral.

The cathedral is open daily from 8am to 5:30pm from April 15 to September 30. Admission is 25 AS ($1.80) per person. Guided tours are conducted daily except Sunday.

After visiting the Cathedral of Gurk, you can take the same road going east and back through Strassburg. Back on E7, and depending on your time and interest, you can either turn north to visit the town of **Friesach** or else go south again, passing through St. Veit en route to Klagenfurt.

If you opt for the Friesach detour, you'll find an interesting old town worth exploring. Friesach may have been your gateway to Carinthia if you came here from Vienna. You enter Friesach after going through Styria. This is an ancient town, whose first mention in historic annals occurred in the mid-9th century. It was once a property of the prince-archbishops of Salzburg, who held on to it until the beginning of the 19th century. Lying in the broad Valley of Melnitz, this was once a major stopover for traders between Venice and the capital of Austria.

Some of medieval Friesach survives, including part of the 12th-century town walls. In one section of town you can see the remains of a moat. The Romanesque Stadtpfarrkirche (town parish church) building, noted for its stained glass in the choir, was constructed in the 13th century. The town has a number of other interesting buildings, including a Dominican monastery from 1673, built on the site of a much older structure and containing a 14th-century church. In summer, open-air plays are performed at the monastery. You can also visit the 13th-century Heiligblutkirche (Church of the Holy Blood) south of the Hauptplatz, the main square of the town.

West of Friesach, a mile-long road or footpath takes you to the hill, **Petersberg,** on which is the Church of St. Peter, dating from the 10th century. Here you can visit a watchtower to see 12th-century frescoes. You can also see the ruins of a castle that belonged to those prince-archbishops of Salzburg. North of the town on another hill is a second castle, partially reconstructed but still much in ruins. Standing on Geiersberg, this schloss is from the 12th century.

I have no accommodations to recommend in Friesach, but you can travel up the Valley of the Melnitz some 24 miles to the mountain summer resort and winter ski area of **Flattnitz** (4,560 feet). It has a circular church in the Gothic style, dating from 1330, built on the site of an earlier Romanesque house of worship.

Flattnitz has some fine hotels with good rooms and excellent food, everything at moderate cost.

Food and Lodging at Flattnitz

Hotel Eisenhut, A-9360 Flattnitz (tel. 04269/218), is a sprawling chalet set at the base of a forested hillside. On the premises are a small indoor pool, a sauna, a bar, and a staff directed by the Rothenpieler family. The hotel offers 26 bedrooms, 17 of which contain private baths. Singles rent for 390 AS ($28.25) to 420 AS ($30.50) daily, with doubles costing 240 AS ($17.50) to 410 AS ($29.75) per person. These tariffs include half board. The hotel is open from December to April and June to September.

Alpenhotel Ladinig, A-9360 Flattnitz (tel. 04269/316), is a generously sized country baroque hotel next to a 12th-century church in an isolated alpine meadow. The renovated interior contains wide hallways with massively handcrafted stairwells and a scattering of sturdy furniture and paneled walls and ceilings. From December to April and June to October, guests are received in the 20 bedrooms, each with private shower. Charges range from 320 AS ($23.25) to 370 AS ($27) per person daily for half board.

A Side Trip to Maria Saal

In the immediate vicinity of Klagenfurt you can visit the pilgrimage church of **Maria Saal,** standing on a hill overlooking the Zollfeld plain, some 6½ miles north of the provincial capital near what was once the Roman city of Virunum, capital of Noricum province.

Maria Saal is a major pilgrimage church of the province. A house of worship was first built here by Bishop Modestus around the mid-8th century. The present church, with its twin towers made of volcanic stone dominating the valley, dates from the early part of the 15th century, when a defensive wall was constructed to ward off attacks from the east. In the latter part of that century the Magyars had a try at taking the fortress-church but were not able to conquer it, nor were the Turks in later years.

One of the church's most outstanding features is a "lantern of the dead" in the late Gothic style at the south doorway. There are some marble Gothic tombstones on the church grounds. See also the **karner** (charnel house), which is octagonal in shape and Romanesque in style, with two tiers of galleries. The church has many objets d'art, but it is the 1425 image of the Virgin inside that has made it the subject of pilgrimage.

An interesting excursion to take from Maria Saal is to the **Herzogstuhl,** or Carinthian Ducal Throne, a mile to the north. A double throne on this ancient site was constructed from Roman stones found at Virunum. The dukes of Carinthia used it as a location from which to grant fiefs in medieval days.

---

2. Lake Wörther

The biggest alpine lake in the province is Wörther See, or Lake Wörther, 10 miles long, lying to the west of Klagenfurt and linked to the city by a channel, mentioned above. In summer it's a mecca for devotees of water sports. In spite of its being an alpine lake, the waters of Wörther See are amazingly warm, its temperature often going above 80° Fahrenheit in midsummer. Beginning in May, Austrians go swimming here, a most unlikely occurrence in most other alpine lakes of other provinces.

The little villages around Wörther See are flourishing summer resorts, especially such centers as Maria Wörth and Velden. Leaving Klagenfurt, we'll go first along the northern perimeter of Lake Wörther, stopping off in the little village of—

KRUMPENDORF

This is just a small stopover along the road, but it contains some moderately priced hotels serving good food. It's also well equipped for water sports. A city bus from Klagenfurt will deliver you to Krumpendorf. This safe, pleasant resort does a thriving family business. Its hotels are spread out, vying for choice spots along the Wörther See.

Food and Lodging

Seehotel Bruckner, Parkweg 3, A-9201 Krumpendorf (tel. 04229/2226), is one of the most appealing hotels on the lake. Located in a small park area, its central building contains a rustically paneled weinstube built in 1496. A newer building, constructed in 1972, accommodates the overflow from the older section. The public rooms are tastefully decorated, and there's a terrace jutting into the water with café tables. Other facilities include a swimming pool, tennis courts, and minigolf. The 84-bed hotel charges 590 AS ($43) to 695 AS ($50.50) per person daily for half board.

Strandhotel Habich, Walterskirchenweg 10, A-9201 Krumpendorf (tel. 04229/2607), set in a parklike garden at the edge of the lake, is administered by members of the Habich family. The exterior looks like a well-appointed private house, and the homey atmosphere inside contributes to that feeling. On the premises are five outdoor tennis courts, a lakeside swimming area with piers for boating, a covered swimming pool, a flowered breakfast terrace, a children's play area, and a rustically paneled interior with woodsy appeal. Rates with half board included are 440 AS ($32) to 730 AS ($53) per person daily. The hotel offers 40 bedrooms with private baths or showers. Rooms are pleasant, attractive, and ideal for summer fun. The hotel is open from the first of April to the middle of October.

PÖRTSCHACH

Known for its promenade along the lakeside, Pörtschach, where many lavish villas have been constructed, is the major resort along the north shore of Lake Wörther and one of the premier resorts in Carinthia. A section of the town juts out on a tiny peninsula, and in summer the promenade is a blaze of flowerbeds. Pörtschach is a sports-oriented resort, with waterskiing, sailing, riding, and golf available.

To the southwest of the resort stands Leonstein Schloss, and in the surrounding area you can take many nature walks or go on scenic drives.

Where to Stay

The first-class **Parkhotel Pörtschach,** A-9210 Pörtschach (tel. 04272/2621), is set in the midst of a 10-acre park on a peninsula bordering a landscape conservation area. From the hotel, a panoramic view opens over the Flower Promenade to Lake Wörther and the Karawanken mountain chain. Guests can enjoy a private lakeside bathing ground with a children's section, and additional outdoor sports activities include windsurfing, waterskiing, horseback riding, tennis (four clay courts), and golfing at a nearby 18-hole course. There's also an indoor recreation center with a swimming pool, a sauna, a solarium, a whirlpool, a fitness center, and a massage area. Further amenities include a beauty center, day care facilities for children, and organized activities. The Palms Restaurant offers musical entertainment along with its varied menu selection. The hotel rents 182 bedrooms, each tasteful and equipped with such amenities as private bath or shower. Rates for half board range from 810 AS ($59) to 1,970 AS ($143.25) per person daily. Open from May to October.

Hotel Schloss Leonstein, A-9210 Pörtschach (tel. 04272/2816). A century ago Johannes Brahms composed his violin concerto here. What you'll see today is a 14th-century, once-fortified castle whose public rooms are tastefully filled with well-chosen furniture. Throughout the establishment are wrought-iron accents, old terracotta tiles, stone detailing, and vaulted ceilings. On the premises are tennis courts, massage and beauty facilities, an assortment of water sports, golf facilities, and cozily elegant bedrooms, some of them duplexes. The hotel rents 35 bedrooms from May to September. With half board included, rates range from 1,010 AS ($73.50) to 1,280 AS ($93) per person daily.

The restaurant offers the sort of a candlelit ambience that many Austrians travel a long way to find. Served either in the courtyard or inside, the food is consistently good, including filet of trout, Valencian fish soup, veal cutlet with cream sauce, and zander filet. The fresh salads complement the homemade desserts, which are often accompanied by live music.

Hotel Schloss Seefels, A-9210 Pörtschach (tel. 04272/2377), is a lakeside collection of elegantly ornate buildings that curve along the shoreline just behind a screen of trees. My favorite of the luxurious sitting rooms contains a massively ornate ceramic stove with laurel garlands, an ornate chandelier, and comfortable chairs upholstered in light-colored fabrics. The 85 elegant and cozy bedrooms are freshly outfitted with decorator colors, discreetly flowered fabrics, and well-polished antiques; rooms are equipped with private baths or showers. With half board, rates range from 1,350 AS ($98.25) to 1,900 AS ($138.25) per person daily. The hotel is open from December to October.

There are dozens of sports facilities, including a sauna with a built-in TV, four outdoor tennis courts, a golf course, indoor and outdoor swimming pools, and a fitness course. The hotel has a handful of bars and an à la carte restaurant. The quays on the premises shelter a small flotilla of motorboats, which go to and from Klagenfurt in three to five minutes.

Seehotel Werzer-Astoria, A-9210 Pörtschach (tel. 04272/2231), is a resort hotel scattering into several buildings of varying ages. One of the most unusual is the 19th-century bathhouse, which extends into the lake, crowned with a latticed tower. On a peninsula jutting out into the lake, the hotel offers big lawns, a private beach, an indoor swimming pool, sauna and massage facilities, a host of boat-oriented water sports, and 11 outdoor tennis courts. The spacious public rooms have big windows and lots of sunlight, and include a wine tavern, a lake-view restaurant, and a terrace with waiter service. Management plays host at Carinthian buffets and dinner dances. The comforts, amenities, and furnishings of the 132 rooms—all with private baths or showers—are worthy of their four-star rating. With half board included, rates range from 1,040 AS ($75.50) to 1,530 AS ($111.25) per person daily. Guests are welcomed only from May to October.

Hotel Rainer, A-9210 Pörtschach (tel. 04272/2300), is scattered among four houses set at the edge of the lake. The older buildings have lots of architectural embellishments—including towers, gables, and porches—from the 19th century. Set on a big, well-maintained lawn, the houses look out over the hotel piers and the private beaches. On the premises are two outdoor tennis courts, water sports facilities (often with instruction), and a range of accommodating public rooms. From April to October, the hotel rents only 32 rooms, each with private bath or shower. Accommodations are tastefully furnished and comfortable, and half board ranges from 1,210 AS ($88) to 2,640 AS ($192) per person daily.

You'll walk through a black entryway before reaching the Lucullus restaurant, which might be the main reason for staying here. The walls are ornamented with dozens of such elegant knickknacks as antique keys and hand-hammered pieces of ironwork. Your meal might include salmon, mussel soup, fresh shrimp, and kiwi sherbet. Fixed-price meals cost from 455 AS ($30). The Lucullus is open from 6:30 to 11pm; closed Sunday and Monday. Barbara and Gerhard Rainer are the diligent owners.

Gasthof Joainig, Kochwirtplatz 4, A-9210 Pörtschach (tel. 04272/2319), is a graceful country house with a hipped and gabled roof, louvered wooden shutters, and masses of summer flowers in boxes. On the premises is a big sun terrace, while the interior contains a collection of wooden furniture and a large bar/café/pastry shop. The 31 smallish bedrooms—26 of which contain private baths or showers—are trimmed with wood and are comfortable. Rooms cost 375 AS ($27.25) to 410 AS ($29.75) per person daily for half board.

Where to Dine

Rainer's, Monte-Carlo-Platz 1 (tel. 04272/3046), is one of the premier dining rooms of the resort. Its immaculately appointed tables provide the right setting for the refined cooking. Rainer Husar, the owner, might tempt you with a Bellini to get things going. As you sip your drink, you can peruse the short and chic menu. It is very much a cuisine de marché place—that is, the ingredients were purchased that day at the food market—and there are no particular specialties. For his inspiration, the chef roams the world. You might try, for example, such dishes as baby onions with mushrooms in a cheese gratinée, or else calves' liver with a smooth herbal sauce, or one of several varieties of seafood. The place is open only six months of the year, from spring to autumn. À la carte meals cost 200 AS ($14.50) to 400 AS ($29), and service is daily from noon to 2:30pm and 6:30 to 9:30pm.

VELDEN

Considered the most sophisticated resort in Carinthia, at the western end of the Wörther See, Velden is called the heart of the Austrian Riviera. The resort has many beautiful parks sweeping down to the lakeside, and from most of the hotel bedrooms you'll have views of the sparkling blue lake with the peaks of Karawanken in the background, marking the Yugoslav and Italian borders.

Naturally, the big attraction here is water sports, ranging from bathing in the warm alpine lake to waterskiing and -surfing. Instruction is available in water activities. The long swimming season begins the first of May and continues until the end of October. Many of the resort hotels have tennis courts, and you can also play golf at an 18-hole course 4 miles from Velden in a beautifully hilly landscape.

Most guests spend their days bathing in the lake and later enjoy dancing. Five o'clock tea dances are popular, and you can also trip the light fantastic to the music of orchestras on lake terraces. Summer festivals are often staged in Velden, and balls and beauty contests keep the patrons of the resort amused. Also, this is a fine center for motoring, with good roads taking you on many scenic routes.

In 1950, the **Casino Velden** (tel. 04274/2064) opened and has since then become the most popular attraction in town. It is open daily year round from 7pm to 2am, offering blackjack, baccarat, stud poker, American and French roulette, as well as slot machines.

Food and Lodging

Parkhotel das Parks, Seecorso 68, A-9220 Velden (tel. 04274/2298-0). You'll find this comfortable 93-room hotel uphill from the center of town, commanding an impressive view into the valley below. The renovated interior contains cozy niches to relax in, along with tastefully appointed bedrooms filled with the modern conveniences. In summer, prices are 1,100 AS ($80) to 1,900 AS ($138.25) per person daily for half board. Winter rates for half board are 740 AS ($53.75) to 1,550 AS ($112.75) per person daily.

The heart and soul of the place lie within the well-recommended restaurant, which is open to nonresidents who make a reservation. A verdant terrace opens through glass doors in warm weather. Chef Hans Senekowitsch concocts a sophisticated array of frequently changing specialties, which might include a mousse of smoked trout with caviar in a champagne-flavored gelatin, river crayfish in a dill-flavored yogurt, a strudel of calves' brains with baby spinach and a mushroom ragoût, cabbage with a truffled cream sauce, and a suprême of freshwater char with tarragon and fresh asparagus. Full meals begin at 300 AS ($21.75) but could go much higher. The hotel has a special winter-sports program that includes skiing, sleighing, ice skating, and ski sailing.

Hotel Schloss Velden, A-9220 Velden (tel. 04274/2655), was built as a home for one of the local aristocrats in 1603. The owner, of course, is long dead, but the ornate towers at each of the building's four corners and the neoclassical extension stretching toward the lake are still painted an ochre yellow and look much the way he built them originally. A Renaissance archway capped with no fewer than three obelisks flanks the entrance to the gardens, while a long L-shaped extension with steeply pitched roofs sweeps off to one side.

On the premises is a modern annex connected to the main building, built roughly in the same style (although vastly simplified), as well as outdoor tennis courts, a musical bar with live music, an elegant red-walled restaurant, a cozy weinstube, and several terraces, some of them with outdoor bars. Water sports are available at the lakeside. The 100 well-furnished bedrooms are equipped with private bathrooms and modern comforts, while the public rooms are filled with luxurious old furniture and elegant accessories. Prices are 770 AS ($56) to 1,150 AS ($83.50) per person daily for a bed and full board. The hotel closes for the winter at the end of September, opening again at the beginning of May.

Seehotel Hubertus Hof, A-9220 Velden (tel. 04274/2676), is a symmetrically designed three-story house with a dignified, restrained façade that emphasizes the curved wrought-iron balconies and its hipped roof. The dignified interior contains comfortable furniture and lots of cozy niches. An equally pleasant second building in the gardens accommodates the overflow from the lakeside house and also contains a café and a big sun terrace. On the premises are a swimming beach, a restaurant, an array of sporting activities, and a small library. From May to October, the hotel rents 48 well-furnished rooms with private baths or showers. Half-board charges range from 810 AS ($59) to 980 AS ($71.25) per person daily. Some rooms have their own balconies. The hotel has a health club with a covered pool, a hot whirlpool, a sauna, a Turkish steambath, and a solarium. The hosts are the Kenney family.

Seehotel Europa, A-9220 Velden (tel. 04274/2770), is a white-walled hotel built in a contemporary format in a tree-dotted area at the edge of the lake. Its pier area contains facilities for water sports, plus a private bar. The nearby tennis courts are floodlit at night for round-the-clock play. On the premises are a dancing bar, a big sun terrace covered by an awning, and a modern dining room with angular chairs. A comfortable annex nearby holds the overflow from the main hotel. The May-to-September hotel earns four stars for the quality of its well-maintained bedrooms, 75 in all, each with private bath or shower. The food is good and generous of portion, so most guests opt for half-board rates, ranging from 900 AS ($65.50) to 1,080 AS ($78.50) per person daily.

Hotel Alte Post-Wrann, A-9220 Velden (tel. 04274/2141). This hotel is partially concealed behind well-positioned plantings in the center of town, close to the casino. Its façade is pierced by stone-trimmed arched windows leading into the bedrooms. A private beach maintained by the hotel is a two-minute walk from the front door. On the premises you'll find a rustic wine tavern called the Reblaus, whose outdoor entrance is marked by massive beams that probably came from a wine press. There's also a paneled restaurant furnished with hunting trophies, a ceramic tile stove, and chandeliers fashioned from deer antlers. Atypically, the hotel is open all year; most other places in the area close for the winter. It rents 39 comfortable bedrooms (each with private bath or shower) at half-board rates ranging from 565 AS ($41) to 665 AS ($48.25) per person daily.

The entrance to the hotel's Wrann restaurant (same phone) is also marked by those massive beams. In summertime it's located in a garden. There, under a canopy of trees, you can order schnitzels, veal in cream sauce, and a range of traditional Austrian and regional recipes, many of them served with homemade spätzle. Open all year, the restaurant suggests that reservations be made.

MARIA WÖRTH

Part of this village, on the southern side of the lake across from Pörtschach, juts out into the Wörther See on a rocky peninsula, providing a good view of the surroundings. From Maria Wörth you can patronize the golf courses in the nearby hamlet of Dellach.

The village's pfarrkirche (parish church) is Gothic with a baroque interior and, to confuse its styles even more, a Romanesque crypt. It's noted for its main altar, dating from the 15th century. The circular karner (charnel house) in the yard, with a round tower, was built in 1278. The church is a pilgrimage sanctuary.

Nearby is another noted church, the Rosenkranzkirche, from the 12th century, often referred to as "the winter church." It has some 11th-century Romanesque frescoes of the apostles.

Food and Lodging

Hotel Astoria, A-9082 Maria Wörth (tel. 04273/2279), is an attractively designed hotel built in several interconnected sections with a pointed tower jutting upward from the center. It sits at the neck of a peninsula extending into the lake, with its own marina and bathing beach as well as two big piers, one of which is covered with deck chairs. The elegant public rooms have lots of sunny space and a scattering of Oriental rugs. On the premises are an indoor pool, a sauna, a masseur, a garage, a bierstube, and two restaurants. Bedrooms are pleasantly furnished and comfortable, each with private bath or shower. From May to September, the 45 rooms rent for ($61.75) to 1,150 AS ($83.50) per person daily, half board included.

Hotel Wörth, A-9082 Maria Wörth (tel. 04273/2276). This balconied chalet sits on a hillside sloping steeply down to the lake. Guests enjoy the sun terrace, the rustically beamed dining and sitting rooms, and the 34 attractively streamlined bedrooms, many of which provide private balconies and a view of the village church a short distance away across the blue waters of a small inlet. The hotel has an attractive beach area and a convenient location in the center. Rates range from 720 AS ($52.25) to 1,010 AS ($73.50) per person daily. Open May to September.

Strandhotel Harrich, A-9082 Maria Wörth (tel. 04273/2228), is a lakeside hotel whose wood-trimmed balconies stretch across a generous expanse of shoreline. The building sits amid a well-planned garden, with an abstractly shaped sun terrace cantilevered above the slope of the hillside. There's also a lakeside grassy area with a scattering of deck chairs. On the premises are an indoor pool, a sauna, a fitness room—and conscientious management. The well-furnished accommodations include apartments and bungalows. From April to October, the hotel rents 35 bedrooms, each with private bath or shower. Half board costs 600 AS ($43.50) to 800 AS ($58.25) per person daily.

---

3. Lake Ossiacher

For the next journey, we'll head west from Klagenfurt, passing through Moosberg and going on to Feldkirchen. Before long I'll introduce you to Lake Ossiacher (Ossiacher See, in German), third-largest lake in the province, some 7 miles long. Its water temperature in summer is only minutely cooler than that of Lake Wörther—a comfortable 79° Fahrenheit.

The lake is ringed with little villages that have been turned into resorts attracting summer visitors, mainly Austrians, who come here to bathe and enjoy water sports.

FELDKIRCHEN

Our first stopover, Feldkirchen, is an old town that was once the property of the Bamberg bishops. At a major crossroads, Feldkirchen grew and prospered from traders passing through the area. (It is not to be confused with Feldkirch in Vorarlberg.)

Segments of the Middle Ages live on in Feldkirchen, especially in its patrician houses and narrow streets. Visit the old quarter to see the Biedermeier façades added in the first part of the 19th century. The village has a pfarrkirche (parish church) in the Romanesque style but with a Gothic choir. If you go inside you'll be rewarded by a look at some frescoes from the 13th century.

In the vicinity of the town are some small lakes worth a visit if time permits.

Food and Lodging

Hotel Rainer, Eppensteinerstrasse 1, A-9560 Feldkirchen (tel. 04276/2097), is an imaginatively designed modern hotel with a flat roof, lots of exposed wood, and a pleasingly geometric format that looks almost Bauhaus. A 36-bed establishment, it offers comfortably furnished rooms filled with streamlined furniture. Guests book in here in summer on half-board terms, paying 410 AS ($29.75) to 420 AS ($30.50) per person daily. On the premises are a big sun terrace and a hospitable dining room, serving generous and good meals.

OSSIACH

This resort on the south side of the lake is small (pop. 650) but it's still the biggest settlement on the Ossiacher See. It has a Benedictine abbey originally built in the 11th century but reconstructed in the 1500s. The monastery was dissolved a century or so ago. Now special events of the Carinthian Summer Festival take place here. On several occasions Leonard Bernstein conducted the orchestra.

SATTENDORF/TREFFEN

On the north shore of the lake, Sattendorf and Treffen, summer and winter resorts, are equipped to receive guests. In summer you can breathe the pure mountain air and wander across alpine meadows and deep into the forest. There's bathing both in indoor pools and in Lake Ossiacher.

From the lake you can go on several easy excursions, including one on the Kanzelbahn cable car, 10 minutes away, and a 20-minute run by car to either Italy or Yugoslavia (if you have a visa). You can also make day shopping trips to either Klagenfurt, already visited, or Villach (see below).

Food and Lodging

Hotel Alpenrose, A-9520 Sattendorf (tel. 04248/2220), is a balconied 29-room chalet partially surrounded by a raised sun terrace dotted with summertime parasols. Built into a hillside, the hotel has two levels of big-windowed public rooms facing guests as they approach the downhill side. The warmly tinted interior has exposed wood and comfortable lounge chairs. On the premises are an indoor pool, a sauna, a restaurant, a dance bar, and several open fireplaces set into attractively textured masonry walls. Guests book in here on the half-board plan, paying 510 AS ($37) to 550 AS ($40) per person daily. The food tends to be excellent, and you can enjoy it from December to March and June to September.

ANNENHEIM

This little lakeside resort is on the north side of Ossiacher See, near the end of the lake. From here a cable car, the Kanzelbahn, will take you to Kanzelhöhe at 4,880 feet. There, an observatory tower offers a panoramic view of the surrounding country.

4. Villach

In the center of the Carinthian lake district, Villach is the gateway to the south. If you get bored, you can always drive over into Yugoslavia (visa required) or Italy for the day. Or if you're heading south already, this would make a good stopover.

An industrial town, Villach, the second-largest town in Carinthia, lies in a broad basin on the Drau River. There was a settlement here in Roman times, and later Villach was the property of the bishops of Bamberg, a distant see near Nürnberg, Germany, from the 11th century until Maria Theresa acquired it for the Habsburgs.

At the center of the **Altstadt** is the Hauptplatz (main square), at the north end of which is a bridge over the Drau. On the southern part is a **pfarrkirche** (parish church) dedicated to St. Jacob. It has three aisles and a mixture of styles, with a baroque altar and Gothic choir stalls. Like most towns of its size, Villach has a **Trinity Column** dating from 1739, commemorating deliverance from the plague.

Theoprastus Bombastus von Hohenheim, Swiss-born chemist and physician better known as Paracelsus, lived here as a youth while his father practiced medicine.

From the heart of the old town it's a 2½-mile drive to **Warmbad-Villach,** known for its thermal swimming pools and mineral springs. This spa, on the southern fringe of Villach, whose waters are said to counteract the aging process, is the only such place where visitors can swim at the source of thermal waters.

In the **Schillerpark,** on Peraustrasse in Villach, you can see a large panoramic relief of the province, which might be helpful before you set out on a tour. It is called *Relief von Kärnten.* You can see the relief from the first of May to the end of October (except Friday, Sunday, and holidays) from 10am to 4:30pm.

Villach is a good center from which to explore the Carinthian lake district, including the Villacher Alpe, an 11-mile journey via a toll road. There are panoramic views in many directions, the best spots for viewing being marked.

At the end of the road it's possible to travel up to the summit of **Dobratsch** (7,100 feet), going partway by chair lift and then by foot. This is one of the most famous views in Austria. Allow about 2¾ hours for this excursion.

WHERE TO STAY

Rich in Carinthian history, the **Romantik Hotel Post,** Hauptplatz 26, A-9500 Villach (tel. 04242/26101), was built in 1500, incorporating many of the rich vaulted ceilings that you'll still see today. The façade is a Teutonic fantasy of carved stone detailing, Ionic columns, and intricately patterned wrought iron. Between 1548 and 1629 this was the town palace of one of the richest families in Carinthia. During that period the building hosted an emperor, a king, an archduke, and later an empress (Maria Theresa). Later still, the nephew of Napoleon I dropped in and signed a registration slip that still belongs to the hotel. On the premises of this historic place are a baronial fireplace, plus an arcaded courtyard shielded from the sun with an ancient collection of chestnut trees, and a host of elegantly furnished bedrooms. Each of these 76 rooms has a private bath or shower, and half-board rates range from 790 AS ($57.50) to 890 AS ($64.75) per person daily.

The establishment pays special attention to its cuisine, much of which is heavily laced with cheese, butter, and cream, following recipes similar to those used in aristocratic homes 200 years ago. These include tafelspitz, schnitzels (sometimes stuffed with cheese and ham), and recipes made from local venison, including soups, pâtés, and stews. Set menus range from 95 AS ($7) to 300 AS ($21.75), with à la carte dinners costing 150 AS ($11) to 450 AS ($32.75).

Hotel Europa, Bahnhofstrasse 10, A-9500 Villach (tel. 04242/26766), is an elegantly detailed corner building in the center of town. The three-story hotel is painted a pale yellow and is accented with white trim and restrained neoclassical detailing. The renovated interior boasts conservative furniture and pleasing tones of grays, reds, and browns. A Viennese-style coffeehouse is on the premises. Forty-four comfortably furnished rooms are rented, each with private bath or shower. Singles range from 570 AS ($41.50) to 690 AS ($50.25) daily, and doubles cost 840 AS ($61) to 990 AS ($72).

Hotel Ebner, Heiligengeist, A-9500 Villach (tel. 04242/23910). Many of this establishment's residents return year after year for the bucolic relaxation that this large house offers. Outfitted in Carinthian style, the place is a few steps from the many footpaths that wind through the nearby forests. There's a swimming pool and a thermally heated spa on the premises, along with comfortable bedrooms. Fifty rooms are rented in all, each with private bath or shower. Rates range from 370 AS ($27) to 440 AS ($32) per person daily, including a buffet breakfast. Guests are received from December to October. Much of the allure, however, derives from the excellent dining room. Many of the dishes are worth the special trip there, including rack of baby lamb, sweetbreads, several kinds of hearty soup, crisply fresh salads, and temptingly caloric desserts.

WHERE TO DINE

Some of the best food in Villach is at the previously recommended Romantik Hotel Post (see above). However, if you like nonhotel dining rooms, try one of the following independent selections.

Koglers Vorspann, Zauchen 16 (tel. 04242/2062), is run by the Kogler family, who offer some of the best food in town. Since Villach is relatively close to international borders, the cooking reflects the influence of not only Austria but also Italy and Slovenia (in Yugoslavia). One Slovakian specialty is pleskavica, actually a fine cut of garlic-studded roast with a cream-and-chive sauce. Dessert might consist of homemade ice cream with fresh figs and a Cointreau sauce, among numerous other choices. À la carte meals cost 100 AS ($7.25) to 275 AS ($20), and service is daily from noon to 2pm and 7 to 9:30pm. The porcelain used at the table might remind you of southern Europe, especially Italy, and the wine cellar is very sophisticated, especially rich in rare Austrian vintages. Reservations are necessary.

Rob Roy, Ossiacher Zeile 46 (tel. 04242/23634). The décor might be British and the list of carafe wine unpretentiously French, but the menu is pure steakhouse. There are many different variations of meat served here, and portions are so generous that you may want to pass over the relatively standardized appetizers. There is also a succulent version of pork in the style of Provence. The traditional dessert is apple pie. Meals are served daily from noon to 2pm and 7 to 9:30pm, costing 150 AS ($11) to 325 AS ($23.75).

FOOD AND LODGING AT WARMBAD-VILLACH

Standing in a large natural park, **Der Karawankenhof,** Kadischenallee 25-27, A-9504 Warmbad-Villach (tel. 04242/25503), is a large modern hotel with a battery of health and spa facilities (it is connected to the latter by an underground passage). The "bath world," as they call it here, consists of whirlpools, indoor and outdoor swimming pools, a fitness center, a gym, a sauna, massage, and other facilities. This four-star hotel rents 80 well-furnished bedrooms, each with private bath or shower. Half-board charges range from 740 AS ($53.75) to 1,000 AS ($72.75) per person daily. The place, open all year, offers an excellent cuisine. Diets are also catered to.

Josefinenhof Hotel, A-9504 Warmbad-Villach (tel. 04242/25531), is a first-class spa, fitness, and conference hotel with evenly spaced rows of big windows and balconies. A sun terrace stretches toward the well-maintained private park area, while a comfortable collection of public rooms offers warmly tinted resting places. This four-star hotel rents 61 comfortably furnished bedrooms. Singles range from 520 AS ($37.75) to 930 AS ($67.50) daily, while doubles cost 610 AS ($44.25) to 1,050 AS ($76.25) per person, with full board included. On the premises are an indoor pool, a bar, an à la carte restaurant, and a host of health and medical services, including facilities for hydrotherapy and a beauty center.

Warmbaderhof, A-9504 Warmbad-Villach (tel. 04242/255010), is a large and elegant hotel closely linked to the town's cure facilities. On the premises is a heated pool with a ceiling shaped like a continuous barrel vault (covered with wood strips) and an abstract mural at the far end. The gardens are visible from the streamlined balconies leading into the comfortable, well-furnished rooms. An angular outdoor pool connects with the waters of the indoor pool. A wide range of sporting activities, many of them organized, are close at hand, including tennis, horseback riding, and walking tours. The management sometimes has evening dances on the big sun terrace. Two restaurants on the premises serve well-prepared food. Each of the 128 rooms has a private bath or shower. Half board costs 750 AS ($54.50) to 1,800 AS ($130.75) per person daily.

LAKE FAAKER

If you're in Villach in summer, you may want to drive over to Lake Faaker (Faaker See, in German), a small body of water that is nonetheless popular with swimmers and devotees of sports such as waterskiing. This is quite a warm lake, with warm temperatures in July and August reaching 79° Fahrenheit.

If you'd like to stay at the lake, you'll find—

Food and Lodging at Faak am See

Inselhotel, A-9583 Faak am See (tel. 04254/2145), is a summertime hotel at the edge of the lake. Its attractive façade has evenly spaced rows of recessed balconies, masses of flowers, and oversize windows. The décor is tastefully contemporary, with stone-flanked open fireplaces, accents of wrought iron, a restaurant serving well-prepared food, and a bar. The hotel is set on an island in the middle of the lake. A motorboat will pick you up at the mainland pier and redeposit you if you want a break on shore. Closed from the end of September until the third week of May, the hotel rents 80 beds. Charges range from 500 AS ($36.25) daily for a single to 2,200 AS ($160) for two persons in a double. You can also take meals here, with set menus costing 140 AS ($10.25) to 300 AS ($21.75).

Da Luciano, Kopeiner Strasse 9, Ledenitzen (tel. 04254/3122), serves some of the finest food along the lake. Specializing in Italian dishes, it offers a popular summer terrace beside the woods where guests can not only enjoy the food but the air. Menu items include minestrone, an array of pasta dishes, and a savory veal schnitzel in Madeira sauce. You can also try the grilled lobster, which goes well with the crispy array of salads. Desserts might be marinated in Grand Marnier. À la carte meals range from 150 AS ($11) to 400 AS ($29). Service is daily from noon to 3pm and 6pm to midnight.

---

5. Spittal an der Drau

Lying west of Lake Millstatter, Spittal, like Friesach in the east, is another "gateway" to Carinthia. It is not to be confused with Spital in Tyrol or Spital am Pyhrn in Upper Austria. This city on the Drau River is one of the leading centers of Upper Carinthia. It's at the foot of the Goldeck, which rises more than 7,000 feet and is reached by cableway.

THE SIGHTS

Spittal is noted for the **Porcia Schloss,** really an Italian palazzo rather than an Austrian castle. It sits next to a park. It was constructed between 1533 and 1597 and is considered the most impressive Italian Renaissance building in the country. Its most striking architectural feature is the courtyard designed in the Italianate style with three-story galleries enclosing three sides.

The **Bezirksheimatmuseum** (regional museum) is on the second floor of the castle. Exhibited here are artifacts of the Drau region, local handcrafts, and regional costumes. It is open mid-May until the end of September from 9am to 6pm, charging an admission of 30 AS ($2.20). It is also open in October from 1 to 4pm.

In the environs, you can visit Teurnia-Ausgrabungen, the **excavations at Teurnia,** 3 miles northwest of Spittal at the village of St. Peter im Holz. The village grew up on the site of a Celtic settlement and, later, Romans lived here, as evidenced by excavation of a forum and a bishop's palace destroyed by the Slavs in the 7th century.

A museum here displays artifacts dug up right before World War I, from the cemetery of a 5th-century church, including mosaics bearing early Christian symbols. The museum is open May to October daily from 9am to noon and 1 to 5pm. Admission is 15 AS ($1.10).

FOOD AND LODGING

Hotel Ertl, Bahnhofstrasse, A-9800 Spittal an der Drau (tel. 04762/2048), is designed in a long, three-story format of cream-colored stucco with detailed trim around the windows. The hotel sits almost on the street, although there's a garden with a sun terrace stretching off to the back, as well as a few café tables set up on the side. The dining room inside is attractively set up with coffered ceilings and brass chandeliers, while the 40 warmly tinted bedrooms (each with private bath or shower) are cozy and appealing. From December to October, the hotel charges guests per-person rates that range from 460 AS ($33.50) to 540 AS ($39.25) daily, including half board. An outdoor pool is on the grounds.

Hotel Alte Post, Hauptplatz 13, A-9800 Spittal an der Drau (tel. 04762/22170), is a traditionally decorated hotel with a streamlined collection of furniture. In the center of town, the 83-bed hotel has rooms that are comfortably furnished and spacious, and charges 520 AS ($37.75) to 585 AS ($42.50) per person daily for half board.

---

6. Lake Millstätter

The second-largest lake in the province, the blue Millstätter See to the east of Spittal is 8 miles long, 1 mile wide, and 460 feet deep. This beautiful lake is set against a backdrop of the forested Seerücken (2,840 feet) to the south and Nockberge to the north. Reflected in the lake are the peaks of the Reisseck and Kreuzeck in the far distance.

MILLSTATT AM SEE

Lying about midway along the northern rim of the lake, Millstatt rivals Seeboden as the principal Lake Millstätter resort.

The average hotel here is open only during the warm months. The highest prices are charged in July and August, when reservations are mandatory at this popular resort. Prices are often reduced in late spring and early autumn, and it's usually easy to find a room at those times. An organ music festival is held here in August.

Millstatt's main sight, other than the lakeside location, is the **Stift** (abbey), founded in 1080 as a Benedictine monastery but taken over by the Jesuits near the end of the 16th century. One part of its buildings has been used as a hotel since 1773—Hotel Lindenhof, once the mansion of the Grand Master of the Knights of St. George.

In the abbey courtyard stands a 1,000-year-old "Judgment" lime tree. The cloister, which has Gothic vaulting and Romanesque arches, is reached from the east side of the court. The abbey contains a fresco of the Last Judgment, considered a masterpiece of Austrian Renaissance art. The abbey church (Stiftskirche) has a Romanesque doorway that is the major architectural attraction of the complex.

Food and Lodging

Hotel am See Die Forelle, A-9872 Millstatt am See (tel. 04766/2050), is an attractive yellow hotel with a façade that includes clean lines and black shutters. The lakeside terrace is sheltered with chestnut trees, while the interior contains bright, light-colored rooms, attractively uncluttered public areas, a bar, and a sunny restaurant. The conservatively furnished bedrooms are filled with tasteful objects and comfortable furniture. On the premises is an outdoor pool plus a big, well-maintained lawn area. The Aniwanter family are the owners of this streamlined hotel. They rent 115 beds, charging from 850 AS ($61.75) to 1,300 AS ($94.50) per person daily, with half board included. Guests are accepted from May to October. The hotel is also known for its excellent cuisine, with set menus ranging from 180 AS ($13) to 400 AS ($29).

Hotel Post, A-9872 Millstatt am See (tel. 04766/2108), constructed around 1900, looks much older. Designed like a baroque country villa, it has ochre walls, dark-green shutters, and neoclassical trim around the windows. The interior is a mixture of Victorian and contemporary furniture. There's an open fireplace plus a restaurant with well-polished knotty-pine paneling and massive chandeliers. The renovated bedrooms are comfortable. New rooms, built in 1985, offer much comfort and have private bathrooms, phones, radios, and balconies facing either south or west. In each of the south-facing rooms, there is a separate recess to sleep one or two children, as well as a stove and a refrigerator. Half board for the 37 rooms costs 580 AS ($42.25) to 880 AS ($64) per person daily. Open from May to October.

The owners of the Post, the Sichrowsky family, also have the **Hotel Postillion,** Am See, A-9872 Millstatt am See (tel. 04766/2552), with a large lawn near the lake reserved for guests of both hotels. If you prefer, you can arrange for full board at either of the hotels or simply for bed-and-breakfast. From April to October, the Postillion rents 22 attractively furnished bedrooms, each with private bath or shower. Charges for half board range from 720 AS ($52.25) to 830 AS ($60.25) per person daily. The Postillion is one of the most tranquil and scenically located hotels in town.

Hotel Alpenrose, Obermillstatt, A-9872 Millstatt am See (tel. 04766/2500), enjoying a splendid scenic setting with a view of the valley and mountains, lies 1½ miles from the center of Millstatt, in the tiny alpine village of Obermillstatt, a few paces from the village church. It is the first "bio-hotel" to open in Austria. The Theuermann family are involved in holistic medicine, macrobiotic diets, and yoga. They also run a good hotel and restaurant in a chalet-inspired building that contains 30 well-furnished bedrooms, each with private bath and balcony. In winter, per-person rates, with a vegetarian half board included, cost from 750 AS ($54.50) daily. In summer the same half-board charges rise to 800 AS ($58.25) to 950 AS ($69) daily. One free massage is included. On the premises is a heated swimming pool, as well as a sauna and an array of carefully monitored new-age programs, including yoga lessons and bio-training in the care of both the body and soul.

Hotel Gasthof Seewirt, A-9872 Millstatt am See (tel. 04766/2110), is a modern four-star hotel with recessed balconies, big windows, and an asymmetrical design. The sunny interior, rustically up-to-date, includes a restaurant. The 30 bedrooms, with many comforts that include private baths or showers, are among the finest at the resort, especially those with a view. Half board costs 570 AS ($41.50) to 700 AS ($51) per person daily. Open from December to October.

Gartenhotel Silberhof, A-9872 Millstatt am See (tel. 04766/2171), is an elegant 19th-century house with dozens of interesting architectural details, including a vertical row of bay windows and half-timbering across the upper floors. The renovated interior is graced with large picture windows that offer a view of the nearby village and the lake. Set a short distance above Millstatt, the hotel is managed and directed by the conscientious Josef K. Silbernagl. He rents 40 bedrooms, charging from 440 AS ($32) per person daily for half board.

SEEBODEN

Many prominent Austrian families have summer villas at this resort on the western side of Millstätter See, using it the way some French families do the Côte d'Azur. Seeboden is quite popular in summer with water-sports enthusiasts who enjoy skiing and boating on the lake.

The major excursion to take from here is along a narrow road for about 6 miles to the Hansbaueralm at 5,635 feet. This is the lower station from which a cable car will take you to the Tschiernock mountain (6,850 feet).

Food and Lodging

Sporthotel Royal Seehof, A-9871 Seeboden (tel. 04762/81714), is composed of two modern buildings set in a grassy park at the edge of the lake. A few steps away, guests enjoy access to six outdoor tennis courts, a sandy beach area, a glass-walled indoor pool that looks somewhat like a big greenhouse, and three indoor tennis courts, each with a sliding roof for ventilation on hot days. The well-furnished interior contains a bar and a restaurant. The Santner family are your hosts, renting 67 well-furnished bedrooms, each with private bath or shower. Half board costs 780 AS ($56.75) to 1,080 AS ($78.50) per person daily. The hotel is open from May to September.

Strandhotel Koller, A-9871 Seeboden (tel. 04762/81245), is a lakefront hotel constructed in two interconnected sections on a well-maintained lawn. Many of the 48 comfortable rooms (each with private bath or shower) have balconies looking over the water, and within view of the old-fashioned cabaña and bathing pier. The woodsy interior has plenty of rustic accents, including open fireplaces, comfortable furniture, and a combination of warm colors. On the premises are a big-windowed restaurant, an indoor pool, a sauna, a large garden, a sunny terrace, and a café/weinstube. A range of sporting facilities is within walking distance. The hotel is open only from Easter until mid-October. Half board costs 590 AS ($43) to 680 AS ($49.50) per person daily. You can enjoy buffet breakfasts, candlelit dinners, and grill parties.

Hotel Pension Klein, A-9871 Seeboden (tel. 04762/81218), is a modern chalet construction with a few regional designs painted across its wood-trimmed, big-windowed façade. Set on a grassy lawn, the hotel offers 29 bedrooms, each with private bath or shower. Guests are accepted from December to February and April to September, and are charged 550 AS ($40) to 580 AS ($42.25) per person daily for half board. Rooms are clean and comfortable.

GMÜND

This small town is in the lower region of the Lieser Valley, at the start of the Malta Valley. It's not on the lake but lies northwest of Seeboden on the road to Salzburg, an easy commute to the Millstätter See. Austrians use it as headquarters for exploring the Nock sector of Carinthia, which lies to the southeast of the town and is visited by mountain climbers in summer and skiers in winter.

The **Altstadt** (Old Town) of Gmünd still has defensive walls pierced by gates erected in the 16th century. Its Old Castle from the 15th century is now mainly in ruins.

A popular excursion from Gmünd is through the **Malta Valley,** taking a toll road beginning to the northwest of the town. This is one of the most enchanting valleys in the country and considered the loveliest in Carinthia. The scenery consists of waterfalls and newly developed artificial lakes along with a nature reserve.

Food and Lodging

Gasthof Kohlmayr, Hauptplatz 7, A-9853 Gmünd (tel. 04732/2149), presents a light-brown façade with restrained white trim to the main square of town. The décor inside is conservative and pleasant, with lots of rustic accessories, occasional antiques, and exposed wood. Rooms are traditional in style, well maintained, and with cozy Carinthian comfort. Twenty-two bedrooms are rented, with private baths or showers, costing 330 AS ($24) to 350 AS ($25.50) per person daily for half board.

Pension Platzer, Vorstadt 26, A-9853 Gmünd (tel. 04732/2745), is a low-lying hotel set at the edge of a small freshwater lake. A garden with well-maintained roses stretches off to the back, while the interior is pleasantly decorated with lots of exposed wood, coffered ceilings, and conservative furniture. Eighteen comfortably furnished bedrooms have private baths or showers. Half board ranges from 295 AS ($21.50) to 315 AS ($23) per person daily, and guests are accepted from December to January and April to October.

7. Bad Kleinkirchheim

A 7-mile drive to the east of Lake Millstätter takes you to Bad Kleinkirchheim, once just a popular summer spa but now a thriving winter ski area as well. Since World War II this resort in the Carinthian Nock mountains has become a mecca for skiers of the not-too-demanding variety. It's about fourth in popularity among Austrian ski resorts, with Tyrol, Land Salzburg, and Vorarlberg centers in the lead. Its winter season is also shorter than those of loftier alpine areas.

Cross-country skiing and winter hiking are popular here, with long runs and even gradients. The Kaiserburg gondola takes skiers to the upper station at 6,250 feet. The satellite resort of St. Oswald, 2½ miles north of the spa, has some good hotels.

Visit the hot springs of Bad Kleinkirchheim, Katharinenquelle, and the pilgrimage church of St. Katharina, which is known for its carvings.

FOOD AND LODGING

Built in 1908 as an elegant way station for clients who came for the cure at the adjacent spa, **Thermenhotel Das Ronacher,** A-9546 Bad Kleinkirchheim (tel. 04240/282), offers a thermal indoor swimming pool, a log-cabin sauna, many physical therapy techniques, a Carinthian thermal garden, a first-class restaurant, a café, and 92 comfortable bedrooms. The interior is luxuriously furnished with pine paneling, ceramic stoves, and open fireplaces, along with comfortably rustic furniture. The bar area affords a rendezvous point, while frequent buffets provide a lavish spread of delicacies. Helga and Günther Ronacher do everything they can to provide a restful environment for their guests. A range of both organized and freely scheduled sporting events is available. Rates, with full board included, range from 765 AS ($55.50) to 1,220 AS ($88.75) per person daily for a double and 825 AS ($60) to 1,200 AS ($87.25) for a single. Prices vary with the season and room assignment.

Hotel Römerbad, A-9546 Bad Kleinkirchheim (tel. 04240/8234), is a well-designed chalet with prominent balconies and attractive contrasts of light and dark detailing. The interior reflects its forested hillside location. It has an open fireplace, wrought-iron appointments, lots of exposed wood, a convivial bar, and big panoramic windows looking out over the forest. A range of sporting facilities is within easy walking distance of this hotel, which is efficiently directed by its owner, Ingrid Putz. She offers 32 well-furnished bedrooms, each with private bath or shower, and keeps her place open from December to October. Half board costs 740 AS ($53.75) to 1,120 AS ($81.50) per person daily.

The dining room here is considered one of the best in town. The cuisine specializes in recipes based on fresh ingredients, many of which come from the region. A typical meal might include a marinated salad, medallions of venison with green noodles and cabbage, and a honeyed dessert parfait with blackberries. Restaurant patrons who are not guests of the hotel are welcome if they make reservations.

Hotel St. Oswald, A-9546 Bad Kleinkirchheim (tel. 04240/482), is an imaginatively designed alpine chalet with an unusual roofline. The interior is luxuriously furnished with wooden ceilings, a scattering of open fireplaces, antique pewter, hand-painted antiques, and brass chandeliers. On the premises are a sunny indoor swimming pool, an accommodating bar with a hand-painted wooden ceiling, dozens of intimate nooks, and a full range of indoor and outdoor sporting facilities. The owners often stage dances with Carinthian music, as well as activities for children, including painting, handcrafts, and short trips. The hotel offers 23 comfortably furnished bedrooms, each with private bath or shower, from December to March and May to October. Half board costs 560 AS ($40.75) to 680 AS ($49.50) per person daily.

Hotel Pulverer, A-9546 Bad Kleinkirchheim (tel. 04240/288), is a carefully designed collection of several chalet buildings arranged into a hotel and athletic complex near the ski lifts. Guests have a wide choice of elegantly decorated public rooms, some of which have vaulted wood ceilings, big windows, and ceramic tile stoves (the chimney of one of these rises more than two stories under a cathedral ceiling in the reception area). There's also a scattering of open fireplaces, along with cozy dining nooks, alpine style, with hunting trophies and antique art objects. Elegance and comfort, all with a woodsy rusticity, are trademarks here. On the premises are an indoor pool and a range of health and beauty regimes. There's also access to lots of sporting facilities. The hotel rents 69 well-furnished bedrooms and 42 apartments (should you desire lots of space). Rates range from 790 AS ($57.50) to 1,020 AS ($74.25) daily for a single, from 800 AS ($58.25) to 990 AS ($72) per person based on double occupancy. Apartments are more expensive.

Hotel Alte Post, A-9546 Bad Kleinkirchheim (tel. 04240/212). This rambling hotel makes a gentle curve around a manicured lawn with an outdoor pool set at the far end. Nearby are several outdoor tennis courts, while indoor courts are a few steps away. The façade is a fancifully detailed ensemble of blue and white paint around arched entrances and rounded windows. The interior is rustically filled with heavy beams, stippled plaster, and open fireplaces. The bar makes a warmly decorated hideaway, while the dancing bar is a rendezvous point for dozens of vacationers. For the 81 well-maintained, comfortably furnished bedrooms, each with private bath, half-board rates range from 720 AS ($52.25) to 980 AS ($71.25) per person daily. The hotel receives guests from December to March and May to October.

Hotel Kirchheimerhof, A-9546 Bad Kleinkirchheim (tel. 04240/278), is a hillside chalet with recessed lattice-work balconies and a low-lying extension cantilevered above the sloping lawn. The view from the sun terrace takes in most of the village, while on a sunny day you might see farm animals grazing not far from the foundations. On the premises is an indoor pool, plus a dancing bar with a high ceiling, along with a cozy series of public rooms (some with open fireplaces) outfitted with rustic paneling and plenty of well-chosen accessories. The 51 bedrooms are of the same high standard, each well maintained and each with private bath or shower. The Hinteregger family charges 560 AS ($40.75) to 780 AS ($56.75) per person daily for half board. Guests are accepted from December to March and May to October.

Hotel Sonnalm, A-9546 Bad Kleinkirchheim (tel. 04240/507), is a chalet with horizontal lines and regionally inspired painted illustrations bordering the outside of the panoramic windows. The sunny interior, which looks out over lawns, has a beamed and paneled interior with lots of carved detailing. An open fireplace is outlined by a rounded travertine arch and capped by an abstractly shaped plaster dome. The emphasis throughout this hospitable place is on comfort. The 24 spacious bedrooms have both private balconies and private baths or showers. Rates are 640 AS ($46.50) to 840 AS ($61) per person from December to October.

NEARBY RESORTS

From Bad Kleinkirchheim you can either stay at or just visit two satellite resorts in the area.

Feld Am See

This tiny resort lies on the shores of Lake Feld (Feldsee, in German), a diminutive lake that's one of the most idyllically situated in Carinthia.

To reach it, drive east from Döbriach, passing through Radenthein. At that village, turn on a secondary road that will take you to Feld am See, where you can enjoy a lakeside holiday or else explore either Brennsee or Afritzersee, two lakes immediately south of Feldsee. The road skirts the shores of both these little lakes. The area is one of the most charming spots in the province.

FOOD AND LODGING The attractive **Hotel Lindenhof,** A-9544 Feld am See (tel. 04246/2274), belongs to the Nindler family. One of the entrances is below a rectangular plaque set with regional designs in colors of terra-cotta and white, while another is set into an old-fashioned façade with country baroque detailing around the shuttered windows. The interior is warmly outfitted with high ceilings, wrought-iron detailing, and lots of cozy comfort as shown to good advantage in the 27 bedrooms, considered the finest in town. Rates, with half board, are 450 AS ($32.75) to 650 AS ($47.25) per person daily. Prices vary with the season. On the premises is a wood-covered bar area illuminated with forgiving light, as well as a restaurant, massage salon, steambath, and sauna. The establishment is open from December to October.

Turracher Höhe

From Bad Kleinkirchheim, take a road northeast to reach this popular spot at an elevation of 5,785 feet, at the pass leading over the Gurktal alpine range into Carinthia. This is sought out as a ski resort in winter and is much visited in summer for its scenic views. You'll be in the vicinity of two lakes, the Schwarzee (Black Lake) and the Turracher See.

A chair lift will transport you to Kornock (6,560 feet). Mountain climbers are drawn here in summer to scale the peaks in the Nock area. Turracher Höhe is on the border of the province of Styria.

FOOD AND LODGING Barbara and Peter Leeb set the tone of this lakeside **Hotel Hochschober,** A-9565 Turracher Höhe (tel. 04275/8213), where casual clothes are the order of the day, where the sporting facilities include an indoor pool, a sauna, massage, bowling, indoor shooting, and where activities feature musical programs in the music room and a disco in the basement. Three mountain lakes in the immediate vicinity provide destination points if you want to go walking. Built in 1929, the hotel looks like the ideal kind of place for a country vacation. The interior is rustically paneled, containing woodsy accessories and open fireplaces, along with plenty of comfortable lounge areas, a bar, and a supervised children's play area. A wing added in 1986 contains beautifully furnished rooms as well as an outdoor warm-hot whirlpool, saunas, and a Turkish steambath. The warmly decorated restaurant serves good food. A total of 83 bedrooms, most with private baths or showers, are rented from December to April and June to October. The hotel charges 700 AS ($51) to 860 AS ($62.50) per person daily for half board.

---

8. Lake Weissen

The fourth-largest lake in Carinthia, Lake Weissen (Weissensee, in German), is also one of the loveliest. On its shores are a few hamlet-size resorts, and more hotels are being built. The lake's major resort is Techendorf (see below). Neusach is another small holiday village.

Of the major lakes visited so far, the Weissensee, southwest of Spittal an der Drau (see above), is the highest. It's about 7 miles long and rather narrow, about 550 yards across. Its waters are warm in summer, more than 75° Fahrenheit.

It's not possible to drive around Lake Weissen. Visitors usually walk to it, although you could get there by boat.

TECHENDORF

As mentioned above, this is the major resort on Lake Weissen, perched on the northwest shore. A bridge spans the lake from here. If you take the bridge you'll find a chair lift to take you up to the Naggler Alm (4,382 feet), which is gaining popularity as a ski area.

Food and Lodging

Sporthotel Alpenhof, A-9762 Techendorf (tel. 04713/2107), is a contemporary chalet with wood-trimmed balconies and low-lying wings stretching off to one side. Built in 1976, with special emphasis on the view available from the panoramic windows, the hotel exudes a rusticity, with warm colors and exposed wood detailing. An adjoining building houses massage and health facilities, which you may not have time for because of the many sporting possibilities within easy reach. Members of the Zöhrer family maintain 28 bedrooms, each with private bath or shower. They charge 700 AS ($51) to 800 AS ($58.25) per person daily for half board, and keep the hotel open from December to October.

Strandhotel Weissensee, A-9762 Techendorf (tel. 04713/2219), is a lakeside chalet whose wood-and-stucco façade is accented with green shutters, patterned balconies, and masses of summer flowers. Set in the midst of a well-maintained garden, the hotel has a sun terrace, a range of nearby water and land sports, a sauna, a bar, an appealing restaurant with a ceramic tile stove and heavy beams, and elegantly simple bedrooms. These often have decorative arches separating the sleeping from the sitting areas, big windows with balconies, and attractively contemporary furniture. Of the 45 bedrooms, 36 contain private baths or showers. Half board costs 700 AS ($51) to 1,050 AS ($76.25) per person daily in winter. In summer, half board goes for 570 AS ($41.50) to 820 AS ($59.50) per person daily. The hotel is open from December to March and May to October.

Hotel Enzian, A-9762 Techendorf (tel. 04713/2221), is an imposingly old-fashioned chalet behind a set of stone columns flanking the path to the main street. Designed with weathered balconies and an attractively hipped roof, the hotel contains simple and attractive accommodations outfitted with warm colors and modern comfort. On the premises are an outdoor tennis court, a big lawn leading up to the lake, a rustic bar, and a restaurant serving well-prepared Austrian specialties. The hotel rents 27 bedrooms (with private baths or showers) from May to October, charging 700 AS ($51) to 780 AS ($56.75) per person daily for half board.

9. The Möll Valley and Mallnitz

Called Mölltal in German, this valley was known in the days of the Romans, with legions passing through it often during their long reign in Carinthia. This is still a much frequented route, as it is now the southern gateway to the Grossglockner Road described in the Land Salzburg section (see Chapter VIII). The valley contains the remains of several castles from the Middle Ages.

The resorts of Heiligenblut and Döllach, described below, lie roughly between Zell am See in Land Salzburg and Lienz, the capital of East Tyrol. Also in this section I'll take you on a detour north of Obervellach to visit the ski resort of Mallnitz, which lies directly to the south of Badgastein in Land Salzburg, although there's no road to there through the towering alpine ranges.

KOLBNITZ

The first stopover I recommend in the Möll Valley, Kolbnitz, is a sunny hamlet set against a mountain backdrop. To reach it, drive northwest from Spittal. This can be the center for many day excursions, either into the Carinthian lake district or to the Grossglockner area. You can even have your car loaded on the train at Mallnitz to go through the tunnel to Badgastein. But the main reason for stopping here is the hotel recommended below.

Food and Lodging

Hotel Marhof, A-9815 Kolbnitz (tel. 04783/2243), played an important role in the feudal politics of the region when it was built in 1150. The founding fathers of this hotel proudly called themselves "free peasants" (as opposed to the masses of serfs in the region), in exchange for which they paid annual revenues to the ruling aristocrat. Much later, when Franz Joseph tried to bestow a title upon a former owner, Joseph Walter, the "free farmer" proudly refused, saying that he preferred the title of his ancestors.

Today the family seat of all this is a prosperous-looking hip-roofed building with a stucco façade and green-and-white chevron shutters. Transformed into a hotel in 1967, the building has a wood-accented interior, unpretentious furniture, an outdoor pool, and a big lawn area for sunbathing. Heinz Walter, the owner, will welcome you into the cozy dining room, where dishes include tafelspitz, beef soups, and Viennese-style food, which, of course, means schnitzels. Fourteen comfortably old-fashioned rooms, each with private bath or shower, are rented at half-board terms costing 350 AS ($25.50) per person daily. The hotel is open from December to March and May to October.

OBERVELLACH

Most of the castles in the Möll Valley are centered around this little village, which also has a late Gothic church known for its 1520 altarpiece by Jan van Scorel, one of the Dutch masters. The artist was a great admirer of Dürer, as evidenced by his works. In the Middle Ages, Obervellach was a gold-mining town.

Among the medieval castles near this village are Oberfalkenstein from the 15th century and Groppenstein from the 12th and 15th centuries.

MALLNITZ

Before you continue your exploration of the Möll Valley, I recommend a detour to Mallnitz, which is both a summer and a winter ski resort. Lying directly north of Obervellach, a 5-mile drive up a steep road, this is a great bargain resort at any time of year.

At an elevation of 3,900 feet, it's so high up that the mountains around it wear permanent ice caps. In summer hikers go on mountain expeditions from this resort, a cable car taking passengers to Elschesattel (8,600 feet). There are several ski lifts and horse-drawn sleigh rides are popular in winter.

Mallnitz lies at the southern end of the Tauern railroad tunnel. Since you can't drive directly from here to Land Salzburg, why not have your car loaded on the train? Otherwise, if you want to go north to that province you'll have to take a long and circuitous highway route.

Food and Lodging

Alpenhotel Mallnitz, A-9822 Mallnitz (tel. 04784/525), is an attractive chalet hotel set in the hollow of a rocky valley. The service is relaxed and cordial, thanks almost entirely to the tone set by the Alber-Berlinger family, who do everything they can to be helpful. Built in 1905, the hotel has richly textured paneling, big windows, lots of rustic accessories, and an impressive collection of hunting trophies. Meals in one of the warmly appealing restaurants could include an array of veal or beef dishes, many of them grilled and covered with savory sauces, tasty soups, cold marinated herring, and homemade desserts. From December to September, guests are received at this 90-bed hotel and charged from 420 AS ($30.50) to 550 AS ($40) per person daily for half board.

Hotel 3 Gemsen, A-9822 Mallnitz (tel. 04784/396), is a 10-room chalet with two floors of shutters, balconies, wood trim, and regionally inspired designs. Just to the left of the front entrance someone has stenciled three deer between the painted dates of both the year of founding and the year of renovation, which are 1758 and 1979, respectively. Inside, the décor is covered with vaulted or beamed ceilings, rustically home-style furnishings as reflected by the bedrooms, and lots of warm colors. On the premises are an alpine bar, a restaurant, and lots of cozy comforts. The Peter Sterz family, the hosts, charge 330 AS ($24) daily per person, with half board included. Fly-fishing for trout in a mountain lake, as well as high-alpine shooting (chamoix and deer), can be arranged. The hotel is open from December to April and June to September.

WINKLERN

This little resort, 19 miles to the west of our stop in Obervellach, stands at an elevation of 3,100 feet. It's north of Lienz, the capital of East Tyrol, and Iselberg. From here you can enjoy a view of some of the highest mountains in Austria.

Winklern has a **pfarrkirche** (parish church) with a watchtower from the Middle Ages.

Food and Lodging

Hotel Defreggerhof, A-9841 Winklern (tel. 04822/252), is an attractively embellished four-story house with gables, balconies, and sunflower-colored illustrations around the borders of its windows. The hotel is a convenient starting point for walks through the surrounding hills. On the premises are a heated indoor pool and a sauna, and there is easy access to the village's sporting facilities. Rates for the 27 well-equipped and maintained bedrooms, each with private bath or shower, range from 380 AS ($27.75) to 450 AS ($32.75) per person daily for half board. Open from December to March and May to October.

DÖLLACH

A gold- and silver-mining center in the Middle Ages, Döllach is now a small Möll Valley resort, its reasonable prices attracting visitors in both summer and winter. Lying 6 miles from Heiligenblut, our next destination, Döllach is at a 3,360-foot elevation, set in an area of some beautiful waterfalls.

Grosskirchheim Castle has artifacts from the town's mining days preserved in a regional museum.

Food and Lodging

Hotel Schlosswirt, A-9843 Grosskirchheim-Döllach (tel. 04825/411), is a well-proportioned 21-room chalet with flowered balconies, weathered siding, and a desirable location at the edge of the forest. The castle is just behind the hotel. All the outdoor sports are available within a few minutes' walk. The interior has a kind of unpretentious elegance that comes mainly from fine woods and careful craftsmanship. The spacious bedrooms have comfortable furniture and lots of horizontal parking. The Sauper family, the hotel's owners, charge 420 AS ($30.50) to 775 AS ($56.25) per person daily for half board. Activities provided for guests include tennis, a sauna, swimming in the pool, horseback riding and trekking tours in Höhe Tauern National Park, and fishing.

On the premises are an attractive bar area and one of the best restaurants in the region. Your meal might begin with cream of trout soup and fresh chives, followed by a juicy pork filet stuffed with Gorgonzola. Dinners range from 140 AS ($10.25) to 250 AS ($18.25). Reservations are suggested. On Sunday, dinner is served in the 500-year-old castle, where you can also have cocktails and enjoy wine-tasting gatherings.

HEILIGENBLUT

If you enter the Möll Valley from the north, coming from Zell am See along the Grossglockner Road, this is the first important little resort you'll reach. It lies at the foot of the southern slope of the Grossglockner. Because of its location there's a lot of traffic through here in summer.

The steeple of the 15th-century **pfarrkirche** (parish church), backgrounded by the lofty mountain, is a much-used subject for illustrations and photographs.

In summer Heiligenblut is the headquarters for a well-known mountain-climbing school. In winter skiers take over.

Food and Lodging

Hotel Glocknerhof, A-9844 Heiligenblut (tel. 04824/2244), is built dramatically on a sloping hillside a stone's throw from the beautifully severe lines of the village church. The hotel's exterior walls are covered with weathered balconies. The interior is rustic, warm, cozy, elegant, and alluring, all at the same time. On the premises are a covered swimming pool, with big windows looking out at a sweeping panorama, an inviting bar, a sauna, a sun terrace, a children's playroom, an open fireplace, a dancing bar, and a host of organized activities, including schuhplatter evenings, dinner dances, and buffet cookouts. Prices range from 500 AS ($36.25) to 1,160 AS ($84.25) per person daily for a double and 630 AS ($45.75) to 1,090 AS ($79.25) for a single, with half board included. Prices vary according to the season. The most expensive accommodations within this price range are small, tastefully furnished apartments. The overflow from the main hotel is housed in one of three annexes operated by the owners, the Pichler family. In all, the hotel rents 52 rooms and 10 suites.

Hotel Post, A-9844 Heiligenblut (tel. 04824/2245), is a pleasant chalet with wrap-around balconies. A wide sun terrace offers a sunny resting place. The paneled interior is accented with wrought-iron chandeliers, warmly tinted fabrics, big windows, and alpine colors of red and forest green. On the premises are an indoor pool, a sauna, a solarium, a steambath, a bar area with massive timbers, and a restaurant serving well-prepared local specialties. Each of the 50 comfortable bedrooms has a private bath, balcony, radio, and phone. Doubles range from 420 AS ($30.50) to 570 AS ($41.50) per person daily, while singles cost 490 AS ($35.50) to 560 AS ($40.75), with half board. The hosts, the Eder family, keep the hotel open from December to September.

Haus Senger, A-9844 Heiligenblut (tel. 04824/2215), is a weathered double chalet, with recessed balconies and a covering almost completely fashioned from wood planks. The cozily rustic interior has massively hewn vertical supports, open fireplaces whose plaster chimneys are crafted into abstract shapes, stone detailing, and lots of cozy niches. The 16 comfortable bedrooms, each with private bath or shower, cost 510 AS ($37) to 770 AS ($56) per person daily in winter for half board. In summer, half board goes for 490 AS ($35.50) to 620 AS ($45) per person daily. Guests are received from December to April and June to October. The hotel also has apartments for rent with rustic living rooms, showers or baths, toilets, balconies, fully equipped kitchens, color TVs, and direct-dial phones.

---

10. The Gail Valley

A lovely valley running parallel to the Valley of the Drau, the Gailtal, as the German-speaking people call it, lies between the Carnic alpine range and the Gail Valley Alps. A trip here will take you into the deepest southern fringes of Carinthia along the Italian border. The resorts here tend to be largely undiscovered, unpretentious, and modestly priced.

HERMAGOR

This is the major town in the Gail Valley, lying to the west of Lake Presseger, which gives it some claim to being a summer resort. Its **pfarrkirche** (parish church) is from the 15th century. In summer Hermagor is popular with hikers and climbers who head for the hills.

Food and Lodging

Hotel Wulfenia and **Hotel Sonnenalpe,** A-9620 Hermagor (tel. 04282/8111), are two sprawling chalets connected to each other by a raised tunnel stretching over the parking area between them. These massive hotels have many facilities,

454 □ FROMMER'S AUSTRIA

including all the usual sporting equipment, as well as comfortable public rooms outfitted with softly glowing paneling, open fireplaces, stone detailing, panoramic
windows, and rustically contemporary furnishings. Bedrooms are streamlined with
many amenities and comforts. The hotels charge 800 AS ($58.25) to 1,100 AS
($80) per person daily for half board, and guests are received from December to
April and June to September. On the premises are a full range of health and beauty
facilities, as well as an indoor pool, whirlpool, sauna, and Turkish steambath. A
bowling alley and outdoor tennis courts are also available. Clients appreciate the
bars, disco, restaurants, and the organized entertainment arranged by the vivacious
hosts, the Pucher family.

KÖTSCHACH-MAUTHEN

With a name like that for your vacation site, no one will know where you're
going if you tell them, but you'll know that this resort is in the upper part of the Gail
Valley. *Mauthen* refers to the toll that was once collected here. The town has a 16th-
century **pfarrkirche** (parish church), known as the "cathedral of the valley."

This little resort is at a major road junction through which you go heading
south to the Plöcken Pass, with Italy as your ultimate destination. From Kötschach-
Mauthen you can go south to the pass for a distance of just under 9 miles, but it's a
narrow, twisting road with gradients of 14%. I consider it suitable only for skilled
alpine drivers who don't mind the numerous hairpin curves. The Italian motorists
coming north don't seem to mind!

Food and Lodging

Kürschner Gesundheits-Hotel, A-9640 Kötschach-Mauthen (tel. 04715/
259), painted a pale yellow with white trim, contains an elegant vaulted reception
area, comfortable bedrooms, and virtually every kind of massage, acupuncture, and
nutritional care available in Austria. On the premises are a big garden with a heated
swimming pool, a tennis court, and a management who frequently organize walking tours, garden parties, and group activities. The 80-bed hotel receives guests from
December to October, charging summer half-board rates of 610 AS ($44.25) to 820
AS ($59.50). Half board in winter goes for 570 AS ($41.50) to 800 AS ($58.25) per
person daily.

Restaurant Kellerwand, Hotel Kellerwand (tel. 04715/269), the dining
room of a four-star hotel at Mauthen, is one of the most elegant in the region. You'll
be greeted by the sounds of classical music as soon as you enter. You'll probably want
a drink at the small, well-appointed bar area before you're led to a beautifully set
table where fresh flowers, silver candlesticks, and painted porcelain along with fresh
bread are *de rigueur*. Menu items include strips of sautéed calves' liver with leaf spinach, trout dumplings, chicken in burgundy sauce, and veal in a sherry sauce. If
you're interested in a dessert after all that, it could be a vanilla ice cream confection
with a Grand Marnier sauce. Closed between mid-October and mid-December, the
restaurant requests reservations and charges from 350 AS ($25.50) on set menus
and from 225 AS ($16.25) on the à la carte menu. Service is daily from 9am to
11pm.

---

11. Lake Klopeiner

The waters of Klopeiner, the warmest lake in Carinthia, can reach 82° Fahrenheit in summer. The lake, surrounded by woodlands and shaped like an
amphitheater, lies to the south of the market town of Völkermarkt. Lake Klopeiner
is fairly small—only 1⅛ miles long and less than half a mile wide at its broadest
point. In summer it's thronged with fun-loving Austrians. The government does
not permit motor-powered craft on the lake, endeavoring to keep its sky-blue waters

free of pollution. The resorts that ring the lake are part of the commune of St. Kanzian.

FOOD AND LODGING

Strandhotel Marolt, A-9122 St. Kanzian (tel. 04239/2236), is an imposing-looking hotel whose different sections are joined together like a series of balconied cubes stretching along the lakeshore. The wood-trimmed façade contains big sliding windows that open into the well-furnished bedrooms, each of which has a private bath. On the premises are a covered swimming pool, several outdoor tennis courts, a bathing pier, a dancing terrace for outdoor parties, and a restaurant. On the spacious grounds around the hotel are a series of at least three annexes to hold the overflow from the main building. The 250-bed hotel is open from April to October, charging 465 AS ($33.75) to 595 AS ($43.25) per person daily for half board.

---

12. The Vellach Valley

Southeast of Klagenfurt, the Carinthian capital, the Vellach Valley leads to the Yugoslav border. It's a place well known in history. Your fellow visitors to this area are likely to be Yugoslavians.

The major stopover in the valley is—

EISENKAPPEL

This town is also known by its Yugoslav name, Selezna Kapla. It lies at the foot of Karawanken, 24 miles from Klagenfurt, or Celovec, as you're likely to hear it called in this valley, the home of a Slovenian ethnic group. Eisenkappel is only 10 miles from the Jezersko Pass, at the Austro-Yugoslav border.

The town is surrounded by centuries-old forests and mineral springs, and it has many cultural and historical curiosities, owing to its position as a frontier town. The southernmost of all the market villages of Austria, Eisenkappel is known both as a summer tourist center and a winter ski resort.

There are many sky-blue lakes and white mountain peaks nearby. Lake Klopeiner, to the north of this town, is the warmest lake in Carinthia, as described above. Five miles to the southwest you'll see Trögerner Gorge.

Food and Lodging

Hotel Obir, A-9135 Eisenkappel (tel. 04238/381), is a striking hotel constructed of red brick with black-framed windows set into its many outside angles. In the center of town close to the thermal baths, the hotel has a big airy format and a simplified interior décor much in keeping with the modern exterior. The 48 comfortably furnished bedrooms, each with private bath or shower, rent for 307 AS ($22.25) to 327 AS ($23.75) per person daily for half board.

STYRIA

The "Green Heart of Austria," Styria (Steiermark, in German) is so called because forests cover about half the land mass, with grassland and vineyards blanketing yet another quarter. The second-largest province in the country after Lower Austria, Styria has many neighbors. It borders not only Yugoslavia and Hungary but also the Austrian provinces of Burgenland, Lower Austria, Upper Austria, Land Salzburg, and Carinthia. Part of Styria takes in the alpine ranges of the Salzkammergut, and some of it (the eastern part) resembles the steppe country of the Great Hungarian Plain.

This land of valleys and rivers, mountain peaks and glaciers, was long an area bitterly fought over, being greedily attacked through the ages by Huns, Hungarians, and Turks, among others. But not all of its suffering from the depredations of battle were in previous centuries. Great damage was inflicted in World War II, particularly in East Styria.

Even in Celtic times the mountains of Upper Styria were known as a prime source of the iron ore on which the tribes depended for their weapons and other valuable implements. The Romans exploited the rich deposits, and the Crusaders used armor made from Styrian iron to fight the "infidel" in the East. Iron resources shaped the economy of Styria, and today it is Austria's leading mining province. Nine-tenths of all the iron ore produced in Austria comes from Erzberg, which means "ore mountain."

Styria is steeped in tradition, more so than any other Austrian province. The distinguishing costume often worn by Styrian men is a case in point. Derived from an original peasant costume, it's made of stout greenish-gray cloth with Styrian green material being used for the lapels and as a stripe down the outside of the pant legs.

Styria is one of the bargain provinces of Austria. Even its top hotels charge prices that would be in the moderate range in most of the major cities of Europe. You can take the train here from either Salzburg or Vienna, and state bus service links all the towns and villages of the province. I think, however, that the ideal way to travel here is by car, since you'll want to be adventurous and head up an unknown valley or drive right up to some castle-fortress.

Styria is good hunting country. In fact, a lot of the game you see on those hunter's menus throughout Austria ran wild in Styrian woodlands during its lifetime. In summer you can fish for trout in the Enns and other rivers. Mountain climbing is another popular summer activity.

In the last decade or so Styria has been entering the winter holiday scene as a ski area, but it still has a long way to go before it will have the facilities of Land Salzburg or Tyrol. Likewise, its après-ski life is not yet nearly on a par with that of already-flourishing Austrian ski centers.

Graz, the capital of Styria, is the second-largest city in the country. In imperial times it was best known as the place to which state officials retired. It even acquired the nickname "Pensionopolis" (City of the Retired) from this fact.

1. Graz

Graz, capital of the iron-rich province of Styria, combines a modern way of life with historical architecture to achieve a harmonious blend of past and present. Its history as a settlement probably dates back to prehistoric times, brought about by its location at the base of a hill at a ford across the Mur River, an important facet of transportation in the beginning of civilization. Romans, Slavs, and Bavarians all took their turn in the development of a town on the northern edge of a plain where the Mur leaves the wooded mountains of central Styria.

Early settlers, fearing flooding, established fortifications on the steep dolomite hill overlooking the river's ford site. The name of the city is derived from the Slavic word *gradec*, meaning "little fortress." This little castle was built on the hill which is now the Schlossberg in Graz. The town is first mentioned in historical documents from early in the 12th century. Graz has come under many governments, among them those of Germany, Bohemia, Hungary, the Babenbergs, the Habsburgs—you name it.

The medieval town developed at the foot of the Schlossberg, and some buildings of the late Gothic period remain, constructed when Emperor Frederick III used Graz as a capital after being forced out of Vienna by the Hungarians. The Burg (castle) and the cathedral of that era, houses that seem to huddle together, narrow-gable roofs, and arcaded courtyards contribute to the city's charm today.

Life wasn't always kind to the people of Graz. In 1480 they must have felt that fate was being extra cruel. In that year of the "Plagues of God," the little town was afflicted by locusts, the Black Death, the Turks, and a threat from the Hungarians.

When the Habsburg inheritance was divided in 1564 into Austrian and Spanish branches, Graz became the capital of "Inner Austria," the residence of Archduke Carl, who ruled Styria, Carinthia, and Italian Habsburg patrimonial lands. Graz was again prosperous. Carl had the town's fortifications strengthened on Italian designs, with bastions and moats.

A Jesuit college and Lutheran foundation school were both active by the end of the 16th century. Johannes Kepler, who gained renown for his mathematical and astronomical knowledge, began his teaching career at the Lutheran school. Fine arts and commerce flourished in Graz, bringing honor and riches to the city, as reflected in palaces and mansions of that period, although when Ferdinand II became emperor, he moved his court to Vienna in 1619. The influence of Italian Renaissance architects made its impact during this period.

The city walls were demolished in 1784, and the area they occupied, the *glacis* (slopes), was planted with trees. Napoleon's armies made three appearances here when he was trying to take over all of Europe, and the defeat of Austria at the Battle of Wagram in 1809 resulted in a treaty that forced Graz to level the battlements of the Schlossberg, in retaliation for the failure of the French troops to seize the citadel earlier that year. Only the Uhrturm (Clock Tower) and the bell tower were saved, rescued by payment of a high ransom by the citizens of Graz. Schlossberg was transformed into the beautiful park on that site today.

World War II saw much destruction by bombers, and the early entry of Russian troops into the city continued the devastation. However, during the occupation Graz was allotted in 1945 to the British and reconstruction began, so that today you can enjoy warm hospitality in the "Garden City" of Austria.

Graz is a city of some quarter of a million inhabitants at present, with such thriving industrial enterprises as breweries, machine factories, trading companies, and service industries. The Graz Fair is a commercial and industrial event of great importance in southeast Europe. Three universities, an opera house, a theater, museums, concert halls, and art galleries are the center of cultural life for Central Styria.

If you're in the vicinity in the fall of the year, you might want to attend the Steierischer Herbst (Styrian Autumn) festival, which features contemporary art, music, and literature.

For an orientation to the geography of Graz, including its landmark squares and major monuments, refer to "The Sights."

TRANSPORTATION IN GRAZ

Streetcar and bus service is operated throughout the city by **Graz City Transport.** Jakomini Square in the city center is the point of intersection of all streetcar lines. To use the network of bus lines, starting points are at Jakomini Square or from terminals of the streetcar lines. For information on any phase of the transport system, telephone 78931.

Radio **taxi** service is available by phoning 983 or 2801.

FAST FACTS

Here are the necessaries for Graz:

AREA CODE: For the city of Graz it is 0316.

AIR TRAVEL: For information, call Thalerhof Airport, south of the city (tel. 0316/291541), or the AUA (Austrian Airlines) city office, Herrengasse 16, Landhaus (tel. 0316/829-64-144). Lufthansa also has a city office, at Herrengasse 6 (tel. 0316/822583).

CAR TRAVEL: If you're traveling by car, Graz is connected to the European highway system, via roads to the southbound and the Pyhrn autobahns as well as to the main road through the Mur and Mürz valleys. The city offers all necessary services to motorists. Ask about this courtesy at the tourist office (see below).

EMERGENCY SERVICES: They are available by telephoning the following numbers: 133 for police, 122 for fire, 144 for an ambulance, and 1900-4566 for medical assistance.

LOST AND FOUND: In an emergency, you can ask at any police station

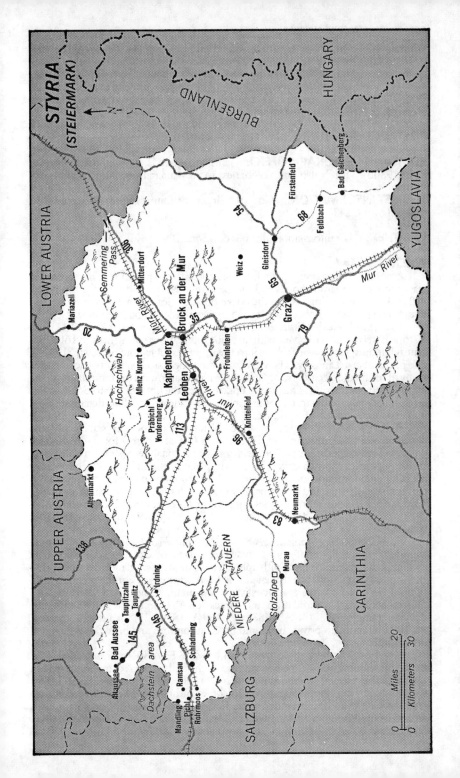

(*wachzimmer*). Otherwise, try the Lost and Found Office, Grabenstrasse 56 (tel. 0316/62279, ext. 57). In criminal cases, apply to the Duty Officer at Police Headquarters, Paulustorgasse 8 (tel. 0316/888-2390).

POSTAL BUS: Information is available at Postverkehrsbüro Graz, Andreas-Hofer-Platz 19 (tel. 0316/811818).

POSTAL CODE: For the city of Graz it is A-8010.

POST AND TELEGRAPH OFFICE: The main one is at Neutorgasse 46 (tel. 0316/9800). There's also a post office next to the main railway station (Bahnhof).

TOURIST INFORMATION: Go to the Graz City Tourist Office, Herrengasse 16 (tel. 0316/835241).

WEATHER: For information, dial 0316/1566.

WHERE TO STAY

Accommodations range from first-class hotels to camping sites. There are many reasonably priced family hotels and inexpensive lodgings, and even the top hotels will strike many as being easy on the pocketbook. I'll lead off with the more expensive choices, and then preview a selection in the middle and budget range.

Alba Hotel Wiesler Graz, Grieskai 4, A-8010 Graz (tel. 0316/91-32-41), is a historic hotel on the River Mur with quayside foundations dating back to 1603. Recent rebuilding has transformed it into the most desirable hotel in town, the only one in the deluxe category. The view from the neoclassical windows encompasses many of the medieval city's baroque spires, which soar toward the mountains on the opposite side of the river. During the upgrading of the hotel in 1985–86, its architects completely reconstructed the lobby with marble and fine detailing in an updated interpretation of art nouveau.

Wiesler's restaurant is a sophisticated blend of good food, crystal chandeliers, paneling, and uniformed waiters. There's a less formal snackbar for sit-down food, plus the Café Jugendstil, where an array of international newspapers supplements the fresh pastries and rich coffee. In the bar, piano music and special drinks tempt residents and nonresidents alike. Many of the 98 rooms and most of the suites contain unusual artwork and sweeping views. After you register, an employee brings fruit and tea to your room. Singles range from 1,420 AS ($103.25) to 1,730 AS ($125.75) daily, with doubles costing 2,050 AS ($149), including a buffet breakfast.

Hotel Daniel, Europaplatz 1, A-8020 Graz (tel. 0316/911080), has a boxy urban look with a flat roof and a sprawling design of concrete and glass. The contemporary interior is filled with upholstered banquettes and modern accessories, and is often frequented by businesspeople from other cities. On the premises are a popular bar area and an elegantly efficient restaurant. A short walk from the Old Quarter at the station plaza, the hotel charges 765 AS ($55.50) to 930 AS ($67.50) daily for a single and 1,140 AS ($83) to 1,460 AS ($106.25) for a double or suite. All 100 units contain private baths and modern comfort, and breakfast is included in the tariffs.

City Hotel Erzherzog Johann, Sackstrasse 3-5, A-8010 Graz (tel. 0316/811616), standing near the pedestrian zone in the Old Quarter, dates from the 16th century. This elegant hotel arranges some of its rooms around a skylit atrium surrounded by curving wrought-iron balconies and plants. There's an array of attractive facilities on the premises, including a contemporary bar area with vivid accents of black and brass, along with a formal restaurant. Reached from the street through a chiseled stone archway, the hotel charges 780 AS ($56.75) to 1,050 AS

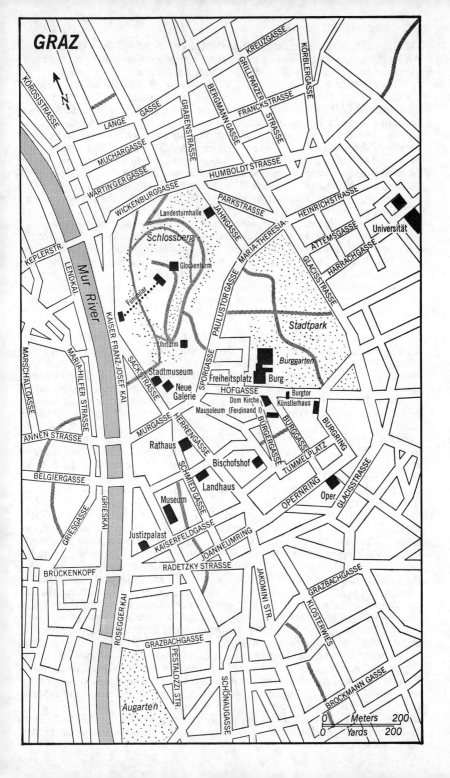

($76.25) daily for a single and 1,250 AS ($91) to 1,550 AS ($112.75) for a double. All 70 bedrooms contain private baths, and the newer rooms tend to be more spacious and tranquil. A buffet breakfast is included in the rates.

Hotel Weitzer, Grieskai 12-14, A-8011 Graz (tel. 0316/913801), has been in the same family for four generations. (It's not to be confused with the previously recommended Alba Hotel Wiesler.) Standing on the River Mur, it consists of two buildings connected by an overhead glass tunnel. The whole 205-room complex, well run and modernized with much contemporary comfort, was completely renovated in 1986 and 1987, with 44 new rooms added. The bedrooms all have private baths, radios, color TVs, minibars, and soundproof windows. Depending on the plumbing, singles range from 910 AS ($66.25) to 1,220 AS ($88.75) daily, with doubles running from 1,320 AS ($96) to 1,910 AS ($138.75).

The Restaurant Casserole on the ground floor is considered by some residents to be among the best in town. Furnished in a modern, warmly tinted style, with waiters formally dressed even at lunchtime, the establishment offers an elegant salad bar with an array of greens, cold marinated vegetables, and varieties of lettuce including the deluxe mâche. The chef's tafelspitz is especially good. Meals range from 150 AS ($11) to 350 AS ($25.50). The hotel also offers the Floriani, a rustic wine tavern, and the Kaffeehaus, in typical Viennese style, along with a lobby bar for cocktails and after-dinner drinks. Facilities include a steambath, solarium, sauna, and massage. The hotel is a member of the prestigious Steigenberger Reservations System. For reservations, call toll free 800/223-5652, or 212/593-2988 collect in New York State.

Schlossberg Hotel, Kaiser-Franz-Josef-Kai 30, A-8010 Graz (tel. 0316/80700). Housed behind a beautifully embellished cerulean-blue façade, this 15th-century baroque inn is my favorite hotel in Graz. Renovated from a decrepit rooming house in 1982 by a former racecar driver, Helmut Marko, the hotel is now one of the most unusual and charming hostelries in town. It was personally decorated by the owner's wife with choice 19th-century furniture. (She has her own antiques business as well as excellent taste.) The hotel offers 54 individually designed rooms, each of which blends the thick original walls with modern comfort. There's an early Biedermeier ceramic stove in the bar area and several pieces of baroque sculpture are set into well-placed niches. There's also a courtyard with a lion's-head fountain. Prices range from 950 AS ($69) to 1,200 AS ($87.25) daily for a single and 1,400 AS ($101.75) to 1,950 AS ($141.75) for a double, these tariffs including taxes and a buffet breakfast. The hotel has a swimming pool, and guests can enjoy drinks on a terrace with a superb view of Graz.

Top Hotel Europa, Bahnhofgürtel 89, A-8010 Graz (tel. 0316/916601). Opened in 1986, this downtown hotel offers easy access from the nearby railway station. The building's mansard roof shelters 120 comfortably modern bedrooms, each of which contains a phone, radio, color TV, minibar, and private bath. Singles cost 850 AS ($61.75) to 950 AS ($69) daily, with doubles renting for 1,300 AS ($94.50) to 1,550 AS ($112.75). After their arrival guests relax in the sauna, whose plunge pool is the chilliest in town, in the solarium, or at the intimate bar. Snacks and drinks are served in the Bistronette restaurant, while more formal meals are available in a plant-festooned restaurant called the Four Seasons (Vier Jahreszeiten). Motorists appreciate the 400-place parking garage and the covered shopping center, both of which are connected to the hotel.

Romantik Parkhotel, Leonhardstrasse 8, A-8010 Graz (tel. 0316/33511), is a large hotel rambling across a gently angled corner of a street near the Opera House, the City Park, and the university. The interior is a combination of baronial accessories (suits of armor and hanging tapestries in the beamed dining room) and modern comforts. The hotel's garage will solve your parking problems. The Florian family charges 700 AS ($51) to 920 AS ($67) daily for a single and 1,000 AS ($72.75) to 1,360 AS ($99) for a double. The 65 traditionally furnished bedrooms offer private baths or showers, radios, and TVs.

Hotel Gollner, Schlögelgasse 14, A-8010 Graz (tel. 0316/82-25-21), the preferred choice of the city's visiting opera stars, is across the street from the Opera House. Its renovated interior has a no-nonsense contemporary décor and 50 often spacious bedrooms. Singles cost 680 AS ($49.50) to 870 AS ($63.25), while doubles range from 1,080 AS ($78.50) to 1,420 AS ($103.25), with breakfast included. The hotel's restaurant serves good, wholesome food, and extra facilities include a sauna and a solarium.

Hotel Mariahilf, Mariahilferstrasse 9, A-8020 Graz (tel. 0316/913163), is a four-story stucco building with a red-tile roof, prominent gables, and modified neoclassical detailing around the windows. Centrally located, the 44-room hotel has an elevator, comfortable public rooms with red leather chairs, and a display of tiny flags from most of the major countries of Europe. The cozy weinstube offers Styrian specialties. With breakfast included, rooms with bath cost 760 AS ($55.25) for a single and 1,000 AS ($72.75) for a double. Bathless rooms cost 350 AS ($25.50) for a single and 625 AS ($45.45) for a double.

Hotel Drei Raben, Annenstrasse 43, A-8020 Graz (tel. 0316/9126-85), near the train station, not far from the Old Quarter, is a contemporary hotel with modern comforts. It rents 58 well-furnished bedrooms, each with private bath or shower. Tariffs, which include a breakfast buffet, are 540 AS ($39.25) daily for a single and 780 AS ($56.75) for a double. Some triple rooms are also rented, costing 980 AS ($71.25).

Hotel Grazerhof, Stubenberggasse 10, A-8010 Graz (tel. 0316/824358), is centrally located on a relatively quiet street in the center of town. The marble-floored lobby offers a group of leather-backed swivel chairs near the reception desk. A popular restaurant offers meals to hotel residents, outside shopkeepers, and shoppers in general. Most of the 26 comfortable bedrooms contain private baths and phones. Singles cost 500 AS ($36.25) to 550 AS ($40) daily, with doubles paying 600 AS ($43.75) to 760 AS ($55.25).

On the Outskirts

Gästehaus/Café zum Kreuz, Kärntnerstrasse 451, A-8044 Graz-Strassgang (tel. 0316/283436), is an ochre-colored guesthouse which has been run by the same family for more than a century. In a suburb south of Graz, the establishment contains only a dozen rooms, as well as a popular restaurant that's often the destination for people from the city who come here for the Styrian wines and the gutbürgerlich cookery. Homemade sausages are a specialty in September and March. The hotel's 12 bedrooms are comfortably furnished and come with private baths or showers. Singles range from 300 AS ($21.75) to 340 AS ($24.70) daily, with doubles costing 460 AS ($33.50) to 500 AS ($36.25).

Hotel/Restaurant Pfeifer zum Kirchenwirt, Kirschenplatz 9, A-8044 Graz-Mariatrost (tel. 0316/391112), in an agricultural suburb about 4½ miles from the center of Graz, is an ochre-colored hotel whose exterior is an appealingly old-fashioned combination of country baroque detailing, hipped roofs, and exposed stone. All 40 comfortable bedrooms have complete baths, phones, and radios; some of the larger, more modern ones have minibars and TVs. The Pfeifer family charges 480 AS ($35) to 580 AS ($42.25) daily for a single and 740 AS ($53.75) to 820 AS ($59.50) for a double, with breakfast and taxes included in the rates. On the premises is a sauna, as well as a gutbürgerlich restaurant with lots of wood trim and daily opening hours of noon to 2pm and 6 to 10pm. Around the corner, guests may want to take a look at the beautiful baroque pilgrimage church of Mariatrost.

WHERE TO DINE

The variety of restaurants is enormous, ranging from first-class establishments to beerhalls to student hangouts. Prices in even the top restaurants are moderate. You can dine in the hotels (which have some of the best food in town) or in cozy pubs and intimate bistros.

My recommendation, for the most part, is to skip the typical international cuisine when possible and concentrate on genuine Styrian specialties. These include wurzelfleisch, a kind of stew, or the different kinds of sterz, a dish made of buckwheat or corn. The homemade sausages in all their infinite varieties are generally excellent. Vienna is noted for its hendl (chicken) dishes, but Graz chefs also do chicken extremely well.

The art of beer brewing is particularly cultivated in Graz. For the local Puntigam or Reininghaus beers, as well as for the Gösser beer, which is brewed in Upper Styria, the people of Graz have a special predilection.

Or you may want to try Styrian wine, which grows on steep slopes exposed to the sun. Important varieties such as Welschriesling, Muskat-Sylvaner, Traminer, but also the Schilcher, which grows only in a limited area in West Styria, have received international recognition.

Many of the wine restaurants of Graz provide background music in the evening.

Hofkeller, Hofgasse 8 (tel. 0316/702439), has a gilt-edged reputation in town as a haven for gourmets. It successfully combines nouvelle cuisine with regional Styrian food. The restaurant, which was formerly a wine and beer tavern, was long ago transformed into an elegant room with refreshing touches of vivid green. The tables are covered with fine napery, good silverware, and beautiful porcelain. The limited menu is augmented by a list of daily specials, whose appearance is heavily dependent on the availability of the ingredients. Your meal might include seafood salad in walnut oil, artichoke hearts stuffed with goose liver and mushrooms, a wide selection of fish, or a savory lamb cut flavored with thyme. Set menus range from 100 AS ($7.25) to 340 AS ($24.75), with à la carte dinners costing 175 AS ($12.75) to 350 AS ($25.50). The place is open from 11am to 2pm and 6pm to midnight; closed Sunday and holidays. Reservations are suggested.

Weincomptoir Stündl, Heinrichstrasse 55 (tel. 0316/33413). With its cerulean façade, lace-covered windows, rows of plants, and geometric patterns, it looks more like a tea room than a restaurant. However, the evening crowd is likely to be among the most sophisticated in Graz. Owner Wolfgang Stündl offers many dishes with nouvelle cuisine flair. Specialties include noodle salad with shrimp and mussels; spaghetti with bacon, mushrooms, and zucchini in a garlic-flavored cream sauce; lamb-stuffed ravioli with thyme butter; trout grilled with a fennel-flavored cream sauce; and chicken with rosemary and creamed cabbage. Full meals cost 320 AS ($23.25) to 380 AS ($27.75), and are served daily except Sunday and holidays from 6pm to 1am. Located on a commercial street, the restaurant is a taxi ride from the center of town.

Gambrinuskeller, Färbergasse 6-8 (tel. 0316/810181). The décor, like the menu, combines elements from rustically conservative Austria with overtones of the Middle East and the Balkans. In addition to lots of exposed wood, the dining rooms contain Oriental rugs which cushion the unyielding surfaces of the banquettes. A large oil painting of a Balkan peasant girl in native headdress dominates one end of the room, while a stainless-steel deli-style case separates the busy kitchens from the dining areas. The unusual menu offers Brazilian, Persian, and Italian foods as well. You might enjoy cevapcici, churrasco of pork, Iranian-style kebabs, Italian pasta dishes, and grilled steaks. Dessert could be anything from baklava to apple strudel. Full meals average around 175 AS ($12.75). Food is served from 10:30am to 11:30pm; closed Saturday and Sunday. In summer, the garden attracts diners and drinkers.

Restaurant Goldene Pastete, Sporgasse 28 (tel. 0316/823416), is housed inside the oldest inn in Graz, constructed in 1571. It's owned by the Patterer family, who have run it for more than a quarter of a century. The restaurant is in a five-story Renaissance building of pink stucco with green shutters and lots of window boxes. The waiters, each dressed in regional garb, are kept busy running from the kitchens to the three dining rooms on three different floors. In addition to 140 places inside, the summer garden holds an additional 60 diners. Open from 10am to midnight every day but Saturday and Sunday, the restaurant serves gutbürgerlich food to all walks of life. The international menu contains an occasional Yugoslav dish, such as cevapcici, but mainly it offers Austrian specialties, including zander (a fish), several noodle dishes, grilled veal, steaks, pork roast in a pepper-cream sauce, and schnitzel Cordon Bleu. Full meals range from 135 AS ($9.75) to 250 AS ($18.25).

Landhaus-Keller, Schmiedgasse 9 (tel. 0316/830276), a dimly lit corridor extends past at least three rustic and authentically Teutonic dining areas (there are six if you count the nooks and crannies). These range from the Hunters' Room to the Knights' Room. A corridor leads to a series of outdoor tables behind the restaurant. This outdoor area opens onto a neighboring courtyard with flowers and a view of the arcade of a baroque church. A sign in the window advertises "delicacies from lakes, rivers, and streams," as well as a wide selection of veal, beef, pork, and both roast and fried chicken dishes.

Specialties are usually from Styria, based on old recipes. You might begin with sour cream soup with burnt polenta, meatballs with sauerkraut, Styrian cheese dumplings in beef broth, and browned omelets with blueberries. Meals cost from 150 AS ($11). Landhaus-Keller is open daily except Sunday and holidays from 10am to midnight. The original building was constructed in the early 16th century, and hosted such famous guests as Metternich, Franz and Eduard Sacher, Field Marshal Esterházy, and the Duke of Wellington.

Kepler Keller, Stempfergasse 6 (tel. 0316/822449), is a wine tavern named after the Renaissance mathematician and astrologer Johannes Kepler, who used to live there. During its lifetime the establishment has served a glass of wine or beer to practically everyone in Graz. The interior is cozily welcoming, done up in an authentic décor of thick paneling and rustic accessories, but my favorite area is the candlelit courtyard, its outdoor tables flanked by a three-story arcade whose repeating arches are supported by chiseled Doric columns accented with cascading flowerboxes.

Live music is usually part of the evening's entertainment, beginning at 6pm. In addition to traditional meals, such as schnitzels, pork, steaks, omelets, cheeses, and salads, the establishment serves carafes of the local wine. The specialty of the house is a Styrian rosé called Schilcher, whose grape only grows south of Graz. The restaurant also serves copious quantities of the Styrian beer called Gösser. It is open daily except Sunday from 6pm to 2am, with the last food orders going in at 1am. Full meals cost from 110 AS ($8) to 225 AS ($16.25).

Krebsenkeller, Sackstrasse 12 (tel. 0316/829377), near the Hauptplatz, is about the closest thing to a total entertainment complex available in Graz. You enter a covered passage that ends in an enclosed courtyard, one side of which has a beflowered loggia. Café tables are usually set up under a grape arbor, although you can choose between an underground "keller," a ground-level stüberl, or a gemütlich restaurant, each of which has different entrances from the courtyard. This labyrinthine arrangement of rooms was built in 1538 by a local official and his wife. Fixed-price menus are a real bargain. They cost 80 AS ($5.75) to 120 AS ($8.75). Menu items include grilled dishes of varying degrees of spiciness, a full range of home-made soups, fresh salads, fresh fish, and wild game from Austria. The cellar is open daily from 9am to midnight.

Pichlmaier, Petersbergenstrasse 9 (tel. 0316/41597), is a citadel for the discerning palate of Graz. Not only do you get a selection of regional dishes, but imaginatively inspired recipes as well. The cuisine is based on market-fresh ingredients, and dishes usually have subtlety, flavor, and eye appeal. Try a filet of beefsteak or a filet of fresh salmon garnished with vegetables. Some low-calorie recipes are prepared without butter. Of course, the finest of Austrian wines can accompany your repast. Service is daily except Sunday from noon to 2:30pm and 6:30 to 9:30pm. À la carte meals cost from 280 AS ($20.25), with set menus offered from 320 AS ($23.25). One, costing around 600 AS ($43.50), is a gourmet delight.

Ringrestaurant Stadtkeller, Andreas-Hofer-Platz 3 (tel. 0316/823354).

Housed in a stucco building with primitive flying buttresses, this gutbürgerlich restaurant can be found on a busy traffic circle near the river. Inside, hanging glass lamps, timbered ceilings, and stenciled wall murals combine with a hearty menu to create a typical Styrian ambience. You can eat here at virtually any price level, from economy to upper bracket. A fixed-price vegetarian dinner is offered for 110 AS ($8). Otherwise, you can spend from 150 AS ($11) to 300 AS ($21.75) for dinner. Menu items come from both the Austrian and the international kitchen, and include a wide variety of pizzas, the most interesting of which is made from "fruits of the sea." There are also Italian pastas, Hungarian dishes, and typically Styrian platters. The terrace overlooks the river and often accommodates a wide variety of local residents, a good sign. Hours are 11am to 11pm daily.

Stadttheuriger, Hans-Sachs-Gasse 8 (tel. 0316/821588). You'll walk down a dark tunnel before reaching the vaulted ceilings of this 400-year-old wine restaurant. Although a bit stark, the locale is clean and bright, ringed with fresh layers of plaster and cream-colored paint. Cold meats, salads, and seafood come from a glass display case, while the Styrian dishes listed on the menu include filet of peppersteak, strudels, pork medallions, and filet steak with mushrooms. Full meals cost from 300 AS ($21.75) and are served daily from 11am to 2am.

THE CAFÉS OF GRAZ

Café Glockenspiel, Glockenspielplatz 4 (tel. 0316/830291), stands on a square filled with neoclassical and art nouveau buildings. In the tower a carillon plays three times a day, at 11am, 3pm, and again at 6pm. The café is on the ground floor of the ornately embellished building, with café tables out front in fair weather. Here, a formally attired waiter will take your order for coffee, light snacks, or sandwiches. The interior has a comfortable décor: serpentine banquettes, mahogany paneling and tables, original lithographs and paintings. Coffee or pastries range from 22 AS ($1.60) to 35 AS ($2.55). The café is open Monday to Friday from 7:30am to 6pm and on Saturday from 8am to 2pm; closed Sunday.

Café am Tummelplatz, Hans-Sachs-Gasse 8 (tel. 0316/821586), connected to the previously recommended Stadttheuriger, is elegant, manicured, well carpeted, and filled with marble tables and well-stocked pastry displays. Waitresses in frilly aprons serve hot chocolate "mit Schlag" (whipped cream). The coffee specialty is named for Maria Theresa. Pastries or coffee costs from 22 AS ($1.60). Service is Monday to Friday from 8am to 8pm, on Saturday from 8am to 2pm; closed Sunday.

Café Leinich, Kaiser-Josef-Platz 4 (tel. 0316/830586). Perfect on a summer day, with a view looking over the activity in the open-air market, this popular institution serves good coffee and homemade pastries. Devotees of the rich concoctions—fresh fruit and berries are used in abundance—include students, workers, and retired people (some of whom plan their afternoon around the time spent here). Coffee and pastries each range from 28 AS ($2.05). Service is Monday to Friday from 7am to 7pm, on Saturday from 7am to 2pm; closed Sunday.

THE SIGHTS

In great part, the **Old Quarter** of Graz is preserved in its original state, and a tour through it is compelling for visitors (see "Tours," below). Major sights include the **Hauptplatz** (main square) in the heart of the city, surrounded by ancient houses with characteristic brown-tile roofs with narrow gables. The most notable is the House of Luegg at the corner of Sporgasse, known for its arcades and façade dating back to the 17th century.

A few steps down Herrengasse, the wide shopping and business street, is the **Landhaus,** seat of the provincial government, a Renaissance masterpiece completed in 1565 by an Italian architect, Domenico dell'Allio. Above the main gate a window is especially highlighted, intensifying the effect of the gate. The courtyard is bounded on the south by an arched arcade traversing the court. The arched Renaissance-style well was poured in bronze near the end of the 16th century.

After that, the next major site is the **Landeszeughaus,** or armory, Herrengasse 16 (tel. 0316/877-2778), next to the Landhaus. Being the capital and main city of the province, Graz was militarily important in earlier times, and for more than two centuries it was a bulwark against the ever-invading Turks. The armory, built during 1642–45 by Anton Solar, dates from the time of the Turkish wars. Its early baroque gate is flanked by statues of the war deities, Mars and Minerva, the work of Giovanni Mamolo. The four upper floors of the building are separated by the original strong wood-beamed ceilings. The cannon hall on the ground floor is vaulted.

Now a museum displaying three centuries of weaponry, the Landeszeughaus contains some 30,000 harnesses, coats of mail, helmets, swords, pikes, muskets of various kinds, pistols, arquebuses, and other implements of war. In 1749 Empress Maria Theresa, in recognition of Styrian military service and strategic significance, allowed this arsenal to remain when others in her empire were destroyed.

You can visit the armory, April to October, Monday to Friday from 9am to 5pm. It closes at 1pm on Saturday and Sunday. Admission is 25 AS ($1.80).

Paulustor, or Paul's Gate, between the remnants of the former rampart of Graz, dates from the time of the fortification of the city by Italian architects. The side of the gate facing the city is plain, the exterior being decorated with large coats-of-arms of Archduke Ferdinand and his first wife, Anne of Bavaria.

Another major attraction is the **Landesmuseum Joanneum,** which has departments at different locations. The natural history displays are at the old Joanneum building, Raubergasse 10 (tel. 0316/877-0). The collections of the Old Gallery and of the arts and crafts department are in the new Joanneum building at Neutorgasse 45 (tel. 0316/877-2457).

The New Gallery on the third floor of the former Herberstein town house, Sackstrasse 16 (tel. 0316/829155), shows art from the 19th century to the present. The Styrian Museum of Folklore is at Paulustorgasse 13 (tel. 0316/830416). Here you'll see stained glass, altarpieces, and important art from the Middle Ages, some going back to the 12th century.

At the Eggenberg Palace (see below) you'll find the department of prehistory and early history, including an extensive collection of Roman stones in an open-air pavilion in the park, the Münzenkabinett, a coin collection, and the Styrian Hunting Museum.

Most Joanneum exhibits are open Monday to Friday from 9am to 4pm, to noon on Saturday and Sunday. Admission is 25 AS ($1.80).

The **Domkirche** (cathedral), between Burgergasse and Burggasse, was originally the Romanesque Church of St. Aegydius, a fortified church outside the town walls, first mentioned in a document in 1174. In the 15th century Frederick III had it converted into a spacious three-bayed city parish church in the late Gothic style, although instead of a Gothic spire the structure later acquired a wooden turret. Archduke Carl of Inner Austria attached the church to his residence, the Burg (castle), and later entrusted it to the Jesuits. After the dissolution of that order in Austria it became the cathedral church of the bishops of Seckau. Inside you'll see two shrines, circa 1475, made in Mantua, and a baroque high altar, the 18th-century creation of Father Georg Kraxner.

Next door on Burggasse is the **Mausoleum of Emperor Ferdinand II,** one of the most remarkable buildings of Graz. Started in 1614 and completed in 1638, it was intended as the tomb of the emperor and his first wife. The church, crowned by a crossing cupola with the tomb chapel also vaulted, is regarded as the best example of mannerism Austria. The high altar is an early work of J. B. Fischer von Erlach, done from 1695 to 1697. The central sarcophagus of the tomb intended for Ferdinand's parents contains only the remains of his mother. His father, Archduke Carl of Inner Austria, was interred elsewhere.

Other than the cathedral, another sightseeing target in Graz is **Mariahilferkirche** (Church of Our Lady of Succor), Mariahilferplatz 3, built for the Minorite brothers on the right bank of the Mur River. Pietro de Pomis carried out reconstruction of the church in the early 17th century and painted the celebrated altarpiece depicting St. Elizabeth interceding with the Virgin Mary. This painting made the church a place of pilgrimage.

Overlooking Graz, **Schlossberg,** the formerly fortified hill, rising to a height of 1,550 feet above sea level, is an island of quiet. As I mentioned above, the fortifications were leveled in 1809 by terms of a treaty Napoleon dictated to a defeated Austria. You can take a cable railway to the restaurant on top or climb the winding stairs. From the top you'll be able to look down on the city and its environs. Guided tours of the citadel are given daily (except in the winter) on the hour from 8am to 5pm, starting from the bell tower opposite the upper station of the cable railway. The cost is 10 AS (75¢) per person.

The **Clock Tower** (Uhrturm) on the citadel is a curiosity above the walls of the former Citizens' Bastion. It acquired its present appearance in 1555–56, when the original Gothic tower was given Renaissance treatment, resulting in a circular wooden gallery with oriels and four huge clock faces.

The **Burg** (castle), northeast of the Hauptplatz in the Old Quarter, is distinguished by its unique double-spiral staircase constructed in 1499 for Emperor Maximilian I.

About 2 miles from the city, you can visit **Schloss Eggenberg** (Eggenberg Palace), Eggenberg Allee 90, a square 17th-century building with towers on its four corners and an accentuated façade over the main gate. The palace sits in a large park now used as a game preserve. The four wings of the baroque structure surround a large court with arched arcades and two smaller courts separated by the palace church. You can take guided tours of the baroque state apartments on the second floor daily from the first of April until the end of October from 9am to 1pm and 2 to 4pm (time of last tour departure). Admission is 25 AS ($1.80). For information, phone 0316/53264.

The ground floor of the south wing houses the Landesmuseum Joanneum's department of prehistory and early history, mentioned above, with a good collection of Styrian antiquities and the coin collections. Visits are possible daily from the first of February until the end of November from 9am to 1pm and 2 to 5pm.

The Hunting Museum, another part of the Landesmuseum Joanneum collections, is on the first floor of the palace, with the same visiting hours.

A major attraction in the environs is about 10 miles north of Graz, at Stübing, the **Austrian Open-Air Museum** (Österreichisches Freilichtmuseum) (tel. 03124/22431), set in a wooded valley branching off from the Valley of the Mur. Here you'll see rustic buildings from all the Austrian provinces, some as much as 300 years old. The 75 authentic structures include a smokeroom house (Rauchstubenhaus) from East Styria and a smokehouse (Rauchhaus) from Land Salzburg, and circular, triangular, and rectangular houses. The museum is open daily except Monday from the first of April until the end of October, charging an admission of 45 AS ($3.25). For information about touring hours, telephone the museum directly.

TOURS

Guided walking tours are offered all year long. From the meeting place at the City Tourist Office, Graz-Steiremark-Haus, Herrengasse 16, you are taken through the Old Quarter (see description under "The Sights" above) to the Landhaus (the seat of the provincial government), Stempfergasse, Glockenspielplatz, Bürgergasse, the Dom (cathedral), the mausoleum, the Burg (castle), the Schauspielhaus (theater), Freiheitsplatz, Hofgasse, Sporgasse, Franziskanerplatz, and the Hauptplatz (main square). In winter, tours depart only on Saturday at 2:30pm.

The guide points out such landmarks as the main post office, the Stadtkeller, the underpass of the main bridge, the electric cable railway to the Schlossberg, Geidorfplatz, Leechkirche (Leech Church), Elisabethstrasse, Landeskrankenhaus (Hospital of the Land Steiermark), Hilm Pond, the university, Heinrichstrasse, Paulustor (Paul's Gate), and the Opera House, among other sights. The tour ends at

Eggenberg Palace, where you can visit the state rooms and the park, after which you're taken at about 12:15pm to the Renaissance courtyard of the Landhaus, concluding the tour. In summer, tours leave on Monday and Thursday at 6:30pm, and Tuesday, Friday, Saturday, and Sunday at 2:30pm. The cost is 40 AS ($2.90) per person.

Bus sightseeing tours are available Monday to Friday all year, departing at 10am and costing 150 AS ($11).

Every Friday afternoon, the tourist office offers trips to **Piber,** 15 miles west of Graz, where visitors see the stud farm where the white Lippizaner stallions are bred and receive their initial training before appearing at the Spanish Riding School in Vienna. Tours depart from the Grazer Congress at 2pm, costing 300 AS ($21.75).

Back in the city, an **electric cable railway** will take you in three minutes some 1,550 feet up from the lower station at Kaiser-Franz-Josef-Kai 38 to the upper station at the Schlossberg Restaurant. This run is made every 15 minutes. The fare is 20 AS ($1.45) for a round-trip for adults. Children under 6 ride free, while those over 6 pay half the adult fare.

Many other tours are offered, by foot, bus, streetcar, car, cable, and even swimming in Graz and its environs. Ask at the tourist office.

SHOPPING

You might begin your shopping expedition at the Hauptplatz, the main square in the center of town. The major shopping streets, including Herrengasse, branch off from here. Of course the major item to buy, if it appeals to you, is Styrian clothing in the famous Styrian grays and greens, a style of dress that has spread all over Austria. Stores offer a good selection of dirndls and hats in particular, as well as local handcrafts and leather clothing.

Steirisches Heimatwerk, Paulustorgasse 4 (tel. 0316/827106), is a large, many-roomed store selling cookbooks, shoes, dirndls, a big selection of regional blouses, dresses, coats, silk, wool, and cotton fabrics, as well as objects made from glass, ceramics, and wood. Every item is made in Austria. Some of the more unusual items include hand-painted depictions of the local saints in small wooden frames. The sales personnel are helpful.

Brühl and Söhne, Am Gsernen Tor 11 (tel. 0316/821616), sells high-quality, but also high-priced, Styrian clothing for men, women, and children. Their inventory includes fashionable dirndls, coats, skirts, hats, vests, suits, and accessories.

Anton Pichler, Herrengasse 28 (tel. 0316/829562), sells hats of all kinds. The varieties range from Tyrolean and Styrian traditional designs to more updated versions, including golfing and hunting hats. The elegant chrome- and marble-trimmed exterior opens to reveal a wood-paneled rectangle with hundreds of hats covering the paneled walls.

The **English Bookstore,** Tummelplatz (tel. 0316/826-2660), sells English and American literature, as well as books on Graz, Styria, and Austria in English. There's also a selection of international newspapers.

GRAZ AFTER DARK

The **Opernhaus** (Opera House), Opernring (tel. 0316/827422), presents both opera and ballet. It is, of course, the leading cultural center of Graz. The building was constructed "in the style of Fischer von Erlach" at the end of the 19th century.

In summer you can often hear concerts in the **Stadtpark,** or city park, which adjoins the northeast side of the citadel.

The **Styrian Autumn,** an arts festival, takes place during parts of September and October. It has a reputation for being avant-garde, presenting everything from jazz to mime.

Sometimes restaurants combine dancing with disco action and nightclub shows, so at one address you might make an evening of it. The cafés often have music as well. Because of the university in Graz, many of the after-dark haunts are heavily frequented by young people.

Haus Gottinger, Strassgang (tel. 0316/281850), offers the best dancing in Graz for an over-30 crowd. When rock groups make special appearances, the charge is slightly more than the regular entrance fee of 50 AS ($3.65). There's a restaurant as well. The place is especially popular on Friday and Saturday nights, and is open daily from 7:30pm to 4am.

The area around Farbergasse-Mehlplatz is the "in" place for all walks of life. Here is centered the greatest cluster of bars and restaurants in the city. The people of Graz refer to it as their "Bermuda Triangle." Most of the establishments charge around 50 AS ($3.65) for a mug of beer. The leading choices include the following.

Altstadtbeisl, Mehlplatz 1 (tel. 0316/828702), is perhaps the most popular place in the Triangle. It is open Monday to Friday from 11am to 1am and on Saturday and Sunday from 6 to 11pm. The house offers Styrian wine and snacks.

Gamlitzer Weinstube, Mehlplatz 4 (tel. 0316/828760), serves a delectable Austrian cuisine, along with Italian specialties, with meals costing from 125 AS ($9). Styrian wine accompanies most meals. It is open daily from 11am to 1am.

Vinothek, Prokopigasse 5 (tel. 0316/810057), has one of the finest selections of wine in the area, including those from Italy and other parts of Austria. Of course, its largest collection centers around Styria's own vintages. Here you can order other drinks as well, along with a selection of snacks. It is open daily from 11am to 11pm.

Bistro, Mehlplatz (tel. 0316/828701), is a restaurant and coffee bar during the day, but at night becomes a much-frequented coffee bar. It is open daily from 11am to 1am except on Sunday, when its hours are 5:30pm to midnight.

---

2. Bad Gleichenberg

The most important summer spa in South Styria, Bad Gleichenberg, lies southeast of Graz near the border of Yugoslavia, in a setting of rolling hills and vineyards. This is one of the most interesting—but little known—parts of Austria to explore. Untersteiermark, or Lower Styria, where this spa is located, was a lot larger in the days of the Habsburgs. Much of its territory was lost to Yugoslavia following the breakup of the empire after World War I.

Bad Gleichenberg's setting is a lovely valley opening to the south. In the area's magnificent parks, you'll see exotic plants, including the giant sequoia. You can partake of the mineral waters of the Emma, Konstantin, and Johannisbrunnen springs and even take a bottle home with you. The spa has an interesting entertainment program, plus special tours in the environs.

You can drive to Bad Gleichenberg, take an express train from Vienna, or a bus from Graz or Vienna.

FOOD AND LODGING

A prosperous-looking white-walled villa, the **Hotel Austria,** A-8344 Bad Gleichenberg (tel. 03159/2205), has shutters and a raised sun terrace. The light coming in from the big old-fashioned windows floods the interior. On the premises is an informal bar area covered with a brick vaulted ceiling, and a collection of public rooms is filled with comfortable furniture in distinguished combinations of white and dark colors. The hotel rents 44 well-furnished bedrooms, each with private bath or shower, and does so from March to November. Half board costs 550 AS ($40) to 620 AS ($45) per person daily.

Hotel Gleichenbergerhof, A-8344 Bad Gleichenberg (tel. 03159/2424), is a modern 12-room chalet set in a forested area with a masonry sun terrace stretching below the white and dark-colored façade. The interior has lots of rustically modern accessories, including a piano bar and an open fireplace. The Kaulfersch family charges from 480 AS ($35) per person daily, based on double occupancy and including half board. All units contain private baths, balconies, and phones.

KAPFENSTEIN
As an alternative to staying in Bad Gleichenberg, you can drive east to this hamlet and its schloss hotel near the Yugoslav border.

Food and Lodging
Schloss Kapfenstein, A-8353 Kapfenstein (tel. 03157/2202), is a solidly built castle with a hipped roof and a curving extension that's almost as old as the main building itself. Set in the middle of forests and rich fields, the castle accepts paying guests in rooms filled with antique furniture and all the modern comforts. The 16-bed hotel charges from 495 AS ($36) per person daily for half board.

The hotel is closed between mid-December and early March. You can eat on the castle's terrace if you wish, as it offers a view of the village below. Every Thursday the Winkler-Hermaden family presents a Styrian buffet; otherwise, specialties are based on regional recipes such as roast hen, homemade blutwurst and sausages, and apple strudel.

---

3. Leoben

In 1797 Napoleon signed a peace treaty in Leoben in Upper Styria, a town built on a loop of the Mur River northwest of Graz and known for its ironworking industries and lignite mining. In fact, it's the seat of a mining college. But because it's industrial, don't assume that the town is without attractions.

The **Altes Rathaus** (Old Town Hall) stands on the Hauptplatz (main square) of Leoben. The **pfarrkirche** (parish church) of the town has two towers dating from the latter 17th century. The **Mautturm,** or toll tower, called the "mushroom tower," is Leoben's most distinguishing landmark, dating from 1615.

If possible, visit the 14th-century **Church of Maria Waasen,** which has some excellent stained glass in the choir. One of its windows depicts the Passion of Christ. This church is west of the town, near the bridge spanning the Mur.

A popular excursion is to **Göss,** 1¼ miles south of Leoben, where Göss beer is produced. The brewery took over what had once been a nunnery, dating from the 11th century. It's considered the oldest nunnery in Styria and still has a Gothic church and a Romanesque crypt.

FOOD AND LODGING
A few doors away from the antique civic buildings in the center of town, the **Hotel Kindler,** Straussgasse 7-11, A-8700 Leoben (tel. 03842/43202), incorporates a richly decorated older structure with a contemporary, big-windowed building just next to it. The hotel is comfortably decorated with modern furniture and tasteful colors in both its public rooms and bedrooms. The hotel offers 43 bedrooms, each with private bath or shower. Bed-and-breakfast costs 345 AS ($25) to 390 AS ($28.25) per person daily.

The Iron Road, no. 115, northwest from Leoben leads to the old market town and ski area of—

VORDERNBERG/PRÄBICHL
The market town of Vordernberg lies at the foot of the Präbichl Pass in the heart of Upper Styria. On its east is the Hochschwab mountain range and on the west the Eisenerz (iron ore) Alps with the romantic Gesäuse canyon. Its alpine location makes this area attractive either as a summer resort or a winter holiday center.

Vordernberg is the oldest center of the Styrian iron industry. Iron mining here is ancient, having been a pursuit of the Celts and the Romans.

On the town's Hauptplatz (main square), you can visit the **Iron Works Museum** (wheel works no. 4). The 17th-century **pfarrkirche** (parish church) has in its graveyard tombs of former hammermill and wheel works owners. The town's **Laurentius Church** is from the 15th century. The **Rathaus** (Town Hall) still has its original tower and stucco ceiling. A richly decorated wrought-iron fountain dates from 1668. There are many splendid burghers' houses in Vordernberg.

The Präbichl, with its Polster and Grubl skiing areas, is well known as a ski center in Styria. A number of ski lifts lead up to the skiing grounds, where well-prepared, avalanche-free slopes allow skiing until April. A ski school, cross-country tracks, toboggan runs, curling and ice-skating rinks, and cleared footpaths are all part of the winter holiday scene.

Summer visitors can take mountain walks and climbs in the Hochschwab area and the Alps, to see the rich alpine flora. From May to October, guests can visit the Styrian Erzberg (Ore Mountain) on guided inspection tours.

---

4. Murau

Lying on both sides of the Mur River at the foot of the Stolzalpe, which rises to nearly 6,000 feet, the old town of Murau is a winter ski region and also the center of many a summer excursion. It's easily reached from Salzburg via the Tauern motorway, as well as from Carinthia, Vienna, and the rest of Styria.

Murau's **pfarrkirche** (parish church) of St. Matthew dates from the 13th century. Note the "lanterns of the dead," a late Gothic sculpture in front of the church. Remnants of the medieval walls of the town can be seen.

Summer visitors enjoy high alpine tours. Two chair lifts will take you through the Murau recreation area. Skiers come here in winter especially for the fine cross-country tracks. The Murau center is a good place for rest and relaxation at any time of the year. It advertises itself as "not intended for the masses." It's a good family vacation spot.

In summer you can take a ride on an old steam-engine train on the narrow-gauge Murtal railway, which goes through the Mur Valley on its run to Tamsweg in the neighboring province of Land Salzburg.

The 900-year-old **Stift St. Lambrecht** (Convent of St. Lambrecht) with fine collections of ecclesiastical art and artifacts is nearby, as is the little romantic village of **Oberwölz**. Both are worth a visit. You can go also a short distance to **Wildbad Einöd** for thermal baths.

FOOD AND LODGING

The solid-looking **Hotel Bräuhaus**, A-8850 Murau (tel. 03532/2437), rents 23 comfortable bedrooms, of which 16 contain private baths or showers. Half-board rates range from 320 AS ($23.25) to 380 AS ($27.65) per person daily. The establishment is better known for its restaurant, serving well-prepared meals on a flagstone-covered terrace or inside in a vaulted dining room. Directed by the Lercher family, the hotel includes a sauna. The location is within an easy walk of the village's sporting facilities.

Murauer Gasthof Hotel Lercher, Schwarzenbergstrasse 10, A-8850 Murau (tel. 03532/2431), is a pleasantly designed, sunflower-colored building with white trim and a generously rambling façade that includes several different sections. In the center of town, the hotel is directed by the Lercher family, who carefully maintain the flagstone-covered entrance hall and the rustically accommodating bar area, along with comfortably furnished bedrooms. Accommodations cost 380 AS ($27.75) to 480 AS ($35) per person per night, with breakfast buffet included. Extra charge for half board is 120 AS ($8.75). The hotel contains 26 bedrooms, each of which has a shower, phone, television, and radio.

---

5. Turracher Höhe

A section of Turracher Höhe was previewed above in the chapter on Carinthia (Chapter XII), but part of it is also in Styria, at the western end of the province on the pass over the Gurktal alpine range that leads into Carinthia. This is both a summer tourist center and a winter ski area.

The mountains surrounding the plateau (5,785 feet) on which Turracher Höhe is situated are excellent for hiking. The Turrachersee (Lake Turrach) is ideal for fishing, windsurfing, sailing, and rowing.

The Nock mountain range (7,875 feet) has wide, carefully prepared ski slopes, cross-country tracks, and marked winter hiking trails. T-bars and chair lifts are available, as is a ski school.

FOOD AND LODGING

Seehotel Jägerwirt, A-8864 Turracher Höhe (tel. 03533/82570) looks like a collection of lakeside chalets carefully joined together with low-lying reception areas and public rooms. The interior is filled with recreational facilities such as a sauna, a children's play area, tennis courts, bars, and restaurants, all of them mixed with a scattering of open fireplaces and rustic furniture. A lakeside terrace covered with flagstones provides a place for outdoor dinners in summer. The Brandstätter family are the accommodating hosts, renting 50 attractively furnished, well-maintained bedrooms, each with private bath or shower, from December to April and June to October. In winter, charges are 575 AS ($41.75) to 945 AS ($68.75) per person daily; in summer, 440 AS ($32) to 650 AS ($47.25) per person daily. Prices include half board and use of the sauna, whirlpool, and indoor swimming pool.

---

6. Dachstein-Tauern

In northwest Styria lies the major ski area in the province. The Dachstein, in the Salzkammergut, is a gigantic alpine mountain range cutting across Land Salzburg, Upper Austria, and Styria, with mammoth glaciers lying between its peaks. The Enns River separates the Dachstein and the Tauern massifs. This is the site of championship ski races and also the place for powder skiing.

The principal Styrian ski resorts, Schladming and Ramsau, are previewed below.

RAMSAU

At the foot of the mighty Dachstein massif, which reaches a height of nearly 10,000 feet, Ramsau is an emerging ski resort, rivaling but not yet surpassing Schladming (see below). The prices here are, in general, lower than those at Schladming. Ramsau lies on a high plateau to the north of Schladming.

Food and Lodging

Sporthotel Matschner, A-8972 Ramsau (tel. 03687/81721), is a double chalet whose identical wings are separated by a collection of flowered balconies. On the premises are an indoor swimming pool and supervised tennis courts with a resident coach. The hotel provides easy access to the many nearby sporting facilities. It offers 60 pleasantly furnished bedrooms, each with private bath or shower, radio, and balcony. Winter half-board rates range from 690 AS ($50.25) to 910 AS ($65) per person daily, with summer half-board charges going from 530 AS ($38.50) to 720 AS ($52.25) per person daily. Prices include participation in the organized sporting activities. Open December to October.

Almfrieden Hotel, A-8972 Ramsau (tel. 03687/81753), is a contemporary chalet with two symmetrical wings joined by an interconnecting section. Set at the base of a rock-strewn mountain, the hotel looks out over a grassy meadow and a nearby sun terrace covered with parasols. The interior is rustically paneled with pine boards and dotted with open fireplaces and mountain chairs. Guests can use the sauna, solarium, TV room, and fitness room; play table tennis and chess; or try marksmanship on the indoor rifle range—all on the premises. With half board included, rates per person range from 525 AS ($38.25) to 775 AS ($56.25) in rooms with private baths. Prices depend on the season and the accommodation.

Alpengasthof Peter Rosegger, A-8972 Ramsau (tel. 03687/81223), is a 13-room chalet surrounded by larches and a grassy field, with a cozy interior of rustic furniture, country chintz, and exposed paneling. Fritz and Barbara Walcher are the owners of this place, charging 620 AS ($45) to 660 AS ($48) per person daily in high season, with a Styrian half board included. On the premises are a sauna, a fitness room, table tennis, and a paneled gaststube with a ceramic stove dating from 1667. There's also a summertime terrace.

Hotel Post, A-8972 Ramsau (tel. 03687/81708), is an attractively detailed chalet with summer flowerboxes, heavy overhanging eaves, and an interior décor of rustic accessories and lots of paneling. On the premises are an indoor pool, a sauna, an elevator, and a restaurant and bar with an open fireplace; there is a cinema nearby. The Lackner family are your hosts, renting 70 inviting, comfortable bedrooms, most with private baths or showers, from December to October. Half board costs from 510 AS ($37) per person daily.

Pension Ennstalerhof, A-8972 Ramsau (tel. 03687/81080), is an attractive chalet with flowered balconies, a pleasant garden, and a warmly rustic interior with autumnal colors, Oriental rugs, big windows, and open fireplaces. The pension rents 14 comfortably furnished bedrooms, charging from 550 AS ($40) per person daily, with half board included.

Hotel Restaurant Pehab Kirchenwirt, A-8972 Ramsau (tel. 03687/81732), is a rambling balconied building in the shadow of the village church in the center of the resort. The pleasantly furnished interior is filled with warm colors, open fireplaces, and wrought-iron accents. On the premises are a bar, two restaurants, and a sauna. There is easy access to the nearby public indoor swimming pool and the ski facilities. The 80-bed hotel offers 37 comfortable, well-furnished rooms with private baths or showers. Rates are 390 AS ($28.25) to 590 AS ($43) per person daily for half board.

SCHLADMING/ROHRMOOS

This skiing center is in the Dachstein-Tauern recreation and winter-sports area on highway no. 308 and the Vienna-Bruck/Mur-Graz rail line, making it easy to reach. The Planai (6,235 feet) and the Hochwurzen (6,070 feet) have fast downhill runs and ski slopes, equipped with a cableway, five double-chair lifts, a connectable three-seat chair lift, ski buses, and 15 ski hoists, at all altitudes. Some 22,000 people per hour can be transported.

The Dachstein-Südward cableway makes skiing at 8,865 feet possible in summer. There are ski schools, and you can leave small children at the kindergarten, which has a children's ski hoist.

Miles of winter footpaths make for good, invigorating walking. You can also enjoy horse sleighing, tobogganing, ski-bobbing, curling, game-feeding trips, and many other winter activities. Cafés and bars offer lively après-ski, as do the hotels. In summer you'll enjoy mountaineering, swimming, tennis, bowling, and a lot of top-quality entertainment, along with warm Styrian hospitality. Golf (an 18-hole course), rafting, and paragliding are other sports practiced in fair weather.

Schladming is an ancient town lying in the upper valley of the Enns River between Dachstein to the north and Schladminger Tauern to the south. It was a silver- and copper-mining town in medieval times. Old miners' houses can still be seen in the town. The pfarrkirche (parish church) is late Gothic. An 1862 church in town is the largest Protestant church in Styria.

Food and Lodging at Schladming

Sporthotel Royer, A-8970 Schladming (tel. 03687/23240), opened in 1975, offers a gracious and contemporary place to stay, with a large collection of sporting facilities. Conceived in a modern design of recessed balconies and angled rooflines, the hotel has a big indoor as well as a heated outdoor swimming pool, two outdoor and three indoor tennis courts, two squash courts, three bowling alleys, pony riding for children up to 14 years old, and children's play facilities. There's easy access to the many outdoor ski and hiking trails in the vicinity. Guests can eat in a 150-seat dining room, in the Rôtisserie Royer Grill, or in the Steirerstüberl.

The warmly furnished bedrooms, 130 in all, rent for 970 AS ($70.50) in high season, based on double occupancy, with half board included. Singles pay a daily surcharge of 180 AS ($13). Each room has a bath, direct-dial phone, radio, minibar, and safe. Most accommodations also have balconies.

Romantik Hotel Alte Post, Hauptplatz 10, A-8970 Schladming (tel. 03687/22571). The first records of this historic restaurant in the center of town date from 1618. The façade is of the symmetrical chalet sort you'd expect in the hills nearby, with a round arched door and dark shutters. The renovated interior, in addition to housing a popular restaurant, offers 40 well-furnished rooms priced from 580 AS ($42.25) to 1,060 AS ($77) per person, half board included. Singles pay a daily surcharge of 120 AS ($8.75).

In the high-ceilinged formal dining room, a sophisticated menu of nouvelle cuisine awaits gastronomes who make a meal here a special event. You might enjoy a mousse of chicken livers with leaf lettuce or a combination of wild salmon and fresh asparagus baked in an orange sauce, perhaps a ragoût of snails or aiguillettes of venison in a creamy sauce. Even if you're staying at the hotel, reservations are advised for full à la carte meals, which average 225 AS ($16.25); or for fixed-price menus, which range from 140 AS ($10.25) to 500 AS ($36.25). Hot food is served daily from 11:30am to 2pm and 6 to 11pm. Less formal meals are available in the rustic Knappenstube. The establishment is closed for most of November.

Haus Barbara, Coburgstrasse 553, A-8970 Schladming (tel. 03687/22077), is an attractively decorated three-story chalet with a picture of a female saint wielding a sword and carrying a chalice painted onto the façade. A short walk from the village, just opposite the Planai cable car, the hotel includes a bar with an open fireplace and a collection of pleasant rooms, each of which has a private bath, phone, and radio. Many of them also contain balconies. No meals are served other than breakfast, which is included in the price of 340 AS ($24.75) to 370 AS ($27) per person daily at this 20-room four-star selection. Facilities include a Turkish bath and a solarium.

Food and Lodging at Rohrmoos

Hotel Rohrmooserhof, A-8970 Rohrmoos (tel. 03687/61455), is an attractively proportioned chalet with long rows of wrap-around balconies and big windows to let sunlight stream into the well-furnished and nicely maintained bedrooms. Set into the slope of an alpine hillside, the hotel has an outdoor pool, a pastry and confectionary shop, and a collection of public rooms accented with lots of wood paneling. Tennis courts and a wide range of sporting activities are close at hand. From January to October, the 48-bed four-star hotel receives international guests, charging 450 AS ($32.75) to 550 AS ($40) per person daily in winter for half board. In summer, half board costs 370 AS ($27) to 400 AS ($29) per person daily.

Gasthof Waldfrieden, A-8970 Rohrmoos (tel. 03687/61487). Built by the

Stocker family in 1964 and renovated in 1976, this hotel is a sprawling chalet with festoons of summer flowers hanging from its wooden balconies and painted decorations around many of its windows. Each of the 40 rooms has its own private bath, balcony, and phone. The in-house restaurant is beamed, with lots of wooden accents. A flagstone-covered terrace provides a mountain vista in summer, while sports-lovers will appreciate the many skiing and hiking facilities in the vicinity. Guests are received from December to October. Half board in winter costs 400 AS ($29) to 500 AS ($36.25) per person daily. In summer, half board ranges from 300 AS ($21.75) to 350 AS ($25.50) per person daily.

Gasthof Sonneck, A-8970 Schladming (tel. 03687/61232), is a balconied chalet with white walls, big windows, and wooden balconies. A flagstone-covered terrace provides a relaxing place for a midafternoon cup of coffee. The interior is pleasantly paneled and rustically outfitted with glowing pine and tasteful furniture. The 20 bedrooms, which look out over the mountains, cost 290 AS ($21) to 390 AS ($28.25) per person in high season for double occupancy, on the half-board plan. Each bedroom has a private bath and a balcony. The hotel offers sauna, a solarium, and table tennis. Open December to September.

Hotel Schwaigerhof, A-8970 Rohrmoos (tel. 03687/61422-0), is an attractively embellished five-story chalet with a prominent eyrie for a stork's nest jutting above the gently sloping roof, as well as a hillside location with a view of the mountains. The interior contains an indoor swimming pool, lots of pine paneling, a bar, and two restaurants. Each of the 39 bedrooms has its own bath, and a host of sporting facilities are available nearby. The Stocker family charges 520 AS ($37.75) to 620 AS ($45) per person daily for half board in winter. In summer, half board costs 320 AS ($23.25) to 420 AS ($30.50) per person daily.

PICHL-MANDLING

Another well-known winter-sports center is composed of Pichl and its neighboring villages of Mandling, Gleiming, Preunegg, and Vorberg. In the Enns Valley, the center has the same accessibility by car, bus, or train as does Schladming/Rohrmoos (see above).

Pichl has avalanche-proof, prepared skiing grounds for everyone from beginner to expert, a cabin cableway, two double-chair lifts, and nine ski hoists. It offers natural toboggan runs, curling rinks, a ski school, and a ski kindergarten. Nonskiers will enjoy walks along the cleared footpaths, folkloric events, and sleigh rides. The area is also a lure for summer visitors, who can explore the mountains on foot, swim, and make trips to surrounding attractions.

Food and Lodging

Alpengasthof-Hotel Pichlmayrgut, A-8973 Pichl-Mandling (tel. 06454/305), is one of the most distinctively styled hotels in the region. It stretches over a sprawling expanse of alpine hillside in various wings, one of which looks like a medieval castle with chevron shutters. A more recent addition is built in roughly the same style, with big windows, a rounded watchtower, and lots of stone masonry. On the premises are an indoor pool, a sauna, a bar, a café, two restaurants, and a host of additional facilities. The 96 bedrooms, each with private shower or bath, are pleasantly and attractively furnished. Half board costs 600 AS ($43.50) to 900 AS ($65.50) per person daily in winter. In summer, half board goes for 500 AS ($36.25) to 700 AS ($51) per person daily. Open from December to October.

7. From Tauplitz to Altaussee

The Styrian Salzkammergut, a section the province shares with both Upper Austria and Land Salzburg, is one of the most beautiful regions of Styria. In the northwest part of the province and long a summer holiday center, this is rapidly developing as a winter ski resort area as well. This area is just to the southwest of the Land Salzburg lake district.

TAUPLITZ/TAUPLITZALM

Ranking among the most popular winter-sports centers and recreation areas in Austria, Tauplitz and its pasture-and-lake district, Tauplitzalm, are also good for summer holidays.

The Tauplitzalm can be approached from Tauplitz by chair lift, and the scenic mountain area is fine country for hiking. You can enjoy swimming, tennis, minigolf, folkloric entertainment, and dancing, plus 5pm tea. The Tauplitzalm can also be reached from Bad Mitterndorf (see below) on the Tauplitzalm alpine road.

In winter the flying ski jump on the Kulm near Tauplitz is a constant attraction. The two places account for more than a dozen ski lifts, ski schools with special children's courses, and long-distance running schools for walking on skis. This is a training center for domestic and foreign national ski teams.

Food and Lodging at Tauplitz

Gasthof/Pension Horst Hechl, A-8982 Tauplitz (tel. 03688/2268), is an imposingly Teutonic-looking building set in front of a tennis court, with an outdoor swimming pool in back. Under its gabled and hipped roof are 20 attractively decorated bedrooms, each with private bath or shower, which cost 400 AS ($29) to 560 AS ($40.75) per person daily for half board in winter. In summer, half board goes for 345 AS ($25) to 415 AS ($30.25) per person daily. The hotel is open from December to October.

Food and Lodging at Tauplitzalm

Sporthotel Tauplitzalm, A-8982 Tauplitzalm (tel. 03688/2306), is a sprawling balconied chalet built into the side of a mountain. Many of the walls are covered with cedar shingles, while the interior is a cozy combination of knotty-pine paneling, fresh colors, and rustic accents. On the premises are a covered swimming pool, a sauna, a day bar, a sun terrace, and 34 tasteful rooms, each with private bath or shower. From November to April and June to September, the hotel charges 680 AS ($49.50) to 750 AS ($54.50) per person daily for half board. In summer, half board goes for 450 AS ($32.75) to 530 AS ($38.50) per person daily.

BAD MITTERNDORF

Long renowned as a health spa in the Salzkammergut, Bad Mitterndorf's proximity to Tauplitz has made it a ski center as well. Lying in the southern foothills of the Totes Gebirge, Bad Heilbrunn, 1¼ miles to the south, is a satellite of Bad Mitterndorf. Salza-Stausee, a lake, is south of the village.

Where to Stay

Kurhotel Heilbrunn, A-8983 Bad Mitterndorf (tel. 06153/2486), is a striking modern 100-room hotel complex that rises from a forested hillside into which it was built. On the premises you'll find both an indoor and an outdoor swimming pool, plus a wide range of physical therapy and spa facilities. Many of the contemporary bedrooms have private balconies and baths, along with all the up-to-date conveniences. Singles range from 670 AS ($48.75) to 920 AS ($67) daily, while doubles run from 740 AS ($53.75) to 990 AS ($72) per person, depending on the exposure, the accommodation, and the season. These prices include full board.

Hubertushof, A-8983 Bad Mitterndorf (tel. 06153/2595), is a well-designed chalet with four floors of balconies, big windows, and wood trim. The tasteful interior is outfitted with rustic furniture, wood ceilings, and earth colors. Bedrooms, 27 in all and each with private bath or shower, are nicely furnished and comfortable.

Half board ranges from 380 AS ($27.75) per person daily. Open from December to March and May to September.

Hotel Kogler, A-8983 Bad Mitterndorf (tel. 06153/2325), has a chalet façade and a T-shaped floor plan. Its balconies are usually draped with summertime flowers, while a garden stretches away from the big windows of the ground-floor reception area. The owners, the Kogler family, rent 31 well-furnished and comfortably appointed bedrooms, each with private bath or shower. They open the hotel from December to March and May to September. In winter, half-board charges go from 350 AS ($25.50) to 550 AS ($40) per person daily. In summer, half board costs 300 AS ($21.75) to 500 AS ($36.25) per person daily.

Pension Lord, A-8983 Bad Mitterndorf (tel. 06153/2553), is an attractive chalet whose uncomplicated design includes wooden balconies stretching across part of the façade and a big picture window piercing through a section of the ground floor. Five minutes on foot from the center of the village, the hotel offers an indoor pool, lots of mountain views, and a rustically modern interior filled with comfortable furniture in both the public rooms and the bedrooms. The pension offers 19 bedrooms, each with private bath or shower, charging 350 AS ($25.50) to 370 AS ($27) per person daily for half board.

Where to Dine

Grimmingswurz'n (tel. 06153/3132), an elegantly rustic restaurant, draws a steady stream of loyal local diners. The menu ranges from regionally inspired to international. Food items include cream of snail soup, plus an array of fish, ragoûts, and meat, particularly veal. Desserts feature a range of seasonally adjusted fruited pastries and sorbets. À la carte meals range from 150 AS ($11) to 450 AS ($32.75), while fixed price menus cost 295 AS ($21.50) to 450 AS ($32.75). The restaurant is open from 11am to 2:30pm and 5pm to midnight; closed on Tuesday and from mid-November to mid-December.

IRDNING

Instead of staying at Tauplitz or Bad Mitterndorf, you might want to take a secondary road leading to one of the most beautiful hotels in Europe, where guests can find facilities for rest and recreation.

Where to Stay

Hotel Schloss Pichlarn, A-8952 Irdning (tel. 03682/2841). Some parts of this sprawling castle are more than 800 years old. Other sections are undeniably modern, including the up-to-date amenities in the comfortable rooms. The entrance is through an arched door covered with chevron designs. The interior is accented with soaring arches, ornate chandeliers, and thick Oriental carpets. The 76 bedrooms, each with private bath or shower, often contain antiques and tasteful colors. Guests are accepted from December to October and charged 1,600 AS ($116.25) to 2,300 AS ($167.25) per person daily for half board in summer. In winter, half board goes from 1,300 AS ($94.50) to 2,000 AS ($145.50) per person daily. The hotel has an elegant dining room, an accommodating bar area, an outdoor terrace, and a range of sporting facilities including an indoor and outdoor pool, a sauna, massage facilities, tennis courts, a tennis and riding hall, and an 18-hole golf course. There is also a beauty salon. If you're just stopping by for a meal, you can have lunch from noon to 2pm and dinner from 7 to 9pm.

BAD AUSSEE

Surrounded by lake, mountains, and woods, Bad Aussee is an old market town and spa in the "green heart" of the Salzkammergut. It lies in the Valley of Traun, with the Totes Gebirge and the Dachstein massif visible in the distance. The ideal time to visit this salt- and mineral-spring spa is in June, when fields of narcissus burst into bloom, one of the most spectacular signs of spring coming to Europe.

Bad Aussee, at the confluence of a pair of upper branches of the Traun River, is considered the capital of the Styrian section of the Salzkammergut. Only 3 miles to the north is Lake Altaussee, with the spa town of Altaussee (see below) on its shore.

In summer this is a good center for walking and climbing in one of the most beautiful sections of Austria. Although Bad Aussee has long been known as a summer spa resort, it has also developed into a winter ski center, with the location of several ski lifts nearby making it attractive to ski enthusiasts.

Bad Aussee's best-known association is with Archduke Johann of the House of Habsburg. In 1827 he married the daughter of a local postmaster, an occurrence that in that era and within the empire was a *cause célèbre* rivaling the later romance of the Duke and Duchess of Windsor. A statue of the "Prince of Styria," Johann, can be seen in the Kurpark.

Incidentally, the Bad Aussee Glaubersalt spring is said to be particularly effective for losing weight.

Food and Lodging

Eurotel Erzherzog Johann, Kurhausplatz 62, A-8990 Bad Aussee (tel. 06152/2507), is a conservatively designed lemon-colored building with stone detailing, forest-green trim, and an arched entranceway in the center of town. The rustic interior offers a handful of winter fireplaces, beamed ceilings, and comfortably up-to-date furniture, as well as easy access to the area's sporting facilities. The spa facilities are connected to the hotel by a covered passageway. The four-star hotel, considered the finest at the resort, offers 62 well-furnished bedrooms, each with private bath or shower. Half board is offered year round for 670 AS ($48.75) to 810 AS ($59) per person daily.

Pension-Villa Kristina, A-8990 Bad Aussee (tel. 06152/2017), is a regionally styled villa about five minutes on foot from the center of town. The steep-roofed, wood-trimmed house is loaded inside and out with dozens of handcrafted details, a scattering of antiques, and all the modern amenities. Surrounded by a flowering park, the 14-room hotel offers shaded terraces as well as balconies adjoining some of the pleasantly furnished rooms. The Raudaschl family, your obliging hosts, charge 525 AS ($38.25) to 600 AS ($43.50) for a single and from 550 AS ($40) per person in a double. The supplement for an apartment is 150 AS ($11) daily. All prices quoted are for half board, the rates varying slightly according to the season.

Hotel Wasnerin, A-8990 Bad Aussee (tel. 06152/2108), was established in 1860 as a hotel for visiting nature-lovers, although the building you see today was constructed in 1934. Built with generously rambling proportions, in a gabled and hip-roofed style with lots of exposed wood and elegantly arched windows looking out on a raised sun terrace, the hotel provides 58 beds from December to October. Twenty-two rooms contain private baths or showers. Half board costs 370 AS ($27) per person daily year round. On the grounds are two tennis courts.

Café Lewandofsky (tel. 06152/2426) welcomes a loyal crowd of clients into its old-fashioned dining room, which serves a wide range of strictly Austrian pastries along with coffee. The summer garden area adjoins the city park and offers a view over the central square of town, as well as of people flocking to the spa facilities for "the cure." Coffee costs from 19 AS ($1.40). Service is daily from 7am to 7pm.

ALTAUSSEE

This is a more tranquil spot for a stopover than nearby Bad Aussee. It also lies in the Styrian section of the Salzkammergut. The Altaussee, facing the Totes Gebirge, is one of the most beautiful bodies of water in Styria. It's about 2 miles long, with rowboats for rent so that you can explore its area. For many decades Altaussee was only a lakeside summer resort, but because of the nearby ski region of Mount Loser (4,995 feet), it now does a winter ski trade as well. From Altaussee you can see the Dachstein glacier.

From Altaussee trips can be arranged in summer to the **Aussee Salt Mines,** 2 miles to the northwest. Conducted tours, lasting about an hour and 25 minutes, are offered from 10am to 4pm daily, except Sunday, costing 90 AS ($6.55). The mines, called Salzbergwerk, were used by the Nazis to store valuable art to prevent its destruction by Allied bombing raids.

Food and Lodging

Hotel Seevilla, Fischerndorf 60, A-8992 Altaussee (tel. 06152/71302), is a romantic villa with arched windows, hipped roofs, and lots of exterior detailing. The interior contains deeply coffered ceilings, exposed wood, and a curving stone staircase leading to the tasteful bedrooms. On the premises are a bathing beach and an indoor pool, as well as a restaurant and café at the lake, and there is access to a wide range of nearby sporting facilities. Each of the units has a private bath, balcony, minibar, radio, and TV hookup. The Maislinger family rents 30 well-furnished bedrooms plus one apartment. In winter, half-board charges range from 650 AS ($47.25) to 730 AS ($53) per person daily. In summer, half-board tariffs go from 630 AS ($45.75) to 700 AS ($51) per person daily, including tax and service.

Gasthof zum Loser, Fischerndorf 80 (tel. 06152/71373), is one of the best restaurants in the region, with a body of local folklore to fill a volume and a loyal clientele that includes actors and poets from as far away as Vienna and California. Many of the fish served here are caught in the nearby lake, and some of the best ones are smoked in the restaurant's own smokehouse nearby. Every Thursday owner Hans Glaser hosts a musical evening, which is the most fun event in town. Glaser himself plays the bass-fiddle. His wife, Heidi, is a visible presence at the restaurant. Framed on the walls of the restaurant are signed photographs of satisfied clients.

In addition to the smoked fish, specialties include wild game dishes, saddle of venison, wild mushroom soup, Styrian-style pork in cabbage, and homemade spätzle. The restaurant closes in summer from May to mid-September. Meals cost from 120 AS ($8.75) to 175 AS ($12.75). As for hours, they are rather happy-golucky, the owners opening whenever they want to, so an advance call is absolutely necessary before heading here.

---

8. Bruck an der Mur

A while back, at Leoben we headed west to take in the resorts and attractions of West Styria. If we had continued north along the Mur River instead, we would have come to Bruck an der Mur, at the point in the Styrian alpine range where the Mur and the Mürz flow together. The ruined fortress of Lanskron looks down on the bustling industrial town of Bruck, where factories process iron ore.

THE SIGHTS

The main attraction of the principal plaza (Hauptplatz) of the town is the **Eiserner Brunne,** a lacy wrought-iron well, done in 1626, one of the finest existing examples of Styrian ironwork.

Also on the Hauptplatz stands the most impressive building in Bruck, the 15th-century **Kornmesserhaus.** Some of it is in the flamboyant Gothic style, while other architectural parts are based on designs of the Renaissance. It has a splendid loggia and arcades.

The **pfarrkirche** (parish church) is on the Kirchplatz (church square). Its major treasure is a sacristy door that, like the fountain just visited on the Hauptplatz, is of wrought iron, circa 16th century.

FOOD AND LODGING

Dating from 1683, **Hotel Bauer** (Zum Schwarzen Adler), Mittergasse 23, A-8600 Bruck an der Mur (tel. 03862/51331), is better known as an inner-village restaurant than as a four-star hotel. It does, however, offer 14 rooms to guests who choose to eat in the restaurant as well. The smallish but well-furnished rooms usually have modern baths and much comfort. Doubles cost 650 AS ($47.25) daily, while singles rent for 450 AS ($32.75), with breakfast included. The restaurant is host to a crowd of local diners, who sit either in the main dining room or in the rustically decorated stüberl. Dishes include venison pâté with Cumberland sauce, an array of roast meats with noodles, and homemade pastries, some of them richly covered with whipped cream. À la carte meals cost 125 AS ($9) to 300 AS ($21.75). Hot food is served daily from 11:30am to 2:30pm and 6 to 9:30pm.

Hotel/Restaurant Bayer, Hauptplatz, A-8600 Bruck an der Mur (tel. 03862/51218), next door to the Rathaus, offers efficient service, comfortable rooms, and good food, right in the heart of town. The bathrooms and many of the furnishings have recently been remodeled or replaced, under the direction of the owners. There are 33 well-furnished bedrooms, of which 16 contain private baths or showers. Half board costs 360 AS ($26.25) to 460 AS ($33.50) per person daily, year round.

FROHNLEITEN

South of Bruck an der Mur you'll come to an Austrian golfing center with an 18-hole international championship course. Long before it discovered golf, however, Frohnleiten was already an ancient town. It has a pfarrkirche (parish church) with rococo embellishments, and to the southwest of town stands a castle from the Middle Ages, **Rabenstein Castle.** It was constructed on the foundations of a Roman fort, and when the baroque craze swept Austria, the castle was not spared.

The town also has an **alpine garden** stretching across 22 acres and exhibiting more than 10,000 species from nearly all the continents of the world where plants grow.

You may want to dine at **Weissenbacher** (tel. 03126/2334), on the road to Graz, which serves well-prepared and traditional Austrian food such as fresh asparagus in season, as well as ham, cheese, beef, and chicken dishes, to a loyal crowd of clients who appreciate the large portions and rich desserts. À la carte meals range from 110 AS ($8) to 250 AS ($18.25). The establishment is open daily from 9:30am to 11pm.

WEIZ

If you're seeking reasonable accommodations in the area, you can drive east from Frohnleiten along a twisting secondary road until you reach Weiz. This is a typical Styrian town—clean and neat, the new blending harmoniously with the old, and mountains forming a backdrop.

Weiz is often visited by Austrians who like to ride on its narrow-gauge railway, running on Saturday from July to September. The twin-towered church here was built in the 1600s as a fortress against Turkish invaders from the east.

Food and Lodging

Romantik-Hotel Modersnhof, Büchl 32, A-8160 Weiz (tel. 03172/3747), looks like an enlarged private house with big arched windows on the ground floor and a long row of cut-out wooden balconies. It actually boasts a history of at least 250 years, and the well-furnished public rooms offer many cozy seating areas with views over the surrounding landscape. A curving iron staircase leads to the seven bedrooms, each of which has a bath, color TV, radio, and hairdryer. Half board costs 1,300 AS ($94.50) daily for a single and 1,075 AS ($78.25) per person for a double. The hotel offers a sauna, tennis court, and swimming pool. The dining room presents a menu considered one of the finest in this part of Austria. The small but well-chosen selections of specialties includes trout filet, veal filet "house style" (with rosemary, mushrooms, and hollandaise sauce), and an array of fresh salads and homemade desserts. Set meals cost from 220 AS ($16). The restaurant is open daily from noon to 2pm and 6pm to midnight.

9. Aflenz Kurort

This is one of the best bases you can find if you want to go mountain climbing in the Hochschwab. It has a reputation as both a summer resort and a winter-sports site. Aflenz Kurort (5,095 feet) can be reached from Kapfenberg in about half an hour.

In winter the attraction is the chair lift to Bürgeralm, which has a ski tow. In summer the chair lift is used by climbers exploring the Hochschwab mountains.

FOOD AND LODGING

The oldest part of the hip-roofed stucco **Aflenzerhof,** A-8623 Aflenz Kurort (tel. 03861/2245), was built in the 15th century, although since then it has been considerably modernized to include vivid colors that complement the thick walls and the vaulted ceilings. Guests who prefer more up-to-date accommodations can stay in the nearby annex, built in a big-windowed modern style with lots of wood trim and pleasant landscaping in a flowered garden. The Schaffenberger family, your hosts, run this 65-bed hotel, offering 28 bedrooms with private baths or showers. Year round, they charge from 390 AS ($28.25) per person daily for half board.

Hotel Hubertushof, A-8623 Aflenz Kurort (tel. 03861/31310), is a dignified stucco house with flowerboxes and green shutters at the windows, as well as a gabled roofline looking out over stately shade trees. The interior is a colorful assemblage of furniture covered with contrasting patterns and country-style accessories. The hotel offers 19 snug and cozy bedrooms, each with private bath or shower, and it is open from December to October. Half board costs 335 AS ($24.25) to 375 AS ($27.25) per person daily.

Alpengasthof Gollner (Bürgeralm), Mariazellerstrasse 20, A-8623 Aflenz Kurort (tel. 03861/2426). In winter this 35-bed alpine hotel can be reached only by chair lift, although if you don't have a car you'll enjoy the ride up even in summer. The interior is pleasantly furnished by the Gollner family, who do everything they can to make guests feel at home. None of the rooms has a private bath, but toilets and showers are easily accessible. The charge per person, with half board included is 275 AS ($20) daily. Open December to April and June to September.

10. Mariazell

Mariazell is the most celebrated pilgrimage center in Austria, in addition to being a winter playground and a summer resort. It is the national shrine of Austria, Hungary, and Bohemia.

The object of pilgrimage is a church dating from the dawn of the 13th century, with three prominent towers. It was originally constructed in the Romanesque style then fashionable, and a Gothic choir was built on in the latter 14th century. The bulbous domes are baroque, a style laid on most of Austria's churches in the 17th century. Fischer von Erlach, both senior and junior, baroque architects by now familiar to readers of this guide, aided in the Mariazell transformation. In the church is the grave of the world-famous Hungarian Cardinal Mindszenty and the Mindszenty Museum. In 1983 Pope John Paul II visited Mariazell and the cardinal's burial place.

In the treasury are votive offerings accrued over some 600 years. The **Chapel of**

Grace is considered the national shrine of Austria. Miracles are attributed to its statue of the Virgin, giving rise to fame that spread all over Europe. The statue is mounted on an altar designed by the younger von Erlach. In summer large groups gather on Saturday night for torchlit processions to the church.

The treasury is open from the first of May until the end of October from 10am to noon. Admission is 15 AS ($1.10).

Over the years Mariazell has attracted much royalty, some of the Habsburgs, in particular, being fond of this village.

Many fathers take their children to Mariazell to teach them how to ski, a generations-old tradition. Here are all the appurtenances of a modern winter-sports and recreation center: avalanche-proof grounds for skiers of all skills, a cableway, a chair lift, numerous ski hoists, a natural toboggan run, a skating rink, a ski school, and a ski kindergarten. Mariazell is a winter holiday center for the whole family.

Its high altitude and good, brisk climate make this a favored summer vacation site, with a multitude of recreational pursuits to choose among. You can go walking on about 125 miles of footpaths, mountaineering, swimming, rowing, sailing, windsurfing, canoeing, fishing, horseback riding, glider flying, and camping, or you can play tennis or golf.

For the most dramatic views in the area, take a chair lift to Gemeindealpe (5,335 feet) or a cableway to Bürgeralpe (4,170 feet), leaving from the center of town. The round-trip fare for the chair lift is 90 AS ($6.55) and for the cableway 80 AS ($5.80). Both modes of transportation operate daily from 9 to 11:30am and 1 to 4:30pm. They are closed in November.

For further information, check with the tourist office, Hauptplatz 13 (tel. 03882/2366).

FOOD AND LODGING

Hotel Feichtegger, A-8630 Mariazell (tel. 03882/2416), is a flat-roofed five-story hotel with evenly spaced rows of recessed balconies. The angularity of the façade is relieved by masses of flowers in the window boxes. Inside is a rustically modern bar area, a restaurant, a paneled tavern, and sunny, comfortable bedrooms. The hotel offers 55 well-furnished bedrooms, each with private bath or shower, charging from 460 AS ($33.50) to 580 AS ($42.25) per person daily for half board. Facilities include an indoor swimming pool and a sauna. Guests are received from December to March and May to October.

Scherfler's Hotel Goldenes Kreuz, A-8630 Mariazell (tel. 03882/2309). The ground-floor façade of this hotel near the basilica has been severely modernized, but the upper stories still retain the rococo detailing and white trim of the year they were built. The interior has lots of elegant accessories, two restaurants (one modern and one regionally paneled), and attractively furnished rooms filled with provincial designs painted on the comfortable furniture. For the 30 bedrooms, each with private bath or shower, the hotel charges 360 AS ($26.25) to 450 AS ($32.75) per person daily for half board.

Hotel Goldene Krone, A-8630 Mariazell (tel. 03882/2583), is an old Styrian house with substantial proportions, stone trim, and a steeply pitched gabled roof next to the basilica. Most of the solidly constructed furniture was added when the hotel was remodeled. On the premises is a contemporary bar area with decorative masonry accents, plus a restaurant and 22 comfortable bedrooms, each with private bath or shower. Half board costs 340 AS ($24.75) to 390 AS ($28.25) per person daily. Open from December to October.

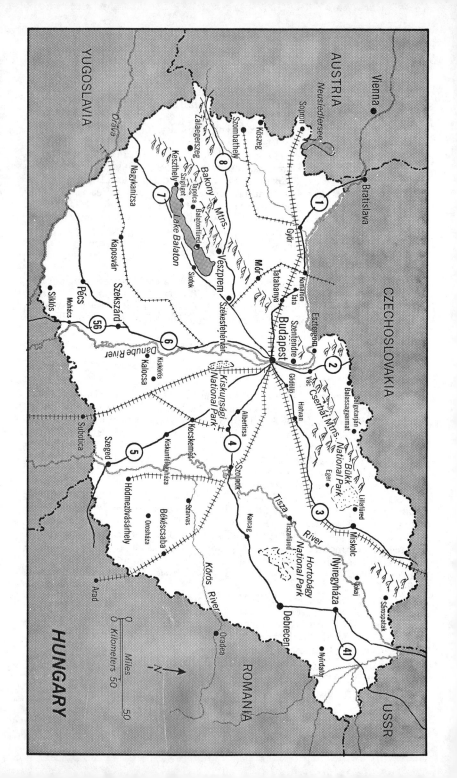

PART TWO

HUNGARY

SETTLING INTO HUNGARY

Hungary is a small country—not quite as big as the state of Indiana. Its neighbors are Czechoslovakia on the north, Austria on the west, Yugoslavia on the south, and Romania and the USSR on the east. The Danube River is a main artery of communications for the country, forming the Czech-Hungarian border from the point at which the river flows in from Austria until it makes its turn south at the Danube Bend to go on to Yugoslavia. To the east of the Danube after its turn is the Great Plain, the Alföld, and the northern middle hills, while to the west lie the Small Plain and Transdanubia. The only important mountain range of the country stretches southwest to northeast, a part of the Carpathians. Transdanubia is a region of small, barren hills, extinct volcanoes, and sloping downs. Both the Great Plain and the Small Plain are fertile regions. Hungary is a land of forests, meadows, and a temperate climate. This is an agricultural country, but efforts are succeeding to achieve a better balance with industrial expansion.

Previously known as the People's Republic of Hungary, the official name of the country was changed in 1989 to the Republic of Hungary to reflect its new status as a Socialist nation and its break with the Communist bloc. Budapest, its capital, idyllically situated on the Danube, was formed in 1873 by uniting three towns that in their early days had developed separately: Buda, built on a hill on the river's west bank; Pest on the plain on the eastern side of the river; and Óbuda, an old city that stands on the right bank of the Danube and is the site of the ancient city of Aquincum, the capital of Rome's province of Pannonia. Today the largest provincial cities outside Budapest are Miskolc, Debrecen, Szeged, Győr, and Pécs.

In Hungary you'll discover a country that in recent years has managed to achieve a fair amount of freedom for its people and a foreign policy based on peaceful coexistence. It is a contemporary country with a diversified economy, but mindful of its history and keen on preserving its architecture, folk music, dancing, arts, crafts and other riches of its past.

You need only sample the Hungarian cuisine and toast your friends with an apricot brandy or Tokay wine to realize that Hungary is a land of hospitality—and of hospitable people. Obey the laws and regulations of the country, as of any other country you visit, and you should have a happy holiday, indeed.

1. Getting Acquainted

What follows is a bit of background—notes on food, history, and other subjects—to give you a running start on your visit.

THE PEOPLE

Originally when I was in Hungary preparing this book and checking on some statistics, I ran across a printed statement by a Hungarian writer which said that the land comprising the country "had never been uninhabited." If the reference was to habitation by humankind, the statement was probably accurate. The discovery in the 1960s at Vértesszöllös of relics of prehistoric man dating back 500,000 years seems to indicate that human beings have been here a good long time. However, the region became demonstrably inhabited when Celts settled along the Danube some 1000 years B.C.

After the coming of the Christian era there were Romans, Huns, Avars from Asia, Greeks, Germans, and Slavs—and probably a few more—who moved in, but the major impact was the coming of the Magyars in the 9th century A.D. The actual origin of the Magyars is long hidden in the mists of prehistoric time, but they probably came from the Ural mountains most recently, and their language is not of Indo-European derivation, as are other Western European tongues, but is Finno-Ugric. That may not mean much to you, but it's the reason Hungarian differs so greatly today from the language of its neighbors. So many Magyars moved in that they rather quickly assimilated the remnants of their predecessors.

Of the almost 11,000,000 inhabitants today, 98% are Hungarian, with a smattering of Germans, Slovaks, Gypsies, and Croatians. The country is predominantly Catholic, 55% (both Greek and Roman), with another 20% following Calvinism and the rest being variously accounted for, some of course being Jewish. Hungarian Jews were not ignored by the Nazis. In 1944, 600,000 of them were rounded up and shipped to concentration camps, where thousands died. Today there are only about 20,000 Jews outside Budapest, with some 80,000 in the capital city.

Traditionally, Hungarian society is male-dominated. Women are honored, but mainly their place is considered to be in the home, or at least secondary to that of males in the marketplace. In rural areas, even quite near large cities, and in villages, women still hand down to their daughters age-old skills in embroidery, spinning, and household chores. This is slowly changing in the large towns, but it's still an important facet of the Hungarian temperament. With the long, long history of warfare in the Carpathian Basin, it's no wonder that the concept of man as the protector of his women and children has survived.

THE HISTORY

Just as throughout Europe—in Switzerland, Germany, Austria, and wherever—the Celtic tribes were followed by the Romans, so it was in the region that is now Hungary. It was a part of the Roman province of Pannonia, and excavations have unearthed a vast number of Roman relics. The Magyars came from the east, as mentioned above, in the 9th century, and after a couple of centuries of conflict with people already here and with outsiders who wanted a piece of the pie, a monarchy was created, headed in the year 997 by Stephen I, who was sent a royal crown by Pope Sylvester II, marking the birth of the kingdom of Hungary under the Árpád dynasty, the first Magyar rulers to adapt to European ways and adopt Christianity.

Stephen I was later to become the St. Stephen (Szent István) whose name you'll see on streets, buildings, and elsewhere in Hungary. As king, he suppressed uprisings aimed at restoring paganism and the clan system, even blinding or exiling his own relatives as necessary.

Establishment of a kingdom and assimilation of a motley crowd of inhabitants as Hungarians wasn't a signal for peace, however. The country (although it was much larger off and on through the centuries) suffered wars and revolutions right up to the present century. Hungary was so situated as to be in the path of many peoples seeking territorial gains—the Mongols in the 13th century, the Turks in the 16th and 17th centuries, and the Habsburgs in 1686—up to World War I and World War II.

The defeat of the Muslim forces and final ouster of the tentacles of the Ottoman Empire from Hungary came when the Habsburgs got tired of having Vienna besieged. In a war that devastated much of the country, the Austrians and their allies finally drove the Turks out of Hungary in 1699. Many Hungarians considered it a very mixed blessing.

There was much dissatisfaction and many uprisings, small and large, by groups wishing total independence from Austria after formation of the Austro-Hungarian Empire with a Habsburg sovereign. Leaders whose names you'll see on squares, streets, and many other places in the country—such as Kossuth, Széchenyi, Rákóczi, and others—had varying degrees of success. Finally, a measure of Hungarian self-determination was achieved when a compromise was reached whereby Hungary and Austria had separate governments although both were under the Habsburgs. This was called dualism. Franz Joseph was still emperor of Austria, but became a king in Hungary.

Many Hungarians never really settled for any sort of royal domination, particularly from outside, and the dualism of the empire created constant bickering that weakened the nation. Being allied with Germany during World Wars I and II added to Hungary's problems.

In World War II, Hungary, in alliance with Nazi Germany, temporarily regained some of its lost territories, including Transylvania and parts of Slovakia (Yugoslavia). Untold suffering followed this ill-fated alliance, as the cream of Hungary's youth lost their lives in the Ukraine and more than three-quarters of the country's Jewish population was massacred. Almost half of the country's wealth had been destroyed by the time the Red Army advanced into Budapest on April 4, 1945. That army was to stay for a long, long time.

After World War II, the Communist Party grew in power, and in 1949 the country became a Socialist republic under the guidance of Soviet Russia. The reins of government were held by persons acceptable to the Kremlin, collective farms were brought into being, and a reign of terror had begun.

Worsening conditions exploded in 1956, when a bloody revolt was stopped by Soviet tanks. This brutal suppression of the short-lived freedom movement sent 200,000 Hungarians into exile. More than 2,000 died. János Kádár—the Hungarian Socialist Workers' Party first secretary—became the number one man in the country and was to rule for many years. He died in 1989. Imre Nagy was hanged for "treason" in 1958 for his role as premier during the uprising. Nagy had formed a multiparty system and had announced Hungarian neutrality. His position was right, only the timing was wrong: much of what Nagy had advocated came true in 1989. His reputation, which had never been tarnished, at least privately among Hungarian citizens, was restored. He is today revered as a national hero.

In 1989 Hungary buried 40 years of Communism and inaugurated a Western-style democracy by proclaiming itself a republic on the 33rd anniversary of the 1956 uprising. This time the proclamation was not crushed by Soviet tanks. The announced intention for the 1990s is to turn Hungary into "an independent, democratic, and legal state." The Communist Party was officially dissolved, and in 1990 Hungary called its first multiparty parliamentary elections since 1947.

GOVERNMENT

Stay tuned for further developments, the new government having just been formed in the early 1990s. Basically, the highest organ of state power is the National Assembly, with the president of the Hungarian Republic being the head of state. There is a multiparty system in the country, which began with the elections of 1990. This election determined the representatives of the various parties who were to constitute the newly created National Assembly, which is charged with electing the new government.

SPORTS

Hungary is a sporting nation, football (soccer), fencing, and swimming being the most popular branches in both spectator and participant activities. Budapest has a fine new sports arena, and provincial towns such as Győr, Szombathely, Székesfehérvár, Debrecen, and Eger have modern stadiums and racing grounds.

Water plays a major role in Hungary's sports scene, and such activities as sailing, windsurfing, rowing, motorboat cruising, swimming, and fishing are popular pursuits.

Sailing vessels are rented in Budapest and at 34 resorts in the Balaton district and around Lake Velence. Windsurfing is also an activity at the two lakes, Balaton and Velence.

All over the country you can find waters good for rowing, canoeing, and kayaking, and facilities for renting the boats and instruction courses are offered. It's also possible to go rafting on the Tisza River. Motorboating is available everywhere except on Lake Balaton, Lake Velence, and the Soroksár branch of the Danube.

Swimming pools and beaches will be found all over the country, many open all year.

Fish are abundant in Hungarian waters, which are much less polluted than those in Western Europe, so that the fish have a chance to thrive. Foreign visitors may purchase a fishing permit, usually issued by local water agencies, on presentation of a passport. At Lake Balaton you can get a permit from travel offices, at your hotel, or from a local fishing association at most settlements. They will also advise you as to restrictions on size and quantity of an allowable catch. You can catch bream, carp, pike-perch, silure, balin, and other varieties in the well-stocked lakes and rivers. There are closed seasons on some fish, and angling is forbidden in Lake Balaton from April 20 to May 20.

Hiking is a popular pursuit in Hungary, with many people going on long walking trips, camping along the way rather than trying to find a hotel. When you're equipped with good hiking boots and a rucksack, you can set forth to see the country's grass roots. One-day excursions are recommended, as there is not an overabundance of tourist accommodations along hiking routes. You can get information, advice, maps, and even help in finding lodgings at the travel offices in county towns.

Horseback riding is big in Hungary, and cross-country riding tours can be arranged by tourist agencies and travel offices. There are also riding schools where you can learn the basics. You are responsible for supplying your own boots and riding breeches.

Both Hungarian and foreign sports hunters find red deer, roe deer, wild pigs, and fallow deer plentiful, with some game birds also popular targets. If you're interested in this sport, you should get in touch with the Hungarian Game Trade Cooperative Enterprise (MAVAD), Uri utca 39, Budapest I (tel. 122-667), before you go to the country.

Tennis, minigolf, and bowling have been gaining in popularity in Hungary in recent years.

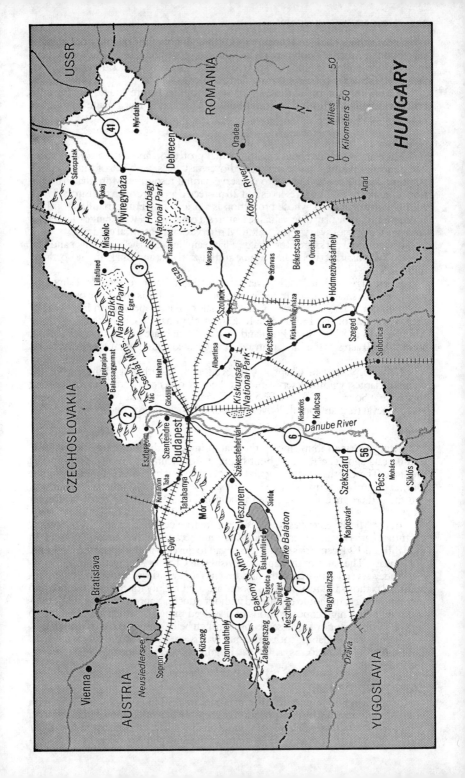

Snow and ice come to Hungary too, although not of the quantity or length of stay found in Austria. Winter sports include skiing, sledging, bobsledding, ice skating, and ice sailing (a popular sport on Lake Balaton), plus riding in an old-fashioned *fakutya*, a chairlike skating sledge.

For information on all these sports opportunities before you go to Hungary, check with IBUSZ Hungarian Travel Bureau, One Parker Plaza, Suite 1104, Fort Lee, NJ 07024 (tel. 201/592-8585).

NATURE

Hungary is serious about environmental protection and nature conservation. "Museums of nature" have been created over vast areas, with 5% of the country's territory coming under the law to conserve natural resources. More than 100 national and nearly 600 local reserves and 28 protected areas are open to visitors. There are three national parks whose protection is a priority by Hungarian law, both to conserve and to display their valuable features. People with a wide range of interests are attracted to the cave systems, wildfowl reserves, and botanical gardens.

The national parks are Hortobágy, a flat plain between the Tisza River and Debrecen; Kiskunság, between the Danube and Tisza rivers; and Bükk, in the northern highlands.

Hortobágy National Park covers about 104,000 acres of woods, fishponds, meadows, marshland, and villages, where thousands of birds either live or visit during migrations. The trees, flowers, and animals of the steppe flourish here. One of the six sections of the 15,000-acre Kiskunság National Park is visited in Chapter XVI, Section 5, "The Great Plain and Puszta." The heart of Bükk National Park, some 70,000 acres, is the Bükk plateau, an unequaled region of caves and symbiotic plants.

Gemenc, visited in Chapter XVI, Section 4, "Southwest Hungary," is the country's largest wildlife reservation, but there are other conservation areas, among them one at Sopron and one at Tihany. Arboretums with exotic plants, rare flowers, and primeval trees are found all over the country, including at Budapest.

SPAS

Hungary has an abundance of thermal springs, which were being enjoyed some 2,000 years ago. The Romans built baths at Aquincum, the capital of Pannonia province. These baths were segregated—not by sex but by civilian or military status. During the turbulent times following Roman domination the baths were destroyed, and today there are only relics, such as beautiful mosaic floors, to recall the former glory.

In the Middle Ages fleshly pleasures were frowned on, but slowly, over a few centuries, baths regained respectability, mainly because of their healing powers. In the 18th and 19th centuries major spas began to develop in Budapest and elsewhere in Hungary. The baths of the capital are visited in Chapter XV, Section 5.

Today several hundred baths and beaches invite visitors, providing entertainment, relaxation, and recuperation. Some are used mainly for treating the sick. No thermal spring bath should be entered without a doctor's approval. Most of the thermal waters have high concentrations of dissolved minerals, which are beneficial to sufferers from a range of illnesses, either through being immersed or by drinking it.

Besides the Budapest baths, thermal waters are found at the following spas: Balatonfüred, Bükfürdö, Eger, Gyula, Hagdúszoboszló, Hárkany, Héviz, Parád, and Zalakaros.

MUSIC AND DRAMA

More than 500 important cultural events are held in Hungary annually, with visitors being attracted by interpretation of the work of world-renowned Hungarian composers Franz Liszt, Béla Bartók, and Zoltán Kodály; by concerts at Keszthely and Martonvasár; by the series of programs of the Budapest Art Weeks or the Szeged

Open-Air Festival; and by the summer cultural events at the Sopron Festive Week, the Gyula Castle Festival, the Szentendre Theater, or the open-air theater on Margaret Island.

Well-known foreign theatrical companies and celebrated guest artists regularly appear on Hungarian stages and at concert halls. Hungarian dance art is known throughout Europe.

Rock concerts, carnivals, balls, and equestrian displays attract many visitors as well as local people.

ART AND ARCHITECTURE

The Scythians in the late Bronze Age and early Iron Age left to Hungary the traditional symbol still used—the golden stag. Some of these, reflecting Oriental influence, decorated the graves of warriors among those early immigrants from the Black Sea plains, a race pushed out of the Danube Basin by the Celts. Later invasion by the Romans is revealed by Pompeian-style mosaics and murals in ruined villas. The Huns and various successors in turn contributed their styles, many marked by Byzantine influence brought in by Mongolian conquerors. Such design motifs were used in church art and sculpture before and in the early days of Magyar (Hungarian) domination of the area. These people achieved a mixed pagan-Christian art form even in ecclesiastical artwork.

Painted panels, illuminated manuscripts, and sculpture proliferated in churches and abbeys in the Middle Ages, with Italian art being a strong influence until the Ottoman Turks moved in in the 16th century. The conquerors destroyed much court art, although some panel paintings can still be seen in museums and cathedrals, and fresco painting was revived in the 17th century. Later Hungarian art took on strong patriotic fervor, a tide that ebbed with the coming of socialism. Painters of note in this century include Kosztka, Károly, and Vasárely, with Borsus, Mikus, and others being notable sculptors. In more than 500 museums of varying sizes, you can see art from ancient to modern, including ecclesiastical works.

Hungarian architecture has ranged from Romanesque through French Gothic (see some of the beautiful churches of this period), late Hungarian Gothic, baroque, neoclassical, and up to the functional modern style without ornamentation.

Folk Art

In Hungary you can see something of the relics of the old life of the peasantry as well as contemporary folk art. The different styles that developed in the architecture, costumes, dancing, handcrafts, and customs in different eras and among people of different ethnic backgrounds are still evident. Of course the oldest original objects of folk art are preserved in museums and other collections, but in folk-art shops you'll find a wide variety of fine items that can be purchased.

Tourists in Hungary find colorful popular art. In different regions artisans carry on time-honored occupations handed down through generations. For instance, they do embroidery in Mezőkövesd, lacework in Kiskunhalas, and fine pottery and dishes in Mezőtúr.

Visitors can participate in occasions like those of the past where forms of folk art originated. You might take part in a Matyo wedding ceremony, a vintage fun gathering, or attend a masked fancy-dress ball. Think what a memorable time you can have enjoying the frolic of a harvest festival to usher in the new bread!

LITERATURE

Hungarian literature had its origins in early pre-Christian poetry, still reflected in some ballads and folk tales. However, these, like other literature of the country, were written down in Latin rather than Hungarian. The country's mother tongue was not developed into a usable literary language until after the Reformation and the conquest by the Turks in the 16th century. The early use of the Hungarian language in literature was in epic poetry and patriotic songs, with novels appearing in the 19th century. Literature of this country has not been widely translated into English, much of it being written for purposes of patriotism and social reform.

FOOD

In Hungary today you can eat better than you can in the other countries of Eastern Europe. The Hungarians have been called "born eaters." It might be conceded that they are restaurateurs as well, and many of them have gone west to establish citadels of cuisine in such places as New York and London. Most but not all restaurants in Hungary are state-run these days, but there are those good souls still around whose parents remember what the food was like under the Habsburgs, when the cuisine of Hungary apparently reached rarefied heights of excellence.

Hungarian cuisine has been able to preserve much from the old, however, even from ancient times, and it has assimilated influences that have reached it in the course of time from immigrant ethnic groups and from abroad. Hungarian cooking has preserved the rich vegetable garnishings as well as several desserts introduced from Renaissance Italy, Turkish spices, and sauces and layered pastries created in Austrian and German kitchens. Many dishes from the surrounding Slavic peoples have been incorporated into Hungarian cookery, while French, Greek, Arab, English, and Indian specialties have added further variety.

Basically, you'll find in Hungary a cuisine in which beef, fish, chicken, pork, or whatever is cooked in lard. Sour cream, onions, and garlic, of course, are tossed in to give the mixture its flavor. The foundation of modern Hungarian cooking is the use of lard, onions, and paprika, and the favorite ingredient is sour cream.

Paprika, often called "the soul of Hungarian cooking," has probably only been in use here since the 16th or 17th century, maybe not that early. Where it came from is uncertain, some authorities believing that the invading Turks introduced it along with other Oriental spices. The Turks did leave behind bags of coffee, which launched the Vienna coffeehouses in Austria, so perhaps they also left behind, after 150 years of rule, bags of the peppers that have become the hallmark of the Hungarian cuisine. However they got here, the handed-down agricultural know-how and the climate have combined to create the paprika industry in the southern part of the Great Plain, east of the Danube. Hungarian cooks use the sweet, brilliant red paprika in many dishes—used sparingly by the better chefs.

Just as the Spanish gave the world paella, so Hungary contributed **gulasch,** or *gulyás* in Hungarian, a dish that seemingly every other cook in America knows how to make, at least in some version. Chefs never seem to agree on how to concoct it, each having an individual interpretation.

Gulyás is a folk dish descended from the Magyars, a belly-warming stew known to have been a menu item in the 9th century. The ingredients could be dried and later prepared out in the open by shepherds and plainsmen. Its basis is cubes of rib or shoulder beef, cooked with finely chopped onion, diced potatoes, and salt, with modern additions of paprika and caraway seeds. Other meats are used by some cooks, even chicken, but true gulyás almost never has sour cream in it.

There are three other categories of Hungarian paprika dishes: pörkölt, paprikás, and tokány. **Pörkölt** is usually made of veal, although beef, mutton, pork, game, goose, or duck may be used. **Paprikás** goes best made with veal or chicken, but lamb, duck, or even fish is sometimes used. Sweet or sour cream is always stirred in. **Tokány,** the fourth of the notable stews of the country, comes in as many varieties as gulasch, and the meat of which it is made ranges from beef to sausage.

Paprika-flavored stews aren't all that Hungarian cooks produce. **Stuffed cabbage** is another favorite, the leaves most often containing bacon, pork, rice, and herbs. Golden-brown suckling pig, chicken fried in breadcrumbs, and soups are worth sampling. Another excellent dish is fogas, a freshwater fish from Lake Balaton, mild tasting and with a firm texture, somewhat like pike-perch. (It appears on German menus as zander.)

Hungary's wonderful sweet pastries compete with Vienna's best. Try the strudel, called **rétes** in Hungary. A variety of fillings provide you with many taste treats. In the provinces they still produce jam-filled **barátfüle,** the **kürtöskalács** (cream horns), and the acclaimed carnival doughnuts, or **fänk.**

DRINK

Hungary has plenty of **coffee** today, after a long scarcity a few decades ago, and the tradition of offering guests a small glass of espresso in homes and offices has been revived. The coffeehouses are back in business. Young and old alike gather again in the innumerable espresso cafés to sip, talk, and make friends. The coffee, however, may not suit you unless you like it strong and thick.

Hungarians are proud of their country's **wines,** the most celebrated being, of course, **Tokay,** from the village of Tokaj (see Chapter XVI, Section 6). It's considered the only great wine made east of the Rhine. One type, Tokaji Aszú, is a syrupy, sweet-tasting wine said to be produced, like a notable sauterne, from "noble mold." Other Tokays vary from sweet to dry.

Egri Bikavér (so-called bull's blood of Eger) is a popular heavy red table wine. Often today this wine is not Hungarian at all but comes from places such as North Africa. I suggest you try the home-grown version while you're here. Exceptional favorites are the Pinôt Noir from Pécs and a burgundy-like wine called Villányi Burgundi from the southernmost city of Hungary, Villány. On the shores of Lake Balaton a grape is grown that is used to produce a rich white wine, Keknyelu (meaning blue stem).

A popular apéritif is **barack,** which is considered the best apricot brandy made in Europe. You may find it too sweet to drink before a meal, but I like a glass of it after dinner. Maybe you will too. Other brandies you may want to sample are plum, cherry, or even rose-hip.

If you want something lighter, try a native brand of **beer.** One of the most popular brand names is Kinizsi. Or you might enjoy one of the country's **mineral waters.**

---

2. Traveling to and Within Hungary

Traveling to Eastern Europe, especially Hungary, is easier than it's been in years. Hungary is eager to attract the Western visitor, and restrictions have been relaxed in recent years. You can visit Hungary either on a package deal or else as an independent traveler. First, I'll discuss the easiest means of—

GETTING THERE

Since around 1960, traveling to Hungary has always been considerably easier than visiting its sister nations in the Eastern Bloc (now, no longer a "bloc," of course). With the openness of the 1990s, a frontier crossing into Hungary presents few complications, other than a visa (see below). Many airlines have initiated (or plan to initiate) routes into Budapest. First, the easiest means of getting there is always by air.

The only commercial airport in Hungary is in Budapest, where there are two terminals servicing international traffic. (Within their premises are a battery of immigration and customs officials.) Unfortunately, there are only two nonstop weekly flights from North America into Budapest, but that is subject to change. Currently, both of these flights are the result of a joint venture between **Malév,** the Hungarian national airline, and **Pan American.** The flights depart every Thursday and Saturday from New York's JFK Airport and arrive just before 9am local time in Budapest the following morning. As we go to press, both **United Airlines** and **American Airlines** have applied for approval for flights to Budapest from Chicago.

Because of the relative infrequency of flights, however, most passengers take alternative routes, booking a transatlantic flight into any one of dozens of gateways in Western Europe and from there transferring to Budapest on one of the national carriers of a particular European country, especially Austrian Airlines. (Vienna has emerged as the principal "gateway" to Budapest.)

One possible option, especially useful for readers of this guide, is to fly to Vienna and then to transfer onto one of several daily connections into Budapest. For example, **Austrian Airlines** offers nonstop service from New York to Vienna every day except Tuesday. In Vienna, the airline provides convenient connections not only to Budapest, but to other capitals in Eastern Europe as well.

If you're already in Europe, at another capital or big city such as London, Paris, Rome, or Amsterdam, you can easily make connections on Malév into Budapest. Perhaps in the lifetime of this edition, Malév will have begun nonstop service on its own between Budapest and Los Angeles, Chicago, and New York. Currently, Malév has offices in those cities, as well as one in Toronto.

For more information on the latest flights offered, consult a travel agent or call one of the various toll-free numbers: **Pan American** at 800/221-1111; **Austrian Airlines** at 800/842-0002; **Malév** at 800/223-6880 (in New York City, 212/757-6446); **United** at 800/241-6522; and **American Airlines** at 800/433-7300.

Fare Options

Most airlines award the least expensive ticket to passengers who reserve their flights long in advance. For the most inexpensive tickets into Hungary, the major airlines usually require a 10-day advance reservation and a stopover of between seven days and six months. Most of them impose a financial penalty for changes in flight dates after the ticket has been issued.

Various price schedules exist for coach class in the airlines. Passengers who want increased comfort and more elegant food and beverage service usually opt for the increased expense of business class or first class if they can afford it. Passengers who can spend a bit of time researching extra savings and then buy unusual combinations of tickets (which lead eventually to their destination) can possibly save a few dollars—if they fly to London, for example, then transfer to an intra-European flight with a carrier such as Austrian Airlines or Malév. However, because of the time, effort, and incidental expenses encountered, this is not always as economical as it first appears. For more information about the subject, see the section on do-it-yourself fares in Chapter I of this guide, "Getting to and Around Austria."

VISAS

To enter Hungary, United States and Canadian citizens must have a valid passport *and* a visa. Visas may be obtained from the Hungarian Embassy, 3910 Shoemaker St. NW, Washington, DC 20008, or the Hungarian Consulate General, 8 E. 75th St., New York, NY 10021. In Canada the Hungarian Embassy is at 7 Delaware Ave., Ottawa, ON K2P 0Z2.

Visas are also issued at the Budapest Airport and at the border if you're traveling by car. However, I advise you to get yours before you leave home if you know you're coming to Hungary. You cannot get a visa at the border if you're traveling by train, nor at the pier if you're coming in by boat or hydrofoil. Visas are valid for six months from the date of issue, for a stay of up to 30 days.

Your travel agent can handle the details of getting a visa for you. If you have questions about obtaining one by yourself, contact IBUSZ Hungarian Travel Bureau, One Parker Plaza, Suite 1104, Fort Lee, NJ 07024 (tel. 201/592-8585).

TRAVELING WITHIN HUNGARY

Now you're in Hungary. If you came by any means other than by private vehicle, chances are you're in Budapest, and now you're wondering how best to get around the country. I'll deal first with what you should know if you're going to be doing your own driving, and then introduce you to the various means of public transport available in this country.

By Car

In Hungary you drive on the right, and the rules of the road used in most of continental Europe are observed. You do not—repeat *not*—drive in this country if you have had a single drink of alcoholic beverage, even a beer. It's also strongly recommended that you not drive after taking a strong tranquilizer or a painkiller before the effects have worn off. Police in Hungary keep a close eye on drivers. The Hungarian Highway Code prescribes that using three-point safety belts in the front seat is required, and children under 6 must ride in the backseat.

On Hungarian roads, with the exception of motorways and limited-access roads, horse-drawn carts, bicycles, and pedestrians are part of the traffic. In the country and on roads through villages you may find livestock using the road too. Although regulations say that horse carts and bicycles must have lights at night, many fail to obey that law, so it's in your own best interest to drive especially carefully after dark. Headlights are required to be on low beam from dark until daylight.

The speed limit on motorways is 75 m.p.h. On other roads outside built-up areas it's 60 m.p.h., and in congested sections, 35. You must yield to pedestrians at zebra-striped crossings and when turning at a road junction.

Accidents must be reported within 24 hours or on the first work day to the **Hungaria Biztosító** (Hungarian International Motor Insurance Bureau), Gvadányi út 69, H-1144 Budapest (tel. 0361/1835-350). Hours are 8am to 6pm on Monday, Thursday, and Friday; 8am to 4pm on Tuesday and Wednesday; and 8am to noon on Saturday. (Be forewarned that you might have to conduct your conversation in German or Hungarian unless an English-speaking employee happens to be there.) If someone is injured, notify the police immediately. If you are stopped for a traffic violation, the police could give you a warning on the spot or impose a fine ranging from 100 Ft. ($1.70) to 500 Ft. ($8.35). Believe me, it's better to admit you were at fault and pay up; otherwise, you'll face a long, involved process that may result in a fine that could go to 5,000 Ft. ($83.30) and cost you valuable time.

The red color and the Áfor emblem of the state-owned Hungarian motor **gas stations** can be recognized from a long way off. In addition, you'll find Shell, BP, and AGIP stations. Stations are usually open daily from 6am to 10pm; in Budapest and on motorways and other busy roads, they're open 24 hours.

For help on the road, the **Hungarian Automobile Club** provides a large number of services. Its headquarters are at Francia út 38B, H-1144 Budapest (tel. 0361/691-831), open Monday to Friday from 8am to 4:30pm and on Saturday from 8am to noon. You can get information in English from the club's information center in its headquarters in Budapest (tel. 0361/152-040). There are several technical service stations at larger towns throughout the country. If you have a breakdown in Budapest, call 0361/691-831 or 0361/693-714 around the clock.

In the country, the "yellow angels," the breakdown fleet of the automobile club, will come to your rescue. This service is free for club members (nonmembers are charged). When you enter the country or visit the Hungarian Automobile Club headquarters, ask for an emergency card. If your car breaks down, just hand the card to a passing motorist who will deliver it to the "yellow angels."

The Hungarian Automobile Club runs a travel agency called Auto Tours. It publishes a booklet entitled *Tours in Hungary for Motorists,* which is available from the MAK headquarters, printed in English and German. This contains information for visiting motorists and includes touring information and details of tours organized by the agency.

CAR RENTALS All you need to rent a car in Hungary is to present a driver's license that has been valid for one year prior to the date of rental. You must also be between the ages of 21 and 70.

As it does in Austria, **Budget Rent-a-Car** maintains offices in Hungary, making car rentals almost as easy as picking up a phone. The type of car and the pricing structure are slightly different from those across the border in Austria, but North Americans will quickly get the hang of the new system. When you arrive at the airport in Budapest, there is a Budget counter to help you pick up your car and to fill out the necessary forms. All major credit cards are accepted. Equally acceptable are a minimum cash deposit of $150 or a cash payment of the estimated rental of a car. If you're arriving in Budapest by train, a representative of Budget will pick you up anywhere in the city (at the train station, your hotel, whatever) and take you to their downtown office at Ferenc Körút 42, H-1094 Budapest (tel. 0361/131-466).

Any of the personnel at Budget's toll-free number will be happy to give further details and reserve a car for you in advance. From points throughout the United States or Canada, call toll free 800/527-0700 and ask for the international department.

Hertz is also well represented in Hungary. You can make reservations worldwide at any Hertz station or directly at either Aranykéz utca 4-8, H-1052 Budapest (tel. 0361/1177-788), or at Kertész utca 24-28, H-1073 Budapest (tel. 0361/1221-471). They also have counters at the airport, which are open daily from 8am to 10pm (tel. 0361/1578-618 for the office in Terminal I, and 0361/1578-606 for the office in Terminal II). Always agree on the tariff at the beginning of the rental. For example, if you're hoping for an unlimited-mileage special, you have to inquire on the spot, not when your use of the car is up. In any event, it always pays to pre-reserve your car through a Hertz office in North America before your arrival. Hertz keeps a well-maintained fleet of cars in Hungary. Its least expensive cars are usually versions of Ladas, but in a slightly more expensive category, you can expect a Peugeot 309-P. BMWs and Volvos, although more expensive, are also available, sometimes with automatic transmission. For toll-free reservations, call 800/654-3001.

If you're a fan of **Avis,** you'll also find them well represented in Hungary. This is the company most often used by IBUSZ, Hungary's most visible official travel agent. The Avis Rent-a-Car office is at Martinelli tér 8, H-1052 Budapest (tel. 0361/1184-158). Business hours are weekdays and Saturday from 7am to 8pm (on Sunday from 8am to 2pm). Because Avis cooperates closely with IBUSZ, a 15% discount is sometimes granted to renters participating in an IBUSZ program. The car-rental company also maintains two offices at Ferihegy airport that are open every day from 7am to 10pm. Many travelers to Hungary prefer to make reservations with Avis in North America before coming to Budapest, and the prudent visitor will do the same. Again, a Lada (the smaller versions) or a small Suzuki are the cheapest cars to ask for if you don't mind the cramped conditions and if you're familiar with manual transmissions. For toll-free reservations, call 800/331-2112.

By Train

Hungary has an extensive, well-developed railway network, with 38 modern express trains daily, linking the larger towns and the capital. Railway tickets may be purchased at the ticket office of any railway station, at IBUSZ Hungarian Travel Bureau ticket offices, or at the **Hungarian State Railways** MÁV-TOURS, MÁV közönségszolgálat (MÁV Central Public Service Office), Népköztársaság utja 35, H-1061 Budapest (tel. 0361/228-049). Because Hungarian State Railways belongs to the European railways reservation system, you can book passage on the trains here from elsewhere. Four pairs of trains run daily between Vienna and Budapest. The traveling time is 4½ hours.

In 1989 Hungary became the first country in Eastern Europe to become part of the Eurailpass agreement—heretofore, the domain of Western European nations. **Eurailpass** for years has been regarded as one of Europe's great travel bargains. For a full discussion of this money-saving pass, along with current rates, refer to the section on Eurailpass in the "Traveling Within Austria," section of Chapter I.

Hungary also offers a **MÁV Tourist Season Ticket,** good for 10, 20, or 30 days of rail travel. It is valid for the whole 8,000-kilometer railway network of the country. MÁV Tourist Season Tickets are available at every booking office in Europe that sells railway tickets to Hungary.

In addition, there are season tickets for traveling on the shore of Lake Balaton, separate ones for the south and the north shores. This ticket provides you unlimited travel on the side of the lake you choose in second class.

It's wise to get your tickets for the whole journey before you start. Seat reservations should be made well in advance, especially during the peak summer season. You can break your journey at any point in Hungary without formalities during international travel.

There are restaurants and snackbars at railway stations where you can have a hot meal and a choice of drinks. There is dining- and buffet-car service on domestic fast and express trains. On long-distance passenger trains, the first-class carriages and dining cars are in the middle of the train. Sleeping cars are only on international trains.

By Bus

Every day, the **Volánbusz** company, the largest passenger road transport system in Hungary, makes 38,000 intertown and 40,000 local bus runs within Hungary, going to all the larger towns and tourist centers of the country. Practically all villages and towns of more than 200 inhabitants with no rail link have a Volánbusz service, and its buses also run to Austria, West Germany, Italy, Poland, Czechoslovakia, and Yugoslavia. Season tickets, usually for a 20% reduction from the regular price, can be bought for 1, 3, and 10 days for stops within Hungary. Tickets for all journeys can be booked 60 days in advance.

Volánbusz also operates Omnibusz Travel Bureau as an agency to take care of travelers needs for accommodations, travel within Hungary by bus at special request, programs of travel, sightseeing tours, and currency exchange.

For travel or other information, get in touch with the **International Bus Terminal** on Engels tér in Budapest (tel. 0361/182-122), or the **Omnibusz Travel Bureau** at the Engels tér bus terminal (tel. 0361/172-369).

By Boat

From April to the end of September, **MAHART,** the Hungarian shipping company, operates hydrofoils between Budapest and Vienna. The journey between the two capitals takes around five hours. MAHART can give you daily departure information in Vienna, Karlsplatz 2/8 (tel. 0222/50-55-644). In Budapest, you should inquire at the MAHART international boat station, Belgrád rakpart–International Landing Place (tel. 0361/1181-953). A one-way fare is around $50 per person.

At Lake Balaton there are regular boat services: rental boats and ferry-boats. The latter run between Szántód-rév and Tihany-rév all year long. From early June to late September, they run every 40 minutes from 6:30am to midnight. The fare is 10 Ft. (15¢) per person, and 69 Ft. ($1.15) for a car with driver.

In Budapest, regular boats operate from Budapest to the Danube Bend as far as Esztergom. In summer, sightseeing boats leave several times daily from Vigadó tér in Budapest, not far from the Forum Hotel.

By Plane

It's simple. You can't travel by air to any Hungarian location except Budapest. **Malév,** Hungarian Airlines, operates service from its private terminal in Budapest between the nation's capital and 39 cities in 26 countries, but none within Hungary.

Malév does provide some special tours and excursions within the country. Especially popular are gastronomic, musical, and professional programs. Malév Airtours' central office is at Roosevelt tér 2, H-1051 Budapest (tel. 0361/189-033). The Malév telephone number at Ferihegy Airport is 0361/575-133.

3. The Grand Tour of Hungary

Most visitors, because of their rushed schedules, allow only a few days for Budapest and almost none for the countryside, except for what they can see on fast excursions into the environs of the capital. With that in mind, I have designed the following tours for the visitor on the run.

BUDAPEST AND NORTH TRANSDANUBIA

This tour takes seven nights and covers some 560 miles in addition to the mileage ticked off traversing Budapest.

Days 1 to 3: Arrival in Budapest is best followed by rest and recuperation, perhaps a folklore show in the evening. Begin the following morning with a three-hour organized sightseeing tour of the city, including its most significant monuments. Lunch at a restaurant in the Buda Hills with a panoramic view of the capital and spend the afternoon visiting Market Hall. Spend Day 3 following up with specific inside visits to attractions that intrigued you on your superficial get-acquainted look. These might include the Hungarian National Museum and other landmarks. In the evening, take a Budapest by Night tour or else go to a restaurant with Gypsy music.

Day 4: Leave for the Danube Bend, one of the most beautiful regions of Central Europe, visiting Szentendre, an artists' town of special character, following with a tour of the former royal seat of Visegrád (Citadel). Proceed to Esztergom, the former capital of Hungarian kings, before motoring west for an overnight stop in Sopron on the Hungarian frontier with Austria.

Day 5: Go sightseeing in the morning in Sopron before visiting the limestone quarry at Fertőrákos. Afterward, call on the Esterházy Palace at Fertőd, 17 miles to the southeast of Sopron. Stay overnight in Szombathely.

Day 6: In the morning go sightseeing in Szombathely, which is rich in Roman ruins and baroque architecture. Take an excursion to Ják to visit its Romanesque church before going on to Székesfehérvár for an overnight stopover.

Day 7: Spend the morning sightseeing in Székesfehérvár, which is rich in art monuments. Take an excursion to Tihany to visit its abbey and the houses of artisans. Return to Budapest via the Roman town of Tác, where you can explore its excavations.

NORTH HUNGARY

This tour takes four nights and covers a distance of some 530 miles.

Day 1: Leave for Eger with a short sightseeing stopover in Gyöngyös on the way. Make an excursion to the Mátra mountains. Stay overnight in Eger.

Day 2: Spend the morning sightseeing in Eger, which is rich in art and historical monuments. Proceed to Miskolc-Tapolca via the Szalajka Valley, where you can stay overnight.

Day 3: Travel to Sárospatak to visit its castle, then drive on to Debrecen via the historical wine region of Tokajhegyalja. Spend the night in Debrecen.

Day 4: Take a sightseeing tour of Debrecen in the morning and lunch at the Hortobágyi Csárda. In the afternoon, go for a horse-drawn carriage drive in the Puszta of Hortobágy. Return to Budapest in the evening.

THE GREAT PLAIN

This tour takes in two nights and covers a distance of some 212 miles.

Day 1: Travel to Kecskemét, one of the most typical towns of the Great Plain and lunch at a local *csárda* (inn). Go sightseeing in the afternoon and spend the night in Kecskemét.

Day 2: Travel to Kiskunhalas to visit the house of lace-making. Then drive to

Szeged, where you can spend an afternoon sightseeing. Stay overnight in Szeged before returning to Budapest the following morning.

SOUTH TRANSDANUBIA

This tour takes four nights and covers a distance of some 440 miles.

Day 1: Travel to Lake Balaton and spend the day relaxing and swimming if the weather is right. Stay overnight in a resort hotel along the shore.

Day 2: Leave for Szigetvár, visiting its local museum and taking in the sights. Proceed to Pécs to visit the Roman and Turkish monuments in the city. Take an excursion to Tettye for a panoramic view of the city in which you'll spend the night.

Day 3: Take an excursion to Uszőgpuszta for a horse-drawn carriage ride. Visit the castle of Siklós and then proceed to Szekszárd via Mohács to see the Turkish cemetery. In Szekszárd, time permitting, visit the game preserve. Stay overnight in Szekszárd.

Day 4: Take an excursion to the town of Kalocsa, which is famous for its paprika and folk art. Return to Budapest in the evening.

TOURS

IBUSZ Hungarian Travel Bureau operates tours in Budapest as well as in the rest of Hungary. A **City Tour** takes you on a three-hour sightseeing bus trip to top attractions, including Heroes' Square, Matthias Church, Fishermen's Bastion, Castle Hill, and the Citadel on Gellért Hill. This tour is given year round leaving from the Engels Square bus station at 10am, in April and September at 10am and 2pm, and from May 1 to August 31 at 10 and 11am and 2 to 3pm. The price is $8.50 (U.S.).

A **Gulasch Party** is a must when you're visiting Budapest. This is an evening tour with Hungarian food and wine, plus a show. They are available every night at 8 from May 1 through October 31, except that there's no Sunday party May 15 to June 15 and October 1 to October 31. The price is $26 (U.S.) per person.

See **Budapest by Night** in a five-hour tour including dinner with floor show, dancing, wine tasting, and Gypsy music. This fun evening is available at 7:30 p.m. May 1 to October 31, on Wednesday and Saturday the rest of the year. The price for all this? Just $38 (U.S.).

Tour **Parliament and the National Gallery** in Buda Castle year round on Wednesday and Friday at 10:30am, with a trip available at 1:30pm from May 1 to October 31. (Some tours may be canceled because of Parliament functions.) The charge is $6.50 (U.S.).

If you're not going to the **Danube Bend** on your own, IBUSZ has a fine half-day tour by bus on the right bank of the Danube. You'll go to Esztergom, the early church center; Visegrád, with its medieval castle with impressive fortifications; and Szentendre, where you'll see the National Village Museum. In good weather lunch is served outdoors. The trip is offered starting at 9am on Tuesday and Friday from May 1 to October 31, on Saturday from November 1 through April 30. The price of this tour is $30 (U.S.).

A full-day excursion to **Lake Balaton,** Hungary's inland sea, by bus leaves at 8am on Monday and Thursday May 1 to October 31. You'll have lunch in the beautiful lake region and go sightseeing among the little villages. This trip costs only $37.50 (U.S.).

One of the most interesting tours from Budapest is a full-day excursion to a world-famous **stud farm** where you'll see a horse show and go riding in a carriage. You can even take a horseback ride if you choose. Lunch at a csárda will be accompanied by Gypsy music. This trip is available at 8:30am on Wednesday and Sunday from May 1 to October 31, on Sunday only from November 1 to April 30, at a cost of $38.50 (U.S.).

A **hydrofoil tour** is available on the Mahart line, with service several times a day to show you the panoramic cityscape of Budapest from the water. For information and tickets, phone Vigado tér pier at 0361/181-223 or Bern Jozsef tér pier at 0361/354-907.

If you'd like a more leisurely **cruise along the Danube,** ask your travel agent about a trip aboard the M.V. *Danube Princess,* a ship designed for special cruises. This ship of the P&O Cruises line travels from Passau in West Germany, stopping at Durnstein, Bratislava in Czechoslovakia, Budapest, Esztergom, Vienna, Melk in Austria, and back to Passau. You can luxuriate in good food, wine, music, and service while you pass along through the beautiful heart of middle Europe.

It's wise to arrange to take any of these tours before you go to Hungary, in order to be sure of having an English-speaking guide. Get in touch with IBUSZ Hungarian Travel Bureau, One Parker Plaza, Suite 1104, Fort Lee, NJ (tel. 201/592-8585).

In Budapest, the main IBUSZ office is at Tanács körút 3C (tel. 0361/423-140).

---

4. Fast Facts for Hungary

Plunging into Hungary, with its language and its government both being totally foreign to the average North American, can be more than puzzling. However, it should help to ease your adjustment to have a few of the basic facts about the country at your fingertips.

CAMPING: There are more than 100 campsites in Hungary, mainly open from the beginning of May to the end of September, most accommodating only camping vehicles, although some rent out tents. Tourists can get information and reserve places in advance from the travel bureau of the **Hungarian Camping and Caravanning Club,** Kalvin tér in Budapest (tel. 0361/177-208).

CIGARETTES: Nearly all the major hotels will sell you cigarettes and other tobacco products. In addition to that, all cities and towns have tobacco shops called *Trafik* or *Dohánybolt.* If you want some hard-to-find foreign brand and your hotel doesn't stock it, chances are you can purchase it at an Intertourist shop, for which you will have to pay "hard currency" (that is, Western).

CLIMATE: The country has a temperate climate with continental, Mediterranean, and Atlantic Ocean influences. The annual mean temperature is 50° Fahrenheit. The coldest month is January with 14° to 30° temperatures, and the hottest is July with about 71° Fahrenheit. The number of hours of sunshine is high—close to 2,000 per year in most of the country.

CLOTHING: In summer, a lightweight jacket, wrap, or sweater may be necessary in the evening. In winter, a moderately heavy coat is advisable.

CREDIT CARDS: Sometimes they're better than having Hungarian currency to pay with. In the larger hotels and restaurants and in certain shops and department stores, American Express, VISA, Carte Blanche, MasterCard, Diners Club, and Eurocard are accepted. However, don't count on being able to use one of the cards in small villages.

CRIME/SAFETY: Whenever you're traveling in an unfamiliar city or country, stay alert. Be aware of your immediate surroundings. Wear a moneybelt and don't sling your camera or purse over your shoulder; wear the strap diagonally across your body. This will minimize the possibility of your becoming a victim of crime

MILEAGE BETWEEN HUNGARY'S MAJOR CITIES
Distance in Miles

	BUDAPEST	Debrecen	Győr	Kecskemét	Miskolc	Pécs	Siófok	Sopron	Szeged	Székesfehérvár	Szombathely
BUDAPEST		140	76	53	111	123	66	130	106	41	138
Debrecen	140		217	118	61	233	206	270	139	181	278
Eger	79	81	156	98	38	202	145	210	152	120	217
Gyöngyös	50	93	126	81	61	172	115	180	135	91	187
Győr	76	217		129	188	149	73	54	182	54	65
Kecskemét	53	118	129		123	109	93	183	53	83	174
Miskolc	111	61	188	123		234	177	242	177	152	249
Pécs	123	233	149	109	234		76	178	117	95	152
Siófok	66	206	73	93	177	76		117	139	27	97
Sopron	130	270	54	183	242	178	117		236	108	43
Szeged	106	139	182	53	177	117	139	236		128	218
Székesfehérvár	41	181	54	83	152	95	27	108	128		97
Szekszárd	89	194	116	76	199	38	56	170	86	62	149
Szombathely	138	278	65	174	249	152	97	43	218	97	
Tata	43	184	37	96	154	140	71	91	149	44	102
Vác	21	156	81	50	112	144	87	135	127	62	146
Veszprém	68	208	48	74	173	103	27	89	149	27	69

It's your responsibility to be aware and be alert even in the most heavily touristed areas.

CURRENCY: There are no restrictions on the amount of foreign currency you can bring into Hungary, and it's wise to keep plenty of dollars on hand, because they won't take their own money for IBUSZ tours or hotel accommodations! They take credit cards (see above) or U.S. currency only. Keep your exchange slip in case you need to trade back when you're leaving the country, as you can't leave with more than 100 **Forints,** the currency of Hungary, which must be in coins, not banknotes. You can change back up to 50% of the officially exchanged sum at the border (but not more than $100). The current rate is 60 Forints (Ft.) to $1 U.S.

Foreign currency can be exchanged only at officially designated places: banks, National Savings Bank branches, travel offices, hotels, and camping sites. Private exchange of currency is forbidden.

One Forint equals 100 **fillérs.** There are banknote denominations of 10, 20, 50, 100, and 500 Forints, and coins worth 1, 2, 5, and 10 Forints, as well as 10-, 20-, and 50-fillér pieces.

CUSTOMS: You can bring goods into Hungary duty free for your own use—in reasonable amounts, of course. If you're over 16, you can carry with you 250 cigarettes or 50 cigars, two liters of wine, and one liter of spirits. Articles of value, such as tape recorders, radios, and cameras, should be declared on entering the country so you can be sure of not being charged duty on them when you leave. You may bring in small gift items worth up to 6,000 Ft. ($100). You may bring 100 Ft. ($1.65) into the country with you, and it must be in coins.

Narcotics, antisocialist literature, pornographic literature or film, explosives, and firearms are prohibited. Sports guns and ammunition and two-way radios require a special entry permit.

ELECTRICITY: Electric current in Hungary is 220 volts AC, 50 cycles.

EMBASSIES: Most major countries have an embassy in Budapest. Here are a few:
United States: Szabadság tér 12, H-1054 Budapest (tel. 0361/1126-450), open Monday, Tuesday, Thursday, and Friday from 8am to 1pm and 2 to 5pm, and on Wednesday from 8am to 1pm.
Canada: Budakeszi út 32, H-1021 Budapest (tel. 0361/1767-711), open Monday to Friday from 8am to 4pm.
Great Britain: Harmincad út 6, H-1051 Budapest (tel. 0361/1182-888), open Monday to Friday from 9am to 1pm and 2 to 5pm.
Australia: Délibáb út 30, H-1062 Budapest (tel. 0361/1534-233), open Monday, Wednesday, and Friday from 9am to noon.

EMERGENCY PHONE NUMBERS: Throughout Hungary, the numbers to call in an emergency are the same. They are: ambulance—04; police—07; and fire—05.

FIRST AID: All foreign visitors are entitled to first aid, which any hospital or medical consulting room will provide.

HITCHHIKING: The government of Hungary does not forbid hitchhiking, but I get the impression that they view it with a lack of enthusiasm.

HOLIDAYS: National holidays are observed in Hungary on January 1, Easter Monday, April 4, May 1, August 20, November 7, December 25, and December 26.

INFORMATION: When you visit a country with a language barrier as forbidding as the Hungarian tongue may seem to you at a glance, it's wise to have sure sources of information beforehand and to know where to get answers in English once you're there. If you have any questions on touring Hungary when you're planning your trip, write to the **Tourist Information Service** at Angol út 22, H-1149 Budapest. While in Hungary, call **Tourinform** (tel. 0361/1179-800), or go personally to the Tourinform Bureau, V. Sütő utca 2, in Budapest.

Both in and outside of Budapest, the IBUSZ Hungarian Travel Bureau can usually help you, with scores of branch offices that can supply you with information and services. In North America, the address for IBUSZ is One Parker Plaza, Suite 1104, Fort Lee, NJ 07024 (tel. 201/592-8585). They'll do all they can to plan all details of your Hungarian trip. The English-speaking staff will offer you brochures, maps, advice, information—virtually everything you'll need for a safe and insightful journey to one of Europe's most interesting countries. This is probably the single most abundant source of information, aside from this book, that a tourist can tap before a trip, especially since the materials IBUSZ provides are in English and are usually free. In Budapest the main office of IBUSZ is at Tanács körút 3C (tel. 0361/423-140). You'll find IBUSZ offices all over Hungary.

Each major town in Hungary has a travel agency bureau and local office of tourism, but you may have difficulty in smaller places getting understandable information in English.

NEWSPAPERS AND MAGAZINES: The *International Herald Tribune* is widely sold in Budapest but much less available in the provinces. Likewise, American news magazines, such as *Time* and *Newsweek*, are for sale at major kiosks, particularly at leading hotels. There's also a bilingual newspaper (in German and English) called the *Daily News*, which is often slipped under your hotel door every morning free.

POST OFFICE: Most city post offices are open from 7am to 8pm Monday to Saturday. At most post offices you can make phone calls and send telegrams. Unlike Western Europe, it is not customary to send your mail poste restante, or general delivery. It's better to have your mail forwarded directly to the hotel where you'll be staying.

REGISTRATION: Citizens of the United States and all other non-Socialist countries must be registered at the local police station within 24 hours of their arrival in Hungary, but you do not need to worry about having to do it yourself if you're staying in a hotel or pension. The management will arrange registration for you. However, if you're staying at a noncommercial accommodation, such as at the home of friends, then be sure to sign in within the allotted time. The head of the family can register for everybody.

STORE HOURS: Consumer-goods shops are usually open Monday to Friday from 10am to 6pm (to 8pm in Budapest and other cities, to 2pm on Saturday). Food shops open earlier and close later. Generally, business offices are open from 8 or 8:30am until 4:20 or 5pm.

TAXES: In January 1988 Hungary made a move that pushed its economy closer to that of most countries of Western Europe. It imposed a value added tax (called "VAT" for short) on most goods and services, including hotel rooms and meals. Merchandise, depending on what it is, carries a value added tax of 8% to 30%. Car-rental charges carry a 25% tax in addition to the fuel. That means that virtually everything in Hungary is more expensive.

TELEPHONES AND TELEGRAMS: I have read in many sources that calls to the West are "almost impossible" to make from Hungary. However, on one recent trip I was able to reach both New York (repeated calls) and Paris and London numbers after a wait of anywhere from 5 to 20 minutes. Try to call at slow periods of the day. If you want to inquire about phone problems, telephone 172-200 in Budapest and an English-speaking operator will come on to assist you. If you're making long-distance calls, either within Hungary or to the West, it's best to go through your hotel switchboard or else use the phone facilities at the post office.

Otherwise, you can go to the international telecommunications center in Budapest, where you can not only make phone calls, but send telegrams and Telex messages. It is at the corner of Petőfi Sándor utca and Martinelli tér, and is open from 7am to 8pm Monday to Friday. On Saturday it closes at 7pm. On Sunday and holidays it's open only in the morning.

In Budapest you'll see a number of phone booths, most characteristically in green and yellow. Inside, easy-to-follow instructions are given about how to make a local phone call. Between 7am and 6pm, the charge for local calls is 2 Ft. (5¢) for each three minutes, which is also the charge for each six minutes between 6pm and 7am. To make a long-distance call within Hungary, dial 06, then the district number (ask the operator) for the town or village you're trying to reach, and then the number you are calling.

To call outside the country, dial 00, then the code number of the country desired, then the area code for the town or village being called, and then the individual number you are calling.

TIME: The clocks of Hungary operate seven hours ahead of Eastern Standard Time in the United States. However, sometime in April the country goes on its own central European summer time, which puts it only six hours ahead of Eastern Standard Time, which of course only lasts until the last Sunday in April, when it becomes Eastern Daylight Saving Time, making seven hours' difference again. However, Hungary goes off the summer time in September, so until clocks in the United States are turned back to standard time on the last Sunday in October there's only the six-hour difference from Eastern time. Understand all that?

TIPPING: During their reign the Communists tried to wipe out the policy of tipping, but they did not succeed. If anything, tipping is now more prevalent than ever. Everyone, seemingly, expects a tip, even the service station attendant. When in doubt, be generous—the Hungarians are, even if they can't afford it. Hotel bills predictably carry a service charge, but extra tipping to those who perform services for you is still expected on top of the service charge. In restaurants, tip at least 10%, and 15% or more in deluxe establishments. Several waiters are likely to have served you, but one blanket tip should cover all. If a Gypsy band should serenade you during dinner, they definitely expect at least 200 Ft. ($3.40). Taxi drivers, hairdressers, and other service workers generally expect a tip equal to 15% of the bill.

TOILETS: All major Hungarian cities and towns have public conveniences. They are found in public parks, museums, metro stations, and in train and bus terminals. Pictures on the door indicate whether the toilet is for men or women. If not, know that *férfi* means men and *nöi* is for women.

BUDAPEST

The lights are brighter, the people have more joie de vivre in Budapest, the most romantic city I've found in Eastern Europe—and I've traveled all the countries except Albania. The Hungarian capital—"pearl of the Danube," as it's been named by people who have traveled the entire 1,700-mile length of the river—is a bustling city of some 2.1 million inhabitants. Its architecture ranges from that left by the Romans to that of the present day. The Buda Castle District alone has been called an open-air museum, with buildings and historic monuments that seem to be an inexhaustible treasury. You see structures of historic character standing on streets with a medieval atmosphere—but you also see modern, well-planned, attractive housing estates and commercial buildings developed in harmony with the legacy of the past.

The ancient city of Buda lies on the gentle wooded slopes of the right (west) bank of the Danube, with the busy, modern metropolis of Pest on the left (east) bank, spread out on the plain.

As in many other parts of the temperate sections of Europe, especially along rivers and lakes, Celtic tribes had settlements on the Danube at this site, and then the Romans moved in. The legions of the Caesars and Romans who followed them settled in Pannonia, today's Hungary, in the first century of the Christian era, building the Pannonia capital, Aquincum, where Buda stands today.

In 896 when the Magyars occupied the country where they live today, one of their strategic settlements was established on one of the islands here in the Danube, Csepel. During the early Middle Ages a new fortified royal town was founded on the hill of Buda, where at the turn of the 14th century the Hungarian kings set up the seat of government that had formerly been based in the ancient coronation town of Székesfehérvár.

The Turkish army slashed its way to power in Hungary in the middle of the 16th century, holding sway until they were driven out a century and a half later, bleeding Buda of its wealth, even converting the largest church, known today as the Matthias Church, into a mosque. After the ouster of the followers of Mohammed, the city was reconstructed under a strong baroque influence in the architecture and decoration.

Pest, just across the river on the plain, grew into a commercial town, and by the beginning of the 19th century the two towns—Buda and Pest—had become the political, business, and cultural center of Hungary, but were still separate entities. In 1849 the towns were connected by the celebrated Chain Bridge, a suspension span built by Adam Clark, a British engineer; and in 1873 Buda, Pest, and Óbuda, the oldest part of Buda, were united under the name Budapest. The Chain Bridge, incidentally, and the other six bridges then linking the two parts of the capital were blown up in World War II and have since all been reconstructed.

There are numerous islands between Buda and Pest, chief among them being Margitziget, or Margaret Island (see below). Budapest is known for its 123 thermal springs, with more than a million gallons of water a day pouring from the dolomite strata beneath the city to earn for it the title of largest spa in the world.

Even in this century Budapest has had its share of trouble, with the World War II demolition of 33,000 buildings and all the bridges (see below) then linking the two parts of the city. It was shaken by a rebellion in 1956 against the rigid Socialist government, put down with much slaughter by Soviet troops. Despite the dark pages of its history, however, Budapest is now a happy city. Splendid reconstruction followed World War II and the troubled times of 1956.

On the Buda side of the river you'll see natural beauty and the wealth of relics of the past, while in Pest, shopping can be your number one priority. Not all you'll see is old and historic, but major efforts have been put forth to make the present harmonious with the past. You'll find the Hungarian food and wines good and the people hospitable at any time of the year.

AN ORIENTATION

Budapest, as mentioned, is really two cities, Buda and Pest. Buda, on the right bank of the Danube, is hilly; Pest, on the left bank, is mainly flat. Pest is still the industrial and commercial center, whereas Buda was historically the fortified royal seat. Buda is certainly not royal anymore, but it is regal in appearance, having been restored after its almost complete destruction in World War II.

The center of Buda is **Castle Hill,** or Várhegy, where the restored royal castle now stands. To its north, a section called Castle District is split by many colorful old streets, for the most part running parallel to each other.

After a long afternoon of exploration, you can get to know the Castle District fairly well, as you traverse its cobblestone streets and take in its historic buildings. It is best covered on foot.

However, learning to find your way around Pest will probably take more time than you plan to spend in Hungary. Most of Budapest's ancient monuments lie within the "Inner City" of Pest, including many of the leading hotels, night clubs, and restaurants, along with the major government buildings such as Parliament.

The **Nagykörút,** or "Great Boulevard," forms a half moon in Pest, stretching for nearly four miles. It takes in all of Pest from Margaret Bridge to Petőfi Bridge, and along the way, it changes its name four times (at one point it is called Lenin körút).

The other major avenue of Pest (and I don't expect you to learn to pronounce it right away) is **Népköztársaság utja,** which was patterned after the Champs-Élysées. It stretches from the Inner Boulevard to the Municipal Park.

Pest also has a pedestrian-only shopping street, called **Kígyo utca,** which is laid out between Váci utca (also good for shopping) and Felszabadulás tér, or "Square of Liberation."

In the center of the Danube lies Margaret Island, a spa garden 1½ miles long.

1. Getting Around in Budapest

Going places in Budapest may be considered a challenge to avid walkers, but if your time is limited, you'll want to know about the public transport network, which is easy to use and cheap. Also, taxis in Budapest are an inexpensive means of traveling around. It will help you if you know some basic facts about transportation in the city.

AIRPORT

If you fly to Budapest, you'll land at **Ferihegy Airport,** which has two terminals, the more modern of which is reserved for Malév flights. This is the only commercial airfield in the entire country, as there are no domestic flights. This is a well-equipped airport, and you can exchange currency here, as well as book hotel rooms or rent a car. Allow about 30 minutes to travel between the airport and one of the hotels in the center of the city. An airline bus costs only 20 Ft. (35¢). However, a trip in by taxi will cost from 500 Ft. ($8.50).

RAILWAY

Budapest has three main stations in the center of the city. The main one (and chances are you will arrive here from Vienna) is **Budapest-Keleti** (Eastern Railway Station), Baross tér 10 (tel. 0361/122-4052 from 6am to 8pm and 0361/113-6835 from 8pm to 6am). Trains not only arrive from Vienna, but go to Berlin, Bucharest, Belgrade, Moscow, Sofia, Warsaw, and other cities, as well as make domestic connections to stations in northern Hungary.

The terminus of the Western Railway Station, **Budapest-Nyugati,** Lenin körut 11, maintains international links with Berlin, Bucharest, Prague, and Sofia, and services stations in western Hungary. For information, call 0361/131-5345 from 6am to 8pm and 0361/149-0115 from 8pm to 6am.

Finally, if you're heading for Lake Balaton or other points in western Hungary, the station to go to is the Southern Railway Station, **Budapest-Déli,** Krisztina körut 37 (tel. 0361/135-1512 from 6am to 8pm and 0361/155-8657 from 8pm to 6am). International connections include such cities as Trieste, Venice, Rome, and Vienna.

A central information service operates in Budapest from 6am to 8pm daily. For international journeys, phone 0361/122-4052; for domestic trips, call 0361/122-4052 or 0361/122-7860.

PUBLIC TRANSPORT

All public transport in Budapest is handled by the Budapest Transport Company—on buses, trams, the suburban railway HÉV, the underground, trolleybuses, the cog-wheel railway, the chair lift, the riverboats. Most tram, trolleybus, and underground lines run from 4am to midnight, a few main lines having all-night service. Buses usually run from 5am to 11pm.

Tram and trolleybus tickets (yellow) and bus tickets (blue) must be purchased in advance, at tobacconist shops, train and bus terminals, railway stations, season ticket offices, terminals of the cog-wheel railway, travel offices, and from automatic machines. There are no conductors on public transport vehicles. You punch your own ticket when you go on board.

The yellow ticket, costing 5 Ft. (9¢), can be used on trams, trolleybuses, the underground, and the suburban railway to the city limits. The blue bus ticket costs 6 Ft. (10¢), and it's valid from one end of the route to the other. If you want to transfer you must get a new ticket. If you're staying in Budapest you can save money by buying season tickets, good for one month.

Up to the age of 6, children are allowed to travel free on practically all public transport vehicles when accompanied by an adult. On riverboats they can travel free up to the age of 2, for half fare up to age 10.

You can get information about public-transport travel on the suburban railway HÉV in Batthyány tér (tel. 0361/370-716); at Déli pályaudvar (Southern Railway

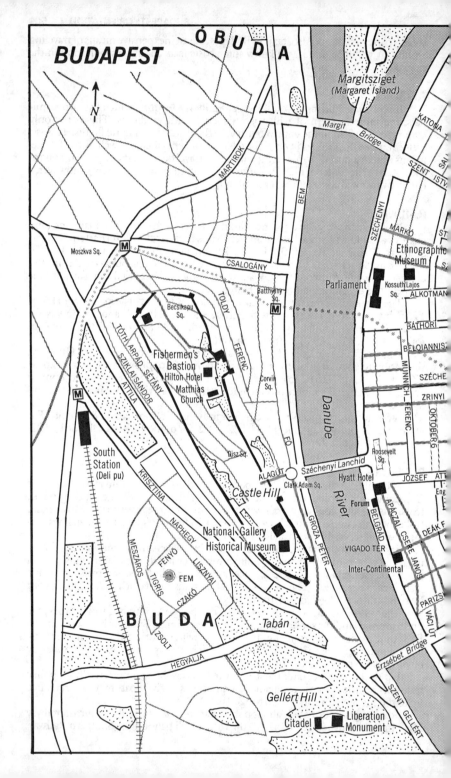

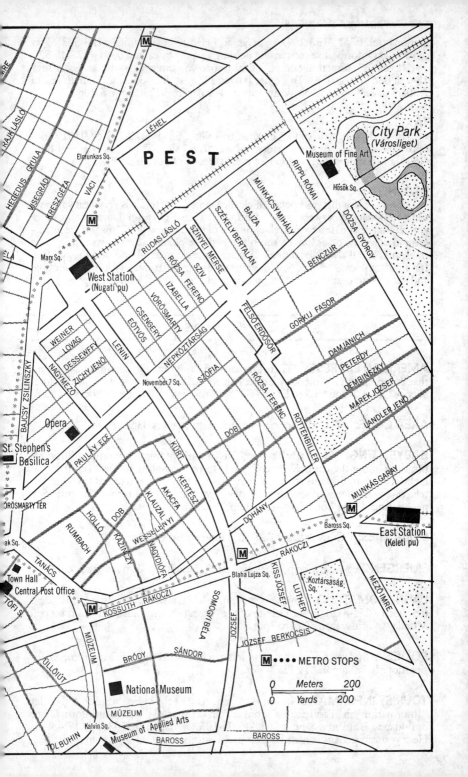

Station) (tel. 0361/153-287); or at Szabó Ervin tér 2 (tel. 0361/183-583). You can also get information concerning public transport by calling 0361/122-40-52.

If you lose something on public transport, you can ask about it at Akácfa utca 18 (tel. 0361/226-613). This office is open Monday, Tuesday, and Thursday from 7:30am to 3:30pm, and on Wednesday and Friday from 7:30am to 6:30pm.

TAXIS

In Budapest, taxis can be ordered by calling 0361/222-222 or 0361/666-666. The vehicles are clearly marked with a "Taxi" sign. The meter begins at 8 Ft. (15¢), and another 8 Ft. is added for every three-tenths of a mile.

DRIVING

If you're driving your own vehicle, be warned that traffic is very heavy in peak times in Budapest, between 6 and 9am and between 2 and 6pm. During those times you might prefer to leave your vehicle in one of the car parks you'll find by the underground stations, or at any of the other parking places in town, and use public transport. You'll always be near a bus, tram, or underground line, and they go fast. It's almost impossible to park in downtown Budapest. You'll be more comfortable and get to your destination more quickly (and cheaply) via public transport.

---

2. Fast Facts

AMERICAN EXPRESS: There is no office for this organization in Budapest (but that could change). American Express affairs are conducted at the IBUSZ Hotel Service Office, Petőfi tér 3 (tel. 0361/118-48-65), which is open 24 hours a day.

AREA CODE: The telephone area code for Budapest is 0361.

BABYSITTING: Need a babysitter? This can be a problem not only in Budapest but throughout the country. There's likely to be a language barrier even if you're lucky enough to find someone to leave with the small fry. Deluxe and first-class hotels often arrange for sitters. Otherwise, you have to do some mighty fine negotiating at your hotel desk—and hope the clerk will have a kindly mother.

EMBASSIES: Consult "Fast Facts for Hungary" in Chapter XIV.

EMERGENCIES: For help, call police at 07, fire at 05, and an ambulance at 04.

LAUNDROMAT: One of the best-positioned laundromats is Patyolat, Rákóczi (tel. 0361/221-840), in the vicinity of the Astoria underground station. It is open Monday to Friday from 7am to 7pm.

POLICE: Budapest police headquarters can be reached for other than emergency situations by calling 0361/1123-456.

TOURIST INFORMATION: In Budapest, contact the same sources listed under "Information" in "Fast Facts for Hungary" in Chapter XIV. The Tourinform Office in Budapest is at Petőfi Sandor út 17-19, H-1052 Budapest (tel. 0361/1179-800). Here you can get answers in English to questions about travel, accommodations, and other data. The office is open Monday to Saturday from 8am to 8pm and on Sunday from 8am to 1pm.

---

3. Where to Stay

As part of the government's energetic program to develop tourism, a glistening collection of elegant hotels has replaced the 19th-century dinosaurs that used to front the Danube. Many of the new hotels are affiliated with chains in the West, including Hilton, Inter-Continental, and Novotel.

However, in spite of this, shortages are reported every season from the first of May until early autumn. Therefore, it's always imperative to secure a reservation. There are many hotels in Budapest that charge far cheaper prices than those I've cited here. The catch is, they're almost always fully booked in spring, summer, and autumn by Eastern European tour groups. Therefore, it's pointless to describe them, since chances are, you wouldn't get in anyway.

All the hotels, including the first-class ones and moderate choices, are reasonable in price when compared with those in Western capitals. Most rates quoted below are in U.S. dollars.

DELUXE CHOICES

Budapest Hilton, Hess András tér 1-3, H-1014 Budapest (tel. 0361/1751-000). Few hotels have created the kind of attention in the design and architectural world that greeted the opening of the Hilton in Budapest in 1977. Critics hailed it as an intelligent and tasteful blend of one of the most historic sections of medieval Buda with a gleaming modern hotel, and a quick walk through its public rooms will show you why. The 700-year-old walls of a 13th-century Dominican church were incorporated into the design, as well as the restored baroque façade of a 17th-century Jesuit university. It is this ornate façade, covered with draping laurel garlands, that guests see first as they walk or drive through the narrow cobblestone streets of Castle Hill.

The hotel is next door to the most potent symbol of the Hungarian nation, the Matthias Church, and just above the Neo-Gothic Fishermen's Bastion. Views across the Danube from the windows of the well-furnished bedrooms encompass panoramas of the Hungarian Parliament and 19th-century Pest. As you walk through the sunny public rooms of this hotel, you can look directly into the partially rebuilt nave of a 13th-century church, which is used as the setting for summer operas, ballets, and musical concerts (you can watch from the huge windows of the glittering lounge area).

Each of the 323 guest rooms contains a color TV set with in-house movies, as well as all the accessories and extras you'd expect from a deluxe modern palace. On the premises are three restaurants, several bars, and a breakfast buffet so plentiful you could skip lunch. There's also a nearby disco, plus a gambling casino. Guests who want to go swimming have free use of the pool at the Thermal Hotel Margitsziget, which is accessible by a hotel bus. The most expensive rooms at the Hilton are on the executive floor. Singles cost $115 to $185 daily, with doubles going for $155 to $224. For more information, refer to my restaurant and nightlife recommendations later in this chapter.

Forum Hotel, Apáczai Csere János utca 12-14, H-1052 Budapest (tel. 0361/1178-0088), on the banks of the river, is a modern palace. Its warmly decorated lobby has lots of niches and intimate seating, with a bar in the rear. The darkly neutral color scheme is subtly lit, bas-relief sculptures in travertine adding abstract patterns. Although this hotel is officially rated below the group of modern palaces that flank it, its services are considered the best in Hungary and among the best in Europe. A battalion of uniformed staff members work hard to make your business or personal adjustment to Hungary as easy as possible. Add to this a dramatic physical plant, and a well-scrubbed health club, sauna, and indoor swimming pool, and you've got a winning combination. (Zsa Zsa Gabor and her mother, Jolie, agree. This is the hotel they've used on return trips to their homeland.)

There's a cozy bar set up in a corner of the lobby, although if you don't want to sit there, you can climb a flight of stairs to a Viennese coffeehouse, where crowds of diners munch rich pastries. Be sure to notice the display cases loaded with petits fours and the handcrafted mural made of intricately carved and painted wood. This represents only one of the many artworks scattered through this plush and unusual hotel. The 408 bedrooms are outfitted with every modern convenience, including in-house movies; many of the units offer sweeping views of the nearby Danube and the historic Chain Bridge. The bedrooms are air-conditioned, with private baths, phones, minibars, radios, and color TVs. Singles go for $135 to $150 per day, with doubles costing $175 to $185.

Atrium Hyatt, Roosevelt tér 2, H-1051 Budapest (tel. 0361/1383-000), occupies one of the most glamorous locations in the city, near the banks of the Danube. Conceived and managed by one of the world's most dynamic hotel chains, it mingles businesslike efficiency with Hungarian charm to create a truly appealing hotel. A favorite of commercial travelers, it rises near the Chain Bridge in a rectangular design of vertically connected rows of jutting bay windows fashioned of bronze-colored metal. As its name implies, it borrowed its design from a Hyatt inspiration already successfully tried elsewhere. The lobby is set up around a soaring atrium design, with what looks like the hanging gardens of Babylon trailing down from nine floors of balconies. You step into a glass-walled elevator that whisks you to your bedroom upstairs.

The 353 bedrooms are comfortable and stylish, all of them monochromatically and restfully outfitted with seating niches nestled into wide-angled bay windows, minibars, TVs with video movies, phones, and many thoughtful extra touches. The rooms cost $120 to $170 daily for a single, $150 to $205 for a double, depending on the accommodation. Included in the price is one of the most copious breakfast buffets in town. The soaring rows of interior balconies are capped with trusses and girders, which support one of the country's most graceful pieces of engineering—a wood-and-canvas reconstruction of the first Hungarian airplane.

On the premises are four restaurants, the best of which, the Old Timer, is recommended separately. There's also a stylish bar along with a business center, a beauty salon, a health club with a sauna, a swimming pool, an underground garage, a collection of boutiques and travel desks, and valet service.

Hotel Duna Inter-Continental, Apáczai Csere János utca 4, A-1364 Budapest (tel. 0361/175-122), in the heart of Pest, was built on a riverfront location affording views of Castle Hill and the stream of the Danube's traffic. This is perhaps the best established of the new palaces along the river. It was built in 1969 as one of the first modern hotels, and changed the face of tourism in Budapest. Three older hotels were demolished to make room for this silver-and-glass 12-story building with views from its hundreds of oversize windows. Since that time it has housed presidents, visiting dignitaries, pop stars, and film celebrities. The side of the hotel facing away from the Danube, toward Pest, is an expanse of stressed concrete, a design that permits each room to have a view of the river. The 340 conservatively tasteful bedrooms have all the necessary accessories and up-to-date amenities to satisfy international patrons. Singles rent for $140 daily, with doubles costing $180. On the hotel's mezzanine is a fitness center with Eastern Europe's first squash court, a swimming pool, sauna, solarium, massage, pedicurist, and pool bar, as well as a sun terrace that is unique among the hotels in the city center. Also on the premises are four restaurants, two bars, boutiques, a beauty parlor, a florist, and an in-house movie system. In addition, the Business Center will handle many of the services a visiting businessperson will need.

Ramada Grand Hotel Margitsziget, Margitsziget, H-1138 Budapest (tel.

0361/111-000). When the hotel was built in 1873, its clientele included the most illustrious names of the Austro-Hungarian Empire, who flocked to its location on an island in the Danube for the curative benefits of the nearby hot springs. With the changing political fortunes of Hungary, its neoclassical white shell grew unkempt until it stood as only a dismal memory of its former self. Completely gutted, the hotel required four years of renovations before it reopened in 1987. It is now the most luxurious and historic of the hotels on Margaret Island.

In fact, it comprises more than a third of the hotel complex whose water-bordered isolation comes as a welcome respite from the bustle of Pest and Buda. The postwar modernism of the thermal baths lies at the end of an underground tunnel. The Ramada Hotel Corporation has adopted this hotel for its own. Employees greet visitors with New World efficiency, yet retain the veneer of politeness and grace of the Old. The most visible remnant of the original hotel is the green marble floor of the lobby. Everything else has been tastefully altered into a conservative and traditional format of exposed paneling, fresh paint, high ceilings, and softly comfortable and safely conservative accessories. The 163 rooms are modernized and up-to-date, with many conveniences, including TV sets, minibars, bathrooms, and phones. Singles range from $79 to $100 daily, with doubles costing $111 to $144.

Thermal Hotel Margitsziget, Margitsziget, H-1138 Budapest (tel. 0361/1321-100), built on top of three thermal springs, stands in this spa park. Proudly occupying a prime location amid the century-old trees on Margaret Island, this glass-and-steel building houses one of Hungary's most impressive spa facilities as well as 206 comfortably furnished bedrooms. You can get a taste of the medicinal waters from one of the four spigots on the modern fountain in the entrance vestibule. The public spaces are vast, sunny areas dotted with chrome and brass sculpture, marble floors, and frequently changing art exhibitions.

You're likely to see a crowd of recuperative patients in bathrobes lounging in the public rooms. Joggers will enjoy the expanses of the botanic gardens a short distance away.

Built in 1979, the hotel offers spacious bedrooms, each of which has its own bath, as well as radio, phone, color TV with in-house movies, balcony, and air conditioning. Doubles rent for $119 to $136 daily, with singles going for $84 to $96.

THE UPPER BRACKET
Hotel Gellért, Szent Gellért tér 1, H-1111 Budapest (tel. 0361/1852-200). The eclectic façade of this time-honored dowager overlooks the Danube at what was once (and might still be) the most fashionable part of town. It's hard to say whether this hotel, which opened in 1918, is designed in art nouveau or Neo-Romanesque. An art nouveau glass-and-iron canopy curves over the entranceway, which leads into a lobby of gray-red stone surrounded by a circular arrangement of marble columns at the edges of a two-story atrium. A tiny bar with unusual sculptures leads off the lobby.

The 235 comfortable but slightly dowdy bedrooms are decorated with combinations of new and old furniture. Rooms rent for $67 to $100 daily for a single, $136 to $146 for a double.

Although its spa facilities may not be the most modern among the several spa hotels in Budapest, they are without doubt the most fascinating. From subterranean depths beneath the hotel, bubbling springs of mineral-rich water are fed into several different pools (some of which are open to the public, others only to hotel guests). The hotel offers several balneotherapeutic programs for medical problems, although healthy guests also enjoy the curative effects. (For more information, please refer to section on baths later in this chapter.)

Novotel Budapest Centrum, Alkotás utca 63-67, H-1444 Budapest (tel. 0361/1869-588). Set amid a complicated series of access roads, this bronze–and–glass-walled affiliate of the ACCOR hotel chain rises in a series of square windows on the edge of the Buda green belt, next door to the Budapest Convention Center. The four-star establishment has several restaurants, bars, an indoor swimming pool, and a big parking area. The brown-colored lobby is glassed in on two sides with an airy bar area that looks out over a raised sun terrace. The 323 soundproof and air-conditioned rooms contain modern furniture and all the necessary amenities. Singles range from $63.25 to $100 daily, while doubles cost $83.25 to $131, depending on the season. The hotel also has six suites. Service, tax, and a buffet breakfast are included.

Hotel Korona, Kecskeméti utca 12, H-1053 Budapest (tel. 0361/1180-999), which opened in 1990, is a modern 10-story building on Kálvin Square, opposite the National Museum. The road leading directly to Ferihegy Airport starts here, and there is an underground station in front of the hotel. Designed in two different sections, the Korona is connected by a "bridge" over Kecskeméti Street; its hipped roof and rows of bay windows evoke memories of the elegant palaces that stood here in the 19th century. The hotel contains 440 bedrooms, each with private bath, soundproof windows, color TV with in-house movies, phone, minibar, and (in most cases) air conditioning. Singles go for $87 daily, and doubles for $113 to $131, depending on the room. The Korona has a parking garage, convention facilities, a business center, a fitness center with a sauna, three bars, and two restaurants.

Flamenco Occidental, Tas veyér utca 7, H-1113 Budapest (tel. 0361/1252-250), is set at the edge of Buda Park Theater, about 3 miles from the rail station. The concrete façade is covered with maroon highlights, while the interior has a décor of soft leather and rough-textured chairs, and various beige, brown, and wood details. The format is streamlined, comfortable, and relaxed, with a rounded bar area and a painted wood sculpture of three flirtatious women occupying a prominent position at the far end of the huge lobby area.

Businesspeople appreciate the convenience and the simplicity of the 360 well-appointed bedrooms, although many tourists come here in summer. Singles go for $98 daily, with doubles costing $121; children under 10 share their parents' room free. Each unit has a tile private bath and a tasteful format of big mirrors, built-in furniture, and color TV with in-house video programs. On the premises are an airy, enormous, and elegant main restaurant, with an impeccably dressed staff, even chamber music. There's also a Spanish-style restaurant, La Bodega.

Hotel Béke Radisson, Lenin körút 97, H-1067 Budapest (tel. 0361/1323-300). An older hotel, built before World War I, stood on the site of the Béke Radisson, which opened for business in 1985 on a busy boulevard in Pest. The architects were careful to incorporate the original façade into the new design, as well as a handful of decorative accessories. One of these is the lobby's massive stairway, the elaborate chiseled masonry of which tapers into a contemporary design of woven brass strips and vertical columns. The lobby level contains an alcove bar and comfortably upholstered chairs; however, many guests gravitate to an inviting perch at the Kupola bar upstairs, with its antique glass–and–ribbed-steel canopy.

Breakfast and lunch are served in the Shakespeare restaurant, where skylit turn-of-the-century murals show romanticized scenes from the Bard's comedies. Breakfast is served daily from 7am to 10am, and lunch daily from noon to 3pm. Dinner is a few steps away in a restaurant ringed with a pair of paintings celebrating the heroism of a 16th-century Hungarian patriot, Szondy. In the glimmer of eight iron chandeliers, within sight of elaborate stained-glass windows, you can sample Hungarian specialties, including grilled trout, crayfish cream soup, and pork steak stuffed with goose liver. There is even a list of 16th-century recipes, supposedly eaten by Szondy and his troops: Turkish wine soup, forcemeat biscuits with rosemary, and kebabs flambé. Reservations are suggested for full meals, which begin at 900 Ft. ($15) and are served nightly from 6pm to midnight.

The 246 up-to-date accommodations—238 rooms and 8 suites—each contain TV, video, radio, phone, alarm clock, tile bath, minibar, air conditioning, and in-house movies. Unusual lithographs by Hungarian artists cover some of the walls. Rates are $100 daily for a single, while doubles and twins go for $124, all with breakfast included. Motorists appreciate the parking garage. There's a swimming pool, plus sauna, solarium, and massage facilities. A high-ceilinged coffeehouse on the second floor emulates the grand conditions of turn-of-the-century Hungarian cafés, although with a modernized décor. The Orfeum nightclub is reviewed separately.

Buda-Penta Hotel, Krist Krisztina körút 41-43, H-1013 Budapest (tel. 0361/1566-333), an imaginatively modern hotel set in a flat area at the bottom of Castle Hill, near the Southern Railway Station. It's separated from a busy thoroughfare by a row of well-placed trees that screens the sunny reception area from the noise of traffic outside. The décor includes low-slung leather chairs, lots of black and orange accents, brown-tile floors, and a labyrinthine arrangement of multilevel bars, coffee shops, and restaurants, all interconnected to one another but separated by short staircases and hedges of verdant plants.

Built in 1982, the Penta offers 394 rooms, each comfortably and simply furnished in wide-striped carpets and neutral color schemes. Each contains a TV, video, minibar, and radio. Singles cost $88 to $100, doubles $113 to $131. The price includes breakfast and access to the indoor pool and sauna. On the premises is one of Budapest's most popular nightclubs, the Horoszkóp (see "Nightlife" later in this chapter), as well as two good restaurants.

MODERATE TO BUDGET

When it was built at the turn of the century, the **Hotel Astoria,** Kossuth Lajos út 19, H-1053 Budapest (tel. 0361/1173-411), was without equal in the capital. It long enjoyed a reputation as the most beautiful, stylish, and fashionable hotel in the city, then entered a sad decline. Now its public rooms and 128 bedrooms have been restored. On a busy traffic artery in the heart of downtown Pest, it is one of the most attractive hotel bargains in its price range. Officials say that only the lack of air conditioning in each room prevents it from being classified as five stars. However, it offers moderate prices. Singles cost $77 daily, with doubles going for $97. The unusually large bedrooms probably have the highest ceilings of any hotel in Budapest, the furniture is French in design, and the bathrooms are modernized. Each unit has a radio, phone, and minibar. Guests register in a lobby floored with green marble and accented with gilt. Through swinging doors lies one of the most comfortably opulent bars in town, along with sitting rooms and restaurants. On the premises is a sauna, along with a nightclub.

Hotel Nemzeti, József körút 4, H-1088 Budapest (tel. 0361/1339-160). Built in 1902, but heavily restored and modernized in 1987, this middle-bracket hotel sports the most beautiful blue-and-white baroque façade in the commercial neighborhood around it. It lies beside a busy traffic artery in the heart of Pest, but because of its thick walls and double windows its units are quiet. Guests register in a marble-floored lobby whose elaborate gilt-accented ceiling was shaped into a Roman-inspired barrel vault. A few steps away, one of the most opulent staircases in Budapest sweeps majestically to the uppermost floors. This is said by the management to be a three-star hotel with four-star facilities. Each of the 76 bedrooms is simply but comfortably furnished, amenities including TV, minibar, and phones. Rates are $61 to $76 daily for a single, $82 to $105 for a double, both with breakfast included. On the premises is an appealing street-level restaurant with an impeccably polite maître d'hôtel and a bar.

Erzsébet Hotel, Károlyi Mihály utca 11-15, H-1053 Budapest (tel. 0361/1382-111), is a streamlined hotel built on the site of an older hotel by an Austrian construction firm in 1985. Few of the details of the original hotel were included in the new design, except for the romantic portrayals of Hungarian patriot Janos Pince, originally painted in 1920, which were moved into the basement beer stube. Each of the 123 comfortable bedrooms contains its own bath, color TV, minibar, radio-alarm, and direct-dial phone. Singles go for $87 daily, with doubles costing $104. Both the inside and outside of the hotel are decorated in neutral shades of brown and white. There's a smallish bar along with a coffeehouse in an annex of the lobby. A contemporary but formal restaurant is a few steps away. Though the hotel lies in a bustling section of Pest, its interior is soundproof.

Grand Hotel Hungária, Rákóczi út 90, H-1074 Budapest (tel. 0361/1229-050). In 1985, one of Hungary's state-owned hotel chains renovated and enlarged an existing property to create the biggest hotel in the country. Since then, the Grand Hungária has welcomed thousands of visitors arriving by car, plane, bus, or train at the Eastern Railway Station lying across the street. Each of the 528 rooms is sound-proofed against the noise of the surrounding district, which bustles with commercial activity. Singles go for $52 to $84 daily, while doubles cost $63 to $105, depending on the season and the plumbing amenities (all rooms have private baths or showers). These rates include an American buffet breakfast.

The architects were concerned with maintaining at least part of the older hotel, so some of the original façade juts out from the painted concrete-and-glass façade of the newer structure. The hotel has three restaurants, a salad bar, two drinks bars, a coffee shop, a nightclub, and a ballroom. Other facilities include a guide service, beauty parlor, fitness center, sauna, rent-a-car, physician, and transfer service. An in-house garage solves an impossible parking situation on the streets above.

Hotel Taverna, Váci utca 20, H-1052 Budapest (tel. 0361/1384-999). A trio of huge bay windows extends from its façade over a lamplit pedestrian walkway in the middle of commercial Pest. Opened in 1985, this hotel was designed in keeping with the latest trends in urban architecture. The color scheme, both inside and out, uses warm shades of brown accented with modest amounts of maroon. Each of the 224 bedrooms contains its own tile bath, color TV, minibar, direct-dial phone, and radio-alarm; each is cozy, well scrubbed, and well upholstered, as well as attractively compact. Singles cost $60 daily, while doubles range from $73 to $85; rates for both include breakfast. There's a fitness center in the basement, as well as two pubs, one of which has its own bowling alley; a wine and champagne bar; and a covered passage-way leading to a downtown shopping mall. Motorists must arrive at the rear entrance of the hotel on a short side street leading off Petőfi utca.

Grand Hotel Royal, Lenin körút 47-49, H-1073 Budapest (tel. 0361/1533-133), opened in 1896, has a name that is not only appropriate but also indicative of high rank. The first decades of its operation were the golden age, when businesspeople and artists made their homes in the hotel, which was and is near many cultural establishments, such as the Conservatory and the Moulin Rouge. The governor of the Philippines once lived here. The old structure was destroyed during World War II, and the rebuilt hostelry opened in 1961, with a rehearsal room for use of the regular artist guests, as well as sauna, solarium, and massage facilities.

Guests in the large and elegant accommodations are given constant attention by the capable staff. The 365 comfortable bedrooms are modernized and cost $34 to $64 daily for a single, $50 to $98 for a double, depending on the season. Off the lobby is a restaurant serving such dishes as Hortobágy crêpes, four kinds of fish, stuffed sour cabbage, tournedos Budapest style, paprika chicken with dumplings, and Gundel-style crêpes. Meals averages 600 Ft. ($10) to 1,000 Ft. ($16.75). The restaurant is open daily from noon to 3pm for lunch, from 6 to 11pm for dinner.

Hotel Expo, Dobi István utca 10, H-1101 Budapest (tel. 0361/1842-130), is an 11-story hotel that opened in 1982 on the grounds of the Budapest International Fair area. Built in a cruciform pattern of aluminum and tinted glass, it offers 160 functional bedrooms and a coffee shop. It pays special attention to businesspeople who choose to make this hotel their stopover point. Singles go for $68 to $75 daily, doubles for $84 to $90.

Hotel Budapest, Szilágyi Erzsébet Fasor 47, H-1026 Budapest (tel. 0361/1153-230). Known throughout Hungary as the circular hotel because of its rounded exterior, the Budapest is designed in the shape of a futuristic, glass-ringed cylinder that almost looks like an enormous power generator. It was entirely reno-vated and modernized in 1985, an event that improved both its image and its interior decoration. Situated on the outskirts of town, at the edge of the Buda Hills, the hotel contains 280 bedrooms, each equipped with bath, radio, color TV, minibar, and a pay-video system. Rates are $68 daily for a single and $84 for a twin, with a buffet breakfast included. Children under 10 stay free in their parents' room. The hotel has a business center and the Budapest Club on the top floor, where guests will also find a sauna and a solarium. There are also a Hungarian restaurant with Gypsy music and a nightclub called the Joker Bar. The Csárda is an example of a real Hungarian wine cellar.

Hotel Stadion, Ifjúság utja 1-3, H-1143 Budapest (tel. 0361/1631-830), is an eight-story modern hotel near the stadium and the Budapest Sports Hall. It's connected directly to the inner city by subway, and is fairly recognizable by its twin towers and rambling emphasis on strong horizontal lines. Inside are a six-alley skittle hall, a swimming pool, a sauna, and 372 bedrooms. The décor is comfortable and functional, and dining facilities include a restaurant, a brasserie, a snackbar, plus a drinking bar. Singles cost $70 daily, and doubles $90.

Hotel Panorama, Rége út 21, H-1121 Budapest (tel. 0361/1750-522), is a hunting-lodge hotel built in the neighborhood of the Szabadság hill. The former Vörös Csillag (Red Star) hotel, it has not only a new name but an improved standard. The hotel offers 36 bedrooms, each with bath, radio, TV, video, phone, and minibar. Rates range from $24 to $53 daily for a single, from $38 to $69 for a twin. The Panorama also operates a bungalow camp with a total of 54 units; prices for two persons begin at $40 daily. On the premises are a cocktail bar, a brasserie, and a hunter-style restaurant decorated with big arched windows, huge antlers, and frescoes by well-known Hungarian painter Molnár Pál. Gypsy music accompanies the meal, which might include both typical Hungarian dishes and regional specialties.

4. Dining in Budapest

We've already previewed the Hungarian cuisine. Now let's lift our forks at one of the following establishments.

THE UPPER BRACKET

Alabárdos, Országház utca 2 (tel. 0361/560-851). Since this restaurant on Castle Hill is connected with a riding school, there's an iron bracket holding a horse's head and the word "Equus" extending over the cobblestone pavement. You'll enter through a brick-floored tunnel lined with chiseled Gothic arches before going into this most charming of Buda restaurants. Near the Hilton Hotel, the restaurant has an impressive decoration of elegant three-foot-thick walls accented with stone arches, ribbed and vaulted ceilings, and a collection of medieval spears and battle axes (*alabárdos* means halberd in English).

The attractively lit interior is the perfect setting for transporting you back into another era, a feeling increased by the discreet lute music played softly by a single musician. Open from 7pm to midnight except Sunday, the restaurant serves well-prepared specialties on Herend china. The English-speaking headwaiter will assist you as you order such delicacies as stewed roebuck with pineapple, roast wild boar, stuffed pork with goose liver, caviar (both red and black), three styles of fogas, two special kinds of steak, and crayfish ragoût with dill. This is one of the best restaurants in the city, with meals priced from 1,200 Ft. ($20.50) and up. Reservations are essential.

The only drawback of the **Restaurant Vadrózsa** (Wild Rose), Pentelei Molnár utca 15 (tel. 0361/1351-118), is its remote location in the prestigious suburb of Rosenhügel, which, before the war, was the most elegant address in the city. A taxi will deposit you in the small but stately garden of a baroque pavilion, the kind an empress might have crafted in the French style as a summer refuge. The interior, however, is modern, with only a pianist in one corner to alleviate the severe angles and the glistening crystal of Venetian chandeliers. It looks much older, but the pavilion dates from 1940, when it was the home of a successful Hungarian actor. It was designed by one of the most famous architects of that era, Tibor Kocsis. Since the early 1970s, the building has been maintained as a restaurant by a pair of charming sisters, Kati Horváth and Margó Vetter. It serves dinner only, and bears the distinction of being one of the most expensive restaurants in Hungary, charging around $50 per person for dinner, which might include beluga or Malossol caviar. It is open from 6pm to midnight daily except Monday (also closed for three weeks in August).

In lieu of a menu, an employee will recite in English the special preparations of the chef. Better yet, enormous and entire goose livers will be brought raw on platters for your examination, as well as fresh fogas from Lake Balaton or meticulously prepared game hens, steaks, or whatever else has been stocked in the larder that night. Whatever you select, be assured that it will be fresh and of the highest quality. The chef will see that it's superb in its flavor and presentation. Reservations (as early as possible) are vital. The location is about a mile northeast of the city center.

Ristorante Marco Polo, Vigadó tér (tel. 0361/1383-354), is the premier Italian restaurant in Hungary—in fact, one of the finest such restaurants in Eastern Europe. You can arrive early to enjoy an apéritif on the ground floor, later climbing the stairs to your well-laid table on the second landing. Opening in the politically explosive year of 1989, the cultivated and elegant establishment was the creation of a trio of Hungarian and Italian entrepreneurs who hired some of Milan's most successful interior designers. They created a chic minimalist décor, a world of cherrywood burl paneling, granite, travertine, and marble floors, and supple black leather couches. Meals are among the most expensive in the capital, costing from 1,200 Ft. ($20) to 2,000 Ft. ($33.50). Lunch is served daily from noon to 2:30pm and dinner from 7:30 to 11pm. The restaurant is closed on Saturday. You can begin with one of the delectable pasta dishes or else a superb choice of antipasti, perhaps even an Italian fish soup. Main course selections include saltimbocca, breast of young chicken with sweet garlic, and risotto with seafood. For dessert, why not try the hot zabaglione with vanilla ice cream?

Légrádi, Magyar utca (tel. 0361/1186-804), meeting place of "haute Pest," is considered the costliest restaurant in Hungary. Owned by the Légrádi brothers and managed by Hungarians who trained at the Budapest Hilton, this is the most socially pretentious restaurant in Pest, a holdover of Habsburgundian consciousness. The sign that identifies its somber entrance is barely visible. You descend a flight of steps into a series of vaulted cellar rooms, filled with romanticized 19th-century paintings and flickering candles, plus a clichéd Gypsy violinist. First, a delectable selection of Hungarian hors d'oeuvres will be wheeled to your table. Go easy here, as the main course portions are huge. You might try, for example, Norman-style goose liver; many different game specialties, including wild boar maison; or stuffed duck served for four persons. Meals cost from $50 and up and are served at dinner from 6pm to midnight Monday to Friday. The restaurant is closed in July and August, and reservations are always needed.

Szindbád, Bajcsy-Zsilinszky út 74 (tel. 0361/1322-749). After descending a short flight of stone steps from a busy commercial street in Pest, you find yourself in the elegantly paneled and vaulted premises of one of the capital's most successful and respected privately owned restaurants. A battalion of young uniformed waiters will help you in your selection of the well-prepared specialties. These might include grilled goose liver with stuffed apples, or braised hare with bread dumplings, perhaps even a Spanish-style paella. You can begin with a sampling of Russian caviar. The cooking is both Hungarian and international. Meals cost from 1,000 Ft. ($16.75). Lunch is served from 11:30am to 3:30pm and dinner from 6:30pm to midnight Monday to Friday. On Saturday and Sunday, only dinner is served, from

6pm to midnight. Part of the restaurant is a plushly upholstered re-creation of a private club used for parties.

Old Timer, Atrium Hyatt Hotel, Roosevelt tér 2 (tel. 0361/1383-000), is one of the leading restaurants of Hungary. Its second-floor position on the banks of the Danube gives diners a sweeping panoramic view not only of the river, but of the Chain Bridge and the Royal Palace. Full meals are served daily from noon to 3pm and 7 to 11pm. Live music from a concert harpist sets the elegant tone. The décor is international and contemporary, but the globe lighting and dark-wood paneling add a 19th-century nostalgic touch, as do the tuxedo-clad waiters.

A fixed-price lunch, costing from 545 Ft. ($9.25), is a sought-after daily event. From a heavily laden circular buffet table, diners select from a battery of salads, appetizers, and pastries, along with fish and meat courses. À la carte meals in the evening are much more elaborate, costing from 1,000 Ft. ($17), a bargain considering the deftness of the kitchen staff and the high-quality ingredients employed. The cuisine is often derived from 19th-century recipes such as roast goose liver with cabbage and ginger or goose liver in paper jackets. A house specialty is filet of beef Atrium style, served with chicken liver and nuts and flambéed at your table with Calvados. My favorite Hungarian soup, a fragrant palosch, is made with spring lamb, green beans, potatoes, cream, tarragon, and paprika. It's at its best here. The chef also does goose liver fried in its own fat, and you can order iced Russian caviar, along with fogas braised in white wine with onions, grapes, and mushrooms. One of the ice cream specialties might be your dessert, perhaps a layered slice of Dobos cake. Reservations are needed.

Silhouette, Forum Hotel, Apáczai Csere János utca 12-14 (tel. 0361/1178-0088), is gaining publicity as one of the best restaurants in Hungary. Many food critics have already acclaimed it as the finest in Budapest. It is set behind the glass walls of the Forum Hotel. The view from your flower-graced table takes in the Danube and the twinkling lights of Old Buda. Although very spacious, the restaurant exudes intimacy, thanks to the engaging pianist and the rows of plants dividing most of the tables from the rest of the dramatically illuminated, plushly upholstered room.

Your meal might include pigeon essence with cheese doughnuts, a selection of smoked fish served with horseradish cream, cold goose liver à la maison, frogs' legs in herb sauce or fried, escargots au gratin with mushrooms, vineyard snails in pottery, filet of fogas with crayfish ragoût flavored with dill, rabbit in a spicy sauce served with green noodles, or braised wild boar with a soupçon of garlic. The strips of beef with brandy and mushrooms will be pan-fried beside your table by a team of waiters at a trolley. Full meals begin at 1,500 Ft. ($25.50) and are served daily from noon to 3pm and 7 to 11pm. Reservations are a must.

Café-Restaurant New York (Hungária), Lenin körút 9-11 (tel. 0361/221-648), is the most famous restaurant in Hungary, a riot of rococo décor on a busy avenue in downtown Pest. It is overly tourist-oriented, which won't please everybody, yet it has its devotees. The reproduced signatures on the front cover of the menu have been called a "time-machine celebrity register," since they contain the names of what were once some of the most important literary and artistic figures in the world, including Charlie Chaplin and Thomas Mann. This is the last of the approximately 30 coffeehouses that between the wars hosted virtually every liberal thinker in Hungary, and provided a setting where much of the Hungarian literature of the 20th century was written. It was christened Café New York because of its home in the branch office of an American insurance firm. The Hungarian government has spent a vast sum restoring the marble-and-gilt interior.

You can order fiery gulasch, a Waldorf salad, fish cocktail, fried strips of carp, paprika chicken, sautéed chicken Marengo style, ribsteak in paprika sauce, sponge cake with chocolate sauce, or pancakes Gundel. There are dozens of places to sit, many below the beige, marble, and gilt-covered capitals that are still emblazoned

"NY," but the best place to dine is in "Deep Water." This is the lowest part of the café, reachable via a wide carpeted stairwell, where vested waiters offer attentive service and where dancers from all parts of Hungary and Gypsy musicians provide evening entertainment. Meals cost from 700 Ft. ($12) and up, and the café is open daily from 9am to 10pm.

Gundel Restaurant, Állatkerti út 2 (tel. 0361/221-002). From the flowery terrace of this landmark restaurant, built near the city zoo in 1873, you can hear the lions roar. In fact, as you approach the symmetrically ornate façade you'll be able to make out the sculpted animal heads emerging from the stonework. A uniformed doorman will usher you into a high-ceilinged reception area surrounded with beautifully etched glass and porphyry trim. The sunny and somber dining room is flooded with sunlight from the big windows and accented with red marble columns, potted palms, and photos of Budapest between the World Wars. The most famous owner of this restaurant was one of Hungarian gastronomy's most important contributors. Dubbed the Hungarian Escoffier, he invented pancakes Gundel, that chocolate-covered flambéed dessert that now appears so often on menus throughout Hungary. Although he is long gone from the premises (which are now directed by a state catering firm), the restaurant is still highly regarded.

If you show up any day of the week from noon to 4pm and 7pm to midnight, you, too, can taste Hungarian specialties that are reputed to be among the best in Budapest. The items, served on the gold-and-white china, include pheasant pie with Cumberland sauce, crêpes stuffed with fowl, Hungarian mushroom soup, Serbian-style carp, gulasch, a stew of prawns and mussels cooked in "the sailors' way," goose breast with a goose-giblet risotto, braised quails, and rosemary-flavored roast of lamb. Count on spending from 1,000 Ft. ($16.25). (The restaurant is closed for Sunday dinner in winter.)

Dominican Restaurant/Restaurant Kalocsa, Budapest Hilton Hotel, Hess András tér 1-3 (tel. 0361/1751-000). Off the lobby of this previously recommended hotel, you'll find a duet of two of the most alluring restaurants in Old Buda. The most visible is the pink and exceptionally comfortable Dominican, named after a monastery that used to stand on the site. It offers an international menu and sweeping views over Fishermen's Bastion, the Danube, and Pest. The house specialty is foie gras, which the chef prepares in many different variations. Other dishes are likely to include fresh pan-fried goose liver with fruit, or grilled filet of pike-perch. Paprika chicken strudel is another popular item. Full meals, costing from 1,200 Ft. ($20.50), are served daily from noon to 3pm and 7pm to midnight. The Kalocsa dining room is outfitted puszta style, with replicas of the elaborate folkloric motifs produced in south Hungary. (Kalocsa is the major paprika-producing area of Hungary.) In this restaurant you're served a selection of Hungarian and international dishes. Meals here also cost from 1,200 Ft. ($20.50). Both restaurants keep the same hours.

Halászbástya Restaurant, Halászbástya (Fishermen's Bastion) (tel. 0361/1853-500), adjoins the Hilton Hotel on Castle Hill. You might consider this an unlikely place for a restaurant, but actually the Neo-Gothic fantasy called Fishermen's Bastion contains enough interior space to shelter a restaurant, and even a disco (see my nightlife recommendations) within its thick stone walls. One of the most charming places in town is the summer terrace. The management has set up tables under the stone vaulting of what almost looks like the ambulatory of a cloister. One side is open to a view of the Hilton and the Matthias Church, while the other looks out over the Danube and virtually everything on the far side of the river.

As you dine, you'll even be sheltered from the river breezes by glass panels set into the pointed arches of the Gothic parapet. Of course, if you prefer to dine inside, there's an attractively decorated restaurant at the bottom of a flight of winding stone steps inside the largest of the bastion's towers. Each of the curved banquettes is covered with sheepskin cushions, and you'll think you've suddenly been transported to the Great Hungarian Plain. The lighting is concealed behind copper wall fixtures, and there's even a scattering of puszta antiques placed throughout the labyrinthine arrangement of rooms inside. Menu specialties include beefsteak Budapest style, fish soup, Danish caviar, and fogas meunière. Expect to pay around 1,200 Ft. ($20.50) for a meal. The indoor restaurant is open daily for dinner from 7pm to midnight.

Barokk Étterem, Mozsár út 12 (tel. 0316/1313-186). To reach this restaurant, you'll probably take a taxi to an unlikely-looking street in the heart of commercial Pest. A door will open into a jewel-like room decorated to the taste of Mozart or Maria Theresa. The restaurant is outfitted with cabriole-legged chairs, fussily ornate cabinets, gold-rimmed crystal glasses, and ornate moldings in shades of white and gold. A young employee, dressed like a footman in a Habsburgundian palace, will hand you a menu with a long list of possibilities that were researched and adapted from 17th-century recipes. Full meals cost from 1,000 Ft. ($17). Try, for example, such dishes as game paste ripened in cognac and delicately spiced, filets of pike-perch in a béchamel sauce, or haunch of vension with rosemary and ginger. Hours are noon to midnight daily.

Fortuna Haz, Hess András tér 4 (tel. 0361/1756-857), was doing a brisk business in the 18th century in a building on Castle Hill that was partially built in the 14th century. Today, greatly restored, this popular restaurant sits across the square from the Hilton behind a stone-trimmed yellow baroque façade. There are several different aspects to this establishment, including a nightclub. It also has a Gothic-style restaurant serving good food. The dining section is reached through a carpeted hallway lined with pointed stone arches whose stonework has been pitted with time. The somber décor is accented with a big stained-glass window, iron chandeliers, and a coffee machine trimmed with Dresden-style china from Pécs. Menu items include carp paprika style with dumplings, crêpes Hortobágy (stuffed with meat), pâté de foie gras, paprika chicken with gnocchi, beef Wellington, shrimp sauté, and filet of fogas. Expect to spend from 1,000 Ft. ($17) for an à la carte meal. The restaurant is open daily for lunch from noon to 3pm and for dinner from 7pm to 1am.

Kárpátia, Károly Mihály 4 (tel. 0361/1173-596). The décor of this unusual restaurant is almost like that of a secularized church. In fact, it combines many of the best features of medieval architecture with good food and attentive service. You'll be ushered through a vestibule into a Gothic fantasy of stenciled walls, ornate hardwood thrones, immaculate sea-green napery, and gilded capitals carved into patterns of grape leaves and animal heads. The high vaulted ceilings are embellished with leaf and vine patterns of red, green, and gold, while the wrought-iron globe lights are fanciful combinations of white glass and black metal. Even the floor is crafted from a combination of black and pink mottled stone, accented with ornate brass trim, which tends to complement the masses of stained glass set into the windows and into the tops of the carved Gothic banquettes.

The restaurant as you see it was constructed in 1925 by a well-known caterer named Charles Spolarich. His culinary standards live on in the brasserie, near the front door, and in the spacious restaurant leading off to the back. Menu items include cold goose liver in its fat, Hortobágy pancakes, Hungarian gulasch soup, fried carp, crisp roasted duck, paprika chicken with gnocchi, and an assortment of strudels. All of this you can enjoy every day of the week for lunch or dinner for around 700 Ft. ($11.75). Gypsy music is provided from 6pm daily, and the restaurant is open from 11am to 11pm.

THE MODERATE RANGE

Mathias Keller (Mátyás Pince), Március 15 tér 8 (tel. 0361/1180-436), was built in 1904, close to the river, near Elisabeth Bridge. This turn-of-the-century restaurant has become a Budapest landmark. It was conceived in a labyrinthine format of stained glass, lots of detailed woodwork, graceful wooden chairs, and a series of wall frescoes of scenes taken from the life of King Matthias Corvinus. You'll enter a spacious vestibule area and leave your coats with the attendant before heading down a long hallway decorated with green-and-beige illustrations from the adventures of Bacchus. The brasserie is on the left and the restaurant on the right, either one of which might strike your fancy. Gypsy music comes from behind a carved zither in a half-paneled area covered with green baize, which you'll enjoy while being waited on by a small army of uniformed waiters. You'll have many rooms to choose from, including an inner sanctum with round wooden columns capped with Neo-Romanesque capitals painted in somber colors.

The Hungarian specialties include crisp roast knuckle of pork, bridegroom's soup, stewed sirloin cutlet with goose liver Budapest style, fisherman's soup in a kettle, and quail with bacon, which could be followed by chocolate pancakes flambé or a cold raspberry strudel. Full meals begin at 1,000 Ft. ($17). The brasserie is open continuously from 11am to 1am, and the restaurant serves lunch daily from noon to 4pm and dinner from 7pm to 1am.

Étterem, Hotel Gellért, Szent Gellért tér 1 (tel. 0361/1852-200). A Hungarian may wander far from home, but he carries with him a fond memory of this place. Whenever he returns, he always schedules a meal here trying to re-create some moment of yesterday. The cuisine, even the décor, hasn't changed much, so he's usually not disappointed. However, first-time visitors shouldn't confuse this restaurant with the Gellért Brasserie, which has its own entrance and outdoor terrace. Head instead through the hotel lobby, up a flight of stairs, and down a hallway to reach the main and more prestigious restaurant. You'll hear the sounds of Gypsy music and quietly conversing Budapesters who sometimes come here for family outings. Full meals, costing from 700 Ft. ($12), are likely to include turtle soup, Hortobágy crêpes, grilled perch or carp, Hungarian veal stew with gnocchi, and pork cutlets with paprika-flavored mushroom sauce. Lunch is daily from noon to either 3 or 4pm; dinner, nightly from 7pm to 12:30am.

Vigadó Café/Beerhall, Vigadó tér 1 (tel. 0361/1181-598). Near Vörösmarty Square on the Pest side of the Danube in the modern Vigadó Concert Hall, this elegantly modern restaurant, despite its name, is more of a light and airy restaurant than a beerhall. The seating is divided among semiprivate modern compartments formed from wood, starched burlap, and rattan accented with brass nails. Although the restaurant is large, you'll get the feeling of being in a much more intimate space thanks to the secluded seating arrangements. The tables are butcher-block constructions, each two inches thick, and will ultimately hold such specialties as carp Dorozsmai style, roast pork with asparagus, chicken in a basket, and smoked pig's leg with horseradish, along with pork Kodály style and rumpsteak with roquefort sauce. Dessert might be a poppyseed parfait or one of three or four other pastries homemade in the kitchen. Meals range upward from 600 Ft. ($10). The place is open daily from noon to 11pm.

Udvarház Hármashatárhegy, Hármashatárhegzi út 2 (tel. 0361/1888-780), lies in the western part of the city and is usually reached by taxi. Budapesters consider dining here worth the excursion. Set in the forested countryside, it is a panoramic place with a summer terrace for dining. The interior is formal, opening onto views of the city and the faraway Danube. A polite staff will usher you into the high-ceilinged and elegantly modern room. When the place was originally built, it was the manor house of a prosperous farm; today it's been completely redesigned. The food tends to be excellent, including such classic Hungarian dishes as paprika chicken, Hungarian veal stew, and smoked breast of goose. For dessert, you have a choice of assorted strudels among other delectable offerings. Full meals cost from 550 Ft. ($9.25), and are served daily except Monday from 11am to 11pm.

Régi Országház Vendéglö (Old Parliament Restaurant), Országház utca 17 (tel. 0361/1751-767). A plaque outside the front door of this yellow baroque house on Castle Hill announces that the building was constructed on the foundations of a medieval house in 1700. You'll enter one of two forest-green doors and walk into a labyrinthine arrangement of rustically decorated rooms, the first of which has about the biggest stucco-domed stove you're likely to see. The ambience is one of candlelit intimacy among local residents, whose faces are dimly lit amid the plaster walls and vaulted ceilings. Throughout your meal a musical trio wanders Gypsy style throughout the rooms. The outdoor terrace is a summer oasis.

The vested waiters usually speak English and serve such specialties as Russian blinis with caviar, roast trout, deer filet with bread dumplings, Serbian salad, green pepper salad, stuffed cabbage with dill sauce, rumpsteak Gypsy style, and turkey breast Kiev. Pike-perch is prepared in many delectable ways. In season, the kitchen also turns out refreshing fruit soups made with peach, cherry, sour cherry, apple, and pear. Expect to spend from 550 Ft. ($9.25) and up for a meal. The restaurant has a wine cellar from the 15th century where you can have dinner if you request it, along with good wines. Food is served Monday to Friday and on Sunday from 11am to midnight, and until 1am on Saturday. Although the restaurant is open for lunch, its food is best appreciated at night.

Fehér Galamb (White Dove), Szentháromság utca 9-11 (tel. 0361/1756-975). On Castle Hill, not far from the Hilton, this restaurant faces a medieval square with a statue of Andras Hadik dating from 1689. The glass door from the street pivots open on a silent central hinge, leading into a small entrance vestibule. The cellar can be reached by going down a winding stone staircase past walls that were once part of the medieval fortress. Today, you can sit at one of the lower level's small tables and reflect on the past.

The same menu is offered on both levels. Specialties in summer include Hungarian gulasch soup, Jokai bean soup, Hortobágy meat strudel, paprika chicken, pork steak Budavar, and Somlói sponge cake. In winter you can enjoy pigeon soup, veal ragoût soup, cold goose liver, deer in red wine, stuffed turkey, or fried lamb, perhaps topped by flamed pancake. The vested staff performs excellent service, and your meal will be serenaded by Gypsy musicians.

The ground-floor restaurant is open daily from 11am to midnight. The wine cellar is open Monday to Saturday from 7pm to midnight. Expect to pay from 500 Ft. ($8.50) for a full meal.

Szechenyi Restaurant, Ramada Grand Hotel Margitsziget, Margitsziget (tel. 0361/111-000). This well-staffed place is especially lovely in summer, when sunlight streams through the leaves of the surrounding trees and large windows. The most elegant restaurant on Margaret Island, it offers an insight into the grand age of the spa vacation. Full meals, costing from 800 Ft. ($13.50), are served daily at lunch from noon to 3pm and at dinner from 7pm to midnight. A diet-conscious menu is offered, but a wide array of other dishes is also available. They are both Hungarian and international in flavor and deftly prepared by a well-trained kitchen crew. Dishes include frogs' legs Provençal, Russian caviar, braised filet of pike, venison chasseur, roast leg of goose with cabbage and wine sauce, and goose liver in its own fat served with spices in an earthenware container.

The Wine Cellar (Borozo), Ramada Grand Hotel Margitsziget, Margitsziget (tel. 0361/111-000). Everything about it is reminiscent of a cozy wine cellar you might find along Lake Balaton or on the Great Hungarian Plain. It sits deep below this 19th-century hotel, which was revitalized by Ramada in 1987. Within one of about a dozen nooks and crannies, surrounded with puszta weavings and thick stucco walls, you can sip Hungarian wine, listen to Gypsy violins, and eat specialties from the centuries-old cuisine of Middle Europe. Menu items include veal ragoût Balaton style, pork cutlets stuffed with chicken liver, and smoked ox tongue with horseradish cream sauce. The dessert specialty is a grape pudding derived from a region of Lake Balaton. The array of wines is wide and impressive. Only dinner, costing from 550 Ft. ($9.25), is served, and it's offered nightly from 7pm to 2am.

Restaurant Platan, Hotel Thermal Margitsziget, Margitsziget (tel. 0361/111-000), is the glistening and spacious restaurant named after the rows of plantain trees that had to be cut down for its construction in 1979. In summer, clients can eat on the outdoor terraces with a view of the adjacent botanical gardens. A huge buffet usually simmers under copper domes on the big central table. The chandeliers are made of modern crystal, the napery is elegant, and the service is excellent. During the course of any particular meal the music might come from a team of Gypsy musicians partially concealed behind a wooden screen. The menu features six Hungarian specialties, including stuffed cabbage, veal paprika, frogs' legs, or filet steak Budapest style (with chicken liver and letcho). If these don't appeal to you, try the pheasant with apple purée, or one of seven kinds of fish. A meal here will cost from 550 Ft. ($9.25) to 600 Ft. ($10.25). Hours for lunch are noon to 3pm; for dinner, 7 to 11pm. Open daily.

BEST FOR THE BUDGET

Kispipa Vendéglő (Little Pipe), Akácfa utca 38 (tel. 0361/422587), is a Pest bistro, the kind that might have existed in that now golden age of "between the wars." On a street running parallel to Lenin körút, Kispipa attracts a wide assortment of clients, all of whom know they get good value for their money here. You pass through a pair of lace-covered glass doors to reach the brightly lit interior of this bistro. A collection of commercial posters from the 1930s adorns the walls. A pianist contributes some desultory melodies, and the food arrives in steaming platters from the overworked kitchen. The chef's specialty is fogas (pike-perch from Lake Balaton), which is prepared in many different ways. You can order baked carp, many venison dishes, or breast of turkey stuffed with goose liver. A fixed-price menu is offered for 190 Ft. ($3.25), or else you can order à la carte for 250 Ft. ($4.25) and up. Open Monday to Saturday from noon to 1am; closed Sunday and when the place takes a much-needed vacation in July.

Apostolok Étterem, Kigyó utca 4-6 (tel. 0361/1183-704). After its frescoes and mosaics were restored by the Hungarian government, this Neo-Gothic restaurant was listed as a historic monument whose interior could never be altered. Dining here exposes a visitor to one of the most amazing décors in Budapest. Each of the elaborately carved oak niches has its own apostle set into gilt-trimmed mosaics. A team of Transylvanian woodcarvers labored for months here in 1902. Even the Virgin Mary is set into the stained glass of some of the table dividers. In a separate section, rows of blue-tinged murals represent cities that once, but no longer, formed part of Hungary.

The menu, printed in four languages, offers smoked knuckle of pork with horseradish, Jokai-style bean soup, sauerkraut soup, pork steak Bakony style, paprika chicken, and both cold and warm goose liver. Fixed-price menus begin at only 180 Ft. ($3), with à la carte meals ranging from 300 Ft. ($5) to 600 Ft. ($10). The restaurant is open from 10am to midnight.

Restaurant Kis-Buda, Frankel Léo utca 34 (tel. 0361/1152-244), lies in a neighborhood known to every Budapester. The street it sits on was the city boundary of medieval Óbuda, and the location of both a medieval cloister and a hospice for the sick and dying. Across the street stood a primitive wine house whose food and drink fortified merchants and passersby. In 1363 the most famous queen of Hungary, Erzsébet, bought the house, the inn, and the land from the innkeeper, donating it to the Sisters of St. Clare. Today, in a building dating from the early 20th century, a re-creation of the original winehouse has been erected, but with an upgrading in décor and facilities. You can dine in darkly paneled comfort, with lots of local color. From Monday to Saturday, the restaurant is open from noon to midnight; but on Sunday, only lunch is served, from noon to 3pm. Meals cost from 350 Ft. ($5.75) and are likely to include such Hungarian treats as grilled filet of salmon or trout, fried frogs' legs, the special carp (served only for two persons), fisherman's soup, blinis with caviar, and eight different preparations of beef. The most popular dish? It's chicken with paprika sauce, the eternal Hungarian favorite.

Duna-Corso, Vigadó tér 3 (tel. 0361/1186-362). You'll enter through a discreet door that faces the red obelisk at the side of the Inter-Continental Hotel. A horseshoe-shaped copper-topped bar near the coatroom is the first thing you'll see, where a changing collection of disco music plays softly. The attractive restaurant is covered with soft red-and-white wallpaper, a stone floor cut into geometric patterns of the same colors, and immaculate napery. You'll be only a stone's throw from the opera and the operetta house, joining the Hungarians who come here for the good value of the inexpensive and well-prepared food. This includes fish soup, zander (pike-perch) filet, oxtail soup, trout, goose liver with mushrooms, medallions of veal Budapest style, half a roast hen with french fries, nine kinds of salad, and six kinds of liver, including baked goose liver with potatoes. For dessert, try a cheese concoction, vargabeles, which originated in Transylvania, or a strudel made with morello cherries. Meals cost from 550 Ft. ($9.25), and are served daily from noon to midnight.

Restaurant Borkatakomba, Nagytétényi utca 64 (tel. 0361/1730-997), lies in Budafok, a suburb of Budapest. More than a century ago, this restaurant was carved into the limestone bedrock as part of a stone vault for the storage of wines. The history of the restaurant was launched with the royal visit of Franz Joseph, head of the Austro-Hungarian Empire, who dined amid the large wooden wine barrels. Today you, too, will be served on tables and benches built out of barrels. Rustic decorations abound, as do the many vintage wines. Regional full-bodied Hungarian food is accompanied nightly by Gypsy music and entertainment. It's good, clean fun. Inexpensive complete meals cost upward from 450 Ft. ($7.50). The restaurant is open daily except Tuesday from 5pm to midnight. Reservations are necessary.

THE CAFÉS OF BUDAPEST

Most of the famous old cafés that were so talked about between the wars are gone. Café life is not as important as it used to be in the pre-television era; however, some of it still flourishes, as reflected by the recommendations below.

Café Gerbeaud, Vörösmarty tér 7 (tel. 0361/1186-823). This old-world establishment is famous through Europe as a sort of twin sister to the celebrated Demel in Vienna. Now nationalized, it is considerably more proletarian than when it was founded in 1858 by the Swiss confectioner Emile Gerbeaud. He had marble tables imported from France, lined the rooms with silk wallpaper, and installed crystal chandeliers. It caters to a diverse crowd of aging women in fur hats, wealthy Austrian tourists, and diverse students from around Europe and the Middle East. But every afternoon it produces the kind of gossip and semichaotic hubbub that seems to mirror the inconsistencies of Budapest itself. There is a long railroad-style layout of at least four separate sitting areas, all of them painted in shades of beige, pastel reds, and greens below reproduction gold-and-white ceilings. Always celebrated for its chocolate, it turns out a chocolate-and-marzipan royal torte that's positively sinful. The aromatic coffee, dispensed from a hand-painted Herend porcelain machine, said to be one of only three on earth, costs from 60 Ft. ($1), with tortes going for 50 Ft. (85¢). The café is open daily from 9am to 10pm in summer, from 9am to 9pm in winter.

Café Ruszwurm, Szentháromság 7 (tel. 0361/1755-284). The government has declared this 17th-century coffeehouse a historic monument. The café on Castle Hill is within an easy walk of Matthias Church, and in summer is mobbed with clients wanting a taste of what is reported to be the finest pastry in Hungary. In tourist season the least crowded time of the day is between noon and 4pm, when you might find a seat on one of the fragile Biedermeier chairs or on one of the gracefully curved striped settees. The café comprises only two intimate rooms, the first of which contains inlaid antique cabinets holding a tempting array of chocolates and pastries, all of which are freshly baked on the premises. In the second room, a waitress whose frilly blouse is trimmed with the same lace as that hanging in the windows will bring you pastries for 25 Ft. (45¢) and coffee for 20 Ft. (35¢). If you're in doubt as to what to order, try the sour cherry strudel or perhaps Ruszwurm's cream bun. The café is open Thursday to Tuesday (closed Wednesday) from 10am to 8pm.

Café Pierrot, Fortuna utca 14 (tel. 0361/1756-971). The trademark of this place is the face of a clown miming an expression made popular in Paris at the turn of the century. It's owned by Ilona Zsidai, who was once the head of press and publicity for Hungar Hotels. Along with her husband, who discovered what had been an abandoned bakery in a house more than 600 years old, she painstakingly created an avant-garde enclave in the middle of Old Buda.

The décor includes Philippine-style cane chairs bent into art nouveau patterns, a well-polished samovar, and an antique oven now painted white. The marble-top tables rest on cane bases, the grand piano is covered Mata Hari style with an Oriental rug, and the walls are dotted with pen-and-ink drawings vaguely reminiscent of Picasso. Above the bar an effigy of Pierrot, the French clown, hangs under one of the plastered ceiling vaults. In addition to the masses of chrysanthemums, you'll be greeted by Elton John's music and a sophisticated crowd. Whether you sit inside or on the summer terrace, you'll enjoy the coffee (dispensed from an Italian espresso machine), French and Hungarian brandies, Irish coffee, and such specialties as an array of crêpes stuffed with goodies like chestnut chocolate and whipped cream. Mixed drinks range from 120 Ft. ($2), crêpes from 80 Ft. ($1.30); and Irish coffee, from 195 Ft. ($3.25). Live piano music is presented daily from 8pm. The café is open Monday to Saturday from 5pm to 1am and on Sunday from 11am to 11pm.

Café Korona, Dísz tér 16 (tel. 0361/1756-139), nestles behind a baroque façade. It is considered one of the watering spots of the Hungarian literati. This might be a destination point after a walk through Old Buda. A few steps from the city ramparts, on your way back from the museums inside the Royal Palace, this coffeeshop offers Hungarian poetry readings as well as illuminated display cases of cakes and pastries, many of them incredibly fancy. My favorite is a chocolate bundt cake with a confectioner's sugar cross on the top. A bigger room off to the side of the vestibule has false marble tables resting on bentwood bases. The waitresses serve a selection of whiskies and wines from a well-dusted rack. Cakes cost upward from 30 Ft. (50¢). The café is open daily from 10am to 9pm.

Café Margaréta, Hilton Hotel, Hess András tér 1-3 (tel. 0361/1751-000), is one of the nicest places in Old Buda for a midsummer cup of coffee. Its entrance is at the rear of the Hilton, the side that faces the Danube. Its interior is a warmly inviting blend of well-worked paneling in two kinds of wood, modern crystal chandeliers, and shield-back upholstered chairs. The best part, however, is the summertime practice of setting up tables in the semicircular depression between the hotel and the Neo-Gothic arches of Fishermen's Bastion. Sheltered by the windbreak created by the architecture around you, you'll surely want to spend time savoring a puszta cocktail, a mixed drink, or a glass of wine, perhaps a beer, which might be accompanied by one of the cold snacks or a fruity strudel. It's open daily from 9am to 9pm in winter, to 11pm in summer. A chef's salad makes a light lunch at 250 Ft. ($4.25), or else you can visit just for a coffee at 45 Ft. (55¢).

Lukács Café, Népköztársaság utja 70 (tel. 0361/321-371), is a turn-of-the-century café that was established by one of Hungary's most famous pastry chefs, Sándor Lukács. You'll be greeted by a huge display case as you enter from the busy commercial street in Pest where it's located. My favorite place to sit is in the "white chamber" on the upper floor, whose gold-trimmed décor has been classified as a national monument. All the pastries you could think of, as well as coffee, are available, costing from 30 Ft. (50¢) for coffee and 35 Ft. (60¢) for pastries. Open daily from 9am to 8pm.

Müvész Café, Népköztársaság utja 29 (tel. 0361/224-606), nicknamed "little Gerbeaud," opened at the turn of the century. It offers a quiet refuge from the activity of this busy street facing the Opera House. The clientele tends to be actors and musicians. The front room is usually more crowded than the back room, so you can choose the ambience you prefer. The walls of this establishment are covered in green silk, and the chairs are cane-backed baroque. Coffee and tortes cost from 35 Ft. (60¢). Open daily from 8am to 9pm.

5. Budapest by Day and by Night

Lively Budapest offers many attractions for visitors, ranging from sightseeing to cultural activities to nighttime entertainment. Whatever your tastes, you're sure to find much to enjoy here.

THE SIGHTS OF BUDAPEST

Don't go looking for skyscrapers in the Hungarian capital—there aren't any. But there are architectural treasures preserved from many eras of the city's history for you to see, as well as beautiful parks and streets, and many museums with displays to intrigue almost everybody.

Hours for the museums in Budapest and throughout Hungary are usually 10am to 6pm. All museums are closed on Monday. Admission is free on Saturday.

If your time is severely limited in Budapest, you may be forced to concentrate on only the highlights. If that is so, then try at least to get around to the following sights: Castle Hill, Gellért Hill, Margaret Island, St. Stephen's Basilica, and the Hungarian National Museum.

These sights are previewed below, together with other attractions you should see if time permits.

A Walking Tour of Old Buda

The district of Castle Hill, on a cigar-shaped platform above the Danube in Old Buda, is regarded as a pedestrian's paradise of cobblestone-covered streets and tree-shaded walkways where traffic is either light or forbidden altogether. You can amble contentedly through the medieval streets, stopping at the sights and panoramas that appeal to you most. Since the entire district is contained within the irregular-shaped oval circumscribed by thick medieval walls, most of the sights lie within a short walk of each other.

If you're hale and hearty, you can begin your walking tour near the Danube at the western end of Széchenyilánchid (Chain) Bridge. Facing Castle Hill, climb the inclined ramp stretching to the left side of the traffic-clogged tunnel. A small stone archway leads from the ramp to a flight of zigzag steps, which will take you to an enormous bronze eagle at one side of the Royal Palace. Or else take bus no. 116 from the Chain Bridge at Clark Adam tér up a winding road to the museums. These museums are accessible via the rear side of the castle (the façade of which faces away from the Danube). They include the Budapest Museum of History, the Hungarian National Gallery, and the Museum of the History of the Working Class. Sweeping vistas of the Danube and Buda's sister, Pest, open during your climb. They'll appear especially dramatic from the statue-dotted terrace in front of the palace.

The Szinhaz utca connects the castle and its museums to the rest of Castle Hill. On it, you'll pass an ochre-colored baroque theater, the Várszinház Galéria, which often presents plays by Shakespeare in Hungarian.

At the Diszt tér, which funnels half of the traffic entering the district, take the right-hand fork, the Tarnok utca, admiring the restored houses along the way. Number 10 contains an antique store, Antikavitás, while no. 18, the Arany Sas (Golden Eagle) houses a medieval pharmacy and a small museum.

Tarnok utca leads into Szentháromság tér, a square focused around a baroque assemblage of ecstatic saints carved in gilt-capped stone. To the right is the most famous monument in Hungary, the Matthias Church, site of the 15th-century wedding of King Matthias and Beatrice of Aragón. Later, Liszt's *Coronation* Mass accompanied the 1867 coronation of Franz Joseph as King of Hungary here.

Turn right along the side of the cathedral for a view of one of the finest bronze castings in Hungary, the equestrian statue of St. Stephen, which is ringed with quadruplicate stone lions and protected from the Danubian winds by the Neo-Romanesque hulk of Fishermen's Bastion. You might revive yourself with a coffee on the Hilton Hotel's sheltered sun terrace if weather permits. Then pass between the mirrored sides of the hotel and the stone carvings of the Matthias Church, admiring the geometric patterns of the tile roof before entering the most famous ecclesiastical portals in Hungary.

When you leave the church, don't turn to the left or right, but walk straight across the square, passing beside the already-visited baroque monument, and continue down Szentháromság utca. On the right you'll pass a tourist information office, then the most historic pastrymakers in Budapest, the Café Ruszwurm. Continue past an equestrian statue of the 18th-century patriot, András Hadik, and walk a few steps down a narrow alleyway.

This leads to the tree-lined path running beside the steep drop-off of the medieval fortifications that surround Castle Hill. Some visitors are so enchanted with this view of the hills of residential Buda that they decide to walk along the footpath for a while, eventually retracing their steps to the András Hadik monument. Your map will show that a trio of roughly parallel streets fans north from this point close to the Matthias Church. Each street deserves its own separate promenade.

Your tour begins with the westernmost street, the Uri utca, which runs past the András Hadik monument. Continue by walking north on the Uri utca, admiring especially the baroque detailing on house nos. 50, 52, and 43. At the street's northern terminus, at the Kapisztran tér, you'll see the restored tower of the Church of St. Mary Magdalene (Magdolna-torony), marking a 13th-century holy site and all that remains of a church destroyed by the Germans in 1945. Only a reconstruction of one of the nave's Gothic windows stands in lonely isolation behind the tower.

Turn right, then take the first right heading south, this time on Országház utca. Here, every other building seems to have been declared a national monument. Rows of well-maintained medieval houses captivate your attention, particularly the ones with semiprivate courtyards. Look for a well-stocked folkloric shop at no. 12.

You'll soon find yourself on familiar territory in Szentháromság square in front of Matthias Church. Turn left when you enter the square and turn left a block later into Hess András tér, passing in front of the architecturally noteworthy Hilton Hotel. Near the bronze statue of a beneficent pope, fork left into the Fortuna utca. You might want to visit the Hungarian museum of catering at no. 4. Admiring the buildings along the way, you'll eventually find yourself in the Bécsikapu tér across from the brooding Gothic hulk of the city archives. Thomas Mann lived at no. 7 on this square between 1935 and 1937. To the right, notice the Vienna Gate with its protective statue. Although what you'll see is a reconstruction of an earlier gate, much of the traffic flowing into Castle Hill passes through here.

Take a hard right around the façade of a baroque church and walk south along Tancsics Mihály utca to finish your promenade over the parallel streets of Castle Hill. Number 26 served as a synagogue in the 14th century.

Number 9 was an 18th-century ammunition dump and a 19th-century prison. Restrained there, among many others, were Hungarian patriot Lajos Kossuth and writer Mihály Tancsics, from whom the street takes its name. The cream-colored baroque palace at no. 7 housed Beethoven in 1800, and is today an archive and a study center for the work of Béla Bartók. If the gate is open, try to see the exquisite courtyard inside. Number 5 contains an attractive art gallery with the works of living Hungarian artists displayed.

Castle Hill

Várhegy, or Castle Hill, a long narrow plateau, is the core of the Buda of the Middle Ages. The streets are still cobbled, and many gardens and courtyards are hidden away along the narrow alleys. Small palaces, mansions, many in the baroque style, and medieval churches have been restored after suffering massive damage in World War II. The Nazis staged the last defense of Budapest in the Castle and Gellért Hill districts, and as a consequence were shelled and bombed by advancing Soviet troops. The district is surrounded by ramparts and once-fortified walls.

In the midst of much controversy, a Hilton Hotel was built right in the center of Castle Hill, the first (and it may well remain the only) hotel in the world incorporating and built around a 13th-century church. This gives the Hilton the unique advantage of being not only a hotel but a sightseeing attraction listed in guidebooks (see my hotel recommendation above).

The major attractions of Várhegy include the **Matthias Church** (Mátyás-templon), which was founded in the 13th century by King Béla IV. It was given the name it bears today after the wedding here of King Matthias and Beatrice of Aragón in the 15th century. The church, originally named Church of Our Lady, has been reconstructed many times since it was built, and the gold-tile-roofed structure shows traces of varying architectural eras.

The Turks, during their 150-year stay in Hungary in the 16th and 17th centuries, converted the church into a Gothic-style mosque. In the Loreto Chapel you'll see a marble statue of the Virgin. The Turks tried to destroy it, but it was too big, so they just sealed it up and apparently forgot it. In the siege of 1686, however, the walls covering the statue fell down. The troops of the pasha considered this sudden emergence of the "Holy Lady" a miracle and did not try to do her further harm.

An important event here was the crowning in 1867 of Emperor Franz Joseph I as king of Hungary. Liszt composed the *Coronation* Mass for this great occasion. The last coronation in this church was that of the last Habsburg emperor, Charles (Karl) IV in 1916, after the death of Franz Joseph in the middle of World War I.

The church has an interesting treasury museum, with many sacred relics and stone carvings from the Middle Ages, replicas of the crown jewels of Hungary, vestments, and Renaissance chalices. Part of the museum is in the crypt. A baroque column outside the church is dedicated to the Trinity in token of deliverance from the plague.

High mass in the "coronation church" is held on Sunday at 10am.

Fishermen's Bastion (Halászbástya, in Hungarian), at the eastern end of Castle Hill, gets its name from the fishermen of the Middle Ages who were assigned the job of protecting the north side of the Royal Palace during any siege that might occur. At the turn of the century builders duplicated a Romanesque version of these ramparts and turrets. The walls were built over an old fishermen's village. No longer used for defense, the bastion provides one of the most dramatic places in Budapest today to take a walk if you're seeing a panoramic view of the Pest side of the Danube embankment. In front of the bastion is an equestrian statue of St. Stephen.

The **Royal Palace** is where the Nazis held sway in Budapest in World War II. The palace had been the headquarters of the controversial Admiral Horthy, but the Führer's occupation forces made it their command post. The Soviets reduced it to rubble in their push against the Nazis.

World War II was not the first time the palace was destroyed. Its construction was ordered by King Béla IV in the 13th century, and it was the ancient seat of the Hungarian kings, called Budavári palota, or Buda Royal Palace. In the siege of 1696 the Turks razed it, and it was rebuilt in baroque style following the liberation of the city from the Muslim yoke by Prince Eugene of Savoy. Today an equestrian statue of the prince stands on the terrace in front of the neobaroque structure, completely rebuilt since 1945 with a healthy respect for its history.

The palace houses two of the most important museums in Hungary: the Historical Museum of Budapest and the Hungarian National Gallery. Before you enter the palace, walk to the edge of the terrace for a panoramic view of the city.

The **Historical Museum of Budapest** (Budapest Történeti Múzeum) is in the south wing of the palace, Szent György tér 2 (tel. 0361/1160-607), accessible from the Szarvas square. Here displays trace 1,000 years of the turbulent history of Budapest from Roman times forward. Magyar saddles and weapons evoke the ancestors of today's Hungarians. Many artifacts and pictures from the Turkish occupation can be seen.

Medieval passageways and fortifications discovered in the war-damaged building and now incorporated into the museum, together with much medieval sculpture. Of interest is the display of the construction of the Royal Palace. Among the furniture, ceramics, and porcelain treasures, outstanding is the Great Gothic and Renaissance Hall with many red and white marble reliefs from the middle and late 15th century palace. One of the most stunning parts of the museum is the Hall of the Knights, with sculpture of knights and heralds from the years 1420 and 1430. The former royal gardens in their present layout are from the 15th century. It is open Tuesday to Sunday from 10am to 6pm, charging an admission fee of 10 Ft. (15¢).

Hungarian National Gallery (Magyar Nemzeti Galéria), Royal Palace, Castle Hill (tel. 0361/1757-533), occupies the heart of the Royal Palace. This museum is devoted solely to the works of Hungarian painters and sculptors from medieval times to today, the major collection showing the panoramic sweep of the work of Hungary's top talent. If you don't have much time to spend here, I suggest that you visit the collection of late Gothic winged altars and see the works of the celebrated painter of the 19th century, Mihály Munkácsy, who lived from 1844 to 1900. Of many of the country's artists who went on to national acclaim, Munkácsy seems to have gained the widest audience. See also the impressionistic landscapes of Pál Színyei-Merse (1845–1920). The gallery is open Tuesday to Sunday from 10am to 6pm. Admission is 10 Ft. (15¢).

The **Hungarian Museum of Commerce and Catering** (Magyar Kereskedelmi és Vendéglátóipari Múzeum), Fortuna utca 4 (tel. 0361/1756-249), is divided into two parts. One section is devoted to the confectioner's art, tracing the history of the Hungarian confection trade from its inception in the Middle Ages, when sweets were sold by chemists. The exhibition acquaints the viewer with the types of goods produced in different periods and the development of furniture and equipment of the confectioners. The other part of the museum traces the commerce of Hungary during the first half of this century up to the beginnings of Socialist commerce. The development was broken by World War I, but displays depict the postwar forms of commerce uniting wholesale and retail trade. Department stores and branch establishments can be traced in a series of showcases. Some exhibits show the different tasks of people engaged in commerce. Cooperative trade flourishing between the two World Wars is also covered. One ticket—costing 6 Ft. (10¢)—admits visitors to both sections of the museum, which is open Tuesday to Sunday from 10am to 6pm; closed Monday. On Saturday there is no admission fee.

Gellért Hill

Gellért-hegy, as it's called in Hungarian, overlooks the Danube from a height of 770 feet above sea level, offering a magnificent vista of both Pest and Buda. The hill was named for St. Gerard, who converted the country to Christianity and was martyred in 1046 by being tossed off this hill into the Danube by pagans who resented his efforts. Gellért Hill, to the south of Castle Hill, is one of the most beautiful parklands in Budapest.

The **Citadel** (or Citadella), constructed by the Habsburg forces during Hungary's struggle for freedom from its link with Austria in 1849, crowns the hill site. The Germans staged a last-ditch effort here before the fall of Budapest to advancing Soviet troops late in World War II, and the fortress had to be reconstructed after the war ended. Its walls are more than nine feet thick. Today it houses a well-known restaurant, with a terrace offering a panoramic view of the city and river.

Visible from almost anywhere in Budapest is the **Liberation Monument,** called Hungary's Statue of Liberty. The monument honors the "heroic Soviet liberators" who freed the city from Nazi occupation. The names of the soldiers of the Red Army who died in the battle are engraved on the monument.

Aquincum

An important Roman city with some 100,000 inhabitants at the peak of its power and prestige, Aquincum was the capital of Rome's province of Pannonia. Its name means "ample waters." It stood on the right bank of the Danube, about 4 miles upstream from the heart of Buda, at the place where Óbuda (Old Buda) was later built. Outside of Italy, the excavations here, begun in the 1930s, have developed into one of the major discoveries of a Roman urban sector.

The **amphitheater,** which dates from the 2nd century A.D., has been reconstructed on the foundations of the old walls. Larger than the Colosseum in Rome, the Aquincum stadium could seat 16,000 bloodthirsty spectators. Gladiators were sent from Rome to amuse the legionnaires stationed at this frontier outpost of the Roman empire and the civilian populace. A fortress was later constructed on the site of the Roman city, and long after that houses were built where the amphitheater had stood.

Some of the artifacts found here are displayed in the **Roman Camp Museum,** Szentendrei út 139 (tel. 0361/804-650). You can see remains of the plumbing and heating system used by the Romans. The museum is open Tuesday to Sunday from 10am to 6pm, and charges 10 Ft. (15¢) for admission.

Margaret Island

Now a resort with two major hotels and a recreation area, Margitsziget, as the Hungarians called Margaret Island, lies in the middle of the Danube and can be reached from both the right and the left banks by the Margaret Bridge. The bridge was reconstructed after being blown up in World War II—not by Allied bombs but by Nazi demolition charges that went off accidentally in 1944 at a time when the bridge was in heavy use.

The island, 1½ miles long and only a few hundred yards wide at its midsection, was once the domain of the elite of the Roman Empire, lying midway between Pest and the Pannonian capital, Aquincum.

The government has turned the island into the biggest park in Budapest, with a big city-owned swimming pool that can accommodate as many as 20,000 people, a zoo where you can see peacocks and deer, and a well-known rose garden where many other flowers flourish in summer. A long-established spa draws people seeking the curative effects of warm thermal waters, which were first brought to the surface in 1866. Summer restaurants are popular here. Busts of some of Hungary's outstanding authors and painters have been placed in the woodlands.

At an open-air theater in the center of the island, theatrical performances, opera, ballet, concerts, and sporting events are likely to be presented during your stay if you're here in summer.

Close by the theater are the ruins of a 13th-century Dominican convent. Margaret, daughter of King Béla IV, was enrolled in the convent at the age of 11 and devoted her life to it. She was later made a saint, and the island was named for her.

A Franciscan church once stood on Margitsziget, but it is now only a lonely archeological "dig." The Premonstratensian Chapel near the Grand Hotel is a modern reconstruction of a 12th-century church. It contains the oldest bell in Hungary in its tower, one that somehow escaped destruction during the Turkish occupation.

The island is closed to cars, but if you're driving, you can cross the Árpád Bridge in the north and go as far as the car park of the Thermal Hotel. Better yet, travel there by public transport.

St. Stephen's Basilica

The two tall spires of Szent István Bazilika, on Bajcsy-Zsilinszky út, dominate the skyline of Pest. Work on construction of this church, the largest in Budapest, holding up to 8,000 worshippers went on from 1851 to 1905, with restoration being necessary after World War II. The 315-foot-high dome collapsed in 1868 and had to be rebuilt.

The hodgepodge of architecture of this church, dedicated to St. Stephen, formerly Hungary's first king, Stephen I, ranges from Renaissance to neoclassical. Two frontal towers grace this architectural mélange, and a bust of St. Stephen, made from Carrara marble, is over the major gate. Leading Hungarian painters and sculptors helped with the decoration.

Actually, St. Stephen's Basilica is a parish church—not properly a basilica, although that's what the people of Budapest call it.

The Bazilika (tel. 0361/111-0839 for information) is open daily from 10am to 4pm. It costs nothing to visit the cathedral, but if you want to view the treasury, the charge is 10 Ft. (15¢).

Parish Church of the Inner City

Speaking of architectural mélanges, take a look at this, the oldest church in Pest, called Belvárosi-templon in Hungarian. The parish church, at the Pest end of the Elisabeth Bridge, at Március tér 15, dates from the 12th century. It even has a Muslim prayer niche.

A 12th-century Romanesque church was originally built here, but it was rebuilt in the 14th century in Gothic style. Two Renaissance alcoves were added in the 16th century. The Turks added their bit when they turned it into a mosque during Ottoman rule in Hungary. During the liberation from the Turks by the Habsburgs, the church was damaged. And after it was gutted by fire in 1723, the baroque architects took over.

Hungarian National Museum

The oldest and most important museum of Budapest is the Hungarian National Museum, Múzeum körút 14-16 (tel. 0361/1134-400), known to the Hungarians as Magyar Nemzeti Múzeum. It even has on display the oldest relic to be found in almost any museum—the skull found at Vértesszőlős, which has been placed in time at about a half million years ago, although one of my sources says 50,000 years. It's old, anyway.

The museum displays the historical and archeological wealth of a much-ravished and -looted country. It's like a storybook of the history of Hungary, with its ancient jewelry and weaponry, a piano owned by Beethoven, and even a 17th-century tent from the Turkish occupation. A major exhibit is a perfectly preserved mosaic floor of a Roman house from the 3rd century B.C. A gold teaspoon that belonged to Empress Maria Theresa and Franz Liszt's gold baton are displayed.

The royal regalia of Hungary are the most outstanding and sought-out exhibit, displayed in the Hall of Honor. In 1945 the retreating Hungarian army, fearful that the royal treasures would fall into Russian hands, turned the regalia, consisting of coronation robes, scepter, gilded 14th-century orb, and crown, over to the advancing U.S. Army.

The royal regalia rested at Fort Knox in the United States until it was returned to Hungary in 1978. The crown, said to have been worn by St. Stephen, the country's first king, is the symbol of national pride in Hungary and is often depicted in paintings. Latter-day experts consider that the crown dates from the 12th century and so could not have been the one used for the coronation of Stephen, but this doesn't diminish the Hungarians' pride in it.

The main collections here date back to 1802, although the building now housing them was constructed between 1837 and 1847. The neoclassical structure with Corinthian columns is surrounded by a spacious garden. It is open Tuesday to Sunday from 10am to 6pm, and charges an admission fee of 10 Ft. (15¢).

Museum of Applied Arts

Since 1896, the Museum of Applied Arts (Iparmüvészeti Múzeum), Üllői út 33-37 (tel. 0361/1175-222), has operated in this highly decorative, domed, art nouveau mansion of brick and ceramic tile near the southern end of the Grand Boulevard (see below). The displays give the history and techniques of handcrafts: gold- and silver-smithing, leatherwork, and the making of ancient textiles and clothing, as well as glass, porcelain, and earthenware, furniture, old fans, book binding, bone and ivory carvings, and enamel works. These are in a permanent exhibition, Arts and Crafts, along with illustrations of weaving, carving, upholstering, and other techniques. There are also temporary exhibits of some of the museum's rich collections from the Renaissance, Mannerist, baroque, and rococo periods, and of 19th- and 20th-century European and Hungarian tapestries. Occasionally, there are international modern exhibitions. Admission is 5 Ft. (10¢). Open Tuesday to Sunday from 10am to 6pm.

The Museum of Applied Arts also operates the following museums:

Hopp Ferenc Museum of Far Eastern Art, Népköztársaság utja 103 (tel. 0361/1228-476), is open Tuesday to Sunday from 10am to 5:45pm, and charges an admission fee of 5 Ft. (10¢).

Ráth György Museum, Gorkij Fasor 12 (tel. 0316/1423-916), is open Tuesday to Sunday from 10am to 6pm, and charges an admission fee of 5 Ft. (10¢). It deserves attention chiefly for its permanent exhibitions of Chinese, Japanese, and Indian objets d'art.

Castle Museum of Nagytétény, Csókásy Pál utca 9, Nagytétény (tel. 0316/1738-547), is open Tuesday to Sunday from 10am to 5:45pm, and charges an admission fee of 5 Ft. (10¢).

Parliament

The domed Neo-Gothic Parliament building (Országház) on the Pest side of the river may remind you of the Houses of Parliament in London, except that here the building looks out over the Danube rather than the Thames. Standing at Kossuth Lajos tér, the Parliament edifice, constructed between 1884 and 1902, evokes the grandeur of the Austro-Hungarian Empire. It was one of the largest buildings in the world at the time it was erected. The dome is the same height as that of St. Stephen's Basilica, 315 feet.

There are 27 gates, 10 courtyards, and 29 stairways, along with 88 statues—a parade of historical figures of Hungary, from kings to generals. Out front is an effigy of Mihály Károlyi, who was president of Hungary during the short-lived republic formed after World War I (Károlyi was forced into exile in 1919).

Individual visitors to the Parliament buildings are not permitted, but travel agencies arrange group tours for foreign visitors.

Ethnographical Museum

Housed in an ornate 19th-century building at Kossuth Lajos tér 12 (tel. 0361/1326-340) is the Ethnographical Museum (Néprajzi Múzeum), the country's most important collection of Hungarian folk art. Included are costumes, daily utensils, decorative objects, tools, textiles, religious icons, and many naïve country paintings. You can also see collections of the art of Oceania, Australia, Africa, and Asia.

The building, completed in the 1890s, was designed as headquarters of the Supreme Court of Hungary. Its main hall has been compared to a railway station. It is open Tuesday to Sunday from 10am to 6pm, and charges an admission fee of 10 Ft. (15¢).

The Grand Boulevard

The street signs read Nagykörút, but calling it the Grand Boulevard probably works better if you're a North American. It's also known as the "Big Ring." Street planners in the 19th century, heavily influenced by Haussmann's boulevards in Paris, laid out this 3-mile thoroughfare, the heartbeat of Pest, to form a half moon, stretching from both ends of the big loop made by the Danube. Road construction was completed in 1896. The boulevard, which traverses one of the most densely populated parts of Pest, is divided into four different sections: Szent Istvan körút, Lenin körút, Jozsef körút, and Ferenc körút.

Long celebrated in song and story, this is a land of theaters, cinemas, and apartment houses, as well as of cafés and nightclubs. As you stroll along the boulevard, much will catch your eye, including a monument to Engels and Marx. You'll pass the Western Railway Station and the renowned Café-Restaurant New York (Hungária) (see my dining recommendations).

People's Republic Road

This broad avenue, considered the most attractive and elegant in Pest, has witnessed much of the turbulent history of Hungary during the some 11 decades of its existence. Laid out in the 1870s and taking the Champs-Élysées as its role model, the avenue goes from the Inner Boulevard to City Park, a distance of almost 2 miles.

I defy you to pronounce the name of the road as it appears on the street signs, unless you're Hungarian. It's Népköstársaság utja now, but it has had many names over the years. Once it was called Radial Avenue, or Sugár út. Then for a long time it was known as Stalin Avenue, and for a brief period during the 1956 Hungarian uprising it was called Avenue of Hungarian Youth. The Gestapo once hung out at building no. 60, which later became the headquarters of the Soviet secret police.

The buildings along the People's Republic Road are an architectural hodgepodge, although most of them are described as neoclassical. They're interesting, often with a mosaic or a frieze on the exterior, perhaps a courtyard with a fountain. The State Opera House, constructed from 1878 to 1884, is on this avenue, and the first underground (metro) system in Budapest, dating from 1896, runs under the roadway.

Heroes' Square

At the end of the People's Republic Road is Heroes' Square (Hősök tére) begun in 1896 to celebrate the millennium of Hungary. A semicircular colonnade, divided by a 118-foot column topped by a winged figure rising in the center, exhibits a pantheon of Hungarian historical figures, including St. Stephen. Seven equestrian statues of ancient Magyar chieftains surround the column. Work on the monument was not completed until 1929.

A stone tablet in front of the Millennial Monument is the simple Hungarian War Memorial on which Margaret Thatcher, the first British prime minister ever to visit Hungary, placed a floral wreath.

Fine Arts Museum

On the northern side of Heroes' Square, at Dózsa György út 41 (tel. 0361/ 429-759), stands the Museum of Fine Arts (Szépmüvészeti Múzeum), where you can see everything from the art of ancient Egypt and Roman vases up to the pictures of European masters, such as Goya, Rembrandt, and Murillo.

The museum, opened in 1906, was designed in eclectic style and is particularly noted for its Department of Western European Paintings. It presents the evolution of painting in Europe from the 13th through the 18th centuries. Italian, Early Netherlandish, Dutch, Flemish, German, French, British, and Spanish pictures are arranged by historical periods and schools. Among the great masters and their works are: Raphael (*The Madonna Esterházy*), Correggio (*The Madonna and Child with an Angel*), Giorgione (*Portrait of a Young Man*), Tiepolo (*St. James the Greater*), Pieter Brueghel the Elder (*The Sermon of St. John the Baptist*), Vermeer (*Portrait of a Woman*), Rembrandt (*A Jewish Rabbi*), Dürer (*Portrait of a Man*), Gainsborough

(*Portrait of Charles Hotchkiss*), Lorrain (*Villa in the Roman Campagna*), Constable (*Waterloo Festival in East Bergholt*), Reynolds (*Portrait of Sir Edward Hughes*), and Velázquez (*Peasants Taking a Meal*), as well as many other masterpieces by noted painters. The museum has seven El Grecos, three Zurbaráns, four Murillos, and five works by Goya.

The Department of Prints and Drawings is an outstanding and varied collection, containing nearly 100,000 prints from the 15th through the 20th centuries. Drawings by such great masters as Leonardo, Raphael, Dürer, Poussin, Rembrandt, Watteau, Delacroix, Manet, Van Gogh, Renoir, and Picasso are displayed.

In the Department of Modern Art, works can be seen by such artists as Corot, Monet, Pissarro, Cézanne, Gauguin, Toulouse-Lautrec, and Chagall, as well as sculpture by Thorvaldsen, Rodin, and many others.

Old sculpture, Greek and Roman antiquities, and an Egyptian collection with works of art reflecting the cult of death are also among the treasures displayed.

Many of the paintings were shipped by rail freight to Germany in 1944, when the Nazi hierarchy was engaged in "collecting" valuable artworks from wherever. Miraculously, the collection from Hungary was somehow spared and sent back.

The building is right at the entrance of the City Park.

The museum is open Tuesday to Sunday from 10am to 5pm, and charges an admission fee of 10 Ft. (15¢).

The Danube Bridges

In an act of dubious military value, the Nazis blew up all the bridges of Budapest in their ignominious retreat from the city. This flagrant destruction took its place among such achievements as blowing up the historic bridges across the Arno in Florence. Before this devastation, Budapest looked with as much pride on its bridges as Londoners take in those spans crossing the Thames or Parisians in the bridges across the Seine.

After the war, Hungarians set about rebuilding the historic spans, and today they form one of the most beautiful sights along the Danube. In the course of your exploration of Buda and Pest you will doubtless cross them many times.

Budapest's two parts are linked by eight bridges, two of them being railway spans. They include:

Margaret Bridge (Margit hid): Built to French designs from the 1870s, it crosses the southern tip of Margaret Island.

Chain Bridge (also called Széchenyi lánchid, named for a Hungarian hero): The first permanent stone bridge linking Pest and Buda, it was originally built by Adam Clark, a British engineer, in 1849.

Arpád Bridge (Árpád hid): A spur of this bridge leads to the northern tip of Margaret Island. It's the longest of the Budapest bridges, about 1.3 miles, and connects the industrial suburbs of Óbuda and Újpest.

Petőfi Bridge (Petőfi hid): Originally built in the 1930, this links the Pest and Buda sides of the Grand Boulevard. It was named for a Hungarian hero-poet.

Liberty Bridge (Szabadság hid, in Hungarian): Once named for the Austrian emperor/Hungarian king, Franz Joseph, this bridge was constructed beginning in 1894. The first span rebuilt after World War II, it was renamed Liberty Bridge.

Elisabeth Bridge (Erzsébet hid): This bridge is not a duplicate of the more ornate one constructed at the turn of the century. When it was opened in 1903, it had the widest span of any bridge in the world.

Excursions

The wooded **Buda Hills** rise to the west of the Danube. You can take the cog railway of the public transport system to Széchenyi-hegy and to Szabadság-hegy (Liberty Hill). The train leaves from the terminus across the street from the Budapest Hotel. The journey takes you through beautiful scenery.

You can take a cable chair lift to the Buda Hills in summer, soaring about a mile, from Zugliget to János-hegy (John's Hill). You can get to either Zugliget or János-hegy by public transport from Moskva tér. The chair-lift trip comes to an end near the top of János-hegy. From there, a few minutes' walk will take you to the summit, where there's a lookout tower at 1,735 feet, providing a panorama of Budapest. If the weather's right you can see for a distance of some 45 miles. The hills are popular for excursions. For another Buda Hills outing, see "Budapest for Children," below.

Beethoven fans may want to take a trip to Martonvásár, some 20 miles from Budapest on Rte. 70. Here stands **Brunswick Castle,** once the home of the Brunswick family whose most celebrated visitor was Ludwig van Beethoven. The castle was originally built in the 18th century, but what you see now is a Neo-Gothic structure into which it was reconstructed in the 19th century.

Music historians say that a number of Beethoven's compositions are connected with the castle and the park. Josephine Brunswick was rumored to have been his "immortal beloved," the woman to whom he wrote his famous love letters. The composer dedicated the *Appassionata* Sonata to the Brunswick family, and it's said that he composed the *Moonlight* Sonata at the castle. A bust of Beethoven is found on a tiny island in a lake.

In the castle on the ground floor a few rooms have been made into a Beethoven Museum, with relics and documents relating to the composer displayed. The rest of the castle is now occupied by an agricultural institute. The museum is open only on Saturday and Sunday from 10am to 6pm.

In summer, open-air Beethoven concerts are given under the trees in the park surrounding the castle.

BUDAPEST FOR CHILDREN

Northeast of Heroes' Square, **Városliget,** or City Park, is a great attraction for children and grownups alike, with its numerous facilities. The park occupies some 250 acres of land, to which the people of Budapest flock in summer to enjoy a big boating lake, open-air swimming pools, and medicinal baths. At or near the top of the list of attractions is the **Zoological and Botanical Garden of Budapest,** Állatkerti körút 6-12 (tel. 0361/1426-303), opened in 1866 under the direction of János Xantus. The zoo is visited yearly by almost two million people. Lectures, guided tours, and biology sessions are held, and the animal garden and riding school are popular. In summer, educational films are shown continuously in the Rock Movie. From October to April, the zoo is open daily except Monday from 9am to dusk. Admission is 20 Ft. (35¢) for adults, 10 Ft. (15¢) for children.

Enter through the main gate and go left to see exhibits corresponding basically to the systematic order of the animal kingdom. The Large Pond is the permanent home of many waterbirds. The Palm House, considered a technical monument, has exotic plants, a tropical aquarium-terrarium, and a crocodile hall. Under the building are the marine and cold-water aquarium, with shoebill storks living nearby. The restored and modernized Bird House, opened in 1985, is occupied by tropical birds and a free-flying hall. Most important is the collection of cranes. Birds of prey are also here, and in the Winter Quarter of Birds, native and tropical feathered specimens are shown. Next to the Rock Garden, the greatest ornament of the zoo, especially in spring, you can see the pelican and penguin colony. Patagonian seals and ice bears are popular, and interesting animals can be observed in their establishment above and below water. The cheetah is among the big carnivores, with the kangaroos and bear collection following. The Africa House and paddock contains Grévy's zebras, gnus, and elands. In the Elephant House, you can see Indian elephants, rhinos, and hippos. An Insectarium, on the side of the Large Rock, is opposite the House of Apes.

Adjoining City Park is an **amusement center,** Állatkerti körút 14-16 (tel. 0361/1221-025), styled after Tivoli in Copenhagen and Luna Park in Berlin, complete with roller coasters and other thrill equipment for people of all ages. From April to September, it's open daily from 10am to 8pm, for an admission fee of 5 Ft.

(10¢). From September to March, when the center is in partial operation, the daily hours are 10am to 7pm, and admission is free.

A fantasy castle, the **Castle of Vajdahunyad,** is a reproduction of a castle that once existed in Transylvania, in that part of its land which Hungary was forced to yield to Romania. Housed in the castle is the Hungarian Agricultural Museum, in which the histories of farming, hunting, and fishing are traced. You can also visit a re-created wine cellar.

American children will be interested in a nearby sight—a statue of George Washington, erected by donations of Hungarians who immigrated to the United States.

The **Municipal Grand Circus,** Állatkerti körút 7 (tel. 0361/428-300), presents performances Wednesday to Sunday.

Budapest's most beautiful park is on **Margaret Island,** previewed above, which has several children's playgrounds, an open-air garden movie theater, a small zoo, swimming pools, a beach, and restaurants.

The **Budapest Planetarium** (tel. 0361/1341-164) lies in a park near the Népliget subway station. Shows are presented five times a day except Monday and Tuesday. Laser shows are given in the evening at 6pm and again at 7:30pm, with an admission fee of 150 Ft. ($2.55). Regular admission to the planetarium is 25 Ft. (35¢).

For an outing to the **Buda Hills,** at Széchenyi-hegy you can take the Pioneer Railway on which, except for the engine driver, all posts are filled by schoolchildren —conductors, switch persons, telegraph operators, and traffic managers. The 1¼-mile train trip takes you across beautiful country to Hűvösvölgy.

SHOPPING IN BUDAPEST

The Budapest shopping center consists of the Grand Boulevard, the "Big Ring," with its four parts (sometimes referred to as rings): Szent István körút, Lenin körút, Jozsef körút, and Ferenc körút. Department stores and shops line both sides of the streets, with a broad selection of merchandise. The real downtown shopping however, is on Kigyó út, Petőfi út, Sándor út, and Váci út. There are three shop networks—Intertourist, Utastourist, and Konsumtourist—that have shops selling goods particularly in demand by foreigners for convertible currency.

Wherever you do your buying, keep any receipt or bill of sale you get here, since it will also serve as your permit to take your purchases out of the country.

Among items you may want to take home with you are hand-embroidered peasant blouses and other handmade goods, dolls in provincial costumes, leather riding whips from the plains, packages of hot paprika, and sheepskin jackets. Albums and tapes of Hungarian and Gypsy music are also on sale. Also offered here are items from Czechoslovakia and Russia that you don't find in the U.S.

Food shops are generally open from 6 or 7am to 6 or 7pm. Other stores usually open at 10 or 11am and close at 6 or 7pm. The larger shops and department stores are open until 8pm on Thursday. On Sunday, only a few sweet shops, florists, and tobacconists are open, mainly in the morning.

Népművészet, Váci utca 14 (tel. 0361/185-844), offers a huge array of regional handcrafts from virtually every section of Hungary. The inventory includes tablecloths, pottery, carved boxes, patterned furniture, and a wide selection of handmade rugs. The store is staffed with an army of pleasant saleswomen. Their selection is about the best in town. The store is open Monday to Wednesday from 10:30am to 6pm, on Thursday from 10:30am to 7pm, on Saturday from 10:30am to 5pm, and on Sunday from 10:30am to 2pm.

Folklore Centrum, Regisposta utca 12 (tel. 0361/1185-840), sells a wide variety of textiles, provincial-style embroideries, tablecloths, and pillows. It is open Monday to Wednesday from 10:30am to 6pm, on Thursday from 10:30am to 7pm, on Saturday from 10:30am to 5pm, and on Sunday from 10:30am to 2pm.

Fimcoop Studióbólt, Apáczai Csere János utca 7 (tel. 0361/183-912), is a consumer outlet for several of Hungary's lesser-known porcelain factories. It sells regional pottery, as well as an entire dinner service of elegant bone china. There's also some etched and engraved crystal. They do not mail purchases, but they do a good job of wrapping whatever you buy. The store is conveniently located behind the Inter-Continental Hotel. Hours are Monday to Saturday from 10am to 6pm.

Hubertus Vadászbolt, Országház utca 18 (tel. 0361/1754-655). This shop is little more than a niche in the wall of a building in Old Buda, but the merchandise makes for an offbeat visit. Beneath a vaulted ceiling are rows of artifacts related in some way to hunting. These include leather goods, trophies, antlers, old weapons, and an occasional piece of antique bric-à-brac. The store is open daily except Sunday from 10am to 6pm.

BATHS

Geneticists say that all of us are descendants of sea creatures, and biologists suggest that we are 90% water. If that's so, it isn't surprising that the natives of a landlocked country such as Hungary should savor their hours in the public baths. Bathing in the mineral-rich waters so abundant in this region is as old as the Roman Empire. Tiberius Nero ordered the first wells dug, and the baths he created were enjoyed and expanded by virtually every conquering race afterward. That includes the Turks who built—what else—Turkish baths at the water sources.

During the heyday of Hungarian nationalism in the 19th century, the opulence of the baths rivaled that of private palaces throughout the rest of Europe. The widespread belief that the waters were good for everything from respiratory ailments (by breathing the fumes) to urinary and digestive disorders (by drinking the waters) to rheumatic and arthritic complaints became even stronger.

Today Budapest is still a city of therapeutic baths, with 123 thermal springs surfacing here, the waters containing large quantities of calcium, magnesium, hydrocarbonates, sulfate ions, and hydrosulfates. The springs from under Gellért Hill are radioactive.

Whether or not you decide to go bathing (and many hygiene-conscious Westerners have given up bathing in public places altogether), you might still want to walk into the Secessionist-style baths. The baths at the **Hotel Gellért,** Kelenhegyi utca 4 (tel. 0361/666-166), are perhaps the most photographed water spa in the world, and with good reason. Brilliantly colored mosaics cover the soaring vaulted ceilings, and the thermally heated waters churn into the swimming areas from the mouths of sea monsters skillfully crafted into dreamlike expressions of grotesquerie. You'll see hundreds of people suffering from all kinds of real and imaginary ailments waiting in turn for what is supposed to be the beneficial action of the mineral-rich waters. The entrance fee is 40 Ft. (70¢). The baths are open Monday to Friday from 7:30am to 7pm and on Saturday and Sunday from 7:30am to noon.

Széchenyi Baths, Állatkerti körút 11 (tel. 0361/1210-310), are one of the largest in Europe. They're combined with open-air swimming pools. This complex of medicinal baths stands in a big park in the heart of the capital. It has a water rich in calcium, magnesium, hydrocarbonates, chlorides, sulfates, and various alkalines, which are said to be beneficial in the treatment of degenerative locomotor disorders. The baths are open daily from 6am to 6:45pm, charging an admission fee of 35 Ft. (60¢).

CULTURAL BUDAPEST

Budapest is the cultural capital of Hungary and a center for the performing arts. Museums and galleries display distinguished permanent collections, as well as having changing exhibits of work by artists both foreign and Hungarian. The Budapest Spring and Autumn festivals are high-standard musical events, with ballet, folk dance presentations, opera, and operetta. The Academy of Music, the Hungarian State Opera House, and the Erkel Theater are open to lovers of classical music. There are 25 indoor theaters in Budapest as well as open-air stage facilities.

From September to the end of June, the Erkel, the Rock Theater, the Municipal Operetta Theaters, and the Opera House function as music theaters, while concerts are given all year long at the Academy of Music, the Pest Concert Hall, and the Buda Concert Hall. Concerts are also held in the Congress Hall of the Hungarian Academy of Sciences and the Banquet Hall of the National Gallery. For information about concerts, call **Országos Filharmónia** (National Philharmonia), Vörösmarty tér 1 (tel. 0361/1176-222). Information about theatrical performances is available from the **Central Booking Office,** Népköztársaság utja 18 (tel. 0361/1120-000). Prices of tickets range from 30 Ft. (50¢) to 600 Ft. ($10) unless the event is considered "outstanding."

In summer, there is a wide range of programs at open-air theaters in Budapest. Among these are the Margitsziget (Margaret Island) open-air theater, Buda Park theater, Varosmajor open-air theater, the Hilton-Dominican Court, and Hild Court. Summer concerts are given at Matthias Church, Fishermen's Bastion, Zichy Castle, and Musical Court.

The **Budapest Spring Festival,** held in late March, is made up of a variety of genres and has a typical Hungarian character. Besides the more serious music and dance offerings mentioned above, the festival now includes a rock show given at the Budapest Sports Hall. For information on the festival, get in touch with the tourist office (see "Fast Facts" above).

NIGHTLIFE

Budapest is the liveliest capital in Eastern Europe. Compared to the after-dark scenes in the capitals of Western Europe, its nightlife is also inexpensive.

Maxim Varieté, Akácfa utca 4 (tel. 0361/227-858), is the most opulent professional cabaret/floor show in the Hungarian capital. You'll be ushered into a large vestibule area whose entrance is illuminated by a Las Vegas–style neon sign above a dark street in commercial Pest. A series of hostesses will lead you to a cloakroom, and after a short wait you'll descend a carpeted stairwell to a bar area and ultimately to your seats. The upholstered semicircular seating area offers multitiered views of the round stage. Service is honest and polite, with a rigid supervision by the Pannonia hotel chain. The performance is of the variety type—a little magic, a little striptease, whatever. Show times are at 9:30pm and 11pm Monday to Saturday, and the club's overall hours are 7:30pm to 3am. You can go before the first show and order dinner if you wish. Admission is 1,050 Ft. ($17), or 1,450 Ft. ($14.75) should you prefer dinner.

Moulin Rouge, Nagymezö utca 17 (tel. 0361/124-492). The theater that houses this titillating revue would be appropriate for some of the grandest theater productions in Europe. It was built as a cabaret in 1895 in a rose-colored format of cavorting cherubs, gilded seashells, and an encircling ring of lushly ornate balconies. Festive streamers hang haphazardly beneath the octagonal tent of the ceiling above a stage whose floorboards have witnessed the passage of history. What you'll see today is an updated version of the kinds of cabaret shows that made Budapest famous "between the wars." Shows times are at 9pm and 12:30am daily, and most hotels will reserve you a table. Performances include revues seemingly inspired by Brazil, New York, and Paris, even the Hungarian puszta. A cover charge of 450 Ft ($7.50) includes the price of two drinks.

Casanova Piano Bar, Batthyány tér 4 (tel. 0361/1351-113), is a warmly accommodating piano bar whose historic premises were said to have been visited by Casanova himself, as well as Emperor Joseph II. The piano has a bar built around it, and the music is nonstop "evergreen" (country to us). The club is open Monday to Saturday from 10pm to 4am, with prices beginning at 200 Ft. ($3.40). The entrance price is 120 Ft. ($2.05). The establishment is in a building that is 225 years old. It was formerly a lodging house on the Buda side of the Danube.

Casino Budapest, Hess András tér 1-3 (tel. 0361/1751-001), was the first gambling casino founded in Hungary. It occupies the tower of the Budapest Hilton, on the sixth floor. The medium of exchange used for gambling is the West German mark, and there's an exchange booth on the premises. The entrance fee of 10 DM ($5.75) is immediately refunded in the form of a chip. The polite English-speaking staff is young and attractive, and games include French and American roulette, boule, blackjack, baccarat, and slot machines (which take only DMs). Winnings are not taxable and may be taken out of the country. Presentation of a passport is required at the door. Open daily from 5pm to 2am.

In 1989 the city of Budapest issued a gambling license to **Schönbrunn Casino,** a converted passenger boat on the Danube at the Chain Bridge (tel. 0361/118-3096). Originally launched just before World War I, the boat was later renovated and transformed into a gambling casino. It is open only in high season from mid-June to October 1, daily from 4pm. The only form of currency accepted is the West German mark. The entrance fee of 10 DM ($5.75) is immediately refunded to you in the form of a gambling chip. You must present your passport to enter.

Faust Wine Bar, Budapest Hilton Hotel, Hess András tér 1-3 (tel. 0361/1751-000), is the premier wine bar of Hungary. A visit to its subterranean depths gives visitors a view of the medieval excavations of Old Buda. To reach it, cut through the lobby of this deluxe hotel and descend into the rocky depths of what legend says has been some kind of wine cellar for 700 years. Today, Hilton and Hungary's largest wine exporter (Hungarovin) maintain more than 75 Hungarian vintages, any of which can be tasted by the glass. Your evening might begin with a glass of sekt (champagne), followed by a choice of white or rosé delicacies, before ending with a strong but subtle Tokaj red. Depending on its vintage, each glass of wine costs from 30 Ft. (40¢) to 70 Ft. ($1.20). The cellar is open daily from 11am to 9pm. No food is served.

Orfeum, Hotel Béke Radisson, Lenin körút 97 (tel. 0361/1323-300). Its linen-covered tables rise in semicircular tiers above the half-rounded stage. This is said to be the most Hungarian of all the nightlife spectacles in town, incorporating a tongue-in-cheek entertainment typical of nightlife "between the wars." You pay a 380-Ft. ($6.25) entrance fee, after which you can drink and dine, depending on your schedule and preference. A scotch and soda costs from 430 Ft. ($7.25). A complete dinner costs from 2,500 Ft. ($41.75) and could feature chateaubriand and/or more Hungarian dishes. Beginning every night except Sunday at 10:45pm, there is a revue that lasts one hour. It includes some discreet nudity, magic and acrobatic acts, a bit of schmaltz, and lots of humor, often with its own kind of charm. Before and after the show, guests dance to live music. A reservation is a good idea.

Lido, Szabadsajtó út 5 (tel. 0361/1182-404). One of Budapest's best cabaret revues combines several entertainment possibilities. At 11pm there's a flashy show with lots of glitter and feathers; at 1am, a folkloric program with Hungarian dances. Unique features include an ice revue with the Lido Girls, plus the performances of guest singers and dancers, some of whom have come from Germany or Britain under short-term contracts. All of this is introduced with plenty of schmaltz by a master of ceremonies. Music is provided by a Gypsy dance band. A fixed-price menu is offered for 900 Ft. ($15), and the cover charge for the revue is 1,200 Ft. ($20). The place is honest, and under the strict supervision of one of Hungary's large hotel chains. For the young at heart, there is also a disco club.

Bellevue, Hotel Inter-Continental, Apáczai Csere János 4 (tel. 0361/1175-122), high on the top floor of one of the best hotels in town, offers incomparable views of the Danube, which might be best enjoyed on a summertime weekend when the monuments are illuminated. The clientele tends to be a conservative, well-dressed crowd out to enjoy the dance band and the changing array of food. Depending on the week of your visit, the cuisine might be Hungarian, Portuguese, Italian, Indian, Greek, or Indonesian. The place is open daily except Sunday from 7pm to 2am, and reservations are suggested. You'll spend 3,000 Ft. ($50) per person and up.

Nightclub Havana, Thermal Hotel Margitsziget, Margitsziget (tel. 0361/

111-000), offers a little bit of Cuba in the middle of the most historic island in Hungary. In fact, this is one of the top nightclubs in town. If you've always wanted to hear Havana-style music and didn't know where to find it, this is the place for you. Housed on the lower level of the Thermal Hotel Margitsziget, the club is reached by going down an elegant marble-walled staircase with mirrors and brass trim into a scarlet vestibule whose doors open into one of the most colorful rooms in Budapest. Curved rows of horseshoe-shaped banquettes with small round tables and quasi–art deco chairs are angled toward the small stage area, which serves as a focal point for the Latin music and the dance floor. It's open every night except Sunday from 10pm until 4am. The entrance fee is 250 Ft. ($4.25).

Halászbástya, Fishermen's Bastion (tel. 0361/1561-446), is a youth-oriented disco, part of the Hilton complex. Guests dance under the vaulted ceiling of a stone-ribbed monument. It's on the upper floor of the biggest tower in Fishermen's Bastion, and might be an amusing stopover point after a late-night walk on Castle Hill. Several side rooms—one of which contains a bar—lead off into medieval chambers whose comfortable settees are often filled with members of Budapest's under-25 crowd. An overhead crystal chandelier accompanies the flashing pin lights, while the music is up-to-date, danceable, and fun. Hard drinks cost from 140 Ft. ($2.35), and no cover is imposed. Dancing is nightly from 10pm to 4am.

Night Club Fortuna, Hess András tér 4 (tel. 0361/1756-857), is a popular nighttime rendezvous on Castle Hill, part of a complex housing the previously recommended Fortuna Haz Restaurant. It is open nightly from 10pm to 4am, charging an entrance fee of 60 Ft. ($10.25). Vaudeville and striptease, among other entertainment, are presented.

Horoszkóp Bár, Buda-Penta Hotel, Krisztina körút 41-43 (tel. 0361/1566-333), is probably the most popular and perhaps the biggest nightclub in Budapest, a labyrinthine arrangement of black-accented, dramatically lit, and plushly decorated rooms. Scattered throughout this elegant place are brass plaques depicting the 12 signs of the zodiac. Trying to find the representation of your particular star sign will give you the chance to explore the entire establishment, even that section with a view of the hotel's indoor swimming pool. The big dance floor stays open daily from 10pm to 4am. Hard drinks begin at 150 Ft. ($2.55), and admission to the 11:30pm show is 200 Ft. ($3.40).

Das Durstige Krokodil (The Thirsty Crocodile), Országház utca 10 (tel. 0361/1561-484). Johnnie Ray sings "Cry" on the tapes, but you'll also hear jollier American songs. This small neighborhood bar on Castle Hill attracts the staff from the nearby Hilton as well as a smattering of low-key locals who enjoy the dimly lit tongue-in-cheek ambience, the mirrored shelves holding an array of liquors, and the off-duty Budapesters celebrating. The beverage range is wide here, from foreign cocktails to Hungarian wines to different brandies and liquors. Hot sandwiches and other snacks are available as well as nonalcoholic cocktails and soft drinks. Most drinks range in price from 110 Ft. ($1.85) to 200 Ft. ($3.40), and hours are 2pm to 3am daily (if the crowd is small, the bar will sometimes close at midnight).

EXPLORING HUNGARY

The colorful provinces of Hungary occupy the greater part of the middle Danube Basin, a fertile plain in most parts, but with mountains, lakes, and rivers along with farming and industrial areas. In the country outside Budapest and its immediate environs, many of the old Magyar customs remain, as well as costumes and lore of other ethnic groups that have added their cultural background to that of the race of people now known as Hungarian.

Resort areas, long the stronghold of the wealthy, have come to be the vacation-land of all the people in Hungary today, as is evidenced by the attractions of Lake Balaton and of the Mecsek, a warm and hilly region to the south. Whether you are bent on seeing the magnificent horses and their riders on the Great Plain, the artists' colonies along the Danube, vineyards and farms, whatever, you'll find it here. Baroque art and architecture abound in many towns from the Carpathian foothills to the section to the south colonized by the Romans as Pannonia. Exploring Hungary can be a rich and rewarding experience, and all visitors should venture out of Budapest to see how Hungarians live in other sections.

1. The Danube Bend

The Danube River flows generally eastward across Austria and between Hungary and Czechoslovakia on its long journey to the Black Sea. A short way north of Budapest in the heartland of Hungary, however, the great river makes a sudden elbow bend, cutting through the Börzöny and Pilis mountains after it leaves the Czech border, to become a southward-flowing waterway. Steeped in history, the Danube Bend, framed by the medieval towns of Esztergom and Visegrád, is a little piece of geography that reflects the turbulent past of the Hungarian kingdom. The banks of the bend are lined with hills hovering over quiet riverfront towns and glorious with blossoming fruit trees in spring. Sheep graze on the slopes in the shade of 1,000-year-old castles brooding over the Danube.

The river, a major transportation artery from prehistoric times, has seen mighty armies marching along its banks since Roman times. Empire builders of the Caesars established a heavily fortified defensive system at the important outpost, the Danube Bend. Good roads linked Pannonia with the rest of the Roman Empire, providing passage for traders and troops. A military road connected the military camps and forts along the Danube between Aquincum (a part of modern-day Budapest) and Esztergom. The roads they built served the Romans and also their succesors in peace and in war.

Visit both banks of the Danube Bend if you have time, but if not, then you'll find the right bank of greater interest. The major towns to see include Szentendre, Visegrád, and Esztergom. On the left bank, the primary town to seek out is Vác.

The most popular tour of this historic region is from Budapest to Esztergom, moving toward the Czech border. Motorists should follow Rte. 11 along the right bank (the west bank out of Budapest), but don't expect to find any bridges in the bend area. You cross the river by ferry.

One of the most romantic ways to explore the area is by boat, taking one of the organized tours previously recommended.

You can visit the Danube Bend in one busy day while you're centered in Budapest, and this is the common method for usually rushed foreign visitors. However, for those with more time, there are a few hotels that merit a stopover or a longer stay.

SZENTENDRE

A resort town some 12½ miles from Budapest, Szentendre lies at the southern gate of the Danube Bend, on the west side after the river turns southward. The Romans built a fortress, Ulcisia Castra, here, followed by a Hungarian settlement as early as the 10th century. The inhabitants were entirely Hungarian until the end of the 16th century. In the course of history the village developed into a town, which was totally destroyed during the wars of the 16th and 17th centuries. After this, in 1690, Serbians immigrated here and rebuilt the ravaged town. Szentendre Island is one of a number of bits of land in the Danube from the bend to Budapest. The town has 14 museums or other exhibition establishments, which mostly display the works of local artists, and there is a gallery in one of the two art colonies for periodic exhibitions.

The heart of the town is Karl Marx tér, which seems like a somewhat inappropriate name for a square flanked by baroque houses, mainly from the 18th century, built by rich Serbian merchants. Szentendre is one of the most colorful towns on the river, with medieval houses and shops painted in pinks, greens, and yellows. Castle Hill is the most storied part of the historic town, but only the Roman Catholic Parish Church is from the Middle Ages.

Ferenczy Károly, the renowned Hungarian artist (1862–1917), who spent from 1889 to 1892 in Szentendre, is honored by the **Ferenczy Museum,** Fő tér 6, which includes several works by the Postimpressionist artist and works of his three children: Váler, a painter and engraver; Béni, a sculptor; and Noémi, a Gobelin tapestry artist. From November 1 to March 31, the museum is open Tuesday to Sunday from 9am to 5pm; from April 1 to October 31, it is open Tuesday to Sunday from 10am to 6pm. Admission costs 5 Ft. (10¢).

The work of my favorite Hungarian artist is shown at the **Kovács Margit Museum** at Washtagh Gy út. Sculptures and ceramics by Margit Kovács, who was born in Györ in 1902, are prized by connoisseurs throughout the world. She often visited Szentendre. Admission to the museum is 10 Ft. (15¢). Open daily from 9am to 6pm.

In summer you can visit the **Serbian Museum of Ecclesiastical History,** Engels út 6, where art from the 18th century is displayed. The museum also has a superb collection of icons, some from the 16th century, and rare books. Open Tuesday to Sunday from 9am to 6pm. Admission is 10 Ft. (15¢).

There are seven Greek Orthodox churches in Szentendre. The first stone church built in the town, the parish church mentioned above, was a 13th-century structure, now the most treasured historic monument here. **Pozharevachka Church** on Kossuth Lajos utca is a baroque building with a Louis XVI tower. Inside is an 18th-century iconostasis (a partition on which icons are hung, separating the sanctuary from the nave). **Blagosestenska Church** on Görög utca is a fine baroque building with 18th-century furnishings. The **Greek Orthodox Episcopal Church** on Alkotmány utca has as its main attraction the rococo wrought-iron gate. The large decorated iconostasis is from 1777–81.

A cultural festival is held in Szentendre every summer, with art and drama highlighted.

Since you'll probably want a restaurant in Szentendre more than a hotel, I'll lead off with the pick of dining selections.

Where to Dine

Restaurant Aranysárkány (The Golden Dragon), Alkotmány (tel. 26/11670), has long been acclaimed the best restaurant in town, and it's popular with writers and filmmakers who in recent years have decided to call Szentendre (Saint André) home. Its name suggests it's an Oriental restaurant, but it isn't. It's a reference to the dragon of St. George, the protector saint of the Serbs. The owner, Attila (yes, that's his real name) Mahr, was a former antiques dealer, as a look around his restaurant reveals: Oriental rugs, copper pots (old ones), and wrought-iron lamps left over from the days of the Habsburg Empire. The restaurant has been compared to the atelier of an artist, which is most appropriate for the artists' town of Szentendre. While eating, diners can view the often frantic activity in the open kitchen. The owner offers only eight tables, which during the regular dining hours always seem to be full. Therefore, it's best to come here during "off-hours," as the place serves continuously from noon to 10pm.

Here you get authentic Hungarian cuisine, and that means lard, so if you're afraid of cholesterol you're in the wrong place. A fat goose and succulent pork are among the favorite items to order. The master chef, Béla Liscsinszky, is skilled at his trade, and even if he uses a lot of sour cream, his dishes are not over-paprikaed or greasy. He turns to the river, the forest, and (in summer) the Great Hungarian Plain with its rich fruits and vegetables for his inspiration. If you're here during game season, you can order pheasant with chestnuts, wild duck with quince, or venison Esterházy (an ancient recipe). On a hot day in July, try the chilled cherry soup laced with cream, then follow perhaps with trout from Piroschka. For dessert, the specialty is "cottage cheese balls from Pilis," which is a town southeast of Budapest. These are actually dumplings coated with a sauce of strawberry jam shipped in from Russia. They are delectable. Meals are reasonably priced, rarely costing more than 350 Ft. ($6).

Vidám Szerzetesek (The Happy Monk), Vöröshasereg út 5 (tel. 26/10544), is the most visibly family oriented restaurant in town. Owned and operated by extended members of the Dvorszky family, it prides itself on its cleanliness, the freshness of its ingredients, and the warmth of its welcome, as well as the quality and wholesomeness of its cuisine. Menus in many languages, including English, are posted both inside and outside the wood-trimmed dining room. You dine within sight of depictions of monks involved in various happy poses, including eating and drinking. Full meals cost from 350 Ft. ($5.75), and are served daily from noon to 10pm. Specialties include trout in the style of the Tokay vine trimmers, stuffed mushrooms, pork cutlets Szentendre style (covered with a sauce of chicken livers, mushrooms, and vegetables), and paprika-flavored veal with dumplings. You can also order tenderloin of beef Dinaria style (with a paste of smoked ham, served with egg-enriched mashed potatoes) and grilled calves' liver in a delicately seasoned fashion created by the owners.

Régimodi Vendéglö, Futó utca 3 (tel. 26/11105), is one of the most charming restaurants in Szentendre, but you'd never know it from its drab exterior. You climb a flight of exterior steps to reach what looks like a second-floor parlor of a private 19th-century house. Owned and operated as a private business by Mrs. Tomkó Béláné, it sits a few buildings away from the Kovács Museum in the center of town. You might examine the rows of antique photographs decorating the walls, the faces of which look like a genetic history of the Great Plain. Even the antique furniture looks as if it had belonged to the family for many generations. The restaurant is open daily from noon to 11pm, and meals cost from 400 Ft. ($6.75). The specialties of the house are prepared from ancient family recipes. You can order such dishes as cold cherry soup with red wine, roast trout, smoked beef tongue with horseradish, and stuffed cabbage in the style of Kolozsvar. The restaurant also has a romantic old wine cellar where you can make many different wine selections or else sample some Hungarian champagne.

Restaurant Görög Kancso (Greek Pot), Görög utca 1 (no phone). This unpretentious stucco and stone-trimmed restaurant serves Hungarian, Greek, and Serbian meals in an ambience of friendly service and low-key local residents. A coal-burning pot-bellied dragon stove is the sole source of heat. The restaurant stands at the bottom of a cobblestone street that runs toward the river. You'll recognize it by the iron doors that close like shutters over the stone arch of the entranceway. Main dishes include pork liver, paprika chicken, and beefsteak with egg. Meals cost from as little as 250 Ft. ($4.25), and service is daily from 10am to midnight.

Where to Stay

Hotel Danubius, Ady Endre utca 28, H-2000 Szentendre (tel. 26/2511), lies just a few yards from the Danube, but many of its clients come for the mineral baths that are found about a 10-minute walk away. Residents of the hotel use the hot and cold baths for free. Built in 1968, but renovated in 1988, the Danubius should not be judged by its lackluster lobby. Its rooms may lack style, but they are clean, cheap, and relatively comfortable. In all, 50 bedrooms are available, each containing a shower, sink, and toilet. Including breakfast, prices are 1,700 Ft. ($28.25) daily for a single, 1,800 Ft. ($30) for a double. The hotel has two restaurants.

A Nostalgic Coffeehouse

Nosztalgia Kávéház (Nostalgic Coffeehouse), Bogdany utca 2 (tel. 26/11660), is famous as a tourist attraction in its own right. Therefore, in summer you may have to wait patiently for a table to become available. It's the creation of one of the region's most imaginative entrepreneurs, Lászlo Bauer, who converted what had been a bakery into a complex of restaurants, open-air theaters, and antiques galleries. You might begin with a foaming cup of the house special coffee, with or without alcohol, and a slice of the many-layered Dobos torte. The setting is richly antique, including dusty Persian carpets, stained-glass windows, and a collection of turn-of-the-century furniture that even your grandmother might have labeled kitsch. Cakes cost 30 Ft. (50¢) to 50 Ft. (85¢); glasses of Hungarian wine, 20 Ft. (35¢) each. In winter additional seating is possible in a stone-vaulted cellar whose entrance lies at the back of the courtyard. The coffeehouse is open Tuesday to Sunday from 10am to 10pm.

Count yourself lucky if you get to attend a production of an English-language operetta for 120 Ft. ($2). Performances are presented in season on a tiny dais in the small enclosed back courtyard. Opened in 1980, the theater is credited with being the first privately owned theater in Hungary to open since the end of World War II.

Heading North for Food and Lodging

Bernadett Panzió (Bernadett Guesthouse), Szabadság tér, H-2022 Tahi (tel. 26/27100). The fact that it was constructed by private funds by a hardworking entrepreneurial family is perhaps a symbol of the growing ranks of privately held businesses within Hungary. It lies behind an impeccably maintained two-story façade brightened with a summer garden. The house contains only 15 well-scrubbed bedrooms. Singles cost 1,200 Ft. ($20) daily, with doubles going for 1,500 Ft. ($25).

There's also a popular but small restaurant with a stand-up bar nestled in one corner. Big windows flood the interior with sunlight and enhance the welcoming smile of the establishment's blonde matriarch, Mrs. Eszter Fejér. Named after her daughter, Bernadett, the place was built in 1985 near the town bridge. Meals in the wood-trimmed street-level dining room cost from 250 Ft. ($4.25) and might include chicken salad, sautéed brains in "Moscow sauce," Hungarian tripe stew, roast duck with orange slices, and—everybody's favorite—Wiener schnitzel. Meals are served nonstop through the day from noon to midnight. The basement contains a pair of bowling alleys and a beer hall.

Pokol Csárda (The Devil's Inn), Tahitofalu, St. Andrew's Island, H-2600 Vác (tel. 26/27111), is a superb choice for a rural outing, but getting there is an excursion. It lies about 6 miles north of Szentendre on the Danube island of St. Andrew, whose farms and fields have been little touched by the 20th century. The restaurant is contained in a tile-roofed stucco-walled inn with geraniums in the windows, a quartet of shady chestnut trees, and a gravel-covered terrace in front. From the terrace (where tables provide outdoor seating in summer), a splendid view of the baroque spires and domes of the city of Vác rise in splendor across the Danube.

The restaurant is open only from March 20 to November 15, and serves meals from noon to 10pm. Inside, guests are surrounded with the accumulated history of the inn's century-old history, as well as by the romance provided by a Gypsy violinist. Full meals cost from 400 Ft. ($6.75), and are reputed to be the best in the region. The fish specialties are carp and pike, but many diners prefer Hortobágy crêpes, a wide array of shish kebabs, or some of the savory pork dishes. The name of the meat specialty is translated as "flaming devil's head," which is nothing more than a paprika-enriched mixed grill flambéed at your table, and served by a waiter wearing a devil's mask. The restaurant is leased by one of the region's most charming entrepreneurs, Attila Kalencsik, who usually greets visitors at the entrance.

VISEGRÁD

It's only a village today, but Visegrád, 28 miles from Budapest and once the site of a Roman fort, was for a few centuries the seat of Hungary's kings. It's about 10 miles up the river from Szentendre. After the conquest of the country by the Magyars, Visegrád became the major center of the Danube Bend, and a **royal citadel,** now in ruins, was built on the hill by the Angevin kings in the 13th century as a defense against the Mongols who kept pressing from the east and the north. The citadel keep housed the coronation insignia of the Hungarian kings. Also here are the ruined crenellations of the military barracks built by King Béla, of the Angevin dynasty, in the 12th century. The ramparts have been reconstructed, and from them you have a magnificent view of the Danube Bend. You can reach the citadel by bus or by climbing the steep slopes.

It was in this citadel that King Matthias Corvinus was born in 1458. When he grew up to be sovereign, Matthias had a **royal palace,** the most magnificent in Central Europe, erected on the river down the hill from the fortress. Most of its bulk was added from a period beginning in 1320, but it reached its height of Renaissance splendor in the 15th century. Impressive even in ruins, the major section of the palace rises from a flat, low-lying area gradually going up a hillside nearby.

The entire complex, including both the citadel and the palace, was destroyed by burning and razing by the Turks in 1541–42. The magnificence of the palace was only a legend of a paradise on earth until excavations started in 1932. The legends proved true, but today this is the kind of monument where so few standing stones are left that only an imaginative re-creation of the era can bring it all to a semblance of life.

The main attraction of the palace ruins is the parade ground with the donjon (the massive inner tower), built around 1250, in the center. Called **Solomon's Tow-**

er, this structure houses some artifacts found in the ongoing excavations. The remains of an original red marble fountain, an outstanding relic of Hungarian Renaissance sculpture, are here.

From May to September, the ruins and excavations are open Tuesday to Sunday from 9am to 4:30pm; from October to April, Tuesday to Sunday from 8am to 3:30pm. Admission is 10 Ft. (15¢).

Where to Stay

Hotel Silvanus, H-2025 Visegrád (tel. 361/113-6063). You'll see this hotel as you drive up toward it from the bottom of a hill. It rises in a modern format of cement, glass, and tile, an attractive contrast to the ruins of the historic fortress a hillock (and a five-minute walk) away. Built in 1971, the 78-room hotel has a marble-trimmed lobby with lots of exposed wood, a combination bowling alley and coffee shop in the basement, and a view of the Danube from the sunny terrace outside. In high season you'll probably find hordes of children and blaring video games as well, but the isolated position and the surrounding woods offer plenty of peace and quiet nonetheless. A double room with bath for one person costs $32 daily. A double room with bath for two persons rises to $45.

There's also a self-service coffee shop, plus a disco bar, tennis courts, and a brasserie. The restaurant is a paneled room with wrought-iron chandeliers fashioned in a design that's solid, heavy, and very Hungarian. Since this is one of the most famous hunting regions in the country, venison is featured on the menu, as well as leg of lamb with tarragon and steamed barley, ground braised beef with mushrooms in white wine, stuffed pike, roast wild boar, and roast wild goose, along with larded pheasant and game stew. On average, a meal costs 400 Ft. ($6.75) without wine.

Where to Dine

Nagy Villámi Vendéglő, Erdészete Park (tel. 26/28-070). A meal here requires a special excursion up a winding forest-bordered road stretching up a hillside in the national park around Visegrád. It's a favorite destination in both winter and summer for hundreds of Hungarian families who turn a meal here into an all-afternoon event. Within a series of conservatively modern rooms, diners look out over the often mist-covered forest that has played such a prominent role in Hungarian history and lore. Full meals, costing from 500 Ft. ($8.50), might include the house specialty of game in season, served in many different ways. These include ragoût of venison and marinated roast of wild boar. Other dishes are likely to include pike-perch from Lake Balaton, served Carpathian style, and the inevitable gulasch soup. The establishment is open daily for snacks and drinks from 10am to midnight, serving full hot meals from noon to either 8 or 9pm, depending on business.

Restaurant Fekete Holló (Black Raven), Fö utca 3A (tel. 22/4180), occupies the cellar of a gingerbread-covered Victorian house built on a flat area between the Danube and the ruins of the royal palace. You enter through an unlikely-looking side door and pass through a smallish bar area. If it's winter, you can warm yourself at a ceramic stove along the way. Meals are served beneath the brick vaulting of the dining room, with its hardwood benches and well-used wood tables. Full meals, costing from 200 Ft. ($3.50), a truly modest value, are served daily from noon to 10pm. Your food might consist of such fare as pork schnitzel with thyme and roast potatoes or else Wiener schnitzel, perhaps pork liver with polenta or cutlets of venison (in season).

Dining on the Outskirts

Restaurant Szökeforrás, Táncsics Mihály utca 1 (tel. Dömös 9 or, from 8am to 4pm, 26/28200), is a modern restaurant that lies at the southernmost point of the bend of the Danube, some 6 miles from Visegrád and 9¼ miles from Esztergom. Meaning "Fair Source," the inn was opened to commemorate the 900th anniversary of the village of Dömös, which is one of the oldest settlements in

Hungary. A spot was selected at the beginning of a footpath through the forest leading to Szökeforrás, a well-known beauty spot. It serves as an attractive stopover for those sightseeing in the region for the day. Its design includes a sloping roof built in several distinctly separated sections, a raised terrace cantilevered above the ground, and large expanses of window walls looking out onto a secluded flat area. The stone floor is laid in small rectangular slabs, while the soaring ceiling is fashioned of heavy blond beams. The menu includes pork cutlet Holstein, rumpsteak with mushrooms, chicken paprika with noodles, and apple strudel. Meals range from around 500 Ft. ($8.25). In summer, select a table on the large terrace, where a panoramic view of the Rám ravine opens before you. The restaurant is open daily from 11am to 10pm, from March 1 to November 15. Music and folk dancing are offered in the evening.

ESZTERGOM

A small city 40 miles upriver from Budapest, Esztergom is across the Danube south from Czechoslovakia, a short distance west from where the river begins its fairly sharp right turn. There was once a bridge across to Czechoslovakia, but it was destroyed by bombs in World War II and has never been rebuilt. A ferry is the only link today.

If you're telephoning, seek operator assistance—you can't call direct.

Esztergom was a significant fortress in Roman days, and it was in this vicinity that Marcus Aurelius, Stoic philosopher, worked on his *Meditations* before he became Roman emperor in A.D. 161. The town became the capital of Hungary in the 10th century, and it was here that Stephen I of the Árpád dynasty was born and was crowned. Considered the cradle of Hungarian Christianity, this is today the seat of the cardinal-primate of Hungary. King Stephen (later St. Stephen) founded an archbishopric here and ordered construction of a basilica on a hill dominating the town.

Esztergom flourished, having its golden age in the 12th century, but it was totally destroyed by the Turks and was not really revived until the 19th century. The present cathedral was built between 1822 and 1860 on the site selected by St. Stephen on Castle Hill, called Várhegy.

The **cathedral,** 390 feet long and the largest church in Hungary, is in the classicist style, with a massive dome. In fact, a prototype of the dome alone was made into a church a short distance away. One of the highlights of the basilica is the **Archepiscopal Treasury,** so rich that the cathedral is called "the Vatican of Hungary." It contains, among other exhibits, golden crosses from the 13th century and royal drinking horns from the 15th century. A celebrated work is the golden Calvary cross of King Matthias Corvinus. Admission to the treasury is 15 Ft. (25¢), and it is open Tuesday to Sunday in summer from 10am to 5pm, and in winter from 10am to 2:30pm.

The southern side of the cathedral, the so-called **Bakócz Chapel,** was built between 1506 and 1511 and survived the Turks. During the construction of the present basilica, it was taken apart and its 1,600 numbered pieces built into the side of the new cathedral. Franz Liszt, the Hungarian composer, conducted a mass he had written for the occasion at the consecration of the splendid house of worship.

The remains of the **royal palace** are side by side with the basilica. Although these digs are only partially worked, Roman and medieval relics are displayed in an open-air lapidarium here. In the palace is the oldest 12th-century living room in Hungary. The most ornate part of the palace is the Royal Chapel. From the reconstructed battlements you get a fine view of the city and the Danube, even looking into Czechoslovakia on the north bank.

Christian Museum (Keresztény Múzeum), in the Primate's Palace, is at Berényi Zsigmond utca 2 (tel. 764), containing one of the finest such collections outside Budapest. Charging 20 Ft. (35¢) admission, it is open Tuesday to Sunday in summer from 10am to 5pm, and in winter from 10am to 2:30pm. You'll see many

Hungarian and Italian panel paintings from the Middle Ages, as well as items of goldsmith and textile art, ceramics, engravings, and medals. Remarkable treasures are the 15th-century altar, a work of Tamás Kolozsvári, and a carved wood St. Sepulchre of Christ. The **Archepiscopal Library** is on Bajcsy-Zsilinszky út in an early eclectic building housing 200,000 volumes of the country's oldest library. Among the contents are more than 700 incunabula. The Water Town Parish Church on the same street is a baroque building erected between 1728 and 1738.

In the midst of all its historic memorabilia, Esztergom is a lively, developing town, the cultural and industrial center of the region. You can enjoy the thermal baths here after strolling through the old streets.

Where to Stay

Hotel Volán, József Attila tér 2, H-2500 Esztergom (tel. 33/11-257). Angular and built of thousands of tons of poured concrete, it looks like a collection of huge cement blocks a giant assembled at the edge of the river. A tree-filled park might block your view of the river, however. The hotel is owned by a Hungarian trucking company and, of its 35 basic bedrooms, only about half contain showers. Toilets are in the hallways, not in the bedrooms. With bath, doubles rent for 788 Ft. ($13.25) a night, with singles costing 693 Ft. ($11.50). Without bath, a double goes for 927 Ft. ($15.50), with a single costing 532 Ft. ($8.75). Built in the 1970s, the hotel has a popular series of stone-floored public rooms, including both a café and a street-level restaurant open daily from 7am to 10pm.

Hotel Fürdő, Bajcsy-Zsilinszky út 14, H-2500 Esztergom (tel. 33/1470), sits behind an ochre-colored façade on the busiest street of town. It enjoys a faded reputation as a grand old hotel. Today a lot of it is in need of repair, but it's a possible choice if you're spending the night. Much of the oldest section is devoted to a series of cavernous cafés, sitting rooms, and restaurants. The 96 bedrooms lie within a modern addition. Bedrooms usually contain tile baths, blandly modern furnishings, and big windows. The better units also offer TV, and a view over the gardens in back. Doubles with bath cost 1,600 Ft. ($26.50) daily; the maximum rate for a single with bath is 1,500 Ft. ($25). In summer visitors can enjoy the waters of the municipal swimming pool nearby. Meals are served in one or another of the hotel restaurants from 7am to midnight.

Where to Dine

Alabárdos Restaurant, Bajcsy-Zsilinszky út 49 (no phone), stands on a busy street to the side of the cathedral behind a modernized baroque façade. It had been little more than a run-down stone-sided house (which city fathers wanted to demolish) until members of the Gindl family restored and enlarged it in 1986. Most of the interior woodwork was crafted by a battalion of cousins, and even the bronze depiction of halberd bearers, crafted from sheet metal, was a creation of a distant relative, Hungarian artist Clara Balatony. In summer you can dine in the terraced garden out back with a view of the spire of the Church of St. Thomas. The establishment serves satisfying meals Tuesday to Sunday from noon to 10pm. Dinners, costing from 300 Ft. ($5), might begin with fruit soup, then follow with Swiss-style liver, Hortobágy crêpes, Gypsy-inspired roast beef, or lamb gulasch.

Anonim Vendéglő, Berenyi utca 4 (no phone). Its founders wanted to name it after St. Stephen, but when the government planning commission objected, everyone began referring to it as the "no name" (anonim) restaurant. It stands near the Christian museum, within low-ceilinged 18th-century walls. You can choose from two dining rooms graced with iron chandeliers and tile floors. In warm weather tables are placed in the walled garden in back. Full meals, served Tuesday to Sunday from noon to 10pm (closed January and February), cost from 300 Ft. ($5). The bill of fare always includes several kinds of beefsteak, pork cutlets, gulasch soup, Wiener schnitzels, and pastries.

DOBOGÓKŐ
Lying some 24 miles from Budapest on the top of the 2,100-foot-high Dobogókő, stands one of the most popular hotels along the Danube Bend (see below). Dobogókő is one of the best-known and oldest winter-sports resorts in Hungary. From the peak, visitors have a splendid view over the nearby Danube Valley and Pilis mountains.

Food and Lodging
Hotel Nimrod, H-2099 Dobogókő (tel. 26/27644). The Danube is not visible from this big-windowed modern 96-room hotel, but the surrounding forests offer plenty of natural interest. It bears the name of the great-grandson of Noah, who was cited as a great hunter in the Bible (Genesis). Renovated in the 1980s, the hotel was built in the early 1970s in a recreational area of villas in an isolated section of the Danube Bend region. Each of the modern bedrooms contains its own bath, and most of the units have balconies as well. A double with bath for one person costs $32 daily, while a double with bath for two persons rents for $45. The hotel has a restaurant and an espresso bar, as well as a swimming pool, sauna, solarium, fitness room, tennis courts, minigolf, and a children's playground.

2. Lake Balaton

The "Hungarian Sea," Lake Balaton, is the summer playground of the nation, with interest in winter activities on the increase. Since Hungary has no seacoast, this lake, 62 miles southwest of Budapest, is the country's Riviera. The Romans knew of the medicinal spas around the shores of the lake, but it took until the 19th century for the sport of swimming to catch on. Since then Lake Balaton has drawn hordes of people to frolic in summer—both Hungarians and thousands of foreign visitors. The waters of the lake and its spas have been praised by all comers, including Rabindranath Tagore, the Indian poet and Nobel Prize winner, who wrote: "I have seen nearly all the world, but nowhere else have I found the wonderful beauty of sky and water more enchanting than here."

Balaton is the largest lake in Central Europe, some 50 miles long, with a shoreline of some 120 miles. It's slightly larger than Lake Geneva, but unlike that deep body of water, this Hungarian lake averages only about 10 feet in depth. On the southern shore the water is shallow, with velvety sands, while in the north the lake's bottom is flat and pebbly, and the water deepens abruptly. The lake is surrounded by plains and vineyards. Blossoming fruit trees draw visitors in spring for drives along the shore, which is studded with small villages where you'll see old churches and thatched cottages. The northern shore is dotted with long-dead volcanoes.

Lake Balaton is almost completely ringed with summer resorts and lakeside houses. The state has taken over many once-private villas as well as some hotels, turning them into holiday homes for workers from throughout the country who look forward eagerly to their summer retreat here. Cutting deep into the lake is the Tihany peninsula, perhaps one of the most scenic parts of the lake. The two shores are connected by ferry service between Szántód and Tihany.

Swimmers prefer the waters off the north shore, although with increasing crowds of vacationers you'll find them everywhere. So many bathers go into the lake that there's a danger of pollution from too much suntan oil!

Motorboats are not allowed on the lake, but it's filled with sailboats. A large program of water sports includes windsurfing and rowing. The lake is rich in fish, and even if you don't want to catch your own, as many people do, you can enjoy fish dishes in the csárdas (inns) along the lake. The most characteristic fish served here is fogas, a kind of pike-perch. Some fogas as large as 21 pounds have been caught in the lake.

In July and August Lake Balaton is vastly overcrowded. Never arrive then without a hotel reservation unless you plan to visit just for the day, returning to Budapest at night. Fast trains from the capital make frequent runs in summer, carrying carloads of holiday-makers, many of whom begin the party as soon as the train leaves the station heading for the lake. I recommend that you go if you can in the late spring or early fall. The water is cooler then, but the conditions are less crowded.

Lake Balaton is not only a summer resort, although that is its main thrust into tourism. In winter, parts of the lake ice over and the winter-sports enthusiasts take over.

Sledging, ice skating, and a winter version of windsurfing called ice sailing are popular. Also, the old-fashioned *fakutya,* a chairlike skating sledge, has made a comeback in recent years. Fishing through holes cut in the ice has a following too.

I'll begin our journey on the north shore of the Balaton, heading west until I have eventually introduced you to the whole lake district.

BALATONALMÁDI

Among the major resorts of Lake Balaton is Balatonalmádi, about 70 miles from Budapest, lying on a bay and surrounded by hills studded with villas dating from the 1880s. You can reach this resort by car on the M7 and on road 71. The center of the little town is to the south of the high road, with an extensive park from which the quay reaches out into the lake.

This is an ideal resort choice for families with children, since the water here is shallow, unlike that at other Balaton holiday centers. Scheduled and charter boats operate regularly from the landing stage, providing transport to other points on the lake.

Roman artifacts have been found in the Almádi area.

Where to Stay

Hotel Auróra, Bajcsy-Zsilinszky utca 14, H-8223 Balatonalmádi (tel. 86/ 38810), is a 14-story glass-and-concrete hotel built on a slight hill above the lake. The interior benefits from the many big windows that flood the earth-colored furniture with light. On the premises are a tennis court, a sauna, a bowling alley, a rose garden, a vaulted tavern called the Kakas Csárda (see the recommendation coming up), a restaurant, and a nightclub. The hotel's private beach rents Windsurfers, and there's a swimming pool on the premises. With half board included, singles go for $54 daily, and two persons pay $63. The hotel is open from the end of April to early September.

Hotel Tulipán, Marx tér 1, H-8223 Balatonalmádi (tel. 86/38317), is a 47-room hotel whose façade angles itself around a street corner in the center of town. Its design includes a central tower and symmetrically hipped roofs. Hungarian specialties are offered in its restaurant. Guests have free use of the private beach of the nearby Hotel Auróra, a five-minute walk away. Try for a room with a balcony opening onto the water. Rooms are comfortably but functionally furnished. With half board included, singles go for $37.25, with doubles costing $43.75. Some units have complete baths, others only showers.

Where to Dine

Kakas Csárda, Hotel Auróra, Bajcsy-Zsilinszky utca 14 (tel. 86/38811). It's hard to believe that such a modern hotel could have such an antique tavern in its cellar, but that's exactly the case with this vaulted restaurant in the basement of the previously recommended hotel. A large part of the inner room is devoted to a trio of

300-liter wine barrels, although there's still plenty of room for the tables, hand-woven napery, and a chattering crowd of vacationing Budapesters. The outdoor terrace includes facilities for barbecuing, as well as tables overlooking the park. A complete dinner, including an apéritif, food, and drink, costs from 500 Ft. ($8.50) per person. Open daily from 3 to 11pm.

Muskátli Restaurant, Marx tér 4 (tel. 86/39111), is a rustically contemporary restaurant whose walls are encircled with pieces of vertical planking, cut into semi-circular curves. Even the ceiling is crafted from strips of the same wood, which produces a décor that is uniquely Hungarian. A garden with thriving summer roses surrounds the building. You might enjoy a drink in the cocktail lounge before heading in for dinner. Specialties are often prepared right at your table, and they feature recipes from different parts of the country. Full meals range from 500 Ft. ($8.50). Open daily in summer from 7 to 11pm (closed October to April).

BALATONFÜRED

This town with narrow, twisting streets is one of the oldest and best-known resorts on the north shore, as well as being a first-class spa of international renown, with nearly a dozen medicinal springs. It's some 80 miles from Budapest and is accessible by either car or train. Balatonfüred's outlying country is one of the major wine-growing districts of Hungary. A promenade along the lake is lined with poplars. The heart of the resort is Gyógy Tér, the spa square.

Rabindranath Tagore, the Nobel Prize–winning Indian poet, came here to recover from a heart attack in 1926, and to commemorate his stay in Balatonfüred he planted a tree that still flourishes in a little park here. The tree planting started a tradition, which was followed by another Nobel Prize winner, the Italian poet Salvatore Quasimodo. Balatonfüred has long been a mecca for persons suffering from cardiac diseases.

The most popular excursion to take from here is to the Tihany peninsula, coming up.

Where to Stay

Hotel Annabella, Beloiannisz utca 25, H-8231 Balatonfüred (tel. 86/42222), has a pleasantly contemporary design of strong horizontal lines and evenly spaced rows of panoramic balconies. Its six stories include simply furnished, comfortable bedrooms, each with private balcony and bath. Some of the suites have wall-size photographs of autumnal forests, as well as separate sleeping alcoves. On the premises are both an indoor and an outdoor swimming pool, a coffee shop, a nightclub, and a colorful and sunny Hungarian restaurant with an excellent kitchen. Open from April till October, the 384 comfortably furnished bedrooms cost $59 daily for a single and $73 for a double, including half board.

Hotel Marina, Széchenyi út 26, H-8231 Balatonfüred (tel. 86/43644), is perhaps the best-known and most up-to-date hotel at the resort. It consists of both a tower building, which soars up above the hilly landscape around it, and a low-lying section containing balconied rooms with views over the tree-dotted beach and the rose garden. The enormous lobby area has a modern airy design of wood paneling and big windows. On the premises are a bowling alley, a large swimming pool, an oval bar in an adjoining snackbar and brasserie, and a wide variety of kiosks and services. This hotel is open from May until October, during which period it's one of the most popular on Lake Balaton. The hotel offers 374 bedrooms, charging guests $65 daily for a single and $80 for a double, including half board.

Hotel Margaréta, Széchenyi út 29, H-8231 Balatonfüred (tel. 86/43824), sits in an isolated field a few minutes' walk from the lake. A three-story covered atrium extends over some of the comfortable and functionally furnished public rooms. This unheralded hotel is a good choice if you prefer a smaller establishment. The 51 bedrooms have good mattresses, private balconies, big bathrooms, four-channel TVs, and three-band radios, all encased in plastic covers. Uniformed waiters with impeccable manners serve ham, cheese, salami, crusty rye bread, and croissants with black coffee for breakfast, in a sunny dining room with white-painted wooden ceiling cut-outs. This is one of the few hotels in the region to remain open all year. Clients have access to the big indoor pool at the nearby Hotel Marina. The rooms go for $86 daily for two persons with half board.

Where to Dine

Baricska Csárda, Baricska dűlő (tel. 86/43105), might be the most popular restaurant on the north shore of Lake Balaton. It sits in the center of rolling hills, within view of the lake. It has a vine-covered terrace for diners who prefer a view of the stars, although the beamed tavern and the vaulted cellars offer traditionally decorated intimate spots for dining in high Hungarian style. The big wine press dates from 1833 and serves as a sort of symbol of the establishment. Baricska Csárda is open daily from April until the end of October, 11am to 11pm. Meals range from 450 Ft. ($7.50). A folkloric program with traditional Hungarian dances and songs, as well as Gypsy music, is presented nightly.

Hordó Csárda, Baricska dűlő (tel. 86/40867). Among rolling vine-covered hills, this low-lying building was once used to store wine. It was also a place to barbecue sausages. A few years ago it was redecorated and expanded into a tastefully colorful restaurant that serves as a focal point of social life on the north shore of the lake. Every evening the management presents a floor show that you can enjoy while tasting such specialties as bean soup with cabbage and pork, gulasch stew, fish soup, and strudel with poppyseed and pumpkin. Full meals cost from 500 Ft. ($8.50). The restaurant is open daily from April to October, 11am to 11pm. It's opposite the Hotel Marina.

Balaton Restaurant, Tagore sétány 5 (tel. 86/40266), built in 1962, is a large and airy restaurant with a high ceiling, potted palms, and a big abstract mural of boats sailing on the lake. A dance band plays in the evening for any guests who might care to trip the light fantastic. Service is polite and efficient, and specialties are typically Hungarian. With meals costing from 500 Ft. ($8.50), the place is open daily from 11:30am to midnight.

Kedves Café, Blaha Lujza utca 7 (tel. 86/43-229), offers a quick stand-up coffee bar, a snackbar on the upper floor, and a more formal café whose décor takes advantage of the building it is housed in, which dates from 1795. The management hosts a Sunday-morning puppet show for children, although many adults seem to enjoy it more. There are regularly scheduled literature readings presented by popular artists and actors (but, alas, only in Hungarian). In the heart of town, the café has a sun terrace whose wicker chairs are a rendezvous point for visiting urbanites and their friends, all of whom seem to enjoy the brilliant sunshine. The café is open in summer from 8am to 10pm. Coffee costs 40 Ft. (60¢), with pastries going for the same.

TIHANY

The most beautiful spot of the entire Lake Balaton region is usually conceded to be the Tihany peninsula. This finger of land, stretching 3 miles into the lake and containing some 90 acres, is a wildlife reserve. Its cone-shaped geyser hills are covered with poplar and acacia trees, and there's a forest of lavender. The main village, also called Tihany, is on the hillside at the top of the peninsula, but the entire area is now a resort. It even has its own little lake, Lake Belső. You can fish in it as well as in Lake Balaton.

The twin-spired abbey, dating back some nine centuries, distinguishes the skyline of Tihany. The Romanesque crypt is all that remains of the building launched by King Andrew I in the 11th century, but I suppose that's enough for him: that's where he's buried. The present church and its adjoining monastery are baroque, resulting from work started in 1719. The abbey is known for its organ, used in summer for concerts.

The monastery houses a museum, and there's also a popular open-air ethnographic display. Summer is always active on the peninsula—and not just on the lake.

You can reach Tihany by car, but if you're traveling by train you'll have to get off at Balatonfüred and take a bus the short distance to the peninsula.

Food and Lodging

Hotel Club Tihany, Tihany-rév, H-8237 Tihany (tel. 86/48088), is the leading holiday complex on Lake Balaton. It opened in 1986, and today has 330 comfortably furnished but functional bedrooms with minibars, color TVs, private baths, and phones. Six rooms are specially designed for handicapped persons. Most guests stay here on the half-board plan, paying $62 daily for a single and $100 for a double. Tennis courts, an array of restaurants, squash, bowling, and skittles are available at the hotel.

Sport Restaurant, Fürdőtelep (tel. 86/48-251). If you dine in this circa-1920 house, you can choose between a seat near the panoramic windows overlooking the lake or a perch near the colorful wall murals painted into regionally inspired patterns by the women of Kalocsa. In good weather tables are set up near the boat landing under the partial shade of a canopy. In the evening part of the establishment becomes a disco. Simple meals, featuring fish soup and other Hungarian specialties, range from 450 Ft. ($7.75). The restaurant is open daily from April to October, serving from 10am to 1am.

Rege Café, Batthyány út 38 (tel. 86/48-280), near the abbey on the hilltop above the lake, is open from March 1 to the end of October. The terrace might be the most popular part of this traditional coffeehouse, where menu items include drinks, coffee, and pastries. Coffee runs from 25 Ft. (40¢) and pastry from 22 Ft. (35¢). The place is open daily from 8am to 9pm.

KESZTHELY

The largest town on Lake Balaton, Keszthely is a place of many charming buildings and old streets. Dating from prehistoric times, this town, lying on the northwestern corner of the lake, attracted the Romans of course, and it was a flourishing market town in the Middle Ages. Its position as a bathing resort was established long, long ago. The first agricultural academy in Europe was founded here in 1797 by György Festetics, who also founded a library.

The most magnificent building in town is the **Festetics Palace,** its southern wing dating from 1750. In the latter 19th century many additions were made to the structure until now it contains some 100 rooms. The Helikon Library, with more than 50,000 volumes, is housed here. Much of the art that once graced the palace walls has been carted off, but some still remains to give the visitor pleasure. The museum of the palace, with a collection of antiques and documents, is of at least passing interest. The palace is open daily from 10am to 6pm.

I most enjoy, however, a walk in the park around the palace, where many sculptures and ornamental plantings please the eye. Summer music concerts are presented here. Much of the aura of the past century still lingers in the park along the pier.

If you're phoning Keszthely, ask for operator assistance.

Food and Lodging

Hotel Helikon, H-8360 Keszthely (tel. 11330). On the water less than a mile from the center of town, this eight-story balconied hotel, opened in 1971, curves gracefully around its own private beach. The big windows of the lobby look out over a winding staircase that leads directly from an upper floor of the hotel onto the center of a small private island a short distance from the shoreline. The interior has red porphyry floors, low-slung leather couches, and an attractive English-speaking staff. In winter the management closes two of the floors, but stays in business despite the reduced flow of clients. On the premises are a restaurant with Gypsy music, a dance café, a big sun terrace, and two bars. The hotel has a swimming pool, bowling alley, sauna, and indoor tennis courts. A double room with bath costs $71 daily, while a double room for single occupancy is $64 a night. Rates include a buffet breakfast. The Helikon rents a total of 232 bedrooms, of which 8 are suites. Amenities include balconies, private baths, toilets, phones, radios, TVs, and minibars.

Restaurant Hungária, Kossuth Lajos út 34 (tel. 12265). The most impressive part about this brasserie and beerhall is the 9-foot-tall arched windows set with gold-and-white stained glass. Each of them is painstakingly set with heraldic shields and depictions of medieval cities. This is a Hungarian/Austrian restaurant, where Gösser beer is a specialty. The room is tastefully wood-paneled and sunny, and the banquettes are comfortably upholstered. A large central bar area with immaculate beer taps curves through the center of this popular restaurant, while an additional country-style room stretches out in back. The service is polite, and the other diners tend to be good friends and workers. Menu items include Serbian bean soup, chicken liver risotto, beef on a skewer, pork filet with mushrooms and rice, and an array of meats. Dessert might be a well-prepared cheese strudel. Full meals cost from 350 Ft. ($5.75), and service is daily from 9am to 11pm.

Now, I'll make a short detour northwest from the shores of Lake Balaton to—

HÉVIZ

The most celebrated spa in Hungary, Héviz, only 4 miles from Lake Balaton, draws many visitors to Lake Héviz, the largest warm-water thermal lake in Europe and second largest in the world (the only other such lake, the larger one, is in New Zealand). The summer temperature of Lake Héviz is 96° Fahrenheit, while in winter it drops to 80°. The sulfide water is radioactive, and the bottom of the lake is covered with a layer of peloid containing mineral and vegetable components. The mud and the lake water both are said to be beneficial to sufferers from a number of ailments, including rheumatism.

Because this is a medicinal lake, one should not go into the water without first checking with a doctor. This is especially true for pregnant women or those suffering from heart diseases.

To reach the resort spa, you can travel by car from Sopron, via Rte. 84. The nearest railway station is Keszthely, from which buses leave every 20 minutes for Héviz.

A variety of excursions and entertainment is available in the vicinity.

To phone Héviz, go through the operator.

Food and Lodging

Thermal Hotel Héviz, Kossuth utca 9-11, H-8380 Héviz (tel. 11-180), built near one of the most famous thermal springs in the country, opened in 1976. Because of its wide-ranging spa facilities, it has more than a 90% occupancy rate year round, and 85% of the clients come for some form of medical treatment, usually from places outside Hungary. The maroon façade adjoins a collection of communal spa hotels that service the needs of Hungarian workers sent by their unions for recuperative therapy. The elegant décor includes a series of marble-floored public rooms with leather armchairs, a plush restaurant with modern upholstered versions of medieval chairs and Gypsy music, a brasserie with handmade ceiling panels of red-and-black patterns over natural grained woods. My favorite is the coffee shop, whose end wall has a mural showing a version of a charioteer in many different kinds of European hardwood.

The 203 rooms are attractively furnished with well-upholstered furniture and all the modern conveniences. They cost $69 to $85 daily for a double and $48 to $59 for a single, breakfast included. Full meals in the restaurant cost from $11. Prices of the rooms cited include only the most basic water treatments; additional therapy will cost more. The gracefully curving roof construction above the thermal pool is an awesome piece of craftsmanship, built entirely of laminated struts and beautifully grained wood planks. The hotel has a casino where the wheel spins from 4pm to midnight. Passports are required.

Back on the Lake Balaton trek, the next stopover is—

SIÓFOK

The largest and most important resort on the lake is Siófok, where an estimated 10,000 bathers can be comfortably accommodated on the beach daily. It was the long, sandy beach, in fact, that was responsible for the early popularity of Siófok. This resort has the best tourist facilities and hotels, as well as the best stretch of beach, to be found on Lake Balaton. In summer you can attend performances at an open-air theater in Dimitrov Park.

Nearly all visitors come to Siófok for the beach and water, but in case of rain you might want to visit the Beszédes József Museum near the Sió bridge. The history of hydroengineering in Hungary is traced here, and you can see relics relating to the history of the town, plus fishing implements.

Every day passenger boats set out on scheduled journeys from Siófok's harbor to other lake resorts. For instance, you can take a ferry to the Tihany peninsula on the north shore (see above) without having to drive around the entire lake, thus avoiding the slow-moving, congested summer traffic. There are opportunities for rowing, sailing, or going on paddle-tandems on the lake. At the Sió channel near Siófok harbor, you can watch the action of the sluice gates, an interesting spectacle.

An Excursion

The most important excursion from Siófok is to Ságvár, 5½ miles to the south, where the remains of a primitive settlement more than 17,000 years old were discovered, as well as artifacts from the Roman village of Tricciana, which was part of the province of Pannonia. Clay pipes and mosaic floors once used in Tricciana have been unearthed. The results of the excavations form a museum open daily except Monday in summer from 10am to 6pm.

Food and Lodging

Hotel Neptun, H-8623 Balatonfölkdvár-Park (tel. 84/40388), is the most modern hotel (1977) on the south shore of Lake Balaton. Equipped with a full range of recreational facilities, the angular building contains 210 balconied rooms, each with phone and radio. On the top floor there's a panoramic nightclub. The hotel also contains tennis courts and a restaurant and bar, and offers free admission to the beach. In season, one person can rent a double room with bath for $60 daily. Two persons can stay here in a room with bath for $74 daily, also including half board.

Hotel Európa, Petőfi sétány 15, H-8600 Siófok (tel. 84/13411), overlooks Lake Balaton. A 12-story modern building, it receives guests from May 1 to October 15. The hotel rents 126 double rooms and 12 suites, each comfortably furnished with private bath, balcony, radio, direct-dial phone, and minibar. One person can stay here in a double room with bath for $73 daily, including half board, the charge rising to $88 for two persons. The hotel has a 240-seat restaurant, the Európa, plus a 150-seat terrace. Its nightclub occupies the uppermost floor and has a panoramic view. An open-air swimming pool and sauna are also on the premises.

Hotel Balaton, Petőfi sétány 9, H-8600 Siófok (tel. 84/10655), stands directly on the lakeshore, a six-story modern building that receives guests from May 1 to October 15. It offers 137 double bedrooms, each adequately furnished and containing a private bath, balcony, radio, and operator-assisted phone. A double for one person costs $52 daily with half board, whereas two persons on the same arrangement pay $73. The hotel offers a 240-seat restaurant, plus a 150-seat terrace. Its services include an open-air swimming pool, a sauna, a hairdresser, and an IBUSZ travel bureau office.

Hotel Hungária, Petőfi sétány 13, H-8600 Siófok (tel. 84/10677), also overlooks Lake Balaton, having been built right on the shore. From May 1 to October 15, it receives guests from all over the world, housing them in 139 comfortably furnished bedrooms, of which 137 are doubles; the other 2 are suites. Each of the accommodations contains a private bath, balcony, radio, and operator-assisted phone. A double rented to a single occupant costs $60 daily, with half board included, whereas two persons pay $74 for the same arrangement. The establishment offers a bar as well as a 240-seat restaurant. Facilities at the hotel include an open-air swimming pool and a sauna.

Hotel Lido, Petőfi sétány 11, H-8600 Siófok (tel. 84/10633), is a six-story modern hotel building rising close to the shoreline of Lake Balaton. From May 1 to October 15, it welcomes masses of visitors from all over the world, especially Germany. These guests are comfortably sheltered in 137 bedrooms, each with private bath, balcony, radio, and operator-assisted phone. One person can rent a double for $62 daily, with half-board included; two persons pay $77 for the same arrangement. The hotel has a hairdresser, an open-air swimming pool, and a sauna. It also offers several dining and drinking facilities, including the Siófok Restaurant, the Lido Brasserie, and a terrace that easily fills up with 150 vacationing guests. In the vicinity are possibilities for tennis, windsurfing, sailing, and riding.

From Lake Balaton, you may want to take some excursions "inland," exploring two of the most historic cities of Hungary. Alternatively, these cities could be explored on your way to the lake from Budapest.

SZÉKESFEHÉRVÁR

Halfway between Budapest and Lake Balaton lies the town of Székesfehérvár, which celebrated its millennium in 1972. For centuries this town, now an industrial center, played an important role in the history of Hungary, and you can see some monuments of historic interest here. The Romans were here of course, and their name for the settlement at this locale was a little simpler than the present-day appellation. They called it Alba Regia.

Before the Turks came in 1526 with fire and sword, Székesfehérvár was the site of the coronation and burial of Hungarian kings. It was the capital of Hungary during the Árpád dynasty, which produced King Stephen I, later St. Stephen. An impressive 11th-century basilica stood here, built between 1016 and 1038, where 38 Hungarian kings were crowned over five centuries, with 18 kings being entombed here also. It was the resting place of St. Stephen until the Turks destroyed his grave. The Ottoman hordes left only the foundations of the basilica.

You can visit an open-air museum daily in the ruins of the former coronation cathedral east of the main square, Szabadság tér. In the **István Király Museum** (King Stephen Museum), at the corner of Népoztársasag and Gagarin tér, archeological finds and folkloric exhibits can be seen. Open Tuesday to Sunday from 10am to 6pm.

The Turks destroyed most of the medieval buildings, and the town was largely rebuilt in the 18th century. The Bishop's Palace, dating from 1790, and the Town Hall are on the main square. You can see the rococo furnishings of the Fekete Sas (Black Eagle) pharmacy, the oldest one in the country dating from 1758, now a pharmacy museum.

Budenz-House on Arany János utca, named for one of the founders of the Finno-Ugrian comparative linguistics institute, has in its cellar the only brick wall in town, which dates back to the Árpád dynastic period.

Food and Lodging

Hotel Alba Regia, Rákóczi út l, H-8000 Székesfehérvár (tel. 22/13484). The name of this concrete-and-glass hotel is the same as the ancient Roman name for the town itself. The façade is dotted with evenly spaced rows of oversize glass windows, which flood the simply furnished bedrooms with light. On the premises are a popular restaurant, a nightclub, and an open-air terrace. The hotel has 104 rooms, most with private baths, and all equipped with radios and phones. Singles go for $41 daily, with doubles costing $53. The hotel is in the center of town near the ancient ruins.

Excursions

Lake Velence about 7 miles east-northeast from Székesfehérvár, just off the M7, has some good beaches and docks along its southern shore, and facilities for water sports are available. Part of the lakeshore is thick with reeds, but you can see its rich bird life from a boat that passes through channels cut into the dense, reedy marshland.

The village of **Tác,** some 8 miles south of Székesfehérvár on the M7, is worth a visit to see the remains of the Roman town of **Gorsium,** an important Pannonian communication center excavated in 1958. The nucleus of Gorsium was a Roman military camp built in the 1st century. Nearby, a Roman burghers' town developed and prospered until the 5th century. An open-air museum displays stone finds, reliefs, excavated sections of streets, commercial buildings, a large villa, an early Christian basilica, and ornate fountains. The cemetery from the 4th and 5th centuries is also interesting. Open for visiting Tuesday to Sunday from 10am to 6pm.

VESZPRÉM

Not actually on Lake Balaton but lying only a few miles from its north shore is Veszprém, Castle District, the capital of the Bakony mountains. This local cultural center is an industrial and university town, some 25 miles to the west of Székesfehérvár.

A town built on five hills, Veszprém is rich in historic monuments, with many narrow streets and dozens of baroque buildings from the late 18th century. The citadel was a favorite residence of Stephen, Hungary's first crowned king, and parts of the one-time royal castle were used in the **Episcopal Palace,** on Tolbuhin Marsall út, built between 1765 and 1776. The first Hungarian bishopric was founded here. Next to the Episcopal Palace is the 13th-century early Gothic Gisella Chapel.

A written record from 1002 actually mentions the cathedral at Veszprém, **St. Michael's.** Originally a Romanesque building consecrated in 1060, it was destroyed many times, making a comeback in different eras in Gothic style, then baroque, and finally, at the beginning of the 20th century, as a Neo-Gothic cathedral.

Next to its northern part are the ruins of the 10th-century **St. George's Chapel.** It was rebuilt in Romanesque style in the 12th and 13th centuries. This is the oldest structure (or remains of a structure) in Castle District. You can also see **Calvary Hill** with its 11th-century cemetery and remains of the St. Nicholas Church, which was built in the 13th century.

The baroque Town Hall of Veszprém stands on Szabadság tér, the so-called Liberty Square, which is the center of town.

---

3. The Western Border Region

This section of Hungary wears the most varied face in the country. It has historical small towns, spas, flowery villages, botanical gardens, forests on the eastern foothills of the Alps, medieval castles, and special folklore. Activity ranges from intensive agricultural production in the river valleys to rapidly developing industry in the large towns. This is an area rich in natural beauty spots and manmade masterpieces. The region embraces three counties, Győr-Sopron, Vas, and Zala, and is bordered by three countries, Austria, Yugoslavia, and Czechoslovakia.

The Hungarians often call this section Transdanubia, which means, roughly, that part of the country lying to the west and south of the Danube. This was a portion of the province of Pannonia in the days of ancient Rome's domination and contains more Roman remains than any other section of Hungary. This area of rich farm country, vineyards, and orchards contains more medieval, baroque, and Renaissance buildings than anywhere else in the country.

If you enter Hungary from Austria moving east from Vienna, you'll probably go through your border formalities at the little town of Hegyeshalom (another important crossing is farther south at Sopron, coming up later). If you do come in on the major artery from Vienna, your first stop in Hungary might be at Győr. Even if you're en route to Lake Balaton or Budapest, this section is easily visited along the way and well merits a stopover.

GYŐR

A county seat and rapidly developing industrial town 80 miles from Budapest on the M1 motorway, Győr is reached about midway in your journey if you're traveling between Vienna and the Hungarian capital. It's called "town of the waters" because it lies at the confluence of the Danube, Rába, Rábca, and Marcall rivers. Győr, which was the town of Arrabona in Roman days, is attractive to visitors today in spite of its heavy industry. Its old core shows a strong baroque influence, and it is known for the Győr Ballet Company.

The **Székesegyhiz** (cathedral), on Martinovics tér, was founded in the 11th century, but many builders have had a hand in working on it in its long and turbulent history. In the 17th century its architects were imbued with the spirit of the baroque, but two centuries later neoclassicism was preferred. The structure suffered much damage in World War II. One of the most ancient parts of the cathedral is the Héderváry Chapel, where you'll see a masterpiece of the medieval Hungarian goldsmith's art, the reliquary of St. Ladislas. The Püspökvar (bishop's castle) also originated in the 11th century.

Also of note is the **Carmelite Church** at Köztarsaság tér (Republic Square), an early 18th-century baroque edifice. The Town Hall on Szbadság tér is a U-shaped, turreted neobaroque building.

Where to Stay

Hotel Rábá, Árpád út 34, H-9021 Győr (tel. 96/15533). You'll find yourself in the interior of a white stone-and-aluminum building that looks out over a parking lot beside a busy commercial street. Nonetheless, the interior is filled with much comfort. The restaurant on the premises has two rooms, high ceilings, modern chandeliers, and a polite staff. Hungarian dishes are served to the accompaniment of folk music. The hotel has 195 rooms, most of which have private baths. Singles cost $35 daily, and doubles $44.

Where to Dine

Vaskakas (Iron Cock), Köztársaság 2-4 (tel. 96/22655). During the Middle Ages residents of Győr used to hide under the vaults of this medieval cellar to avoid the Turkish bombardments that used to shake the city ramparts. Today one of the city's most unusual restaurants lies behind the arched façade whose entrance is marked with a statue of a rooster. In the evening the stone vaults will be pierced with the sound of Gypsy music, which echoes off the white marble floors. The tables are flanked with rustically modern chairs adapted (I was told) from a medieval design. This place stands on a baroque square near the Rába River.

The formally dressed waiters will bring well-flavored dishes laced with paprika and pickled vegetables. These include pork gulasch, a Parisian-style schnitzel, veal medallions Hungarian style, and an array of roast meats. For dessert, try not to miss the Gundel crêpes, covered with chocolate sauce and flamed in cognac at your table. Meals cost from 300 Ft. ($5) and are served daily around the clock.

Jereván Kioszk, Tolbuhin sétány 1 (tel. 96/12686). Considered more a snackbar than a traditional restaurant, this popular establishment sports brick walls, hanging lamps, and a long bar area. Menu items include foods from Armenia, Bavaria, Slovakia, and Thuringia, as well as traditional Hungarian favorites. A coffee bar with a big tree-shaded terrace is on the upper level. Meals cost from 250 Ft. ($4.25) and are served Monday to Saturday from 11am to 11pm in winter and summer. As part of the complex, the establishment operates a Chinese dining room, which also charges from 250 Ft. ($4.25) for a meal, and does so daily from noon to 11pm.

PANNONHALMA

About 13 miles southeast of Győr on Rte. 82 sits a centuries-old **Benedictine abbey and abbey church** (tel. 96/70022). This has been the center of the Benedictine order in Hungary for some 1,000 years. The first Benedictine monks came here and took up habitation on the hill site in A.D. 996, building the first stone church in 1137. Construction of the abbey began in the 13th century. It was rebuilt in baroque style during the centuries, but the foundations of the original cloisters remain, a legacy of the Árpád dynasty, which ruled the kingdom of Hungary in its infancy.

One of the most important libraries in the country is at the abbey. With 320,000 volumes laboriously assembled over the centuries, it houses a priceless object, the foundation deed of an abbey on the Tihany peninsula overlooking Lake Balaton, dating from 1055. What makes it significant is that it's the first document extant that contains Hungarian words inserted into the Latin text. The library, largest in the world in the hands of a single religious order, is adorned by 150 carved cherrywood bookcases and a balconied upper level.

The abbey church, which was transformed into a mosque when the Turks occupied Hungary, is all that remains of the early Gothic churches of the country. It was rebuilt in the 19th century on medieval foundations. The three-nave Romanesque crypt is the oldest part, dating from around 1200. It's said that the abbot's chair in the crypt contains slivers of wood from the chair used as the throne by St. Stephen, the first crowned king of Hungary. The king's coronation robes are in a glass case at the far end of the library. A bronze statue in the courtyard is of Astrik, the man who carried the crown from Pope Sylvester II in Rome to Hungary for the crowning of Stephen.

One section of the monastery, a barracks during the Turkish period, is filled with Benedictine memorabilia. There is a rich collection of paintings, including a masterpiece, *Fête in Brussels,* by David Teniers, 15th-century works by Fra Angelico, and some polychromed religious statues.

Stephanie, who was the wife of Crown Prince Rudolf of Austria when he allegedly committed suicide at Mayerling for love of another woman, is buried in the crypt here. She and her second husband came to Pannonhalma in 1945, fleeing the Russians and bearing more than 8,000 rare books and dozens of manuscripts. Before she died she willed this treasure to the monastery.

Of interest, too, are some stone carvings set into a tunnel inside the complex leading under one of the buildings. These are from the Forum in Rome, the gift of the Italian foreign minister under Mussolini. A museum displays Bronze and Stone Age implements, Roman amphorae, and ancient glass jewelry, plus some Bronze Age hair clips and bracelets, as well as a grisly collection of swords and halberds.

Today in this severe-looking complex of old and new buildings—reminiscent of Mont-Saint-Michel on its hilltop, with steeply buttressed walls looking out over a sweeping valley—some 300 students are housed, and a home for old people is maintained. Concerts are held in the basilica from spring to autumn.

The establishment is open Tuesday to Sunday from 8:30am to 4pm. The admission fee is 40 Ft. (65¢), and monastery rules require that you be accompanied by a guide, costing 200 Ft. ($3.35).

Where to Eat

Restaurant Pannonhalma, Szabadság tér 1 (tel. 96/70175), attracts visitors from all over the world to its modest precincts. It's an ideal place to visit after a tour of the monastery, and is open daily from 8am to 11pm, with meals costing from 200 Ft. ($3.35). Dishes, which are most often accompanied by Hungarian wines, are likely to include gulasch, fish soup, paprika chicken, and other traditional favorites from the Hungarian kitchen.

TATA

Before going on to Budapest, 45 miles distant, I'd like to veer south on Rte. 100 for another stopover, Tata, a well-known baroque spa town and equestrian headquarters on the shores of a lake. Called the town of old watermills and springs, Tata, once the scene of royal hunting parties, lies between the Gerecse and the Vértes mountains, with other lakes nearby. The town reached its heyday in the 15th century, with King Sigismund rebuilding the royal castle near here. The Diet met at Tata under King Matthias in 1510.

Jakob Fellner, an 18th-century architect known throughout Europe, lived and worked here for a long time and was responsible for the reconstruction of the town, with the use of baroque and rococo styles for many of the buildings. An example of his work is the parish church on Kossuth tér. The Esterházy Palace on November 7 tér was also designed by Fellner, this one in Louis XVI style.

About 1½ miles to the north of Tata is the **Fenyes spa,** where you can bathe in sulfurous, slightly radioactive spring water. The lakes of the area are popular recreation spots. A national park surrounds the lake of Tata, and a riding school here is known throughout the country.

Another historic castle, **Oregvár,** lies on the shore of a nearby lake. After destruction by both the Turks and the Habsburgs, it was reconstructed in a romantic style.

Food and Lodging

Hotel Diana, H-2890 Tata-Remetesegpuszta (tel. 34/80388), occupies the 15th-century Esterházy mansion, which since its 1971 conversion into a hotel has added a nearby annex. The building includes an angular brick-trimmed tower extending off to one side from the main building and an exterior of baroque yellow with red-tile roofs. On the premises are a first-class game restaurant serving meals from 7am to 10pm daily, a wine cellar with Gypsy music, a pizzeria, a tennis court, and dozens of walking paths. Open all year, the hotel is about 3 miles from the center of town. There are nine rooms in the manor house, all with private baths, TVs, radios, and minibars. The tourist annex has 21 rooms, all with showers; however, 7 of these don't have toilets. In the castle two persons pay $50 daily with breakfast. In the annex the charge for a double with bath is $29.

SOPRON

Lying right on the old Hungarian-Austrian border, Sopron, once the capital of the province of Burgenland, is one of the most history-rich cities of the western border region of Hungary. When the Austro-Hungarian Empire was split up after World War I, a plebiscite was taken and Sopron, then called Ödenburg, voted to be part of Hungary, while the rest of the Burgenland province chose to be part of Austria (see Chapter VI). Sopron today is one of the best-preserved cities of Hungary, with much work being carried out to protect national monuments and avoid problems with devastation from outside.

Sopron, known to the Romans as Scarbantia, is between Lake Fertö (Neusiedlerse, or Lake Neusiedl, in Austria) and the Sopron Mountain, 130 miles from Budapest, 44 miles from Vienna, and 5 miles from the Austrian frontier station, Klingenbach. It's an important holiday resort town of Hungary.

The Sights

The inner city, enclosed by the medieval city wall, has as its landmark the **Fire Tower** (Tűztorony, in Hungarian), where 125 steps take you up to an observation level. The lower part of the tower is in Romanesque style, the midsection in Renaissance, and the upper portion in baroque. Next door to the tower is a museum of Roman artifacts.

The main square of town is Fő tér, where you are literally surrounded by historic buildings. In the middle of the square is the **Trinity Column,** constructed at the beginning of the 18th century. Its three-tier spiral columns decorated with angels make it an outstanding example of Hungarian baroque sculpture. The Town Hall looks more like a national theater. On this square also is the Patika Museum, at no. 2, a pharmacy with all the old paraphernalia.

The once Gothic Benedictine **Kecske-templom,** called the Goat Church because of the goats carved into the crests on the structure, was built on the square between 1280 and 1300. Its tower is from the 14th century. The church is known for its rococo main altar and altarpieces around the pulpit.

At no. 8 on the square, the **Storno House** is a beautiful Renaissance structure built in the 15th century. A rare private collection of paintings and other treasures of the Storno family is on display here. Everybody from King Matthias to composer Franz Liszt has stayed here.

At Szent György utca 16 is **Erdődy Palace,** a flamboyant rococo-style building. Two medieval **synagogues** stand at Uj utca 11 and 22, from the 14th and 13th centuries. **St. Michael's Church,** Szentmihály út, is a Gothic building from the Middle Ages, with beautiful interior sculptures and paintings. In the churchyard at the back is the oldest building of the town, the Romanesque-Gothic St. James's Chapel, built in the mid-13th century.

The names of celebrated musicians are known here, and important events in the town's music life are connected with the name of Franz Liszt. The composer made his piano debut here as a child prodigy. Liszt fans will gravitate to the **Liszt Ferenc Museum,** Május tér 1 (First of May Square), where many fine-art and handcraft displays are on view. The museum (tel. 99/11463) also traces the history of Sopron over the years. It is open Tuesday to Sunday from 8am to 5pm, and charges an admission fee of 5 Ft. (10¢).

Two other composers of note who spent time in Sopron were Franz Joseph Haydn and Johann Strauss Jr. Haydn, who was a protégé of the Esterházy princes (see below), often stayed at what was then the White Horse Inn on the main street of

Sopron at no. 55. The street is now Lenin körút. Strauss composed a section of his *One Night in Venice* during a stay in this city.

A popular recreation area in the vicinity is the **Lővérek,** an extension of the Alps with a subalpine climate, rich in woods and pine forests. On the north shore of Lake Fertő, 5½ miles from Sopron, in the underground halls of the monumental limestone quarry at Fertorákos, classical music concerts are held and Greek tragedies performed in summer.

Good red wines are produced from grapes grown on the hills around Sopron, the best known being the Kékfrankos.

Where to Stay

Hotel Lővér, Várisi utca 4, H-9400 Sopron (tel. 99/11061). Many Austrians from across the nearby border retreat here for weekends. The hotel stands in the middle of the Sopron forest, in a modern format of several different wings extending at angles from a central core. The lobby is a sunny, high-ceilinged expanse of crafted stone and woodwork, with comfortable chairs for reading and an attentive staff ready to assist you. On the premises are a swimming pool, a fitness room, a sauna, a fine restaurant, a bar, and a sporting center with tennis courts less than a kilometer away. The hotel was recently renovated and enlarged to contain 203 bedrooms, which are furnished with simple attractive pieces and minibars. The accommodations also contain phones, radios, TVs, and private baths, with balconies opening onto the enveloping forest. Singles cost $44 daily, with doubles going for $57. Open all year, the hotel maintains a wintertime ski lift.

Hotel Palatinus, Uj utca 23, H-9400 Sopron (tel. 99/11395), presents a simple white façade to one of the city's best-preserved historic squares. The interior is a blend of modern textiles and wooden furniture. In summer a terrace offers a place to sit outdoors. The in-house restaurant is open from 7am to 11pm.

This family-style hotel has 32 basic rooms with radios and phones, but not always private baths. Singles cost $27 daily, and doubles $41.

Where to Eat

Cézar Wine-Cellar, Hátsókapu utca 3 (tel. 99/11337), dating from the 17th century, is outfitted inside with soaring vaulted ceilings, some of which are trimmed with stone, along with massive sections of an antique wine press. The menu is well known for its good selection of local wines, as well as its simple Hungarian cold foods. You'll sit on three-legged stools at tables set against the whitewashed plaster walls. You'll recognize the restaurant by its location inside a centrally located baroque building whose façade is painted a pastel green. Tabs average about 250 Ft. ($4.25), and the cellar is open daily from 10:30am to 10:30pm.

Generalis/Corvinus Complex, Fő tér 7 (tel. 99/14841), on the main square of town, is a successful joining of a coffee shop, a pizzeria, and a cellar beer bar. The original part of the establishment, the snackbar, is in a 17th-century baroque building with an inner courtyard filled with Gothic relics. The coffee shop is in the first room, while an informal restaurant with high plaster arches and a grill are toward the rear. In the famous Storno House next door, the complex has been extended to contain the pizzeria, offering Hungarian dishes as well as Italian, and the cellar bar, where guests can order specialties of the house. Meals cost from 300 Ft. ($5). The pizzeria is open daily from 10:30am to 10:30pm; the Corvinus beer cellar daily from 11am to 11pm; and the coffeeshop and snackbar, daily from 9am to 9:30pm.

Hungária Snack Bar, Lackner Kristóf utca 60 (tel. 99/14036). Just after crossing the border, many Austrian tourists profit from the attractive prices both at this warmly contemporary restaurant and at the adjacent Shell gasoline station. There's no reason why you shouldn't do the same thing. The glass building offers tourist services as well as currency exchange offices. The restaurant serves a wide variety of Hungarian and international foods in a décor of barrel chairs and hanging amber-colored lights. Meals cost from 350 Ft. ($5.75) and are served daily from 8am to 8pm.

Nightlife

The third casino in Hungary lies near the Austrian border, presumably to profit from those Viennese looking for a nearby gambling outlet. Opened in 1989, **Casino Sopron** (tel. 36/99-14475) offers French and American roulette, black jack, and slot machines. Open daily at 3pm, the casino insists that only West German marks be used as legal tender. Entrance is 10 DM ($5.75), which is immediately refunded in the form of a gambling chip. You must present your passport to enter.

FERTŐD

The major excursion from Sopron is 17 miles to the southeast to the **Esterházy Palace** (tel. 94/45971) at Fertőd. It is the most outstanding (also the most mammoth) baroque palace in the country and has been called "the Versailles of Hungary." The horseshoe-shaped palace suffered damage in World War II, since repaired. What became a 126-room imperial palace was a hunting lodge until Miklós Esterházy, a prince of the Holy Roman Empire, effected the change. Construction on the transformation started in 1760 and lasted a decade.

Visitors approach the palace through magnificent wrought-iron gates. This memorial to the opulence of other days stands in ochre-colored splendor since its restoration, with the ornate interior making noticeable the lack of furnishings of the period, the result of visits by Soviet soldiers who pillaged the palace in 1945. There are a few reminders of the finery the baroque structures once contained—fine chinoiserie panels, some old decorated stoves, and now and then a few pieces of china. The restoration of the rooms has brought back the 18th-century grandeur of gilded walls, rich paneling, and particularly the elegant floors of marble, parquet, and hardwoods in other intricate designs. (Visitors are required to put on felt overshoes to protect these floors.)

As mentioned in Chapter VI on Burgenland, Haydn was conductor for the court of the Esterházy family. When the noble court was in residence at Fertőd, the composer lived in the baroque Music House, which was part of the palace complex, conducting concerts in the three-story gilt concert hall. You can see the concert hall and Haydn's Music House, preserved as a memorial to the composer, on guided tours.

In summer, concerts are given in memory of Haydn in the baroque concert hall or in the palace gardens.

The palace is open Tuesday to Sunday from 8am to 5pm and charges an admission fee of 30 Ft. (50¢).

KŐSZEG

The old walled town of Kőszeg has been a border outpost throughout its long history, standing today only a few miles from the Austria border station of Rábafüzes. A holiday resort enjoying a subalpine climate, Kőszeg was inhabited as far back as the Avar times in the 6th and 7th centuries, long before the coming of the Magyars.

The town was often embroiled in conflicts between the armies of Austria and Hungary. Its "finest hour" came in 1532, when the people of the town staged a heroic defense against the invading Turkish hordes. The odds were, at a rough estimate, 200,000 Turks to 1,000 defenders. Kőszeg held out for some 22 days, delaying the western sweep of the Ottoman Empire, and, it is believed in these parts, thus saving Vienna. The Wellington-like hero was Capt. Miklós Jurisich. The central square of the town bears the name of the valiant captain.

Jurisich tér (Jurisich Square), once defended by walls and a watchtower, has preserved its medieval townscape to the present day. The square has a number of notable buildings, including the Town Hall and a 17th-century baroque church, St. Emerich's, as well as St. James's Church. Although St. James's dates from as recently as the 19th century, it stands on the site of an early Minorite church from the 13th century, one of the most significant Gothic historic monuments in the country. A baroque altarpiece is from 1693. There are many historic churches in Kőszeg.

The 14th-century Kőszeg castle played an important role in the battles against the Turkish invaders. It has two towers left from the Middle Ages, and the western wing has a decorative Renaissance row of windows from the 15th century. The eastern wing houses the Jurisich Miklós Museum, where you can see much weaponry, some from the 17th century, and many antiques. Over the centuries architects have used varying styles for the castle, including Gothic, Renaissance, and baroque. Reconstruction work has been under way since 1958. The castle (tel. 94/60240) is open Tuesday to Sunday from 10am to 5pm, and charges an admission fee of 10 Ft. (15¢).

Food and Lodging

Your best choice out of a limited selection is **Hotel Irottkő**, Kőztársaság tér 4, H-9730 Kőszeg (tel. 94/60373), which lies in the heart of this old-fashioned city near the principal plaza, Jurisics tér, center of the historic building district. Rooms are adequately furnished, and might be suitable for an overnight stop if you're touring in the area. There are 52 bedrooms, each with private bath or shower. Prices, including a Continental breakfast, are 1,040 Ft. ($17.25) daily for a single, rising to 1,850 Ft. ($30.75) for a double. The hotel also makes a good dining choice, as its restaurant serves an array of Hungarian regional food daily. There is also a bar.

If you'd like to find an independent restaurant, you can join dozens of visiting Austrians from across the border and head for **Bécsikapu**, Rajnis József utca 5 (tel. 94/60297). Lying in the vicinity of the previously visited castle, the restaurant offers simply prepared food, both traditional Austrian and Hungarian favorites, even pizza. Try one of the game dishes, perhaps venison or wild boar in wine sauce. You can also order Hungarian-style steaks. The restaurant has high Gothic-style windows, and an atmosphere that some visitors describe as medieval. Meals cost from 200 Ft. ($3.25), and are served daily from 9am to 10pm. Annual closing is from January 11 to 28.

SZOMBATHELY

There's been a town at the site of Szombathely on the Rába River for a long, long time. In fact this is said to be the oldest town in Hungary. It may well be, since it apparently was something more than a village when the Romans made it the capital of their province of Upper Pannonia. They called the town Savaria. It was an important trading center at the time, situated on the Amber Road, a busy trade route used by the Romans. Remnants of the road are visible in the **Garden of Ruins** discovered here in 1938.

Szombathely has yielded many archeological treasures. The Garden of Ruins mentioned above, between the present-day school and the cathedral, was named for Istvá Járdányi Paulovits, who led excavations carried out here. You can see the remains of the one-time imperial palace with its 20-yard mosaic floor, a significant relic of 4th-century Pannonia. The Basilica of St. Quirinus was the largest Christian building in Pannonia.

The **Isis shrine,** on Rákóczi út, is the largest sanctuary of the Isis cult, a religion of Egyptian origin, unearthed in Pannonian territory. It was restored in the 1960s. Every August opera performances are presented at the shrine, and there's a small museum here of Roman artifacts.

Caesar Palace, Alkotmany utca 1-15, is in the center of the old Roman city of Savaria. The rebuilt ruins with mosaic pavements are from the 4th century.

On a more recent note, a Franciscan church on Savaria tér was rebuilt in the baroque style in the 17th and 18th centuries. The Dominican church on Talbuhin út is a baroque structure dating from about 1670, its interior being from the 17th and 18th centuries.

The **cathedral** on Berzsenyi Dániel tér, one of the most significant Louis XVI–style buildings in Hungary, can hold 5,000 worshippers. Construction on it began at the end of the 18th century, and heavy damage was inflicted in a U.S. Air Force bombing raid in 1945. However, it has been restored.

The largest town in western Transdanubia, Szombathely is one of the main tourist centers of West Hungary. It's 138 miles from Budapest and 12½ miles from Kőszeg, just visited.

On the northern edge of this city lies the village of Kámon, where you can visit the **Arboretum** with its 2,000 shrubs and trees, including a rose garden with flowers named for such "goddesses" as Sophia Loren.

WHERE TO STAY

Hotel Claudius, Bartók Béla körút 39, H-9700 Szombathely (tel. 94/13760), in the center of the resort, has evenly spaced rows of curved borders encircling the big glass windows of the five-floor façade. Each of the 97 comfortable rooms has its own balcony, a view of the surrounding park area, as well as a décor that tries vaguely to evoke the region's connections with ancient Rome. On the premises are two restaurants, a coffee shop, and a nightclub. The rooms are equipped with minibars, baths, phones, and radios; a few have TVs. Tennis courts and a sauna are on the premises. Singles go for $47 daily, with doubles costing $49.

Hotel Isis, Rákóczi utca 1, H-9700 Szombathely (tel. 94/14990), rises like a streamlined cube from its location in the heart of town, near the site of the Isis shrine. Its glass-covered façade is accented with wide black bands stretching horizontally across the front, while the entryway is under a heavy concrete parapet built off to one side. The simple and colorful interior contains a bar, a restaurant with Gypsy music, and a coffee shop that doubles as a disco in the evening. The hotel rents 72 comfortable bedrooms, costing $22 daily for a single, $36 for a double.

Hotel Savaria, Máritírok tére 4, H-9700 Szombathely (tel. 94/11440). Its name derives from the ancient Latin name of the town surrounding it. Originally built in 1912, the hotel is imbued with a unique form of art nouveau that only Hungary produced. After years of neglect, the building was renovated and reopened in 1985 in an upgraded format of contemporary bedrooms and streamlined public rooms. Most of the 90 comfortably furnished bedrooms contain TVs, radios, and private baths. Singles with baths cost $47 daily, with doubles costing $49.

Where to Eat

Most visitors pass through here on a day trip and therefore won't need a hotel, but a good restaurant might be in order. Try **Kispityer Halászcsárda,** Rumi út 18 (tel. 94/11227), about 10 minutes from the center of town. Its summer terrace is a magnet in fair weather, especially for visiting Austrians. The establishment is known widely for its way with fresh fish, all of which are caught in Hungarian waters. You might try, for example, a fish soup made from local carp, followed by pike-perch (the famous Hungarian fogas), even salmon. At least 100 different dishes make up the menu, the house specialty being the Kispityer plate, consisting of fogas, frogs' legs, medallions of pork, escargots, and tender goose liver. Meals cost from 225 Ft. ($3.75) to 300 Ft. ($5), and are served daily from 11am to 11pm. Gypsy music is provided in the evening from 6 to 11pm.

Excursion to Ják

Some 10 miles southwest of Szombathely is the abbey church of Ják, a masterpiece of Hungarian Romanesque architecture and one of the oldest churches in the country. It was built in the first half of the 13th century as a church with basilica-type nave and aisles. Two towers flank its façade, and rich sculptures decorate the portal. Visits are Monday to Saturday from 9am to 6pm. Admission is 20 Ft. (35¢).

SPA HOTELS IN THE WEST

Nestled among the trees of an arboretum, **Thermal Hotel Sárvár,** Rákóczi utca 1, H-9600 Sárvár (tel. 96/16088), offers easy access to Nádasdy Castle. It lies on the road between Sopron and Lake Balaton. The hotel was built on the site of a pair of thermal springs, which bubble out of the ground nearby. To take advantage of this, a complete spa facility was designed, including all the massage and hydrotherapy treatments believed to be helpful for gynecological and respiratory disorders. The property contains 136 rooms, each of which has its own balcony, private bath, phone, color TV, and radio. Singles cost $43 to $53 daily, with doubles running from $64 to $74. The hotel has both a bar and a restaurant, serving Hungarian specialties. Full meals cost around $8.

Thermal Hotel Bük, H-9740 Bük (tel. 94/58500). The elevated mineral content of the very deep springs of Bük was the motivation that Danubius Hotels needed to erect this modern spa facility in 1986, containing a superb fitness center with a swimming pool and thermal baths. Its waters are considered healthy for digestive and respiratory ailments, as well as for rheumatism. The establishment contains 200 bedrooms, each of which has a private bath, balcony, phone, radio, minibar, and color TV with in-house video. The Roman and baroque monuments of Ják and Szombathely, as well as the medieval attractions of Kőszeg, are nearby. The well-furnished and comfortable accommodations go for $58 (single) and $84 (double). Full meals are priced from $11. The hotel contains a first-class restaurant with a terrace and a bar, along with a nightclub and game room. Bük is 15½ miles from the Austrian border, about 35½ miles from the Transdanubian city of Sopron.

4. Southwest Hungary

The Celts liked it, the Romans liked it, and through the centuries Southwest Hungary, once a part of the Roman province of Pannonia, has been a plum that numerous territory-hungry plunderers have tried to gobble up. The vicissitudes of war and migration have left their mark on the area. The Magyars came here too, when they moved westward and took over a broad swath of what is now Hungary. However, during the Turkish conquest the Hungarian population dwindled, and Yugoslavs and Germans settled in the region in the 17th century. After World War II, Moldavians and Slovakian Hungarians moved in.

To this day a significant number of the inhabitants here speak German, with people of other nationalities and ethnic groups using the language and carrying on the traditions and folk art of their ancestors. You can see how the colorful Sárköz embroidery with its many motifs is produced and visit the folk art cottages in Decs and Sióagard. In Bátaszék and Ófalu, German folk art predominates, while in South Baranya, a section of Southwest Hungary, women still weave Yugoslavian designs. Presbyterian churches in Kóros, Kovácshida, and Drávaivány have fine examples of Ormánság folk art.

The Mecsek region of Southwest Hungary, lying mainly to the south of Lake Balaton, has one of the mildest climates in the country. Rivers and streams slice the terrain, and the shores of its lakes and the depths of the woodlands are quiet and serene. Many Yugoslavs view Mecsek as their vacationland.

Southwest Hungary is a good place to sample dishes from a cookery that is a result of many ethnic specialties.

PÉCS

The Mecsek region is the site of my favorite provincial city in all of Hungary, Pécs, the largest city in the district and fourth largest in the country, 123 miles from Budapest. Its warm climate gives it a Mediterranean aura.

Pécs is 2,000 years old, although that hasn't always been its name. The Romans built a town on the slopes of the Mecsek mountain, naming it Sopianae and using it as the capital of eastern Pannonia province. This area was ruled by the Romans for four centuries. By the time the Magyars appeared in Transdanubia, the town was no longer called Sopianae but was referred to in a 9th-century document as "Quinque Basilicae," the town of five churches. It's believed that the churches alluded to were really memorial chapels from Roman times.

The Sights

The oldest architectural relics of Pécs are the 4th-century **tombs** found in the Roman cemetery whose center is where Cathedral Square (Dom tér) was built in the Middle Ages. Some of the tombs are frescoed vaults with chapels erected over them. Those on the higher ground of the Mecsek slopes which survived the Dark Ages probably looked like churches to travelers approaching the city. Evidence has been found of four of these chapels for which this must have been true. An entrance has been opened in the eastern buttress of the Dom tér so that you can see one of the wall-painted chapel crypts, the decoration of which shows that it was the burial place of a Roman Christian family. The town's atmosphere today shows a heavy influence of Mediterranean culture, and the only other similar painted crypts are in Italy. The tombs are open daily except Monday from 10am to 6pm, charging an admission fee of 20 Ft. (35¢).

In the Middle Ages the city walls of Pécs encircled a larger area than that of contemporary Vienna. One of the most valuable medieval historic monuments in Hungary is the four-spired Romanesque **cathedral,** founded in the 11th century by St. Stephen, the country's first king, in the Dom tér. It has since seen many rebuilders and restorers, but the spatial concept has been preserved through the centuries. The five-nave undercroft is part of the original construction. The spire-capped towers date from the 11th and 12th centuries. The cathedral is rich in frescoes and carvings by outstanding Hungarian ecclesiastical artists. During Turkish rule, 1543–1686, the cathedral was turned into a mosque and storehouse, a stain removed when the area was returned to Christian sovereignty.

The **bishop's palace** stands on the west side of the Cathedral Square, near where Christian catacombs were found. This palace originated in the Middle Ages but received its present look in the mid-19th century.

The first university in Hungary, founded in Pécs in 1367, made the town a citadel of humanism in the 15th century, a situation that was greatly changed by the Turkish occupation. After a 17-year siege the followers of Mohammed moved in as rulers in 1543, staying for 143 years and leaving their indelible mark on Pécs. The main square of the town, Széchenyi tér, is a curious cultural mélange, with many historic buildings of varying provenance.

Here you'll see the **Pasha Kasim Mosque,** the largest building in Hungary from the Turkish era, now used as the inner-city parish church. Its minaret was demolished in the 18th century. Restorers of the mosque have uncovered some of the calligraphy on the walls, but a crucifix now occupies the former Muslim mihrab, or prayer niche. Charging no admission, the mosque is open daily from 6am to 8pm.

Also on this square is the archeological collection of the **Janus Pannonius Museum.** In seven rooms of exhibits, you see artifacts dating from the Stone Age to the Magyar takeover of the country in the 9th century. The glass cases of the museum, named for the 15th-century humanist scholar and renowned poet Janus Pannonius, occupy five other buildings in the town besides the one on Széchenyi tér. The museum is open Tuesday to Sunday from 10am to 4pm. Price of admission is 20 Ft. (35¢). For information, telephone 72/24822 and ask for the museum.

All visitors to Pécs will want to see the **Eosin Fountain,** symbol of the town, in front of the one-time Ignorantine Church dating from the 1720s. This fountain was donated by the well-known Zsolnay Porcelain Factory, founded here in 1870. A **Zsolnay Museum** with 8,500 items on display occupies the oldest house in Pécs, a former private home at Káptalan utca 2 from pre-Turkish days. The house survived the Muslim occupation because it was chosen by the Turkish chief mufti as his private quarters. Displays in the museum include what may well be the most sophisticated porcelains in Central Europe, plus ceramic sculptures, pottery, and tiles. The museum is open Tuesday to Sunday from 10am to 6pm. Admission is 10 Ft. (15¢). For information, dial 72/24822 and ask for the museum.

You can see the only surviving mosque-minaret combination in Hungary at the **Yakovali Hasan Mosque,** built in the 16th century and now housing a museum. The mosque has been restored to its original atmosphere, and the museum shows a cross section of life and culture of the Hungarian Turkish period. You'll see a collection concerning the life of dervishes who had a monastery nearby. After the Turks were driven out in 1686, Bishop Nesselrode had the mosque rebuilt (1702–1732) for use as a chapel and hospital. The mosque is open Thursday to Tuesday (closed Wednesday) from 10am to 6pm, and charges an admission fee of 20 Ft. (35¢).

All Saints Church, Tettye utca, built on the Tettye plateau outside the city walls, survived the Turk occupation. Constructed as a one-nave Romanesque church in 1157, it was given three naves in a 15th-century restoration.

Art-lovers will seek out the **Tivadar Csontváry Museum,** Janus Pannonius utca 11 (tel. 72/10544). Here you can see the works of this internationally acclaimed artist—the "Rousseau of the Danube"—Tuesday to Sunday from 10am to 6pm for an admission fee of 20 Ft. (35¢). Much of the world became acquainted with the paintings of this artist at the Paris World's Fair. Works by other Hungarian artists are also displayed.

Some works by Hungary's most celebrated modern artist are displayed in the **Vasarely Museum,** Káptalan utca 3 (tel. 72/24822; ask for the museum). It is open Tuesday to Sunday from 10am to 6pm, charging an admission fee of 10 Ft. (15¢). The works of Victor Vasarely, who was born in this house, show him to be one of the founding fathers of kinetic art and a pop-art practitioner.

Pécs is an important cultural center of Hungary, with a summer theater program in July, including opera, ballet, pantomine, drama, and concerts.

A short journey will take you to the Tettye plateau, from which the road leads through the Mecsekkapu (gateway of the Mecsek) to a zoo and pioneer railway, then up to Missinatető, where the **television tower** is a major attraction. You can take an elevator to its lookout terrace and café, from which you have a magnificent view of the Mecsek, the city of Pécs, and the Zsolnay eosin-tiled roof of the post office, and even as far as to the fortress of Siklós (see below) and Harkány, a thermal resort. For information about the tower, telephone 72/12044. From April to October, the tower is open daily from 9:30am to 8pm. Off-season, it's open Tuesday to Sunday from 11am to 6pm. Admission is 30 Ft. (50¢).

Where to Stay

Hotel Palatinus, Kossuth Lajos út, H-7621 Pécs (tel. 72/330220), provides among the finest accommodations in Pécs. Rooms are modern, well maintained, and comfortable. You don't get grand style here, but you'll probably get a good night's sleep. In the 88 rooms (with private baths) guests are housed for $44 daily in a double and $42 in a single. You can dine in the formal restaurant, serving some of the best food in town for 300 Ft. ($5) and up, or else less expensively in the beerhall for 150 Ft. ($2.50). Also available are bowling facilities and a sauna.

Hotel Hunyor, Furisics Miklós utca 16, H-7624 Pécs (tel. 72/15677), is a two-star hotel that would have three stars if it had an in-house restaurant. A quick visit, however, reveals that this is only a technicality, since a pleasant restaurant run by another company lies only a few steps away (see "Where to Dine"). Thus, because of this bureaucratic requirement, you get one of the least-publicized hotel values in Hungary. A short distance from the center of town, the Hunyor stands on a hillside, its foundations tapering gracefully upward to terraces. The building, which opened in 1984, is covered with white ceramic tiles. It is clean and modern, its staff personable. Each of its 53 accommodations has a private bath, southern exposure, radio, and an open-air balcony or terrace. Several units offer minibars, and most have glistening wood floors. Singles or doubles cost 1,300 Ft. ($21.75) to 1,900 Ft. ($31.75) daily, with suites going for 1,800 Ft. ($30) to 2,600 Ft. ($43), including breakfast. A bar and TV lounge are near the lobby.

Hotel Pannónia, Rákóczi út 3, H-7621 Pécs (tel. 72/13322), is a three-star hotel lying a mile from the railway station. Its jutting porch is angled into a series of zigzag lines that are repeated in the design of the decorative tiles on each of the balconies. Inside, it has 108 bedrooms, all doubles with private baths, costing $53 a night. Built in 1976, the hotel also has a restaurant serving well-prepared Hungarian dishes. Other facilities include a night bar and terrace, and there is free admission for hotel guests to a nearby swimming pool.

Hotel Fönix, Hunyadi út 2, H-7621 Pécs (tel. 72/11680). Built in 1985, and now owned by an insurance company, this hotel is small, with 14 functional but comfortable bedrooms. It lies on an old street near the center amid 18th-century ochre-walled villas. An iron cut-out of the hotel's symbol, a phoenix, juts out from one corner. Its exterior incorporates puzsta-inspired Magyar themes into its modern stucco and brickwork for an attractively updated twist. Each of the bedrooms has a shower and a sink, but only one has a toilet. Those on the uppermost floors, near the opening of the massive chimneys, have slanted ceilings and sloping skylights. Doubles are 1,810 Ft. ($30.75) daily and singles 1,310 Ft. ($22.25). To register, guests ascend a spiral staircase from the street-level entrance whose décor motifs were inspired by Hungarian art nouveau themes. There's no formal restaurant on the premises, but a pizzeria next door is a popular meeting place for the city's youth.

Where to Dine

Elefánts Ház Étterem/Elefánt Söröző (The Elephant), Jókai tér 4-6 (tel. 72/13449), is the most historic restaurant in Pécs, and also, in the opinion of some, the best. In 1669, after the Turks were driven out, it was constructed as a blacksmith's shop. In 1830 the street-level arches and the second story were added, the place hosting balls and fêtes of the town's bourgeoisie. In the 1850s someone added a shop selling difficult-to-obtain luxuries. But then it fell into dusty neglect, but was reopened in 1984. Almost immediately it became the most popular dining place in town. The location is a short block from the main square on a historic street whose ancient buildings are enhanced with the statues of the elephant jutting out over their front entrances.

A café and a wine bar lie to the left and right of the entrance. Visitors looking for more substantial fare head to the top of a wide stone staircase facing the entrance. There, a team of tuxedo-clad waiters offer you a table in the high-ceilinged restaurant. Food is served Monday to Saturday from noon to midnight, on Sunday from noon to 4pm. Full meals cost from 300 Ft. ($5), and the menu includes such choices as caviar with butter, stuffed cabbage, paprika salad, cheese and noodle casserole, and pan-fried slices of goose liver.

Szőlőskert Étterem, Kisszkókó utca 3 (tel. 72/15886), lies within a separate annex a few steps downhill from the previously recommended Hotel Hunyor. Built as a glass-sided octagon, with big windows and lots of exposed wood, it might have been perched on the ski slope of an alpine resort. But regional weavings, Gypsy music, and paprika-laden specialties give it Hungarian flair. A member of a nationwide chain, this place prides itself on its reasonable prices and good food. You can order such dishes as sautéed chicken, grilled pork cutlets, beefsteak, and Hungarian sausage grilled inside a portion of mutton. Dessert might be crêpes Gundel. Meals cost from 200 Ft. ($3.25), and food is served Monday to Saturday from noon to 11pm, on Sunday from noon to 3pm.

Bástya Söröző, Landler Jenö utca 12 (tel. 72/11706), owned and operated by a local brewery, is another good choice. Its vaulted ceiling and thick masonry walls nestle in the oldest part of the foundations of the medieval fortress (the Var) of Pécs. A musician dispels some of the cavelike ambience with cheery music that emanates from one corner. You dine at trestle tables on such Hungarian specialties as gulasch stew Bástya style, bierbraten, pork schnitzel imperial style, ham schnitzel with brains, and creamed noodles with bacon. Full meals, served from noon to 11pm, cost from 200 Ft. ($3.25). Naturally, the preferred beverage is the excellent beer of the brewer owners, but an array of Hungarian wines is also available.

Dom Vendéglő, Kossuth Lajos utca 3-5 (tel. 72/10732). The unlikely-looking covered alleyway leading up to this restaurant empties into one of the main square's most important arteries. Swinging doors open to reveal a very popular restaurant whose tables are scattered amid a sturdy timber framework that forms a room-size miniature of the Pécs cathedral. Spreading over the entire room is one of the most beautiful ceilings in Pécs. Go here for either a drink or a meal. Specialties include a variety of fish, beef, pork, and poultry dishes, all prepared in the Hungarian style. Full meals cost from 150 Ft. ($2.50). Fixed-price lunches are a bargain at 60 Ft. ($1). The restaurant is open daily from 11am to 10pm, with the fixed-price lunches served Monday to Friday from noon to 3pm.

Minaret Étterem, Szalai utca 1 (tel. 72/13322), is reached by going through a labyrinth of stairs and hallways. The restaurant lies in the basement of a centuries-old monastery, which, after the advent of socialism, was converted into a low-cost but run-down hotel—understandably not recommended. But its restaurant offers good food and about the least expensive prices in town. You dine at trestle tables on hard wooden benches while looking at photos of turn-of-the-century Pécs. From May 1 to September tables are placed in a garden. A fixed-price menu is offered for only 60 Ft. ($1), but regular à la carte meals start at 200 AS ($3.25). Menu items include dill soup, deer ragoût in rice, two varieties of fish soup, filet of carp, and ham-flavored risotto. Open daily noon to 10pm.

On the Outskirts

Kastély Fogadó (Castle Inn), Üszögpuszta, H-7601 Pécs (tel. 72/10311), lies 3 miles southeast of Pécs, amid rolling farmland and good horse-breeding country. To reach it, you pass through imperial-looking gates and a bronze statue of a pair of battling stallions. The sprawling ochre-colored villa was built at the end of the 18th century by some of the most famous Hungarian patriots of their day, the Batthyány family. Today the hotel and its annexes contain 21 year-round rooms, all with baths, supplemented in summer with 5 outlying bungalows. Two persons, depending on their room assignment, can pay anywhere from 1,000 Ft. ($16.75) to 2,260 Ft. ($37.75) a night. Frankly, only a smattering of the place's original grandeur has remained after several modernizations, but many guests view this as an affordable and accessible country inn for the passage of a quiet weekend.

On the premises is a spacious and sun-flooded restaurant, outfitted with modern furniture and a high ceiling. Full meals, costing from 500 Ft. ($8.25), are served daily from 7am to 9pm. Menu specials include pork schnitzels, several preparations of chicken, game-filled crêpes, and fried cheese with rice and tartar sauce. In season, game dishes are offered.

Excursion to Mohács

One of Hungary's largest river docks is on the Danube in the Baranya County town of Mohács, about 25 miles west-southwest of Pécs, where the Hungarians lost a bloody battle against the Turks in 1526. This was a prelude to the 143-year occupation of the country, dating from 1543. You can see the **Mohács Historical Garden of Monuments** with carved grave posts and wooden statues.

Medieval times are brought back to life here each year with springtime festivals called *busójárás,* which originated from the Sokác Slavonic ethnic group.

SIKLÓS

The fortress town of Siklós, about 20 miles south of Pécs, is another settlement dating back to Roman times. It lies in Villány, the major wine-producing district of Southwest Hungary. The fortified castle, built here after the Mongol invasion of 1241, escaped the fate of other such castles in the country, which ended as ruins. This remnant of the Middle Ages, **Siklós Fortress** (Siklós Var) was remodeled somewhat in the 15th century and then was almost in ruins in 1686, when the Turks abandoned it. It was given by the Austrian emperor to one of his generals, who re-built it in the 18th century and installed his coat-of-arms above the narrow entranceway leading up a hill into the inner courtyard. The 18th-century look was retained in a 1969 restoration.

Aside from a hotel built into one of the oldest parts and an underground restaurant (see my hotel and restaurant recommendations, below), the fortress has an unusual church, a torture chamber, a summer café on the ramparts, a museum, and a gift shop.

The austere chapel is the only intact Gothic structure in south Transdanubia. You'll see a "web net" ceiling of chiseled stone ribs and a private balcony leading directly into the living quarters of the lord and lady of the castle. The holy water near the chapel door is contained in a basin that the occupying Turks also used as a font. Near the entrance is a gift shop, selling handmade jewelry, textiles, and a striking variety of black porcelain with flowers done in shiny black paint against a black matte background. In summer you may hear Gregorian chants emanating from a recording played in the chapel.

Once you're inside the castle, look for a small wooden door braced with iron that leads down to the torture chamber, equipped with uniquely Hungarian instruments of torture. In another underground cellar that used to house the guards who defended Siklós, locals operate the restaurant described below. The living quarters of the noble owners can be visited. You can almost circumnavigate the ramparts in good weather, looking out over the vineyards surrounding this ancient brick and stone stronghold.

The most memorable woman to live here as lady of Siklós Var was Dorothy Kanizsai, who is much celebrated in Hungarian legend. It was she who took on the grisly and unhappy task of burying the dead after the disastrous battle of nearby Mohács in 1526, when the Turks slaughtered the Hungarian troops. With a handful of serfs helping, she laid to rest the bloodied bodies of the Hungarian dead in the graveyard at Satorhely, today a memorial park (see above). It's open from 9am to 6pm April 1 to October 30 (closes at 4pm in winter), charging 20 Ft. (35¢) admission. The fortress is closed on Monday. For information, telephone 73/11433.

Siklós hosts an annual ceramic symposium and exhibition, Castle Festival and Brass Band meetings, and a summer cultural program.

Food and Lodging

Hotel Tenkes, Siklós Fortress, H-7800 Siklós (tel. 72/270), is built into the stone superstructure of the castle itself. The entrance through the courtyard leads into an airy, stone-floored lobby with a high ceiling and a riserless stairway climbing to the rooms of the upper floors. Many of these ring the exterior wall of the fortress, offering views of the ramparts and the vineyards beyond. The 27 bedrooms are attractively simple, almost beautifully severe. Many of them have 15-foot ceilings, stucco walls, big closets, and lots of plants. Some of the larger rooms have interior stairwells leading to sleeping lofts. A single room goes for 1,050 Ft. ($17.50), a double for 1,400 Ft. ($23.25). Each of the rooms has a private bath.

Guests of the hotel are allowed to patronize the Restaurant Tenkes, where meals cost from 350 Ft. ($5.75). The guard quarters used to be under the vaults of this brick-and-stucco cellar with a red stone floor. Today it's a restaurant where Hungarian specialties are served on green-and-white Herend china. Gypsy music plays every evening to an appreciative crowd of local community members and visiting tourists. Open daily noon to 2:30pm and 6 to 10pm.

SZEKSZÁRD

This is the capital of the county of Tolna, which is about 95 miles from Budapest and almost 40 miles from Pécs in Southwest Hungary, its eastern border formed by the Danube River. People have inhabited the site of Szekszárd for many centuries. The Roman town of Alisca sat on what is now Béla tér (Bela Square), where King Béla I established a Benedictine abbey in 1061. Romans ruins are on view here.

The County Hall on Béla tér is worth seeing. It was built between 1828 and 1832 in the classical style. Interesting houses stand on Geray tér. The archeological and ethnographical collections at the Béri Bologh Adám Museum are particularly rich.

The hill region around Szekszárd and Bálazék, another Tolna County town, produces some excellent wines, the best known of which are red Kadarka, Bull's Blood, and Cabernet.

Food and Lodging

Hotel Gemenc, Mészáros Lázár utca 1, H-7100 Tolna (tel. 74/11722), is a modern balconied hotel built out of reinforced concrete and glass. A minute's walk from the center of town, it offers comfortably simple bedrooms and a big sunny restaurant with stone floors, black-tile accents, and an impressive collection of hunting trophies. The hotel has 92 bedrooms, 88 of which are doubles (the other 4 are suites). Each of these has a private bath, balcony, and radio. A double for one person costs $31 daily, whereas two persons are charged $43. The hotel also has an array of drinking and dining facilities, including a 250-seat restaurant and a beer garden. Also on the premises are an ice-cream garden, a confectionery, a drinks bar, and a nightclub.

Excursions

The **Sötét Valley,** between the townships of Szekszárd and Kakasd, is a nature reserve of 2,471 acres, with footpaths, benches, and a rowing pond, a popular spot for quiet and relaxation.

The **Gemenci Forest,** 8 miles from Szekszárd, is a national nature reserve situated in a former flood area of the Danube called Sárköz. In the 25,000 acres is almost every species of Hungary's birds and wild animals, as well as grass and leafy trees. Rare animals can be seen in their natural habitat or at the Hunter's Lodge. Guided tours, with English commentary, of the game reserve are possible from Szekszárd in summer, going by miniature railway or by boat on the backwaters of the Danube. Trips are arranged by the county tourist office.

DECS

The biggest village in the Sárköz, Decs (don't confuse it with Pécs, a city), is known for its **Sárközi tájház,** Kossuth út 35, a combination museum and cooperative crafts store in the middle of a farm community. Here you can purchase local crafts products, especially hand-woven materials.

The museum contains artifacts that would have been in a puszta farmer's house 100 years ago. It includes a collection of small, thick-walled rooms filled with furniture, photos of poker-faced wedding couples in all their hand-embroidered finery, cooking utensils, decorative national costumes, and pottery.

You can visit every day except Monday from 10am to noon and 1 to 6pm, but this place isn't easy to find—the entrance is on a bleak street and isn't very distinctive.

KALOCSA

About 4 miles east of the Danube, lying to the northeast of Szekszárd, is Kalocsa, the folkloric capital of Hungary, noted for its paprika and its "painting women," who are especially known for their wall painting. In fact, Kalocsa has a **Paprika Museum** (a first for me!), on the Marx tér, across from an open-air fruit and vegetable market. The tiny museum traces the history of paprika farming and the process by which it is turned from a vegetable into the spicy red powder.

The historic heart of the town, which was rebuilt in the 18th century, is Szabadság tér, where you'll see a baroque cathedral from the time of the rebuilding, the fourth house of worship on that spot. A three-story archbishop's palace is also on the square.

One of the interesting sights in town is the **Károly Viski Museum** at István út. In various rooms, the life of the region around Kalocsa is re-created. Of more recent vintage is the **Nicholas Schöffer Memorial House,** created in the birthplace of the well-known artist.

If it's folklore you came here for, head for the **Kalocsa Folk Art Cooperative,** which has both a small museum with farm implements and antiques, and a gift shop selling the renowned pottery and flower-embellished embroidery of the area.

---

5. The Great Plain and Puszta

Hungary's Great Plain and puszta region takes up about half the country, beginning almost at the outskirts of Budapest and reaching the frontiers of Yugoslavia and Romania. The Tisza River divides the plain, a nearly flat expanse that is considered the most typical Hungarian landscape—or at least the best known.

This is a land of legend, celebrated in poetry and song. It's known for its *csikós,* or riders, of the Great Plain and their magnificent horses. In the puszta areas you can get glimpses of ancient Hungarian shepherd traditions. Many of the sleepy little villages are still living happily in the past, enjoying the untouched simplicity of peasant life.

In days of yore the Great Plain was almost like the American prairie, a wild, untamed land, except that back then it consisted mainly of swamplands and puszta. The sand of the plain was driven by the wind for centuries, until the peasants tied it down with acacias and made it fertile. Now vineyards grow on the reclaimed acres, and cattle graze on meadowland.

Two major routes are followed in the exploration of the plain—one southwest to Szeged, going via Kecskemét, and the other directly to the east of Budapest all the way to Debrecen, not too far from the Romanian border.

KECSKEMÉT

Once a quiet farm town, Kecskemét has been irrevocably altered by progress. For a long time the town was charmingly intact (and much of it still is), as it was never bombed in any war, although it did suffer many medieval fires. During recent years the single-story houses of the old town have been replaced by modern housing estates, and industry has gained a leading role in the town's economy. Two squares —Kossuth tér and Szabadság tér—join to form the core of the town. In the center of the region between the Danube and Tisza rivers, 53 miles southeast of Budapest, Kecskemét was a settlement at the time of the Magyar invasion of Hungary in the late 9th century.

The Sights

There's still much of the old town to be seen, including three churches opening onto Kossuth tér. Oldest is the **Franciscan church,** which has wall pillars dating from the 13th to the 15th centuries. It was later remodeled in the baroque style. The **Calvinist** (Protestant) **church** is from the 17th century. The **"Old Church,"** a neo-classical Catholic house of worship, was begun in 1774. A synagogue, built in 1862 in Neo-Byzantine style on Szabadság tér, is now occupied by the House of Technology.

Kecskemét was the native town of the 20th-century composer Zoltán Kodály, who pioneered in the field of music education. The International Kodály Seminar is held here every two years (in the odd years) at the beginning of August. The **Zoltán Kodály Institute of Music Education** is housed in the former monastery of Franciscan friars.

Late in the 19th century Hungary wanted to create a typically Hungarian architectural style, and a countrywide competition was held. The winning design was what you see today at the three-story **Town Hall,** a style designated Hungarian art nouveau or Hungarian Secessionist. This gaudily painted, vaulted fantasy has dozens of architectural details, many incorporating Kecskemét's symbol of a standing goat, but the structure looks more Gothic Revival than anything else. The ceremonial hall on the second floor, used now for an occasional wedding ceremony, is graced with frescoes done by Bertalan Székely in 1896. The entire room is covered with peasant-inspired designs in beige, pink, and green pastels. From the ceiling hangs what may be the most magnificent chandelier you'll see in Hungary.

Another building of the Hungarian Secessionist school of architecture is **Cifrapalota** (Cifra Palace), Rákóczi út 1 (tel. 76/21776), where the **Kecskemét Gallery** is to be found. A significant collection of Hungarian art of the 19th and 20th centuries is exhibited, along with works of art of Menyhért Tóth (1904–80). Contemporary and historical materials are the subjects of temporary exhibits. The gallery is open in summer Tuesday to Sunday from 10am to 5pm. In winter it is open Thursday, Friday, Saturday, and Sunday from 10am to 5pm. Admission is 10 Ft. (15¢).

The **József Katona Museum** (tel. 76/21281) is named for the playwright who was born in Kecskemét. Today it houses a rich local, historical, archeological, and ethnic collection. It is open Tuesday to Sunday from 10am to 1pm and 2 to 5pm. It shuts down from mid-December to March. Admission is 10 Ft (15¢) except on Thursday, when it is free. **Theater Katona József,** also honoring the native son who died in 1967, is used for concerts and plays. It's baroque yellow with a red-tile roof and has decorative urns on its corners. Michael York has performed here, and filmmakers have for decades used it for scenes in movies, including *The Phantom of the Opera.* It was used in the European TV series on the lives of Berlioz and Wagner, in which Richard Burton played Wagner.

You might want to go shopping in Kecskemét, and I recommend trying the Hungarian Intourist shop, the Zoltán Kodály book and music store, and the Amphora glassware, china, and ceramics emporium for good buys. Of course, there are lots of souvenir shops throughout the town. Kecskemét is in the center of an apricot-growing region that turns out one of the most celebrated of all Hungarian drinks, barack, an apricot brandy you may want to sample and take home.

Where to Stay

Hotel Aranyhomok, Széchenyi tér 3, H-6000 Kecskemét (tel. 76/20011), is a six-floor rectangular hotel in the center of town near the yellow baroque church. In Hungarian its name means "Golden Sands." If you're sightseeing you might want to stop for a snack in the ground-level café. On the premises is an upstairs bar with a solid wall of stained glass, plus a nearby two-level restaurant with enormous windows, lots of plants, Gypsy music, and a slanted ceiling studded with chrome detailing and hanging lamps that look vaguely Chinese.

Menu items include fried filets of goose liver, medallions of pork Hungarian style, Russian salad, crêpes stuffed with pork and served with a paprika sauce, Hungarian beef stew in red wine, and a dessert that might be crêpes Gundel or a strudel. You can eat a full meal for 350 Ft. ($5.75). Each of the 103 rooms (all doubles) is balconied and contains a phone and radio. Those with private baths also have refrigerators. Doubles go for $45.50 nightly.

Három Gúnár Fogadó (The Three Geese), Batthyány út 7, H-6000 Kecskemét (tel. 76/27077), behind a baroque façade in the center of town, was originally built in the late 1800s as a private villa. In 1986 it opened as one of the most appealing hotels in Kecskemét after a nearby chicken-producing communal farm and the country tourist board purchased the property jointly. Accommodations include color TVs, minibars, and phones, and several units have sloping ceilings, adding to the coziness. A modern extension was added. Today the hotel has 45 comfortably furnished rooms, 7 with private baths and the rest with showers. Singles cost 1,800 Ft. ($30) daily, doubles go for 2,200 Ft. ($36.75). Other facilities include a bowling alley in the cellar, and a drinks bar open until 2am.

Where to Dine

Három Gúnár Fogadó, Batthyány út 7 (tel. 76/27077), is a popular and decent modern restaurant, the hipped roof of which vaguely reflects the baroque lines of the 18th-century villa that houses its sister, a hotel (see "Where to Stay"). The all-glass walls of the restaurant offer views of the rear of some of Kecskemét's most imposing buildings. In summer the gardens come alive, and you can order some goose cracklings, which go well with the beer and wine served in liberal quantities. Specialties include a goose platter (for two diners), chicken Kiev, chicken livers with game sauce and bread dumplings, roast duck with tangerine, and gizzard stew with gnocchi. Meals cost from 250 Ft. ($4.25). Open Monday to Friday and on Sunday from 6:30 to 11pm, and on Saturday from 6:30pm to midnight. The place lies about two blocks from the town theater.

Kis-Bugaci Csárda, Munkácsy utca 10 (tel. 76/24174), is one of the most authentic puszta-style restaurants around, but it's in the heart of Kecskemét. It lies about a 10-minute walk north of the town center on a sidestreet off the Lugossy István utca, running into the main road to Budapest. Students from the Kodály Music Institute are among the most frequent visitors to this place. The csárda was established some 40 years ago in a low-slung white-walled villa containing four different dining areas, each partially filled with puszta weavings and stuffed birds from the Great Plain. In warm weather, diners enjoy an outdoor terrace. A liter of wine costs only 130 Ft. ($2) and no one minds if you come with friends to enjoy it. Full meals, going for 350 Ft. ($5.75) each, include such fare as pork cutlets grilled with chicken livers, turkey breast stuffed with cheese, and rumpsteak with goose liver. The restaurant is open Sunday to Thursday from noon to 1am, on Friday and Saturday from noon to 2am.

Dining on the Outskirts

Szélmalom (Windmill) **Csárda** (tel. 76/22166). You'll notice the vanes of this transplanted windmill from far across the plain as you drive from Kecskemét toward Szeged on the E5 highway, near kilometer stone 91. The interior is a round room with thick wooden tables arranged like the spokes of a wheel, each radiating toward a circular bar area in the center. Each seating area has its own small arched window of double-paned glass, a bouquet of flowers, and puszta furniture that is pegged, not nailed, together. A vested waiter will place a hand-woven mat in front of you and serve such specialties as "drunken piglet with sauerkraut," or bean soup with sour cream. Meals cost from 300 Ft. ($5), and are served daily in summer from 8am to 11pm and in winter from 8am to 10pm.

Erdőkert Csárda (tel. 76/43127) lies in a forested area close to Hwy. **44,** about 9¼ miles outside Kecskemét. Built in a former farmhouse, the red-tile building has a paneled interior décor of warmly finished pine, with animal skins, embroidered napery, and antique farm implements hanging from sections of white plaster. Both the recipes and the crockery that they're served on come from the Hungarian Plain. Open daily in season from 6am to 10pm, the csárda serves meals that average around 300 Ft. ($5).

Excursions in a National Park

The most important excursion you can take from Kecskemét is to the **Bugac-puszta,** the most frequently visited of the six separate regions of the Kiskunság National Park. The park contains some 100 square miles of landscape set aside by the government for protection. Much of it is windswept desert, with sandstorms in early spring sometimes enveloping Kecskemét, 15 miles away. In the Bugac are tiny salt lakes, marshes, dense forests, sand dunes, and wildflower meadows. Featured is the Pásztormuzeum (peasants' museum), showing relics of the Bugac peasant life.

The traditional rigid animal husbandry is pursued today as a tourist attraction. The ancient Hungarian gray forked-horn cattle, twisted-horn Racka sheep, "mangalica" pigs with curly bristles, and the renowned Hungarian half-breed horses will be found here. Besides the flora and fauna, the Bugac farmsteads are of interest.

Tours can easily be arranged at the tourist office in Kecskemét or at the leading hotel, Aranyhomok. Visitors go first to the Bugac Csárda, a wayside inn, from which they're taken by horse carriages along dirt roads. Along the way you'll get to see some cowboys, puszta style, called *pasztorok,* wearing baggy white trousers.

The excursion ends back at the Bugac Csárda, where local specialties and wine from the grapes produced in the sandy soil are served.

SZEGED

Sweet paprika, salami, fish soup, and the summer theater festival are major productions of Szeged, the economic and cultural center of Hungary's southern Great Plain. On the banks of the Tisza River, this was the first planned city in Hungary, others just growing up haphazardly. Szeged in its early days may have done just that, but when the town was destroyed by flood in 1879, Franz Joseph, emperor of Austria and king of Hungary, personally visited here and ordered the town redesigned and rebuilt. The inner boulevard bears the name of Lenin, but the outer ring uses names of the various cities that contributed to the rebuilding, such as Paris, Vienna, and Rome.

The main square of the town, Széchenyi tér, is like a municipal park, one of the country's finest squares, occupying about 12 acres. There's also a Roosevelt tér (square) in Szeged, honoring the American wartime president.

The landmark of the town is the **Votive Church** on Dom tér (Cathedral Square), a neo-Romanesque, two-towered church completed in 1930. Its attraction is an organ with five manuals and 10,180 pipes, the second-largest such instrument in Europe after that of the Milan Cathedral. Beside the Votive Church stands the medieval **St. Demetrius Tower.** When construction started on the new church in 1913, the builders tried to blow up the old tower to make way for the new edifice. They failed, and the people of the town considered this divine intervention, so the tower was allowed to remain.

The **Greek Orthodox Serb Church** behind the Votive Church is a richly ornamented baroque building with a Louis XVI steeple. Inside there's a Byzantine-style iconostasis (a partition on which icons are hung, separating the sanctuary from the rest of the church). The **Lower Town Parish Church** on Mátyás Király tér is a valued historic building with a sacristy from the 15th century.

Szeged draws many visitors in summer to its **Open-Air Theater Festival,** held annually in July and August, when Hungarian and international opera and drama are presented by native-born and foreign stars. Performances are on Cathedral Square on a stage before the Votive Church.

You can go boating on the Tisza in summer and swim in a cold-water pool or the open-air facility in the park. Both holiday visitors and locals go to the hydropathic establishment on Kálvin Square, where they can bathe in thermal spring water.

Szeged is a convenient place to stop if you're on your way to Transylvania, once a part of Hungary but now in Romania, or else to Belgrade in Yugoslavia.

Where to Stay

Hotel Hungária, Komócsin Zoltán tér 2, H-6720 Szeged (tel. 62/21211), is a modern 10-story hotel on the bank of the Tisza River. It has a uniformed staff and a fire-engine-red corner bar just off the big lobby area. Its huge dining room might happen to be hosting a tour group from Siberia during your visit, but the ambience created by the musical group playing 1940s-style big-band music lightens the mood considerably. Next to the Szeged National Theater, the 138-room hotel charges $47 daily for a single and $49 for a double. Rooms contain private baths. The hotel has a good restaurant, serving (among other dishes) halászle, the famous fish soup.

Hotel Tisza, Wesselényi utca 1, H-6720 Szeged (tel. 62/12466), the oldest hotel in town, has an elegantly ornate 19th-century façade. Parts of the interior have been renovated, however, and little of the original detailing remains. The big dining room makes a pleasant oasis, flooded here and there with sunshine from the skylight and the oversize windows; huge wall murals with stylized human figures cover two opposite walls. Béla Bartók used to perform in the concert hall on the ground floor of this historic place. The recently renovated hotel rents 81 rooms with radios and phones (some with private baths). Singles cost $26.50 daily, with doubles going for $42.50.

Hotel Royal, Kölcsey utca 1, H-6720 Szeged (tel. 62/12911), is a centrally located medium-size hotel (110 rooms) near many of Szeged's architectural treasures. This is a satisfactory stopover in the center of town, with an interior covered with reddish slabs of polished stone. Most of the façade is old, ochred, elaborately 19th century (and slightly in need of repair), but that doesn't influence the comfort of the simple rooms or your treatment by the English-speaking staff. Some of the bedrooms have private baths, and each unit contains a phone and radio. Rates are $48 daily for a single, $49 for a double. The bar leading off the lobby has a dimly lit décor of high ceilings and modern stained-glass ceiling lamps.

Where to Dine

Restaurant Alabárdos, Oskola utca 13 (tel. 62/12914). The bronze panels on the front door facing the street depict mythological scenes that will make you search through your memory of ancient religions. An inner set of doors glows with carefully set stained glass. You'll enter a vestibule and find a brasserie with a vaulted ceiling off to the right. There will usually be students from the nearby university talking quietly in a good-natured ambience of darkly lit intimacy. If you turn left after entering, you'll see a long series of vaulted rooms whose walls are hung with medieval weapons that almost make you shudder.

You'll quickly forget your fears when you see the fragile Herend china, the fine crystal, and the elegant cutlery, along with wildflowers clustered in vases. In one of the rooms a large millstone topped with a mound of multicolored candle drippings and a single burning taper gives a Gypsy-like aura of the puszta. No lunch is served, but in the evening a Gypsy band provides music as you are served such specialties as mixed fish soup of Szeged, paprika chicken with sour cream and dumplings, pork gulasch with noodles, fried goose liver with tartar sauce, "robber's meat" on a spit, sautéed frogs' legs, and Hungarian veal stew. Expect to spend from 500 Ft. ($8.25). The restaurant is open Monday to Saturday from 6pm to midnight, and on Friday and Saturday it stays open till 2am.

Virág Café, Klauzál tér 1 (tel. 62/11459). In summer a terrace extends into the baroque square in front, although in winter you'll have to sit amid the dozens of old-world details that fill this Central European–style coffeehouse. The furniture is from the turn of the century, including pink marble tables and cabriole-legged chairs. The crystal chandeliers are each slightly different, my favorite being a brass-trimmed art nouveau fantasy. As long as you're looking around, be sure to notice the porcelain-trimmed coffee maker from Pécs. Come here for ice creams, coffee, and the best pastries in town. Pastries cost from 30 Ft. (50¢), and are served daily from 7am to 10pm.

DEBRECEN

The cultural and economic center of eastern Hungary, near the Romanian border, is Debrecen, a largely industrial city that is nevertheless an up-to-date resort. Already the third-largest city in Hungary, Debrecen is one of the country's most rapidly developing towns. The main thoroughfare is the Vörös Hadsereg utja.

This site must be a good place to live. Evidence shows that there were people here in the Stone Age, and in the 14th century Debrecen was a bustling market town on an important trade route. It has long been a seat of learning and culture, known for its **university** in Memorial Gardens. The seat of learning was established in the Middle Ages, the present building being from the early 19th century. Its library contains one of the biggest public collections in the country.

The largest Calvinist church in Hungary is here. The **Great Church** on Kossuth tér (square), the heart of the city, is one of the finest examples of Hungarian classicist architecture in the country. It has a colonnaded façade and tall twin towers, the tower on the left containing a five-ton bell, the largest in Hungary. St. Anne's Church on Béke út is a baroque structure erected between 1719 and 1746.

You might also visit the **Déri Museum,** on Múzeum utca (tel. 52/17577), which is rich in East Asian artifacts and also has some Etruscan items. Many 19th-and 20th-century works of art are on display. See *Ecce Homo* by Mihály Munkácsy, one of Hungary's outstanding artists. The museum also has a re-creation of a typical East Hungary peasant room, complete with a four-poster bed. The museum is open Tuesday to Sunday from 10am to 6pm, and charges an admission fee of 15 Ft. (25¢).

The Csókonai Theater on Liszt Ferenc utca is one of the most important examples of 19th-century Romantic eclecticism built outside Budapest.

Debrecen has long been known for its fierce spirit of independence. Groups formed here in 1849 to oppose the Habsburgs and again in 1944 to fight the Nazis.

Food and Lodging

Arany Bika (Golden Bull), Vörös Hadsereg utca 11-15, H-0253 Debrecen (tel. 52/16777), is a historic hostelry dating from 1699 and standing diagonally across from the "Great Church" in the heart of town. Over two centuries later, the 270-room hotel was completely modernized and made ready for occupancy in 1914, just in time to catch the beginning of World War I. Art nouveau in style, it's celebrated for its cuisine, said to be the best outside Budapest. It has as its principal dining room an area rich in nostalgia; chandeliers hang from a stained-glass ceiling three stories high. Here, excellently prepared food is served, with meals costing from 400 Ft. ($6.75), which makes them great bargains considering the quality of the cuisine.

Depending on the plumbing, singles range from $25 to $36 daily, with doubles costing $40 to $45. Breakfast is included.

The Golden Bull takes its name from an innkeeper who had a sign put up in memory of the former owner, János Bika. The sign depicted a golden bull.

---

6. The Northern Highlands

This is the section of Hungary perhaps least explored by North Americans, yet it's one of the most rewarding in terms of natural sightseeing attractions. In the northeastern section of the country, the highlands border on Czechoslovakia and the Soviet Union. Occasionally you'll see a ruined castle standing on top of a hill, a reminder of all the conquering hordes who have passed through this part of Hungary.

Parts of the highlands are heavily forested with beech, hornbeam, pine, and oak trees. The area contains some state game reserves, where you may chance to spot a wild boar. Certainly you'll see herds of deer. The Hungarian eagle also still lives in these parts.

The highest mountain peak in Hungary, 3,300 feet, is at Kékestető. The Hungarians use this area for winter sports, although many cross the border into Czechoslovakia to ski where the mountain ranges are much higher. Most Western visitors will enjoy the highlands more in summer, exploring the many vineyards, caves, and lakes. The major wine-producing regions are Tokaj, Eger, and Gyöngyös.

EGER

This city, northeast of Budapest, lies on the banks of the little Eger River at the meeting point of the Mátra and Bükk mountains. Known for its thermal springs and baths and its wines, Eger is rich in historic monuments. It was already an old town when the Mongols invaded in 1241, with a bishopric founded by St. Stephen, the first king of Hungary, who donned the crown in A.D. 1000.

The Sights

The Mongols and later the Turks were particularly cruel to the people of Eger, but the cruelty bred heroism among the townsfolk. Eger Castle was built after the Mongol invasion, and it played its most important role against the Turks. Every Hungarian knows of the heroic defense of the castle in 1552 by István Dobó and Gergely Bornemissza, who, with a handful of men, defeated the massive Turkish army, thought before that to be invincible.

However, some 34 years later the Turks came back, this time capturing the town and turning it into one of the regional capitals of the Ottoman Empire. For almost a century Eger was the northernmost outpost of Muslim might. The Turks erected mosques, baths, and the **Kethuda Minaret,** which has been restored in recent years. This 14-sided, 130-foot-high Turkish building, now one of the small city's main attractions, stands on Dobó István tér, the square named for the commander who led the successful 1552 defense of Eger. The mosque of Knézich Károly, beside which the minaret was originally built, was torn down in 1841.

The **castle-fortress** has been much restored, with little remaining from the original 15th-century edifice, but it's worthwhile having a look at the vast system of subterranean casemates, and the view from here is the best in Eger. The material excavated from the underground of the old castle is displayed in the Castle Museum, which occupies a Gothic building of the former episcopal palace. Exhibited is a lot of weaponry from both sides in the 1552 siege. The town was reclaimed for the kingdom of Hungary in 1687. The fortress (phone 36/12-744 for information) is open Tuesday to Sunday from 9am to 5pm, and charges an admission fee of 20 Ft. (35¢).

The **Minorite Church,** on Dobó István tér, is an 18th-century baroque building colored pink and ivory with green-topped towers. The **Cathedral of Eger,** on Szabadság tér, the second-largest church in the country, is in Greek temple style, built between 1831 and 1836. On its façade a tympanum rests on a Corinthian column.

You don't really need to be directed to specific sights in the old town of Eger, as this baroque city has much of interest for you to discover just by walking around through the little winding streets at the foot of the castle. The most interesting street is Kossuth Lajos utca, filled with buildings in the baroque and rococo styles.

As a curious side note to your touring, take a look at the 18th-century Lyceum, now a secondary school for girls. This is the largest baroque building of its type in the country, complete with a museum on the upper floor and an astronomical observation tower.

Wine connoisseurs will want to sample the renowned wine, **Egri bikavér,** or Bull's Blood, product of the valley of Szépasszony. The old taverns in the heart of town proudly sell this wine.

Where to Stay

Hotel Eger, Syálloda utca 1, H-3300 Eger (tel. 36/13233), and **Hotel Park,** Klapka utca 8, H-3300 Eger (tel. 36/13233), differ radically in architectural style. The Park, the oldest hotel in town, is decidedly the more modest, appealing to the budget-minded and rating only two stars; the Eger, on the other hand, is a three-star hotel and the best in town, its rooms divided between "Eger I" and "Eger II"—the latter a more modern construction.

The Park has an arched and hip-roofed exterior; the entrance is bordered with ornate vases and an elaborate stone wall. The hotel contains only 39 rooms, some a little threadbare. Singles go for $51 daily, with doubles costing $53. The restaurant has a big terrace serving regional wines and Hungarian specialties. In season, Gypsy music entertains the diners.

The two Egers are connected to the Park by a covered walkway. Their 172 modern bedrooms look out over balconies to a view partially encompassing the old town. The modern façade is embellished with a series of curved panels set between each window, giving the impression that the windowpanes are eyes staring through holes in evenly spaced masks. Singles range from $29 to $46 daily, with doubles going for $40 to $53.

Hotel Senator Ház, Dobo tér 11, H-3300 Eger (tel. 36/20466), is the gem of the town, lying in a historic early 17th-century building in the monumental old town. Restored and modernized, it is now an excellent small hotel—snug and cozy. Its 11 attractively furnished bedrooms all come with baths. Prices are $35 a day for a double, lowered to $27 for a single. Breakfast is provided in a café in the adjoining building.

Where to Dine

Fehér Szarvas Csárda (White Stag), Klapka utca 8 (tel. 36/13233, ext. 28), in the cellars of the Hotel Park, has an intimately rustic ambience of coffered ceilings, warmly tinted paneling and exposed brick, along with an impressive collection of hunting trophies. The overall effect is almost like that of a hunting lodge, especially with the evening Gypsy music. As you'd expect, the house specialty is venison in many different forms, ranging from soups to gulasch. You'll also find wild boar soup served with sour cream and various forms of poultry cooked on a spit. Meals cost from 500 Ft. ($8.25). The place is open from 6pm to midnight every day but Tuesday.

Kazamata Étterem Borozó, Márítork tér (tel. 36/11538), is a restaurant, nightclub, and drinks bar popular with tourists and locals. The establishment is directly below the cathedral. The restaurant serves Hungarian national and regional dishes, with such specialties as Jókai bean soup, Janicsár (Turkish soldier) soup, Mátra highwayman soup, cellar gulasch, stuffed joint à la Captain Dobó, steak à la

Eged mountain, roast pork à la Heves County, and beef cutlets stewed in Bull's Blood. Prices are moderate, a three-course meal costing from 200 Ft. ($3.50). The restaurant is open Sunday to Thursday from 11am to 11pm, on Friday and Saturday from 11am to midnight. The bar, serving a full choice of Hungarian Törley champagne, is open daily from 9pm to 3am. In summer you can have a drink either under the ancient trees of the park in front of the cathedral or on the terrace of the restaurant.

Dobos Café, Széchenyi utca 6 (tel. 36/13335), a city landmark, also offers the best pastries in town. Established in the 19th century by one of Hungary's leading confectioners, who named the establishment after himself, it is now a popular rendezvous point. The elegantly colorful décor includes red stone floors set into differently shaped rectangular slabs, marquetry paneling, and cabriole-legged chairs. The crystal chandeliers and wall lights date from the age of Maria Theresa. The specialty of the house is a richly caloric dessert called Dobos cake, although there are also ice cream and coffee.

Pastries range upward from 20 Ft. (35¢), and drinks begin at 28 Ft. (45¢). In summer the café is open from 7:30am to 9pm every day except Tuesday, when it closes at 4pm. (It closes at 8pm in winter.)

MISKOLC-TAPOLCA

Miskolc is the second-largest city of Hungary and the center of northern Hungarian economic and industrial life. Lying about 111 miles from Budapest, Miskolc holds little interest for tourists. However, Miskolc-Tapolca, at the eastern foot of the Bükk Mountains, is a busy tourist center, with numerous resort and spa facilities. Its thermal cave bath, called **Cave Lake,** draws year-round interest. In summer a beach and a boating lake are popular favorites with vacationers. The Miskolc-Tapolca area is also good for hiking.

From Miskolc, excursions can be made to **Diósgyőr Castle** and to **Lillafüred,** to admire its waterfall and caves, as well as **Lake Hámori.** A narrow-gauge railway runs from Miskolc through the forest. Another thermal bath, **Castle Bath,** is near Diósgyőr Castle at the foot of the mountain. Bathers can rent swim suits, deck chairs, toys, and rocking chairs, and patronize a snackbar.

Food and Lodging

Hotel Juno, Csabai utca 2-4, H-3519 Miskolc-Tapolca (tel. 46/64133). The glass-and-concrete perimeter of this streamlined hotel juts skyward above clusters of venerable trees. To reach it from the road, you'll have to drive over a rushing stream, then past a public swimming pool and a manmade pool into which funnel thermally heated waters. One of the hotel's biggest attractions is the nearby cave baths. Elevators lead from the airy lobby of the hotel to the glass-sided upstairs hallways. Each of the 108 comfortably modern rooms has its own balcony and private bath. Singles cost $45 daily, doubles around $47.

Hotel Pannónia, Kossuth Lajos utca, H-3525 Miskolc (tel. 46/16434), standing in the heart of this industrial city, dates from the turn of the century but was renovated and reopened in 1987. Today it offers 33 comfortably furnished rooms with private baths. Rates are $26 daily for a single, rising to $39 for a double. The hotel also offers a beer cellar, breakfast room, and the ground floor Rorariusz Confectionery.

AGGTELEK

This village stands at the western end of one of the biggest and loveliest systems of caves in all of Europe—the **Baradla Caves,** the greatest natural phenomenon in Hungary. The whole passage stretches a distance of some 14 miles, part in Czechoslovakia. Foreign visitors must have their passports to visit the Czechoslovakian passage, although the border crossing is actually at Bánréve, about 24 miles from Aggtelek. Bones found deep inside the caves show that prehistoric bears and Stone

Age humans inhabited these subterranean chambers—but probably not at the same time.

The so-called Hall of the Giants is one of the largest caverns in Europe. In summer, concerts are presented in another gigantic room, the Concert Hall. One formation is fancifully called "The Leaning Tower of Pisa"; another, "The Observatory," is one of the biggest stalagmites in the world. A lake formed in the caves can be crossed by rowboat if the water level is right.

The caves were once torchlit, which must have made exploration pretty spooky. Now professional guides take you through, and a good lighting system lets you see the full beauty of the grottoes. Tours are of varying length, depending on a party's stamina and interest. It's possible to take a short tour, lasting one hour, beginning at Aggtelek. Dress warmly and wear good, sturdy walking shoes. The temperature inside is around 50° Fahrenheit even in midsummer.

The caves are open daily from 9am to 4pm, charging an admission fee of 40 Ft. (60¢). For more information, phone 48/12-700.

TOKAJ

The best-known little town in Hungary is Tokaj, but its product—"the wine of kings and the king of wines"—is **Tokay,** renowned since the Middle Ages. Tokaj lies some 30 miles east of Miskolc, at the confluence of the Bodrog and Tisza rivers, in the heart of one of the great wine-growing regions of the country. The ideal time to visit in the countryside around Tokaj is in autumn at harvest time.

No other country, including France, has been able to produce Tokay wine successfully. This vintners' pride has been enjoyed by such personages as Maria Theresa, Voltaire, Goethe, Beethoven, and Frederick the Great, and in the wine cellars of Tokaj you can discover what all the excitement is about.

The most exciting cellar to visit is **Rákóczi cellar,** said to contain some 450,000 gallons of wine. The entrance is at Kossuth tér 13. Built centuries ago, the cellar has more than two dozen labyrinthine passageways and a total length of almost a mile. In the country's fight for independence from the Habsburgs in the 19th century, this cellar was often the scene of secret partisan meetings.

You can also visit a wine museum which has been installed in a former wine cellar. You will see, among other exhibits, a 19th-century grape press. The museum is open daily except Monday from 9am to 5pm.

Food and Lodging

Hotel Tokaj, Rákóczi út 5, H-3910 Tokaj (tel. 46/58), is a modern hostelry in a region where accommodations have been few. The architect designed it with vivid horizontal lines in a spectrum of colors across its roof. These, combined with Space Age balconies and repeated lollipop-style lamps, make it one of the most distinctive hotels in the region. The establishment has 30 fine double rooms with balconies and baths, plus 12 doubles with showers. They cost from $18 to $19 daily, depending on the plumbing. The hotel has a restaurant, open from 7am to 10pm, with meals accompanied by a Gypsy orchestra; there is also a small drinks bar. In back of the hotel the Bodrog River falls into the Tisza River, and guests can swim, fish, row, or canoe.

SÁROSPATAK CASTLE

Finally, you can visit one of the most outstanding castles in the area, Sárospatak Castle, considered one of the greatest monuments in Hungary. To reach it, you take Rte. 37 from Miskolc.

Construction on this fortified castle, which lies in a park near the Czech border, spread across the centuries, but the oldest part is the red tower, rising six floors, dating from the latter part of the 15th century. Many Italian architects worked on the building.

Guided tours are conducted through the fortress, during which you'll see a display of religious art and a system of cellars. See, in particular, a loggia from the 1640s, a shining example of Renaissance art in Hungary. You can visit one of the largest Gothic hall churches in East Hungary, the core of which is from the 14th century.

Like all other historic monuments in Hungary, the castle is closed on Monday but open otherwise from 10am to 6:30pm, charging 15 Ft. (25¢) for admission. For information, phone 41/11-83.

AUSTRIAN VOCABULARY AND MENU TERMS

A. Austrian (German) Vocabulary

		Pronounced
Hello	**Guten Tag**	goo-ten-tahk
How are you?	**Wie geht es Ihnen?**	vee gayt ess ee-nen
Very well	**Sehr gut**	zayr goot
Thank you	**Danke Schön**	dahn-keh-shern
Good-bye	**Auf Wiedersehen**	owf vee-dayr-zayn
Please	**Bitte**	bit-tuh
Yes	**Ja**	yah
No	**Nein**	nine
Excuse me	**Entschuldigen Sie mir**	en-school-di-gen zee meer
Give me	**Geben Sie mir**	gay-ben zee meer
Where is?	**Wo ist?**	voh eest
the station	**der Bahnhof**	dayr bahn-hohf
a hotel	**ein Hotel**	ain hotel
a restaurant	**ein Restaurant**	ain res-tow-rahng
the toilet	**die Toilette**	dee twah-let-tuh
To the right	**Nach rechts**	nakh reshts
To the left	**Nach links**	nakh leenks
Straight ahead	**Geradeaus**	geh-rah-deh-ous
I would like	**Ich möchte**	ikh mersh-ta
to eat	**essen**	ess-en
a room	**ein Zimmer**	ain tzim-mer
for one night	**für eine Nacht**	feer ai-neh nakht
How much is it?	**Wieviel kostet?**	vee-feel kaw-stet
The check, please	**Zahlen, bitte**	tzah-len bit-tuh
When?	**Wann?**	vahn
Yesterday	**Gestern**	geh-stern
Today	**Heute**	hoy-tuh
Tomorrow	**Morgen**	more-gen
Breakfast	**Frühstück**	free-shtick
Lunch	**Mittagessen**	mi-tahg-gess-en
Dinner	**Abendessen**	ah-bend-ess-en

B. Austrian Menu Terms

SOUPS

Erbsensuppe pea soup
Gemüsesuppe vegetable
Griessnockerlisuppe dumpling
  soup
Gulaschsuppe thin Hungarian
  gulasch
Hühnerbrühe chicken soup
Kartoffelsuppe potato soup
Königinsuppe cream of chicken

Kraftbrühe consommé
Leberknödlsuppe liver dumpling
  soup
Linsensuppe lentil soup
Nudelsuppe noodle soup
Ochsenschwanzsuppe oxtail soup
Schildkrötensuppe turtle soup
Rindsuppe beef broth

MEATS AND POULTRY

Aufschnitt cold cuts
Backhendl breaded fried chicken
Bauernschmaus sausages, pork,
  sauerkraut, and dumplings
Beinfleisch boiled beef
Brathuhn roast chicken
Bratwurst grilled sausage
Deutsche Beefsteak hamburger
  steak
Eisbein pigs' knuckles
Ente duck
Gans goose
Gefüllte Kalbsbrust stuffed breast
  of veal
Gulasch stew
Hammel mutton
Hirn brains
Kalb veal
Kaltes Geflügel cold poultry

Kassler Rippchen pork chops
Lamm lamb
Leber liver
Natur schnitzel unbreaded veal
  cutlet
Nieren kidneys
Ragout stew
Rinderbraten roast beef
Rindfleisch boiled beef
Sauerbraten sauerbraten
Schinken ham
Schweinebraten roast pork
Tafelspitz boiled beef with
  vegetables
Taube pigeon
Truthahn turkey
Weiner schnitzel breaded veal cutlet
Wurst sausage

FISH

Aal eel
Forelle trout
Hecht pike
Karpfen carp
Krebs crawfish

Lachs salmon
Makrele mackerel
Rheinsalm Rhine salmon
Schellfisch haddock
Seezunge sole

EGGS

Eier in Schale boiled eggs
—mit Speck with bacon
Rühreier scrambled eggs

Spiegeleier fried eggs
Verlorene Eier poached eggs

SANDWICHES

Käsebrot cheese sandwich
Schinkenbrot ham sandwich

Schwarzbrot mit Butter rye bread
  and butter
Wurstbrot sausage sandwich

SALADS

Gemischter Salat mixed salad
Gurkensalat cucumber salad

Kopfsalat lettuce salad
Rohkostplatte vegetable salad

VEGETABLES

Artischocken artichokes
Blumenkohl cauliflower
Bohnen beans
Bratkartoffelin fried potatoes
Erbsen peas
Grüne bohnen string beans
Gurken cucumbers
Karotten carrots
Kartoffelbrei mashed potatoes
Kartoffelsalat potato salad
Knödel dumplings
Kohl cabbage

Reis rice
Rote Rüben beets
Rotkraut red cabbage
Salat lettuce
Salzkartoffelin boiled potatoes
Sauerkraut sauerkraut
Spargel asparagus
Spinat spinach
Steinpilze mushrooms
Tomaten tomatoes
Vorspeisen hors d'oeuvres
Weisse Rüben turnips

DESSERTS

Blatterteiggebäck puff pastry
Bratapfel baked apple
Kaiserschmarren sugared jam
  omelet
Käse cheese
Klöss dumpling
Kompott stewed fruit
Obstkuchen fruit tart

Obstsalat fruit salad
Palatschinken sugared pancakes
Pfannkuckhen sugared pancakes
Pflaumenkompott stewed plums
Salzburger nockerlin soufflé
Teegebäck tea cakes
Torten pastries

FRUITS

Ananas pineapples
Apfel apples
Apfelsinen oranges
Bananen bananas

Birnen pears
Kirschen cherries
Pfirsiche peaches
Weintrauben grapes
Zitronen lemons

BEVERAGES

Bier beer
Ein Dunkles a dark beer
Ein Helles a light beer
Milch milk
Rotwein red wine
Sahne cream

Schokolade chocolate
Eine Tasse Kaffee a cup of coffee
Eine Tasse Tee a cup of tea
Tomatensaft tomato juice
Wasser water
Weinbrand brandy

CONDIMENTS AND OTHERS

Brot bread
Brötchen rolls
Butter butter
Eis ice
Essig vinegar

Pfeffer pepper
Salz salt
Senf mustard
Zitrone lemon
Zucker sugar

COOKING TERMS

Gebackt baked
Gebraten fried
Gefüllt stuffed
Gekocht boiled

Geröstet broiled
Gut durchgebraten well done
Nicht durchgebraten rare
Paniert breaded

HUNGARIAN VOCABULARY AND MENU TERMS

A. Hungarian Vocabulary

		Pronounced
Good morning	jó reggelt	yaw raig-gailt
Good afternoon	jó napot	yaw noppawt
Good evening	jó estét	yaw aishtayt
Good-bye	Viszontlátásra	veesawntlaataashro
Yes	Igen	eegain
No	Nem	naim
Please	Kérem	kayraim
Thank you	Köszönöm	kersernerm
You're welcome	Szívesen	seevaishain
How are you?	Hogy van?	hawd' von
Very well, thank you	Köszönöm, nagyon Jól	kersernerm, nod'awn yowl
Excuse me	Bocsásson meg	bawchaash-shawn maig
I'm hungry	Ehes vagyok	ayhaish vod'awk
Breakfast	Reggeli	raig-gailee
Lunch	Ebéd	aibayd
Dinner	Vacsora	vochawro
The check, please	Kérem a számlát	kayraim o saamlaat
Where is the?	Hol van?	hawl von
restaurant	az étterem	oz ayt-airaim
station	a vasútállomás	o voshootaallaw-maash
Where are the toilets?	Hol vannak az illemhelyek?	hawl vonnok oz eellaimhai'aik
How much?	Mennyi?	main'ee
How many?	Hány?	haan'
When?	Mikor?	meekawr
Who?	Ki	kee

B. Hungarian Menu Terms

SOUPS

burgonyakrémleves cream of potato soup
erőleves húsgombóccal consommé with meat dumplings
gombaleves mushroom soup
gulyásleves Hungarian gulasch

kalocsai halászlé fish soup in red wine
paradicsomleves tomato soup
spárgakrém leves cream of asparagus soup
tejfeles bableves bean soup with sour cream

MEATS AND POULTRY

bárányhús lamb
borjúhús veal
csirke chicken
disznóhús pork
fácán pheasant
fasirozott meatballs
galamb pigeon
kacsa duck
kolbászfélék sausages

liba goose
máj liver
marhahús beef
nyelv tongue
nyúl rabbit
őz venison
pulyka turkey
sonka ham
szalonna bacon

FISH

csuka pike
fogas local pike-perch
pisztráng trout

ponty carp
viza sturgeon

VEGETABLES

burgonya potatoes
fehérrépa turnips
gomba mushrooms
hagyma onions
káposzta cabbage
kelbimbó Brussels sprouts
karfiol cauliflower
paprika pepper
paradicsom tomatoes

saláta lettuce
sárgarépa carrots
spárga asparagus
spenót spinach
sültkrumpli french fries
uborka cucumber
zeller celery
zöldborsó peas

DESSERTS

almás palacsinta apple pancake
aranygaluska sweet dumpling
csokoládéfánk chocolate doughnut
fagylalt ice cream
gesztenyepüré tejszinhabbal chestnut purée with whipped cream

képviselöfánk cream puff
mákosrétes poppyseed strudel
somloi galuska sweet cookies with chocolate sauce
szilvás rétes plum strudel

FRUITS AND NUTS

alma apple
ananász pineapple
banán banana

citrom lemon
cseresznye cherries
eper strawberries

körte pear
málna raspberries
mandula almonds
narancs orange
őszibarack peach

sárgabarack apricot
sárgadinnye honeydew melon
szilva plum
szőlő grapes

BEVERAGES

almalé apple juice
ásványviz mineral water
bor wine
gin gin
grepfruit-lé grapefruit juice
gyümolcslé fruit juice
kávé coffee
kóla cola drink
konyak cognac
narancslé orange juice
pálinká brandy
paradicsomlé tomato juice

rum rum
sör beer
barna sör dark beer
vilagos šor light beer
szódaviz soda water
tea tea
tej milk
üditőital soft drink
whisky whisky
viz water
vodka vodka

CONDIMENTS AND OTHERS

borse pepper
cukor sugar
ecet vinegar
kenyér bread
ketchup ketchup

mustár mustard
kifli crescent roll
sajt cheese
só salt
vaj butter

COOKING TERMS

dinsztelve braised
félig nyersen rare
főve boiled
közepesen kisütve medium
pörköltnek stewed slowly

rántva breaded
grillezve grilled
roston sütve roasted
sütve fried

INDEX

GENERAL INFORMATION

Austria

Hungary

DESTINATIONS

Austria

Key to Abbreviations (Accommodations): *D* = Deluxe (5-star); *FC* = First Class (4-star); *M* = Moderate (2- or 3-star); *B* = Budget (1-star); *P* = Pensions. (Restaurants): *E* = Expensive; *M* = Moderate; *B* = Budget.

Hungary

Key to Abbreviations (Accommodations): D = Deluxe (5-star); FC = First Class (4-star); M = Moderate (2- or 3-star); B = Budget (1-star); P = Pensions. (Restaurants): E = expensive; M = Moderate; B = Budget.

FROMMER BOOKS
PRENTICE HALL PRESS
15 COLUMBUS CIRCLE
NEW YORK, NY 10023
212/373-8125

Date_____

Friends:
Please send me the books checked below.

FROMMER'S™ GUIDES

(Guides to sightseeing and tourist accommodations and facilities from budget to deluxe, with emphasis
on the medium-priced.)

☐ Alaska	$14.95	☐ Germany	$14.95
☐ Australia	$14.95	☐ Italy	$14.95
☐ Austria & Hungary	$14.95	☐ Japan & Hong Kong	$14.95
☐ Belgium, Holland & Luxembourg	$14.95	☐ Mid-Atlantic States	$14.95
☐ Bermuda & The Bahamas	$14.95	☐ New England	$14.95
☐ Brazil	$14.95	☐ New York State	$14.95
☐ Canada	$14.95	☐ Northwest	$14.95
☐ Caribbean	$14.95	☐ Portugal, Madeira & the Azores	$14.95
☐ Cruises (incl. Alaska, Carib, Mex, Hawaii, Panama, Canada & US)	$14.95	☐ Skiing Europe	$14.95
		☐ South Pacific	$14.95
☐ California & Las Vegas	$14.95	☐ Southeast Asia	$14.95
☐ Egypt	$14.95	☐ Southern Atlantic States	$14.95
☐ England & Scotland	$14.95	☐ Southwest	$14.95
☐ Florida	$14.95	☐ Switzerland & Liechtenstein	$14.95
☐ France	$14.95	☐ USA	$15.95

FROMMER'S $-A-DAY® GUIDES

(In-depth guides to sightseeing and low-cost tourist accommodations and facilities.)

☐ Europe on $40 a Day	$15.95	☐ New York on $60 a Day	$13.95
☐ Australia on $40 a Day	$13.95	☐ New Zealand on $45 a Day	$13.95
☐ Eastern Europe on $25 a Day	$13.95	☐ Scandinavia on $60 a Day	$13.95
☐ England on $50 a Day	$13.95	☐ Scotland & Wales on $40 a Day	$13.95
☐ Greece on $35 a Day	$13.95	☐ South America on $35 a Day	$13.95
☐ Hawaii on $60 a Day	$13.95	☐ Spain & Morocco on $40 a Day	$13.95
☐ India on $25 a Day	$12.95	☐ Turkey on $30 a Day	$13.95
☐ Ireland on $35 a Day	$13.95	☐ Washington, D.C. & Historic Va. on	
☐ Israel on $40 a Day	$13.95	$40 a Day	$13.95
☐ Mexico on $35 a Day	$13.95		

FROMMER'S TOURING GUIDES

(Color illustrated guides that include walking tours, cultural and historic sites, and other
vital travel information.)

☐ Amsterdam	$10.95	☐ New York	$10.95
☐ Australia	$9.95	☐ Paris	$8.95
☐ Brazil	$10.95	☐ Rome	$10.95
☐ Egypt	$8.95	☐ Scotland	$9.95
☐ Florence	$8.95	☐ Thailand	$9.95
☐ Hong Kong	$10.95	☐ Turkey	$10.95
☐ London	$8.95	☐ Venice	$8.95

TURN PAGE FOR ADDITONAL BOOKS AND ORDER FORM

0690

FROMMER'S CITY GUIDES

(Pocket-size guides to sightseeing and tourist accommodations and facilities in all price ranges.)

☐ Amsterdam/Holland	$8.95	☐ Montréal/Québec City	$8.95
☐ Athens	$8.95	☐ New Orleans	$8.95
☐ Atlanta	$8.95	☐ New York	$8.95
☐ Atlantic City/Cape May	$8.95	☐ Orlando	$8.95
☐ Barcelona	$7.95	☐ Paris	$8.95
☐ Belgium	$7.95	☐ Philadelphia	$8.95
☐ Boston	$8.95	☐ Rio	$8.95
☐ Cancún/Cozumel/Yucatán	$8.95	☐ Rome	$8.95
☐ Chicago	$8.95	☐ Salt Lake City	$8.95
☐ Denver/Boulder/Colorado Springs	$7.95	☐ San Diego	$8.95
☐ Dublin/Ireland	$8.95	☐ San Francisco	$8.95
☐ Hawaii	$8.95	☐ Santa Fe/Taos/Albuquerque	$8.95
☐ Hong Kong	$7.95	☐ Seattle/Portland	$7.95
☐ Las Vegas	$8.95	☐ Sydney	$8.95
☐ Lisbon/Madrid/Costa del Sol	$8.95	☐ Tampa/St. Petersburg	$8.95
☐ London	$8.95	☐ Tokyo	$7.95
☐ Los Angeles	$8.95	☐ Toronto	$8.95
☐ Mexico City/Acapulco	$8.95	☐ Vancouver/Victoria	$7.95
☐ Minneapolis/St. Paul	$8.95	☐ Washington, D.C.	$8.95

SPECIAL EDITIONS

☐ Beat the High Cost of Travel	$6.95	☐ Motorist's Phrase Book (Fr/Ger/Sp)	$4.95
☐ Bed & Breakfast—N. America	$11.95	☐ Paris Rendez-Vous	$10.95
☐ California with Kids	$14.95	☐ Swap and Go (Home Exchanging)	$10.95
☐ Caribbean Hideaways	$14.95	☐ The Candy Apple (NY with Kids)	$12.95
☐ Honeymoon Destinations (US, Mex &		☐ Travel Diary and Record Book	$5.95
Carib)	$14.95	☐ Where to Stay USA (From $3 to $30 a	
☐ Manhattan's Outdoor Sculpture	$15.95	night)	$10.95

☐ Marilyn Wood's Wonderful Weekends (CT, DE, MA, NH, NJ, NY, PA, RI, VT) $11.95
☐ The New World of Travel (Annual sourcebook by Arthur Frommer for savvy travelers) $16.95

GAULT MILLAU

(The only guides that distinguish the truly superlative from the merely overrated.)

☐ The Best of Chicago	$15.95	☐ The Best of Los Angeles	$16.95
☐ The Best of France	$16.95	☐ The Best of New England	$15.95
☐ The Best of Hong Kong	$16.95	☐ The Best of New York	$16.95
☐ The Best of Italy	$16.95	☐ The Best of Paris	$16.95
☐ The Best of London	$16.95	☐ The Best of San Francisco	$16.95

☐ The Best of Washington, D.C. $16.95

ORDER NOW!

In U.S. include $2 shipping UPS for 1st book; $1 ea. add'l book. Outside U.S. $3 and $1, respectively.
Allow four to six weeks for delivery in U.S., longer outside U.S.
Enclosed is my check or money order for $_____

NAME_____

ADDRESS_____

CITY_____ STATE_____ ZIP_____

0690

AMERICAN EXPRESS CAN DELIVER CASH
AND A REPLACEMENT CARD TO YOU WITHIN 24 HOURS,
AS LONG AS YOU'RE IN THIS GENERAL AREA.

No matter where you are in the world, if you lose your wallet, we can get a new American Express® Card and cash in your hands usually within 24 hours.*

If you're truly in the middle of nowhere, say the African Outback, it might take a little longer. Depending upon how many wandering hippos and fallen trees our local courier must contend with.

But more often than not, you'll have a new Card and cash the next day. Something you'd expect from American Express.

So carry the American Express Card. And no matter where on earth you go, you'll never leave civilization behind.

For assistance, call your nearest American Express office, or in the U.S. call our 24-hour number 1-800-252-3650; everywhere else call collect 602-954-1225. Don't leave home without it.®

MEMBERSHIP HAS ITS PRIVILEGES.℠

 TRAVEL RELATED SERVICES *Delivery time may vary in some areas depending on transportation availability, existence of war or civil strife or other factors beyond our control. For U.S. Cardmembers only.

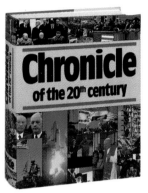
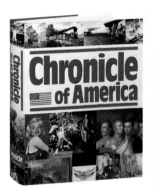